THE
ST.
JAMES

OPERA

ENCYCLOPEDIA

THE
ST.
JAMES

OPERA

edited by
John Guinn and Les Stone

ENCYCLOPEDIA

A Guide to
People and Works

VISIBLE
INK
PRESS

DETROIT • NEW YORK • TORONTO • LONDON

The St. James Opera Encyclopedia: A Guide to People and Works
Edited by John Guinn and Les Stone

Copyright © 1997 Visible Ink Press™
Visible Ink Press is a division of Gale Research
835 Penobscot Building
Detroit, MI 48226

Most Visible Ink Press™ books are available at special quantity discounts when purchased in bulk by corporations, organizations, or groups. Customized printings, special imprints, messages, and excerpts can be produced to meet your needs. For more information, contact Special Markets Manager, Gale Research, 835 Penobscot Bldg., Detroit, MI 48226. Or call 1-800-776-6265.

Cover Photo: Placido Domingo; courtesy of UPI/Bettman
Cover Design: Pamela A. E. Galbreath

Library of Congress Cataloging-in-Publication Data

St. James opera encyclopedia : a guide to people and works / editors, John Guinn, Les Stone.
    p. cm.
  Includes indexes.
  ISBN 0-7876-1035-6 (alk. paper)
  1. Opera—Dictionaries. I Guinn, John. II Stone, Les.
ML102.06.S7 1996
782.1'03—dc2096-22877
  CIP
  MN

ISBN 0-7876-1035-6
Printed in the United States of America

10 9 8 7 6 5 4 3 2 1

contents ≡ OPERA

introduction OPERA

"A bizarre affair made up of poetry and music in which the poet and the musician, each equally obstructed by the other, give themselves no end of trouble to produce a wretched work."

You probably wouldn't have to look far to find people who would agree with that observation, made by French critic Charles Saint-Evremond in the late seventeenth century. For, despite its regular presence on public television, despite the expanding popularity of those three tenors (with their noticeably uneven talents), despite the proliferation of operatic arias and duets as background music in films and television commercials, opera is still seen by many as an idiotic pastime of the wealthy who, in order to maintain their status, stoically submit themselves to listening to a 300-pound diva shrieking in some foreign tongue about being rejected by a short tenor whose girth indicates his appetite matches hers. Yet people continue to pack opera houses. In fact, at a time when some commentators are direly predicting the demise of so-called serious music because of aging audiences, opera companies report their audiences are steadily increasing. Why the apparent contradiction? Why does an art form so outlandish it continues to be the subject of parody also continue to intrigue more and more people? Why, to bring it down to a personal level, would you be interested in finding out more about it through a book like the one you hold in your hands?

There are a number of reasons. For one thing, opera incorporates many different art forms: literature, drama, singing, acting, costuming and scenery, orchestral playing, often dancing. Witnessing all those arts coming together into a unified whole is something not experienced elsewhere, and, providing it is done well, it offers a special satisfaction.

There's also the lure of the famous. Major opera companies attract big-name experts to take part in their productions. Luciano Pavarotti and Placido Domingo regularly take time from their stadium spectaculars to sing at New York's Metropolitan Opera. Italian filmmaker Franco Zeffirelli *(Romeo and Juliet)* stages operas there. American playwright Arthur Miller (once wed to Marilyn Monroe, perhaps the most recognizable celebrity of the century) has been contracted to write the libretto for an opera based on his play, *A View from the Bridge,* for the 1999-2000 season of the Lyric Opera of Chicago. American composer William Bolcom is writing the music for the opera; filmmaker Robert Altman will stage it. The prospect of witnessing the work of such notables certainly attracts audiences.

Another reason for the increasing popularity of opera is that some of its so-called impediments are actually myths. It is a myth, for instance, to claim that you won't be able to understand what is happening in operatic performances because the words are sung in foreign languages. In fact, operas are sung in many different languages, including English, and some American companies perform foreign-language operas in English translations. More to the point, though, is that every major American opera company (and most minor ones) have adapted a practice first developed by the Toronto-based Canadian Opera Co. whereby English translations are projected above the stage or, in the case of the Metropolitan Opera, on the backs of seats, thus doing away with the language problem once and for all. Not every word is projected, but there is enough of the text to keep you informed as to what is going on. Should you not care, the projected titles are quite unobtrusive, and don't interfere with the onstage proceedings.

A beneficial side effect of projected translations is that most singers no longer feel the need to exaggerate stage gestures in order to communicate with their audiences. That means the level of operatic acting, which has been improving steadily with the advent of comparatively svelte singers who look more like their characters, continues to become more believable.

Another myth is that everyone dresses up to go to the opera. In a country where few dress up for anything any more, you'll find people wearing every-thing from tails and evening gowns to jeans and T-shirts mingling in opera house lobbies. And when it's time for the lights to go down, you're apt to see as many jeans as tails heading for the more expensive seats.

Then there's the myth that operatic plots are important. In some cases they are; in most they should be looked upon primarily as fragile progenitors of major emotional manifestations. Take Verdi's *Rigoletto.* In its final scene Rigoletto, the hunch-backed court jester with the gorgeous daughter named Gilda, thinks he's dragging across the stage a sack filled with the dead body of the Duke of Mantua, his overbearing employer and the seducer of his daughter. But this is a tragedy, so Rigoletto's vengeance will be short-lived. As Rigoletto prepares to drop his sack into the river, he hears the Duke singing his signature tune, "La donna e mobile," offstage. If the Duke is singing, who is in the bag? Daughter Gilda, of course, who is, of course, dying. But before Gilda dies she sings for several minutes, in the process producing some pearly high notes that could only come from an unusually healthy soprano's throat. You would think such convoluted proceedings would cause stifled snickers, if not outright guffaws. Instead, there's usually not a dry eye in the house as the curtain descends on the woebegone father screaming "Ah, la maledizione!" ("Ah, the curse!") over his daughter's corpse.

Why? As an opera composer, Verdi was able, perhaps more than any other composer, to write music that could transcend an absolutely improbable situation by conveying universal emotions. Tears rather than laughter are produced by the scene containing Gilda's swan-song because Verdi's music conveys with such great strength the utter despair Rigoletto feels at losing the only beautiful thing in his life.

That is what great operatic music can do. It can transform the ridiculous into the meaningful, the outrageous into the logical, the mundane into the memorable. And that is why, ultimately, it is the music that matters most. Opera lovers will put up with inadequate acting, overweight singers, impossible plots, misdirected staging and drab sets and costumes, providing the music is worthwhile and well-served. If it isn't, the performance is a failure, no matter how successful the remaining elements are.

Should you decide to give in further to the temptations that have lured you to this odd art, you'll understand more and more how its apparent contradictions are really proofs of its unique artistic integrity. And you'll be hooked.

One person who understood that well was Rudolf Bing, former general director of the Metropolitan Opera. "If theater is an insane asylum," Bing once quipped, "opera is the ward for incurables."

Ready to be committed?

John Guinn

picture acknowledgments ⊟OPERA

Photographs and illustrations for entries in the *St. James Opera Encyclopedia* have been used by permission of the following organizations and individuals:

AKG Photo, London: Auber, Bartók, Bizet, *La bohème,* Britten, Cherubini, *Les contes d'Hoffmann,* Debussy, Destinn, Donizetti, *Elektra,* Farrar, *Der fleigende Holländer,* Flotow, Gershwin, Christoph von Gluck, Humperdinck, Korngold, London, Mascagni, Massenet, Melchior, Meyerbeer, Mussorgsky, *Parsifal,* Penderecki, *Porgy and Bess,* Puccini, Ravel, *Salome,* Scarlatti, Smetana, Strauss, Tchaikovsky, *Thaïs,* Wagner, Weber, Weill

Culver Pictures: Albani, Alda, Bori, Caruso, Chaliapin, De Luca, Eames, Flagstad, Alma Gluck, Lauri-Volpi, Milanov, Pasta, Patti, Ruffo, Scotti, *Turandot*

Donald Cooper/Photostage: *Anna Bolena,* Baker, *Il barbiere di Siviglia, The Cunning Little Vixen,* Ewing, Kraus, *Lady Macbeth of Mtensk District, The Love for Three Oranges,* Pavarotti, *Simon Boccanegra,* Te Kanawa, Verrett

Giancarlo Costa Photography, Milan: Bellini, *L'elisir d'amore,* Ponchielle, Rossini, *Semiramide, La sonnambula,* Verdi

Siegfried Lauterwasser, Überlingen am Bodensee: Behrens, Jones, *Lohengrin, The Makropoulos Case, Die Meistersinger,* Price, *Siegfried, Der Rosenkavalier, Tristan und Isolde, Il trovatore*

Mary Evans Picture Library, London: Lind, *Aïda, Roméo et Juliette*

Metropolitan Opera Archives, New York: Marian Anderson, *La fanciulla del West, Lakmé,* Tibbett, *Il trittico, Vanessa*

Royal Opera, Stockholm: *The Consul*

a OPERA

Adams, John

Composer. Born 15 February 1947, in Worchester, Massachusetts. Initially studied clarinet with his father, then with Felix Viscuglia; B.A. (magna cum lauda) 1969, and M.A. (in composition), 1971, Harvard University, where he studied with Leon Kirchner, David Del Tredici, Roger Sessions, and Earl Kim; an accomplished clarinettist, he played the solo part in Walter Piston's Clarinet Concerto, Carnegie Hall, 1969; head of composition department, San Francisco Conservatory, 1971-81; Guggenheim fellowship, 1982; new music adviser, San Francisco Symphony Orchestra, beginning in 1978, composer in residence, 1982—85; creative chair, St. Paul Chamber Orchestra, beginning in 1988.

Operas *Nixon in China.* Alice Goodman, Houston, Houston Grand Opera, 22 October 1987; *The Death of Klinghoffer,* Alice Goodman, Brussels, Théâtre Royal de la Monnaie, March 1991.

Adams studied composition at Harvard University with Leon Kirchner, Roger Sessions, Earl Kim and Mario di Bonaventura. While at Harvard he distinguished himself as the first undergraduate permitted to submit a musical composition as his required senior thesis. He completed a BA in 1969 and an MA in 1971. During the summer of 1970 he served as composer-in-residence at the Marlboro Festival in Vermont. In 1972, he became director of the "New Music Ensemble" at the San Francisco Conservatory of Music, a post which he held until 1982.

Adams' association with the San Francisco Symphony Orchestra began in 1978, when he became the new music advisor for the orchestra under Edo de Waart. Under the auspices of that orchestra, he founded and directed the "New and Unusual Music Series," which served as a model for the nationwide "Meet the Composer" program. In 1982, under this residence program, Adams was appointed composer-in-residence with the San Francisco Symphony Orchestra and served until 1985.

Particularly important from this collaboration are his early works using voices: *Harmonium* and *Grand Pianola Music*. These pieces, although still influenced by minimalistic principles, show Adams as a composer with a commanding gift for sweeping lyrical melody, and the ability to combine modern and classical idioms with superior craftsmanship.

Harmonium (1981), commissioned by the San Francisco Symphony Orchestra, sets the poems of John Donne and Emily Dickinson. Of the young composer's first work for chorus, Alan Rich of *Newsweek* (March 18, 1985) said that the cantata was "among the major choral works of the era." Rich especially admired the "amazing range of sound" that Adams was able to elicit from the chorus. In *Grand Pianola Music* (1983) scored for wind, brass, two pianos, percussion ensemble, and three female vocalists, Adams abandoned pure minimalism for material that is reminiscent of early twentieth-century American popular music, particularly marches and player-piano music. Although *Grand Pianola Music* was not well received, the EMI/Angel recording went on to be a best seller.

Adams' opera *Nixon in China* (1985) represents a major contribution to late twentieth-century opera. Based on President Richard Nixon's historic seven day trip to the People's Republic of China in February of 1972, the opera was created in collaboration with American producer Peter Sellars and the poet/librettist Alice Goodman. The idea for the opera was offered by Sellars, a director whose imaginative and unusual settings of classical plays and operas have won critical respect. In 1984, the three collaborators gathered in Washington D.C. to study news reports and television footage of the historic visit. Adams told Stephanie Buchau in an *Opera News* interview (October 1987) that they had focused on Nixon's "more heroic aspects," finding Nixon an "interesting character" because of his vulnerability. Alice Goodman's beautifully written libretto succeeds in focusing on the heroic qualities of each character.

The opera is uniquely constructed in that its structural units decrease proportionally throughout the opera. There are three scenes in the first act, two scenes in the second act and one scene in the third act. The dramatic plot parallels the diminishing size of the acts in that it moves from a larger public sphere to a smaller personal one throughout the course of the opera.

Despite his foundations in minimalism, as a composer of opera, Adams uses melodic material in dramatic rather than repetitive ways. K. Robert Schwartz (*Fanfare,* June 1985) suggests that the dramatic requirements of Adams's music transcend the "deliberate austerity" inherent in minimalistic music. Adams has not abandoned the repetition and arpeggiation of minimalism; he simply relegates them to the orchestral accompaniment, and by doing so makes the vocal lines stand out in dramatic relief. This preservation of minimalistic elements in the orchestral scoring allows a freedom of vocal writing previously not seen in minimalistic opera.

Nixon in China was premiered on October 22, 1987, by the Houston Grand Opera. Two months later the production traveled to the "Next Wave Festival" at the Brooklyn Academy of Music and the Kennedy Center in Washington D.C. These performances took place amidst a storm of publicity and strongly divided critical controversy. The production was also mounted at the Netherlands Opera in Amsterdam (June 1988) and at the Edinburgh Festival (August 1988).—PATRICIA ROBERTSON

L'Africaine [The African Maid]

Composer: *Giacomo Meyerbeer.*

Librettist: *Eugène Scribe.*

First Performance: *Paris, Opéra, 28 April 1865 [posthumous; final revisions by Fétis].*

Roles: *Ines (soprano); Selika (soprano); Vasco da Gama (tenor); Nelusco (baritone); Don Pedro (bass); Don Diego (bass); Anna (mezzo-soprano); Don Alvar (tenor); Grand Inquisitor (bass); High Priest of Brahma (baritone); chorus (SSAATTBB).*

But for a stroke of fate, *L'Africaine* might have been Meyerbeer's third opera composed for Paris, following *Robert le diable* and *Les Huguenots* and preceding *Le prophète*. Whenever possible, the composer wrote his music for specific voices, and in the person of Cornélie Falcon, who had triumphed as Valentine in *Les Huguenots*, he had found a remarkable soprano, possessor of a voice that must have somewhat resembled, in expressive range if not in timbre, those of Shirley Verrett or Régine Crespin in our time. It was a voice capable of both secure projection in the high mezzo register and solid extension into the lyrico-dramatic. With Falcon's voice in mind, Meyerbeer turned to a libretto by Eugène Scribe in which a humble Spanish sailor falls in love with an African princess.

But when Falcon, who in her brief six-year career gave her name to a specific type of voice, the "sopran falcon," lost her voice three years after the premiere of *Les Huguenots*, Meyerbeer laid the larger project aside, after having completed a piano score to the *L'Africaine* libretto in 1840 to satisfy his contract with the Opéra. According to the research of John H. Roberts, he turned to it again in 1849, following the success of *Le prophète*, and on the advice of a friend Meyerbeer asked Scribe to move the scene from Africa to India. Scribe finished the new libretto in 1853, having altered the story to conform more closely to his successful formula of building fictional stories around historical personages. The Spanish sailor became the Portuguese explorer, Vasco da Gama, sole survivor of an expedition seeking lands beyond Africa; the African princess, Selika, now inhabited a Hinduized Madagascar and was in love with Vasco, who had purchased her at a slave market. He, however, loves the noblewoman Ines. Imprisoned by the Inquisition, Vasco is freed when Ines agrees to marry his rival, Don Pedro, who then sets sail for the Indian Ocean, followed by Vasco. Thanks to Selika's jealous slave Nelusko, Don Pedro's ship is sunk. Vasco comes ashore to the beautiful new land, where he faces death until Selika swears he is her husband. But Ines, too, has survived, and Selika sends the lovers off. She commits suicide by inhaling the poisonous fumes of the hallucinatory flowers of the manchineel tree.

Meyerbeer died after having scored more than enough music for the evening's entertainment, leaving the musicologist Francois-Joseph Fétis to pare it to manageable proportions, consigning over an hour's worth to a companion volume of the performance score. For the most part, his excisions and inclusions reflect what Meyerbeer would probably have done in rehearsal. As Roberts notes (in an informative essay for San Francisco's 1988 program booklet) he changed both the text and orchestration of the most famous single piece of the score, Vasco's "O paradiso," which should, at least for comparison, be recorded in its original scoring.

Despite its posthumous construction, *L'Africaine* has been rightly judged Meyerbeer's most mature score. It echoes and surpasses the best of his previous efforts in most respects. He had made the chorus a protagonist in *Les Huguenots*, contrasting Catholic and Protestant in the tavern scene of act III. In *L'Africaine's* first act, the liberal and conservative factions of the Grand Council debate the veracity of Vasco's story in a fiery exchange, punctuated by the sinister threats of the Grand Inquisitor's entourage. His tenors from *Robert le diable* onward had won applause with dramatic ariosos rather than full-fledged arias; "O paradiso" successfully integrates the melodically-varied arioso with traditional aria structure, even adding a conventional but rousing cabaletta, "Conduisez-moi vers ce navire." Perhaps having learned something from Verdi's *Rigoletto*, Meyerbeer gives the baritone a remarkable two-part aria, and at the conclusion of the fifth act, when Selika inhales the hallucinogenic fumes of the deadly manchineel, he constructs a mini-symphony of vocal movements comparable to Fides' "O prêtres de Baal" in *Le prophète* or Dido's "Adieu, fiere cité" from Berlioz' *Les Troyens,* which itself owes much to Fides' scena.

Perhaps Fétis' only real error lies in his introduction of Nelusko, who has secretly loved Selika, in that finale. Both musically and dramatically his appearance is anticlimactic. Scribe has been unjustly blamed for other perceived flaws, predominantly the title, as the opera no longer has much to do with Africa; but Fétis argued that Paris had been waiting for a Meyerbeer opera called *L'Africaine* for a quarter-century, not for one titled *Vasco da Gama*. Scribe has also been criticized for Vasco's apparent fickleness, his falling into Selika's arms as soon as he thinks Ines is dead; but key lines explaining that he has drunk a love potion were truncated in the performance version. Even with its questionable revisions, *L'Africaine,* when played in French by a stellar cast, can overcome its dramatic deficiencies as effectively as does Verdi's *Il trovatore* to provide a moving evening of musical theater.—WILLIAM J. COLLINS

Aida

Composer: *Giuseppe Verdi.*

Librettist: *Antonio Ghislanzoni (after a scenario by François Auguste Ferdinand Mariette as sketched in French by Camille du Locle).*

First Performance: *Cairo, New Opera House, 24 December 1871.*

Roles: *Aida (soprano); Amneris (mezzo-soprano); Radames (tenor); Amonasro (baritone); Ramfis (bass); Pharaoh (bass); Priestess (soprano or mezzo-soprano); Messenger (tenor); chorus (SSATTTTBBB).*

Aida, the daughter of King Amonasro of Ethiopia, has been taken captive in an Egyptian war and made to serve as a slave in Memphis to the Pharaoh's daughter Amneris. She has kept her royal status secret, and fallen in love with the soldier Radames, who is ironically chosen to lead the Egyptian forces against her people. Amneris, also enamored of Radames, tricks Aida into revealing her concealed passion for him. Radames is victorious in war, and brings home as one of his captives Aida's father, who has kept his true identity secret. The Pharaoh announces that Radames will have as his victor's reward the hand of Amneris in marriage. Aida, in despair, meets Radames on the banks of the Nile and, induced by her father, convinces her lover that they must flee together. He unsuspectingly reveals the military secrets the concealed Amonasro has wanted to hear. Amneris has also overheard. She sends a guard after Amonasro, who is killed. Aida escapes. Radames, to save his honor, surrenders, and Amneris repents of her jealousy when Egypt's priests, led by the implacable Ramfis, condemn Radames to be buried alive. Sealed in his tomb, Radames finds that Aida has already found her way there to die with him. As Amneris prays in the temple above, Aida and Radames sing below that their souls are flying upwards to eternal day.

Archaeology was an exciting new science when *Aida* was written. Heinrich Schliemann unearthed Homer's Troy the very year of *Aida*'s premiere, and other excavations were revealing much of ancient Egypt itself. Verdi wanted archaeological correctness in his Egyptian opera. Specifically, he wanted on stage the long, straight, valveless instrument that was the only trumpet known to antiquity. He had six of them specially made in Milan to play his triumphal march, which called for just six brassy notes (the four a bugler plays in "Taps" plus two passing notes).

Verdi was careful to ensure that his archaeological correctness would sound, not embarrassingly primitive, but grandly barbaric: after three of his long trumpets have played the tune in the key of A flat, he has the other three, pitched a tone-and-a-half higher, repeat it from across the stage in the higher key of B natural; then he restores the march to its earlier key and, in a simple but very telling effect, has the two sets of trumpets play together, using as a descant the only note the second set has in common with the first. The effect was as grand as anything Meyerbeer had done for Paris. And without knowing it, Verdi was archaeologically right about the trumpets. When King Tut's tomb was opened in 1925, two trumpets were found within, one tuned in A flat, the other in B—incredibly, the very two keys Verdi had used.

Verdi had to be persuaded to write *Aida*. He had twenty-three operas behind him, regarded the old battles as won, and wanted to retire to his farm. But one of his Paris librettists, Camille du Locle, eventually interested him in a four-page synopsis for an opera for Cairo, to be

Aida, Paris, 1880

set in ancient Egypt, written—so du Locle implied—by the Khedive of Egypt himself, the munificent Ismail Pasha, first of the three viceroys appointed by the Ottoman empire to rule Egypt during and after the construction of the Suez Canal.

Du Locle probably got the synopsis from Auguste Mariette, a cataloguist at the Louvre who had found archaeological fame in the Egyptian sands and was given the title of Bey and made Inspector General of Monuments by the Khedive. Mariette had the beginnings of *Aida*'s story in his own experience: he had actually uncovered a walled-up skeleton when excavating his Serapeum.

Du Locle visited Verdi on his Italian farm, and in less than a week the four-page scenario became, between the two of them, the four acts of *Aida,* in French prose. Verdi then had the French translated into Italian verse by the man who had already helped with the revision of *La forza del destino,* Antonio Ghislanzoni. We have thirty-four of the letters that passed between the composer and librettist, so we can still read how Verdi bullied Ghislanzoni till he got, instead of libretto language, the simple, heartfelt dialogue he wanted. Sometimes, tired of waiting, Verdi simply wrote his own Italian lines and set them to music. So in effect, Verdi is the librettist of *Aida*. He also suggested some of the best details in the staging, including the split levels in the last act.

The music of *Aida* is of a new richness and complexity, yet accessible even when heard for the first time. Act III, the Nile scene, contains solos and duets as impassioned and beautifully wrought as anything in opera. The scene is also a master textbook on how to write evocatively for woodwinds. Flute and oboe, clarinet and bassoon, wave and undulate in intricate patterns and conjure up the steamy, shimmering night, the ebb and swell of the river with all its creatures. But Verdi surpasses everything that has gone before in the duet "O terra, addio" in the last act. This grandest of operas ends, as it began, with music that is quiet, luminous, and delicately nuanced. The lovers voice their farewell to earth in a great, spreading arc of melody while the whole orchestra seems to quiver in one vast, cosmic tremolo. In no other music is there anything quite to equal this feeling of leaving earth for sky, of quietly walking through space.

Since the Cairo premiere, delayed for almost a year when the Franco-Prussian war broke out and Mariette and all the scenery were closed off in beleaguered Paris, *Aida* has become one of the most popular operas in the world. But a great operatic success does not always mean triumph and fulfillment for its creators. For the creators of *Aida,* it was almost as if they had inherited the curse laid on those who opened King Tut's tomb. The Khedive was dismissed by the Ottomans for administrative incompetence. Mariette lost his wife and five of his children to cholera and most of his records to the Nile when it flooded his house. Du Locle took over the management of the Opéra-Comique in Paris, saw it go bankrupt with the initial failure of Bizet's *Carmen,* and had a temporary but bitter falling out with Verdi over money. Ghislanzoni wrote over eighty other librettos, but never had a success remotely like *Aida*.

Finally, Verdi was angered that his new work, while widely admired, reminded some critics of Wagner. "If only I had never written *Aida!*" he said, ruefully. "To end up, after more than thirty-five years in the theater, an imitator!" We, with hindsight, have come to see *Aida* as not Wagnerian at all, but as crafted dramatically along the lines of French grand opera and musically the vindication and renewal of Italian vocal art in the face of the onslaughts of German symphonic drama. But Verdi was so saddened about being praised for the wrong reasons that he went into another period of virtual retirement. When he resurfaced sixteen years later, in his late seventies, after Wagner's death, it was to write the two greatest of all Italian works for the musical stage, the ultimate reconciliation in opera of the vocal and the orchestral—*Otello* and *Falstaff*.—M. OWEN LEE

Albanese, Licia

Soprano. Born 22 July 1913 in Bari, Italy. Married Italian-American businessman Joseph Gimma, 1945; studied with Emanuel De Rosa in Bari and with Giuseppina Baldassare-Tedeschi in Milan; professional debut in 1934 at the Teatro Lirico in Milan, replacing a soprano who had become ill during the first act in the part of Cio-Cio-San in Madama Butterfly; *debut at Parma as Cio-Cio-San, 10 December 1935; Metropolitan Opera debut in the same role, 9 February 1940; received Order of Merit in Italy; received from Pope Pius XII award of the Lady Grand Cross of the Equestrian Order of the Holy Sepulchre; final Metropolitan Opera performance on 16 April 1966; a noted Puccini singer, her other roles include Marguerite in* Faust, *Violetta in* La Traviata, *and Desdemona in* Otello.

Licia Albanese had what she called "tricks for beauty": vocal and histrionic effects that were entirely legitimate, apposite, heartfelt, and uniquely hers, ways in which she shaped phrases ineffably and unforgettably, and movements (never, in her case, anything as obvious as the stock operatic "gesture") that both illuminated a character's deepest emotions and profoundly stirred those of her hearers.

Nowhere was Albanese's mastery of her art more palpable than during the moments that required her to "expire" onstage, something she invariably accomplished with the most exquisite expressivity, whether called upon to demonstrate a gradual, quiet fading away (Mimì, *La bohème*), a final feverish outburst (Violetta, *La traviata*), an intense losing battle to cheat death (Manon Lescaut), or an act of unbearable poignancy such as the suicide of Butterfly.

The effect Albanese made as Cio-Cio-San in *Madama Butterfly* after she had sung the geisha's final words, made all the ceremonial preparations for her hara-kiri, committed the act behind the shoji, and knocked the screen over to writhe and die before our eyes, remains one of the most indelible visual memories ever created by any opera singer. With her legs bound according to ritual, Butterfly's arms were still free to express both the pain of her mortal wound and the ascendancy of her spirit, which exults because she has redeemed her disgraced honor by making the ultimate sacrifices: giving up her son to his father and taking her own life. In a specially designed kimono with very large, beautifully colored sleeves, Albanese was in fact a butterfly, fluttering—but not melodramatically—until the moment there was no life remaining. She appeared to respond to the offstage voice of Pinkerton calling her name while at the same time making it clear that the temporal world was fast sliding away from her and that the voice might actually be one summoning her to the next plane—an altogether remarkable achievement.

Albanese was the fifth of seven children in a close-knit southern Italian family, all of whom had good voices. She was the one with ambition, instinct, and passion, and she began to study singing in her teens. She flourished under the tutelage of Giuseppina Baldassare-Tedeschi in Milan and at twenty-two won the first Italian government-sponsored vocal competition over three hundred other entrants. Her initial operatic appearance (Teatro Lirico, Milan, 1934, as an emergency substitute) and her "official" debut (Parma, 1935) were as Butterfly. She was soon

a

OPERA

championed by such artists as Gigli (who requested her for Mimì when he was about to record *La bohème*) and Muzio, whom she succeeded as Italy's principal interpreter of the title role of Refice's *Cecilia*. In the first five years of her career, Albanese sang at Teatro alla Scala, Covent Garden (debut 1937, Liù), and the Rome Opera, while working regularly in smaller houses in order to perfect her repertory. She went as far as to sing Elsa in *Lohengrin* at Modena but learned that Wagner, even in Italian, was not for her.

In 1939, when a number of distinguished Italian artists left New York for Italy to fulfill their engagements at the Teatro alla Scala, unaware that Mussolini would forbid them to leave the country again, Albanese went in the opposite direction. Seeking a career in America, she managed to get herself to Portugal and onto a boat for the United States, armed only with the enthusiasm of youth and her great talent.

Almost from the moment of her American debut at the Metropolitan (9 February 1940, again as Cio-Cio-San) a special rapport existed between her and the New York public. Despite the fact that this was the Metropolitan's 246th performance of *Madama Butterfly*, Albanese was only the third Italian soprano to perform the part with the company (and her two predecessors, Claudia Muzio and Augusta Oltrabella, had only sung it once each). Albanese struck an authentic chord not previously touched, and no singer ever became more beloved by the Italian-American opera audience. She endured until the closing of the old Metropolitan Opera House in 1966 in spite of the fact that her bright, penetrating, emotionally charged voice, with its strong top, was not really large enough to fill that huge theater as historically great voices have done. Albanese nonetheless made her points unequivocally, with the most detailed and nuanced artistry, and her most delicate moments registered clearly. Although remembered most vividly for her Puccini heroines and her Toscanini-endorsed Violetta, she also loved to sing Mozart, and brought a Mediterranean warmth and piquancy to his operas that was quite beyond the "Viennese School" singers.

Through the Puccini Foundation, begun with her late husband, Joseph Gimma, Albanese works tirelessly for the furtherance of those artistic values she considers indispensable to the survival of opera as an art form. In 1985 and 1987 she stepped out of retirement to enjoy a personal triumph in New York and Houston revivals of Sondheim's *Follies,* singing "One More Kiss" with prodigal tone and definitive understanding.—BRUCE BURROUGHS

Albani, Emma (born Marie Louise Cécile Lajeunesse)

Soprano. Born 1 November 1847 in Chambly, near Montreal. Died 3 April 1930. In 1878 married impresario Ernest Gye, who became lessee of Covent Garden after his father's death. Educated at Couvent du Sacré-Coeur at Montreal; soloist at St Joseph's Church in Albany, New York; in 1868 she began lessons with Duprez in Paris; in 1870 she studied in Milan with Francesco Lamperti, who dedicated his treatise on the trill to her; professional debut at Messina as Amina in Bellini's La sonnambula *in 1870; debut at Covent Garden on 2 April 1872, where she continued to sing until 1896; debut at Metropolitan Opera as Gilda in 1891; farewell concert at Albert Hall, 1911; premieres include Elgar's* The Apostles *and* St Elizabeth*; Dame Commander of the Order of the British Empire June 1925.*

The first Canadian performer to achieve an international reputation, Emma Albani became one of the most acclaimed divas of the late nineteenth century. In a career that spanned four decades, she sang more than forty operatic roles of remarkable stylistic diversity.

In her autobiography, *Forty Years of Song,* Albani attributed her celebrated facility for assimilating music to her early training with her father. Under his strict tutelage, she became a proficient composer, pianist, organist and harpist as well as singer. Her position as soprano soloist, organist and choir director at St. Joseph's church in Albany, NY (1865-1868) further contributed to her highly developed general musicianship. She traveled to Europe in 1868 where her teachers included Gilbert-Louis Duprez in Paris and Francesco Lamperti in Milan. The latter in particular was an important mentor, and she always subscribed to the "Lamperti method."

Her highly successful debut as Amina in Bellini's *La sonnambula* (Messina, 1870) marked the beginning of her public career. It was at this time that she assumed her stage name of Albani. In 1872, she repeated the role of Amina for her debut at Covent Garden in London. The critic for the *Musical Times* (May 1872) recognized the presence of "a genuine soprano voice, a facile and unexaggerated execution, and a remarkable power of *sostenuto* in the higher part of her register." These characteristics continued to earn critics' admiration; her natural and ingenuous stage manner also won the devotion of audiences, and even of royalty (she was a personal favorite of Queen Victoria). In 1878, she married Ernest Gye, who had just taken over from his father the position of manager of Covent Garden.

While continuing to sing at Covent Garden almost every season until 1896, Emma Albani also performed in many other countries, including France, Russia, Germany, the United States (where she sang several times at the Metropolitan Opera), and her native country, Canada. Her success as an opera diva was matched by her fame as a singer of oratorios and cantatas; for many years she sang to great acclaim at the English festivals. After retiring from the opera stage near the end of the century, she continued to tour and perform until 1911, when she gave her farewell recital at the Royal Albert Hall in London. Her final years, clouded by financial strain, were spent teaching and even singing in music halls. In recognition of her contribution to British music, she was made a Dame Commander of the British Empire in 1925.

Albani's vocal style changed significantly in the course of her career. Her earliest roles—such as Amina (*La sonnambula*), Lucia (*Lucia di Lammermoor*) and Elvira (*I puritani*)—required a light coloratura, but in the mid 1870s she expanded her repertoire to include the more dramatic vocal roles of Wagnerian opera. Always a believer in thor-

Emma Albani (Culver Pictures)

ough preparation, she traveled to Germany to study the methods and practices of German opera with the conductor and coach, Franz Wüllner. She became especially celebrated for her interpretation of Wagner; one of her last great triumphs was a performance of *Tristan und Isolde* with Jean and Edouard de Reszke (1896).

The noted critic Herman Klein commented dispassionately and at some length on Albani's 1874 performance in *Lucia di Lammermoor,* observing that: "Her voice, a soprano of considerable range, with fine notes in the head register, was then clear and resonant if somewhat thin in timbre; perhaps more remarkable for its flexibility and a remarkable *sostenuto* (due to perfect breath-control) than for that peculiar sweetness and charm which haunts the ear. Neither then nor subsequently was there much power in the chest and lower medium notes."

The only known recordings of Albani's voice to survive are a handful of pieces recorded on wax cylinder in the first years of this century, some of which have been reissued. Keeping in mind that these date from the end of her career when she was in her late fifties, the recordings show a very clear voice, with great agility and a delicate *mezza voce.* They can only hint at the qualities that made her one of the most distinguished singers of her time.—JOAN BACKUS

Albert Herring

Composer: *Benjamin Britten.*

Librettist: *Eric Crozier (after Maupassant).*

First Performance: *Glyndebourne, 20 June 1947.*

Roles: *Lady Billows (soprano); Florence Pike (contralto); Miss Wordsworth (soprano); Mr. Gedge (baritone); Mr. Upfold (tenor); Superintendent Budd (bass); Sid (baritone); Albert Herring (tenor); Nancy (mezzo-soprano); Mrs. Herring (mezzo-soprano); Emmie (soprano); Cis (soprano); Harry (boy soprano).*

The life expectancy of comic operas is appallingly brief. Few outlive their composers. The effervescent tunes soon go flat (even if the singers stay on pitch), and the porous characters turn stale after an airing or two. To survive, comedy needs more than bubbles and yeast. If the characters are necessarily shallow, their postures and reactions must ring true. Some vicariously fulfill our egoistic wishes suppressed by mores and conventions. Don Giovanni, Figaro, Dr. Dulcamara, Falstaff, and Gianni Schicchi all live by their wits and do as they please, propriety be damned.

The hero of *Albert Herring* could hardly match wits with this rogues gallery. Feckless and obtuse, he nonetheless has his way in the end, subverting his mother's will and shocking the village dignitaries. Benjamin Britten and his librettist Eric Crozier caricature Albert's adversaries while satirizing puritanism, Victorian music and manners, operatic clichés, ceremonious busybodies, and anything decorously British. Irony is their ultimate weapon, and with it they impugn formality and expose hypocrisy. Britten especially delights in piercing the flatulent rhetoric of high-minded prigs with musical absurdities until their despotic pronouncements dwindle to flurries of self-righteous indignation. Unburdened and unimpressed, Albert walks away from them and the town of Loxford a free man.

In conceiving the libretto for *Albert Herring,* Crozier transplanted Maupassant's story "Le Rosier de Madame Husson" to Loxford (close to Britten's home in Aldeburgh), gave it a lighthearted ending, and Anglified everyone and everything. In act I, the imperious Lady Billows and a committee of distinguished citizens are attempting to select a virtuous girl as Loxford's Queen of the May. Several names are advanced, but none of the candidates meets Lady Billows' rigorous standards. Finally the Police Superintendent suggests a King of the May instead, and nominates Albert Herring, a young man with no vices, whose mother shelters and dominates him. Despite initial misgivings, Lady Billows enthusiastically endorses this modest proposal.

Scene ii shows us Albert tending his mother's grocery shop. The action contrasts him with the butcher's boy Sid, his girlfriend Nancy, and three rambunctious children who swipe fruit behind Albert's back. All accentuate the servile young man's stifled and joyless life. Abstemious, scrupulous, and lonely, Albert wonders why he alone has no fun. When the May Day delegation arrives to tell Albert how they plan to honor him, his mother is at first skeptical, but approves wholeheartedly after learning that the crown comes with twenty-five pounds from Lady Billows. Albert demurs, however, incurring his mother's wrath. Affronted by his protests and calling him ungrateful, "Mum" forcibly sends Albert to bed as the onlooking children taunt him in song.

As the second act curtain rises, the ceremonies are about to begin. In one of the opera's funniest bits, Miss Wordsworth, head teacher at the Church School, rehearses the children in a song of praise she has composed for King Albert. Sid furtively spikes Albert's glass of lemonade with rum. Finally King Albert himself arrives wearing a white suit and a crown of orange blossoms. To the copious speeches and presentations, he flatly responds, "Thank you very much." His loyal subjects acclaim him nonetheless, but Albert has a sudden attack of hiccups, prompting gratuitous remedies from all sides until Lady Billows bids the celebrants get on with the feast. Albert, meanwhile, upon witnessing an intimate scene between Sid and Nancy, decides to go in search of romance himself.

The next afternoon (act III), everyone is searching for Albert under the disgruntled Superintendent's direction. Already grieving for her son, "Mum" faints when Albert's crown is retrieved from a well. This unpropitious discovery inspires a threnodic ensemble climaxed by Albert's timely or untimely return. After a little grilling, he tells his astounded mourners that he has been out all night drinking, and has spent three pounds of the prize money. Scandalized, the upright citizens stalk out, and "Mum" retreats upstairs in near hysterics. Cheered on by Nancy, Sid, and the children, Albert sails the remains of his crown out over the heads of the audience.

Britten composed *Albert Herring* for the newly formed English Opera Group as a companion piece to *The Rape of Lucretia*. Like its predecessor, it is a chamber opera with an orchestra of single strings including harp, single woodwinds, one horn, and a versatile percussionist. There is no chorus. The conductor accompanies the recitatives on a piano. Although the more conventional scoring sometimes begs for a larger ensemble, it interchanges with more resourceful color schemes better suited to the small instrumental forces.

Like Schubert, Britten had a keen ear for adroitly applying inventive harmony. He also matched Debussy's skill in linking melodic fragments of disparate tonality. His style is at once practiced and original, protean but carefully pruned. The reticular vocal ensembles demand absolute precision, though some are intentionally jumbled to produce the "cocktail party effect."

Albert Herring is unpretentious entertainment about pretentious people. Its bland, humorless protagonist escapes Loxford's hyperbolic populace, leaving the provincial luminaries to spout platitudes and venerate banalities. Britten, however, broadened the parody to include opera itself, a genre long encumbered by conventions and affectations. Like Albert, the

a OPERA

composer went his own way, taking English opera with him. Pedantic thunder resounded from Loxford to Covent Garden, but he never looked back.—JAMES ALLEN FELDMAN

Alda, Frances

Soprano. Born 31 May 1879, in Christchurch, New Zealand. Died 18 September 1952, in Venice. Married Giulio Gatti-Casazza, manager of the Metropolitan Opera, in 1910 (divorced in 1928). Studied with Mathilde Marchesi in Paris; debut as Manon at Opéra-Comique in Paris, 1904; appearances at Brussels, 1905-08, Covent Garden, 1906, and Teatro alla Scala, 1908; debut as Gilda at the Metropolitan Opera, where she sang more than 250 performances until 1930; premiered Damrosch's Cyrano *(1913) as Roxanne, Herbert's* Madeleine *(1914), and Hadley's* Cleopatra's Night *(1920); also appeared in Buenos Aires, Boston, and Chicago.*

It was Alda's misfortune to sing at the Metropolitan Opera during what can be seen in hindsight as a golden age of sopranos. Lacking the charisma (and American birth) which made Geraldine Farrar a superstar, too outspoken and acerbic to win the hearts of colleagues and critics, and handicapped in her career by her ill-advised marriage to the Metropolitan's General Manager, Giulio Gatti-Casazza, Alda had to work harder than most to maintain her position. Her success was a tribute to her fighting qualities and to the genuineness of her talent.

Frances Alda (Culver Pictures)

That Alda deserves to rank amongst the leading lyric sopranos of her day is attested by some 130 gramophone recordings which she made for the Victor Company between 1909 and 1928. These show her clean attack and elegant line, and the sheer beauty of her voice. To quote J.B. Steane in *The Grand Tradition* (London, 1974), "she is probably the most consistently satisfying lyric soprano on pre-electrical records."

The most immediately notable aspect of Alda's recordings is her scrupulous attention to matters of rhythm, intonation and phrasing. She was undoubtedly better schooled in musicianship than many of her colleagues. Born into one of Australia's most notable operatic families, she was thoroughly grounded in piano and violin before she ever had a singing lesson. Her technical security and beautiful head tones were largely the product of her studies with Mathilde Marchesi prior to her European debut in 1904. Also characteristic of the Marchesi schooling is her forward voice production; she uses a tremendous amount of head resonance, and deliberately brightens her vowels to assist in this. At times the process adversely affects her diction, as in the charming recording of "A Perfect Day" from Victor Herbert's *Madeleine,* in which the word 'day' emerges as 'dee' throughout. On the other hand, few sopranos of any era can match the clean, clear figuration, free of intrusive aspirates, which she displays in negotiating the difficulties of "L'altra notte" from Boito's *Mefistofele.* Made in 1920, this was one of her own favorite recordings.

Another fine example of her art is "Ah, dunque" from Catalani's *Loreley,* where her technical security and excellent intonation in an aria beset with awkward intervallic leaps excites admiration. The recording is one of many which display her particularly close and precise trills. As a performance, "Ah, dunque" is amongst her most passionate. However, musical feeling rather than passion is the hall-mark of her interpretations. While her private life was colorful, on stage and on record she excelled in portraying lyrical, gentle, and often doomed heroines. Mimì in *La bohème* was her favourite. She sang the role at the Metropolitan more often than any other soprano, partnering all the leading tenors of her day—from Caruso to Gigli.

Desdemona in Verdi's *Otello,* Massenet's Manon and Puccini's Manon Lescaut, Marguerite in Gounod's *Faust,* Lady Harriet in *Martha,* and Nannetta in Verdi's *Falstaff* were other roles in which she made her mark. Her recordings of excerpts from Puccini's *Madama Butterfly* show that she was equally suited to that role, but opportunities to sing it were denied her once she moved to America. The lyricism of Micaela's aria (*Carmen*) and Lauretta's "O mio babbino caro" (*Gianni Schicchi*) fall naturally within her compass, and in recordings of both she displays a lovely warmth of tone allied to tasteful restraint. By applying the same care to popular music as she did to the finest operatic arias, she lent distinction to her many recordings of ballads and other lighter repertoire.

The modern listener needs to make few stylistic concessions in listening to an Alda recording. She generally concentrates on singing the notes the composer wrote, while emotional tricks, such as over-indulgence in portamento, are foreign to her style. Alda was an early advocate of radio broadcasting, which she described as "the greatest medium the world has ever seen for disseminating culture, particularly musical culture." She also felt that the movies were the only medium in which one would ever be able to see perfect operatic productions. In 1937 Alda completed her autobiography, *Men, Women and Tenors,* which is notable for its lively style and forthright views on contemporary singers and singing.—ADRIENNE SIMPSON

Allen, Thomas

Baritone. Born 10 September 1944 in Seaham Harbour, County Durham, England. Married Margaret Holley, 1968 (one son). Studied at the Royal College of Music, London, 1964-8; professional debut at the Welsh National Opera as Figaro in Il barbiere di Siviglia, *1969; Covent Garden debut as Donald in* Billy Budd *in 1971 and joined company the following year; appeared at Glyndebourne as Papageno in* Die Zauberflöte *in 1973, returned as Figaro in 1974, Guglielmo in 1975 and Don Giovanni in 1977; created role of count in Musgrave's* The Voice of Ariadne *at 1974 Aldeburgh Festival; Metropolitan Opera debut as Papageno, 1981; appeared at Salzburg in* Il ritorno d'Ulisse, *1985; in English National Opera's production of Busoni's* Doktor Faust, *London Coliseum, 1986.*

Hailed by the *Guardian* as the best English baritone of his day, Thomas Allen reached fame in his mid-twenties with his portrayal for the Welsh National Opera of Figaro in Rossini's *Il barbiere di Siviglia*. His musicianship, vocal elegance and flexibility were never in doubt, and after taking on this buffo role he also quickly proved his further range as a singing actor by playing such Mozart roles as the Count in *Le nozze di Figaro*, the officer-lover Guglielmo in *Così fan tutte* and the simple bird-catcher Papageno in *Die Zauberflöte*. His good looks and stage presence also made a considerable impression as Britten's handsome, doomed, young sailor in *Billy Budd* in a production by the same company that helped to make him the best interpreter of this demanding role for nearly two decades. In fact, Allen appeared as Budd in the late 1980s for English National Opera and BBC Television when he was already in his forties, admitting with some humor that soon he would have to give it up on account of his age alone.

At Covent Garden from 1971, Allen widened his experience by singing some supporting roles such as the politician Paolo Albiani in Verdi's *Simon Boccanegra* and the musician Schaunard in Puccini's *La bohème,* and he brought the same sense of good natured comedy to the role of Marcello, the hero Rodolfo's other artist friend in the same opera. He was a vivid soldier and would-be lover as Belcore in Donizetti's *L'elisir d'amore*. His experience as Mozart's Count Almaviva, a more complex character and a mature man, must have stood him in good stead when he took on the challenging Mozart role of Don Giovanni in 1977 for Glyndebourne. It was also in the 1970s and at another British venue, Benjamin Britten's Aldeburgh, that he proved again his ability to convince in new music when he created the role of the Count in Thea Musgrave's *The Voice of Ariadne*. He played the cynical but perhaps likable apothecary Ned Keene in the Philips recording of Britten's *Peter Grimes* that was made in the late 1970s; perhaps he thought himself (or was thought) unsuitable to take the older role of Captain Balstrode.

Thomas Allen possesses both vocal flexibility and an alert stage personality. Together these have given him a wide range, and made him good casting in operetta, for example Johann Strauss's *Die Fledermaus* at the New York Metropolitan Opera. As he approaches fifty, he seems to be concentrating on character roles such as Mozart's Count and Don Giovanni, and he has also sung the Count in Strauss's *Capriccio*, Faust in Busoni's *Doktor Faust* and the Forester in Janáček's *The Cunning Little Vixen*. This latter performance was recorded (EMI), and besides Mozart's Almaviva and Don Giovanni he has also recorded his portrayals of the somewhat unsympathetic Onegin in Tchaikovsky's *Eugene Onegin,* the heroine's brother Valentin in Gounod's *Faust,* the hero's friend Albert in Massenet's *Werther,* the unhappy, guilt-ridden Orestes in Gluck's *Iphigénie en Tauride* and Prince Hector in Tippett's *King Priam.*

Although it might be a disappointment to Thomas Allen that his baritone range largely prohibits him from playing strictly Romantic roles, he has nonetheless championed much of the Romantic repertory. He has appeared as Strauss's wealthy and idealistic "Croatian landowner" Mandryka in *Arabella,* and, being capable of a high baritone register, as Debussy's doomed young hero Pelléas in *Pelléas et Mélisande.* Allen has also played the Trojan Prince Aeneas in Purcell's *Dido and Aeneas,* but though this is nominally a romantic lead, the role is quite small and dramatically unsatisfying. Allen sang it opposite Jessye Norman in a recorded performance conducted for Philips by Raymond Leppard and brought to the vacillating Prince a touching quality of flawed nobility. He was no less dignified as yet another Prince, the romantic widower Andrei in Prokofiev's *War and Peace.* His vocal finesse has also allowed him to succeed as a lieder singer and in oratorio, and here too his recorded repertory is wide-ranging.—CHRISTOPHER HEADINGTON

Alva, Luigi (born Luis Ernesto Alva Talledo)

Tenor. Born 10 April 1927, in Lima, Peru. Studied with Rosa Morales in Lima, with Emilio Ghirardini in Milan and with Ettore Campogalliani; opera debut in I pagliacci *in Lima, 1950; European debut at Teatro Nuovo in Milan as Alfredo, 1954; sang Paolino in* Il matrimonio segreto *at the opening of Piccola Scala in Milan, 1955; debut at Teatro alla Scala as Almaviva, 1956; debut at Salzburg, 1957; debut at Covent Garden, 1960; debut as Fenton at the Metropolitan Opera, 1964, where he sang more than 80 performances in 8 roles until 1976; also sang in Chicago, Glyndebourne, Edinburgh, Vienna.*

Few singers have been able to match the cheerfulness, delicacy and gentle melancholy that Luigi Alva brought to his performances of leading tenor roles in late eighteenth- and early nineteenth-century comic opera. Alva was a lyric tenor of great musicality and sweetness of voice—characteristics he shared with his contemporary Peter Schreier. Although Alva did not have Schreier's vocal power and dramatic urgency, he often surpassed his German colleague in the warmth and charm of his interpretions and in the pure beauty of his voice. Like Schreier, Alva specialized in Mozart; but the Mozart operas represented an exception for both singers: Alva's repertory was mostly limited to the works of Italian composers while Schreier limited himself primarily to operas in German.

Early in his career Alva revealed his talents in a memorable portrayal of Paulino, the secret newly-wed in Cimarosa's *Il matrimonio segreto*. Near the end of his career he returned to the role with as much success as earlier. Although this reflects well on Alva's strength, it also suggests that he was not the type of singer-actor who could easily develop new repertory and new kinds of characters to portray as he got older. He sang young, rather innocent lovers throughout his career, never making a full transition to more mature tenor roles such as Mozart's Idomeneo.

Alva's interpretations of Rossini's young romantic leads won him great applause through-out his career. In a recording of *Il barbiere di Siviglia* under Abbado we can hear Alva's Almaviva. The voice is light and clear, sometimes (especially in dialogue and ensembles, when Alva is not trying to project his voice) with a distinctly (and perhaps to some listeners annoyingly) boyish quality. He rarely strains his voice: his high notes are strong without being forced. He spins out strands of coloratura with ease and grace, although his tendency to aspirate each syllable in runs might strike some listeners as mincing and effeminate. As Lindoro in *L'italiana in Algeri,* recorded under Silvio Varviso, Alva projects much the same character as he does in *Il barbiere:* he is the same gentle, young lover. In the big aria "Languir per una bella" Alva's excellent breath control allows him to stretch out the opening slow melody to wonderful effect. He attacks the many high B-flats in the fast section with confidence and conquers them with rich, full-blooded tones. This is splendid, virile singing; this is Alva at his lyric best.

Although he is primarily remembered today as an interpreter of Mozart and Rossini, Alva's repertory was considerably more diverse than that. His performance of the role of Oronte in Handel's *Alcina* (as recorded under Bonynge) makes one wish that he had devoted more attention to Baroque opera. He is a spirited Handel singer, bringing to arias like "Semplicetto! a donna credi?" and "È un folle" a strong sense of character, vividly conveying each aria's meaning to the listener.—JOHN A. RICE

Amahl and the Night Visitors

Composer: *Gian Carlo Menotti.*

Librettist: *Gian Carlo Menotti.*

First Performance: *National Broadcasting Company, 24 December 1951; stage premiere, Bloomington, Indiana, 21 February 1952.*

Roles: *Amahl (soprano); His Mother (mezzo-soprano); King Kaspar (tenor); King Melchior (baritone); King Balthazar (bass); Page (bass); chorus (SATB).*

Menotti calls *Amahl and the Night Visitors* "an opera for children, because it tries to capture my own childhood." Having agreed to write the first opera ever commissioned for television, Menotti drew upon memories of happy childhood Christmases which were triggered by a chance encounter with Hieronymus Bosch's painting, *The Adoration of the Magi,* in New York's Metropolitan Museum of Art. The score and libretto arose instinctively and remained mostly free of alterations, as if the composer himself recognized that it could not be bettered. The original orchestral score bears not only Menotti's handwriting but also that of Samuel Barber, who had to assist in readying the work for rehearsals and the impending premiere.

A crippled boy who plays his shepherd's pipe and is possessed of a grand imagination, Amahl lives with his mother in a hut amid great poverty. The Three Kings, following the Star to find the Christ Child, knock at the door, seeking a brief rest on their way. When the Mother can finally be persuaded that Amahl is not spinning another foolish tale, she welcomes the Kings, and soon afterward the neighboring shepherds appear, singing and carrying baskets of fruit and vegetables, from which they present gifts to the visitors. Encouraged by the Mother to dance for the guests, the shepherds shyly begin a faltering folk dance that moves with increasing confidence from *lento, ma non troppo* to a whirling, excited *tarantella,* with music extracted from a string quartet Menotti wrote as a young student. When the neighbors leave, everyone is soon asleep, except for the Mother, who sings the only aria in the opera, a soliloquy reflecting on how she could help her son with just a piece of "all that gold." As she reaches for the gold, the aroused Page seizes the Mother, whereupon Amahl in great distress rises at once to her defense and tries to beat off the Page with his crutch. King Melchior tells the Mother she may keep the gold, for "the Child we seek doesn't need [it] . . . On love alone He will build His kingdom." The Mother sinks to her knees in tears, and wishes she could afford to send a gift of her own. Amahl breaks in and offers his hand-made crutch as a present to the Christ Child. Eagerly lifting the crutch, he steps toward the Kings, and in a dramatic hush, they all realize that he is walking without it for the first time. The Kings are awed by this "sign from the Holy Child," and when the procession departs, Amahl goes with them, to take his gift personally to the Child.

Amahl and The Night Visitors immediately became a classic among music for the Christmas season. Translated into more than twenty languages, it remains Menotti's most popular work, and the most frequently performed. The starkly simple stage requirements and modest instrumentation provide a wide choice of locale in which to perform it; Menotti chose to think of "a stage within a stage," and ignored the unique capabilities of television. With repeated melodic motives and the use of major triads at emotional climaxes, the unified elements of music and libretto produce in this work a strong emotional response that is by no means confined to children.—JEAN C. SLOOP

Anders, Peter

a **OPERA**

Tenor. Born 1 July 1908, in Essen. Died 10 September 1954, in Hamburg. Studied with Grenzenbach and Lula Mysz-Gmeiner in Berlin; in chorus of Reinhardt's La Belle Hélène in 1931; engaged at Heidelberg, 1932; Darmstadt, 1933-34; Cologne, 1935-36; Hanover, 1937-8; Munich, 1938-40; Berlin, 1940-48; Hamburg, 1948-54; sang Tamino at Salzburg, 1943; Bacchus in Ariadne auf Naxos at Edinburgh Festival in 1950; Walther in Die Meistersinger at Covent Garden in 1951.

The era of the 1930s and 40s may justly be regarded as a golden age of the German lyric tenor. The period also coincided with the development of the electrical recording process and produced an embarassment of riches that has served record collectors handsomely. Through the recording medium names like Richard Tauber, Julius Patzak, Helge Roswaenge, Josef Schmidt, Walther Ludwig, Herbert Ernst Groh and Marcel Wittrisch became famous throughout the world as exponents of opera, operetta and German Lied. The list would not be complete without the name of Peter Anders.

Anders made his operatic debut in 1932 in Heidelberg. In 1938 the noted conductor Clemens Krauss engaged him for the Munich Opera and subsequently Anders became a principal tenor at the Berlin Staatsoper during the war years. After the war, he sang principally at the Hamburg Opera. In 1950 he appeared at the Edinburgh Festival under Sir Thomas Beecham, who also conducted his Covent Garden appearance the following year as Walther von Stolzing in *Die Meistersinger.*

His earliest recordings date from 1933 for Telefunken, and he continued his association with that label through 1951. He then made a few recordings for Electrola, and his last recordings were issued by Deutsche Grammophon. He is also featured on a number of recordings from Berlin Radio published on Acanta and BASF. He recorded one role in a complete opera set, that of Lionel in *Martha*. At present two CDs are available, one on Electrola and one on Acanta.

His repertoire, typical of the German tenors of his generation, was wide ranging— German opera from Mozart to Wagner, Italian opera from Donizetti through Verdi to Mascagni and Puccini, operetta and German lied. Like his contemporaries he sang almost exclusively in German, the only exceptions being an "Una furtiva lagrima" and a "Funiculì-funiculà" in Italian. He was a serious and cultivated artist and recorded little from the popular song repertoire.

His early recordings reveal a lyric tenor voice with a distinctive bright, metallic timbre, combined with an excellent technique, faultless intonation and exemplary breath control. He was a dependable singer, always correct and eminently musical. His voice was not particularly flexible, although he manages the long run in "Il mio tesoro" (sung in German) on one breath. He did not have an extreme top range and therefore perhaps unwisely recorded the "Postillion lied" from *Le postillion de Longjumeau* without the climactic high D.

The Telefunken series of recordings are undoubtedly his best. The vocal quality is equalized throughout the range and is always used artistically. He disdained any use of *falsetto;* the vocal quality ranged from a pure head voice in soft passages through *mezza-voce,* to a ringing *forte* chest voice. A. G. Ross, writing in *Record News,* notes that Anders "took his Lehar, Millocker and Johann Strauss seriously and treated them with understanding and respect, giving a virile straightforward presentation of these melodies without Schmalz or egotistic virtuosity."

The statement also applies to his operatic recordings, but paradoxically the virtues of his approach to music also reveal its weakness. The drawback is that his singing is mechanical, always musically correct, but lacking a distinctive personality.

Toward the end of his career he attempted the transformation from lyric to dramatic tenor. In his prime his voice was basically lyrico-spinto. Since his life was cut short by an unfortunate automobile accident, it is not possible to know whether or not he would have achieved success as a dramatic tenor. The evidence of his late recordings, however, suggests the possibility of decline. They reveal a loss of focus and evidence of strain in the high notes as well as a forced baritone-like quality in the middle register. The distinctive ease of production of his earlier records has vanished.

On the whole his Electrola recordings are probably his least successful, and unfortunately they have been the ones that have been released on CD. Close miking is a part of the problem, for it emphasizes the strained quality of his singing during this late period. The Deutsche Grammophon recordings are not entirely successful either, although the *Meistersinger* and *Undine* selections come off well.

His consumate musicality served him well in his recordings of Lieder. Like most of his contemporaries, his recordings from the Italian repertoire suffer from the use of the German text, and the exception, the 1944 "Una furtiva lagrima," is not successful. In fact, his 1942 version of the aria in German shows that he is more comfortable in his native language.

Critical evaluation of vocal quality is, of course, entirely subjective. The recordings of Peter Anders, particularly those by Telefunken, will always satisfy those who admire a clear, bright tenor voice used with taste and discernment. But that is also the drawback—they merely satisfy, they do not thrill. What Anders lacks is that spark of individualty and personality, that "egotistic virtuosity," that separates the great singer from the very good one.—BOB ROSE

Anderson, June

Soprano. Born 1955, in Boston. Studied with Robert Leonard, New York. Debut as Queen of the Night with New York Center Opera, 1978; Rome debut as Rossini's Semiramide, 1982; appeared in Verdi's Il corsaro, San Diego, 1982; performed Rossini's Armida at Aix-en Provence and Maometto II in San Francisco, 1988; Metropolitan Opera debut as Gilda in Rigoletto, 1989; has sung at the Teatro alla Scala, Vienna, Rome, Paris, and Chicago.

Born in Boston, Massachusetts, June Anderson graduated from Yale University with a major in French Literature. She studied voice in New York City with Robert Leonard, and made her American debut in 1978 at the New York City Opera singing the Queen of the Night in Mozart's *Die Zauberflöte.* She made several other appearances with the New York City Opera, including Gilda in Verdi's *Rigoletto,* Rosina in Rossini's *Il barbiere di Siviglia,* Elvira in Bellini's *I puritani* and a concert version of Wagner's *Die Feen.* During the 1981-82 season she began to attract considerable critical attention. Theodore W. Libbey, Jr. of the *New York Times,* reviewing Anderson's *I puritani* at the New York City Opera, described her coloratura as "effortless" and with "touching vocal expressiveness." John Rockwell, also of the *New York Times,* reviewing Anderson's performance of Wagner's *Die Feen,* compared her coloratura and agility to that of "an early Anja Silja."

After a number of appearances in the United States, she moved to Italy, where she quickly achieved a series of successful performances which helped to launch her international career. In quick succession, she performed *Semiramide, Lucia di Lammermoor* and *Il barbiere di Siviglia* during the 1982-83 season at the Rome, Florence and Palermo Operas, respectively. Throughout this period she continued to perform in festivals in the United States and Canada.

Her Venice debut in April 1984, in Bellini's *La sonnambula* is particularly noteworthy in that the role of Amina had not been heard in the Teatro Malibran since Maria Malibran herself had sung it in 1835. In her *Opera News* (July 1984) review, Elizabeth Forbes described Anderson's voice as one which combined "flexibility, firmness of line and purity of tone in ideal proportions for this music." She also admired her characterization and "expressive strength."

By her own admission, Anderson has learned to say "no" to offers that do not fit the direction she has chosen for her career, even though this has meant turning down "performances in major places, major theaters with major conductors." This strategy has not seemed to hurt her prospects as she continues to strengthen her hold on the "bel canto" heroines. She recently performed a concert version of Rossini's *Semiramide* at Covent Garden with Marilyn Horne and Samuel Ramey.

Among her recordings are some unusual and less well-known works, such as Rossini's *Mosè in Egitto* and *Maometto Secondo* for Philips, Wagner's *Die Feen* for Orfeo and Bizet's *La jolie fille de Perth* with Alfredo Kraus for EMI/Angel. Her disc "Live from the Paris Opera," with Alfredo Kraus, contains a stunning version of "Bel raggio lusinghier" from Rossini's *Semiramide* which is, to date, the most representative recorded example of her ability and formidable talent.—PATRICIA ROBERTSON

Anderson, Marian

Contralto. Born 17 February 1902, in Philadelphia. Died 8 April 1993, in Portland, Oregon, from complications of a stroke. Studied with Giuseppe Boghetti in New York. First African-American soloist to appear in a major role at the Metropolitan Opera, as Ulrica in Un ballo in maschera, *1955; retired 1965; primarily known as a concert artist.*

When Marian Anderson returned to the United States for the 1935-36 concert season after her successful European tour, Olin Downes (*NYT,* 1/21/36) acclaimed her as "a born singer and a very sincere and thoughtful musician . . . She is a person of natural dignity and distinction . . . distinction, intelligence and taste are invariably reflected in her singing. The voice is a rare one, a deep contralto, rich in color and of a sensuous quality, save in the upper tones, which have a measure of nasality not displeasing . . . The middle register is best developed of all. The lowest octave has depth and beauty which haunt the ear and the memory." Downes lauded her artistic integrity: "[Miss Anderson] never distorts a rhythm or the contour of a phrase and is fortunately far from that type which stresses a high note or hangs on some advantageous effect in order to arouse the audience. It is not necessary for Miss Anderson so to attempt to arouse an audience, and she would not dream of doing so. She has palpably a real knowledge of her score in all its details, a fine control of breath, a knowledge of the laws of singing."

Noel Straus (*NYT,* 4/13/37) concurred with Downes, crediting Anderson with "the humbleness of spirit and unaffected simplicity which seem invariably to accompany greatness in

**Marian Anderson as Ulrica in *Un ballo in maschera*,
Metropolitan Opera, New York, 1955**

any field of endeavor." At Carnegie Hall in 1937, he found that "the effect of her work was heightened by the sincerity and directness of her approach. . . . When the contralto employed mezzavoce in sustained passages . . . her singing was at its best. When used at its full power, the voice was less perfectly produced, often losing that perfection of sound which marked it in softer work. But as interpreter, Miss Anderson was ever impressive, whatever the mood and content of the selection."

Throughout her career, Anderson continued to impress critics by not allowing her extraordinary success to lead her into complacency. "The expressive capacities of her voice are constantly expanding," Downes wrote in 1939 (*NYT,* 1/7/39), "and she is becoming always more skilled in employing it for purposes of dramatic interpretation. . . . Miss Anderson can bridge registers and blend the tone of one into the other when that is her purpose. At the same time the dark color of the low octave and the degree of reediness which occurs higher up represent only two of the natural tone colors which are at her disposal. Add to this her control and reserve of breath, and the quality, always vibrant and emotional of the voice itself. It has been developed . . . by the most serious and thoughtful work." Likewise Howard Taubman in 1942 (*NYT,* 1/6/42): "Marian Anderson's art grows deeper and richer with the years, even though the voice has not quite the magnificent lustre of half a dozen years ago . . . [She] sings with more restraint now, and with even greater variety of color effects. She can still let the voice out in stirring climaxes, but she saves these properly for big moments."

In addition to artistic and dramatic sincerity, the concert presentation of spirituals became an Anderson trademark. Again, Olin Downes commented that "Miss Anderson sings music by classic masters not as a lesson learned, or a duty carefully performed, but as an interpreter who has fully grasped and deeply felt the import of the song. When she interprets . . . Negro spirituals, she invests them with extraordinary distinction . . . One would not call this mere singing in the folk manner. The old folksongs were re-interpreted by an artist with special gifts that served to heighten and make the more complete expression of the things which had inspired the unknown composer of the melody."

Both Taubman and Downes expressed some disappointment, however, when Anderson ventured beyond Lieder and spirituals. "She is at her greatest in songs of profound compassion and soaring ecstasy; she can also manage a light, lyrical song with grace and sweetness"; but "when she tackles an operatic aria she leaves something to be desired," wrote Taubman. On the occasion of an appearance with the Philharmonic Orchestra in 1946, Downes (*NYT,* 4/5/46) conceded that "it may be that Miss Anderson is a singer primarily for the recital platform. Her rich voice fascinated the ear; her musicianship and her sincerity were unquestionable, but she sang apparently with constraint and inhibitory caution with the orchestra. No one would accuse her of musical misrepresentation, but the conviction as well as the mastery of nuance which is hers when she is accompanied by a piano was rather lost in the orchestral shuffle." Of course, because of limited operatic opportunities for African-American artists prior to her celebrated Metropolitan Opera debut in 1955, the solo recital platform was in fact her primary venue during the height of her concertizing years—it is not surprising that the more large-scale performances reflected a lack of experience.

Anderson's debut at the Met elicited a storm of praise, but also criticism at the tardiness of the event. "[The engagement] comes late—at least 15 years late. Miss Anderson's beautiful voice is not now in its prime" (Downes, *NYT* 10/17/54); "it would have been even happier as the tenth anniversary of an honor she richly merited long before, when she had vocal youth on her side as well as artistic experience" (Irving Kolodin, *Saturday Review,* 1/22/55); the performance "was long overdue, not only as far as the Metropolitan was concerned but also as far as Miss Anderson herself was concerned. And because of this I found the evening an occasion for sadness as well as rejoicing. Miss Anderson's voice—once so lovely, limpid, and unforgettably evocative—is far past its prime . . . She showed, understandably, considerable nervousness . . . and even when this initial nervousness had worn off, she failed to produce the brilliant result that the historic event seemed to demand. The audience gave her a thundering ovation, but I'm afraid that its applause was for the principle of the thing, and not for the specific artistic contribution she made. Her voice was unexpectedly small and tremulous in the vast spaces of the Metropolitan, and her stage personality . . . was timid and lacking in authority. The event should have occurred years before; coming at this time, it was hardly more than a gesture" (Winthrop Sargeant, *New Yorker,* 1/15/55).

Ronald Eyer (*Musical America,* 1/15/55), on the other hand, was thoroughly impressed by Anderson's Metropolitan Opera performance. "The contralto was a little unsettled at the beginning . . . but the powerful controls of a great and long-experienced artist took hold and she was singing with all her accustomed security, richness and warmth of tone and innate musicianship. Particularly notable was her contribution to the exacting quintet at the end of the act. Notable, too, was the deep penetration of the text, the meaning of the words given her to sing. For all the attention she gave to mood, inflection and tone coloration, she might have been singing the subtlest of lieder." Finally, Olin Downes again, who had followed Anderson's career for two decades: "there was no moment in which Miss Anderson's interpretation was common-place or repetitive in effect. In Ulrica's one half-act, Miss Anderson stamped herself in the memory and the lasting esteem of those who listened."

Marian Anderson is also renowned as an exemplary humanitarian as well as musician. When she was nominated to the United Nations delegation in 1958, Harold Schonberg wrote about "The Other Voice of Marian Anderson" (*NYT* Mag, 8/10/58) and how "she has always represented something that transcends singing and embraces humanity . . . Bolstered by faith, by a love for people and by a sincere desire to see and understand the other person's point of view . . . she manages to communicate that faith, love and sincerity as much through her meetings with people as through her singing."—KIKO NOBUSAWA

Andrea Chénier

Composer: *Umberto Giordano.*

Librettist: *Luigi Illica.*

First Performance: *Milan, Teatro alla Scala, 28 March 1896.*

Roles: *Maddalena di Coigny (soprano); Chénier (tenor); Carlo Gérard (baritone); Contesse di Coigny (mezzo-soprano); Bersi (mezzo-soprano); Madelon (mezzo-soprano); Pietro Fleville (bass or baritone); Mathieu (baritone); Incredibile (tenor); Roucher (bass or baritone); Majordomo (bass); Fouquier-Tinville (bass or baritone); Schmidt (bass); Abbé (tenor); Dumas (bass); chorus (SSSSAATTBB).*

A report in *Opera* from a 1986 conference in Verona on Umberto Giordano and nineteenth-century *verismo* made the rather surprising point that ninety years after its Teatro alla Scala premiere, *Andrea Chénier* can still, in Italy at least, be the occasion of fiercely partisan controversy rather than the subject of cool critical appraisal. In most other operatic centers Giordano's best known work has, by and large, secured for itself a place in the ongoing repertory, while his other operas, except for an occasional performance of the later *Fedora,* have disappeared. Few critics regard *Andrea Chénier* as an unqualified masterpiece; indeed the then-editor of *Opera,* Harold Rosenthal, questioned the need for Covent Garden's 1983 revival on the grounds that the opera is "contrived." Nevertheless, despite gaps caused by the absence of suitable singers—the work requires three big Italianate voices—most houses now see it as worthy of periodic revival. And indeed, most audiences, untroubled by the critics' reservations, tend to respond enthusiastically to a good performance of the work.

Giordano had written three operas, *Marina, Mala vita,* and *Regina Diaz*—the latter two of which experienced some success—before being offered the libretto for *Andrea Chénier* which Luigi Illica had committed himself to write while still working on the libretto for what was to become Puccini's *La bohème.* Based very approximately on the life of the historical André Chénier, a poet who was first a supporter and then a victim of the French Revolution, the libretto is tautly effective in its condensation of the pertinent action into four acts. The first act, a kind of prelude to the other three, is set in the ballroom of the Comtesse de Coigny in 1789 on the eve of the Revolution. The three primary figures are clearly established: Carlo Gérard, a budding revolutionary but as yet still a servant, who secretly loves the daughter of the household, Maddalena di Coigny; she, in her turn, falls under the spell of one of the guests, the poet Andrea Chénier, when he responds to her challenge to improvise on the theme of *amor* by singing of his love for his country ("*Un dì, all'azzuro spazio*"). The unyielding insensitivity of the idle nobility toward the oppressed poor and the portents of the retribution about to come are vividly depicted. The remaining three acts, set in the Paris of the Reign of Terror five years later, depict Chénier's final days. In act II Chénier succeeds in meeting a mysterious woman who has been writing to him. It is Maddalena, hunted and threatened, sustained and protected only by Bersi, her faithful mulatto servant; she has continued to love Chénier since that first evening in her mother's home. The spy, Incredibile, reports their meeting to Gérard who is also searching for Maddalena; Gérard and Chénier fight, the former is wounded but recognizing Chénier whispers to him to escape because the Tribunal is seeking him. Act III takes place in the court of the Tribunal where Gérard, after initial hesitation, signs the warrant against Chénier, his rival. In a moment of self-disgust, he reflects on the degeneration of his Revolutionary ideals ("*Nemico della patria*"), but when Maddalena appears looking for Chénier who has now been arrested, he reveals his passion for her. She offers herself in exchange for Chénier's safety but, moved by her description of what she has undergone ("*La mamma morta*") and her love for the poet, he tries unsuccessfully to save Chénier from the Tribunal. Awaiting execution in act IV, Chénier sings an apostrophe to spring and new life ("*Come un bel dì di Maggio*"); he is joined by Maddalena, who has bribed a guard to let her change places with a condemned woman. Absorbed totally in each other, singing a magnificently climactic duet ("*Vicino a te*"), they move joyfully towards execution as the sun rises and a new day begins to dawn.

Andrea Chénier, though it is a thoroughly *verismo* work, has little of the earthiness of feeling or setting of the *verismo* prototype, *Cavalleria rusticana* (1890); its mixture of literary Romanticism and overtly passionate lyricism derives more from the example set by *Manon Lescaut* (1893). The characters, the "literary" language, the epoch, the situations all belong to the high Romantic school and are based on the well-worn premise that "*Amor* is all." However, the premise, taken as seriously and absolutely as it is in *Tristan und Isolde,* lacks the philosophical and intellectual strength necessary to give it total conviction. The result is a persuasion, dramatic

a

OPERA

and musical, which never gets beyond the rhetorical; it convinces for the moment but fails to make any lasting effect. Giordano's chief instruments in effecting this persuasion are, first, a cunning sense of pace which structures each act and aria towards an effective climax: and second, a gift for creating passionately lyric outpourings which provide thrilling moments of emotional release for an audience. In *Andrea Chénier* at least, Giordano's gifts rarely fail.—PETER DYSON

Anna Bolena [Anne Boleyn]

Composer: *Gaetano Donizetti.*

Librettist: *Felice Romani (after Pindemone and Pepoli).*

First Performance: *Milan, Carcano, 26 December 1830.*

Roles: *Enrico (bass); Anna (soprano); Giovanna (mezzo-soprano); Ricardo Percy (tenor); Lord Rochefort (bass); Smeton (contralto); Sir Harvey (tenor); chorus (SSATTB).*

In Felice Romani's libretto of *Anna Bolena,* Anna has been supplanted in the affections of Henry VIII (Enrico) by Jane Seymour (Giovanna), her lady-in-waiting. Enrico invites Riccardo Percy to return to court from exile in order to compromise his unwanted wife. Mark Smeaton (Smeton), a page who is in love with Anna, comes to her defense, with the result that all three— Anna, Percy, and Smeton, as well as her brother Lord Rochefort—are imprisoned. Despite

Joan Sutherland and Suzanne Mentzer in *Anna Bolena*, Royal Opera, London, 1988

Giovanna's impassioned attempts to save Anna, a corrupt council of ministers declares the queen guilty of adultery. In the Tower of London Anna recalls her childhood happiness and her adolescent love for Percy. Hearing the tumult of Enrico's marriage to Giovanna in the street outside, she recovers her senses and goes to the block with dignity amid the laments of her ladies.

Anna Bolena not only brought Donizetti his first taste of international fame, but also assembled all the necessary strands of his maturing talent: dramatic flexibility, an instinct for musical eloquence, and a seemingly limitless melodic flow. It marked that moment in the career of the composer when all the ingredients for triumph were at hand.

The year 1830 was a turning-point for Donizetti, but *Anna Bolena* was far from being his first successful opera. Many of the novelties ascribed to *Anna Bolena* had been tried out earlier, most notably in the opera *Imelda de' Lambertazzi* which immediately preceeded it. Donizetti made no sudden stylistic breakthrough; his ascent to mastery was unusually gradual and perfectly deliberate.

The genesis of *Anna Bolena* was long and painful. In collaborating with Felice Romani, Donizetti risked the ire of Bellini, whose star was at its zenith in the wake of several Bellini/Romani scores which had brought the Italian peninsula to a pitch of excitement unknown since Rossini's departure. If Donizetti elected to write an ultra-dramatic opera, he was, in part, avoiding the latter's ultra-lyrical trademarks.

Anna Bolena is also the most important serious opera of Donizetti's early career. In it, he depicts real people instead of the operatic stereotypes familiar to audiences at that time, and for the first time he displays his taste for *"il vero,"* that elusive veracity which obsessed Giuseppe Verdi for the whole of his musical lifetime. It is this quality that raises the emotional temperature of many of Donizetti's subsequent scores, such as *Lucia di Lammermoor* (1835), *Roberto Devereux* (1837), *Le duc d'Albe* (unfinished 1839), and *Maria di Rohan* (1843), all of which transcend the cardboard characters and feeble texts of the day with music of exceptional flair and dramatic insight.

True to the Romantic age, both Romani and Donizetti were increasingly committed to exact portraiture instead of the vague generalizations of their predecessors. In arias like Anna's "Come innocente giovane," when she bursts into Smeton's sentimental ditty, the composer begins to probe a complex personality far more pointedly than ever before in a scene that perhaps is fiction but is dramatically credible. Many of the subsidiary roles, however, remain inert: Percy is a vignette (the usual yelping tenor of Italian opera), Smeton lacks real motivation, and Rochefort scarcely exists. Anna's act II confrontation with Giovanna, however, is magnificently conceived, displaying two fully-rounded portraits. Enrico, though deprived of a showpiece aria, is also brilliantly drawn as the perfect depiction of tyranny, quite repellently true to life.

Anna's final *scena* was recognized to be a major offering on first hearing. Giuditta Pasta, who created the role of Anna, transfixed audiences with this long series of *arie* and *ariosi* punctuated with orchestrally supported recitative. The three sections, the larghetto "Al dolce guidami," the lento "Cielo a'miei lunghi spasimi" (based, perhaps, on what Donizetti thought of as a Sicilian air), and the traumatic cabaletta "Coppia iniqua"—furious, and leaping to the extremes of register in painful anguish too poignant to be borne. This was music which reinvested Italian opera with meaning; *Anna Bolena* not only brought the composer to the

a

OPERA

attention of the world but reasserted the validity of *dramma per musica* once and for all.—ALEXANDER WEATHERSON

Antony and Cleopatra

Composer: *Samuel Barber.*

Librettist: *F. Zeffirelli (after Shakespeare).*

First Performance: *New York, Metropolitan Opera, 16 September 1966; revised, with libretto revisions by C. Menotti, 1975.*

Roles: *Cleopatra (soprano); Antony (bass); Caesar (tenor); Enobarbus (bass); Octavia (soprano); Charmian (mezzo-soprano); Iras (contralto); Dolabella (baritone); Mardian (tenor); Soothsayer (bass); Thidias (tenor or high baritone); Agrippa (bass); Lepidus (tenor); Maecenas (baritone); Eros (tenor); Candidus (baritone); Demetrius (tenor); Scarus (bass); Decretas (bass); A Rustic (baritone or bass); Messenger (tenor); Alexas (bass); Voice offstage (soprano); chorus (SSATB).*

Samuel Barber's opera *Antony and Cleopatra* has achieved notoriety as one of the twentieth century's most heralded, lavish, and expensive operatic failures. Commissioned for the opening of New York City's new Metropolitan Opera House at Lincoln Center for the Performing Arts, the opera was conceived on a grand scale. Its creators undoubtedly aspired to present a work which captured the glamour and magnificence of the new house. They chose their subject well in the entanglement of the exotic, seductive Egyptian queen, Cleopatra, with the power and grandeur of ancient Rome embodied in Marc Antony. Yet *Antony and Cleopatra* fell victim to its own press—it could not hope to meet the inflated expectations of such a hyped audience—and a mismatch of creative talents.

It would not steal from Barber's achievements as a composer to partially attribute the opera's failed reception (and subsequent dearth of productions) to the composer's idiom. Barber, trained as a singer, developed a lyrical style that was well-suited to intimate vocal forms, less well-suited to extended symphonic structures. His language, which used tonal materials in a highly chromatic manner, seems to lack the potential for convincing large-scale dramatic structure that successful operatic writing requires. Dramatic momentum was achieved mostly through lengthy sequential developments, which, through their ubiquity, rapidly descend to mannerism and thus lose expressive power.

The best music of the opera is found when Barber evokes the contrasts between the principal locales of the drama. The opening scene, in which the chorus of Romans chides Antony for his decadence, is marked by skilled contrapuntal invention and harmonic clarity. With its hammered rhythms and furious quality, the scene establishes an energy which, sadly, is not maintained in subsequent scenes. In Cleopatra's first solo scene (act I, scene iii) the music evokes the allure of ancient Egypt through dazzlingly colorful orchestration and sinuous melody. Barber's evocation of the exotic stands in sharp contrast to the stolid, abrupt music of the Romans.

Overall, Barber's skillful orchestration and clear text-setting clarify the action of the libretto compellingly. Thus the weaknesses in the libretto are made more glaringly apparent. Barber's own compositional strengths underscore the opera's weaknesses.

Antony and Cleopatra was extensively revised after its premiere. The currently published score and the recording each reflect the revisions. Franco Zeffirelli, who wrote the first libretto and staged the first production, adapted Shakespeare's play for the operatic stage mostly by cutting characters, switching the sequence of the play's lines, and shrinking and rearranging scenes. This editing was necessary because the extreme length of Shakespeare's play rendered it far too cumbersome even for a full-length grand opera. Zeffirelli maintained Shakespeare's Elizabethan English, causing Barber some consternation; he was afraid that the language would compel him to write in a mannered style. In addition, a huge chorus was added, compromising the intimacy of the web of relationships between the principle characters in the drama.

Menotti's revisions clarify the text considerably, lessen the amount of spectacle, and eliminate many tangential characters, streamlining the cast and clarifying relationships. The action was made more compact, relationships between principal characters strengthened, and crucial lines of the libretto underscored.

Perhaps the most damaging addition to Shakespeare's drama is the central love duet sung by Antony and Cleopatra, "Oh take, oh take those lips away." No such love scene appears in Shakespeare's play; Barber's setting of these words, to a languid and melodramatic tune, colors the scene with shallow emotion and seems more suited to operetta than opera. The first version of the opera lacked a love scene between Antony and Cleopatra, and this omission was felt by many critics to be seriously detrimental to the opera's success. In heeding the advice of his critics Barber weakened the expressive thrust of the work, lowering it to bathos.

Shakespeare's rich language suffers from the librettist's deletions. The characters often speak lines which are cryptic and rhythmically awkward: for example, note Caesar's statement in act I, scene ii, "You have broken/the article of your oath, which you shall never/Have tongue to charge me with." In the absence of a strong text, the composer is forced to rely on surface portrayals of turbulence. In this case, as mentioned above, tension is too often weakly suggested by the use of literal sequences of melodic/harmonic progressions that, being highly chromatic, possess a basic neutrality.

Other composers writing post-tonal opera in the twentieth century have relied on strong associative techniques to convey drama. One need only consider Berg's operas or Bernd Alois Zimmerman's *Die Soldaten* to see that opera can achieve high drama without tonality. Yet in these examples a strong libretto was given, and the composers were willing to utilize expressionistic effects in their orchestrations and vocal writing, stylistic elements that Barber, by nature a conservative, eschewed.

While Barber was a skilled musical craftsman, possessed of a facile and strong technique, long-range structural drama was not his strong suit. While many passages of *Antony and Cleopatra* are engaging, beautifully lyrical and moving in expression, overall the work is not particularly compelling. Perhaps if the libretto had been more engaging Barber's gifts would have served him better.—JONATHAN ELLIOTT

Arabella

Composer: *Richard Strauss.*

Librettist: *Hugo von Hofmannsthal.*

First Performance: *Dresden, Staatsoper, 1 July 1933.*

Roles: *Count Waldner (bass); Adelaide (mezzo-soprano); Arabella (soprano); Zdenka (soprano); Mandryka (baritone); Matteo (tenor); Count Elemer (tenor); Count Dominik (baritone); Count Lamoral (bass); Fiakermilli (soprano); Fortuneteller (soprano); several small roles from chorus; chorus (SATB).*

Arabella was the last opera of the Strauss/Hofmannsthal collaboration. The idea for the opera arose in November 1927, after which events moved quickly. By December 1928 the complete text was in Strauss's hands and, during the spring of 1929, a painstaking revision of act I was satisfactorily accomplished. Sadly, Hofmannsthal never knew how much this had delighted the composer: after his fatal heart attack of July the 15th, 1929, Strauss's congratulatory telegram was discovered, unopened. Hofmannsthal's revised first act is, indeed, a masterpiece of lyric theater offering the composer a musical challenge to which he rose magnificently. It is fashionable to criticize acts II and III, with whose text, in homage to the dead Hofmannsthal, Strauss refused to tamper. In fact, despite a somewhat looser dramatic organization, both acts work very well, giving Strauss openings for some of his most memorable music, including the Arabella/Mandryka meeting, and Arabella's farewell to her suitors in act II, and the marvellous "staircase" music of the final scene of act III.

The opera is set in 1860s Vienna. The Waldners aim to revive their fortunes by marrying off Arabella. Matteo, rejected by Arabella, is loved by her sister, Zdenka, (masquerading as a boy), who falsely encourages his suit with forged letters in her sister's hand. Of Arabella's current suitors, Elemer is the most eligible: time is short, and despite dreams of an attractive stranger she has encountered in the street, Arabella resigns herself to her fate. Now Waldner, to his delight, has an unexpected visitor, Mandryka, nephew of a rich former colleague, who seeks Arabella's hand. The two are introduced at the "Cabbies" ball; Arabella recognizes her stranger and begins to think dreams can come true. Mandryka socializes; she bids farewell to erstwhile suitors. Later, he overhears Zdenka offering Matteo the key to (supposedly) Arabella's room. Outraged, he creates an ugly scene before leaving in search of her. Fresh from his rendezvous (Zdenka has impersonated her sister in the darkness) Matteo is surprised to find Arabella in the hotel lobby. Mandryka enters, and upon seeing them together his suspicions are confirmed. He accuses; she protests. A duel is averted by a repentant (now female-clad) Zdenka, who confesses her guilt. Matteo is charmed. Ashamed, Mandryka intercedes on the lovers' behalf. All save Mandryka retire—Arabella, re-enacting an old Slav custom, descends from her room with a glass of water; he drinks exultantly before smashing the glass to seal their betrothal.

After a critically chequered career, *Arabella* is now firmly established in the repertoire. Nevertheless, accusations of triviality persist, and the work has too often, in some quarters, been dismissed as a pale reflection of *Der Rosenkavalier*. Critics seldom define their terms, but the substitution of "charm" for "triviality" (a commodity no opera was ever the worse for) gives perhaps a more faithful picture. Furthermore, it is a mistake to view this delightful opera as mere imitation; it constitutes the refinement of a process that, indeed, commenced with *Der Rosenkavalier,* but which led through the "parlando" experiment of the *Ariadne* "Vorspiel," via *Intermezzo* to reach ultimate fulfilment in *Capriccio* and the orchestral music of Strauss's last years. Leaner and conciser than *Der Rosenkavalier,* less innovative than *Intermezzo,* its generic importance lies in a successful attempt to capture the natural intimacy of Viennese spoken theater for the musical stage. The work springs naturally from the Viennese comedy tradition, already celebrated by Hofmannsthal's stage plays, *Der Schwierige* (*The Difficult Man,* 1921) and *Der Unbestechliche* (*The Incorruptible Man,* 1923). It provided the poet with an opportunity to exploit the musicality dormant in his prose writing, while the musician gloated with anticipatory relish over an essentially modern, absolutely realistic domestic character comedy, which would avoid previous mistakes and "longueurs."

There is, then, a new subtlety apparent in *Arabella*. Structurally better proportioned than *Der Rosenkavalier,* its slimmer format is also more easily damaged by those seemingly now statutory cuts which too often bedevil the final act. Handled with a delicacy born of the *Ariadne/ Intermezzo* experience, the orchestra offers an imaginative solution to the problems of accompanimental balance, allowing much greater audibility to the text. This ideal balance between words and music was built into the Strauss/Hofmannsthal concept of music-theater: it was defined by the poet as "less of music, where the lead, the melody would be given more to the voice, where the orchestra would accompany . . . and be subordinate to the singers." It is this operetta-like, communicable human warmth, this lightness of touch and lyric subtlety, often sought but not always achieved in this long-standing partnership, which makes *Arabella* such a fine example of its genre.

Both *Der Rosenkavalier* and *Arabella* sprang from a pressing post-*Elektra* need to "detour around" the "Wagner mountain." One must, however, accept the work on its own merits—for its stage-worthiness, for its musical delights and Viennese authenticity, and for its charm of character and gently humorous situations. It demonstrates the refinement of an idiom, as well as being arguably among the most mature manifestations of a unique collaborative genius. Historically it is representative of a new species, the "conversation" opera, of which, as a supreme example, it occupies a significant place in the development of twentieth-century music theater.—KENNETH W. BIRKIN

Araiza, Francesco

Tenor. Born 4 October 1950, in Mexico City. Studied at the University of Mexico City, where he sang in University choir; concert debut in Mexico City in 1969 and subsequently sang in opera there; joined Karlsruhe Opera in 1974; lessons in Munich with Richard Holm and Erik Werba; appeared as Ferrando in Così fan tutte *at Aix-en-Provence Festival, 1977; Metropolitan Opera debut as Belmonte in* Die Entführung aus dem Serail, *1984; other roles include Tamino in* Zauberflöte *in 1980, Title role in* Faust *and Pong in* Turandot *in 1982, Ramiro in* Cenerentola *in 1986; appearances with opera houses in Zurich, Düsseldorf, Stuttgart, Munich, and the Salzburg Festival.*

After declining for 150 years, vocal virtuosity is on the upswing. Twenty-five years ago few tenors sang roulades or high Cs. Today the number who do so is steadily burgeoning, though their singing sometimes lacks personality, passion and charm.

The differences between Nicola Monti on a Melodram recording of a Naples performance of *La cenerentola* in 1958 and Francisco Araiza on a CBS studio recording of the opera from 1980 are representative of the typical differences between tenors then and now. Monti is sunny and ingratiating, his mezza voce caressing. But he omits the trills, smudges the coloratura at conductor Mario Rossi's fast clip and sounds uncomfortable in the high register. The technical demands are beyond him and his range is simply too narrow: had the more difficult high passages not been cut, he probably would have been unable to sing the part.

Araiza sings it uncut, hitting all the notes except the trills, which he too avoids. He has marvelous agility and velocity, and the high Cs hold no terrors. But despite his proficiency, he is charmless and mechanical. There is little evidence that anyone in Rossini's day produced a tone as does Araiza, with the locus of resonation far forward in the face.

Compared to such turn-of-the-century interpreters of the part of Almaviva in *Il barbiere di Siviglia* as Fernando de Lucia and Alessandro Bonci, Araiza is less inspired in his treatment of rhythm. Their singing abounds in rubato; his is comparatively four square. De Lucia admittedly imposes his period's romanticism on the music, underscoring with accentuation and rubato its nascent romantic trends, overstepping stylistic boundaries expressively. He is heuristic. No less sensitive to the music, Bonci is less extreme in his liberties—as is his successor Dino Borgioli.

Araiza is probably the best recent Belmonte in *Die Entführung aus dem Serail.* At a 1984 performance at the Metropolitan Opera, he hit most of the notes dead on, with big, bright tones so well focused as to make intonation lapses more noticeable. In the notoriously florid "Ich baue ganz," he was accurate in the stepwise passages but less so in the arpeggiated ones. He interpolated a small cadenza before the repeat, followed by a little ornamentation—and a few extra breaths. He pronounced German well (unusual in an Hispanic singer) and acted energetically. But his singing was more impressive than beautiful, and he did not arouse interest. His dynamics were sometimes random, sometimes inert. He failed to emphasize melodic climaxes and to distinguish melody from ornamentation and sang with little tenderness. He hardly ever shaded his tone and managed to be vigorous yet dull.

To obtain precise articulation of florid passages Araiza aspirated. Many listeners—and some reviewers—find aspiration unendurable, yet musicologists and performers point to period writings suggesting that in the seventeenth and eighteenth centuries aspiration, or at least "detached" singing, was accepted practice. Admittedly the clarity of articulation achievable with aspiration can prove useful in certain contexts. In the quartet in Rossini's *La scala di seta,* for instance, the tenor sings triplets against the others' duplets, and aspiration helps him to clarify the rhythms. In *Die Entführung,* however, Araiza aspirated too heavily for my taste.

Singers sustain interest through temperament no less than through careful planning: Luciano Pavarotti does so through charisma; Tito Schipa, through charisma, charm and musical sensitivity; Giuseppe Di Stefano, through passion and feeling for words; Enrico Caruso, through warmth and emotion. Araiza isn't endowed with an extraordinary supply of these qualities. On a recording of lirico-spinto warhorses made in 1986, he relies instead on musical effects, such as contrasting soft singing with loud. His interpretations of the album's two Puccini pieces, "Che gelida manina" and "E lucevan le stelle," are satisfying, for in addition to alternating dynamics, he sings with tenderness and fervor. But in the aria from *Eugene Onegin,* one misses Dmitri Smirnoff's plaintive quality, his wistful yearning. In the *Arlesiana* aria, Araiza lacks both bitter melancholy for the opening and desperation and *slancio* (surge, "oomph") for the end—as well as punch and substance on the high As, where the voice is unassertive and veiled, particularly on dark vowels. Perhaps the recording's most underinterpreted selection is "Ah! fuyez, douce image," where Araiza sings as if he hadn't considered the importance of the notes in relation to each other or thought about which leads to which. In the middle voice he produces a strong round tone, but he doesn't imbue the high B-flats with longing, pleading and desperation, nor is he able, in the alternative, to trumpet them forth; however, on higher notes, such as the *Bohème* aria's C or the interpolated high D at the end of "Possente amor," the voice takes on brilliance. Stylistically he is an anomaly: a Latin singer with a German sound who achieves legato in the

German manner since World War I—almost without portamento. The music on the record, mostly from the late nineteenth century, was first performed by singers who used portamento generously.

Araiza is never tasteless. At his worst he is earthbound, offering conscientious observance of markings in the score without going beyond them. At his best he is an excellent singer who just misses striking sparks.

Since 1983 he gradually has undertaken more dramatic repertory, although he has said that it may force him to abandon high parts. Having already performed Rodolfo, Faust and Lohengrin, he is scheduled for Chénier and wants to sing Alvaro, Don Carlo, Manrico (*Il trovatore*) and Max. He succeeded in florid repertory by virtue of technical prowess. In these parts, however, his relatively bland vocal personality probably will tell against him. Further, he may be producing a more heroic sound at the expense of vocal gleam. On a recent recording of *Maria Stuarda,* his tone is brassier but also thicker and coarser—the classic tradeoff.

Araiza has said that Neil Shicoff and Luis Lima are at the same point in their careers as he and are performing much of the same repertory. Of the three, Shicoff has the prettiest middle voice but is the least expressive and musically secure, Lima has the greatest emotional intensity and Araiza the most proficiency.—STEFAN ZUCKER

Argento, Dominick

Composer. Born 27 October 1927, in York, Pennsylvania. Studied with Nicolas Nabokov, Henry Cowell, and Hugo Weisgall at the Peabody Conservatory (B.A. 1951); studied with Dallapiccola at the Conservatorio Cherubini in Florence; studied with Bernard Rogers, Howard Hanson, and Alan Hovhaness at the Eastman School of Music, where he was awarded a Ph.D. in 1957; two Guggenheim fellowships, 1957, 1964; on the faculty of the University of Minnesota since 1958; in 1964, co-founder of the Center Opera Company, now the Minnesota Opera; Pulitzer Prize for his song cycle From the Diary of Virginia Woolf, *1975; elected a member of the American Academy and Institute of Arts and Letters; member of the American Academy of Arts and Sciences, 1980.*

Operas   *Sicilian Lines,* New York, 1 October 1954; *The Boor,* J. Olon-Scrymgeour (after Chekhov), 1957, Rochester, 6 May 1957; *Colonel Jonathan the Saint,* J. Olon-Scrymgeour, 1958-61, Denver, Denver Opera Company, 31 December 1961; *Christopher Sly,* J. Manlove (after a scene from Shakespeare, *The Taming of the Shrew*), 1962-63, Minneapolis, University of Minnesota, 31 May 1963; *The Masque of Angels,* J. Olon-Scrymgeour, 1963, Minneapolis, 9 January 1964; *The Shoemaker's Holiday,* J. Olon-Scrymgeour (after the comedy by Thomas Dekker), 1967, Minneapolis, Center Opera Company, 1 June 1967; *Postcard from Morocco,* J. Donahue, Minneapolis, Center Opera Company, 14 October 1971; *A Water Bird Talk,* Argento (based on Chekhov, *On the Harmful Effects of Tobacco,* and J.J. Audubon, *The Birds of America*), 1974, Brooklyn, New York, 19 May 1977; *The Voyage of Edgar Allan Poe,* Charles M. Nolte, 1975-76, Minneapolis, 24 April 1976; *Miss Havisham's Fire,* J. Olon-Scrymgeour (after Dickens, *Great Expectations*), 1977-78, New York, New York City Opera, 22 March 1979; *Miss Havisham's Wedding Night,* J. Olon-Scrymgeour (after Dickens, *Great Expectations*), 1980,

Minneapolis, 1 May 1981; *Casanova's Homecoming,* Argento, 1980-84, St Paul, 12 April 1985; *The Aspern Papers,* Argento (after Henry James), Dallas, November, 1988.

Dominick Argento was studying at Peabody Conservatory in the mid 1950s when he turned away from writing sonatas, quartets and symphonic pieces and began to focus his attention on writing for the voice with the composition of *Songs About Spring.* From that point forward his compositional output was dominated by works for the voice. His operatic emphasis was secured not only as a part of his normal studies, but through his private work with Hugo Weisgall, who was artistic director of the Hilltop Opera in Baltimore.

Over the years Argento has composed over one dozen operas, the first of which was a chamber opera, *The Boor,* completed in 1957. His first full-length opera was *Colonel Jonathan the Saint,* which was composed during his Guggenheim Fellowship between 1958-61. It was not premiered until 31 December 1961 by the Denver Opera Company. *Christopher Sly* is a comic opera based on the opening of Shakespeare's *The Taming of the Shrew.* It was first performed at the University of Minnesota in 1963 and was quite well received. The following year Argento became co-founder of the Center Opera in Minnesota, which was later renamed the Minnesota Opera. During the company's first season they premiered Argento's religious comedy, *The Masque of Angels,* for chorus and small orchestra, which was met with critical acclaim. This was followed three years later with the ballad opera, *The Shoemaker's Holiday,* adapted from the comedy of Thomas Dekker, and in 1971 by *Postcard from Morocco.* Argento received national attention when he received the 1975 Pulitzer Prize in music for *From the Diary of Virginia Woolf,* which was introduced in Minneapolis on 9 January, 1975 by Dame Janet Baker. In commemoration of the American bicentennial Argento completed *The Voyage of Edgar Allan Poe,* based upon a libretto by Charles M. Nolte which describes the last crazed days of Poe's life. *A Water Bird Talk,* a one-act opera for baritone and twelve instrumentalists, was produced in Brooklyn, New York on 19 May 1977. The libretto is loosely based upon Chekhov's *On the Harmful Effects of Tobacco* and J. J. Audubon's *The Birds of America.* Within two years, his two-act opera with prologue and epilogue, *Miss Havisham's Fire,* was premiered by the New York City Opera on 22 March 1979. It is based on Charles Dickens's *Great Expectations* with the libretto by John Olon-Scrymgeour.

Argento's compositional style has its roots in the voice. He has a deep respect for the human voice and does not view it as just another instrument. As he once explained, "It is a *part* of the performer rather than an adjunct to him." Thus, it is only natural that we find his writing focussed upon melodic line with a typically dramatic character that is unashamed of deep emotion. Argento views himself as a traditionalist "in the broadest sense . . . If you want a school, include me in the Mozart, Verdi, Mussorgsky school." His melodic and harmonic vocabulary is versatile, including such diverse elements as Gregorian chant, quotes from Wagner, folk music, jazz, and serialism.

Almost all of his operas deal with the underlying theme of self-discovery and self-knowledge. Over the years the plots of his operas have manifested these themes in a variety of ways. Argento describes them as follows: "*Christopher Sly* elaborates it farcically: a drunken ne'er-do-well is discovered unconscious, he is taken to a fine home, dressed as a Lord, supplied with a wife and servants. When he comes to, they convince him that his past life has all been a dream, that he is wealthy, respected, etc. For a long time he believes the prank to be reality, but eventually he learns who he really is, and in turn pulls a prank on the pranksters. The *Masque of*

Angels puts the theme in a religious context; *Postcard From Morocco* treats it surrealistically; *The Voyage of Edgar Allan Poe* does it fantastically; *A Water Bird Talk* handles it tragi-comically; and *Casanova's Homecoming* does it very deliberately."—ROGER E. FOLTZ

Ariadne auf Naxos [Ariadne on Naxos]

Composer: *Richard Strauss.*

Librettist: *Hugo von Hofmannsthal.*

First Performance: *Stuttgart, Court Theater, 25 October 1912; revised, Vienna, Court Opera, 4 October 1916.*

Roles: *Ariadne (soprano); Bacchus (tenor); Zerbinetta (soprano); Composer (soprano); Music Master (baritone); Dancing Master (tenor); Naiad (soprano); Dryad (contralto); Echo (soprano); Harlequin (baritone); Brighella (tenor); Scaramouche (tenor); Truffaldin (bass); Lackey (bass); Officer (tenor); Wigmaker (bass); Majordomo (speaking part).*

The first version of *Ariadne auf Naxos* (1912) was intended as a short *divertissement,* to be appended to Max Reinhardt's production of Molière's *Le bourgeois gentilhomme.* Strauss and Hofmannsthal felt that the little opera would serve two functions at once: it would be an offer of thanks to Reinhardt, whose last-minute attention had saved the Dresden premiere of *Der Rosenkavalier* the year before, and it would allow Strauss and Hofmannsthal to work on a small piece as they developed ideas more suitable for a grand opera. This rather inauspicious beginning for *Ariadne,* the most elliptical of their operas, was ironic, for it would prove the most protracted and problematic fruit of the legendary collaboration. Indeed, the often stormy letters between Strauss and Hofmannsthal around the writing of *Ariadne* (a situation quite singular in their normally placid correspondence) attests to the significance of the work, and to its special place in their hearts.

The original *Ariadne auf Naxos* (connected to *Le bourgeois gentilhomme* by means of a prose scene written by Hofmannsthal) was generally met by critics and public with incomprehension. A rewrite was in order. The result was a full-length version of *Ariadne,* in which the prose scene was replaced by an extended musical prologue, which also shifted the action to eighteenth-century Vienna. The full-length *Ariadne auf Naxos* was first presented in 1916 to better response, but still there was a sense that the new opera was rather odd, something of a hybrid, most certainly a piece for highly specialized tastes. This reputation continues, and although *Ariadne* has found a place in the repertoire of international opera houses, it has never achieved the popular success of *Der Rosenkavalier* or even *Elektra.*

The lack of *Ariadne's* general appeal is due in great part to its complex plot, which juxtaposes in a seemingly arbitrary way the political and social attitudes of characters who exist in several unrelated historical contexts (eighteenth-century Vienna, Greek antiquity, Renaissance Italy). Critical interpretation of the enigmatic libretto has fallen rather generally into two different, and perhaps opposing, readings. The more prevalent focuses on the idea of an "allomatic transformation," a notion put forward by Hofmannsthal himself in his celebrated "Ariadne letter" of 1911, and suggesting that Ariadne herself, through her suffering and loss, is genuinely purged and transformed, or reborn. This interpretation accounts for the presence of Zerbinetta chiefly as a dramaturgical device to provide contrast: her "false" understanding of transformation as an ever-present element of courtship and sex serves to underscore the "truth"

33

of Ariadne's renewal. At the other extreme, formalist critics see *Ariadne*'s meaning in its multiple settings; in this view, the juxtaposition of historically and socially disparate elements represents a pluralistic world without a fixed reality.

There certainly is room for further interpretation. The turmoil and evolving social order of Strauss and Hofmannsthal's own *fin-de-siècle* Vienna have intriguing parallels with the eighteenth-century world of *Ariadne*'s prologue and its *nouveau-riche* nobleman who undertakes sponsorship of the little *opera seria*. The role of the chimerical Composer in the prologue offers marvelous insights into Strauss and Hofmannsthal's own attitudes to the process of artistic creation. And the very different perspectives on male/female relations offered by Ariadne and Zerbinetta make the work ripe for a feminist reading. Yet such notable critics as Herbert Lindenberger and Catherine Clement have largely ignored *Ariadne auf Naxos* in their recent books on opera; the work remains under-appreciated by the scholarly community as well as by the general public.

Such popular acclaim as *Ariadne* has received is due, no doubt, to its superb score. The multiple contexts of the story gave Strauss an opportunity to blend the lush romantic style of his "Vienna operas" (*Rosenkavalier, Arabella, Intermezzo*) with the more dissonant chromatic writing we find in his settings of mythological and ancient subjects (*Salome, Elektra, Die Frau ohne Schatten*). The resulting admixture—orchestrated with Strauss' typical mastery—is among the most piquant and unusual sound-worlds in opera. Interestingly, the orchestra in *Ariadne*— the score calls for thirty-six players—is one of Strauss' smallest. This poses some difficulties to theaters presenting the opera, for the chamber-sized instrumental ensemble suggests one kind of opera house, while the nearly-Wagnerian vocal demands of the score seems to call for quite another.

Strauss' great gift for creating character through music is never better displayed than in *Ariadne auf Naxos*. The trouser role of the Composer, written in a conscious attempt to capitalize on the success of the similar character of Octavian in *Der Rosenkavalier,* is actually an improvement on its predecessor, and is crowned by a monologue on the nature of writing music ("Musik ist eine heilige Kunst"), which is one of the most beautiful and moving in the Strauss canon. The small ensembles for the comedians who support Zerbinetta and the three nymphs who comfort and serenade Ariadne are endlessly imaginative and elegant. And if, in this context, the tenor music for Bacchus is stiffer than one expects, that is entirely in keeping with the artificial and one-dimensional nature of the character.

The marvelous parts of the *prima donne* are two of Strauss' most superb musical portraits. Ariadne's monologues are sombre, elevated, fashioned in a neo-classical style reminiscent of Gluck's music for Alceste or Orphée, while at the same time the arching vocal line and autumnal glow of the orchestrations are unmistakably Strauss. By contrast, Zerbinetta's music makes use of the highly virtuosic coloratura conventions of *bel canto* Italian opera, culminating in an aria ("Grossmächtige Prinzessin"), nearly ten minutes in length, which is probably the most difficult and exacting music for soprano in our century. In one of the opera's cleverest devices, the monologues of the two women are juxtaposed so as to maximize a sense of rivalry and to galvanize the audience into factions. At the premiere of the revised *Ariadne auf Naxos* in 1916, the combination of the great Maria Jeritza as Ariadne and the equally-famous Selma Kurz as Zerbinetta created a furor; in recent years, the comparable star casting of Jessye Norman and Kathleen Battle in the roles has also stirred audience interest, and has ensured the opera a well-deserved place on the roster of the Metropolitan Opera, Covent Garden, and other major theaters.—DAVID ANTHONY FOX

Arroyo, Martina

Soprano. Born 2 February 1937, in New York. Studied with Joseph Turnau at Hunter College, New York; co-winner with Grace Bumbry of the 1958 Metropolitan Opera Auditions; professional debut in Pizzetti's Assassinio, *Carnegie Hall, 1958; Metropolitan Opera debut as Celestial Voice in* Don Carlos, *1959; also sang in Vienna, Frankfurt, Berlin, and under contract in Zurich in 1963-68, returning to the Metropolitan Opera in 1965; at Covent Garden, 1968—80; other roles include Butterfly, Gioconda, Liu, Santuzza, and Elsa.*

Martina Arroyo was one of several outstanding African American singers to figure prominently on the roster of the Metropolitan Opera during the 1960s and 1970s. Leontyne Price was the pioneer and role model among the sopranos, and to a great extent Arroyo has lived up to the high standards established by Price in certain roles. Both excelled in the great Verdi operas calling for a lirico-spinto soprano voice, notably Aïda, Amelia in *Un ballo in maschera,* Leonora in *La forza del destino* and the *Messa da requiem;* and both were superb Mozarteans as Donna Anna and Donna Elvira in *Don Giovanni.*

Arroyo has recorded a number of the above roles. The concensus is that on her recordings as on the stage, Arroyo displays extremely beautiful vocalism with healthy, rounded tone, but that she is seldom dramatically involved. Ethan Mordden has described her Donna Anna under Colin Davis as "gutlessly beautiful" and her *Forza* Leonora as "temperate and smoothed-out in the modern manner." Yet her recorded *Forza* is dark, opulent, and soaring and she provides an effective *messa di voce* for the opening of "Pace, pace, mio Dio," capping the aria with a fine high B-flat. She has also recorded Donna Elvira with Karl Böhm; in this role, too, she does little characterization with the voice, but the singing is thrilling as pure sound and the technical demands are executed in masterly fashion. On balance, the timbre of the voice is perhaps better suited to Donna Anna, although Arroyo, like many other big-voiced sopranos, finds "Non mì dir" a bit treacherous and sings "Or sai chi l'onore" without tension and urgency. Similarly, her recording of Valentine in *Les Huguenots* under Richard Bonynge finds her in sumptuous voice but dramatically unconvincing. In the recording of *I vespri siciliani* in which she filled in for Montserrat Caballé, the "Bolero" is performed in a perfunctory manner, carefully, as though it were a vocalise, lacking the requisite sparkle in the fioriture and missing tonal nuances when the music changes mode. As with *Forza,* her singing of Amelia in *Un ballo* with Muti is very strong, yet if one compares her delivery of the dramatic recitative in "Ecco l'orrido campo" with that of Callas, Arroyo seems tentative and rather lacklustre.

In short, Arroyo was a truly stunning vocalist, one of the great voices of our time, but her recordings do not present stage portraits. Much the same criticism has been leveled at her stage performances. Andrew Porter noted of her Amelia in the 1974 Chicago Lyric Opera production of *Simon Boccanegra* that she "merely produced imposing and beautiful sounds" and of her *Forza* Leonora at the Metropolitan in 1975 that she "made some sweet, full sounds, but her performance did not have much character." In that same year at the Metropolitan, her first Gioconda fulfilled similar expectations, but her fourth Gioconda was "passionate, both amply and powerfully sung," according to Porter, who also has a memory of an Arroyo-Shirley Verrett *Il trovatore* in which they sang and acted so well as to eliminate mid-scene applause. Reasons for Miss Arroyo's usual lack of dramatic verve might be her own temperament and the basically sweet, rounded tone of her voice, which lacks "bite" and incisiveness, especially in the low register.

Onstage Arroyo performed many more roles than she recorded. After winning the Metropolitan Auditions of the Air along with Grace Bumbry in 1958, she spent her early career in Germany and Austria, where she sang Aida, among other roles. In 1965 she returned to the Metropolitan, her principal operatic home, as Aida and appeared in 1966 in *Don Carlos*. Other performances include Selika in Meyerbeer's *L'Africaine,* Rezia in Weber's *Oberon,* Senta in *Der fliegende Holländer,* Elsa in *Lohengrin,* the lyrical Puccini roles, Rossini's *Stabat mater,* Beethoven's Ninth Symphony, and such twentieth-century masterpieces as Stockhausen's *Momente* and Schoenberg's *Gurrelieder.*—STEPHEN WILLIER

The Aspern Papers

Composer: *Dominick Argento.*
Librettist: *Dominick Argento (after Henry James).*
First Performance: *Dallas, November 1988.*

Dominick Argento has composed several highly evocative operas, including *The Aspern Papers.* The plot is of course based on Henry James' short story of the same name, but Argento (who wrote his own libretto) has opened up the original considerably, showing us characters and scenes merely alluded to in James, their existence being only a distant memory of the protagonist Juliana Bordereau.

Simultaneous to this broadening of the tale's scope and compass, Argento has made its content more operatic; Aspern himself is no longer a Byronesque author but rather a leading composer of the bel canto era. Thus Juliana is not merely his paramour but also a famous diva of the time and creatrix of his leading roles. The treasured papers which she so zealously retains of the dead composer are now not merely a stray love letter or two, but the manuscript of Aspern's final and long-suppressed opera, *Medea.*

All these events, including Aspern's betrayal of Juliana with the young opera singer Sonia and their dealings with the impresario Barelli, are shown in scenes occurring in the summer of 1835. These episodes are interwoven with others from 1895 in which Juliana is an old lady living with her shy and unattractive spinster niece, Tina. This part of the story comes from James' original novella, whose prose Argento has closely followed. A young scholar of Aspern's life and works (known only as The Lodger) arrives at the ladies' villa and, hoping to use Tina as a means of getting his hands on the ancient Juliana's trove of manuscripts, woos the ungainly woman. When the old lady dies, Tina offers the young man the surviving papers on condition that he agree to marry her. Shocked, he refuses and bolts from the scene, but shortly returns. Tina tells him she has destroyed the papers, and in agony he leaves for a second and final time. Then, all alone, Tina withdraws the score of *Medea* from its hiding place and burns it, page by page, as we simultaneously see a vision of all the *Medea* characters (Juliana costumed as the title role, etc.) going up in flames.

The opera is a real *tour de force* for the two female leads, with Elisabeth Söderström as Juliana (both old and young: a particularly challenging part) and Frederica von Stade as Tina in the Dallas premiere of this work in November 1988. Argento's texture is through-composed, but the opera still separates into noticeable musical numbers. Especially memorable are the love duet of Juliana and Aspern in act II and the barcarolle (supposedly written by Aspern) whose melody permeates the score at several crucial moments. Argento's subtle attention to the nuances of his text suggests the Debussy of *Pelléas et Mélisande,* but there is also an Italianate richness to his melody. While it is obviously too soon to comment on the opera's staying power, it certainly is as good as any other score to emerge in the last few years and a good deal better than most.—DENNIS WAKELING

Attila

Composer: *Giuseppe Verdi.*

Librettists: *Temistocle Solera and Francesco Maria Piave (after Z. Werner).*

First Performance: *Venice, La Fenice, 17 March 1846.*

Roles: *Odabella (soprano); Foresto (tenor); Ezio (baritone); Attila (bass); Uldino (tenor); Pope Leo I (bass); chorus (SSAATTBB).*

Verdi's version of the Attila story presents the King of the Huns fresh from his victory at Aquileia and poised to march on Rome. The plot is mainly concerned with his courageous albeit barbarian greatness pitted against three rather unsavory and scheming Italians, a surprising structural balance given the patriotic furor it incited on the peninsula.

The amazon-like Odabella, as close to being a Valkyrie as any character Verdi ever created, wins Attila's trust and favor through her courage and warlike prowess. The Roman general Ezio first tries to cut a deal with Attila to share the world between them, only to join the conspiracy against him when rebuffed. The patriot Foresto, Odabella's lover, is first seen with refugees from Aquileia in the grand act of founding the city of Venice. His next entrance, however, places him in the thick of plot and counterplot, whence he never re-emerges.

In the opera's strongest sequence, Attila describes a dream in which he is turned back at the gates of Rome by a saintly vision. Soon thereafter the vision turns to reality when Pope Leo I bars his way in a scene reproducing the famous fresco by Raphael in the Vatican. The remainder of the opera is devoted to the schemes of the Italian trio until in the end Odabella stabs Attila in the heart, claiming that she thus has avenged her father.

This strange and brutal mishmash of an opera is the result of the work of two librettists. In 1845 Verdi, badly in need of a success after the dismal reception accorded *Alzira,* turned for a text to Temistocle Solera, who had proven a tried and true collaborator with *Nabucco* and *I Lombardi.* However, his version of the original play (a flamboyant and mystical farrago entitled *Attila, König der Hunnen* by Zacharias Werner) was not well received by Verdi, especially the final act. A break between the two men occurred, and the composer called his faithful Francesco Maria Piave onto the scene to patch up the ending. The result is a work of brusque noisiness in an epically broad manner with an utterly mismatched finale in which Verdi tries through intimacy to humanize his cardboard characters, to little avail. Yet it must be noted that *Attila* was in fact wildly popular in its day, representing a sort of culmination for Verdi of his "Risorgimento" style. When Ezio offered Attila to "Take the universe, but leave Italy to me" ("Avrai tu l'universo, resti l'Italia a me") an audience battlecry was born. Likewise, the founding of Venice with its attendant sunrise effect was praised, especially by Venetian audiences at the premiere, this despite its oxymoronic chorus of hermits.

In our renewal of interest in the early Verdian canon, *Attila* has not fared so well as other works. While moments such as Attila's dream and the ensemble with Pope Leo, some of Odabella's solos, and the tenor/baritone duet still evoke enthusiasm, the abrupt and formulaic simplicity of much of the rest, plus the two-dimensional characterization of all save the title role, sits poorly on a public ready to savor, say, the woes of a Doge Foscari or even the cross-cultural clash of an Alzira. *Attila,* therefore, will probably remain on the fringes: often unsatisfactory yet worthy of a revival when a basso of great vocal and histrionic gifts is seized by an understandable yen to perform the title role.—DENNIS WAKELING

Auber, Daniel-François-Esprit

Composer. Born 29 January 1782, in Caen. Died 12 May 1871, in Paris. Student of Ladurner and Cherubini. In London in his teens, where his vocal compositions met with success; in Paris, 1803; first dramatic work the comic opera L'erreur d'un moment, *1805; first opera publicly performed* Le séjour militaire, *1813; first successful opera* La bergère châtelaine, *1820; the grand opera* La muette de Portici, *upon which much of his reputation is based, premiered in 1828; succeeded Gossec as a member of the Académie in 1829; appointed director of the Paris Conservatoire in 1842 by Louis Philippe; given the title of* imperial *maître de chapelle in 1852 by Napoleon III.*

Operas   *L'erreur d'un moment,* Jacques Marie Boutet de Monvel, Paris, Salle Doyen, 1805; *Jean de Couvin,* Népomucène Lemercier, Belgium, Château de Chimay, September 1812; *Le séjour militaire,* Jean Nicolas Bouilly and Emanuel Mercier-Dupaty, Paris, Opéra-Comique, 27 February 1813; *Le testament et les billets-doux,* François Antoine Eugène de Planard, Paris, Opéra-Comique, 18 September 1819; *La bergère châtelaine,* François Antoine Eugène de Planard, Paris, Salle Feydeau, 27 January 1820; *Emma, ou La promesse imprudente,* François Antoine Eugène de Planard, Paris, Opéra-Comique, 7 July 1821; *Leicester, ou Le château de Kenilworth,* Eugène Scribe and Anne Honoré Joseph Mélesville (after Scott), Paris, Opéra-Comique, 25 January 1823; *La neige, ou Le nouvel éginard,* Eugène Scribe and Casimir Delavigne, Paris, Opéra-Comique, 8 October 1823; *Vendôme en Espagne* (with Hérold), Adolphe Joseph Simonis d'Empis and Edouard Mennechet, Paris, Opéra, 5 December 1823; *Les trois genres* (with Boieldieu), Eugène Scribe, Emanuel Mercier-Dupaty, and Michel Pichat, Paris, Odéon, 27 April 1824; *Le concert à la cour, ou La débutante,* Eugène Scribe and Anne Honoré Joseph Mélesville, Paris, Opéra-Comique, 3 June 1824; *Léocadie,* Eugène Scribe and Anne Honoré Joseph Mélesville (after Cervantes, *La fuerça del sangre*), Paris, Opéra-Comique, 4 November 1824; *Le maçon,* Eugène Scribe and Casimir Delavigne, Paris, Opéra-Comique, 3 May 1825; *Le timide, ou Le nouveau séducteur,* Eugène Scribe and Xavier Boniface Saintine, Paris, Opéra-Comique, 30 May 1826; *Fiorella,* Eugène Scribe, Paris, Opéra-Comique, 28 November 1826; *La muette de Portici* (*Masaniello*), Eugène Scribe and Casimir Delavigne, Paris, Opéra, 29 February 1828; *La fiancée,* Eugène Scribe, Paris, Opéra-Comique, 10 January 1829; *Fra Diavolo, ou L'hôtellerie de Terracine,* Eugène Scribe, Paris, Opéra-Comique, 28 January 1830; *Le dieu et la bayadère ou La courtisane amoureuse* (opera-ballet), Eugène Scribe, Paris, Opéra, 13 October 1830; *Le philtre,* Eugène Scribe, Paris, Opéra, 20 June 1831; *La*

Marquise de Brinvilliers (with Batton, Berton, Blangini, Boieldieu, Carafa, Cherubini, Hérold, and Paer), Eugène Scribe, and François Henri Joseph Castil-Blaze, Paris, Opéra, 31 October 1831; *Le serment, ou Les faux-monnayeurs,* Eugène Scribe, and Édouard Joseph Ennemond Mazères, Paris, Opéra, 1 October 1832; *Gustave III ou Le bal masqué,* Eugène Scribe, Paris, Opéra, 27 February 1833; *Lestocq, ou L'intrigue et l'amour,* Eugène Scribe, Paris, Opéra-Comique, 24 May 1834; *Le cheval de bronze* (opéra féerique), Eugène Scribe, Paris, Opéra-Comique, 23 March 1835; revised as opéra-ballet, 21 September 1857; *Actéon,* Eugène Scribe, Paris, Opéra-Comique, 23 January 1836; *Les chaperons blancs,* Eugène Scribe, Paris, Opéra-Comique, 9 April 1836; *L'ambassadrice,* Eugène Scribe, Paris, Opéra-Comique, 21 December 1836; *Le domino noir,* Eugène Scribe, Paris, Opéra-Comique, 2 December 1837; *Le lac des fées,* Eugène Scribe and Anne Honoré Joseph Mélesville, Paris, Opéra, 1 April 1839; *Zanetta, ou Jouer avec le feu,* Eugène Scribe and Jules Henri Vernoy de Saint-Georges, Paris, Opéra-Comique, 18 May 1840; *Les diamants de la couronne,* Eugène Scribe and Jules Henri Vernoy de Saint-Georges, Paris, Opéra-Comique, 6 March 1841; *Le Duc d'Olonne,* Eugène Scribe and Xavier Boniface Saintine, Paris, Opéra-Comique, 4 February 1842; *La part du diable,* Eugène Scribe, Paris, Opéra-Comique, 16 January 1843; *La sirène,* Eugène Scribe, Paris, Opéra-Comique, 26 March 1844; *La barcarolle, ou L'amour et la musique,* Eugène Scribe, Paris, Opéra-Comique, 22 April 1845; *Les premiers pas* (with Adam, Carafa, and Halévy), Alphonse Royer and Gustave Vaëz, Paris, Opéra-National, 15 November 1847; *Haydée ou Le secret,* Eugène Scribe (after a Russian story translated by Prosper Merimée, *Six et quatre*), Paris, Opéra-Comique, 28 December 1847; *L'enfant prodigue,* Eugène Scribe, Paris, Opéra, 6 December 1850; *Zerline, ou La corbeille d'oranges,* Eugène Scribe, Paris, Opéra, 16 May 1851; *Marco Spada* (first version: opéra-comique), Eugène Scribe and Casimir Delavigne, Paris, Opéra-Comique, 21 December 1852; *Jenny Bell,* Eugène Scribe, Paris, Opéra-Comique, 2 June 1855; *Manon Lescaut,* Eugène Scribe (after Prévost), Paris, Opéra-Comique, 23 February 1856; *La circassienne,* Eugène Scribe, Paris, Opéra-Comique, 2 February 1861; *La fiancée du Roi de Garbe,* Eugène Scribe and Jules Henri Vernoy de Saint-Georges, Paris, Opéra-Comique, 11 January 1864; *Le premier jour de bonheur,* Adolphe Philippe d'Ennery and Eugène Cormon, Paris, Opéra-Comique, 15 February 1868; *Rêve d'amour,* Adolphe Philippe d'Ennery and Eugène Cormon, Paris, Opéra-Comique, 20 December 1869.

From the 1820s until his death during the Paris Commune of 1871, Auber retained a pre-eminent position in the field of French *opéra comique*. In his hands this genre shed the frequently stiff, classicizing traits of the preceding generation (Dalayrac, Méhul, Cherubini, Le Sueur); at the same time it shed its more earnest dramatic ambitions of the Revolutionary period in favor of a witty, sophisticated entertainment suited to the tastes of Restoration society and the "bourgeois monarchy" of Louis-Philippe. The historical significance of his grand opera *La muette de Portici* (1828)—an important prototype in the development of that new genre—was realized through its influence on others rather than in the composer's own subsequent works.

Auber was born into relatively comfortable circumstances, and spent some time in London as a youth in preparation for a mercantile career. Only after the failure of his father's business (as a print dealer) in 1819 did Auber turn to music as a profession. Before this, however, he had already studied with Cherubini, composed several concertos and a mass, and had the opportunity of mounting informally two small-scale stage works under the aegis of an aristocratic family acquaintance, the Prince de Chimay. Auber achieved his first public success with the 3-act *opéra comique, La bergère châtelaine,* at the Salle Feydeau in 1820. Three years later he entered into what became a life-long association with the gifted and prolific man of the theatre, Eugène Scribe (*Leicester ou Le château de Kenilworth* after Scott and, more successful from the dramatic point of view, *La neige*). Both of these scores remain strongly in the thrall of Rossini, whose athletic vocal writing and other mannerisms were more easily imitated than was his genuine, but elusive, melodic charm. With *Le maçon* in 1825 the torch of French *opéra comique* was passed, so to speak, to Auber from Boieldieu, who celebrated his last and most enduring success in that year with *La dame blanche* (both had texts by Scribe). The plot of *Le maçon*—based on a supposedly factual account of a rich Turk living outside Paris who tries to foil his daughter's elopement by kidnapping a local mason and locksmith to seal up his *château*—exemplifies Scribe's ability to fashion clever, colorful librettos from the most varied sources. The posthumous fame of Auber's first and most significant grand opera, *La muette de Portici,* rests especially on the report that the patriotic fervor of the tenor-baritone duet in Act II ("Amour sacré de la patrie") set off the ultimately successful struggle for Belgian independence from Holland in 1830. *La muette* was the first of three operas of this period (with Rossini's *Guillaume Tell,* 1829, and Meyerbeer's *Robert le diable,* 1831), which together established a musical and dramaturgical model for the historical-spectacular 'grand opera' type that would remain influential through the 1880s. The novelty of a mute heroine (Fenella, played by a dancer to passages of orchestral pantomime) inspired Scribe and Auber to collaborate on the opera-ballet *Le dieu et la bayadère,* principally conceived as a vehicle for the famed dancer Marie Taglioni. *Gustave III ou Le bal masqué* of 1833 was already Auber's last attempt at a full-scale grand opera (here designated an *opéra historique* by Scribe), except for the relatively unsuccessful biblical drama, *L'enfant prodigue,* of 1850. *Gustave III* has of course been eclipsed by the musically tauter, much more dynamic treatment of the material by Verdi as *Un ballo in maschera.*

After their comic masterpiece, *Fra Diavolo* (1830), the next two most enduring creations of the Scribe-Auber team in the genre of *opéra comique* were two equally lighthearted works in Iberian settings: *Le domino noir* (1837) and *Les diamants de la couronne* (1841). Auber's swan song was *Le premier jour de bonheur,* produced (without Scribe, who had since died) in 1868, at the age of 87. In the meantime he had continued to provide a steady stream of works for the Parisian musical stage, although his production tapered off somewhat (understandably) after 1850. Among the other later works deserving mention are *Haydée ou le secret* (1847, after a Russian story translated by Prosper Merimée) and an *opéra comique* version of Prévost's *Manon Lescaut* from 1856. The aria from the latter work known as "L'éclat de rire" remained a favorite coloratura vehicle into the early age of recording, while the closing scene (death of Manon)

Daniel Auber

represents a "unique page in the works of Auber for its simple grandeur and deeply felt emotion," according to Charles Malherbe.

Auber's achievement in *La muette* may not consist so much in the creation of a "new form" of opera (which would in any case have owed as much to Scribe's contribution) as in the synthesis of elements from the *opéra comique* with others from Rossinian *opera seria*. To the extensive, vocally demanding solo and duo scene structures of the latter, he—and Scribe—added the colorful historical setting, characteristic chorus and dance numbers (Barcarolle, Tarantella, etc.), a more active musical and dramatic role for chorus, all within the context of a compelling dramatic plot. The preponderance of jaunty, dotted rhythms and the tendency to foursquare phrase structures in this score also betray its proximity to *opéra comique*. Wagner, who was well acquainted with the work from his youth, praised its "drastic concision and economy" of form and the vibrant, vital energy of the musical style, which seemed to make all previous efforts at "serious" opera obsolete at one stroke. Franz Liszt also wrote approvingly of the work, although he felt it to be less substantial than Rossini's *Guillaume Tell*; and, like Wagner, registered disapproval of the essential frivolity of Auber's musical nature as manifested in most of his other works.

It was, nonetheless, the charm, grace, and wit of his lighter works on which Auber's reputation ultimately rested. A number of critics noted his increasing dependency on the rhythms and phraseology of the popular dance (contredanse, quadrille, waltz) in his later works. Berlioz complained of this already in *Les diamants de la couronne* (1841). But on the foundation of such simplistic rhythmic structures Auber was able to float a supple, naturalistic musical dialogue that won the admiration of Eduard Hanslick, who pointed to the opening trio (ball scene) in *Le domino noir* as a "classic example" of Auber's virtuosity in passing freely between *cantabile* and declamatory styles to create a true "musical conversation" style.—THOMAS S. GREY

a OPERA

OPERA b

Baccaloni, Salvatore

Bass. Born 14 April 1900, in Rome. Died 31 December 1969, in New York. Attended Sistine Chapel Choir School, then studied with Giuseppe Kaschmann from 1921. Professional debut as Bartolo in Il barbiere di Siviglia *in Rome, Adriano, 1922; sang at Teatro alla Scala, 1926-40, specializing in buffo roles; debut at Covent Garden as Timur in* Turandot, *1928; United States debut in Chicago as Melitone in* La forza del destino, *1930; debut at San Francisco as Leporello, 1938; debut at Metropolitan Opera as Bartolo, 1940, and he appeared in almost 300 performances there until 1962; roles include Don Pasquale, Dulcamara, Varlaam, Gianni Schicchi, Osmin, and Falstaff.*

Salvatore Baccaloni reigned from the 1920s to the 1950s as one of the twentieth century's leading comic basses. He made his debut in Rome in 1920, in the role of Bartolo in Rossini's *Il barbiere di Siviglia,* a role to which he often returned. During the 1920s he sang mostly in Italy, building a reputation that soon brought him requests to sing in many countries. The following decade was the most hectic of his long career. Baccaloni travelled widely, making many appearances at the Teatro Colón in Buenos Aires as well as in several theaters in North America and in Europe. He sang at Covent Garden from 1928; from 1936 to 1939 he sang at Glyndebourne. The last two decades of Baccaloni's career were a little more sedentary. From 1940 until the end of his singing career in the early 1960s he sang at the Metropolitan Opera in New York as a regular member of the company.

Baccaloni's repertory, like that of his successors, Italian comic basses Rolando Panerai and Sesto Bruscantini, was limited almost exclusively to opera in Italian. (All three of these singers were more limited in dramatic, linguistic, and musical range than the German bass Walter Berry; which is not to say that they did not rival or even excell Berry in some parts of their chosen repertory.) Baccaloni specialized in Mozart's buffo roles as well as in those of Rossini and Donizetti; perhaps his greatest role was that of the title role in Donizetti's *Don Pasquale.* Among his other roles were Geronimo in Cimarosa's *Il matrimonio segreto,* the title role in Puccini's *Gianni Schicchi,* and Uberto in Pergolesi's *La serva padrona.*

Conrad L. Osborne's discussion (in *High Fidelity*) of Baccaloni's portrayal of Leporello in the recording of Mozart's *Don Giovanni* made by Fritz Busch at Glyndebourne in 1936 points to the strengths and weaknesses of Baccaloni as a buffo artist: "He had a fluent, fruity light bass of true singing properties, and is up to a piece of serious work here, quite different from all those later Met evenings of slithering pitch and corn-pone antics (*polenta,* I guess it'd be, and lots of it) . . . . this ranks with the best of the Leporellos." The recording shows Baccaloni to have been a fine musician and singer who conveyed emotions vividly. He was capable of a wide range of vocal colors and used this variety with great dramatic effectiveness. Late in his career, in the 1950s, Baccaloni's vocal powers declined. Osborne's criticism refers to the comic exaggeration that Baccaloni increasingly depended on at the Metropolitan as his voice grew weaker. Yet even then his commanding stage presence did not desert him; a report in *Opera* about a performance of Mozart's *Entführung* at the Teatro alla Scala in 1952 (with Callas as Constanze) praised Baccaloni's Osmin. The fifty-two year old bass, "despite having very little voice left, showed that he is still a master of the stage."—JOHN A. RICE

Bailey, Norman

Baritone. Born 21 March 1933, in Birmingham, England. Married Doreen Simpson in 1957 (divorced 1983; two sons, one daughter); married the singer Kristine Ciesinski in 1985. Studied at Rhodes University in South Africa and at Vienna Music Academy with Adolf Vogel, Josef Witt, and Julius Patzek; professional debut in Rossini's La cambiale di matrimonio, *Vienna Chamber Opera, 1959; sang in Linz (1960-63), Wuppertal (1963-64), Dusseldorf (1964-67), and Sadler's Wells (1967-71), especially in Wagner roles; Teatro alla Scala debut as Dallapiccola's* Job, *1967; debut in New York as Hans Sachs for New York City Opera (1975) and Metropolitan Opera (1976); made CBE in 1977.*

During 1973 the English baritone Norman Bailey sang no fewer than eight different major roles from the Wagnerian repertory. This extraordinary achievement confirms his affinity with Wagner, but it would be misleading and grossly unfair to label him a specialist, since his career places him as a leading exponent of a wide range of roles and styles.

Norman Bailey was born in Birmingham, but studied at Rhodes University, South Africa after his family emigrated to that country. Having diverted his studies from theology to music, he spent a further two years at the Vienna Academy of Music, and this enabled him to launch his career in Austria. His professional debut was as Tobias Mill in the Vienna Chamber Opera's 1959 production of Rossini's *La cambiale di matrimonio,* and a year later he became a member of the company at the Landestheater, Linz. There he performed many contrasted roles ranging through the German and Italian repertories. Further experience in Germany, mainly at Wuppertal and with the Deutsche Oper am Rhein in Düsseldorf, preceded his membership of the Sadlers Wells (now English National) Opera in London, from 1967 until 1971.

When he took the part of Hans Sachs in the celebrated 1968 performances of *Die Meistersinger* under Reginald Goodall, he immediately impressed as a Wagnerian singer of major importance. Soon he was able to confirm the fact through his appearances at Covent Garden and Bayreuth, at Hamburg, Brussels and Munich.

When the English *Ring* was launched at the Coliseum in January 1970, Bailey's Wotan proved the ideal complement to Rita Hunter's Brünnhilde and Alberto Remedios's Siegfried. The magisterial command he brought to the role was impressive indeed, while at Bayreuth and other centers he extended his reputation in Wagner with successful portrayals of Günther and Amfortas.

Inevitably these years brought a concentration of roles, Bailey tending to reserve himself for the *Heldenbariton* rather than the higher Italianate style, of which also he had already shown himself an adept interpreter. But in 1972 he responded positively to a request from English National Opera to sing the Count di Luna in the new production of Verdi's *Il trovatore;* and, soon after, he took on the role of Ford in the same composer's *Falstaff* for BBC television. The result was that his career gained in flexibility, and his voice confirmed its ability to cope with a high *tessitura,* even if the singer admitted that he was under strain unless he felt in perfect health. Other notable successes, beyond Wagner, have included Jochanaan (*Salome*) and Pizarro (*Fidelio*), while some critics regard his performance as Kutuzov in the English National Opera's production of Prokofiev's *War and Peace* as the most spectacular of all his achievements. Certainly it was typical of the commanding stature and the depth of characterization with which Bailey brings roles to life. This rare ability, which he shares with but a handful of singers, was found to the full in this remarkable portrayal of Balstrode in Britten's *Peter Grimes* at Covent Garden, which was played alongside Jon Vickers's intense realization of the title role.

Only careful preparation and complete dedication can bring about the standards for which Norman Bailey is known. His vocal timbre, firm but not rich, does not always help to fill large halls, but in terms of clarity and musical intelligence few singers have been able to match him, while he has consistently displayed his mastery of dramatic understanding. Above all, his career reflects his commitment to the medium of opera itself, for he continues to explore new roles at the same time as confirming his stature in those with which he has become firmly identified.—TERRY BARFOOT

Baker, Janet

Mezzo-soprano. Born 21 August 1933, in Hatfield, Yorkshire. Married James Keith Shelley in 1957. Studied with Helene Isepp in 1953 and later with Meriel St Clair, and at Salzburg Mozarteum; won second prize in the Kathleen Ferrier Awards, 1956; opera debut as Roza in Smetana's The Secret, *Oxford University Club, 1956; Eduige in Handel Opera Society's Rodelinda (1959), also Ariodante (1964) and Orlando (1966); debut with English opera group as Purcell's Dido at Aldeburgh, 1962; Covent Garden debut as Hermia in* Midsummer Night's Dream, *1966; Scottish Opera debut as Dorabella, 1967; other roles include Pippo in* La gazza ladra, *Gluck's Orfeo (1958), Strauss's Octavian; Britten composed the part of Kate Julian in the 1971 television opera* Owen Wingrave *for her; Hamburg Shakespeare prize, 1971; honorary degrees from universities of London, Birmingham, and Oxford; made Commander of the Order of the British Empire in 1970 and Dame Commander in 1976.*

The career of the English mezzo-soprano Janet Baker has been equally remarkable in its three different aspects: the opera house, the Lieder recital and the concert hall. Her distinctive and beautiful voice has thus proved itself a flexible instrument, and her sure technique and warm personality have together made her the singer the British musical public has taken most closely to its heart since the days of Kathleen Ferrier.

In 1956 Janet Baker won second prize in the Kathleen Ferrier Competition; that same year she sang in the chorus at Glyndebourne and made her solo opera debut as Roza in Smetana's *The Secret* for the Oxford University Opera Club. Her operatic work rapidly developed, though at all times she has been careful in her selection of roles. She sang her first Orpheus (Gluck) in 1958, following it the next year with Eduige in the Handel Opera Society's production of *Rodelinda*. This association with pre-classical opera she maintained throughout her career, and her understanding of style and her commitment to the expressive nature of such works produced a series of memorable performances.

Though less frequently linked with Monteverdi, Baker has shown a clear sense of this style also: in Ottavio's solos in *L'incoronazione di Poppea,* such as the Act I lament and, in Act III, "Addio Roma," where the natural grandeur of her voice was enhanced by the most subtle colorings. Such things were even more true of her Purcell, Gluck and Handel performances. Her emotional commitment to Purcell's Dido, for instance, was matched by that to Gluck's Orpheus.

In 1962 Baker made her debut with the English Opera Group at Aldeburgh, where the following year she sang Polly in Benjamin Britten's realisation of *The Beggar's Opera*. She has written of the remarkable intensity created in the Aldeburgh environment, dominated by Britten and Peter Pears, and of the special influence it had on both her career and her musical personality: ". . . the debt I owe those two wonderful men is incalculable. Most performers who went through the experience of Aldeburgh must have known this feeling of being burned at the sacred fire. We survived the ordeal or we did not; but if we did, we were always changed, and I feel I was changed for the better. Ben and Peter gave us standards which turned us from national to international performers, and the alteration in status which British performers are now accorded, the respect we are unreservedly given all over the world, is due in large measure to them." (*Full Circle,* 1982)

Baker's special feeling for Britten's music was particularly evident in her performances in *The Rape of Lucretia;* and the composer recognised her achievement in creative terms, for in 1971 he wrote the part of Kate Julian for her in his television opera *Owen Wingrave*. Here her very positive sense of characterization was shown in a new way, for her Kate was a personality at once cold and unpleasant, whose outlook provided the necessary expression to emphasize Owen's situation as the outsider in an unsympathetic society.

Janet Baker in *Julius Caesar,* **London, 1979**

Baker's 1967 Scottish Opera Dorabella (*Così fan tutte*) preceded her magnificent portrayal of Berlioz's Dido (*Les Troyens*) with the same company. This success she repeated at Covent Garden, and her feeling for the emotion and the fundamental nature of the tragic Queen enabled her to rise to one of the heights of her career. During these years her work expanded further: the double role of Diana-Jupiter in Cavalli's *La Calisto,* Penelope in Monteverdi's *Il ritorno d'Ulisse in patria,* Vitellia in Mozart's *La clemenza di Tito.*

Through the 1970s, Janet Baker maintained close links with three companies: Glyndebourne, Covent Garden and English National Opera. For the latter her Charlotte in Massenet's *Werther* was especially moving, and confirmed her strength in the French repertory; but her appearance as Donizetti's Mary Stuart perhaps reached even greater heights.

Baker first sang Mary Stuart at the Coliseum in 1973, and nearly ten years later she did so again in a performance which has been preserved in a memorable recording. 1981-2 was in fact the season she chose to retire from the opera house, giving farewell performances also with Covent Garden, in Gluck's *Alceste,* and at Glyndebourne in Gluck's *Orfeo.* That season she chose to preserve her experiences in the form of a diary under the title *Full Circle,* a reference to the fact that her operatic career ended at Glyndebourne, the place where it had begun. In the text her thoughts return to the theme of the pressures opera places on the singer, to the demands of performing at the highest level; and certainly the expressive commitment for which she was noted must have been demanding in the extreme.

Janet Baker has in recent years, therefore, concentrated on the concert hall, but her work in the theatre has made its indelible mark on operatic life. Her achievements have been wide-ranging, through three hundred years of music, through many varying styles, through tragic and comic roles. In all these fields she was outstanding: Janet Baker must be ranked as one of the finest artists of recent times.—TERRY BARFOOT

Balfe, Michael William

Composer. Born 15 May 1808, in Dublin. Died 20 October 1870, in Rowney Abbey, Hertfordshire. Married: the Hungarian singer Lina Roser (1808-88); one daughter, Victoire, also a singer. Violinist in his youth; in London, 1823, and a member of the Drury Lane Theatre orchestra; in Rome, 1825, where he lived with his patron Count Mazzara and studied with Paer; in Milan, he studied counterpoint with Federici and singing with Filippo Galli; first dramatic work, the ballet La Pérouse *(1826); met Rossini in Paris, sang Figaro in* Le Barbier de Séville *(1827); continued singing in Italy in Palermo and Milan, and sang with Malibran at La Scala; in London 1833; manager of the Lyceum Theatre, 1841-42; composed English operas 1835-41, as well as one Italian opera for the London stage (*Falstaff, *19 July 1838); continued his career as both singer and opera composer in Paris, London, Berlin, St. Petersburg, and Trieste between 1841 and 1864. Balfe's English opera* The Bohemian Girl *(1843) was translated into German, Italian, and French, and continued throughout his life to be an international success.*

Operas   *Atala,* after Chateaubriand, Paris, 1827 [lost]; *I rivali di se stessi,* A. Alcozor (after Le Brun), Palermo, 1829; *Un avvertimento ai gelosi,* G. Foppa, Pavia, 1830; *Hamlet,* after Shakespeare, 1832 [unfinished; lost]; *Elfrida,* intended for Paris, 1832 [unfinished; lost]; *Enrico IV al passo della Marna,*

Milan, Teatro alla Scala, 19 February 1833; *The Siege of Rochelle*, E. Fitzball (after Mme de Genlis), London, Drury Lane Theatre, 29 October 1835; *The Maid of Artois*, A. Bunn, London, Drury Lane Theatre, 27 May 1836; *Catherine Grey*, G. Linley, London, Drury Lane Theatre, 27 May 1837; *Joan of Arc*, E. Fitzball, London, Drury Lane Theatre, 30 November 1837; *Diadeste, or The Veiled Lady*, E. Fitzball, London, Drury Lane Theatre, 17 May 1838; *Falstaff* (in Italian), S. Maggione, London, Her Majesty's Theatre, 19 July 1838; *Keolanthe, or The Unearthly Bride*, E. Fitzball, London, Lyceum Theatre, 9 March 1841; *Le puits d'amour*, Eugène Scribe and J.H. Vernoy de Saint-Georges, Paris, Opéra-Comique, 20 April 1843 (performed in English as *Geraldine, or The Lover's Well*, translated by G.A. à Beckett, London, Princess's Theatre, 14 August 1843); *The Bohemian Girl*, A. Bunn (after J.H. Vernoy de Saint-Georges), London, Drury Lane Theatre, 27 November, 1843 (performed in Italian as *La zingara*, London, Her Majesty's Theatre, 6 February 1858); *Les quatre fils Aymon*. Eugène Scribe and J.H. Vernoy de Saint-Georges, Paris, Opéra-Comique, 29 July 1844 (performed in English as *The Castle of Aymon, or The Four Brothers*, Leuwen and Brunswick, London, Princess's Theatre, 20 November 1844); *The Daughter of St. Mark*, A. Bunn (after J.H. Vernoy de Saint-Georges), London, Drury Lane Theatre, 27 November 1844; *The Enchantress*, A. Bunn (after J.H. Vernoy de Saint-Georges), London, Drury Lane Theatre, 14 May 1845; *L'étoile de Séville*, H. Lucas (after Lope de Vega), Paris, Opéra, 17 December 1845; *The Bondman*, A. Bunn (after Dumas), London, Drury Lane Theatre, 11 December 1846; *The Maid of Honour*, E. Fitzball, London, Drury Lane Theatre, 20 December 1847; [untitled work], after Hugo, *Le roi s'amuse*, 1848 [unfinished]; *The Sicilian Bride*, A. Bunn (after J.H. Vernoy de Saint-Georges), London, Drury Lane Theatre, 6 March 1852; *The Devil's In It*, A. Bunn (after Eugène Scribe), London, Surrey Theatre, 26 July 1852; *Pittore e duca*, F.M. Piave, Trieste, 21 November 1854 (performed in English as *Moro, or The Painter of Antwerp*, W.A. Barrett, London, Her Majesty's Theatre, 28 January 1882); *The Rose of Castille*, A. Harris and E. Falconer (after D'Ennery and Claireville) London, Lyceum, 29 October 1857; *Satanella, or The Power of Love*, A. Harris and E. Falconer (after Le Sage), London, Covent Garden Theatre, 20 December, 1858; *Bianca, or The Bravo's Bride*, P. Simpson (after M.G. Lewis), London, Covent Garden Theatre, 6 December 1860; *The Puritan's Daughter*, J.V. Bridgeman, London, Covent Garden, 30 November 1861; *Blanche de Nevers*, J. Brougham (after Le Bossu), London, Covent Garden, 21 November 1862; *The Armourer of Nantes*, J.V. Bridgeman, London, Covent Garden, 12 February 1863; *The Sleeping Queen, Mazeppa*, H.B. Farnie, London, Gallery of Illustration, 31 August 1864; *The Knight of the Leopard*, A. Matthison (after Scott, *The Talisman*), unfinished, arranged by Costa as *Il talismano*, G. Zaffira, London, Drury Lane Theatre, 11 June 1874.

England's relationship with opera, from its beginnings through the early twentieth century, involved both acceptance and envy of the continental product and fitful attempts at the development of an indigenous approach to the vocal art form. Dr. Samuel Johnson had characterized Italian opera, as exemplified by Handel and Piccini, as "an exotick and irrational entertainment." The success of ballad operas, drawing for their music on popular tunes of the street, drove Handel into oratorio and English opera composition into a hybrid form which reflected middle-class rather than "elite" taste, more comparable, despite the sophisticated contributions of Thomas Arne and Stefano Storace, to the mid-twentieth century's Broadway and West End musicals than to the Italian, German, and French models at hand.

The success of Carl Maria von Weber's *Oberon*, to a preposterous English libretto, and the reform of the theatre patents by Parliament in 1843 combined to renew the demand for a musical drama which would reflect both the sophistication of continental opera and the ingenuous appeal of the ballad opera. Of those who advanced to the fore in this endeavor, none was as particularly gifted for the task as Balfe. Born in Ireland, he had trained as a violinist, playing in the Drury Lane Theatre orchestra before traveling to Italy to begin a short but successful career as principal baritone, singing the works of Mozart, Rossini, and Bellini, in the major Italian opera houses.

He volunteered to compose a short opera during an engagement in Naples when a chorus strike nullified the scheduled large-scale works. In his third opera, *Enrico Quarto,* he became the only well-known composer to create a major role in his own opera, a feat he repeated in England in *Geraldine, or the Lover's Well* (he later also sang in his own *The Siege of Rochelle* and *Catherine Grey,* but was not part of the original cast).

Others besides Balfe had musical credentials with which to challenge him for English opera supremacy, but they lacked his ability to merge the best in continental ensemble music with arias that echoed the native ballad opera tradition. Edward Loder proved too sophisticated, though his *The Night Dancers* (based on the plot of Adam's ballet, *Giselle*) and *Raymond and Agnes* are probably, as a whole, musically superior to any of Balfe's operas. But Loder also lacked the talent for prolific output which Balfe possessed to a Rossinian degree; John Barnett and George MacFarren, other talented contemporaries, also suffered this defect.

Balfe himself contributed the first major English opera without spoken dialogue, *Catherine Grey*. The success of *The Bohemian Girl* eight years later confirmed his place as the foremost composer of English opera, which, to his death, in spite of challenges by Julius Benedict and William Vincent Wallace, he retained.

Balfe's reputation today rests almost solely on *The Bohemian Girl,* the only one of his operas that continues, though with increasing infrequency, to be given on provincial stages. What popularity it has comes from the ballad arias, Arline's "I dreamt I dwelt in marble halls," Thaddeus' "When other lips," and Count Arnheim's "The heart bow'd down." Ballad arias celebrated in his own time, such as "With rapture dwelling" and "The light of other days," introduced by Maria Malibran in *The Maid of Artois,* and "When I beheld the anchor weigh'd" from *The Siege of Rochelle* have been totally forgotten, as have his most ambitious operas, *The Daughter of St. Mark, The Talisman,* and *Satanella.*

Balfe's choice of libretti, especially those by Alfred Bunn and Edward Fitzball, reflect a conscious choice to respond to the socio-economic preconceptions of his audience. At a time when Meyerbeer was setting his own highly successful Parisian operas to libretti reflecting sophisticated religious and political themes, Verdi was beginning to investigate the influence of such great themes on individuals caught in their forces, and even the musically conservative Lortzing was celebrating labor unrest in his *Regina,* Balfe was setting simplistic class-conscious fairy tales which the British public sought out as an antidote to reality.

It appears to have become difficult if not impossible for most contemporary listeners to judge the music of a simple melodist such as Balfe (or Auber, Marschner, the Ricci brothers, etc.) on its own merits, laying aside both the sophistication of hindsight and a sense of frustration that he did not use his considerable gifts in more challenging ways. If he did not, after all, establish an ongoing tradition of English opera (that would await the coming of Benjamin Britten a century later), his is the most representative response to one chapter in the quest for a national approach to an international art form, fascinating on a sociological level and naively charming

musically.—WILLIAM J. COLLINS

The Ballad of Baby Doe

Composer: *Douglas Moore.*

Librettist: *J. Latouche.*

First Performance: *Central City, Colorado, 7 July 1958.*

Roles: *Baby Doe (soprano); Augusta (mezzo-soprano); Horace Tabor (bass-baritone); William Jennings Bryan (bass); Mama McCourt (contralto); Sam (tenor); Bushy (tenor); Barney (bass); Jacob (bass); Sarah (soprano); Mary (soprano); Emily (contralto); Effie (contralto); McCourt Family (soprano, alto, tenor, bass); Four Washington Dandies (tenors, basses); many bit parts which may be doubled or tripled; chorus (SATB).*

The story of *The Ballad of Baby Doe* has its roots in the American West of a century ago, and its chief characters are fashioned from actual historical figures. Horace Tabor, a rich owner of silver mines in Colorado, becomes infatuated with the much younger Elizabeth "Baby" Doe (Mrs. Harvey Doe). Horace's wife Augusta discovers her husband's secret liaison and threatens to drive her rival from town. She fails, and the affection between Horace and Baby Doe grows stronger. After both are divorced, their wedding is celebrated in Washington, D.C., with the President of the United States in attendance. Yet reputable folk continue to snub them, and Horace starts to encounter financial reverses. His career ends in ruins despite an attempt to recoup by supporting new political allies. After Horace's death Baby Doe's unshakable devotion leads her to live out her lonely days near one of his abandoned mines.

The very title of *The Ballad of Baby Doe* hints at the simplicity and the reliance on convention that mark the work both in its tone and in the dramatic content. Horace, Augusta, and Baby Doe exemplify an archetypal love-triangle in the plainest way—a hero caught between women who represent respectively the power of love and the demands of social obligations. The characters themselves are almost reducible to humors. Horace is all ardor and ambition, Baby Doe radiant sweetness, and Augusta possessiveness and embitterment.

These characters, creatures more of feeling than of thought, exist at some remove from the political issues that are introduced midway in the opera, including the question of whether gold or silver should be the proper monetary standard for American currency. Crowd scenes set about dealing with this question through slogans rather than argument; the operatic equivalent of poster art conveys the politics of the day. Thus the level of stylization here matches the work's formulaic approach to characterization.

Douglas Moore's music skillfully delineates the nature of each character. The vocal parts for the two leading women especially stand in sharp relief. Baby Doe's placid charm displays itself in easy songfulness and flurries of coloratura writing, while Augusta's resentment finds expression in more jagged melodies and unexpected rhythms. In addition, Moore had the gift of creating a role that makes the singer appear to best advantage. For instance, Baby Doe has as her most prominent numbers three well-placed arias—a "willow song" in the second scene, a hymn of sorts "to the silver moon" during the first-act finale, and the opera's epilogue, a piece of almost Handelian serenity—and all three are guaranteed applause-getters. The epilogue is a home-spun Liebestod, though musically it is akin to the close of Wagner's *Tristan und Isolde* mainly in its choice of key, B major. To set its opening words, "Always through the changing of sun and shadow, time and space," Moore has come upon a melody like the one Arthur Sullivan uses in

49

setting other thoughts on the passing of the years, namely, "Silvered is the raven hair," from Gilbert and Sullivan's *Patience.*

During the nineteenth century, German composers were sometimes advised to strive for "ballad tone" in their works and, *mutatis mutandis,* this is what Moore achieves in *Baby Doe.* His score overflows with pieces in American popular, so-called vernacular, styles from a hundred-or-so years before. Marches and dances (in particular, several notable waltzes), sentimental airs suitable for the front parlor and rousing songs like some of Stephen Foster's comic efforts press in on one another throughout the opera. Even the more operatic numbers, however spiced with dissonance, always avoid the intense complexity of twentieth-century musical modernism; they have lucid tonal harmonies and concise formal shapes. And when once-heard music reappears in later scenes, its recurrence resembles as much a Broadway musical's reprise of tunes as it does an insistent Wagnerian Leitmotiv.

In a masterful fashion Moore, together with John Latouche, simplified and mingled traditional ingredients in *The Ballad of Baby Doe.* It is a singers' opera that has memorable melodies, elements of spectacle, points of national and historical interest, including musical Americana, and time-honored characters and plot.—CHRISTOPHER HATCH

Un ballo in maschera [A Masked Ball]

Composer: *Giuseppe Verdi.*

Librettist: *Antonio Somma (after Eugène Scribe, Gustave III).*

First Performance: *Rome, Apollo, 17 February 1859.*

Roles: *Riccardo (tenor); Renato (baritone); Amelia (soprano); Oscar (soprano); Ulrica (contralto or mezzo-soprano); Samuel (bass); Tom (bass); Judge (tenor); Silvano (baritone or bass).*

Due to all sorts of difficulties with censors, Verdi and his librettist for *Un ballo in maschera* twice found it necessary to change the title as well as the names of characters and locales from Scribe's *Gustave III* in order to get permission for performance. First they changed the title to *La vendetta in domino,* and the setting to seventeenth-century Stettin. Then, again at the censor's demand, the title became *Un ballo in maschera,* and the setting, seventeenth-century Boston. In the process, King Gustavus, the original victim of regicide, becomes Riccardo, variously Earl of Warwicke, or Governor of Boston. Anckarström, the original assassin, becomes Renato, and his wife, Countess Anckarström, becomes Amelia, or even sometimes Adelia. Oscar, a page, remains constant, as do other minor characters; but the two main conspirators appear as Tom and Sam, consigned to the Boston scenario, which Verdi was forced to adopt for the first Roman production.

After a synoptic overture, which forecasts the dramatic development of the opera by presenting the main dramatic themes, Count Riccardo, who has fallen in love with the wife of his secretary, Renato, holds audience to receive proof of the loyalty and love of his subjects. Among those present, lurking in the background, are Samuel and Tom, negroes who conspire with other dissidents in a plan to murder Riccardo. Also present is Ulrica, a black fortune-teller, who is to be banished from the realm as a witch if Riccardo accepts the recommendation of his ministers.

Listening to the light-hearted advice of his page, Oscar, he decides that he will first visit Ulrica in disguise, that very night, before making a final decision.

Dressed as a common fisherman, Riccardo briefly observes Ulrica's black magic before quickly hiding when Renato's wife, Amelia, arrives seeking a magical solution to her problem. As he listens, Riccardo learns that she has come to find a cure for the love she feels for him. For remedy, Ulrica directs her to go at midnight to pick a plant growing under a gibbet just outside town. Riccardo plans to meet her there, but first hears Ulrica's prophecy that he will be murdered by the next person whose hand he shakes. Renato arrives just then, and the two shake hands.

Amelia, heavily disguised, arrives at the gibbet just before midnight, and is startled by the sudden appearance of Riccardo, who soon persuades her to confess that she does love him indeed, which disclosure unleashes a glorious love duet. Meanwhile the assassins have discovered Riccardo's whereabouts. But before they can actually accost him, Renato, unaware of the budding love affair and still loyal to Riccardo, arrives to warn him of the danger that threatens. He agrees to escort to safety the veiled figure who actually is his wife, while the count escapes to safety. Only later, when he and his disguised wife are accosted by Tom and Sam, does Renato discover her true identity.

Renato, increasingly furious, soon joins the conspiracy against Riccardo. At home the next day, Renato tells his wife she must die. Then, relenting a little, he forces her to draw lots to decide which of the conspirators will actually assassinate Riccardo. Renato wins. Despite a warning to stay away from the ball, Riccardo attends, is inadvertantly identified by the page, Oscar, and fatally stabbed by Renato. He dies, forgiving all.

Un ballo in maschera shares several characteristics with four other operas Verdi wrote in the 1850s, *Luisa Miller, Rigoletto, Il trovatore,* and *La traviata.* In the first place, the libretto is dramatically convincing, and the story it tells is interesting and credible. This last named quality stems from the realism which *Un ballo in maschera* shares with the above named, except, possibly, for *Il trovatore.* Musically, it measures up to the new high standards Verdi had achieved in these operas, particularly with regard to melody, tonal adventurousness, and rhythmic vitality. In musical characterization Verdi introduced a new type in the role of Oscar, and in orchestration he found new finesse, variety, and power of expression, anticipating in these the great orchestral mastery of his late works. In short, *Un ballo in maschera,* with its successful premiere in Rome on 17 February 1859, marked a fitting close to a remarkable decade of creative growth for Verdi.—FRANKLIN ZIMMERMAN

Bampton, Rose

Soprano, mezzo-soprano. Born 28 November 1909, in Lakewood, Ohio, near Cleveland. Married: conductor Wilfrid Pelletier, 1937. Educated at the Curtis Institute; studied with Horatio Connell, Queena Mario, Martha Graham, Elena Gerhardt, and Lotte Lehmann; debut as Siebel in Faust, *Chautauqua, 1929; minor roles with Philadelphia Opera, 1929-32; Metropolitan Opera debut as Laura,* La gioconda, *1932; sixteen roles with the Metropolitan Opera, including Aida and Amneris in* Aida, *Donna Anna in* Don Giovanni, *the title role in* Alceste, *and a number of Wagnerian heroines; soprano debut as Leonora in* Il trovatore; *Covent Garden debut as Amneris in* Aida, *1937; also sang with the New*

York City Opera; retired 1950. Taught at the Manhattan School, North Carolina School of the Arts, Drake University, the Juilliard School.

Rose Bampton's mother was born in America of German descent; her father came from Great Britain. Both were music-lovers, and the mother was an accomplished pianist, but their son, who studied the violin, decided not to pursue music professionally. Though born just outside Cleveland, which had a thriving musical life, Bampton did not study music until after the family had moved to Buffalo, New York. There her first voice teacher, a church organist named Seth Clark, recommended that the girl attend the Curtis Institute in Philadelphia, an all-scholarship institution, and she was accepted there, studying with Horatio Connell and later Queena Mario.

At first her voice was judged to be a coloratura soprano, and by studying the appropriate repertory she acquired technical agility, but she suffered uncertainty as to her rightful vocal range, and Curtis, thinking her too tall for the opera stage, gave her little preparation for opera. During student years she sang solo as a contralto in some concerts with the Philadelphia Orchestra under Stokowski; with him she recorded the "Wood Dove" in Schoenberg's *Gurre-Lieder* for RCA Victor. An appearance as Siebel in *Faust* at Chautauqua in 1929 actually preceded her Curtis studies, and while at Curtis she made a few appearances with the Philadelphia Opera in minor roles, 1929-32.

Invited to audition for the Metropolitan Opera as a result of the *Gurre-Lieder* recording, she sang mezzo-soprano repertory but was diagnosed as a soprano by the conducting staff, including Wilfrid Pelletier, whom she later married (in 1937). His coaching proved invaluable to her career, as did work in stage deportment with the dancer Martha Graham and the Greek tragedienne Margaret Anglin. She was also coached in the Lieder repertory by Elena Gerhardt during a visit to England and later by Lotte Lehmann in California.

Starting at the Metropolitan as Laura in *La gioconda* on 28 November 1932, she eventually assumed sixteen roles with the company, appearing sixty-eight times at the Opera House and twenty-six times on tour before retiring with the advent of the Rudolf Bing administration in 1950. Her transition from mezzo to soprano was signaled by taking on Aida instead of Amneris, though as late as 1940 she sang both roles in the same season when Bruna Castagna, the scheduled Amneris, was taken ill. At Covent Garden she had sung Amneris to Eva Turner's Aida in 1937. Her other major roles at the Metropolitan included Leonora in *Il trovatore,* Donna Anna in *Don Giovanni,* Gluck's Alceste and four Wagner heroines—Sieglinde, Elisabeth, Elsa and Kundry. She was chosen by Arturo Toscanini for his 1944 National Broadcasting Company Symphony broadcasts of *Fidelio,* later released on records; her other recordings consist mainly of arias.

From these records it is possible to judge Bampton's scrupulous musicianship and thorough stylistic coaching, though not the sheer size of her voice, which amply filled the large Metropolitan. In matters of detail, such as vowel elision and arbitrary breath breaks, where Italian-trained singers are apt to fall back on "tradition" and expediency, Bampton was more likely to adhere to the composer's original. Yet her singing possessed ample feeling and temperament, together with an aptitude for classical restraint and nobility, notably in the *Alceste* arias. Hers was not the heart-on-sleeve artistry that appeals to the gallery, but it benefited from uncommon intelligence, solid musical discipline and adaptability to different musical styles.

Both in her extensive recital and radio work and in the theater, Bampton exemplified the sort of well-trained all-round singer for which America became increasingly known after World War II. Herself a teacher at the Manhattan School, North Carolina School of the Arts, Drake University and finally at the Juilliard School, she has passed on to younger singers her belief in a broad-based knowledge of music and practical experience before the public in a wide variety of repertory.—JOHN W. FREEMAN

Barber, Samuel

Composer. Born 9 March 1910, in West Chester, Pennsylvania. Died 23 January 1981, in New York. Nephew of contralto Louise Homer. Studied composition with Rosario Scalero, piano with Isabelle Vengerova, singing with Emilio de Gogorza, and conducting with Fritz Reiner at the Curtis Institute of Music, graduating 1932; taught at Curtis, 1939-1942, honorary doctorate awarded 1945; American Prix de Rome, 1935; Pulitzer Scholarships, 1935, 1936; his Symphony No. 1 became the first American work to be presented at the Salzburg Festival of Contemporary Music, 25 July 1937; served in the United States Army Air Force, 1942-45; Post Service Guggenheim Fellowships, 1945, 1947, 1949; Critics Award for his Cello Concerto, 1946; consultant at the American Academy in Rome in 1947 and 1948; Pulitzer Prize for Vanessa, 1958; honorary doctorate, Harvard University, 1959; Pulitzer Prize for his Piano Concerto, 1962. Barber's works have been performed by many major orchestras, including the Boston Symphony under Serge Koussevitzky and the Philadelphia Orchestra under Eugene Ormandy.

Operas   Publisher: G. Schirmer. *The Rose Tree*, A.S. Brosius, 1920; *A Hand of Bridge*, C. Menotti, 1953, Spoleto, 17 June 1959; *Vanessa*, C. Menotti, 1956-57, New York, Metropolitan Opera, 15 January 1958; *Antony and Cleopatra*, F. Zeffirelli (after Shakespeare), New York, Metropolitan Opera, 16 September 1966; revised, with libretto revisions by C. Menotti, 1975.

Lyricism seems almost synonymous with the music of the American composer Samuel Barber. He is represented on the concert platform today more by his instrumental works than by his songs or operas, but one senses in all his pieces—even in the most abstract, and even in those few that hint at twelve-tone serial techniques—an expressive urge best satisfied through deeply meaningful melody. He was a "conservative" composer throughout his career. The several works that are deliberately angular and atonal—the 1939 Violin Concerto, the 1942 *Second Essay for Orchestra*, the 1949 Piano Sonata—stand out in marked contrast from the rest of his output; Barber flirted with musical modernism, and he did so successfully, but he never strayed far from the tonal harmonic language and basically diatonic melodic style to which he had early on pledged his allegiance.

His two best-known operas are the 1958 *Vanessa*, with a libretto by his long-time associate and companion Gian Carlo Menotti, and the 1966 *Antony and Cleopatra*, with a libretto by Franco Zeffirelli after the Shakespeare play; both were written for and produced by New York's Metropolitan Opera. *Vanessa*, a stormy drama about an older woman attempting to recapture her youth by means of a romantic involvement with a younger man, won the Pulitzer Prize for Music and it has enjoyed a fair number of subsequent productions; *Antony and Cleopatra*, commissioned for the opening of the Met's new opera house at Lincoln Center, was generally a failure as much with critics as with the public. Barber also wrote a one-act chamber opera titled *A Hand of Bridge,* for Menotti's Festival of Two Worlds in Spoleto, Italy, in 1959; among the many works he produced as a child is a still unpublished opera—written at age ten—titled *The Rose Tree.*

As noted, Barber's instrumental music—in particular the 1933 *School for Scandal* overture, the *Adagio for Strings* extracted from his 1936 String Quartet, the 1962 *Piano Concerto,* the first two of the three *Essays for Orchestra* (from 1937 and 1942) and the 1955 *Summer Music* for wind quintet—is in general heard more frequently than his vocal pieces. Among the latter, the most enduringly popular seem to be the 1931 *Dover Beach,* for string quartet and mezzo-soprano or baritone, and the 1947 *Knoxville; Summer of 1915,* for soprano and orchestra, based on the prologue to James Agee's novel *A Death in the Family.*—JAMES WIERZBICKI

Il barbiere di Siviglia (Almaviva, ossia L'inutile precauzione) [The Barber of Seville]

Composer: *Gioachino Rossini.*

Librettist: *C. Sterbini (after Beaumarchais and G. Petrosellini).*

First Performance: *Rome, Torre Argentina, 20 February 1816.*

Rossini's *Il barbiere di Siviglia*, Royal Opera, London, 1990

b

OPERA

Roles: *Rosina (soprano); Count Almaviva (tenor); Figaro (baritone); Dr. Bartolo (bass); Basilio (bass); Berta (mezzo-soprano or soprano); Fiorello (baritone); Sergeant (tenor); Ambroggio (bass); Notary, Magistrate (mute); chorus (TTB).*

No less an operatic authority than Giuseppe Verdi once said: "For abundance of real musical ideas, for comic verve, and for truthful declamation, *Il barbiere di Siviglia* is the finest *opera buffa* in existence." No one has ever seriously disputed Verdi's appraisal. Rossini himself realized the scope of his achievement, for in his later years he remarked: "I hope to be survived by, if nothing else, the third act of *Otello,* the second act of *William Tell,* and the whole of *The Barber of Seville.*" Rossini's *Otello,* alas, has been effaced by Verdi's; *Guillaume Tell* lives on principally as an overture; only *Il barbiere* has never worn out its welcome on the world's operatic stages.

Rossini composed it when he was twenty-four and already regarded as a budding genius, with *Tancredi* and *L'italiana in Algeri* already to his credit. The libretto (by Cesare Sterbini) was drawn from *Le barbier de Séville* of Beaumarchais, the French playwright whose *Le mariage de Figaro* had already provided Mozart with an excellent operatic subject.

Figaro, that most ebullient of barbers, also is the centerpiece of Rossini's comedy. The Count Almaviva, a Spanish grandee, has arrived in Seville disguised as a poor student named Lindoro, to serenade and otherwise lay siege to Rosina, the ward of the pompous Dr. Bartolo, who plans to marry her himself. Almaviva, after his opening serenade, runs into his former attendant Figaro and enlists him in his campaign. On Figaro's advice, Almaviva makes two forays into Bartolo's house to woo Rosina, in act I pretending to be a drunken soldier and in act II a singing teacher replacing her regular instructor, the slippery Don Basilio. Rosina, who detests Dr. Bartolo, encourages Almaviva. Despite all of Bartolo's machinations, Almaviva (who reveals his true identity at the last minute) manages to marry Rosina, while Figaro, his work done, happily extinguishes his lantern.

Out of deference to Giovanni Paisiello, then seventy-five years old, who had written a *Barbiere* also based on Beaumarchais some thirty-five years previously, Rossini decided to entitle his opera *Almaviva, ossia L'inutile precauzione* (*The Useless Precaution*). It was, as you might say, a useless precaution, for Paisiello's supporters effectively sabotaged the opening of Rossini's opera at the Torre Argentina Theater in Rome on 20 February 1816, turning it into a fiasco. By the third night, however, Rossini's opera was a roaring success, casting poor Paisiello's version quite into the shade, where it has remained ever since.

The American author James M. Cain, in his novel *Serenade,* has an operatic baritone describe Rossini's overtures this way: "Rossini loved the theater, and that's why he could write an overture. He takes you into the theater—hell, you can even feel them getting into their seats, and smell the theater smell, and see the lights go up on the curtain." In fact, Rossini liked some of his overtures so much that he recycled them from opera to opera. The sparkling and beautifully scored *Barbiere* overture, which seems so admirably suited to setting the mood for the buffoonery that follows, had already seen service in two earlier operas called *Aureliano in Palmira* and *Elisabetta, regina d'Inghilterra.*

From start to finish *Il barbiere* is so marvellously crafted, brilliantly inventive and uproariously funny that it becomes, as Verdi indicated, the ultimate *opera buffa.* Rossini once observed that he could set a laundry list to music, but far more important, he also knew how to create characters. Figaro, the mercurial barber himself, seems molded out of music. His rippling rhythms, agile phrases, infectious melodies, acrobatic leaps, even his repetitions and reiterations, all describe his character with a clarity that pages of descriptive text could scarcely match. He hardly needs words—indeed, at times in that most dazzling of all patter songs, the "Largo al factotum" in which he introduces himself, he actually gives language up in favor of a string of "la-la-la-la-las."

Similarly, Rosina's music admirably meets the requirements of both a kittenish young woman expressing the joys of first love and an operatic soprano seeking to make a brilliant impression. Rossini's first Rosina, Maria Giorgi-Righetti, was a contralto, so the role authentically belongs, if not to contraltos, at least to mezzo-sopranos. However, the role nowadays is perhaps most frequently sung by high sopranos, permitting some dazzling vocalizations in Rosina's introductory aria "Una voce poco fa." Rosina also has a chance to shine in the act-II "Lesson Scene," in which the supposed singing master, Almaviva in disguise, invites the girl to present a song of her choice. Rossini actually wrote an aria to be used at this point, but that hasn't prevented *prima donnas* from inserting selections of their own, ranging from the mad scene of *Lucia di Lammermoor* to "Home, Sweet Home."

Almaviva, with his impersonations of a drunken soldier and the unctuous music master, comes across more strongly than many a romantic lead, while Doctor Bartolo is a tonal image of inane pomposity, as in his aria "A un dottor della mia sorte," and the artful intriguer Don Basilio discloses both his intentions and his character in his "Calumny" aria.

Yet for all its individual depictions, *Il barbiere* is essentially an ensemble opera, with its duets, trios, and larger groupings that manage to be farcical and touching at the same time. Also very much in evidence throughout are the "Rossini crescendo," in which the music increases dizzily in tempo and volume, and the "ensemble of perplexity," in which the various personages in overlapping combinations insist melodiously and repeatedly that the situation is most vexing and they really don't know what to do. Somehow, they always manage to do something, and it usually turns out for the best.

Il barbiere di Siviglia even drew praise from Beethoven, who counseled Rossini, however, not to try anything but *opera buffa*. "Wanting to succeed in another style would be to stretch your luck," he said, adding: "Above all, make a lot of *Barbers*." One, as it turned out, was enough.—HERBERT KUPFERBERG

Barbieri, Fedora

Mezzo-soprano. Born 4 June 1920, in Trieste, Italy. Married impresario Barzoletti. Studied at Trieste with Luigi Toffolo and at school of Teatro Comunale, Florence with Giulia Tess; debut in Florence as Fidelma in Matrimonio segreto *in 1940; created Dariola in Alfano's* Don Juan de Manara *in 1941 at Florence Festival; Teatro alla Scala debut as Meg Page in* Falstaff *in 1942, and sang regularly at the Teatro alla Scala from 1946; Metropolitan Opera debut in 1950 as Eboli in Verdi's* Don Carlos *on opening night of Sir Rudolf Bing's regime, and appeared there 1950-54, 1956-57, and 1967-68; sang at Covent Garden with Teatro alla Scala tour in 1950, and as guest, 1957-58 and 1964; created the Wife in Chailly's* L'idiota *at the Rome Opera.*

One of the voice types that seem to be missing from stages today is the earthy, voluptuous mezzo/contralto: a voice born to sing Verdi's Azucena with as much naturalness as ease of power. Chloë Elmo had such a voice, and she was followed by Fedora Barbieri. Others sing these roles, but who really followed Elmo and Barbieri? Giulietta Simionato's sound was gorgeous but more refined in timbre.

The "meaty" vocal lines of such characters from Italian opera as Laura, La Principessa di Bouillon, Ulrica (*Un ballo in maschera*), and especially Dame Quickly were not Barbieri's only successes; her repertoire was large and extremely varied. She had a style and technique that encompassed Gluck, Handel, Cherubini, Rossini and Bellini, as well as Verdi. She was also a noted Carmen.

After her 1940 stage debut in Florence, her career enjoyed a steep upward rise, aided in part by her marriage to the director of Florence's Maggio Musicale. Successful debuts in many international houses came in rapid succession: she first sang in London with an Italian ensemble in 1950, and in the same year she debuted as Eboli (*Don Carlos*) in Rudolf Bing's original opening night at the Metropolitan, with Björling and Siepi. She subsequently sang eight roles at the Metropolitan; the final one, Quickly, in 1967 when she returned after several years' absence. Barbieri immediately became a favorite with audiences everywhere she appeared.

Barbieri's portrayal of Adalgisa (*Norma*) was often given with Maria Callas as Norma. She also sang that role with Zinka Milanov, with whom she also appeared in *Aïda*. Del Monaco was often her partner in *Carmen*.

Commercial recordings do not abound with Fedora Barbieri, and that is a definite loss. The best known are the two complete operas with RCA, *Trovatore* and *Aïda*, making up the dream operatic quartet of Milanov, Barbieri, Jussi Björling and Leonard Warren. In spite of magnificent singing and vocal style, the recorded performances are somewhat marred because the principals strive for perfection at the expense of visceral excitement. If a "pirate" copy of the Met's *Don Carlo* with Björling, Robert Merrill and Cesare Siepi can be found, certainly listen to that. "Pirate" copies of *Norma* with Callas and Barbieri are generally available. Late in her career, James Levine called on Barbieri to sing Berta in his recording of *Il barbiere* but intonation problems do not help the memory of her triumphs.

We still await the true successor to Fedora Barbieri.—BERT WECHSLER

The Bartered Bride [Prodaná nevěsta]

Composer: *Bedřich Smetana.*

Librettist: *K. Sabina.*

First Performance: *Prague, Provisional Theater, 30 May 1866.*

Roles: *Mařenka (soprano); Jeník (tenor); Krušina (baritone); Ludmilla (soprano); Micha (bass); Hata (mezzo-soprano); Vašek (tenor); Kečal (bass); Circus Manager (tenor); Esmeralda (soprano); Circus Indian (tenor); chorus (SATB).*

After a bustling overture, the action of *The Bartered Bride* opens on a spring holiday in a Bohemian village. At once we are introduced to the young lovers Mařenka and Jeník, who are shocked by the news that Mařenka's parents have promised her in marriage to the "only" son of their rich neighbor Micha, whom she has not even met. (There has been another son from a first marriage, but he has left home). Mařenka confesses her pledge to Jeník; after a vigorous exchange with the marriage broker Kečal and her parents, she remains defiant, and the act ends with a festive polka danced by the villagers.

Act II begins with a drinking song, with contributions in praise of money by Kečal and in praise of love by Jeník, while the villagers dance a vigorous *furiant*. Now at last we meet Vašek, Kečal's choice to be Mařenka's husband, a shy, simple, but good-natured lad with a stammer. He is terrified at the thought of marriage and by chance confesses this to Mařenka, who does not identify herself but seizes the opportunity to tell him that his prospective bride is flighty and that there is a prettier and nicer girl who loves him. In the meantime Kečal offers Jeník three hundred guilders if he will give up Mařenka, and surprisingly he agrees on the condition that she shall marry only Micha's elder son. When Kečal exits, Jeník tells us why: he is Micha's long-lost son, and now not only can he marry Mařenka, he can get her a dowry as well! Now the marriage contract between Mařenka and Vašek is read out publicly together with Jeník's renunciation of her, but when Kečal mentions the money the villagers, angry that Jeník should abandon Mařenka for gain, turn on him.

In the meantime, poor Vašek is searching anxiously for the nice girl who gave him good advice, in a comic aria marked *lamentoso*. He is cheered by the arrival of circus entertainers with a beautiful dancer called Esmeralda and a performing bear. But the man who should be in the bearskin is drunk, and Vašek, who agrees to take his place so as to dance with Esmeralda, starts practicing some steps, escaping from his parents who want him to meet the dreaded Mařenka. She in turn appears, furious at the news that Jeník has deserted her for money. When Vašek comes back to learn with delight who she really is, and all four parents urge her to marry him, she becomes even more confused, and after a touching ensemble she is left alone to bewail her situation. The appearance of Jeník provokes her to fury, and she cannot understand why he remains so cheerful. The dénouement comes when the official betrothal is to take place. Jeník, recognized by his father as his long-lost elder son, offers himself to Mařenka to the happiness of all present save Kečal.

For most operagoers, *The Bartered Bride* is the quintessential Czech national opera, although Smetana himself regarded his *Dalibor* and *Libuše* as more seriously nationalistic and was occasionally somewhat dismissive about this most popular of his works. He said that in writing it his model had been Mozart, and certainly the overture has the same vivacity, while the light-hearted intrigues of plot and counter-plot also owe something to Mozart (both *Le nozze di Figaro* and *The Bartered Bride* feature the rediscovery of a long-lost son), as well as perhaps such Italian composers as Rossini and Donizetti. As for Kečal, Smetana may have modeled him on the character Van Bett in Lortzing's *Zar und Zimmermann*.

It took some time before *The Bartered Bride* reached the form in which we know it today, for after the premiere Smetana made a number of major revisions that took him four years in all, not the least of which was the addition of the dances in each act—the polka that ends act I, the *furiant* in act II, and the circus clowns' *skočná* in act III. Another addition was the drinking song in praise of beer as "a gift from heaven" at the start of act II. Although the dances needed to be added for a planned Paris production—the French insisted on it—their incorporation is a gain in every way, while they and the drinking song also give the villagers more to do than simply observe and comment.

Good humor and *joie de vivre* abound in *The Bartered Bride*. But there is much more to the opera than this, with such touching moments as the quintet (later sextet) near the end, where it seems that Mařenka really must marry a man she does not love. The scheming broker Kečal provides comedy and has some effective scenes of frustration and anger too. But it is Vašek who provides the really inventive comic figure; here is a youth who is too sympathetic to be merely a figure of fun, and as sung by Peter Pears in 1943 in a Sadler's Wells production he provided the librettist Eric Crozier with a model for the Suffolk lad Albert Herring in Britten's comic opera of that name four years later.—CHRISTOPHER HEADINGTON

Bartok, Béla

Composer. Born 25 March 1881, in Nagyszentmiklós, Hungary (now Sînnicolau Mare, Rumania). Died 26 September 1945, in New York City. Married: 1) the pianist Márta Ziegler (two sons); 2) Ditta Pásztory (died 21 November 1982). A child prodigy on the piano, he was initially taught by his parents, then by Ferenc Kersch, Ludwig Berger, and László Erkel; studied harmony with Anton Hyrtl; studied composition with János Koessler and piano with István Thomán at the Budapest Royal Academy of Music, 1899-1903; interested in folksongs as both an ethnomusicologist and a composer—commissioned by the Hungarian Academy of Sciences in 1904 to edit a folksong collection of 13,000 items; taught piano at Budapest Royal Academy of Music from 1907-1934; moved to New York City in 1940; honorary doctorate, Columbia University, 1940; worked on a collection of Yugoslavian folksongs at Columbia University, 1941-1942. Bartók's only opera is Duke Bluebeard's Castle *(1918).*

Operas *Duke Bluebeard's Castle (A Kékszakállú herceg vara)*, Béla Balázs, 1911 (revised 1912, 1918), Budapest, Budapest Opera, 24 May 1918.

Bartók composed only one opera, *Duke Bluebeard's Castle,* based on the "mystery play" by the contemporary poet Béla Balász. It was also his first vocal work, and the text was offered to him at a highly appropriate time, both in his musical and in his personal development.

By 1911 Bartók had devoted several years to an intensive study of Hungarian folk music, and the fruits of this work had begun to emerge in his own music, in particular in the First String Quartet and the Violin Concerto no. 1. It gave him the courage to throw off the early influences on his style, especially that of Liszt, and he became fascinated by the music of Debussy, who also employed the lydian and whole-tone scales, which are frequently found in Hungarian folk-music.

Bartók had passed through a period of introspection in 1911. An intensely private and self-contained person, he had been obliged first by his unrequited love for the violinist Stefi Geyer, and then by marriage to his young pupil Márta Ziegler, to brood on the violation of individuality which is involved in any close relationship between man and woman. Balász's text is a direct symbolic dramatization of his idea.

The musical style of *Bluebeard* was partially influenced by Debussy's approach to the setting of Maeterlinck's *Pelléas and Mélisande*. Like Debussy, Bartók often uses his large orchestra to create coloristic tone-pictures of setting and landscape. He also displays an acute

59

Béla Bartók

sensitivity to word-setting; the vocal line follows the intonations and cadences of the spoken Hungarian language, and totally avoids melismas.

Bartók's voice parts are far more passionate than those in *Pelléas,* and the declamation is often of Wagnerian power. The orchestra also plays a role in *Bluebeard* which is opposed to Debussy's aesthetics, despite his influence on its sound. Bartók employs impressionistic devices to evoke the contents of the first six rooms (and memorably adapts the sustained triads of *La cathédrale engloutie* to his own purposes in the climactic revelation at the fifth door), but the overall conception of his opera is post-Straussian. Bartók broke with Strauss in an adverse review of *Elektra* shortly before composing *Bluebeard,* but his one act opera is akin to Strauss' in its grandeur, power, and harmonic savagery. It is also composed on the same principle, as a symphonic poem with an ending which recapitulates the opening (to reflect the movement on stage from darkness to light and then back into utter darkness).

The use of tonal symbolism is also Straussian. Bartók's opera is dominated by a conflict between Judit's tonality of F natural and Bluebeard's F sharp; and this conflict is reinforced by the repeated use of a dissonant *leitmotif,* consisting simply of a repeated minor second, to portray the blood that Judit finds throughout the castle.

The violence and emphatic statement of many passages in the score of *Bluebeard* remove it decisively from Debussy's aesthetic. The debt to Strauss is also transcended by the features which gives Bartók's score its greatest individuality—the folk melancholy of the exquisite woodwind solos which establish the atmosphere in the opening sections of the work, and the predominantly linear, rather than vertical, harmonic procedures.

Bartók submitted *Duke Bluebeard's Castle* to a competition for a new opera; it was unsuccessful, and remained unperformed until 1918. His ballet *The Wooden Prince,* also to a text by Balász, was acclaimed on its first production in 1911, but rarely performed thereafter, and the pantomime *The Miraculous Mandarin*—one of Bartók's greatest scores, if also his most ferocious—was withdrawn after one performance in Cologne in 1926, and not heard in Hungary during the composer's lifetime.

These experiences partially explain why Bartók never wrote another opera, and his personal and financial situation was for many years so precarious that after *The Miraculous Mandarin* he wrote only one more work for orchestra (the *Cantata Profana*) without a commission.

Bartók's musical thinking also became more appropriate to concert than to stage music. During the 1920s and 1930s he was increasingly preoccupied with symmetrical construction, complex numerically based structures, counterpoint and fugue, approaches to composition which are not easily combined with a flexible response to text and stage action.

Hindemith and Berg, among others, have shown that these formal means can be employed successfully in opera. Bartók's reasons for not returning to this medium lie elsewhere. The difficulties he had encountered in achieving performance for his three stage works undoubtedly deterred him, but the fundamental reason is that in *Duke Bluebeard's Castle,* he had found a text which allowed him to express the one subject to which he wished to give lyric and dramatic expression.—MICHAEL EWANS

Bartoli, Cecilia

Mezzo-soprano. Born in Rome, 1966. Studied with her parents, Silvana Bazzoni and Angelo Bartoli, both professional singers, and attended the Conservatorio di Santa Cecilia. Roles include Rosina in Il barbiere di Siviglia, *Angelina in* La Cerentola. *Awards: Grammy Award for Best Classical Vocal Album for her* Italian Lieder *album; Deutsche-Schallplatten Preise, La Stella d'oro (Italy), the Caecilia Award (Belgium), the Diapason d'or Award (France).*

Just when many observers were ready to concede that the proliferation of competent but faceless singers moving through the 1980s and 90s was destined to become a distinguishing characteristic of late-20th century singing, along comes Cecilia Bartoli to prove them wrong. Bartoli is an authentic vocal phenomenon. Her mezzo-soprano is stamped with a uniquely affable personality that is welcome rain following the troublesome vocal drought that preceded it; hers is a voice meant for the ages, a one-in-a-million vehicle whose intense character proves once and for all that there is more to singing than getting the notes right.

Trained primarily by her mother, Bartoli sings with disarming naturalness. Her technique, which includes impeccable coloratura capabilities and an unusually wide and apparently seamless range, is solid enough to negotiate the fiercest demands of Rossini, the composer with whom she has achieved her greatest successes to date.

The effervescent Bartoli clearly loves to sing, and she brings an infectious enthusiasm to that process. How fabulous, she seems to be saying, that the black-and-white shapes composers scatter across staff paper can be translated through the voice into such moving sequences of sounds. Part of Bartoli's charm is this naive wonder. Despite the strong musical personality that informs her singing, she gives the impression that she is as mystified by the high-calibered results as her listeners are.

Her mezzo is not a large one, and some believe she may be less effective in giant houses like the Metropolitan Opera. That has not been the case to date, partly because her training has equipped her with the means to magnify her sound without straining it, and partly because her art is so precious it causes audiences to become uncharacteristically quiet during her performances. Heard in a 1994 recital from the rear portion of the main floor of a 4,000-seat auditorium, Bartoli was able to project intimate subtleties of her singing—a sudden staccato at the end of a phrase, for instance, or a slight increase in volume on a prominent note—with no trouble. It would be inaccurate to say that her voice filled the hall; it would be equally inaccurate to say that her talent didn't. Bartoli's special gifts also come through with surprising strength on her recordings.

What the future holds for such a singer can only be imagined. Provided she takes care of her instrument, Bartoli should continue to be proof of the startling difference between a greatly gifted singer and a merely adequate practitioner. She may find that the best way to do that is to devote herself primarily to recitals and recordings, with only occasional forays into gargantuan opera houses. On the other hand, her voice may deepen and grow larger as she moves into her 30s and 40s. If that happens, and if her current technical attributes remain intact, she may develop into one of the major operatic singers of the next century.——JOHN GUINN

Battistini, Mattia

Baritone. Born 27 February 1856, in Rome. Died 7 November 1928, in Colle Baccaro, near Rome. Studied briefly with Venceslao Persichini and Eugenio Terziana; traveled in Russia and to South America, but never visited United States; debut at the Torre Argentina, Rome in 1878; Covent Garden debut as Riccardo in Bellini's I puritani, *1883; Teatro alla Scala debut in 1888 as Nelusko in* L'africaine; *St Petersburg debut as Hamlet, 1893, thereafter visited Russia annually until 1914; roles include Rigoletto, Don Giovanni, Simon Boccanegra, Wolfram, Telramund; sang until 1926.*

Battistini was one of the first generation of great singers to leave behind a significant recorded legacy. His career, lasting fifty years—the length of his adult life—began and ended at the top. His debut was in late 1878 as King Alfonso in *La favorita* at the Torre Argentina in Rome. It was an enormous success and was followed within a few months by leading roles in *Il trovatore, La forza del destino* and *Rigoletto*. Although he was to sing in various Italian towns during the next decade culminating in his first Teatro alla Scala season in 1888, Battistini's international career was to begin almost immediately. During 1881 and 1882 he sang extensively in South America, returning there in 1889. In addition to appearances in both London and Paris he also sang frequently in Madrid and Lisbon.

In many ways the decisive step in Battistini's career was his journey to Russia in the winter of 1893 for his first performances in St. Petersburg and Moscow. In both he was to become an enormous favorite. For the next twenty years, until the First World War, the regular pattern of his year was to perform in St. Petersburg and Moscow during the winter months and in Warsaw en route in spring, autumn or both. He appeared in many other Russian cities as well as in Berlin, Vienna, Bucharest, but his performances in Italy were relatively few and far between.

Levik's memoirs include marvellous descriptions of Battistini's Russian appearances: "Battistini was particularly rich in overtones which continued to sound long after he had ceased to sing. You saw that the singer had closed his mouth, but certain sounds still held you in their power. The unusually attractive timbre of his voice caressed the listener, as though enveloping him in warmth." Levik also makes an important point which may help explain the length of Battistini's career: "If Battistini's greatest asset was his voice, then his second was his marvellous training. He attached great importance to work on his voice."

After his youthful journeys to South America Battistini never again crossed the Atlantic and thus never appeared in the USA. His first appearances at Covent Garden were in 1883, but neither then nor later in 1905 and 1906 did he make quite the same impact as he did further East. He was clearly effective in the first London performances of *Eugene Onegin,* but the opera itself had little success. P.G. Hurst claims that in *La traviata* he overshadowed Caruso and Melba, but this was probably not a widely held view. Much later in the 1920s he appeared in several concerts in London and the critics, marvelling at the longevity of his career, vied with each other in a battle of superlatives.

"My school is in my records." Clearly Battistini was very aware of the importance of his recorded legacy. His first records were made in Warsaw in 1902, but while historically fascinating, they do not demonstrate the best in the singer's art. His 1906 series, however, include some of the greatest records ever made.

Battistini recorded until the early 1920s and it becomes easy to appreciate the sobriquet "King of baritones and baritone of kings." The style seems aristocratic; vocal production seems easy; there is a finely flowing legato line; the overall effect is frequently of rare beauty. We have to remember that this style of singing has long since vanished for it reflects the age in which Battistini learned his trade. Expression is as important as legato and the singer is profligate with ornamentation which might not be acceptable today. Certainly it seems inappropriate in Mozart and verismo, but Battistini is simply superb in Bellini, Donizetti and early Verdi and, if acceptable in Italian, Massenet and Thomas. All his recordings from *La favorita* are fine. If the legato cannot quite match Renaud, Battistini has the edge in expression. His 1906 recording of "Il mio Lionel" from *Martha* seems the acme of perfection, whilst there is regal splendor to the wonderful series from *Ernani*. In all his records Battistini seems to be tireless. A less well-trained artist could not have sustained such a career, with almost fifty years devoted to eighty different roles.—STANLEY HENIG

Battle, Kathleen

Soprano. Born 13 August 1948 in Portsmouth, Ohio. Studied with Franklin Bens at Cincinnati College-Conservatory (B.M. 1970; M.M. 1971); professional debut at Spoleto Festival in Ein Deutsches Requiem, *1972; sang Susanna with New York City Opera, 1976; debut at Metropolitan Opera as Shepherd in* Tannhäuser, *1978, and has sung over 100 performances there, including Strauss's Zdenka, Rossini's Rosina, Despina, Zerlina, Blondchen, Susanna, Cleopatra in first Metropolitan Opera performance of Handel's* Giulio Cesare *in 1988, and Pamina in 1991; received Laurence Olivier Award for the Best Performance in a New Opera Production for her Covent Garden debut as Zerbinetta in* Ariadne auf Naxos; *has also appeared with Opéra of Paris, Vienna State Opera, and Lyric Opera, Chicago; honorary doctoral degrees from the University of Cincinnati, Westminster Choir College in Princeton, New Jersey, Ohio University in Athens, Ohio, Xavier University in Cincinnati, and Amherst College.*

Soprano Kathleen Battle has established herself as one of the leading *leggero* sopranos of the 1980s and 1990s. This term designates the vocal type situated between the agile coloratura and the slightly weightier lyric. Throughout her career Battle has remained within her voice category, although she has sung some lyric roles and, with her facility in fioritura, a few coloratura ones as well, choosing roles that require some agility and do not necessitate a particularly large instrument. She has avoided the tendency common in lyric sopranos to venture into the heavier, vocally dangerous spinto roles—roles that can take a physical and emotional toll on a singer.

Battle's repertoire includes Susanna in Mozart's *Le nozze di Figaro*, Blondchen in Mozart's *Die Entführung aus dem Serail*, Despina in Mozart's *Così fan tutte*, Pamina and Papagena in Mozart's *Die Zauberflöte*, Zerlina in Mozart's *Don Giovanni*, Norina in Donizetti's *Don Pasquale*, Adina in Donizetti's *L'elisir d'amore*, Sophie in Massenet's *Werther*, Sophie in Richard Strauss's *Der Rosenkavalier*, Zerbinetta in Richard Strauss's *Ariadne auf Naxos*, Zdenka in Richard Strauss's *Arabella*, the Shepherd in Wagner's *Tannhäuser*, Elvira in Rossini's *L'italiana in Algeri*, Rosina in Rossini's *Il barbiere di Siviglia*, Oscar in Verdi's *Un ballo in maschera*, and Cleopatra in Handel's *Giulio Cesare*.

Although Battle has sung extensively with the Metropolitan Opera (where she made her debut in 1978), she has also sung in the opera houses of Zurich, Chicago, San Francisco, Paris, London, and at the Salzburg Festival. She has also participated in concert performances of Handel's *Semele* and Verdi's *Falstaff* (as Nannetta) at Carnegie Hall.

Battle's voice is pure, light, and lyrical, and it is marked by an exceptional beauty of tone. The purity of her voice is not marked by a "whiteness," the characteristic vibratoless sound of some voices of its type. Although she does not have great power, she has the ability to float high pianissimo notes. Her high range is extended, encompassing the highest notes of Zerbinetta's aria, although it thins out somewhat at the very top. Her voice has been described as ravishing, radiant, and silvery, with effortless high notes of soaring purity; her voice is secure and well controlled. Within a relatively limited dramatic range, she is capable of expressive singing through nuances of tone color, and is able to convey coquetry and charm as well as deeper feelings. Her acting is aided by her clear diction and close attention to the words.

Critics have sometimes found her singing too beautiful for certain of her roles, and they note an excessive coyness in her manner, with the natural sweetness of her voice becoming cloying. Some critics have made reference to her tendency—to use their evocative term—to coo. They have noted that in some roles she emphasizes the soubrettishness of the character at the expense of the wisdom and wit that lie beneath the surface.

Battle has made recordings of some of her roles, including Elvira in Rossini's *L'italiana in Algeri* (under Scimone), Oscar (under Solti), Adina (under Levine), Zerbinetta (under Levine), Papagena (under Lombard), Despina (under Muti), Zerlina (under Karajan), Blondchen (under Solti), Susanna (under Muti), and the Woodbird in Levine's complete recording of Wagner's *Der Ring des Nibelungen*.—MICHAEL SIMS

The Bear

Composer: *William Walton.*

Librettist: *P. Dehn (after Chekhov).*

First Performance: *Aldeburgh, 1967.*

Roles: *Mme Popova (mezzo-soprano); Smirnov (baritone); Luka (bass); Cook (mute); Groom (mute).*

The Bear was William Walton's second opera. The first, *Troilus and Cressida*, was composed in 1954 in the "grand" tradition of the nineteenth century. *The Bear*, which stands at the other end of the scale from this earlier work, is more closely related to a vaudeville than to grand opera. The libretto was skillfully adapted from Anton Chekhov's one-act play *The Bear* by Paul Dehn and the composer. The action takes place in the drawing room of a young widow, Madame Yeliena Ivanova Popova. The time is 1888. Madame clings to her widowhood, vowing to remain faithful to the memory of her late husband, who was anything but a paragon of virtue. Luka, her bailiff/manservant, announces the arrival of Gregory Stepanovitch Smirnov, a middle-aged landowner to whom Popova's late husband owed 1,300 rubles for oats for the family horse, Toby. Smirnov has come to collect. Popova assures him that her bailiff will pay at the end of the week, but Smirnov insists that he needs the money immediately. Popova exits. Smirnov carries on, moving from lamentation to shouting. Popova re-enters, bothered by the shouting. After an argument, Smirnov challenges her to a duel and she accepts. She gets her husband's pistols. While they brandish pistols and threaten one another, Luka alternately begs Smirnov to leave and prays to God for mercy. Just before shots are fired, Smirnov declares his love for the widow. They embrace.

The music, essentially diatonic, is composed in a style more akin to the music of Walton's *Façade* in its various versions. With such a light-hearted libretto, Walton is able to indulge himself, revealing the extent of his wit and tongue-in-cheek attitude towards his characters. He revels in parody. The music itself is a masterful interweaving of original composition, quotations, and allusions to other composers' works (not to mention a subtle snippet from Walton himself from time to time).

For instance, critics have often suggested that early in the work, while Madame Popova is contemplating a photograph of her late husband, the music is at times pure Tchaikovsky. A more blatant allusion is apparent during the exchange between Popova and Smirnov, when she admonishes him about his lack of manners, declaring that he is coarse and ill-bred while she is a lady. Smirnov's response is in the style of a French singer; the music strongly suggests Fauré. Smirnov's use of French, of course, is pure conceit, given that the use of that language by nineteenth-century Russians signified refinement and breeding. Critics have also detected bits of Strauss, Offenbach, Verdi, and Britten, in addition to Walton's quotes from himself.

The Bear exhibits a strong rhythmic drive. The action is pushed along by the music, punctuated quite dramatically at appropriate times in the score. Although the instrumentation is light (including a single woodwind, one horn, one trumpet, one trombone, percussion, harp, piano and strings), the composer's skill is evident in the changes of texture that accompany changes of mood in the libretto.

The Bear has been described as "high-spirited" and "rollicking"; it is a farce from start to finish. It is also one of a small number of one-act operas that lend themselves to performance by amateurs as well as professionals. It is effective in its own right, not necessarily requiring all the trappings of elaborate sets and costumes.—CAROLYN J. SMITH

Beatrice di Tenda [Beatrice of Tenda]

Composer: *Vincenzo Bellini.*

Librettist: *Felice Romani (after a novel by Carlo Tebaldi Fores and a ballet by Antonio Monticini).*

First Performance: *Venice, La Fenice, 16 March 1833.*

Roles: *Filippo (baritone); Beatrice (soprano); Agnese (soprano); Orombello (tenor); Anichino (tenor); Rizzardo del Maino (baritone or bass); chorus (SSATTBB).*

The plot of *Beatrice di Tenda* is propelled by each of the principal characters loving someone who does not return his or her love. Filippo Visconti, a fifteenth-century Duke of Milan and husband of Beatrice di Tenda, through whom he rose to power, loves Agnese del Maino, Beatrice's lady-in-waiting. Agnese, while aware of Filippo's feelings, is in love with Orombello, Lord of Ventimiglia. Orombello, however, loves Beatrice. Beatrice, although she complains of Filippo's ingratitude, seems to love neither Filippo nor Orombello; she sings affectionately about her deceased husband. The plot moves through a series of accusations and betrayals. In act I, Orombello foolishly reveals to Agnese that he loves Beatrice. Filippo accusingly confronts Beatrice with a bundle of compromising secret papers, which Beatrice claims are petitions from her loyal subjects. Orombello begs Beatrice to run away with him and rally her supporters to overthrow Filippo, who has failed her both as a husband and as a ruler. Beatrice refuses and orders Orombello to leave, but at that moment they are surprised by Filippo and his retinue. Filippo has them both arrested.

The two main scenes of the second act are a trial scene and the final scene preceding Beatrice's execution. At the trial Beatrice does not defend herself against the accusations but rather questions the legality of being tried by her own vassals. Orombello who, offstage, had confessed under torture, retracts his confession before the judges. Both Agnese and Beatrice express sympathy for his sufferings. Filippo attempts to call off the trial, but now the judges declare that Beatrice must undergo torture. Agnese pleads with Filippo to pardon Beatrice and Orombello, but an attempted uprising by Beatrice's followers convinces Filippo that Beatrice is too great a threat to him. In the final scene Agnese begs Beatrice for forgiveness. Beatrice adds her forgiveness to Orombello's and bravely goes to her death.

Beatrice is the work of the mature Bellini, but it is not Bellini at his peak. The story suggests that the characters are driven by political desires as well as emotional ones. But rather than enhancing the drama, the overabundance of motives just diffuses the focus. Does Filippo believe Beatrice to be guilty of treason or adultery?—or both? or neither? With his motives unclear, both his decision to forgive Beatrice and to condemn her seem equally contrived. Beatrice's inner life is likewise opaque to the audience. What is the source of her abundant courage and fortitude? She has two full-scale arias—one in each act—but the musical effect of these numbers is routine, and when she has sung them our knowledge of her and sympathy for her do not increase much. It is possible that, in creating Beatrice, Bellini set out to generate a character who would outdo Norma in nobility and stature. Unfortunately, he formed a passionless character whom it is hard to care about.

Compared to several of his earlier operas, *Beatrice* has fewer of the long, long lines for which Bellini is so justly famous. A large number of melodies are constructed by accumulating repetitions of a single motive. There are also several open-ended melodies, which are responsible for much of the propulsive force of the opera, but also for a certain sense of incompletion and frustration. Probably the two most successful numbers in the opera are both ensembles of reconciliation—the quintet in act II beginning with Beatrice's text "Al tuo fallo" and the trio at the end of the second act, "Angiol di pace." Bellini borrowed the melody for "Angiol di pace" from one of his earlier operas, *Zaira*.—CHARLOTTE GREENSPAN

Béatrice et Bénédict [Beatrice and Benedict]

Composer: *Hector Berlioz.*

Librettist: *Hector Berlioz (after Shakespeare, Much Ado about Nothing).*

First Performance: *Baden-Baden, 9 August 1862.*

Roles: *Béatrice (mezzo-soprano); Hero (soprano); Bénédict (tenor); Ursula (contralto); Somarone (bass); Claudio (baritone); Don Pedro (bass); Leonato (mute); Messenger (speaking part); Scrivener (speaking part); Two Servants (speaking parts); chorus (SSATTBB).*

Don Pedro returns from defeating the Moors to stay with the governor of Sicily, Leonato. Among his officers are Claudio, who is betrothed to the governor's daughter Hero, and Bénédict. After a celebratory chorus and Hero's meditation on her love, Hero's cousin Béatrice and Bénédict resume their long-standing war of words in a duet; but aside they admit their fascination with each other. Pedro and Claudio rail at Bénédict's intention to die a bachelor. They plot to have him fall in love with Béatrice; their success leads to his aria of gleeful acquiescence. The first act ends with a nocturnal duet for Hero and her maid Ursula. After a roistering drinking-song, a parallel plot causes Béatrice to fall in love with Bénédict. Following a great internal struggle, revealed in her magnificent aria and a trio with Hero and Ursula, she and Bénédict join Hero and Claudio in a double wedding.

An unkind summary of this slender plot would be *Much Ado about Nothing* without the much ado; the main thread of Shakespeare's drama, the conspiracy against Hero's virtue, is omitted. Instead of the comic police Berlioz invented the Kapellmeister Somarone, affectionately if rather heavily pilloried in his act I fugal epithalamium and act II drinking song. The dialogue is mostly taken from Shakespeare, but the opera suffers from the difficulty singers find in speaking verse, while singing actors certainly cannot manage such sophisticated music.

The tale of Béatrice and Bénédict contains just enough dramatic substance to keep the work afloat, but performance is justified mainly for the sake of the music. The brilliant overture is intricately built on several themes from the opera, yet it forms a secure sonata-form with introduction, enlivened with counterpoint of theme against theme and exuberant modulations. The arias for the title-roles and Hero, and several ensembles of biting wit (notably the act I duet and the men's trio) and delicate sentiment (the Nocturne and the women's trio in act II) form a substantial dramatic score. They are framed by good choruses: the celebration of victory; the pedantic epithalamium; the drinking-song "improvised" by Somarone; a distant chorus with guitar accompaniment which softens Béatrice's heart; and a sturdy processional march. There is also a delicious Siciliano which Berlioz based on a song of his youth.

The most enchanting number, although it stands outside the plot, is the Nocturne for Hero and Ursula, a piece of unsurpassed instrumental delicacy and melodic bloom. But the spirit of Berlioz's swan-song is best summed up in the final Scherzino-duettino (which provides the main theme of the overture). Amid the sparkle of the orchestra the lovers swear to become enemies tomorrow, but through their very levity the brittle textures and deceptive rhythms convey a sense of the gravity of existence which has only previously been hinted at in the melting Nocturne and Béatrice's fiery aria.—JULIAN RUSHTON

Beethoven, Ludwig van

Composer. Born 15 or 16 December 1770, in Bonn. Died 26 March 1827 in Vienna. Basic music instruction with his father, then piano lessons with Tobias Friedrich Pfeiffer; keyboard and music theory instruction with Gilles van Eeden; violin and viola lessons with Franz Rovantini; enrolled at the University of Bonn, 1789, but never finished his formal training; composition study with Christian Gottlob Neefe; appointed deputy court organist by the elector Maximilian Franz, 1784; violinist in theater orchestras, 1788-92; studied with Haydn in Vienna, 1792; counterpoint lessons with Johann-Georg Albrechtsberger, 1794-95; lessons in vocal composition with Salieri, 1801-02; Prince Karl von Lichnowsky a benefactor, beginning 1800; first public appearance in Vienna, 29 March 1795, playing one of his piano concertos; performance of his works and competitions in Prague, Dresden, Leipzig, Berlin, and Vienna, 1796-1800; "Heiligenstadt Testament," 6 and 10 October 1802 [Beethoven's document concerning his growing deafness]; composition of Symphony No. 3, *"Eroica," 1803-04; asked by Emanuel Schikaneder in 1803 to set his libretto,* Vestas Feuer (The Vestal Flame), *which he began but did not finish; began work on* Fidelio, *first performed 1805; numerous concerto, chamber, and solo piano works composed 1802-14;* Symphony No. 9, *1824; last string quartets (op. 127, 130, 131, 132, 133, 135), 1824-26.*

Operas *Fidelio, oder Die eheliche Liebe,* J. Sonnleithner (after J.N. Bouilly, *Léonore ou L'amour coniugal),* 1804-05, Vienna, Theater an der Wien, 20 November 1805; revised 1805-06, Vienna, Theater an der Wien, 29 March 1806; revised 1814, Vienna, Kärntnertor, 23 May 1814.

In the face of Beethoven's extensive output in the other leading genres of his day—five piano concertos, nine symphonies, sixteen string quartets, thirty-two piano sonatas—his one completed opera *Fidelio* in many ways stands as an anomaly. Why only one, and one existing in three versions and with no less than four different overtures? Although many critics have suggested a lack of empathy for the art form, a more compelling answer is to be had in the composer's lifelong adherence to the tenets of the Enlightenment, a philosophy that, among other things, taught that humans can overcome the antagonisms that separate them one from another, that any problem can be overcome by sufficient and untrammeled use of reason, that nature provides an unerring source of joy and wisdom, and, as Immanuel Kant (a philosopher Beethoven greatly esteemed) proclaimed in 1784, that happiness can be granted to all who would "dare to be wise."

Beethoven's faith in the tenets of the Enlightenment is reflected on the one hand in his attraction to philosophically idealistic literary works in general and on the other hand in the texts he set to music. A telling, albeit extreme case in point is his thirty-year fascination with Friedrich Schiller's 1785 poem "An die Freude" ("To Joy"); first documented in 1793, when the Bonn jurist B. L. Fischenich wrote to the poet's wife reporting the twenty-three year-old composer's desire to set the poem to music as well as his dedication to the "great and the sublime," it was not until the choral finale of the Ninth Symphony in 1824 that the ambition bore fruit. In a sense, then, *Fidelio* is but one chapter within a much larger creative undertaking, one in which Beethoven's dedication to the poetically exalted impelled him to ever "strive," as he wrote to Christine Gerhardi in 1797, "toward the inaccessible goal which art and nature have set us."

A cursory survey of just a few of the many operatic librettos Beethoven rejected bears this out. Heinrich Collin's 1809 proposal for an opera on *Bradamante* was abandoned because the composer found it had "a soporific effect on feeling and reason." Emanuel Schikaneder's 1803 *Vestas Feuer* (The Vestal Flame) was discarded after Beethoven had completed the opening scene because he found the "language and verses" were of the sort "such as could only proceed out of the mouths of our Viennese apple-women." The plan for an opera on Goethe's *Faust,* first broached in 1808, was squelched when Beethoven met Goethe in 1812 and formed the opinion that the venerated poet enjoyed the trappings of the courtier "far more than is becoming to a poet." "Glitter," Beethoven grumbled to his publishers Breitkopf & Härtel, was more important to Goethe than being the "leading teacher of a nation." (For his part Goethe found the composer "an absolutely uncontrolled personality.") The same high-mindedness underlies his assessment of the subjects other composers deemed worthy of operatic treatment. Thus he found the story of Mozart's *The Marriage of Figaro* ridiculous and that of *Don Giovanni* offensive. And although in 1822 he praised Rossini's comic opera *The Barber of Seville,* he advised him to stay away from serious opera as it was "ill suited to Italians. You do not possess sufficient musical knowledge to deal with real drama."

Needless to say, a taste for the idealistic does not a satisfactory opera make, particularly if the ethical values are pursued at the expense of character development or musical interest. In addition, there is always the risk the allied philosophy will gain the upper hand, or—far worse— ring insincere, which the American critic and composer Virgil Thomson obviously believed Beethoven succumbed to now and again when he berated him (in his once-famous essay "Mozart's Leftism") as "an old fraud who just talked about human rights and dignity but who was really an irascible, intolerant, and scheming careerist." Yet Chopin, surely the Romantic composer least influenced by Beethoven but one who knew well the full possibilities of musical expression, maintained that "Beethoven embraced the universe with the power of his spirit."

For all Thomson's vituperative spleen-venting, it is Chopin's pronouncement that rings with greater authority. The reason why—apparent especially in *Fidelio,* a work with a text that makes clear its meaning—is that Beethoven succeeds so well in musically realizing the philosophical implications of the libretto. Joseph Kerman has persuasively put forward the notion that starting with the "Eroica" Third Symphony (composed two years before the first version of *Fidelio*) "Beethoven's compositions become to a cardinal degree pointed individuals," individuals moreover that "one meets and reacts to . . . with the same sort of particularity, intimacy, and concern as one does to another human being." While the principal characters of *Fidelio* may occasionally strike us as of the cardboard variety, the concerns and emotions they voice nevertheless are expressed with universal persuasiveness, a manifestation of the composer's abiding interest in humanity as a whole. Indeed, one is moved to agree with Beethoven's own statement made in 1814 that the opera succeeds in speaking to and in turn engendering "kindred souls and sympathetic hearts for that which is great and beautiful."

Far from displaying a lack of empathy for opera, Beethoven, in aspiring to the "great and beautiful" in *Fidelio,* succeeded not only in that, but also in creating a work steeped in mastery of the medium. One need not doubt that the author of the glorious canon quartet "Mir ist so wunderbar," Leonore's "Abscheulicher! Wo eilst du hin?," the prisoner's chorus "O welche Lust!," the gradually-mounting intensity of Florestan's recitative and aria "Gott! welch ein Dunkel hier!," or the ecstatic duet "O namenlose Freude," sung by Leonore and Florestan in

69

celebration of their long-awaited reunion, was anything less than an operatic composer of the first rank.—JAMES PARSONS

The Beggar's Opera

Composer: *Johann Christoph Pepusch (and others).*

Librettist: *John Gay.*

First Performance: *London, Lincoln's Inn Fields, 28 January 1728.*

Roles: *Mr. Peachum (bass); Mrs. Peachum (mezzo-soprano); Polly (mezzo-soprano); Captain Macheath (tenor); Filch (tenor or speaking); Lockit (baritone); Lucy (soprano); Mrs. Trapes (contralto); Beggar (speaking); Player (speaking); several lesser roles for all voice ranges; chorus (SATB).*

The Beggar's Opera is a "ballad opera," so called because the structure involves dialogue alternating with familiar tunes. The style grew out of a French vaudevillian practice of ridiculing grand opera; as French touring companies visited England, the genre gained instant popularity, and the practice was quickly adopted. For years England had subsisted on mostly Italianate opera that was considered effete by the general public. Singers were imported from many countries who might sing in their own language; also, most lead roles in Italian opera were given to castrato singers. The English considered the practice of castration barbaric and disliked the sound produced by castrati, and foreign opera came to be considered affected and unnatural.

A ballad opera by Scottish composer Allan Ramsay entitled *The Gentle Shepherd* had been published around 1725. This work, which contained verse in Scottish dialect and songs set to Scottish tunes, was not performed in England until the year following the success of *The Beggar's Opera.* The published score of *The Gentle Shepherd,* however, was well known among intellectual circles in London, and came to the notice of a group including Alexander Pope, Dean Swift, and John Gay. Pope later wrote that Ramsay's pastoral was on Swift's mind when he suggested that their mutual friend Gay should write a set of Quaker Pastorales, or a pastoral set in Newgate (the notorious London prison which held suspects awaiting trial) among the whores and thieves. From this comment supposedly arose the idea for the opera, although Gay changed the form from a pastoral to a comedy.

The plot deals with the intrigues of several characters associated with Newgate prison: Mr. Peachum (a receiver of stolen goods and an informer), his "wife" and their daughter Polly; Lockit (the keeper of Newgate); his daughter, Lucy; Captain Macheath (a highwayman); Filch (Peachum's young assistant); and assorted male and female criminals. In a prologue, a beggar explains to a player that the opera was written for a celebration of the marriage of two ballad singers, Moll Lay and James Chanter. The beggar then goes on to satirize and ridicule foreign opera.

In the first scene Peachum and Filch are discussing a jailed woman when Mrs. Peachum enters and expresses her concern about Polly and Macheath. Filch reveals that Polly and Macheath have been secretly married. Polly enters and they chide her for this indiscretion. Finally, they decide that Macheath must hang in order to keep the reward in the family (as well as Macheath's knowledge of Peachum's operations). Polly protests, but to no avail; she is sent to hang him, but decides instead to warn him.

Macheath's gang have been drinking in their hideout, where Macheath tells them that he must go into hiding. They leave, and Macheath, proclaiming his love for women, sends for some dancers. The women gradually seduce Macheath, removing his weapons playfully. When he is disarmed, Peachum enters and takes Macheath prisoner. Macheath is fettered in Newgate, where he must pay extortion money for a lighter set of irons. Lucy Lockit enters and berates him for his marriage. (Macheath is a rake who is chasing both Polly and Lucy.) He denies that he is already married and promises Lucy that he will marry her.

Meanwhile, Peachum and Lockit are quarreling about sharing the reward for Macheath. Lucy tries unsuccessfully to bargain for Macheath's release and returns to his cell with the bad news. Macheath suggests a bribe. Polly enters, insists that she is Macheath's legal spouse, and begins to fight with Lucy. Peachum drags Polly off, after which Macheath makes more promises to Lucy, who steals the key and sets him free.

There is a short scene in a gaming house, followed by a scene in which Lockit and Peachum learn of Macheath's escape. Lucy tries to poison Polly; meanwhile, Macheath is recaptured, but warns his gang against Peachum and Lockit. Polly and Lucy visit Macheath to say goodbye. He advises them to go to the West Indies to get married. The Jailer announces that Macheath has five more wives (each with a child) waiting to say goodbye; Macheath announces that he is quite ready to be hanged immediately.

Finally, the beggar and player re-enter. The player insists that the beggar can't hang Macheath; the beggar retorts that he can and will. The player insists that that would make the opera into a tragedy, and that it must end happily because it is a comedy; the beggar concurs, and Macheath is saved.

The Beggar's Opera is distinguished by several innovations. All of the characters in it were expected to both sing and act, unlike the performers of the masques of the time, and there was a total absence of recitative, unlike the practice in Italian operas. The music was almost entirely borrowed—twenty-eight of the tunes are Old English, fifteen Irish, five Scottish and three French songs with the remaining eighteen tunes by individual composers; three by Henry Purcell, two each by John Barrett, Henry Carey, Jeremiah Clarke and G.F. Handel, and one each by G.M. Bononcini, John Eccles, G. Frescobaldi, F. Geminiani, J.F. Pepusch, Lewis Ramondon, and John Wilford. (A list of the sources and attributions of the sixty-nine airs can be found in Edward J. Dent's edition of *The Beggar's Opera,* London, Oxford University Press, 1954.) *The Beggar's Opera* provoked much controversy on the grounds of immorality, and its immediate success was phenomenal—during the first season, ending in June 1728, it received sixty-two performances.—MEREDITH WYNNE

Behrens, Hildegard

Soprano. Born 9 February 1937, in Oldenburg. Law degree from the University of Freiburg; studied voice with Ines Leuwen at Freiburg Music Academy; debut as Countess in Le nozze di Figaro, *Freiburg, 1971; sang at Deutsche Oper am Rhein in Düsseldorf, 1971; in Düsseldorf and Frankfurt she sang Fiordiligi in* Così fan tutte, *Agathe in Weber's* Der Freischütz, *Elsa, Musetta, Katya Kabanova, and Marie in Berg's* Wozzeck; *Salome at Salzburg, 1977; debut as Giorgetta in* Tabarro *at Covent Garden and Metropolitan Opera in 1976; sang Brünnhilde at Bayreuth, 1983.*

German dramatic soprano Hildegard Behrens has had a successful career as a Wagnerian soprano. Many would argue, however, that her chief strengths lie elsewhere, that her voice is basically unsuited to the demands of the Wagnerian roles. Known as an intelligent and committed singer, Behrens has demonstrated that a lyric instrument can be employed in heavier repertoire, but at a cost. She has shown that dramatic involvement and dedication can carry a singer through even when the purely vocal requirements cannot fully be met.

Behrens's breakthrough came in 1977 with her performance of the title character in Richard Strauss's *Salome* in Salzburg under Herbert von Karajan. Since then she has performed Elettra in Mozart's *Idomeneo* (a role for which she is more suited dramatically than vocally), Elena in Janáček's *The Makropoulos Case*, Katya Kabanová, Isolde in Wagner's *Tristan und Isolde,* and the Empress in Richard Strauss's *Die Frau ohne Schatten,* as well as Richard Strauss's Ariadne. She first sang the three Brünnhildes in 1983 at Bayreuth under Georg Solti's baton.

Known as an intelligent singer (she studied law at the University of Freiburg), Behrens researches her characters before she performs them for the first time. Her performances are rarely less than interesting, and Behrens's intentions are generally clear even when they are not completely realized. She is best at portraying psychologically complex characters. An instinctive actor, she objects to directors who impose outlandish concepts on the operas. She sees opera as a medium for catharsis, the revelation of truth to the audience. Few would question Behrens's dedication; her performances possess a riveting intensity, combining vocal frailty and dramatic power. At its best, her singing has a majesty and stateliness.

Hildegard Behrens as Brünnhilde in *Siegfried,* Bayreuth, 1983

Behrens's strength has always been in her gleaming, powerful top notes, notes that have remained stunningly effective even while the rest of her voice has shown signs of wear. Her assumption of roles that put excessive strain on her voice has undoubtedly contributed to the vocal problems critics have noticed in some of her performances. Defects that were incipient in her early years, and which were concealed by her many virtues, have, inevitably, become more prominent. Even early in her career, her voice had an unfocused, tremulous quality in its middle register, an unsteadiness that may have contributed to her ability to portray vulnerable characters but that can be disconcerting for the listener.

Although much of her career has been founded on the Wagnerian heroines—Sieglinde, Brünnhilde, Isolde—it is arguably in two Richard Strauss roles, Salome and Elektra, that she has created her greatest achievements. Her Elektra, especially as heard in concert performances with the Boston Symphony, is an astonishing welding of dramatic and vocal qualities, both in the bloodcurdling portrayal of Elektra's obsession and in the tenderness of the recognition scene, as well as in the heartbreaking moment when Elektra recalls the beauty she once possessed. This role, in which the title character holds the stage from her first appearance a few minutes after the rise of the curtain until the end, allowed her to demonstrate what she has described (in another context) as the necessity for both the passion and the steel of a role to be there from the beginning.

Behrens's Wagnerian characterizations have been well received, largely because of her combination of effective acting—she is able to convey searing passion as well as vulnerability—and the necessary strong high notes. She is relatively deficient in such aspects as stamina (the effort sometimes shows) and the sense of being in possession of unlimited resources; although she generally rises to the occasion, the listener may find it difficult to relax in the confident belief that Behrens will not run out of voice. She also lacks the ideal smoothness of the middle register and solidity of tone for Wagnerian roles.

Her recordings of complete operas, other than ones taken from staged performances, include the roles of Salome (under Karajan), Brünnhilde in James Levine's complete *Ring* cycle, Isolde (under Bernstein), Agathe in *Der Freischütz* (under Kubelik), Truth in Magnard's *Guercoeur* (under Plasson), and the Dyer's Wife in Richard Strauss's *Die Frau ohne Schatten* (under Solti).—MICHAEL SIMS

Bellini, Vincenzo

Composer. Born 3 November 1801, in Catania, Sicily. Died 23 September 1835, in Puteaux, near Paris. Studied with his father, Rosario Bellini, and grandfather Vincenzo Tobia Bellini, and at the Real Collegio di Musica di San Sebastiano (Naples) with Giovanni Furno, Giacomo Tritto, Carlo Conti, Girolamo Crescentini and Niccolò Zingarelli; Il pirata commissioned for Teatro alla Scala, Milan, 1827; various successes in Milan and Venice, 1827-31; unsuccessful production of Beatrice di Tenda, *Venice, 1833; in London and then Paris, where, on the recommendation of Rossini, he was commissioned to write I* Puritani *produced at the Théâtre-Italien in 1835. His principal librettist was Felice Romani; he was closely associated with the tenor Rubini from 1827, and the soprano Giuditta Pasta from 1830.*

73

Operas *Adelson e Salvini,* Andrea Leone Tottola, Naples, Teatrino del Collegio San Sebastiano, January 1825; *Bianca e Gernando,* Domenico Gilardoni, Naples, Teatro San Carlo, 30 May 1826; *Bianca e Fernando* (second version of *Bianca e Gernando*), Felice Romani (after Gilardoni), Genoa, Teatro Carlo Felice, 7 April 1828; *Il pirata,* Felice Romani (after M. Raimond, *Bertram ou Le pirate*), Milan, Teatro alla Scala, 27 October 1827; *La straniera,* Felice Romani (after Victor—Charles Prévost, vicomte d'Arlincourt, *L'étrangère*), Milan, Teatro alla Scala, 14 February 1829; *Zaira,* Felice Romani (after Voltaire), Parma, Teatro Ducale, 16 May 1829; *I Capuleti ed i Montecchi,* Felice Romani (after Scevola, *Giulietta e Romeo* and Ducis, *Roméo et Juliette,* Venice, Teatro La Fenice, 11 March 1830; *Ernani,* Felice Romani, late 1830 [unfinished]; *La sonnambula,* Felice Romani (after a ballet-pantomime by Eugène Scribe and Jean-Pierre Aumer), Milan, Teatro Carcano, 6 March 1831; *Norma,* Felice Romani (after Louis Alexandre Soumet), Milan, Teatro alla Scala, 26 December 1831; *Beatrice di Tenda,* Felice Romani (after a novel by Carlo Tebaldi Fores and a ballet by Antonio Monticini), Venice, Teatro La Fenice, 16 March 1833; *I Puritani,* Carlo Pepoli (after Jacques-Arsène Ancelot and Josèph Xavier Boniface *Têtes rondes et cavaliers,* Paris, Théâtre-Italien, 24 January 1835.

Vincenzo Bellini may be considered the most efficient of the Italian operatic composers of the first half of the nineteenth century in that he made the greatest impact with the smallest product. Rossini composed about thirty-eight operas in about twenty years, Donizetti sixty-five operas in twenty-seven years and Verdi twenty-eight operas in fifty-four years. Bellini composed only ten operas in a ten year period, but on the basis of these works (or, in fact, a subset of these works), his importance in the history of opera and his value to lovers of opera is secure.

The principal events of Bellini's development as a composer were his acquisition of the eighteenth-century Neapolitan heritage, his mastery of the musical style of his day (shaped in part by Rossini's legacy and subject to currents of romantic thought), and finally his formulation of a unique personal style. His ten operas may be viewed in four stylistic categories.

Bellini's first two operas, *Adelson e Salvini* (1825) and *Bianca e Gernando* (1826) are well-crafted copies of already out-of-date stylistic models. *Adelson e Salvini,* Bellini's graduation piece, composed in his last year at the Naples Conservatory, is an *opera semiseria* having among the characters a noble lover, a comic servant who speaks Neapolitan dialect, and an impulsive artist. The libretto of *Bianca e Gernando,* with noble characteristics and a tyrant bloodlessly deposed at the conclusion, suggests a conservative *opera seria.* Musically, however, *Bianca* shows Bellini coming to terms with a more modern, Rossini-influenced musical style, particularly in the construction of multi-tempo arias.

Bellini's next two operas, *Il pirata* (1827) and *La straniera* (1829), are his most innovative, progressive works. They were composed for Milan, a city in which opera-goers were less steeped in and reverent towards eighteenth-century styles than in Naples. They were composed to librettos written by Felice Romani, Bellini's partner in the creation of all his mature operas except for *I Puritani.* These two operas show clear Romantic tendencies both in text and music. Both operas derive their stories from nineteenth-century depictions of medieval times. *Il pirata,* set in thirteenth-century Sicily, is based on a melodrama, *Bertram, ou le pirate,* by M. Raimond (possibly a pseudonym for Isadore Taylor) first performed in Paris in 1826. *La straniera,* set in thirteenth-century Brittany, is based on a novel by Victor-Charles Prévost, vicomte d'Arlincourt. In both operas the characters are propelled to their doom by overwhelming passions. Gualtiero in *Il pirata* and Arturo in *La straniera* both die at their own hands when they recognize they cannot be united with the women they love. For these works Bellini developed a melodic style, sometimes called *canto declamato* and sometimes *canto d'azione* which, standing somewhere between recitative-like and aria-like vocal writing, allowed a more flexible progression of the drama. Emotional texts were declaimed in a more direct, less embellished way. Formal shapes of the arias are more varied. In the case of Arturo in *La straniera*, the aria is abandoned entirely as a means of presenting the character.

Bellini's next two operas, *Zaira* (1829) and *I Capuleti ed i Montecchi* (1830) represent a kind of retrenchment from Romantic strivings with respect to texts, although Bellini continued to work with increasingly fluid and flexible melodic ideas between the borders of recitative and aria. *La sonnambula* (1831)

Vincenzo Bellini, c. 1825

and *Norma* (1831) attain a superb classical equipoise, a perfect balance between musical means and dramatic ends. In Bellini's last two operas, *Beatrice di Tenda* (1833) and *I Puritani* (1835), this balance is once more disturbed. *Beatrice,* with a tenor who is dragged onstage after undergoing torture, would seem to adumbrate the *verismo* violence of *Tosca*. But one gets the impression that neither Romani's nor Bellini's heart was in this work. *I Puritani,* which, like *La sonnambula,* has a last-minute happy ending, moves on emotional ground more comfortable for Bellini. Unfortunately, Bellini was deprived of Romani's skills and support when he composed *I Puritani*. Thus, although *I Puritani* is among Bellini's richest and most advanced musical scores, the effect of the opera is weakened by an amateurish libretto by Carlo Pepoli.

One of Bellini's most significant distinguishing features, setting him apart from and in some ways above Rossini and Donizetti, was his sensitivity to the text he was setting. Bellini himself was the first to recognize and proclaim his dependence on good texts, specifically good texts written by his preferred poet, Felice Romani. In 1828, when Bellini's friend Francesco Florimo suggested that Bellini might set a libretto by Rossi, Bellini responded, "however much Rossi could make a good libretto for me, nevertheless he never, never, could be a poet like Romani, and especially for me, for I am so reliant on good words." In 1835, after a breach with Romani had led Bellini to set a libretto by another poet (*I Puritani* by Carlo Pepoli) Bellini again wrote to Florimo, "I shall try to make peace with Romani; I have great need of him if I want to compose for Italy again; after him nobody else can satisfy me." Richard Wagner who, of course, thought a good deal himself on the interrelations of words and music in musical drama, recognized Bellini's skillful handling of texts. He told Florimo, in 1880, "Bellini is one of my predilections: his music is all heart, closely, intimately linked to the words."

However, to say simply that Bellini was sensitive to his texts could be misleading. He cared about texts on the level of poetry and within the bounds of the single scene. All evidence indicates that Bellini viewed a libretto as a collection of parts—scenes or set numbers. He seems not to have thought of a libretto as a whole as having a structural integrity or dramatic consistency. After a story had been decided on, Bellini began composing when he had the texts for the first few scenes; he did not wait to see a completed libretto before he began composing. Similarly, work on an opera stopped when Bellini had composed three to four hours worth of music. *Norma* and *I Puritani* both shorten the endings of their source plays, at least in part because enough music had already been composed.

It is also a mistake to think that good texts were necessarily the inspiration of Bellini's fine melodies. Bellini routinely wrote wordless melodies—vocalises or *solfeggietti*—as a kind of compositional exercise. Many of his operas make use of melodies borrowed from earlier works. Thus, what Bellini sometimes needed from Romani was not a text to inspire him, but a text that would flawlessly fit a pre-existing melody.

No Bellini opera is performer-proof. Without a sympathetic and informed performance, his operas may fail to make a strong effect. Bellini himself seemed aware of and comfortable with his dependence on good singers for successful performances. When negotiating with representatives of various opera houses about the composition of a new work, Bellini's first concern was the singers who would give the premiere. (That Romani would provide the libretto for the new opera was not a negotiating point but a given.) When Bellini found satisfactory singers he was loyal to them. Bellini composed *La sonnambula, Norma,* and *Beatrice di Tenda* fully mindful of the talents of the prima donna Giuditta Pasta. The roles of Gernando in *Bianca e Gernando,* Gualtiero in *Il pirata,* Elvino in *La sonnambula,* and Arturo in *I Puritani* were composed for the unique vocal talents of Giovanni-Battista Rubini. Antonio Tamburini was Bellini's baritone in the revised *Bianca e Fernando, Il pirata, La straniera,* and *I Puritani;* Luigi Lablanche his bass in *Bianca e Gernando, Zaira,* and *I Puritani.* For his leading ladies, Bellini preferred singers with considerable dramatic gifts. He admired Pasta and also Maria Malibran, whom he heard perform *La sonnambula,* in English, in London. He considered Giulia Grisi, who created the role of Adalgisa in *Norma* and Elvira in *I Puritani,* a rather cool singer.

Musicologists disagree as to where to place Bellini on the classic-romantic continuum. Simon Maguire emphasized Bellini's classical roots, Gary Tomlinson calls Bellini an "ambivalent Romantic," while Friedrich Lippman characterizes Bellini as "a composer who took a strong sensual delight in sound, and who in passages of ecstatic sonority proved himself a Romantic *par excellence.*" Certainly, particularly at the beginning of his career, Bellini was pleased to think of himself as an innovator and as a composer with a distinct personal style.

In 1834 Bellini wrote to Carlo Pepoli, "opera, through singing, must make one weep, shudder, die." This remark may be taken as the composer's credo. Curiously, if one reads through Bellini's letters for examples of the composer's own evaluation of his works, one can find him most often praising a cleverly conceived chorus or a good stroke of orchestration. After the premiere of an opera he often pointed to the good effect this or that number had when this or that singer performed it. The instances in which he praises one of his melodies, as such, are rare. Nevertheless, Bellini's contributions to the art of melody must be considered his most important artistic legacy. Tomlinson has commented, "no later Italian composer, and least of all Verdi, failed to be touched by the sweeping changes in melodic style that he more than any other single composer brought about. These changes included, in addition to his lyricism of heavenly lengths—his *"melodie lunghe lunghe lunghe"* in Verdi's famous phrase—the incisive *canto declamato* and enhanced recitative styles." Bellini fashioned a style of melodic utterance which, denuded of coloratura ornamentation, could have a direct emotional impact even in the space of a phrase or two.

An important innovation of Bellini's with regard to melodic structure was his placement of the climax close to the end of the piece. "Qui la voce" in *I puritani* is a particularly exquisite example of this type of construction. Interestingly, this change in the placement of the melodic climax parallels a change in dramaturgy in Italian Romantic opera; the climax of the drama is pushed as close to the final curtain as comprehensibility will allow. As the hero or heroine walks or plunges to his or her death, no time is allowed for a final peroration given by a secondary character or by the chorus. The audience is given just enough time to react emotionally, not to reflect. One may return to Bellini's statement that "opera, through singing, must make one weep, shudder, die," not consider, draw conclusions, intellectualize.—CHARLOTTE GREENSPAN

Benvenuto Cellini

Composer: *Hector Berlioz.*

Librettists: *Léon de Wailly and Auguste Barbier (after Cellini's autobiography).*

First Performance: *Paris, Opéra, 10 September 1838.*

Roles: *Balducci (bass); Teresa (soprano); Benvenuto Cellini (tenor); Ascanio (mezzo-soprano); Fieramosca (baritone); Pompeo (baritone); Francesco (tenor); Bernardino (bass); Innkeeper (tenor); Officer (baritone); chorus (SATTBB).*

On the last Monday of Carnival, the Papal treasurer Balducci is grumbling at having to pay Cellini for work on an unfinished statue. Meanwhile Cellini serenades Balducci's daughter Teresa. Fieramosca, an inferior sculptor but the suitor preferred by Balducci, overhears Cellini make an assignation with Teresa; but he is caught hiding in her bedroom and ejected as a libertine. On Shrove Tuesday, Cellini and his men have nothing to drink until his apprentice Ascanio brings the Pope's money, reminding him that the statue is already overdue. They sing a hymn to their art, repeated at the end of the opera. During the Carnival Cellini has Harlequin pillory Balducci; then he tries to elope with Teresa. Fieramosca rashly intervenes but is humiliated by Ascanio while his friend Pompeo is killed by Cellini. The extinction of lights at midnight, marking the start of Lent, allows Cellini to escape.

On Ash Wednesday Cellini and Teresa are reunited in his workshop, but he is denounced by Fieramosca, Balducci, and finally the Pope (whom the censors insisted should be merely "the Cardinal"). But the Pope is more interested in the great statue of Perseus; and when Cellini threatens to destroy the mould he is granted the rest of the day to save his skin by finishing it. After difficulties with workmen and materials the statue is cast, Cellini's enemies fawn on him, and art and love are triumphantly vindicated.

Berlioz planned *Benvenuto Cellini* with spoken dialogue, and with a major climax to each act: the Carnival and the casting of Perseus. The Paris Opéra required recitatives, retained in the three-act Weimar version, for which he divided the first act and shortened the original second. In the latter the Weimar version alters the order of scenes, improbably allowing Cellini an hour rather than a day to finish Perseus; Berlioz also abbreviated the sextet with the Pope and the casting scene, which in the original version are magnificently developed, and cut the beautiful slow movement of the lovers' duet. Although it presents difficulties in the theater, the first version is musically preferable, and it is represented on the only recording. The Carnival makes, perhaps, too brilliant a first climax, anticipating *Die Meistersinger* in its handling of a stage filled with principals and a festive crowd which turns ugly. In both versions the final act contains excellent numbers (Ascanio's aria, a prayer heard against a passing procession of monks, Cellini's narration), but in neither is it as cogent as the earlier scenes. These unexpectedly reveal Berlioz as a master of comedy. The serenade interrupted by the furious grumbling of Balducci make a hilarious introduction, and the trio in which Fieramosca overhears the lovers perfectly blends enchanting music with farce. The overture and Fieramosca's aria, where he practices duelling in mixed metres, exemplify the explosive and capricious rhythmic inventions abounding in a score which is still, to some palates, over-rich for the opera house.—JULIAN RUSHTON

Berg, Alban

Composer. Born 9 February 1885, in Vienna. Died 24 December 1935, in Vienna. Married: Helene Nahowski, May 1911. Little musical training before meeting Schoenberg in October of 1904; in his youth, he was friends with Zweig, Kraus, Klimt, Loos, Altenberg, and Kokoschka; saw a performance of Büchner's Woyzeck *in May of 1914, and immediately began sketches for a musical setting of the play; army service from 1914-1918; part of* Wozzeck *completed during a period of leave from the army in 1917; management of Schoenberg's Verein für Musikalische Privataufführungen in 1918; act I and first two scenes of* Wozzeck *completed in 1919, short score completed in autumn of 1921, orchestration completed in the spring of 1922, published by the composer in 1923; performance of* Drei Bruchstücke aus "Wozzeck" *in Frankfurt, June 1924; premiere at the Berlin Staatsoper, 14 December 1925;* Lyric Suite *published 1927; composition of* Lulu *from 1929-1935: short score completed spring 1934;* Symphonische Stücke aus der Oper "Lulu" *performed 30 November 1934; work on* Lulu *interrupted by composition of the Violin Concerto in 1935;* Lulu *suite performed in Vienna on 11 December 1935; orchestration of* Lulu *only through the beginning of act III; posthumous premiere in Zurich, 2 June 1937, but with only the parts of act III found in the* Lulu *suite. The materials for* Lulu, *act III, were withheld by Berg's widow until her death in 1976, and publication of the complete vocal score was in 1979, in an edition by the Viennese composer Friedrich Cerha, who completed the full score as well; first complete performance of* Lulu *24 February 1979.*

Operas *Wozzeck,* libretto arranged by the composer (after Georg Büchner), 1917-22, Berlin, Staatsoper, 14 December 1925; *Lulu,* libretto arranged by the composer (after Frank Wedekind's *Erdgeist* and *Die Büchse der Pandora*), 1929-35, incomplete performance Zurich, 2 June 1937; first complete performance, Paris, Opéra, 24 February 1979.

Berg's natural feeling for the voice is heard in the many songs which were his first essays in composition. Written both before and during his period of study with Schoenberg, these show a secure command of late-Romantic Viennese musical language and a gift for lyrical word-setting through sensitivity of melodic contour and rhythmic characterisation. Understandably, one of his teacher's main aims was to encourage Berg towards a more instrumental style, less dominated by melody, more motivic in material and polyphonic in texture. Schoenberg also introduced his pupil to the expanded harmonic resources through which he himself was moving determinedly towards a psychological break with the conventions of tonality.

Though dominated throughout his life by the personality of Schoenberg, Berg remained true to his own instincts through the strength of his innate sensibility. Accepting Schoenberg's criticism of the brevity of the *Altenberg Lieder* and the *Four Pieces* for Clarinet and Piano, he composed the *Three Orchestral Pieces* in a style which, while reaping the benefits of Schoenbergian expressionism, owes a more direct debt to Mahler. Another irony of this work is that Schoenberg himself was unable to sustain music in larger forms at this time. Arguably, having found for himself a path through the impasse that Schoenberg had identified, Berg was from now on to prove the more artistically consistent and successful composer of the two.

Berg's major works number just twelve, composed over a span of nearly thirty years. His operas are thus better understood within the chronological progression of his output in all genres than by considering them together as a pair. At the same time, his tendency towards conservatism and his responsiveness to inspiration from sources beyond Schoenbergian modernism demand that his work be placed in a broader context. Thus while *Wozzeck* may be seen to follow the musical style of the *Three Orchestral Pieces* in all essentials, and was for many years thought of as the most successful "atonal" opera, its musical language in fact retains many links with the extended tonality developed by Strauss and others (including Schoenberg) during the first decade of the century and also restores to some extent the primacy of melody Berg had shown in his earliest compositions. In line with other developments in post-war music, the opera is notable for its use of conventional forms within the framework of a through-composed music-drama, and the revival of works by Zemlinsky and Schreker has confirmed *Wozzeck* as a work rooted in the time and place of its composition.

Moving towards serial technique in the mid 1920s under the inescapable influence of Schoenberg, Berg nonetheless maintained the prominence of tonalistic devices in his later works. Even more than *Wozzeck's* blend of artificial formal construction with an eclectic mix of late-Romantic and post-Expressionist musical languages, these works constantly explore the historical tension between the conventions of tonal Romanticism and modernist musical constructivism, in contrast to Schoenberg's clear but uncertain commitment to the latter aesthetic.

Berg's last years were dominated by his work on *Lulu*. This task remained incomplete at his death, having been interrupted by the composition of the concert aria *Der Wein* and the *Violin Concerto,* both of which were undertaken for financial reasons. These three works are linked stylistically by an overt tonalism which makes their musical language more accessible than that of *Wozzeck*. At the same time, this is complemented by an ingenuity of construction which, particularly in *Lulu,* anticipates the 'tonal serialism' of the 1950s, while being all the more remarkable for its virtual inaudibility—an art which conceals art. The link between music and drama in *Lulu* is less onomatopoeic than in *Wozzeck,* however, and the subject matter less immediately appealing. The title role, for coloratura soprano, makes extraordinary vocal demands, and until the release in 1979 of Friedrich Cerha's realization of its third act the opera could only be performed as a fragment. All these factors prevented its proper appreciation for many years after Berg's death, during which period his reputation was carried largely by *Wozzeck* and the *Violin Concerto*.

The fuller acquaintance with *Lulu* which has become possible in recent years has been central to a revision of critical attitudes towards the composer. His earlier reputation for approachability through artistic compromise has now been replaced by a fascination with his ability to combine serialism with tonalistic elements, and an attractive sound-world with a

b

OPERA

forbidding array of hidden complexities in construction. Berg's second opera has found its place through the pluralistic climate of post-Modernist criticism. At the same time, there can be little doubt that the reputation of *Wozzeck* will in due course be restored to equal heights. For many musicians, these two operas stand alongside some by Strauss and Puccini, and perhaps a handful of other works, as the greatest of their century.—ANTHONY POPLE

Berganza, Teresa

Mezzo-soprano. Born 16 March 1935. Married to the composer Felix Lavilla. Studied with Lola Rodriguez Aragon; won singing prize at Madrid in 1954; operatic debut as Dorabella in Così fan tutte *at Aix-en-Provence Festival, 1957; debut at Piccola Scala as Isolier in* Comte Ory, 1958; *Glyndebourne debut as Cherubino in* Le nozze di Figaro, 1958; U.S. *debut at Dallas, 1958 appeared at Covent Garden as Rosina, 1960; Chicago as Cherubino, 1962; Metropolitan Opera debut as Cherubino, 1967.*

Teresa Berganza specialized in Italian opera of the 17th, 18th and early 19th centuries. With few roles in the operas of Verdi and Puccini for her sweet, light mezzo-soprano voice and gentle stage personality she explored earlier repertory. She sang with great success some of the best roles in baroque opera, including works by Monteverdi, Purcell, and Handel. Although she is best known today for her performances in comic opera, especially those of Mozart and Rossini, Berganza's work in baroque opera showed that she was also capable of bringing tragic characters such as Ottavia (*L'incoronazione di Poppea*) and Dido (*Dido and Aeneas*) to life.

A recording of Handel's *Alcina* under Bonynge shows how fine Berganza was as a singer of baroque opera. Berganza's Ruggiero is strong and heroic. With perfectly executed coloratura she portrays him as a dashing, almost reckless figure (as, for example, in the brilliant aria "Bramo di triomfar"). Yet Ruggiero is also thoughtful and gentle; Berganza reveals this side of his character most beautifully in slow, lyrical arias like "Col celarvi", "Mio bel tesoro" and the famous "Verdi prati, selve amene".

One of Berganza's first professional roles was that of Dorabella (*Così fan tutte*), at Aix in 1957; she went on to sing several other Mozart roles. She won much applause for her portrayal of Cherubino at Glyndebourne in 1958; fourteen years later, she was still delighting audiences with the same role (Salzburg, 1972). Her performances of the role of Sesto in Mozart's *La clemenza di Tito* in two recordings (under Kertesz and Böhm) show that she was as effective in evoking the tragic and heroic aspects of Mozart as she was the comic.

It was especially as an interpreter of Rossini's comic heroines that Berganza revealed the full extent of her musical and dramatic talents. Her many performances of Rosina (*Il barbiere di Siviglia*) and Cinderella will long be remembered for their wit, charm and polished musicality. A recording of *Il barbiere* under Abbado shows Berganza to be a fine Rosina after singing the role for more than a decade. In her performance of "Una voce poco fa" one can hear the strength and flexibility of her voice; she attacks the sudden high notes (as she names Lindoro) with confidence and perfect accuracy without shouting or screeching; her voice blends beautifully with the orchestra. Her low notes are rich and strong. One could complain only that the performance is a little hurried, a little stiff. The pure beauty of Berganza's voice makes one wish that she took more time at fermatas; she seems to rush through coloratura where she might have slowed a little and let listeners savor her voice. Berganza's performance of Isabella (*L'italiana in Algeri*) as recorded under Silvio Varviso lacks some of the heroic and mock-heroic qualities that Marilyn Horne could bring to the role (especially in the aria "Pensa alla patria" and the recitative that precedes it). But the sweetness of her voice, the deftness of her coloratura, the beauty of her appearance and the liveliness of her acting all combine to make Berganza's Isabella one that can hardly be bettered.—JOHN A. RICE

Bergonzi, Carlo

Tenor. Born 13 July 1924, in Polisene, near Parma. Studied with Edmondo Grandini in Brescia and under Ettore Campagalliani at Boito Conservatory in Parma, 1945-48; imprisoned for anti-Nazi activities during World War II; began career in baritone roles, singing Schaunard in Catania, 1947, and Rossini's Figaro in Lecce, 1948; tenor debut as Andrea Chénier in Bari, 1951; created role of Napoli's Masaniello for his Teatro alla Scala debut in 1953; sang Alvaro in La forza del destino for his London debut at Stoll Theatre in 1953, and for his Covent Garden debut in 1962; Metropolitan debut as Radames, 1956, and sang at the Metropolitan Opera until 1983 in 249 performances of 21 roles, including Alfredo, Manrico, Pollione, and Nemorino.

"A great Verdi stylist" is a description most often accorded to Carlo Bergonzi. In fact, Bergonzi has epitomized more of the essential qualities of an outstanding Verdi interpreter than most of the important tenors of the post-War period. In that respect he is the legitimate heir of a long line of Verdi stylists, and the logical successor to Pertile and Lauri-Volpi.

Though lacking the ringing top and heroic qualities of a Corelli or the dark, robust coloration of a Vinay, Bergonzi has managed, by sheer dint of hard study and a lifelong dedication to his art, to encompass the qualities necessary for the ideal Verdi interpreter. He is justly proud of his achievement of recording, after a nearly thirty year career, all the tenor arias of the Verdi repertoire in a 3-disc set for Philips: an outstanding achievement recognized as such by the awards of the Deutscher Schallplattenpreis, the Premio della critica discografica Italiana and the *Stereo Review* "Record of the Year."

How has Bergonzi achieved this reputation as a great Verdi stylist? In some respects his sympathy for Verdian style is to a large extent innate, as he was born and raised in the same area as Verdi himself. But added to this is a superlative vocal technique wedded to a beautiful voice used with sensitivity, superior musicality and intelligence. These qualities have enabled him to surmount many of the difficulties presented by Verdi's arias, many of which sound deceptively easy to sing. Much of Verdi's writing is around the *passaggio,* the notes E, F and G, where the male voice encounters a natural 'break' between the chest and the head registers. The tenor must learn to bridge these notes and "cover" (protect) the voice from this break if it is to last throughout a long career.

Bergonzi himself feels that an essential requirement of the Verdi specialist is to find the correct vocal color for each of his tenor roles. The color needed for the carefree, licentious Duke of Mantua is quite different from that appropriate for the heroic Radames. This is one reason why he has never attempted one of the most difficult of Verdi's tenor roles: Otello. He feels Otello demands a dark color that could never be his, either by nature or by study.

A somewhat stolid figure on stage, Bergonzi nevertheless succeeds in conveying the character he is portraying by vocal means, a factor which has no doubt been significant in his success in transferring his greatest Verdi roles to disc.

Yet, it is not just in Verdi's operas that Bergonzi has been acclaimed. He has sung many of Puccini's tenor roles: Cavaradossi (*Tosca*), Des Grieux (*Manon Lescaut*), Calaf (*Turandot*) and Rodolfo (*La Bohème*), has been acclaimed in the music of Giordano (*Andrea Chénier*), Boïto (*Mefistofele*), Catalani (*La Wally*), Massenet (*Werther*) and Ponchielli (*La Gioconda*) and is in much demand as a recitalist. Few tenors have demonstrated such versatility during the course of a career of more than forty years.

In his sixties, Bergonzi was still singing beautifully. He remains a testimony to the value of a sound technique and the wisdom of realising the capabilities of the voice and remaining within those limitations.

His association with Verdi remains, for in Verdi's birthplace, Busseto, he has formed a singing-school and shows a keen interest in passing on his experience and technique to young singers. He is also the driving force behind the "Concorso internazionale di voci verdiane," a competition dedicated to the furtherance of Verdian art. Perhaps from this enterprise a worthy successor to the master's crown will arise. Certainly Bergonzi's career is one of which any singer could be proud, and an inspiration to any young artist.—LARRY LUSTIG

Berio, Luciano

Composer. Born 24 October 1925, in Oneglia, Italy. Married: 1) singer Cathy Berberian, 1950 (divorced 1966; one daughter); 2) Susan Oyama, 1964 (divorced 1971; one son, one daughter); 3) Talia Pecker, 1977 (two sons). Studied composition with Ghedini and conducting with Giulini at the Milan Conservatory (composition degree, 1950); studied composition with Dallapiccola at Tanglewood; contacts with Darmstadt school, 1954; interest in electronic music and directorship of Studio di Fonologia Musicale, 1955-61, Milan; editor, Incontri Musicali; worked with Pierre Boulez at the Institut de Recherche et de Coordination Acoustique/Musique (IRCAM), Paris; on the faculty of the Juilliard School (1965-72), the Tanglewood Festival, and Harvard University since 1960; moved to the United States in 1963, returned to Italy in 1972; Artistic Director, Maggio Musicale, Florence, 1984; honorary member of the Royal Academy of Music, London, 1988; British Broadcasting Company Berio Festival at the Barbican, London, 1990.

Operas *Opera*, Berio, U. Eco, and F. Colombo, 1969-70, Santa Fe, New Mexico, 12 August 1970; revised, 1976; *La vera storia*, Italo Calvino, 1977-81 Milan, Teatro alla Scala, 9 March 1982; *Un re in ascolto*, Italo Calvino, Salzburg, 7 August 1984.

Luciano Berio was born into a family of musicians in Northern Italy. He is, with Luigi Nono, one of Italy's leading composers and intellectuals. Berio is first and foremost a musician, followed closely by the activities of pedagogue, lecturer, conductor and musical innovator.

Berio studied with Dallapiccola in the United States and Ghedini in Italy. He has been on the faculty of the Juilliard School of Music in New York, and taught at Harvard and Tanglewood as well. One of the earliest proponents and exponents of electronic music, he has worked alongside Pierre Boulez at IRCAM (Institut de Recherche et de Coordination Acoustique/Musique) at the Pompidou center in Paris, and ran a series of broadcast workshops on electronic music for RAI (Italian State Radio) in the late fifties and early sixties.

Berio's extraordinarily wide intellect has, over the years, brought him into contact, and in many cases close friendship with the leading Italian intellectual and literary figures of our day. His fascination with literature from Shakespeare to James Joyce has provided endless and fertile ground for seemingly limitless musical innovation, especially for the voice.

His marriage to the great American soprano Cathy Berberian produced a rare partnership in avant-garde music. Berberian had a voice of incredible range and flexibility which, combined with an exciting theatrical stage presence, was to lead to some of Berio's most original and memorable early work.

Partnerships have always played a major role in Berio's career. Most of these collaborations are with writers, but he has worked with other composers (Bruno Maderna and Mauricio Kapel for example) and choreographers. The music for Maurice Béjart's ballet *I Trionfi* was created in 1974 and was premiered in Florence. Much of his concert music has been used by choreographers in the modern dance idiom.

Luciano Berio's preoccupation with the voice verges on an obsessional interest. In his opera *Un re in ascolto* (A King Listens), the composer almost requires the audience to participate in the action by actually "listening" as well as "hearing" the work. Despite the fact that in the Italian language the word is the same for both concepts, it is Berio's particular interest in semantics and linguistics that helped create this intriguing opera.

Un re in ascolto was the second opera Berio composed in collaboration with the great Italian writer Italo Calvino (who died in 1985), the first being *La vera storia,* first staged at La Scala in 1982. It is typical of Berio that the first idea for *Un Re* came from an essay by the French intellectual Roland Barthes, was further influenced by W.H. Auden's writings on "The Tempest," and had program notes by Umberto Eco in the Royal Opera House program when the opera was produced there in 1989.

Luciano Berio loves the open-mindedness of the young, and has a strong following. In today's world he remains one of the most approachable (in human terms), challenging and prolific composers. With such a brilliant mind and eclectic approach to all cultural activity his many disciples, both professional and amateur can look forward with eager anticipation to further stimulus and possible provocation in the years to come.—SALLY WHYTE

Berlioz, (Louis-) Hector

Composer. Born 11 December 1803, in La Côte-St.-André. Died 8 March 1869, in Paris. Married: 1) Harriet Smithson, actress, 3 October 1833 (died 1854; one son), 2) Marie Recio, singer, 1854 (died 1862). Studied flute with Imbert and guitar with Dorant in Grenoble; self-taught in theory; medical student in Paris, 1821-24; studied composition with Jean François Le Sueur and counterpoint and fugue with Anton Reicha at the Paris Conservatoire, 1826-30; wrote for several Paris journals from 1823-63, including Le Rénovateur, Gazette Musicale *(later merged with* Revue Musicale*),* Le Corsaire, *and*

Journal des Débats, *among many others; sang in the chorus at the Théâtre des Nouveautés; awarded the Prix de Rome for his cantata* La mort de Sardanapale *in 1830; order of the Légion d'Honneur, 1839; Assistant Librarian 1839-50 and Librarian 1850 at the Paris Conservatoire; frequent concert engagements in Germany, Austria, and England, from 1842; visited Russia, 1847; in England, 1848; replaced Adolphe Adam at the Institute, 1856.*

Operas *Estelle et Némorin,* Gerono (after Florian), 1823 [not performed; score lost]; *Les francs-juges,* Humbert Ferrand, 1826 (revised 1829, and 1833 as *Le cri de guerre de Brisgaw,* T. Gounet) [not performed; only overture and five movements survive]; *Benvenuto Cellini,* Léon de Wailly and Auguste Barbier (after Cellini's autobiography), composed 1834-37, Paris, Opéra, 10 September 1838; revised 1852 for Weimar, 17 November 1852; *La nonne sanglante,* Eugène Scribe, 1841-47 [unfinished]; *Les troyens,* Berlioz (after Virgil), 1856-58, Paris, Théâtre-Lyrique, 4 November 1863; revised 1859-60; divided into two parts, 1863; *Béatrice et Bénédict,* Berlioz (after Shakespeare, *Much Ado about Nothing*), composed 1860-62, Baden-Baden (in German), 9 August 1862.

Berlioz's first eighteen years were passed remote from any major cultural center. His earliest experience of music was in small genres: chamber-music, to which he contributed nothing in his maturity; songs, including operatic arias arranged for the drawing-room; provincial examples of church and municipal music; folk-music. He fed his imagination on literature, thoughts of distant climes, and lives of great composers, but not until he came to Paris to study medicine did he experience theater, symphonic music, and opera.

Although nineteenth-century Paris was host to an unprecedented variety and richness of artistic achievement, opera remained the dominant art-form. Berlioz's contemporaries and friends included representatives of a great epoch in literature and spoken theater (Hugo, Nerval, Dumas, Balzac, Gautier, Vigny) and at least one great painter (Delacroix), as well as musicians who concentrated on the piano (Chopin, Thalberg, Liszt). But opera combined poetry, the music of voices and instruments, and the spectacle of elaborate scenery and dancing in the most fascinating of total experiences; and as in the age of Louis XIV it was both art and business, the cultural flagship of a rapidly developing nation. The Mecca of aspiring singers, dancers, and composers, Paris boasted three major opera companies: the Opéra itself, dominated by the grand operas of Rossini, Halévy, Meyerbeer, and later Verdi; the Opéra—Comique of Boieldieu, Hérold, Auber and Adam; and the Italian theatre which both imported and commissioned works by Rossini, Donizetti and Bellini.

Opera was at the center of Berlioz's livelihood, but he seldom took the parts he desired, of conductor and composer. He first attended the opera as an outspoken enthusiast, then as a newspaper critic and essayist whose judgment was respected and whose wit was feared. His comments, elegantly conveyed in *Les soirées de l'orchestre* (in which orchestral musicians tell stories during dull or pretentious operas), are harsh, but history has tended to bear out his verdicts. He conducted a number of operas in London and Germany, and concert extracts from many more, but he was constantly passed over for posts in Paris for which, as a musician, he was the best qualified candidate.

His career as a composer was always primary for him, but his training and habits of thought were unconventional, and his greatest successes fell outside prevailing trends. No pianist, he was fascinated by the expressive instrumental music of Beethoven, and his earliest

b

OPERA

successes were in the unfashionable genres of concert overture and symphony. He gave concerts in France, Belgium, Germany, Russia, and England throughout his career, which were often highly successful, but they did little to further his operatic ambitions. The success of his innovative programmatic works, notably the *Symphonie fantastique* (1830) and *Harold en Italie* (1834), combined with a reputation for eccentricity and extravagance fed by such pieces as his huge (but state-commissioned) *Requiem* (1837), combined to make the Parisian establishment of Conservatoire and theater wary of him; nor did his reputation as a critic help acceptance of his own compositions.

For his time, Berlioz had unusual and decided tastes in opera. Despite his love of Weber and his sympathetic understanding of the best contemporary work, such as Meyerbeer and Verdi, he based his operatic aesthetic on Gluck and his successor Spontini. At the inception of his career he appeared as a flagrant romantic before Romanticism was widely acceptable; by the time the public and establishment had caught up with him, he had embraced a very personal form of neo-classicism. As a result none of his operas fitted with prevailing tastes, and none was remotely successful in his lifetime.

Berlioz's only completely romantic opera was his first, *Les francs-juges* (1826, revised 1829), to a libretto by his close friend Humbert Ferrand. This tale of sinister political violence in medieval Germany never reached the stage. He later destroyed much of the score, finding a place for its best ideas in other works; enough remains to show his ready assimilation of the French pre-Romantics, Méhul and his own teacher Le Sueur, as well as the recent and controversial works of Weber. The overture still holds its place in the concert-hall.

Frustrated in his attempts to obtain a theater commission, Berlioz could still develop his dramatic gifts in the annual competition cantatas for the Rome Prize, notably *Herminie* (1828) and *Cléopâtre* (1829), and in a group of *Eight Scenes,* using lyrics from Nerval's translation of Goethe's *Faust* (1829). He finally won the prize in 1830, subsequently destroying the winning cantata, *Sardanapale,* which he claimed to have written in a deliberately conventional style. After the required sojourn in Italy, where he denounced the quality of music and performance in opera as well as church music, he carved out a place for himself in Parisian concert life, promoting his own works at huge expense of money and effort.

He remained at heart a dramatic composer. In 1833 he married Harriet Smithson, whose assumption of the roles of Ophelia and Juliet had moved him, and all Paris, in 1827. His love and understanding of Shakespeare emerged in an entertaining fantasia on *The Tempest* (1830), the stirring *King Lear* overture (1831), and the huge 'dramatic symphony' *Romeo and Juliet* (1839). Meanwhile he had at last achieved a staged performance when *Benvenuto Cellini,* loosely based on the memoirs of the Florentine goldsmith and sculptor, was given at the Paris Opéra late in 1838. The libretto was a collaboration, Berlioz having a controlling hand; inexperience led to serious dramatic weaknesses in construction, notably a too-episodic final act following a brilliant climax in the previous finale, the Roman Carnival from which Berlioz later derived a popular concert overture. The semi-serious genre, mingling comedy with violence and the expression of artistic idealism, also created difficulties. But the reasons for its perhaps predictable failure are more mundane. The libretto was naturalistic in its language, evading the usual operatic euphemisms; the musicians, including the tenor Duprez and the conductor Habeneck, could not grasp Berlioz's electric rhythms and complex melodic phrasing. There were only four complete performances until *Benvenuto Cellini* was revived in London and Weimar in the 1850s, eventually with extensive revisions; the German performances obtained the success that the music deserved under the committed direction of Liszt.

In the 1840s Berlioz was persuaded to compose recitatives to Weber's *Der Freischütz* for the Opéra, and accepted a libretto from Scribe, *La nonne sanglante*. He never finished the music; the libretto was withdrawn and eventually set by Gounod. The main work of this period is the concert-length "dramatic legend" *La damnation de Faust* (1846), incorporating the earlier *Eight Scenes*. Despite being conceived for the concert-hall, much of this masterpiece is overtly operatic; partly because of this generic mix, *Faust* is the last of Berlioz's works which might be considered romantically extravagant. A project to adapt it for the London stage (1847) came to nothing, but the 20th century has seen several operatic productions. Its style of dramatic presentation is designed to appeal to the visual imagination rather than to complement a spectacle, and some scenes, notably those in hell and heaven, are near-impossible theatrically. It was while working on *Faust* that Berlioz became his own librettist; he never again relied on other poets, writing his own texts for the successful oratorio *L'enfance du Christ* (1850-54) and his last two operas.

Les Troyens (1855-9) was written without a commission, under the influence of a lifelong passion for Virgil's *Aeneid,* and upon persuasion from Liszt's mistress Carolyne Sayn-Wittgenstein. Nevertheless, always practical, Berlioz designed it for the resources of the Paris Opéra. Its huge scale, its ritual and processional scenes involving chorus and dancing (especially in the first and third acts), the spectacular effects required (the fall of Troy, the royal hunt and storm, the vision of imperial Rome), and the centering of a wide-ranging action upon noble, suffering women align it superficially with grand opera. But in essence it is deeply opposed to the prevailing bourgeois aesthetic; it is a work of idealism, tracing its stylistic ancestry to Gluck and Spontini rather than the fashionable Italians and Meyerbeer. It is no accident that in this period Berlioz produced his most-often performed stage work, an adaptation of Gluck's *Orpheus* for Pauline Viardot-Garcia which retained the revisions and enlargements made for Paris while restoring the key-scheme with the vocal tessitura of the original Vienna version.

Les Troyens is a classical epic, remote in spirit from the historical and religious subject-matter favoured by Grand Opera. Berlioz was under no illusions about the likely reaction of the public, but he had every right to expect immediate interest in his longest work; instead, unfounded rumors began to circulate about its absurd length and colossal instrumentation. In fact it is chastely scored, reserving large forces for ceremonial scenes, and is no longer than contemporary works of Meyerbeer and Wagner. The indifference of the authorities, including the Emperor Napoleon III, was unpardonable; soon after its completion the Opéra tried to repair its fortunes by calling in Wagner for *Tannhäuser*. Finally a magnificently unified conception was shattered by division into two operas, *La prise de Troie* (Acts I and II) and *Les Troyens à Carthage* (Acts III to V). Only the latter was performed in Berlioz's lifetime (1863), savagely cut, at the inadequately equipped and funded Théâtre Lyrique, but with enough success to enable him to give up criticism; his last article is a warm appraisal of Bizet's *Les pêcheurs de perles*.

After finishing *Les Troyens* Berlioz contemplated a Cleopatra opera, and was asked for one on a Thirty Years' War subject. Successive bereavements and declining health make it doubtful that he would have had the strength for major projects; the gaps between his larger works had been growing since 1840, and his production of lesser pieces also declined. However, his friendly relationship with the impresario at Baden led him to agree to write his last and shortest opera, for which he returned to his beloved Shakespeare. "A caprice written with the point of a needle" was Berlioz's summary of *Béatrice et Bénédict,* as fresh and surprising an end to his career as is Verdi's *Falstaff.* But it is no surprise to find that he conceived an opera on *Much Ado about Nothing* in the productive 1830s, although there is no evidence of composition prior to 1860. Although it is ostensibly an opéra comique with spoken dialogue, *Béatrice et Bénédict* bears little resemblance to that genre as generally understood in Paris; it is designed as a sophisticated entertainment for a spa audience, and performing it in a large theatre is as damaging as putting on *Les Troyens* in a small one.

Throughout his career, Berlioz dreamed, conducted, and planned opera, but was continually frustrated in his efforts to create successful works for the stage. We cannot now regret the abortion of *La nonne sanglante* and the absence of other works on conventional librettos, but for Berlioz the refusal of the powers that were to recognize his operatic potential was a life-long tribulation. He understood the theatre thoroughly, and given intelligent singing and production his operas can all hold the stage; *Benvenuto Cellini* has unquenchable fire and spirit, *Béatrice et Bénédict* a uniquely intricate charm, and modern performances and recording have shown *Les Troyens* to be among the greatest works of the entire century.—JULIAN RUSHTON

Bernstein, Leonard

Composer/Conductor. Born 25 August 1918, in Lawrence, Massachusetts. Died 14 October 1990, in New York. Married: Felicia Montealegre, actress, 9 September 1951 (died 1978). Studied piano with Helen Coates and Heinrich Gebhard; studied orchestration with E. B. Hill and counterpoint and fugue with Walter Piston at Harvard University, 1935-39; studied orchestration with Randall Thompson, piano with Isabella Vengerova, and conducting with Fritz Reiner at the Curtis Institute; studied conducting with Serge Koussevitzky at Tanglewood, summers of 1940 and 1941; Assistant Conductor, 1943, and Music Director, 1958-69, New York Philharmonic; guest conducting with Vienna Philharmonic and London Symphony Orchestra, among many others; awarded Order of Merit, Chile, 1964; Chevalier of the French Legion of Honor, 1968; Cavaliere, Italy, 1969; Austrian Honorary Distinction in Science and Art, 1976; Albert Einstein Commemorative Award in the Arts; International Education Award; George Foster Peabody Award; honorary doctorate of letters, University of Warwick, England, 1974. Bernstein's stage works include the musicals On the Town, *1944,* Wonderful Town, *1953,* Candide, *1956, and* West Side Story, *1957.*

Operas *Trouble in Tahiti,* Bernstein, Waltham, Massachusetts, Brandeis University, 12 June 1952; *A Quiet Place,* S. Wadsworth, Houston, Houston Grand Opera, 17 June 1983 [revised 1984].

Leonard Bernstein devoted much of his career to various aspects of the opera and musical theater. He composed works for the Broadway stage that straddle the fine line between musical comedy, opera, and operetta; he composed works that adhere much more closely to the traditional European concept of opera; and he conducted major engagements at many of the world's most respected and renowned opera houses.

Whereas Bernstein's Broadway shows frequently contain operatic elements, such as the aria "Glitter and Be Gay" from *Candide* (1956), which requires a highly-developed and flexible operatic voice, in general they conform most closely to the forms and idioms established by his musical comedy predecessors Jerome Kern, Irving Berlin, Cole Porter, George Gershwin, and Richard Rodgers. His earliest collaborations for the Broadway stage, including the ballet *Fancy Free* (1944) and its musical comedy companion *On the Town* (1944), surely helped prepare him to some extent for the operatic stage. The popular song idiom, which inspired much of his first opera, clearly derives from his early Broadway and Tin Pan Alley song-writing experience.

Bernstein's two works that best represent traditional European opera are the one act *Trouble in Tahiti* (1952) and its sequel *A Quiet Place* (1983, which incorporates *Trouble in Tahiti* as two flashbacks). However, to call these two essentially autobiographical works traditional in any sense stretches considerably the accepted boundaries of opera. Elements of the popular theater and the conventional opera house merge and contrast throughout to create a hybrid form of musical theater. Bernstein has stated about *Trouble in Tahiti:* "It's a lightweight piece. The whole thing is popular-song inspired and the roots are in musical comedy, or, even better, the American musical theater." Certainly some of the roots may lie in musical comedy, but Bernstein's statement seems unusually reserved and restrained. Both the nature of the subject matter and its musical setting clearly reveal a genre that skirts the middle ground between traditional opera and musical comedy. And his allusion to "a lightweight piece" really misrepresents both *Trouble in Tahiti* and *A Quiet Place*. These two works attempt to convey substantially more serious subject matter than the typical Broadway musical; they are composed throughout, and they include musical techniques, forms, and idioms far removed from the Broadway theater. Even *Candide* represents an exception to his Broadway works because through various revisions and transformations it too now seems most at home in the opera house.

Although by no means best known as a conductor of opera, Bernstein enhanced his international reputation markedly through his association with individual operatic productions. In 1953 he became the first American to conduct at the Teatro alla Scala in Milan when he conducted Maria Callas in a production of Cherubini's *Médée*. He has also introduced some of the major operatic works of the twentieth century to the American public. For example, in the summer of 1946 he conducted the American premiere of Benjamin Britten's *Peter Grimes* at the Berkshire Music Center.

The predominant conflict in Bernstein's career as a theatrical composer has been whether to write popularly influenced music or music more closely allied with mainstream opera. In fact, this conflict between his obvious talent for the Broadway stage and his attraction to the European tradition represents the crucial dilemma of Bernstein's entire composing career. *A Quiet Place* would seem to be his partial response to those critics who have questioned his operatic credentials, since it attempts to reconcile the two seemingly incompatible idioms. While the sections based on *Trouble in Tahiti* (only a few passages of which were modified for the new work) utilize a language heavily influenced by popular musical techniques, the newly composed sections of *A Quiet Place* employ a musical language derived largely from the musical idioms of contemporary opera. The integration and juxtaposition of the contrasting styles creates a unique, if somewhat precariously balanced, theatrical composition.

Bernstein's most important theatrical contributions will almost certainly be remembered as those written specifically for the Broadway stage. Although both *Trouble in Tahiti* and *A Quiet Place* introduce some startlingly fresh elements to American opera, such as the biting commentary on contemporary life and the attempt to blend popular and contemporary musical idioms, they are undoubtedly not as innovatory or influential as the Broadway shows, particularly *West*

Side Story (1957). While Bernstein should not be regarded among the foremost American composers of opera, his two works should find and retain a secure place in the repertory of American opera.—WILLIAM THORNHILL

Berry, Walter

Bass-baritone. Born 8 April 1929, in Vienna. Married Christa Ludwig in 1957 (divorced 1970). Studied with Hermann Gallos at the Vienna Academy. Joined Vienna State Opera in 1950. Metropolitan opera debut as Barak in Strauss's Die Frau ohne Schatten, *1966; from 1952 was a regular soloist at the Salzburg Festival, creating roles in Liebermann's* Penelope *(1954), Egk's* Die Irische Legende *(1955), and Einem's* Der Prozess *(1953).*

Walter Berry is one of the most accomplished bass-baritones of the second half of the twentieth century. With a beautiful, rich voice, accuracy of intonation, and unusual vividness of characterization, Berry has brought memorably to life roles as diverse as Leporello (Mozart's *Don Giovanni*), Pizarro (Beethoven's *Fidelio*), Kurwenal (Wagner's *Tristan*), Barak (Strauss's *Die Frau ohne Schatten*) and the title role in Berg's *Wozzeck*.

Berry's talents won praise from the beginning of his international career in the 1950s. In a recording of *Don Giovanni* made in the mid-1950s under Rudolf Moralt, Berry's Leporello stands out for its clear enunciation, its wit and sense of style. A later recording of the same opera, under Klemperer, shows Berry in even better form. Notice, in "Notte e giorno faticar," the extraordinary energy that Berry brings to the music, his alertness to the meaning of the words. Leporello's annoyance and impatience could hardly be expressed in a more lively, entertaining manner.

Another Mozart role in which Berry has been successful is Papageno (*Die Zauberflöte*). In the recording conducted by Sawallisch, Berry presents Papageno with plenty of high spirits and a wonderful variety of vocal color, while the clarity of Berry's enunciation breathes life into the music. Papageno's strophic songs benefit especially from Berry's musical and dramatic skills. In "Der Vogelfänger bin ich ja" Berry brings out individual words with subtle variations of vocal color; there is something new and interesting in each repetition of the melody. Yet the richness and sophistication of his performance does not keep Berry from remaining very much in character: his Papageno remains a simple, good-hearted man throughout.

Berry has won much praise for his many performances in the operas of Richard Strauss. His portrayal of Baron Ochs (*Der Rosenkavalier*) is celebrated. When he performed the role in Vienna in 1972 critics admired his diction, his *parlando,* and applauded him for never exaggerating; all of these features of his performance can be heard in a recording of an excerpt from act II, conducted by Heinrich Hollreiser (issued in 1967). Berry brings his accustomed energy and variety to his performance, expressing with subtle gradations of dynamics and tone color a wide spectrum of emotions. Berry's Ochs is a real person, not a caricature. The same recording shows that Berry could bring to life with equal vividness Strauss's Barak and Orest (in *Elektra*). Also recorded (under Leinsdorf) is Berry's fine portrayal of the Music Master in *Ariadne auf Naxos.*

Berry has devoted much more attention to twentieth-century opera (in addition to Strauss) than many opera singers. His gripping portrayals of Berg's Wozzeck have been acclaimed by critics and audiences alike. Among the many less familiar twentieth-century operas in which he has sung is Werner Egk's *Irische Legende*. Berry's fine performance was not enough in itself to save the opera from failure when it was performed in Salzburg in 1955, but there are other recent operas (Liebermann's *Penelope* and Einem's *Der Prozess,* for example) whose success owed much to Berry's talents.—JOHN A. RICE

Billy Budd

Composer: *Benjamin Britten.*

Librettists: *E.M. Forster and Eric Crozier (after Herman Melville).*

First Performance: *London, Covent Garden, 1 December 1951; revised 1960.*

Roles: *Edward Fairfax Vere (tenor); Billy Budd (baritone); John Claggart (bass); Mr. Redburn (baritone); Mr. Flint (bass-baritone); Lieutenant Ratcliff (bass); Red Whiskers (tenor); Donald (baritone); Dansker (bass); Novice (tenor); Squeak (tenor); Bosun (baritone); First Mate (baritone); Second Mate (baritone); Maintop (tenor); Novice's Friend (baritone); Arthur Jones (baritone); Four Midshipmen (boys' voices); Cabin Boy (speaking part); chorus (TTBB).*

Based upon Herman Melville's *Billy Budd, Sailor,* Benjamin Britten's opera is set on board ship during the French wars, shortly after the mutinies of 1797. Edward Fairfax Vere is Captain of HMS Indomitable, and John Claggart is its Master at Arms. Billy Budd, a young seaman, is impressed from a passing merchantman; he is a paradigm of beauty and goodness, his only flaw being his stammer. He excites the envy and hatred of the evil Claggart, who schemes to destroy him by falsely accusing him of mutiny. When, however, Vere arranges a confrontation between Billy and Claggart, Billy's stammer prevents him from answering the charges, and he strikes Claggart a fatal blow. The officers, bound by the Articles of War, find Billy guilty of murder, and sentence him to death. Vere accepts the verdict, and, behind closed doors, conveys this to Billy in a manner left to the audience's imagination. That night Billy, in chains, unflinchingly accepts his fate in a searching meditation; then, facing a dawn execution, is moved to cry before the assembled ship's company, "Starry Vere, God bless you!" He is hanged at the yard-arm while the officers quell an incipient mutiny against the injustice. A Prologue and Epilogue show Vere in old age reflecting on his experiences. Now convinced that the execution had been a tragic mistake, he is assured that, blessed by Billy, he has found salvation and the love that passes understanding. Originally in four acts, the opera also provides graphic episodes depicting both the brutality and the comradeship of life on board, the excitement of impending battle and a ship's muster which elevates Vere as a patriotic commander. The latter scene was omitted when, for the revival of 1960, the opera was re-arranged in two acts.

The librettists, E.M. Forster and Eric Crozier, wrote in prose, though often a "heightened" prose, which Britten found well suited to musical setting. Musically the opera marks a development in Britten's style, embodying the complex inter-relationships of many short motifs in an overall structure which has been described as "symphonic." There is a developed symbolism in the use of tonal centers: for example, the ambiguity of the opening bars, rocking between B flat major and B minor, symbolic at once of the mist and of Vere's uncertainty, finds a final triumphant resolution in the blazing chord of B flat major in the Epilogue, as Vere affirms his assurance of salvation. The use of intervals, such as the fourth to mark Claggart's depravity, can be equally symbolic. All Britten's skill, both in characterizing individuals and in portraying different moods, from the intimate to the spectacularly grand, is evidenced, and so skilful is the writing even for a large orchestra, that the confinement of the vocal range to male voices only is hardly noticed. Particularly moving is the solemn succession of thirty-four variously orchestrated triads which marks the veiled interview between Billy and Vere.

The drama reflects a contest between fate and love. Forster saw in Melville's tale a prophetic utterance, "reaching back into the universal." It is pervaded by ineluctable fate—seen in the cruelly flogged novice, in Claggart's sense of predestination, in the "We've no choice" of the officers at the trial, in Billy's final reflection on the inevitability of Claggart's death and his own. The ship is an image of mankind "lost on the infinite sea." But strength to overcome this predicament is found through love, even though love perverted (in Claggart) can also destroy.

Though indirectly conveyed, the love which in their different ways Claggart and Vere feel for Billy is thus pivotal. For Claggart, that love is so deeply repressed and frustrated that it issues in a diabolical desire to destroy its object. But Vere is also drawn to the handsome sailor, and recent research has shown how in successive libretto drafts the relationship between Vere and Billy was developed far beyond Melville's portrayal of the Captain as an aloof disciplinarian. He is emotionally involved with the young man, while Billy responds with the ardor of personal devotion to Vere's goodness. The tragedy for Vere lies in the conflict between his love for Billy and his overriding sense that naval discipline requires the execution of the death sentence.

The love implicit in these relationships is symbolized in a recurring harmony of consecutive thirds and sixths. This harmony transforms the emotional atmosphere in the duet between Billy and Vere (act II, scene 2). It is also heard in the agitated quarter-deck interview between Claggart and Vere, with Claggart's innuendo that Vere is unduly moved by the young seaman's beauty. But at the climax it is the love between Billy and Vere (the "far-shining sail"—identified as love in a surviving note by Forster) which provides the strength to withstand fate. The point is made musically when Billy's melody for the far-shining sail is underpinned by the consecutive thirds/tenths of love: and when, at the hanging, the fearful orchestral fortissimo dissolves into tranquil high sixths, as forgiveness eclipses pain. In this context, reinforced by the recurring thirds in Vere's melodic line and Billy's arpeggio-like motif, the "Interview Chords," which reiterate the thirds of the common triad, are to be heard as the affirmation of a love which strengthens both Billy (in the darbies) and Vere (at the execution) in their resolve to hold to the path of duty. The Epilogue, in its combination of the Interview Chords with the tenths of the far-shining sail, confirms, however paradoxically, that this love has brought salvation.

Many other themes emerge from this inexhaustible score: the universal struggle of good and evil; the vulnerability of innocence; the power of forgiveness, with Billy seen as a Christ-figure; the misery, injustice and oppression, as well as the heroism and camaraderie, of life in Nelson's navy; the evil of war. Britten himself indicated that his interest was kindled by the conflict in Vere's mind. Perhaps only the obligatory reticence about homosexual desire inhibited a more overt statement of this theme in the opera as a conflict between love and duty.—CLIFFORD HINDLEY

Bizet, Georges

Composer. Born 25 October 1838, in Paris. Died 3 June 1875, in Bougival, near Paris. Married: Geneviève Halévy (daughter of the composer), 1869 (one son). Bizet's father was a voice teacher and composer, and his mother was a pianist; initially he studied with his parents, then fugue and composition with Zimmerman at the Paris Conservatory from the age of 9, where he also studied piano with Marmontel, organ with Benoist, and composition with Halévy; became a prodigious pianist, and was praised by Liszt. His cantatas David (1856) and Clovis et Clotilde (1857) won second and first prizes (Charles Colin was also awarded a first prize in 1857), respectively, in the competition for the Prix de Rome; in 1857, Bizet tied with Lecocq for first place in a competition sponsored by Jacques Offenbach for the composition of a one act stage work, Le docteur miracle; in Rome from January 1858-1860; Les pêcheurs de perles (Paris, 1863) praised by Berlioz; the well known incidental music to Daudet's L'Arlésienne was composed in 1872; Bizet died during the initial run of Carmen (1875), which did not achieve critical success until after his death. Bizet was made Chevalier of the Légion d'Honneur in 1875.

Operas *La maison du docteur* (opéra-comique), Henry Boisseaux, c. 1854-55; *Le docteur miracle* (operetta), Léon Battu and Ludovic Halévy, 1856 or 1857, Paris, Théâtre des Bouffes-Parisiens, 9 April 1857; *Don Procopio* (Italian opera buffa), Carlo Cambiaggio, 1858-59, posthumously produced in Monte Carlo, 10 March 1906; *L'amour peintre*, Bizet (after Molière), 1860 [unfinished]; *La prêtesse* (operetta), Philippe Gille, c. 1861?; *La guzla de l'émir*, Jules Barbier, Michel Carré, 1862; *Les pêcheurs de perles*, Michel Carré and E. Cormon, 1863, Paris, Théâtre-Lyrique, 30 September 1863; *Ivan IV*, F. H. LeRoy and François-Hippolyte Trianon, 1862-63?, revised 1864-65, posthumously produced in Württemberg, Möhringen Castle, 1946; *Malbrough s'en va-t-en guerre* (with Legouix, Jonas, Delibes), Paul Siraudin and William Busnach, 1867, Théâtre de l'Athénée, 13 December 1867; *La jolie fille de Perth*, Jules-Henry Vernoy de Saint-Georges and Jules Adenis (after Walter Scott), 1866, Paris, Théâtre-Lyrique, 26 December 1867; *La coupe du roi de Thulé*, Louis Gallet and Édouard Blau, 1868-69; Completed Halévy's biblical opera *Noë*, 1869; *Clarisse Harlowe* (opéra-comique), Philippe Gille et Adolphe Jaime the younger (after Richardson), 1870-71 [unfinished]; *Grisélidis* (opéra-comique), Victorien Sardou, 1870-71 [unfinished]; *Djamileh* (opéra-comique), Louis Gallet, 1871, Paris, Opéra-Comique, 22 May 1872; *Sol-si-ré-pif-pan* (operetta), William Busnach, 1872, Château d'Eau, 16 November 1872; *Don Rodrigue*, Louis Gallet and Édouard Blau (after Guilhem da Castro, *La Jeunesse du Cid*), 1873 [unfinished]; *Carmen*, Henri Meilhac and Ludovic Halévy (after Mérimée), 1873-74, Paris, Opéra-Comique, 3 March 1875.

Bizet is often credited with helping to introduce realism into opera with *Carmen,* now widely popular but largely rejected by the Parisian critics in 1875 both for its harsh libretto and the colorful score. Bizet influenced his contemporaries in less obvious ways, too, as they learned from his virtuoso orchestration techniques or from ideas they borrowed (Tchaikovsky clearly modeled the boys' march in *The Queen of Spades* [1890] on a similar piece in act I of *Carmen*). Bizet, however, did not leave direct descendants in opera, partially because he died so soon after achieving true artistic maturity. Furthermore, he did not establish new forms or revolutionize the concept of scene structure; instead, Bizet absorbed influences from Italian, German and French composers and, within the number opera tradition, combined these with his own innate gifts for melody and orchestration. At their best his scores combine a vital dramatic sense with colorful, tuneful, sometimes exotic-sounding music and create unforgettable passages that may range in their depictions from wittiness to tragic passion.

Though Bizet died at thirty-six, only three months after the controversial *Carmen* premiere, his operas span twenty years. In addition to his operatic projects and the incidental music for Daudet's tragedy *L'Arlésienne,* he also wrote songs, choral works, piano pieces, two symphonies and other orchestral pieces. Thus, Bizet's development as a composer can not be summarized in a single genre, and even for an assessment of his achievements in opera, it is necessary to study all the manuscripts, since a number of his works were abandoned or failed in the theater and were then either issued or reissued in untrustworthy, posthumous editions.

Georges Bizet

While still a student at the Paris Conservatoire in the 1850s, Bizet turned to writing opera, but his individual musical personality took time to assert itself with consistency. These unpretentious early works show that he had successfully absorbed the lighter styles then current in France and Italy and had mastered a sparkling orchestration technique. Even his earliest opera, *La maison du docteur,* has some melodic charm, but it was never scored and was probably prepared for an informal performance with his Conservatoire friends. *Le docteur miracle,* with a standard comic plot featuring thwarted young love and disguise, won a competition and was staged at Offenbach's theater in 1857. Within the light comic style Bizet wrote fresh-sounding tunes for his solo numbers and several appealing ensembles; he responded to the most intriguing dramatic opportunity with a masterful and deliciously witty quartet, "Voici l'omelette." After winning the Prix de Rome later that year, he left for Italy and claimed to have changed his tastes in music. "I am more than ever convinced that Mozart and Rossini are the two greatest musicians. Though I still admire Beethoven and Meyerbeer with all my faculties, I feel that my nature is inclined more toward loving pure and accessible art than that of dramatic passion," he wrote to his mother in October 1858. Not surprisingly, *Don Procopio* quite convincingly appropriates the manner of Rossini and Donizetti, and incorporates Italianate accompaniment figures and an attractive vocal style. The more even and accomplished score was praised by the Academy of Fine Arts: "This work is distinguished by an easy and brilliant touch, a youthful and bold style, valuable qualities for the genre of comedy toward which the composer has shown a marked propensity."

In the 1860s Bizet expanded his range and absorbed the more dramatic and grandiose styles. His operas of this period incorporate and juxtapose elements derived from Gounod, Félicien David, Meyerbeer, Weber and even Verdi; however, more and more passages also strike the ear as distinctive to Bizet's personal style. A music critic's remark on *Djamileh* in 1872 describes Bizet and his two staged operas of the 1860s, *Les pêcheurs de perles* and *La jolie fille de Perth*: "The composer who stumbles in taking a step forward is worth more attention than a composer who shows how easy it is to take a step backwards." This statement applies as well to the abandoned *Ivan IV,* where Bizet turned to Meyerbeer as a model for grand opera. Though the orchestration and massed effects are at times overblown and the pacing not always well controlled, the score teems with good ideas which Bizet quarried for years thereafter. *Les pêcheurs de perles* also attempts grandiose effects in some scenes, but here there are more lyrical moments, especially for the soloists, and effective use of musical exoticism.

Surprisingly large portions of *La jolie fille de Perth* sound like pre-echoes of the *opéra-comique* style that would flower in *Carmen*. Although the influence of Weber and Verdi's *Rigoletto* lingers in the background, there are passages of wit, tunefulness and masterfully delicate orchestral effects that could only have been written by Bizet. Despite important style consolidation, however, he also made concessions to fashion in an Italianate coloratura part, and could not consistently find inspiration in the weakest libretto he ever set.

Perhaps the greatest loss of the 1860s is *La coupe du roi de Thulé,* submitted to an Opéra competition in 1869; even the surviving fragments of this manuscript reveal much originality and dramatic power. More abandoned projects followed. Two *(Clarisse Harlow* and *Grisélidis)* were intended for the Opéra-Comique; another, the grand opera *Don Rodrigue,* for the Opéra. Even though sketches and drafts for these operas permit some understanding of Bizet's intentions, his theater works that have not gone through the rehearsal process are far from finished. During the *Carmen* rehearsals, for example, Bizet greatly improved the pacing of the work, rewrote three of the four finales, cut and reworked a great deal of music for the chorus, removed most of the *mélodrames,* and even wrote solo material as striking as the Habanera.

Both of Bizet's staged operas from the 1870s feature exotic subjects, masterful scoring, interesting harmonies, and unforgettable melodies. The libretto of *Djamileh* has quite lovely poetry but is dramatically weak, with little action and a hero whose appeal remains a mystery to all but Djamileh herself. Perhaps these weaknesses have kept the lovely, one-act score from the wide popularity that it richly deserves. *Carmen,* on the other hand, is supported by one of the half-dozen best libretti ever written. Bizet recognized the quality of his work and wrote to a friend: "They claim that I am obscure, complicated, tedious, more fettered by technical skill than lit by inspiration. Well, this time I have written a work that is all clarity and vivacity, full of color and melody."

Bizet correctly assessed his skills and should be regarded as one of the greatest melodists and orchestrators of France. His themes may be traditional and four-square (as the main theme of the famous tenor/baritone duet "Au fond du temple saint" from *Les pêcheurs de perles*) or spun-out with phrases run together so seamlessly that they form an indivisible sentence (as in the "flower song" from *Carmen*) or sinuous and exotic. Even many of the youthful melodies have an ageless charm and freshness.

Generalizations about Bizet's melodic style are complicated by his practice of borrowing from his earlier works that had not been publicly performed. The graceful flute duet in the prelude of *La jolie fille de Perth* was written several years earlier for *Ivan IV.* Most of Don José's flower song was rescued from a baritone piece abandoned in the sketches for *Grisélidis.* Only occasionally does the melodic style betray a borrowing, as in the old-fashioned choral passage "Ah, Chante, chante encore" (close of act I, *Les pêcheurs de perles*), which was pulled from its context in *Don Procopio.*

Bizet's skill at orchestration is also evident throughout his career. Except in a few blatantly Meyerbeerian passages his scores sparkle with woodwind color and the occasional brass accent. Strings serve as the foundation of his orchestral sound. A favorite Bizet combination, flute and harp, opens one of the loveliest orchestral pieces in opera, the entr'acte before act III in *Carmen*. Later in the score, flutes and bassoons play a delicate counterpoint to Frasquita's and Mercédès' warning to Carmen that Don Jose is nearby the bullring. The examples of imaginative and striking scoring could go on and on.

Bizet's music is perhaps most characteristic when he is creating an exotic atmosphere. Although in *Carmen* he used several real Spanish tunes, he had basically one generic exotic mode; thus, he felt it appropriate to take a bolero from his ode symphony *Vasco da Gama* (1860) and place it in the mouth of the young Bulgarian called upon to entertain Ivan IV with a song from his homeland. The exotic vocabulary often includes chromatic harmonies and sinuous or chromatic melodies over the tonal security of a pedal note (as near the end of each strophe of Djamileh's "Ghazel"). The laughing figure that represents Carmen and is later transformed into the "fate" motif may be called exotic since it incorporates the distinctive sound of an augmented second. In Bizet's exotic mode accompaniment figures focus on a repeated rhythm (often involving drone fifths or syncopation); harmonies shift ambiguously between major and minor. Bizet's harmonic experiments are probably most noticeable within this style, but are not confined to these pieces. The opening of Carmen's séguedille dances along without solidly confirming the tonic for twenty-nine bars; but in the next act the feather-light quintet, squarely within the *opéra comique* tradition, slides effortlessly from a distant G major to the tonic D-flat major. Accented dissonances, on the other hand, like those in Djamileh's lamento probably gave fuel to Bizet's contemporary critics, who hurled the epithet "Wagnerian" at his scores.

In the combination of drama with music Bizet achieved a unique and highly successful balance, at first only in individual numbers, then in the entire second act of *La jolie fille de Perth*, then in much of *Djamileh* and virtually all of *Carmen*. Though Bizet received few libretti of high quality, he did work with his librettists to try to refine the dramatic impact of each scene. The quality of the text and the interest of the situation was strongly linked to the quality and interest of his musical response. Witty and ironic situations appealed to him, as evidenced by the imaginatively scored "marche et choeur des gamins" of *Carmen* where children parody the adults' ritual. In *La jolie fille de Perth* an elegant minuet backstage wryly comments on the insincerity of the Duke of Rothsay's practiced seduction technique as he attempts to seduce his old mistress disguised as another. Given the quality of his invention in humorous dramatic situations, we might wish that Bizet had had the opportunity to write a full-length comic opera in the 1870s.

At the other end of the spectrum, Bizet also found inspiration in intense or desperate situations and in the pure flame of tragic passion. The final tragic duet of *Carmen* combines drama and music so convincingly that at moments a listener can also forget that there are two arts combined, and the unbearable intensity removes any distance between audience and performers. Though it is one of the greatest of operatic duets, it cannot be successfully excerpted because it is so wedded to the dramatic situation. Bizet's success with dramatic situations is by no means confined to his last work. At her investiture Léila, the high priestess of *Les pêcheurs de perles* refuses in a line of flexible recitative worthy of Carmen ("Je reste ici quand j'y devais mourir") to back away from an equally impossible situation. On the other hand, religious ceremony may also stimulate a more conventional response. Here Bizet may depend on Meyerbeer, and such passages sound curiously dated next to the exotic portions of his scores. Tenderness and conventional love tend to inspire a derivative (Gounodesque) style. It is not by chance that the duet of Marie and the young Bulgarian (act I of *Ivan IV*) and of Catherine and Smith (act I of *La jolie fille*) sound much like the act I duet of Micaela and Don Jose.

The works of the 1850s reveal much skill and appealing charm but only glimpses of Bizet's individuality; in the 1860s they are more original but also more eclectic; and in the 1870s they are too few in number. But Bizet has left a body of work that maintains its vitality and appeal. It demonstrates, too, a surprisingly wide range—from wit to tragic passion, from delicacy to dramatic power—and at its best a balance of music and drama that few have equaled.—LESLEY A. WRIGHT

Björling, Jussi

Tenor. Born 5 February 1911, in Tuna, Sweden. Died 9 September 1960 in Stockholm. Married soprano Ann-Lisa Berg, 1935—and sometimes sang opposite her. Entered Stockholm Conservatory in 1928, studied with Joseph Hirlop and John Forsell; appeared as Lamplighter in Manon Lescaut, *but official debut as Don Ottavio, both in Stockholm in 1930; sang regularly in Stockholm until 1939; Vienna debut as Manrico, 1936; Chicago debut in* Rigoletto, *1937; Metropolitan Opera debut as Rodolfo, 1938, and appeared with Metropolitan Opera until 1959 as Manrico, Faust, Riccardo (in* Un ballo in maschera), *Don Carlos, and Romeo, among others; San Francisco debut as Rodolfo, 1940.*

Arguably the finest lyric tenor of the century, Jussi Björling was one of a long line of eminent Swedish singers whose musical achievements have contributed immeasurably to opera. Jenny Lind, Kirsten Flagstad, Lauritz Melchior, Christine Nilsson, Birgit Nilsson, Karin Branzell, Astrid Varnay, Nicolai Gedda, John Forsell, and many others have all helped to establish Sweden as a major source of vocal genius. Yet few have come to define a benchmark of such supreme musical taste, secure vocal production, and disciplined performance as that set by Björling. His remarkable achievement was the result of a fortuitous combination of the gift of a voice with a timbre of rare beauty and the advantage of a long, careful musical tutelage that provided a pedagogical foundation of uncommon soundness. Björling, though often compared inappropriately with Caruso, certainly should be considered the great singer's successor as the preeminent tenor of his time. For it would be difficult to bring forth another candidate who could clearly exceed Björling's artistic and commercial success.

Björling was born into a musical family, the atmosphere of which contributed substantially to his early growth. His father, David, had studied voice early in the century at the Metropolitan Opera School, and later at the Vienna Conservatory. He relinquished a modest opera career in Sweden to devote himself to the education of his sons, Olle, Jussi, Gösta, and Karl (the youngest). With the older three, David formed the Björling Male Quartet, which concertized until the latter's death in 1926. The elder Björling evidently was a gifted and patient pedagogue, for it is clear that much of the sound, disciplined approach to fundamentals of vocal production that characterized the mature Jussi Björling was owed in no small way to his father's influence. Evidently his father would not allow him to sing one note without his personal supervision.

Björling's musical development was assisted considerably by his early association (1928) in Sweden with John Forsell, director of the Royal Opera in Stockholm, and gifted teacher. It would be difficult to overestimate the value of Forsell's guidance. His was a disciplined school which stressed musical expressivity; slow, careful development of technique; ease of vocal production; and memorization of a wide variety of basic repertoire.

Securely under Forsell's wing, Björling made his first operatic appearance in 1930 as the Lamplighter in *Manon,* but almost immediately made a far greater impact in his debut roles as Ottavio in *Don Giovanni* and as Arnold in Rossini's *Guillaume Tell.* The latter role, with its demanding *tessitura* and *coloratura,* evidently was a perfect vehicle for Björling's secure high register and technical prowess and is revealing of the nature of his early capabilities. During the next few years at the Royal Opera in Stockholm, Björling sang over 50 roles—early evidence of his reliable memory, which perhaps explains his well-known distaste for rehearsing. He took pride in his absolute knowledge of his parts and his ability to sing them at a moment's notice.

After the beginning of his international career in 1936, his active repertoire decreased considerably. He ultimately narrowed his efforts to a dozen familiar works, most of which are available on recordings and establish his unerring mastery of the Italian style. His gift for singing in the Italian language (although he did not speak it) and his supreme execution of its characteristic *cantabile* lines clearly sustained his judgment in restricting his artistic purview.

Of his operatic roles, Björling expressed a preference for des Grieux in *Manon,* and it must be said that his performances in this role were particularly well done. Late in his career Björling declared an interest in singing more performances as Radames (*Aïda*), as well as in the roles of Lohengrin and Otello. To those dubious as to the suitability of these heavy parts for his lyric voice, he characteristically dismissed the challenge as of no consequence for him. Björling had an implicit faith in the ability of a singer with a mastery of technique to sing "anything." Nevertheless, it must be said that on the whole he chose his operatic roles with discretion, notwithstanding the frequent performances of *Il trovatore,* which many consider to have been less than ideal for his voice. Appropriately, the demands of a stage performance of *Turandot* held no allure for Björling, though he often performed "Nessun dorma" in recital. It is a commonplace to speak critically of Björling's acting ability, and it must be admitted that he often performed with an undeniable dramatic stiffness that belied his otherwise complete command of the requisite skills of a world-class lyric tenor. Nevertheless, most agree that on the stage his consummate musicianship and expressive delivery usually more than atoned for this deficiency.

To various degrees the voices of all great singers may be characterized as distinctive. Of no one may this be said more truly than of Björling. His timbre was unique and his voice distinguished throughout its range for an uncommon evenness of production. Personally, he dismissed the concept of vocal "registers," and maintained that the voice should never have a break in the scale. He possessed an extraordinary *mezza voce,* but derided the cultivation or use of *falsetto.* Though some critics have pointed to a brightness of tone that could become tiresome or even a bit harsh, Björling is known for his pure vowels and a youthful quality that he preserved throughout his career. He did acknowledge some change in his sound as he aged, describing it as possibly a "lyric *spinto,*" and, not surprisingly, the repertoire of his maturity eschewed the Rossini *coloratura* of his youth. His was never an exceptionally powerful voice, and there were those who questioned its carrying power in the larger houses. Nevertheless, whatever it lacked in this respect was strongly countered by its fundamental focus and clarity. In comparison with his peers he possessed superior control, maintaining pitch and tone quality in the most demanding of melodic lines—regardless of dynamic constraints. Like many, he occasionally pushed pitch on the highest notes, but this was not a constant problem. In his remarks on singing he always stressed correct and appropriate breathing—not only for support

b

OPERA

of the production, but for intelligent musical and poetic phrasing. He was quick to condemn poor phrasing that garbled and distorted the meaning of the words and his own style was exemplary in avoiding that. He possessed an adroit command of shading of tone and of the use of *legato* in spinning out a melodic line. His mastery of the Italian style in vowels, diction, and tone quality was accompanied by disciplined approach to rubato and phrasing not often matched by other leading tenors. Finally, he rarely indulged himself at the expense of the composer. He acknowledged that the conductor with whom he sang so frequently, Grevillius, helped inculcate this all-too-rare attitude.

Not yet fifty years of age when he died, Björling not only immeasurably enriched his times, but, thanks to an abundance of recordings, continues to generate admiration as each generation encounters his legacy. His artistic accomplishment stands as a model for those who value integrity, moderation, and discipline in interpretation; who respect deft surety in technical execution; and who prize uncommon beauty of tone. Although his remarkable gift was innate, Björling's devotion to its assiduous preparation and intelligent use serves as a peerless example.—WILLIAM E. RUNYAN

Blitzstein, Marc

Composer. Born 2 March 1905, in Philadelphia. Died 22 January 1964, in Fort-de-France, Martinique. Married: Eva Goldbeck (died 1936). Studied composition with Rosario Scalero at the Curtis Institute; studied piano with Alexander Siloti in New York; studied with Nadia Boulanger in Paris, 1926-27 and with Schoenberg in Berlin, 1927; Guggenheim fellowship, 1940; stationed in England with United States Armed Forces during World War II. At the time of his death, Blitzstein was working on an opera on the subject of Sacco and Vanzetti, composed under the aegis of the Ford Foundation for performance at the Metropolitan Opera in New York.

Operas *Triple Sec,* R. Jeans, 1928, Philadelphia, 6 May 1929; *Parabola and Circula* (opera-ballet), G. Whitsett, 1929; *The Condemned* (choral opera), Blitzstein, 1932; *The Harpies,* Blitzstein, 1931, New York, 25 May 1953; *The Cradle Will Rock,* Blitzstein, 1936, New York, 16 June 1937; *No for an Answer,* Blitzstein, 1937-40, New York, 5 January 1941; *Regina,* Blitzstein (after Lillian Hellman, *The Little Foxes*), 1946-49, New York, 31 October 1949; *Reuben Reuben,* Blitzstein, 1949-55; *Juno,* J. Stein (after S. O'Casey, *Juno and the Paycock*), 1957-59; *Sacco and Vanzetti,* Blitzstein, 1959-64 [unfinished]; *The Magic Barrel,* Blitzstein (after B. Malamud), 1963 [unfinished]; *Idiots First,* Blitzstein (after B. Malamud), 1963 [unfinished]; completed by L. Lehrman, Ithaca, New York, August 1974.

One of the most important American composers from the late 1930s through the 1950s, Marc Blitzstein is now remembered for only a few works: *The Cradle Will Rock,* his opera with Orson Welles and the Federal Theatre Group that the government tried to ban in 1937; *Regina,* an opera based on Lillian Hellman's *The Little Foxes,* which has been unlucky in revivals; and the *Airborne Symphony,* a cantata for male voices which has seen sporadic performances. But those more familiar with Blitzstein know a much richer body of work: the agitprop opera *No for an Answer,* his 1950s cold war Faust story *Reuben Reuben,* and his late musical version of Sean O'Casey's *Juno and the Paycock.*

Blitzstein was one of the few composers of his time who used his works to make social statements, considering this more important than plots that would guarantee box office success. His stage works of the thirties and early forties took up labor issues and were written so they could be performed by the very people he was writing about. Even when he turned to a more difficult, operatic style in *Regina* and his later works, Blitzstein took on unpopular subjects: racial issues, alienation, and the position of women in society. Blitzstein stayed with a tonal idiom throughout his career to keep his message accessible to audiences.

The 1941 opera/musical *No for an Answer* shows a move forward from some of the Weill-like numbers and the lack of variety in *The Cradle Will Rock* of four years before. Although still a stage work for and about the masses, *No for an Answer* used a variety of styles: the patter in the clever "Penny Candy"; full-blown lyricism in "Secret Singing"; a *Lehrstück* (teaching piece), "The Song of the Bat"; and a marvelous torch song, "Fraught." "Fraught," with its clever text and sophisticated nightclub idiom, is the best number in the show and one of the best Blitzstein ever wrote. Blitzstein attempted an interesting experiment in the love duet, "Francie," in which the male role Joe keeps repeating his love Francie's name. It is not entirely successful because the repeated vocal line requires a little more development to avoid monotony, but it shows the composer willing to depart from the standard Broadway conventions of his day. Blitzstein developed a better sense of line and phrasing in his later stage works, perhaps helped by his composition of the *Airborne Symphony,* a work for male chorus, in the 1940s.

Reuben Reuben, which closed in 1955 before it reached Broadway, is truly a through-composed opera, as opposed to Blitzstein's next work, *Juno. Juno* has discrete musical numbers separated by spoken dialogue and thus is akin to other Broadway musicals of its era. *Reuben* has musical numbers, listed as such in the program, but most of the dialogue between these numbers is underscored by music. Blitzstein uses unaccompanied dialogue only for important points in the story. To illustrate how Blitzstein creates a scene: in the first scene Reuben's exposition of his past is spoken over music. When he is unable to give directions because of his aphonia, the music stops. A song for Reuben, "Thank You," comes next, followed by circus-like music under a partly spoken, partly sung scene with some pickpockets. A lyrical duet for an argumentative couple expands into a trio with a girl asking directions and into a quartet with Reuben joining in ("Never Get Lost"). The music stops again when Reuben contemplates dying like his father. A jazzy interlude leads into the next scene in a bar.

This through-composed style in *Reuben* is an advance from that in *Regina*. Much of the dialogue in *Regina* had been set to music for the second production, and it occasionally sounds like interpolations. The music in *Reuben,* on the other hand, has a more developed flow and a better unity. This is an extravaganza of a score, with the boisterous scene at the street fair, the villain Bart's brooding music, another successful nightclub number, and the lovely duet "There Goes My Love." In this opera Blitzstein composes those developed, arching melodic lines that are missing in places in his early work. Although his book would need extensive reworking, this is a score that deserves to be resurrected.

One of the greatest hindrances to Blitzstein's career was his insistence on writing his own libretti. He claimed that he could not find any suitable collaborators, but working alone also allowed him to procrastinate, where a partner might have forced him to focus his work. Blitzstein achieved his best results when he used preexisting plays, in *Regina* and *Juno*. Reviewers commented on his problem with dramatic construction in *No for an Answer,* based on an original idea. Years later Blitzstein's muddled plot crippled the musically accomplished *Reuben*

Reuben. His unfinished opera about Sacco and Vanzetti was held up by his insistence on working on his own and by other projects. This piece had the potential for being his greatest work, both as a social statement and as music drama. It is our loss that Blitzstein was killed before he could finish it.—DAVID E. ANDERSON

La bohème

Composer: *Giacomo Puccini.*

Librettists: *Giuseppe Giacosa and Luigi Illica (after Mürger).*

First Performance: *Turin, Regio, 1 February 1896.*

Roles: *Rodolfo (tenor); Marcello (baritone); Schaunard (baritone); Colline (bass); Benoit (bass); Mimi (soprano); Musetta (soprano); Alcindoro (bass); Parpignol (tenor); Customs Guard (bass); chorus (SATB).*

During the second half of the nineteenth century, a new movement appeared in the arts which was to have profound repercussions throughout Europe. The social upheaval resulting in the Revolution of 1848 in France brought about radically new approaches in artistic expression as well. Endowed with a new social awareness, many artists now saw it as their primary mission to depict the world "as it really was," with no idealizing tinsel attached. Painters such as Courbet and Millet produced "realistic" paintings, showing ordinary working people in lifelike settings.

La bohème, title page of piano score, 1895, illustrated by Adolfo Hohenstein, who also designed the sets and costumes for the premiere

While the first dramas of Dumas *fils* can be seen as early examples of realism in the work of a French writer, it was Émile Zola during the last third of the century whose novels became the prime representatives of "realism" in French literature.

A more localized version of "realism" came about in Italy as well. Referred to as *verismo,* its foremost representative was the novelist Giovanni Verga, whose short stories and novels dealt primarily with rural characters, placed in realistic settings, who find themselves in extraordinary crises which result in violent outbursts of emotion. It was this display of crude passion which had a particular appeal to the realists in both France and Italy.

One of Verga's Sicilian short stories, included in his collection *Vita dei campi* (1880), was *Cavalleria rusticana.* It served as the model for the opera with the same name by Pietro Mascagni, a work, premiered in 1890, which is now considered the first Italian *verismo* opera. The great success of this work gave rise to a number of operas in

b

OPERA

the same mold by composers such as Spinelli, Giordano, Cilèa, and Leoncavallo, whose *I pagliacci* (1892) had won the Sonzogno opera competition, as Mascagni's *Cavalleria rusticana* had before.

Giacomo Puccini is often listed among these "veristic" composers as well, and specific reference is made to his *Tosca* and *Il tabarro,* mainly for the spine-chilling display of crass emotions and deadly violence in these operas. But the portrayal of common, real-life characters in a realistic setting was of concern to Puccini in other operas as well in which no connection can be seen with the more local tradition of literary *verismo*. This is true, more specifically, for *La fanciulla del West, Madama Butterfly,* and *La bohème.*

The model for Puccini's *La bohème* is the novel *Scènes de la vie de bohème* by the French writer Henry Mürger, originally published in various episodes in the magazine *Le Corsair* between 1845 and 1848. In 1849, a stage adaptation of the story by Théodore Barrière and Henry Mürger followed, which was a great success. In 1851, the novel was reissued in book form. It is not a structurally unified novel, but rather a collection of vignettes presenting the joys, woes, and aspirations of young people, mostly artists, and their struggles to survive. In portraying characters from the lower social strata, without any effort at concealing the less pleasant aspects of their existence, Mürger hit upon a raw nerve among his readers. Given the new vogue for "veristic" operas in the early 1880s, it is thus not surprising to find Puccini attracted to the "realistic" story of *La bohème*. The libretto by Giuseppe Giacosa and Luigi Illica is based primarily on the novel, and not the stage play.

The opera, set in Paris around 1830, tells the story of four Bohemians, the poet Rodolfo, the painter Marcello, the philosopher Colline, and the musician Schaunard, who are chronically without money and live in the most wretched conditions in a shared attic apartment. In act I, Rodolfo meets his neighbor Mimi, who knocks on his door to ask for a light for her candle. She has an ominous cough and does not seem at all well. During their conversation, Rodolfo and Mimi fall in love. It is Christmas eve, and they decide to join the other Bohemians, who had gone out to celebrate at the Café Momus.

Act II takes place later the same day. Rodolfo and Mimi have joined the other Bohemians at the Café, and shortly thereafter Musetta, a vivacious woman and former love of Marcello's, appears in the company of a wealthy paramour, Alcindoro, for whom she shows no respect at all. As she still loves Marcello, she sends Alcindoro away on a pretext, and no sooner is he gone than she and Marcello immediately make up.

In act III, Rodolfo has left Mimi after a quarrel. Mimi tells Marcello of Rodolfo's jealousy, but when she overhears that Rodolfo is despairing over her failing health, she is deeply moved. Although Rodolfo and Mimi feel that their relationship is coming to an end, they decide to stay together until the spring.

In act IV, both Rodolfo and Marcello have ended their affairs with Mimi and Musetta. In the garret, the four Bohemians are having a Spartan meal consisting of a herring and some bread. Trying to cheer one another up, they engage in some exaggeratedly farcical activities, including a courtly dance and a mock duel. Unexpectedly, Musetta bursts in and announces the arrival of Mimi, whose health has further deteriorated. All past grudges are forgotten as everyone gathers around Mimi. While the others go off to fetch a doctor, some medicine, and a muff for Mimi's cold hands, Rodolfo and Mimi have a chance to express their feelings for each other. But Mimi is more ill than anyone had thought. When the others have returned to the room, she dies.

Comparison of the opera and Mürger's novel reveals, of course, both similarities and discrepancies. To analyze what the opera has retained, what is has discarded, and what it has transformed, provides important insight into the aesthetic choices made by Puccini and his librettists. The manner in which the opera deals with its "realistic" subject also provides a reference point vis-à-vis some of the "veristic" operas written at about the same time.

While Mürger's *Scènes de la vie de bohème* is one of the earliest examples of French "realist" literature, one would be hard-pressed to detect any explicit social criticism, and in this respect Mürger differs drastically from Zola or Verga. Mürger's Bohemians struggle not *against* the system, but rather for success *within* it; his characters do not seem to suffer from or resign themselves to the sociological and economic conditions; rather, they can almost be seen as taking a sort of sardonic, bitter-sweet pleasure in it. Mimi's death does not strike us so much as the shocking result of society's injustice, but rather as the product of her own carelessness. In their excessive lifestyles, the Bohemians are still very much "romantic"; new in Mürger is the insight that these romantics have to face up to a "real world."

Puccini's *Bohème* in its non-violent presentation of the story captures Mürger's brand of realism therefore very well; the opera is devoid of social criticism and commentary, yet full of attention to realistic detail. Great care was taken to create an ambience that seems as lifelike as possible, and the dialogue between the characters has none of the traditional poetic diction of Italian opera, but indulges instead in unabashed colloquial speech. Nevertheless, the differences between the novel and the opera reveal how far Puccini and his librettists were willing to take "realism" on the opera stage. Mimi, for instance, is by no means an altogether sympathetic character in Mürger's book; she shows, in fact, some rather unpleasant personality traits. In the opera, however, Mimi is a transformed, "purified" character, and this transformation brought her closer to operatic tradition as a heroine with whom the audience could identify. Realism notwithstanding, Puccini was not willing to risk an opera in which the tragic character would not be a sympathetic one whose fate would arouse pity. More than that: in the novel, Mimi dies abandoned in a charity hospital. Her body, after being subjected to experiments in an anatomy class, was buried in a pauper's grave. Clearly, this end was out of the question for Puccini and his librettists.

While the opera retains much of the essential character of the novel, a significant reversal of priorities has occurred: whereas love, or "amorous episodes," in Mürger's novel do not play the dominant role (the friendship of the Bohemians and their artistic aspirations are rather the main theme), Puccini's *Bohème* places love, more specifically the love between Mimi and Rodolfo, at the center of attention. Mürger and Barrière felt it necessary to do the same in their stage adaptation. Clearly, friendship or artistic ambition was not felt to be apt for dramatic development.

Structurally, *Scènes de la vie de bohème* can be seen to reflect "realism" in the seemingly random order of the episodes. Tragic, comic, and "sober" elements are freely juxtaposed—just as in real life. This structural principle had a formative influence on Puccini's *La bohème*. In the preface to the libretto, Giacosa and Illica pointed out, among other things, that they have strived to reproduce the spirit of the novel; to remain faithful to Mürger's characters; and to follow Mürger's method of presenting the story in distinct tableaux. Indeed, the four acts of the opera do represent four distinct tableaux, and they show only a vague dramatic connection with each other. With this, Giacosa and Illica had stepped onto new ground. In fact, it was this lack of dramatic unity which prompted considerable criticism at the premiere.

The free juxtaposition of tragic and comic, serious and not-so-serious episodes in the novel is masterfully reflected in the opera in those instances when such sentiments are fused together. This can be observed during Musetta's waltz, *"Quando me'n vo' "* (act II), where Puccini weaves the sentiments of Marcello, Alcindoro, Mimi, Rodolfo, Schaunard, and Colline into the musical structure. Similarly, the closing scene of act III shows Mimi and Rodolfo deciding to stay together until spring, and their emotional conversation is perpetually interrupted by the ranting argument between Musetta and Marcello. Arguably the most striking instance of this sort of juxtaposition occurs when, in act IV, Musetta bursts into the room and interrupts the silly behavior of the four Bohemians with the announcement of the arrival of the ailing Mimi.

How is "realism" reflected in Puccini's music? One would have to say, not very well, but this answer would be misleading. The very fact that in opera all the text is sung, with accompaniment by an orchestra, is in itself "unrealistic": in real life, people don't sing to each other, but talk. In this respect, all "veristic" operas are unrealistic. It is not coincidental, therefore, that in those moments when the "veristic" composers wanted to be as realistic as possible—namely at the point of heightened tension, when raw passion comes to the surface—the characters often stop singing and start screaming. This type of "lyricism," often referred to as *aria d'urlo,* became one of the trademarks of *verismo* operas. There is such a moment in *La bohème* as well, namely at the very conclusion of the opera, when the tragedy unfolds. In that moment of terrible recognition, all singing stops, and Rodolfo starts screaming as he finds out that Mimi has died.

Another way in which *verismo* composers attempted to infuse realism into their scores was by incorporating folkloristic songs, such as "ordinary" people might sing. Giordano did this in his *Mala vita,* which incorporates several popular Neapolitan tunes. Such real-life quotes are absent from Puccini's score, except for the military tattoo marching across the stage in act II (as Mosco Carner has pointed out, it is based on an authentic French march of the time of King Louis Philippe). But Puccini creates atmosphere by paying close attention to dramatic details. There is a good bit of descriptive music, illustrating, for instance, the flickering of the fire in the stove in act I, or the snowfall at the beginning of act III. His orchestration pays close attention to the dramatic situation as well. The more intimate the scene is, the more chamber-like is the orchestration. The full orchestra is dutifully employed for the portrayal of the crowd scenes in act II.

What impresses most about Puccini's score, however, is the virtually perfect pacing of the music. There is never a dull moment in the music, and Puccini abstains from musical verbosity. The result is a score consisting of musical units which say exactly as much as needed, and then move on to the next unit. Each act is relatively short as well: Puccini presents precisely what is needed, and not more. There is never a moment of boredom.

Whereas Puccini's first opera, *Le villi,* as well as his third, *Manon Lescaut,* revealed decided traces of Wagnerian influence, no Wagnerisms can be detected in *La bohème.* The tonal language is predominantly diatonic, and chromatic counterpoint is virtually non-existent. Even though Puccini does make use of extended harmonies, the tonal center is rarely in question. But above all, melody is the most important ingredient of the score, and in *La bohème* Puccini's genius for melodic invention has come to full fruition.

La bohème was arguably the work which established Puccini as the leading voice in Italian opera, indeed as one of the foremost opera composers anywhere around the turn of the century.

b

OPERA

Despite an initially cool reception, *La bohème* has always maintained itself in the repertoire, and may well have been performed more often than any other opera ever written. While the work reflects the general preoccupation with realistic subjects in opera at the time, it illustrates a marked detachment from some of the baser aspects of *verismo* opera.—JÜRGEN SELK

The Bohemian Girl

Composer: *Michael William Balfe.*

Librettist: *A. Bunn (after J.H. Vernoy de Saint-Georges).*

First Performance: *London, Drury Lane Theatre, 27 November 1843.*

Roles: *Arline (soprano); Thaddeus (tenor); Queen of the Gypsies (contralto); Devilshoof (bass); Count Arnheim (bass); Florestein (tenor); Captain of the Guard (bass); Officer (tenor); Buda (soprano).*

The Bohemian Girl, Michael William Balfe's most enduring opera, has been described as a work of "charming sentimentality." Both words are apt. The music has undeniable charm, if little sophistication, a quality it does not, after all, seek. Alfred Bunn's libretto reflects the nineteenth-century middle-class preference for the highly sentimental, and in this Bunn succeeds where other of Balfe's librettists failed, striking the precise note that would inspire the composer to his best effort.

Bunn has rightly been accused of both banality and oversimplicity. His plot is a *mélange* of elements from familiar works. Thaddeus, a Polish soldier hiding from Austrian authorities disguised as a gypsy, saves the life of little Arline, the Count of Arnheim's daughter. When the gypsies are threatened with punishment for disloyalty to the Austrian flag, the gypsy Devilshoof kidnaps Arline. Twelve years pass, during which time Arline's memory of her former life seems to her only a dream, but her love for Thaddeus, and his for her, is real. Thaddeus, however, is also desired by the Queen of the Gypsies, who gives Arline an amulet she knows will be recognized as stolen, causing Arline's arrest. The plan works, but Arline is recognized by the count as his long-lost daughter. She is restored to her estates, but her love for a gypsy, Thaddeus, cannot be tolerated. He meets Arline secretly, but is betrayed by the queen. Thaddeus reveals to the count that he is no gypsy; he too has noble blood, which fact is enough for the count to accept him. Her plot foiled, the queen menaces Arline, but is shot dead by Devilshoof, leaving the lovers to rejoice.

Certainly Bunn's libretto appeals to the most obvious, uncomplicated emotions. But aside from the jarring transition at the close of act III—Devilshoof's shooting of the Queen leading directly into a chorus in praise of the young lovers (ameliorated in the 1978 Central City production by director Robert Darling's interpolation for the count: "Let not this awesome event mar our joy")—Bunn provided a clear story, one whose assumptions its public shared. Thaddeus is worthy of Arline not because he saved her life or has loved her regardless of her station, but because, as it turns out, he too is of her social class. When his right to Arline's hand is questioned by the count, he relies not on his goodness but on his blood to justify his suit. The gypsies are lighthearted but treacherous (as the audience knew all gypsies to be). Arline and the count are stereotypes, as is Florestein, the count's inept nephew. There are no surprises in this libretto, except to the characters on stage.

But a libretto cannot make an opera by itself, nor overly mar one written by a composer upon whom genius is smiling. Verdi converted the ridiculous book of *Il trovatore* into the quintessential Italian romantic opera, while far superior libretti (Boito's to Faccio's *Hamlet,* for example) lie forgotten, wedded to unmemorable music. Balfe poured into *The Bohemian Girl* some of his best ideas and created for it perhaps his three best arias. If the opera ever becomes as totally forgotten as those of his contemporary (some would suggest, superior), Edward Loder, the last notes of Balfe to be heard will surely be those of Arline's "I Dreamt I Dwelt in Marble Halls," whose haunting descending cadences possess a charm that only the most determinedly intellectual listener can reject. The quintessential Italian tenor of the century, Beniamino Gigli, recognized the visceral appeal of Thaddeus' "When Other Lips" (for some reason better known by its closing words "Then You'll Remember Me"), while the absence of the Count's "The Heart Bow'd Down" from contemporary baritone recitals and recordings perhaps reflects more a fear of being thought old-fashioned than an adverse judgment on the aria's singability or capacity to please an audience. In the concerted passages, Balfe advances the action with an undeniable skill and innate conviction, though without building a musical structure anywhere as interesting as the ensembles in his own *Satanella* or in Loder's *The Night Dancers.*

Beyond the unsophisticated pleasure its music can give, *The Bohemian Girl* has the unsought burden of being the only example of English romantic opera one is likely to encounter in live performance (though even these are becoming rarer). As one of the best and most representative (the two are not always synonymous) works of its subgenre, it requires a production (such as those of Covent Garden in 1951 and Central City in 1978) which does not flinch in taking the opera seriously and reproducing it without deconstruction or irony. Given such a production, the opera has much to tell us about the taste of a vanished age. *The Bohemian Girl* has an uncomplicated honesty that transcends its banality, and tests our capacity to participate in a relentlessly unsophisticated pleasure, so very alien to our own age, in responding to it.—WILLIAM J. COLLINS

Boito, Arrigo

Composer/Librettist. Born 24 February 1842, in Padua. Died 10 June 1918, in Milan. Studied composition with Alberto Mazzucato and Ronchetti-Monteviti at the Milan Conservatory, 1853-61; in collaboration with Faccio, the composition of two cantatas (1860-61) won for them a two year travel grant from the Italian government, with which Boito travelled to Paris, Poland, Germany, Belgium, and England; wrote the text for Verdi's cantata Inno delle Nazioni, *and later for Verdi's* Otello *and* Falstaff; *served in Garibaldi's army, 1866; first production of his* Mefistofele *at the Teatro alla Scala in 1868 was controversial and consequently unsuccessful, but his revisions of the original score led to later successful runs in Italy and elsewhere; appointed inspector general of Italian conservatories by the King of Italy, 1892; honorary doctorates from Cambridge and Oxford Universities; made a senator by the King of Italy, 1912. Boito also published verses under the pen name Tobia Gorrio, as well as translations of operas (Wagner's* Rienzi *and* Tristan und Isolde*), opera librettos for various composers (most notably Verdi), and novels.*

Operas   *Ero e Leander; Nerone,* 1862-1916; revised for performance by Toscanini, Milan, Teatro alla Scala, 1 May 1924; *Mefistofele,* Boito, Milan, Teatro alla Scala, 5 March 1868.

Librettos: *Amleto,* F. Faccio, 1865; *Un tramonto,* G. Coronaro, 1873; *La falce,* A. Catalani, 1875; *La Gioconda,* A. Ponchielli, 1876; *Ero e Leandro,* G. Bottesini, 1879; L. Mancinelli, 1897; *Simon Boccanegra* (after F. Piave), G. Verdi, 1881; *Otello,* G. Verdi, 1887. *Falstaff,* G. Verdi, 1893; *Semira (La regina di Babilù)* [not performed]; *Pier Luigi Farnese* [not performed]; *Iràm* [not performed]; *Nerone,* Boito, 1924 [posthumous]; *Basi e bote,* R. Pick-Mangiagalli, 1927.

Arrigo Boito (1842-1918) was a significant opera composer, librettist, and man of letters. He is best known today as the composer of *Mefistofele* (1868; revised 1875 and 1881) and as librettist for Verdi's *Otello* (1887) and *Falstaff* (1893) and Ponchielli's *La Gioconda* (1876).

Although Boito was a composition graduate of the Milan Conservatory, he composed relatively few musical works, the bulk of his creative output being in the literary domain. Boito managed in his long lifetime to compose only two operas, *Mefistofele* and *Nerone* (first performed in 1924) of which only the former was completed.

Boito was associated in the 1860s and 1870s with the *Scapigliatura* (literally translated, the "disheveled ones"), a loosely-knit group of young Italian intellectuals and artists. The members of the *Scapigliatura* emphasized the darker side of human nature and exhibited a penchant for extreme pessimism, resembling in certain respects the earlier *Weltschmerz* movement in Germany and the naturalism evident in the contemporaneous works of the French. It was precisely this pessimistic streak that attracted Boito to the ambivalent character of Faust and the malevolent Nero.

Ironically, it is with the opera *Mefistofele* that Boito scored both his greatest disaster and triumph as a composer. The literary-minded Boito wanted to set both parts of Goethe's *Faust,* not just a truncated version of Part I as is the case with Gounod's *Faust.* The original version of *Mefistofele* was six hours in length and was very poorly received when it was premiered at the Teatro alla Scala on 5 March, 1868. Boito then began a lengthy process of revision in which half of the opera's original material was excised. *Mefistofele* was first performed in its revised version in 1875, was well received, and remains to this day as part of the standard opera repertoire.

Boito's experience with *Mefistofele,* while revealing his limitations as a composer, clearly demonstrated his formidable powers as a librettist. He was able to condense the many strands and subplots of Goethe's drama into a workable size for an opera, reducing the complexities of the original drama to an essential conflict between the real (as symbolized by Margherita) and the ideal (as represented by Helen of Troy). This ability to condense a complicated literary work to its essence also proved invaluable when Boito collaborated with Verdi on *Otello* and *Falstaff.* The latter opera, in fact, skillfully combines three Shakespeare plays, *Henry IV,* parts I and II, and *The Merry Wives of Windsor.* Another important factor in Boito's greatness as a librettist was his outstanding ability as a linguist. Being able to read Goethe and Shakespeare in their original languages gave Boito a distinct advantage over his colleagues since he was able to comprehend not only the author's precise poetic meanings but also the rhetoric and cadences of their languages. Finally, Boito's knowledge of musical composition gave him an intimate knowledge of the ways in which music and words are able to be combined successfully (or unsuccessfully as the case may be).

For all of his shortcomings as a composer, Boito did leave behind one masterpiece in *Mefistofele,* although it may be argued that this is the result of the opera's total effect being greater than the sum total of its musical, literary, and dramatic aspects. It is primarily as a librettist that Boito will be remembered and it is in this category that he ranks with such notable figures as Lorenzo da Ponte and Hugo von Hofmannsthal.—WILLIAM E. GRIM

Bolcom, William

Composer. Born 26 May 1938 in Seattle. Married: 1) Fay Levine, 1963 (divorced 1967), 2) Katherine Agee Ling, 1968 (divorced 1969), 3) Joan Clair Morris, 1975. Entered University of Washington at age 11, studied composition with George Frederick McKay and John Verrall, earned B.A. there, 1958; further studies with Darius Milhaud at the Aspen Music Festival (1957), at Mills College (1958-61) and in Paris at the Conservatoire de Musique, 1959-61 and 1964-65; completed doctorate in composition at Stanford, 1964; won Deuxieme Prix in composition at Paris Conservatoire, 1965; has taught composition at University of Michigan, Ann Arbor since 1973, full professor since 1983, named Ross Lee Finney Distinguished University Professor of Music, 1994; awarded Guggenheim fellowships, 1965 and 1968; awarded Koussevitzky Foundation Awards, 1976 and 1993; elected to American Academy of Arts and Letters, 1992; awarded Pulitzer Prize in Music, 1988 for "12 New Etudes for Piano;" regularly performs as pianist with Joan Morris in recitals devoted to American popular music from the 19th century to today.

Operas *Dynamite Tonite* (cabaret opera), Arnold Weinstein, 1960-63, New York, Actors Studio, 21 December 1963; *Greatshot* (cabaret opera), Arnold Weinstein, 1966, New Haven, Yale University, 15 May 1969; *The Beggar's Opera* (completion of adaptation begun by Darius Milhaud in 1937), John Gay, 1978, Minneapolis, Tyrone Guthrie Theater, 27 January 1979; *Theater of the Absurd* (paraphrase), Bolcom, 1969-70, San Francisco, Conservatory of Music, 2 March 1979; *Casino Paradise* (operatic tragifarce), Arnold Weinstein, 1986-90, Philadelphia, Play and Players, 4 April 1990; *McTeague,* Arnold Weinstein and Robert Altman, Chicago, Lyric Opera of Chicago, 31 October 1992; *View from the Bridge,* Arnold Weinstein and Arthur Miller (work in progress, commissioned by the Lyric Opera of Chicago for premiere in October, 1999).

William Bolcom may be the most American of late 20th century American operatic composers. His music—intentionally difficult to pigeon-hole, eclectic to a sometimes exasperating extent, technically masterful, consistently clever, never solemn, often quirky and almost always enticing—pays a strong debt to that composed by his iconoclastic fellow countryman, Charles Ives, whom he has cited as the major influence on his compositions.

Bolcom's initial forays into musical theater show his preoccupation with fitting nontraditional operatic styles into traditional operatic forms. Both the 1963 *Dynamite Tonite* and the 1966 *Greatshot* are described as "actors operas"; the 1979 *Theater of the Absurd* is called "a paraphrase for live actor, taped actors, electronic tapes, wind quintet, piano and mechanized eyeballs"; the 1990 *Casino Paradise* is subtitled "An Operatic Tragifarce."

With *McTeague,* the first opera commissioned from an American composer by the Lyric Opera of Chicago and premiered there in 1992, Bolcom plunged into the big-time world of grand opera. Based on Frank Norris 1899 novel about a "sometime dentist" and his greedy wife, the two-act opera is set to a libretto by Arnold Weinstein, a longtime Bolcom collaborator, and filmmaker Robert Altman, who also staged the work. True to form, Bolcom brought most of his stylistic quirkiness with him to *McTeague*. He describes the work as "an eclectic mix, from simple to complex, atonal to tonal." There are set pieces, including some forthright arias and ensembles. Most of the music is tonally centered, and some of it flirts with folksiness.

Bolcom was generous in his vocal writing in *McTeague*. The title role was written for a voice of heldentenor proportions (sung admirably in the world premiere performances by Canadian tenor Ben Heppner); the part of Trina Sieppe, McTeague's wife (sung with equal success by American soprano Catherine Malfitano) is also meaty.

While each of the initial 10 performances of *McTeague* was sold out at the Lyric, the opera was not an unqualified success. To a certain degree its stylistic eclecticism worked against its impact. There were also places—a scene where Trina becomes so obsessed with the gold coins she has hoarded that she tries to make love to them, for instance—where Bolcom's music fell short of matching the dramatic situation. The opera has yet to be taken up by another major professional company, although it was "revived" at the Indiana University School of Music in February, 1996.

No one could fault Bolcom's craftmanship, though, or his unabashed desire to reach his listeners. The Lyric Opera obviously continues to be impressed with his efforts: the company commissioned a second opera from him for the 1999-2000 season. This one is based on Arthur Miller's *A View from the Bridge,* with Miller and Weinstein collaborating on the libretto.

That it would be nearly impossible to predict the sort of music Bolcom will bring to Miller's play is further proof of the uniquely American qualities that continue to be perhaps the foremost hallmark of his considerable talent.—JOHN GUINN

Bori, Lucrezia [Lucrecia Borja y Gonzalez de Riancho]

Soprano. Born 4 December 1887, in Valencia. Died 14 May 1960, in New York. Studied at Valencia Conservatory and with Melchiorre Vidal in Milan; debut as Micaela in Carmen *in Rome, 1908; at Teatro alla Scala in 1909; sang in Paris in 1910; New York Metropolitan Opera debut in* Manon Lescaut, *1912; singer at Metropolitan Opera, 1912-36; on the board of directors of the Met, 1935-60.*

The greatest triumph of Lucrezia Bori's career, notwithstanding the myriad times that the love of her exceptionally affectionate public flowed toward her across the footlights, actually took place offstage. This protracted victory over adversity began in 1915, when nodules developed on the twenty-eight-year-old soprano's vocal cords and the inescapable operation to remove them proved unsuccessful, or at least unskillful. A Milanese surgeon tried another procedure in 1916, and afterwards told Bori that a long silence was the only hope for restoration of the voice. Her lengthy ordeal and eventual return to singing with absolutely unimpaired resources constitutes one of the most famous chapters in operatic lore.

Lucrecia Borja y Gonzales de Riancho was born in Valencia, where her initial studies took place at the local conservatory. After further instruction in Italy, she made her operatic debut in Rome in 1908 as Micaela in *Carmen*. Here she adopted the Italian spelling of her first name and altered that of the last in order to minimize her connection with the sinister Borgias, from whom she was in fact one of the many Spanish descendants.

Bori did not have to struggle for recognition of her special, though fragile, gifts. She was at the Teatro alla Scala within a year of her debut (and sang Octavian in the Italian premiere of *Der Rosenkavalier* there in 1911), and on the Metropolitan Opera's first European visit in 1910 she was engaged to replace Lina Cavalieri as Manon Lescaut in five performances in Paris. This role served as well for her American debut with the company on opening night of the 1912 season.

The virtues that won for Bori the deep affection of the American audience were evident from the outset in what Henry Krehbiel, reviewing her first New York performance, called "the real fineness of her vocal art . . . an exquisite exhibition of legato singing . . . exquisite diction, impeccable intonation and moving pathos."

Bori's last appearance prior to her surgery was with the Metropolitan in Atlanta (Fiora in *L'amore dei tre re,* 30 April 1915). After the second operation, she had the devotion and the discipline to remain completely silent for an entire year and to speak in no more than a whisper for most of the next, so that healing might be without further intervention or incident. A deeply devout Roman Catholic—despite rumors of a romantic entanglement with tenor and later Metropolitan Opera general manager Edward Johnson, Bori is believed to have been celibate—her faith sustained her through the anguish and uncertainty of her period of enforced silence. Whatever brought on the problem (which developed shortly after she took on the title role of Mascagni's *Iris*), when Bori was able to return to singing she consecrated her life completely to her art and to her public. She tested the waters first in the 600-seat theater at Monte Carlo in 1919 (as Zerlina in *Don Giovanni*) and returned to New York as Mimì (*La Bohème*) on 28

January 1921. Every performance thereafter was for her the repayment of a nonreimbursable debt to God and to those who gave her their devotion by coming to hear her sing. The love affair between Bori and the American public (her career after this was almost exclusively in the United States) continued unimpeded until her formal farewell to the stage on 29 March 1936. At that time, W. J. Henderson called her "America's opera sweetheart" and said that "there was every reason for thanksgiving that we had all been so fortunate as to live in Miss Bori's time." (She actually sang once more, a Mimì four days later with the Metropolitan in Baltimore.)

The soprano's recordings reveal a voice of warm and beautiful timbre, an unfailingly affecting delivery, some brilliance when necessary (though her preference was for repertory short on this requirement), a complete understanding of style, emotional power in tragedy, and a quite irresistible charm that suffuses every measure. In the theater she was recognized as a superb and nuanced

Lucrezia Bori as Giulietta in *The Tales of Hoffmann*

actress-interpreter equally at home as Mélisande and Despina, Mimì and Mignon, no less persuasive in *Peter Ibbetson* than in *La vida breve*.

When the Great Depression hit, Bori was still a prominent artist in the company, but she spent all of her free time campaigning for funds to save the Metropolitan and "keep opera going." She became an indefatigable letter-writer and an ardent speech-maker who would appear at any meeting or before any group, and opera lovers heard her speaking voice for the first time in eloquent appeals over the radio. Even before retirement, she became the first singer *and* the first woman elected to the Metropolitan's board of directors. After she stopped singing, she fulfilled her vow to serve the company for the rest of her life by doing so up until the very day of her death from a brain hemorrhage. She remained on the board until that day, and was also honorary chairman of the Metropolitan Opera Guild (1936-60, with a term as active chairman 1943-48). Moreover, she was for many years president of the Bagby Music Lovers Foundation, which provided financial assistance to her less fortunate colleagues in retirement.

She remembered her own people as well, and worked tirelessly to raise relief funds following the devastating floods in Valencia in 1957. Three years later, thousands lined the streets there to pay homage and watch the soprano's funeral cortège, in a demonstration as great as that for any political figure. Franco bestowed upon her posthumously the Gran Cruz de la Beneficencia, the highest honor awarded in Spain for charitable work. "It is because of her that I have a roof over my head" said one mourner. Anyone working inside the old Metropolitan Opera House that day could legitimately have said the same thing.—BRUCE BURROUGHS

Boris Godunov

Composer: *Modest Musorgsky.*

Librettist: *Modest Musorgsky (after Pushkin and Karamzin).*

First Performance: *St Petersburg, Maryinsky Theater, 8 February 1874; revised posthumous production, Leningrad, 16 February 1928.*

Roles: *Boris Godunov (bass-baritone); Fyodor (mezzo-soprano); Xenia (soprano); Nurse (contralto or mezzo-soprano); Prince Shuisky (tenor); Brother Pimen (bass); Gregory Otrepiev, later The Pretender, Dimitri (tenor); Marina Mnishek (mezzo-soprano or soprano); Rangoni (baritone or bass); Varlaam (bass); Missail (tenor); Innkeeper (mezzo-soprano); Simpleton (tenor); Shchelkalov (baritone); Nikitich (bass); A Boyar (tenor); Lavitsky (bass); Cherniavsky (bass); Officer of Frontier Guard (bass); Mityukh (baritone); A Woman (soprano); chorus (SSAATTBB).*

The intriguing sound of Musorgsky's *Boris Godunov* has captured the attention of audiences for well over one hundred years. Yet the opera in its initial form (1869) was considered inadequate by the Board of Directors of the Imperial Theater. The Committee's rejection of the 1869 version had to do primarily with the absence of a significant female role.

Soon after Musorgsky received word of the committee's criticism, he added the Polish act, which revolves around the Princess Marina. Though the act set in Poland appears only in the revision of 1872, there is evidence that Musorgsky had thought of it from the beginning. In addition to the Polish act, Musorgsky added the Revolution scene (act IV, scene i), also known as the "Scene Near Kromy." He deleted the St Basil scene and rewrote most of act II (Boris and his children).

After completing the revisions of 1872, Musorgsky won the approval of the Committee for a performance of *Boris,* which took place on 8 February 1874 at the Maryinsky Theater in St Petersburg, with Melnikov as Boris. According to David Lloyd-Jones, the definitive version of the opera was performed only twenty-six times between 1874 and 1882 in St Petersburg, the Revolution scene being omitted in the last fourteen of these; and then ten times in Moscow between 1888 and 1890.

In commemoration of Paul Lamm's 1928 edition of *Boris Godunov,* a performance of it was given on 16 February 1928 in Leningrad. One of the photographs of scenes from this production is entitled: "The Square by the Cathedral of St Basil at Moscow. The starving people implore the Czar to give them bread." The St Basil scene which Musorgsky excluded from the premiere performance of the opera in 1874 made its debut in the 1928 performance in Leningrad. Originally the St Basil scene came in the last act, just before the death of Boris. In the 1872 version, however, the St Basil scene was replaced by the Revolution scene, which Musorgsky placed after Boris' death. Except for the not very long lament of the Simpleton, almost the same in both versions, there is little in common between these scenes in dramatic or musical content. Still, they share some elements of style, modal textures being the more prevalent. Both close with the Simpleton singing, "Weep, weep, Russian folk, poor starving folk." In productions which include the St Basil scene (1869) as well as the Revolution scene (1872), the song of the Simpleton, which appears in both scenes, becomes a kind of ritornello mourning the vicissitudes of Mother Russia.

The St Basil scene is closer to Pushkin than the Revolution scene. In musical style, the Revolution scene is closer to the Polish act, both having been added for 1872. The death of Boris, composed in 1869, is in turn stylistically closer to the St Basil scene, also composed in 1869. Just before Boris dies, the static harmonies of the Coronation scene are heard; through rhythmic transformation they become his death knell, reminding us also of the chiming of the clock. The music introducing Boris' Coronation is unusual for the feeling of stasis created by two chords of like quality repeated over and over, imitating the sound of clanging bells.

The 1869 version, then, is the more individualistic and original in style. On the other hand, the 1872 version is dramatically more complete and musically more varied. The composer has expanded his scheme of events, adding the clock scene, the Innkeeper's song, the Polish act, and the Revolution scene, all of which increase the scope and human interest of the work. Cosmopolitan musical style makes the revised score more varied, interesting, and accessible to a general audience.—MAUREEN A. CARR

Borkh, Inge

Soprano. Born Ingeborg Simon, 26 May 1917, in Mannheim. Married the singer Alexander Welitsch. Studied acting in Max Reinhardt seminary in Vienna and singing in Milan and at the Salzburg Mozarteum; debut in Lucerne, 1940 or 1941, and was engaged there 1941-44; first major success as Magda Sorel in The Consul *in Basel, 1951; appeared in Munich, Vienna, Berlin, Stuttgart and London; U.S. debut in San Francisco as Elektra in 1953 and she returned to San Francisco as Verdi's Lady MacBeth in 1955; debut at*

Metropolitan Opera as Salome, 1958; Dyer's wife in first Covent Garden performance of
Die Frau ohne Schatten, 1967.

Had Inge Borkh been singing at almost any other time in recent history, it seems certain
that her fame would have been far greater. But it was perhaps her misfortune that she appeared
on the scene during what may have been the last golden age for dramatic sopranos. Much of her
Strauss and Wagner repertoire was shared with, among others, the internationally-celebrated
Birgit Nilsson, whose clarion trumpet of a voice is certainly unique in our time, as well as with
Astrid Varnay, whose vocal gifts were not the equal of Nilsson's, but whose intensely charismatic
theatricality was much beloved by critics and audiences alike. And the years during which Borkh
sang much of the Italian lyrico-spinto repertoire were also the years of Callas and Tebaldi,
Milanov and Price. In this very distinguished company Borkh's own achievements tended to get
lost, and she seemed a less immediately distinctive artist than these other singers.

Yet as we listen to the recordings which Borkh has left us, we realize that she possessed a
rare excellence all her own. The breadth of her repertoire especially impresses; few singers have
performed both German and Italian roles with equal security, and Borkh sounds absolutely
idiomatic in both. She is one of a very small number of German sopranos who might actually be
mistaken for an Italian when she performs Italian music; the language, although slightly
accented, is stressed and the words pointed with the fluency and ease of a native speaker. Even
more, Borkh's positive and natural way of sculpting the musical line is in the grand tradition of
true bel canto singing. Recorded recitals preserve arias from *Un ballo in maschera, Andrea
Chénier, Macbeth, Cavalleria rusticana* and more—a broad cross-section of the lyrico-spinto
and dramatic repertoires. In all of these, Borkh's performances are warmly voiced and boldly
projected. The tone itself is less immediately recognizable than some of the more famous voices
of the time, but ironically Borkh's performance may in fact be better sung and as strongly
characterized as several of the others. Her complete recording of *Turandot* is a good example of
Borkh's artistry in Italian music. While Borkh lacks the gleaming top notes which are so exciting
in Nilsson's performance of the role, she presents a more specific and in many ways more
interesting interpretation of the troubled princess. And on the other hand, if Borkh's handling of
text is almost inevitably less detailed than that of Maria Callas, her handling of the fearsome
tessitura is far more secure.

As formidable as many of Borkh's performances in Italian music are, it is in the German
repertoire that she especially excelled, and here her recordings need fear no comparisons. A
radio transcription of her Sieglinde is predictably strongly sung and touchingly characterized,
with Borkh skillfully projecting the fragility and nervousness of the young girl. She is even more
impressive in an off-the-air performance of Salome from the Metropolitan Opera, excitingly
conducted by Dimitri Mitropolous. Critics who saw Borkh perform this role in the theater
invariably speak of her very fine acting, and this certainly comes through on purely aural terms. A
comparison with the celebrated Salome of Ljuba Welitsch is revealing—where Welitsch is more
overtly dramatic (sometimes rather too much so), her electrifying performance is achieved
through some of the most idiosyncratic singing in memory; in truth, she often allows the musical
line to all but vanish in search for "character." Borkh is equally vivid and her singing is far more
consistent and true to Strauss' score. Her musical scrupulousness is, in fact, one of Borkh's great
distinctions in this repertoire—like Callas, she never alters or abandons the musical line for
dramatic effect and instead chooses to create character through the written notes.

Nowhere are these virtues more welcome than in the role of Elektra, and this portrayal was probably Borkh's crowning achievement. There exists a famous record of scenes conducted by Fritz Reiner, as well as a complete performance of the opera under Karl Böhm and several live recordings which are in wide circulation. In all of them Borkh distinguishes herself first by truly singing the difficult Strauss music, the tone always rich and firm, the awkward intervals meticulously observed. And once again always within the confines of her vocal achievement, Borkh is among the most intense and heart-wrenching of Elektras. Her performance is a splendid achievement, setting a standard for many years to come in this most difficult and exacting of operatic roles.—DAVID ANTHONY FOX

Britten, (Edward) Benjamin

Composer. Born 22 November 1913, in Lowestoft, Suffolk. Died 4 December 1976, in Aldeburgh. Studied viola with Audrey Alston and composition with Frank Bridge; studied piano with Arthur Benjamin and Harold Samuel, and composition with John Ireland at the Royal College of Music, 1930; Fantasy Quartet *performed at the International Society for Contemporary Music in Florence, 5 April 1934; film scores from 1935-1942; organized the English Opera Group, 1947, and the Aldeburgh Festival, 1948; Companion of Honour, 1952; Order of Merit, 1965; made a Lord by Queen Elizabeth II, 1976.*

Operas *Paul Bunyan,* W.H. Auden, 1941, New York, Columbia University, Brander Matthews Hall, 5 May 1941; *Peter Grimes,* M. Slater (after a poem by Crabbe), 1944-45, London, Sadler's Wells, 7 June 1945; *The Rape of Lucretia,* Ronald Duncan (after A. Obey), 1946, Glyndebourne, 12 July 1946; revised, 1947; *Albert Herring,* Eric Crozier (after Maupassant), 1947, Glyndebourne, 20 June 1947; *The Little Sweep, or Let's Make an Opera* ("entertainment for young people"), Eric Crozier, 1949, Aldeburgh, Jubilee Hall, 14 June 1949; *Billy Budd* (revised 1960), Forster and Crozier (after Herman Melville), 1951, London, Covent Garden, 1 December 1951; *Gloriana,* W. Plomer, 1953, London, Covent Garden, 8 June 1953; *The Turn of the Screw,* M. Piper (after Henry James), 1954, Venice, Teatro La Fenice, 14 September 1954; *Noye's Fludde* (children's opera), Orford Church, 18 June 1958; *A Midsummer Night's Dream,* Britten and Pears (after Shakespeare), 1960. Aldeburgh, Jubilee Hall, 11 June 1960; *Curlew River* (church parable), W. Plomer, 1964, Orford Church, 12 June 1964; *The Burning Fiery Furnace* (church parable), W. Plomer, 1966, Orford Church, 9 June 1966; *The Prodigal Son* (church parable), W. Plomer, 1968, Orford Church, 10 June 1968; *Owen Wingrave,* M. Piper (after Henry James), 1970, broadcast premiere: BBC, 16 May 1971; stage premiere: London, Covent Garden, 10 May 1973; *Death in Venice,* M. Piper (after Thomas Mann), 1973, Snape Maltings, 16 June 1973.

In the opening of *A Time There Was,* the filmed profile of Benjamin Britten's life directed by Tony Palmer, American composer/conductor Leonard Bernstein is quoted saying that Britten was "a man at odds with the world . . . ." At that time, shortly after Britten's death, it sounded strangely incompatible with the general impression of the composer's seemingly charmed life. Britten was, after all, the most prominent musician in England, and was hailed by many as the greatest English composer since Henry Purcell. Closer examination of his early life, however, reveals clues to the darker side to which Bernstein alludes, and Britten's life-long struggle is manifested in the themes and character of his vocal music, in particular the operas.

Benjamin Britten with Peter Pears, 1939

By the time Britten was in his mid-twenties, several personal and professional circumstances coalesced that are fundamental to a deeper understanding of his life and work. First, Britten, who exhibited a prodigious musical talent early on, felt unappreciated by the conservative English musical establishment of the 1920s and 1930s. Second, as a pacifist, Britten found himself aligned with the minority who opposed England's increased involvement in the approaching war. Third, Britten was a homosexual at a time and in a place that offered him little recourse but repression. Together, these circumstances resulted in overwhelming feelings of isolation, alienation, and oppression, feelings with which Britten struggled for the rest of his life, and about which, through his operas, he spoke eloquently.

It is not surprising, then, that Britten fled to America as World War II began, as did many European artists. He desired to live and work in an atmosphere free from social and political pressures, and one more conducive to creative expression. It was in the United States that his first operatic venture, *Paul Bunyan,* was written and produced (to decidedly less than enthusiastic reviews), along with other works, though it was not long before he realized that England, in particular that part of East Anglia close to his birthplace, was indeed the source of his creative roots and inspiration. Britten returned to England in 1942, along with a commission for an opera (which was to become *Peter Grimes*) from Serge Koussevitzky, and made Aldeburgh, on the North Sea coast, his home. He never ventured very far away, for any length of time, from then on.

Interestingly, his decision to return to England did not signal an end to his feelings of isolation. His continued hypersensitivity to criticism, and his (relative) physical isolation in Aldeburgh, surrounded by a protective shield of friends and close colleagues, at least suggest unresolved personal and creative issues. It is possible even to view the forming of the English Opera Group and the Aldeburgh Festival, both populated with close associates, as an attempt to ensure a certain artistic distance.

The themes of Britten's operas are quite personal, and in them one catches more than just a glimpse of their creator. Britten wrote about people and their relationships rather than about events, and this drew him to a wide variety of sources for libretti. Many, like Melville's *Billy Budd* or Henry James's *The Turn of The Screw,* were considered too problematic for operatic treatment, yet all contained the textual resources to meet Britten's thematic criteria. The result is a legacy of dramatic works, rich in formal variety, but unified in their examination of isolation, alienation and oppression.

Britten's musical style is eclectic. His vocabulary and techniques come from composers of all periods, though he assimilated them into an expression that is uniquely his own. He clearly favors those composers whose styles reflect the clarity of form and texture associated with "classicism" over the thicker texture and more harmonically dense "romanticism" of others. Purcell, Mozart, Schubert, Mahler and Shostakovich were particular favorites of Britten's and influential in forming his style. He was also thoroughly conversant with the techniques of the twelve-tone (dodecaphonic) school of composers, and utilized them when, as in *The Turn of the Screw* and *A Midsummer Night's Dream,* for example, they served his purpose. To this must be added the influence of music from the Far East, experienced most directly during Britten's tour of Japan and Bali in 1955-56, although Britten was first introduced to Balinese music in the late 1930s by fellow composer and authority on Balinese music, Colin McPhee. From Britten's exposure to Far Eastern music came an increased interest in the expressive potential of percussion instruments, and a more economical, linear texture in his subsequent works.

Among the compositional processes that Britten mastered, the principle of variation was central to his style, from the earliest compositions through nearly six decades of creativity. This ranged from large scale theme and variation structures, as in *A Boy Was Born, Variations on a Theme of Frank Bridge* and even the opera *The Turn of the Screw,* to the smallest, most elemental use of the process, such as basing a whole composition on a melody or motive that becomes the source for musical ideas and development. One observes this especially in Britten's later (post-1964) works, such as the church parables *(Curlew River, The Burning Fiery Furnace, The Prodigal Son), Owen Wingrave,* and *Death in Venice.*

The most characteristic use of the variation principle in Britten's music is through the passacaglia (variations above a repeated harmonic/melodic foundation). Virtually all of his operas contain at least one extended passacaglia, placed in significant dramatic situations. The most recognizable, perhaps, is the orchestral passacaglia in *Peter Grimes* (Interlude IV) which is based on the melody and harmonic implications of Grimes's climactic and prophetic cry, ". . . and God have mercy upon me!" in act II, scene 1. Equally important are those found in *Albert*

Herring ("The Threnody" in act III), the "chase" scene in *Billy Budd* (act II, scene 1), the final scenes in *The Turn of the Screw* and *The Rape of Lucretia,* and act II, scene 9 ("The Pursuit") in *Death in Venice*.

In addition to his skills as a composer, Britten was an extraordinary pianist and gifted conductor. His musical collaborations with artists like Peter Pears, Dietrich Fischer-Dieskau, Mstislav Rostropovitch, and many others, are legendary, and his consummate musicianship is widely acknowledged. His popularity as a composer is in some measure reflected by the large number of his works that have remained in the repertoire. In terms of quality and quantity, the works of Benjamin Britten have dominated the post-World War II operatic stage, through the composer's keen sense of what works theatrically, his gift for melody and vocal writing in general, and his thorough craftsmanship.

In his acceptance speech upon being chosen the first recipient of the Aspen Award in the Humanities in 1964, Britten articulated those "human" characteristics which were so much a part of his conscious compositional process (his friend, the writer E.M. Forster, called it Britten's "Confession of Faith"): "I certainly write for human beings—directly and deliberately. I consider their voices, the range, the power, the subtlety, the colour potentialities of them. I consider the instruments they play—their most expressive and suitable individual sonorities . . . . I also take note of the *human* circumstances of music, of its environment and conventions; for instance I try to write dramatically effective music for the theatre—I certainly don't think opera is better for not being effective on the stage (some people think that effectiveness *must* be superficial)" (from *On Receiving the First Aspen Award,* London, 1978). By his personal testimony, Britten did not write for posterity, wisely pointing out that to try to do so would be impossible. Rather he wanted his music to be performed and enjoyed for the present, leaving others to worry about its place in music history. Assuming, though, that truly great music demands sufficient subjective (and emotional) response *and* objective (intellectual, analytical) appeal, Britten's operas of dramatic power, beauty, and technical skill argue impressively for inclusion in that category.—MICHAEL SELLS

Bumbry, Grace

Mezzo-soprano and soprano. Born 4 January 1937, in St. Louis. Married the tenor Erwin Jaeckel in 1963. Studied at Boston University, Northwestern University and with Lotte Lehmann in Santa Barbara, 1955-58; winner (with Martina Arroyo) of the Metropolitan Opera auditions, 1958; operatic debut as Amneris in Aida *at the Paris Opera, 1960; first black artist to appear at Bayreuth, 1961; debut at Covent Garden as Eboli, 1963; debut at Chicago as Ulrica, 1963; debut at Salzburg as Lady Macbeth, 1964; debut at Metropolitan Opera as Eboli, 1965, where she appeared in more than 170 performances; first soprano role was Santuzza in 1970.*

Grace Bumbry was one of several African American female singers to arrive on the international operatic stage in the 1960s. Her emergence to this position progressed through a series of events that began in her childhood—singing both in her church and school choirs, beginning formal vocal study, entering local talent competitions, and appearing and winning first prize by singing the aria "O don fatale" from Verdi's *Don Carlos* on Arthur Godfrey's Talent Scouts in 1954 after her graduation from high school in St. Louis, Missouri. The singing of this aria allowed her to be heard by many Americans. The role of Princess Eboli in *Don Carlos* has continued to be one of her most successful endeavors on the operatic stage.

A scholarship enabled Bumbry to attend Boston University, but her true progress as a student of voice did not come about until she met and sang for Lotte Lehmann in a series of Master Classes in 1955, after transferring to Northwestern University near Chicago. It would appear that Lehmann was immensely impressed with Grace Bumbry because she was able to entice Bumbry to begin a very thorough and intensive three and a half years of study with her at the Music Academy of the West in Santa Barbara, California. She was, during her study, the recipient of a Marian Anderson Scholarship and a John Hay Whitney Award. During her final year of study with Lehmann, she was a joint winner (with Martina Arroyo) of the Metropolitan Opera Auditions of the Air. Even after this prestigious award, it was still not easy for her to launch a creditable career in the United States. Lehmann took her to England and Europe in 1959, where her most significant success took place at the Paris Opéra with her portrayal of Amneris in *Aïda*. The acclaim she received in Paris helped her secure a three-year contract with Basel Opera in Switzerland. She began to add numerous roles to her repertory there.

Bumbry reached true international status in 1961 with her performance in Wagner's *Tannhäuser* for the Bayreuth Wagner Festival. She became the first African American artist ever to sing in this great house. Her opportunity to portray the role of the traditionally blond-headed goddess was the result of a recommendation from the conductor Wolfgang Sawallisch to Wieland Wagner. In spite of protests from racist groups and neo-Nazi factions, Bumbry received thunderous applause. Critics were quick to make predictions about her future. For example, Ronald Eyer, writing in the *New York Herald Tribune,* prophesied that she would be the first great African American Wagnerian. She did make a repeat appearance in Bayreuth later in the year in the same opera and for companies in Lyons and Chicago; but these prognostications did not completely materialize, in spite of her development into a singer of dramatic soprano roles. Her debuts at Covent Garden in 1963 and at the Metropolitan Opera in 1965 were both as Princess Eboli in *Don Carlos*. Reviewers were lavish in their praise of her commanding presence on stage (at 5 feet 7 inches with weight of 140 pounds, she is extremely striking in appearance), and critics lauded the excitement and dramatic qualities she brought to roles she interpreted for the stage.

Bumbry's singing also captured the hearts of spectators and reviewers, as is evidenced by statements such as those made by Alan Rich in the *New York Herald Tribune* of her debut at the Metropolitan Opera: "It is a big voice, but flexible and beautifully focused."

After 1970 when Bumbry began to perform soprano roles, conductors such as Karajan, Böhm, and Solti encouraged her upon hearing the way her top tones were developing. Her debut as Santuzza in Mascagni's *Cavalleria rusticana,* her first soprano role, came with the Vienna Staatsoper. She continued singing soprano repertoire as Salome in the same year (1970), and in 1971 she sang her first Tosca at the Metropolitan Opera. She performed the same role at Covent Garden in 1973. Reviewers and audiences have not been as consistent in their praise of her singing since her transition from a mezzo-soprano to a dramatic soprano. Notes in her upper range are not always as warm and resonant as those in her middle and lower tessituras. Other critics fault her languages and ability to execute phrases effectively. Despite such criticism, Bumbry, with her ability to exude magnetism from the stage, is still in 1992 singing in the major opera houses throughout the world. Because of her mastery of both mezzo-soprano and soprano roles, she has been successful as both Elisabetta and Eboli in *Don Carlos,* the roles of

117

Venus and Elisabeth in *Tannhäuser*, and the Aïda and Amneris in *Aïda*—she sang both of these roles in a 1975 British Broadcasting Corporation telecast of *Aïda*. Her first major recording was with Joan Sutherland in Handel's *Messiah* in 1961. Opera discs that followed include *Aïda*, Bayreuth *Tannhäuser*, *Orfeo*, *Carmen*, and *Il trovatore*, to name a few.—ROSE MARY OWENS

Busoni, Ferruccio

Composer. Born 1 April 1866, in Empoli, near Florence. Died 27 July 1924, in Berlin. Married: Gerda Sjostrand (two sons). Child prodigy as a pianist; studied with Wilhelm Mayer in Graz, 1877; a member of the Academia Filarmonica in Bologna, 1881; studied Bach's music in Leipzig, 1886; professor of piano, Helsingfors Conservatory, where Sibelius was a student of his; first prize in the Rubinstein Competition for his Konzertstück *for piano and orchestra, 1890; piano teacher at the Moscow Conservatory, 1890-91; professor at the New England Conservatory of Music, 1891-94; concert tour of Russia, 1912-13; director of the Liceo Musicale in Bologna, 1913; received the order of Chevalier de la Légion d'Honneur from the French government, 1913; in Zurich, 1914-1920, then Berlin until his death. Among Busoni's piano students were Brailovsky, Rudolf Ganz, Egon Petri, Mitropoulos, and Percy Grainger; among his composition students were Kurt Weill, Jarnach, and Wladimir Vogel. Busoni greatly influenced the works of Edgar Varèse.*

Operas *Sigune, oder Das stille Dorf,* F. Schanz (after a fairy tale), 1885-9 [never orchestrated]; *Die Brautwahl,* Busoni (after E.T.A. Hoffmann), 1906-11, Hamburg, 12 April 1912; *Arlecchino, oder, Die Fenster,* Busoni, 1916-17, Zurich, 11 May 1917; *Turandot,* Busoni (after Carlo Gozzi), 1916-17, Zurich, 11 May 1917; *Doktor Faust,* Busoni (after the Faust legend and Marlowe), 1916-24 [unfinished; completed by Philipp Jarnach, first performed Dresden, 21 May 1925].

Busoni may still be better known as a transcriber of Bach (as in the "Bach-Busoni" Chaconne and many other keyboard recreations) than as a composer in his own right, but his music and thinking have been a seminal influence in the 20th century. A searching, speculative mind, a mystic and an ironic humorist, he was an inspired synthesizer of opposites, impaled from his earliest years upon the conflicting poles of Italian and German musical and linguistic culture. (His operas are all in German despite their imaginative infusions of Mediterranean warmth and clarity.)

Busoni's earliest influences were in fact the massive formal and contrapuntal logic of Bach (which his father, an itinerant clarinet virtuoso, forced him to study), and the *bel canto* melodic style of Italian opera (his father's repertoire consisted chiefly of operatic fantasies). These he soon combined with Brahmsian romanticism and the revolutionary harmonic thinking (and troubled spiritual atmosphere) of late Liszt: the results can be seen in the spacious virtuosity and startling stylistic juxtapositions of Busoni's huge *Piano Concerto* of 1904, with its final Lisztian "chorus mysticus."

From the *Piano Concerto* on, his idiom became increasingly exploratory. A profound and stimulating writer, in his *Aesthetic der Tonkunst (Sketch for a New Aesthetic of Music)* (1907), Busoni proposed the 12-note chromatic scale as the basic unit of tonality, with the abolition of "consonance" and "dissonance"; he also forecast microtonal systems and the invention of new instruments, including electronic ones. His own music passed through a period of eerily disembodied chromaticism that issued at length in a neo-Mozartian manner Busoni termed *junge Klassizität*—"renewed [literally, "youthful"] classicality"—which ultimately signified the rejection of all competing systems of composition, and the unself-conscious (but masterly) employment of whichever artistic means were most appropriate to a given artistic situation.

Busoni had decided views on the role and proper subject of opera. In a 1913 essay, *The Future of Opera,* he stated most categorically that opera: ". . . should take possession of the supernatural or unnatural as its only proper sphere of representation and feeling and should create a pretence world in such a way that life is reflected in either a magic or a comic mirror, presenting consciously that which is not to be found in real life. The magic mirror is for grand opera, the comic for light opera. And dances and masks and apparitions should be interwoven, so that the onlooker never loses sight of the charms of pretence or gives himself up to it as an actual experience." Busoni's personal aesthetic was resolutely antipathetic to Wagner, and this dual stress on the importance of the fantastic and the magical, and on its ironic distancing, ultimately derived from his admiration for Mozart's *Don Giovanni* and *Die Zauberflöte.* In his own work, this aesthetic leads in apparently contradictory directions—on the one hand toward mythic, metaphysical fantasy with an almost religious dimension, and on the other toward an adumbration of Brechtian "alienation." The latter impulse is clearly developed in the stage works of Busoni's pupil Kurt Weill; the former finds perhaps its most resonant echo in the operas of a later admirer, Luigi Dallapiccola. But Busoni's own operas—above all *Doktor Faust*—matchlessly reconcile spiritual yearning and pungent irony, producing a uniquely potent and troubling atmosphere that makes the unseen almost palpable, and eludes easy popularity or facile classification.

Busoni wrote five operas, although the earliest, *Sigune, oder das stille Dorf* (*Sigune, or the Quiet Village*), composed 1885-89 on a fairy-tale subject, was never orchestrated. The others all belong to the exploratory and consolidatory periods of his last two creative decades. *Die Brautwahl* (*The Bridal Choice*), composed 1906-11 as Busoni's musical language was beginning to develop new attitudes toward melody and harmony, is by his own above-quoted criteria only a limited success. In this three-act "musical-fantastical comedy," closely based on a tale by E.T.A. Hoffmann (on whom Busoni was an acknowledged authority), comedy and magic are curiously intermingled as the petit-bourgeois society of 1820s Berlin is subverted by the action of magicians—and presented at a length that suggests grand rather than comic opera. Very rarely performed, *Die Brautwahl* contains much fascinating and attractive music, but displays problems of scale and stagecraft. It is both over-leisurely and almost too full of incident; it modulates alarmingly between farce, high seriousness and diablerie, and the libretto (in which Busoni was anxious to alter Hoffmann's dialogue as little as possible) remains undeniably wordy.

Far more successful (because it is concise, fast-moving and unified) is the one-act "theatrical capriccio" *Arlecchino* (*Harlequin,* 1916-17), a mercurial neo-Mozartian comedy, inspired by the artificiality of marionette-theater. The libretto—Busoni's own—involves the traditional characters of the *Commedia dell'arte* in a satirical anti-war fable, with the trickster Harlequin now in the magician's role, upsetting and energizing the complacent burghers of Bergamo. The 'Chinese fable' *Turandot,* in two short acts, was also composed in 1916-17—to be performed with *Arlecchino* as a double bill. A comparatively minor work, it is built up from extensive incidental music Busoni had written in 1905 and 1911 for Gozzi's play, which is here turned in the direction of studied artificiality, a "light and unreal tone" and fairy-tale exoticism (increased by the use of some actual oriental elements). It thus stands at the furthest possible remove from Puccini's opera on the same subject.

Busoni's choice of subjects and libretti reflect his fascination—and identification—with the powerfully symbolic figures of the magician, or the great artist: indeed, the magician is ultimately a symbol for the artist as seen at the most daring phase of creativity. At various times Busoni projected operas on the subject of the Wandering Jew, of Merlin (Karl Goldmark's opera *Merlin* was an early inspiration), and of Leonardo da Vinci (apparently foreshadowed in Leonhard, the good magician of *Die Brautwahl*). He published a libretto *Die mächtige Zauberer* (*The Mighty Magician*) for which he wrote no music, and also wrote, in 1918, the libretto of an *Arlecchino Part II, or the Geese of the Capitol,* which remains unpublished. A bitter and fantastical satire on contemporary art and society, this libretto reputedly introduces a powerful figure who is at once Leonhard, Leonardo—and Faust. In fact, it is in Busoni's *Doktor Faust,* whose libretto was written between 1910 and 1914, that the summation of his life-work is to be found.

Busoni composed the music of *Doktor Faust,* his last opera, between 1916 and his death in 1924, at which point two portions of the work, including the final scene, remained unfinished (completions have been made by his pupil Philipp Jarnach and by Anthony Beaumont). Most of his other compositions during this period have been viewed as "studies" for *Faust,* and many were eventually woven into the opera's fabric in whole or in part. The view, sometimes expressed, that this renders *Faust* some kind of compilation or palimpsest, however, is utterly wrong. The result is Busoni's masterpiece and testament. Based not on Goethe but on the ancient puppet-plays, it is a profoundly, even achingly spiritual work, unsettlingly unattached to any conventional religious purpose save the protagonist's desperation to transcend his human condition. With seeming familiarity it expresses the extremes of mortal terror and spiritual radiance: a religious ardor directed, like that of the Renaissance alchemists, toward a new and magical world, symbolized by the naked youth born from the body of the dying Faust. Its message of psychic struggle, which still intermittently haunts the music of later generations, defines one of the most potent ambiences in 20th century opera.—MALCOLM MACDONALD

Caballé, Montserrat

Soprano. Born 12 April 1933, in Barcelona. Studied at Barcelona Conservatorio del Liceo and with Eugenia Kemeny, Conchita Badia and Napoleone Annovazzi; awarded Liceo Gold medal in 1954; debut in La serva padrona *at Reus, near Barcelona; appeared in Basel and Vienna in the late 1950s; debut at Teatro alla Scala as Flowermaiden in* Parsifal, *1960; in Massenet's* Manon *in Mexico City, 1964; achieved international fame in concert performance of Lucrezia Borgia at Carnegie Hall, 1965; sang Marschallin in* Der Rosenkavalier *and Countess in* Le nozze di Figaro *at Glyndebourne, 1965; debut at Metropolitan Opera as Marguerite in* Faust, *1965; debut in Chicago as Violetta, 1970; Covent Garden debut as Violetta, 1970; other roles include Luisa Miller, Desdemona, Ariadne and Tosca.*

Montserrat Caballé is one of a handful of the greatest prima donnas of the twentieth century. Her limpid tone, seemingly inexhaustible breath capacity, ethereal, high, floated *pianissimi,* and sensitive musicality all combine to make her an exquisite vocalist, one with the ability to drive audiences into a frenzy. As a child she listened to recordings played by her father of Miguel Fleta, who was able to float high notes extremely softly, and she decided that a female could master that also. André Tubeuf has called Caballé's "a slow voice . . . spreading out like a becalmed sea," and Rupert Christiansen has characterized her as "fuller-voiced than Milanov, more individual than Tebaldi, more versatile than Leontyne Price," conceding that "even on an off-night [she] can produce *belles minutes* of a splendor that none of her contemporaries can match." Caballé's ability to spin out a pure legato line in an effortless manner comes from the many years (from age eight through age twenty) she studied at the Liceo Conservatory in her native Barcelona. She was taught breath control by Eugenia Kemeny, who trained her pupils as if they were long-distance runners—they had to learn how to spend the breath to have enough to finish the phrase, the aria, the opera with plenty to spare. At the Conservatory, Caballé learned her first operatic roles—Fiordiligi (*Così fan tutte*), Susanna in *Le nozze di Figaro*, Lucia, and the Queen of the Night (*Die Zauberflöte*)—from its music director, Napoleone Annovazzi. After leaving her studies with the Gold Medal for Singing, Caballé unsuccessfully made the rounds of auditions in Italy. She began her career in Basel, where she stayed for three years, singing an astonishing number and variety of roles, among them Mimì (when another soprano fell ill), Nedda (*I pagliacci*), Marta in d'Albert's *Tiefland,* Pamina (*Die Zauberflöte*), Marina in *Boris Godunov,* Salome, all three heroines in Offenbach's *Les contes d'Hoffmann,* Leonora in *Il trovatore,* twenty-six Aïdas in the second season, and numerous Donna Elviras (*Don Giovanni*). From there she went to Bremen, where she added Violetta (*La traviata*), Ariadne, Tatiana, Armida, and Rosina (*Il barbiere di Siviglia*). Altogether Caballé sang forty-seven different roles in seven years in the late 1950s and early 1960s. She won a prize from the Vienna Staatsoper for her performance of Salome, her "very favorite" role and one that she has recorded stunningly for RCA Victor under Leinsdorf. Her Teatro alla Scala debut came in 1960 as the First Flower Maiden in Wagner's *Parsifal.* In 1962 she sang for the first time at the Teatro del Liceo in Barcelona, where she met her future husband, the tenor Bernabé Martí. He was Pinkerton to her Butterfly. A wealthy Barcelona family, the Bertrands, had helped the young Caballé, born during the Spanish Civil War, to finance her studies; for this Caballé promised them she would appear every season at the Barcelona theater. Recent undertakings there have included Sieglinde in *Die Walküre,* Respighi's *La fiamma*, Salome, and Isolde.

Caballé has a vast repertoire, ranging from Mozart and before through Bellini's *Norma,* the *non plus ultra* of soprano operatic endeavors, to Wagner and Strauss and beyond. As a young singer she preferred Strauss (there is an exquisite Strauss Lieder recital on RCA with Miguel Zanetti accompanying) and Mozart above all, never intending to tackle the bel canto operas of Rossini, Bellini, and Donizetti. Elisabeth Grümmer was Caballé's idol in Mozart singers. When the opportunity came for Caballé to make her New York debut at Carnegie Hall, substituting for the pregnant Marilyn Horne in Donizetti's *Lucrezia Borgia,* she decided to approach the music as if it were Mozart—whose music she considers a tonic for the voice—but with the proper early-nineteenth-century style. Her success was overwhelming and she has since revived such bel canto rarities as Bellini's *La straniera* and Donizetti's *Caterina Cornaro, Parisina d'Este,* and *Gemma di Vergy.* All of these are available on "live" recordings, the *Gemma di Vergy* from a Carnegie Hall performance in March of 1976 under Eve Queler that captures the soprano at her transcendant best. The final half hour is a model of magical, rapt bel canto singing of a very rare kind. Likewise, few have done more than Caballé to bring to life the early works of Verdi—*Il corsaro* and *I masnadieri* among them, both recorded on the Philips label.

Although Caballé has recorded extensively, rivaled among sopranos only by Joan Sutherland, and even though many of her performances are easily found on "pirates," there remain certain gaps that frustrate her many admirers. There should have been commercial recordings of three Verdi roles with which she had a great success—the Leonoras in *Il trovatore* and *La forza del destino* and Desdemona in *Otello.* Fortunately there are "live" recordings available of the two Leonoras. There is, however, much to be thankful for; in Verdi recordings alone, aside from the early operas mentioned, there is a fine *Traviata* (Caballé being one of the few sopranos after Callas who was a successful Violetta) under Prêtre, a *Don Carlos* under Muti that could hardly be bettered (included in the cast are Domingo and Verrett), a *Luisa Miller* with Pavarotti that outstrips all recorded competition, an *Aïda* under Muti with Domingo and Cossotto with an appropriately ethereal Tomb Scene, and a *Messa da requiem* under Barbirolli (with Cossotto, Vickers, and Raimondi) that is sheer perfection exactly where Verdi demands it— on the ultra-soft high B-flat in the "Libera me." Other recordings that stand out among the many that she has made are a *Così fan tutte* under Colin Davis, in which she and Janet Baker blend beautifully (this is the only commercial example of Caballé's Mozart, when there should have been a Countess and a Donna Elvira, the latter of which she sang over four hundred times); an early *Lucrezia Borgia* on RCA that displays her astonishing coloratura technique, the only hole in which is a weak trill (the live performance of her New York debut is also available); a definitive reading of Bellini's seminal *Il pirata;* and numerous recital discs, among them Puccini arias, French opera arias, duets with Martí, duets with Verrett, and Spanish song literature, which she studied with Conchita Badia.

In the last several years Caballé's career has been confined mainly to Europe. The Metropolitan Opera has not particularly served her well, giving her roles such as Tosca, when she would have been better as Semiramide or the Marschallin. Due to her sound early training Caballé has had a long career with no great deterioration in vocal quality. She attributes this in part to singing so much Mozart early in her career. Of her singing in Salieri's *Les Danaïdes* in Perugia in 1984 the correspondent for *Opera* wrote that "The most warmly applauded singer was Montserrat Caballe, an imposing yet very sweet Hypermestra, torn between love for her father and her lover, and distinguished for her sensitive *mezza-voce* singing and some powerful vocal outbursts." Numerous cancellations because of ill health have in the last decade marred an otherwise glorious career.—STEPHEN WILLIER

Callas, Maria

Soprano. Born Cecilia Kalogeropoulos, 3 December 1923, in New York. Died 16 September 1977 in Paris. Married Giovanni Battista Meneghini, 1949 (divorced 1959). Studied in Greece with Maria Trivella at National Conservatory, 1937-39; student debut as Santuzza in Cavalleria rusticana, *Athens, 1939; sang Beatrice in* Boccaccio, *Tosca, Marta, Santuzza, and Fidelio in Greece; Italian debut as Gioconda in Verona Arena, 1947; Elvira in* Puritani *and other florid parts in Venice, 1949; Teatro alla Scala debut as Aida, 1950; joined La Scala in 1951; Covent Garden debut as Norma, 1952; Chicago debut in* Norma, *1954; Metropolitan Opera debut, 1956; recital tour with di Stefano, 1973-74.*

Had Maria Callas been able to cope as effectively with persons and events as she did with the scores she absorbed and the roles she re-created, her life might not have ended prematurely in a tragedy of almost Greek proportion.

Cecilia Kalogeropoulos was born in New York in 1923, the second of two daughters of an emigré Greek family. She returned to Greece with her mother and sister in 1937, a spotty, short-sighted, over-weight adolescent with thick, ungainly legs, but she had an untrained voice of extraordinary potential and great determination to become a singer.

Elvira de Hidalgo, a once celebrated Spanish soprano who became a professor at the Athens Academy of Music, took Maria as her personal pupil free of charge. De Hidalgo perceived that the girl had three disconnected voices: a rich, veiled lower one; an insecure middle one; and an upper voice placed at the back of the throat and likely to go out of control when too much pressure was put upon it. All these voices needed to be brought together with no 'gaps' between them, and to be made to sound pleasant, if not beautiful, all the time. They never were.

De Hidalgo strongly advised her pupil to use the flexibility in her voice to its best advantage by concentrating on bel canto roles (for which de Hidalgo herself had been admired).

123

This would be the best way of allowing the voice time to become strong enough in all its three registers to take on heavier roles later. So Maria, with great willingness and ability for intense concentration, quick study and endless patience, applied herself to the heroines of Bellini, Donizetti and Rossini.

Before she was eighteen years of age, Callas yielded to the first of many damaging temptations by accepting four roles with the Athens Opera during the German occupation of Greece: *Boccacio, Cavalleria rusticana,* Tosca, and Leonore in *Fidelio.* She was determined to sing any major role offered in spite of de Hidalgo's advice and warnings. Such stubbornness—and foolishness—was later seen as one of Callas's ineradicable characteristics.

In 1947 she made her first important debut at the Verona Arena as La Gioconda in Ponchielli's opera. There was still much wrong with the voice: noticeable breaks between the registers, a general unevenness of tone and some very crudely placed notes at the top. But her performance was ecstatically received and she was marked as a singer of high quality indeed.

Callas's conductor in Verona was Tullio Serafin, experienced director and voice-trainer who had founded the Verona Festival. He was greatly excited by Callas's voice and ability, and wanted her to profit from his instruction. He was to have both a good and a malign influence upon her career and began by encouraging her to sing the *Walküre* Brünnhilde and Kundry in *Parsifal,* side by side, as it were, with *I puritani, Il Turco in Italia, La traviata;* then Isolde, Norma and Turandot. In retrospect, it is difficult to understand what prompted Serafin to do such a thing, but he gave Callas the advantage of support and confidence which she so much lacked and seemed to find only from much older men. One of these, thirty years her senior, was an industrialist called Giovanni Battista Meneghini. He was old enough to be her father and rich enough to give her the security and pampering she sought. He attentively chaperoned her until they married and then gave up his business interests to become her sole agent and manager, although he was temperamentally unsuited to the task.

Callas went on singing, conquering audiences in Europe and America, blazing her own trail and becoming richer every time her husband maliciously doubled her fee. She began to live more than ever on her nerves instead of nursing her natural physical and vocal resources. When she was not singing in opera houses, she was making more recordings than any other singer of her time. She managed—some say "contrived"—to upset her family, her friends and colleagues, and as "The Tigress" she was grist to the newshounds whenever and wherever she caused a stir: public aggressiveness, cancelled performances, even poorer performances than her best (which would have gone unremarked in other singers) all made "La Callas" a merciless target for adverse publicity.

After ten years she had slimmed and was now very beautiful indeed. She had conquered the Teatro alla Scala, Milan, the Met, Covent Garden, Vienna and was tired of old Meneghini. The multi-millionaire Aristotle Onassis took her up, divorced his wife Tina, and gave Callas the entrée to the highest of High Society. She was fêted, adored, followed everywhere but sang less, because she had allowed her voice to get into a precarious state. All she wanted now was to settle down peacefully and have a child, but this was not what Onassis wanted. In 1968 he suddenly told her that he was "marrying Jackie Kennedy" (widow of the assassinated US President) "in two days' time." Her last hope of security and support instantly vanished and the physical and mental shock to Callas was deep-seated.

Most of the final artistic events in her career pale before the early achievements and are best overlooked, except for two. In 1971 and 1972 she gave exceptional and vivid master classes at the Juilliard School, New York. Fortunately they are preserved in book form and on tape/disc, and they indicate much of the deep natural perception she had acquired for a variety of operatic roles—and not only her own—as well as how to sing them. Callas was not an intellectual. Her innate understanding of her forty or so different operatic roles coupled with her extraordinary vocal quality, make those assumptions unique.

Maria Callas died suddenly in her Paris house in 1977. It was really a mercy for her. She was only fifty-four, but her voice was worn out and consequently there was nothing for her to live for. Those who heard her in her prime will not—cannot—forget the impression which she made; nor will memory of her perish because of the many records which she left as proof of her fine, flawed genius.—ALAN JEFFERSON

Calvé, Emma

Soprano. Born 15 August 1858, Décazeville. Died 6 January 1942, Millau. Married tenor Galileo Gaspari. Studied with Jules Puget, 1879-82, Mathilde Marchesi in 1882, and Rosina Laborde in 1887; debut as Marguerite in Gounod's Faust, *Brussels, 1881; performed at the Opéra-Comique, Paris, in 1880s; debut at Teatro alla Scala in Samara's* Flora Mirabilis, *1887; created Suzel in Mascagni's* L'amico Fritz, *Rome, 1891; debut at Metropolitan Opera as Santuzza, 1893; performed 61 Carmens at Met as well as Boito's Marguerite and Elena, Ophélie in Thomas's* Hamlet *and the title role in* Messaline; *Massenet composed Anita in* Navarraise *(1894) and Fanny in* Sapho *(1897) for her; at Manhattan Opera, 1907-09; Boston, 1912; and Nice, 1914.*

Admonishing young singers in a 1922 essay entitled "Practical Aspects on the Art of Studying Singing," soprano Emma Calvé outlined the binding principle that guided her own extraordinary career: "People do not go to the opera or the concert hall merely to hear solfeggios, trills and runs. They want to hear a human message from a human being who has experienced great things and trained the mind and soul in finer discipline than mere exercises. The singer must be a personality, must understand the bond of sympathy with mankind which, even more than a beautiful voice, commands the attention and interest of the audience." Emerging at a time when verismo was at the height of its international popularity, when the standard operatic repertory was in a state of transition and the demands made upon singers were being reassessed, Calvé was a uniquely resourceful performer, and summoned in great abundance the flexibility to adapt. She was among the most accomplished singers of her generation, perhaps its most inspired actress, and certainly one of its most celebrated personalities. She had little sympathy for the kind of theatrical posturing that prevailed in the opera house—the "false and conventional standards of lyric expression," as she described them, and looked instead to the dramatic stage for inspiration. The brilliant tragedian Eleanora Duse (1859-1924), in particular, had a profound effect on Calvé: "All my life," she wrote in her 1922 autobiography, "I have loved and admired her [Duse] deeply . . . Hers was the spark that set my fires alight. Her art, simple, human, passionately sincere, was a revelation to me." Just as Duse had triumphed as Santuzza in a dramatization of Verga's *Cavalleria rusticana,* Calvé's impersonation of the role in Mascagni's musical setting was equally successful, and brought her immediate recognition. Marveling not so much at the shrewdness of her stage business as at the integrity of its every detail, Herman Klein called her "the first *real* Santuzza" he had ever seen, bringing to the opera "the Sicilian atmosphere of Verga's story, just as Duse had brought it into the theater." Similarly, Bernard Shaw, an unabashed admirer of Calvé during her heyday at Covent Garden, described her Santuzza as "irresistibly moving and beautiful, and fully capable of sustaining the inevitable comparison with Duse's impersonation of the same part."

Until her first brief retirement from the operatic stage in 1904, she enjoyed great success in the standard repertory of Mozart, Bellini, and Donizetti, and was associated with the premieres of many important contemporary works—several of them written for her. But her fiery portrayals of Santuzza and Carmen made an even more lasting impression, and led to prestigious engagements at Covent Garden and the Metropolitan Opera. Carmen especially came to dominate her career and to compromise her early versatility, and to this day she remains inseparably linked to the role. London and New York were both shocked and delighted by her brooding portrayal, leaving critics in the challenging position of remaining detached from the ensuing hysteria: in his review of her first Carmen at the Metropolitan Opera in December, 1893, W. J. Henderson wryly observed that "the audience was much moved by Mme. Calvé's Carmen, but what will be thought of it in the calmer light of the morning's remembrance, it is not easy to tell." Shaw wrote with some ambivalence of Calvé's Carmen and her brutalization of the character, making clear his displeasure in seeing the restraint and subtlety that so distinguished her Santuzza yielding to such extravagance. "Her death-scene," he concluded, "is horribly real. The young lady Carmen is never so effectively alive as when she falls, stage dead, beneath José's cruel knife. But to see Calvé's Carmen changing from a live creature . . . into a reeling, staggering, flopping, disorganized thing, and finally tumble down a mere heap of carrion, is to get much the same sensation as might be given by the reality of a brutal murder." Just as her compulsion to embody Santuzza had gone deeper than simply immersing herself into the coarse realism of the drama and the excesses of the score, the preparations for her first Carmen at the Opéra-Comique in 1891 led her to Granada to observe life among the gypsies. She later wrote that the "absorption of one's personality in a role requires adaptability, a chameleonlike change of one's whole aspect and being." Even her costumes—whether Italian peasant rags or Spanish gypsy garments—were entirely authentic in both spirit and detail.

Herman Klein described Calvé's voice best as having "the somber quality of a contralto miraculously impinged upon the acute timbre and high range of a soprano . . . the ideal voice," he added—perhaps in deference to the general nature of her repertory—"for the expression of mental anguish, suffering, pleading, and despair." Its compass was extraordinary. She had the naturally high range of a lyric-spinto, aided by an almost falsetto-like upper extension, but the more striking disposition of a true dramatic soprano, with a sumptuous middle register and dark, alluring chest tones.

Calvé's range allowed her to cultivate a diverse repertory that often included more than one prominent role in the same opera—she appeared variously as Salomé and Hérodias in Massenet's *Hérodiade,* and was a notable interpreter of both Margherita and Elena in Boïto's *Mefistofele.* The different registers of her voice were more dissimilar in texture than in temperament, but the warmth and resonance of the tone remained the same throughout her natural scale. Her passage between the extremes—often exhibited with virtuosic force in her recordings—was always calculated wisely for dramatic effect. An exquisitely controlled head voice, if indeed it was that (Calvé called it her "fourth voice"), produced with her mouth shut in

OPERA

coloratura fashion, allowed her virtually seamless access above the staff. She claimed to have learned its secret from Domenico Mustafà (1829-1912), last of the Sistine Chapel's virtuoso castrati, and though it was rather small and distant in context, she used it unhesitatingly even on the stage, as we can hear in one of the *Faust* fragments recorded live from the stage of the Metropolitan Opera in February, 1902. It is featured prominently and very effectively in many of her studio recordings as well.

Her records disappoint only insofar as they present a rather limited repertory further circumscribed by the repetition of some of the least substantial titles. They offer only a glimpse of the drama that contemporary critics insisted was as much a part of her singing as it was her acting. The voice itself recorded with great fidelity, leaving a splendid account of its size, its range, and its silvery tone. Apart from the five Mapleson cylinder fragments recorded at the Metropolitan Opera during the 1901-1902 season, and a few irretrievable Bettini cylinders from about 1900, there are just over fifty records made for four commercial companies between 1902 and about 1919. Of these, only fifteen titles are operatic. There is surprisingly little from *Cavalleria rusticana* and *Carmen:* in addition to three Mapleson ensembles, her Santuzza is represented by only four recordings of "Voi lo sapete"; from Carmen there are four recordings of the "Habanera," two each of the "Chanson Bohème" and "Seguidilla," a single "Card Scene" reduced to a solo, and a second-act duet recorded with tenor Charles Dalmores in March, 1908— her only commercially recorded duet. The Victor discs, made in 1907, 1908, and 1916 offer the finest account of her voice and her best operatic interpretations, and seem to represent the singer's most serious efforts to preserve something of herself for posterity. Her last recordings as a singer, made for the Pathé Company in Paris in about 1919 when she was past sixty, suggest that her voice and technique were largely unimpaired by age. Richard Aldrich, reviewing her Aeolian Hall recital of February, 1915, noted that the voice seemed "to have lost little in its high ranges, and even to have gained something in the rich lower tones of a purely contralto quality." It still showed "remarkable power, brilliancy and beauty of quality and the evidence of firm control and easy mastery of it." Deplorable as they are from a technical standpoint, the Pathés bear this out, especially the *Carmen* excerpts, the haunting "Pendant un an je fus ta femme" from *Sapho* (her only "creator" recording), and the lovely "L'Heure exquise" of Reynaldo Hahn, all of which are among her most effective and hauntingly memorable recordings. A poignant spoken excerpt from her autobiography, long thought to have been recorded on her deathbed, appeared shortly after Calvé's death, but was probably made in Millau, Aveyron in 1940, in the wake of the German offensive.—WILLIAM SHAMAN

Caniglia, Maria

Soprano. Born 5 May 1905, in Naples. Died 15 April 1979, in Rome. Married: Pino Donati, 1939. Studied at the Conservatory San Pietro a Maiella, in Naples; debut as Chrysothemis in Elektra, *Turin, 1930; Teatro alla Scala debut as Maria in Pizzetti's* Lo straniero, *1931; sang in Rome, 1930—51; created the roles of Manuela in Montemezzi's* La notte di Zoraïma, *Milan, 1931; Roxanne in Alfano's* Cyrano de Bergerac, *Rome, 1936; and the title role in Respighi's* Maria Egiziaca, *1937; Covent Garden debut, 1937; Metropolitan Opera debut, 1938.*

Caniglia

To the 1940s generation of collectors, Maria Caniglia was the foremost spinto voice of complete recordings of Italian opera: Gigli's soprano in *Tosca, Andrea Chénier, Un ballo in maschera, Aïda,* and the Verdi *Requiem,* and Leonora in the only *La forza del destino* then available. On the Italian stage she had her rivals—Iva Pacetti, Gina Cigna, Giuseppina Cobelli, and Lina Bruna Rasa among them, and in America there were Zinka Milanov and occasionally Stella Roman on the radio, but when you wanted to hear in modern sound some of the classic operatic confrontation scenes—the second act of *Tosca,* the third of *Andrea Chénier,* or the second of *La forza del destino,* say—you had to go to Caniglia. Her tone itself was a dramatic statement: an unforgettable mass of rubies and brass. She could attack the ear without offending it; the pain itself could be bewitching and the quality was uniquely weighty and lyrical at once.

Caniglia began her career at the height of the *verismo* approach and, like Magda Olivero, carried on with it to her retirement, in the early 1960s. By that time she had sung for twenty years at the Teatro alla Scala and an additional ten in Rome. Her idols had been Muzio and Cobelli and her self-chosen coaches were often such earlier singing actresses as Carmen Melis and Gilda dalla Rizza. Caniglia's records recreate that *verismo* world. Moments—indeed, entire passages—of crudeness have been noted, from her day through our own. She could obliterate a phrase on first attack, thrash a vocal line into submission, and play the lady baritone at the drop of a betrayal. Her Magnani manner might destroy a character: Caniglia's Aïda, for example, has a toughness at odds with everything we are told about that heroine. When she was tired her top voice could be metallic, colorless, and flat, and in the quest for drama she could forget whatever she knew about legato. Others sang more beautifully and some more movingly, but few had her theatrical sting, her sweeping sense of dramatic line, and, when she worked at it, her instinct for vibrant delicacy.

One sees her working at this last in *Andrea Chénier,* when at the start she really tries for an abstracted, youthful tone, in act II for fragility, and in "La mama morta," where Maddalena describes her degradation during the French Revolution, for sorrowful vulnerability. Her voice hasn't the poetry of Muzio's but the impulses are the same. Her greatest accomplishments, though, are as Tosca and Leonora, both possessed of an unique theatrical vibrance and dramatic range. In *Tosca* the voice is luscious. She manages some flirtatiousness at the start but really comes into her own in her first bitter confrontation with Scarpia. The second act is played with a brilliant impression of spontaneity. The rich, biting voice and her vibrant defenselessness are made for the music and the murder, and she handles the *parlando* closing with extraordinary believability. In act III, the narrative of Scarpia's death has a welcome lyricism, the love duet both languor and animal vigor, and the final scene a *verismo* conviction unsurpassed on records. The *Forza* Leonora is, all told, her masterpiece, and reveals her gifts more fully than any other recording. Here she appears both powerful and touchingly distraught. The few coarse moments are never cheap, and she is quite equal to the lyric grandeur of the role. In the long and difficult scene with Padre Guardiano, the voice is radiant with hope, and the prayer at the end (Caniglia worshipped this music) voiced with an earthy purity unique to this artist. "Pace, pace, mio Dio" shares this quality; no faceless beauty here. Caniglia at her best struck both the senses and the heart.—LONDON GREEN

Cappuccilli, Piero

Baritone. Born 9 November 1929 in Trieste, Italy. Married Graziella Bossi. Studied with Luciano Donnaggio in Trieste, 1970-75; debut as Tonio in I pagliacci at Teatro Nuovo in Milan, 1957; debut at Teatro alla Scala as Enrico in Lucia di Lammermoor, 1964; first Covent Garden appearance in La traviata, 1967, then sang Otello (1974) and Un ballo in maschera (1975) there; first Chicago appearance, 1969; sang the role of Don Carlos in 1975 Salzburg Festival under Herbert von Karajan.

Piero Cappuccilli has been one of the leading baritones of the Italian repertoire of the past three decades, with a special affinity for the roles of Verdi. After studying with Luciano Donaggio in Trieste, he made his debut as Tonio in Leoncavallo's *Pagliacci* at the Teatro Nuovo, Milan, in 1957. The following year he sang in Verdi's *I vespri siciliani* in Palermo, where conductor Tullio Serafin was impressed by his performance and signed him to record the part of Enrico in Donizetti's *Lucia di Lammermoor,* the role of his Teatro alla Scala debut in 1964.

Cappuccilli has sung at the major opera houses of Italy, in roles including Nottingham in Donizetti's *Roberto Devereux*; Ernesto in Bellini's *Il pirata*; Don Carlo di Vargas in Verdi's *La forza del destino*; Simon Boccanegra; Iago in Verdi's *Otello*; Verdi's Rigoletto; and Rodrigo in Verdi's *Don Carlo*. Outside of Italy he has appeared as Filippo in Bellini's *Beatrice di Tenda* in Monte Carlo, 1986; Riccardo in Bellini's *I Puritani* in Chicago, 1969; Miller in *Luisa Miller* at the Edinburgh Festival, 1963; Rodrigo at the Salzburg Festival, 1975 (under Herbert von Karajan); and Di Luna in Verdi's *Il trovatore* in Paris, 1973.

Cappuccilli was hastily signed by the Metropolitan Opera as one of three baritones hired to take on roles that needed to be filled upon the death of Leonard Warren on the Metropolitan Opera House stage in March 1960. He sang a single performance, Germont *père* in Verdi's *La traviata* on 26 March 1960 and has not returned (he was announced for Verdi's *Rigoletto* in the 1984-85 season but canceled his appearances).

His Covent Garden debut was as the elder Germont in Verdi's *La traviata* in 1967; he later sang Iago in Verdi's *Otello* (1974) and Renato in Verdi's *Un ballo in maschera* (1975).

Cappuccilli may be described as a singer in the central tradition of Italian baritones, with a solid technique and a highly intelligent approach to the music. The possessor of a voice that some consider not intrinsically beautiful, he is capable of producing a warmth of sound when it is needed. Cappuccilli is most successful at portraying the fatherly Verdi figures, such as Rigoletto, Francesco Foscari and—especially—Simon Boccanegra, where his dignity, nobility, authority, and sturdiness of voice complement the maturity of the characters. He is also a fine Macbeth, vocally and dramatically refined, but with a trace of a snarl in the voice to add a touch of instability to the character. The color of his voice conveys the melancholy of many of Verdi's father-figures and lends an aura of pathos to his portrayals; it also contributes to his singing of villainous parts. The more romantic figures take less well to his vocal quality. As a vocal actor he has developed greater expressiveness in his singing. His earlier performances exhibited a tendency toward interpretive blandness and portrayals that were somewhat generalized. He can convey character without histrionic excess through careful attention to the words. His sure breath control facilitates his legato phrasing and his mastery of the long line, an important asset in the arching contours of Verdi's writing. He is also capable of sustained high *pianissimi* (as, for example, on the word "*figlia*" at the end of the Boccanegra-Amelia duet in his second *Simon Boccanegra* recording). He is less adept at the roles of Bellini and other composers who demand skill in florid singing.—MICHAEL SIMS

Capriccio

Composer: *Richard Strauss.*

Librettists: *Clemens Krauss and Richard Strauss.*

First Performance: *Munich, Staatsoper, 28 October 1942.*

Roles: *The Countess (soprano); The Count (baritone); Flamand (tenor); Olivier (baritone); La Roche (bass); Clairon (contralto); Monsieur Taupe (tenor); Italian Singers (soprano, tenor); Majordomo (bass); Servants (four tenors, four basses).*

It is hard to decide what is most remarkable about *Capriccio,* Richard Strauss' fifteenth and final opera: that it was premiered amid the air-raids on Munich during the height of World War II; that, especially given its unveiling during that period of unparalleled conflagration and clashing world-views, it takes as its anachronistic and seemingly irrelevant setting the aristocratic salon-life of the *ancien régime* in France, at which time social civility allowed people of a certain class the leisure to discuss abstract artistic theories; or that Strauss should still be able, in his late 70s, to write a work of such compositional savvy, intellectual rigor, unhackneyed wit, and glowing humanness.

Since Strauss no doubt intended *Capriccio* as his operatic testament, he used the opportunity to fill the work with a multitude of forms: arias, scenas, small ensembles, large ensembles, dances, fugues, orchestral interludes, self-contained chamber music. It's as if Strauss were re-inventing the "number opera" of his beloved Mozart by incorporating it into the continuous texture of his perhaps even more beloved Wagner to produce a one-act synthesis termed by its authors "a conversation-piece for music."

The subject matter of *Capriccio*—whether words or music are more important in opera— was suggested by Stefan Zweig, Strauss' librettist for *Die schweigsame Frau,* who happened across a copy of the libretto to *Primo la musica e poi le parole* that the Abbé Casti had written for Antonio Salieri (the opera of which was first performed on a double bill with Mozart's *Der Schauspieldirektor* in 1786). When Zweig, who was Jewish, necessarily fell from political acceptability with the newly installed Nazi Régime, Strauss turned first to Joseph Gregor (librettist for *Friedenstag, Daphne,* and *Die Liebe der Danae*), whose literary attempts on the project were unsatisfactory to Strauss, and then to the conductor Clemens Krauss, with whom he finally collaborated on the text.

Capriccio takes place about 1775 in the salon of a château near Paris, where a birthday celebration for the Countess Madeleine is being planned by the composer Flamand, the poet Olivier, the theater director La Roche, and the count, brother of the countess and himself an amateur actor. Flamand has written an instrumental sextet, Olivier a sonnet-play, and La Roche is conceiving a large-scale spectacle in two parts. Clairon, an actress, arrives from Paris to participate in the rehearsals, and La Roche brings along a dancer and two Italian singers.

Flamand and Olivier, in addition to vying with each other over the intrinsic merits of music and words, are each seeking the hand of the countess, a still-young widow. The artistic sparks begin to fly when Olivier recites a sonnet to Madeleine and the sonnet is impetuously set to music by Flamand. Madeleine realizes the new life that the sonnet now assumes, and though Flamand presses her to make a decision—music or words, Flamand or Olivier—Madeleine asks for a day to decide.

Meanwhile La Roche, the practical man of the theater, ridicules both Flamand and Olivier for their remote and high-minded notions, and demonstrates with his dancer and Italian singers what entertainment is meant to be: melodious and understandable, not abstruse and arcane. The center of the opera is devoted to La Roche's passionate espousal of the direct and unforced allure of his brand of theater. (There's more than a little autobiographical comment here by Strauss, who, over the preceding thirty years, had seen his own musical palette patronized and discredited by the more "advanced" twentieth-century composers.)

Arguments ensue among all those present, from which the count makes the suggestion that an opera be created based on the events of that very day. Now Olivier needs to know what ending to write: he or Flamand. Life has, in a modernistic twist, become art. Madeleine likewise puts Olivier off until the next day, and the opera ends, in an extended monologue, with her inability to choose.

Though a few sections of *Capriccio* bog down into flavorless recitative (the characters of the count, Clairon, and even Olivier are, musically, not very richly defined, perhaps because they represent words, not music), the rest of the opera comprises one glorious musical inspiration after another: the opening sextet; the sonnet and, especially, the trio that develops out of it; Flamand's love scene with Madeleine; the neo-Baroque dances; the Italian singers' duet (at once a scathing parody and an affectionate homage); the laughing and quarreling ensembles; and La Roche's monumental *cri du coeur.* And just when it appears that Strauss may have wound down comes the dessert: the marvelously funny servants' ensemble, the wry appearance (in mixed metres) of the prompter, the moonlit orchestral intermezzo, and the countess' neo-*Rosenkavalier* monologue of tender introspection.

There are hundreds of places in this wise and witty score where Strauss must have, at the 1942 premiere, chuckled to himself in barely containable glee. His famous statement that "Isn't this D-flat major the best possible conclusion to my life's work in the theatre?" seems utterly and self-knowingly genuine. He had ended his cycle of fifteen operas in the same luminescent tranquility of D-flat major as Wagner had ended his cycle of the four *Ring* operas. For Strauss, there could have been no greater fulfillment.—GERALD MOSHELL

I Capuleti ed i Montecchi [The Capulets and the Montagues]

Composer: *Vincenzo Bellini.*

Librettist: *Felice Romani (after Scevola,* Giulietta e Romeo *and Ducis,* Romeo et Juliette).

First Performance: *Venice, La Fenice, 11 March 1830.*

Roles: *Capellio (bass); Giulietta (soprano); Romeo (mezzo-soprano); Tebaldo (tenor); Lorenzo (bass); chorus (SATB).*

The libretto of *I Capuleti ed i Montecchi* is Romani's revision of his *Giulietta e Romeo,* written for Nicola Vaccai in 1825. The immediate source for the story was not Shakespeare but a play *Giulietta e Romeo* by Luigi Scevola of 1818. The action in the libretto for Bellini is as follows. Giulietta and Romeo have already met and fallen in love before the opera begins. Act I: Romeo, disguised as a messenger, offers peace between the warring families, to be cemented by the marriage of Giulietta and Romeo. However, Giulietta is promised by her father Capellio, leader of the Capuleti, to his ally Tebaldo. Although Giulietta is distraught over her impending marriage to Tebaldo, she rejects Romeo's entreaties to run away with him. The wedding festivities are interrupted by the sound of the Montecchi attacking. Romeo again tries to convince Giulietta to flee, is confronted by Capellio and Tebaldo, and is rescued by the Montecchi. Act II: Lorenzo, a physician, gives Giulietta the potion that will make her appear dead. Romeo and Tebaldo meet and are about to fight when they hear the funeral procession approaching. At the tomb, Romeo takes poison. Giulietta awakens, and the lovers bid each other farewell. As Romeo dies, Giulietta falls lifeless upon him. The Montecchi, Lorenzo, and Capellio enter and discover the tragedy.

Despite the inevitable unfavorable comparison between the libretto and Shakespeare's play (Berlioz is particularly scathing), Romani's drama is concise and well constructed. In part, the concision is the result of accident: Romani had to supply the libretto quickly because Bellini received the commission at the last minute after another composer had defaulted. Whatever the reason, the drama proceeds fairly logically, with the tragedy growing out of the irreconcilable conflicts of Romeo's ardor, Giulietta's vacillation between love and filial loyalty, and Capellio's stubbornness. (We are, however, left asking why Romeo is not recognized as the messenger of the opening scene and why Giulietta would refuse to run away with him but agree to take the potion.) There are no superfluous characters and subplots.

The haste required of Romani also affected Bellini, and just as the librettist reused old material, so did the composer. His previous opera, *Zaira,* had been a failure, and Bellini adapted many of its melodies for *I Capuleti.* However, in the majority of cases the text in *I Capuleti* bears little resemblance to the text in *Zaira* that had served for the same melody; they differ in poetic form or dramatic context or both. The process of adaptation sometimes led to awkward results, as in Romeo's aria at Giulietta's tomb, "Deh! tu, bell'anima," in which the composer had to repeat the opening words of each line to make the text fit the music ("Deh! tu, deh! tu, bell'anima /A me, a me rivolgiti" ["Ah! you, ah! you, fair spirit /Turn to me, to me"], etc.). In addition to the self-borrowings, Bellini relied on the example of Vaccai in using a mezzo-soprano in the role of Romeo and in forming the two finales, numbers whose structures lie outside the usual conventions of bel-canto opera.

In modern times *I Capuleti ed i Montecchi* has not had the popularity of the two operas that followed it, *La sonnambula* and *Norma.* And indeed the score is uneven. After a slow start, the opera comes to life with Giulietta's entrance to a beautiful horn solo that will also accompany part of the ensuing recitative (several of the most striking melodies in the score are instrumental introductions; in addition to this horn solo, there is one for violoncello that opens act II and one for clarinet before the confrontation between Romeo and Tebaldo). This is followed by her elegiac *romanza* "Oh! quante volte, oh! quante" ("Oh! how many times"), whose melody, borrowed from his first opera, *Adelson e Salvini,* is testimony to the presence of Bellini's melodic gift even in his earliest works. Most of the remaining pieces in *I Capuleti,* while rarely reaching the heights of lyrical beauty attained in *Norma,* are attractive and dramatically apt. One might single out Giulietta's solo in the finale to act I, with its unsettling syncopated accompaniment, and the following duet with Romeo. Of the longer, more formal melodies, the slow section of the earlier Giulietta-Romeo duet in act I and both tempi of Giulietta's aria in act II are especially effective.

For most observers, the greatest scene of the opera is the finale, at the Capulets' tomb. It is unconventionally constructed of recitative, a one-tempo aria for Romeo, more recitative, a brief duet, and an even briefer conclusion after the lovers' deaths. The recitatives are particularly expressive; note the surge of melody when Romeo addresses Giulietta's corpse and the despairing fall of an octave when Romeo informs Giulietta that he will be staying in the tomb forever. Romeo's aria has a moving simplicity, despite the problems of text-setting mentioned above. And the duet, "Ah! crudel! che mai facesti?" ("Ah! cruel one! what did you do?")—whose structure Bellini derived from Vaccai but which he imbued with far greater musical power—is heart-rending with its brief spurts of lyricism defeated by the bleak changes from major to minor when Romeo starts to feel the effects of the poison and again as he enters his death throes. Unfortunately, because Vaccai's finale is somewhat more brilliant for Romeo, Maria Malibran in 1832 began the practice of using it in place of Bellini's, thereby depriving the audience of Bellini's finest dramatic achievement to date and perhaps contributing to the opera's descent into oblivion, from which it has only recently begun to emerge.—CHARLES S. BRAUNER

Cardillac

Composer: *Paul Hindemith.*

Librettist: *Ferdinand Lion (after Hoffmann, Das Fräulein von Scuderi).*

First Performance: *Dresden, Staatsoper, 9 November 1926; revised by Hindemith (after Lion's libretto), first performed Zurich, Stadttheater, 20 June 1952.*

Roles: *Cardillac (baritone); His Daughter (soprano); Apprentice (tenor); First Singer at Opera (soprano); Officer (bass); Young Cavalier (tenor); Klymene (contralto); Phaeton (tenor); Apollo (bass); Rich Marquis (mute); tenors; chorus (SATB).*

Paul Hindemith's first full-length opera, *Cardillac,* is also the first of a trilogy of works for the stage, which span three different periods of his dramatic writing. *Cardillac, Mathis der Maler,* and *Die Harmonie der Welt* all deal with the problem of the creative artist's relationship to his work and to society.

During the 1920s the alienation of the artist was a prevailing theme, and at this time Hindemith himself, pondering new directions for his dramatic writing, was experiencing a turbulent period in his development. Hence E.T.A. Hoffmann's novella of 1820, *Das Fräulein von Scuderi,* with its artist-in-society subject matter, proved to be a very attractive and challenging topic for the composer's first major confrontation with the problems of 20th-century opera.

At Hindemith's request, Ferdinand Lion, the Alsatian poet and essayist, produced a terse, theatrical libretto, freely based on Hoffmann's compelling portrait of the gifted, but psychotic goldsmith, René Cardillac, a highly renowned artist but isolated member of society in the Paris of Louis XIV. His obsessive self-identity with his creations and his pathological compulsion never to become separated from them, impel him to murder his clients in order to recover the precious objects they have purchased. Interwoven in this tale of terror is a love story of Cardillac's daughter and a young man, which interlocks with the dark side of the life of the father and heightens the pathos and tragedy as Cardillac is finally exposed and killed by the mob.

In his desire to maintain a creative distance from the explosive text, Hindemith avoided writing psychological music by supporting his architectonic concept with terse, dissonant, strict polyphony, thus controlling the psychological tensions of the work through the discipline of the orchestral music, and by placing the two stylistic elements—musical and literary—on different levels. In the rehearsals for the 1926 premiere under Fritz Busch, Hindemith insisted that the production not be static, but generate its own dramatic tensions with strong stage movement in contrast to the concertante orchestral music. As Felix Wolfes observed after the first performance, "The main attraction of this remarkable work consists in the curious union of dramatically forceful musical full-bloodedness with the strictest formal and stylistic asceticism, almost without parallel in opera." David Neumeyer, in his analysis of the 1926 *Cardillac* published in 1986, regards the work as "the most characteristic German opera in modern style of the mid and late twenties," because only *Cardillac* represents the "new objective" manner: i.e., through musical formal principles, subjective-psychological powers become objective-musical. Music and drama, in a juxtaposition of stylistic and expressive components, stand in a new relationship.

However, the "revolutionary élan" of the young Hindemith for "new objectivism" in opera as a counter force against the romanticism of Richard Strauss and Wagner, prevented him from recognizing the romanticism within his own nature, and ironically, against his intentions, the romantic element endemic to the subject matter returned strongly in the concept of the opera, resulting in a revision twenty-five years later.

Adaptations, revisions, new settings are not unusual in the history of opera. However, Hindemith's 1952 revision was so drastic that except for the title, some leading characters, and a few musical scenes, the new version had very little in common with the original. Moreover, the libretto was replaced by the composer's own text. In addition to adding new characters and scenes, Hindemith enlarged the work to four acts by creating a new act (act III, a "play within a play") which includes the performance of part of Lully's *Phaeton*. This insertion not only provides a virtuosic, declamatory scene, which brilliantly contrasts with the lugubrious environment of the impending crime, but this injection of baroque music into the drama with another level of activity increases the observational objectivity of the work.

As in most revisions, a certain amount of stylistic unity is sacrificed in Hindemith's effort to approach a new esthetic principle, and critical response varied. Some felt the emphasis placed on the expressionistic, abstract qualities of the score weakened the dramatic power of the work; others thought the philosophy and terror of the piece were not well combined. There were complaints that the vocal line was mostly declamatory, while the orchestral music carried the "tunes." Nevertheless, Hindemith ordered his publisher to permit only the revised score for performance, and not until the composer's death was the original version made available again. A champion of the original version in spite of the composer's wishes was the conductor Joseph Keilberth, who shortly before his death in 1968 initiated for Cologne Radio an authoritative recording, which Deutsche Grammaphon issued as the first commercial recording of the work in either version—an invaluable documentary event.—MURIEL HEBERT WOLF

Carmen

Composer: *Georges Bizet.*

Librettists: *Henri Meilhac and Ludovic Halévy (after Mérimée).*

First Performance: *Paris, Opéra-Comique, 3 March 1875.*

Roles: *Carmen (mezzo-soprano); Don José (tenor); Escamillo (baritone); Micaëla (soprano); Frasquita (soprano); Mercedes (mezzo-soprano); Le Remendado (tenor); Le Dancaire (tenor); Zuniga (bass); Morales (baritone); chorus (SATTBB), chorus (children).*

Hostile reviews and talk of scandal greeted the 1875 premiere of *Carmen,* Georges Bizet's best known work, which was to become the world's most popular opera. For Bizet, *Carmen*'s debut was a bitter disappointment. He had worked for two years on the score, and he expected a hit: "People make me out to be obscure, complicated, tedious, more fettered by technical skill than lit by inspiration. Well, this time I have written a work that is all clarity and vivacity, full of colour and melody. It will be entertaining. . . ." While these qualities may account for *Carmen*'s subsequent success, it's less-than-enthusiastic initial reception could be attributed, in part at least, to the frustrated expectations of the middle-class families that regularly attended the performances of the Opéra-Comique. A passionate affair between a wanton Gypsy and a weak soldier set in the company of smoking working girls, lighthearted smugglers and ribald soldiers was hardly the kind of love story or social milieu that reflected the values of this bourgeois public. Moreover, the on-stage stabbing at the conclusion of the work broke the conventions of dramatic decorum, further offending the audience's sense of propriety. The original *Carmen* was composed of a Prélude followed by twenty-seven pieces that were separated by scenes in spoken dialogue, but it was an amended version produced in October 1875 at the Vienna Opera, after Bizet's death, that was to become the *Carmen* in the Grand Opera tradition now performed throughout the world. In its new format, the spoken dialogues were replaced by recitatives composed by Ernest Guiraud.

Stationed in Seville, far from his native Basque country, Corporal Don José arrests Carmen, the beguiling Gypsy, accused of attacking another woman during a fight in the tobacco factory. In exchange for a rendez-vous, José allows her to escape, and he is sent to prison. Upon his release, José arrives at the tavern of Lillas Pastia to meet Carmen. Their evening comes to an abrupt end when José hears the bugle sound the retreat and decides over Carmen's objections to go back to the barracks. As he is about to leave, Lieutenant Zuniga comes in with the express purpose of courting Carmen's favors; the two soldiers exchange words and draw their swords; they are separated by Carmen's Gypsy companions. His military career now jeopardized, José joins up with Carmen and her friends. When Micaëla, José's former sweetheart, fetches him at the request of his dying mother, Carmen, tired of their relationship and José's constant jealousy, begins a liaison with the toreador Escamillo. On the day of the corrida, outside the bullfighting arena, José urges Carmen to come back to him. In spite of his pleas and his threats, Carmen refuses to follow him, affirming that she would rather die than not be free to live and love as she pleases. As the shouts of the public in the background announce the victory of the toreador over the bull, José stabs her.

For the libretto, which is based on a short story by Prosper Mérimée published in 1845, Georges Bizet relied on two seasoned dramatists, Henri Meilhac and Ludovic Halévy, who had previously authored the libretti of Jacques Offenbach's very popular *opera bouffes.*

Bizet's *Carmen* changed the traditions of the French lyrical stage by blurring the distinctions between operatic genres. For example, Micaëla and Escamillo, whose roles were invented by Meilhac and Halévy, are stock characters in the Opéra Comique tradition—as are Carmen's companions—but the impossible love story between the Gypsy and the soldier is a tragedy that belongs to Grand Opera. In this story of romantic passion, the incompatible protagonists never sing of love in unison. Carmen's lower range mezzo and José's lyrical tenor are also mismatched, for the usual coupling of voices in nineteenth-century opera casts a soprano as the tenor's lover. In the aria "Ma mère, je la vois!" Micaëla's soprano blends with José's voice in a traditional duet which only calls attention to the unconventional nature of Carmen's and José's relationship. Bizet introduced another innovation when he insisted on a realistic staging that respected the opera's dramatic unity and that transformed the then motionless chorus into kinetic performers, and turned the lead singers into actors.

Tchaikovsky described *Carmen* as "a masterpiece in the fullest meaning of the word, that is to say, one of those rare works that translates the efforts of a whole musical period," and Nietzsche wrote to his friend, the composer Peter Gast, that Bizet's opus was "the best opera that existed . . . the opera of operas." Bizet's score offers a dazzling variety of moods and textures from the most delicate and hauntingly seductive to the tackiest of tunes, as in the case of the Toreador Song. For Richard Strauss, Bizet's composition stands as a masterpiece of orchestration. "If you want to learn how to orchestrate," he writes, "study the score of *Carmen*. What wonderful economy, and how every note and rest is in its proper place." *Carmen* has been hailed by pro- and anti-Wagnerians alike, and admired by a variety of composers, including Brahms, Gounod, Wolf, Debussy, Puccini, Stravinsky, Grieg, and Prokofiev.

Because the last act makes the bullfighting arena the referential backdrop of the story, the corrida has been the most commonly used critical topos for the interpretation of the opera. A fight to the death between man and beast, the corrida has been seen as a test of manly courage, and also as an event that averts the latent violence inherent in society through the ritual sacrifice of a scapegoat. But bull and matador can also be viewed as mirror images of each other, both torturer as well as victim, and the reversibility of their positions leaves open the possibility of divergent, even contradictory, interpretations. Thus, while critics in the past have judged Carmen's death to be a just retribution for causing a man's downfall, today a feminist critic, Catherine Clément, eulogizes Carmen as a heroine "who chooses to die before a man decides it for her." For Nietzsche, Bizet's work illustrated the war between the sexes, but a contemporary public might feel that it is Micaëla and Escamillo who better represent their sex—and there is no interaction between them—rather than the protagonists who seem equally distant from ideals of femininity and masculinity. A story about unrequited love, Bizet's *Carmen* demonstrates the tragedy of passion as a form of desire that negates the desire of the other.

From sexual politics to partisan causes, *Carmen* has often been used to represent political ideologies. In a 1984 production by Frank Corsaro at the New York City Opera, the opera is set during the Spanish Civil War with Carmen portrayed as a freedom fighter who falls in the struggle against fascism; yet, in a similar staging performed in Pforzheim during the Third Reich, Bizet's opera may have served rather to remind Nazi soldiers of the dangers awaiting those who fraternized with so-called "non-aryan" women. For Theodor Adorno, the greatness of Bizet's opera resides in its oppositional structure which continuously challenges the ascription of any fixed meaning, making it possible for the story of Carmen to become a myth. From the exotic temptress and the bewitching vamp to the incarnation of the modern free woman, the popularity of Bizet's *Carmen* launched a cultural industry which has already produced over thirty films, several ballets, and numerous plays bearing the unofficial trademark of her name.—NELLY FURMAN

Carreras, José

Tenor. Born 5 December 1946 in Barcelona. Studied with Jaime Puig at Barcelona Conservatory and with Juan Ruax; debut as Flavio in Norma, *Barcelona, 1970; sang Gennaro in* Lucrezia Borgia, *1970; London debut in concert version of* Maria Stuarda; *at New York City Opera, 1972-75; San Francisco debut, 1973, as Rodolfo in* La bohème; *Metropolitan Opera debut, 1975; Salzburg debut as Don Carlos, 1976; Chicago debut as Riccardo, 1976.*

José Carreras has recently made a return to public performance after a bout with leukemia. He is evidently still a very affecting singer but the strain the illness has had on his vocal apparatus is apparent. Carreras in any case always tended to push his naturally lyric tenor voice to the limit, singing Andrea Chénier, Calaf, and even Radamès; the first role he sang gloriously as a young poet and artist, the others with only partial success. His dark, rich timbre, he claims, "can be dangerous because at times it makes me seem to have a bigger voice than I really do." Herbert von Karajan principally persuaded him to sing many of the heavier roles in his repertoire. Carreras is vocally, physically, and temperamentally a perfect Rodolfo in Puccini's *La bohème.* Yet even if there was some sense of vocal strain as he went from the essentially lyric roles in *La bohème, Luisa Miller, La traviata, Rigoletto,* and *Lucia di Lammermoor* to heavier ones in *Andrea Chénier, Don Carlos, Carmen, Il trovatore, La forza del destino,* and *Turandot,* there was a corresponding improvement in Carreras's acting ability and believability on stage. One role that Carreras always sang with particular success was Don José in *Carmen,* a part that he performed with Agnes Baltsa alone over one hundred times. Of Carreras's José, Alan Blyth wrote in *Gramophone:* "Carreras's Flower Song, ending with a marvelous *pianissimo* high B flat, is a thing of light and shade, finely shaped, not quite idiomatically French either in verbal or tonal accent, but very appealing." Of the above list the only role that has positively eluded him has been Radamès with Karajan, a role that Carreras immediately dropped.

The Barcelona native who, like Corelli and Domingo, is largely self-taught, was discovered at age 22 by Montserrat Caballé's brother Carlos. The soprano quickly recognized the young tenor's great talent, and Caballé and Carreras have subsequently appeared together numerous times both in live performance and on recordings. Carreras's official stage debut took place in 1970 in Barcelona as Flavio to Caballé's Norma. That same year he and Caballé appeared together at the Liceu in Donizetti's *Lucrezia Borgia.* In 1971 Carreras sang Rodolfo in Parma, where he won the International Verdi Competition in that year, and in 1972 he made his debut as Rodolfo at the New York City Opera. There he was given a three-year contract and learned eleven new roles in sixteen months. Debuts in important opera centers around the world followed. Carreras has been especially active in Salzburg, Vienna, and at Covent Garden. His collaboration with Karajan began in 1976 with a Verdi *Messa da Requiem* at the Salzburg Easter Festival and a recording and stage performances of Verdi's *Don Carlos.*

Carreras not only pushed his voice but appeared on stage with great regularity. He has likewise had a prolific recording career, even as a "crossover" artist, having recorded not only Spanish and Italian folk and love songs but also *West Side Story* with Bernstein himself conducting (he was Bernstein's third choice and it was not a particularly happy collaboration) and *South Pacific,* both of these musicals with Kiri Te Kanawa. In the opera repertoire Carreras has been especially active recording the works of Verdi, not only the well-known masterpieces but also the less often performed earlier works such as *Un giorno di regno, Il corsaro, I due Foscari,* and *Stiffelio,* all for Philips. Carreras sings elegantly in *Il corsaro* with Caballé and Norman and is perhaps at his very best in *I due Foscari,* impassioned and gorgeous of tone in the prison scene. He has recorded a superb *Otello* of Rossini with von Stade under López Cobos on Philips. His Edgardo in *Lucia di Lammermoor* with Caballé is suitably ardent, reminiscent of the young Giuseppe Di Stefano. Carreras sings a high E at the conclusion of "Verrano a te." In *Il trovatore* under Colin Davis on Philips, Carreras follows Verdi's markings scrupulously, singing "Con espressione" in "Ah si, ben mio," and performing "Di quella pira" in the correct key of C major topped by a thrilling high note. His Don Carlos on EMI under Karajan is an ideal youth burning from unrequited love and political fervor; he is likewise ardent as Riccardo in *Un ballo in maschera* with Caballé under Davis, but here another similarity with Di Stefano is evident in that the voice shows signs of strain. Carreras's Cavaradossi in *Tosca,* likewise on Philips with Caballé and conducted by Davis, is sung heroically with a glorious thrust and a breathtakingly slow tempo for "E lucevan le stelle" that Carreras sustains beautifully, but the *Turandot* on which he sings Calaf (Caballé is Turandot) is marred by Alain Lombard's dull conducting. With Caballé there are also a number of live recordings, notable among them a 1974 *Maria Stuarda* from the Salle Pleyel and a 1977 *Roberto Devereux* from Aix-en-Provence. These give a good account of Carreras in his prime.

Blessed with a highly individual voice of a dark hue, superb physical looks, and intelligence, Carreras has had a thrilling international career, if not quite on the par with his contemporary tenor superstars Domingo and Pavarotti. Carreras appears in a number of videos of complete operas including a visually appealing Zeffirelli production of *La bohème* with Teresa Stratas as Mimi, a film about the Spanish tenor Julian Gayarre, the tenor "with the voice of an angel" who lived from 1844 to 1890, and in 1991 a compact disc of the songs of Andrew Lloyd Webber.—STEPHEN A. WILLIER

Caruso, Enrico

Tenor. Born 25 February 1873, Naples. Died 2 August 1921 in Naples. Two sons by singer Ada Giachetti. One daughter by Dorothy Park Benjamin. Studied with Guglielmo Vergine, 1891-94, and Vincenzo Lombardi; debut in L'Amico Francesco *in Naples, 1895; created Maurizio in* Adriana Lecouvreur, *Loris in* Fedora *and Dick Johnson in* La fanciulla del West; *sang at Teatro alla Scala, 1900-02; Covent Garden debut in* Rigoletto *with Nellie Melba, 1902; debut at Metropolitan Opera in* Rigoletto, *1903, and sang there for eighteen seasons; operation for node on vocal cords in 1909.*

Enrico Caruso had just turned twenty-two when he made his professional debut in Domenico Morelli's new opera, *L'amico Francesco,* on 15 March 1895. During the engagements that followed, mostly in the provincial Italian theaters, he built a repertory at an astonishing rate. The record shows that he learned 16 major roles in two years. With each successive and successful engagement Caruso's name gained currency. In 1897, he sang in the world premiere of *L'Arlesiana,* and upon the sudden death of Roberto Stagno for whom Giordano composed

Fedora, Caruso was chosen to take his place at the world premiere on 17 November 1898. As he later said: "After that the contracts descended on me like a big rainstorm." It marked the beginning of his rise through the ranks of Italian tenors to preeminence.

After tours of Russia (1899 and 1900) and Buenos Aires (1899, 1900, 1901), his ascendancy began to accelerate. The series of important debuts that followed included Teatro alla Scala (1900), Teatro San Carlo of Naples (1901), Covent Garden (1902), Paris (1904), and Vienna (1906). In retrospect, Caruso's most important debut was with the Metropolitan Opera, as the Duke in *Rigoletto* on 23 November 1903. The Met became his artistic home for the rest of his career; he sang 628 performances in the house including galas, and 234 at the Brooklyn Academy of Music, in Philadelphia, and on tour. During his 18 seasons with the Met he was featured in 17 opening nights; he performed 39 of the 64 roles in his repertoire, among them Canio (*I pagliacci*), Radames (*Aïda*), Manrico (*Il trovatore*), Samson, Faust, Don José, Lionel, Cavaradossi, Rodolfo, the Duke of Mantua, and Riccardo. His only Wagnerian role was Lohengrin (three performances, Buenos Aires, 1901) and his only Mozart role Don Ottavio in *Don Giovanni* (Covent Garden). During his career he took part in ten world premieres, and he created Dick Johnson in *La Fanciulla del West*.

By his mid-thirties, Caruso became the most sought after and highest paid singer in the world. His fees at the Metropolitan eventually rose to $2,500 a performance, a fee limited, rather than set, by the tenor himself. His cachet elsewhere was much higher, $10,000 a performance in Cuba (1920) and $15,000 in Mexico City (1919). His last Victor contract (scheduled to run until 1934) guaranteed him an annual minimum of $100,000 in royalties, and his two silent movies (*My Cousin* and *A Splendid Romance*, 1918) allegedly brought him $100,000 each.

Caruso made his first recordings in 1902. The ten sides he recorded for the Gramophone and Typewriter Company in Milan on 19 April 1902 were so successful that Caruso has been generally credited with turning the gramophone, until then regarded as a toy, into a musical instrument. He signed an exclusive contract with the Victor Talking Machine Company in 1904, and all of his subsequent records were made either in New York City or in Camden, New Jersey. The majority of these acoustic recordings have never been out of the catalog, and despite the sonic deficiencies, his entire recorded legacy has been repeatedly reissued on long playing records and compact discs.

Although Guglielmo Vergine was Caruso's only singing teacher, conductor Vincenzo Lombardi helped him conquer his difficulties with his high notes, and he received help from his common-law wife, Ada

Enrico Caruso as Manrico in *Il trovatore* (Culver Pictures)

Giachetti, herself an accomplished conservatory-trained singer and pianist. Thereafter, he firmed up his own technique by daily practice. His voice, initially light and lyrical, grew heavier and more dramatic with age. The baritone timbre and the solid lower range had been there from the beginning; in fact, in his youth he had some doubts whether he was a baritone or a tenor. His recordings show that he was able to sing a high D flat ("Cujus animam" from *Stabat Mater*) and color his voice to deliver a beautiful rendition of the bass aria "Vecchia zimarra" from *La bohème,* the latter commemorating the occasion when he sang the aria onstage for an indisposed Andrès de Segurola (23 December 1913). Remarkably, the two recordings were made only three years apart.

In stylistic terms, Caruso represented the bridge between the bel canto tenors of the late 19th century—Angelo Masini, Francesco Marconi, Fernando de Lucia, Alessandro Bonci—and the more robust verismo singers who followed him. Caruso did not abandon the merits of the old school but rather built on them, combining the old with the new style of singing. He would not distort the music, but allow the weight and meaning of the words to dominate the vocal line, thereby achieving a dramatic involvement and communicative effect greater and more immediate than any of his contemporaries. An example that bears out this assertion is his three *fortissimo* outbursts of "Sangue!" in the duet from *Otello* with Titta Ruffo. He is possibly the only singer on record who actually sings—not screams—these words.

Aurally, Caruso's voice had a sensuous appeal, "carnal," as described by Geraldine Farrar. His vocal production was flawless: a solid column of air supported an unwavering sound of exceptional beauty. The quality of the voice has been consistently described in many languages as "golden" and "velvet." It had a caressing warmth, a heroic ring, and sufficient flexibility to respond to the singer's demands. In his best years he could produce at will a *diminuendo,* piano, head tone, falsetto, or *voce mista* with the same ease as a forte or fortissimo. He took pride in his ability to color his voice according to the character of the music—light for Nemorino, heavy for Radames or Samson. Although his voice darkened and grew more robust, his increasingly "muscular" singing near the end appears to have been a matter of choice rather than limitations. His light and playful "'A vucchella" recorded in September 1919, shows the singer still in full control of his *mezza voce.*

He worked on his interpretations throughout his career. In some of his roles—Canio, the Duke of Mantua, Radames, Eléazar (*La Juive*)—he established standards that have not been equaled, much less surpassed. His style, modern if compared with that of any of his contemporaries, had a lasting influence on operatic singing in this century. His initially crude and elementary acting improved over the years, culminating in Eléazar in *La Juive,* his last role, which was uniformly regarded as a great histrionic as well as vocal achievement.

Caruso was a serious man in private, and a kind, gregarious, fun-loving person in company. His warm humanity endeared him to his public, his generosity was legendary. Always ready to extend a helping hand, he is said to have supported or helped over a hundred friends and relatives with monthly checks. The international publicity he generated was unsought and unpaid; it came of itself, the product of his accomplishments and celebrity and the love of his public.

Dying at the relatively young age of 48, Caruso had a professional career that spanned only 26 years. Although he performed in opera and concert in most countries of Europe, North and South America, a single televised concert of present-day superstars can reach more listeners than all the audiences who heard Caruso in his lifetime. He has been dead for seventy years, yet his name is synonymous with opera and great singing throughout the entire civilized world. Some authorities maintain that toward the end of his life, Caruso's voice showed signs of decline. Bearing in mind a chronic chest cold he could not shake in the fall of 1920, and conceding the effects of the inevitable aging process, it was still the Caruso voice. Mount Everest has eroded several feet over the enturies; it is still the tallest peak in the world.—ANDREW FARKAS

Catalani, Alfredo

Composer. Born 19 June 1854, in Lucca. Died 7 August 1893, in Milan. Studied with his father, and then studied counterpoint with Fortunato Magi at the Istituto Musicale Pacini in Lucca, 1872; studied composition with Bazin and piano with Marmontel in Paris, 1872; returned to Italy, 1873; studied composition with Bozzini at the Milan Conservatory, 1873; professor of composition at the Milan Conservatory, 1886, where he met Toscanini.

Operas *La falce,* Arrigo Boito, Milan, Milan Conservatory, 19 July 1875; *Elda,* Carlo D'Ormeville, Turin, Teatro Regio, 31 January 1880; *Dejanice,* Angelo Zanardini, Milan, Teatro alla Scala, 17 March 1883; *Edmea,* Antonio Ghislanzoni, Milan, Teatro alla Scala, 27 February 1886; *Loreley,* Angelo Zanardini (after D'Ormeville), Turin, Teatro Regio, 16 February 1890; *La Wally,* Luigi Illica (after the novel by Wilhelmine von Hillern), Milan, Teatro alla Scala, 20 January 1892.

As a composer of Italian opera, Alfredo Catalani was something of an anomaly. Representing an independent current in the history of nineteenth century Italian opera, Catalani's style had little in common with Giuseppe Verdi's or Giacomo Puccini's. Catalani's style remained surprisingly free of Verdi's direct influence. The Verdian aspects of Catalani's style largely derived from the operas of Amilcare Ponchielli, which were important models in the Milan of the 1870s and 80s, particularly during the period of Verdi's hiatus following the composition of *Aïda.* Even more striking was Catalani's resistance to the contemporary "naturalist" currents and French operatic dramaturgy that animated Puccini and other young Italian composers of Puccini's generation, this despite an enthusiasm for Émile Zola dating from Catalani's year as a student at the Conservatoire in Paris. In some respects, Catalani may be viewed as a spiritual heir of Vincenzo Bellini, and commentators have often remarked a Bellinian *morbidezza* (morbidity) in Catalani's work, although Bellini could hardly have exerted much of a direct influence, given Catalani's birthdate. Above all, it may have been Catalani's fascination with early German Romanticism and all things Northern, his allegiance to Arrigo Boïto (composer of *Mefistofele* and librettist for Verdi's *Otello* and *Falstaff)* and the *Scapigliatura* movement, that lent his operatic output its distinctive character.

Through Antonio Bazzini, his teacher at the conservatory in Milan, Catalani gained entrée to the salon of the countess Clara Maffei, where he was befriended by Boïto and the composer/conductor Franco Faccio, who would later lead the premiere of Verdi's *Otello.* Boïto and Faccio were active in the bohemian *Scapigliatura* (from the Italian for "dishevelled") movement, essentially a literary movement along the lines of the French "decadence" formed during the period of disillusionment among intellectuals following the unification of Italy. The *Scapigliatura* championed various ultramontane Romantic and avant-garde movements from Goethe and the

141

Lake Poets to Wagnerism, but Boïto and Catalani were less than perfect Wagnerites. If his scores bespeak a real familiarity with Wagner's *Lohengrin,* Catalani resented the charges of "Wagnerism" and "*avvenirismo*" ("futurism") that were routinely laid at his doorstep, and, like Boïto, he was at least as enamored of Carl Maria von Weber as of the master of Bayreuth. Boïto prepared an Italian translation of Weber's *Der Freischütz* for its Teatro alla Scala premiere in 1872, while Weber's influence on Catalani's style of early German Romantic opera was palpable and abiding. This is directly reflected in Catalani's choices of subject matter for his first and last full-length operas, *Elda* and *La Wally;* the former is based on the legend of the Lorelei, the latter on a German novella set in the Tyrol.

Catalani's mature style is best reflected in the rustic drama of *Edmea,* despite a crippling libretto by Ghislanzoni, the librettist of Verdi's *Aïda;* in *Loreley,* an extensively revised version of *Elda;* and in *La Wally,* his last and best-known work. With *Dejanice,* Catalani tried his hand at Italian grand opera in the manner of Ponchielli. Ponchielli's *La Gioconda* (with a libretto by Boïto after Victor Hugo) was the more or less explicit model for *Dejanice.* Both operas freely avail themselves of the *convenienze* (conventions or conventional layout) of Verdian *melodramma* and Meyerbeerian French grand opera with their abundant opportunities for striking set pieces of various kinds. Like Wagner's, however, Catalani's was primarily an art of transition, and in the later operas, some of the most original music is to be found in the fluid developments linking the set pieces with their subtle and flexible use of *arioso* and *parlando.* Catalani's quasi-symphonic developments with their references to *ländler,* horn calls, and other effects of local color are so effective that the set pieces can seem like throw-backs to an earlier aesthetic, however successfully they may be elided in context. Consequently, the most successful set-pieces in Catalani's operas tend to be either atmospheric orchestral passages evoking natural or, in *Loreley,* supernatural phenomena, or genre scenes in which atmosphere and local color impinge on the dramatic transaction, as with the hushed and effective funeral procession in *Loreley* or the *Walzer del bacio* (Waltz of the kiss) in *La Wally.*

Catalani exploited his rich harmonic and orchestral palettes with real mastery. His mature works are orchestrated in a "symphonic" manner remote from that of earlier Italian opera. Catalani's instrumentation was beholden to the German symphonic tradition, to Beethoven and Weber—Beethoven's Seventh Symphony is evoked at one point in *La Wally*—and like them Catalani employed combinations of clean primary colors rather than Wagner's subtly shifting and imperceptibly blended timbres. Catalani exploited his harmonic language with great originality and with all of the flexibility that harmony had acquired in the later nineteenth century.

In Catalani's operas there is an odd amalgam of Italian conventions and German Romanticism, numbers opera and symphonic continuity, Italianate lyricism and motivic development that is not always perfectly reconciled. If he was no more fully successful in his particular quest for that late-nineteenth-century chimera, continuous opera, than many other composers of the period, on the basis of the finest pages in *Loreley* and *La Wally,* we can endorse Verdi's summation of Catalani as "brav'uomo ed eccelente musicista" ("a brave fellow and an excellent musician").—DAVID GABLE

Cavalleria rusticana [Rustic Chivalry]

Composer: *Pietro Mascagni.*

Librettists: *G. Targioni-Tozzetti and G. Menasci (after Verga).*

First Performance: *Rome, Costanzi, 17 May 1890.*

Roles: *Santuzza (soprano); Turiddu (tenor); Lola (mezzo-soprano); Alfio (baritone); Lucia (mezzo-soprano or contralto); chorus (SSATTB).*

Cavalleria rusticana is universally regarded as the archetype of operatic *verismo,* a term which defined the literary source of the libretto and was also adopted for the musico-dramatic structures of the opera. Stripped of all its operatic embellishments, *Cavalleria,* set in a Sicilian village, is about a case of adultery, with the complication of a seduced girl who triggers off the revenge of the betrayed husband.

A critical assessment of the opera should first distinguish between the veristic literary source—Giovanni Verga's one-act play *Cavalleria rusticana* (1884)—and the libretto arranged by Targioni-Tozzetti and Menasci. Subtitled "Sicilian popular scenes," Verga's text marked a turning point in the theater of post-unity Italy for the originality of the subject and its innovative dramatic conception.

The play is organized as a series of duets encompassed by two choral scenes. The action takes place on Easter Sunday. Alfio is the Sicilian "man of honor," the stern believer in an unwritten code of conduct which empowers a wronged man to take justice into his own hands with no need of intermediaries. The silent presence of two *carabinieri* (policemen) in the first and last scenes acquires a special relevance in the context: Alfio's own justice is set against the law and order established in Sicily by the new Italian state. An old-time mafioso component surfaces in the characterization of Alfio and Turiddu. It is exemplified by the ritual and public challenge of the bite on the ear-lobe. Turiddu's death in the ensuing off-stage duel is accepted by the villagers as the right punishment for someone who infringed the common law that defends the family and condemns adultery as a threat to its integrity. The spine-chilling cry signaling the catastrophe: "Hanno ammazzato compare Turiddu!" ("Turiddu has been killed!"), phrased in the impersonal form, relates the final act of violence to a well-defined social context.

In the libretto, the skilfully coordinated movement of well individualized villagers is lost. Mascagni does manage to suggest a festive atmosphere in musical terms, opening with resounding church bells and adding, later on, organ music and Latin hymns, but these devices tend to remain exterior and decorative. They do not permeate the people on stage. In fact, Verga's villagers are gone. Their place has been taken by a chorus of blissful peasants who are made to sing an incongruous, anodyne work-song full of "birds," "myrtles," "oranges," and "humming spindles." From the crude dialect of the opening *Siciliana*—a sort of folkloric token of what is about to unravel on stage—we are taken back to the world of Arcadia.

Alfio is no longer the modest, hard-working carter of the play. His entry, modeled on Escamillo's first appearance in *Carmen,* shows us a vociferous local hero who braves icy winds, rain and snow, and boasts about his wife's faithfulness. On the other hand, Santuzza is very much the desperate and passionate peasant girl of the original story. Yet the last scene of the opera contains an incongruity that distances the opera, once more, from the *verismo* of the play: Santuzza reappears at the very end and throws herself into Lucia's arms. In the last scene of the play, instead, Verga leaves Turiddu's mother, Lola, and the minor characters on stage but keeps Santuzza well out of the way. She is left alone with her shame and sense of guilt. She is not only "dishonored" but *scellerata* (wicked), since, by exposing Lola's adultery, she has indirectly sentenced Turiddu to death. Her expiration begins with her seeing herself as an outcast in her own village. Her despair can hardly be shared with the mother of the man she has caused to be killed.

As remorse and isolation await Santuzza, institutional justice pursues Alfio, the murderer. At the end of the play, the two *carabinieri* dash off towards the place of the duel. In the opera the presence of policemen patrolling the village square would have spoilt the picturesqueness of the Sicilian setting and made it all too realistic, so there is no trace of that.

Having removed or distorted some essential, realistic features of the story, Mascagni and his librettists introduced their own pseudo-veristic ingredients: the serenade in Sicilian dialect inserted in the orchestral prelude, Lola's *stornello* (flower song, more Tuscan than Sicilian) and Turiddu's drinking song. These pieces of on-stage music, as well as the mellifluous intermezzo, spaced and enhanced the lyrical numbers of the opera such as Santuzza's romanza "Voi lo sapete, o mamma" ("You know that, mother") or Turiddu's farewell to his mother. The result was an intriguing melodrama where the thrill of novelty was balanced by the warm melodiousness of the Italian operatic tradition.

Mascagni's coarse-grained, impassioned music introduced a realistic, "earthy" dimension that was easily seen as a new style, indeed as the transposition of *verismo* from literature into opera. No less alluring was the veristic interpretation of Gemma Bellincioni and Roberto Stagno as Santuzza and Turiddu in the Roman premiere of *Cavalleria*. Their agitated confrontations, their dramatic gestures, such as Santuzza's curse "A te la mala Pasqua!" ("An evil Easter to you!"), helped establish a new vocal style and led to similar interpretations even in operas, such as *Carmen*, that belong to a different genre (i.e. *opéra-comique*). The casual encounter with literary *verismo* would be of little consequence in Mascagni's later production. *Cavalleria rusticana*, however, was to remain his greatest success, and the genre it inaugurated in 1890 would be primarily linked to this composer.—MATTEO SANSONE

Cavalli, Francesco

Composer. Born Pietro Francesco Caletti, 14 February 1602, in Crema. Died 14 January 1676, in Venice. Married: Maria Sozomeno, 1630 (died 1652). Studied with his father, Giovanni Battista Caletti, who was the maestro di cappella at Crema; taken to Venice for further musical study by the Venetian nobleman and mayor of Crema, Federico Cavalli, whose name Cavalli adopted; joined the choir of San Marco, under the direction of Claudio Monteverdi, 1616; second organist at San Marco, 1639; first opera Le nozze di Teti e di Peleo, *1639;* Il Xerse *(1654) performed for the marriage of Louis XIV, 1660; principal organist at San Marco, 1655, and maestro di cappella, 1668.*

Operas *Le nozze di Teti e di Peleo,* Orazio Persiani, Venice, San Cassiano, 20 January 1639; *Gli amori d'Apollo e di Dafne,* Giovanni Francesco Busenello, Venice, San Cassiano, Carnival 1640; *La Didone,* Giovanni Francesco Busenello, Venice, San Cassiano, Carnival 1641; *L'amore innamorato,* Giovanni Battista Fusconi (after G. F. Toredan and P. Michiel), Venice, San Moisè, 1 January 1642 [lost]; *La virtù de' strali d'Amore,* Giovanni Faustini, Venice, San Cassiano, Carnival 1642; *L'egisto,* Giovanni Faustini, Venice, San Cassiano, fall 1643; *L'Ormindo,* Giovanni Faustini, Venice, San Cassiano, Carnival 1644; *La Doriclea,* Giovanni Faustini, Venice, San Cassiano, Carnival 1645; *Il Titone,* Giovanni Faustini, Venice, San Cassiano, Carnival 1645 [lost]; *Il Giasone,* Giacinto Andrea Cicognini, Venice, San Cassiano, 5

January 1649; *L'Euripo,* Giovanni Faustini, San Moisè, 1649 [lost]; *L'Orimonte,* Nicolò Minato, Venice, San Cassiano, 20 February 1650; *L'Oristeo,* Giovanni Faustini, Venice, Sant' Apollinare, Carnival 1651; *La Rosinda,* Giovanni Faustini, Venice, Sant' Apollinare, 1651; *La Calisto,* Giovanni Faustini, Venice, Sant' Apollinare, 28 November 1651; *L'Eritrea,* Giovanni Faustini, Venice, Sant' Apollinare, 17 February 1652; *La Veremonda, l'Amazzone di Aragona,* arranged by Luigi Zorzisto [G. Strozzi] (after G. A. Cicognini, *Celio*), Venice, SS. Giovanni e Paolo, 28 January 1653; *L'Orione,* Francesco Melosio, Milan, Regio, June 1653; *Il Xerse,* Nicolò Minato, Venice, SS. Giovanni e Paolo, 12 January 1654; *Il Ciro* [music by Francesco Provenzale, originally performed in Naples; Cavalli composed changes for Venice], Giulio Cesare Sorrentino, Venice, SS. Giovanni e Paolo, 30 January 1654; *La Statira, principessa di Persia,* Giovanni Francesco Busenello, Venice, SS. Giovanni e Paolo, 18 January 1655; *L'Erismena,* Aurelio Aureli, Venice Sant' Apollinare, 30 December 1655; *L'Artemisia,* Nicolò Minato, Venice, SS. Giovanni e Paolo, 10 January 1656 [lost]; *L'Antioco,* Nicolò Minato, Venice, San Cassiano, 25 January 1659 [lost]; *L'Hipermestra,* Giovanni Moniglia, 1654, Florence Teatro della Pergola, 18 June 1658; *Elena,* Giovanni Faustini and Nicolò Minato, Venice, San Cassiano, c. 1659-60; *Ercole amante,* Francesco Buti, Paris, Tuileries, 7 February 1662; *Scipione affricano,* Nicolò Minato, Venice, SS. Giovanni e Paolo, 9 February 1664; *Mutio Scevola,* Nicolò Minato, Venice, San Salvatore, 26 January 1665; *Pompeo magno,* Nicolò Minato, Venice, San Salvatore, 20 February 1666; *Eliogabalo,* anonymous libretto completed by Aurelio Aureli, composed for SS. Giovanni e Paolo, 1668; not performed; *Il Coriolano,* Cristoforo Ivanovich, Piacenza, Ducale, 28 May 1669; *Massenzio,* G. F. Busani, composed for San Salvatore, 1673; not performed [lost].

Unquestionably the most prolific Italian opera composer of the seventeenth century, Francesco Cavalli wrote more than thirty operas. Indeed, his contemporaries so admired this achievement that they attributed to him several operas by other composers. Together with his principal librettists, Giovanni Faustini, Giovanni Busenello, and Nicolò Minato, Cavalli vitalized the musical theater through a sympathetic regard for the dramatic sense of the word and by a flair for creating compelling scenic action.

In recent years Cavalli has been overshadowed as an opera composer by his older contemporary, the magnificent Claudio Monteverdi. However, it is Cavalli who can be credited with the formulation of the normal operatic divisions of scenes within acts, the interlocking of recitative with aria, the insertion of the plaintive lament, and the interjection of choral comment by large or small groups. Cavalli was also responsible for exporting this Venetian operatic style to other European cities after his works had achieved unparalleled success in public and private court theaters throughout the Italian peninsula.

During his lifetime Cavalli was respected not only as a composer of operas but of church music as well. Additionally, he was a performing artist throughout his musical career, having achieved success as a tenor singer and organist at the Church of San Marco in Venice. Eventually he earned the rank of maestro di cappella at San Marco and, as part of his duties in this capacity, furnished a considerable number of ceremonial works for liturgical use. Prominent and significant as Cavalli was as a church musician, however, his contribution to church music remained a local Venetian one.

Opera for the public arrived in Venice in 1637 with the opening of the Teatro San Cassiano. The proliferation of additional theaters throughout the city during the 1640s inaugurated a vivid and colorful world of singing actors, impresarios, and librettists. Cavalli succumbed to the enticements of this atmosphere and recognized its opportunities for the advancement of his own talent. With his 1639 debut opera, *Le nozze di Teti e di Peleo* (*The wedding of Thetis and Peleus*), at the Teatro San Cassiano, Cavalli was acclaimed by his Venetian contemporaries as a theatrical composer of exceptional imagination. Although most of his operas—and indeed all the earliest ones—were written on commission from one or another of the public Venetian opera houses, most of them received performances by traveling troupes or by resident court companies in other major Italian cities, such as Milan, Naples, Palermo, Rome, and Bologna.

The success of his earliest operas, especially *La Didone* (*Dido*), written to a libretto by Busenello, and *Egisto* (*Aegisthus*) and *Ormindo,* both written to libretti by Faustini, caused Cavalli to be praised throughout the Italian peninsula as a paragon among composers and a genius of the musical theater. International recognition followed when *Egisto* was repeated in Paris. *Giasone* (*Jason*), with its fiery libretto by G. A. Cicognini, was probably the most frequently performed opera during the seventeenth century. It became a brilliant symbol of a new demand for opera in Italy. *Xerxes* continued the exultant reception accorded the earlier works and was eventually chosen for performance at the Court of Louis XIV of France. While Cavalli was toasted in France and Austria, his success continued in Italy. One of Cavalli's latest and finest operas, *Scipione Affricano* (*Scipio Africanus*) and his ubiquitous *Giasone* were performed at the opening of the Teatro Tordinona in Rome at the behest of Queen Cristina of Sweden.

Cavalli's operas are meant to divert and entertain through music devised to complement word and story. Short vivacious arias and pungent, often colloquial, recitatives cleverly illuminate situations of comedy or mock heroism. Although the plots must certainly be fraught with political significance, the insinuations are lost to us through the passage of centuries. One general tendency can be appreciated for its immediacy: the presence of two sets of characters, one set historical, heroic or godlike, and the other group lower in social status and usually emanating from the servant class. The latter set of characters exhibits shrewdness, incisive wit, and admirable practicality, all of which engagingly illuminate and propel the action. These sprightly servants demand our sympathy through their shrewd dominance over their masters and their fates. Nobles and gods, on the other hand, act as genial commentators or revel in the agonies of love as they bemoan the paralysis brought on by their destinies.

Cavalli and his later librettists have occasionally been dismissed as superficial by a few recent critics for what they consider an unfortunate surrender to weak plots and the inferior poetic structures preferred by "public taste." One may agree that such a change in emphasis from the noble to the mundane does not represent a positive development; however, the action did become more lively, the scenic shifts more deft and ingenious, and the music more concise as it smartly underscored the characters' emotions. The result is immediate identification with plot and character on the part of Cavalli's audience—during both his time and ours. His works thus can be considered significant harbingers of the popularity accorded eighteenth-century opera buffa and dramma giocoso.—MARTHA NOVAK CLINKSCALE

Cendrillon [Cinderella]

Composer: *Jules Massenet.*

Librettist: *Henri Cain (after Perrault).*

First Performance: *Paris, Opéra-Comique, 24 May 1899.*

Roles: *Cendrillon (soprano); Pandolphe (bass); Madame de la Haltière (contralto); Noémie (soprano); Dorothée (mezzo-soprano); Fairy Godmother (soprano); Prince (tenor); Majordomo of Entertainment (baritone); Dean of Faculty (tenor); King (baritone); Prime Minister (bass); Herald (speaking); chorus (SSATTBB).*

After decades of neglect, Massenet's *Cendrillon* has enjoyed a revival since the late 1980s, to the pleasure of audiences and critics alike. *Opera* magazine called it "a lightweight piece, using the Cinderella story as a vehicle for gorgeous ceremonial, seductive melody and dazzling virtuosity, with snatches of neo-Baroque archaism and nursery rhyme to ensure a fairy-tale flavor." Critics agree that it makes a charming departure from "the usual depressing parade of Carmens and Cavallerias."

The libretto by Henri Cain remains true to the original tale by Charles Perrault with only slightly more emphasis on magic and fairies. The opera opens in the house of Madame de la Haltière—Cinderella's stepmother—as the Madame and her two daughters prepare for the Prince's ball. After the family leaves, Cendrillon, who is of course not included, sits by her hearth bemoaning her fate to the only live creatures around, the crickets, before falling asleep. She dreams of going to the ball; the fairies and sprites change her rags into a magnificent ball gown, give her jewels to wear and a carriage to ride in. She joyfully rushes away to the ball while the fairies warn her to return by midnight.

The second act presents the Prince's ball. The Prince stands miserably alone; he has not chosen his bride as he was supposed to, and is quite annoyed by the attentions of Cendrillon's two step sisters. None of the fair maidens delight him until Cendrillon arrives and he falls instantly in love with her. He courts her all evening and she tells him she is his, but she behaves mysteriously. She refuses to tell him her name, and then races out at midnight. She loses a glass slipper in her haste; he picks it up and tries to follow her, but the fairies prevent him.

The third act begins in Madame de la Haltière's house. Cendrillon, who has already returned from the ball, sits weeping. Her stepmother and stepsisters return and tell her of the scandalous arrival of a stranger, and lead her to suspect that the Prince doubts her innocence. Upset, she decides to run away to the farm where she and her father were happy before he married his second wife. The scene changes to the forest of the fairies. Cendrillon asks the fairies for help and comfort. The Prince then finds Cendrillon and declares his love for her, offering her his heart as proof of his sincerity. The fairies send them both to sleep. She awakens months later—in act IV—and is told she is recovering from a long illness after being found unconscious in the woods. In response to her questions, her father tells her that during her fever she mumbled incoherent words about love and shoes. On the street below, a herald announces that the Prince is searching for the girl who lost her slipper, and Cendrillon begins to realize that all has not been a dream. She goes to the Palace. A crowd has gathered to watch the procession of young ladies. The Prince watches anxiously as girl after girl tries on the slipper unsuccessfully. At last the fairies lead Cendrillon to him; she carries the heart he gave her in the woods, whereupon the Prince recognizes her, and everyone rejoices.

Cendrillon was born in the Cavendish hotel where Massenet and his librettist, Henri Cain, were staying for the London premier of *Le Cid*. After hours of discussion, they settled on Perrault's story as the right vehicle for their next venture. Months later when he finished the music, Massenet then worked with the director of the Opéra-Comique in Paris, Albert Carré, to fashion the costumes, scenery, and staging. The result was a glittering production perfectly suited to this romantic tale of fairies. The contemporary French critic Willy was amazed at the spectacle: "The clever composer has spared nothing to make this operetta of apparitions successful—neither the iridescent polychrome of fairie's wings, nor humming choruses, nor castanets, nor the Mustel organ, nor the abundance of fourths and sixths, nor real turtledoves, nor the pizzicati of mandolas, nor *buffo* ensembles in the Italian manner, nor the archaic prettiness of imitation minuets . . ." The rich costumes, the splendid scenery, and the elaborate stage machinery required to transform the local setting into a world of magic, all guaranteed the opera's success with the French public.

In his music, Massenet always aimed to please his public; his compositions were rarely innovative. One critic in *Opera* magazine found it "distressing to read the score through and see how few original ideas he has. . . ." Critics claim that *Cendrillon* is musically flawed: the overture is "wooden," the chorus is "dull," and the work is "overburdened with repetitive musical schemes." Yet the music is also charmingly lyrical and expressive. To give his work a slightly old-fashioned flavor, Massenet used eighteenth-century musical styles. He matched the glittering fairy world on stage with gossamer-light textures from the orchestra. Cendrillon's magical fairy-godmother sings sparkling coloratura. The beauty of the melodies serve to hide any problems the work might have, and audiences have loved the work from the beginning.

The first production of *Cendrillon* ran for sixty performances at the Opéra-Comique in Paris; when it opened in Milan shortly afterwards, it did as well. The critic Willy witnessed opening night and said: "It would have been impossible to understand if, with so many aces in his hand, M Massenet had lost the game: he has won it triumphantly. To deny it would be dishonest." As new works replace old works, *Cendrillon* was dropped from the repertoire. In the 1980s during a general Massenet revival, opera companies discovered its charm and wondered why they had waited so long to perform it. In 1988, *Opera* magazine wrote: "Massenet's *Cendrillon* is a rarity in Britain. It is difficult to understand why this delicate, late romantic opera should apparently be so unattractive to those who plan the repertory of our opera companies, particularly at Christmas time." Audiences loved the contrast this light opera made to the traditional repertoire of tragic and *verismo* works.—ROBIN ARMSTRONG

La Cenerentola, ossia La bontà in trionfo
[Cinderella, or The Triumph of Goodness]

Composer: *Gioachino Rossini.*

Librettist: *G. Ferretti (after Perrault, Cendrillon; C.-G. Etienne, and F. Fiorini).*

First Performance: *Rome, Valle, 25 January 1817.*

Roles: *Don Ramiro (tenor); Dandini (bass); Don Magnifico (bass); Clorinda (soprano); Tisbe (mezzo-soprano); Angelini, known as La Cenerentola or Cinderella (mezzo-soprano); Alidoro (bass); chorus.*

From 1815 to 1823 Rossini was composer and musical and artistic director for the Royal Theater of San Carlo in Naples, engaged largely in composing serious operas. His contract permitted him to accept commissions from other theaters, and among those compositions are found *Il barbiere di Siviglia* (Rome, 20 February 1816) and *La Cenerentola*. The eleven months between them saw the premieres of two operas in Naples (*La gazzetta,* 26 September 1816, and *Otello,* 4 December 1816). With such a schedule it is no wonder that legends arose about the speed with which Rossini composed. In the case of *La Cenerentola,* legend and fact seem to be in agreement, for the theme was chosen on 23 December 1816, and the opera had its premiere a month later.

The original commission from the Teatro Valle had specified a different libretto, but the Roman censors caused so much difficulty that Rossini requested an entirely new subject. The shortness of time prevented Ferretti from writing an entirely new text; rather he adapted two previous libretti on the same topic. Most of the familiar fairy-tale elements (wicked stepmother, fairy godmother, pumpkin and mice transformed into coach and horses) are absent from those sources and thus from Ferretti's libretto. Even the glass slipper is missing, its place being taken by a pair of matching bracelets.

Need for haste also affected the music. Rossini re-used his overture to *La gazzetta* and, as frequently happened, assigned all the *secco* recitative and three numbers (a chorus and arias for Alidoro and Clorinda) to a Roman musician, Luca Agolini. In 1821 Rossini replaced the Alidoro aria with a new one of his own composing, "Là del ciel nell' arcano profondo" (There from heaven in profound mystery).

The opera presents the fairy-tale transformation of a scullery maid into a princess. Cinderella herself sets the sentimental theme in her opening song about a king who chose as his bride a kind-hearted girl rather than a beautiful one ("Una volta c'era un Re": Once there was a King). She demonstrates her own kindness by giving some food to a beggar, who is actually prince Ramiro's tutor Alidoro in disguise. Heralds announce the prince's imminent arrival: he will choose a wife from among the women he will invite to a ball. The beggar foretells that Cinderella will be happy by the next day. Clorinda and Tisbe, Cinderella's stepsisters, awaken their father, the impoverished Don Magnifico, who envisions himself as grandfather of kings.

Ramiro, having exchanged clothing with his valet Dandini in order to travel incognito, enters the house, and he and Cinderella immediately fall in love. When Alidoro, now functioning as royal tutor, asks Don Magnifico about his daughters, the father acknowledges only two, saying the third died; the tutor invites Cinderella to the ball.

At the ball Clorinda and Tisbe scornfully mistreat Ramiro, believing him to be the squire. A veiled lady, strangely resembling Cinderella, arrives, and Ramiro asks her to be his wife. She tells him he must seek for the mate of the bracelet she gives him; if he still loves her when he finds it, she will marry him. When Ramiro goes in search of the mysterious lady his carriage overturns in front of Magnifico's house—a happy accident arranged by Alidoro. Cinderella and Ramiro recognize each other. At the wedding banquet the father and stepsisters are forgiven so that all may live happily ever after.

Rossini uses a variety of musical styles to develop the sentimental love story and its various comic interludes. Cinderella's arias range from the folk-like opening song to the elaborate *rondò finale,* "Nacqui all'affano e al pianto" (I was born to grief and weeping). Equally ornate is Ramiro's second-act aria ("Sì, ritrovarla, io giuro": Yes, I will find her, I swear it), a piece that would not be out of place in an *opera seria.* For Don Magnifico, Rossini writes a standard comic patter song; however, Dandini, who spends much of the opera pretending to be the prince, has a grand mock-heroic cavatina, *buffo* declamation alternating with coloratura. In his duet with Dandini, Magnifico babbles in confusion; the following sextet, "Questo è un nodo avviluppato" (This is a tangled knot), is among the most wonderful of Rossini's ensembles.—PATRICIA BRAUNER

Chaliapin, Feodor Ivanovich

Bass. Born 13 February 1873, near Kazan. Died 12 April 1938, in Paris. Studied in Tbilisi (1892-93) with D.A. Usatov; joined chorus of traveling opera at age fourteen; debut as Stolnik in Halka, *Ufa, 1890; belonged to Imperial Opera at Mariinsky Theater, St Petersburg; first major successes with Mamontov's company in Moscow, 1896-99, where he sang Boris, Dosifey in* Khovanshchina; *Ivan the Terrible in* Maid of Pskov, *created Salieri in* Mozart and Salieri; *associated with Bolshoi, 1899-1914; at Teatro alla Scala in Boito's* Mefistofele, *1901; created Massenet's Don Quichotte, 1910; debut at Metropolitan Opera as Mefistofele, 1907; director of Mariinsky Theater from 1918 to 1921; sang every season at the Metropolitan Opera 1921-29; appeared in films* Tsar Ivan the Terrible *(1915) and* Don Quixote *(1933).*

Chaliapin was one of the greatest singers, not only of Russia but of all time. Possessing a deep lyrical bass voice of very wide range, he stressed vocal declamation, being much aware of the relationship between words and music. Contemporary accounts speak of the "exceptional softness and beauty of timbre," combining "sincerity with depth and power." He was able to convey extremes of emotion, being capable of warm tenderness to lofty tragedy and biting sarcasm. In preparing himself for a role, Chaliapin would go to immense trouble, not only reading historical literature about the character in question but visiting museums and art galleries. Thus, when undertaking the part of Ivan the Terrible in Rimsky-Korsakov's *The Maid of Pskov,* he studied the various portraits of the tsar by Shvarts (Schwarz), Repin, Vasnetsov and the sculptor Antokol'sky. Before applying his make-up, he would make sketches of the role in question, paying special attention to costume and other details. In fact, his ability to think himself psychologically into a particular part was such that it influenced the work of the great Russian producer, Konstantin Stanislavsky, who based his own theories of acting and performances on Chaliapin's stage roles. Nijinsky, too, is said to have watched Chaliapin's performances from the wings. Chaliapin himself was a true disciple of the Russian realist school, manifest in Russian literature by such writers as Gogol, Dostoevsky, and Gorky (with whom he had a close friendship), painters such as Repin, and, of course, with composers such as Borodin and Musorgsky; indeed, his performance of Tsar Boris in Musorgsky's *Boris Godunov,* still remains unsurpassed to this day. But Chaliapin was never content simply to rest on his laurels and repeat himself *ad*

Chaliapin as Don Quixote (Culver Pictures)

nauseam. Striving incessantly for self-improvement, he often sought to interpret standard roles in new ways. That this was the case is evidenced by the many surviving accounts in a multitude of foreign languages describing his performances as Don Basilio in Rossini's *Il barbiere di Siviglia,* Leporello in Mozart's *Don Giovanni,* Mephistopheles in both Gounod's *Faust* and Boito's *Mefistofele,* Oroveso in Bellini's *Norma* and a host of other characters, whilst his renderings of great Russian parts such as Galitsky, Igor and Konchak in Borodin's *Prince Igor,* Farlaf in Glinka's *Ruslan and Lyudmila,* Boris and Pimen in Musorgsky's *Boris Godunov* and Dosifey in the same composer's *Khovanshchina* have all served as paradigms for subsequent performers. Whether tsar or peasant, passionate lover or mad miller, all were infused with living power so that in Chaliapin's hands they were not motley stage figures but vital beings of flesh and blood. His interpretation of Salieri in Rimsky-Korsakov's much neglected *Mozart and Salieri* was said to be electrifying. No doubt Chaliapin was helped in all this by his own fine profile and excellent physique, which served him well up to his final years, as may be heard from recordings made as late as 1931; even though the voice is no longer in its prime, his magnetic personality and passionate intensity are still evident. Chaliapin was also an excellent chamber singer and had a repertoire of some 400 pieces. Critics praised in particular his performance of Schubert's "Der Doppelgänger," Schumann's "Die beiden Grenadiere," selected songs of Glinka, Dargomyzhsky, Rimsky-Korsakov and Rubinstein, his singing of Musorgsky's "Song of the Flea" becoming world famous. In all his work his excellent sense of phrasing, subtle nuances and awareness of the meaning of the text enabled him, as one writer has put it, "to imbue each musical phrase with imagery and profound psychological meaning." His performances of Russian folk-songs, especially "The Volga Boatmen" and "Dubinushka," which he sang on 26 November 1905 in the Bol'shoy Theater at the height of the revolutionary uprising, have never been forgotten. Finally it should be mentioned that he was both a stage director, giving Massenet's *Don Quixote* (1910), *Khovanshchina* (1911), and Verdi's *Don Carlos* (1917), and a screen actor appearing in the films *Tsar Ivan Vasil'evich Grozny* (based on Rimsky-Korsakov's *The Maid of Pskov*) in 1915 and *Don Quixote,* with music by Ibert, in 1933. His surviving drawings, paintings, sketches and sculptures reveal still further facets of his remarkable personality as well as his autobiography, translated as *Man and Mask.*—GERALD SEAMAN

Charpentier, Marc-Antoine

Composer. Born c. 1634 in Paris. Died 24 February 1704, in Paris. Studied music with Carissimi in Italy; collaborated with Molière in the production of the comédie-ballets Le mariage forcé *(1672) and* Le malade imaginaire *(1673) at the Théâtre-Français, and stayed with the company after Molière's death (1673) until 1685; appointed maître de chapelle to the Dauphin, c. 1679; granted a pension by Louis XIV, 1683; maître de musique and music teacher to Mlle. de Guise, c. 1670s-1688; intendant to the Duke of Orléans; maître de musique of the Jesuit Maison-professe, 1684; maître de musique of Sainte-Chapelle, 1698.*

Operas/Pastorales Operas—*Les amours d'Acis et de Galatée,* Châlet M. de Rians, Paris, January 1678; *Endimion,* Paris, 22 July 1681; *La descente d'Orphée aux enfers.* c. 1685; *Les arts florissants.* 1685-86; *Celse Martyr,* Collège Louis—le—Grand, 1687 [lost]; *David et Jonathan.* Collège Louis—le—Grand, 1688; *Médée* (tragédie lyrique), Thomas Corneille, Paris, 4 December 1693; *Philomèle* (with the

Duke of Chartres), Paris, Palais-Royal. Pastorales—*Le sort d'Andromède*, c. 1670; *Petite pastorale*, c. 1675 [incomplete]; *Le retour de printemps* [lost]; *Le jugement de Pan* [lost]; *La fête de Rueil*, 1685; *Actéon*, 1683-85; revised as *Actéon changé en biche*, 1683-85; *Les plaisirs de Versailles*, c. 1680; *Sur la naissance de notre Seigneur Jésus Christ*, 1683-85; *Pastorale sur la naissance de notre Seigneur Jésus Christ*, 1683-85; *La couronne de fleurs*, 1685; *Dialogue de Vénus et Médor*.

It is an odd twist of fate that French Baroque opera has been more or less defined by an Italian, Jean Baptiste Lully, while the Italian Baroque style was represented by a Frenchman, Marc-Antoine Charpentier. Charpentier was a respected composer in seventeenth-century France, but it was Lully who became the major court composer—a virtual musical monarch—in the court of King Louis XIV. He was *the* dominant French opera composer. Further, Lully obtained royal decrees in 1671, 1672, and again in 1685, giving him a musical monopoly which made it possible for him to completely dominate French theater and restrict any competition. Marc-Antoine Charpentier's operatic output was therefore somewhat limited; the majority of his compositions, including dramatic ones, are sacred works, for which he was highly esteemed.

A prolific composer of over 550 works, Marc-Antoine Charpentier was rediscovered only in the twentieth-century (musicologist H. Wiley Hitchcock is particularly known for his work on the composer). There is a remarkable lack of primary information about Charpentier. Much of the biographical material about him is based on secondary sources and comparative speculation. The date of his birth, for example, has been estimated to be as early as 1634 and as late as 1645 (1643 is now considered to be the probable year). We know nothing of his appearance or personality. Only the details of the latter part of his life can be determined with certainty.

As a young man, Charpentier spent several years studying in Italy, notably with Carissimi. His work as a composer for drama began in collaboration with the playwright Molière and his company, the Comédiens du Roi, in 1672 (*La Comtesse d'Escarbagnas, Le mariage forcé*). Though Molière died in 1673 after the fourth performance of *Le malade imaginaire,* Charpentier continued to compose for what in 1680 became the Comédie-Française until the mid 1680s. Thomas Corneille, brother of famous dramatist Pierre Corneille, and Donneau de Vise, editor of the *Mercure galant* newspaper, became Charpentier's two principal dramatic collaborators. A particularly notable production which required stage machines was Thomas Corneille's elaborate play, *Circé* (1675).

During the time he provided music for the Comédie-Française, Charpentier also worked for Marie de Lorraine, the Duchess de Guise. She employed a number of musicians in what became a remarkable musical establishment. For her, Charpentier composed at least eight secular dramatic works, including *La descente d'Orphée aux enfers.*

From 1679 or 1680 until about 1683, Charpentier served as musical director for the chapel of the Grand Dauphin. The Dauphin was probably the source of a commission to write music for two stage works, *Les plaisirs de Versailles* and *La fête de Rueil.* In 1683 Charpentier was a candidate for a post of *sous-maître* of the royal chapel, but could not complete the competition due to illness.

From about 1684 to 1698, Charpentier was employed by the Jesuits at the Collège Louis-le-Grand and at the Église St. Louis (called "l'église de l'opéra" by his contemporary, Le Cerf de la Vieville). For the Jesuits and their colleges Charpentier wrote sacred French opera as well as

Latin church music. The opera *David et Jonathan* (1688), perhaps the most important of these works, was his first dramatic work to be written without the limitations of Lully's monopoly.

The death of Lully in 1687 opened up the "official" Parisian musical scene to other composers. In 1693, Charpentier's most famous dramatic work, the opera *Médée* (libretto by Thomas Corneille), was commissioned and produced by the Académie Royale de Musique. In 1694, the publisher Ballard printed the score to *Médée,* the only major publication of Charpentier's music during his lifetime.

In the early 1690s, Charpentier was employed to teach music to Philippe, Duke of Chartres, a nephew of the King who in 1701 became the Duke of Orléans and from 1715-1723 was Regent of France. For him, Charpentier wrote treatises on composition and accompaniment. Teacher and student collaborated on an opera, *Philomèle* (now lost), which was performed three times in the royal palace.

Of Charpentier's over 200 motets, thirty-five are classified by H. Wiley Hitchcock as dramatic motets. Sometimes referred to as oratorios because of their specific characters and structure, these diverse works were designated by the composer's terms *motet, historia, canticum,* and *dialogus,* and were designed for use in church services. Topics include biblical stories (Abraham and Isaac, Joshua, Esther, the prodigal son, etc.), church history (such as the 1576 plague of Milan), and several Christmas works. From these compositions comes one of Charpentier's last works, *Judicium Salomonis* (*The Judgment of Solomon*), written in 1702 for the "Messe Rouge" "Red Mass," because of the red robes of the officials) at the opening of the French Parliament.—DONALD OGLESBY

Cherubini, Luigi

Composer. Born 8? September 1760, in Florence. Died 15 March 1842, in Paris. Married: Anne Cécile Tourette, 12 April 1794 (one son, two daughters). Studied music with his father, then with Bartolomeo Felici and his son Alessandro, Pietro Bizzarri, and Giuseppe Castrucci; sent to Bologna and Milan by Duke Leopold of Tuscany to study with Sarti, 1778-81; in London, 1784-86; composed sacred music and operas, 1778-88; settled in Paris, 1787; conductor and composer at the Théâtre de Monsieur (later the Théâtre de la rue Feydeau), 1789-1800; appointed inspector at the Paris Conservatory, 1 November 1794; inspector and professor at the Paris Conservatory, 1794-1822; in Vienna, 1805-06; in London, 1815; composed French operas, 1788-1814; surintendant of the royal chapel, 1814-30; member of the Institut de France, 1814; Chevalier of the Légion d'honneur, 1814; director of the Paris Conservatory, 1822-42; Commander of the Légion d'honneur, 1841. Cherubini's students include Auber and Halévy.

Operas *Amore artigiano* (intermezzo), Fiesole, San Domenico, 22 October 1773 [lost]; *Il Giocatore* (intermezzo), Florence, 1775; Untitled intermezzo, Florence, Serviti, 16 February 1778; *Il Quinto Fabio,* Apostolo Zeno, Alessandria, Paglia, fall 1779 [lost]: revised, Rome, Torre Argentina, January 1783; Untitled opera, 1781 [unfinished]; *Armida abbandonata,* Jacopo Durandi, Florence, Teatro della Pergola, 25 January 1782; *Adriano in Siria,* Metastasio, Livorno, Teatro degli Armeni, 16 April 1782; *Mesenzio, re d'Etruria,* Ferdinando Casori, Florence, Teatro della Pergola, 6 September 1782; *Lo sposo* *di tre e marito di nessuna,* Filippo Livigni, Venice, San Samuele, November 1783; *Olimpiade,* Metastasio, 1783; *L'Alessandro nell'Indie,* Metastasio, Mantua Nuovo Regio Ducale, April 1784; *L'Idalide,* Ferdinando Moretti, Florence, Teatro della Pergola, 26 December 1784; *Demetrio* (pasticcio) Mestastasio, London, King's Theatre, 1785 [four pieces by Cherubini]; *La finta principessa,* Filippo Livigni, London, King's Theatre, 2 April 1785; *Il Giulio Sabino,* London, King's Theatre, 30 March 1786; *Ifigenia in Aulide,* Ferdinando Moretti, Turin, Regio, 12 January 1788; *Démophon,* Jean François Marmontel (after Metastasio, *Demofoonte*), Paris, Opéra, 5 December 1788; *Marguerite d'Anjou,* 1790 [unfinished]; *Lodoïska,* Claude-François Fillette-Loraux (after Jean-Baptiste Louvet de Couvrai, *Les amours du chevalier de Faublas*), Paris, Théâtre Feydeau, 18 July 1791; *Koukourgi,* Anne-Honore-Joseph Duveyrier [=Melesville], Paris, written for the Théâtre Feydeau, 1793 [not performed; part of the music used for *Ali Baba*]; *Sélico,* 1794 [fragments only]; *Le congrès des rois* (pasticcio), A.F. Eve Desmaillot, Paris, Favart, 26 February 1794 [lost]; *Eliza, ou Le voyage aux glaciers du Mont St-Bernard,* Jacques-Antoine Saint-Cyr, Paris, Théâtre Feydeau, 13 December 1794; *Médée,* François Benoît Hoffman, Paris, Théâtre Feydeau, 13 March 1797; *L'hôtellerie portugaise,* Étienne Saint-Aigan, Paris, Théâtre Feydeau, 25 July 1798; *La punition,* Jean-Louis Brousse Desfaucherets, Paris, Théâtre Feydeau, 23 February 1799; *La prisonnière* (with Boieldieu), Victor Joseph Étienne de Jouy, Charles de Longchamps, and Claude Godard d'Aucour de Saint-Just, Paris, Théâtre Montansier, 12 September 1799; *Les deux journées,* Jean-Nicolas Bouilly, Paris, Théâtre Feydeau, 16 January 1800; *Epicure* (with Méhul), Charles-Albert Demoustier, Paris, Théâtre Favart, 14 March 1800; Untitled opéra-comique, 1802 [unfinished]; *Anacréon, ou L'amour fugitif* (opéra-ballet), R. Mendouze, Paris, Opéra, 4 October 1803; *Les arrêts,* 1804 [unfinished]; *Faniska,* Josef von Sonnleithner (after René-Charles Guilbert de Pixérécourt, *Les mines de Pologne*), Vienna, Kärntnertor Theater, 25 February 1806; *La petite guerre,* 1807 [unfinished]; *Pimmalione,* Stefano Vestris (after Antonio Simone Sografi's Italian version of Rousseau's *Pigmalion*), Paris, Tuileries, 30 November 1809; *La crescendo,* Charles Augustin de Bassompierre [=Sewrin], Paris, Opéra-comique, 1 September 1810; *Les abencérages, ou L'étendard de Grenade,* Victor Joseph Étienne de Jouy (after Jean Pierre Claris de Florian, *Gozalve de Cordoue*), Paris, Opéra, 6 April 1813; *Bayard à Mézières* (with Boieldieu, Catel, and Isouard), E. Dupaty and R.A. de Chazet, Paris, Opéra-comique, 12 February 1814 [lost]; *Blanche de Provence, ou La cour des fées* (with Berton, Boieldieu, Kreutzer, and Paër), M.E.G.M. Théaulon and de Rancé, Paris, Tuileries, 1 May 1821; *La marquise de Brinvilliers* (with Auber, Batton, Berton, Blangini, Boieldieu, Carafa, Hérold, and Paër), Eugène Scribe and François Henri Joseph Blaze [=Castil-Blaze], Paris, Ventadour, 31 October 1831 [lost]; *Ali Baba, ou Les quarante voleurs,* Eugène Scribe and Anne-Honoré Joseph Duveyrier [=Melesville], Paris, Opéra, 22 July 1833 [part of music from *Koukourgi*].

In an era when the freer, more liberalizing forms of *opera buffa* and *opéra comique* were coming to the fore, Cherubini seemed to be more interested in *opera seria* and *tragédie lyrique.* It is difficult to assess his contribution to *opera seria* because of the present inaccessibility of the original scores. (Although originally housed in the Deutsches Staatsbibliothek in Berlin, the manuscripts of Cherubini's early works were among those sent to Poland during World War II and are now kept in the Jagellonian Library, Cracow.) A brief look at what is available and a referral to contemporary criticism does indicate that Cherubini belonged to the "reform" school.

Cherubini's first interest in opera was probably due to his father, Bartolomeo. As he was *maestro al cembalo* at the Teatro della Pergola in Florence, his son must have been a frequent spectator there. Luigi's choice of Giuseppe Sarti (1729-1802), a reknowned composer of *opera*

OPERA

seria, as his teacher would indicate that, at the age of eighteen, he already had a preference for dramatic music. He frequently contributed arias to Sarti's operas as part of the learning process, so that, by the time of the appearance of his first *opera seria, Il Quinto Fabio,* in 1779, he was already showing a predilection for the new school of Italian dramatic music as espoused by Niccolo Jommelli (1714-74), Tommaso Michele Francesco Saverio Traette (1727-79), Antonio Maria Gaspero Gioacchino Sacchini (1730-86), as well as his teacher Sarti. In this first opera, Cherubini showed signs of uncommon use of orchestral color through imaginative instrumentation. The score of *Armida abbandonata* (1782) reveals the use of the orchestra to heighten dramatic moments, even to the detriment of the vocal line. In *Adriano in Siria* (1782), the instrumentation is somewhat unusual in its use of flutes, oboes, bassoons, French horns, trumpets, and kettle drums in addition to the strings.

Luigi Cherubini, engraving after a portrait by Ingres

By 1783, Cherubini was already finding the *opera seria* form restrictive in its limitations. In that year, he wrote his first *opera buffa, Lo sposso di tre e marito di nessuna.* He returned to *opera seria* with *L'Alessandro nell'Indie* (1784), where he first used the "recall-motive." There are several places in the text where the poet has characters refer to previous events or feelings, and Cherubini uses musical recall to emphasize these moments. Further, the instrumentation continues to be interesting: flutes, oboes, English horn, bassoons, trumpets, and four French horns. Cherubini also made use of the recapitulation aria, but not necessarily with a tonal progression of tonic-dominant-tonic.

By now, Cherubini was feeling stifled in his native Italy and decided to travel. He went first to London, where the *opera buffa La finta principessa* and the *opera seria Il Giulio Sabino* (1786) were presented. The latter was a fiasco. The critics blamed the disaster on the singers' inadequacy, but the fault was also Cherubini's, as he was still experimenting with *opera seria* form and was not yet sure of the direction he wished to take. During the summer of 1785, he visited Paris where he met his compatriot Jean-Baptiste Viotti (1755-1824). Except for a visit to London at the end of 1785 and one to Italy for the performance of his next operatic creation, he spent the rest of his life in France.

The culmination of Cherubini's *opera seria* output was *Ifigenia in Aulide* (1788). The single most important element which differentiated this work from previous ones was Cherubini's use of music to delineate character. Perhaps it was his thorough grounding in counterpoint which suggested to him this musical interpretation of character; perhaps it was a personal trait which allowed him to empathize more fully with a libretto that demanded development of the text through music. Whatever the reason, Cherubini's most successful operas were always those requiring the revelation of character traits through dramatic, out-of-the-ordinary situations. It must be assumed that *opera seria* was more suited to the demands of Cherubini's musical genius. It appears also that he preferred the Greek and Roman plots typical of *opera seria,* or perhaps historical subjects in general, to more mundane situations.

When Cherubini arrived in France, he was offered the music directorship of the Théâtre de "Monsieur," which opened its doors to the public in the Tuileries on 26 January 1789. He jumped at the chance, and for good reason. In 1786, he had accepted a commission to write an opera for the Académie royale de musique on a libretto by Jean François Marmontel (1723-99). Despite lack of experience in dealing with the difficult French metrical texts, he made his debut in Paris with *Démophon* on 5 December 1788. The results were mediocre. The critics complained that Cherubini did not yet possess the necessary technique to set a French text properly. His directorship would provide him with a job while he familiarized himself with the French language and acquired a name amongst French music lovers. His post obliged him to add arias and ensembles in a musical style currently in vogue to the mediocre and sometimes outdated Italian operas presented by the company.

In 1792, Cherubini signed a new contract with the Théâtre de la rue Feydeau (the reincarnation of the earlier Théâtre de "Monsieur") which paid him 6,000 livres a year for the continuation of his duties, plus 2,000 for the first two completely new operas written by him each year and another 4,000 for each additional opera. The result was a ten-year period of creativity which produced the following works: *Lodoïska* (1791), *Eliza ou Le voyage aux glaciers du Mont St-Bernard* (1794), *Médée* (1797), *L'hôtellerie portugaise* (1798), *La punition* (1799) and *Les deux journées* (1800). Work was also begun on *Koukourgi* (1793) but was never finished. The music was later reused and completed as *Ali-Baba ou les quarante voleurs*. In essence, the Théâtre de la rue Feydeau gave Cherubini financial stability and a stage which he used to experiment with the *opéra comique* form.

The first of this series of *opéras comiques, Lodoïska,* was also the first of a shorter series of "rescue" operas which included *Eliza,* and *Les deux journées*. Even *Médée* fits into this category, in which the action culminates with the rescue of one or more of the main protagonists from a sticky situation. Although the libretto of *Lodoïska* was not a masterpiece, the music was beautiful and effective and the stage devices were sensational. Its success was assured because of its flowing vocal lines, its unusually new and expanded orchestral elements, and its romantic plot which seized the imagination of revolutionary Paris by portraying the righteousness of heroism, liberty, and fraternity as opposed to the evilness of tyranny. With this opera, Cherubini embarked on a course of development of the *opéra comique* form which would lead to the eradication of almost all differences between it and *opera seria,* except for the spoken dialogue. The simple strophic ariettes become fully developed emotive arias, the ensemble becomes the norm rather than the exception, and the orchestration acquires symphonic proportions.

This trend continued with *Eliza,* which drew large audiences to view the onstage depiction of an avalanche. The musical numbers are no longer pauses in the plot allowing a character to sing quickly a couple of stanzas expressing his sentiments; they are scintillating with action and display a continuity which sometimes makes the spoken dialogue seem intrusive. This piece is considered by some to be the most consciously romantic of Cherubini's operas. *Médée* was the culmination of this style of Cherubini's dramatic development. In spite of the spoken dialogue, this is musically closer to a true *tragédie lyrique* than most of the works presented at the Académie.

With *Les deux journées,* Cherubini returned to a happier, if less interesting, compositional style, and he experienced a success which he never repeated in his lifetime. This was partly due to the libretto, judged by Beethoven and Goethe to be one of the finest of the period. Beethoven considered Cherubini the greatest living operatic composer based on his knowledge of this opera, and Mendelssohn remarked that the first three bars of the overture were worth more than all of the Berlin opera's repertory. Musically, it was successful because Cherubini conformed to the French concept of the *opéra comique*—short musical numbers with an emphasis on spoken dialogue and ensemble. Only two of the fifteen musical items are arias. Although this was Cherubini's most popular dramatic work, it contains none of the innovations characterizing his other efforts in this genre.

With his move to France, the logical continuation of Cherubini's developments of *opera seria* would be in the exploitation of *tragédie lyrique*. However, he was never able to break into the clique which ruled the tastes of the Académie royale (or impériale) de musique and his three works in the form—*Anacréon* (1803), *Les abencérages ou L'étendard de Grenade* (1813) and *Ali-Baba ou Les quarante voleurs* (1833)—were never successful. As well, Cherubini was unable to overcome two problems of the *tragédie lyrique* form—the use of recitative and the need for ballet, even if it did not fit into the plot. Consequently, all his most important contributions to nineteenth-century opera took place within the mold of *opéra comique*. In fact, almost half a century before Wagner, Cherubini evolved an operatic style which was criticized for being unsingable, unmelodic, for putting emphasis on the orchestra and making it play loudly, and for creating long musical numbers which slowed down the action even if they did underline the emotions and actions of the protagonists.

Although Cherubini stopped composing for the stage almost entirely after 1813, his dramatic sense was evident in other musical forms. His Symphonie (1815), composed for the Royal Philharmonic Society of London, has been described as a play without words. His numerous settings of the Mass continued the operatic tradition begun by Mozart. And his two *Messe des morts* established a new style for this form which culminated in Verdi's *Requiem*. The intrigues of the world of French opera defeated Cherubini but did not stifle the dramatic qualities of his creativity.

Many books and musical dictionaries have mistakenly hypothesized that Cherubini had no effect on future schools of composition. The names of his pupils, friends, and visitors read like a musical Who's Who of the nineteenth century: Bellini, Berlioz, Chopin, Donizetti, Fétis, Halévy, Hérold, Liszt, Mendelssohn, Meyerbeer, Rossini, Schumann, just to mention the most important and obvious. But his influence extended beyond the circle of his personal acquaintances. His developments in *opéra comique* were continued by Halévy (1799-1862) and Hérold (1791-1833) and culminated in Bizet's *Carmen;* in Germany, Carl Maria von Weber (1786-1826) examined every work of Cherubini that he could find, and the new style of *Singspiel* owed its origin in some part to the French master. In the *tragédie lyrique,* Spontini copied most of what his colleague had done, and thus, starting with Rossini and Meyerbeer, a direct link with Romantic Grand Opera, which pervaded the French stage during the mid-nineteenth century, was established. Later musicians who studied Cherubini included Brahms, Bruckner, Bülow and Wagner. German Music Drama, as epitomized by the works of Wagner, can also trace its existence directly to Cherubini.

There are good reasons why Cherubini's works disappeared from European stages after his death, despite their affinity with the romantic era: his *opéras comiques* were soon surpassed by those of his pupils and admirers, and his *tragédies lyriques* were too long and boring to excite much interest, especially after the subsequent reforms of Rossini and Meyerbeer. More importantly, he was unlucky in his librettists, and the music of the majority of his lyric works outdistances their texts. However, it is impossible to study operatic development in the

157

nineteenth century without acknowledging Cherubini's place. A judicious editing of many of his stage compositions would render them agreeable to contemporary ears, thus assuring Cherubini's rightful survival as one of the principal architects of Romantic opera.—STEPHEN C. WILLIS

Christoff, Boris

Bass. Born 18 May 1914, in Plovdiv, Bulgaria. Died 28 June 1993 from complications from a stroke. Received a law degree from the University of Sofia, then sang with Gussla Choir and Sofia Cathedral Choir where King Boris heard him and provided him with funds to study with Riccardo Stracciari in Rome; later studied with Muratti in Salzburg, 1945; opera debut as Colline in Reggio Calabria, 1946, then sang in Rome at the Teatro alla Scala as Pimen, 1947; U.S. debut in San Francisco as Boris, 1956; Chicago, 1957-63.

In a career that lasted from 1946 until well into the 1980s, Bulgarian bass Boris Christoff sang with most of the major opera companies of the world, with the notable exception of the Metropolitan Opera. His earliest successes occurred in Italy; his debut was as Colline in Puccini's *La bohème* in Reggio Calabria, but his first major roles were as Pimen in Musorgsky's *Boris Godunov* in Rome in 1946 and at the Teatro alla Scala in 1947, and as King Marke at the Teatro la Fenice in Venice in late 1947. He was scheduled to sing King Philip II in Verdi's *Don Carlos* in the inaugural production of Rudolf Bing's regime at the Metropolitan Opera (1950). Christoff was prevented from entering the country, however, because he had a Bulgarian passport (which, under the terms of the McCarthy period's McCarran Act, was an insurmountable problem), and he never appeared there.

Christoff did, however, sing King Philip at Covent Garden in 1958, and it proved to be one of his most memorable portrayals. His Covent Garden career had begun in 1949, and its problematic beginnings evaporated in the light of his subsequent triumphs there. His first performance, as Boris Godunov, was preceded by three conflicts that threatened its cancelation: Christoff insisted on singing the role in Russian (in the event, the rest of the cast sang in English, even though mixed-language performances were contrary to policy); Christoff knew, and insisted on following, the Rimsky-Korsakov version of the score (he was allowed to employ this version while the rest of the cast followed the original Musorgsky); and he disagreed with director Peter Brook—not his only disagreement with a director—over several aspects of the staging, including a giant clock that he feared would dwarf his own efforts (general manager David Webster's intervention was needed to appease Christoff). Christoff's career came to a temporary halt in 1964 when it was discovered that he was suffering from a brain tumor, but Covent Garden was the first to rehire him, in 1965, for another Boris.

Musorgsky's tsar also served as the role of Christoff's San Francisco debut in 1956. He made frequent appearances in Chicago between 1957 and 1963, including performances of Verdi's *Don Carlos* in 1957 and Verdi's *Nabucco* in 1963. His New York debut came in a concert version of Rossini's *Mosè*.

Many considered Christoff to be Chaliapin's successor. Like that of his great Slavic predecessor, Christoff's singing was marked by an authority and an intensity, as well as substantial theatricality. It was a well-schooled, sonorous voice of substantial size, powerful and imposing, with a true legato, but it was not a richly honeyed, Italianate sound (the voice was a bit lacking in the warmth characteristic of that style). Despite this, he became a notable interpreter of Verdi's bass roles (he was more successful in this repertoire than Chaliapin had been), including, in addition to Zaccaria and King Philip, Ramfis in Verdi's *Aida,* Fiesco in *Simon Boccanegra,* and Procida in *Les vêpres siciliennes.* Other roles include Agamemnon in Gluck's *Ifigenia in Aulide,* Oroveso in Bellini's *Norma,* Count Rodolfo in Bellini's *La sonnambula,* Seneca in Monteverdi's *L'incoronazione di Poppea,* Méphistophélès in Gounod's *Faust,* Rocco in Beethoven's *Fidelio,* Gurnemanz in Wagner's *Parsifal,* Handel's Giulio Cesare, Massenet's Don Quichotte, and Boito's Mefistofele.

Voluminous but not especially large, Christoff's voice had the distinctive character frequently associated with Slavic singers. It possessed an inherent dignity and nobility that were significant assets in his portrayals of kings and tsars. To this was added an ability simultaneously to convey menace and evoke sympathy. Besides his apparent technical command and his exemplary breath control, Christoff had substantial stage presence, was capable of realistic acting, and demonstrated an admirable ability to project the text. Much of his acting was distinguished by its naturalness, its authority, and especially by its introspective quality. Only occasionally, as in his traversal of the role of Méphistophélès in *Faust,* was he guilty of exaggeration, even overacting.

Christoff's impersonation of King Philip II was perhaps his greatest role. It offered him the opportunity to demonstrate his ability to portray a multidimensional character, distinguishing between the public and private sides of the man. It also exhibited, in the great monologue "Ella giammai m'amo . . . Dormirò sol nel manto mio regal," his ability to produce a sustained pianissimo line, conveying the introspection and revealing the most personal thoughts of the character. It showed Christoff's ability to convey the sadness and resignation of the character as well as his essential nobility in a detailed, well-rounded portrait of the king.

In addition to numerous recordings of individual arias, Christoff participated in several recordings of complete operas. These include Fiesco (under Santini, 1957); Philip II (under Santini, 1954, 1961); Ramfis (under Perlea, 1955); Méphistophélès (under Cluytens, 1954, 1958); Pimen, Varlaam, and Boris in the same recording (1952, under Dobrowen; 1962, under Cluytens); and Galitzky and Konchak in Borodin's *Prince Igor* (1967, under Semkow).—MICHAEL SIMS

Le Cid

Composer: *Jules Massenet.*
Librettists: *Adolphe Philippe d'Ennery, Louis Gallet, and Edouard Blau (after Corneille).*
First Performance: *Paris, Opéra, 30 November 1885.*
Roles: *Chimène (soprano); The Infanta (soprano); Don Rodrigue (tenor); Don Diègue (bass); Don Fernand, The King (baritone); Don Gomès (bass); Saint Jacques (baritone); The Moorish Ambassador (bass); Don Arias (tenor); Don Alonzo (bass); chorus.*

Le Cid followed immediately after Massenet's great triumph with *Manon,* and, for a time, rivaled it in popularity, although by the early years of this century it had begun to flag and eventually disappeared from the repertory. This is probably because, despite its contemporary success, it is something of a hybrid and suffers from an inadequate libretto. There have been at least twenty-six operas based on the Spanish national hero, many of them Italian, including one by Paisiello whose attempt on the Cid was to be outdistanced by Massenet.

The libretto for *Le Cid* is based on a French source, the great classical tragedy by Corneille. The three librettists interpolated many of the poet's original lines into their own dialogue. Additionally, Massenet insisted on putting in not only an extra scene inspired by his reading of the work but also a fifth act of another tragedy which he rescued from the bottom of a drawer somewhere. The result is a plot of clumsy dimensions and clumsier language, where Corneille's stolen gems shine all the more incongruously for being surrounded with paste of the most derisory nature.

Massenet was probably not the ideal choice for composing an opera on this subject. Much of the opera's initial success was due to the brilliance of the stars Jean and Edouard De Reszke, the two brothers who had served Massenet well before, and of Fidès Devriès as the heroine Chimène. Quite apart, however, from the shortcomings of the libretto, the music is rarely at one with the setting and the characterization. Heroic attitudes and Castilian haughtiness were strangers to Massenet's music. He lacked ability to convey the fierce and passionate emotions which *Le Cid* demanded, and his insight into Spanish music was by no means as profound as Debussy's or even Bizet's. All that remains today of *Le Cid* is the showpiece aria "Pleurez, pleurez mes yeux," sung by Chimène. Yet even this, effective as it is when considered in isolation, is not wholly appropriate, for, while it is neatly written in the style of *Manon,* it strikes a false note in a score which ought to be striving for something else.

One other legacy of *Le Cid* may be mentioned, and that is the suite of ballet music which was drawn from it and which may still be heard today. It is an appealing example of Massenet's gift for light music and for the picturesque. He heard the tune of the *Castillane* while traveling in Spain as a young student, and, faithful to his thrifty habit, carefully noted it down. Guitars and flutes had played the theme to accompany a wedding celebration, and he had already used it, though less adroitly, in his second opera, *Don César de Bazan*. If, on the whole, *Le Cid* is not an example of Massenet at his best, at least one fine aria and a charming ballet suite survive.—JAMES HARDING

Cigna, Gina

Soprano. Born 6 March 1900, in Angères. Studied at the Paris Conservatory; debut at Teatro alla Scala, 1927; sang there every season from 1929 to 1943; Metropolitan Opera debut as Aida, 1937; returned to Milan as a voice teacher; abandoned her singing career following an automobile accident in 1947; taught at the Royal Conservatory in Toronto, 1953-57.

Gina Cigna reigned the opera stages of Italy and beyond during the 1930s. Between her debut at La Scala in 1927 and an automobile accident that ended her stage career in 1947, she specialized in heavy, dramatic Italian heroines, particularly those of Verdi and Puccini, Mascagni and Zandonai, Giordano and Ponchielli.

Her debut as Aida at New York's Metropolitan Opera was broadcast in February 1937. The performance was representative of Gina Cigna at midpoint in her career. We hear from her a serious, concentrated, controlled, often exciting performance, an honest, restrained, somewhat generalized dramatic intensity. Her voice is a naturally clean, sensitively colored instrument with a sound redolent of trumpets and violas, modulated by a prominent, pleasing vibrato. She demonstrates an alertness to pulse and rhythm in setting a context for careful shaping of phrases, draping upon that scaffold a simple, unforced, natural-sounding rubato.

Cigna's voice was not always perfectly even and connected throughout its range. She would at times exploit the break between the middle and lower registers, pouncing on that low note and relishing it with a growl for a dramatic effect. As Cigna's career progressed, those notes would tend more often to escape capture. She would on occasion simplify a low fioratura, covering it with a stylized, aspirant, dramatic "point."

An example of a positive employment of Cigna's vocal articulations can be heard in her rendition of "Morrò, ma prima in grazia," from *Ballo in maschera,* in which Amelia is waiting to be put to death at the hands of her husband as punishment for a supposed infidelity. A hardening of tone on the low notes at the ends of phrases, a subtle sharpening of the rhythm pointing to these cadences conveys, beyond sadness and desolation, an underlying bitterness, resentment, and strength in the character. This impression is a result of Cigna's deliberate interpretive choices.

One of Cigna's most celebrated roles was as Bellini's Norma. Considering today her account of that part can perhaps teach us something of the performance values of a past era. In the aria "Casta diva," while the singing is often beautiful, it is not universally so. We don't hear her sustaining a smooth, even, controlled legato. The long line is subdivided into shorter phrases of characteristically Verdian length, although each of these phrases is endowed with definition and vitality. But the voice as a whole seems not to be supported, tones are not sustained, and dynamics are not controlled according to the tenets of *bel canto* familiar to us. An important element of Bellini's expressive universe is compromised.

Norma's soliloqy in which she contemplates murdering her children is potent and splendid as delivered by Gina Cigna: it is a valid and consistent interpretation in its context, but not as highly inflected—not hair-raising—as we can hear from other divas. Arguably, Cigna's most satisfactory work in *Norma* comes out in the ensembles. Here her singing is focussed, deliberate, responsive; earnest and intense, intelligent, she listens to the performance around her. Her character stands out in these conflicts and contrasts. It is an integrated conception: with the conductor, she imparts a monumentality that serves the performing ensemble and the piece as a whole rather than primarily advancing the character of a particular *prima donna.* It also serves a particular conception of opera as a form of musical drama, a conception that deemphasizes the role of the beautiful voice in favor of what that voice might express, something more sensational, perhaps more accessible to that audience.

It is probably easier to hear Cigna's interpretive strengths in the later, more overtly dramatic composers who point to *verismo*—a different musical style in which the contrasting emotions are simple, ardent, clearly laid out, together with more directed, less ornamented melodic shapes and more fluid musical forms.

When Cigna's Gioconda sings to us of her impending "Suicidio!" a hot, contained rage sears across the footlights, but with such mastery of vocal resources, with such flexibility, craft, and impetus, that the aria gains a generative nature, the momentum of which carries us through the final act. As Cigna's Gioconda shows us many faces among complex emotional layers, these she will also present to her protagonists in the remaining thirty minutes of the opera.

In "La mamma morta" from *Andrea Chénier,* Maddalena recounts her mother's murder at the hands of the Revolution, flight with her maid and subsequent adversities, and finally describes a benediction bestowed by a celestial voice personifying her earthly love. These shifts of contrasting mood and meaning are depicted by Gina Cigna with striking clarity through musical means—modulating tone, tempo, consonants, vowels, discarding pitch altogether for a line or two when appropriate for expressing the agitated sense of the text, all used to express unspeakable (but singable) loss and despair, a turbulent journey from innocence to worldliness through pain and fear. She achieves a sense of resolution and closure in the final lyrical section by increasing her vocal weight and expanding the tone, creating a second voice for this second section of the aria.

We can see from these examples—and others in which she demonstrates a gorgeously controlled and inflected cantabile—that she had the vocal resources and intelligence to control her interpretive options, at least early on in her career. It is in this context that we consider the centrality of the role of Turandot in her career. Cigna's detached, intellectual, idealized sense of "dramatic" expression she so often projects in many ways weaves through the fundamental conception of Puccini's *Turandot* as opera; this is an illustration of several currents of aesthetic elements coinciding in a single event. *Turandot* was considered New Music at that time.

Her characterization of the Princess is imperious, competitive, hugely scaled, gestures tremendous, appropriate for a festival occasion. Part of our thrill in this spectacle may be inadvertent, based on our awareness that Cigna's control over her voice is not absolute. The sense of latent vulnerability resounds in the real-life soprano as well as the stage character, all contributing to our experience of suspense in the outcome of the Riddle contest.

The core in Turandot's part is her narrative "In questa reggia," the still center of the opera where the drama reposes for a short while, plot and motivations are explained, and the stage is reset, literally and figuratively, for the subsequent conflict to take off again. The form and meaning in this aria are shifting, restless, linear, in which an ancient history and the present of the opera performance, as well as constant vertical layers of meaning, interchange consecutively but freely, all through the voice of the soprano. Gina Cigna presents these various moods in many ways as a series of masks, each powerfully and richly portrayed, yet revealed statically, one by one. Here the externalized sense of drama is made clear, in which stage histrionics begin to take on independent meanings of their own, and all reverberating, through performer and audience, across experience and memory, against all the other grand, controlled, stylized gestures—in other performances, in other operas—this soprano has shared with us.—MICHAEL CHERNISS

Cilea, Francesco

Composer. Born 23 July 1866, in Palmi, Calabria. Died 20 November 1950, in Varazze. Studied piano with Beniamino Cesi and composition with Paolo Serrao at the San Pietro di Majella Conservatory in Naples, 1881-89; knight of the Order of the Crown of Italy, 1893; piano teacher at the Naples conservatory, 1894-96; taught harmony at the Istituto Musicale in Florence, 1896-1904; member of the Reale Accademia Musicale in Florence, 1898; head of the Bellini Conservatory in Palermo, 1913-16; director of the San Pietro di Majella Conservatory in Naples, 1916-35.

Operas *Gina,* Enrico Golisciani, Naples, Conservatory, 9 February 1889; *La Tilda,* Angelo Zanardini ["A. Graziani"], Florence, Pagliano, 7 April 1892; *L'Arlesiana,* L. Marenco (after Alphonse Daudet), Milan, Lirico, 27 November 1897; revised 1898, 1910, 1937; *Adriana Lecouvreur,* Arturo Colautti (after Scribe and Legouvé), Milan, Lirico, 6 November 1902; *Gloria,* Arturo Colautti, Milan, Teatro alla Scala, 15 April 1907; revised 1932 (with libretto revisions by E. Moschini); *Il matrimonio selvaggio,* G. di Bognasco, 1909 [not performed]; *La rosa di Pompei,* E. Moschini [unfinished].

Modest, shy, and retiring, Francesco Cilèa was a conscientious musician who, on first appearances, would seem to have been suited by temperament more to academic than to theater life. As happened to so many composers-to-be, his family wished to see him in a career in law or medicine, but Cilèa was attracted early to music, his motivation supported by his maternal aunt's tenacious approval of the boy's desires. Overcoming opposition, he entered the San Pietro di Majella conservatory in Naples in 1881. His greatest inspiration there was Francesco Florimo, the librarian as well as a teacher, who also helped reconcile Cilèa's family to the boy's aim of having a musical career. Among other teachers particularly influencing the future composer were Cesi, Serrao, and Martucci. Cilèa proceeded rapidly and steadily in his studies, and, while still pursuing them, he became a student master, the first step along the way to his later calling as an educator. In 1889 he graduated, but straightforth became an auxiliary professor of harmony and piano, thereby launching his long professional teaching career, in which he achieved much distinction quite apart from his accomplishments as a composer.

Cilèa's first opera, an idyll in three acts to Enrico Golisciani's text, was a student work, *Gina,* first given 9 February 1889 at the conservatory in Naples. This score already was notable for the warmth, refinement, and fresh, copious melody that would characterize Cilèa's mature works. It also drew the attention of Edoardo Sonzogno, the publisher, who encouraged Cilèa to set *Tilda* (three acts, libretto by Angelo Zanardini writing under the pseudonym "A. Graziani"). *Tilda* was first mounted at the Teatro Pagliano in Florence on 7 March 1892 and quickly made a modest rounds of some theaters in and outside Italy. *Tilda* was a full-fledged work in the *verismo* idiom, remaining, however, the only one of the composer's stage works that could be so described. Tilda herself, in this mode of theatrical realism, is a prostitute, whose self-denying efforts to save her rival result in her own stabbing. The subject was not truly congenial to Cilèa's inclinations as a composer, and he had not yet developed the skill in composition to surmount the hurdle of setting such a subject convincingly. His last staged work, *Gloria,* itself on a stiff and conventional subject little to Cilèa's bent, was an artistic success despite its libretto, due to the composer's acquired skill and stagecraft, but *Tilda* was too premature to so succeed.

With his next libretto, however, Cilèa found a text ideally suited to his particular dramatic gifts. Leopoldo Marenco based his libretto for *L'Arlesiana* on Alphonse Daudet's French play, *L'Arlésienne.* Although ostensibly about matters of love and passion among people of humble origin, concerns true to the *verismo* movement's charter of realism, the libretto provided Cilèa the many moments of intimacy and reflection best calculated to engage his real sympathies and his talent for elegiac expression. Premiered in 4 acts in Milan on 27 February 1897, it appeared at the same theater, the Teatro Lirico, in a three act revision, with greater success, on 22 October 1898. Cilèa undertook the revision due to pressure from Sonzogno's firm, which was manifesting a lack of enthusiasm in promoting the work, but the changes were at the expense of the music's integrity.

Cilèa kept working away at the score of *L'Arlesiana* over the years, in 1910 restoring some of the music previously cut, and *L'Arlesiana* began to approach its familiar form by the time of the 1912 revival at the Teatro San Carlo, Naples. Cilèa added the aria, "Esser madre è un inferno" in the 1910 revision, as well as a scene for the same character (Rosa Mammai) with the "Innocente." The 1936 production at the Teatro alla Scala, Milan, did much to enhance the reputation of the opera through the efforts of a superb cast (Carosio, Schipa, Pederzini, Basiola). Even after that production, Cilèa continued to tinker at *L'Arlesiana,* in 1937 adding a new prelude to the score. The result of these changes was to strengthen the work's structure, which had been too rambling and diffuse.

L'Arlesiana remains essentially a lyrical work, lovably but perhaps too unrelievedly elegiac and melancholy in sentiment. It persisted as Cilèa's favorite among his own operas. Two arias from *L'Arlesiana* have held their place in the recital repertoire, "Esser madre è un inferno" and "Anch'io vorrei dormir così" (the famous "Lamento di Federico"); they typify the lyrical beauty of the work. Indeed, one can say that the simple strophic bipartite structure (AA') of the "Lamento di Federico" influenced Puccini to use the same formal device in his operas from *Tosca* onwards, which all postdate Cilèa's *L'Arlesiana.*

After *L'Arlesiana,* Cilèa, discouraged at its spotty reception, accepted a position as harmony instructor at Florence's musical institute. At about the time that he was losing heart, however, Sonzogno offered him *Adriana Lecouvreur,* which would prove a more decisive success, and a more enduring one, than *L'Arlesiana.* Arturo Colautti based his libretto, in four acts, on the play by Scribe and Legouvé. Certain ambiguities in the action, which have caused the libretto to suffer derision from some, actually derive from the perceived need to compress not only the play but also the draft of Colautti's text of the libretto, originally rather intricate but at least minimally logical, for the needs of the lyric stage. The subject exerted a strong grip on the composer, having many of the elements that kindled his imagination, including a sympathetic artist-heroine of deep feeling and sensitivity, as well as much humor and aristocratic etiquette to which Cilèa's elegance of style were well suited.

Adriana Lecouvreur saw its premiere on 6 November 1902 at the Teatro Lirico, Milan, with Caruso, Pandolfini, and De Luca, under Cleofonte Campanini's direction. *Adriana Lecouvreur* quickly became Cilèa's one sure success and justly remains at least on the margins of the standard repertory. It was immediately staged all over Italy, and within five years had spread from Lisbon (1903) west to Buenos Aires (1903), New Orleans, and New York (both 1907), as well as east to St. Petersburg (1906).

After *Adriana Lecouvreur,* Cilèa considered setting D'Annunzio's *Francesca da Rimini,* but negotiations over the libretto failed; the composer also pondered Renato Simoni's libretto to *Ritorno d'amore,* but rejected it. Cilèa settled on *Gloria,* to another three act libretto by Colautti. The text was already undeniably old-fashioned at the time of the work's composition. Its tale of heroic valor, love-instigated war and politics is redolent of the kind of libretto which Cammarano or Solera had cobbled for such works of Verdi as *Il Trovatore* or *I Lombardi.* There is little room in Colautti's text for character development, beyond Gloria's capitulation to her feelings for Lionetto. In spite of this, Cilèa, the complete professional, threw himself whole-heartedly into his work on the opera, clothing this turgid tale with music of the splendor and color needed to bring its creaking plot to life.

Toscanini conducted the premiere of *Gloria* on 15 April 1907 at the Teatro alla Scala. After *Gloria,* Cilèa resumed teaching more actively than ever, leaving Palermo for Naples in 1916 to teach at the San Pietro di Majella conservatory until 1935. He fashioned a revised version of *Gloria,* with the libretto revised by E. Moschini, for a production in Naples (20 April 1932). The fact that *Gloria's* subject was not conducive to Cilèa's refined and delicate sensibilities, however, may account for the opera's lack of any truly memorable set pieces, despite considerable beauties in the score. All is well accomplished, and the orchestration, especially, has many felicities, such as the depiction of surging water in the fountain scene and the imitation of bells tolling in the wedding scene. The choral writing in *Gloria,* as usual with Cilèa, is exquisite.

Gloria's music is on a large scale and, taken as a whole, very impressively clothes the grand scenes of public ritual, battle, and similar happenings. Perhaps Cilèa's only real miscalculation is in the handling of Bardo's assassination of Lionetto, after which the action bustles along to other matters too quickly for such an important turn of the plot to register its impact fully enough. *Gloria,* although a solid success at the 1907 premiere, has held the stage less well than either *L'Arlesiana* or *Adriana Lecouvreur.* When *Gloria* has been revived occasionally, it is the 1932 score that has been used.

Cilèa set his last completed opera, *Il matrimonio selvaggio,* to a text by G. di Bagnasco in 1909, but the work was never staged or published. Cilèa broached one last opera, *La Rosa di Pompei,* to a text by E. Moschini, but left off work on it in a very preliminary stage. Although *Gloria* had terminated his career as a composer for the stage, Cilèa kept on composing while pursuing his calling as a teacher, even after his retirement. He had always devoted himself to instrumental music and continued to do so. His vocal works after *Gloria,* besides the two unstaged operas, include songs, a *Canto della vita* (a symphonic poem for solo voice, chorus, and orchestra, 1913) and the *Vocalizzi da concerto* (a wordless concerto for voice, 1932).

Cilèa is accounted one of the "Giovane Scuola" or, less aptly labelled, *verismo* school figures. He shared the fondness of his contemporaries (Giordano, Zandonai, Mascagni, et al.) for the "costume drama" (e.g. his own *Adriana Lecouvreur* or Giordano's *Andrea Chénier*) and, less widely perceived among these men, a late-blooming Mannerist sensibility, more than a real affinity for these composers' occasional forays into the realism known in Italian opera as *verismo.* Cilèa's *Tilda* and, to some extent, *L'Arlesiana* are his contributions to *verismo,* per se. On the whole, Cilèa leans towards the Mannerist aspect, with its cultivation of a refined but very expressive aestheticism, rather than the merely intermittent *verismo* of the "Giovane Scuola." What Cilèa does share with his contemporaries, for all his refined sensibility, aloof temperament, and his more elegantly diaphanous orchestration, is their harmonic language, exploitation of richly sensual orchestral palette, and highly charged lyricism.

Cilèa's experience in chamber music and instrumental writing is obvious in the finesse and refinement of much of his orchestration. Cilèa's harmony and orchestration, even more so than with others of the "Giovane Scuola," reflect the influence of the French school of the period. Cilèa, like many Italian composers both of his own time and before, did succumb perhaps too often to the use of *tremolandi* and arpeggiation to flesh out his orchestration at times, but such devices only rarely appear to any really crude or arbitrary effect. Cilèa carefully gauged the voicing of his harmonies (a concern no doubt influenced by study of French scores), each added or altered note making its fullest impact by being situated in the instrumental section or taken by an individual instrument which would most highlight its harmonic color and desired degree of prominence. While not so daring as Puccini, neither was Cilèa so reticent as Giordano in exploiting new harmonic pathways in his time.

Cilèa made more than passing use of the motif (something readily observable in *Adriana Lecouvreur*) as a unitary and dramatic device, even if his handling of motifs, often bits from arias or other musical numbers, was like that of many *veristi*, rudimentary compared to Wagner. As were most Italian composers (Puccini excepted) Cilèa was content to repeat motifs rather than to develop or modify them through symphonic synthesis.

More distinctive than even his harmonic style or orchestration, however, are Cilèa's melodies. At their best, they are noteworthy for their elegiac lyricism, melancholy, and for their sinuously decorative contours. Cilèa could write music powerful and blunt in effect, as, for example, the music with which he provides the formidable Princesse de Bouillon in *Adriana Lecouvreur*. In many ways, Cilèa summed up in one last, glorious burst the abundant lyricism of Naples and of southern Italy, with a strongly Gallic harmonic language (from the influence of such masters as Gounod, Bizet, and Massenet) underpinning it. The structure, dramatic and musical, of Cilèa's operas is at times faulty, but the rich melodic invention and fragrant orchestration more than compensate in holding the listener's attention and interest.—C. P. GERALD PARKER

Cimarosa, Domenico

Composer. Born 17 December 1749, in Aversa, near Naples. Died 11 January 1801, in Venice. First music teacher was Polcano, organist of the monastery overseeing the charity school of the Minorites; scholarship to the Conservatorio Santa Maria di Loreto, where he studied singing with Manna and Sacchini, counterpoint with Fenaroli, and composition with Piccinni, 1761-72; his oratorio Giuditta *performed in Rome, 1770; first opera,* Le stravaganza del conte *performed in Naples, 1772; in Rome and Naples, 1778-1781; succeeded Paisiello as court composer at St Petersburg, 1787-91; success in Florence, Vienna, and Warsaw on the way to St Petersburg; Kapellmeister of the court at Vienna, 1791; Cimarosa's* Il matrimonio segreto *a huge success in Vienna, 1792, and later Naples, 1793; in Venice, Rome, and Naples, 1794-1801. Cimarosa went to prison in Naples in 1799 for his open support of the French republican army.*

Operas *Le stravaganze del conte,* P. Mililotti, Naples, Teatro dei Fiorentini, carnival 1772; *La finta parigina,* F. Cerlone, Naples, Nuovo, carnival 1773; *I sdegni per amore,* P. Mililotti, Naples, Nuovo, January 1776; *I matrimoni in ballo,* P. Mililotti, Naples, Nuovo, January 1776; *La frascatana nobile,* P. Mililotti, Naples, Nuovo, winter 1776; *I tre amanti,* Giuseppe Petrosellini, Rome, Valle, carnival 1777; *Il fanatico per gli antichi romani,* Giovanni Palomba, Naples, Teatro dei Fiorentini, spring 1777; *L' Armida immaginaria,* Giovanni Palomba, Naples, Teatro dei Fiorentini, summer 1777; *Gli amanti comici, o sia La famiglia in scompiglio.* Giuseppe Petrosellini, Naples, Teatro dei Fiorentini?, 1778?; *Il ritorno di Don Calandro,* Giovanni Petrosellini?, Rome, Valle, carnival, 1778; *Le stravaganze d'amore,* P. Mililotti, Naples, Teatro dei Fiorentini, 1778; *Il matrimonio per raggiro,* c. 1778-79?; later performance in Rome, Valle, 1802; *L'italiana in London,* Giuseppe Petrosellini, Rome, Valle, carnival 1779; *L'infedeltà fedele,* Giovanni Battista Lorenzi, Naples, Teatro del Fondo, 20 July 1779; *Le donne rivali,* Rome, Valle, carnival 1780; *Caio Mario,* Gaetano Roccaforte, Rome, January 1780; *I finti nobili,*

Giovanni Palomba, Naples, Teatro dei Fiorentini, Carnival 1780; *Il falegname,* Giovanni Palomba, Naples, Teatro dei Fiorentini, 1780; *Il capriccio drammatico,* Giuseppe Maria Diodati, Turin?, 1781?; *Il pittor parigino,* Giuseppe Petrosellini, Rome, Valle, 4 January 1781; *Alessandro nell'Indie,* Pietro Metastasio, Rome, Torre Argentina, carnival 1781; *L'amante combattuto dalle donne di punto,* Giovanni Palomba, Naples, Teatro dei Fiorentini, 1781; *Giunio Bruto,* G. Pindemonte ("Eschilo Acanzio"), Verona, Accademia Filarmonica, autumn 1781; *Giannina e Bernardone,* Filippo Livigni, Venice, San Samuele, November 1781; *Il convito,* Filippo Livigni, Venice, San Samuele, 27 December 1781; *L'amor costante,* Rome, Valle, carnival 1782; *L'eroe cinese,* Pietro Metastasio, Naples, San Carlo, 13 August 1782; *La ballerina amante,* Cesare Augusto Casini and/or Giovanni Palomba, October 1782, Naples, Teatro dei Fiorentini, 1782; *La Circe,* D. Perelli, Milan, Teatro alla Scala, carnival 1783; *I due baroni di Rocca Azurra,* Giovanni Palomba, Rome, Valle, February 1783; *Oreste,* L. Serio, Naples, San Carlo, 13 August 1783; *La villana riconosciuta,* Giovanni Palomba, June 1783, Naples, Teatro del Fondo, fall 1783; *Chi dell' altrui si veste presto si spoglia,* Giovanni Palomba, Naples, Teatro dei Fiorentini, 1783; *I matrimoni impensati,* Rome, Valle, carnival 1784; *L'apparenza inganna, ossia La villeggiatura,* Giovanni Battista Lorenzi, Naples, Teatro dei Fiorentini, spring 1784; *La vanità delusa,* Carlo Goldoni, Florence, Teatro della Pergola, June 1784; *L'Olimpiade,* Pietro Metastasio, Vicenza, Eretenio, 10 July 1784; *I due supposti conti, ossia Lo sposo senza moglie,* Angelo Anelli, Milan, Teatro alla Scala, 10 October 1784; *Artaserse,* Pietro Metastasio, Turin, Reggio, 26 December 1784; *Il marito disperato,* Giovanni Battista Lorenzi, Naples, Teatro dei Fiorentini, 1785; *La donna sempre al suo peggior s' appiglia,* Giovanni Palomba, Naples, Nuovo, 1785; *Il credulo,* Giuseppe Maria Diodati, Naples, Nuovo, carnival 1786; *Le trame deluse,* Giuseppe Maria Diodati, Naples, Nuovo, 1786; *L'impressario in angustie,* Giuseppe Maria Diodati, Naples, Nuovo, 1786; *Volodimiro,* G. Boggio, Turin, Regio, January 1787; *Il fanatico burlato,* Saverio Zini, Naples, Teatro del Fondo, 1787; *La felicità inaspettata.* Fernando Moretti, St Petersburg, Hermitage, March 1788; *La vergine del sole,* Fernando Moretti, St Petersburg, Hermitage?, 1788?; St Petersburg, Kamennïy, 6 November 1789; *La Cleopatra,* Fernando Moretti, St Petersburg, Hermitage, 8 October 1789; *Il matrimonio segreto,* Giovanni Bertati (after Colman and Garrick, *The Clandestine Marriage*), Vienna, Burgtheater, 7 February 1792; *Amor rende sagace,* Giovanni Bertati, Vienna, Burgtheater, 1 April 1793; *I traci amanti,* Giovanni Palomba, Naples, Nuovo, 19 June 1793; *Le astuzie femminili,* Giovanni Palomba (after Bertati, *Amor rende sagace*), Naples, Teatro del Fondo, 26 August 1794; *Penelope,* Giuseppe Maria Diodati, Naples, Teatro del Fondo, carnival 1795; *Le nozze in garbuglio,* Giuseppe Maria Diodati, Messina, Monizione, 1795; *L'impegno superato,* Giuseppe Maria Diodati, Naples, Teatro del Fondo, 1795; *La finta ammalata,* Lisbon, San Carlo, 1796; *I nemici generosi,* Giuseppi Petrosellini, Rome, Valle, carnival 1796; *Gli Orazi ed i Curiazi,* Antonio Simone Sografi, Venice, La Fenice, 26 December 1796; *Achille all' assedio di Troia,* Rome, Torre Argentina, carnival 1797; *L'imprudente fortunato,* Rome, Valle, carnival 1797; *Artemisia regina di Caria,* Marcello Marchesini, Naples, San Carlo, 25 June 1797; *L'apprensivo raggirato,* Giuseppe Maria Diodati, Naples, Teatro dei Fiorentini, 1798; *Il secreto,* Turin, Carignano, autumn 1798; *Artemisia* (left unfinished by the composer; finished for production by an unknown hand), Giovanni Battista Colloredo ("Cratisto Jamejo"), Venice, La Fenice, carnival 1801.

It was in his native Naples that Cimarosa first attracted attention as an opera composer. The established presence of Piccinni and Paisiello prevented him from making a significant breakthrough for several years, however, for it was not until these two composers both left the city in 1776—for Paris and St. Petersburg respectively—that Cimarosa's qualities were fully recognized. Soon his operas were heard in all the major Italian centers, beginning with the intermezzo *I tre amanti,* which was staged in Rome in 1777.

Within a few years Cimarosa's reputation had become international, and he responded by writing operas of various stylistic types. His first serious opera was *Caio Mario,* performed in Rome in 1780 in the two-act design he had by then come to prefer. Seven years later Catherine II invited him to take up the post of maestro di capella at her court in St. Petersburg, and there he remained until 1791. During these years his style developed toward the contemporary trend of complex finales containing a variety of musical structures, and each of the three operas he wrote in St. Petersburg moved impressively to a closing chorus.

Cimarosa chose to leave Russia once his contract there expired, making his way to Vienna, where he was well received by the Emperor Leopold II. Such was his reputation that Cimarosa was soon appointed Kapellmeister, and his creative response was the opera which posterity has judged to be his masterpiece, the opera buffa *Il matrimonio segreto.* With due respect for his new artistic environment, he worked with the Viennese Imperial Court Poet, Giovanni Bertati, as his librettist. Bertati was an experienced librettist who had previously worked with Salieri and Paisiello, and his plot concerning a wealthy merchant's daughter's secret marriage to her father's employee proved an excellent vehicle for Cimarosa's lively and entertaining music. So pleased was the Emperor that he treated the entire cast to dinner after the premiere, in order that they could perform the opera again for him that same evening.

Leopold died soon after the premiere of *Il matrimonio segreto* and Cimarosa responded to the many invitations he received from his native Italy by returning to Naples in 1793, soon presenting a new opera, *I traci amanti.* His creative strength remained, and he returned successfully to serious opera three years later with *Gli orazi ed i curiazi.* In this, probably his best such work, he wrote skilfully and dramatically not only for solo voices but also for the chorus, which in fact plays a prominent and integral part in the evolution of the plot. An unusual feature of this opera is that the chorus is for male voices only.

During 1799, Naples was occupied by republican forces, and Cimarosa publicly sympathized with their cause. When the city was regained by King Ferdinand, the composer was arrested and spent a few months in prison. The intervention of eminent friends eventually secured his release, and he moved on to Venice, where he began composing a new opera, *Artemisia.* He did not live to complete it, however, for he died in January 1801. Throughout his career, in the course of which he completed more than sixty operas, Cimarosa was an accomplished master of dramatic pacing and of the depiction of individual characters. For these reasons he excelled in comic opera, writing in a style that reflected the prevailing taste but that also had integrity. His orchestral writing was skilful and well balanced, using contrasts of instrumental groupings and rhythmic phrases to enhance the movement of the plot. A typical feature, found generally in this style of opera, is how it is conveyed by means of short repetitive figurations. In his later works especially, his lyrical writing could be most expressive, and not merely in the vocal line, for his sense of orchestral color grew more acute, as did the range of his harmony. Accordingly, Cimarosa's later operas enhance their dramatic content with subtlety.

In the last decade of his life Cimarosa became the leading international exponent of Italian opera. He was ultimately more successful in comic opera than in serious works, though the latter cannot be judged insignificant. Only the arrival of Rossini would eclipse him.—TERRY BARFOOT

La clemenza di Tito [The Mercy of Titus]

Composer: *Wolfgang Amadeus Mozart.*

Librettist: *Caterino Mazzolà (after Metastasio).*

First Performance: *Prague, National Theater, 6 September 1791.*

Roles: *Tito (tenor); Sesto (contralto or mezzo-soprano); Vitellia (soprano); Servilia (soprano); Annio (countertenor or tenor); Publio (bass); chorus (SATB).*

Mozart's setting of Metastasio's *La clemenza di Tito* is perhaps his most controversial opera. Written for the coronation of Leopold II as King of Bohemia in Prague, *La clemenza di Tito* had a lukewarm reception. The empress' barb condemning the work as a "porcheria tedesca" (German dirty trick) after she heard it was supported by many early nineteenth-century writers, who (while avoiding such out and out slander) found the work sterile, lacking in invention and creativity. That hardly reflects its proper evaluation, however, for soon after the composer's death the opera steadily gained popularity. It is now seen as an important culmination of Mozart's dramatic compositions and as revealing his affinity for serious opera; it is not like his Da Ponte comedies, but neither ought it to have been. It is a different genre, written for different circumstances, exhibiting different aesthetic proprieties.

Mozart's early biographer Niemetschek (1798) claimed that *La clemenza di Tito* was composed in eighteen days; that fact, along with Mozart's illness, was often offered as justification for shortcomings in the work. Recent studies have shown that Mozart probably began composing as early as July of 1791, with his attention directed first to the ensemble pieces and the arias for Tito. The other arias were written later. The work *was* written in a short time, therefore, and some compromises were made: it is fairly certain that Mozart's student, Sussmayr, set the recitatives (yet this practice was fairly common, as can be seen in the scores of such composers as Cimarosa and Paisiello).

This was the third time that Mozart had set a Metastasio text to music, but his last attempt (*Il rè pastore,* for Salzburg) had occurred over fifteen years earlier. Metastasio's *Tito,* loosely inspired by the reports of Titus's magnanimity in Suetonius and other Roman historians (but more directly modeled on several plays by Corneille and Racine), was one of his most popular texts. *La clemenza di Tito* was first set in 1734 by Caldara, and over seventy other settings preceded Mozart's 1791 version. Caterino Mazzolà—who served as Dresden court poet from 1782 until the spring of 1791, when he came to Vienna as court poet (replacing Da Ponte)—was engaged as the arranging librettist for Mozart's production by Guardasoni, the impresario. Mazzolà followed the pattern he had set in Dresden, altering Metastasio's texts to conform to the *dramma giocoso* model, i.e., collapsing the three acts into two (largely by deleting twelve scenes from the second act) and supplying a variety of extra ensembles (two duets, three trios), including act-ending finales, by then a tradition well established in comedies. His ideas pleased Mozart, who called his arrangement a transformation of the out-of-date Metastasio original into "vera opera," and whose musical setting underscores the integrity of Mazzolà's ideas.

The plot revolves around the disturbance of the natural order caused by Vitellia's irascible jealousy. Vitellia, the daughter of the deposed Roman emperor Vitellio, loves Tito, but, believing that he is about to marry another, swears Sesto (confidant to the emperor and her ardent admirer) to slay him. Too late, she learns of her error; the palace is in flames and reports bear news of Tito's death. Fate has turned the tables, however: the wrong man was struck down. Annio,

Sesto's friend and engaged to Sesto's sister, Servilia, at first appears to bear the blame, but the evidence soon shows Sesto the author of the conspiracy. Tito mourns for his friend and desperately hopes for some explanation, some new evidence. When that fails, he decides to forgive him, yet at the last moment Vitellia reveals her own fault. Still, Tito proclaims that his clemency is stronger than the irrational acts of passion now repented and forgives all. He proclaims that he will have no other consort but Rome, and all join in praise of Tito's virtue.

The act-ending ensembles for both acts are reminiscent of other operas from the 1780s. That for the first act, which culminates in the revelation of Sesto's guilt, is particularly effective. Unified tonally in E-flat, its harmonic plan strays abruptly to support dramatic events: Publio's declaration that Tito is feared dead is underlaid with diminished seventh chords; and the final chorus, in E-flat, is colored by movement to the minor subdominant and all its borrowed chords to underscore such emotive text as "tradimento" and "dolor." Mozart's lifelong sensitivity to his text setting is also well evident in his solo numbers. Sesto's aria, "Parto, ma tu ben mio," shows a three-part division of the two stanza Metastasio text. Each section accelerates the tempo (a not uncommon device in general), but with textual repetition that creates a truly rising passion. The basset horn obbligato part, written for Anton Stadler, is one of Mozart's most beautiful settings.—DALE E. MONSON

The Consul

Composer: *Gian Carlo Menotti.*

Librettist: *Gian Carlo Menotti.*

First Performance: *Philadelphia, 1 March 1950.*

Roles: *Magda Sorel (soprano); John Sorel (baritone); Mother (contralto); Secretary (mezzo-soprano); Secret Police Agent (bass); Mr. Kofner (bass-baritone); Foreign Woman (soprano); Anna Gomez (soprano); Vera Boronel (contralto); Nika Magdaoff (tenor); Assan (baritone).*

The Consul is a disturbing political opera about the plight of a woman trying to obtain a visa to leave a totalitarian state. Following the tradition of its predecessor, *The Medium,* it is a true "musical drama" in three acts and six scenes. It was Menotti's first full-length work, and its libretto is one of his finest.

Magda Sorel is a woman left stranded in a police state, when her husband, John Sorel, barely escaping capture, flees across the frontier to gain asylum in a neighboring country. Trying to obtain a visa for her family, Magda virtually haunts the foreign consulate but is endlessly thwarted by red tape. The consul himself never makes an appearance. He is represented by his secretary, who is the personification of governmental indifference and intrigue. At the consulate, Magda waits with other impoverished people, among them Nika Magdaoff, a magician with hypnotic powers.

As time passes, Magda's situation grows steadily more desperate. The secret police agent interrogates her, hoping she will betray other patriots. He watches her movements constantly, setting her up as bait in a trap for her husband. Magda's child dies of undernourishment, and the health of John's mother deteriorates from despair and worry. Assan, the window mender, is the only real contact Magda has to the underground; he brings news of her husband.

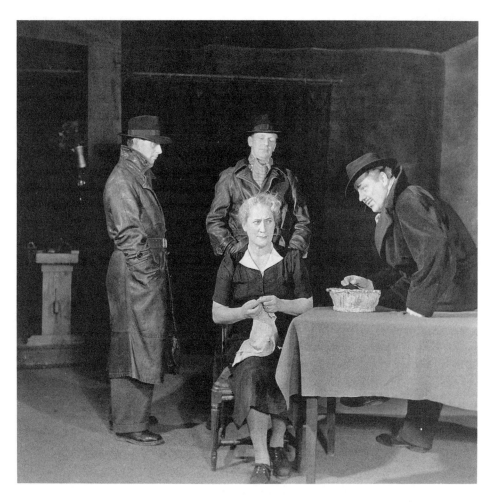

Menotti's *The Consul,* Royal Opera, Stockholm, 1952

In the end, the pressure from Assan and the underground acts as the catalyst to real tragedy. Assan is concerned about the lives of all the underground members should John try to return and risk capture. He pleads with Magda to find a way to prevent John from rescuing her; John must not come back or the underground will be exposed. Magda agrees and resolves to end her life in order to eliminate any need for John to return.

In the last scene, Magda lies down by the gas stove while the telephone rings in the background; the unanswered call bears new of her husband's capture. As she drifts toward death, she dreams—of her husband as he comes to woo her, of John's mother still young, and of the magician saying "Look into my eyes, look into my eyes. You feel tired. You want to sleep. Breathe deeply." The visions recede; the room is empty; Magda falls back unconscious. The telephone continues to ring as the curtain falls.

The Consul, like it's predecessor *The Medium,* was presented on Broadway at the Ethel Barrymore Theater on March 15, 1950. The actual premiere took place two weeks earlier in

Philadelphia. This original production, which was extremely well cast, ran for 269 performances, almost eight months. Among the cast can be found names such as baritone Cornell MacNeil, making his opera debut as John Sorel, soprano Patricia Neway, riveting as Magda Sorel, and contralto Marie Powers, who created the title role in *The Medium,* as the mother. Olin Downes of the *New York Times* (March 16, 1950) said each member of the cast "blended so excellently in the dramatic ensemble" that none was inadequate to the task. Speaking of Magda's "nobly fashioned" second act aria, he said it "simply stopped the show."

The Consul received The New York Drama Critics' Circle Award for the Best Musical of the Year and the Pulitzer Prize for Music in 1950. Productions were mounted in London, Zurich, Berlin, Vienna, and Italy in 1951, in Hamburg in 1952, and at Sadler's Wells, London, in 1954. It has since become standard operatic fare and has been translated into twelve languages. Though Menotti does not identify the police state in which his drama is set, it was a timely subject that remains current today.

Although originally a theater piece, it is opera in the finest tradition, and Menotti's training is clearly seen in the manner in which he creates musical shapes for the human voice. The melodies are tonal and easily remembered. Melodic repetition is common but with a sense of natural speech-like inflection. His melodic passages are often Puccini-like in their expanse of line and their singing quality. Recitative, ensemble, and aria seem to flow together with such ease that there are only two excerpts which can be pulled from the score without difficulty: the grandmother's lullaby to the dying child, and Magda's tragic recitative and aria from the second act.

Menotti is often compared to Puccini because, like Puccini, he is sensitive to techniques that make the dramatic intentions of the music stand out. He is not afraid of using musical techniques and devices—the dramatic levels of a Mozartian ensemble, the verismo of Puccini, or even the dissonance and atonality of the twentieth century—to create and sustain his dramatic purpose.—PATRICIA ROBERTSON

Les contes d'Hoffmann [The Tales of Hoffmann]

Composer: *Jacques Offenbach [unfinished; completed by Guiraud].*

Librettist: *J. Barbier.*

First Performance: *Paris, Opéra-Comique, 10 February 1881.*

Roles: *Hoffmann (tenor); Lindorf, Coppélius, Dappertutto, Dr. Miracle, four manifestations of Hoffmann's evil genius (should be sung by the same bass-baritone); Stella (speaking); Olympia (soprano); Giulietta (mezzo-soprano); Antonia (soprano); Spalanzani (tenor); Crespel (bass or baritone); Pitichinaccio (tenor); Schlemil (bass or baritone); Frantz (tenor); Nicklausse (mezzo-soprano); A Voice (mezzo-soprano); Muse (speaking); Luther (bass or baritone); Hermann (bass or baritone); Wilhelm (tenor or baritone); Nathaniel (tenor); Andres (tenor); Cochenille (tenor); chorus (SATTBB).*

All his life Jacques Offenbach wanted to be accepted as a serious composer, though the bulk of his output had consisted of a lifelong flood of light comic operettas. Many of these had been extremely successful, but Offenbach wanted to write something that would gain him the respect of the serious musical establishment. He finally got his wish, albeit posthumously, with

Les contes d'Hoffmann. In this his last opera, he strove for a level of seriousness seldom if ever evident in the operettas; Antonia's lovely, mournful "Elle a fui, la tourterelle," (The Turtledove has flown) is one of the few sad songs Offenbach ever wrote.

Offenbach had used E.T.A. Hoffmann as a literary source once already, with *Le roi carotte,* based on the story of "Kleinzaches, gennant Zinnober." Having seen a play based on some short stories of Hoffmann by Jules Barbier and Michel Carré, writers who had written other librettos, Offenbach decided to use it for an opera. The composer worked more slowly than usual, wanting this to be a serious piece of work. But he continued to turn out lighter pieces, and died without finishing the score. Léon Carvalho, director of the Opéra-Comique, was eager to mount the show anyway. Ernest Guiraud was asked to complete and orchestrate the work, and Carvalho himself made extensive alterations. As a result, there have been many conflicting editions appearing over the years. Although it is impossible to reconstruct it fully, since Offenbach always made changes depending on the audience's reaction to the first performance, *Les contes d'Hoffmann* remains his most popular work.

The opera is loosely based on three short stories by E.T.A. Hoffmann, in which the main character is Hoffmann himself, living out his own peculiar adventures. This arrangement is justified by Hoffmann's practice of modeling his fictional characters after himself. A lengthy prologue introduces Hoffmann in a tavern with a rowdy group, drinking and singing ("Glug, glug, glug, I am wine, Glug, glug, glug, I am beer!"). A performance of Mozart's *Don Giovanni* is going on next door. The subject of women comes up, and Hoffmann promises to tell the story of three women whom he has loved: Olympia, Giulietta, and Antonia. But there is a sinister twist to each story.

Act I, drawn from *Der Sandmann,* details Hoffmann's adventure with Olympia, falling madly in love only to learn that the woman is an automaton, smashed in the end by a disgruntled co-creator. Based on *Die Abenteuer der Sylvester-Nacht,* act II introduces the courtesan Giulietta, who, working for Dapertutto, steals the enamored Hoffmann's reflection; she is poisoned with drugged wine intended for Nicklausse. Act III features Antonia from *Rat Krespel;* she is a girl with a lovely voice who becomes ill and fevered when she sings. She agrees to renounce singing, but the evil Dr. Miracle invokes the portrait of the girl's dead mother, tempting Antonia to sing, whereupon she collapses and dies.

Throughout these adventures, Hoffmann is accompanied by his one faithful friend, Nicklausse, who tries to protect him. The epilogue returns to the tavern, where Hoffmann's three loves are revealed as incar-

Les contes d'Hoffmann, with Melanie Kurt and Jean Nadolovitch, Berlin Opera, 1905

nations of Stella, who leaves with Lindorf. Nicklausse, on the other hand, reappears as the Muse, who consoles the despondent Hoffmann. "And what of me, your faithful friend, whose hand has dried your tears? I love you, Hoffmann! Be mine!" He replies: "Beloved Muse, I am yours!"

The opera is unified by parallel figures in each act, beginning with Hoffmann's three ill-advised loves, each a manifestation of Stella. (The four roles are often played by the same singer.) Within each of the stories, there is also someone to prevent Hoffmann from being with the woman he loves: Coppélius destroys Olympia, Dapertutto plants the poisoned wine that kills Giulietta, and Dr. Miracle causes Antonia to sing herself to death. In the epilogue, Hoffmann's rival Lindorf intercepts Stella. Each of these is a parallel manifestation of the devil (again, usually sung by the same singer).

The libretto does not always live up to the promise of the source. If the women seem shallow, it is perhaps due to their nature as figments of Hoffmann's imagination. But the incarnations of the devil, while increasingly threatening through the course of the three acts, are not always convincing. The evil nature of Lindorf, who appears in the epilogue and prologue, is made ridiculous through self-aggrandizement. "I have the spirit of a devil, of a devil! My eyes flash lightning, and my whole appearance become diabolic," he sings.

Nor is Hoffmann's characterization in the opera profound; he is a pathetic and lonely spirit, yearning in vain for the ideal human woman but not achieving the level of the heroic, tortured Romantic soul. His persona is developed through brief references to a few well-known facts about E.T.A. Hoffmann's life, such as his love of Mozart (which Offenbach shared) and his Romantic reinterpretation of *Don Giovanni,* or veiled references to the beloved Julia Marc. Offenbach sought, and to a degree found, serious legitimacy by using Hoffmann as a source, but the opera does not fully escape the composer's habit of parody.

Whatever the shortcomings of the opera, especially when compared with the genius of E.T.A. Hoffmann, it is redeemed by Offenbach's brilliant music. The harmony is often standard, though there are also inspired touches of chromaticism. But Offenbach's typical tunefulness is raised to new dramatic heights, as in the setting of the prologue, when Hoffmann's dreamy reverie interrupts his energetic description of the mis-shaped dwarf Kleinzach. Again, the thrilling act III ensemble finale with Antonia, Dr. Miracle, and the mother is a well-constructed dramatic admixture of accompanied recitative, lyricism, and trio as the three voices sing increasingly in step with one another. *Les Contes d'Hoffmann* has been acknowledged as Offenbach's masterpiece, and it has gained him more respect and historical attention than would have been the case without it. Offenbach would undoubtedly have been pleased.—ELIZABETH W. PATTON

Corelli, Franco

Tenor. Born 4 August 1921, in Ancona. Married singer Loretta di Lelio. Attended Liceo Musicale, Pesaro. Debut as Don José in Carmen, *Spoleto, 1951; Teatro alla Scala debut as Licinio in* Vestale, *1954, and continued to sing there until 1965; Covent Garden debut as Cavaradossi in* Tosca, *1957; Metropolitan Opera debut as Manrico, 1961, and sang there regularly until 1975; appeared at Berlin Städtische Oper, 1961, Vienna Staatsoper, 1963, and Paris Opéra, 1970.*

Some operatic voices suggest color associations or personalities. Franco Corelli's voice is unusual in that his recordings have an immediacy which suggests actual physical presence. Some admire Pavarotti's flexibility and strength; others may appreciate Domingo's clarity or Carreras's refinement. Corelli was of a different breed. A contemporary of del Monaco and di Stefano, this tenor was one of the most remarkable, with a ringing and potent force that sounds as if its possessor could sustain his notes indefinitely. It is also a beautiful voice offering great strength as well as heart-breaking tenderness.

Compared to many other singers, Corelli came to opera rather late in his life: he began to study voice at twenty-three. He comes from the same region of Italy by the Adriatic Sea as Tebaldi, del Monaco, Cerquetti and Gigli, and according to all sources, the people of Ancona have long said "Beautiful voices are born in this area." The Corelli family did not have a particularly musical background, and Franco began his young adulthood as a student of naval engineering. Impressed with his natural ability, friends encouraged him to train his voice, and after some study at the Pesaro Conservatory of Music, he entered and won a vocal competition at the Maggio Musicale in 1951.

At this point, his study took an unusual turn. Twice he studied with voice teachers, once before and once after winning the vocal competition; he found vocal studies unsatisfactory. Deciding he was his own best teacher, he became virtually self-taught. He learned about vocal technique from the recordings of Caruso, Lauri-Volpi and Gigli, gleaning from them details of style and projection to complement his natural technique. He apparently memorized roles through the phonograph, making him purely a tenor of the recording age. Singers traditionally rely on one or two mentors to guide their development. Since a recorded voice provides no critique or interaction, it may seem like an ineffective teacher. However, the results are impressive in Corelli's case. By shaping his voice along the lines of legendary tenors of the past, Corelli perfected a style of singing suited to the age of the long-playing record. It is certainly no wonder that his voice suggests physical presence.

The "physical presence" of his voice stems from his surety, firmness and phenomenal reserves of power. One is tempted to attribute his dramatic capabilities to his non-musical background, and correlate the strength he shows on stage to his resolution and determination to teach himself. Mainly, though, his voice carries the drama in a role. Though reviewers periodically claimed he was stiff in performance and substituted posing for acting, the roles in which he specialized do not call for intricacies of feeling. However, videotapes reveal him to have been a performer who concentrated on creating drama rather than just projecting voice. He is very satisfying. Many of his numerous performances spanning the 1950s and 1960s are available on broadcast tapes, and he has been credited with reviving many obscure operas including Donizetti's *Poliuto* and Allegra's *Romulus*.

Four roles show off Corelli's power, stamina and vibrancy to their best advantage: the title role in Giordano's *Andrea Chénier,* Manrico and Radamès in Verdi's *Il trovatore* and *Aida,* and Calaf in Puccini's *Turandot.* These are such operatic standards that the singer who can make them distinctive stands out from other tenors. Corelli differentiates himself from others in these works, and fills the roles superbly with ample, free-flowing voice. Although many can perform them, few can sound as if they inhabit Calaf or Manrico by sheer vocal force. As an example of that force, Corelli is in peak form in the recording of *Turandot* with Birgit Nilsson as his voice manifests the exuberance and hubris of Calaf.

Corelli certainly had his detractors, though, who note a sameness to his approach in various roles, a tendency to hold high notes too long, and, as Paul Henry Lang wrote in the *New York Herald Tribune* in the early 1960s, "inadequate" legato and pianissimo. While much of the criticism of his career is well-founded, he has inspired a core group of admirers who believe the strength and magnitude of his voice render such criticism superfluous. While he does sound miraculous in a specialized repertory, his voice is not so pliable that he can assume any tenor role with equal results.

Corelli has, not surprisingly, what some consider the most Italianate of traits, the tendency to embed a note with a throaty sob. Perhaps the greatest example of this is his recording of Leoncavallo's *I pagliacci*. Both detractors and admirers focus on this ability. Often critics maintain his way with a sob sacrifices music for the sake of cheap effect. But for music in which sentiment precedes other considerations, the sob is appropriate. His recording of the most familiar of Neapolitan songs, " 'O sole mio," bears this out. The poem equates the sun in the daytime to a lover's eyes at night, and while the conclusion has not the all-out sob you hear in "Vesti la giubba," the result is nonetheless compelling.

Corelli is nearly always compelling, and to hear him at his best, one should listen to his three recordings with Birgit Nilsson: *Turandot, Aida,* and *Tosca.* These show him off as the perfect match for another singer with a big voice and great reserves of power. Any operatic recording will reveal his individual timbre and exciting presence, but his readings of Neapolitan songs have an authority and charming conviction that are telling, too. Even if one is bothered by his tendency to sob, or his lack of pianissimo, the richness, vibrancy and presence of his voice place it among the most satisfying.

In Corelli we hear how a voice can be as individual as a face, and how that individuality transforms some of the most-performed roles in the tenor repertoire into fresh experiences.—TIMOTHY O. GRAY

Corena, Fernando

Bass-baritone. Born 22 December 1916. Died November 1984, in Lugano. Studied for holy orders in Fribourg University, but won a music competition, and studied music in Geneva, 1937-38, and with Enrico Romani in Milan; Italian debut in Tricote, 1947; appeared regularly throughout Italy; sang in 1949 premiere of Petrassi's Cordovano *at Teatro alla Scala; debut at Metropolitan Opera as Leporello, 1954; debut at Covent Garden as Rossini's Bartolo; sang Osmin in* Die Entführung aus dem Serail *at Salzburg, 1965.*

The basso buffo tradition began in Naples in the early eighteenth century with the Casaccia family, who dominated buffo singing there for four generations, generally performing in dialect. Some members went in for broad comedy. Stendahl had this to say of Carlo Casaccia in connection with his appearance at the city's Teatro dei Fiorentini in Pietro Carlo Guglielmi's *Paolo e Virginia* in 1817: "[T]he famous Casaccia ... is enormous, a fact that gives him opportunity for considerable pleasant buffoonery. When seated, he undertakes to give himself an appearance of ease by crossing his legs; impossible; the effort that he goes through topples him onto his neighbor; a general collapse. This actor, commonly called Casacciello, is adored by the public; he has the nasal voice of a Capuchin. At this theater, everyone sings through his nose."

During the eighteenth century two types of buffo emerged: the "buffo nobile," or noble comic, and the "buffo caricato," or exaggerated comic. The same singers who undertook "basso cantante" or non-comic lyric bass roles also frequently sang those for buffo nobile, for they are similar in vocal demands, often requiring virtuosity. Buffo caricato parts, on the other hand, were a specialty, calling for falsetto singing in imitation of women and, above all, patter singing or chatter. Beauty of tone is of small consequence for a buffo caricato, mastery of comic effect essential. The part of Don Basilio in *Il barbiere di Siviglia* is for buffo nobile, that for Don Bartolo in the same opera for buffo caricato. The florid passages for Mustafà in *L'Italiana in Algeri* are not very different than those for Assur in *Semiramide,* and in fact both roles were written for Filippo Galli, who moved comfortably between the nobile and cantante genres. On the other hand Taddeo in *L'Italiana* is a patter part.

Fernando Corena had wonderful flair as a buffo caricato, and his best role was Bartolo—at first grand and expansive, exuding self-importance and pomposity, then sputtering with outrage. He invariably stole the show. But when he crossed over into parts for basso cantante, such as Il conte Rodolfo in *La sonnambula* or those for buffo nobile, such as Mustafà, he sounded ungainly—labored in coloratura and spread in pitch. Still, his voice was truer than that of Salvatore Baccaloni, his immediate predecessor. Corena was able to swat out Mustafà's Gs, beyond the range of many basses; however, particularly in later years, he sounded strained in the high tessitura of the *L'elisir d'amore* entrance aria, with its many Es. His voice retained substance no matter how quickly he chattered. And he was masterful at caricaturing women in falsetto, for example, at the interpolated words "sul tamburo" in *Barbiere.*

On stage, Baccaloni, a comedian, was never out of character. He claimed to have prepared five ways to play each moment, once remarking, "I choose. Only a fool improvises." Corena, a clown, often improvised—and frequently amused himself by playing pranks on other singers. He was better at expressing extroverted feelings than deep dark emotions. Portraying Falstaff as a clown, he failed to capture the character's reflective side. As Leporello (*Don Giovanni*) he was a delight in the "Catalogue" aria, somewhat of a disappointment toward the opera's end. As Don Pasquale he was a triumph—except in those passages calling for pathos. Above all, Corena excelled at detailing foibles and pomposity. He was pre-eminent in his repertoire from the mid-fifties until the late seventies.—STEFAN ZUCKER

Corigliano, John

Composer. Born 16 February 1938 in New York City to a musical family (his father, John, was concertmaster of the New York Philharmonic, 1943-66); Columbia University, BA 1959, studied with Otto Luening; later studied with Vittorio Giannini at the Manhattan School of Music and privately with Paul Creston; music programmer for WQXR-FM and WBAI-FM, 1959-64; associate producer of music programs for CBS television, 1961-72; music director of Morris Theater in New Jersey, 1962-64; composition teacher at several New York schools including Manhattan School (from 1971), Lehman College of the City University of New York, where he is distinguished professor of music (from 1974) and the Juilliard School of Music (from 1991); has received commissions from major organiza-

*tions like the Metropolitan Opera (*The Ghosts of Versailles, *1991), New York Philharmonic (clarinet concerto, 1977, and* Fantasy on an Ostinato, *1985), Chicago Symphony Orchestra (*Symphony No. 1, *1991), the Cleveland Quartet (*String Quartet No. 1, *1995); film score he composed for* Altered States *was nominated for an Academy Award, 1981; Guggenheim fellow, 1968; composer-in-residence, Chicago Symphony Orchestra, 1987-90; received Grawemeyer Award and two Grammy awards for Symphony No. 1, 1991; elected to American Academy and Institute of Arts and Letters, 1991; received the Composition of the Year Award from the first International Classic Music Awards for "Ghosts of Versailles," 1992.*

Operas   *Naked Carmen* (electric rock opera based on Bizet), Corigliano and David Hess, issued on recording only, 1970; *The Ghosts of Versailles,* William A. Hoffman, 1987, New York, Metropolitan Opera, 19 December 1991.

John Corigliano is, next to Philip Glass, the most successful American operatic composer of the late 20th century, despite the fact that he has composed only one full-scale grand opera. That's because the opera, *The Ghosts of Versailles,* made such an unprecedented impact on audiences, management and most critics. Commissioned by the Metropolitan Opera (the first new opera to be performed there in a quarter-century), *Ghosts* became an instant hit. All seven performances of the initial run were sold out; it was subsequently televised nationally and released on VHS and laser disc by Deutsche Grammophon.

The opera, set to a libretto by playwright William Hoffman, was revived to renewed acclaim at the Met during the 1994-95 season, and achieved further praise when it joined the repertory of the Lyric Opera of Chicago during the 1995-96 season.

The Met world premiere featured major singers like Teresa Stratas, Marilyn Horne and Hakan Hagegard. It was conducted by James Levine and staged by Colin Graham. The work's unabashedly tonal melodies, most often set amidst contemporary harmonic and orchestral schemes, proved that it is quite possible for modern opera to move audiences, provided it reaches out to them directly.

Corigliano's only other claim to operatic fame has never been staged. *The Naked Carmen,* a 1970 one-act "electric rock opera," was created in collaboration with record producer David Hess directly for LP on the Mercury label. Featuring such diverse performers as Melba Moore, the Detroit Symphony Orchestra led by Paul Paray, a children's chorus dubbed "The Universal Military Bubblegum Band," kazoos and, at one point, the voice of Spiro T. Agnew, *The Naked Carmen* is a highly inventive period piece, an amalgamation of Bizet's music with late-1960s thoughts about love, freedom and conflict. (Sample lyrics for the "Habanera:" "When Love is Free, then Love's for Me.") The work's sincerity and youthful vigor continue to ring true more than 25 years later.

Intense lyricism, a strong dramatic component and a firm desire to reach out to listeners are basic elements of Corigliano's style. His highly charged *Symphony No. 1,* commissioned by the Chicago Symphony Orchestra and dedicated to friends who died of the AIDS virus, has been performed by more than 30 orchestras around the world and garnered for him the 1991 Grawemeyer Award. The Chicago Symphony's recording of the work for the Erato label was at the top of the Billboard charts for 69 weeks.

At present Corigliano's catalogue leans toward one-time efforts: single concertos for piano, flute and oboe, a single string quartet, a single symphony, a single full-length opera. Given his proven ability to attract and hold audiences, one would hope he turns his ample talents to second attempts at such forms, especially to opera. For while there has been at least a minor explosion of operatic activity by contemporary composers, too many of their efforts seem to have become one-shot deals, mildly interesting on first encounter but lacking the staying power that signals masterpiece status. With *Ghosts,* Corigliano has shown that he has the ability to create operatic music that endures. We need to hear more from him.—JOHN GUINN

Così fan tutte, ossia La scuola degli amanti [All Women do Thus, or The School for Lovers]

Composer: *Wolfgang Amadeus Mozart.*

Librettist: *Lorenzo Da Ponte.*

First Performance: *Vienna, Burgtheater, 26 January 1790.*

Roles: *Fiordiligi (soprano); Dorabella (soprano): Guglielmo (baritone); Ferrando (tenor); Despina (soprano); Don Alfonso (bass); chorus (SATB).*

Così fan tutte was Mozart's fourth opera since moving to Vienna, and his third major collaboration with the librettist Lorenzo Da Ponte (1749-1838). It has often been perceived as "problematic": there were few performances during the nineteenth century, and the opera gained recognition only in the more sympathetic climate of the 1920s. Even today, many feel uneasy with the work.

The question of immorality that so exercised the Romantics merits some exploration. Two pairs of lovers—Fiordiligi and Guglielmo; Dorabella and Ferrando—swap partners with feigned or (and increasingly) real conviction and then abruptly shift back (we assume) to their original attachments. This belies what are often felt to be crucial messages in Mozart's operas, the moral and emotional power of love and fidelity, and the significant place of women in the commonwealth of humanity. Moreover, the cynical machinations of Don Alfonso—the puppet-master of the intrigue—and the maid Despina are not what we expect in Mozart. Why should he have chosen such a frivolous plot for some of his greatest music?

Mozart's choice of subject (if the choice was his) is difficult to explain: there is little evidence on the genesis of *Così* either in Mozart's letters, Da Ponte's *Memoirs,* or other contemporary records. Moreover, the opera has no clear basis in pre-existing literary or dramatic sources. Mozart's first collaboration with Da Ponte, *Le nozze di Figaro* (1786), reworked a fashionable play by Beaumarchais, and their second, *Don Giovanni* (1787), involves characters with a clear history in seventeenth- and eighteenth-century drama. In both cases, contemporary audiences would have been sufficiently informed about the characters to understand and assess their motives, actions, and dramatic significance.

But the sources for *Così* are unclear. Certainly, the characters are rooted in the *commedia dell'arte,* as are the trappings of the plot (Albanian disguises, playful references to Mesmerism, a maid dressing up as a medical, then legal, quack). Similarly, fickle relationships can be traced back to classical myth—Procris and Cephalus offer one source—and the didactic message presented by this "School for Lovers" (the subtitle of *Così*) echoes Ovid's *Ars amatoria.* The action also had contemporary resonances: some commentators claim origins for the plot in a recent scandal at the court of Emperor Joseph II, and even in Mozart's own currently fraught relationship with his wife, Constanze Weber (he had originally fallen in love with her sister, Aloysia). Moreover, the Albanian elements (compare with Mozart's "Turkish" *Die Entführung aus dem Serail*) evoke Joseph II's recent military campaigns in the Balkans. But none of the characters in *Così* has the clear history of, say, Figaro or Don Giovanni. Thus they have a pasteboard quality, making it difficult for us to empathize with their predicament. And even when Mozart does explore his characters—Fiordiligi's wholehearted submission to Ferrando (in the magnificent duet "Fra gli amplessi in pochi istanti" in act II) well illustrates how he could focus on the human psyche—this seems the exception rather than the rule.

A second criticism of *Così fan tutte* is that Mozart's music is surprisingly and unusually inconsistent in terms both of style and quality, and of matching music to drama. Differences between the profound trio "Soave sia il vento" (act I) and Guglielmo's rather vapid "Donne mie, la fate a tanti" in act II sit uneasily in our minds. Further difficulties are caused by the parody-like nature of much of the opera: Fiordiligi's "Come scoglio immoto resta" (act I), a glorious pastiche of an *opera seria* aria, is only the most obvious example. Is this satire, irony, or real emotion? It is difficult to tell.

Of course, one can find explanations, or at least excuses, for the problems of *Così*. The original cast contained singers of whom Mozart was not particularly fond. Adriana Ferrarese del Bene (Fiordiligi) was Da Ponte's mistress, and Mozart disliked both her and her voice. Similarly, Francesco Bussani (Don Alfonso: his wife, Dorotea Sardi, played Despina) had proved unhelpful to the composer and librettist during their difficult careers in Vienna (he was Bartolo and Antonio in *Figaro,* and Masetto and the Commendatore in *Don Giovanni*). Moreover, his voice was apparently in decline: witness the absence of a *bona fide* aria for him. As for Ferrando, although Mozart could rely on the acknowledged talents of Vincenzo Calvesi, the composer never seems to have liked writing for a tenor voice (compare Don Ottavio in *Don Giovanni*). And although Guglielmo was played by that Mozart stalwart, Francesco Benucci (the first Figaro and Leporello), even his presence may not have been enough to attract Mozart to do his best in *Così*.

Another explanation for *Così* may lie in the generally unfavorable reception afforded to Mozart's operas in Vienna: *Figaro* had only nine performances in 1786, and *Don Giovanni,* an opera conceived with Prague tastes in mind, was hardly successful when staged in Vienna in 1788. To be sure, multiple performances of operas in Vienna were less the norm than an exception: opera was an essentially transitory entertainment. But contemporary audiences did not always take kindly to the questionable politics of *Figaro,* the confusing mixture of genres in *Don Giovanni,* and, in general, the apparent complexity of Mozart's operatic style: Joseph II's comment on *Die Entführung*—"Too beautiful for our ears, and far too many notes, my dear Mozart"—may be apocryphal, but it represents a common view of the composer. Thus Mozart was perhaps struggling to meet the tastes of an audience that had failed to appreciate his best efforts: the work has by far the simplest plot of the three Mozart-Da Ponte operas, and the music, too, exhibits concessions to somewhat frivolous Viennese tastes.

It is convenient to blame the problems of *Così* on his singers and audience. But perhaps this misses a crucial point: the undoubted inconsistencies in the music of *Così* may instead reflect Mozart's changing perception of the nature and function of operatic music. In both *Figaro* and *Don Giovanni,* he had transfered essentially symphonic styles to the stage. This is most obviously apparent in his use of sonata-form structures: sonata form, often found in, say, the first movements of symphonies, is based on the establishing and resolution of tonal dissonances between different keys (often tonic and dominant), and also on thematic repetition for the sake of balance. But thematic repetition seems fundamentally unsuited to dramatic situations, where the action (and therefore the music) must look forwards rather than backwards. This creates problems for a composer seeking to use sonata form in an operatic context.

It is striking, however, that there is an almost total absence of sonata form in *Così fan tutte*. At several points where, were this *Figaro*, one might have found a sonata-form movement (e.i., the act I sextet, "Alla bella Despinetta," or "Fra gli amplessi in pochi istanti," Mozart produces instead more processive structures to match the forward-march of the action. Something is lost in the process (thematic unity and tonal coherence suffer) but the result is a more operatic, rather than symphonic, mode of dramatic composition.

The notion of Mozart experimenting with new kinds of operatic writing may seem an abstruse explanation of the musical problems of *Così fan tutte*, but it is entirely consistent with Mozart's own compositional development: his brief life encompassed an extraordinarily rapid growth in musical technique and emotional perception. But one might equally argue that the difficulties of the opera are due less to Mozart than to our own misguided expectations. Neither the drama nor the music of *Così fan tutte* are untypical of contemporary *opera buffa*— Domenico Cimarosa's *Il matrimonio segreto* (1792) provides a useful comparison—and its general opera embodies an aristocratic, slightly cynical and detached wit that is entirely consistent with late eighteenth-century aesthetics. We would perhaps do better to accept things for what they are rather than expect them to be what they are not. But is that not the lesson of this "School for Lovers"?—TIM CARTER

Cossutta, Carlo

Tenor. Born 8 May 1932, in Trieste. Studied with Manfredo Miselli, Mario Melani, and Arturo Wolken in Buenos Aires; debut as Cassio at Teatro Colón, Buenos Aires, 1958, where he spent five seasons; created Ginastro's Don Rodrigo there in 1964; Chicago debut as Cassio, 1963; Covent Garden debut as Duke of Mantua, 1964; debut at Metropolitan Opera as Pollione, 1973.

The tenor voice is relatively rare among male singers: the *tenore robusto* (dramatic tenor) is rarer still. The voice type is characterised by a dark, baritonal timbre, often of considerable size and ideally combined with a ringing upper register and innate histrionic ability. For such singers were written roles such as Radames (*Aïda*), Manrico (*Il trovatore*), Don Alvaro (*La forza del destino*), many of Wagner's tenor parts and the ultimate role in the *robusto* repertoire, Otello. We do not usually look to the dramatic tenor, however, for the subtlety, style or sensitivity more usual in his lighter-voiced colleagues. Rarely, a robusto combines all these qualities; the result is an exceptional artist indeed.

Carlo Cossutta *is* such an artist, yet his career and achievements have been curiously undervalued. His career has been steady rather than spectacular and, most regrettable of all, he has been sadly neglected by the record companies. The result is that his exceptional art will be preserved for posterity in not even a handful of recordings, while some of his less accomplished colleagues record roles for the second or even a third time.

It is difficult to understand why a singer of such accomplishment has not had a more illustrious career, but even so, Cossutta's success has been considerable. In the late 50s and early 60s, as house tenor at the Teatro Colón in Buenos Aires, he was entrusted with leading roles but often also sang Cassio there to many of the most famous Otellos of the day, experience that was to prove invaluable in the future. As the voice darkened during the next decade, he became one of the most sought-after dramatic tenors, and eventually for his own assumption of the role of the Moor. Few tenors have combined all the requirements of this colossus amongst tenor roles more successfully than he.

It is in the singing of Verdi that Cossutta has most excelled. Few dramatic tenors have so exceptionally risen to every requirement of Verdi's writing for the tenor voice. Cossutta's technique permits adaptation of style from the most dramatic to the finest lyricism, while always demonstrating musicality and the scrupulous observation of the directions in the score. Exceptionally for this type of voice, he can sing pianissimo when required, as demonstrated in his commercial recording of the Verdi Requiem. During his career, Cossutta has been admired not only in such Verdi roles as the Duke of Mantua (*Rigoletto*), Radames, Don Alvaro, Gabriele Adorno (*Simon Boccanegra*) and Riccardo (*Un ballo in maschera*) but also in Puccini's, as Rodolfo (*La Bohème*) and Dick Johnson (*La Fanciulla del West*).

However, it will always be for the role of Otello that Cossutta will be best remembered. Perhaps there have been Otellos more gifted histrionically, but few have sung the part more beautifully or have been so technically the equal of one of the most difficult roles in the tenor repertoire. His commercial recording of Otello is a little disappointing. Though well-sung, Cossutta is not successful in compensating for the lack of a stage persona that makes his interpretation all the more convincing in the theatre.

Cossutta is possibly one of many exceptionally gifted singers in operatic history who have lacked the temperament and relentless ambition necessary to strive for the very highest operatic accomplishment. He has in addition eschewed the frenetic career tolerated by some of his colleagues, preferring to limit the number of his performances. Perhaps this may to some degree explain why Cossutta has never achieved just recognition. But, whatever the reason, it is unlikely that those who heard this fine singer in the theater would have been unaware of hearing an artist of anything other than the first rank.—LARRY LUSTIG

Cotrubas, Ileana

Soprano. Born 9 June 1939 in Galati, Romania. Married Manfred Ramin, 1972. Studied with Constantin Stroescu at Bucharest Conservatory and at Vienna Music Academy. Debut as Yniold in Pelléas *in Bucharest, 1964; won first prize in the 's-Hertogenbosch competition, 1965; joined Frankfurt Opera, 1968; Glyndebourne debut as Mélisande, 1970; Vienna Staatsoper debut at Vienna, 1971, as Violetta; Covent Garden debut as Tatiana, 1971; Chicago debut as Mimi, 1973; Teatro alla Scala (1975) and Metropolitan Opera (1977) debuts in same role.*

The Romanian soprano Ileana Cotrubas won the admiration and affection of opera lovers throughout the world during her relatively short career on the international operatic stage. Her roles were many and varied, extending chronologically from Cavalli's *Callisto* to Debussy's

Mélisande. Her voice was not heavy enough for Wagner, making his operas one of the few major parts of the standard repertory into which she rarely ventured. Truly cosmopolitan in her repertory, she sang Mimi (Puccini's *La bohème*, Tatyana (Tchaikowsky's *Eugene Onegin*) and Micaela (Bizet's *Carmen*) with equal success. Her many recordings represent a valuable testament to her musical and dramatic skills.

In general Cotrubas tended towards the portrayal of good characters. There was something gentle and sweet in her stage personality that encouraged opera directors to cast her in the roles of young, innocent and essentially virtuous heroines, such as Ilia (in *Idomeneo*), Susanna, and Pamina, among others. She rarely had the opportunity to sing such villainous roles as Mozart's Queen of the Night (*Die Zauberflöte*), Electra (*Idomeneo*) or Vitellia (*La clemenza di Tito*).

When she sang Pamina at Covent Garden in 1979 her portrayal won praise from one critic as "a delectably phrased and coloured Pamina." Her performance of Ilia at the Metropolitan Opera, opposite Frederika von Stade's Idamante, can be admired on a video tape recorded in 1982 under the direction of James Levine. The opera opens with a big solo *scena* for Ilia in which we can see Cotrubas's strengths and her weaknesses. Among her strengths is the beautiful, uniform sound of her voice as well as her effective use of gestures and facial expressions to communicate feelings. Her excessive vibrato, however, often distorts the pitch. In the aria "Padre, germani, addio" a wider variety of vocal timbres would be welcome: it seems that Cotrubas's uniformity of tone comes at the expense of dramatic color. At the words "Grecia, cagion tu sei" (Greece, it is your fault), Mozart's music and Cotrubas's gestures and face express the intensity of Ilia's feelings, but Cotrubas's voice does not.

Among Cotrubas's best roles in nineteenth-century Italian opera was Norina in Donizetti's *Don Pasquale*. When she portrayed Norina at Covent Garden in 1979 a critic described her as "enticing", and praised the "effortless flow of liquid tone" with which she executed Donizetti's coloratura. She also won much praise for her performances of two of Verdi's best soprano roles, Violetta in *La traviata* and Gilda in *Rigoletto*. One critic who heard her perform Gilda at Covent Garden in 1976 called her portrayal "ideal," not only vocally but also in the way in which she conveyed the innocent and youthful personality of her character. Two years later a critic at Covent Garden described her Gilda as "peerless."—JOHN A. RICE

The Cradle Will Rock

Composer: *Marc Blitzstein.*
Librettist: *Marc Blitzstein.*
First Performance: *New York, 16 June 1937.*

The text of Marc Blitzstein's *The Cradle Will Rock*, biting and satirical, involves the efforts of the workers in Steeltown, USA to unionize, as well as the actions of the capitalistic establishment to thwart them. Mr. Mister controls Steeltown and its citizenry. In order to stop the workers, he organizes a so-called "Liberty Committee," comprised of stereotypical "good people" of the community; they are symbolic representations of the Press, the Groves of Academe, the Medical Establishment, the Church, the Arts, and the Legal Profession. The action takes place in a night court, and the plot unfolds through a series of flashbacks.

Mr. Mister's efforts to thwart the union include bribing the local newspaper to help frame Larry Foreman, the union organizer, and using his leverage as owner of the mortgage of Harry Druggist's drug store to coerce the mild-mannered apothecary to help frame the innocent Gus Polack for the bombing of union headquarters. Polack and his wife Sadie, who is expecting a child, are to be killed in the blast. The Druggist's son, Steve, in an effort to prevent the tragedy, is himself killed along with the young couple. In the end, however, all the workers unite; virtue triumphs.

In this, his first full-length stage work, Blitzstein was clearly influenced by Kurt Weill, Bertolt Brecht, and Hanns Eisler. Aaron Copland aptly characterized *The Cradle Will Rock* as "something of a cross between social drama, musical review, and opera." The musical material includes parody and satire as well as popular songs in the style of Weill's *Three-Penny Opera*.—DAVID Z. KUSHNER

Crespin, Régine

Soprano. Born 23 March 1927, in Marseilles. Married writer Lou Bruder, 1962. Debut as Elsa in Mulhouse and at Paris Opera, 1950; Bayreuth debut as Kundry, 1958; Glyndebourne debut as Marschallin, 1959-60; Covent Garden debut as Marschallin, 1960; Chicago debut as Tosca, 1962; in Buenos Aires since 1962; Metropolitan Opera debut as Marschallin, 1962; entered mezzo repertory after 1971.

Régine Crespin is undoubtedly the greatest mid–twentieth-century singer produced by France; she is also, according to Henry Pleasants in *The Grand Tradition*, "one of the great singers on record." She is all the more remarkable that, like her great predecessor Germaine Lubin, she made her reputation in the German repertoire. Crespin's singing, however, is not to everyone's taste. Some critics, while recognizing the eloquent artistry of her dramatic soprano, have called the voice itself "flawed"; indeed, even Pleasants thinks of her as an "acquired taste that becomes addictive."

Crespin, in fact, had what may be almost thought of as two careers. Her busy international round of appearances as a dramatic soprano was interrupted by a personal crisis in the late 1960s and early 1970s which brought, in its turn, a vocal crisis about which she herself has written most frankly and movingly in the autobiographical *La vie et L'amour d'une femme* in 1982, and about which she has talked freely in interviews. As a result of the crisis she stopped singing during 1973-74 and reworked her vocal technique from the ground up with a "vocal rehabilitator," as she describes him, in Cologne. When she resumed her career in 1974 she moved toward (or returned to) roles more associated with mezzos (though continuing to sing them as a soprano): Carmen, Charlotte in *Werther*, and the Old Prioress in *Dialogues des Carmelites*, enjoying great success in them in New York and elsewhere.

But it was in what she calls *"les Wagneriennes blondes,"* that she began her career, making her debut in 1950 as Elsa at Mulhouse, quickly following that by her debut in the same role at the Paris Opéra. Seven years of singing such diverse roles as Tosca, Desdemona, Amelia (*Un ballo in maschera*) and the Marschallin in France brought her to Bayreuth in 1958 to work with Wieland Wagner as his "Mediterranean" Kundry. This marked the start of an international career which quickly took her to the major houses of Europe and North and South America where she won great renown in other Wagner roles: Elizabeth, Senta, Sieglinde (a special favourite with herself and audiences), the *Walküre* Brünnhilde—with Karajan only, for the recording and for nine live performances; in major Verdi roles; and as Fidelio, Ariadne and Pizzetti's *Fedra* among others. Her French roles included the role of the Second Prioress (which Poulenc wrote for her) in the Paris premiere of *Dialogues*, Fauré's Pénélope, Berlioz's Marguerite and Dido, as well as a number of Offenbach roles. Her debut at the Metropolitan Opera (1962) was as the Marschallin, for which she was coached by Lotte Lehmann.

Crespin could dominate the stage even when not actually singing, rivetting one's attention from her entrance. While her voice sometimes acquired a slightly acidulous quality under pressure, the use she made of it assures her a high place in the history of vocal art. Her striking femininity and personal elegance were reflected in the refinement of her singing; high intelligence and profound emotional comprehension lay behind her exquisite diction, her subtle phrasing, and the variety of her tone color. At her best the voice was lustrous, smooth, seductive, strong and even throughout its range; her high pianissimo was of a beauty and eloquence few of her rivals could approach. She could transform herself onstage into a magisterial Marschallin; a Sieglinde matching Lehmann's in its tender womanliness; a Carmen full of stark fatalism, humour, insouciance, sexiness; a Grande Duchesse of witty élan; an Old Prioress—a role she performed frequently towards the end of her career—of elemental power.

Crespin was a notably accomplished recitalist, singing Schumann and Wolf with subtle insight. The French repertoire, notably Berlioz, Fauré, Duparc, Ravel and Poulenc, provided some of her greatest moments in the concert hall. Some of them—not nearly enough—along with Brünnhilde, Sieglinde and Marschallin, provide some of her greatest testimonials on record. Her *Nuits d'Été,* not yet surpassed, contains many exquisite moments, not least the ethereally gentle expiration on the final word of the song, *"jalouser"* (*"que tous les rois vont jalouser"*).

Wit, intelligence, sensitivity, integrity, dramatic concentration, all working through a voice capable of expressing noble defiance or exquisitely tender resignation—this was the art for which Régine Crespin will be long remembered.—PETER DYSON

The Crucible

Composer: *Robert Ward.*

Librettist: *B. Stambler (after A. Miller).*

First Performance: *New York, 26 October 1961.*

Roles: *John Proctor (baritone); Elizabeth Proctor (mezzo-soprano); Abigail Williams (soprano); Reverend John Hale (bass); Judge Danforth (tenor); Reverend Samuel Parris (tenor); Tituba (contralto); Rebecca Nurse (contralto); Giles Corey (tenor); Mary Warren (soprano); Ann Putnam (soprano); Thomas Putnam (baritone); Ezekiel Cheever (tenor); Francis Nurse (bass); Sarah Good (soprano); Betty Parris (mezzo-soprano); Ruth Putnam (soprano); Susanna Walcott (contralto); Mercy Lewis (contralto); Martha Seldon (soprano); Bridget Booth (soprano); chorus (SATB).*

In 1962 Robert Ward received both the Pulitzer Prize and the New York Critics Circle Citation for *The Crucible*. The opera, a large work in four acts, was based on Arthur Miller's play of the same name with the libretto adapted by Bernard Stambler. Ward's setting of Miller's powerful play about the witch trials of Salem, Massachusetts of the 1690s was a success at its New York premiere on 26 October 1961. The play and opera recreate the frenzy and anguish of the witch hunts of that strange period in American history. Winthrop Sargeant, writing in the *New Yorker* after the premiere, stated: "[Ward's] music, though quite accessible to the average listener, is everywhere dignified and nowhere banal. It is continuously expressive, and it intensifies all the nuances of the drama. . . . he has created an imposing work that will, I suspect, take its place among the classics of the standard repertory."

The central theme of the plot concerns the love affair between Abigail Williams and John Proctor. John, married to Elizabeth Proctor, will eventually be discovered for his adulterous behavior. The story opens with the Reverend Samuel Parris kneeling distraught at the bed of his daughter Betty. Betty and her cousin Abigail had been found dancing in the woods the night before. Abigail enters to tell him that the town is whispering about witchcraft. Accusations are made about compacts with the devil, and the citizens claim that these evil spirits must be removed from the community. The Reverend Hale, the leading inquisitor, arrives and begins his trials to seek out those who are bewitched. John Proctor and Rebecca Nurse are accused of witchcraft and sentenced to be executed.

Since its premiere performance, the opera has become one of the most frequently performed of American operas. Ward skillfully combines modern dissonance with his conservative tonal musical style. The result is a terse musical texture which creates great tension and anxiety for the unfolding drama. Ward utilizes a recitative-like style throughout the opera with occasional moments of lyricism. The orchestra provides much color and rhythmical punctuation to the quick-paced dramatic action. Ward's lyrical skill is especially evident in the close of act I. A hymn-like melody in 7/8 is sung by all the main characters beginning with the words, "Allelulia. Jesus, my consolation, . . . " bringing the first act to a dramatic conclusion. The melody also reappears in the last three acts and provides motivic cohesion for the entire work.

The Crucible remains Ward's outstanding opera. His conservative tonal style with occasional incursions into twentieth-century dissonance was an ideal musical style for this historical drama. The story is one that will continue to hold an audience's attention. This work gives Ward an important role in the development of American opera.—ROBERT F. NISBETT

The Cunning Little Vixen [Príhody Lišky Bystroušky]

Composer: *Leoš Janáček.*

Librettist: *Leoš Janáček (after Rudolf Těsnohlidek).*

First Performance: *Brno, National Theater, 6 November 1924.*

Roles: *Forester (baritone); His Wife (contralto); Schoolmaster (tenor); Priest (bass); Harasta (bass); Vixen/Bystrouska (soprano); The Fox, Goldenmane (tenor or soprano); Lapák, Forester's Dog (mezzo-soprano); Pasak (tenor); His Wife (soprano); Badger (bass); Rooster (soprano); Hen (soprano); Screechowl (contralto); Jay (soprano); Woodpecker (contralto); various animals; chorus (SATB).*

The Cunning Little Vixen is a striking example of Janáček's pantheism. His patchwork methods of story-telling are used less to form a coherent plot than to create a certain ambience, or to develop a vitalist philosophy. It is no coincidence that the most beautiful music of the opera occurs in the love scene between The Fox, Goldenmane, and The Vixen, Bystrouska, and in the finale, in which Forester pronounces a benediction on the beauty of nature, and the eternity of Life itself.

Janáček's musical setting for this story is remarkable. He avoids long melodic lines at almost all points in the score. As is now well known, Janáček believed that all music finds its ultimate source in the spoken word. This crucial aspect of his music is often misrepresented. He was as interested in reflecting the psychological realities of speech as he was in recreating the particular accents and other characteristics of the language. Like the composer's other operas, *The Cunning Little Vixen* contains a great deal of melodic writing, but it is usually of the short rhapsodic sort, as would be expected from the naturalistic word setting described here.

The orchestra for this opera is large and has a special luminosity that is even more pronounced than in most of Janáček's other operatic works. Janáček's orchestra is one of alternating choirs and brilliant colors, rarely blended in the nineteenth-century style; it is sharp, clean, and utterly personal. He has a liking for wide orchestral spaces, often using extreme registers both in combination and alternately. Although the orchestra is very active, its scoring makes it quite easy for voices and words to be heard.

Superficially, it is possible to make a comparison between Janáček's methods and those of Wagner. It was the great German who militantly rejected (but not always) the "number opera." He also opted for a more naturalistic kind of expressive recitative. In the narrow sense, this could also describe the methods used by Janáček. But he goes further; each person is represented by music which reflects *his* particular use of language, governed by his personality and its particular idiosyncrasies. The criterion for Janáček was what the character would sound like if he were only speaking the lines.—HARRIS CROHN

The Cunning Little Vixen, with Thomas Allen as the Forester, Royal Opera, London, 1990

OPERA ≡d

Dal Monte, Toti

Soprano. Born Antonietta Meneghel, 27 June 1893, in Magliano Veneto. Died 26 January 1975, in Treviso. Married singer Enzo de Muro Lomanto, one daughter. Studied with Barbara Marchesio for five years; debut at Teatro alla Scala as Biancofiore in Francesca di Rimini, *1916; engaged by Toscanini to sing Lucia at La Scala, 1921; Metropolitan Opera debut as Lucia, 1924; Covent Garden debut as Lucia and Rosina, 1926; retired from the operatic stage in 1949, but continued to act.*

Toti dal Monte is one of those rare and fortunate singers who made her debut at the foremost opera house of Europe. After five years of study with the celebrated mezzo-soprano Barbara Marchisio, and following a series of auditions with the leading conductors of the day, dal Monte was engaged for three months at the Teatro alla Scala, at ten lire a day. She made her debut as Biancofiore in Zandonai's *Francesca da Rimini* on 22 February 1916. Her colleagues were Rosa Raisa (another Marchisio pupil), Aureliano Pertile, and Giuseppe Danise. During rehearsals conductor Gino Marinuzzi suggested that she should change her name, Antonietta Meneghel. She chose her nickname—Toti—and her grandmother's maiden name.

After this promising start, dal Monte spent the next three years building a repertoire and gaining much needed experience in the lesser theaters of Italy. Her new roles included Norina, Oscar, Lisette in Puccini's *La Rondine*, Gilda, Nedda, the title role of Mascagni's *Lodoletta*, Zerlina in Auber's *Fra Diavolo*, Musetta, Leila in the *Les pêcheurs de perles,* and Lauretta in *Gianni Schicchi*. She sang her first Cio-Cio-San in *Madama Butterfly* on 14 September 1918, at the Teatro Lirico of Milan; after a total of six performances she did not assay the role again until 1938. Her tours soon made her a favorite of audiences everywhere, and her reputation grew accordingly.

During her first foreign engagement she sang Gilda, Philine *(Mignon),* Nannetta in *Falstaff,* the Countess in Gomes' *Lo Schiavo,* and Musetta in *La bohème* in the major South American cities of Argentina, Uruguay, and Brazil. Between her first two South American seasons she returned to La Scala in June 1922, as a soloist in Beethoven's Ninth Symphony under the baton of Arturo Toscanini. The Maestro then invited her for the following season to sing Gilda opposite Carlo Galeffi and Giacomo Lauri-Volpi in the cast. This endorsement and her success established her as a permanent member of that illustrious company. Her assignments at La Scala included the plum roles of the coloratura repertory: the title roles of *Lucia di Lammermoor, La sonnambula, La fille du régiment,* and *Linda di Chamounix,* along with Rosina, Gilda, and Norina. She also sang Rosalina in the world premiere of *Il re,* on 29 January 1929, a role Giordano had expressly composed for her.

Established as a major artist of international caliber, she received many invitations from the major operatic centers of the world. Among the many cities where she performed, her most important engagements were her debuts at the Teatro Colón in Buenos Aires (1923), Paris Opéra (1924), Metropolitan Opera (1924), Covent Garden (1925), San Carlo in Naples (1929), and the Verona Arena (1934). In 1924 and 1928, Nellie Melba took her on the Melba-Williamson tours to Melbourne and Sydney. In 1926 she was engaged for a four-month concert tour of Australia and New Zealand, and in 1929, when Toscanini took the La Scala company on tour to Germany and Austria, dal Monte was his choice for the title role of *Lucia di Lammermoor* in Berlin and Vienna. Another five-month concert tour took her in 1931 from Moscow to Hong Kong, Manila, Shanghai, and five cities in Japan. She sang only two Lucias and one Gilda in her single season at the Metropolitan (1924-25), but she was a member of the Chicago Civic Opera Company from 1924 to 1928, and toured the United States coast to coast.

Later in her career she took on heavier roles: Mimi, Butterfly, Manon, Violetta. In spite of her initial apprehensions, Cio-Cio-San became one of her most successful and most often requested roles. In her own words, "I could have sung nothing else, so many were the requests." A list of her partners through her career read like the operatic who's who of the period: Gigli, Pertile, Lauri-Volpi, Schipa, Battistini, Stracciari, Galeffi, Chaliapin, Pinza. Her last operatic engagement was a series of Rosinas in four small Italian cities in 1947, and she continued to give recitals until 1950. She also appeared as an actress in speaking roles on stage (in Goldoni's *Buona madre*) and in films, among the latter *Il carnevale di Venezia* (1940), *Fiori d'arancio* (1944), *Una voce nel tuo cuore* (1950) and *Cuore di mamma* (1955). Following her retirement, she taught singing in Milan, Rome, Venice, and the USSR. Her pupils included Gianna d'Angelo (*née* Jane Angelovic) and Dolores Wilson.

Dal Monte credited her teacher, Marchisio, with developing her voice, giving it power and agility, extending its range, and teaching her correct breathing and an exceptional coloratura technique. Light, clear, and brilliant, dal Monte's voice had more weight than the coloratura sopranos who preceded her or were her contemporaries. In fact, at first she thought of herself as a light mezzo, and was able to darken her voice sufficiently to persuade the management to let her sing Lola in *Cavalleria rusticana,* her second role at La Scala in 1916. The spectrum of her vocal palette and her sound musical instinct enabled her to shade her voice according to the dramatic demands of the role. Her well-executed coloratura ornamentations and *staccatti* as preserved on disc are accurate but not flashy, more devices of expression than vocal exhibitionism. Her voice had great purity; she could float a note and produce a well-supported, focused tone at any pitch or dynamic level. She was an accomplished actress, and although small and plump, her attractive face, expressive and beautiful large eyes, charm, grace, and innate femininity made her impersonations credible and appealing.

d OPERA

Dal Monte's recordings for Victor and His Master's Voice command respect among collectors. Writing in the *Gramophone,* the well-known author, critic, and voice teacher Herman Klein had high praise for her mad scene from *Lucia* (DB 1015): "The vocalization is worthy of Toti dal Monte at her best. . . . The duets with the flute are flawlessly executed; but even more astonishing to my ear are those long, gigantic E flats in *alt.*" Upon the release of her *Carnevale di Venezia* (DB 1004) Klein wrote "That this gifted *soprano leggiero* is the best singer of her class Italy has produced since Tetrazzini there can be no manner of doubt." Her only complete recording—*Madama Butterfly* (His Master's Voice, 1939), with Beniamino Gigli—was received with some ambivalence. Dal Monte purposefully and successfully colored her voice in the first act to create the vocal image of the fifteen-year-old geisha, a sound not associated with the role as sung by other sopranos. Her approach is well-conceived, her delivery honest, and her dramatic involvement complete.

Dal Monte suffered from high blood pressure all her life and she retired because of it. In January 1975 she was hospitalized in Florence and treated for circulatory problems. She died at Pieve di Soligo, on 26 January 1975. Her entertaining autobiography, *Una voce nel mondo,* first appeared in 1962; it was posthumously republished under the editorship of Rodolfo Celletti, with an added chronology and discography.—ANDREW FARKAS

Dantons Tod [Danton's Death]

Composer: *Gottfried von Einem.*
Librettists: *Boris Blacher and Gottfried von Einem (after Büchner).*
First Performance: *Salzburg, 6 August 1947; revised 1955.*
Roles: *Georges Danton (baritone); Camille Desmoulins (tenor); Herault de Sechelles (tenor); Robespierre (tenor); St. Just (bass); Lucille (soprano); Herrmann (baritone); Simon (bass); Julie (mezzo-soprano); Simon's Wife (contralto); Young Man (tenor); Two Executioners (tenor, bass); Woman (soprano); chorus (SATB).*

The successful premiere of Gottfried von Einem's opera *Dantons Tod* at the 1947 Salzburg Festival and its quick staging by European houses were due to more than the strong drama of Einem's score. The production of an opera by a young Austrian composer, one who had not collaborated in the former regime's cultural policies, was a first step toward the rehabilitation of German musicians after the war. *Dantons Tod* dramatizes legalized governmental terror, a plague which the world at that time realized had not been eradicated with the end of the war.

Dantons Tod was adapted from Georg Büchner's play by Einem and his teacher, composer Boris Blacher. The protagonist is Georges Danton, a leader in the French government during the Revolution. When he turned against Robespierre's tactics—including the Terror—he was guillotined in April 1794. The opera's first act establishes Danton's confrontation with Robespierre. In the first scene, Danton and Camille Desmoulins express, to a group of their friends playing cards, their desire for an end of the daily executions. Scene ii introduces the volatile crowd. Robespierre enters and in an aria sways the crowd and promises more executions. Danton confronts him. After Danton leaves, Robespierre and his colleague Saint-Just decide that he and Camille must be killed. In the last scene of the act Danton announces to Camille and his wife Lucille that he is to be arrested, but he refuses to flee.

Act II depicts Danton's trial and death. Two scenes before the Revolutionary Tribunal are separated by one with Danton and Camille in prison. Lucille comes to see Camille; she has lost her reason. In the trial scenes the crowd swings between demanding Danton's death and falling under the spell of his eloquent oratory. At the end, in the Place de la Revolution, the condemned prisoners sing the Marseillaise in counterpoint to the crowd dancing the Carmagnole. Danton and Camille are guillotined. After the crowd disperses, Lucille enters and sits on the steps of the guillotine. She cries "Es lebe der König" (Long live the king) and is arrested as the curtain falls.

Einem and Blacher collapse the four acts of Büchner's play to two. Most of their changes in the first act consist of pruning speeches and removing minor scenes and characters. The second act contains more substantial dramatic changes, the scenes with the crowd and in the prison being moved before the tribunal scene. Most of the newly penned lines in the opera occur in the passage where Lucille calls to Camille in prison. In making these changes, the authors unfortunately removed much explanatory material. For example, at the end of the trial scene with Danton's soaring oratory and acclaim by the crowd, one would think that he would be released, but in the next scene we find him at the guillotine. This is one of those historical- and literary-based operas with which it is helpful to be familiar with either the historical background of the plot or else the play on which it is based.

The power of Einem's musical expression makes up for the failings in the libretto. Throughout his career his chosen idiom has been tonal, "post-romantic." The most noticeable influence is Stravinsky, heard in the repeated wind chords and in the liberally sprinkled "wrong" notes over a diatonic foundation. In this opera Einem follows the stage works of Hindemith more than those of Berg or Strauss; he does not use a leitmotif complex. *Dantons Tod* is clearly conceived in terms of the orchestra: each scene is based around a clearly defined orchestral figure, as in the scene before the court with the sixty-fourth-note runs. Orchestral interludes between scenes play an important role in the mood of the opera and in conveying the progress of the drama. The quiet interlude before the chaotic counterpoint of the Carmagnole and the Marseillaise is a masterstroke. As Strauss used the waltz as an anachronism in *Der Rosenkavalier,* here Einem favors the tango, a dance form also found in other of his compositions.

Although the orchestra is predominant, the vocal line is not reduced to an expressionist recitative. Einem lets the voice take over in lyrical and dramatic moments: Robespierre's aria, the scenes for Lucille, Danton's address to the court. In his declamatory lines one hears the influence of Hindemith, Hugo Wolf, Othmar Schoeck, and others. His later practice of setting text to one repeated note is occasionally found here. One fault may be that at many points the orchestra is more interesting than the voice, although in Robespierre's aria, for example, Einem shows he can spin out an exquisite cantilena. Einem makes the crowd into a major character in the opera, but it often seems that it is better delineated than some of the characters.

Einem revised the score slightly after the premiere, replacing an orchestral prelude with the chords that now open the opera, cutting an orchestral passage after Danton's death, and revising the final scene with Lucille. These changes make for a more dramatic beginning and ending and add to a score that deserves more frequent revivals than it has seen to date.—DAVID ANDERSON

Daphne

Composer: *Richard Strauss.*

Librettist: *J. Gregor.*

First Performance: *Dresden, Staatsoper, 15 October 1938.*

Roles: *Peneios (bass); Gaea (contralto); Daphne (soprano); Leukippos (tenor); Apollo (tenor); Four Shepherds (baritone, tenor, two basses); Two Maids (sopranos); chorus (SATB).*

Daphne was the second opera of the Richard Strauss/Joseph Gregor collaboration. Unlike the Zweig inspired *Friedenstag,* its immediate predecessor and team running-mate, Gregor was responsible both for the initial concept and for its textual working out. Zweig had withdrawn from collaboration with Strauss in the mid-1930s, pledging himself to monitor Gregor's librettist activities, but his retreat to England and subsequent self-exile in Brazil inevitably reduced both the opportunity for active participation and the level of his commitment. Gregor's original design ran parallel to that of *Friedenstag,* envisaging a similarly oratorio-like conclusion which portrayed the transformed Daphne as mediator between gods and men. The ultimate solution, as it emerged over the months of collaboration, was more complex owing to an injection of new ideas by the composer who, a life-long admirer of Nietzsche's *The Birth Of Tragedy,* re-interpreted Gregor's symbolism in terms of Nietzschean (Apollo/Dionysos) theory. It was these additions that contributed to the excessive combined length of *Daphne* and *Friedenstag,* which have, after the Dresden joint-premiere of 1938, generally been performed separately.

Daphne, daughter of Peneios (river) and Gaea (earth), is wooed by the shepherd Leukippos, her childhood playmate. She, however, eschews earthly passion, identifying with nature and glorying in sunlight, which she worships. Shepherds gather to celebrate the feast of Dionysos where bacchanalian rites are traditionally enacted. Leukippos, disappointed at his rejection, plans to approach Daphne in female disguise during the festal dances. Meanwhile, the sun god Apollo, also enamored of Daphne, takes human form, pressing his suit disguised as a cowherd. At first intrigued, she is shocked by his passionate embrace. During the feast, Apollo observes Leukippos' successful ruse to partner Daphne in the dance. In a fit of jealousy he exposes his rival's deceit. Leukippos replies in kind, enraging the god, who deals him a mortal blow. Daphne, distraught, mourns her lost playmate. Praying for death, she decks Leukippos' bier with flowers. Overcome with remorse, Apollo intercedes with Zeus to grant Daphne's innermost nature longings: during the course of a wondrous orchestral postlude she is transformed into a flowering laurel tree.

Strauss's revived interest in ancient Greek mythology is not without significance. Increasingly isolated by events and official attitudes in the political climate of the mid-1930s, he perhaps found safety and greater security in a symbolic means of expression. Without doubt it was disillusionment with the contemporary world that led him, through re-identification with his cultural roots, to reaffirm his allegiance to the great German/European tradition which he saw in danger of eclipse. To this end, as a result of a profound inner compulsion, he set himself a comprehensive re-reading schedule which embraced Nietzsche, Wagner and, in chronological order, the entire Goethe opus.

Under the circumstances it is hardly surprising that the final group of operas, written between 1935 and 1942, reflect, comment on, and relate to an artistic heritage which he deemed, culturally, of paramount importance and which he set out, in practice and application, to preserve for future generations. The intensely autobiographical *Die Liebe der Danae* summarized the inheritance in terms of Mozart and Wagner. *Friedenstag,* modeled on *Fidelio,* had an explicit message to the world from which Strauss had ostensibly withdrawn, since it celebrates the peace and brotherhood of mankind—a fitting corollary to Daphne's mediation between the gods and men. The *Daphne* symbolism as Strauss eventually conceived it, however, goes much further than this. Opening with an inspired woodwind pastorale and sun invocation, the opera concludes with the wordless, hushed serenity of Daphne's transformation. "Touched by both Apollo and Dionysos," she is, as Strauss himself pointed out, representative, in the Nietzschean sense, of the perfect, the eternal, art work.

Within the framework of this consistently lyrical and almost perfectly structured opera, the Apollonian conflict is played out granting the composer ample opportunity for those illustrative effects in which he reveled and which so delighted his audiences. The Daphne role itself embodies some of Strauss's finest writing for soprano, while for once, it seems—in the case of Leukippos and Apollo—he conquered his wonted antipathy to the tenor voice. As the composer pointed out, each of his stage works inhabits its own sound world, each responds directly to the individual qualities, atmosphere, and ethos of its text. *Daphne* is no exception. Its perceived balance and lucidity of form, its linear plasticity dominated by the high lyric timbre of soprano and tenor voice, combine with radiantly glowing orchestral textures to personify that popular Germanic concept of Hellenism so dear to the composer's heart. It is this idiomatic serenity and restraint that presages the refined instrumental manner of Strauss's final years.—KENNETH W. BIRKIN

Davies, (Sir) Peter Maxwell

Composer. Born 8 September 1934, in Manchester. Attended Leigh Grammar School, then the Royal Manchester College of Music and Manchester University; in Rome on a scholarship from the Italian government, where he studied with Goffredo Petrassi, 1957; Olivetti Prize for his orchestral work Prolation, *1958; director of music at Cirencester Grammar School, 1959-62; in the United States on a Harkness fellowship, where he studied with Sessions, 1962; joined the UNESCO Conference on Music in Education, and toured the world lecturing, 1965; composer-in-residence at the University of Adelaide, Australia, 1966-67; organized the Pierrot Players (renamed The Fires of London, 1970) with Harrison Birtwistle, 1967; professor of composition, Royal Northern College of Music, 1975-80; organized the annual St Magnus Festival on the Orkney Islands, 1977; honorary doctorate of music from Edinburgh University, 1979; successor to Sir William Glock as director of music at Dartington Summer School, 1979; named Composer of the Year by the Composers' Guild of Great Britain, 1979; commissioned to write a symphony for the Boston Symphony Orchestra for their centennial, 1981; associate conductor, Scottish Chamber Orchestra, 1985-. Davies was knighted in 1987.*

Operas/Masques *Cinderella. Blind Man's Buff* (masque), Davies (after G. Büchner, *Leonce und Lena*), 1972, London, Round House, 29 May 1972; alternate version, 1972, London, The Place, 24 November, 1972; *Taverner,* Davies, (libretto written 1956-64; set 1964-70), London, Covent Garden, 12 July 1972; *Notre Dame des fleurs* (mini-opera), Davies, 1966, London, Queen Elizabeth Hall, 17 March

1973; *The Martyrdom of Saint Magnus,* Davies (after G. MacKay Brown), 1976, Kirkwall, Orkney, St Magnus Cathedral, 18 June 1977; *The Two Fiddlers* (children's opera), Davies (after MacKay Brown), 1978, Kirkwall, Orkney, 16 June 1978; *Le jongleur de Notre Dame* (masque), Davies, 1978, Kirkwall, Orkney, 18 June 1978; *The Lighthouse,* Davies (after a story by Craig Mair), 1979, Edinburgh, 2 September 1980; *Resurrection,* Davies, Darmstadt, 25 September 1988.

As a composer, Peter Maxwell Davies has been both remarkably prolific and remarkably versatile, composing works in a wide variety of forms and even a wide range of styles. Six of his works (as of this writing) are operas, each of them a unique and original work, though some common threads do exist among them. But any account of his operas must also make some mention of his ten or so other dramatic works, including music-theatre pieces (the most famous of which is *Eight Songs for a Mad King*), the 1984 *No. 11 Bus,* and the 'mono-drama' *The Medium:* all these incorporate operatic elements.

Davies's operas may be grouped into three classes: first, the two large-scale works *Taverner* and *Resurrection;* next, the chamber operas *The Lighthouse* and *The Martyrdom of Saint Magnus;* and finally, the two operas *Cinderella* and *The Two Fiddlers* written to be played and sung entirely by children.

Certainly the most celebrated of these works is *Taverner,* the story of John Taverner (1490-1545), a man in crisis with both his art and his religion. Davies began work on this composition, one of the most important of his early years, in 1956; it was first performed in 1972. In *Taverner,* the composer makes use of music by Taverner (principally his *In Nomine*), weaving it in and out and permuting it throughout the opera. Renaissance and medieval compositional forms appear in the work alongside highly contemporary music. *Resurrection,* Davies's most recent opera, was commissioned by the city of Darmstadt and premiered there 25 September 1988. As in the case of *Taverner,* the composer wrote his own libretto. *Resurrection* is centered around a character, the "Hero," portrayed by a dummy. The Hero is tormented by the endless pressures and shallow values of contemporary society, represented by various characters and events (for instance, twenty-four television commercials and eight popular songs are included). Eventually, he is "resurrected" into an acceptable conformist, a truly "modern" man. The work calls for eight solo singers, an electronically amplified vocal quartet, dancers, a rock group, a Salvation Army band, and a main ensemble of 17 players.

Davies's two chamber operas are also very different in character from one another. *The Martyrdom of Saint Magnus* launched the first Saint Magnus Festival when it was premiered in the Cathedral of Saint Magnus in Orkney, 18 June 1977. Again, Davies provided his own libretto (basing it on the novel *Magnus* by George MacKay Brown, an author whose writings have served as the basis for a number of Davies's works). The musical material is open, bare, and stark: again, as in *Taverner,* a somewhat medieval treatment. Davies's other chamber opera, *The Lighthouse,* strikes quite a different note: it is the composer's interpretation of an event in a story by Craig Mair which tells the story of three lighthouse keepers who vanished from the Flannon lighthouse in December 1890. Davies overlays the events with religious imagery and ghosts; the lighting directions included in the score, as well as the spare scoring, serve to convey an aura of mystery and horror.

The two operas for children reflect Davies's interest in and concern with producing quality music for children to perform, as well as his commitment to music education. *The Two Fiddlers,* based on another novel by George MacKay Brown, is a moral tale, cautioning against the dangers of complacency, laziness, and succumbing to popular culture and fads. Its delightful score includes folk and folk-like themes, such as a square dance accompanied only by a solo violin; there is also a good deal of modal writing. *Cinderella*, composed for the Kirkwall Grammar School, is a retelling of Perault's classic fairy tale. The music, including a small ensemble consisting of three recorders, various percussion instruments and a string quintet, is primarily tonal and quite accessible to young performers. Rather than try to deal with expensive sets and props, the composer has thoughtfully included in the score directions calling for the use of cardboard cut-outs for such props as the carriage. In these two operas for young people, the same attention to detail found in all Davies's music is much in evidence: nothing is left to chance.—CAROLYN J. SMITH

d

≡OPERA

Death in Venice

Composer: *Benjamin Britten.*

Librettist: *M. Piper (after Thomas Mann).*

First Performance: *Snape Maltings, 16 June 1973.*

Roles: *Gustav von Aschenbach (tenor); Traveller (baritone); Elderly Fop (baritone); Old Gondolier (baritone); Hotel Manager (baritone); Hotel Barber (baritone); Leader of the Players (baritone); Dionysus (baritone); Voice of Apollo (counter tenor); Polish Mother (dancer); Tadzio (dancer); Two Daughters (dancers); Governess (dancer); Jaschiu (dancer); Hotel Porter (tenor); Lido Boatman (baritone); Hotel Waiter (baritone); Strawberry-seller (soprano); Guide (baritone); Glass-maker (tenor); Lace-seller (soprano); Beggar-woman (mezzo-soprano); Newspaper-seller (soprano); Strolling Players (soprano, tenor); English Clerk (baritone); Two Acrobats (dancers); Russian Mother and Father (soprano, bass); Russian Nanny (soprano); German Mother (mezzo-soprano); Gondoliers (tenor, baritone).*

Benjamin Britten and his librettist Myfanwy Piper follow, in *Death in Venice,* the plot and theme of Thomas Mann's novella closely. The plot begins in Munich, where Gustav von Aschenbach (Mann gave him the first name and physical description of Mahler) is walking, taking a break from his work. He is known as an accomplished writer of prose fiction which emphasizes formal perfection of language and thus requires great concentration and self-discipline from the author. Seeing a strange figure in a graveyard, Aschenbach is overcome suddenly by an uncharacteristic desire to travel to the South. He soon arrives in Venice, where he begins to observe a Polish family on vacation—a mother, daughters, and an extremely beautiful boy. The boy, Tadzio, becomes a symbol of absolute beauty for the writer, and calls to his mind the Greek ideal of beauty discussed in Plato's *Phaedrus.* In spite of his pleasure in the boy's beauty, however, his vacation does not seem to be working out; Venice is too hot and seems somehow sinister. Aschenbach decides to leave. But at the last minute he finds he cannot leave the boy and aborts his departure. Remaining in Venice, then, Aschenbach becomes more and more interested in the boy as the days pass, and finally realizes that he has rather ridiculously fallen in love with him. Belatedly he also comes to understand, after various inquiries, that a cholera epidemic has struck the city. The visitors at the hotel have begun to leave, in spite of the efforts of the city officials to keep knowledge of the sickness hidden. Aschenbach stays on because of his infatuation with Tadzio, however; at last the boy's family decides to leave but it is too late for Aschenbach. He dies, presumably of the cholera, lying in his beach chair watching the boy walking on the beach.

Mann's story is usually interpreted as an exploration of the radical effects of separating reason and feeling. Britten adopts this interpretation, adding the offstage voices of Apollo and Dionysus to articulate the ideas of the story. As his opening aria makes clear, Aschenbach has always been an Apollonian artist, interested in form, reason, and restraint. But as the opera progresses, his love for Tadzio begins to allow him to see that passion is closely related to beauty, and finally, in a dream sequence, he understands that the irony of his life has been that the worship of beauty and perfection of form, removed from feeling, is not possible. He grasps at last that his life-long devotion to formalism is in its own way a type of sensualism, and leads one to submit to passion as surely as does a more direct love of beauty. Aschenbach learns inevitably that even the most disciplined artist cannot avoid passion or feeling, and that the more repressed passion is, the greater strength it has when it finally surfaces.

Britten makes these ideas clear in seventeen short scenes, with the overture inserted after the second scene. The fatigue and self-discipline with which Aschenbach works are indicated musically in the opening scene by a cell of melodic half-steps, a motif that returns frequently. The vague threat of the strange people Aschenbach meets is indicated dramatically by the fact that all—the man in the graveyard, the gondolier, a grotesque old fop he meets on the way to Venice, the barber who near the end makes Aschenbach up to resemble the fop, the hotel clerk—are played by the same actor and use the same musical motif, one that Aschenbach himself, after his admission of love for Tadzio, takes up. The sea has its own motif, of large intervals and rhythmic sweep, which near the end is transformed as it too becomes associated with the sensuality that begins to overwhelm Aschenbach. The boy Tadzio and his family are also indicated by their own music, and the boy is always accompanied by the vibraphone when he is on stage. In addition, the family are dancers, not singers, emphasizing the lack of communication between them and Aschenbach; several times the writer tries to naturalize his relationship with them simply by opening a conversation, feeling that would end his infatuation. But he is unable to do so, since Tadzio occupies a different world. Casting Tadzio as a dancer also allows for several dance scenes that make clear just how physical Aschenbach's attraction is and points up the body/mind dichotomy in which he is caught. For finally the opera shows that Aschenbach has tried to deny the body, not only to suppress passion, but to suppress even the body's natural desire for recreation and rest. The story suggests from the beginning the artificiality of this denial; self-discipline begins to break down in the first scene, when the mind inexplicably desires the South as a symbol of relaxation and sensuousness, and continues in the infatuation with the boy. Finally the South comes to represent the revenge of the senses, and Aschenbach succumbs to a death wish—pleasure and death become one for him. *Death in Venice* suggests that the radical separation of mind and body, reason and feeling, work and social life so common in Western culture is untenable and leads finally to total disintegration of the individual.—SANDRA CORSE

Debussy, (Achille-) Claude

Composer. Born 22 August 1862, in St-Germain-en-Laye. Died 25 March 1918, in Paris. Married: 1) Rosalie Texier, 19 October 1899 (divorced, 2 August 1904); 2) Madame Emma Bardac, 15 October 1905 (daughter; died 14 July 1919). Studied with Madame de

OPERA

d

Fleurville, a student of Chopin; studied piano with Marmontel, solfeggio with Lavignac, and harmony with Emile Durand at the Paris Conservatory, 1872-1880; became the family piano teacher to Madame Nadezhda von Meck, Tchaikovsky's patron, and travelled to Switzerland, Italy, and Russia with her family, 1880-82; in Moscow, became acquainted with the music of Borodin and Mussorgsky; second Prix de Rome, 1883; Grand Prix de Rome for his cantata L'enfant prodigue, *1884; heard* Parsifal *in Bayreuth, 1888; returned to Bayreuth in 1889; interest in Oriental music, which was presented at the Paris Exposition, 1889; his only opera,* Pelléas et Mélisande *composed between 1892 and its premiere at the Opéra-Comique on April 30, 1902; most of his well known orchestral compositions composed between 1892-1908; contributions to numerous journals, including* La revue blanche, Gil Blas, Musica, Le mercure de France, Le Figaro, *and others between 1901-17; various conducting engagements in Paris, Vienna, Budapest, Turin, Moscow, St Petersburg, The Hague, Amsterdam, and Rome between 1910-14; Debussy's last public appearance on 5 May 1917, when he played the piano part of his* Violin Sonata *with Gaston Poulet.*

Operas *Axël,* Auguste de Villiers de L'Isle—Adam, c. 1888 [one scene only]; *Roderigue et Chimène,* C. Mendès (after G. de Castro and Corneille), 1890-92 [unfinished]; *Pelléas et Mélisande,* Debussy (after Maeterlinck), 1893-95, 1901-02, Paris, Opéra-Comique, 30 April 1902; *Le diable dans le beffroi,* Debussy (after Poe), 1902-11 [unfinished]; *La chute de la maison Usher,* Debussy (after Poe), 1908-17 [unfinished].

Despite the fact that Debussy's total output in the genre of opera was quite limited, he made an immense impact on opera with his monumental work, *Pelléas et Mélisande.* Although none of his other operatic works survive in their complete form, Debussy worked on a number of opera projects throughout his life.

Debussy's early aborted opera projects include passages from two comedies of de Banville, *Hymnis* and *Diane au Bois,* which are both unpublished works, and a scene from Villiers de L'Isle—Adam's *Axël,* which is also unpublished. After working on these scores, Debussy realized he had overextended his abilities, which may be why he chose to abandon the works. Some say that the use of the dream world in *Diane,* in a general sense, foreshadows *L'Apres-midi d'un faune.*

After *Axël,* Debussy wrote *Rodrigue et Chimène,* a grand opera with a libretto by Catulle Mendès. The work remains in an unfinished, unpublished short score. Supposedly, Debussy undertook the project due to parental pressure, with the personal hope that his association with Mendès would open doors for him at the Paris Opéra. After two years of work on the project, however, he abandoned it, claiming that the manuscript had been destroyed in a fire.

Debussy's only completed opera score was set to the libretto, *Pelléas et Mélisande,* a slightly adapted version of Maeterlinck's play. Debussy began working on *Pelléas* in 1893, and the work was completed a decade later. *Pelléas et Mélisande* represents the height of Debussy's art and is one of the monuments in post-Wagnerian opera.

Opinions on *Pelléas et Mélisande* tend to be divided into two schools. Igor Stravinsky once said that it is "a great bore on the whole, in spite of many wonderful pages." On the other

Claude Debussy, c. 1900

hand, Oscar Thomson once said that "*Pelléas et Mélisande* is of all lyric dramas the most objective and the most convincingly human."

Despite Debussy's admiration for Wagner, he rejected Wagner's symphonic method of composing operas. Debussy once had a conversation with his teacher, Guiraud, in which he stated that, "Music in opera is far too predominant. My idea is of a short libretto with mobile scenes, no discussion or argument between the characters, whom I see at the mercy of life or destiny." This aesthetic principle is in direct opposition to the ideas of Wagner. To compare the two, Wagner tended towards opera as symphonic poem, Debussy towards opera as sung play. Critics have generally compared *Pelléas et Mélisande* to Wagner's *Tristan und Isolde,* saying that *Pelléas* is the more refined, self-conscious, constrained work; *Tristan* is much more radical, much more difficult to come to terms with. Both of these operas are significant, however, for an understanding of the famous operatic "reform" of the nineteenth century.

After *Pelléas et Mélisande,* Debussy devoted a great deal of time to two operas: *Le diable dans le beffroi* and *La chute de la maison Usher.* Both of these are tales of Poe. In *Le diable,* Debussy was attempting to find a style of writing that embraced the conglomerate sentiments found in a crowd. In addition, Debussy decided to have the part of the Devil whistled rather than sung. The opera was never completed.

La chute is a study of pathological melancholia. It has been written that Debussy, to some extent, saw himself mirrored in the oversensitive person of Roderick Usher in *La chute.* In 1908 Debussy wrote to his editor: ". . . there are times when I lose contact with my surroundings and if Roderick Usher's sister were suddenly to appear I should not be all that surprised."

It is difficult to summarize either Debussy's contribution to the genre of opera or his musical process. As Debussy himself once said: "We must agree that the beauty of a work of art will always remain a mystery, in other words we can never be absolutely sure 'how it's made.' We must at all costs preserve this magic which is peculiar to music and to which, by its nature, music is of all arts the most receptive."—KATHLEEN A. ABROMEIT

Delibes, (Clément-Philibert-) Léo

Composer. Born 21 February 1836, in St-Germain-du-Val, Sarthe. Died 16 January 1891, in Paris. Enrolled in the Paris Conservatory, 1847; studied solfège with Tariot (first prize in 1850), organ with Benoist, and composition with Adam; organist of St Pierre de Chaillot and accompanist at the Théâtre-Lyrique, 1853; chorus master of the Paris Opéra, 1864; professor of composition at the Paris Conservatory, 1881; member of the Institut, 1884. Delibes is renowned for his ballets Coppelia, ou La fille aux yeux d'émail *(1870), and* Sylvia, ou La nymphe de Diane *(1876), as well as for his operas.*

Operas *Deux sous de charbon, ou Le suicide de bigorneau,* J. Moinaux, Paris, Théâtre des Folies-Nouvelles, 9 February 1856; *Les deux vieilles gardes,* Villeneuve and Alphonse Lemonnier, Paris, Théâtre des Bouffes-Parisiens, 8 August 1856; *Six demoiselles à marier,* E. Jaime and A. Choler, Paris, Théâtre des Bouffes-Parisiens, 12 November 1856; *Maître Griffard,* Mestépès and Adolphe Jaime, Paris, Théâtre-Lyrique, 3 October 1857; *La fille du golfe,* C. Nuitter [vocal score published 1859]; *L'omelette à la Follembuche,* Marc Michel and Eugène Labiche, Paris, Théâtre des Bouffes-Parisiens, 8 June 1859; *Monsieur de Bonne-Étoile,* Philippe Gille, Théâtre des Bouffes-Parisiens, 4 February 1860; *Les musiciens de l'orchestre* (with Offenbach, Erlanger and Hignard), de Forges and A. Bourdois, Paris, Théâtre des Bouffes-Parisiens, 25 January 1861; *Les eaux d'Ems,* H. Crémieux and L. Hálevy, Ems, Kursaal, July 1861; *Mon ami Pierrot,* Lockroy, Ems, Kursaal, July 1862; *Le jardinier et son seigneur,* M. Carré and T. Barrière, Paris, Théâtre-Lyrique, 1 May 1863; *La tradition* (prologue), H. Derville, Paris, Théâtre des Bouffes-Parisiens, 5 January 1864; *Grande nouvelle,* A. Boisgontier [vocal score published 1864]; *Le serpent à plumes.* Philippe Gille and Cham, Paris, Théâtre des Bouffes-Parisiens, 16 December 1864; *Le boeuf Apis,* Philippe Gille and Furpille, Paris, Théâtre des Bouffes-Parisiens, 25 April 1865; *Malbrough s'en va-t-en guerre* (with Bizet, Jonas, and Legouix), Paul Siraudin and William Busnach, Paris, Théâtre de l'Athénée, 13 December 1867; *L'écossais de Chatou,* Adolphe Jaime and Philippe Gille, Paris, Théâtre des Bouffes-Parisiens, 16 January 1869; *La cour du roi Pétaud,* Adolphe Jaime and Philippe Gille, Paris, Théâtre des Variétés, 24 April 1869; *Fleur-de-lys,* H. B. Farnie; *Le roi l'a dit,* Edmond Gondinet, Paris, Opéra-Comique, 24 May 1873; *Jean de Nivelle,* Edmond Gondinet and Philippe Gille, Paris, Opéra-Comique, 8 March 1880; *Lakmé,* Edmond Gondinet and Philippe Gille, Paris, Opéra-Comique, 14 April 1883; *Kassya* (unfinished: scoring and recitatives by Massenet), Henri Meilhac and Philippe Gille (after L. von Sacher-Masoch, *Frinko Balaban*), Paris, Opéra-Comique, 24 March 1893 [posthumous performance]; *Le Don Juan suisse* [lost]; *La princesse Ravigote* [lost]; *Le roi des montagnes* [sketches]; *Jacques Callot* [unfinished].

Léo Delibes is one of those figures in the history of French music in the nineteenth century whose reputation rests securely on but a few compositions, namely, three ballets, one opera, and several songs. He was talented enough to be admitted to the Paris Conservatory at the age of twelve but sufficiently unremarkable so as to pass four years as a composition student without distinction. Yet, such was his level of competency that when only sixteen he secured a position as staff accompanist at the Théâtre Lyrique where he tried his hand at operetta composition; several of these efforts were modestly successful and enjoyed a modicum of popularity. In time, he joined the choral staff at the Opéra and simultaneously held a similar position at the Théâtre Bouffes-Parisiennes, Offenbach's theater.

Delibes' disciplined training at the Conservatory served him admirably, and he learned the intricacies of the music theater inside out. His keen sensitivity to the taste of the middle class audience of the day enabled his continuing success, however modest, until almost by accident he was engaged by a leading Polish dancer to prepare a ballet score. *La Source,* 1866, was enormously successful and was followed a little over three years later by an even more esteemed work, *Coppelia.* It has been noted that Delibes's musical abilities were as *ballabile* (dance worthy) as Italian opera was *cantabile* for the singer. With another enormously successful ballet, *Sylvia,* in 1876, Delibes reached the apex of his fame in the dance theater.

Finally, in 1883, after many years of effort, Delibes achieved the critical success in opera which had long eluded him. *Lakmé* was a triumph at its premiere and within twelve years had

199

been performed 200 times at the Paris Opéra; it celebrated its 1000th appearance in 1931 and continues to be produced on occasion in France.

The story of *Lakmé* was ready-made for a respectably bourgeois clientele. The scene is India, and the work redounds with elements of the fashionable orientalism of the time as found in many Gerôme paintings and operas by Bizet (*Pearl Fishers*) and Saint-Saëns (*Samson and Delilah*). Lakmé, the beautiful daughter of a Brahmin priest, falls in love with an English officer. Determined to avenge this dishonor her father uses Lakmé to lure Gerald into the open in order to kill him (the seductive song employed for this purpose in act II is the famous "Bell Song" beloved by many a soprano since its premiere). Gerald is seriously wounded, and Lakmé nurses him back to health. Their secret haven is discovered by a fellow officer who persuades Gerald to rejoin his regiment. Lakmé, heart broken, commits suicide in a bower of poisonous datura plants.

This slightly scandalous tale was sufficiently genteel to be acceptable to late nineteenth-century French audiences. Delibes was not to repeat this success, but he had the honor of being elected to the Institut de France in 1884 to fill the vacancy left by Victor Massé. To his end he remained the epitome of the fashionable musician, confident in his craft, esteemed for the elegance and charm of his fashionable music, and conservative to the core with respect to compositional practice.—AUBREY S. GARLINGTON

Delius, Frederick

Composer. Born 29 January 1862, in Bradford. Died 10 June 1934, in Grez-sur-Loing, France. Married: the painter Jelka Rosen, 1903. In Solana, near Jacksonville, Florida, 1884, to manage an orange plantation bought by his father; met and studied with the organist, Thomas F. Ward; taught in Danville, Virginia, 1885; studied counterpoint and harmony with Reinecke, Sitt, and Jadassohn at the Leipzig Conservatory, 1886, and met Grieg there; in Paris, 1888; in Grez-sur-Loing, near Paris, 1897; Companion of Honour awarded by King George V, 1929; honorary Mus.D. by Oxford, 1929. Sir Thomas Beecham organized a Delius festival in 1929.

Operas *Irmelin*, Delius, 1890-92, Oxford, New Theatre, 4 May 1953; *The Magic Fountain*, Delius, 1893-95; *Koanga*, Charles Francis Keary (after George Washington Cable, *The Grandissimes*, 1895-97, Elberfeld, Stadttheater, 30 March 1904; *A Village Romeo and Juliet*, Delius (after Gottfried Keller, *Romeo und Julia auf dem Dorfe*), 1900-01, Berlin, Komische Oper, 21 February 1907; *Margot la Rouge*, Mme Rosenval, 1902; *Fennimore and Gerda*, Delius (after Jens Peter Jacobsen's novel *Niels Lyhne*), 1909-11, Frankfurt am Main, Opernhaus, 21 October 1919.

The subject-matter of Delius's first operatic experiment, *Irmelin* (1890-92), seems now more English and Victorian than the composer's later iconoclastic cosmopolitanism might have countenanced: a fairy-tale princess hears a "voice in the air" that encourages her to long for a fairy-tale prince, who duly arrives in the form of Nils, a dispossessed prince who has been reduced to acting as swineherd to a Nordic robber-lord. In the final scene their individual fantasies entwine and love blossoms; the sun rises as they wander playfully, hand in hand, into the forest "like two children." The later revised *Irmelin Prelude* captures the essence of the opera's evanescent lyricism, focussed by the idyllic vision of the young men and women Irmelin sees running into the forest at sunset. She is bound by duty and her lack of a partner to watch from afar in this essential Delian moment: the "free" young folk distantly singing and dancing their dreamy "tra-la-la" in an archetypally "English" nine-eight rhythm. Irmelin's own music, however, is typically cast in a slower tempo, its rhythm and manner that of the sentimental ballad of discreetly repressed Victorian ladies.

Although repeatedly criticized for the monotony of his declamation, Delius's idealistic purpose was to transform this manner into an ever more subtle reflection of a certain kind of bourgeois subjectivity in an art uncluttered by the inauthentic formulae and clichés of what he regarded as arid musical convention. His aim was for unbroken melodic continuity in his vocal lines, and he deliberately avoided the realism that might have been attained by more rapid vocal delivery over the complex orchestral underlay which was in itself consistently admired before the First World War in Germany for its subtly nuanced post-Wagnerian lyricism.

The "fantasy" Delius avowedly aimed for in his composition was influenced by memories of his Florida experiences. In his next two operas, Delius explored the late-Victorian tendency to link the Romantic Idyll with the lost freedom of oppressed colonial peoples like the American Indians or the black slaves. The improvised harmony of black field hands, heard in the distance at sunset, remained with Delius as an intense musical image of paradise recalled, and inspired him to write a trilogy of operas based respectively on the Indians, the negroes and the gypsies. The first of these was *The Magic Fountain,* through whose elaborate, filmic scene-changes we follow the shipwrecked Spanish explorer Solano and the Seminole Indian girl Watawa in search of the Fountain of Eternal Youth. Once found, its powerfully magical waters kill the unprepared couple, for whom love had blossomed out of initial racial suspicion (Watawa had intended to kill the white man as symbolic oppressor of her people).

That the problems of *Irmelin* were only partially solved in *The Magic Fountain* (neither was staged in Delius's lifetime) makes all the more remarkable the achievement of *Koanga.* This "negro" opera was indeed opera in a much more fully realized sense of the term. Above all Delius had found the pretext for a really integrated role for the chorus, whose richly harmonized spirituals and work-songs contribute to the strong effect of this drama. The story concerns Koanga, a Voodoo prince captured as a slave and "tamed" by his Mississippi owner, who offers him the beautiful mixed-race Palmyra as a wife. Other whites conspire to prevent the marriage, however, and the enraged Koanga escapes with followers into the swamps after placing a curse upon the plantation. The structurally-defining choruses of the slave workers and the fine set-piece "wedding" (including the dance-episode "La Calinda") are succeeded by a magnificent scene of Voodoo invocation. However, Koanga's remorseful longing for Palmyra leads the slave back to his capture and death. Palmyra commits suicide after denouncing Koanga's killers and their Christian faith.

In *Koanga* the Romantic Idyll is doubly historicized: first, as the memory of an oppressed people whose troubles are manifest in the forces that separate Koanga and Palmyra, and secondly, in that the three-act opera itself is framed by a prologue and epilogue in which "Uncle Joe" is persuaded by the daughters of a southern plantation house owner to retell the old story. As a key late-nineteenth-century expression of liberal-colonial Romanticism, it is only to be regretted that the opera's inept and historically naive libretto (by Keary after George Cable—it has been "improved" with some success in a new edition by Douglas Craig and Andrew Page), combined with unintentional racist implications, makes it unlikely that it will be revived, although it is arguably a masterpiece of its kind.

There should really be no argument about *A Village Romeo and Juliet,* which Delius deliberately called a "Lyric Drama in six scenes" (*Lyrisches Drama in sechs Bildern*—like *Koanga* and *Fennimore and Gerda,* this opera was first performed in German). The scenes are of varying length and avoid larger "act" divisions; they present six episodes from Gottfried Keller's tragic tale of Sali and Vrenchen, children of two farmers who get into conflict over an overgrown field whose rightful owner is a strange gypsy (The Dark Fiddler). Jealousy and litigation separate and finally ruin the two farmers whose grown-up children fall passionately in love with each other. Symbolically denied access to the luxuriantly overgrown "wildland" where they had played long ago, and recoiling from the sexual freedom of the gypsy folk, they finally consummate their love in a river barge which they deliberately sink as the opera concludes. Filled with strongly characterized music of considerable variety, it includes some of Delius's most successfully judged melodic declamation, but also functions as a seamlessly rhapsodic orchestral fantasy, whose initial descending motif of summer childhood abandonment is slowly replaced by the rising arpeggio whose apotheosis comes in the famous interlude between scenes five and six (which accompanies the partly-mimed "walk to the Paradise Garden," symbolic name of a country tavern). More than any other, this work clarifies Delius's conception of operatic fantasy as embodied dream in which the symbolic and the real meet in the musical language of subjective experience. Delius's stage characters are created *by* the impulse of his music, which has secondary concern for individual characterization.

Neither the one-act *Margot la Rouge* (a nevertheless interesting Delian interpretation of *verismo,* set amongst Parisian "vagabonds" of the kind that Sali and Vrenchen shun) nor the structurally problematic but stylistically flawless *Fennimore and Gerda* (1909-11) significantly extended Delius's range as an opera composer. Already by 1919, when *Fennimore and Gerda* was premiered in Frankfurt, his style had become that of a past era before it had ever fully been appreciated.—PETER FRANKLIN

Della Casa, Lisa

Soprano. Born 2 February 1919, in Burgdorf, near Berne. Married Dragan Debeljevic, 1947 (one daughter). Studied with Margaret Haeser in Bern and Zurich; debut as Cio-Cio-San in Solothurn-Biel, 1941; sang in Zurich, 1943-50; debut at Salzburg as Zdenka, 1947; British debut at Glyndebourne as Countess, 1951; joined Vienna State Opera, 1947-73; debut at Metropolitan Opera as Countess, 1953, where she sang for fifteen seasons until 1968.

From the 1950s to the early 1970s, Swiss-born soprano Lisa Della Casa shared repertoire with some of the centuries finest singers: her contemporaries include Elisabeth Schwarzkopf, Sena Jurinac, and Elisabeth Grümmer. Della Casa's natural vocal gifts were probably not comparable, but her willowy, raven-haired beauty and telling muscial artistry earn her a place in even this elite pantheon.

Della Casa's lyric soprano was a fascinatingly inconsistent instrument—Giacomo Lauri Volpi's famous description of Claudia Muzio's voice ". . . made up of tears and sighs" is equally appropriate here. Her voice was never completely equalized; the upper notes were always gloriously light and easy, but the bottom of the range was rather tinny and weak, and the middle voice—not dependable nor strong even in her earliest recordings—became increasingly threadbare over time. Yet it was Della Casa's gift to manipulate this rather patchy tone to a positive end, lending an ageless, touchingly frail and feminine quality to her performances. She seemed at once innocent and experienced, young and old, and Della Casa was able to turn what was a natural limitation into an asset.

That these fragile means could serve so well in a wide variety of music was again a tribute to Della Casa's artistry. She pushed her limited resources to encompass with some success the difficulties of Strauss' Chrysothemis in *Elektra* and even *Salome,* although she wisely limited her appearances in these roles. Della Casa greatly enjoyed singing Italian opera—her repertoire included Gilda in *Rigoletto,* Mimì in *La bohème,* Tosca and Butterfly, but she was rarely cast in these roles in international opera houses. Some German language highlights recordings of the latter two may explain why; the singing is lovely and Della Casa's touching femininity is much in evidence, but a curious reticence and reserve leave the listener unsatisfied, and finally a warmer, more Italianate sound is needed.

Della Casa was in great demand as an interpreter of Mozart, though the lack of homogenous tone color was noticeable in this demanding music. She frequently performed and recorded the roles of Donna Elvira in *Don Giovanni,* the Countess in *Figaro,* and Fiordiligi in *Così fan tutte.* In each she exhibits lovely tone color, a clean sense of line and some personal charm, but all three performances lack the technical perfection of her contemporary Elisabeth Schwarzkopf. In the operas of Richard Strauss, Della Casa was something of a specialist—in addition to the two roles previously noted, her repertoire included Zdenka in *Arabella,* Ariadne, the Countess in *Capriccio* and all three principal parts (Octavian, Sophie and the Marschallin) in *Der Rosenkavalier.* Some exerpts from *Der Rosenkavalier,* recorded perhaps a bit too late to show Della Casa at her best are nonetheless a worthy souvenir of her fine Marschallin, altogether more youthful and natural than Schwarzkopf's, less specific in her word painting but always expressive and alive to nuances.

But no comparisons are necessary in judging Della Casa's assumption of the title role of Strauss's *Arabella,* of which she is the century's acknowledged master interpreter, and both of her complete recordings (Decca, 1957 and DG, 1963) more than adequately preserve this renowned portrayal. No other singer has negotiated the climactic high pianissimo phrases of "Und du wirst mein Gebieter sein" with such radiance. No other singer has invested the little "Aber die richtige" duet, in which Arabella dreams of a perfect lover, with more poignancy, and none has invested the oddly ambivalent character with such compassion—even the slightly chilly, aloof quality which limited some of Della Casa's portrayals was wholly consistent with this strange, serious, romantic girl.

Lisa Della Casa virtually owned the role of Arabella after she sang it for the first time; it is altogether appropriate and fitting that it was as Arabella that Della Casa performed for the last time in 1974.—DAVID ANTHONY FOX

Del Monaco, Mario

Tenor. Born 27 July 1915, in Florence. Died 16 October 1982, in Mestre. Largely self-taught before brief study with Melocchi at Pesaro Conservatory, Rome Opera School, 1935; debut as Turiddu in Pesaro, 1939; international appearances (including Mexico City, Buenos Aires, Rio) 1945-46; United States debut in San Francisco as Radames, 1950;

debut at Metropolitan Opera as Des Grieux, 1950; sang more than one hundred performances at the Met in the 1950s; retired from the stage in 1973.

Mario Del Monaco was a leading Italian dramatic tenor in the period from the 1940s to the early 1960s. Those who believe that the Italian dramatic tenorial ideal is represented by loud, intensely powerful, full-throated, virile singing in which emotion is at the forefront—the epitome of the verismo style—may hear its realization in his voice. Others, desiring elegance, subtlety, and nuance—approaching the so-called bel canto style—may perceive Del Monaco as monotonous, coarse, and insensitive. The true nature of his voice resides somewhere in between, although Del Monaco's reputation is of a singer employing the former style.

Del Monaco made his professional debut in 1940 as Turridu in Mascagni's *Cavalleria rusticana* in Cagli, Italy. His first major performance was as Pinkerton in Puccini's *Madama Butterfly* in Milan at the Teatro Puccini in 1941. Subsequent performances, especially those at the Verona Arena as Radames in Verdi's *Aida* and with the San Carlo opera company on tour at Covent Garden during the 1945-46 season, established Del Monaco's international career. He first appeared at the Teatro alla Scala as Pinkerton in 1945. His American debut was as Radames opposite Renata Tebaldi's Aida (in her American debut) in San Francisco in 1950, and he then sang extensively with the Metropolitan Opera in New York.

Del Monaco has often been described as a singer of unremitting loudness and unrelenting intensity, more the warrior than the philosopher. His most frequently cited fault was a disinclination (or apparent inability) to sing below mezzoforte. Critics complained that he demonstrated force without subtlety, and a brash, hard vocal quality. As one critic has remarked, he frequently gave the impression that the character he was portraying was not taking time to think; his style has been called the vocal equivalent of machismo. Some have found his singing boring because of an insufficient variation of tonal color and a lack of suppleness in the phrasing; others complain of a whining quality. He was also capable of sloppy, undisciplined singing, with excessive sliding between notes and some carelessness about pitch.

At times, however, Del Monaco displayed sufficient virtues to justify, at least in part, the high reputation he held in Italy. His voice had a bright, attractive surface with substantial body of tone and occasional moments of vocal splendor—a vibrant, heroic sound with strong visceral appeal. He had the ability to produce the kind of thrilling high notes that sustain listeners through the monotonous stretches. Del Monaco employed a firm legato and sense of line to produce an even flow of rich tone. Despite his voice's size and power he was able to sing beautifully, even sensitively, when required. Recordings show he was capable of some delicacy, and in his prime he managed to execute diminuendos, although his *piano* singing lacked body. He demonstrated a sense of drama and was able to convey honest emotion, not being afraid to be crude when the role demanded it and able to generate animal excitement when it was required (if also, frequently, when it was not). Toward the end of his career his voice became thinner and more nasal. As with many singers, however, he improved in artistry as his vocal prowess began to decline, making dramatic advantage out of increasing vocal difficulties. He never developed into a great actor—the relative inflexibility of his voice was probably a limiting factor.

Verdi's Otello was probably his greatest role; in it he combined dramatic power with depth of feeling. Other roles span the dramatic roles of the Italian and French repertoire: Don José in Bizet's *Carmen,* Aeneas in Berlioz's *Les Troyens,* Canio in Leoncavallo's *I pagliacci,*

Verdi's Ernani, Don Alvaro in Verdi's *La forza del destino,* Radames, Pollione in Bellini's *Norma,* Samson in Saint-Saëns's *Samson et Dalila,* Manrico in Verdi's *Il trovatore,* Des Grieux in Puccini's *Manon Lescaut,* Dick Johnson in Puccini's *La fanciulla del West,* Giordano's Andrea Chénier, and Enzo Grimaldo in Ponchielli's *La gioconda,* the last two being especially well suited to his style. He also was successful, remarkably so for an Italian tenor, in two Wagnerian roles—Lohengrin and Siegmund (in *Die Walküre*), the latter of which he sang in its original language.

Many of these roles were recorded, often with the partnership of Renata Tebaldi: Canio in 1953 under Erede, Des Grieux in 1954 under Molinari-Pradelli, Otello in 1954 under Erede and in 1960 under Karajan, Don Alvaro in 1955 under Molinari-Pradelli in 1955, Manrico in 1956 under Erede, Enzo Grimaldo in 1957 under Gavazzeni, Andrea Chénier in 1957 under Gavazzeni, Dick Johnson in 1958 under Capuana, and Don José in 1962 under Schippers. Other recorded performances include Turiddu in Mascagni's *Cavalleria rusticana* in 1953 under Ghione, Calaf in Puccini's *Turandot* in 1955 under Erede, Maurizio in Cilèa's *Adriana Lecouvreur* in 1961 under Capuana, Luigi in Puccini's *Il tabarro* in 1962 under Gardelli, Loris in Giordano's *Fedora* in 1969 under Gardelli, and Hagenbach in Cilèa's *La Wally* in 1969 under Cleva.

Del Monaco's studio recordings are, in general, more disciplined than the recordings made at staged performances, as if the presence of an audience brought out the aggressive qualities of his singing.—MICHAEL SIMS

De Los Angeles, Victoria

Soprano. Born Victoria Lopez Cima, 1 November 1923, in Barcelona. Married Enrique Magrina, 1948 (two sons). Studied with Dolores Frau at Barcelona Conservatory to 1944; debut as Mimì in Barcelona, 1941; formal debut as the Countess in Le nozze di Figaro *at Teatro Liceo in Barcelona, 1945; won Geneva International Singing Competition, 1947; debut at Paris as Marguerite, 1949; Teatro alla Scala debut as Ariadne, 1950; Covent Garden debut as Mimì, 1950; Metropolitan Opera debut as Marguerite, 1951, and she sang more than one hundred performances there until 1961; appeared as Elisabeth at Bayreuth, 1961-62.*

With a musical family background, Victoria de Los Angeles seems to have first learned to sing as a mere natural expression of childhood happiness. Although the Spanish Civil War shadowed her formative years it did not interrupt her development, and after university and conservatory study it was clear that her future lay in opera, so much so that in 1941 she was invited at the age of eighteen to sing Mimì in *La bohème* at the Teatro Victoria in her native city of Barcelona. With surprising maturity, she refused the offer because she felt herself unready. Her official debut came four years later in another theater in the same city, as the Countess in Mozart's *Le nozze di Figaro*—an older role, which suggests that her voice and stage personality were already recognized as mature for her years.

In the immediate post-war years, helped by her success in the Geneva Singing Competition in 1947, de Los Angeles quickly gained international acceptance. British audiences were among the first outside Spain to appreciate her vivid personality and fine musicianship, not least in a 1949 British Broadcasting Corporation broadcast in which she played the fiery heroine

Salud in Falla's *La vida breve*. Though Spanish music was an obvious field for her, she must have known from the start that it was limited, and she soon gave evidence of her mastery of several languages and a wide repertory, playing at Covent Garden as Mimì, Cio-Cio-San in *Madama Butterfly*, Nedda in *I pagliacci*, Santuzza in *Cavalleria rusticana*, Manon in Massenet's opera of that name and two Wagner roles, Elsa in *Lohengrin* and Eva in *Die Meistersinger*. She also sang the role of Rosina in Rossini's *Il barbiere di Siviglia*.

It has been said that "a voice is a person," but as an opera singer de Los Angeles had to be not just herself but also a singing actress, and during her career of more than two decades she gave abundant and consistent evidence of dramatic force and presence, together with real imaginative flexibility. The accompanist Gerald Moore declared that she sang with "total involvement in the emotions" as well as a lovely voice and keen musicianship. She gave further evidence of her musical and dramatic range in her performances of roles as diverse as Debussy's elusive Princess Mélisande in *Pelléas et Mélisande*, the virtuous but vocally agile Marguerite in Gounod's *Faust* and the loving and too-trusting Desdemona in Verdi's *Otello*. There was some suprise in Britain when the conductor Sir John Barbirolli chose her to sing (in English, alongside British singers) the role of Dido, the ill-fated Queen of Carthage in his recording of Purcell's *Dido and Aeneas*, but she rose magnificently to the occasion and did memorable justice to Purcell's style and the tragic role.

De Los Angeles' voice was sweet and vibrant as well as somewhat Mediterranean in quality, with a rich lower register. The upper soprano range was not quite so easy for her, particularly later in her career, and there could be a touch of hardness in some notes, but she could nearly always vary her tone so as to suit the music and her characterization of a role. By 1970 she had more or less brought her stage appearances to an end, but she continued with concert work and recordings. Her recording career was remarkably full, with no less than twenty-two operas committed to disc as well as an even larger number of recitals. Her personality seems to have been easy-going; she was charmingly modest in the British Broadcasting Corporation's long-running *Desert Island Discs* program in which she was invited to choose favorite records—in contrast with some other singers who have seemed only interested in their own voices. On the other hand, she was firm where artistic standards were concerned, and once refused to continue with a recording of Bizet's *Carmen* under Sir Thomas Beecham until she was given what she felt to be adequate recording time; Beecham took her side, and their famous 1960 recording offers proof of their successful collaboration. Perhaps it took her some time to get inside this particular role of a Spanish *femme fatale;* she did not sing it on stage until fairly late in her career.—CHRISTOPHER HEADINGTON

De Luca, Giuseppe

Baritone. Born 25 December 1876. Died 26 August 1950. Studied with Venceslao Persichini in Rome and with Contogni; debut in Piacenza as Valentine in Faust, *1897; created Michonnet in* Adriana Lecouvreur, *Milan, 1902; debut at Teatro alla Scala as Alberich, 1903; created Gleby in Giordano's* Siberia, *1903, and Sharpless, 1904; Covent Garden debut as Sharpless, 1907; Metropolitan Opera debut as Rossini's Figaro, 1915, and sang there until 1935; created Paquiro (in* Goyescas*) and Gianni Schicchi, 1918; taught at Juilliard.*

d

OPERA

Baritone Giuseppe De Luca may not have been the last authentic exponent of bel canto as legend would have it, but he was certainly one of its most celebrated spokesmen, and a formidable representative of its principles long after most other bel canto singers had vanished. During De Luca's 1947 Golden Jubilee Concert, soprano Frances Alda commented "I've heard many voices *bigger*. . . Amato, Titta Ruffo, Battistini, and many others—but none of them could compare with the magnificent *bel canto* of De Luca." Few would dispute her. In 1946, as De Luca was undertaking a final wave of recitals, Irving Kolodin offered a similar assessment of him with even greater precision, observing that "There were some who considered the amount of voice he had to work with a small part of its original splendor; but they remember incorrectly. It was never a voice distinguished by size, rather by quality and the deftness with which it was used." To be sure, De Luca's was not an especially large voice, but it was beautifully modulated,

Giuseppe De Luca in *Rigoletto* (Culver Pictures)

effortlessly produced and skillfully handled. It may have lacked some of Ruffo's flexibility, but his singing was altogether more refined; it did not have Amato's dramatic consistency, but in the repertory that suited it best, it was sweeter and more sympathetic. Only Battistini can perhaps be seen as having been the more cultivated artist, possessing as he did an instrument of unrivaled agility. De Luca's was a low baritone of great dramatic potential, without Battistini's vast upper resources. It had considerably less weight in the first decades of his career, and seemed then to be propelled by a vibrant, almost tremulous intensity later absorbed into the darker, full-bodied timbre of his authentic prime. His technique was immaculate, capable of transforming the humblest material into a virtuosic display of classical phrasing and exemplary legato. Recordings make it equally clear, however, that De Luca's voice was neither small nor second-rate, any more than his artistry was simply a triumph of technique and interpretation.

De Luca cultivated and maintained a large and varied repertory throughout his career, but did so cautiously. He certainly made no attempt to dominate so commanding a repertory as many of his contemporaries did, choosing instead to adopt only those roles which his voice could accommodate with complete authority. Avoiding the kind of destructive shouting that prematurely ruined the voices of Ruffo and Amato, his career—like Battistini's—was unusually long. Although he had created major roles of Giordano, Cilèa, and Puccini during his stay at the Teatro alla Scala, and continued to perform others as dramatically demanding as Tonio (*I pagliacci*) during his prime, his patronage of the verismo repertory was more or less incidental. His scant Wagnerian repertory, which consisted of Alberich (*Das Rheingold*), Wolfram (*Tannhaüser*), and Beckmesser (*Die Meistersinger*), though it brought him much success, was abandoned when he left the Teatro alla Scala after the 1914-1915 season. It was in fact with misgivings that he first performed Beckmesser under Toscanini's direction during a 1903 South American tour, complaining to his agent that such roles were ruinous to the voice. He eventually settled into the earlier nineteenth-century Italian repertoire, was a notable interpreter of Mozart, and gained his greatest recognition in the leading early and middle Verdi baritone roles. Here the size and disposition of his voice, as well as his skills as an actor—most notable, contemporary accounts suggest, in the extremes of high melodrama and buffo comedy—were particularly well suited. Hence his renown as Rigoletto, Germont (*La traviata*), Malatesta (*Don Pasquale*), and Rossini's Figaro (*Il barbiere di Siviglia*). Over the course of his career he also created a number of important roles, including the Devil in the 1902 Italian premiere of Massenet's *Griselda*, Michonnet and Gleby in the world premieres of Cilèa's *Adriana Lecouvreur* (1902) and Giordano's *Siberia* (1903), Sharpless in the chaotic first production of Puccini's *Madama Butterfly* (1904), and at New York's Metropolitan Opera, Paquiro in Granados' *Goyescas* (1916) and Puccini's Gianni Schicchi (1918). His American stage premieres—the title role in *Eugene Onegin* (1920), Guglielmo in *Così fan tutte* (1922), Ping in *Turandot* (1926), and the elder Bruschino in Rossini's *Il Signor Bruschino* (1932)—were equally impressive. He was also Don Carlos in *La forza del destino* (1918), Rodrigo in *Don Carlos* (1920), Sancho Panza to Chaliapin's Don Quixote in Massenet's *Don Quixote* (1926), and Miller in *Luisa Miller* (1929) in the first Met presentations of these works. De Luca was a commanding interpreter of song as well, his vast repertory accommodating Italian, French, English and Russian works spanning four centuries. With characteristic ease and assurance, he was able to invest in these the same evocative details that distinguished his operatic interpretations.

Like Battistini (and very briefly, Ruffo), he was a pupil of Venceslao Persichini (1827-1897), with whom he studied for five years at Rome's Academia di Santa Cecilia. He made his professional debut as Valentin (*Faust*) in Piacenza in 1897, and by 1904 had already embarked upon successful starring seasons at the Teatro Lirico, the Teatro San Carlo, and the Teatro alla Scala, where he remained for eight illustrious seasons. Giulio Gatti-Casazza, for whom De Luca sang both at the Teatro alla Scala and the Met, recalled him with restrained appreciation in his memoirs: "our admirable singer of *bel canto*," he wrote of him, ". . . a reliable, versatile and serious artist, and distinctly a fine stylist." De Luca spent much of the first two decades of the century touring the major operatic centers of the world, enjoying particular success in Eastern Europe and South America. Prior to his coming to New York in 1915, he sang three guest seasons at Covent Garden between 1907 and 1910, yet he returned there only once for a single appearance as Figaro in 1935. At the Met he flourished for nineteen consecutive seasons, singing fifty-two roles in some 700 performances. Like a number of other notable Met imports, he went back to Europe in the midst of the Depression, but returned briefly in 1940 for performances of works closely associated with him—*La traviata, Rigoletto, Il barbiere di Siviglia* and *La Bohème*. He was again in fleeting residence at the Teatro alla Scala in 1936 and 1937 for performances of *Manon, L'elisir d'amore,* and *Don Pasquale*.

After nearly four decades of unceasing professional activity, he spent the war years at his estate in Italy. "For five years I was playing cards," he told a *Time* interviewer in March, 1946, "I refused to sing because I was not in a good humor." But in fact, he did manage to perform sporadically throughout the hostilities. Returning to America in 1945, he gave a number of well-received concert performances in New York, culminating in a poignant farewell recital at New York's Town Hall on 7 November, 1947 in celebration of the "Golden Jubilee" of his career. He continued broadcasting and recording up until the year of his death at age 73. His professional activities never really allowed him to devote his energy entirely to teaching as he had anticipated, and we are only left to wonder at the vast influence he might have exerted had he lived to enjoy a long retirement.

De Luca recorded prolifically over a period of forty-eight years, leaving 156 published commercial recordings, forty-five live concert items, and nine surviving broadcasts. His first recordings were made in Milan for the Gramophone & Typewriter Ltd. in December, 1902, and his last, issued on a long-playing disc by the Continental Record Company of New York, in the winter of 1950. His principal output, made for Victor during his years at the Met, amounted to nearly seventy published titles. Few other major singers enjoyed such extraordinary artistic endurance, or managed to produce a recorded legacy as satisfying. The only significant gap in his recording activities was between 1908 and 1915, rendering inaccessible the transition into his prime. Several of his most important roles—Rigoletto, Germont (*La traviata*), Rossini's Figaro, are documented rather sparsely, though fortunately, there is an ebullient "Largo al factotum" among his three Vitaphone films of 1927 and 1928 to illustrate just how irresistible his Figaro must have been. Less fortunate is the fact that, apart from three published versions of Michonnet's Monologue from the first act of *Adriana Lecouvreur,* and three exerpts from *Siberia,* he was somehow never induced to record from the many important roles he created. Even among his American and Metropolitan Opera premiere vehicles, there remains only a handful of scenes from *La forza del destino* and *Don Carlos.* He left only one Wagner title, a 1907 "O tu bell' astro" from *Tannhäuser,* leaving little by which to judge his early success in this repertory.

It is only after the Second World War, in the commercial recordings he made for Decca (1946) and Continental (1950) and in the 1947 Town Hall recitals, that we begin to see signs of serious vocal decline. His last important recordings, duets from *Rigoletto* and *Il Barbiere di Siviglia* with Lily Pons, were recorded for Victor in March, 1940, and these, along with two Met broadcasts from the 1939-1940 season, give astonishing testimony to the fact that forty years of singing were powerless to diminish the stylistic vitality that so distinguished him among his contemporaries.—WILLIAM SHAMAN

De Reszke, Edouard

Bass. Born 22 December 1853, in Warsaw. Died 25 May 1917, in Garnek. Studied with Ciaffei in Warsaw, and with his brother, the tenor Jean de Reszke; also studied in Italy with Steller and Alba in Milan, and Coletti; debut as the King in Aïda *under Verdi's direction at the Théâtre des Italiens in Paris, 1876; appeared in Paris for two seasons, then at Teatro alla Scala; sang in London 1880-84; American debut as the King in* Lohengrin, *Chicago, 1891; Metropolitan Opera debut as Frère Laurent in* Roméo et Juliette, *1891; greatest role was as Méphistophélès in* Faust, *the last act of which he sang for his last appearance, at a Metropolitan gala in 1903.*

The De Reszke family is legendary in *fin de siècle* operatic history. Of the two brothers and one sister who had important careers, Josephine was a soprano, Jean a tenor, and Edouard, arguably the most gifted of the three, was a bass.

Edouard's voice, according to contemporary reports, was a high bass, capable of singing the bass-baritone repertoire with considerable sonority in the lower register. Its size was remarkable, and not long after his debut he was already being compared with the great Lablache, who was endowed with a similarly phenomenal organ.

The De Reszke brothers were inseparable. Together they conquered the major opera houses of the world but were especially admired at the Metropolitan Opera and at Covent

Garden, where they both appeared practically every season during the 1890s. Edouard was a gentle giant of a man and a character of considerable bonhomie, a quality for which he was loved by his colleagues. His *laissez-aller* attitude and lack of discipline might easily have become his eventual artistic undoing. But the very qualities which he lacked were to be found in abundance in Jean, who watched over and guided his career with brotherly affection.

Edouard merely needed to find a role congenial to want to perform it. His technique and vocal range afforded him considerable versatility, a quality which also endeared him to managements. He appeared with considerable regularity in a great variety of roles. In his first New York season, for example, he appeared in fourteen different roles in less than five months. He could turn with ease from a florid Rossini role like Assur (*Semiramide*) to the heaviest Wagnerian role, but was particularly happy in those parts where his personality and enormous voice could be allowed their full rein, such as Méphistophélès (*Faust*), Mefistofele in Boïto's opera of that name and Leporello (*Don Giovanni*). According to the critic of the *New York Times,* he was as Leporello "simply superb. It is a joy without alloy to hear him read the recitative with all the skill of a perfect actor and vocalist, and with such brimming and unctious humour that every line is funny. As for his 'Madamina', it is one of the most admirable of all achievements in the art of buffo singing."

No doubt Jean's increasing forays into the Wagnerian repertoire were responsible also for Edouard's assumption of many of Wagner's bass roles in the latter part of his career. He continued to elicit high praise from the critics in roles such as Hagen (*Götterdämmerung*), König Marke (*Tristan und Isolde*), Hans Sachs (*Die Meistersinger*) and Wotan (*Siegfried*).

If the operatic careers of the De Reszke brothers could be described as unique, lamentable would be an appropriate description of their recording careers. Jean made two test recordings, disliked what he heard and forbade their release. Edouard was coaxed into the studios of Columbia in 1903, but by then the voice was well past its best. Though he was only forty-nine (an age at which the bass voice should be at its most mature), a career of overworking the voice and frequent appearances had obviously taken its toll. Matters are not improved by the technically poor nature of the recording. The results are perhaps the most disappointing records ever to have been made by a singer of major importance. The voice as recorded sounds weak, the lower register colorless and the breath short. There were just three titles: the best of them is probably Plunkett's aria from *Marta,* which at least shows agility, an excellent trill and evidence of obvious good schooling. The others, Tchaikovsky's Don Juan's Serenade and the aria "infelice" from *Ernani,* do not even begin to give an idea of the voice of one of the finest basses in operatic history.—LARRY LUSTIG

Dernesch, Helga

Soprano and mezzo-soprano. Born 3 February 1939, in Vienna. Studied at Vienna Conservatory, 1957-61; debut in mezzo-soprano role of Marina in Boris Godunov, *Berne Opera, 1961, where she performed until 1963; appeared in Wiesbaden and Cologne, 1965-69; at Bayreuth, 1965-69; shifted to soprano roles; appeared with Scottish Opera, where she sang Gutrune (1968) and Leonore in* Fidelio *(1970); Salzburg debut, 1969; made her Chicago (1971) and Vienna Staatsoper (1972) debuts in* Fidelio; *returned to mezzo roles, 1979; Metropolitan Opera debut as Marfa in* Khovanschina, *1985.*

Helga Dernesch is one of the few singers to have considerable success as both a soprano and a mezzo-soprano. Though the voice itself has never achieved a particularly individualistic sound, it is a more than adequate vehicle for an exceptional musical and dramatic intelligence. With her handsome appearance, this theatrically thrilling artist is able to make even minor character roles take on a dominating force in any given opera. This is perhaps why she is best experienced onstage rather than on recordings. Similarly, her broad strokes and bold characterizations have made her more of an operatic than a concert artist.

Dernesch's early years as a Wagnerian soprano under Herbert von Karajan brought her to some of the finest opera capitals of the world. Yet in listening to her recordings of Brünnhilde in *Götterdämmerung* and Isolde in *Tristan und Isolde,* it seems inevitable that she would eventually be a mezzo. Her high notes never had the ease and openness of a true soprano.

This is not to minimize her achievements in the soprano repertoire. Though her *Ring* recordings have a certain interpretive blandness that afflicts many of Karajan's opera recordings, her Isolde, also under Karajan, is a memorable interpretation that alone guarantees her a chapter—albeit a brief one—in the history of 20th-century dramatic sopranos. She has an unsparing, dramatic fearlessness that gives Isolde's curse in act I ample dramatic weight, even if she lacked the heft or color to make such a moment convincing from a purely vocal standpoint. Though she loses some of the more ecstatic aspects of the role because of the limitations in her upper range, her "Liebestod" is unusually articulate. Rather than simply letting the music carry the moment, she infused the words with meaning and conveys a feeling of being overwhelmed with the forces of passion more than anyone since Lotte Lehman.

Following a vocal breakdown of sorts during rehearsals for *Die Frau ohne Schatten* in Hamburg in 1979, Dernesch went home to Vienna on the advice of conductor Christoph von Dohnanyi and reworked her voice in the mezzo-soprano range. She did so with such remarkable speed and vigor, it's fair to say that her career as a mezzo-soprano has been considerably more interesting than her soprano career. She has embraced a wide range of roles, including Herodias in *Salome,* Adelaide in *Arabella* and Marfa in Mussorgsky's *Khovanchina,* and sung in the original Russian. Her interpretations of these extremely different roles—a decadent queen, a penniless socialite and a religious fanatic—are all so complete in their own way, it is sometimes difficult to imagine another singer in them.

Her most important legacy came out of her relationship with the 20th-century composer Aribert Reimann, whose Requiem (1983) and operas *Lear* (1978) and *Troades* (1986) she premiered. Though Reimann's idiom is atonal and frequently thorny (in keeping with the subject matter he chooses), Dernesch maintained a dramatic sense in her vocal lines, as is apparent in her performance as Goneril in *Lear.* In the first scene when she proclaims her love for her father, her slightly exaggerated stylization of the wide-leaping vocal lines tell the listener she is not being sincere. Her background as a Wagnerian was particularly appropriate in this role. As she shuts her father out into the stormy night, she does so with a steely confidence perhaps only a Wagnerian could muster. Though the role does not have a great emotional range, Dernesch gives even the most hysterical moments a musical dignity that reveal her character as a cool manipulator, even in the most emotionally charged situations.

Possibly her finest achievement with Reimann is *Troades,* a retelling of the Trojan war whose score is more spare and vocal lines more graceful than its predecessors. Her voice was in prime condition for the premiere at the Bavarian State Opera, and the role of Hekabe, the mother of Hector, offered her monologues with only spare accompaniment from the tympani and lower brass, gives her a tailor-made platform for her sense of theatricality. She dominates the opera, culminating in an immolation scene, the comparisons with the Wagnerian counterpart illustrating how much she has grown in dramatic depth from her early years with Karajan, and suggesting that her career as a soprano is perhaps best considered a period of preparation for her real career as a mezzo.—DAVID PATRICK STEARNS

Destinn, Emmy

Soprano. Born Ema Pavlinâ Kittlová, 26 February 1878, in Prague. Died 28 January 1930, in Česke Budějovice. Married air force officer Joseph Halsbach, 1923. Studied with Marie Loewe-Destinn, whose name she adopted; debut as Santuzza in Berlin Kroll Opera, 1898, launched her international career; remained in Berlin until 1908, where she sang the first Salome in 1906; her debut as Senta at Bayreuth in 1901; Covent Garden debut as Donna Anna, 1904, and returned every season until 1914; debut at Metropolitan Opera as Aida, 1908, and sang regularly at Met until 1916 and in 1919-21; created Minnie in La fanciulla del West, *Met, 1910; Chicago debut as Gioconda, 1915; return to native Bohemia during World War I; arrested for her Czech nationalist views during war; wrote the drama* Rahel *as well as novels and poetry; also a composer.*

Emmy Destinn ranks as one of the very greatest dramatic sopranos of the twentieth century. Born Ema Kittlová she adopted the name Destinn as a tribute to her teacher Marie Loewe Destinn. In this she was probably impelled by a need in the German operatic world to divert attention from her Czech origin. She remained a fervent Czech nationalist and after the creation of independent Czechoslovakia in 1918 she used the name Destinnova.

After being rejected by the Czech opera in Prague and at Dresden, she was engaged by the Berlin Opera and made her debut in the role of Santuzza in *Cavalleria rusticana* in 1898 at the age of 20 at the Kroll Theater. She was hailed by critics and compared favorably to the great Bellincioni, who had created the role. She soon appeared at the main Berlin house, the Hofoper and was to remain there for a decade, appearing in more than fifty different roles, usually singing several times a week. Throughout her career Destinn was a prodigous worker. She was later to complain of infrequency of appearances during her time with the Metropolitan Opera and looked back blissfully to singing several times a week in Berlin. In fact she appeared in 339 Metropolitan performances between 1908 and 1920, extensively at Covent Garden during the same period, and still giving some guest performances in Berlin and a few elsewhere. It seems probable that in her career on the operatic stage Destinn gave well over 1500 performances.

Destinn's versatility was also remarkable. Her debut in Berlin was in verismo. In 1901 she sang the role of Senta in *Die fliegende Holländer* at Bayreuth. According to the critic Oskar Bie her "silver toned instrument, full of sensuous charm throughout its entire compass was allied to impeccable technique in attack." In 1904 her first role at Covent Garden was Donna Anna in *Don Giovanni*. Hermann Klein thought her very nearly perfect—"surely, I thought, an artist capable of success at the outset in this most exacting of roles will one day stand in the royal line of dramatic sopranos." Although Destinn was to become an enormous popular favorite at Covent Garden, her career did not proceed quite in the direction anticipated by Klein. She was to appear in nearly 200 performances of 17 operas, with 60 performances as Cio-Cio San in *Madama*

Butterfly, which she was the first to sing in London. Her debut in the USA was in yet another operatic role as Aïda. According to Sydney Homer, whose wife Louise was singing Amneris that night, Destinn's was "a new and unique voice . . . the medium like some new woodwind instrument . . . a legato like a river of sound."

The year 1908 stands out as a kind of *annus mirabilis* in Destinn's career. In that year she had to break with the Berlin Hofoper when she was refused leave to sing with the Metropolitan Opera. Before crossing the Atlantic for the first time, she returned in triumph to Prague. She had left in 1898 unable to secure a contract and had given only a smattering of performances there since, but now returned as an international star. She appeared in *Aïda, Der fliegende Holländer, The Bartered Bride, Cavalleria rusticana, I pagliacci* and *Dalibor.* In the dungeon scene of *Dalibor* she was "strong, heroic, carrying all before her . . . voice ringing out like a church bell." During the same year Destinn also made 83 records—a third of her total output.

The voice on the best of her records is instantly recognizable. There is a warm throb in the middle of her voice allied to an exciting dramatic intensity, much in evidence in a recording of Tosca's prayer. Evenness throughout the register is demonstrated in early recordings, particularly as Donna Anna and Aïda. There is a rare lyric beauty in one of the lesser known arias from *Der Freischütz* "Und ob die Wolke." By way of contrast there is incredible verve and bite in Destinn's rendition of Milada's aria from *Dalibor*—the Czech language version has a peculiarly blazing intensity.

Emmy Destinn as Carmen, Königliche Oper, Berlin, 1906

Destinn gave prodigously of her talents. The war had a considerable impact on her life and career and for a time she was interned by the Austro-Hungarian government as a Czech national sympathizer. She returned to Covent Garden in 1919 but without the same success as previously. She made a number of appearances at the Czech National Opera in Prague, and there were also concerts although this was hardly the medium for Destinn's talents.

Evidence of a singer's status can be derived from records and published criticism. But a further acid test of status lies in the testimony of fellow artists. Geraldine Farrar commented on Destinn's fine voice and musicianship. Lotte Lehmann was "nearly distracted (as) I had listened to that angelic voice." Frances Alda remarked: "hers was one of the greatest voices and she was one of the greatest singers . . . nobody ever sang Butterfly as Destinn did . . . her manner of singing was so perfect, her voice so divine . . . all these made her unforgettable."—STANLEY HENIG

The Devils of Loudon [Diably z Loudon]

Composer: *Krzysztof Penderecki.*

Librettist: *Krzysztof Penderecki (after Huxley/Whiting).*

First Performance: *Hamburg, Staatsoper, 20 June 1969.*

Roles: *Sister Jeanne of the Angels (soprano); Urbain Grandier (baritone); Father Barré (bass); De Laubardemont (tenor); Father Rangier (bass); Adam (tenor); Mannoury (baritone); Ninon (contralto); Philippe (soprano); Prince Henri de Condé (tenor); Gabrielle (soprano); Claire (mezzo-soprano); Louise (contralto); Father Mignon (bass); Father Ambrose (bass); Bontemps (bass-baritone); Mayor Jean D'Armagnac (speaking); Guillaume de Cerisay (speaking); chorus (SATB).*

The Devils of Loudon, Krzysztof Penderecki's first opera, was commissioned by the Hamburg Opera, which premiered it on 20 June 1969. The composer wrote his own libretto based on Aldous Huxley's documentary novel *The Devils of Loudon* (published in 1952 with a translation by Erich Fried) and John Whiting's play *The Devils,* first produced in London at the Aldwych Theatre in 1961. Although Penderecki depended substantially on Whiting's dramatization, he kept close to historical facts rather than the dramatic means employed by the playwright.

Penderecki's penchant for seeking momentous subject matter for his compositional activity suggests the impact on his social consciousness of many tragic events in the contemporary world. In *The Devils of Loudon* he addresses such topics as intolerance, the manipulation of truth, and the persecution of the individual by external forces and by the ignorance and injustice of society. The composer prefaced his score with the political and religious truth "DAEMONI, ETIAM VERA DICENTI, NON EST CREDENDUM (The devil cannot be believed even when he tells the truth)." The tragedy of all men is present in the intolerance shown to one man.

The story deals with the witchcraft trial, torture, and execution of Father Urbain Grandier, who was burned at the stake in Loudon on 18 August 1634. Ostensibly, Grandier was found guilty because of his confession under torture (actually, he refused repeatedly to confess despite the fact that his legs were smashed until the marrow ran from his bones); but in reality, it was Grandier's self-destructive egotism and powerful political prowess, dangerous to both church and state in seventeenth-century France, which condemned him.

According to Huxley's study of the morbid psychology underlying the circumstances, Grandier's flaunting of his sexual adventures, his making personal enemies with his cutting wit, enraging the Carmelites and Capuchins with his pulpit eloquence, and assuming an oppositional political position, all led him to martyrdom. Ironically, he was accused of demonic possession by a neurotic hunchbacked prioress he had never even met. Enticed by the rumors of his sexual indiscretions, she had invited Grandier to take a position in her convent. When Grandier rejected her, her love turned quickly to hate and vengeful action.

Thus Penderecki's highly charged libretto supports many levels of action and characterization interwoven with multifarious political, religious, and social ramifications. In an interview published in *Opera News* (1969), the composer explains that he approached writing the libretto like a movie script. Attracted to dramatic-literary sources, he wrote any number of scores for film and theater from 1955 to 1966. For his first operatic venture he stretched his various musical, dramatic, and linguistic resources completely, often to the most extreme ends.

Penderecki decided to work with the Erich Fried translation since German is an operatic language and the work would be premiered in a German opera house. (In the American premiere at Santa Fe, the English version adapted from Whiting's play was used.) However, Latin is always the language of the chorus in every version, not only because phonetically it was attractive to the composer, but also because it gave him an aesthetic distance from the text, which he needed in order to project its multi-functional and actively atmospheric role, reminiscent of Greek tragedy.

In his search for the creation of an authentic musical environment as background for the dramatic action, Penderecki describes his use of quotations from a Black Mass, which he found "on a dusty shelf of a monastery in Cracow," as well as from the Mass Book, "The Gruesome *Litany of Christ's Blood*," which is sung during the torture scene.

Penderecki finds nothing irreligious in his opera, although some audiences took exception to the love scene between Grandier and the young Widow Ninon, naked in an old bath tub. The nudity in this scene and in the exorcism sequence, during which the nuns rip off their habits, shocked some viewers (particularly after the Stuttgart premiere) and prompted criticism of the composer for seeking sensational effects.

Although the opera was commissioned after the premiere and worldwide acclaim of his *St Luke's Passion,* Penderecki stated that he had contemplated this opera long before the *Passion* and that both works are, in a sense, related in their focus on the elements of religious mystery and exorcism. The passion of St Luke, conceived as Stations of the Cross, parallels the passion of Grandier.

In the flow of the opera's thirty brief, self-contained scenes (suggestive in concept of Berg's *Wozzeck*), each vignette presents the composer with a vehicle for the fullest exploitation of his dynamic and expressionist musical language. According to Penderecki, of paramount importance is the creation of an atmosphere with a spectrum of sound supportive of the dramatic environment and circumstances in which the individual characters find themselves. However, critically speaking, against this intensely illustrative sonic background, character definition tends to become unfocused instead of being developed. It is as if this spectrum of sound as an extended musical means proportioned according to the great range of dramatic situations becomes an essential and powerful constituent to heighten the effect of the drama and to clarify

215

the complexities of the plot. However, it often overshadows the characterization of the human participants.

Vocally, in addition to both free and rhythmically measured dialogue and monologue, declamatory recitative, solo and ensemble singing, Penderecki requires the chorus to scream, roar, laugh, chatter, as well as intone Gregorian chant. The huge orchestra—forty-two strings, thirty-two wind instruments including saxophones, a large battery of percussion plus organ, harmonium, piano, harp, electric guitar—is seldom used at full strength but provides a plethora of musical sound-painting with its individual instrumental combinations, tone clusters in quarter tones, glissandi, extreme ranges, and is designed to respond to whatever intensity or expressivity is demanded. The invention of special notational signs by the composer was necessary in order to accommodate his innovative vocal and instrumental techniques. Thus, having exploited and developed new sonic resources originated by Boulez, Xenakis, Stockhausen, and other avant-gardists, as well as his extensions of microtonality and the post-serialism of the Vienna School, Penderecki has been called the complete eclectic.

Predictably, the climax of this music drama is reached in the Aristotelian manner of a catharsis of fear and pity. At the end, the protagonist Grandier, who had previously squandered his honor, is prepared to endure excruciating agony and go to the stake forgiving his enemies for the sake of his own self-respect. Moreover, according to Huxley's socio-psychological theory of transcendence, Grandier's search for God, which led him to pursue life experience at all of its levels, is finally realized, in his passion for the truth.—MURIEL HEBERT WOLF

Dialogues des Carmélites [Dialogues of the Carmelites]

Composer: *Francis Poulenc.*

Librettist: *Francis Poulenc (after Georges Bernanos).*

First Performance: *Milan, Teatro alla Scala, 26 January 1957.*

Roles: *Blanche de la Force (soprano); Prioress (contralto); Madame Lidoine (soprano); Mother Marie (mezzo-soprano); Sister Constance (soprano); Chevalier de la Force (tenor); Marquis de la Force (baritone); Mother Jeanne (contralto); Sister Mathilde (mezzo-soprano); Father Confessor (tenor); Two Officers (tenor, baritone); Jailer (baritone); Thierry (baritone); M Javelinot (baritone); chorus (SSAATTBB).*

In March of 1953, Francis Poulenc arrived in Milan while on a brief concert tour with Pierre Fournier, the cellist for whom he had written a 1948 sonata. He called at the offices of Ricordi to discuss a ballet on the life of Saint Margaret of Cortona, which the publishing company had commissioned from him for a premiere at the Teatro alla Scala. He informed the director that Saint Margaret simply did not inspire him; Ricordi countered with George Bernanos' *Dialogues des Carmélites,* a play Poulenc had seen. Suddenly, it seemed like the perfect libretto: "I can see myself sitting in a café, devouring Bernanos' drama, and saying to myself at each scene, 'But of course, it's made for me, it's made for me.' "

Poulenc made the few cuts he felt were necessary to adapt the play into a libretto during his train ride back to Paris. He then immersed himself in the lives and thoughts of the Carmelite nuns, reading extensively about them and visiting their convents. His letters to friends during the fall of 1953 reveal his obsession with the subject matter: "I am working like a madman—I don't go out, I see no one—I am composing a tableau (scene) each week. I no longer recognize myself. I am so obsessed with my subject that I am beginning to believe that I knew these women."

The "women" were the entire order of Carmelite nuns from the Compiègne convent, who, having been found "enemies of the people," were publicly guillotined in Paris on 17 July 1794, during the last days of the Reign of Terror. Their story leading up to this execution is contained in the memoirs of Mother Marie, the only member of the order not to face the blade that day. Her memoirs were expanded into a novella, *Die Letzte am Schafott* (*The Last on the Scaffold*), by the German novelist Gertrud von Le Fort. In 1947, the Reverend Raymond Bruckberger and French producer Philippe Agostini decided to make a film version of Le Fort's novella. They called upon Georges Bernanos to write the dialogue, and he agreed reluctantly, for he had never before worked in the film medium. But the producers soon canceled the project, expressing dissatisfaction with the screenplay. Bernanos' "dialogues" survived, however, and were arranged for the stage after his death by his friend and executor, Albert Beguin.

Bernanos's story focuses on a fictitious character, the aristocratic Blanche de la Force, who enters the Carmelite convent to seek refuge from the horrors of the French Revolution and her own fear of death. As Sister Blanche of the Agony of Christ, however, she struggles to cope with the exigencies of religious life, with the death of her beloved Mother Superior, and with an imposed vow of martyrdom. She makes the ultimate sacrifice in a stirring conclusion, joining her fellow Sisters as they are beheaded while singing a Salve Regina which fluctuates from a quiet, sensual prayer to a sweeping cry of anguish. In a brilliant *coup de théâtre,* Poulenc has the nuns' voices drop out one by one as the blade falls, leaving Blanche's friend Constance alone as Blanche dramatically joins the procession. As the blade descends for the final time, the hushed crowd murmurs a final minor seventh chord, a harmonic "signature" of Poulenc.

The dedication of the opera tells us much about the musical sources of *Dialogues:* "to Debussy, who inspired me to compose, and to Claudio Monteverdi, Giuseppe Verdi, and Modeste Mussorgsky, who served here as my models." The emphasis on interior, psychological drama, as well as the consistently subdued mood, recall Debussy's masterful *Pelléas et Mélisande.* Furthermore, Poulenc's vocal style, which occupies a middle ground between accompanied recitative and lyric aria, owes much to the extended arioso style developed by Debussy.

The influence of Monteverdi appears in several passages, such as the introductions to act I, scene ii and act III, scene i, which are reminiscent of early seventeenth-century Italian music. In the case of Musorgsky, the influence is felt particularly in the harmonic style—various chord progressions can be traced directly to *Boris Godunov.* The same can be said of Stravinsky, a pervasive influence on Poulenc who was probably not mentioned because it was such instrumental works as the *Symphonies of Wind Instruments* (see the opening of act I, scene iii) rather than Stravinsky's operas which influenced *Dialogues.*

The imprint of Verdi is the most significant, for *Dialogues* is clearly singers' opera in the best Italian tradition. Everything in the opera is designed to glorify the solo voice: the orchestra is subtle and subdued, there is little action to detract from the singing, and ensembles are avoided (in fact, there are only two short choruses before the final choral scene). Even when an obvious opportunity for a duet presents itself, as in the scene between Blanche and her brother, Poulenc

217

resolutely retains a dialogue format. His thirty-five years of experience as France's leading art song composer certainly served him well in this opera.

Three other striking musical characteristics of *Dialogues* bear mentioning. The opera is irrepressibly tonal, though many of the harmonies are highly colored, and parallel diminished seventh chords create an ambiguity in some of the less lyrical passages. Secondly, several phrases have taken on the role of unifying leading motives, referring, for example, to Blanche's father, to the imminence of danger, or to the concept of redemption through grace. These motives are entrusted to the orchestra, and each appears in several different tonalities. The orchestra also sets the mood for many of the twelve scenes with short preludes or more substantial interludes, reminding the listener of Britten's *Peter Grimes*.

In fact, like *Grimes, Dialogues des Carmélites* is one of the last great tonal operas in the nineteenth-century tradition. It provided Poulenc with a fine outlet to express his deep, personal religious fervor, and it remains a viable dramatic stage work with a place in the standard repertoire.—KEITH W. DANIEL

Dido and Aeneas

Composer: *Henry Purcell.*

Librettist: *Nahum Tate (after Virgil).*

First Performance: *London, Josias Priest's Boarding School for Young Ladies, Chelsea, December 1689.*

Roles: *Dido (soprano or mezzo-soprano); Aeneas (baritone); Belinda (soprano); First Woman (soprano); Second Woman (mezzo-soprano); Sorceress (mezzo-soprano); First Witch (soprano); Second Witch (soprano); Sorcerer (soprano); Sailor (tenor); chorus (SATB); chorus (SATB).*

Dido and Aeneas is Henry Purcell's only opera with continuous music. More than that, it is his only theatrical work in which the main characters are delineated directly through musical expression. His other theatrical compositions, such as *The Fairy Queen* and *King Arthur*, consist rather of a spoken play with musical interpolations of varying relevance to the drama. *Dido and Aeneas,* however, is not merely exceptional for its period and for Purcell's oeuvre in terms of its form; it is also exceptional for all time in terms of its literary and musical quality.

The libretto of *Dido and Aeneas* was written by Nahum Tate based on the original story in Virgil's *Aeneid*. In Virgil, Aeneas leaves the destroyed city of Troy with a band of devoted followers in hopes of founding a new state in Italy. After seven tempest-tossed years, the ragged and diminished fleet takes harbor at the city of Carthage. Aeneas and the Queen of Carthage, Dido, quickly fall in love, due at least in part to the interference of the goddesses Juno and Venus. When Jove (the king of the gods) discovers Aeneas's dalliance, he sends his messenger Mercury to remind him of his destiny to found a kingdom at Rome. Although stunned by this order, Aeneas obeys. He leaves Dido, and she, in despair, kills herself on his sword.

Tate's libretto makes a number of changes in this outline, of which two stand out. He replaces the mythological characters who are aware of and concerned with Aeneas's destiny with a Sorceress and a coven of witches who plot Dido's downfall. Secondly, he omits Dido's violent suicide, replacing it with a scene in which the Queen dies from grief. Both changes had been previewed in Tate's play *Brutus of Alba* (1678), which as Tate himself writes in the preface was "begun and finish . . . under the Name of *Dido and Aeneas.*" *Brutus of Alba* is thus the direct source for *Dido and Aeneas,* the major differences between the two texts being that the play is much longer, has more characters, and is written in decasyllabic blank verse (unrhymed lines of ten syllables), whereas the libretto limits the actions and characters to the main story and is written in rhymed verse with varied but generally shorter line lengths appropriate for musical setting. Despite his stature as poet laureate (which position he attained three years before *Dido and Aeneas*), Nahum Tate has not been kindly treated by posterity. He is especially criticized for his adaptation of Shakespeare's *King Lear,* in which he gives the play a happy ending. However, Tate's ability to write dramatic English verse well-suited to musical setting is rivaled by none in the seventeenth century.

Because no definitive source for this opera survives, questions have been raised about its original content and form. The only seventeenth-century source is an undated, printed libretto that is assumed to derive from the original performance, thought to have taken place in 1689. The earliest musical score dates from no earlier than 1777. These two sources present sometimes strikingly different versions of the work. The libretto contains an allegorical prologue depicting the arrival and ascension of William and Mary, King and Queen of England (21 April 1689). No musical setting of this survives. The remainder of the libretto is divided into three equal acts, whereas the musical sources contain a lopsided division into three acts that indicates an underlying division into two equal parts. Many lines in the libretto are assigned differently in the musical sources, and a chorus and dance at the end of the second act in the libretto are lacking altogether. Because of these and other discrepancies, it is impossible to recreate an absolutely authoritative version of this work.

Some modern writers have interpreted all of *Dido and Aeneas,* like its prologue, as a political allegory. According to one such theory, William, the Dutch Prince of Orange, was (like Aeneas) a foreign king whose allegiance to Mary, the native queen (like Dido), might be questioned. The libretto might therefore illustrate "the possible fate of the British nation should Dutch William fail in his responsibilities to his English queen." Alternatively, the libretto has been seen to illustrate the Protestant fear that the Catholics (represented by the Sorceress and her witches) would undermine the joint sovereignty of William and Mary (Dido and Aeneas) and reestablish the Catholic James II on the throne. However, given that it was written for a girls' school in Chelsea and never performed publicly, it is also possible that the opera was intended as a morality play for the female performers and the audience. The Epilogue, written by Thomas D'Urfey and spoken by Lady Dorothy Burke, significantly asks "Great Providence . . . To save us from those grand deceivers, men."

Dido and Aeneas illustrates Purcell's particularly sensitive setting of English text through word painting, dissonance, and proper rhythmic declamation. For example, in "Whence could so much virtue spring," the word "storms" is set with hurried runs of sixteenth notes, while "valour" receives a pompous dotted note figure. Dissonance is used to express the pain of "woe" and "distress." Most distinctive to the modern ear, however, is Purcell's use of short-long rhythmic patterns (with the short note accented) to set the many English words, such as "pity" and "stubborn," with this accentuation.

Purcell's opera is also justly famous for its use of ground bass (repetitive bass patterns). Such pieces would seem to have a built-in rigidity, as the regularity of the repeated bass exerts a powerful influence over harmony, melody, and phrase structure. Purcell, however, takes this apparent compositional limitation and creates continually different and imaginative solutions. The four ground bass pieces in the opera: "Ah, Belinda," "The Triumphing Dance," "Oft she visits," and "When I am laid in earth" (Dido's Lament), are all remarkable in different ways. Dido's Lament particularly stands out. The voice line never coincides with the regular cadences of the five-bar recurring bass until the last word, when Dido, echoed by the music, meets her fate.—ELLEN T. HARRIS

Di Stefano, Giuseppe

Tenor. Born 24 July 1921, near Catania, Sicily. Educated in Sicily. Studied with Adriano Torchi and Luigi Montesanto in Milan; three years of military service, then escaped to Switzerland, 1943, interned as refugee; debut as Massenet's Des Grieux, Reggio Emilia, 1946; Teatro alla Scala debut in same role, 1947; Metropolitan Opera debut as Duke of Mantua in Rigoletto, *1948; appeared at Met 1948-52, 1955-56 and 1964-65; San Francisco debut as Rodolfo, 1950; at La Scala 1952-60, often appearing with Callas; created Giuliano in Pizzetti's* Calzare d'Argento; *Chicago debut as Edgardo, 1954; British debut at Edinburgh, 1957; Covent Garden debut as Cavaradossi, 1961; world tour with Callas, 1973-74.*

Giuseppe di Stefano's beautiful, warm voice places him among the best lyric tenors since World War II. In fact, di Stefano's voice may easily be rated one of the best tenor voices of this century. In the late 1940s he began to make some of the best recordings by a lyric tenor in some two decades. Unfortunately the voice had lost its youthful freshness by 1960 and along the way there had been blatant problems. Like his contemporary Franco Corelli, di Stefano could sometimes be crude, singing with open vowels, lifting to notes, shouting, and aspirating. "A te, o cara" from the *I Puritani* recording of 1953 with Maria Callas already shows some clear faults. Yet at his best—as Pinkerton, Cavaradossi, and Rodolfo (the latter two also recorded with Callas), in some early aria discs, and in Neapolitan songs and in tunes from his native Sicily—di Stefano was incomparable. Above all, there was the warm, ardent sound, the embodiment of how an Italian tenor should sound. However, di Stefano was too prodigal, singing on the edge, giving away far too much too quickly.

It was a large enough voice, yet di Stefano took on a number of roles that were too heavy for him. These included Manrico (preserved in a fine recording with Callas), Riccardo in *Un ballo in maschera,* and Enzo in a recording with Milanov in which di Stefano performs at the limit of his capabilities. As is common with a voice of such richness and beauty, di Stefano's high notes never sound effortless. In this regard Placido Domingo is his closest contemporary counterpart.

After a number of radio broadcasts, di Stefano made his operatic debut in 1946, in a production of Massenet's *Manon* with Mafalda Favero at Reggio Emilia. His Metropolitan Opera debut came in 1948 and it was in 1951 that he sang with Callas for the first time, a partnership that became legendary both in the opera house and on recordings throughout the 1950s, sadly revived in a worldwide recital tour in 1973-74. A number of the recordings he and Callas made together were conducted by Tullio Serafin; others were led by Victor De Sabata, Antonino Votto, and Herbert von Karajan. The 1953 *Tosca* with Callas, di Stefano, and Gobbi, conducted by De Sabata, is still considered not only the most stirring *Tosca* ever committed to discs, but also one of the finest opera recordings ever made.

Although di Stefano continued to sing for many years after his voice began showing signs of deterioration in the late 1950s, eventually limiting himself to Viennese operetta, he was never the same artist. Incipient flaws previously masked by the almost erotic warmth of his sound could no longer be disguised or ignored. Aspirating seemed to become a necessity to make it through even the most elementary of florid passages, lifting to notes became more pronounced, as did register breaks. He took on increasingly heavier roles throughout the 1950s and mid-1960s, including Radames, Alvaro, Calaf, and Otello. One serious consequence of the overuse and abuse of the voice was di Stefano's eventual inability to sing, not *piano,* but even *mezzo-forte:* the later recorded examples are painfully stentorian. This tendency can be heard on the "live" recordings made by di Stefano and Callas on their 1973-74 tour and on a duet album of 1974 with Montserrat Caballé. The general feeling was that one of the most glorious Italian tenor voices of the century had been misused to the point of early destruction. Yet without this prodigality, this outpouring of passion, would he have been such a sensation in his prime? In his willingness to give everything with little regard to the future he was the perfect match for Callas; perhaps working with her alerted him to dramatic possibilities and refinements, although, as in the famous 1957 Teatro alla Scala production of Verdi's *La traviata,* di Stefano voiced loud complaints about the long, painstaking rehearsal process.

The final impression of di Stefano must be a positive one. Even with the faults there is still much to praise: the earliest aria recordings, such as "Ah dispar, vision" from *Manon,* are stunning and even in the 1960s, with all the problems, the tone is still gorgeous on many notes. The ever-present ardor, the yearning sound, the "tears in the voice" made di Stefano incomparable.—STEPHEN WILLIER

Doktor Faust

Composer: *Ferruccio Busoni [completed by Busoni's pupil Philipp Jarnach after Busoni died in 1924].*

Librettist: *Ferruccio Busoni (after Marlowe and other treatments of the Faust legend).*

First Performance: *21 May 1925.*

Roles: *Doktor Faust (baritone); Mephistopheles (tenor); Nightwatchman (tenor); Wagner (baritone); Duchess of Parma (soprano); Duke of Parma (tenor); Master of Ceremonies (bass); Girl's Brother (baritone); Lieutenant (tenor); Three Students (tenor, two bass); Theologian (bass); Jurist (bass); Doctor of Natural History (baritone); Four Students (four tenor); Gravis (bass); Levis (bass); Asmodus (baritone); Beelzebub (tenor); Megarus (tenor); chorus (SSATTBB).*

Doktor Faust is considered by most critics to be Ferruccio Busoni's masterpiece. The composition of this opera occupied the last fifteen years of the composer's life, and many of his earlier compositions were conceived as studies for the technical problems he thought he would encounter in *Doktor Faust.* Busoni first contemplated Leonardo da Vinci as the subject of this opera, abandoned that idea in favor of Merlin before finally settling upon Faust. Through his acquaintance with Arrigo Boito and his knowledge of the latter's great difficulties with *Mefistofele,* Busoni wisely decided to eschew setting Goethe's *Faust* and instead fashioned a libretto based upon the traditional Faust *Puppenspiel.* The opera was fully complete at the time of Busoni's death except for the final scene, which was realized by the composer's protégé Philipp Jarnach.

The opera is prefaced by a prologue in which Busoni's operatic philosophy is recited in verse. Faust is first seen in his study and is visited by three students who present him with a book of magic, a key, and a deed assigning ownership of the items. Faust then invokes the Devil who appears in six manifestations, the final being Mephistopheles. After Faust requests Mephistopheles' assistance in disposing of his creditors and pursuers, a pact is signed to the ironic accompaniment of the Easter Chorus. Valentine, the brother of the unnamed girl Faust has seduced, is killed in church. Faust and Mephistopheles then intrude upon the wedding festivities of the Duke of Parma. After conjuring up the images of various historical personages, Faust runs off with the Duchess before the wedding is complete. The scene then shifts to a tavern in Wittenberg in which rival groups of Protestant and Catholic students are holding forth in an intellectual debate. Faust thinks wistfully of the Duchess whom he has abandoned. Mephistopheles arrives and announces that the Duchess has sent Faust a child, whose dead body Mephistopheles drops at Faust's feet; however, Mephistopheles transforms the corpse into straw which is then burned and transformed into a vision of Helen of Troy, which vanishes as Faust attempts to embrace it. The three students from Cracow return and demand their gifts back, but Faust is unable to honor their request because he has lost them. The three students prophesy Faust's death at midnight and depart. In the final scene, Wagner has been named Rector of the University and now resides in Faust's former house. Faust sees a beggar woman who turns out to be the Duchess. She gives Faust their dead child and tells him that there is still time to complete his task. Kneeling before a cross, Faust is unable to remember any prayers. He puts the child on the ground and makes a magic circle. In his last living act, Faust transfers his will to the child who rises up and flies across the town. Mephistopheles, in the guise of a night watchman, sees Faust's body and asks rhetorically: "Sollte dieser Mann verunglückt sein?" ("Has this man met with some misfortune?").

Busoni's conception of the Faust legend is both dramatically effective and conspicuously modern. Influenced by the philosophy of Friedrich Nietzsche, Busoni has altered the traditional Faust story from the level of morality play to an examination of a being truly beyond good and evil, a musical *Bildungsroman* of the *Übermensch* as it were. Busoni's atheistic impulses, indeed his rejection of both the sacred and the demonic, is most forcefully in evidence in that portion of Faust's final monologue which was left unset at his death and which Jarnach felt too controversial to realize, especially the lines: "So let the work be finished,/in defiance of you,/of you all,/who hold yourselves for good,/whom we call evil,/who, for the sake of old quarrels/take mankind as a pretext/and pile upon him/the consequences of your discord./Upon this highest insight of my wisdom/is your malice now broken to pieces/and in my self-won freedom/expire both God and Devil at once."

Unlike other Faust operas, Busoni never allows other characters to dominate Faust, nor is there even a suggestion of sentimentality in the opera. This latter phenomenon is seen in the downplaying of the "Gretchen" episode to the point that it is only mentioned as already having occurred; the woman seduced by Faust is never seen nor mentioned by name, and the episode's only pretext in the opera is to provide a motivation for the appearance and eventual murder of Valentine. Additionally, the episodic dramaturgy of *Doktor Faust,* while reminiscent of Berlioz's *La damnation de Faust* and other works, suggests on the part of Busoni an awareness of the editing techniques of cinema.

From a purely musical standpoint, *Doktor Faust* is remarkable for the composer's rejection of the Wagnerian leitmotif. Although the music of the opera is continuous in the Wagnerian sense, there are no meaningful repetitions of melodic fragments in conjunction with readily identifiable characters, objects, ideas, or emotions. Indeed, in his theoretical writings, Busoni emphasized his belief that the organic development of the music and the text of an opera should not be contingent upon one another. Unlike other Faust operas, Busoni's *Doktor Faust* employs almost no word-painting except for a few instances of melodic tritones (the "diabolus in musica") at appropriate places in the text. From a stylistic standpoint, *Doktor Faust* is indicative of the hyper-romantic sensibilities of the late nineteenth-early twentieth-century period which led to the collapse of the traditional system of harmonic relationships and provided the impetus for the development of expressionist and dodecaphonic techniques. Busoni utilizes a curious admixture of the old and new in *Doktor Faust;* modern chromatic harmonies are placed within the context of traditional musical forms and techniques such as the sarabande and the fugue.

Although seldom performed, *Doktor Faust* deserves its place of honor alongside other breakthrough operas of the early twentieth century, such as Berg's *Wozzeck* and the *Salome* and *Elektra* of the Strauss-Hofmannsthal collaboration.—WILLIAM E. GRIM

Domingo, Plácido

Tenor. Born 21 January 1941, in Madrid. Lived in Mexico from age seven. Studied singing with Iglesias and Morelli in Mexico City. Debut as Borsa in Rigoletto *in Mexico City, 1959; United States debut in Dallas, 1961; with Israel National Opera in Tel Aviv, 1962-65; operatic debut at Metropolitan Opera as Maurizio in* Adriana Lecouvreur, *1968; Teatro alla Scala debut as Ernani, 1969; appeared at Covent Garden as Cavaradossi, 1971; appeared at Salzburg as Don Carlos, 1975; created title roles of Morena Torroba's* El poeta *(Madrid, 1980), and Menotti's* Goya *(Washington, DC, 1986); has appeared in films of* La traviata *(1983),* Carmen *(1984) and* Otello *(1986).*

Plácido Domingo is the most gifted all-around operatic artist of his generation, combining musical, vocal and dramatic talents to a rare degree. Although specializing in late nineteenth-century Italian and French opera, Domingo has a vast repertoire (including more than eighty operas) that ranges from light romantic Spanish "zarzuelas" and the songs of popular composers like Andrew Lloyd Webber to some of the most demanding roles of Wagner. No other basically "Italianate" tenor in this century has worked with such consummate success through so wide a repertoire.

Domingo's voice quality is in many ways reminiscent of the later, darker Caruso (minus the "protruding jaw" mannerisms and with a cleaner *portamento*): a powerful, burnished, often almost baritonal sound which Domingo characteristically uses with impeccable musicianship. In this integration of qualities, he is the natural successor to Bjorling. With his tall, dark good looks and powerful stage presence, Domingo is superb in the standard romantic tenor parts: Hoffmann, Don Carlo, Cavaradossi in *Tosca,* Don José in *Carmen,* Gustavo (or Riccardo) in *Un ballo in maschera,* Rodolfo in *La bohème,* Radames in *Aïda.* A conscientious actor, Domingo is capable of making each role develop during performance. There is a twinkle in the eye, and in the voice, in the opening scenes of an opera like *Ballo* or *Bohème,* for example, that makes the tragic final scenes of these operas all the more poignant. In *Carmen,* Domingo will typically portray a shy young man whose nervous infatuation grows gradually towards a homicidal passion.

The part with which Domingo has come to be most associated is the title role in Verdi's *Otello*. His assumption of this role is essentially a lyrical, internalized interpretation in contrast to the stentorian vocalism of Mario del Monaco, the eye-popping madness of James McCracken, or the terrifying desperation portrayed by Jon Vickers. Domingo's Otello retained greater dignity than these, a quality of yearning after the unattainable that suggested tragedy on an epic scale. The only Domingo performance of *Otello* in which frenetic movement took the place of inner turbulence was the one filmed by Franco Zeffirelli.

Domingo has made a number of operatic films, and is also one of the most recorded classical artists in the history of the gramophone. He has committed the entire standard operatic repertoire to disc, much of it two or three times. In addition, he has recorded a number of operas that are only rarely performed (Charpentier's *Louise,* Montemezzi's *L'Amore dei Tre Re* and Mascagni's *Iris,* for example) and a great many light and popular songs in English, French, German, Italian and Spanish. Domingo has also starred in well over fifty operatic videos and telecasts. He has also given some 2,500 live performances during a quarter century on the operatic stage.

Inevitably an artist so exposed will lay himself open to criticism. Some have found Domingo's performances undifferentiated, his Cavaradossi too like his Andrea Chénier, his Canio too like his Otello. There is certainly a recognizable Domingo style of stagecraft: the quick, short steps as a way of suggesting energy or resolve, or the furrowed brow, stooped shoulders and buckled knees to indicate yearning or pleading. Vocally, too, Domingo's invariably covered tone, his characteristic qualities of legato phrasing and clean *portamento,* are evident whether he is singing *Lohengrin* or *L'elisir d'Amore.* Even in Domingo's lighter, more popular recordings—zarzuela, German operetta or the songs of John Denver, Henry Mancini or Lloyd Webber—his characteristic style is in evidence, including a reluctance either to press the voice too hard or to resort too often to head tones. Critics have asked whether an occasional slide or tear in the voice, a suggestion of desperation (or even of vulgarity), perhaps, would add an extra dramatic *frisson?* These questions miss the point. Domingo's art, for all the magnetism of the man and the muscular glory of his vocalism, is essentially that of a refined and sensitive artist who uses his voice as an instrument in the service of music rather as Casals treated his cello.

At the height of his career, Domingo was criticized by some for spreading himself too thin—taking on too many operatic commitments, appearing on too many television chat shows, recording popular music unworthy of his talents, etc. His energy, and ubiquity, are legendary. Was Domingo motivated by a desire for fame? For money? Some supposed he was goaded by the growing celebrity of Luciano Pavarotti, his supposed rival, into these undertakings. Domingo's own answer is unequivocal: he was brought up in an atmosphere of popular song, and he liked the music he sang. He also felt that by reaching out to a wider audience he could help bring millions to opera. Domingo is by no means the first top-level opera singer to perform a more popular repertoire.

He is, however, the first major operatic singer with serious aspirations as a conductor. A versatile musician quite capable of teaching himself difficult operatic roles at the piano, Domingo has conducted something like a dozen different works and appeared on the podium in most of the world's major opera houses. He has also begun conducting symphonic repertoire.

Domingo's calling card as a conductor is Johann Strauss' *Die Fledermaus* (which he has recorded), and he has also conducted a number of the operas with which he is associated as a singer, including *Tosca* and *Bohème.* He has a large, clear, somewhat curvilinear beat, with a tendency to use more arm and less wrist or eye than might be ideal. Performances tend to be thoroughly professional, though lacking the kind of freedom from the page that he regularly achieves as a singer.

Into his fifties, Domingo shows little sign of reducing his commitments, though he is scheduling more concerts than formerly, some in places new to him like Norway, Belgium, and Australia. But there is perhaps a greater change, both in the man and in the artist: more Wagner and fewer press and television interviews. Domingo is Artistic Consultant to the Los Angeles Opera and has become increasingly identified over the years with the Hispanic world, devoting time to Mexican earthquake relief, singing Spanish and Latin American music, and helping to direct the ambitious musical programme for the 1992 Seville International Festival. The greatest singer-actor of recent times clearly enjoys the emerging role of operatic elder statesman.—DANIEL SNOWMAN

Don Carlos

Composer: *Giuseppe Verdi.*

Librettists: *François Joseph Méry and Camille du Locle (after Schiller, W.H. Prescott, History of Philip II, and E. Cormon, Philippe II, roi d'Espagne).*

First Performance: *Paris, Opéra, 11 March 1867; translated into Italian by A. de Lauzières and A. Zanardini for Milan, Teatro alla Scala, 10 January 1884.*

Roles: *Elisabeth de Valois (soprano); Princess Eboli (mezzo-soprano); Don Carlo (tenor); Rodrigo (baritone); Philip II (bass); Grand Inquisitor (bass); Friar (bass); Theobaldo (soprano); Count of Lerma (tenor); Royal Herald (tenor); Celestial Voice (soprano); Countess of Aremberg (mute); chorus (SATB).*

Verdi's *Don Carlos* is, in its original French version, the longest of Verdi's operas. The work was to be a showpiece for the Paris Opéra during Napoléon III's 1867 Universal Exhibition and was thus for Verdi a challenge to produce French grand opera in the Meyerbeerian manner in Paris itself. When Verdi's French publisher, Léon Escudier, brought the scenario for *Don Carlos* to Sant' Agata for Verdi's perusal in 1865, the composer was extremely enthusiastic but wanted to add some elements of spectacle, an important component of French grand opera. In addition to the act I scene at Fontainebleau and the appearance of the emperor Charles V, Verdi, who played a large role in shaping this libretto, also demanded a scene, found in Schiller, between Philip and the blind and aged Inquisitor, and a duet between Philip and Rodrigo. One of the most spectacular scenes of the entire opera was the coronation-*auto da fé* in act III.

As befitting the French grand opera mould, the opera is in five acts. Act I begins in the forest of Fontainebleau. The Infante Don Carlo of Spain is to wed Elisabeth, daughter of Henri II of France. Carlo has come to France incognito to see her; they meet in the Fontainebleau forest and fall passionately in love. The scene ends, however, with the news that Elisabeth is not to wed Carlo, but his father, Philip II. Act II, scene i is set at the cloister of the monastery of San Yuste, to which Carlo's grandfather, Charles V, has retreated from earthly cares. Carlo meets his friend Rodrigo, the Marquis of Posa, who has just returned from Flanders. Carlo tells of his love for

Elisabeth, and the two men swear friendship and devotion to liberty in a rousing duet. In scene ii, outside the gates of the convent, Princess Eboli sings the "Veil Song" with the court ladies as chorus. Elisabeth and Rodrigo join them; the latter distracts Eboli's attention so that Elisabeth may read a note from Carlo. Rodrigo leads Eboli away, Carlo enters to talk to Elisabeth, but he ends up delirious; when she reminds him that she is now his mother he leaves in despair. Philip and Rodrigo have a long exchange in which the latter criticizes the king's cruelty to the Flemings. The king confesses his suspicions about the queen and his son to Rodrigo and asks him to pay attention to the situation.

Act III begins in the queen's gardens in Madrid. Carlo is reading a letter about a midnight tryst. He thinks Elisabeth wrote it, but it was actually Eboli, who becomes extremely angry and swears vengeance. Scene ii shows Philip's coronation in conjunction with an *auto da fé*. During the procession a group of Flemish deputies, led by Carlo, asks for pity for Flanders. Carlo draws a sword on his father, but is persuaded to yield it to Rodrigo. In act IV, scene i Philip reveals in soliloquy that his wife never loved him. The Grand Inquisitor enters: Philip speaks of sacrificing his own son, and the Inquisitor asks for Rodrigo's life. Philip eventually acquiesces. Elisabeth enters, distraught that her jewel-case is missing; Philip has it, with the picture of Carlo inside. The queen swoons. Eboli, left alone with her, confesses that she was the one who betrayed her to the king because of her own love for Carlo. Elisabeth forgives her this, but when Eboli then confesses to being Philip's erstwhile mistress, Elisabeth forces her to choose between exile and the veil. Eboli chooses the latter, but in the one day left to her she vows to save Carlo. In scene ii Carlo is visited in prison by Rodrigo. Incriminating letters have been found on Rodrigo; he must die and Carlo, freed, must go to save Flanders. Rodrigo is then killed by a shot, the king enters to free his son but Carlo recoils from him. Act V takes place at the cloister again. Elisabeth addresses the tomb of Charles V, recalling her happiness at Fontainebleau. Carlo comes to bid her farewell; he will go to Flanders and they will meet in another world. Philip and the Inquisitor interrupt them and the gates of Charles V's tomb open as the Emperor appears to lead Carlo back into the cloister with him.

Both Schiller's play and Verdi's operatic setting have had the charge of historical inaccuracy leveled against them, yet accuracy was not a primary consideration for either. In 1883 Verdi wrote a letter to Giulio Ricordi addressing this issue: "In short, nothing in the drama is historical, but it contains a Shakespearean truth and profundity of characterizations." Previously, in 1876, he had remarked to Andrei Maffei that "To copy truth can be good, but to invent truth is better, far better." Typical Verdian themes that are found in *Don Carlos* are the depiction and criticism of ecclesiastical narrowness and cruelty (also found in *La forza del destino, Aida,* and *Simon Boccanegra*) and the destruction of personal lives against the background of larger forces: religious, political, and dynastic. Thus *Don Carlos,* as with other Verdi operas, e.g., *La forza del destino, Un ballo in maschera, Aida,* and *Otello,* and as with French grand opera and Metastasian *opera seria,* is revelatory of personal happiness destroyed by exigencies of public duty.

A number of versions of *Don Carlos* exist. Because of the length of the original and the need for the Parisian audiences to catch the last train back to the suburbs, cuts were already being made during Opéra rehearsals for the premiere. Those passages cut—among them a prelude and introduction, a duet for Elisabeth and Eboli, and a duet for Carlo and Philip that eventually became the "Lacrymosa" of the *Messa da Requiem*—were never published. They were physically cut from the score; in 1969 Andrew Porter and David Rosen discovered and reconstructed them from 1867 performance materials. Verdi made small revisions in 1872 and revised the score heavily in 1882, with a Viennese revival in mind. Aims of this revision were first to cut a very long opera, and also to repair some of the damage of the 1867 cuts and to bring the drama closer to Schiller (a goal of Verdi's from the very beginning), and finally to excise purely musical moments that impeded the action. With these in mind, Verdi cut out all of act I, placing Carlo's *romanza* in act II so that he would not be without a solo aria; cut the ballet (which had been obligatory for Paris) and the mask-changing episode preceding it; shortened the great act IV quartet; and recomposed the ending insurrection in act IV in a much more concise manner. These revisions were completed in February of 1883 and the result was published both in French (du Locle had helped Verdi) and in Italian; this version premiered at the Teatro alla Scala in Italian in January 1884 with Francesco Tamagno in the title role. Two years later another version was performed and published in which, with Verdi's consent, the 1867 Fontainebleau act preceded the four acts of the 1883 revision. This 1886 version is the one most often performed and recorded today. It is well to keep in mind that Verdi actually composed none of *Don Carlos* to an Italian text. Although this opera was not always appreciated, *Don Carlos* is now considered by many to be one of Verdi's greatest operas.—STEPHEN WILLIER

Don Giovanni (Il dissoluto punito)

Composer: *Wolfgang Amadeus Mozart.*

Librettist: *Lorenzo Da Ponte.*

First Performance: *Prague, National Theater, 29 October 1787.*

Roles: *Don Giovanni (bass-baritone); Leporello (bass); Donna Anna (soprano); Don Ottavio (tenor); Donna Elvira (soprano); Masetto (bass or baritone); Zerlina (soprano); Commendatore (bass); chorus (SATB).*

The Don Juan theme had appeared in Western literature even before Tirso de Molina (if indeed it was he) immortalized the great seducer's legendary powers in *El burlador de Sevilla* (*The Prankster from Seville*) around the turn of the sixteenth century. It was part of a corpus of tales inherited from the late middle ages, which included also the story of the quasi-historical Don Juan Tenorio, and may be seen as counterpart to another great legend of masculine prowess, that of Dr. Faustus, which also harks back to medieval times.

The story line was primitively simple in the beginning, merely describing Don Juan's unending series of sexual exploits. But it grew deeper and more complicated as the tradition grew, as did the character of Don Juan himself. Originally merely a libidinous womanizer, Don Juan in time took on new psychological dimensions, offering a basis for philosophical speculations on the daemonic in romanticism, on the universality of the Don's persuasion, and so forth, as the tradition developed.

By 1787, when Lorenzo Da Ponte prepared a libretto for Mozart to set as *Don Giovanni, ovvero il dissoluto punito* (*Don Juan, or the Roué punished*), both the play and its principal character had reached maximum depth and complication. Truth to tell, these qualities were virtually copied from a libretto which Giovanni Bertati had produced in 1775 for a setting by Gazzaniga with the title *Don Giovanni Tenorio, o sia Il convitato di pietro* (*Don Juan Tenorio, or The Stone Guest*). Indeed, Da Ponte's recommendation that Mozart set his new libretto was probably prompted by his close familiarity with Bertati's script, which gave him basis for a new libretto with minimum labor on his part.

Mozart's Overture sets in motion both tragic and comic elements of this *dramma giocoso,* as the composer named it, building these upon two basic motives. The tragic element is expressed throughout by an ominous scalar figure in d-minor, which recurs as a psychological flashback at a key point in the drama, when Donna Anna first suspects that Don Giovanni is the mysterious rapist who murdered her father. The same scalar motive, with its aura of the supernatural, returns again at the end when Don Giovanni is consumed by hell-fire after his last encounter with the stone statue of the Commendatore. The second motive is a light-hearted tune which captures the merriment that brightens festive scenes throughout the drama.

Act I of the tragicomedy opens in the garden of the Commendatore, where Leporello, Don Giovanni's serving man, laments his underprivileged social status as he stands guard, while his master attempts to seduce Donna Anna, the Commendatore's daughter. How he longs to achieve the Don's status! Suddenly, much to Leporello's disquietude, a commotion begins as Don Giovanni appears, still masked, and hotly pursued by Anna, the angry object of his seduction. Awakened by the disturbance, the Commendatore enters, sword in hand, to challenge the intruder, who promptly dispatches the old man. Leporello, commenting on the fact that neither father nor daughter asked for what they got, flees with his master, as Donna Anna returns with Don Ottavio, her fiancé, to find her father already dead. It is a remarkable opening scene, introducing the two basic topics that are treated in the opera: Don Giovanni's ruling passion for sexual conquest, and Leporello's revolutionary aspiration for equality. However, nothing in this opening scene is more remarkable than Mozart's music, which vividly mirrors every nuance of human feeling, every psychological reaction, with utmost reality. The musical portrayal of the dying Commendatore is one of the most masterful expressions of a human condition in all of operatic literature.

As Leporello and his master escape to make their way back to Seville, a brief duo-recitative reflects their ambivalent relationship. Don Giovanni is jubilant and unremorseful for his most recent acts, but nevertheless shows a strange dependence upon his minion, Leporello, who remains in the Don's service. The tone of the recitative veers suddenly as Don Giovanni senses a female presence and all his instincts are awakened.

Scene ii reveals Donna Elvira, whose presence had aroused the Don's hopes for another romantic adventure—hopes intensified when he hears her singing of finding the villain who had ruined her, "to carve out his heart." He does not recognize that Elvira is a former conquest until the end of her song, when she turns and recognizes him, the man who had ruined her life. In her surprise, her feelings of vengeance falter, giving way to soulful entreaty that they resume their old relationship. Don Giovanni, unheedful of the strength of character revealed in her virtuoso aria, slips away, after charging his servant to acquaint her with his illustrious record of sexual conquest. Leporello complies, singing a mocking "catalog aria," classifying, characterizing and enumerating all his exploits, nation by nation: there were 640 in Italy, 231 in Germany, 100 in France, 91 in Turkey, but 1003 in Spain! Mozart's music again subtly delineates every psychological nuance, with orchestral *bizzarrie* which catch the mocking tone of Leporello's aria most adroitly.

Even as Elvira, shocked by the Don's sheer effrontery, reaffirms her feelings of vengeance, the amorous Don is off on another romantic adventure, as Zerlina and Masetto, a peasant pair, enter to celebrate prenuptial festivities. Don Giovanni, deciding at once to exercise his *"droit de seigneur"* where Zerlina is concerned, orders Leporello to invite the wedding party to his castle, at the same time instructing him to keep Masetto well occupied. Immediately, he applies his seductive arts to Zerlina, and wins her over in a lively duet that faithfully mirrors her ebbing resistance and eventual capitulation. He is about to set off with her to a convenient cottage nearby, when Donna Elvira catches up with him, preventing the seduction. She warns Zerlina with the voice of bitter experience and upbraids the Don, still arguing passionately for reconciliation. Donna Anna and Don Ottavio arrive to witness the end of this scene. Disbelieving Don Giovanni's explanation that Donna Elvira is love-mad, they join forces with her, in growing doubt of his credibility. As he leaves, Donna Anna suffers a feeling of *deja vu,* as the music recalls the scene of her father's death. At that moment she recognizes Don Giovanni as the rapist who killed her father.

Still intent on seducing Zerlina, and perhaps a dozen more that same evening, Don Giovanni gloats over prospects created by the great ball he has organized at his palace. Meanwhile, Zerlina manages at least partially to quiet Masetto's fears concerning her fidelity. But just as she does, Don Giovanni returns, and her reactions awaken all his fears again. So he decides to hide and watch; but the wily Don dissimulates, inviting both to the ball, now in full swing in the palace. Just then Donna Anna, Don Ottavio, and Donna Elvira arrive in masks, and Leporello, upon his master's instructions, invites them all to the ball. Inside, as the dance begins, Leporello again keeps Masetto occupied, while Don Giovanni dances off into a nearby bedroom with Zerlina. No longer compliant, she screams for help as he attempts to force her, and the crowd comes to her rescue. Cleverly, the Don emerges prodding Leporello forth at sword's point and branding him as the would-be rapist. No one is fooled, but Don Giovanni nevertheless makes good his escape in the confusion.

As act II begins, Leporello serves notice on his master: He will quit unless his master gives up women altogether. "Impossible," says the Don, "I need them more than the food I eat, more than the very air I breathe." He then quickly persuades Leporello to aid him with his next conquest. Don Giovanni now has settled his amorous attention upon Elvira's maid-servant. To lure Elvira away that evening, he disguises Leporello as himself by exchanging hats and cloaks, then stands behind his gesticulating servant while he sings a seductive aria underneath her window. Taken in by the ruse, Elvira descends to disappear into the shrubbery with Leporello, who under cover of night now undertakes the pleasant task of seducing her.

Meanwhile, Don Giovanni, dressed in Leporello's clothes, openly serenades Elvira's maid. But his seduction is forestalled by Masetto, at the head of a posse of peasants who seek to capture the aristocratic felon. Taking advantage of the darkness and using his servant's disguise, the Don pretends to join forces with the band and immediately sends off all the other peasants on various missions, tricking Masetto to give up his musket and pistol, with which he promptly beats him before making good his escape. Zerlina arrives with a lantern to find Masetto sorely wounded, and offers to cure him, magically, with a certain balm she carries with her always. As usual, Mozart's musical accompaniment is apt and highly suggestive.

Meanwhile, Donna Elvira, still mistaking Leporello for Don Giovanni, seeks what she supposes to be an amorous reconciliation, while he desperately tries to escape. Suddenly, Donna Anna and Don Ottavio come upon the pair, and they too mistake the servant for the master. To save his skin, Leporello reveals his true identity, then quickly runs off, leaping over the wall of the cemetery in which the Commendatore lies buried, to find Don Giovanni there before him. As the Don chortles over his latest conquest, a sepulchral voice interrupts, commanding both to be silent. Leporello is terrified, but Don Giovanni remains nonchalant, forcing his servant to read the inscription on the Commendatore's tomb: "Revenge awaits the villain who killed me." The Don, laughing, orders Leporello to invite the statue to dine with him that same evening. To the latter's dismay, the statue accepts. In the next scene, inserted after the first performance, Don Ottavio upbraids Donna Anna for postponing their wedding day by a year, but at last accepts her decision.

In the final scene, Don Giovanni, well entertained by music from several operas, including one of his own, prepares to dine in his apartment as Leporello waits to serve him. Just then Donna Elvira rushes in, vainly urging the Don to repent. As she departs in total distress, the statue from the Commendatore's mausoleum treads heavily up the steps to the Don's apartment. He too urges the Don to repent, and, upon his resolute refusal, consigns him to his fate. The flames of hell rise up to surround him, and Don Giovanni falls headlong, to join the infernal chorus.

In a brief epilogue, all the remaining characters arrive to question Leporello about his master. When they learn of his fate, Donna Anna and Don Ottavio rejoice, Donna Elvira retires to a convent, Zerlina and Masetto go home to have their dinner, and Leporello goes off in search of a new master. Before going their several ways, they all sing a final chorus on the fate of evildoers, whose punishment always suits their crimes.—FRANKLIN B. ZIMMERMAN

Donizetti, (Domenico) Gaetano (Maria)

Composer. Born 29 November 1797, in Bergamo. Died 8 April 1848, in Bergamo. Married: Virginia Vasselli, 1828 (died 30 July 1837). Studied singing with Salari, piano with Gonzales, and harmony with J.S. Mayr at the Bergamo school of music; studied counterpoint with Pilotti and Mattei at the Bologna Liceo Filarmonico, 1815; 30 operas between 1816-29; Anna Bolena *(1830) a huge success; visited Paris, 1835; succeeded Zingarelli as the director of the Naples Conservatory, 1837;* Poliuto *not performed in Naples due to censorship; numerous successful productions in France, including* La fille du régiment, *and* La favorite, *1840; in Rome and Milan, 1841; court composer and master of the imperial chapel, Vienna, 1842; a stroke suffered in 1845 led to his death.*

Operas *Il Pigmalione* (scena drammatica), 1816, Bergamo, 13 October 1960; *L'ira d'Achille,* 1817 [not performed]; *Olimpiade,* Metastasio, 1817 [unfinished]; *Enrico di Borgogna,* B. Merelli (after Kotzebue), Venice, San Luca, 14 November 1818; *Una folia,* B. Merelli, Venice, San Luca, 15 December 1818 [also performed as *Il ritratto parlante*]; *Le nozze in villa,* B. Merelli, 1819, Mantua, Vecchio, carnival 1820-21 [also performed as *I provinciali*]; *Il falegname di Livonia, o Pietro il grande, czar delle Russia,* G. Bevilacqua-Aldovrandini (after A. Duval), Venice, San Samuele, 26 December 1819; *Zoraida di Granata,* B. Merelli (after F. Gonzales), Rome, Torre Argentina, 28 January 1822; revised, with libretto revisions by J. Ferretti, Rome, 1824; *La zingara,* A.L. Tottola, Naples, Nuovo, 12 May 1822; *La lettera anonima,* G. Genoino, Naples, Fondo, 29 June 1822; *Chiara e Serafina, o I pirati,* Felice Romani (after R.C.G. de Pixérécourt, *La cisterne*), Milan, Teatro alla Scala, 26 October 1822; *Alfredo il grande,* A.L. Tottola, Naples, San Carlo, 2 July 1823; *Il fortunato inganno,* A.L. Tottola, Naples, Nuovo, 3 September 1823; *L'ajo nell'imbarazzo, o Don Gregorio,* Ferretti (after G. Giraud), Rome, Valle, 4 February 1824; revised, 1826 and 1828; *Emilia di Liverpool,* Scatizzi, Naples, Nuovo, 28 July 1824;

revised 1828; also performed as *L'eremitaggio di Liverpool*. *Alahor in Granata*, Palermo, Carolion, 7 January 1826; *La bella prigioniera*, 1826 [unfinished]; *Elvida*, G.F. Schmidt, Naples, San Carlo, 6 July 1826; *Gabriella di Vergy*, Tottola (after Du Belloy), 1826; second version composed 1838; *Olivio e Pasquale*, Ferretti (after A.S. Sografi), Rome, Valle, 7 January 1827; *Otto mesi in due ore, ossia, Gli esiliati in Siberia*, D. Gilardoni (after Pixérécourt, *La fille de l'exilé*), Naples, Nuovo, 13 May 1827; revised 1833; *Il borgomastro di Saardam*, D. Gilardoni (after A.H.J. Mélesville, J.T. Merle, and E. Cantiran de Boire), Naples, Nuovo, 19 August 1827; *Le convenienze ed inconvenienze teatrali*, Donizetti (after Sografi), Naples, Nuovo, 21 November 1827; revised 1840; *L'esule di Roma, ossia Il proscritto*, D. Gilardoni, Naples, San Carlo, 1 January 1828 [also performed as *Settimio il proscritto*]; *Alina, regina di Golconda*, Felice Romani (after S.J. de Boufflers), Genoa, Carlo Felice, 12 May 1828; revised 1833; *Gianni di Calais*, D. Gilardoni (after C.V. d'Arlincourt), Naples, Fondo, 2 August 1828; *Il Giovedì Grasso, o Il nuovo Pourceaugnac*, D. Gilardoni, Naples, Fondo, fall 1828; *Il paria*, Gilardoni (after C. Delavigne), Naples, San Carlo, 12 January 1829; *Elizabeth, o Il castello di Kenilworth*, A.L. Tottola (after Hugo, *Amy Robsart*; Scribe, and Scott, *Leicester*) Naples, San Carlo, 6 July 1829; *I pazzi per progetto*, D. Gilardoni (after Scribe and Poirson), Naples, Fondo, 7 February 1830; *Il diluvio universale*, D. Gilardoni (after Byron, *Heaven and Earth*, and Ringhieri, *Il diluvio*), Naples, San Carlo, 28 February 1830; *Imelda de' Lambertazzi*, A.L. Tottola (after Sperduti), Naples, San Carlo, 23 August 1830; *Anna Bolena*, Felice Romani (after Pindemonte and Pepoli), Milan, Carcano, 26 December 1830; *Gianni di Parigi*, Felice Romani (after Saint-Just), 1831, Milan, Teatro alla Scala, 10 September 1839; *Francesca di Foix*, D. Gilardoni (after Favart and Saint-Amans, *Ninette à la cour*), Naples, San Carlo, 30 May 1831; *La romanziera e l' uomo nero*, D. Gilardoni, Naples, Fondo, 18 June 1831; *Fausta*, D. Gilardoni and Donizetti, Naples, San Carlo, 12 January 1832; *Ugo, conte di Parigi*, Felice Romani (after Bis, *Blanche d'Acquitaine*), Milan, Teatro alla Scala, 13 March 1832; *L'elisir d'amore*, Felice Romani (after Scribe, *Le philtre*), Milan, Canobbiana, 12 May 1832; *Sancia di Castiglia*, P. Salatino, Naples, San Carlo, 4 November 1832; *Il furioso all'isola di San Domingo*, Ferretti (after an anonymous *Don Quixote* play), Rome, Valle, 2 January 1833; revised 1833; *Parisina*, Felice Romani (after Byron), Florence, Teatro della Pergola, 17 March 1833; *Torquato Tasso*, Ferretti (after G. Rosini), Rome, Valle, 9 September 1833 [also performed as *Sordello il trovatore*]; *Adelaide*, 1834 [unfinished; partly used in *L' ange de Nisida*]; *Lucrezia Borgia*, Felice Romani (after Hugo), Milan, Teatro alla Scala, 26 December 1833; revised 1840; *Rosamonda d' Inghilterra*, Felice Romani, Florence, Teatro della Pergola, 27 February 1834; revised as *Eleonora di Gujenna*, Naples, 1837; *Maria Stuarda*, G. Bardi (after Schiller), 1834 [for Naples], Milan, Teatro alla Scala, 30 December 1835; second version [new libretto, Naples music], *Buondelmonte*, P. Saltino, Naples, San Carlo, 18 October 1834; *Gemma di Vergy*, E. Bidera (after Dumas, *Charles VII*), Milan, Teatro alla Scala, 26 December 1834; *Marino Faliero*, E. Bidera (after C. Delavigne and Byron), Paris, Théâtre Italien, 12 March 1835; *Lucia di Lammermoor*, S. Cammarano (after Scott), Naples, San Carlo, 26 September 1835; revised 1839; *Belisario*, S. Cammarano (after J.F. Marmontel), Venice, La Fenice, 4 February 1836; *Il campanello di notte*, Donizetti (after L.L. Brunswick, M.B. Troin, and V. Lhérie, *La sonnette de nuit*), Naples, Nuovo, 1 June 1836; *Betly, ossia La capanna svizzera*, Donizetti (after Scribe, *Le chalet*), Naples, Nuovo, 24 August 1836; revised, 1837; *L' assedio di Calais*, S. Cammarano (after Du Belloy), Naples, San Carlo, 19 November 1836; *Pia de' Tolomei*, S. Cammarano (after Sestini), Venice, Apollo, 18 February 1837; revised with libretto revisions by Sinigaglia, 1837; *Roberto Devereux, ossia Il conte de Essex*, S. Cammarano (after F. Ancelot, *Elisabeth d'Angleterre*), Naples, San Carlo, 29 October 1837; *Maria di Rudenz*, S. Cammarano (after Anicet-

Bourgeois and Mellian, *La nonne sanglante*), Venice, La Fenice, 30 January 1838; *Le duc d'Albe*, Eugène Scribe and Duveyrier, 1839 [unfinished]; *Poliuto*, S. Cammarano (after Corneille), 1838, Naples, San Carlo, 30 November 1848; second version, *Les martyrs*, Eugène Scribe, Paris, Opéra, 10 April 1840; *La fille du régiment*, J.H.V. de Saint-Georges and J.F.A. Bayard, Paris, Opéra Comique, 11 February 1840; *L'ange de Nisida*, A. Royer and G. Vaëz, 1839 [not performed]; also as *Silvia*; revised as *La favorite* [below]; *La favorite*, A. Royer and G. Vaëz (after Baculard d'Arnaud, *Le comte de Comminges*), Paris, Opéra, 2 December 1840; revised and expanded from *L'ange de Nisida* [above]; *Adelia, o La figlia dell' arciere*, Felice Romani and G. Marini (after an anonymous French play), Rome, Apollo, 11 February 1841; *Rita, ou Le mari battu*, G. Vaëz, 1841, Paris, Opéra-Comique, 7 May 1860 [also performed as *Deux hommes et une femme*; *Maria Padilla*, G. Rossi (after Ancelot), Milan, Teatro alla Scala, 26 December 1841; *Linda di Chamounix*, G. Rossi (after D'Ennery and Lemoine, *La grâce de Dieu*), Vienna, Kärntnertor, 19 May 1842; revised 1842; *Ne m'oubliez pas*, J.H.V. de Saint-Georges, 1842 [unfinished]; *Caterina Cornaro*, G. Sacchero (after Saint-Georges, *La reine de Chypre*), 1842, Naples, San Carlo, 18 January 1844; *Don Pasquale*, G. Ruffini and Donizetti (after A. Anelli, *Ser Marc'Antonio*), Paris, Théâtre Italien, 3 January 1843; *Maria di Rohan*, S. Cammarano (after Lockroy [J.P. Simon], *Un duel sous le cardinal de Richelieu*), Vienna, Kärntnertor, 5 June 1843; revised 1844; *Dom Sébastien, roi de Portugal*, Eugène Scribe (after Barbossa Machado, *Memoires . . . o governo del Rey D. Sebastiao*), Paris, Opéra, 13 November 1843.

The reputation of Gaetano Donizetti has undergone remarkable fluctuations. At the outset of his career he was regarded as merely one of a number of people imitating Rossini; later, even in the first years after *Anna Bolena* had made his name known in Paris, London, and Vienna, he was apt to be ranked as inferior to Bellini. It was not until *Lucia di Lammermoor,* which ironically had its premiere three days after Bellini's untimely death, that Donizetti became generally recognized as the leading Italian composer of his day, and this was in part because *Lucia* spoke persuasively to the romantic sensibility of its time.

Until his death, Donizetti was the most widely performed composer of the day, even though his declining health cut short his active career in 1845. His reputation lost ground during the remaining years of the nineteenth century, in part because of the influx of newer works (by Verdi, Wagner, and the *veristi*) and in part because singers capable of doing full justice to his music were becoming scarcer. Up through the time of World War II, he had come to be regarded as hopelessly old-fashioned, a composer for canaries. It was not until the 1950s that the tide began to turn, and today he is generally acknowledged as one of the most important Italian composers of his time and a key figure in the development of Italian opera.

The reasons for this shift are not hard to find. Most importantly, since World War II the influx of new works that enter the repertory and are performed internationally with any frequency has so shrunk as to become barely perceptible. To introduce variety into their offerings, the directors of large, expensive-to-run opera houses found no alternative but to turn to neglected works from the past. Further, in those years after World War II there emerged a number of singers, sopranos principally, with Maria Callas heading the procession, who made a popular and artistic success of revivals of some largely forgotten operas by Donizetti, among them *Anna Bolena, Maria Stuarda,* and *Lucrezia Borgia*. Further, the case for opera composers in particular has been boosted considerably by the emergence of newer and handier methods of not merely auditory recording but visual recording as well, improvements which make a whole cornucopia of attractive material easily accessible to a steadily increasing public. Donizetti's reputation has profited from these developments because of the sheer number of viable operas in the whole gamut of genres to be found in his extensive *oeuvre.*

The conditions under which Donizetti was forced to pursue his career were unfavorable in certain respects. In his time composers were primarily concerned with providing material for singers, tailored to show off their strong points and disguise their weak ones. In those days before the repertory concept was well established, the opera houses of Italy constantly demanded new material, preferably fresh but not too far out, much in the way television requires it today. By training, Donizetti was equipped better to meet this requirement than most of his contemporaries, but what raised him above them was his craftsmanship, his good taste, and his deep concern with dramatic values.

In Italy in Donizetti's time every new stagework had to conform to the stringent limits imposed by

Gaetano Donizetti, portrait by Girolamo Induno

religious as well as political censors, imposed in the rather naive hope that if theaters were places that uplifted morals they would also affirm the status quo politically. This purpose rather seriously limited the subjects available for musico-dramatic treatment. As actively as he could as a private citizen dependent upon state-regulated theaters for his livelihood, Donizetti waged a campaign to try to liberalize these censorious restrictions in the interest of providing powerful dramatic fare in the form of romantic lyric tragedies. In Naples both *Maria Stuarda* and *Poliuto* were banned before they received what would have been their first performances. *Lucrezia Borgia,* to cite another instance, was regarded as such a volatile subject (its heroine a pope's daughter who is presented as a mass poisoner) that two years elapsed after its successful premiere in Milan before another Italian opera house would stage it and then only in a bowdlerized form. Also at Milan, then slightly more liberal than Naples, Maria Malibran sought to get away with using the pre-censored text and action of *Maria Stuarda,* with the result that the opera was banned there as well after only a handful of performances.

As a composer, Donizetti excelled both in tragic works and comic, the most consistently popular of the latter being *L'elisir d'amore, La fille du régiment,* and *Don Pasquale,* but serious works dominated his last decade of activity. He was particularly famous for his skill at writing powerful ensembles, the most famous of them being the "sextet" from *Lucia,* but there are a number of others that are equally effective: the whole temple scene from *Poliuto* (which anticipates many of the effects of the triumphal scene in Verdi's *Aïda*) and the septet in act IV of *Dom Sébastien.* One of his greatest achievements, serious or comic, is the quartet-finale to act II of *Don Pasquale.*

Donizetti frequently experimented with modifying the convention of quadri-partite structure he inherited from Rossini. This pattern consisted of: 1) *tempo d'attacco* or active build-up, 2) *cantabile,* a static lyric section (often reflective), 3) *tempo di mezzo,* active, shift of mood (often a message arrives or a decision is reached), and 4) *cabaletta* or *stretta,* a static piece, often a two-statement aria with opportunities for vocal display, or, in an ensemble, involving the intensification of some confrontation. This four-section pattern could be employed in solo arias, duets, and large ensembles. In its totality the mad scene from *Lucia* is a familiar example of this structure. Donizetti, however, frequently modified this basic pattern. As one who was much concerned with dramatic values, Donizetti shifted the whole emphasis of the mid-point finale in *Maria Stuarda,* for example, to the third section, the confrontation between Queen Elizabeth and Mary, Queen of Scots. Sometimes he would introduce a second voice into what would traditionally have been a solo, as when he inserts a mezzo-soprano line into the entrance aria of the heroine of *Rosamonda d'Inghilterra*. In two of his later works, *Linda di Chamounix* and *Caterina Cornaro,* he experimented with eliminating or telescoping parts of this compound structure, even dividing its sections between different soloists, all in the interest of sustaining dramatic tension and momentum.

One characteristic peculiar to his style was his ability to write sad elegiac numbers using major instead of minor tonalities: Edgardo's 'Tu che al Dio spiegasti l'ali' from the tomb scene in *Lucia* is a good example of this, as is the arioso for the dying Gennaro in the final scene of *Lucrezia*. In many ways, Donizetti can be seen to anticipate certain aspects of Verdi's practice: increased importance of baritone parts, as with the title roles in *Il furioso, Torquato Tasso,* and *Belisario*. There is a general movement away from the emphasis on solo arias toward confrontational duets as points of major focus: the encounter between the Duke of Nottingham and his wife Sara at the beginning of act III of *Roberto Devereux,* for instance, or the father-daughter encounter in act II of *Linda,* or the tragic duet that climaxes act IV of *La favorite*. The treatment of the voices in the famous trio in *Lucrezia Borgia* provided a model that lingered in the back of Verdi's mind as late as *Otello*. Indeed, *Lucrezia Borgia* was receiving its first round of performances at the Teatro alla Scala when Verdi came to Milan to study composition, and the impact of this work upon his formative imagination is difficult to overestimate.

It used to be wondered at that a few of Donizetti's works stubbornly survived even when his reputation was at its lowest ebb. Prejudices and fashions have modified the repertory in the century and a half since his death. As the so-called "music of the future" (a phrase associated with the introduction of Wagner's works) has receded into the past and, later, various anti-romantic stances have come to seem mere posturing, the musical consistency and unfailing good taste of Donizetti have come to seem more valuable virtues than once they did. The operatic repertory we have grown accustomed to today is more extensive chronologically than it was even a quarter of a century ago. In its context the combination of vocal melody, solid structure, and dramatic intensity to be found in a surprising number of Donizetti's operas have won him new respect and admiration.—WILLIAM ASHBROOK

La donna del lago [The Lady of the Lake]

Composer: *Gioachino Rossini.*

Librettist: *A.L. Tottola (after Scott, The Lady of the Lake).*

First Performance: *Naples, San Carlo, 24 September 1819.*

Roles: *Elena (soprano); Malcolm (mezzo-soprano); Rodrigo (tenor); Uberto (tenor); Douglas of Angus (bass); Albina (soprano); Serano (tenor); Bertram (tenor); chorus.*

La donna del lago, one of Rossini's most frequently revived operas in the nineteenth century, was premiered at the Teatro San Carlo in Naples on 24 September 1819. It is an *opera seria* in two acts with a libretto by Andrea Leone Tottola based on Sir Walter Scott's poem *The*

Lady of the Lake. In the original cast, the title role was sung by Isabella-Angela Colbrán, who created a number of Rossini's heroines. The action takes place in Scotland during the time when the Highlanders were in conflict with James V, who was planning to subdue them. *La donna del lago* is thus one of the several Italian operas from the early nineteenth century with a Scottish setting. In act I, Elena, the "lady of the lake" and daughter of the rebel leader Douglas of Angus, sings pensively of her love for Malcolm as she crosses the lake. Elena's father, however, has promised her to Rodrigo. Elena encounters Uberto, who is actually the king in disguise, separated from his hunting party, and offers him shelter. He falls in love with her practically at first sight and is mistakenly convinced that she returns his feelings. As Elena is about to be married to Rodrigo, Malcolm arrives with forces to repel the advancing royal army. In act II, Elena is forced to tell Uberto the truth about her feelings for him; he gives her a ring that he claims will obtain for her anything she wishes from the king. Rodrigo surprises them and challenges Uberto to a duel, which Rodrigo loses. The rebels are defeated and Elena's father, Douglas of Angus, is captured. Elena recognizes Uberto's true identity, the king releases Douglas and gives Elena in marriage to Malcolm.

La donna del lago, the first opera in Italy based on a work by Walter Scott was a landmark opera in its use of such romantic elements as local color and characteristic choruses. Scott's poem seemed to cry out for operatic treatment: it had a strong narrative line, vividly contrasting characters, picturesque lake and mountain scenery, in addition to numerous cues for choruses and folk songs, ballads, and laments. Ellen's "Ave Maria" was set by Franz Schubert and became one of his most popular songs. The focus on landscape, atmosphere, and setting is captured by Rossini especially well in the large ensembles at both the beginning and the end of the first act. The orchestral prelude consists of a mere sixteen bars before the chorus of countrymen begin to sing. Pastoral-idyllic elements such as a chorus of shepherds and hunters are evoked by lyrical music and by the prominence of hunting-horns. Elena appears in a boat on the lake, a stage picture that prompted the following response from Stendahl in his *Life of Rossini:* "The décor of the opening scene showed a wild and lonely loch in the Highlands of Scotland, upon whose waters, the *Lady of the Lake,* faithful to her name, was seen gliding gracefully along, upright beside the helm of a small boat. This set was a masterpiece of the art of stage-design. The mind turned instantly towards Scotland, and waited expectantly for the magic of some Ossianic adventure." The conclusion of the first act features the Scots bards singing a hymn to a harp accompaniment as suggested by Scott's "Harp of the North! that mouldering long hast hung/On the witch-elm that shades Saint Fillian's spring." The warriors sing a martial chorus to a brass band accompaniment; eventually the two melodies are contrapuntally combined.

La donna del lago was not well received at its premiere. The second night's audience was considerably more responsive, however, and the work quickly became appreciated. Colbrán's powers were on the decline at this time; Rossini thus gave Elena only one brilliant solo scene (the finale, "Tanti affetti") and relatively little ensemble singing. On the other hand, the two tenors must sing a number of high Cs, several C-sharps, and extensive coloratura passages. When Rossini wrote the role of Elena's lover, Malcolm, for a mezzo-soprano, he was employing an operatic convention that was already outmoded. There is general agreement that *La donna del lago* begins better than it finishes. The static second act was labeled a "costume in concert" by the nineteenth-century English critic, Henry Chorley.—STEPHEN WILLIER

Don Pasquale

Composer: *Gaetano Donizetti.*

Librettists: *G. Ruffini and Gaetano Donizetti (after A. Anelli, Ser Marc' Antonio).*

First Performance: *Paris, Théâtre-Italien, 3 January 1843.*

Roles: *Don Pasquale (bass); Ernesto (tenor); Dr. Malatesta (baritone); Norina (soprano); Notary (tenor, baritone, or bass); chorus (SATB).*

The last of Donizetti's comic operas, *Don Pasquale* is also the last work in the original *opera buffa* tradition to have remained in the repertory. It was written for the Théâtre-Italien, where it enjoyed immediate success, thanks to the supple wit of its score and a cast including the greatest stars of the international Italian opera circuit: Lablache, Tamburini, Grisi, and the tenor Mario. Luigi Lablache's characterization of the portly old Pasquale trying to play the gallant suitor in act II was especially appreciated. The text was a re-working by Giovanni Ruffini of an 1810 *buffa* libretto, *Ser Marc'Antonio,* with an unusual amount of input from Donizetti himself.

Don Pasquale is determined to disinherit his nephew, Ernesto, who has refused the sensible liaison proposed by his uncle. To effect this disinheritance, he decides to get married himself, with the help of his doctor and confidant, Malatesta. The doctor assures him that he has the perfect candidate in the person of his sister, "Sofronia," a meek and obedient girl fresh from the convent. In the meantime he contrives with the high-spirited Norina, the real object of Ernesto's affection, to have her play the part of the sister in such a way as to cure Pasquale of his matrimonial ambitions forever. Norina arrives with Malatesta, feigning the utmost timidity until the moment the (sham) contract is signed. Thereupon she immediately begins to play the brazen hussy, to the consternation of Pasquale and the amusement of Ernesto, who is present as a witness.

In act III "Sofronia" compounds her new-found impertinence with outrageous extravagance. Don Pasquale is finally defeated when his uncontrollable new wife delivers him a slap in the face on her way out to the theater, where she goes in defiance of his commands. Now Pasquale is ready to fall in with the next stage of the plot against him. Dr. Malatesta arranges a rendezvous between Sofronia/Norina and a secret admirer for that evening in the garden and alerts her husband to this assignation. Pasquale tries to snare his guilty wife. Although he fails even at this, the masks are soon dropped, and in his relief the old man quickly assents to the marriage of the young lovers.

The enduring popularity of *Don Pasquale* is probably due to several factors. The work is simple and concise without being vapid. The vocal roles and the orchestration are grateful and elegant but not over-taxing (with the possible exception of the consistently high tessitura of the tenor role). The comic situations are well-defined and easily conveyed, whether in Italian or in translation, as, for example, Norina's sudden character reversal in the act-II finale, her clowning with Malatesta as they rehearse her role as Sofronia, or the ever-popular Rossinian patter style of Malatesta and Pasquale as they plot to surprise the guilty lovers in act III. All of the roles (again with the exception of Ernesto) offer ample opportunity for engaging comic acting. Donizetti usually provides these situations with foolproof cues by means of apt declamatory inflections and gestures in the vocal line. Yet every character is afforded at least one opportunity for expansive lyricism, even the affable prankster Malatesta ("Bella siccome un angelo," act I), and the cunning, roguish Norina (her opening cavatina and the "notturno" with Ernesto in the garden scene of act III).

Although Donizetti claimed to have completed *Don Pasquale* in eleven days—fast work even for this facile composer—the evidence suggests that this figure does not include the time spent on orchestration and—in the case of Ernesto's principal number, "Cercherò lontana terra"—even a considerable amount of sketching and revision. Some time was saved by means of the typical procedure of borrowing earlier material: Don Pasquale's bouncy 3/8 cabaletta, "Un foco insolito," was transposed down from a tenor aria in *Gianni di Parigi* (1831), and the final ensemble rondo is a re-working of a *mélodie* for voice and piano, "La bohémienne" (1842).

The characters in *Don Pasquale* are all clearly drawn from stock buffa types: the over-aged suitor, the strong-willed and rebellious young woman, the young tenor lover prone to amorous lament, the neutrally situated figure directing the course of the intrigue. Naturally, the style of their music is also indebted to the analogous vocal types and styles, such as the characteristic syllabic patter of the *basso buffo* in ensemble contexts, or the pert coloratura *soubrette* of Norina, immediately recalling Rosina in *Il barbiere di Siviglia*. The element of pathos, often cited as a trademark of Donizetti's mature comic operas, is focused here in the A-minor larghetto, "E finita, Don Pasquale," in act III. The following section, in C major (with Norina), is notable for its expressive excursions into the neapolitan-relation of D flat. The "Mozartean" quality that has been attributed to Donizetti's last *opera buffa* may reside in the intimacy and deftness of its musical characterizations in general, or in the specific musical character of such passages as the bustling D-major "vivace" ending act II, whose rhythmic and melodic gestures suggest a deliberate evocation of the finales of Mozart or Cimarosa. On the other hand, Donizetti also makes repeated use of a quick, 3/8 or 6/8 waltz rhythm (e.g., Norina's "Via, caro sposino," the chorus's "Quel nipotino," and the rondo-finale, "Bravo, bravo, Don Pasquale!" all in act III), lending the score a distinctly "modern" imprint. This contrast of styles seems appropriate to a work standing, as it does, at the end of a tradition.—THOMAS S. GREY

Don Quichotte [Don Quixote]

Composer: *Jules Massenet.*

Librettist: *Henri Cain (after Jacques Le Lorrain, Le chevalier de la longue figure).*

First Performance: *Monte Carlo, Opera, 19 February 1910.*

Roles: *Don Quixote (bass); Sancho (baritone); Dulcinea (contralto); Juan (tenor); Pedro (soprano); Garcia (soprano); Rodriguez (tenor); Two Servants (baritones); Bandit Chief (speaking); Four Bandits (speaking); chorus (SAATTBB).*

Don Quichotte is a late work taken from a contemporary poetic drama by Jacques Le Lorrain, which in turn was based on the Spanish masterpiece by Cervantes. In this operatic version Don Quixote becomes a champion of goodness and idealism, while Dulcinea is transformed from a tavern servant into a sophisticated lady of fashion. The famous windmill incident is preserved from Cervantes, but the main episode concerns Quixote's gallant retrieval of the lady's necklace from a gang of bandits: they are so moved by his blessed simplicity that they meekly hand it over to him. When the haughty Dulcinea rejects his offer of marriage, the old man realizes his futility and dies, lance in hand, leaning against a tree.

This "comédie héroïque," as Massenet called it, has a genial warmth that sets it apart from his other works. The brilliance of *Manon* and *Thaïs* is replaced by a more relaxed mood, and the music he wrote for Dulcinea in particular strikes a delicate balance between irony and true emotion. Sometimes his touch is so light that the style hints at operetta, although Don Quixote himself is always portrayed with sympathy. Written as a starring role for Chaliapin, the central character is given many opportunities himself, among them the famous mandoline serenade which is a tender statement of romantic idealism and which returns at various points throughout the action.

The humor of the score expresses itself in various different ways. One example is Sancho Panza's boisterous diatribe against women, "those hussies, those jades!" Another, more subtle and reaching a plane where idiocy becomes sublime, is Quixote's aria when he attacks the windmills. By the fifth act, however, which shows him dying in the starry night, sympathetic amusement at him has turned into pity. The faithful Sancho addresses him, "O mon maître, O mon Grand!" (O my master, O my Great One), in a few bars of pathetic *grisaille,* and the knightly apotheosis takes place to a flowing accompaniment which repeats the fourth-act motif of Dulcinea's regret that the time of love has flown.

To a certain extent the original drama on which the opera is founded presents a self-portrait of its author Jacques Le Lorrain, foolhardy to the point of nobleness, eccentric to a degree of genius. His version of the knight of the doleful countenance inspired a late flowering of Massenet's art, as mellow as it is attractive. The music written for Dulcinea shows an advance on his earlier techniques of constructing his heroine's melodic lines: particularly noticeable are the plangent tones of her lament referred to above ("Lorsque le temps d'amour a fini"), which gains still more from the contrast it makes with the bright festive music immediately before and after it. Only in the fourth act, where she gently disabuses the amorous knight, does the too-expansive bloom seem a little out of place. This is only a small blemish on a score which in general is remarkable for its sustained charm and attractiveness. Although much of its initial success was due inevitably to the presence of Chaliapin, revivals of *Don Quichotte* have shown that the opera can stand on its own merits and that the music still preserves its vitality and its ability to move the listener.—JAMES HARDING

Die Dreigroschenoper [The Threepenny Opera]

Composer: *Kurt Weill.*

Librettists: *B. Brecht and E. Hauptmann (after John Gay, The Beggar's Opera).*

First Performance: *Berlin, Theater am Schiffbauerdamm, 31 August 1928.*

Roles: *Jenny (chanteuse-style singer); Polly (soprano); Macheath (tenor); Mr. Peachum (bass); Mrs. Peachum (mezzo-soprano); Lucy (soprano); Streetsinger (tenor); Tiger Brown (bass); chorus (SATB).*

Die Dreigroschenoper, the second collaboration of Bertolt Brecht and Kurt Weill (they had already completed the *Mahagonny Songspiel*), not only created a new style somewhere between opera and popular theater, but was to set the type for much of Brecht's later theatrical practice. Although based on John Gay's *The Beggar's Opera* (in a German translation provided for Brecht by Elisabeth Hauptmann), *The Threepenny Opera* differed in spirit from its original;

d OPERA

musically, it owes much not only to Pepusch's ballads, but also to operatic models such as *Die Zauberflöte* and *Fidelio*, German cabaret styles, and American jazz.

The story follows the outlines of Gay's play but with a Brechtian twist. Macheath, affectionately known as Mack the Knife (Mackie Messer) has married, in a mock ceremony, Polly Peachum, the daughter of a man who runs a front for beggars in Victorian London. In doing so, however, Macheath angers not only her parents but also his former lover, the prostitute Jenny, who with Mrs. Peachum conspires to turn him in to the authorities for his many crimes. However, this is not easy, since Macheath has a long-standing agreement with the Chief of Police, Tiger Brown, who overlooks his crimes in return for payoffs. Peachum, however, forces Brown to arrest Macheath this time by threatening to organize a march of beggars to disrupt the Queen's coronation. Macheath escapes, but he is betrayed and arrested again. Brought to the gallows, he sings a ballad asking forgiveness for his crimes but is rescued at the last moment by operatic convention—Peachum announces that the opera demands a better ending. Promptly a Riding Messenger from the Queen arrives and announces Macheath's reprieve in an elaborate burlesque of rescue operas. All characters then step forward and sing a final chorale prelude, ironically exhorting the audience to combat injustice, but in moderation.

The theatrical and operatic style, which owes much to the moralistic commentary in *Die Zauberflöte* as well as *The Beggar's Opera,* is intended to provide what Brecht later called estrangement (*Verfremdung*). He and Weill intended not simply to parody operatic conventions but to provide social commentary which engages the audience in new ways, later elaborated by Brecht as part of what he called epic theater. The songs consciously interrupt the action, their titles announced on letter boards and the actors stepping out of character in order to sing; the singing style is rough, with many lines spoken "against" the music rather than sung with it. The texts of the songs, influenced by François Villon and Rudyard Kipling, comment on the action, though often very obliquely. The point is to disallow the usual identification an audience has with the characters in illusionist theater and to force the audience to view them as actors and to see theater as social space. Brecht and Weill attempt to call into question the easy middle-class assumptions of audience members; the songs emphasize the injustice and pain of a bourgeois world in which every person is a commodity.

Gay's opera depends on the motivations of individual characters. For Brecht and Weill, the individuals are, rather, examples of an economic system which forces them to become property, things to be bought and sold. For example, Macheath wants Polly less for herself than for her business acumen; he plans to turn in his followers and go into banking (the obvious point is that there is no difference between thieves and bankers). Similarly, Peachum uses the beggars to provide his own income, forcing them to exploit the inadequate pity of the middle class by donning false limbs and rubber wounds. Jenny sells Macheath just as he, her pimp, sells her; the other prostitutes, like Peachum's beggars and Macheath's thieves, sell themselves and their work. Though this work is usually classified as pre-Marxist Brecht, the message is clear: bourgeois society is structured on the exploitation of the workers, who reproduce their own exploitation by failing to question the discrepancy between the easy sentimentality advocating justice and love, ironically presented in the songs, and their own reality. The final parody of baroque opera's *deus ex machina* points out that the bourgeois system cannot fail its own members: Macheath is needed by the Queen to keep the system of commodification going, so he is spared.

Musically, Weill's score places itself firmly in the various movements in Germany in the twenties to renounce an individualist and elitist aesthetic for a new style of music that included popular and dance elements, a simplification of musical means, and an overall montage effect which highlights the artificiality of each of its elements. The music is characterized by a ballad style, beginning with the famous opening *Moritat* (a type of ballad sung by street singers who illustrated their lurid tales with pictures, which may have suggested Brecht's use of title-boards for the songs throughout). Weill's music employs monotonous Alberti basses, simple melodic lines, texts and melodies that often don't quite "fit" together, small melodic ranges in keeping with the untrained voices of the actors, and dance and jazz rhythms. The music was described by Adorno as surrealist, designed to shock the decadent bourgeoisie, as was the text. However, the work was and remains extremely popular with exactly the middle-class audience it was supposed to shock.—SANDRA CORSE

I due Foscari [The Two Foscari]

Composer: *Giuseppe Verdi.*

Librettist: *Francesco Maria Piave (after Byron, The Two Foscari).*

First Performance: *Rome, Torre Argentina, 3 November 1844.*

Roles: *Francesco Foscari (baritone); Jacopo (tenor); Lucrezia Contarini (soprano); Jacopo Loredano (bass); Barbarigo (tenor); Pisana (soprano); Officer of the Council of Ten (bass); Servant of Doge (bass); Messer Grande (mute); Two Small Sons of Jacopo (mute); Officer (mute); Jailor (mute); chorus (SATB).*

I due Foscari (1844) was Verdi's sixth opera, coming immediately after his Venice triumph earlier the same year with *Ernani*. The opera is based on Lord Byron's play, *The Two Foscari,* which is a rather static exploration of the hidden malevolence of fifteenth-century Venice. It nevertheless attracted Verdi, who described it to his librettist Francesco Piave as "a fine subject, delicate and full of pathos," while noting that it would need some changes since it didn't quite have the "theatrical grandeur needed for an opera." The work was enthusiastically received at its opening performances in Rome and appeared everywhere until the 1870s, when it fell into disfavor. Dismissed, usually by critics who had never seen it, in the 1930s and 40s as an inferior work that could never be resuscitated, it began, as part of a reawakening interest in early Verdi, to reappear onstage to favorable audience and critical response only in the 1950s.

The action, set in the Venice of 1457, traces the final stages in the misfortunes of the elder Foscari, the Doge, and his last living son, Jacopo, who has been brought back out of exile to stand trial for further crimes against Venice. An enemy of the Foscari family, one Loredano, a member of the Council of Ten, pursues father and son relentlessly for injuries he believes the Foscari have done his family. The old Doge, urged on by Jacopo's wife, Lucrezia, desires to aid his son, but is rendered impotent by his duty (and perhaps his weakness) to uphold the laws of Venice. Jacopo is again unjustly condemned by the Council to further exile but dies as he sets sail, while his father, crushed by this loss of his last son and forced by the Council (urged on by Loredano) to abdicate, collapses and dies as he hears the bells of San Marco saluting his successor, at which Loredano is observed to write in his notebook, "I am paid."

There are three dramatic drawbacks to the work which, while causing difficulty, by no means render it ineffective: first, being no Iago, the villain Loredano and his hatred, which is the driving force of the action, remain unfocused both dramatically and musically; second, the struggle between the old Doge's paternal desire to save his son and the restrictions imposed on him by his position as Doge is not clearly articulated until late in the opera, leaving his motivation unclear; and third, the dramatic situation is such that it has no direction in which to develop. Jacopo begins and ends condemned; the struggle to save him is merely a series of stops and starts. Important moments are not part of the stage-action: Jacopo's condemnation by the Council happens between the scenes; the arrival of the letter from Erizzo (whoever he may be since he figures otherwise not at all in the drama) absolving Jacopo of guilt is given no context; indeed, the death of Jacopo himself is merely reported—and in a perfunctory manner—by his long-suffering wife. The scenes which stir the excitement of the audience, e.g., act I, scene iv, in which Lucrezia pleads with her father-in-law, the Doge, to save her husband, have musical but not dramatic momentum. Other stageworthy moments such as Lucrezia's sudden appearance with her children before the Council to plead for her husband allow an exciting musical climax which fails to carry the action forward. There is little overall sense of dramatic necessity. Not surprisingly perhaps, Verdi, who tended to be dismissive of his past accomplishments, described *Foscari* a few years later as too unvarying in color.

Nevertheless, *I due Foscari* is stageworthy; recent productions have shown that whatever the dramatic problems, the music makes it eminently viable. No one can hear it in the theater without recognizing that Verdi has caught the sombre gloom of the Venice conjured up by Byron's drama. Sensitive from the beginning to the dramatic function of orchestral coloring, Verdi makes an advance in *I due Foscari* in his use of woodwinds to create atmospheric darkness and, in combination with harp and strings, to produce moments (e.g., the prison scene of act II) of the most delicate texture. The level of workmanship throughout is high; stylistically the work marks a movement toward the intimate style which Verdi was later to develop in *Luisa Miller* and, especially, *La traviata*. The duet between Lucrezia and the Doge points toward the latter while the prison ensembles point toward *Rigoletto;* if the comparisons are apt to highlight the shortcomings of *I due Foscari,* they also place this earlier work in a line of major Verdian development.

The musical characteristic of *I Due Foscari* most often pointed out is Verdi's use of quasi-*Leitmotivs,* not developed systematically in the Wagnerian manner but used almost as static signature tunes. Their success is variable. For example, the motiv associated with most of Lucrezia's entrances constantly suggests her haste and energy without adding to her stature; meanwhile the Doge's motiv does precisely that, establishing him in his first appearance ("Eccomi solo alfine") as a figure of suffering majesty far more than Piave's text would appear to warrant; suggestions of that later Doge, Simon Boccanegra, are unmistakable.

I due Foscari contains a number of fine Verdian numbers: Jacopo's opening aria with its evocative accompaniment suggesting the Venetian waterside; Lucrezia's act I cavatina ("Tu al cui sguardo onnipossente") and cabaletta in which the solo voice is most effectively floated above the chorus; the tender duet ("No, non morrai") for Lucrezia and Jacopo in the prison which evolves into a magnificent trio at the entrance of the Doge; and the Doge's splendid outpouring ("Questa dunque") to the Council when they demand his resignation.—PETER DYSON

Duke Bluebeard's Castle [A Kékszakállú herceg vara]

Composer: *Béla Bartók.*

Librettist: *Béla Balázs.*

First Performance: *Budapest, Budapest Opera, 24 May 1918.*

Roles: *Judith (soprano or mezzo-soprano); Bluebeard (bass-baritone); The Bard (speaking part); Bluebeard's Three Former Wives (mute); ballet.*

Béla Bartók's opera, *Duke Bluebeard's Castle,* is exemplary of the radical transformation in opera that occurred during the first decade of the twentieth century. Despite its status as the first genuinely Hungarian opera, *Bluebeard* did not find national public support in its early years, a condition which was largely due to the conservative tastes of the Hungarian public. It was originally rejected in a competition for a national opera in 1911 because its true Hungarian qualities were unrecognizable to an audience accustomed to hearing Italianate and Germanized settings of Hungarian texts. *Bluebeard* finally had its premiere in Budapest on May 24, 1918, but, with the collapse of the post-war revolutionary regime in 1919, the opera was banned because of the political exile of its librettist, Béla Balázs, and was not performed again in Budapest until 1937.

As part of an evolution toward new musical styles and techniques in the early part of the century, this opera, based on the symbolist play by Maurice Maeterlinck, is far removed from the ultra-chromaticism of German late-Romantic music as well as from the major-minor scale system of Classical functional tonality. Originating in the pentatonic-diatonic modality of Hungarian peasant music, it is inevitable that the musical language of *Bluebeard* should reveal irreconcilable differences from the prevailing supranational German and Italian operas of the nineteenth century in details of phrase, rhythm, and pitch organization as well as large-scale formal construction. In its general stylistic and technical assumptions, one finds fundamental connections rather with the musical impressionism of Debussy's *Pelléas et Mélisande* (1893-1902), another revolutionary opera from the same symbolist trilogy by Maeterlinck. An affinity between *Bluebeard* and *Pelléas* is partly suggested in their common absorption of pentatonic-diatonic modality into a kind of twelve-tone language, a fusion which is revealed by Bartók's own statement: "it became clear to me that the old [folk] modes, which had been forgotten in our music, had lost nothing of their vigor. Their employment made new rhythmic combinations possible. This new way of using the diatonic scale brought freedom from the rigid use of the major and minor keys, and eventually led to a new conception of the chromatic scale, every tone of which came to be considered of equal value and could be used freely and independently." Bartók realized that Debussy's music was based on the same "pentatonic phrases" that he had found in his own Hungarian folk music, and he attributed this to the influences of folk music from Eastern Europe, particularly Russia.

With the reaction around the turn of the century against the naturalism of nineteenth-century theater, many authors began to develop a new interest in psychological motivation and a level of consciousness manifested in metaphor, ambiguity, and symbolism. In his symbolist plays, Maeterlinck was to transform the internal concept of subconscious motivation into an external one, in which human action is entirely controlled by fate. *Bluebeard* represents a significant manifestation of this transformation. Theodor Adorno's assessment of musical modernism is particularly relevant to the *Bluebeard* idiom, in which "the concept of shock is one aspect of the unifying principle of the epoch. . . . Through such shocks the individual becomes aware of his nothingness." Bartók's opera, limited to a bare minimum of characters, introduces the shock element and a level of reality entirely steeped in metaphor. "Blood," as a symbol of Bluebeard's inner soul, vividly appears in each of his chambers as the seven doors are forced open by Judith, who relentlessly pries into her husband's hidden life. Judith herself represents the "fatalistic" element of relentless time and Bluebeard's inevitable move toward "endless darkness."

Bartók's personal symbolist musical language is set within a clearly architectural framework in both its overall form as well as local phrasal details, an approach which is in keeping with the composer's understanding of the folk-music structures themselves. The entire opera consists of distinct forms (often based on folk-like quatrain structures that sometimes suggest a rondo type of format) within scenes. Furthermore, much of the melodic and harmonic fabric is generated by means of modal elaboration and transformation, a principle that appears to be derived from the process of thematic variation found in the folk-music sources. From the modal material of the opera, Bartók derives the basic leitmotifs and pitch cells, which are central in generating the musico-dramatic fabric. The basic "Blood" motif, characterized by half-steps, is gradually manifested in the intrusion of this dissonant element into the opening pentatonic folk mode as Judith becomes aware of blood on the castle walls. However, psychological tension in the unbroken musical fabric is created not so much by the manifest details, but by the latent symbolic and metaphorical questions that these details invoke with regard to our own perception of reality. Such questions are explicit in the Prologue: "The curtains of our eye-lids are raised. But where is the stage? In me? In you?"

Psychological development, which is also fundamental to the symbolic meaning of the opera, is realized by means of two inextricably connected and overlapping formal concepts, one sectional, and the other unfolding the dynamic spiritual evolution and transformation of the two characters. Sándor Veress has shown how the large-scale form of the opera is a closed symmetrical construction, an arch-form in three parts: (1) an introduction initially established by a folk-like, brooding, F-sharp pentatonic theme and the "menacing" motif; (2) seven scenes demarcated by Doors I-VII, which peak at the uncovering of Bluebeard's vast domain behind Door V in the contrastingly bright key of C major (the most distant key from the opening F sharp); and (3) a recapitulation of the "menacing" motif and F-sharp pentatonic. The shape of the sectional arch-form is heightened by the dramatic psychological process. The distinct vocal styles and personalities of the two characters are established at the outset. Judith's first vocal entry, a prominent (whole-tone related) wide-ranging figure in a characteristically strong Magyar rhythm, contrasts with Bluebeard's reserved (pentatonic-diatonic) repeated-note line in even durational values. By the time Door V (opening on Bluebeard's vast domain) is reached, this contrast is reversed: the man has progressed from quietness to increasingly intense and passionate utterance, while the woman has moved in decrescendo toward her own extinction. Only with the inevitable loss of Judith does Bluebeard become emotionally resigned.

The symbolism of *Bluebeard* is derived directly from that of Debussy's *Pelléas,* both operas belonging to the same dramatic trilogy of Maeterlinck. The woman as "fatalistic" symbol—the siren of destruction—is first evident in the Debussy opera. This is represented musically by the intrusion of the whole-tone scale ("fate" motif) into the diatonic sphere ("human" motifs); the interaction between these two types of pitch-sets also underlies the same dramatic symbolism in Bartók's opera. Bluebeard's opening vocal sections are primarily diatonic, Judith's primarily whole-tone, Judith thus "fatalistically" intruding into Bluebeard's inner life. The subject of *Bluebeard* suggests the eternally problematical relation of the two sexes. The relation between the two as depicted in the opera is one that the contemporary feminist movement would deplore, but all the more do we have to understand this relation. There are only two characters, a man and a woman. The man is the central character, who is reticent to reveal his inner self, while Judith symbolizes the passionate and demanding woman who, through her love, is in the man's power.

Both the Debussy and Bartók operas also find common ground in their approaches to the relationship between music and language. Both operas are based on a kind of contemporary "recitative" style pioneered by Debussy. The music-text relationships of both operas are based on special premises that could only have been established by the liberation of meter and rhythm that became possible after the disappearance of traditional tonal functions in the early twentieth century. In Bartók's case, exploration of the old Hungarian folk tunes permitted him to break with the established nineteenth-century tradition of translating Western languages into Hungarian for opera performance, a tradition which had inevitably led to distortions in Hungarian accentuation. Just as Debussy had been faithful to the French language in his musical setting, Bartók strictly preserved the Hungarian language accents in his musical setting of the Balázs libretto, in which the archaic syllabic structure is set almost entirely in the old "parlando-rubato" folk style. The Hungarian text—and this is true of the orchestral phrases as well—is appropriately based on eight syllables per line, which is one of the isometric stanzaic patterns that the composer found in the oldest of the Hungarian folk melodies. Thus, as the intended inception of a new and genuinely Hungarian tradition based on the fusion of folk elements and French impressionism, the *Bluebeard* idiom permitted an expansion of the possibilities for symbolic representation that were first manifested in Debussy's opera.—ELLIOTT ANTOKOLETZ

Dvorak, Antonín

Composer. Born 8 September 1841, in Mühlhausen. Died 1 May 1904, in Prague. Married: Anna Cermáková, 1873 (7 children). Studied with Pitzsch at the Prague Organ School; violist in the orchestra of the National Theater in Prague, 1861-71; Austrian State Prize for his Symphony in E-flat, 1875; organist at St Adalbert's Church in Prague; professor of composition at the Prague Conservatory; in London, 1884; commissioned to write a new work for the Birmingham Festival of 1885 (The Spectre's Bride); made honorary Mus. D. by Cambridge University, and honorary Ph.D. by the Czech University in Prague, 1891; headed the National Conservatory in New York, 1892; symphony From the New World premiered by the New York Philharmonic, 15 December 1893; artistic director of the Prague Conservatory, 1901; life member of the Austrian House of Lords.

Operas   *Alfred*, K.T. Körner, 1870, Olomouc, Czech Theater, 10 December 1938; *King and Charcoal Burner* [*Král a uhlíř*], B.J. Lobeský, 1871, Prague, National Theater, 28 May 1929; revised, 1874; further revised and performed, 1887; *The Stubborn Lovers* [*Tvrdé palice*], J. Štolba, 1874, Prague, New Czech Theater, 2 October 1881; *Vanda*, V.B. Šumavský (after J. Surzycki), 1875, Prague, Provisional, 17 April 1876; revised 1879, 1883; *The Cunning Peasant* [*Šelma sedlák*], J.O. Veselý, 1877, Prague, Provisional, 27 January 1878; *Dimitrij*, Červinková-Riegrová, 1881-82, Prague, New Czech Theater, 8 October 1882;

revised 1883, 1885, 1894-95; *The Jacobin* [*Jakobin*], Červinková-Riegrová, 1887-88, Prague, National Theater, 12 February 1889; revised, 1897; *Kate and the Devil* [*Čert a Káča*], A. Wenig (after Czech fairy tale), 1898-99, Prague, National Theater, 23 November 1899; *Rusalka*, J. Kvapil, 1900, Prague, National Theater, 31 March 1901; *Armida*, J. Vrchlický (after Tasso, *Gerusalemme liberata*), 1902-03, Prague, National Theater, 25 March 1904.

Of all Dvořák's operas, *Rusalka* is the only one which has achieved a degree of international recognition. Why this is so is complicated, but a major part of the reason is the rather long period of development which Dvořák seemed to need.

Dvořák reached the point of total mastery in the genre of opera with *The Jacobin,* a product of the mid 1880s, which was further revised in the late 1890s. Before that, we observe Dvořák running from his roots, so to speak, in an attempt to address a wider audience. The results were often striking, as in *Vanda,* a story about the Polish nobility that takes place in the 16th century. It has many affecting moments as well as much fine vocal writing, but it also has a curiously static, even formal quality.

One might be critical of the formal quality of *Vanda,* but it is a fact that Dvořák wrote it that way deliberately. The Prague National Opera was to have a triumphal opening in 1876, and the call went out to create something new and impressive. Smetana had just finished his positively statuesque masterpiece, *Libuse,* and there is evidence that Dvořák had seen the score. He countered with *Vanda,* and its "static" quality was almost an exact duplication of the style found in *Libuse.* In any case, if it was indeed a contest between Prague's two best composers, Smetana won, and his was the first opera presented at the new opera house. It should be said that Smetana (older and more experienced) was a past master at this kind of ceremonial music, whereas for Dvořák, it was a new departure. Consequently, it is hardly surprising that, on balance, *Libuse* is the more effective work.

After *Vanda,* Dvořák was preoccupied with *Dimitrij,* the story of which can be characterized as a quasi-historical sequel to Mussorgsky's quasi-historical opera, *Boris Godunov.* In *Dimitrij,* as in almost all of Dvořák's operas, there are wonderful choruses, as well as vocal parts which are quite demanding, but also quite effective dramatically. *Dimitrij* and *Vanda* are spoken of by many of today's critics with great respect, even though both are marginally uneven, and yet they have been performed rarely, even in Czechoslovakia.

Kate and The Devil was written just prior to *The Jacobin* and approaches it in quality. Here the potent mix of peasants, a ruling aristocracy, a tenor hero, Hell, and the admirable, plain but rude Kate create a mix of comedy, pathos, and social conflict which seems to have excited Dvořák's imagination. This is a serio-comic opera in which the music is consistently strong, and the frequently used technique of through-composition works really well. There are some problems, however. The libretto, though effective, is occasionally unclear and it all but eliminates Kate, one of the title characters, before the last act begins.

The problems of the earlier operas are notably absent from *The Jacobin.* Written at the same general time as his 7th and 8th symphonies, this opera shares the strengths of those works and gives us the quintessential Dvořák. The story is a good one, involving a pair of young lovers, an older man of high station who threatens the young pair with his libidenous demands on the young girl, a father who has denounced his son and daughter-in-law, and, oddly pivotal to the rest, the choir-master Benda, who speaks constantly of ideals, particularly those of the "devine"

245

art of music. This latter element seems to have inspired Dvořák to compose a veritable flood of gorgeous music, utilizing brilliant orchestral sonorities, and some of his finest melodies.

Rusalka, based on a Czech re-working of the old Undine legend, marks a rather new path for the composer. It is a fairy-tale-fantasy-opera for adults, and is in many ways the most Romantic music Dvořák penned. He was, of course, a Romantic composer, but his music retained the formal clarity, and clean-limbed rhythmic drive of an earlier period. In *Rusalka,* these stylistic fingerprints are modified by a kind of aural voluptuousness. The opera, a grand tragedy, provides many opportunities for exquisite vocalism, as well as the kind of high drama of which Verdi might have been proud. In spite of some minor difficulties in the matter of sustained musical invention, *Rusalka* is a masterpiece, and has become known as such throughout the world.

In the 1930s and 40s not much of Dvořák's music was known. For whatever reasons the situation today has changed markedly. Dvořák is now one of the most respected and performed composers of the instrumental repertoire. One is reminded of what Gustav Mahler once said: "My time will come." Perhaps Dvořák's operas will find their "time" soon.—HARRIS CROHN

Eames, Emma

Soprano. Born 13 August 1865, in Shanghai. Died 13 June 1952, in New York. Studied with Clara Munger in Boston and Mathilde Marchesi in Paris. Debut as Juliette in Gounod's Romeo et Juliette; *Covent Garden debut as Marguerite, 1891; Metropolitan Opera debut as Juliette, 1891; sang over 250 performances at Metropolitan Opera until 1909; after her retirement from the Met she made concert tours with her second husband, the baritone Emilio de Gogorza.*

Emma Eames' career on the operatic stage was relatively short, only twenty years, and her activities were confined largely to New York and London, but there were few singers of the "Golden Age" who wore the mantle of *prima donna* with greater authority. Between 1891 and 1901 she sang more than a dozen leading roles in eight seasons at Covent Garden, although her celebrated rivalry with Nellie Melba did not allow her to enjoy the kind of absolute domination over her repertory that she felt was her due. She fared better in her sixteen seasons at the Metropolitan Opera as one of the highest paid artists on the roster, singing some twenty-one roles in more than 250 performances. She did not have an especially large repertory, but she was certainly the most versatile of the star Marchesi pupils. In addition to the predictable lyric heroines of Gounod, Bizet and Massenet, she quickly assumed a number of heavier roles which eventually came to include Aïda, Leonora (*Il trovatore*), Alice Ford (*Falstaff*), and Amelia (*Un ballo in maschera*). In December 1902 she added *Tosca* to her growing dramatic repertory, following Milka Ternina in the title role. She was also entrusted with the first Met productions of Mascagni's *Cavalleria rusticana* and *Iris*. Her Desdemona, which she sang in both New York and London to the Otello of Francesco Tamagno, the role's creator, received stunning reviews, and as early as 1891 she made her way with great assurance into the Wagnerian repertory, first as Elsa in *Lohengrin*, and later as Elisabeth (*Tannhäuser*), Eva (*Die Meistersinger*), and most remarkably, Sieglinde (*Die Walküre*). Throughout her career, she was a notable interpreter of Mozart as well, singing the Countess (*Le nozze di Figaro*), both Donna Elvira and Donna Anna (*Don Giovanni*), and Pamina (*Die Zauberflöte*).

Few *prima donnas,* even of that era, went to such lengths to compose so stern and defensive a public profile as did Eames. With certain determination she offered this sober prelude to her 1927 autobiography, *Some Memories and Reflections:* "Great fixity of purpose, absolute absorption in the task at hand, and a complete obsession concerning the duty to be accomplished, have been the fundamental laws governing my career and life." Her career, forged by self-denial and nurtured by self-discipline, is portrayed as a constant challenge of temptations, met with a consuming suspicion of all external forces beyond her control. "I was so obsessed and absorbed by my work," she commented in 1939, "that it proves to me that the wisest course is to mind one's own business exclusively. I had to detach myself from outside influences in order to find simplicity, sincerity, and truth in my interpretations."

In spite of her subsequent rejection of Mathilde Marchesi's instruction and her merciless public recriminations of her as a teacher, Eames possessed in abundance virtually all of the stylistic characteristics associated with the Marchesi method. Like Melba's, hers was a perfectly sculpted instrument, with an exquisite, even scale, a highly disciplined precision of attack, immaculate intonation, and the fluidity necessary to cope with the most demanding passage work. It was only in the upper extremes that she seemed to have lacked Melba's consummate fluency, and this proved a burden from the outset of her career. Bernard Shaw pointed it out in his review of her Covent Garden debut in April, 1891, noting that the upper register, "though bright, does not come so easily as the rest," and her recordings demonstrate—in some cases, painfully—that she was never able to fully overcome this deficiency.

Eames has been unjustly labeled a cold and unfeeling singer, an accomplished yet

unemotional interpreter. Shaw found her an "intelligent, ladylike" actress, but "somewhat cold and colorless . . . The best that can be said for her playing in the last two acts [of *Faust*] is, that she was able to devise quietly pathetic business to cover her deficiency in tragic conviction." He later wrote of her: "I never saw such a well-conducted person as Miss Eames. She casts her propriety like a Sunday frock over the whole stage." Even her celebrated beauty and her patrician bearing were conveniently summoned in contrast to her staunch emotional reserve, especially by colleagues making light of their many unpleasant encounters with her. Eames scurried to her own defense in a February 1939 New York radio broadcast, using some of her recordings as tools of reconciliation. She described her Gounod numbers in particular as "documents as well as interpretations . . . for with him," she explains, "I studied at the beginning of my career, *Faust, Mireille,* and *Roméo and Juliette.*" Her 1906 recording of the "Jeux vivre dans ce rêve" from *Roméo et Juliette* is offered as an exam-

Emma Eames as Elsa in *Lohengrin* (Culver Pictures)

ple "sung as Gounod taught it to me, absolutely in time and without the meaningless holds and *retards* that one so often hears," as if to caution against mistaking what she felt was purity and authority of style for lack of involvement. But like most of her recorded performances, the "Waltz" is in fact saturated with all of the affectations she professes to eschew, just as the tempo she invokes is breached throughout by clear and frequent departures.

Her last appearances in opera, single performances of *Tosca* and *Otello* at the Boston Opera, were made in December, 1911, two years after her official retirement from the stage. She continued to give occasional recitals for several years, but these were not always received enthusiastically.

Like so many other brilliant-voiced lyric sopranos of her day (the Marchesi pupils in particular), Eames was not well-served by the acoustical method of recording. She fully realized the consequences of her activity in the primitive studios and lived longer than most to regret it. She disliked the process of record making: "With even the most satisfactory results," she felt, "my voice would be diminished and deformed, and the softer vibrations eliminated completely." But in spite of her fears, the brilliance and warmth of her voice are still unmistakable. The recordings certainly attest to the fact that there was little in Eames' singing of the "monotony of beautiful, even tones" that dissuaded Geraldine Farrar from studying at the *École Marchesi* on Melba's advise.

Between 1905 and 1911, Eames made nearly fifty commercial recordings, resulting in thirty-five published titles divided almost equally between opera and song. Only a few of the dramatic roles with which she was associated—Tosca, Leonora, and Santuzza (*Cavalleria rusticana*)—are represented by major arias, along with a good deal of the Mozart and Gounod. There is even a faint but persuasive sample of her Elsa in the second-act duet "Du Ärmste kannst wohl" from *Lohengrin,* sung with contralto Louise Homer. In addition, there are five Mapleson cylinders recorded live from the stage of the Met in 1902 and 1903, the most remarkable of these being four excerpts from the last act of *Tosca*. The most sympathetic performances, however, are drawn from her extensive repertory of French and Italian song. While her manner with songs was neither vibrant nor caressing, it was rarely wanting of color and warmth of expression. She recorded works of Hermann Bemberg, George Henschel, Horatio Parker, and Charles Koechlin in 1908, and as early as 1905, songs of Amy Beach, Reynaldo Hahn and Schubert. Her final recording sessions of November, 1911 yielded a superb rendition of Tosti's "Dopo," and what may be the definitive acoustical recording of Schubert's "Gretchen am Spinnrade." Had she left nothing else in the way of recorded evidence, these would dispel any doubt as to her contemporary stature.—WILLIAM SHAMAN

Edgar

Composer: *Giacomo Puccini.*

Librettist: *Ferdinando Fontana (after A. de Musset, La coupe et les lèvres).*

First Performance: *Milan, Teatro alla Scala, 21 April 1889; revised, Ferrara, 28 February 1892; further revised, Buenos Aires, 8 July 1905.*

Roles: *Edgar (tenor); Gualtiero (bass); Frank (baritone); Fidelia (soprano); Tigrana (mezzo-soprano); chorus.*

First staged at the Teatro alla Scala in 1889, *Edgar* was withdrawn after its third performance. Like Puccini's *Le villi* of 1884, it suffered from a weak libretto by Ferdinando Fontana, who adapted Alfred de Musset's play *La coupe et les lèvres* (1832). Fontana reset the tale in medieval Flanders rather than the Tyrol, creating four exaggerated leading characters who have little in common with those of Musset's original. Puccini attempted to improve the libretto but to no avail, since Fontana was adamant about the quality of his verse. Although the composer later revised the work in 1892, compressing acts III and IV into one, this later version was no more successful.

Act I begins at daybreak in a Flemish village. The opera opens as Fidelia, a pure and innocent girl, expresses her love for the sleeping Edgar. She withdraws at the approach of Tigrana, a gypsy girl who was abandoned as a child and brought up by Fidelia's father. Tigrana tries to convert Edgar to her own sensual way of life, but he denounces her and returns home. The gypsy insults Fidelia's brother Frank, who secretly loves her. After he departs she reappears, this time outraging the approaching congregation with her taunts about religion and her defence of the erotic life. Edgar, by now besotted with Tigrana, protects her against the hostile crowd. He resolves to take her away from the village and, in a gesture of defiance, sets fire to his own house. Following a fight with Frank, Edgar flees with Tigrana.

The second act, which takes place at night on the terrace of a palace, concerns the deteriorating relationship of Edgar and Tigrana. Although Tigrana adores him, Edgar now finds her tiresome. Towards the end of this short act, Frank and some soldiers appear. He and Edgar resolve their quarrel and depart together. Tigrana, deserted, swears vengeance.

Act III, set in a fortress, opens with a choral *Requiem aeternam* during which a suit of armor is borne in, supposedly Edgar's coffin. As Frank proclaims Edgar a hero, he is interrupted by a monk who accuses Edgar of villainy, so that all but Fidelia turn against him. As the people depart, Frank and the monk try to tempt Tigrana to discredit Edgar. She is eventually persuaded when jewels are put in front of her. The monk calls back the crowd. His claim that Edgar had betrayed his country is confirmed by Tigrana. As the people break into the suit of armor, the monk tears off his costume, revealing himself as Edgar. Condemning Tigrana, he embraces Fidelia, who is stabbed by her rival. All demand Tigrana's execution and the curtain falls as Edgar, in despair, throws himself on Fidelia's dead body.

If it were not for the quality of the music, an opera with such an inane plot would be forgotten. From the opening bars Puccini's superior talent is clearly apparent. His melodies have a character that is both sensuous and haunting, while his use of lower instruments to double high-lying vocal lines gives them a unique quality. It is a sign of the general excellence of his melodies that he was able to reuse one aria, discarded from the 1892 version, in *Tosca* as Cavaradossi's leading final aria "Amaro sol per te." He avoided the standard number system, making the music continuous. Puccini's choral writing is fluent, frequently conceived in the contrapuntal manner. Some, indeed, is borrowed from his earlier *Messa di gloria* (1880). The chorus plays an important part in generating the necessary dramatic power, in particular at the climax of act I and the beginning of act III.

One weakness can be found in Puccini in extreme dramatic moments when the music accompanies the *verismo* passages of violent and realistic action in an over-indulgent manner, for example as in the fight near the end of act I, or at the end of the work, in Frank's summary condemnation of Tigrana to execution.

The most effective section of the whole opera is in act II, where the growing disharmony between Tigrana and Edgar is expressed in a passage comparable with the best of *La bohème*. Such moments outweigh the opera's occasional crudities, making it well worthy of occasional revival.—ALAN LAING

Einem, Gottfried von

Composer. Born 24 January 1918, in Bern, Switzerland. Studied at Plön, Holstein (Germany); opera coach at the Berlin Staatsoper; arrested by the Gestapo in 1938, imprisoned for four months; studied composition with Boris Blacher in Berlin, 1941-43; resident composer and music adviser, Dresden State Opera, 1944; visited the United States in 1953; settled in Vienna; professor at the Hochschule für Musik, 1965-72.

Operas *Dantons Tod,* Blacher and von Einem (after Büchner), 1944-46, Salzburg, 6 August 1947; revised 1955; *Der Prozess,* Blacher and von Cramer (after Kafka, *The Trial*), 1950-52, Salzburg, 17 August 1953; *Der Zerrissene,* Blacher (after Nestroy), 1961-64, Hamburg, 17 September 1964; *Der Besuch der alten Dame,* Dürrenmatt, 1970, Vienna, 23 May 1971; *Kabale und Liebe,* Blacher and L. Ingrisch (after Schiller), 1975, Vienna, 17 December 1976; *Jesu Hochzeit,* L. Ingrisch, 1980, Vienna, 18 May 1980; *Der Tulifant,* L. Ingrisch, 1989-90, Vienna, 30 October, 1990.

Austrian composer Gottfried von Einem emerged in the aftermath of World War II as one of Europe's most promising opera composers. Beginning with *Dantons Tod* in 1947 and progressing through *Der Prozess* (1953), *Der Zerrissene* (1964), *Der Besuch der alten Dame,* *Kabale und Liebe* (1976), and *Jesu Hochzeit* (1980), Einem produced a series of stage works popular with European audiences, although they have not proved to be popular exports.

Einem did not join the serial juggernaut but continued composing in an unashamedly romantic style, probably one major reason for his success. His style has always demonstrated strong neoclassical influences, especially that of Stravinsky. The spirit of the dance is felt in many of his compositions, which doubtlessly also contributed to the success of Einem's ballet scores. Another factor in Einem's favor with Cold War audiences is his choice of libretti. Throughout his career he has shown an interest in themes of alienation and of the individual against the crowd— witness Danton, Josef K. in *Der Prozess,* and Alfred Ill in *Der Besuch*.

Einem's early works, *Dantons Tod* and *Der Prozess,* are heavily indebted to Hindemith and Berg rather than to Strauss and Wagner. Einem has never been one to use leitmotifs (leading motives) or tone rows in his operas; he depends more on symphonic development within self-contained scenes. In *Dantons Tod,* he shows himself to be at an early stage of this procedure, with individual orchestral figures often the basis of blocks of a scene; for example, the ornament-like figure in the first scene before the tribunal. Einem exhibits his ability here to construct effective scenes for chorus—the first crowd in act I, the scenes before the tribunal, and the final frenzy at Danton's death are all vividly portrayed. Large-scale orchestral interludes are also important, as in his later operas, to the progression of the drama as much as for covering scene changes.

Der Prozess incorporates Einem's first large-scale use of singers singing long passages of text on a single tone, a technique which he improved on in later operas and songs. This opera

OPERA

251

also shows an advancement in developing and contrasting orchestral materials within a scene, perhaps furthered by Einem's work in purely symphonic idioms in the years since *Dantons Tod*. *Der Zerrissene* is lighter in character, tending more toward a Singspiel style appropriate for Nestroy's farce. *Der Besuch* is still divided into self-contained scenes, separated by interludes, but the scenes are now thoroughly through-composed and demonstrate Einem's fully developed, personal style. *Kabale und Liebe* is notable for his identification of instruments with characters in the opera. In *Jesu Hochzeit,* his "mystery opera" with a text by his wife Lotte Ingrisch, Einem turned more toward a chamber style, one of his interests in his purely instrumental works of the last decade.

Einem's *Der Besuch der alten Dame* enjoyed one of the composer's greatest successes at its Vienna premiere in 1971, but it seems unlikely that it will demonstrate lasting success. Most of the opera's strength comes from the libretto by Friedrich Dürrenmatt, adapted from his play. Einem, in all of his operas, gives the orchestra the primary musical and dramatic impetus, but the unevenness of his ideas here causes the drama to unravel to some extent. The score almost seems to be a series of studies or excerpts from Einem's orchestral compositions of the 1950s or early 1960s. Often it demonstrates a peculiar detachment from what is happening on stage, especially when the composer falls back on his ever-favorite dance figures and rhythms. *Der Besuch* illustrates one problem encountered when a composer is not using a "system" such as a motif-complex—namely, how to ensure both musical cohesion and dramatic portrayal.

As in other Einem operas, the chorus is often given the most interesting material, but the *Totentanz* (dance of death) at the end, which should be the apotheosis of the chorus/townspeople, is barely half the length it needs to be. To Einem's credit, his percussion interludes between scenes and when Ill meets his fate are brilliant. *Der Besuch* may be the contemporary "winner" among his operas, but one suspects that posterity will judge his fine first work, *Dantons Tod,* to be his best.—DAVID E. ANDERSON

Elegy for Young Lovers

Composer: *Hans Werner Henze.*

Librettists: *W.H. Auden and C. Kallman.*

First Performance: *Schwetzingen, 20 May 1961; English Premiere, Glyndebourne, 13 July 1961.*

Roles: *Gregor Mittenhofer (baritone); Hilda Mack (soprano); Elisabeth Zimmer (soprano); Carolina (contralto); Dr. Wilhelm Reischmann (bass); Toni (tenor); Joseph Mauer (speaking part); Servants (mute).*

Elegy for Young Lovers is the first of the two opera collaborations between composer Hans Werner Henze and librettists W.H. Auden and Chester Kallman. The story takes place in 1910 at the mountain inn "The Black Eagle" at the base of the "Hammerhorn." Every summer the great poet Gregor Mittenhofer comes here to receive inspiration from the visions of the inn's proprietress, Hilda Mack. Hilda's husband disappeared on the mountain on their wedding day forty years before, and since then she believes she hears his voice and that he will return one day. Mittenhofer is a supreme egoist who manipulates those around him—Hilda and his entourage—to get material for his poetry. This year his doctor's son Toni has joined them. When Toni is introduced to Mittenhofer's mistress, Elisabeth, Hilda has a vision in which she foresees the fate of Toni and Elisabeth.

The opera revolves around Mittenhofer's writing of his poem and Toni and Elisabeth's falling into an illusory love. The body of Hilda's husband is found by the retreating glacier, left exposed, on the mountain, and her visions leave her. After Elisabeth falls in love with Toni, Mittenhofer wins her back with a powerful monologue in which he expounds on the joys and sorrows of being a poet. This and the ensemble reading of his poem-in-progress later in the act form the central points, dramatically and musically, of the opera. Mittenhofer sacrifices Toni and Elisabeth to a sudden blizzard, so he can call his poem an elegy. His secretary, Carolina, acquiesces in the deed and slips into madness. In the last scene, Mittenhofer gives a reading of his newest poem, based on the fate of the young lovers. As he reads, the voices of all who played a part in the poem's creation are heard in a wordless ensemble.

Auden and Kallman's libretto tackles the romantic myth of the artist as isolated hero who uses all those around him to create his art. Mittenhofer has more than a little of Auden himself drawn in him (tongue in cheek for the most part), with his secretary/patroness, his doctor with daily medications, and his overbearing attitude. The librettists fashioned the libretto on Italian models: Felice Romani's stanzas for the *Lucia di Lammermoor* mad scene are parodied for Hilda's; each act and each scene is given a title, usually prefigured in the last line of the preceding scene; there is a "servant number," here the duet early in act I for Carolina and the doctor, Reischmann. The second act, except for Mittenhofer's central monologue, is taken up with ensembles.

Henze's score uses twelve-tone techniques, although not strictly applied; many passages could better be described as atonal, almost tending toward tonality, rather than dodecaphonic. The orchestration is delicate and complex, and the vocal writing is carefully differentiated between the various characters. Hilda's line uses leaps of wide intervals and coloratura, for example. Henze meticulously distinguishes between spoken lines, singing speech or *Sprechstimme,* "rhythmically fixed speech without definite pitch," and "rhythmically fixed speech on three levels of pitch (high, middle, low)." There are many passages of breathtaking beauty and great dramatic power: the ensemble reading of Mittenhofer's poem is an example of the former; Mittenhofer's showpiece aria, of the latter.

If the opera is marred by a certain consistency of tone in many places, this is an unfortunate result of the twelve-tone style Henze employs. Even at this late date in musical history, listeners find it easier to distinguish between major and minor than among various pitch class sets. Henze's later opera, *Der junge Lord,* shows a more tonal emphasis that has contributed to its wider acceptance. Dramatically, *Elegy for Young Lovers* would benefit by a cut or cuts toward the end of the last act. We know that Elizabeth and Toni are going to die in the blizzard; the "playing house" scene on the mountain that Auden and Kallman gave them is anticlimactic. Revising or cutting part of the scenes on the mountain would strengthen the ending.

Elegy for Young Lovers requires a strong ensemble—particularly in Mittenhofer and in Hilda, who emerges as his nemesis—and a skilled conductor. Many companies have probably been frightened away from the work by its poorly received English premiere at Glyndebourne. But this is a powerful opera. It is distinguished by a libretto laden with both humor and pathos, by ravishing lyrical passages in nontonal settings, and marvelous orchestration.—DAVID ANDERSON

e

OPERA

Elektra

Composer: *Richard Strauss.*

Librettist: *Hugo von Hofmannsthal.*

First Performance: *Dresden, Court Opera, 25 January 1909.*

Roles: *Elektra (soprano); Chrysothemis (soprano); Klytemnestra (mezzo-soprano); Aegisthus (tenor); Orestes (baritone); Klytemnestra's Confidante (soprano); Trainbearer (soprano); Overseer of Servants (soprano); Young Servant (tenor); Old Servant (bass); Guardian of Orestes (bass); Five Maidservants (two sopranos, two mezzo-sopranos, contralto); chorus (SATB).*

In *Elektra,* Strauss creates a new level of demands for female voices and for singers remaining on-stage for extended periods of time. For example, after the short opening scene in which the servants describe her, Elektra is present on stage for the rest of the opera. The size of the orchestra and the ways in which it is used require singers who can project well in the lower registers more so than in his other operas. In fact, with its leitmotivic use of themes, the orchestra itself becomes another character in the drama. Because of the orchestra, the singers must on several occasions employ "Sprechstimme" (speaking in the direction of the pitch of a melody line) rather than actually sing the notes as they ordinarily would.

The first production of *Elektra*, Berlin, 1909, with Marie Götze as Klytemnestra and Thila Plaichinger as Elektra

The plot, adapted from the Greek plays of Aeschylus, is continuous, without changes of stage. In scene i the servants describe Elektra as insanely blood-thirsty, eager to avenge her father Agamemnon's death. Scene ii opens with Elektra's entrance and first words, "alone" (melodic intervals which occur again after her death) and connects to scene iii with her sister, Chrysothemis. In scene iv Elektra confronts her mother, Klytemnestra, and both receive the false news of Orestes' death. Scene v is another Elektra-Chrysothemis conflict with Elektra demanding that Chrysothemis help her avenge their father's death. Scene vi is the gentle recognition scene between Elektra and her brother, Orestes; but it connects with the off-stage vengeance—Klytemnestra's death for Agamemnon's murder. Scene vii is between Aegisthus (Klytemnestra's lover and now husband) and Elektra; he too goes off-stage to be killed. The final scene shows Elektra claiming her triumph. Chrysothemis calls on their brother Orestes with the same two melodic intervals Elektra sang in her first scene; but Elektra is dead; and the Agamemnon and the murder motives end the opera.

Elektra, Chrysothemis, and Klytemnestra are required to have two-octave ranges in order to be able to project the text, especially in the lower register. Strauss, a master of orchestration, generally reduces the orchestration when he writes for the singers' lower registers. However, due to the symphonic poem aspects of the orchestra-as-character in this work, occasionally the singers are secondary to the orchestra. Since this orchestra-as-character continually states both the Agamemnon and murder motives, the opera could almost be retitled *Agamemnon*. The dead king dominates the opera musically through the orchestra.—SAMUEL B. SCHULKEN, JR.

Elias, Rosalind

Mezzo-soprano. Born 13 March 1930, in Lowell, Massachusetts. Studied at New England Conservatory, Boston, and at the Accademia di Santa Cecilia, Rome; joined the Metropolitan Opera, 1954; sang role of Erika in premiere of Barber's Vanessa, *1958.*

Rarely, but by good fortune every so often, a singer and a role come together as one entity for posterity. Of all the roles she has sung on the world's stages in a long career, mezzo-soprano Rosalind Elias will always be associated with Erika, the niece of Vanessa in the Samuel Barber-Gian Carlo Menotti opera of that name. *Vanessa* premiered at the Metropolitan in 1958, and received limited performances at the Salzburg Festival (where critics were upset about having to hear an American opera). Elias's single-minded intensity and her identification with Erika became almost legendary even in those relatively few appearances.

American-born and almost completely American trained, Elias has sung all manner of roles, large and small. At the Metropolitan Opera, where she debuted in 1954, she has sung the Second Esquire in *Parsifal,* Octavian, the Second Peasant Girl in *Le Nozze di Figaro* and Carmen. (To round out a trio of "seconds" she has also sung the Second Lady in *Die Zauberflöte.*) She branched out at the Metropolitan to sing Zerlina (*Zauberflöte*), a role not usually recognized as part of the mezzo's repertoire. She has sung over 45 roles in the New York house alone.

In Europe Rosalind Elias has appeared from Hamburg to Lisbon, and at many festivals, including Glyndebourne. She has also appeared at the Teatro Colón in Buenos Aires. She became part of Leonard Bernstein's traveling casts, singing his works with him or under other conductors. She has also concertized extensively. While never known as a reigning star, Elias was always recognized as a reliable, hard-working artist—and a survivor.

First among her recordings is with the "original cast" on RCA (now BMG) of Barber's *Vanessa* with Eleanor Steber, Regina Resnik, Nicolai Gedda, and Giorgio Tozzi, conducted by Dimitri Mitropoulos, which duplicates the original performances. Elias also appears on other RCA complete opera recordings such as *La forza del destino, Il trovatore,* and *Falstaff* in roles of varying sizes. There are also excerpts from *Werther* with Elias as Charlotte opposite Cesare Valletti in the title role, conducted by René Liebowitz, which show off her vocal and dramatic gifts to fine advantage.—BERT WECHSLER

L'elisir d'amore [The Elixir of Love]

Composer: *Gaetano Donizetti.*

Librettist: *Felice Romani (after Scribe, Le philtre).*

First Performance: *Milan, Canobbiana, 12 May 1832.*

Roles: *Dr. Dulcamara (bass); Adina (soprano); Nemorino (tenor); Sergeant Belcore (baritone); Gianetta (soprano); chorus (SATTB).*

Gaetano Donizetti wrote dozens of tragic and dramatic operas and created the most durable of all musical madwomen, Lucia di Lammermoor. But he also was a comic genius, producing three warm and cheerful works, *L'elisir d'amore, La fille du régiment* and *Don Pasquale,* which have spread sunshine through the operatic world for a century and a half.

Of these, *L'elisir d'amore* was the earliest, and the only one composed in Italian, the others being designed originally for production in Paris and set to French texts (though they have long been given in Italian versions). Donizetti had already written thirty-five operas when, at the age of thirty-four, he completed *L'elisir d'amore* in two weeks' time. Showing no signs of haste in its graceful melodies and sparkling ensembles, it was an instant hit when given on 12 May 1832 at the Teatro della Canobbiana, a rival of the Teatro alla Scala in Milan.

Its plot was adapted—not to say stolen—by the librettist Felice Romani from *Le philtre,* a successful French opera by Auber with a text by Eugène Scribe. In the Donizetti version, a young

and rather simple villager named Nemorino is hopelessly in love with Adina, daughter of a wealthy landowner and a flighty girl much given to reading romances, such as that of Tristan and Isolde. A quack doctor named Dulcamara arrives in town, genially peddling an elixir guaranteed to cure all ills from aches to love-sickness. Nemorino eagerly buys a flagon, hoping it will work like Isolde's love-potion. A troop of soldiers arrives, led by Sergeant Belcore who promptly pays court to Adina. She promises to marry him that very night, mainly to spite Nemorino, who has deliberately begun acting indifferently to her while he waits for the potion to exercise its magic. Shocked by the impending nuptials, Nemorino purchases a second bottle, raising the money by enlisting in Belcore's regiment for "venti scudi"—twenty crowns. Suddenly word arrives that Nemorino's uncle has died leaving him a fortune, but even before hearing this news, Adina relents, buys back Nemorino's enlistment contract, and confesses that she loves him. The villagers, led by Dulcamara, rejoice in the happy outcome.

Luigi Lablache and Giovanni Mario in *L'elisir d'amore*

Donizetti's buoyant score became a favorite wherever it was presented; in Paris, for example, it played at the Théâtre des Italiens while Auber's *Le philtre* continued to be given at the Opéra. When someone suggested to Auber that the two versions be presented on the same evening as a double-bill he replied: "That's an idea. But it might suit Donizetti better than me." And indeed, *Le philtre* has long since evaporated while *L'elisir* has never lost its potency as one of the supreme achievements of opera buffa.

L'elisir d'amore is something more than a straight comedy, however; thanks to Donizetti's lyric gifts, it also is a warm and touching story about people who, while they may not be particularly original or strikingly individual in character, nevertheless represent some thoroughly recognizable and sympathetic human types. Lovesick tenors, for instance, are anything but an operatic rarity, yet Nemorino turns out to be one of the most likable of the species. Long before he gets to sing his famous aria "Una furtiva lagrima" in the second act, he has the audience on his side; clearly he is far more entitled to get the girl than the belligerent Belcore. As for that mellifluous aria just named, beloved of tenors from Caruso to Pavarotti, we owe it strictly to Donizetti the composer rather than Romani the librettist, who objected that a melancholy *romanza* might dampen the comic spirit of the work. But Donizetti insisted and prevailed, thus producing one of Italian opera's all-time hit numbers.

Adina is a more conventional figure; her opening aria, in which she mockingly reads the story of Tristan and Isolde from a book, establishes her as a mixture of the worldly and the romantic, but we never quite see the reason for her obduracy in refusing to accept her village swain—except, of course, to establish some sort of excuse for the young man to grasp so avidly at Dr. Dulcamara's magical drink.

Dulcamara himself—"quel gran medico, Dottore enciclopedico," as he portentously announces himself—is a true descendant of the basso buffo line, as pompous as any, friendlier than most, and, at the end, an honest man—for has his elixir, after all, failed to deliver the promised goods? He is one of Donizetti's supreme creations, and he is blended into the musical landscape with consummate ease and mastery. Observe, for instance, the act I scene between Dulcamara and Nemorino when the quack is selling the youth his magical bottle of "bordo" wine, all the time commenting on his gullibility. The episode builds up from a *recitativo secco* (with keyboard) to accompanied recitative (with the orchestra joining in) to a full-fledged comic duet with the two voices intertwining in a splendid example of Italian patter ensemble.—HERBERT KUPFERBERG

The Emperor Jones

Composer: *Louis Gruenberg.*

Librettists: *Louis Gruenberg and K. de Jaffa (after Eugene O'Neill).*

First Performance: *New York, Metropolitan Opera, 7 January 1932.*

Roles: *Brutus Jones (baritone); Henry Smithers (tenor); An Old Nativewoman (soprano); Witch-Doctor (dancer); several non-singing parts; chorus.*

The importance of *The Emperor Jones* in the history of American opera cannot be underestimated. After the opera's premiere in 1932, the consensus of opinion was that the work was the most epoch-making of all attempts at an American opera up to this time. Olin Downes, writing in *The New York Times,* stated "The Emperor Jones, an American opera, American in its dramatic and musical origins, its text, its swiftness and tensity, and all the principle elements of the interpretation, was given its world premiere, with instant and sweeping success." Soon after this first performance Gruenberg was given the David Bispham Medal for his contributions in American opera. This distinguished award brought Gruenberg into national prominence and established his reputation as an important operatic composer.

In adapting Eugene O'Neill's play into an opera, Gruenberg was confronted with a very difficult task. The play, O'Neill's earliest success, had a continuous run of 204 performances in 1920. O'Neill intensified the drama by requiring the steady beat of a tom-tom throughout the play. Thus Gruenberg was undertaking a text which already had musical effects as part of the stage directions. The story is that of an ex-Pullman porter who makes himself emperor of a West Indian island by combining an appeal to superstition with the white man's cunning. Jones cynically exploits the natives, until they rebel and he is forced to flee. Making his escape into the jungle, Jones loses his way, panics, and returns in a circle to where he began and is shot by his rebelling subjects. Most important is O'Neill's expressionistic treatment of the torment Jones undergoes when he escapes into the jungle, with the result that he is gradually destroyed by fear.

The libretto differs only slightly from the original play. For the most part Gruenberg uses O'Neill's text verbatim with an occasional omission or repetition of dialogue for emphasis. Other important changes include the use of a chorus that comments on the events taking place (with text written by Gruenberg), the insertion of the Black spiritual "It's Me, O Lord," and the manner in which Jones dies. Gruenberg's treatment of Jones' death is a significant alteration from the original play. Rather than having the natives kill him, Gruenberg has Jones commit suicide. This changed ending brought forth a mixed reaction but was accepted by many critics as an important element that contributed to the opera's dramatic success. Throughout the opera the orchestra provides a background of syncopated dissonances to the fast moving drama. Except for one lyrical, dramatic moment when Jones sings the interpolated spiritual, the singers recite and shout their words in a speech-like manner. The demands of the title role are great, and in the premiere Lawrence Tibbett received rave reviews for his portrayal of Jones.

The Emperor Jones remains Gruenberg's most important opera. Although the work enjoyed immediate recognition after its premiere, performances have become infrequent and rare in recent years, partly owing to the work's controversial subject matter—the exploitation of Blacks by a Black—and the difficulty in casting the lead role of Brutus Jones.—ROBERT F. NISBETT

L'enfant et les sortilèges [The Bewitched Child]

Composer: *Maurice Ravel.*

Librettist: *Colette.*

First Performance: *Monte Carlo, 21 March 1925.*

Roles *(some of the following may be doubled): The Child (mezzo-soprano); Mama (contralto); The Bergère (soprano); The Chinese Cup (mezzo-contralto); The Fire (soprano); The Princess (soprano); The White Cat (mezzo-soprano); The Dragonfly (mezzo-soprano); The Nightingale (soprano); The Bat (soprano); The Screech-owl (soprano); The Squirrel (mezzo-soprano); A Country Lass (soprano); A Herdsman (contralto); The Armchair (bass); The Comtoise Clock (baritone); The Teapot (black Wedgwood) (tenor); The Little Old Man; The Black Cat (baritone); A Tree (bass); The Tree*

Frog (tenor); The Bench, The Sofa, The Stool, The Wicker Chair (chorus of children); The Numbers (chorus of children); The Shepherds, The Herdsmen (chorus); The Tree Frogs, The Animals, The Trees (chorus).

Ravel—like Satie, Stravinsky, Milhaud, Hindemith, Weill, and many other European composers—was fascinated by the chic vitality of the popular music (mostly ragtime and jazz) coming from the United States in the 1910s and 1920s. In writing *L'enfant et les sortilèges*, Ravel consciously tried for a style akin to the feel of American musical-comedy and operetta. And while *L'enfant* bears little resemblance to, say, the Gershwin or Kern shows being produced in the mid-1920s, there remain the lightness, the satire, the genuine but unwrenching emotion that wed American spunk to French sentimentality.

America, to Europeans, was a young, restless country, and it suited Ravel's musical aims that his librettist, Colette, took as the central character a naughty little boy who hasn't been doing his homework. (Though the scene is set in Normandy, might not the choice of subject have been inspired by the little American girl in Satie's *Parade*?) His mother confines him to his room to reflect on his poor behavior. And what should happen? His behavior gets worse, as he flies into a rage, smashing and abusing everything around him (and all the while feeling triumphantly wicked).

Magically, the objects of his fury come to life, and, in retribution, begin to taunt him. The first scene of the one-act opera takes place in the boy's room, while the second scene whisks us out into the moonlit garden, where the insects and animals continue the harassment only, by accident, to discover the boy's fundamental goodness.

Constructed something in the manner of French eighteenth-century opera-ballet, with its series of "entrées" (Colette's original title for the opera was *Ballet pour ma fille*), *L'enfant* moves from one essentially self-contained episode to another. Unfortunately, the supernatural succession begins with the least interesting vignette of the entire work, the duet for chair and sofa, but following this tentative beginning, the opera continues at an amazingly high level of musical and dramatic inspiration.

The wonderfully comic "ding, ding, ding" of the grandfather clock from which the Boy yanked the pendulum gives way to the jaunty fox-trot of the black Wedgwood teapot (who struts around in the manner of an American boxer) and the Chinese cup. Ravel and Colette use pidgin American and Chinese here to charming effect ("How's your mug?" "Rotten"; "I knock out you, stupid chose, I marm'lade you"; "Hara-kiri, Sessue Hayakawa"), with the polytonal jazziness of the teapot's music (one of the few overt Americanisms of the score) juxtaposed with the parallel-4th pentatonicisms of the cup.

Next, from the fireplace, appears Fire, who, as a coloratura soprano, informs the Boy that she warms good boys but burns the bad ones. The shepherds and shepherdesses slip off the torn wallpaper in a mournful little dance, which Ravel imbues with a centuries-old flavor by means of Renaissance modalism. The Princess emerges plaintively from out of the pages of the ripped storybook (another soprano, accompanied only by flute), followed by little Mr. Arithmetic, complete with a squadron of numerical demons who menace the boy with insoluble mathematical problems. (Even the Boy's homework is getting back at him.)

Two cats croon a meowing duet (considered scandalously suggestive at the opera's premiere), whereupon we find ourselves transported to the garden, in which trees cry out in pain and in which frogs, dragonflies, bats, owls, and squirrels commingle. When the animals, as a group, finally attack the Boy (as he utters the strange word "Maman") and a squirrel is injured in the mélée, the Boy demonstrates compassion by binding its wounds. The animals' anger toward the Boy now abates, and the work ends with a fugal chorus in praise of his goodness and wisdom. The Boy calls out one final time to his mother.

What makes *L'enfant* so refreshing and absorbing to modern audiences is its combination of impudence and warmth, communicated through its continually varied set of musical episodes. Ravel uses a large orchestra mostly for the range of colorings it offers him, and he for the most part eschews tutti scoring in favor of chamber-music-like settings. His restraint is nowhere more apparent than in the opera's opening bars, where two oboes play langorously in parallel 5ths and 4ths until they are joined by a single string-bass. The orchestral coloring changes with each vignette, never more enchantingly than in the "night music" and dances in the garden. It is also here that the opera takes an unexpectedly expressionist turn: the animals, stunned at the boy's show of humanity, sing in choral *Sprechstimme*. Schoenberg's influence on Ravel dates back to *Pierrot Lunaire,* and moonlit Pierrot makes a symbolic appearance here in *L'enfant's* moonlit garden. The expressionist tone of this one episode deepens and enriches the psychological resonance of the entire work.

It is well known that Ravel, unmarried throughout life, held his mother in especial reverence and that he, small in stature, had an affinity for child-like simplicities. It is thus particularly understandable that Colette's libretto should have brought out in Ravel the choicest and most poetic compositional thoughts of his entire career. *L'enfant* is sometimes ranked, after Alban Berg's *Wozzeck,* as the finest and most irreplaceable twentieth-century opera. That ranking hardly seems amiss.—GERALD MOSHELL

Die Entführung aus dem Serail [The Abduction from the Seraglio]

Composer: *Wolfgang Amadeus Mozart.*

Librettist: *J. Gottlieb Stephanie, Jr (after C.F. Bretzner, Belmonte und Constanze).*

First Performance: *Vienna, Burgtheater, 16 July 1782.*

Roles: *Constanze (soprano); Blonde (soprano); Belmonte (tenor); Pedrillo (tenor); Osmin (bass); Pasha Selim (speaking); chorus (SATB).*

Posterity has agreed that the operas Mozart composed during the last decade of his life surpass those of his contemporaries. *Die Entführung aus dem Serail,* the first of these operas, is a *Singspiel,* in other words, an essentially German treatment of a plot, although the story has an exotic setting in a Pasha's palace in Turkey. The *Singspiel* tradition, which in some ways continues in modern musicals, also demanded that many of the exchanges between the characters be in speech rather than music, thus dispensing with the rather artificial use of recitative that belonged to Italian-language operas including Mozart's own. However, the singers made up for this when they did have solo numbers, duets, and ensembles, for since these tended to occur at key points of the drama, they were often powerful and florid. The remark made by the Austrian Emperor after the first performance, "Too many notes, my dear Mozart," has gone down to posterity unexplained: it may well be that he felt there were too many sung numbers relative to speech, or that they were too long. He may also have thought Mozart's orchestra too big, for the composer had used "Turkish"-type instruments (piccolo, triangle, cymbals and bass drum) in addition to the normal ones of the orchestra in order to set the scene already in the first bars of the overture.

Much of the story—though not the ending—pokes fun at the Ottoman Empire, something the Austrians always enjoyed doing. At the start of act I, the Spanish nobleman Belmonte is outside the house of the Pasha Selim (a speaking role), seeking his beloved Constanze, who has been taken captive with her English maid, Blonde. The name Constanze was that of the composer's own wife, and it suggests too that the character in the opera shall prove herself to be faithful: indeed, the Pasha courts her but respects her virtue. Pedrillo is Belmonte's servant just as Blonde is Constanze's, and he loves Blonde; he aids his master in a plan for the rescue of Constanze, and Belmonte meets the Pasha in the guise of a visiting architect. In the meantime the Pasha's comic chief servant Osmin is at odds with Pedrillo, who has also gained admittance to the house, and with Blonde herself, whom he fancies. Act II includes a vivid exchange between Osmin and Blonde as well as Constanze's large-scale aria "Martern aller Arten" ("Martyrs of all kinds"), in which she tells the Pasha that death itself shall not make her give herself to a man she does not love. Pedrillo devises a plan to make Osmin drunk and facilitate the escape of both couples, which he does after overcoming his adversary's religious scruples, and he and Belmonte reassure themselves of the ladies' virtue in a quartet with Constanze and Blonde.

But the unhurried preparations of the two couples are overheard by a guard. Osmin is awakened and appears to sing a celebrated aria of comic and gloating rage, "Ha! wie will ich triumphieren" ("Oh, how I will triumph"). The Pasha enters and pronounces a sentence of torture on Belmonte, now revealed as the son of an old enemy. Belmonte and Constanze are left to sing a duet, "Welch' ein Geschick" ("What fate is this"), in which they bravely face punishment and parting, but now the Pasha returns to tell them that he has decided on clemency: he will not carry out his sentence and they are free to go. The opera ends with an ensemble of general happiness.

The busy plot of *Die Entführung*, together with the essentially light-hearted nature of the *Singspiel* tradition in which Mozart wrote, makes it a thoroughly entertaining opera, and it is well supplied not only with memorable arias (such as those already mentioned as well as Belmonte's fearful "O wie ängstlich, o wie feurig" in act I and Pedrillo's charming act III serenade "Im Mohrenland") but also with ample stage action together with broad comedy as provided by Pedrillo and Osmin. But Osmin is especially well drawn, a fearsome character as well as a comic one, and his aria of triumph in act III requires a bass singer to offer a range of over two octaves upwards from a low D. Carl Maria von Weber said of *Die Entführung* that in this opera Mozart reached maturity: "With the best will in the world he could not have written another *Entführung*."—CHRISTOPHER HEADINGTON

Ernani

Composer: *Giuseppe Verdi.*

Librettist: *Francesco Maria Piave (after Hugo, Hernani).*

First Performance: *Venice, La Fenice, 9 March 1844.*

Roles: *Ernani (tenor); Don Carlo (baritone); Don Ruy Gomez de Silva (bass); Elvira (soprano); Giovanna (soprano); Don Riccardo (tenor); Jago (bass); chorus (SSATTBB).*

Accustomed as we are nowadays to all manner of theatrical fare, it seems hard to believe that a play such as Victor Hugo's *Hernani* could ever have been deemed even potentially seditious. Yet at its 1830 Paris premiere it very nearly provoked a riot. And why? The list of infractions against tradition in the name of Romanticism, or "Liberalism in literature" as Hugo preferred to put it, was lengthy: flagrant disregard for the classical unities of time and place; mixing the comic and the tragic; irregular verse forms; and, arguably the greatest sacrilege of all in the precarious political climate in France immediately preceding the July 1830 revolution against King Charles X, portraying a nobleman turned bandit (Don Juan of Aragon, better known as Hernani). But for Verdi in 1843, buoyed by the recent success of his *Nabucco* and *I Lombardi,* the freedom of expression *Hernani* offered must have seemed heaven-sent, particularly since he was then bent on expanding his horizons—heretofore limited to Milan's Teatro alla Scala— by accepting the commission of northern Italy's other leading opera company, Venice's Gran Teatro la Fenice.

Radical though *Hernani* surely was, then, at bottom what it offered Verdi and his librettist Francesco Maria Piave was the utterly fundamental conflict between love and honor—what Verdi called "immensely good theater." Or, to take a different tact as has the daringly unorthodox but perceptive Verdi critic Gabriele Baldini, the "story" afforded the pretense for "an ideal musical subject" that "requires nothing but the vaguest explanation. . . . A youthful, passionate female voice is besieged by three male voices, each of which establishes a specific relationship with her." Baldini continues, "the siege is fruitless. The male voices, or rather registers, meet with various fates, and each is granted a relationship with the woman, although on different levels. This relationship varies in intensity of passion according to the distance between the soprano register and the particular male voice" (*The Story of Giuseppe Verdi,* 1980). What an inventive way to make the point that *Ernani* is first and foremost an opera about *music,* and incredibly forceful music at that. Small wonder, too, that George Bernard Shaw was moved to write of Verdi's first collaboration with Piave: "*Falstaff* [Verdi's last opera] is lighted and warmed only by the afterglow of the fierce noonday sun of *Ernani.*"

Verdi and Piave tailored their reworking of Hugo's amatory quadrangle into four acts, each of which bears a subtitle: "The Bandit," "The Guest," "The Pardon," and "The Mask." The first introduces all four principals, the tenor Ernani, the soprano Elvira, the baritone Don Carlo (King of Spain), and the bass Don Ruy Gomez de Silva. While all three men have designs on Elvira, she has pledged to marry her uncle Silva though she loves Ernani alone. The complications generated by the four-way romantic entanglement continue in act II with an interrupted impromptu rendezvous between Elvira and Ernani on the eve of her marriage to Silva, Silva learning that the king is also a suitor for the lady's hand, and the unexpected alliance between Ernani and Silva against Carlo. The act is capped, however implausibly, by Ernani giving his hunting horn to Silva as a token of good faith, promising to kill himself whenever the old man sounds it. Silva is given a reason to do exactly that when in act III Carlo is elected Emperor Charles V of the Holy Roman Empire; among his first acts is to condone the marriage of Ernani and Elvira. In act IV the two do marry yet their happiness is brief; hardly has the ceremony taken place when Silva sounds the horn. Ernani pleads for a moment of happiness at the end of his life of misery, but Silva insists the pact be honored forthwith. Offered a dagger, Ernani slays himself and falls dying into Elvira's arms.

Shaw's judgment of *Ernani* was not misplaced. Indeed, the score abounds with a special kind of memorable and highly-charged music aptly characterized by his phrase "fierce noonday sun." The first evidence of this comes in the second scene of act I, in Elvira's impassioned "Ernani, involami" when she dreams of being carried away by her beloved. As Baldini nimbly characterizes this showcase of vocal bravura that demands of the soprano a range of over two octaves (from high C to B-flat below middle C): "So overwhelming is the expressive force here that the passion seems to consume and destroy the woman." Other instances from among the many in this, one of Verdi's most tune-drenched of scores, include the baritone's third-act "O dei verd' anni miei," the conspirator's chorus "Si ridesti" and Elvira's "Ah! signor, se t'è concesso" in the same act, and—as an example of what could be called the very substance of early Verdi— the whole of the last-act trio.

Perhaps surprisingly, given Verdi's well-known diatribes against mere "entertainment, artifice and the system" when it threatened to obscure what to him was "art," on at least two occasions he deigned to supply *Ernani* with insert arias, one of the chief mediums by which singers traditionally sought to assert their dominance in the "system" that was nineteenth-century Italian opera. The first, the addition of the cabaletta "Infin che un brando vindice" for Silva in act I, was made in order to make the role more appealing to star bass singers; in the event, Verdi's authorship has been questioned, although the piece appeared in printed scores of the opera during his lifetime. Unequivocally authentic, however, is the act II double aria for Ernani that begins "Odi il voto, o grande Iddio." The aria was commissioned by none other than Gioacchino Rossini who had shortly before taken on the role of mentor for the tenor Nicola Ivanoff; the latter first sang the new number 26 December 1844 in a performance of the opera in Parma. Luciano Pavarotti revived the piece in 1983 at the Metropolitan Opera. Verdi's autograph for the aria is preserved at New York's Pierpont Morgan Library.—JAMES PARSONS

Erwartung [Expectation]

Composer: *Arnold Schoenberg.*

Librettist: *Marie Pappenheim.*

First Performance: *Prague, Neues Deutsches Theater, 6 June 1924.*

Roles: *A Woman (soprano or mezzo-soprano).*

Erwartung, which Schoenberg himself called "a monodrama in one act," was written in a seventeen-day period between 27 August and 12 September 1909 using a libretto written for Schoenberg by his friend Marie Pappenheim, a physician in Vienna. The premier, however, did not take place until fifteen years later in Prague on 6 June 1924 at the second International Society for Contemporary Music Festival at the Neue Deutsche Theater with Marie Gutheil-Schröder, soprano, and conducted by Schoenberg's teacher (and brother-in-law), Alexander von Zemlinsky. It was performed subsequently in Wiesbaden on 22 January 1928, in Berlin on 7 June 1930, and in Brussels on 6 May 1936 in a French translation by J. Weterings. More recent performances include those in London on 4 April 1960, with Heather Harper, and the American stage premiere in Washington, D.C. on 28 December 1960 with Helga Pilarczyk, conducted by Robert Craft.

While the term "nightmare" is often used to describe this opera, Schoenberg's "Angst-traum" is more precise. Lasting only twenty-seven minutes, it is comprised of four scenes marked by the entrance and exit of a solitary woman. The plot, if we may use the term at all, unfolds by memory association as if the woman were a patient on an analyst's couch. The woman enters, walking along the moonlit path of the garden, searching for "the man." The night is full of sinister intimations, but she finds the courage to rush into the wood in her search. In the second scene she is deep in the forest's interior darkness; she sees apparitions, imagines she hears strange noises and is being attacked. Suddenly calmed, she ventures deeper still. The speech now becomes in part a dialogue with the imagined man, and in part a confession. As the scene closes, she stumbles into a tree trunk which she mistakes for a body. The third scene brings her to a clearing. She is even more frightened by the specters of the night and now identifies "him" as her lover. She imagines him calling; a shadow reminds her of his shadow on a wall. She complains because he must leave her so quickly, and plunges deeper into the wood, crying for her lover's protection against the imagined wild beasts.

The final scene presents a dark and shuttered house. She stumbles in, dress torn, face and hands now bleeding. Now the night symbolizes death. There is no living thing, no breath of air, no sound. Only death and the pallid, bloodless moon. She approaches a bench but fears that a strange woman will chase her away. Her foot strikes something—a bloody corpse. She swoons as she recognizes the body of her lover, and attempts to call him awake in a hymn-like passage. We learn that of late the beloved's attentions have slacked off, and she suspects him of betraying her with another, the white-armed woman. The kisses and embraces with which she first greeted the imagined corpse (there is no corpse in Schoenberg's stage directions; everything is imagined) turn to kicks and jealous tantrums. Finally, as dawn colors the sky, she rises, exhausted, saying "I was seeking . . ." and slips away into the shadows, the quest unsatisfied, and her memory already slipping away from her conscious mind. The music ends with one of the most amazing passages ever written—an orchestral "shiver" which seems not to stop but to vanish beyond audible sound.

Although direct connections between Schoenberg and Freud are difficult to make, *Erwartung* can surely be called the first psychoanalytic opera. The reality plumbed in the short, intense drama is purely psychological, and the only dramatic event is the discovery of the body. This occurs quite early in the opera, and the remainder of the monologue passes from recall of the past love through heightened emotions and ends in a kind of posthumous reconciliation brought about by exhaustion. There is only a vestigial sense of real time. Past and present seem to cross and recross in a way that mirrors the confused state of mind of the nightmare victim. Conventional tonal music could not have convincingly supported the interplay of conflicting emotions. Although there are identifiable repetitions of musical themes—the ostinato figures used as the woman walks along the path, for instance—the score appears athematic. The level of repetition is so subtly disguised within the surface fabric that whatever repetition exists contributes but little to the overall coherence of the music. Certainly this is Schoenberg's most daring and furthest venture into athematicism, a path he chose not to pursue further.

The extreme compression of this work, both in actual time and in the almost continuous level of harmonic intensity, seem somehow inexorably tied to the subject matter itself: the confused state of the hysterical mind. It is not generally known that the librettist, Marie Pappenheim, was the cousin of "Anna O." (Bertha Pappenheim, whose initials were transposed backward one place to arrive at the name Freud used in his case study, the first classic documented case of hysteria). While the symptoms displayed by Anna O. differ markedly from those apparitions and phantoms that appear in the opera, comparing the cases tempts one to make suppositions that Schoenberg knew at least something about Freud's investigations. On the other hand, Schoenberg himself was no stranger to the tortured state of mind. Furthermore,

Viennese culture was fixated on repression, despair, and suicide, and any number of plays, poems, and other art works can be identified that spring from these dark psychic roots. We may never know exactly which influences were uppermost in Schoenberg's mind as he worked so feverishly on this opera, but there is no doubt that *Erwartung* is a direct expression of its time and place.—ROBERT H. DANES

Eugene Onegin [Evgeny Onegin]

Composer: *Piotr Ilyich Tchaikovsky.*

Librettists: *K. Shilovsky and Piotr Ilyich Tchaikovsky (after Pushkin).*

First Performance: *Moscow, Maliy, 29 March 1879.*

Roles: *Tatyana (soprano); Lensky (tenor); Eugene Onegin (baritone); Madame Larina (mezzo-soprano); Olga (contralto); Filippevna (mezzo-soprano); Prince Gremin (bass); Triquet (tenor); Zaretski (bass); A Captain (bass); Gillot (mute); chorus (SSAATTBB).*

When a singer named Elizaveta Lavrovskaya first suggested Pushkin's *Eugene Onegin* to Tchaikovsky as a subject for an opera, he thought the idea peculiar. But a short time later, reading over the poet's popular "novel in verse," he changed his mind, and eagerly sketched out a scenario for the opera that is largely a blueprint for the finished product.

Tchaikovsky had tried his hand at opera many times with varying degrees of success. He set ten librettos and considered many other subjects that never came to anything. But this time, something clicked. Pushkin's verses about a naive young girl named Tatyana, cruelly spurned by the worldly, sophisticated Onegin, fired his imagination as had no other source.

In a letter from 1877 he wrote, "How delightful to avoid the commonplace Pharaohs, Ethiopian princesses, poisoned cups and all the rest of these dolls' tales! *Eugene Onegin* is full of poetry. I am not blind to its defects. I know well enough the work gives little scope for treatment, and will be deficient in stage effects; but the wealth of poetry, the human quality and simplicity of the subject, joined to Pushkin's inspired verses, will compensate for what it lacks in other respects."

Pushkin's *Eugene Onegin,* a "novel in verse," is imbued with his special sarcastic touch. He had started the tale intending a satire on Byron's *Don Juan,* but over the years it took him to complete it, the work developed instead into a merciless satire on Russian society of Pushkin's time. The narrator's snide remarks and long asides create an ironic distance, discouraging deep sympathy for the characters on the part of the reader. By poking fun at the troubles of his characters, Pushkin made his tract an anti-Romantic caricature of emotional idealism.

Tchaikovsky by contrast identified deeply with the characters, especially the sensitive Tatyana. In constructing the libretto, he eliminated the ironic tone of the original. A great deal of Pushkin's beautiful poetry is used as written, but with the narrator's asides excised or restated as the words of the characters. For example, Lensky, who was "in the flower of youthful looks and lyric power," "mourned the wilt of life's young green, when he had almost turned eighteen." The first phrase appears in the libretto, but the comical remark about the jaded youth's real age does not. By thus eliminating the sarcasm, the characters' emotional vagaries are accepted at face value.

These were calculated changes made by a composer who knew the language of opera to be one of strong, visceral feeling. Operatic characters must be larger than life and experience intense emotions: hence the importance of Tatyana's love. Pushkin's dry, intellectual sarcasm had exactly the opposite effect. Pushkin deflated his characters; Tchaikovsky re-inflated them.

In the opera, Madame Larina has two daughters, Olga and Tatyana. Lensky, who is courting Olga, brings his friend Eugene Onegin to meet the girls. Tatyana is immediately attracted to the worldly Onegin. Later, in private, she writes him a long letter confessing her love. Tatyana is devastated when Onegin rebuffs her love coolly, telling her that he is unsuitable for marriage and suggesting that she learn to control her emotions.

Act II opens with a ball. Irritated with Lensky after overhearing gossip about himself and Tatyana, Onegin flirts and dances with Olga, who is not unresponsive to his attentions. The fiery Lensky is furiously jealous and challenges Onegin to a duel. When Lensky is killed in the duel, Onegin is grief-stricken. Act III takes place three years later, when Onegin by chance meets Tatyana at another ball. Now married to Prince Gremin, Tatyana is transformed from a naive girl into a sophisticated lady. It is Onegin's turn to be smitten. But when he professes his love, Tatyana in turn rejects his overtures, saying that whatever her true feelings she must remain faithful to her husband.

Pushkin's tale has little to recommend it to grand theatrical effects, a problem of which Tchaikovsky was keenly aware. Acknowledging the non-dramatic nature of his work, the composer did not even call it an opera, but rather "lyric scenes in three acts." Some of the rewriting of the libretto, such as the contrived confrontation between Onegin and Lensky at the ball, was designed to inject a bit of drama. But significant portions of the story are left out entirely, making the plot a little confusing. The disjointed progression is particularly noticeable in the gap between the second and third acts. Tchaikovsky could safely assume that most of his listeners would be familiar with Pushkin's novel, but today, for non-Russian audiences, such familiarity is unlikely.

The most important of the scenes, and the first that Tchaikovsky wrote, was the crucial letter scene from act I. Freed of Pushkin's long preamble, which in the novel trivializes Tatyana's distress, Tchaikovsky makes it into a drama in miniature of the rollercoaster ride of the girl's emotions. Tatyana boldly begins the letter, then falters, tears it up, and starts again. After pouring out her feelings, she finally finishes writing, throwing herself on Onegin's mercy. This scene underscores the heights to which Tchaikovsky fanned Tatyana's passion, supported musically by the obsessive sequential repetitions of a chromatic descending four-note theme.

Throughout his creative life, Tchaikovsky was usually involved in some way with dramatic music. He found his subjects in sources as varied as Shakespeare (*Hamlet*), Joan of Arc (*The Maid of Orleans*), and mythology (*Undine*). But that was not where Tchaikovsky's strengths lay. His powers lay in characterization, not in depicting the fantastic, and his lyric gifts were most effective in direct emotional expression. It was with *Eugene Onegin,* a tale of ordinary people and real passions, that Tchaikovsky achieved his greatest success and created a staple of the Russian operatic repertory.—ELIZABETH W. PATTON

Euryanthe

Composer: *Carl Maria von Weber.*

Librettist: *H. von Chezy.*

First Performance: *Vienna, Kärntnertor, 25 October 1823.*

Roles: *Euryanthe de Savoy (soprano); Eglantine de Puiset (mezzo-soprano); Count Adolar de Nevers (tenor); Count Lysiart de Forêt (baritone); King Louis VI of France (bass); Rudolph (tenor); Bertha (soprano); chorus (SATTBB).*

Euryanthe, a "grand heroic-romantic opera," as Weber called it, has an entirely implausible and fanciful libretto. Even such an admirer of the composer as Mahler made some cuts in the score when he conducted it in Vienna, with the intention of making the drama more convincing. But it now seems that the opera should be accepted on its own terms as a kind of pageant.

The time is the twelfth century. Act I is set in the French court of King Louis VI. Adolar de Nevers loves Euryanthe and sings a troubadour song in her praise, but Lysiart de Forêt cynically tells him that he can prove she lacks virtue, persuading Adolar into a bet of their respective estates pledged upon her fidelity and chastity. In the second scene we meet Euryanthe herself in the castle at Nevers, telling her guest Eglantine of her love for Adolar, revealing foolishly to Eglantine that she and Adolar share the guilty secret (which they have sworn to keep) of his sister Emma's suicide and that the ghost of Emma cannot rest until the tears of an innocent maid have been shed on her ring, lying in her tomb. Eglantine, who has also loved Adolar, is jealous and determines to obtain the ring and show him that his beloved Euryanthe has betrayed the secret. Lysiart arrives to escort Euryanthe back to court and is welcomed by her and her peasants.

In act II Lysiart quickly realizes that his bet is vain and hopeless, recognizing the goodness of Euryanthe, though in an angry aria he vents feelings of frustration and a desire to avenge himself. Learning of Eglantine's plot, he tells her that he will aid her in the betrayal of Euryanthe and that they will marry and together enjoy the possession of Adolar's lands. Scene ii reveals Adolar alone, singing rapturously of Euryanthe. When Euryanthe enters, the lovers unite in a lyrical duet. But now the king and court enter, and Lysiart announces that he has won his bet, producing the dead Emma's ring and saying that he knows the precious secret on which Euryanthe and Adolar had vowed eternal silence. The court accepts what Lysiart says, and even Adolar is now convinced that his rival has seduced her; but instead of abandoning her, he leads her away to kill her.

The last act begins in a wilderness. Adolar reproaches Euryanthe, who protests her innocence and love but is left in the desert. Alone, she awaits death, but the king and court now appear on a hunt, and she convinces the king that she is guiltless. He assures her that Adolar will be restored to her, and the act ends with an ecstatic short aria for Euryanthe in which the chorus echoes her happiness. However, at the end of the scene she collapses. Scene ii shows us Lysiart and Eglantine in possession of Nevers and its lands, and preparing for their wedding in dances and a joyful chorus. But when Adolar reappears, the peasants pledge their renewed loyalty to their former lord. In the meantime, the guilty Eglantine is visited by a vision of the dead Emma. The king arrives just in time to prevent Adolar and Lysiart from fighting. He tells them that Euryanthe is dead, and on hearing this Eglantine confesses her plot and is at once killed by Lysiart. Adolar says that his own guilt is worse, but when a revived Euryanthe is restored to him, her tears falling on Emma's ring assure us, together with smooth harmonies, that the troubled ghost of Emma may at last rest.

Euryanthe's qualities are mainly musical rather than dramatic, although several commentators have suggested that the story of Wagner's *Lohengrin* owes something to this work. The overture sets the tone by foreshadowing later music such as Adolar's aria of love in act II and the ghostly muted string harmonies associated with the dead Emma and her ring; and among the memorable numbers that follow are Adolar's troubadour-style song and Eglantine's confession of jealous anger (both in act I), Adolar's loving soliloquy in act II and some of the choruses such as the wedding chorus in act III. The opening of this final act, set in the wilderness, is remarkable for its uncannily shifting harmonies which create an eerie atmosphere.

It is such imaginative touches that make *Euryanthe* special. In 1847 Schumann called the music "noble," indeed the noblest that Weber could offer. But it was Liszt—who though not himself an opera composer knew more about it than most—who perceptively said that here was "a marvelous divination of the future shaping of the drama and the endeavour to unite with opera the whole wealth of instrumental development"—in other words that Weber, with his rich instrumental imagination, showed future composers, and Wagner above all, how to make the operatic orchestra itself part of the drama.—CHRISTOPHER HEADINGTON

Evans, (Sir) Geraint (Llewellyn)

Baritone. Born 16 February 1922, in Pontypridd, Wales. Died 20 September 1992, in Bronglais, Wales. Married: Brenda Evans Davies, 1948 (two sons). Military service in Royal Air Force, then studied with Walter Hyde at the Guildhall School of Music, with Theo Hermann in Hamburg, and with Fernando Carpi in Genoa; debut at Covent Garden as Night Watchman in Die Meistersinger, *1948; sang at Glyndebourne, 1950-61; San Francisco debut as Beckmesser, 1959; debut at Teatro alla Scala (1960) and Vienna Staatsoper (1961) as Figaro; debut at Chicago as Lem in Giannini's* The Harvest, *1961; Salzburg debut as Figaro, 1962; debut at the Metropolitan Opera as Falstaff, 1964; debut at Paris Opera as Leporello in* Don Giovanni, *1975; created Flint in* Billy Budd *(1951), Mountjoy in* Gloriana *(1953); Evadne and Antenor in Walton's* Troilus and Cressida *(1954); began to produce operas in mid-1970s.*

The compact but energetic figure of Geraint Evans became a familiar one on the British operatic stage and in many other centers during a career which lasted not much short of forty years. Like so many British singers, he began his professional life in oratorio, but his studies in Hamburg and Geneva revealed to him that his strengths lay in opera. From the start his typically Welsh vitality and confidence, together with a mercurial sparkle, made him a future star in a profession where such stardom is often reserved for tenors rather than baritones—although not always so, as the case of Tito Gobbi reminds us.

The mention of Gobbi makes it worth saying that Evans was a different kind of artist from that Italian baritone. His innate geniality, a vocal matter as well as one of physical presence, made him less than convincing in the role of Scarpia, the cruel and corrupt police chief in Puccini's *Tosca*, a role in which Gobbi excelled—but it is also fair to say that however well Evans had acted, his public might not have accepted him as a villain. Nor would they see him as a darkly brooding, wronged and vengeful Rigoletto, Verdi's court jester; and although his musicianship allowed him to sing Berg's downtrodden soldier protagonist in *Wozzeck* he may have found it hard to portray a man so weak and wanting in initiative. By contrast, his wit and bravado made him an ideal Figaro in Mozart's *Le nozze di Figaro.* After he had sung this role at Covent Garden in the 1949-50 season he became closely identified with it, and it was not surprising that Herbert von Karajan singled him out to sing it at the Teatro alla Scala, Milan, in 1960 and he sang it again at the Vienna Staatsoper.

At this time, Evans was approaching forty and at the height of his powers, having already had considerable experience. Somewhat earlier Benjamin Britten, always more interested in vocal personality than mere vocal beauty, saw Evans' warmth and essential goodness and wanted him in the title role of *Billy Budd* in its first performance in 1951 but the singer thought the music lay too high for his voice (he sometimes referred to himself as a bass-baritone). Instead he sang the sailing master Mr. Flint in what the producer Basil Coleman later called "a performance full of individuality and character." However, he did sing Mountjoy in the premiere of Britten's *Gloriana.*

It is above all for his skilful acting of genial and comedy roles that Evans remains famous. He was a playful yet believable Papageno in Mozart's *Die Zauberflöte* and a likably cynical Leporello in *Don Giovanni.* As Beckmesser in Wagner's *Die Meistersinger* he was pompous but comic, while he was a kindly American consul Sharpless in Puccini's *Madama Butterfly.* He was best of all in middle-aged roles, particularly where humor was to the fore. His portrayal of the title role in Verdi's *Falstaff* was one of his finest, and it was as Shakespeare's fat knight that he made his Metropolitan Opera debut in 1964, while in 1973 he returned to Covent Garden to play Donizetti's crusty old bachelor Don Pasquale with vigour and relish.

Evans' voice was unfailingly pleasant in tone and carried well although it was not exceptionally powerful. In later years he continued to work as a producer and operatic coach and he held some effective master classes for television, including some on Britten's *Peter Grimes,* which showed his enthusiasm and ability to communicate with young students.—CHRISTOPHER HEADINGTON

Ewing, Maria

Soprano. Born 27 March 1950, in Detroit. Married producer Peter Reginald Frederick Hall, artistic director at Glyndebourne (one daughter). Studied with Eleanor Steber at the Cleveland Institute of Music, and later with Jennie Tourel and Otto Guth; appeared at Meadowbrook Festival, 1968; debut at Ravinia Festival with Chicago Symphony Orchestra, 1973; Metropolitan Opera debut as Cherubino, 1976, where she has also sung Zerlina, Dorabella, Rosina, and Carmen, among others; debut in Pelléas et Mélisande *at Teatro alla Scala, 1976; at Glyndebourne from 1978; Covent Garden debut as Salome, 1988.*

The story of Maria Ewing's career is still unfolding with great interest and an element of surprise. Born in 1950 (in Detroit, Mich.), she has left a distinguished reputation as a mezzo-soprano behind, and is now singing roles such as Salome and Tosca.

American trained, she studied in Cleveland with two superb teachers, Jennie Tourel and Eleanor Steber, both of whom were concerned not only with singing but also with dramatic

Maria Ewing in *Carmen*,
Royal Opera, London, 1991

declamation and acting. Ewing's professional debut was at the Ravinia Chicago Symphony Summer Festival in 1973. Her Metropolitan Opera debut came three years later, as Cherubino in *Le nozze di Figaro*.

Throughout several seasons, her appearances at the Metropolitan were unfathomably spotty: Blanche in *The Dialogue of the Carmelites* alternating seasons in French and English, an extremely funny Dorabella (*Così fan tutte*) and a *Barbiere* Rosina in the same mold, an impassioned *Ariadne* Composer, and a poorly received Carmen (the production was excoriated in the New York press) that had originated at Glyndebourne. Once a protégée of Music Director James Levine, but long chafing at his refusal to cast her more extensively and more often, Ewing publicly denounced him and left the Metropolitan Opera. Her American appearances are now only with other opera companies or as soloist with symphony orchestras.

She has long been a favorite at Glyndebourne: among the roles she has sung there are Carmen and Monteverdi's Poppea (*L'incoronazione di Poppea*), both later released commercially on video tape. She has sung Zerlina and recorded Donna Elvira in different productions of *Don Giovanni*. As early in her career as 1976, she sang Mélisande at the Teatro alla Scala. Ewing has appeared at the Salzburg Festival, the Paris Opéra, Brussels, and sang a particularly successful Perichole in Geneva.

Maria Ewing is a dedicated artist whose voice can be velvety and can negotiate florid passages. She is a striking woman with a particularly sensuous face who is not afraid to look a bit daft, should the role call for it, or should her interpretation of the role require it. She can be hilarious or a spitfire. Her Salome actually removes the seventh veil, as well as the other six.

Ewing's recorded Donna Elvira has its faults, but the videos from Glyndebourne, including the *Carmen* so hated in New York, are superb. She is a Poppea, in or out of the stage bath, for whom any Caesar would leave home.

More is to be heard and seen from Maria Ewing.—BERT WECHSLER

OPERA *f*

Falstaff

Composer: *Giuseppe Verdi.*

Librettist: *Arrigo Boito (after Shakespeare, The Merry Wives of Windsor and King Henry IV).*

First Performance: *Milan, Teatro alla Scala, 9 February 1893.*

Roles: *Sir John Falstaff (baritone); Mr. Ford (baritone); Mrs. Ford (soprano); Nanetta (soprano); Dame Quickly (mezzo-contralto or contralto); Fenton (tenor); Mrs. Page (mezzo-soprano); Dr. Caius (tenor); Bardolph (tenor); Pistol (bass); Host (mute); Robin (mute); chorus (SATB).*

After the disastrous failure of his first comic opera, *Un giorno di regno* in 1840, Verdi had been naturally reluctant to try another. However, following the satisfaction of successfully completing the Shakespearean *Otello* with librettist Arrigo Boito in 1887, and, with the sense at the age of almost eighty of little to lose and the gifted services of Boito on which to draw, the composer once again turned to comedy. Boito actually suggested the subject and sent Verdi a proposed scenario in the summer of 1889: it was a study of another powerful old man, the Shakespearean character of Falstaff as he appears in the *Merry Wives of Windsor* and the *Henry IV* histories. The subject attracted Verdi immediately, possibly because it promised the composer a broad, career-summing opportunity to comment on life through the extravagant, comic alter ego of Falstaff.

The plot is as follows: Sir John Falstaff has written the same love letter to two different married women of Windsor, Alice Ford and Meg Page, in the hope of seducing them and thereby gaining access to their husbands' money as well. His comrades Bardolph and Pistol refuse to carry the letters, and instead reveal his plans to the husbands, who then plot revenge against the ridiculous fat knight. Meanwhile, the wives have compared the love letters and also plan comic revenge with the other women of Windsor, including Dame Quickly, who is engaged to set up an appointment between Sir John and Alice. In the midst of the planning, Alice's daughter

Nannetta steals moments of love with young Fenton, although her father wants her to marry his friend Dr. Caius.

In act II, Falstaff receives Dame Quickly's instructions to attend Alice at their home between two and three o'clock, when her husband will be out. He also receives a visit from Ford, in his disguise as Mr. Fontana, a man who wants to pay Falstaff to seduce Alice, after which he hopes to have an easier time doing the same. Laughing at the poor cuckolded husband in the affair, Falstaff reveals that he already has an appointment with Alice, leaving husband Ford (unaware of the women's plot) in a jealous rage. When Falstaff follows Quickly's instructions and attends Alice, Ford unexpectedly comes home to catch them in the act, but the women hide Falstaff in a laundry basket. Instead of Alice and Falstaff making love, Ford finds Nannetta and Fenton, and the servants accidentally dump Falstaff, still in the laundry basket, out the window into the stream below.

In act III, Falstaff drinks away his shame and falls for another trap when Dame Quickly tells him to meet Alice in Windsor forest at midnight, dressed as the legendary Black Hunter with horns. Falstaff meets Alice as instructed, but they are interrupted by The Queen of the Fairies and her band (Nanetta and the disguised Windsorites), who beat and insult the frightened Falstaff until he finally admits his stupidity. Now Ford proposes his plan, a wedding between his friend Caius and the Queen of the Fairies, and he in turn agrees to his wife's request of a marriage for two other disguised lovers. To Ford's chagrin, when the wedding is over and the disguises are off, the mates turn out to be Caius and Bardolph—now dressed as the Queen of the Fairies instead of Nanetta—and Nanetta and Fenton; after which Ford admits to being as big a fool as Falstaff, and all join in a final fugue, "Tutto nel mondo e burla" ("All the world's a joke").

In terms of musical language, *Falstaff* is a marvelous culmination of Verdi's career-long experimentation and evolution, beginning out of the singer-oriented, *bel canto* traditions of the early nineteenth-century, moving towards a more organic, dramatically-oriented approach to musical theater. In *Falstaff* Verdi's expressive vocal lines work together with the words, the scenography, and the orchestral accompaniment to convey the composer's dramatic ideas, very often through the lightning-quick action and conflict of duets and ensembles. The square thematic phrase groups of Verdi's middle period give way in *Falstaff* to a more flexible syntax of irregular phrase-groups, which in turn are given larger-scale coherence through a combination of thematic and motivic recurrence, and harmonic symmetry. Perhaps the best example of this flexible syntax is found in the delightfully concise scene ii of act I, where the composer makes a unified whole of amazingly disparate characters and incidents, ending in a simultaneous polyphonic reprise of mens' and womens' choruses as they plot their separate revenges against Falstaff.

Another unique aspect of *Falstaff* is Verdi's success at focusing attention on the central words of Boito's libretto with deft musico-poetic imagery and repetition. Thus in act II, scene i, for example, the ornamental flourish and repetition of Dame Quickly's line "reverenza" ("your reverence") captures both Falstaff's grandiosity and Quickly's mocking of it in a single musico-poetic image, which, in its repetitions, helps to infuse the whole scene with dramatic color and unity. Moreover, the orchestration of *Falstaff* is the most careful and evocative of Verdi's career, especially in the act III tone paintings of Falstaff's drunken trance and the sublime fairy scene in Windsor forest.

f

OPERA

Falstaff had a successful premiere run at the Teatro alla Scala with twenty-two perform-ances, a European tour, and subsequent appearances at every major opera house in the world, with translations into every modern European language. Nonetheless, audiences and critics gradually cooled to the opera, uncomfortable with the lightning-quick complexity of the musical language. Verdi made revisions for the Rome and Paris productions of April 1893 and 1894 respectively, but he gradually gave up hopes for an ultimate triumph, particularly after a difficult run in Genoa in the winter of 1894-95. Still, the conductor of that run, Arturo Toscanini, continued to program and perform *Falstaff* as often as he could during his influential career, featuring it eight seasons in a row during his reign as artistic director at La Scala in the 1920s. Today *Falstaff* is widely recognized as a work of greatness, and although it requires an unusual number of exceptional singers, among other heavy production demands, it has become a solid part of the operatic repertory.—CLAIRE DETELS

La fanciulla del West [The Girl of the West]

Composer: *Giacomo Puccini.*

Librettists: *Guelfo Civinini and Carlo Zangarini (after David Belasco, The Girl of the Golden West).*

First Performance: *New York, Metropolitan Opera, 10 December 1910.*

Roles: *Minnie (soprano); Dick Johnson/Ramerrez (tenor); Jack Rance (baritone); Nick (tenor); Ashby (bass); Sonora (baritone); Trin (tenor); Sid (baritone); Handsome (bari-tone); Harry (tenor); Joe (tenor); Happy (baritone); Larkens (bass); Billy Jackrabbit (bass); Wowkle (mezzo-soprano); Jake Wallace (baritone); Jose Castro (bass); Courier (tenor); chorus (TTBBB).*

Based on a play by David Belasco, *La fanciulla del West* has only recently been getting the attention it deserves. After a highly successful premiere at the Metropolitan Opera in New York in 1910, it quickly sank out of sight. Since the 1960s, on the other hand, the opera has been regularly revived—often for a particular soprano who wants to sing the role of Minnie—and regularly appreciated.

Act I takes place in the Polka Saloon in California during the Gold Rush. The men are miners who come to the saloon to forget their loneliness through gambling and drink. Minnie, the owner of the saloon, conducts a Bible class there for the miners, who enjoy it very much. Minnie tries to protect the miners' gold by guarding it in the saloon, but she also tries to remind them of religion and God. The miners are also hunting for one Ramerrez, a bandit and outlaw. Jack Rance, the town sheriff, is especially eager to hang Ramerrez and also to win Minnie for a wife. Ramerrez enters, disguised as Dick Johnson, and Minnie is immediately attracted to him and invites him to dinner the next night.

Act II occurs in Minnie's log cabin. Dick Johnson enters, while Jack Rance and the other miners are hunting the woods for the bandit Ramerrez. During their dinner together, Minnie and Dick seem to fall in love, but then Johnson leaves suddenly and, recognized as the bandit by the sheriff, is shot. Johnson once again enters Minnie's cabin, bleeding from his wound. Jack Rance enters, demanding possession of Dick Johnson. Minnie offers to play a hand of poker for him, and she wins, but only by cheating.

In Act III, set in a California forest, Johnson has been caught and is brought onstage by the miners to be lynched. The noose is around his neck, and just as Jack Rance orders his execution, Minnie rushes in to save him. The opera ends with Minnie and Dick riding off into the dawn, seeking a new life away from the greed of the California Gold Rush.

Aside from its thriller plot, the opera contrasts the materialism of the California Gold Rush with the spiritual qualities of Minnie, who seeks a more religious and less materialistic life. On another level, the opera is also a comic parody of Wagner's *Ring* cycle, which also contrasts material with spiritual values. The opera has some lovely arias, but its ensemble singing, use of chorus, and orchestration remain especially remarkable.—JOHN LOUIS DIGAETANI

Farinelli

Soprano castrato. Born Carlo Broschi, 24 January 1705, in Apulia. Died 15 July 1782, in Bologna. Studied with Nicolo Porpora; first public performance in 1720 in Naples, in Angelica e Medoro by Porpora; sang in Naples and Rome, 1720-34; sang in London, 1734-37; sang in Paris, 1736; sang at the court of the Spanish Kings Philip V (1700-46) and Ferdinand VI (1746-59), 1737-59; retired to Bologna in 1759.

The premiere of *La fanciulla del West*, Metropolitan Opera, New York, 1910, with Enrico Caruso (center) as Dick Johnson

Perhaps the most famous of all castrato singers, Farinelli appears in literature, letters and art to such an extent that even non-musical members of the public had heard of him well before the middle of the 18th century. At fifteen he had already made a successful debut as a soprano in an occasional cantata by his teacher Porpora, with whom he was later associated in Rome and London.

Contemporary reports on his singing emphasize particular features of his tone and technique. Giambattista Mancini, court singing-teacher in Vienna, found his voice powerful, sonorous and rich throughout its range. A supreme master of ornamentation, he exploited it to the full, ever inventing new flourishes and conceits which contributed vastly towards his reputation. His breathing seemed little short of miraculous, for he was able to take in quietly and sustain almost endlessly an air supply more than adequate for the most elaborate and taxing of arias.

His other qualities included evenness of voice, total control of the *messa di voce* (swelling out and back again on one long note), *portamento* (gliding lightly from one note to another) and a truly remarkable trill. At first an exponent of the heroic style, full of brilliance and bravura, he later cultivated a gentler aspect of his art, in which the voice became an instrument of pathos and simplicity.

It was these features which caused an abrupt change in his career, when after experiencing triumphs in Italy, France and England he set his sights on Spain, intending only a fleeting visit. In fact this lasted for almost twenty-five years, as chamber singer and first favorite at the royal court. His duties in alleviating the melancholic disposition of Philip V might be termed monotonous, since he sang the same few songs whenever the king required them, but his spare time saw him actively engaged in politics, the importation of Hungarian horses and the redirection on the river Tagus. Aside from this, he greatly influenced the music performed at the royal chapel and opera house, altogether wielding powers such as few ministers ever enjoyed. Such was his acceptance that he remained there in the reign of Ferdinand VI and continued to receive a generous pension from Charles III, who nevertheless asked him to leave in view of the political importance of dealing with Naples and France, to which Farinelli was opposed.

He lived the last twenty years of his life at a magnificent villa near Bologna where he developed his considerable gallery of paintings and played on his collection of instruments, which included the viola d'amore, harpsichord, and fortepiano. Burney and others visited him there, commenting on his courtesy and hospitality. George Sand mentions him in her novel *Consuelo,* and Voltaire obviously had him in mind when he wrote in *Candide* that the Neapolitan castrato who survived the operation could look forward to fame, fortune and political power. Among those who painted his portrait were Jacopo Amigoni and Bartolommeo Nazari, while caricatures exist by such artists as Zanetti, Ghezzi and Hogarth. Stage works about his life and adventures have been written by August Roeckel, Hermann Zumpe, and Auber, in whose operetta *La part du diable* the part of Farinelli is sung by a soprano.—DENIS STEVENS

Farrar, Geraldine

Soprano. Born 28 February 1882, in Melrose, Massachusetts. Died 11 March 1967, in Ridgefield, Connecticut. Studied voice with Mrs. John H. Long, Emma Thursby, Trabadello, Francesco Graziani, and Lilli Lehmann; studied stage presentation with Sarah Bernhardt,

David Belasco, Jules Massenet. Operatic debut as Marguerite in Faust, *Berlin Royal Opera, 1901; sang in first performance of Mascagni's* Amica, *Monte Carlo, 1905; Metropolitan Opera debut as Juliette in* Roméo et Juliette, *1906; sang in American premiere of* Ariane et Barbe-bleue, *1911; created the roles of the Goose Girl in Humperdinck's* Königskinder, *1910, and Louise in Charpentier's* Julien, *1914; twenty-nine roles at the Metropolitan Opera, 1906-22, including Butterfly, Tosca, Thaïs, Zazà, Gilda, Manon, and Carmen; frequent partner of Enrico Caruso; retired 1922; also worked in silent films and as a radio commentator.*

From 1906 until 1922, Geraldine Farrar was the Metropolitan Opera's most popular prima donna. Convinced that music must always serve the drama, she often sacrificed tonal beauty to dramatic effect. Nevertheless, Farrar was a superb singer, possessing a beautiful lyric soprano voice, as evidenced on her numerous recordings. She studied singing in Boston with Mrs. John H. Long, in New York with Emma Thursby, in Paris with Trabadello, and in Berlin with Francesco Graziani and later Lilli Lehmann. But it was in large part due to Lehmann's training that Farrar was to be noted for the evenness of her voice, vibrant forward production, and impeccable diction.

On 15 October, 1901, Farrar made her operatic debut at the Berlin Royal Opera as Gounod's Marguerite. She was an instant success. Contracts followed in Monte Carlo, Paris, Munich, Warsaw and finally New York. The beautiful and magnetic young singer opened the Metropolitan Opera's 1906/1907 season on 26 November as Gounod's Juliette. During her sixteen year reign as the Metropolitan's leading singing actress, Farrar performed 493 times in twenty-nine roles, the most popular of which were Puccini's Madama Butterfly and Tosca, Humperdinck's Goose Girl, Bizet's Carmen and Leoncavallo's Zazá.

Farrar was meticulous in the preparation of her roles. She studied Madama Butterfly with the Japanese actress, Fu-ji-Ko; Tosca with the French actress Sarah Bernhardt, for whom Victorien Sardou had written the play upon which the opera's libretto is based; Zazá with the stage version's director and producer, David Belasco; and Manon with its composer, Jules Massenet. Farrar's characterizations were highly individualized. She frequently introduced radically new staging and costuming into her performances of the standard repertory. Her acting was noted for its intensity and realism. Farrar's voice was sufficiently flexible for the rapid vocal passages of Gounod's Juliette and yet adequately powerful for the dramatic outbursts of Wagner's Elisabeth. Her vocal range was extensive, with the brilliant upper register

Geraldine Farrar as Cho-Cho-San in *Madama Butterfly,* **1907**

necessary for the high tessitura of Puccini's Madama Butterfly and the rich middle and lower registers required for Bizet's Carmen. She could produce almost limitless contrasts of tonal coloration, from the soft caressing notes of Massenet's Manon, to the raucous laughs of Dukas' la Fille. Despite a tendency to force the upper register of her voice during moments of emotional intensity, she was a brilliant vocal technician.

With petite figure, refined features, and warm sympathetic personality, Farrar was ideally suited to the romantic heroines of the Italian, French and German lyric repertoires. Visually and emotionally, she virtually embodied Gounod's Marguerite, Puccini's Madama Butterfly, and Humperdinck's Goose Girl, imbuing them with her own grace and charm. Farrar, however, was not limited to these roles alone. In later years she won acclaim for a flamboyant Carmen and Zazà as well as for a realistically brutal Dukas' la Fille. She was a versatile actress both on stage and in films.

Farrar's frequent operatic partner was the tenor Enrico Caruso. Their joint performances of *Madama Butterfly, Tosca, Manon* and *Carmen* guaranteed sold-out houses. They were undoubtedly the most dynamic duo in the annals of the Metropolitan.

Farrar's farewell performance at the Metropolitan Opera on 22 April 1922, as Zazà occasioned one of the most tumultuous demonstrations in the history of American opera. During the 1934/1935 season, she was intermission commentator for the Metropolitan Opera's Saturday afternoon broadcasts. Her first autobiography, *Geraldine Farrar: the Story of an American Singer by Herself,* was published in 1916, and her second, *Such Sweet Compulsion,* in 1938.—ELIZABETH H. NASH

Farrell, Eileen

Soprano. Born 13 February 1920, in Willimantic, Connecticut. Married: Robert V. Reagan in 1976; one son and one daughter. Studied with Merle Alcock and Eleanor McLellan; professional debut with Columbia Broadcasting Company, 1941; opera debut as Santuzza in Mascagni's Cavalleria rusticana *with the San Carlo Opera in Tampa, Florida, 1956; San Francisco debut as Leonora in Verdi's* Il trovatore, *1957; Metropolitan Opera debut as Alceste in Gluck's* Alceste, *1960; Distinguished Professor of Music at Indiana University's School of Music, 1971-80; Distinguished Professor of Music at the University of Maine, 1984.*

Eileen Farrell possessed one of the most powerful and beautifully agile dramatic soprano voices of the second half of this century. Her parents, of Irish descent, both had successful careers in vaudeville and church music. As a child, Farrell received informal but serious training in singing from her mother. Her mother also arranged for her to study with Merle Alcock, former Metropolitan Opera contralto, after Farrell's graduation from high school and a brief stint in an art school in 1939. She remained under the stern tutelage of this teacher until she began to study with Eleanor McLellan, to whom she has given almost total credit for her subsequent successes.

Farrell's breakthrough as an artist came when James Fassett of CBS made her a member of the choruses and ensembles of that broadcasting company. In 1941 she sang on a program in which she impersonated Rosa Ponselle, a soprano to whom she would be most favorably compared in future years. This appearance eventually led to the establishment of her own radio program, *Eileen Farrell Sings,* where she presented operatic arias, art songs, and popular music to eager listeners. In the late 1940s she began singing in numerous concert appearances—both as a recitalist and as a soloist with orchestra. Her close association with the New York Philharmonic allowed her to establish a record sixty-one appearances with this famed ensemble during the 1950-1951 season. She distinguished herself by singing with the Philharmonic in American premiere performances of Milhaud's *Les Choëphures* and Berg's *Wozzeck.* It was her concert performances and recordings of Wagner with this and other orchestras that encouraged fans of opera to anticipate Farrell's entering this arena. Her first appearance singing in a complete work did not come until 1955, however; and it was not a staged performance but rather a concert version of Cherubini's *Medea* by the American Opera Society in New York's Town Hall. Critics wrote lavish praise of this performance and a new era in her career appeared to have begun.

Although she appeared as Santuzza in a staged production of Mascagni's *Cavalleria rusticana* in Tampa, Florida, in 1956, it was later in that same year that she made her first appearance with a major company, the San Francisco Opera. Her performance there of Leonora in Verdi's *Il trovatore* brought her rave reviews. She made subsequent appearances in San Francisco and in Chicago with the Chicago Lyric Opera. Her entry to the New York stage occurred on Staten Island with the Richmond Opera Company production of *Il trovatore* in 1959. Her debut at the Metropolitan Opera came in Gluck's *Alceste* late in 1960 some fifteen years after Edward Johnson, then managing director of the Metropolitan, had invited her to sing. In addition to this role, Farrell appeared at the Metropolitan as Santuzza in *Cavalleria rusticana,* La Gioconda in Ponchielli's opera by the same name, Leonora in *La forza del destino,* and Maddalena in Giordano's *Andrea Chénier.* Her career began in the old opera house, but her contract was not renewed when the company moved into its new quarters at Lincoln Center.

The fact that Farrell was never heard in a staged production of Wagnerian opera is a loss to opera-goers, but Rudolf Bing, managing director of the Metropolitan opera during her tenure, did not like Wagner. Farrell did not have the professional temperament to propel herself into performing more than excerpts from these roles on recordings and in concert. Had she determined to do so, Farrell could have had an enormous impact upon the international scene even without recording, because her concert appearances in Berlin, London, Spoleto, and South America were well received.

Very frequently artists who successfully perform in opera are consumed by it and never become satiated, but this has not been the case with Farrell. Despite having the talent for such a challenging career, her priorities lay in her devotion to family life rather than to learning and performing additional roles on a regular basis. Her performing satisfaction came in other musical mediums—the dubbing of her voice in the motion picture *Interrupted Melody,* a biography of the life of Marjorie Lawrence, is but one example. Of large stature, she may have been self-conscious about her appearance on stage, but her weight apparently never detracted from her effectiveness in the roles she portrayed and would have served her well in Wagner. Her work with radio gave her a clarity of diction envied by many on the operatic stage, and her earlier association in New York with William Scheide's Bach Aria Group gave her interpretative powers an added dimension.

Farrell's singing career has been complemented by one in teaching, with positions as Distinguished Professor of Music at Indiana University from 1971-1980 and at the University of Maine, Orono, from 1984. She has also been the recipient of several honorary doctorates and other awards.—ROSE MARY OWENS

Fassbaender, Brigitte

Mezzo-soprano. Born 3 July 1939, in Berlin. Studied with her father, baritone Willi Domgraf-Fassbaender, at Nuremberg Conservatory, 1957-61; debut as Nicklausse in Les contes d'Hoffmann *at Bayerische Staatsoper, Munich, 1961; debut at Covent Garden as Octavian, 1971; debut at Salzburg as Fricka in* Das Rheingold, *1973; debut at Metropolitan Opera as Octavian, 1974; has sung in Paris, Milan and Vienna; made a Bavarian Kammersängerin, 1970.*

Opera singers, like sports figures, usually achieve fame and critical recognition while they are young. The prime years of a career generally fall between the ages of twenty-five and forty-five, and a singer with a beautiful voice may make a great impact on the musical world right away. Sadly, it also often happens that as a voice inevitably loses youthful beauty and bloom, the singer's career itself may lose some of its lustre, and critics and audiences turn their attentions elsewhere—to other, younger, artists.

Rarer and more treasurable is the performer whose artistic imagination and musicianship grows year by year, so that reputation and appreciation also increase over time. Such is the case of the remarkable German mezzo-soprano Brigitte Fassbaender. In the decades following her 1962 debut, Fassbaender has matured steadily from one of a rather large number of capable though perhaps not especially distinctive mezzos into the magnificent singing-actress that she is today. At the time of this writing, Fassbaender is just over fifty years old, yet today she is widely regarded as the finest female Lieder singer on the concert stage, and her increasingly infrequent appearances in opera are celebrated by critics and public alike.

That Fassbaender's great fame has been somewhat late in coming may be explained in part by a voice which, while highly distinctive and skillfully deployed, is not conventionally beautiful. Hers is a rather lean, reedy sound, with a pronounced vibrato; the high notes in particular are not always easily nor cleanly produced. Fassbaender cannot muster the sheer power and plush sense of amplitude of Christa Ludwig, for example, much of whose repertoire she shares. Nor has she the silvery sheen which is such an essential and delectable part of the voice of Frederica Von Stade, her near-contemporary. And, over time, Fassbaender's vocal idiosyncracies have become more exaggerated, so that now in louder musical passages the voice can take on a pronounced beat and sound threadbare and hollow; high notes frequently turn sour and have an almost "wailing" quality in the tone.

Perhaps this is a reason that Fassbaender has recorded so few of the standard operatic roles with which she was associated in her early career. Carmen, Princess Eboli in *Don Carlo*, Cherubino in *Le nozze di Figaro*, Sextus in *La clemenza di Tito*, Rosina in *Il barbiere di Siviglia*, Amneris in *Aïda*—all of these she performed with critical success yet recorded none of them. She was probably the premier Octavian in *Der Rosenkavalier* of her generation, yet this splendid portrayal too was not recorded commercially, although a much-heralded televised performance under Carlos Kleiber is available and confirms her great reputation in the part.

Not that Fassbaender made few records—quite the contrary, for from very early on recording played a major part in her career. It is instead that she turned her attention primarily to concert music and in particular the Lied, where her outstanding musicality and interpretive gifts were best displayed—and where, perhaps, her purely vocal limitations mattered less. In recitals of the songs of Schubert, Schumann, Brahms and others, Fassbaender demonstrates an actor's natural ability to color and inflect words and phrases, as well as a surprising boldness; she always shapes music in a startling and individual way, yet such is her skill that these performances never sound forced or mannered. As time has passed and Fassbaender's vocal gifts have waned, her interpretive mastery continues to grow; like Maria Callas in a much different repertoire, Fassbaender is able to capitalize on her own weaknesses, to make the odd and sometimes infirm sounds seem to be artistic choice rather than enforced limitations.

In the last several years, Fassbaender's operatic career has focused on Wagner: she has sung Fricka in *Das Rheingold* and *Die Walküre,* Waltraute in *Götterdämmerung,* Brangaene in *Tristan und Isolde,* all with great success. Much of this music is extended narrative, and to it Fassbaender brings her Lieder singer's sense of detail and word painting; rarely have these passages seemed so acted, the texts so illuminated. She has also sung to acclaim some of the character mezzo roles in the operas of Richard Strauss—in particular Klytemnestra in *Elektra* and Herodias in *Salome*—where these same gifts are even more welcome.

Fassbaender's explorations of the song repertoire continue, and with each new recital it seems that her already exalted critical reputation increases. Recently, in collaboration with pianist and composer Aribert Reimann, she has performed Schubert's *Die Winterreise,* the bleak, epic song cycle which is the Lieder singer's ultimate challenge. Few women have attempted this monumental work; fewer still have met with success. For Fassbaender it has been a triumph. She brings an operatic sense of size and scope to the twenty-four songs, vividly characterizing the narrative of the wanderer, achieving through varied tone color and an ever-attentive rhythmic sense an almost unbearable pathos as well as a remarkable feeling of perspective—for once we really sense the time and progression of the cycle. In Fassbaender's singing, and in the highly individual accompaniment of Aribert Reimann, *Die Winterreise* sounds almost modern, and rarely if ever has seemed more heartbreaking. Brigitte Fassbaender's recording of this cycle is one of the remarkable records of recent years, and a fitting document of this extraordinary vocal artist.—DAVID ANTHONY FOX

Faust

Composer: *Charles Gounod.*

Librettists: *Jules Barbier and Michel Carré (after Goethe).*

First Performance: *Paris, Théâtre-Lyrique, 19 March 1859; revised to include recitatives, Strasbourg, April 1860, and ballet, Paris, Opéra, 3 March 1869.*

Roles: *Faust (tenor); Mephistopheles (bass or bass-baritone); Marguerite (soprano); Valentine (baritone); Martha (mezzo-soprano or contralto); Siebel (mezzo-soprano or soprano); Wagner (baritone); chorus (SSAATTBB).*

Faust is arguably the most popular opera of all time. By 1934, it had been performed over 2,000 times in Paris alone, and the work was the first opera performed at the Metropolitan Opera House (New York City) on the occasion of its opening on 22 October 1883. For all of its popularity with general audiences, *Faust* has been reviled as an unliterary perversion of Goethe's *Faust,* a work so estranged from its original source that it is commonly referred to in German-speaking countries by the title *Margarete.*

Act I begins with Faust alone in his study, lamenting his loss of youth and lack of love. A chorus singing the glories of nature does nothing to rouse Faust from his spiritual torpor. Still despairing, Faust cries out for Satan to appear. Mephistopheles appears, offers to wait upon Faust in exchange for his soul, and entices Faust with a vision of Marguerite at her spinning wheel. Faust then signs the demonic pact and is transformed into a young man. The setting switches to a village fair with a festive peasant chorus performing. Valentine (Marguerite's brother), Wagner (Faust's assistant), Siebel (a youth infatuated with Marguerite), and Mephistopheles appear at the fair. The "Song of the Golden Calf," the "Chorale of the Swords," and the "Waltz and Chorus" ensue. Faust sees Marguerite and immediately falls in love with her.

Act II shows Siebel proclaiming his love for Marguerite before Faust in turn sings her praises. He leaves a box of jewels for Marguerite, who sings the "King of Thule" and "The Bijou Song." Faust meets Marguerite at an encounter arranged by Mephistopheles and Martha, Marguerite's friend and neighbor. Faust and Marguerite become enamored of one another and pledge eternal love.

Act III begins with Marguerite lamenting her loss of innocence, and a chorus informs the audience that Marguerite has been abandoned by Faust. She then sings the dolorous "Spinning-Wheel Song." Siebel arrives and tells Marguerite that he will avenge her honor. Marguerite goes to church where she is accosted by a chorus of demons. Valentine returns with his fellow soldiers and follows Siebel to the church where Marguerite is praying. Valentine engages in swordplay with Faust in order to avenge his sister's honor. Faust's sword, however, is guided by Mephistopheles, and Valentine is mortally wounded. Before dying, Valentine curses Marguerite and tells her to repent. Act IV commences with Faust and Mephistopheles' attendance at the "Walpurgis Night." Faust, however, desires to return to Marguerite, who is now in prison for the murder of her child by Faust. Faust attempts to rescue Marguerite, but she rejects his offer. Marguerite prays for forgiveness, dies, and ascends to Heaven.

Although it has become a commonplace of operatic criticism to disparage the libretto of *Faust,* in fairness to Barbier and Carré we must consider their work in relation to the unique demands of opera. Barbier and Carré only utilized portions of eight of the twenty-six scenes of Part I of Goethe's *Faust.* Those who criticize the libretto often deplore the omission of the "Prologue in Heaven," whereby Goethe altered the traditional Faust story from a personal relationship between the supplicant Faust and the procurer Mephistopheles into a cosmic "wager" between God and the Devil. Goethe's lofty conception is lost in the libretto, but there is a very important practical reason for doing so. In Goethe's *Faust* the full implications of the "Prologue in Heaven" are not realized until the final scene of Part II, some 12,000 lines later. Including Part II would not only have been too vast an undertaking, but it would also have proved to be especially problematic in view of the religious sensibilities of the potential audience. Goethe's Faust never begs for forgiveness, yet he is saved. Gretchen's rediscovery of her moral substance (and her subsequent transcendence) along with the melodramatic nature of her descent into sinfulness, were precisely those features of the Faust legend that appealed most directly to the conventional (and public) morality of the opera-going bourgeoisie.

Barbier and Carré also give increased emphasis to characters and situations which are only briefly utilized by Goethe. The most notable example is the importance given to the character Siebel. In Goethe's drama, Siebel (along with Altmayer, Brander, and Frosch) is one of Faust and Mephistopheles' student drinking companions at Auerbach's Tavern. Barbier and Carré have transformed Siebel from a drunken collegian into a youthful defender of Marguerite's honor. He is completely ineffectual but his intentions are entirely noble.

Other additions to the opera include choral sections designed to be crowd-pleasing spectacles, such as the "Song of the Golden Calf" and the "Chorale of the Swords." But this type of material is precisely what was required by Parisian audiences of the time, for it not only satisfied the audience's appetite for visual spectacle, but also provided the extravagance of heightened emotionality that is opera's métier.

Barbier and Carré also change drastically Goethe's conception of the title character. Youth and love are all that Gounod's Faust wants from life. The lofty conception of the struggle for perfection exemplified in Goethe's phrase "verweile doch, du bist so schön," the desire for a truly transcendent moment of being, is completely absent. Faust does enjoin Marguerite to linger during their duet "Il se fait tard," but the relationship between Gounod's opera and Goethe's drama has become so attenuated that the text of the duet cannot be considered as anything more than the importuning of a desperate lover.

From a musical standpoint Gounod does adhere to Goethe's preference for strophic settings of poetic texts; this is seen particularly in Gounod's settings of Goethe's song lyrics. Although Gounod does not generally employ tonalities in a unifying and consistent manner, there are a few notable exceptions; for instance, when Marguerite recalls in prison her first meeting with Faust, a short reprise of the waltz music from their initial encounter is given.

Sometimes, however, the demands of the music alter Goethe's staging intentions. In Gounod's setting of Goethe's "Garden" scene ("Seigneur Dieu"), Faust, Mephistopheles, Marguerite, and Martha at times sing simultaneously. This type of ensemble is very popular with audiences and has a long history in opera, yet it effaces the original concept of Goethe's in which two couples (Faust-Gretchen and Mephistopheles-Martha) were to stroll in a circular pattern and alternately come into view and listening range of the audience.

Ultimately, the critical dilemma that *Faust* presents, its overwhelming popularity in the face of severe and long-standing criticism, belongs more to the realm of *Rezeptionsgeschichte* than to the criticism and history of opera per se. For better or worse, Gounod's *Faust* is a permanent fixture in the operatic repertory; its beautiful arias live separate existences on the concert stage, and its affective qualities are such that authors as diverse as Ivan Turgenev (in *Faust: A Story in Nine Letters,* 1856) and Estanislao del Campo (in *Fausto,* 1866) have utilized the opera as the catalyst for profound emotional and spiritual upheavals in their literary protagonists.—WILLIAM E. GRIM

La favorite [The Favorite]

Composer: *Gaetano Donizetti.*

Librettists: *A. Royer and G. Vaëz (after Baculard d'Arnaud, Le comte de Comminges).*

First Performance: *Paris, Opéra, 2 December 1840 [revised and expanded from L'ange de Nisida, 1839].*

Roles: *Leonora di Guzman (soprano or mezzo-soprano); Alfonso XI (baritone); Fernando (tenor); Baldassare (bass); Don Gaspare (tenor); Ines (soprano); Gentleman (tenor); chorus (SATB).*

La favorite

It was with *La favorite* that the *French* Donizetti finally emerged. In this opera, the Italian composer had, in Wagner's opinion, acquired a "skill and dignity that you would search for in vain in the other works of the inexhaustible maestro." He had had an eye on Paris since 1830 or so, when Rossini's residence there and the vogue for *grand-opéra* captured the attention of all Europe. His first tentative effort had been *Marino Faliero* at the Théâtre-Italien in 1835, but this had proved an unappreciated sacrifice at the Parisian alter. In 1838 he moved to the French capital more or less for good. Operas with French texts, *La fille du régiment* and *Les martyrs* (both 1840), soon followed, but these were thoroughly Italianate in everything except language. It was *La favorite* that actually realized Donizetti's Parisian ambitions to the full. It has a four-act score, with a properly integrated ballet, replete with the processions, the scenic wonders, the adultery, cloisters, cowls and religiosity that made the Meyerbeerian exemplar so fascinating to all aspiring Italian *maestri* seeking international fame. But *La favorite* was far from being an original score; the opera showed that a really professional operatic composer could add and subtract any number of ingredients to the musical stew and still end up with a perfect assimilation of flavors. *La favorite* was cobbled together in haste from two unfinished scores, *Adelaide* of 1835, and *L'ange de Nisida* of 1839, to which were added some fragments from other operas, and six or seven new pieces.

The opera is set in Castille in 1340. Fernando, a novice in the Monastery of Santiago de Compostela, protests his love for the beautiful Leonora before his Father Superior (who is incidentally his own father). But Leonora, unbeknownst to Fernando, is the mistress of the king, Alfonso XI.

Expelled from the monastery, Fernando goes off to seek fame and fortune and the hand of Leonora. With notable cynicism, Alfonso renounces Leonora, who marries Fernando. When the nature of his misalliance is explained to him, Fernando breaks his sword before the court and returns to the cloister. After taking orders, he is horrified to discover the disguised Leonora at his knees begging forgiveness. Repentant, she dies in his arms.

To those familiar with Donizetti's Italian scores, the music of *La favorite* is at once plainer, lower-keyed, more expansive melodically, eschewing predictable transitions and cadences, and with a grander orchestration. Indeed, Donizetti employed as many Parisian mannerisms as he dared. Even the *vocalità* has been pruned: Italian in volume and sheen, it is Gallic in its choice of range. Leonora is a *falcon;* Fernando a tenor inching up into an *haut-contre* register; Alfonso is a baritone honeyed as never before. All these roles are devoid of superfluous ornament, and there are only some isolated passages of florid singing. The lyrical flow is nearly unbroken throughout. Everything is flexible, more responsive to words and setting, and arias are not allowed to obtrude out of context.

Even a relatively seamless score can have its sterling moments. *La favorite* has three great arias to its credit: Alfonso's *andante* section of the act III trio, "Pour tant d'amour"; Leonora's *air* which almost immediately follows, "O mon Fernand" (both composed especially for the opera and not derived from earlier music); and Fernando's "Ange si pur" (famous also as "Spirto gentil" in the various bowdlerized Italian versions of the opera), taken from the unfinished *Le duc d'Albe* of 1839. It is, however, the ballet music, used by Carlotta Grisi to make her sensational stage debut in Paris, that shows Donizetti at his most versatile, his most truly adaptable, relishing France and its traditions, even embracing with enthusiasm the dilution of this music with a "ballabile," at home a task given to lesser composers.—ALEXANDER WEATHERSON

Fedora

Composer: *Umberto Giordano.*

Librettist: *A. Colautti (after Sardou).*

First Performance: *Milan, Lirico, 17 November 1898.*

Roles: *Princess Fedora Romazoff (soprano); Count Loris Ipanoff (tenor); De Siriex (baritone); Countess Olga Sukarev (soprano); Grech (bass); Borov (baritone); Cirillo (baritone); Lorek (baritone); Dimitri (contralto); Desire (tenor); Little Savoyard (mezzo-soprano); Baron Rouvel (tenor); Boleslao Lazinski (mime); chorus (SATB).*

Fedora was written toward the end of the *verismo* decade opened by Mascagni's *Cavalleria rusticana,* and remained in the repertories as Giordano's most successful opera after *Andrea Chénier* (1896). It displays the composer's unerring sense of the theater and his ability to create suspense and convey strong emotions while exercising restraint and formal control over his musical resources.

Sardou's four-act play exploiting a fashionable subject (love among Russian aristocrats) is turned into a tight, action-packed, operatic thriller. The wealthy princess Fedora Romazoff is to marry count Vladimir Andreyevich, but he is wounded in a shooting and dies. Count Loris Ipanoff is named as a strong suspect and Fedora vows to pursue the murderer by herself. At a reception in her Paris house, Fedora makes Loris fall in love with her and extorts a confession of guilt from him. Loris promises to return after all the guests have departed and reveal his good reasons for the murder. Meanwhile Fedora writes a letter to the police authorities in Petersburg accusing Loris and his brother Valeriano who has been mentioned as an accomplice by a Russian agent. Loris returns and explains that Vladimir was having an affair with Loris' own wife Wanda, so his murder was in fact an act of revenge. As a proof, he shows Vladimir's love letters to Wanda; in one of them Fedora reads that her fiancé was marrying her only for her money. All this turns Loris from a murderer into her own avenger. Fedora takes him to her retreat in the Bernese Oberland. But her dilatory letter reaches the police in Petersburg and Valeriano Ipanoff is arrested. In the fortress on the Neva the waters rise overnight and drown the young prisoner. His old mother dies of a shock. The idyll in the Oberland is soon shattered by such tidings. Fedora admits her responsibility to Loris, takes poison and dies in the arms of her distressed lover.

Giordano's approach in devising a suitable musical medium was to support the quick pace of the action and enhance the well calculated theatrical effects of Sardou's drama. This resulted in a tense orchestral continuum interspersed with few recurring motifs which either identify a character (e.g., Fedora's love theme in act I) or provide dramatic depth for crucial narrative sequences (e.g., the sombre figure of the strings accompanying the account of Valeriano's drowning and his mother's death in act III). Loris and Fedora are given very short lyrical solos fully integrated in the action: e.g., Fedora's fond description of Vladimir as she contemplates his photograph in act I ("O grandi occhi lucenti di fede"—"Oh large, shining, truthful eyes"), or Loris' passionate statement "Amor ti vieta di non amar" ("Love forbids you not to love," act II); its warm, straightforward melody is then used as an orchestral interlude to distance Loris' second meeting with Fedora, and quoted at the end of the opera to counterbalance Fedora's dramatic *parlato* in her death scene.

The first two acts of *Fedora* have none of the turgid orchestration and vocal paroxysm of a Mascagni opera. The musical comment is always neat and adroit. The dialogue between Fedora and Loris (act II), in the course of which he confesses his killing of Vladimir, has no orchestral accompaniment. A simple and effective solution is adopted by Giordano to add realism and tension to the scene and avoid the conventional form of a duet. The main attraction of the reception in Fedora's Parisian residence is a young Polish pianist who plays a pseudo-Chopin nocturne. The orchestra stops and the guests listen attentively while, in the foreground, Loris and Fedora keep themselves apart from the stage audience and sing *a mezzavoce,* in a subdued tone. Their conversation is thus indirectly supported by the piano solo and terminates on the last, slightly ironic, virtuoso passage of the nocturne. A totally different treatment is chosen for the second part of the dialogue which closes the act: the description of the murder, Fedora's realization of Vladimir's deceitfulness and her response to Loris' love are built up into a duet with impassioned, soaring phrases shared by the full orchestra. In act III, Loris' vocal outbursts supported by string tremolos and the predictable, picturesque, off-stage mountain songs fall within the common practice of *verismo* composers.

Fedora ranks with other minor nineteenth-century operas for its conventional harmonic language, but it also exhibits an individual character in the dynamic, agile structures anticipating, at their best, the future techniques of film music.—MATTEO SANSONE

Fidelio, oder Die eheliche Liebe [Fidelio, or Conjugal Love]

Composer: *Ludwig van Beethoven.*

Librettist: *J. Sonnleithner (after J.N. Bouilly, Léonore ou L'amour conjugal).*

First Performance: *Vienna, Theater an der Wien, 20 November 1805; revised 1805-06, Vienna, Theater an der Wien, 29 March 1806; revised 1814, Vienna, Kärntnertor, 23 May 1814.*

Roles: *Florestan (tenor); Leonore (soprano); Don Pizarro (bass-baritone); Rocco (bass); Marzeline (soprano); Jaquino (tenor); Don Fernando (bass); chorus (SATTBB).*

Although the story of Beethoven's only completed opera is based on a 1798 French libretto by Jean-Nicolas Bouilly (set to music by Pierre Gaveaux and subsequently by two Italians, Ferdinando Paer in 1804 and Simone Mayr in 1805), Beethoven's interest in that story may be traced to his arguably larger fondness for a subcategory of operatic entertainment immensely popular with French audiences for some two decades following the French Revolution: the "rescue opera." More often than not such works were based on actual historical incident, the plot typically centering on a comparatively defenseless person who challenges the unjust use of power and ancient privilege on the part of another, one moreover who not only defies that power but triumphs over it in the end. But what saves the victim is the strength and ingenuity of another, prompted into action by the conviction of his or her personal feelings—variously love, compassion, gratitude or loyalty. Indeed, Beethoven's admiration for such operas—and for French opera in general—was very great. Of the master of the genre, Luigi Cherubini, he declared as late as 1823: "I value your works more highly than all other compositions for the theater"; elsewhere we know that Beethoven considered Cherubini the greatest living composer. As it happens, Cherubini was to a large extent the originator of the "rescue opera" as well, having brought out *Lodoïska* in 1791, *Eliza* in 1794, and *Les deux journées* in 1800, each one involving the deliverance of an individual from some injustice. And when *Lodoïska* and *Les deux journées* arrived in the Austrian capital in 1802, Beethoven, like the rest of Vienna, must have been startled by the sureness of technique and contemporary realism expressed in both works, traits worlds removed from the conservatism of most Viennese operas.

The rescue opera in general together with the story of *Fidelio* seem fated to have appealed to Beethoven, who held fast to the Enlightenment ideals of a benevolent social order devoted to spiritual and physical freedom as well as to secular reform. True to most of the details of Bouilly's libretto, Beethoven and his librettist Joseph Sonnleithner concerned themselves with an account of how the brave wife Leonore disguises herself as a man—thereby assuming the name Fidelio— in order to rescue her husband Florestan from the dungeon of the tyrant Pizaro. While the story is set in Spain, the plot nevertheless was drawn from a true event that had taken place in France during the Reign of Terror, a period of particular cruelty in the first turbulent days of the French Revolution.

Yet for all Beethoven's devotion to the subject, in the end he would see the opera through three separate versions and four different overtures over a period of ten years. (Stephan von Breuning was called in as librettist for the 1806 version, Georg Frierich Treitschke for that of 1814.) In the event, the premiere in 1805 was less than encouraging given that a great many of the composer's friends, as well as most of the aristocracy, had fled Vienna in the wake of Napoleon's occupation of the city; after only three performances the opera was withdrawn. The critics were decidedly unenthusiastic. The few friends of Beethoven's who did hear the work urged that it be severely revised, particularly the first act, which was judged too long and static. Thus Beethoven and Breuning combined acts one and two (reducing the work from the original three acts to two), condensed several numbers and removed others. The 1806 version was performed twice but again failed to find favor. Profoundly disappointed, Beethoven accused the theater management of having cheated him and angrily withdrew the work with the remark: "I don't write for the galleries!" Following an eight-year hiatus, he was induced to take up the opera a third time when he learned three singers wished to revive it. Insisting on still further changes, he wrote his third and final librettist Treitschke: "I could compose something new far more quickly than patch up the old. . . . I have to think out the entire work again. . . . This opera will win for me a martyr's crown. If you had not given yourself so much pains with it and revised everything so successfully . . . I would scarcely have been able to bring myself to it. You have thereby saved some good remainders of a ship that was stranded." The outcome, especially in the first act, was well worth the toil, a point reflected on the one hand in the success accorded the 1814 version and, on the other, in the fact that it is in this version most listeners know the opera today. (Nevertheless, as revivals have convincingly shown, the 1805 version is not the slight work it is oftentimes claimed; in fact, for many listeners—especially scholars and critics—it expresses individuality of character far better than do the subsequent versions.) If the opera (i.e., the 1814 version) has not become a repertory staple, it is not because it is musically or dramatically ineffectual (far from it), but rather because it lies outside the norm of operatic tradition. *Fidelio* is an exceptional work, one in which character delineation is secondary to the larger goal of addressing a philosophical ideal: namely faith in the nobility of the human spirit and the unswerving conviction that good will triumph over evil.

As for the various overtures Beethoven supplied for the opera, *Leonore* no. 2 was composed for the November 1805 premiere while *Leonore* no. 3 was written for the 1806 revival. The misleadingly-entitled *Leonore* no. 1 was composed in 1807 for a hoped-for yet never realized performance of the opera in Prague. The *Fidelio* overture dates from the 1814 version.

The practice of performing *Leonore* no. 3 between the two scenes of act II was inaugurated by Gustav Mahler and followed by Toscanini and Klemperer as well as many other conductors.—JAMES PARSONS

The Fiery Angel [Ognennïy angel]

Composer: *Sergei Prokofiev.*

Librettist: *Sergei Prokofiev (after V. Bryusov).*

First Performance: *act II concert performance, Paris, 14 June 1928; complete concert performance, Paris, Champs-Elysées, 25 November 1954; staged, Venice, La Fenice, 14 September 1955.*

Roles: *Ruprecht (baritone); Renata (soprano); Mephistopheles (tenor); Faust (baritone); Innkeeper (mezzo-soprano); Fortune-teller (soprano); Jacob Glock (tenor); Agrippa (tenor); The Inquisitor (bass); Laborer/Matthew (mute); Abbess (mute); Physician (mute); Innkeeper (mute); Count Heinrich (mute); chorus (SATB).*

The Fiery Angel was written in the period 1919-1923. Based on a novel by the Russian Symbolist writer Valery Bryusov (published in 1907), the opera in its original form consisted of three acts and eleven scenes, though Prokofiev subsequently altered this to five acts and seven scenes. Though some parts of the opera were performed at a concert conducted by Koussevitsky in Paris in 1929, the first complete performance did not take place until 25 November 1954, when it was given at the Théâtre des Champs-Elysées under Charles Bruck. The full stage premiere occurred at the Venice Festival in 1955.

The action of *The Fiery Angel* is set in sixteenth-century Germany. In act I Ruprecht, a wandering knight, takes a room at an inn, but is disturbed by a woman's cries in the next room. Her agitation is so great that Ruprecht breaks down the door and discovers a young girl, Renata. Ruprecht calms her and she tells him her story: since childhood she has been in love with an angel, Madiel, who encouraged her to do good deeds. When she was seventeen, however, she asked him to love her physically, upon which the angel glowed in anger but finally promised to return in human form. Renata met Count Heinrich von Otterheim, whom she believed to be the angel, and they lived together for a year before he left her. Since then she has searched for the Count without success, and she begs Ruprecht to help her find him.

In act II Renata and Ruprecht are in Cologne. Ruprecht has fallen in love with Renata, who, still infatuated with Heinrich, repels his advances. They attempt to invoke Heinrich's spirit by means of sorcery, but though three knocks are heard (the thought that it is Heinrich excites Renata to the point of hysteria), there is no one there. Ruprecht decides to consult the famous magician, Agrippa von Nettesheim, and, following a short orchestral interlude, Ruprecht finds himself in the necromancer's room. Agrippa, fearing the power of the Inquisition, will not help Ruprecht.

In act III Ruprecht returns to discover that Renata has found Heinrich, who has spurned her; she pleads with Ruprecht to avenge her. Heinrich is not Madiel, she says, but an impostor. The hapless Ruprecht fights an impossible duel with Heinrich and is severely wounded. In act IV Ruprecht has almost recovered and is living with Renata, who tells him that she must enter a convent in order to save her soul. At this point Faust and Mephistopheles enter and provide a bizarre comic scene (which is sometimes cut). In the final act Renata is in the convent, where she is accused of being possessed by the devil and brought before the Inquisitor. In a scene of indescribable frenzy, perhaps unparalleled in opera, the nuns are possessed and Renata is condemned by the Inquisitor to be burnt at the stake.

The fact that Prokofiev devoted so much time to composing *The Fiery Angel* suggests that the theme had a special fascination for him. *The Fiery Angel* is a brilliant, enigmatic, psychological study in which the theme of erotic schizophrenia is enhanced by orchestral music that is strident, dissonant, energetic and vital.—GERALD SEAMAN

La fille du régiment [The Daughter of the Regiment]

Composer: *Gaetano Donizetti.*

Librettists: *J.H.V. de Saint-Georges and J.F.A. Bayard.*

First Performance: *Paris, Opéra-Comique, 11 February 1840.*

Roles: *Marie (soprano); Tonio (tenor); Sulpice (bass); Marquise of Birkenfeld (mezzo-soprano); Duchess of Krakentorp (speaking part); Hortensio (bass); Corporal (bass); Peasant (tenor); Notary (mute); chorus (SSATTB).*

Gaetano Donizetti's *La fille du régiment* was the composer's first attempt at French comic opera. The setting, as in a number of comic operas of the period, is a Swiss village. In act I, set in the Marquise of Birkenfeld's castle, Sulpice, sergeant in the Savoyard regiment, arrives with Marie, the young *vivandière,* the "daughter of the regiment." Marie had been found in a battlefield and raised by the soldiers. Young Tonio has been following the troops out of love for Marie. He is arrested as a spy, but Marie intervenes and relates how Tonio saved her from falling over a precipice. When the regiment insists that she may only marry a grenadier, Tonio enlists and becomes one of them. Sulpice recounts that years ago a certain Captain Roberto de Birkenfeld had entrusted Marie to the soldiers before his death. Upon hearing this, the Marquise declares that Marie must be her niece and takes her off to the castle to be raised properly. Marie is sad to leave the regiment, especially Tonio.

Act II takes place in a salon in the castle. Marie is dressed so elegantly that Sulpice barely recognizes her. She enjoys the luxury of living in the castle but loathes having to learn singing and dancing. There is a hilarious singing lesson with the Marquise during which Marie rebels, preferring fanfares to the poignant love songs she is forced to learn. The Marquise has arranged for Marie to marry the Duke of Krakentorp; she has confided to Sulpice that she is actually Marie's mother. Upon hearing this, Marie decides that she must comply with her mother's wishes and marry the Duke. The Marquise, however, realizes how much Marie and Tonio love each other and allows them to be married.

At the time of the premiere of *La fille du régiment,* a number of other operas by Donizetti were playing in Paris, a situation that prompted Berlioz to write in the *Journal des débats:* "What, two major scores at the Opéra, *Les Martyrs* [a French reworking of his *Poliuto*] and *Le Duc d'Albe,* two others at the Renaissance, *Lucie* [*sic*] *di Lammermoor* and *L'Ange de Nisida,* [really his *La favorite*], two at the Opéra-Comique, *La Fille du régiment* and another whose title is unknown, and still another for the Théâtre-Italien, will have been written or transcribed in one year by the same composer! M. Donizetti seems to treat us like a conquered country; it is a veritable inva-

f

OPERA

sion. One can no longer speak of the opera houses of Paris, but only of the opera houses of M. Donizetti!" Berlioz' diatribe notwithstanding, *La fille* was a great popular success: it was given at the Opéra-Comique forty-four times in 1840, eleven in 1841, achieving a total of 1044 performances at that theater alone by the turn of the century. In France it became customary, because of the opera's lively military tunes and jingoistic nature, to perform it on Bastille Day. It has always been more popular in France than in Italy; for the Italian version that premiered at the Teatro alla Scala in December of 1840, the French text was adapted by Callisto Bassi, and Donizetti supplied recitatives to replace the spoken dialogue.

Despite its great success with the French public, *La fille* was nearly a failure at its premiere, a situation recounted by the great tenor Duprez in his *Souvenirs d'un chanteur* (*A Singer's Recollections*). Apparently there was a French cabal organized against Donizetti. Berlioz judged the opera's defects thus: "The score of *La fille du régiment* is not at all one that either composer or the public takes seriously. There is some harmony, some melody, some rhythmic effects, some instrumental and vocal combinations; it is music, if one will, but not new music. . . . One discovers the style of M. Adam next to that of M. Meyerbeer." Nor was the music of *La fille*, despite the fact that it was Donizetti's first essay in the opéra-comique genre, new in terms of his own style and output. The combination of vivacious comic musical style and *larmoyante* arias (exemplified by "Il faut partir" in this score, sung when Marie must leave the regiment to live in the castle) is a hallmark of Donizetti's comic operas, traits found as well in his Italian operas *Don Pasquale* and *L'elisir d'amore* (*The Elixir of Love*). Giuseppe Verdi was evidently greatly influenced in a general way by Donizetti's operatic style; one specific instance is surely the model of "Il faut partir" for Violetta's "Ah fors'è lui" in act I of Verdi's *La traviata*: both arias begin in F minor and, through a series of short, detached phrases, proceed to F major, at which point a broad, descending melody begins from the F at the top of the stave.

La fille du régiment has been favored by some of the most famous "nightingales" in opera history, including Jenny Lind, Henriette Sontag, Marcella Sembrich, Toti Dal Monte, and Lily Pons. Recent revivals have featured Mirella Freni and, especially successfully, Joan Sutherland, who has also recorded the role for London-Decca. It was Tonio's "Pour mon âme quel destin" with its string of high Cs that helped to bring the young Luciano Pavarotti to international prominence.—STEPHEN WILLIER

Fischer-Dieskau, Dietrich

Baritone. Born 28 May 1925, in Zehlendorf. Studied in Berlin with Georg Walter and Hermann Weissenborn; in German army; prisoner of war in Italy, 1945; concert debut in Ein deutsches Requiem, *in Freiburg, 1947; opera debut as Posa in* Don Carlos; *in Berlin, 1948, in Vienna and Munich from 1949 and Salzburg from 1952; appeared at Bayreuth, 1954-56 as Herald in* Lohengrin *(1954); Covent Garden debut as Mandryka in* Arabella, *1965; created Mittenhofer in Henze's* Elegy for Young Lovers, *Schwetzingen Festival 1961.*

While there are now a few Anglo-Saxon critics/record reviewers who are hesitant to grant Dietrich Fischer-Dieskau even the status of one of the greatest Lieder singers of the twentieth century, there are still more, it seems, who are wary of ranking him among the most distinguished operatic baritones of the century. The reasons for this prejudice in the USA and Great Britain are varied, but stem possibly from his relatively rare operatic appearances on

British stages and his complete absence from American ones. His operatic performances have therefore to be judged from the limited cultural experience of his many recordings; only the Germanic countries have seen him in countless stage productions.

It has always been the custom in German-speaking countries for Lieder singers also to appear regularly in opera. Frieda Hempel, Lotte Lehmann, Hans Hotter, Heinrich Schlusnus, Elisabeth Schumann, Elisabeth Schwarzkopf and many others enjoyed great reputations in the opera houses of the world as well as in the concert halls. Dietrich Fischer-Dieskau is no exception; from his first operatic appearance as Posa in Verdi's *Don Carlos* in the Berlin Städtische Oper on 18 November 1948, he has been a regular member of the great opera houses in Berlin, Munich and Vienna, and has sung all the leading baritone roles in the repertoire. Britain has seen him only as the Count in *Le nozze di Figaro,* as Mandryka in Strauss' *Arabella,* and as a very controversial Falstaff at Covent Garden in February 1967. Although some critics have since written that the faults (mainly the overdone "stage business") in that *Falstaff* production were to be laid at the door of the producer rather than at that of the singer, Fischer-Dieskau was sufficiently disgusted by the views of the critics to wish never to return to Covent Garden—in opera, at any rate. A recording of *Falstaff* (January 1967) had been made during the six performances in Vienna where Fischer-Dieskau had been compared to "the Falstaff of the century," Mariano Stabile. It is a performance full of fire, wit and pathos crowned by a superb rendition of Falstaff's great "Ehi! Taverniere!" monologue at the beginning of Act III which proves that Sir John was indeed *the* creative spirit of the opera: "L'arguzia mia crea l'arguzia degli altri" ("My cleverness creates the cleverness of others"). Many felt that the Covent Garden performance retained that vocal magnificence.

Of his many other Verdian performances, I should select his 1970 Italian version of *Macbeth,* where his ability to depict the text and his knowledge of Italian gained from his two years' imprisonment in Bologna during 1945-1947 enabled him to create a chilling interpretation of the great Scottish rogue. All his skills as a great interpreter of Lieder went into the moving performance of Macbeth's last aria and, in particular, of that melting phrase "sol la bestemmia, ahi lasso! la nenia tua sarà" ("Blasphemy alone, alas, shall be your epitaph!") where Fischer-Dieskau's celebrated *mezza voce* served to underline his oft-repeated reminder that Verdi worshipped Schubert and his heartfelt melodies "based on rhythm."

As in the Britain of Carl Rosa's and Sadler's Wells' times, opera in German-speaking countries is often given in the native tongue, and there are many recordings of Italian operas in German, unknown to the largely non-German speaking Anglo-American public, which feature Dietrich Fischer-Dieskau. He has also recorded almost every lyric baritone role (and some *Heldenbariton* ones as well) in the Wagner repertoire. German speakers rate highly his Wotan for Karajan's *Rheingold* (1968), and I was always most impressed by the majesty of the performance which Karajan himself (in a private letter to the singer) felt had "the fascination of a late Renaissance prince." The re-issue of the celebrated *Tristan und Isolde* recording of 1952, with Flagstad and Suthaus, conducted by Furtwängler, allowed the younger record reviewers who had grown up to accept Fischer-Dieskau as an aging wonder now a little *passé* to marvel at his Kurwenal which, as one of them wrote, "is what Wagner singing is all about."

The major recent criticism of Fischer-Dieskau concerned his practice of highlighting specific words and the overly forceful, emphatic delivery of much of his singing. A great singer, however, lives a role whether in opera or in song and will emphasize a word with special meaning for him or her as one would do in speech. ("Oh, how *lovely . . .*!). Listen for example to

f

OPERA

Fischer-Dieskau's caressing of the erotic "gioiello mio" phrase in the introduction to his duet with Zerlina in *Don Giovanni*. The second objection was dealt with by Suvi Raj Grubb in his book *Music on Record,* where he describes how difficult Fischer-Dieskau's voice is to record and to balance because of its enormous dynamic range, "much greater than that of any other singer I have recorded" (p. 106). I am sure that this is the major cause of many of the reviewers' complaints since one is not aware of this "fault" in concert hall or opera house. The voice is simply an enormous one, with the range of a Titta Ruffo.

Is *all* perfection then? By no means; perfection is unattainable. Some of Fischer-Dieskau's rather weak notes at the top and bottom of the range have always disappointed his admirers, and his willingness to record almost every genre of music, his unwillingness to say "No" to an agent or a record-producer, has led him into recording music unsuited to his particular, if impressively versatile, genius. One thinks of roles such as Handel's *Giulio Cesare* or Golaud in Debussy's *Pelléas et Mélisande,* where the voice and the delivery do not seem to be quite right.

However, when one looks back over a career now spanning over forty years and listens, for example, to Fischer-Dieskau's matchless Count in *Le nozze di Figaro,* his Mandryka in *Arabella,* his Rigoletto, his Amfortas in *Parsifal,* his magisterial Hans Sachs in *Die Meistersinger,* recorded at the age of fifty, among his countless operatic roles, then one is inclined to wonder, with John Steane, whether Fischer-Dieskau has ever sung anything "without shedding some new light on it." Such a thought alone surely places a singer among the greatest artists of his day.—KENNETH WHITTON

Flagstad, Kirsten

Soprano. Born 12 July 1895, in Hamar. Died 7 December 1962, in Oslo. Studied voice with her mother and with Ellen Schytte-Jacobsen in Christiana; debut as Nuri in d'Albert's Tiefland, Oslo, 1913; sang throughout Scandinavia until 1933, when she began to sing minor roles at Bayreuth; first major success as Sieglinde, Bayreuth, 1934; Metropolitan Opera debut as same, 1935; Covent Garden debut as Isolde, 1936; guest appearances at San Francisco Opera, 1935-38, and Chicago Opera, 1937; returned to Nazi-occupied homeland to be with her husband, 1941; resumed her career after the war; sang Leonore and Isolde at Metropolitan Opera, 1951; director of the Norwegian Opera, Oslo, 1958-60.

Kirsten Flagstad's career took her to a position as one of the greatest Wagnerian sopranos of the mid-20th century. But it started slowly, and it was some twenty years from her Oslo debut at eighteen in d'Albert's verismo opera *Tiefland* (when she played the young girl Nuri) to her first Isolde in *Tristan und Isolde* in Oslo in 1932. However, during these years she gained vast stage experience in operetta, musical comedy and even revues, though singing nearly always in Norwegian. But as Isolde she sang in German, and her fellow Scandinavian Ellen Gulbranson, Bayreuth's regular Brünnhilde in Wagner's *Ring* cycle from 1897-1914, heard her and recognized her potential, recommending her to the management at Bayreuth. Flagstad was now approaching forty and had recently married for the second time, and she had even contemplated retirement from active singing. But now instead she found herself catapulted into a new start in different surroundings, and small roles at Bayreuth during 1933 and 1934 led to her going to the New York Metropolitan Opera in the following year to sing Sieglinde in *Die Walküre* and Isolde in *Tristan und Isolde*. From now on, she was in demand internationally. Soon she added

Brünnhilde to her Wagner roles, singing this one as well as those of Isolde and Senta in *Der fliegende Holländer* at Covent Garden in London.

Kirsten Flagstad as Brünnhilde in *Die Walküre* **(Culver Pictures)**

The Second World War found Flagstad in the United States, but her return to occupied Norway in 1941 and her husband's arrest as a collaborator after the end of the war cast a temporary cloud over her career, though this resumed in the late 1940s when she sang a memorable Isolde at Covent Garden and she continued to please British and American audiences in the major Wagnerian soprano roles (including now the enchantress Kundry in *Parsifal*) until her last appearance as Isolde at the age of fifty-five in 1951. Her British following also gave her an opportunity in new repertory when she was offered the chance to play Dido, the tragic Queen of Carthage in Purcell's opera *Dido and Aeneas,* in a production that took place in the small Mermaid Theatre in London, which was directed by the actor-producer Bernard Miles. This is traditionally a somewhat mature role (though it is unclear why this should be so) and she brought to it a tremendous presence and pathos, not least in the final Lament over a ground bass which crowns her role and which precedes the final suicide. It was as Dido that she made her farewell to the operatic stage in 1953. However, she continued to sing occasionally in concerts, for example in the songs of Grieg and Sibelius, and went on to direct the Norwegian State Opera. She also recorded *Dido and Aeneas* and a Wagner role new to her, that of the god Wotan's wife Fricka in *Das Rheingold,* the first opera in the *Ring* tetralogy.

Beside the Wagner roles already mentioned, Flagstad's career also included Elsa in *Lohengrin* and Elizabeth in *Tannhäuser.* But her powerful and splendidly focused voice made her suited above all to heroic roles, and another such by Beethoven was that of Leonore (disguised as the young man Fidelio) in *Fidelio.* Unfortunately, she did not record the complete role of Brünnhilde, but her recordings include a famous performance as Isolde, opposite Ludwig Suthaus as Tristan, that was conducted by Wilhelm Furtwängler. Here she is heard at her best and most characteristic, as a Northern princess of great dignity and depth of feeling, with a voice of remarkable and inimitable natural beauty which stood up magnificently to the demands Wagner placed upon it.—CHRISTOPHER HEADINGTON

Der fliegende Holländer [The Flying Dutchman]

Composer: *Richard Wagner.*

Librettist: *Richard Wagner (after Heine, Aus den Memoiren des Herrn von Schnabelewopski).*

First Performance: *Dresden, Königliches Hoftheater, 2 January 1843; revised, 1846; revised, 1852; revised, 1860.*

Roles: *Senta (soprano); The Dutchman (baritone); Daland (bass); Erik (tenor); A Steersman (tenor); Mary (mezzo-soprano); chorus (SSAATTBB).*

Cursed by Satan, the Dutchman is doomed to sail the seas forever, unless he can find a woman who will be faithful to him until death. He hopes to have found his redeemer in Senta, who agrees to marry him out of compassion. Overhearing and misunderstanding a conversation between Senta and Erik, the Dutchman assumes she has been unfaithful and sets sail. Senta declares her loyalty and leaps into the sea; the Dutchman's ship sinks with all hands. The transfigured forms of Senta and the Dutchman rise from the sea and soar upward.

Der fliegende Holländer revolves around three central elements: cosmic conflict, redemption, and transfiguration. The dramatic/musical relevance of these concepts is intimately connected with the opera's compositional history.

In early May 1850, Wagner drafted a prose scenario for a one-act opera based upon the legend of the Flying Dutchman. Hoping for a commission from the Paris Opéra, he submitted this draft to the librettist Eugène Scribe. Sometime before the end of July, he composed three numbers from the projected opera for a Paris audition: the chorus of Norwegian (originally Scottish) sailors, the "phantom chorus" of the Dutchman's crew, and Senta's ballad. Wagner did not require a libretto in order to give musical expression to three of the drama's crucial elements: the world of everyday reality (sailor's chorus), the realm of the supernatural (phantom chorus), and redemption through eternal fidelity (Senta's ballad). Apparently he had conceived the dramatic argument in essentially musical terms from the very beginning.

When he realized that the Opéra was not about to offer him a contract, Wagner sold his scenario to the Opéra's director, Léon Pillet, but not before he had finished his own libretto. He

Der fliegende Höllander, Städtische Oper, Berlin, 1933

then composed two more numbers—the Steersman's Song and the Spinning Chorus—each of which depicts yet another facet of the "normal" everyday world. These five songs, all cast in three-verse strophic form, lie at the heart of the opera's musical structure, and form the basis of the following discussion.

In act I, Daland's steersman whiles away his watch by singing the first of the opera's five strophic songs, about a sailor returning home to his sweetheart. He sings the first verse to a tune whose regular phraseology and melodic symmetry evoke the mundane, everyday world. Beginning the second verse, he gradually succumbs to drowsiness; the orchestra fills in his involuntary pauses with agitated storm music signaling the arrival of the Dutchman's ship. Thus Wagner musically depicts the interpenetration of the normal world by the spectral realm. After the Dutchman's apocalyptic aria and his buffa-like duet with Daland, the sailors round out the act by vigorously declaiming the long-awaited third verse of the Steersman's Song—now revealed as a trite parody of the Dutchman's tremendous quest for salvation.

The Spinning Chorus which opens act II is a female counterpart to the Steersman's Song: encouraged by Mary, the girls sing about the return of their seafaring lovers. Unable to bear this "stupid song" any longer, Senta angrily interrupts its third verse to sing the ballad of the Flying Dutchman, whose brooding portrait hangs on the wall. By doing this, Daland's daughter verbally and musically summons the spectral, storm-tossed world into her father's comfortable sitting room. Each of Senta's three verses begins in a rather agitated manner but concludes with a lyrical theme expressing the promise of redemption. At the end of the third verse, the maidens alone sing this tune as Senta sinks back exhausted. Suddenly inspired, the girl leaps to her feet and interrupts her own song to declare, in a passionate variant of the "Redemption" theme, "Let me be the one who through her faith redeems thee!" Although Senta has presumably sung the ballad before, this represents the first time she has attempted to catapult herself into the legend, to become a part of the story she unfolds.

At the opening of act III, the drama's cosmic conflict erupts into a duel of song between the Norwegian sailors and the Dutchman's crew. After the former have sung the first verse of a rollicking C major tune, their girlfriends appear bearing refreshments, and the merrymakers comment upon the unnatural silence of the Dutch ship. To calm their jitters, the sailors sing verse two above an increasingly restless accompaniment. Suddenly the Dutchmen interrupt and roar out two verses of their own grisly song, in a demonic b minor. Both crews sing their third verses simultaneously, C major and b minor fighting for supremacy. This tremendous tonal conflict is finally resolved in favor of b minor, as the terrified Norwegians quit the deck and the Dutchmen burst into shrill laughter. The demonic element has triumphed.

The catastrophe follows swiftly. After Senta leaps into the sea and the Dutchman's ship sinks, the variant of the "Redemption" theme with which Senta interrupted her own ballad reappears in D major, followed (in the original version of the opera) by a sonorous major-mode rendition of the Dutchman's motive. However, the final tableau—the transfigured forms of Senta and the Dutchman rising from the sea in close embrace—at first found no counterpart in the music.

In 1860, Wagner changed the ending of the overture for a Paris concert. Originally the overture ended like the opera, with no hint of transfiguration. However, by 1860 Wagner had composed *Tristan und Isolde,* whose transfigured lovers transcend the physical world and become one with each other and the universe. He replaced the ending of the *Holländer* overture with an ecstatic development of the "Redemption-Variant"; its rising sequences and "celestial" orchestration express the couple's transcendence of both the natural and the supernatural world. He then grafted the final portion of this ending, with its Tristanesque plagal cadence, onto the end of act III, whereby the concept of transfiguration—previously present in the stage directions alone—finally received full musical expression.

Although some critics have denigrated *Der fliegende Holländer,* recent scholarship has begun to reveal what a fascinating, multifaceted work it really is. Of all the composer's pre-*Rheingold* operas, this one alone contains a dramatic-musical expression of cosmic conflict, redemption, transfiguration, and transcendence—elements Wagner was later to work out on a colossal scale in *Der Ring des Nibelungen.*—WARREN DARCY

Flotow, Friedrich

Composer. Born 27 April 1813, in Teutendorf. Died 24 January 1883, in Darmstadt. In the choir at Gustrow; studied piano with J.P. Pixis and composition with Reicha at the Paris Conservatory, 1829; collaborations with various composers on a number of operas produced in Paris, 1836-39; first big success Alessandro Stradella, *1844; intendant at the grand ducal court theater in Schwerin, 1855-63; in Austria and then Germany, 1873.*

Operas *Pierre et Cathérine,* J.H. Vernoy de Saint-Georges, 1831-32; performed in German, Ludwigslust and Schwerin, 1835; *Die Bergknappen,* Theodor Körner, c. 1833; *Alfred der Grosse.* Theodore Körner, c. 1833; *Rob Roy,* P. Duport and Pierre Jean Baptiste Choudard Desforges (after Walter Scott), Paris, Royaument Castle, September 1836; *Sérafine,* Pierre Jean Baptiste Choudard Desforges (after Soulier), Royaumont Castle, 30 October 1836; *Alice,* Comte de Sussy and D. de Laperriere, Paris, Hôtel de Castellane, 8 April 1837; *La lettre du préfet,* E. Bergounioux, Paris, Salon Gressler, 1837; revised 1868; *Le comte de Saint-Mégrin* (*La duchesse de Guise*), F. and C. de la Bouillerie (after Dumas, *Henri III et sa cour*), Royaumont Castle, 10 June 1838; revised as *Le duc de Guise,* Paris, Ventadour, 3 April 1840; German translation, Schwerin, 24 February 1841; *Le naufrage de la Méduse* (with Grisar), Hippolyte and Théodore Cogniard, Paris, Théâtre de la Renaissance, 31 May 1839; revised and enlarged as *Die Matrosen,* Hamburg, 23 December 1845; *L'esclave de Camoëns,* J.H. Vernoy de Saint-Georges, Paris, Opéra-Comique, 1 December 1843; second version: *Indra, das Schlangemädchen,* Gustav Gans zu Putlitz, Vienna, 18 December 1852; third version: *Alma, L'incantrice* (*L'enchanteresse*), J.H. Vernoy de Saint-Georges, Paris, Théâtre-Italien, 6 April 1878; fourth version: *Die Hexe,* 1879; *Alessandro Stradella,* F.W. Riese, Hamburg, Stadttheater, 30 December 1844 [recomposed from incidental music to the play by P.A.A. Pittaud de Forges and P. Duport]; *L'âme en peine* (*Der Förster*) (*Leoline*), J.H. Vernoy de Saint-Georges, Paris, Opéra, 29 June 1846; *Martha, oder, Der Markt zu Richmond,* F.W. Riese (after the Ballet, *Lady Harriette*), Vienna, Kärntnertor, 25 November 1847; *Sophia Katharina, oder Die Grossfürstin,* C. Birch-Pfeiffen, Berlin, Hofoper, 19 November 1850; *Rübezahl,* Gustav Gans zu Putlitz, Retzien, 13 August 1852 (private performance); Frankfurt am Main, 26 November 1853; *Albin, oder Der Pflegesohn,* Salomon H. Mosenthal (after *Les deux savoyards*), Vienna, Kärntnertor, 12 February 1856; revised as *Der Müller von Meran,* Königsberg, 1859, Gotha, 15 January 1860; *Herzog Johann Albrecht von Mecklenburg, oder Andreas Mylius,* Hobein, Schwerin, 27 May 1857; *Pianella,* Emil Pohl (after Federico, *La serva padrona*). Schwerin. 27 December 1857; *La veuve Grapin,* P.A.A. Pittaud de Forges, Paris, Théâtre des Bouffes-Parisiens, 21 September 1859;

performed in German, Vienna, Theater am Franz-Josephs-Kai, 1 June 1861; *Naida* (*Le vannier*) translated into Russian from J.H. Vernoy de Saint-Georges and Léon Hálevy, St. Petersburg, 11 December 1865; *La châtelaine* (*Der Märchensucher*), M.A. Grandjean, Vienna, Karl Theater, September 1865; revised K. Treumann as *Das Burgfräulein*. *Zilda, ou La nuit des dupes,* J.H. Vernoy de Saint-Georges, Henri Charles Chivot, and A. Duru, Paris, Opéra-Comique, 28 May 1866; *Am Runenstein,* Richard Genée, Prague, 13 April 1868; *Die Musikanten* (*La Jeunesse de Mozart*), Richard Genée, Mannheim, 19 June 1887; *L'ombre,* J.H. Vernoy de Saint-Georges and Adolphe de Leuven, Paris, Opéra-Comique, 7 July 1870; German translation as *Sein Schatten,* Vienna, Theater an der Wien, 10 November 1871; *La fleur de Harlem,* J.H. Vernoy de Saint-Georges (after Dumas); in Italian as *Il fiore di Harlem,* Turin, 18 November 1876; *Rosellana,* c. 1878, Achille de Lauzières de Thémines [unfinished]; *Sakuntala,* c. 1878-81 C. d'Ormeville (after Kalidasa).

Although Flotow was born in Mecklenberg, and composed his two most famous works, *Martha* and *Alessandro Stradella,* to German libretti, it would be a mistake to judge him as a "German" composer. Of an ancient aristocratic family, he came to Paris at the age of sixteen to study under Anton Reicha, whose other pupils would include Berlioz, Gounod, and César Franck. Except for a short time in 1830 when he returned home in the aftermath of the 1830 Revolution against Charles X, Flotow was seldom far from Paris for almost two decades. He knew the foremost French composers of the day, Auber, Cherubini, and Halévy, as well as the two Germans who redefined French theater music in the mid-19th century, Meyerbeer and Offenbach.

Most of Flotow's earliest works were written for, and in the style preferred by, the salons of the rich and titled, where talented amateurs performed them. His stylistic influences were not Beethoven, Weber, and Marschner, but Boieldieu, Auber, and Cherubini. As his two best-known operas show, he was not unmindful of the tradition within which his German contemporaries Lortzing and Nicolai were writing successfully, but musically his allegiance was to France (and, to a lesser extent, to the Rossinian influence from Paris).

Alessandro Stradella, Flotow's first international success, reveals both his strengths and his weaknesses. Like the later *Martha,* it contains one unforgettable aria, the eponymous tenor's "Jungfrau Maria," a prayer he has composed to the Virgin, the performance of which saves him from assassins. Otherwise, the score demonstrates Flotow's capacity to produce facile melody, his thoroughly professional orchestral writing, and his unevenness of invention. Some of the arias and ensembles, notably the quartet "Italia, mein Vaterland," have an undeniable charm, but they are linked by other numbers which, though pleasant, possess little individuality.

With *Martha,* an expansion of music he had previously composed for a cooperative ballet, Flotow found a subject which inspired him to compose his most consistently inventive score. Using a succession of finely-wrought duets and intricate ensembles punctuated only three times by solo arias (the tenor's "Ach so

Friedrich von Flotow

fromm," Lady Harriet's "The Last Rose of Summer," and Plunkett's drinking song), he paces the work masterfully, leading up to the third act finale, its main melody heard earlier in the conclusion of the overture, "Mag der Himmel euch vergeben."

His international reputation assured in his thirty-fifth year, Flotow continued to write for both the German and French stages until his death. Whereas his contemporary Meyerbeer explored the dramatic possibilities of the orchestra as protagonist, and massive changes were being wrought by Wagner and Verdi, Flotow was content to reflect the conservative simplicity which had served him so well. There are no neglected masterpieces among his forgotten works, though *L'âme en peine* (1846), which contains the first use of the "Ach so fromm" melody, the once highly popular *La veuve Grapin* (1859), and his last success, *L'ombre* (1870), deserve an occasional hearing. The latter especially is much superior overall to the overrated (at least at one time) *Stradella,* and is an outstanding example, perhaps the last of its genre, of the kind of opéra-comique produced by Auber and his school.—WILLIAM J. COLLINS

Floyd, Carlisle

Composer. Born 11 June 1926, in Latta, South Carolina. Studied composition with Ernst Bacon at Syracuse University, A.B. 1946, M.A. 1949; private lessons with Rudolf Firkusny and Sidney Foster; on the staff of the School of Music, Florida State University at Tallahassee, 1947; professor of music at the University of Houston, 1976; his opera Susannah *received the New York Music Critics Circle Award as the best opera of 1956.*

Operas *Slow Dusk,* Floyd, 1949, Syracuse, New York, May 1949; *The Fugitives,* Floyd, 1951, Tallahassee, Florida, 1951; *Susannah,* Floyd, 1954, Tallahassee, Florida, 24 February 1955; *Wuthering Heights,* Floyd (after Brontë), 1958, Santa Fe, 16 July 1958; revised, 1959; *The Passion of Jonathan Wade,* Floyd, 1962, New York, 11 October 1962; *The Sojourner and Mollie Sinclair,* Floyd, 1963, Raleigh, North Carolina, 2 December 1963; *Markheim,* Floyd (after Stevenson), 1966, New Orleans, 31 March 1966; *Of Mice and Men,* Floyd (after Steinbeck), 1969, Seattle, Washington, 22 January 1970; *Bilby's Doll,* Floyd (after E. Forbes, *A Mirror for Witches*), 1976, Houston, 29 February 1976; *Willie Stark,* Floyd (after R.P. Warren, *All the King's Men*), 1981, Houston, 24 April 1981.

Carlisle Floyd's career spans over thirty years and includes nine full length productions, yet his place in the history of American opera remains unclear. Despite several critical successes, including *Susannah,* which won the New York Critics Circle Award in 1956, he has not attained the status level of other prominent American composers. As Andrew Porter has noted (*New Yorker* 5 April 1982), "If there is a national repertory to be discerned here, it is—at any rate, on the far shores of the Hudson—founded largely on Floyd's work. . . . [Yet] there is something about Floyd's operas that pleases the public but often inhibits simple, unreserved praise from critics." Though Floyd's own librettos often excel in the ability to convey high drama, according to most critics the composer has never succeeded in developing a bold music language which sustains its own internal development and momentum.

At their best, Floyd's works offer a compelling and complete drama centered around highly charged scenes. He focuses on American themes, and the plots usually pit an individualistic protagonist against society's norms with tragic results. The subject matter may often relate directly to profound conflicts within contemporary America: *The Passion of Jonathan Wade,* in which a Northerner works in the South during Reconstruction, appeared at the onset of the civil rights movement in the early 1960s. The music is often eclectic in style and combines traditions and techniques such as American folk music, Wagnerian leitmotif effects, Puccini's lyrical sense, and sometimes even Broadway. Winthrop Sargeant (*New Yorker* 27 October 1956) wrote of *Susannah:* "This style owes a great deal to the homely idioms of real American religious and folk music, but Mr. Floyd's work is by no means the dreary essay in musical ethnology that American 'folk operas' have usually turned out to be. The language he employs in telling a story that moves forward with enthralling intensity is clearly his own, and he uses it with the intellectual control and the theatrical flair that bespeak both the serious composer and the born musical dramatist."

Some critics, however, find that this eclecticism leads Floyd astray. Irving Kolodin, who was enthusiastic about *Susannah* as well, expressed disappointment with *The Passion of Jonathan Wade:* "My conclusion is that Floyd is conducting a search for identity which has led him into a kind of musical Everglades. What he needs is the vantage point of perspective from which one can chart the way out of such dilemmas, artistic as well as geographic." (*Saturday Review* 27 October 1962).

Floyd's operas pose aesthetic problems beyond the merely technical. In his writings, Floyd displays a greater concern over the libretto than the music. He states (*Opera News* 10 November 1962) that "Perhaps the greatest advantage enjoyed by a composer-librettist is his tremendously increased awareness of dramatic elements, a general sharpening of his theatrical acuity. By necessity he is forced to think in dramatic terms, both in structure and content." Concerning *Wuthering Heights,* (*New York Times* 13 July 1958) "I have tried to tackle head-on with this opera a basic aesthetic difficulty that composing music for this medium presents us with. That is, I have tried to strike a balance between two polarities, symphonically conceived music on the one hand that is essentially theatrical effect on the other." Not surprisingly, Floyd has also been directly involved in the stage direction. As Frank Merkling of *Opera News* (1 December 1962) has perceptively commented: "*The Passion of Jonathan Wade . . .* suggests that there are two Carlisle Floyds. One writes plays; the other wants to compose stirring operas."

Critics echo Floyd's conception of music as "theatrical effect", but often find the results to be less than satisfying. Thus, Andrew Porter has written of *Susannah* that "most of the time the music is an accompaniment to the drama, not really dramatic in itself. To justify that charge, I'd point (as I did when writing about *Bilby's Doll*) to the reluctance of the harmonies to move, to impel and not merely follow the drama; and also to the way that Floyd, when he gets hold of a good idea, works it out thoroughly, doggedly, without the flights of imaginative fancy that suggest the music has taken on a life of its own. . . . . *Susannah* depends a lot on its acting. In elaborate rubrics, Floyd spells out what his music alone does not convey."

This charge has been repeated with *Of Mice and Men,* adapted from the Steinbeck novel. Robert Commanday (*New York Times* 1 February 1970) found that "Floyd's orchestral score does not develop the deeper more powerful qualities that should comment on the drama; this is still opera dominated by text and vocal line—a musical play. It's as if the prose and melody had been set and the orchestral music created as accompaniment." And Phillip Gainsley (*Opera News* 12 December 1970) specifically pointed out how "Part of the blame falls on the lack of melody and the repetition of phrases in the score. Crescendoes and sudden changes in tempo, even in the more subdued scenes tend to vitiate the compassion and sensitivity of the libretto. Thus, whether a particular work succeeds, depends seemingly on one's critical view point, and the extent to which the music integrates into the drama, rather than perhaps the other way around."

The issue recurred with Floyd's last full length score *Willie Stark*. Here, Floyd employs long passages of dialogue over a small thirty-six piece Broadway-style orchestra, and at the premiere preferred lightly amplified singers to a full voice production. The most vitriolic response came from Donal Henehan of the *New York Times:* "Mr. Floyd's work . . . retold Mr. Warren's many-leveled tale in a one-dimensional Broadway musical style, which relied for most of its appeal on period flavor and tricky staging ideas. The music was pushed into the background rather effectively." Not all critics disliked the overall effect, however, and Andrew Porter felt it to be "a dexterous and accomplished piece," noting that "*Willie Stark* is a political opera that picks up some threads from Marc Blitzstein's political operas, some of its dramaturgy (I think) from *Evita,* and some of its musical manners from Broadway ballads. It is a bold and adventurous work. Over the air . . . it seemed to me brilliant."

Though critics have yet to agree on Floyd's work, *Susannah* and *Of Mice and Men* continue to be performed and remain among the most successful and popular of American operas. Despite some aesthetic confusion and the lack of consistent critical success, "Floyd's music speaks to the contemporary American operagoer" (Frank Warnke, *Opera News* 14 March 1970).—DAVID PACUN

La forza del destino [The Force of Destiny]

Composer: *Giuseppe Verdi.*

Librettist: *Francesco Maria Piave (after Angelo Pérez de Saavedra, Don Alvaro, o La fuerze de Sino, and Schiller, Wallensteins Lager).*

First Performance: *St Petersburg, Imperial Theater, 10 November 1862; revised, libretto by A. Ghislanzoni, Milan, Teatro alla Scala, 27 February 1869.*

Roles: *Leonora (soprano); Don Alviro (tenor); Don Carlo (baritone); Padre Guardiano (bass); Preziosilla (mezzo-soprano); Curra (soprano); Trabucco (tenor); Fra Melitone (baritone); Alcalde (bass); Surgeon (baritone); Marquis di Calatrava (bass); chorus (SSSATTTBBB).*

With the sole exception of *Don Carlos,* none of Verdi's operas is on the epic scale of *La forza del destino.* The action takes place over an indeterminate number of years in both Spain and Italy and requires a large cast. Unlike several operas of middle period Verdi, such as *La traviata, Rigoletto* and *Luisa Miller, Forza* is not really about people. The theme of the opera is fate, which determines the lives of the three major protagonists. Heroic characters in a tragedy seek to determine their destinies but are undermined by their own character faults. *Forza* is not like this: Leonora, Don Alvaro, and Don Carlos have no control over circumstance.

It is sometimes suggested that the opera is made unwieldy by Verdi's mixing of sources. The opera is formally based on a play by the Duke of Rivas, but the encampment scene which involves a major enhancement of the role of the gypsy, Preziosilla, is derived from Schiller's Wallenstein plays. The very length of the opera and its apparent unwieldiness have inspired editors to make various cuts, but Verdi knew his business. It is, of course, the case that the "high born" and "low born" characters know little about each other and probably care less. But if Don Alvaro knows nothing of Melitone's soup kitchen, he has little more appreciation of Don Carlos' motivations, and in the first version of the opera he has little time for Padre Guardiano's sanctimoniousness. The opera has been described as a long duet, but in the first-act love scene and the later duel scenes the protagonists communicate at, rather than with, each other. Only between Guardiano and Melitone is there some real communication and, perhaps, a little understanding.

The ending was a problem for Verdi. There were simply too many dead bodies for the critics at the first performance in St Petersburg and in early productions in Italy. Verdi's 1869 revision introduces the fine last trio in which Alvaro is urged by Guardiano to accept God's comfort. Perhaps to make this a more likely denouement Verdi removed Alvaro's "blood and thunder" aria from the end of act IV—a real musical loss—and also re-arranged the sequencing of acts III and IV, making the dramatic flow even less comprehensible. However, various small compositional changes were almost all for the better. The famous 1869 overture replacing the 1862 prelude is probably Verdi's masterpiece of the genre.

Once the 1869 version entered the repertoire, the original version was almost forgotten. Producers tampered with the order of events in the middle scenes and made various cuts, but surprisingly in an age of interest in the first thoughts of composers there was no interest in the 1862 *Forza*. However, in the early 1970s the British Broadcasting Corporation gave a studio performance. In 1990 The Scottish National Opera mounted a production including the 1862 prelude, Alvaro's "additional" aria and the original ordering of acts III and IV, but otherwise using the musical score of 1869. The result was a performance of great musical and dramatic impact.—STANLEY HENIG

Four Saints in Three Acts

Composer: *Virgil Thomson.*

Librettist: *Gertrude Stein.*

First Performance: *Hartford, Connecticut, 8 February 1934.*

Roles: *St Teresa I (soprano); St Teresa II (mezzo-soprano); St Settlement (soprano); St Chavez (tenor); St Ignatius (baritone); Commère (mezzo-soprano); Compère (bass); St Plan (bass); St Stephen (tenor); small chorus of named saints with solo lines (SATB); large chorus (SATB).*

Despite its name, Virgil Thomson's first opera features approximately thirty saints in a prologue and four acts. Set in Spain, the plotless and free-wheeling work with its vivid stream-of-consciousness libretto by Gertrude Stein is, according to Thomson in his autobiography, about "the religious life—peace between the sexes, community of faith, the production of miracles." Lacking a logical story progression, the opera presents a course of tableaux and processions which are dominated by two major saints, Teresa of Avila and Ignatius Loyola. An uninhibited blend of gravely devout episodes and theatrical choruses, piety and circus parades, sense and nonsense, the work amuses and amazes. As John Cage explains in his *Virgil Thomson: His Life and Music*, the hearer of *Four Saints in Three Acts* must "leap into that irrational world from which it sprang, the world in which the matter-of-fact and the irrational are one, where mirth and metaphysics marry to beget comedy."

It would have been interesting indeed to have been with Thomson in Paris during the work's composition. In the mornings he sat at his piano, text before him, and sang, improvising act by act. He wrote nothing down until an act had been repeated several times in the same way, placing great faith in the ability of his unconscious mind to shape the music to the text, including the stage directions which he felt formed a part of the poetic whole. Thomson's score is mainly diatonic and filled with snatches drawn from a wide musical range: Anglican chant, popular songs, ballads, nursery tunes, and dance melodies. The work often has a tongue-in-cheek resonance as Thomson weaves these varying musics into witty parodies of the conventional arias, recitatives, choruses, and ballets of grand opera. Moments of grandeur do surface here and there, but there is also much musical wit amidst the word play of Stein's poetry. Ever sensitive to prosody, Thomson's declamation is superb; he imbues the startling and seemingly incoherent text with energy. Having previously set Stein's "Susie Asado" and "Capital, Capitals," Thomson was in tune with her sensibilities and delighted by her poetic ear, finding her words quite often closer to music than to speech. The two were an imaginative, compatible team that could scarcely fail to produce a work of originality, flair, and odd magic.

The resounding success of the premiere was more than a parlor trick, however. The strange but tonal music and unorthodox libretto jarred the 1934 season and toppled the conventions of opera. With its famous and innovative collaborators, its all Black cast, and its sets of cellophane, feathers, shells, lace, and glitzy colored lights, *Four Saints in Three Acts* catapulted its composer into fame and fashion. Store windows imitated the sets, and the names of both the composer and the work were buzzwords among the society and intellectual sets that year. The opera toured in New York and Chicago, but Thomson went back to Paris a few months after the premiere and continued to compose and write extensively. It would, however, be more than a decade before he and Stein worked together again on his second opera, *The Mother of Us All.*—MICHAEL MECKNA

Francesca da Rimini

Composer: *Riccardo Zandonai.*

Librettist: *G. d'Annunzio (abridged by T. Ricordi).*

First Performance: *Turin, 1914.*

Roles: *Francesca (soprano); Samaritana (mezzo-soprano); Ostasio (baritone); Gianciotti (baritone); Paolo (tenor); Malatestino (tenor); Biancofiore (soprano); Garsenda (soprano); Donella (soprano); Altichiara (mezzo-soprano); Smaragdi (mezzo-soprano); Ser Toldo Berardengo (tenor); Jester (baritone); chorus (SSAATTBB).*

Zandonai's fourth opera, based on d'Annunzio's play of the same name from 1900, is the composer's most popular work, and the only one to have made any lasting international impact. The reduction of the play into a libretto was done by Tito Ricordi, after the rights had been secured from the poet at the enormous cost of twenty-five thousand lire. Later, when the composition was in progress, Zandonai and Ricordi together went to visit d'Annunzio in France to request and receive a new text for the third-act duet between the two lovers.

The setting of the opera is Italy at the end of the thirteenth century. Francesca, the daughter of Guido Minore da Polenta, is to be married to one of Malatesta da Verucchio's three sons. The husband chosen for her is the lame Giovanni lo Sciancato (Gianciotti), but she is tricked into believing that she will marry the handsome Paolo il Bello. After the marriage has taken place, Francesca and Paolo are unable to deny their love for each other, and drawing together while reading a tragic story, they kiss. The wicked third brother, Malatestino dall'

Occhio, himself makes advances to Francesca and when she rejects him he tells Gianciotti of his suspicions about Paolo. Acting on this information, Gianciotti surprises the two lovers and kills them both.

The influences of recent operas on both librettist and composer are fairly audible in this work. Nevertheless, with the rhetoric and archaicism of d'Annunzio's text, the result is a satisfyingly confident example of the rosy-tinted view of the Renaissance current at the time (the designs for the premiere, in which Renaissance palaces were subtly transformed into bourgeois early twentieth-century homes, were striking).

As with other operas of the period, the immediate points of reference for *Francesca da Rimini* are Verdi's last two operas, *Otello* and *Falstaff*. (Zandonai, according to his biographer Vittoria Tarquini, intended the libretto to be the equal of Boito's text of *Falstaff*.) The sonata structure of the opening scene of Verdi's opera and the tossing of motifs between orchestra and singers set the standard for the composers of the *verismo* period and their successors.

Zandonai's method, developed from this model, relies on a network of significant themes, and he is more likely to favor the orchestra rather than the singer's line in driving a dramatic point home. Thus the *coup de théâtre* of the first act is the moment when Francesca and Paolo see each other for the first time and gaze in silence from either side of a gate. Above a static open chord in the bass and murmuring strings on top, a viola shapes a broad, rhapsodic theme as a wordless comment on the scene. When text does appear and voices re-enter, it is only Francesca's ladies singing yet another quaint song.

Strauss and Debussy are frequently named as the composers with most recognizable influence on Zandonai's scores, yet the influence has been absorbed into a fundamentally Italian musical idiom. The rhythmic fluidity of Debussy is missing, as is the sheer energy and free tonality of Strauss, whose *Elektra*, first performed in Italy in 1909, influenced the violent first scene of Zandonai's fourth act. One other work which resonates through *Francesca da Rimini* is Wagner's *Tristan und Isolde*, not simply in the subject matter, but also in the sonorous B-major close to the love duet.

Perhaps the most interesting element of Zandonai's writing in *Francesca* is his harmonic idiom. He rarely writes a key signature, but where he does (and usually it is one of exaggerated sharpness or flatness), the major-key tonality arrived at is emphasized in its plainness, after a period of troubled chromaticism. Vocal and instrumental lines often move in tritones, and the composer exploits this interval and the whole tones contained in the French 6th chord, which will often be extended for many bars before resolving.

Elsewhere, relations at the third are used to propel the harmonic sense forward. These can be interspersed with chords created by adding whole tones to an existing harmony. The progression in the last scene on Francesca's words "Perdonami! /Un sonno duro più d'una percossa /mi spezzò l'anima" is typical in this respect. Zandonai, however, is not able to break out of conventional four-square melodic and harmonic periods to anything like the extent of *Elektra*. In addition, the self-conscious archaic quality of the text is often simply illustrated with apt music, rather than providing a springboard for the music to take flight. The exceptions are the mime at the end of the first act, the long love duet, and the two scenes of the fourth act. And sometimes Zandonai provides colorful touches of his own (a tiny sketch of the sea at the words "Guardate il mare come si fa bianco") which show him to be a composer with a keen theatrical imagination.—KENNETH CHALMERS

f

OPERA

Die Frau ohne Schatten [The Woman without a Shadow]

Composer: *Richard Strauss.*

Librettist: *Hugo von Hofmannsthal.*

First Performance: *Vienna, Staatsoper, 10 October 1919.*

Roles: *The Emperor (tenor); The Empress (soprano); The Empress' Nurse (contralto); Barak, the Dyer (baritone); The Dyer's Wife (soprano); Spirit Messenger (baritone); Falcon (soprano); Hunchback (tenor); One-Eye (bass); One-Arm (bass); Apparition of Youth (tenor); Keeper of Temple (soprano); chorus (SSAATTBB).*

Die Frau ohne Schatten, completed in 1917 and first performed in 1919, represents a climax of sorts for Strauss and Hofmannsthal. This elaborate allegorical fairy tale follows on the heels of *Ariadne auf Naxos,* and, like its predecessor, mixes mythology and domestic drama, although *Die Frau ohne Schatten* attains a size and scope that are unique in the Strauss-Hofmannsthal canon. After *Die Frau,* composer and librettist would abandon this intriguing mix of elements in favor of more straightforward works with less overtly symbolic references. Their subsequent operas are primarily settings of contemporary and historical domestic themes: the autobiographical *Intermezzo* (1924), and *Arabella* (1933), their final collaboration, are little more than a gloss on *Der Rosenkavalier.* Strauss and Hofmannsthal would return only once to the grandeur of a mythological theme, with *Die ägyptische Helena* (1928), a stiff and awkward piece which met with less than rapturous public acclaim. So *Die Frau* is the last of Strauss and Hofmannsthal's truly ambitious works, and it also serves as a critical transitional piece in our understanding of the team: in the vivid words of Ernst Kraus, *Die Frau ohne Schatten* "rears up like an immense mountain massif between the one-act tragedies of the first decade of the century and the sunlit slopes of the later operas."

It seems scarcely possible to imagine a more grandiose conception than that which lies behind this opera. Hofmannsthal's libretto drew on an immense and complex series of sources, from Grimm fairy tales and folk stories of China, Persia, and India, to the works of Goethe, Rückert, and other German Romantic poets. Strauss' music is of Wagnerian proportions: even heavily cut (as the opera invariably is in performance), it can run nearly four hours in length, and requires five star singers of almost superhuman stamina and power. These elements, coupled with the need for extraordinary and spectacular production effects, have prohibited *Die Frau* from being presented by any but the most ambitious opera companies—although in truth, even if the staging requirements were less limiting, the abstract and often murky symbolism of the opera probably rules it out for most popular tastes.

Hofmannsthal's libretto is a tale of two mythical couples—in particular, of two wives. One is a fairy empress who is too much a part of the spirit world: she has not achieved humanity. The other, the dyer's wife, is a mortal who is too much bound by earthly desires. For both women, their inability to integrate spiritual and human values is exemplified by their barrenness: the empress cannot have children, and the dyer's wife will not. The latter character, in fact, offers her shadow (a representation of fertility) to the empress in return for worldly riches. What follows in the action of the opera is a series of trials and rituals of purification for the two couples which resemble those undergone by Tamino and Pamina in Mozart's *Die Zauberflöte,* an opera which served as a conscious model for Strauss and Hofmannsthal in *Die Frau ohne Schatten*, just as in *Der Rosenkavalier* seven years before the two had paid homage to *Le nozze di Figaro*.

As with *Die Zauberflöte*, the densely allegorical nature of *Die Frau ohne Schatten* invites complex interpretation. Critics have written extensively on the meaning of Hofmannsthal's libretto, often giving particular significance to the fact that the opera was composed so soon after World War I, and suggesting that the ability to conceive, an issue so central to *Die Frau*, should be read broadly as referring to the survival of mankind rather than as a representation of purely personal fulfillment. In this view, the themes of creation, humanity, and survival are inexorably linked: perpetuation of the species can be ensured only by uniting the earthliness of man with the higher values of the spiritual realm. Hofmannsthal's letters to Strauss make clear that this idea was a primary theme in his libretto, but—again as with *Die Zauberflöte*—the end result is not wholly satisfying as an allegory. Too much of *Die Frau ohne Schatten* is merely obtuse and heavy-handed; worse, equating women's worth with childbearing, even in this special historical context, is depressingly antiquated and bourgeois, even—in light of the often overblown libretto—pretentious. Strauss himself questioned the wisdom of overlaying the text so heavily with symbols, insisting that the central issues were really quite clear and simple.

Hofmannsthal's response, as it always was when he felt Strauss had misunderstood a crucial point, was to despair that his composer was not a real intellectual. It is especially ironic, then, that Strauss' score seems to complement Hofmannsthal's libretto perfectly and in truth the music often more successfully realizes the scope and size of the poet's intention than the text itself does. In keeping with the Wagnerian style of *Die Frau ohne Schatten*, Strauss uses leitmotifs to define characters and ideas, and it is these themes which illuminate and clarify the story, guiding listeners through the often convoluted plot.

The music itself is some of Strauss' lushest and most demanding, combining the long melismatic vocal lines which are typical of his later operas with the jagged, often dissonant writing found in his early settings of mythology. The dense orchestration, reminiscent of Mahler and Wagner, further emphasizes the large scale of the work, and—coupled with the difficult vocal parts—makes extraordinary demands on the singers.

Strauss is justly celebrated for his ability to write marvelous music for sopranos, and *Die Frau* certainly has its share. The three female leads—the empress, the dyer's wife, and the nurse—are each given highly individualized treatments, but they share the gorgeous chromatic harmonies which are a Strauss trademark. The superb music for the male characters in *Die Frau* is more of a surprise. Most of Strauss' music for men's voices is of the character or buffo variety; he rarely seemed interested in composing for a principal tenor or baritone. Yet the roles of the emperor and Barak, the dyer (tenor and baritone respectively) are executed with the same detail and sense of melody which characterize their spouses; the resulting duets and ensembles are quite beautiful.

It is the music of *Die Frau ohne Schatten* which is responsible for its continued place in opera theaters. And as difficult as the principal roles are to sing, several opera stars in recent years have made something of a specialty of the work. Leonie Rysanek was strongly identified with the part of the empress, and Christa Ludwig and Walter Berry had a joint triumph in performances as the dyer and his wife. Occasionally, these three singers came together, as in a now-legendary production at the Metropolitan Opera during the 1960s. Such performances, and the memory of them, ensure that *Die Frau ohne Schatten* will retain a place in the repertoire, but it is highly unlikely that this odd and difficult work will ever displace *Der Rosenkavalier* or *Elektra* in the public's affections.—DAVID ANTHONY FOX

Der Freischütz [The Free-Shooter]

Composer: *Carl Maria von Weber.*

Librettist: *J. F. Kind (after J.A. Apel and F. Laun, Gespensterbuch).*

First Performance: *Berlin, Schauspielhaus, 18 June 1821.*

Roles: *Agathe (soprano); Aennchen (soprano); Max (tenor); Caspar (baritone); Kilian (bass); Cuno (bass); Prince Ottokar (baritone); Hermit (bass); Bridesmaid (soprano); Samiel (speaking); chorus (SATTTBB).*

The seventh of Carl Maria von Weber's ten operas, *Der Freischütz* is a *Singspiel,* an alternation of musical numbers and spoken dialogue. Weber and his librettist, Johann Friedrich Kind (1768-1843), recount the legend of the marksman who makes a pact with the forces of evil to obtain magic bullets. The plot unfolds in the great Bohemian forest shortly after the end of the Thirty Years' War (1618-48). Local custom dictates that the young hunter Max must pass a shooting trial in order to marry his beloved Agathe. Caspar, a hunter in league with the heathen world represented by Samiel, persuades Max to use "free bullets," which streak magically to their targets. Casting such bullets involves forbidden rites conducted in a terrifying abyss, the Wolf's Glen. Samiel controls one of these bullets. Caspar expects it to strike Agathe; instead it mortally wounds him. For Max's transgression, Prince Ottokar decrees banishment. A hermit, who represents the Christian world, recommends clemency. The secular ruler accepts heaven's will. The shooting trial is abolished. Max, if he proves worthy, can marry Agathe in a year. The opera ends with general rejoicing.

For the libretto (1817), Kind consulted earlier versions of the tale, chiefly a short story in the *Gespensterbuch* (Book of Ghosts, 1810) by Johann August Apel and Friedrich Laun [Friedrich August Schulze] and *Der Freyschütze* by Franz Xaver von Caspar (1812; 1813; music by Carl Neuner). He adds bridesmaids and huntsmen, the villain Caspar, the soubrette Aennchen, and the peasant Kilian, reduces the number of magic bullets from sixty-three to seven, shifts the forbidden rites from a crossroads to the Wolf's Glen, and substitutes a happy ending (Apel's story ends tragically, as does Caspar's 1813 version). Weber contributed various details and, over Kind's objections, accepted his fiancé Caroline's recommendation to eliminate two opening scenes involving the hermit. Thus, the action begins *in medias res* with the entire village assembled at a shooting contest.

Simple, brave, and motivated by love, the well-intentioned Max is an early Heldentenor. Agathe, pure, patient, domestic, faithful, and pious, is nicely complemented by Aennchen, her charming, lively, good-natured relative. Beyond the individual characters stands a lovingly portrayed community of simple folk. This community, in turn, exists within the vast forest, an environment both hospitable and threatening.

"There are in *Der Freischütz* two principal elements that can be recognized at first sight— hunting life and the rule of demonic powers as personified by Samiel." In this bit of conversation with J.C. Lobe, Weber underscores the chief dramatic theme of the opera: a struggle between the forces of good and evil. Important also are the themes of religion, love, and nature: its dark, sinister side (the Wolf's Glen); its idealized side (the huntsmen and the farmers); and its ordered, beautiful side (nature in harmony with God and humanity).

Having contemplated a *Freischütz* setting as early as 1810, Weber enthusiastically set Kind's libretto during the years 1817-20, adding in 1821 the Romance and Aria for the first Aennchen, Johanna Eunicke. Not only was the material consonant with Weber's own personal triad of God, family, and music; it also afforded him a welcome opportunity to create the kind of opera he thought Germans desired: "an art work complete in itself, in which the partial contributions of the related and collaborating arts blend together, disappear, and, in disappearing, somehow form a new world" (Weber, "On the Opera 'Undine'," trans. Strunk).

Weber drew inspiration from several musical traditions: the *Singspiel,* to include Beethoven's *Fidelio;* Italian opera, as in Max's great scene, waltz and aria, "Durch die Wälder, durch die Auen" (no. 3, Through the Forests, through the Meadows), and Agathe's scene and aria, "Wie nahte mir der Schlummer" (no. 8, How tranquilly I slumbered); *opéra comique,* with its realistic out-of-doors scenes, choruses and dances, and soubrette roles; and folksong, drawn into the realm of art and functioning intrinsically, not incidentally. He incorporated actual melodies, for example, the refrain of the Bridesmaids' Chorus (no. 14) and "Marlborough," embedded in the Huntsmen's Chorus (no. 15). Conversely, original Weber tunes, such as the opening of the Huntsmen's Chorus, quickly became popular songs. Whatever the influence of the moment, vocal production ranges from speech and melodrama (speech accompanied by the orchestra) at one extreme to exquisite lyricism at the other.

Reinforcing the opera's dramatic plan and the dark-light curve it suggests are unifying musical plans of motive, tone color, and key. Identified with characters or states of mind, certain themes and harmonies recur throughout the opera. Weber explained his tone color plan as follows: for the forest and hunting life, horns; for the dark powers, "the lowest register of the violins, violas and basses, particularly the lowest register of the clarinet, which seemed especially suitable for depicting the sinister, then the mournful sound of the bassoon, the lowest notes of the horns, the hollow roll of drums or single hollow strokes on them" (Warrack, *Carl Maria von Weber,* p. 221). Commentators have tended to exaggerate Weber's key architecture. C minor does indeed represent a specific force in the opera, the demonic. Otherwise, the most that can realistically be said about tonal planning is that good generally is associated with bright major keys, evil with minor keys.

Distributed throughout the three acts are an overture and sixteen musical numbers: an introductory complex, an entr'acte, simple songs, ariettas, elaborate arias, ensembles, choruses, and two great ensemble finales. In evoking the forest, the demonic powers, Max, Agathe, and the triumph of love and faith, the overture is a symphonic synthesis of the drama. Within the *Singspiel* format, Weber builds some remarkable structures by combining separate components into large form-complexes, as in the introduction (no. 1; see also the linking of Caspar's drinking song [no. 4], which Beethoven admired, with his aria of rage and triumph [no. 5]). "Half the opera plays in darkness. . . . These dark forms of the outer world are underlined and strengthened in the musical forms." The Wolf's Glen scene (no. 10) dramatically illustrates Weber's observation. Elements of chorus, recitative, aria, melodrama, and symphonic music coalesce into an innovative, yet unified whole. Here, where the work reaches its profoundest depth before the resolution into light, he realized musically a "real, palpable, and unmistakable scene of horror" (report of his son, Max Maria von Weber).

Count Carl von Brühl, the Berlin Intendant and Weber's friend, oversaw the preparations for the premiere. Although some negative criticisms were voiced, by Hoffmann, Zelter, Tieck, and Spohr, for example, *Der Freischütz* was fabulously successful from the outset. For a host of commentators, it epitomizes German Romantic opera. Indeed, Kind and Weber have emphasized nature and the "folk," blurred the distinctions between humans, nature, and the supernatural, integrated the overture with the opera, allotted the orchestra a role in the drama, and aimed the music at the listener's emotions. But is the opera a high Romantic product, in the manner of the Hoffmann-Fouqué *Undine* of 1816? Given its basic format of innocence, fall, and redemption, does it offer a questioning, probing, and expansive world view? Is it even truly nationalistic? Without diminishing the importance or stature of the opera, one specialist has argued persuasively that *Der Freischütz* has as its goal the reinforcement of established norms: "Man remains oriented towards the church and hence towards a universal conception of man" (Doerner, "The Influence of the 'Kunstmärchen' on German Romantic Opera, 1814-1825"). As a mixture of morality play and melodrama, Doerner argues, it illustrates a later, more tamed phase of Romanticism, a blend of Romantic and Enlightenment values: "dogma and religious moralizing take the place of a complex secular philosophy. . . . The jubilation expressed at the conclusion . . . is focused on the modest prospect of a more secure and comfortable worldly existence." Whatever its interpretation, in Austria and Germany especially, *Der Freischütz* continues to hold the stage.—MALCOLM S. COLE

Freni, Mirella

Soprano. Born 27 February 1935, in Modena. Married: 1) Leone Magiera (one daughter); 2) bass Nicolai Ghiaurov in 1981. Studied at Mantua and at Bologna Conservatory with Ettore Campogalliani; debut as Micaela in Carmen *at Modena, 1955; sang with Netherlands Opera; Covent Garden debut as Nannetta in* Falstaff, *1961; Teatro all Scala debut in same role, 1962 and has appeared there regularly since; Metropolitan Opera debut as Mimì, 1965; appeared at Salzburg, 1966-72 and 1974-80.*

In the 1960s Mirella Freni emerged as one of the world's leading sopranos; she has maintained her preeminent position during the following two decades. Much of her early career was devoted to eighteenth-century opera and to some of the lighter roles in opera of the nineteenth century, but as her voice and acting ability have matured she has gradually taken on heavier nineteenth-century roles. At the same time she has managed to maintain a youthful face and figure, causing one critic who witnessed her performance of Elisabetta in Verdi's *Don Carlos* in 1979 to call her "something of a miracle, since she does not seem to get older."

A recording of *Don Giovanni* made in the mid 1960s under Klemperer shows the young Freni in good voice. As Zerlina she sings with attractive clarity and freshness. In the duet "La ci darem la mano" her singing is simple and beautiful; it perfectly conveys Zerlina's sweetness, and at the same time hints at her seductive power. We understand why Don Giovanni is attracted to her. Freni's arias are just as charming, though "Batti, batti" is marred by an annoying mannerism: Freni's excessive scooping eventually wears on the listener's patience.

Freni brought all her youthful talents to bear in another great eighteenth-century role, this one much less familiar to today's opera-goers. She is perfect in the title role of Picinni's *La buona figliuola* (or *La Cecchina*), as recorded under Franco Caracciolo in the 1960s. In her beautiful, sentimental showpiece "Una povera ragazza" she sings with moving tenderness and simplicity. Even more memorable is her performance of the aria "Vieni, il mio seno," sung by Cecchina as she goes to sleep. Freni sings the aria's long lines with exquisite delicacy.

Another recording from early in Freni's career reveals her as a fine singer of baroque opera: Handel's *Alcina,* recorded under Bonynge. In the role of Oberto, Freni stands out as an outstanding declaimer of recitative. She sings recitative as if it means something: there is real pathos in Oberto's words as he tells of his attempt to find his father. Freni's arias are no less vivid. In "Chi m'insegna il caro padre" one can hear a fresh, light soprano voice of beautiful tone. Gliding over melismas with ease and grace, Freni seems to caress Handel's melodies.

Freni's versatility in the performance of nineteenth-century opera is extraordinary. Whether the opera is in Italian, French or Russian, she is able to bring her character to life with unsurpassed vividness and musical perfection. One of her best roles is Tatyana in Tchaikovsky's *Eugene Onegin*—"the Tatyana of one's dreams," one critic raved after her performance of the role in Bordeaux. The subtlety and variety that she brings to this role have astonished and delighted audiences in many of the world's leading opera houses. One of the Verdi roles in which Freni has been particularly successful is the title role of *Aida.* She triumphed in the role at Salzburg, winning praise for her rich tone, her intelligent, expressive phrasing, and for the intensity of her acting. Freni has been equally successful as Desdemona, a role she has sung in Salzburg and elsewhere. She has brought to lighter, more cheerful roles in nineteenth-century opera as much energy as she brings to her portrayals of the great tragic heroines, winning praise for her many performances of Micaela in Bizet's *Carmen* (the role with which she made her operatic debut in the mid 1950s), Nannetta in Verdi's *Falstaff* and Marie in Donizzetti's *La fille du régiment.*—JOHN A. RICE

Frick, Gottlob

> *Bass. Born 28 July 1906, in Olbronn, Württemberg. Studied with Neudörfer-Opitz and at Stuttgart Conservatory. Debut as Daland in* Der fliegende Holländer *at Coburg, 1934; sang in Freiburg and Königsberg, then in Dresden, where he created Caliban in Sutermeister's* Die Zauberinsel *and the Carpenter in Haas's* Die Hochzeit des Jobs, *1941-52; at Berlin State Opera, 1950-53; Bavarian State Opera from 1953; Metropolitan Opera debut as Fafner in* Das Rheingold, *1961; appeared as Sarastro at Salzburg, 1955; Bayreuth from 1957.*

In an era rich in dark-voiced bassos, Gottlob Frick possessed his own distinctive majesty and greatness. Born in 1908, Frick studied voice in Stuttgart and in 1927 became a member of the Stuttgart Opera Chorus. His solo debut was as Daland in Coburg, in 1934, beginning a distinguished career as a leading Wagnerian bass.

After further seasons in Freiburg and Königsberg, Frick joined the Dresden company where he remained a valued member until 1950, singing repertoire roles and appearing in several world premieres. He then moved to the Berlin Opera and in 1953 became a member of the Munich and Vienna companies, and a regular guest in Hamburg. In 1951 he first appeared at Covent Garden where he sang Rocco (*Fidelio*) and important Wagner bass roles during the next twenty years.

In 1953 he was in Rome participating in the grand recording of Wagner's Ring under Furtwängler for Italian Radio. He was a regular at the Bayreuth Festival. At the Salzburg Festival, Frick sang Mozart, Pfitzner, and Egk. He was a guest at the Teatro alla Scala, the Paris Opéra, and in Amsterdam and Brussels.

Frick first came to the Metropolitan Opera in 1961 for a Ring cycle under Erich Leinsdorf. This engagement was belated perhaps due to the plethora of fine basses at the time.

Frick officially retired from the stage in 1970, but actually continued to appear. Further roles were Philip in *Don Carlos* and Padre Guardiano in *La forza del destino* of Verdi, Kaspar in *Der Freischütz*, Osmin in *Die Entführung aus dem Serail*, Kezal in *The Bartered Bride*, and van Bett in *Zar und Zimmermann*.

From his Dresden days, Gottlob Frick is represented on recordings of Dvorak's *Rusalka*, *Tristan*, *Fra Diavolo*, Hugo Wolf's *Der Corrigidor*, and Goetz' *The Taming of the Shrew*. He appears in performance recordings from Bayreuth, and in other commercial complete Wagnerian opera accounts. He also sings in complete recordings of *Entführung*, *Zar und Zimmermann*, *The Merry Wives of Windsor*, *Fidelio*, *Don Giovanni* and is especially delightful in Orff's *Die Kluge*.

Frick had a well-schooled, even voice, and was noted for his interpretive ability. He was equally at home and enjoyable as a villain or as a comedian.—BERT WECHSLER

From the House of the Dead [Z mrtvého domu]

Composer: *Leoš Janáček.*

Librettist: *Leoš Janáček (after Dostoevsky).*

First Performance: *Brno, National Theater, 12 April 1930 (posthumous; revised and reorchestrated by O. Chlubna and B. Bakala).*

Roles: *Goryančikov (baritone); Alyei (tenor); Šiškov (baritone); Shapkin (baritone); Skuratov (tenor); Commandant (bass); Prostitute (soprano or mezzo-soprano); Four Men and Four Women (mute); chorus (TTBB).*

The House of the Dead (1860-62) was Dostoevsky's first novel. He was arrested in 1849 as a political prisoner, and—after a mock execution and reprieve—was sent to Siberia for ten years. The novel is a thinly disguised autobiographical record in which Dostoevsky repeatedly shows how the strength of the human heart and the quality of the soul may transcend humiliation and oppression. This was the aspect of the novel which appealed to Janáček, who summed up the whole of his life's work in *From The House of the Dead*, completed just after his 74th birthday. It was far ahead of its time in its musical style, its brevity, the absence of a coherent plot and the composer's disregard for most of the conventions of opera.

Janáček entitled his opera *From the House of the Dead*, and the message which he brings from the prison to his audience is summed up in the motto: "in every creature a spark of God." The quest to understand the human soul, and vindicate our existence by seeking that "spark of God" even among convicted murderers, is the essence of the opera. There is a tension throughout (most eloquently expressed in the orchestral introduction) between the music of *f* **OPERA**

oppression and human suffering and the exultant music in which Janáček asserts and celebrates the essential, inner freedom of all humanity.

Janáček had focused four of his previous operas—*Jenůfa, Katia Kabanová, The Cunning Little Vixen* and *The Makropoulos Case*—on the developing character of one central female figure. In *From the House of the Dead,* by contrast, there are no women (except a raddled prostitute who sings a few bars in act II). There is also no plot, in any conventional sense. Janáček developed still further the discursive, almost cinematic narrative techniques with which he had experimented in *Osud* and *The Excursions of Mr. Brouček.* He wrote no formal libretto, but simply excerpted episodes, narratives and anecdotes from Dostoevsky's novel and arranged them, sometimes synthesizing characters and incidents, to create his text.

The fortunes of one character, the political prisoner Alexandr Petrovič Goryančikov, form a loose framework. He is admitted into the prison and savagely flogged early in act I; the opera ends with his release. There is also an implied sequence of seasons or moods; act I is set in winter, act II in spring, and act III, after opening in the gloom of the prison hospital at night, escapes for the final scene, in which Goryančikov is freed, into the light of a sunny day.

Dostoevsky observed the prisoners' habit of obsessively telling their own stories to one another. From *Jenůfa* onwards, Janáček had crystallized the meaning of each of his tragic operas through the medium of a monologue just before the close. In *From the House of the Dead* he used his gift for narrative more extensively, and gave a strangely compelling unity to this opera by setting in each act a prisoner's story of the events which led him to be imprisoned.

This device introduces into the camp glimpses of the normal, outside world. Each story is more expansive than the one before, and Šiškov's narrative in act III, in the prison hospital, leads to the central climax of the opera. One of the more depraved and brutal convicts tells how, tormented by his young wife Akulina's declaration of love for one Filka Morozov, he cut her throat. As the story ends, another convict dies, and Šiškov recognizes him in death as Filka.

Šiškov curses the corpse repeatedly, but an old convict comments that "even he was some mother's child." Janáček used these words as the springboard for a music which expresses his compassion for and understanding even of men like Šiškov and Filka. By comprehending acts of violence which are almost incomprehensible, Janáček finds the "spark of God" in the most apparently worthless of human beings, and so vindicates our own common humanity.

To match this extraordinary subject-matter, Janáček devised an extraordinary musical style. It proved to be beyond the understanding even of his own pupils; two of them reorchestrated the opera for the posthumous premiere, and substituted a jubilant closing chorus in praise of freedom for Janáček's grimmer finale, in which the prisoners are forced to march back to work. This adaptation seriously distorts the composer's meaning; the sound of the whole opera is softened, and the ending imposes a sentimental idealism where the original has taught us to accept the cruel realities of separation and imprisonment, and to glory in the tenacity of the human spirit. In recent years performances have reverted more to Janáček's original scoring.

Janáček's orchestration in *From the House of the Dead* is extremely spartan, with often bizarre combinations between extremes of pitch and timbre. The music is more dissonant than any of his earlier works; and there is a striking alternation between the stylized use of the prisoners as a chorus and the realism—heightened almost to the level of expressionism by Janáček's laconic, gestural style—in the interchanges between individuals.

From the House of the Dead

Despite its forbidding title and almost all-male cast, *From the House of the Dead* has attracted memorable productions both inside Czechoslovakia and elsewhere. Many theatrical styles have proved effective, ranging from the detailed realism of Colin Graham's version when Charles Mackerras first conducted the score in England for Sadler's Wells Opera to the stylization and abstraction of Götz Friedrich's production for the Berliner Staatsoper. This is certainly Janáček's most original score, and possibly his greatest opera.—MICHAEL EWANS

Gadski, Johanna

Soprano. Born 15 June 1872, in Anklam, Prussia. Died 22 February 1932, in Berlin. Studied with Schroeder-Chaloupka in Stettin; debut in Lortzing's Undine *at the Kroll Opera, Berlin, 1889; American debut as Elsa in* Lohengrin *at Damrosch Opera Company's season at the Metropolitan Opera, 1895, and remained with company for three years; engaged by Covent Garden, 1898-1901; debut as a member of Metropolitan Opera Company as Senta in* Der fliegende Holländer, *1900, and remained at Met until 1917; concert tours of the United States, 1904-06; appeared in Munich, 1905-06; appeared at Salzburg in 1906 and 1910; after 1917 did not appear in opera until 1929, when she was leader of a Wagnerian touring company.*

Although recorded only on pre-electronic records which sound tinny and fuzzy to modern ears, Johanna Gadski is still a pleasure to hear more than fifty years after her death. J.B. Steane called her "one of the most sensitive and musical singers of her day." Yet Gadski did not always receive such praise in live performance. Audiences loved her, but the critics were less impressed. The reviews were so mixed that sometimes it seemed as if the critics were contradicting each other, and themselves, with each subsequent report. Her reputation, like that of many artists, has fared better after death than during her life.

Gadski debuted at age seventeen in Lortzing's *Undine* at the Kroll Opera in Berlin; she sang in Germany between 1889 and 1894 before her United States debut in 1895 with the Damrosch Opera company in *Lohengrin* at the Metropolitan Opera House in New York. She joined the Metropolitan Opera Company in 1900. While she was one of their leading Wagnerian sopranos, her repertoire was not limited to Wagner. She had roles in Verdi's *Aïda, Il trovatore,* and *Rigoletto,* Meyerbeer's *Les Huguenots,* Mozart's *Zauberflöte* and *Le nozze di Figaro;* she sang in Mahler's production of *Don Giovanni* at the Met in 1908 as well as in Toscanini's revival of *Orfeo,* and performed in some lesser known works such as Ethel Smyth's *Der Wald,* Boieldieu's *La Dame Blanche,* Mancinelli's *Ero e Leanero,* and Damrosch's *Scarlet Letter.* She sang recitals as well as opera, programming Mozart and Wagner arias, and German lieder; she was one of the few recitalists of her day to regularly include songs by American composers. The burgeoning record industry saw her potential early. She was one of the first Victor Red Seal artists, and made almost 100 records during her career. In 1917, when German nationals had grown out of political favor during the first world war, she was asked to leave the Met. In the 1920s, she formed her own opera company in Germany and toured the United States several times before her death in an auto accident in 1932.

Her live performances received mixed reviews and contradictory criticism. Richard Aldrich, reviewing for the *New York Times,* wrote of a recital in 1904 "She is, first of all, a singer in the real sense of the word; an uncommonly beautiful voice, in which the evidences of full control and skillful use are rarely lacking, is at her disposition. She has the dramatic instinct, guided by intelligence and artistic understanding, and she has sincere sentiment and a serious view of the artist's task." Audiences agreed, and she was an extremely popular recitalist. Aldrich had less positive things to say as well, however. He continued in the same article in a less complimentary vein that "with much that is beautiful in her singing she has not always a perception of the finer differences of values, [nor] the subtler elements of characteristic expression that go to the proper singing of songs." Eleven years later he reviewed her again and complained that her voice was not what it used to be and that she was "not infrequently at variance with the pitch." Another New York critic, W.J. Henderson, did not like her at all. In 1917, he attributed her retirement from the Metropolitan Opera, a purely politically-induced move, to "the deterioration of Mme Gadski's voice and art." He said she was merely "an honest, hardworking . . . soprano" who has had "much admiration from easy going opera patrons." Yet when she toured in the United States after the war, he wrote that she was in "astonishingly good condition." While one critic maintained that she did not have "the creative imagination of an interpreter," Herman Klein in London disagreed: "[She is] the finest Eva we have had in London . . . [due to her] rare vocal and histrionic attainments."

Gadski fared better in recordings than she apparently did in live performance, for her recordings are considered vocal classics. They reflect her versatility: she recorded the lieder of Schubert, Mendelssohn and Strauss, Rossini's *Stabat Mater,* operas of Wagner, Strauss, Verdi, and Mozart, and American songs. She had a large voice with a beautifully pure tone. She could sing strongly when needed without the "Bayreuth Bark" of some other Wagnerians. Her "*Liebestod,*" "Immolation," and "Battle Cry" all ring out with power and vibrancy, yet she could also float her tones when warranted; her performance of Pamina was young and light. While she showed an occasional tendency towards shrillness at the top of her range, she also had a lovely, round, high pianissimo. Her chest voice was well blended and even. In most of her recordings, at least, her musicianship was unquestionable. Even in the most difficult of passages, her accuracy showed her thorough knowledge of her scores.

During her life, Gadski's critics accused her of expressive monotony. Aldrich wrote that she had a very limited emotional range. One modern critic labeled her "worthy if not exciting." Yet her recordings prove her to be a sensitive interpreter with a real depth and frankness of emotion. Critics of her live performances complained of her stolid and unchanging interpretations, but her records belie this. She recorded some pieces more than once; the differences and variety of these performances are striking. She shaded and colored her tone to create moods. Her expressive use of the *portamento* lent a tragic inflection to her singing. She could command a driving energy, or a tender pathos.

Her later records also illustrate that some of the criticisms received were justified. Towards the end of her career she lost some of her vocal consistency. Her middle register occasionally sounded colorless; her vibrato grew wider and more fluttery. Sometimes her highest notes went flat, and her phrasing seemed slightly short breathed. Her rubato occasionally gave way to rhythmic inaccuracies. But as J.B. Steane concluded, "with so many strengths, . . . she can carry a few weaknesses."

Modern listeners are fortunate that the early days of the recording industry caught Gadski for posterity. The recordings that have been periodically reissued have kept her voice alive and have given us the pleasure of evaluating her singing and the criticism she received. Recordings, which have insured immortality to many musicians, provided a new vehicle for Gadski—a second, if posthumous, career, which has fared better and been less controversial than the reception of her live performances.—ROBIN ARMSTRONG

Galli-Curci, Amelita

Soprano. Born 18 November 1882, in Milan. Died 26 November 1963, in La Jolla, California. Married Luigi Curci, 1910 (divorced 1920) and pianist Homer Samuels, 1921. Studied piano at Milan Conservatory. Took up singing at Mascagni's suggestion. Studied briefly with Carignani and Sara Dufes, but mainly self-taught; debut as Gilda at Trani, 1906; then appeared in Italy, Spain, and South America; in Rome she appeared in premiere of Bizet's Don Procopio, *1908; United States debut as Gilda in Chicago, 1916, where she remained until 1924; Metropolitan Opera debut as Violetta, 1921, and became a regular member of Metropolitan Opera until 1930; underwent surgery for a goiter, 1935; attempted to return to stage in* La bohème, *Chicago, 1936.*

Originally trained as a pianist at the Milan Conservatory, Amelita Galli-Curci was encouraged to become a singer by the opera composer Pietro Mascagni, who admired the unique timbre of her voice. It appears that her preparation for a career in opera consisted of a few voice lessons, the study of opera scores, and her own natural ability to imitate the serene singing of birds outside her home. She made her operatic debut as Gilda, singing a series of *Rigolettos* in Trani and Rome.

During the next decade she carefully selected roles which would highlight her natural agility and bird-like timbre. She consistently performed that group of heroines which we now consider to be the property of the coloratura soprano. She sang Rosina in Rossini's *Il barbiere di Siviglia,* Amina in Bellini's *La sonnambula* and Donizetti heroines *Lucia di Lammermoor* and *Linda di Chamounix.* She also included in her repertoire such roles as *Lakme, Dinorah* and *Manon.* In his book *The Great Singers,* Henry Pleasants suggests that Galli-Curci, as well as her contemporary Luisa Tetrazzini, succeeded in distinguishing themselves from other sopranos of their time by specializing in these particular roles and creating a new phenomenon by "crowning" their performances with the electrifying high notes (E-flat, E and F) that we have come to expect from "coloratura" sopranos. Although she sang primarily these roles, from time to time she did perform more lyrical repertoire, including Sophie in *Der Rosenkavalier,* Mimi in *La bohème* and Violetta in *La traviata.* She performed continually during these early years, but did not really achieve international status until her American debut in 1916.

She sang in the United States for the first time on 18 November 1916 in a performance by the Chicago Opera. She again chose Gilda as her debut vehicle. Her performance there electrified the unprepared audience and she was an overnight sensation. Critics and audiences alike adored her. During her first season with the Chicago Opera she sang *Lucia di Lammermoor, Roméo et Juliette,* and *Il barbiere di Siviglia* as well as *Rigoletto.*

She had come to the United States, after a performance tour in South America, primarily because she had a letter of recommendation to Victor Records in New York City. She would record throughout these next few years on the Victor Records label, and some of her best recordings are from this early acoustic period. After her Chicago triumph, a quickly arranged tour of American cities solidified her popularity in the United States. Her phonograph records, distributed in huge editions, sold as fast as they reached the dealers; "Caro nome" sold 10,000 copies of the first edition in Chicago alone.

Two years later, during a tour designed to show off the roster of the blossoming Chicago Opera, Galli-Curci performed at the Lexington Theater in New York City. Singing Meyerbeer's *Dinorah* for this much-publicized New York performance, she took the town by storm. The audience demanded twenty-four curtain calls after the "Shadow Song" and sixty curtain calls at the end of the opera. She was heard five more times during this rather lengthy season in New York, each performance drawing more patrons than the theatre could hold. In addition to a second Dinorah, she sang Lucia, Gilda, Rosina and Violetta. James Alfonte in his *Opera News* tribute to Galli-Curci (March 1958) relates the incredible circumstances surrounding her last appearance at the Lexington Theater. Undaunted by the fact that the performance was "long since sold out," 10,000 hopeful admirers remained outside the theater, and the capacity crowd inside simply "refused to go home" until "a piano was wheeled on stage" and Galli-Curci serenaded them from the piano. The unprecedented reaction of the public to these and other performances demonstrates the astounding effect of Galli-Curci's voice and personality. Her Metropolitan Opera debut, this time as Violetta, took place on 14 November 1921. From 1921 until 1924 she was a permanent member of both the Metropolitan and Chicago Operas, but after that she made the decision to remain permanently in New York and withdrew from the Chicago roster.

Throughout her career Galli-Curci's popularity never flagged. However, many critics commented about her increasing tendency to sing under pitch. We can only assume that she sang better, at least more consistently, earlier in her career. It is important to note that the height of her career came well before her actual Metropolitan debut, and that at this age, she was in all probability feeling the first effects of a thyroid condition which would worsen as the years progressed.

Her voice, most often described as "limpid" and "natural," was said to have been of remarkable beauty. She had the ability to produce sustained tones with a seemingly effortless floating quality. The unique timbre is said to have been reminiscent of birds and not necessarily the metallic quality that one hears on recordings. The crystalline quality of her upper notes remained unspoiled despite the increasing intonation problems. She was said to have an extraordinary, warm and graceful stage presence.

A throat ailment, diagnosed as a goiter, compelled her to bring her career to a temporary end. She was operated on in 1935 and in November of the following year she attempted a comeback with the Chicago Opera as Mimì. She then went into complete retirement in California, where she remained until her death in 1963.—PATRICIA ROBERTSON

Galuppi, Baldassare

Composer. Born 18 October 1706, on the island of Burano, near Venice. Died 3 January 1785, in Venice. Studied with his father; first opera, La fede nell' incostanza, *performed in Vicenza, 1722; studied with Lotti in Venice; appointed maestro del coro at the Ospizio dei Mendicanti, 1740; in London, 1741-43; second maestro at San Marco, Venice, 1748; principal maestro at San Marco, 1762-64; maestro del coro, Ospedali degl' Incurabili, 1762; maestro to the Russian court, 1765-68; returned to Venice. Galuppi and the librettist and playwright Carlo Goldoni pioneered a number of important techniques in comic opera; Galuppi taught a number of Russian singers and composers, including Bortniansky.*

Operas *La fede nell' incostanza, ossia Gli amici rivali,* Neri?, Vicenza, Teatro delle Grazie, 1722; *Gl' odi delusi dal sangue* (with Pescetti), Lucchini, Venice, Sant' Angelo, 4 February 1728; *Dorinda* (with Pescetti), Benedetto Pasqualigo?, Marcello?, Venice, San Samuele, 9 June 1729; *L'odio placato,* Silvani, Venice, San Samuele, 27 December 1729; *Argenide,* Giusti, Venice, Sant' Angelo, 15 January 1733; *L'ambizione depressa,* Papis, Venice, Sant' Angelo, Ascension 1733; *La ninfa Apollo,* Lemene (with additions by Boldini), Venice, San Samuele, 30 May 1734; *Tamiri,* Vitturi, Venice, Sant' Angelo, 17 November 1734; *Elisa, regina di Tiro,* Zeno and Pariati, Venice, Sant' Angelo, 27 January 1736; *Ergilda,* Vitturi, Venice, Sant' Angelo, 12 November 1736; *L'Alvilda,* Zeno (with additions by Lalli), Venice, San Samuele, 29 May 1737; *Issipile,* Metastasio, Turin, Regio, 26 December 1737; *Alessandro nell' Indie,* Metastasio, Mantua, Nuovo Arciducale, carnival 1738; *Adriano in Siria,* Metastasio, Turin, Regio, January? 1740; *Gustavo primo, re di Svezia,* Goldoni, Venice, San Samuele, 25 May 1740; *Oronte, re de' Sciti,* Goldoni, Venice, San Giovanni Grisostomo, 26 December 1740; *Berenice,* Vitturi, Venice, Sant' Angelo, 27 January 1741; *Didone abbandonata,* Metastasio, Modena, Molzo, carnival 1741; *Penelope,* Rolli, London, King's Theatre in the Haymarket, 23 December 1741; *Scipione in Cartagine,* Vanneschi, London, King's Theatre in the Haymarket, 13 March 1742; *Enrico,* Vanneschi, London, King's Theatre in the Haymarket, 12 January 1743; *Sirbace,* Stampa, London, King's Theatre in the Haymarket, 20 April 1743; *Ricimero,* Silvani, Milan, Regio Ducal, 26 December 1744; *La forza d'amore,* Panicelli, Venice, San Cassiano, 30 January 1745; *Ciro riconosciuto,* Caldará, Milan, Regio Ducal, 26 December 1745; *Antigono,* Metastasio, London, King's Theatre in the Haymarket, 24 May 1746; *Scipione nelle Spagne,* Piovene, Venice, Sant' Angelo, November 1746; *Evergete,* Silvani and Lalli, Rome, Capranica, 2 January 1747; *L'Arminio,* Salvi, Venice, San Cassiano, 26 November 1747; *L'Olimpiade,* Metastasio, Milan, Regio Ducal, 26 December 1747; *Vologeso,* Zeno, Rome, Torre Argentina, 13 or 14 February 1748; *Demetrio,* Metastasio, Vienna, Burgtheater, 16 or 27 October 1748; *Clotilde,* Passarini, Venice, San Cassiano, November 1748; *Semiramide riconosciuta,* Metastasio, Milan, Regio Ducal, 25 January 1749; *Artaserse,* Metastasio, Vienna, Burgtheater, 27 January 1749; *L'Arcadia in Brenta,* Goldoni, Venice, Sant' Angelo, 14 May 1749; *Il conte Caramella,* Goldoni, Verona, Teatro dell' Accademia Vecchia, 18 December 1749; *Il Demofoonte,* Metastasio, Madrid, Teatro del Buon Retiro, 18 December 1749; *Olimpia,* Trabucco, Naples, San Carlo, 18? December 1749; *Alcimena, principessa dell' Isole Fortunate, ossia L'amore* *fortunato ne' suoi disprezzi,* Chiari (after Molière, *Princesse d'Élide*), Venice, San Cassiano, 26 December 1749; *Arcifanfano, re dei matti,* Goldoni, Venice, San Moisè, 27 December 1749; *Il mondo della luna,* Goldoni, Venice, San Moisè, 29 January 1750; *Il paese della Cuccagna,* Goldoni, Venice, San Moisè, 7 May 1750; *Il mondo alla roversa, ossia Le donne che comandano,* Goldoni, Venice, San Cassiano, 14 November 1750; *La mascherata,* Goldoni, Venice, San Cassiano, 26? December 1750; *Antigona,* Roccaforte, Rome, Teatro delle Dame, 9 January 1751; *Dario,* Baldanza, Turin, Regio Ducal, carnival 1751; *Lucio Papirio,* Zeno, Reggio Emilia, Teatro del Pubblico, fair 1751; *Artaserse,* Metastasio, Padua, Nuovo, 11 June 1751; *Le virtuose ridicole,* Goldoni (after Molière, *Les précieuses ridicules*), Venice, San Samuele, carnival 1752; *La calamità de' cuori,* Goldoni, Venice, San Samuele, 26 December 1752; *I bagni d'Abano* (with Bertoni), Goldoni, Venice, San Samuele, 10 February 1753; *Sofonisba,* Roccaforte, Rome, Teatro delle Dame, c. 24 February 1753; *L'eroe cinese,* Metastasio, Naples, San Carlo, 10 July 1753; *Siroe,* Metastasio, Rome, Torre Argentina, 10 February 1754; *Il filosofo di campagna,* Goldoni, Venice, San Samuele, 26 October 1754; *Il povero superbo,* Goldoni, Venice, San Samuele, February 1755; *Attalo,* Papi?, Silvani?, Padua, Nuovo, 11 June 1755; *Le nozze,* Goldoni, Bologna, Formagliari, 14 September 1755; *La diavolessa,* Goldoni, Venice, San Samuele, November 1755; *Idomeneo,* Rome, Torre Argentina, 7 January 1756; *La cantarina,* Goldoni, Rome, Capranica, 26 February 1756; *Le pescatrici,* Goldoni, Modena, Rangoni, carnival 1756; *Ezio,* Metastasio, Milan, Regio Ducal, 22 January 1757; *Sesostri,* Zeno and Pariati, Venice, San Benedetto, 26 November 1757; *L'Ipermestra,* Metastasio, Milan, Regio Ducal, 14 January 1758; *Adriano in Siria,* Metastasio, Livorno, spring 1758; *Melite riconosciuto,* Roccaforte, Rome, Teatro delle Dame, 13 January 1759; *La ritornata di Londra,* Goldoni, Rome, Valle, c. 19 February 1759; *La clemenza di Tito,* Metastasio, Venice, San Salvatore, Ascension 1760; *Solimano,* Migliavacca, Padua, Nuovo, fair 1760; *L'amante di tutte,* Antonio Galuppi, Venice, San Moisè, 15 November 1760; *Li tre amanti ridicoli,* Antonio Galuppi, Venice, San Moisè, 18 January 1761; *Il caffè di campagna,* Chiari, Venice, San Moisè, 18 November 1761; *Antigono,* Metastasio, Venice, San Benedetto, carnival 1762; *Il marchese villano,* Chiari, Venice, San Moisè, 2 February 1762; *L'orfana onorata* (intermezzo), Rome, Valle, carnival 1762; *Il re pastore,* Metastasio, Parma, Ducal, spring 1762; *Viriate,* after Metastasio, *Silface,* Venice, San Salvatore, 19 May 1762; *Il Muzio Scevola,* Lanfranchi-Rossi, Padua, Nuovo, June 1762; *L'uomo femmina,* Venice, San Moisè, fall 1762; *Il puntiglio amoroso,* Carlo or Gasparo Gozzi, Venice, San Moisè, 26 December 1762; *Arianna e Teseo,* Pariati, Padua, Nuovo, 12 June 1763; *Il re alla caccia,* Goldoni, Venice, San Samuele, fall 1763; *La donna di governo,* Goldoni, Prague, 1763; *Sofonisba,* Verazi, Turin, Regio, carnival 1764; *Caio Mario,* Roccaforte, Venice, San Giovanni Grisostomo, 31 May 1764; *La partenza il ritorno de' marinari,* Venice, San Moisè, 26 December 1764; *La cameriera spiritosa,* Goldoni, Milan, Regio Ducal, 4 October 1766; *Ifigenia in Tauride,* Coltellini, St Petersburg, court, 2 May 1768; *Il villano geloso,* Bertati, Venice, San Moisè, November 1769; *Amor lunatico,* Chiari, Venice, San Moisè, January 1770; *L'inimico delle donne,* Bertati, Venice, San Samuele, fall 1771; *Gl'intrighi amorosi,* Petrosellini, Venice, San Samuele, January 1772; *Montezuma,* Cigna-Santi, Venice, San Benedetto, 27 May 1772; *La serva per amore,* Livigni, Venice, San Samuele, fall 1773;

Baldassare ("Baldissera" in Venetian records) Galuppi was, for a time in the 1750s and early 1760s, the most performed composer of Italian opera in Europe. While he has long been praised for his collaboration with Goldoni in the development of the *dramma giocoso,* he is now known to have played a central role in serious opera as well.

His first opera, composed at age 16, was *Gli amici rivali* (*La fede nell' incostanza* at a later performance); its poor reception (a "scandal") led him to approach Benedetto Marcello for advice. Galuppi committed himself to extended study with the first organist in San Marco, Antonio Lotti, and to abstain from the stage for three years. The boy was arranging operas and composing substitute arias (as well as playing cembalo) for theaters in Venice and Florence before two years were out, however, and his career rose steadily through the 1730s and 40s.

In 1741-43 he was in London, where he oversaw the production of numerous operas, both his own works and many arranged from other composers. Horace Walpole and Handel criticized his music, but his light, tuneful melodies captured much public attention; his music was printed and reprinted by London publishers, and his operas continued to be staged after his return to Italy. Back in Venice, he took up his old professions of arranging, performing, and composing, and his prestige continued to climb.

His genius fully blossomed only late in the 1740s. In *opera seria* he saw enormous success. *L'Olimpiade* (Milan, 1747) and *Vologeso* (Rome, 1748) were followed by *Demetrio* and *Artaserse*, both for Vienna, which broke all box office records. While he remained within the traditional formal constraints of the opera of the day, both in recitatives and arias, his charming and graceful melodies were everywhere praised. His orchestration (he was a hard taskmaster over those orchestras under his control) was always clear and unobtrusive.

His success proved only to be an omen of greater things to come, for 1749 saw the beginning of his collaboration with the father of Italian comedy, Carlo Goldoni. Their first joint venture in comic opera, *L'Arcadia in Brenta* (Goldoni had supplied Galuppi with two serious librettos in 1740, neither of which was particularly successful), was rapidly followed by a long series of similar works, all of which were quickly adapted and performed throughout Europe. Goldoni's elegant poetry, witty dialogue, and sometimes biting satire were ideally matched with Galuppi's remarkable comic pacing, his facile, tuneful melodies, and his lucid orchestration. Together they largely pioneered the development of the ensemble finale (or "chain" finale), in which all aspects of the musical structure, including tempo, mode, key, accompaniment, formal design, etc., shift fluidly and easily according to the dictates of the drama; ensembles and solo sections freely alternate, usually presenting a variety of comic situations, and (particularly) the reactions of the protagonists to these changing developments. The second act finale of *La diavolessa* (Venice, 1755) is a good example; here a farcical seance evoking dark spirits is juxtaposed with pointed laughter, amazement, ridicule, and confusion when the lights go out. Similarly, the sneezing ensemble that closes the first act of *L'arcadia in Brenta* (Venice, 1749) is a masterpiece of comic effect.

In both his serious and comic compositions, Galuppi was particularly sensitive to the needs and abilities of his singers, and in this he enjoyed the collaboration of the finest singers of his day, including two of the most gifted comic performers: Francesco Baglioni and Francesco Carrattoli. Among his serious cast members were Caffarelli, Manzuoli, Gizziello, Gabrieli, Guadagni, and Amorevoli. His vocal writing changed to suit the abilities and inclinations of his singers; it was at times brilliantly florid, and at other times subdued, but always elegant and refined.

Climaxing his unimpeded rise to international prominence over the 1750s and 1760s, Galuppi accepted the post of maestro di coro of St. Marks in Venice in April, 1762 (with a high salary), and was elected maestro di coro at the Ospedale degli' Incurabili. Despite his advanced years, Galuppi petitioned the Venetian senate in early 1764 to allow his travel to Russia, which was reluctantly granted a year later. He served both in St Petersburg and Moscow from September 1765 to late in 1768, completing his *Ifigenia in Tauride* and reviving *Didone abbandonata* and *Il re pastore,* all to great success, while arranging other operas and providing religious and occasional music. Upon his return to Venice, laden with many gifts, he dedicated himself exclusively to sacred music until his death.—DALE E. MONSON

The Gambler [Igrok]

Composer: *Sergei Prokofiev.*

Librettist: *Sergei Prokofiev (after Dostoevsky).*

First Performance: *Brussels, Théâtre de la Monnaie, 29 April 1929.*

Roles: *The General (bass); Pauline (soprano); Alexey (tenor); Grandmother (mezzo-soprano); Marquis (tenor); Mr. Astley (baritone); Blanche (contralto); Prince Nilsky (tenor); Baron Wurmerhelm (bass); Potapich (baritone); several bit roles which may be doubled; chorus (SATB).*

Prokofiev shared with Tchaikovsky both a lifelong passion for opera and a high failure-rate in the genre. Three Prokofiev operas, *Maddalena* (1911-13), *Khan Buzay* (1942) and *Distant Seas* (1948), were abandoned unfinished. Three more, *The Fiery Angel* (1919-27), *War and Peace* (1941-52) and *The Story of a Real Man* (1947-48), were denied complete staged performances in his lifetime. Following decades of neglect, the reputation of *The Gambler* has been much enhanced by recent revivals.

Prokofiev long had it in mind to compose an opera based on Dostoevsky's novel *Igrok* or *The Gambler*—the first such Dostoevsky adaptation. Rebuffed by his patron Sergey Diaghilev, he took the project to the Maryinsky Theater where there was a real prospect of operatic performance from the end of 1915. Aware that a sensation was expected of him and eager to restore a fluid, theatrical dimension to the form, Prokofiev reacted sharply against operatic convention. He put together his own text and opted for a supple conversational style, leaving no room for anything as orthodox as an aria to hold up the action.

The story (a curtailed version of Dostoevsky's) is set in the imaginary German spa town of Roulettenburg, where a retired Russian general eagerly awaits the news that Babulenka, a rich relative, has died leaving him her fortune. He is surrounded by a crowd of fellow-gamblers, plus his young children, his step-daughter Pauline, and Alexey, the children's tutor. Alexey is in love with Pauline, while Pauline has in the past had a liaison with the marquis from whom the general has had to borrow large sums of money. Unfortunately for the family finances, Babulenka turns up in her wheel-chair. Reports of her death have been greatly exaggerated. She too becomes infected with the passion for roulette and loses a fortune before leaving for home. Now Pauline is faced with marriage to her father's creditor, the marquis. In order to rescue her from this situation, Alexey vows to win the money for her at roulette. He has fantastic luck and breaks the bank. But when he brings her the cash, she throws it back in his face, crying that money is an insulting payment for love. The opera ends with Alexey raving, lost to his obsession.

For too long, *The Gambler* was generally dismissed as a problem piece. The drama lacks any genuinely sympathetic characters, and its almost relentless cynicism is not for all tastes. On the other hand, Prokofiev builds to a stunning last act: "I make bold to believe that the scene in the gambling-house is totally new in operatic literature both in idea and structure. And I feel that in this scene I succeeded in accomplishing what I had planned," he wrote. Instead of treating the gamblers and croupiers as a chorus, Prokofiev gives them individual lines and characters. The effect is appropriately feverish: the track of mounting tension will culminate in hysteria and madness. It would be absurd to present a non-political composer as having revolutionary ambitions, yet the collective intoxication of Russia on the brink is aptly symbolized in this idiosyncratic score. Prokofiev's *Gambler* seems to hold up a mirror to a society corrupted by the pursuit of easy money and racing toward oblivion.

The work's chequered career was not unaffected by the spirit of revolution. Rehearsals began at the Maryinsky in January 1917. But, as the press reported, "The prevailing sentiment among the artists is that Prokofiev's opera *The Gambler* should be dropped from the repertory, for while this cacophony of sounds, with its incredible intervals and enharmonic tones, may be very interesting to those who love powerful musical sensations, it is completely uninteresting to the singers, who in the course of a whole season have scarcely managed to learn their parts" (*Vecherniye Birzheviye Vedomosti*, 10 May 1917). By the time of the world premiere, given in French at the Théâtre de la Monnaie, Brussels, in April 1929, Prokofiev had revised the work thoroughly, softening the edges in the process. *The Gambler* had to wait until 1962 for its first British performance, given in Serbo-Croat by a touring company of Belgrade Opera. And until Gennady Rozhdestvensky's pioneering radio broadcast of March 1963, it was unknown in its native Russia. In April 1974, *The Gambler* finally entered the repertoire of the Bolshoi and, in 1983, David Pountney's brilliantly effective production came to English National Opera, giving UK opera-goers their first real chance to assess one of Prokofiev's most compelling operatic achievements.—DAVID GUTMAN

Garden, Mary

Soprano. Born 20 February 1874, in Aberdeen. Died 3 January 1967, in Inverurie. Studied in Chicago with Mrs. Robinson Duff and in Paris with Sbriglia, Bouhy, Trabadello, Marchesi, and Fugère; debut as replacement in Louise *at Opéra-Comique, 1900; at Covent Garden, 1902-03; Hammerstein's Manhattan Opera House debut in United States premiere of* Thaïs, *1907; Chicago debut as Mélisande, 1910, and remained with Chicago for twenty years; director of Chicago's 1921-22 season; last Chicago appearance as Jean in Massenet's* Le jongleur de Notre Dame, *1931; appeared in Cleveland, 1932; appearance at Opéra-Comique, 1934; in United States for Debussy recital-lectures in 1934-35, and Debussy lectures, 1949-55; created roles in Massenet's* Chérubin, *Pierne's* La fille du Tabarin, *d'Erlanger's* Camille, *Leroux's* La reine fiammette, *and Debussy's* Pélleas et Mélisande.

Once, when confounded by a critic's comment that her upper notes were like the snakes in Ireland, Mary Garden turned to her father for an explanation. "Why, Mary," he responded, "there are no snakes in Ireland." The story may be apocryphal, but it illustrates the problems Garden faced with critics throughout her professional life. Mary Garden was known as a "singing-actress" long before the term was popularized by Maria Callas. The stress was on "actress," and Garden professed to be enamored of the dramatic stage just as much as the operatic. Like Callas, however, she was not an actress per se, as both discovered when they attempted straight drama in unsuccessful films.

In order to appreciate Garden better, we must depend on contemporary reviews of her performances which constantly drive home the fact that for her word and gesture were paramount. Garden's voice followed along like an obedient servant ready to bow to her will to make the note telling, the scene more riveting. Was this not Callas's aim also? The analogy is apt since both aspired to the same end—the vivid recreation of a character according to the composer's intentions. The comparison can be extended even further since Callas possessed a hauntingly beautiful voice finely schooled in the art of bel canto, and Garden (at least toward the beginning, if one judges by the recordings prior to 1926) one of gleaming silver, perhaps less well schooled than Callas's, but no less effective.

In her own time Garden was unique. When other sopranos were emulating the legendary Adelina Patti in their tonal perfection, Garden, by her own admission, was trained (albeit briefly) in all the finer points of vocal techniques, but left most of what she learned in the studio. We must take this statement on faith, however, since apart from her recording of "Semper libra" (in French) which she executes unembellished but quite neatly, we have no other example of what she could do with florid singing. Her recordings, in general, reveal only a small part of what was the essential Mary Garden. Without the visual element, we can only guess at what she looked like on stage. Her voice is nonetheless telling, from the purity of "Mes longs cheveux" from *Pelléas et Mélisande,* which so eloquently and simply captures the childlike quality of Debussy's waif, to the dark, tortured tones of Katusha's aria from *Risurezzione* (again, sung in French), which so pointedly depicts the despair of a woman facing an emotional crisis.

Another source for capturing a glimmer of what Garden was like are her photographs. The pains she took to resemble the character she portrayed are clearly reflected in these—from the steely stare of a hoydenish Carmen, the aloof beauty of Thais, black-clad Marguerite "after the fall", the Renaissance grace of Mélisande, the jeweled gossamer dress of Salome to the plain, simple Jongleur. The photograph of Garden's Katusha is arguably the most telling, and after one has viewed the torture in her eyes, the unkempt hair, the haggard face, one has almost been witness to Garden on stage.

Today Teresa Stratas most closely resembles Garden in intent. It is doubtful that the two sopranos mirror one another's acting style, for styles change, though their purpose remains the same. When one has seen Stratas bare her soul as Suor Angelica or suffer the grand passions of Violetta in *La traviata,* one has also fit another piece in the Garden puzzle. Even if Garden's films were available, they would not give more than a hint as to what she was like; they were silent films and, like her recordings, therefore, tell us only half the story.

Where does all this leave us? The art of Mary Garden is as elusive as the voices of Jean de Reszke or Emma Eames, Adelina Patti in her prime or Jenny Lind, or the great castrati. Although there are those who can still recall the rose strewing Thaïs of their youths, there are a multitude who can not. The disembodied voice of Garden only begins to tell the story.—JOHN PENNINO

Gedda, Nicolai

Tenor. Born Harry Gustaf Ustinoff, 11 July 1925, in Stockholm. Married Anastasia Caraviotis, 1965 (one son, one daughter). Studied with his father in Leipzig, in Stockholm

with Carl Martin Oehmann, and later in New York with Paola Novikova; military service, then worked in a bank for five years; debut in Stockholm as Chapelou in Adam's Le postillon de Longjumeau, *1952; debut at the Teatro alla Scala as Don Ottavio, 1952-53; debut at Paris Opéra, 1954; Covent Garden debut as Duke in* Rigoletto, *1954; Metropolitan Opera debut as Faust, 1957; created role of the Bridegroom in Orff's* Il trionfo d'Afrodite *and Anatol in Barber's* Vanessa.

Throughout his long career, tenor Nicolai Gedda has been known for his versatility, style, intelligence, and taste, characteristics in small supply in the stereotypical operatic tenor. He made his operatic debut in 1952 as Chapelou in Adam's *Le postillon de Longjumeau* in Stockholm; his success was such that he was invited almost immediately to make his first recording, as Dmitri in Musorgsky's *Boris Godunov,* a recording that starred Boris Christoff in the title role (and that cut one of Dmitri's arias).

Gedda's debut at the Teatro alla Scala, as Ottavio in Mozart's *Don Giovanni,* followed in 1953. He created the role of the Bridegroom in Orff's *Il trionfo dell' Afrodite* at the composer's request. He made his debut at Covent Garden (as the Duke in Verdi's *Rigoletto*) and at the Paris Opéra (as Huon in Weber's *Oberon*) in 1954, followed quickly by his debuts in Rome (in Stravinsky's *Oedipus Rex*) and Vienna. He gave his first performances at the Metropolitan Opera (as Gounod's Faust) and Salzburg in 1957; at the Metropolitan he created the role of Anatol in Barber's *Vanessa* in 1958 and, in its American premiere, sang Kodanda in Menotti's *Le dernier sauvage* in 1964.

A highly accomplished singer, Gedda is renowned for his musicianship, insight, sensitive phrasing, and attention to detail. A specialist in the lyric and spinto tenor repertoire who rarely attempts heavier roles (although he sang Wagner's Lohengrin in Stockholm in 1966 and has sung and recorded Don José in Bizet's *Carmen*), Gedda possesses a voice that can be described as sturdy, sweet, centered, and firmly focused. His proficiency with languages (he is fluent in Swedish, Russian, English, French, and German) and excellent diction, combined with his apparent intelligence and taste, have been significant assets in his unusually extensive repertoire. He has the ability to convey or suggest personality through his singing. His acting is vivid and enthusiastic yet nuanced; his ability to sing mezzavoce and even pianissimo is a skill that contributes to his vocal acting ability. He generally follows the composer's score markings scrupulously. At his best, his tone is liquid, limpid, his phrasing aristocratic, his interpretations stylish, charming, even bewitching.

This intelligent approach has led some critics to fault Gedda for what they consider to be overstudied, unspontaneous interpretations, ones imposed from without rather than growing naturally out of the words. He is sometimes more reliable than exciting; his singing can be mannered, the enunciation exaggerated, the characterizations too sophisticated. He has also been criticized for a lack of smoothness in his line, for an explosive attack on certain notes that disrupts the flow. In later performances he has sometimes sounded cautious and labored, unable to conceal the effort of singing. Even in his prime he was sometimes criticized for a lack of Italianate tone in his Italian roles, a result of his rather lean timbre.

Gedda is especially associated with the French repertoire, including such roles as Des Grieux in Massenet's *Manon,* Hoffmann in Offenbach's *Les contes d'Hoffmann,* Berlioz's Benvenuto Cellini, Gounod's Faust and Roméo, and Raoul in Meyerbeer's *Les Huguenots.* Among his Slavic roles are Gherman in Tchaikovsky's *Queen of Spades,* Jeník in Smetana's *The*

Bartered Bride, Dmitri, and Lensky in Tchaikovsky's *Eugene Onegin.* His Mozart portrayals include Don Ottavio in *Don Giovanni,* Belmonte in *Die Entführung aus dem Serail,* and Tamino in *Die Zauberflöte.* In the Italian lyric repertoire he has sung Nemorino in Donizetti's *L'elisir d'amore,* Ernesto in Donizetti's *Don Pasquale,* Edgardo in Donizetti's *Lucia di Lammermoor,* and, among Verdi roles, the Duke in *Rigoletto,* Alfredo in *La traviata,* and Riccardo in *Un ballo in maschera.* His Puccini roles include Rodolfo in *La bohème* and Pinkerton in *Madama Butterfly.* He has also performed and recorded operettas, particularly Johann Strauss's *Die Fledermaus* and *The Gypsy Baron,* and Lehar's *The Merry Widow.*

Lensky in Tchaikovsky's *Eugene Onegin* is arguably Gedda's greatest role, and was the role that marked his debut in Russia in 1980. He brings to it both the youthful ardor and the sadness and resignation of Pushkin's character.

Gedda has been a prolific recording artist; he has perhaps recorded a greater range of works than any other tenor. Among the roles he has performed in complete opera recordings are Gounod's Faust, Don Narciso in Rossini's *Il turco in Italia,* Orfeo in Gluck's *Orfeo ed Euridice,* Pinkerton, Eisenstein in Johann Strauss's *Die Fledermaus,* Don José, Rodolfo, Tamino in Mozart's *Die Zauberflöte,* Don Ottavio, Hoffmann, Belmonte, Max in Weber's *Der Freischütz,* Des Grieux in Massenet's *Manon,* Alfredo, Benvenuto Cellini, Arturo in Bellini's *I Puritani,* Mozart's Idomeneo, Ferrando in Mozart's *Così fan tutte,* Nicias in Massenet's *Thaïs,* Auber's Fra Diavolo, and Vaudémont in Tchaikovsky's *Iolanta.*—MICHAEL SIMS

Gershwin, George

Composer. Born Jacob Gershvin, 26 September 1898, in Brooklyn, New York. Died 11 July 1937, in Beverly Hills, California. Studied piano with Ernest Hutcheson and Charles Hambitzer in New York; studied harmony with Edward Kilenyi and Rubin Goldmark; studied counterpoint with Henry Cowell and Wallingford Riegger; also studied with Joseph Schillinger in the last years of his life. Gershwin enjoyed enormous success throughout his career; song Swanee *sold over a million copies, 1917;* Rhapsody in Blue *conducted by Paul Whiteman with Gershwin playing the solo part, Aeolian Hall, New York, 12 February 1924; numerous orchestral compositions, including* Piano Concerto in F, An American in Paris, Cuban Overture, *and* Variations for Piano and Orchestra *on his song, "I Got Rhythm," 1925-1934, as well as many musicals.*

Operas *Blue Monday* (retitled *135th Street*), Globe Theater, 28 August 1922; *Song of the Flame* (operetta), O. Hammerstein II and O. Harbach, New York, 44th Street Theater, 30 December 1925; *Porgy and Bess,* DuBose Heyward (after Dubose and Dorothy Heyward), New York, Alvin Theater, 10 October 1935.

Irving Berlin said of Gershwin: "He is the only songwriter I know who became a 'composer.'" For Gershwin, to be a "composer" meant to accomplish much more than achieving phenomenal commercial success as a tunesmith for Broadway's musical theater scene. It meant engaging larger, more traditional forms such as ballet, opera and the symphony, and it meant producing music—contrary to the Broadway norm—in which every note would in fact be written by him. Through Charles Hambitzer, with whom he took piano lessons from 1912 to 1914, he had been exposed early on to the world of classical music. Later he studied composition with, among others, Wallingford Riegger, Joseph Schillinger, Rubin Goldmark and Henry Cowell. But his involvement with composition teachers was typically intermittent and short-lived. For the most part, Gershwin was self-taught in both songwriting and in what he regarded as his "serious" work.

Products of the latter include the 1924 *Rhapsody in Blue* for piano and jazz band, the 1925 *Concerto in F* for piano and orchestra, the 1928 tone-poem *An American in Paris,* the 1931 *Second Rhapsody for Piano and Orchestra,* the 1932 *Cuban Overture,* the 1934 set of *Variations for Piano and Orchestra* based on his song "I Got Rhythm" and—perhaps his best-known work—the 1935 opera *Porgy and Bess.* All of these have been, and continue to be, performed in orchestrations other than Gershwin's. Except for *Rhapsody in Blue* (written by Gershwin only in "short score" and then arranged, originally for Paul Whiteman's jazz band and later for full orchestra, by Ferde Grofé), however, all of them do have scores that are entirely Gershwin's own.

Commissioned and premiered by Walter Damrosch and the New York Symphony Orchestra, *An American in Paris* proved enormously popular, and its reception prompted New York's Metropolitan Opera in 1929 to commission a full-length theatrical work from Gershwin. A contract was signed for "a Jewish opera" to be titled *The Dybbuk,* but the commission was never fulfilled. *Porgy and Bess,* based on a play by DuBose Heyward, with libretto by Heyward and lyrics by Gershwin's brother Ira, was not a commissioned work; its first production, heavily invested in by Gershwin himself, took place in New York's Alvin Theater. It ran only for 124 performances and was considered a financial failure.

George Gershwin with DuBose Heyward and Ira Gershwin, 1935

Gershwin died less than two years after the premiere of *Porgy and Bess,* the victim—at age 38—of a brain tumor. Along with a ballet titled *Swing Symphony,* a string quartet, another piano concerto and a classically structured symphony, his plans included a second full-length opera to be made in collaboration with Heyward.—JAMES WIERZBICKI

Ghiaurov, Nicolai

Bass. Born 13 September 1929, in Lydjene, near Velingrad, Bulgaria. Married Mirella Freni in 1981. Studied with Christo Brambarov at Sofia Conservatory, 1949-50, and Moscow Conservatory, 1950-55; debut as Basilio in Il barbiere di Siviglia, *Sofia, 1955-56; Bolshoi Opera debut as Pimen, 1957-58; Teatro alla Scala debut as Varlaam, 1959; appeared at Covent Garden as Padre Guardiano in* La forza del destino, *1962; Chicago debut as Mephistopheles, 1963-64; Metropolitan Opera debut in* Faust, *1965.*

During his long and highly successful career Nicolai Ghiaurov has established a firm reputation as one of the leading basses of the second half of the twentieth century. His repertory is restricted chronologically: he has sung comparatively few roles composed before 1850 or after 1900. Nor is he particularly effective in comic roles. But in serious operas of the second half of the nineteenth century Ghiaurov is unsurpassed in the richness and power of his deep voice and the vividness of his acting.

One can hear the qualities that have brought Ghiaurov such success in one of his rare eighteenth-century roles, the title role of *Don Giovanni* (as recorded under Klemperer). Ghiaurov is a strong, threatening Don Giovanni; the power of his voice seems to convey an almost superhuman strength against which all resistance by women (or men) is futile. And yet he can be lyrical and suave. When he praises Zerlina's face in the recitative preceding "La ci darem la mano," he caresses her with his gentle words. We can understand how Zerlina (sung in the recording by Mirella Freni, later to become Ghiaurov's wife) allows herself to be seduced.

Ghiaurov has sung many Verdi roles. As Fiesco in *Simon Boccanegra* (Paris, 1978) he won praise for his "rich bass tone and great dignity," and at the Teatro alla Scala he was greatly applauded in the same role. A recording of the opera under Abbado shows why Ghiaurov has been so successful a Fiesco. His performance of the great aria "Il lacerato spirito" is deeply felt, and intensely lyrical (in spite of an imperfection in the voice that produces thin, hard-edged tones on the syllable "o"; listen, for example, to the second "o" in "dolore" as Ghiaurov holds this syllable). His low register is rich and strong; he uses it to wonderful effect in the duet "Vieni a me, ti benedico."

Among Ghiaurov's other Verdi roles are Philip II in *Don Carlos* and Ramphis in *Aida* (his Ramphis as recorded under Muti was praised by one critic as "magnificent") He has sung several more unusual Verdi roles as well, winning applause as Silva in *Ernani* (Chicago) and as Banquo in *Macbeth* (La Scala).

Ghiaurov's roles are not limited to opera in Italian. He has achieved considerable success in nineteenth-century French and Russian opera. One of his early international triumphs, at La Scala in 1962, was in the role of Marcel in Meyerbeer's *Les Huguenots.* In the title role of Massenet's *Don Quichotte* at Chicago he was praised as a "funny—yet very unfunny—and lovable Quixote." Less successful was his portrayal of Mephistopheles in a recording of

Gounod's *Faust;* a critic found fault with the "worn patches" in Ghiaurov's tone (perhaps alluding to the same weakness mentioned above). He is one of the best recent portrayers of the title role in Mussorgsky's *Boris Godunov;* he has also sung the role of Gremin in Tchaikovsky's *Eugene Onegin.* Reviewing a recording of Tchaikovsky's opera a critic praised Ghiaurov as "a tower of strength"; but when he sang the role in Chicago in 1984 a critic pointed out that Ghiaurov's voice had lost some of its former richness.—JOHN A. RICE.

The Ghosts of Versailles

Composer: *John Corigliano.*

Librettist: *William A. Hoffman.*

First Performance: *New York, Metropolitan Opera, 19 December 1991.*

Roles: *Woman with Hat (mezzo-soprano), Louis XVI (bass), Marquis (tenor), Trio of Gossips (soprano, soprano, alto), Opera Quartet (soprano, alto, tenor, bass), Beaumarchais (baritone), Marie Antoinette (soprano), Figaro (baritone), Susanna (soprano), Count Almaviva (tenor), Rosina (soprano), Leon (tenor), Florestine (coloratura soprano), Begearss (tenor), Wilhelm (speaking part), Cherubino (mezzo-soprano), Suleyman Pasha (bass), British Ambassador (baritone), Samira (mezzo-soprano).*

The Ghosts of Versailles is concerned with a love affair between two ghosts: Marie Antoinette, the French queen guillotined during the French Revolution, and Pierre-Augustin Caron de Beaumarchais, the man best known as the author of the plays on which Mozart's *Marriage of Figaro* and Rossini's *Barber of Seville* were based.

The opera's characters are borrowed from *La mere coupable,* the third play in Beaumarchais' Figaro trilogy. It is simultaneously set in three different worlds: the historical, the ghostly, and the theatrical. Beaumarchais, a ghostly presence at Versailles, has fallen in love with fellow ghost Marie Antoinette. He tells her that his art can change history, and offers to create a new opera he claims will prevent her beheading. While her fellow ghosts applaud the idea, Marie Antoinette remains unconvinced. In the opera-within-an-opera, Figaro, Susanna, Almaviva, Rosina, Cherubino and their cohorts plot to ransom Marie Antoinette from the revolutionaries. Incensed by Beaumarchais' attention to his wife, Louis XVI challenges him to a duel and kills him, which changes nothing since they are both ghosts. Ultimately, Beaumarchais' plan to spare Marie Antoinette fails, undone by the Figaro he creates, who sees fit to abandon his revolutionary ways, and by Marie Antoinette herself, who is intent on letting history proceed unchanged so she won't lose Beaumarchais. The opera ends with the ghostly Beaumarchais kissing Marie Antoinette's ghostly hand.

At its premiere, *The Ghosts of Versailles,* described by its composer as "a grand opera buffa," made an unprecedented impact on audiences, management and most critics. Here was a work, commissioned by the Metropolitan Opera and the first new opera to be performed there in a quarter-century, that offered an irresistible melange of gorgeous melodic invention, side-splitting comedic antics and heart-wrenching dramatic situations involving major historical figures, all placed within a swirling pool of contemporary devices set to remind audiences that it is still possible to compose memorable music as the century ends. Many of the reviews were rapturous. "This is a brilliant, beautiful score from a composer who continues to surpass himself," wrote a reviewer in *Newsday.* " In short, *The Ghosts of Versailles* is a masterpiece," agreed the commentator for *New York Daily News*. *Opera News* called it "an amazingly accomplished work." The work was televised nationally on PBS and released on VHS and laser disc on the Deutsche Grammophon label.

Typical of Corigliano's style, the music for *Ghosts* is a pastiche, running the gamut from Mozart-like tunes to 12-tone rows, with Turkish parodies and quarter-tone intervals and lots of impressionistic overlays to match its ghostly setting. While there is a sense of control throughout the score—the opera ends on an "A," for example, the same note with which it begins—there are also improvisatory elements, especially in the orchestral part, where players are often given instructions to take liberties like varying the lengths of passages and, at one point, to "make a slow and even rallentando, ignoring the conductor."

The music is blessedly free of the aimless fodder some composers substitute for a lack of imagination. Some set pieces grab your attention instantly. Marie Antoinette s first aria, "Once there was a golden bird," (its plaintive melody returns at the opera's end) is a bittersweet masterpiece. "Look at the green here in the glade," which begins as a duet between Rosina and Cherubino and, with the addition of Marie Antoinette and Beaumarchais, expands into a quartet, is filled with ethereal beauty. There is high hilarity in Samira's cavatina near the end of Act I, its mock-solemn music set to an unusually zany text: "I am in a valley and you are in a valley. I have no she- or he-camel in it. In ev'ry house there is a cesspool. That s life!" The Rossini-like chase scene that ends the act can leave you breathless. And the "Aria of the Worm," a sinister tribute to that slimy creature sung by the treacherous villain Begearss, is at the least a small masterpiece.

Ultimately, *Ghosts* works so well because it does precisely what great opera is meant to do: It attracts your attention, keeps you fascinated and leaves you with a desire to return to it again and again. When he received the commission from the Met to compose the opera, Corigliano described the experience as like being offered "the Hope diamond, complete with curse. It's so glorious you cannot turn it down, even though you know it's going to kill you." Fortunately, for him and for us, the curse turned instead into a precious operatic blessing.—JOHN GUINN

Gigli, Beniamino

Tenor. Born 20 March 1890, in Recanati, Italy. Died 30 November 1957, in Rome. Married Costanza (one daughter, singer Rina Gigli; one son, Enzo; and three other children). Studied with Agnese Bonucci in Rome, and at Liceo Musicale with Antonio Cotogni and Enrico Rosati; debut as Enzo in La gioconda, *Rovigo, 1914; appeared in Bologna and Naples as Boito's Faust, 1915; appeared in same role under Toscanini at the Teatro alla Scala, 1918; at Metropolitan Opera, 1920-32, and returned for 1938-39 season; Covent Garden debut as Andrea Chénier, 1930, and sang there in 1931, 1938, and 1946; appeared primarily in concert after World War II; final tour of North America, 1955; appeared in seventeen films.*

The foremost Italian operatic tenor of the 1920s, 30s, and 40s, Beniamino Gigli is said to have possessed "the finest lyric tenor voice of this century." His voice was indeed one of extraordinary beauty; its texture was warm, lush, velvety, and mellifluous. It was also a large voice, and Gigli could sing with passion and vigor and with ringing, thrilling top tones. To these qualities can be added his excellent diction, his absolutely accurate sense of pitch, and his perfect breathing technique. One critic noted that he sang "as naturally as a gamecock fights." He best exhibited his talents when a role called for both lyricism and dramatic vitality. While his stage acting was old-fashioned, he was capable of expressing through his singing a wide range of emotions. One might say that he acted with his voice. To all his roles and performances he brought a conviction, an emotional intensity, and a total commitment that never failed to electrify his audiences.

In addition to his appearances all over Italy, he was leading tenor at the Metropolitan Opera between 1920 and 1932, returning for a few performances in 1939. He sang often at Covent Garden. As a young man he sang in Spain and in South America; he returned to enthusiastic audiences in Rio de Janeiro and Buenos Aires after World War II. He was a popular recitalist as well as an opera singer. More than 300 commercial recordings are to his credit and perhaps an equal number of recordings not to be bought on commercial labels, including complete or substantially complete operas that were recorded sometimes from live performances. He also appeared in several films.

Gigli's repertoire was enormous, although it was primarily within the vast realm of Italian opera and song. He might have said as did Andrea Chénier, "Colla mia voce ho cantato mia patria!" (With my voice I have sung my country!). The most notable exceptions were his excursions into French opera, which he sang usually in Italian. Early in his career he sang Des Grieux in Massenet's *Manon,* and later he excelled in Gounod's *Faust,* as his fine recording of "Salve, dimora casta e pura" bears witness. After World War II he sang Don José in *Carmen,* with his daughter Rina, a highly gifted soprano, in the role of Micaela. To this list one can add the tenor roles in Gounod's *Romeo and Juliet,* Thomas's *Mignon,* and Lalo's *Le roi d'Ys.*

Gigli's recitals were full of Italian songs ranging from those of the 16th-, 17th-, and 18th-century masters through the traditional Neapolitan songs to those of contemporary composers. These pieces endeared him to his audiences and were a delightful appendage to his truly herculean accomplishments in opera, where his fame chiefly rests.

As an interpreter of Puccini roles, Gigli has not been surpassed. The complete recordings on 78 of *La bohème, Tosca,* and *Madama Butterfly,* made in the late 1930s, have set a standard for all future tenors. Although we have no complete commercial recording of *Manon Lescaut,* the arias that he recorded and a live performance from Rio in 1951 indicate that Puccini's Des Grieux was one of his best roles. His artistic temperament is best exemplified in the scene at Le Havre leading into the impassioned aria "No! Pazzo son! Guardate." The excessive sobbing for which he was frequently criticized is very appropriate here as Des Grieux implores the captain to let him board the ship to go with Manon to Louisiana. The captain agrees, and there is a crashing E-major chord in the orchestra, to which Gigli interpolates a high B sung to the name "Manon." The effect is absolutely electrifying; it is vintage Gigli.

Among Verdi operas one should first cite *La traviata,* in which Gigli's fine lyricism stood him in good stead as Alfredo. A complete live performance from Covent Garden (in 1939) has come down to us in which Gigli sings with Maria Caniglia, a favorite partner, in the title role. The war-time commercial recording of *Un ballo in maschera* (1943), again with Caniglia and under the baton of Serafin, is another testimony of Gigli's excellence. He and Caniglia also had sung solo parts, along with Ebe Stignani and Ezio Pinza, in Serafin's 1939 complete recording of the *Requiem.* Gigli sang Radames in the 1930s and 1940s and recorded a complete *Aïda* (1946), the last of the complete commercial operatic recordings, but in *Aïda,* as well as in *Il trovatore* and

OPERA

Rigoletto, he shares honors with other great tenors. Heroic tenors like Caruso and Mario del Monaco come first to mind when one thinks of Alvaro in *La forza del destino,* but Gigli's recording from 1927 with Giuseppe de Luca of the famous tenor/baritone duet, "Solenne in quest'ora," is an everlasting monument to his memory; never has Verdi's beautiful tenor line been sung so expansively and with such vocal splendor.

In Leoncavallo's *I pagliacci* Gigli's inspired rendition of "No, Pagliaccio non son" is unforgettable; a complete commercial recording was made in 1939. Unfortunately we have no complete recordings of his performances in *La gioconda* and *Mefistofele;* the arias and excerpts that do exist suggest that he has no peer. There is no question that his complete commercial recordings of *Cavalleria rusticana* (1940), with Mascagni conducting, and of *Andrea Chénier* (1941)—his favorite role, for which he received high praise from Giordano himself—will remain the standards by which all later interpretations can be measured.

Two of Gigli's interpretations of Donizetti are particularly noteworthy: *L'elisir d'amore* and *Lucia di Lammermoor.* Gigli was singing Nemorino as late as 1953, with daughter Rina as Adina. Although the complete recording has rather bad sound, the celebrated aria "Una furtiva lagrima" and the aria from Act I have been well preserved in earlier studio recordings. Gigli's finest electrical 78 RPM recordings also include the Sextette from *Lucia* and the entire Tomb Scene, with Pinza. The Fountain Scene (from Edgardo's entrance to the end of the act) exists on a private label; Gigli sings with Marion Talley in this collector's item from 1927.

Gigli also starred in famous operas that are seldom performed today, including Meyerbeer's *L'Africaine* and Flotow's *Martha;* his recordings of "O Paradiso" (1928) and "M'appari" (1929) are superb. Finally, he sang the leading tenor roles in operas not well known outside of Italy; these include Mascagni's *Iris* and *L'amico Fritz* (of which there is a complete recording), Giordano's *La cena delle beffe* and *Fedora* (Gigli sang "Amor ti vieta" extremely well), and operas by Catalani, Cilèa, and Montemezzi.

In April of 1955 at the age of 65, Beniamino Gigli returned to New York, after an absence of sixteen years, for three farewell recitals at Carnegie Hall. Although his vocal prowess was beginning to wane, as is evident from the RCA Victor recording, his adoring audiences called him back on stage for encore after encore, one of which was "E lucevan le stelle." While he had recorded *Tosca* completely and the aria separately when in his prime, his rendition of the famous aria on these memorable occasions—especially the poignant closing line: "E non ho amato mai tanto la vita, tanto la vita!" ("And never have I loved life so much!")—would have thrilled Puccini as much as it did everyone present, judging from the spontaneous burst of enthusiastic applause before he finished.—JEROME MITCHELL

La Gioconda [The Joyful Girl]

Composer: *Amilcare Ponchielli.*

Librettist: *Tobia Gorrio [=Arrigo Boito] (after Hugo, Angelo, tyran de Padoue).*

First Performance: *Milan, Teatro alla Scala, 8 April 1876; revised, Venice, Rossini, 18 October 1876; final revision, Milan, Teatro alla Scala, 12 February 1880.*

Roles: *La Gioconda (soprano); Laura (mezzo-soprano); La Cieca (contralto); Enzo (tenor); Barnaba (baritone); Alvise (bass); Zuane (bass); Isepo (tenor); Pilot (bass); A Monk (bass); Two Streetsingers (baritones); Two Voices (tenor, bass); chorus (SSATTBB).*

Amilcare Ponchielli's *La Gioconda* was premiered at the Teatro alla Scala on 8 April 1876 but did not assume precisely the form we know it in today until 1880, when Ponchielli made the revised, definitive version. The libretto is by Tobia Gorrio, an anagram of Arrigo Boito. The action is set in Venice in the seventeenth century. In act I, set in the courtyard of the ducal palace, a traveling singer, La Gioconda, rejects the advances of Barnaba, a spy of the Council of Ten. In retaliation he accuses her blind mother, La Cieca, of being a witch. If Enzo Grimaldo, a Genoese prince whom La Gioconda secretly loves, had not intervened, Gioconda's mother would have been killed by the crowd after Barnaba's accusation. Enzo had been banished from Venice but has returned in disguise because he is in love with Laura Adorno, wife of Alvise Badoero, one of the chiefs of the Venetian state inquisition. Alvise arrests La Cieca despite Enzo's intervention, but Laura obtains a pardon for her. In gratitude La Cieca gives Laura a rosary. Meanwhile, hoping to keep Enzo away from La Gioconda, Barnaba promises to help him elope with Laura. When La Gioconda discovers this, she determines to kill her rival.

In act II, La Gioconda hides in the ship in which Enzo and Laura plan to escape. As La Gioconda is about to stab Laura, she notices her mother's rosary and realizes that it was Laura who saved La Cieca. La Gioconda now resolves to help the lovers escape. Alvise appears; as Laura and La Gioconda flee together, Enzo sets fire to the ship and swims ashore.

Act III begins at the Ca' d'Oro in Laura's room. A magnificent ball is taking place while Alvise accuses his wife of adultery and demands that she drink poison. La Gioconda, however, substitutes a sleeping draught for the poison; she instructs Laura to drink it and merely pretend to be dead. After the ball, during which the famous ballet, "Dance of the Hours," is heard, Alvise raises a curtain to show the shocked guests Laura lying, as it were, dead. The masked Enzo is at the ball, but when he sees Laura thus he betrays himself and is arrested. To save Enzo, La Gioconda realizes her only recourse is to give in to Barnaba's lust in exchange for Enzo's safety. Barnaba agrees but hauls away La Cieca as a hostage.

In act IV, La Gioconda has the sleeping Laura brought to a ruined palace. Because she has lost both her mother and Enzo, La Gioconda contemplates suicide. With Barnaba's help Enzo has escaped from prison; although he is grateful for La Gioconda's sacrifices, he nevertheless leaves with Laura. Barnaba arrives to claim his part of the bargain from Gioconda; she pretends to consent but instead stabs herself. He cries out that he has killed her mother, but La Gioconda is past hearing.

La Gioconda is the only opera by Ponchielli still to be heard on a regular basis. It is an old-fashioned standard grand opera with a full complement of voice types, each given a solo aria, a large chorus that adds local color, a lengthy ballet, and several instances of theatrical spectacle. In fashioning the libretto Boito drew on Victor Hugo's play *Angelo, tyran de Padoue* (1835); although it was not one of Hugo's stronger dramas, it also served as the basis for operas by composers as diverse as Mercadante (*Il giuramento* of 1837) and César Cui. Boito changed the locale to Venice, where there were greater opportunities for intrigue and spectacle than in Hugo's Paduan setting. Boito's libretto featured the play of sharply drawn opposites and the portrayal of one of the first genuinely evil characters in Italian opera—Barnaba—whom one cannot help seeing as a model for Iago in Boito's libretto for Verdi's *Otello*.

It has been said that Boito's libretto for *La Gioconda* relies heavily on coincidence and hysteria, and in general terms it has been so roundly criticized as to make his assumption of an anagram of his own name readily understandable. Boito and Ponchielli were in many ways an ill-matched pair: Boito's literary conceits were not ideal for the rather unsophisticated Ponchielli, as he himself recognized. "I compose more easily when the verse is more common-place. The public wants smooth, clear things, melody, simplicity." At Ponchielli's request, Boito constantly had to revise and simplify. He was asked to make changes, however, that were not always improvements. In cutting La Gioconda's aria in act III, scene ii (in which she explains why she has shown up at Alvise's party) in favor of the long ballet, for example, dramatic motivation is lost. When *La Gioconda* was given in Rome (December 1877) and in Genoa (December 1879) it was substantially altered from the original. The final version, representing the work as we know it today, was staged in Milan at the Teatro alla Scala on 12 February 1880. With each revision much of the complexity of the story and the music was discarded.

For Ponchielli was indeed a master of "melody, simplicity." His opera, with its melodramatic situations, its expressive arias (full of wide leaps and vocal acrobatics), and its masterly handling of huge crowd scenes, all against the backdrop of the Venice of opulent palaces and sinister little alleys, is extremely popular with the public but loathed by the snobs. It is a remarkably well-crafted piece. Rather than compose separate numbers, in *La Gioconda* Ponchielli joined arias and ensembles and *declamato* passages so skillfully that each act holds together as an entity. Act I, for example, is skillfully wrought in introducing the six main characters, showing the relationships among them, and portraying the vitality and shifting moods of the Venetian crowds. In act II the music vividly heightens the scenic element, and in act III there is the famous ballet, "Dance of the Hours." If *La Gioconda* leans heavily on the incredible, the music, although not to everyone's taste, compensates handsomely.—STEPHEN WILLIER

Giordano, Umberto

Composer. Born 28 August 1867, in Foggia. Died 12 November 1948, in Milan. Studied with Gaetano Briganti in Foggia, and with Paolo Serrao at the Naples Conservatory, 1881-90; his opera Marina *given honorable mention at the Sonzogno competition, 1888; opera composition until 1929. Giordano was elected a member of the Accademia Luigi Cherubini in Florence.*

Operas *Marina,* E. Golisciani, 1888; *Mala vita,* N. Daspuro (after Salvatore Di Giacomo), Rome, Torre Argentina, 21 February 1892; revised as *Il voto,* Milan, Lirico, 10 November 1897; *Regina Diaz,* G. Targioni-Tozzetti and G. Menasci (after Lockroy, *Un duel sous le cardinal de Richelieu*), Naples, Mercadante, 5 March 1894; *Andrea Chénier,* Luigi Illica, Milan, Teatro alla Scala, 28 March 1896; *Fedora,* A. Colautti (after Sardou), Milan, Lirico, 17 November 1898; *Siberia,* Luigi Illica, Milan, Teatro alla Scala, 19 December 1903; revised 1921, Milan, Teatro alla Scala, 5 December 1927; *Marcella,* L. Stecchetti (after H. Cain, J. Adenis), Milan, Lirico, 9 November 1907; *Mese Mariano,* Salvatore Di Giacomo, Palermo, Massimo, 17 March 1910; *Madame Sans-Gêne,* R. Simoni (after Sardou and Moreau), New York, Metropolitan Opera, 25 January 1915; *Giove a Pompei* (with Franchetti), Luigi Illica and E. Romagnoli, Rome, La Pariola, 5 July 1921; *La cena delle beffe,* S. Benelli, Milan, Teatro alla Scala, 20 December 1924; *Il Re,* G. Forzano, Milan, Teatro alla Scala, 12 January 1929; *La festa del Nilo,* Sardou and Moreau [unfinished].

Giordano's early operas can appropriately be defined by the term *verismo,* which has been loosely applied to the production of the Young Italian School. *Verismo* should be understood, however, as indicating a new musico-dramatic conception not necessarily connected with a particular subject matter.

Like his colleagues Mascagni and Leoncavallo, Giordano first achieved success with a low-life story, *Mala vita* (*A wretched life*), derived from a veristic play by the Neapolitan poet Salvatore Di Giacomo. Written in the wake of the sensational success of *Cavalleria rusticana,* it was the first opera to deal with the superstitions and moral weaknesses of the Neapolitan working classes.

A dyer suffering from tuberculosis vows to marry and redeem a prostitute so that God may help him recover his health. In the event, his former mistress does not let him keep his word and the young prostitute he has chosen returns to her brothel while the whole city revels in the Piedigrotta festival. *Mala vita* has an authentic Neapolitan flavor not simply for its musical folklore (a fiery "tarantella" and some songs skillfully inserted in the action) but for the unabashed realism of its characters and situations.

Sung by the first interpreters of *Cavalleria,* Gemma Bellincioni and Roberto Stagno, the opera was well received in Rome but failed hopelessly on its first and only performance in Naples (San Carlo, 26 April 1892) where the audience and the press took it as an insult to the city and its glorious opera house. Away from its natural milieu, *Mala vita* enjoyed an ephemeral popularity. In September 1892, it was presented at the Vienna International Theater and Music Exhibition with other veristic operas such as *Cavalleria* and *Pagliacci.* In his review, the critic E. Hanslick pointed out what would become a typical characteristic of Giordano's music: "[it] makes its effects through its rough-hewn ability to achieve a tone appropriate to the situation . . . the music is the obedient, all too eager servant of the dialogue." A few years later, Giordano tried to reshape *Mala vita* and tone down its pungent *verismo.* The revised version, presented as *Il voto* (*The vow*) at the Teatro Lirico of Milan in 1897, with E. Caruso and R. Storchio in the leading roles, no longer moved or outraged anybody and the opera was soon forgotten.

In 1910 Giordano turned again to the vernacular theater of Di Giacomo for a one-act opera with a Neapolitan setting, *Mese mariano* (*Our Lady's month*). It featured nuns and children in a poor-house. Pathos, diatonic harmonies and an intimate conversation style characterized the music of this short lyrical episode. It was not a belated return to the youthful *verismo* of *Mala vita,* but rather a disavowal of its sensational, cruder connotations.

Giordano made a more appreciable and lasting contribution to *verismo* with two operas written in the late 1890s, *Andrea Chénier* and *Fedora.* A poet guillotined during the French Revolution and a fictitious Russian princess should be clear evidence of a shift of Giordano's taste and interests. In fact, Sardou's four-act drama *Fedora* had been a pet project of the composer's since he had seen it played by Sarah Bernhardt in Naples where he was a student at the Conservatory. In 1894, fruitless negotiations with the French playwright on *Fedora* determined the choice of an alternative subject.

Luigi Illica's libretto on Chénier had originally been intended for Alberto Franchetti who then sold his rights to Giordano. Borrowing from various sources (the Goncourts, Barbier, Houssaye, Méry, Renan), the skilled librettist managed to strike the right balance between fiction and history, individual feelings and collective moods, and produced four "tableaux" with strong, dramatic situations: i. reception at the castle of the Countess of Coigny (1789); ii. Paris under the Reign of Terror (1794); iii. revolutionary tribunal; iv. prison of St. Lazare. After their first meeting at the castle, Chénier and Maddalena of Coigny go through the horrors of the Revolution and fall victim to the machinations of Gérard, formerly a servant in the Coigny household and secretly in love with Maddalena, then a revolutionary leader. Chénier is sentenced to death and Maddalena volunteers to die with him taking the place of a female prisoner. Reunited in prison the night before the execution, they sing a passionate hymn to love and death, and move "with enthusiasm" to the guillotine.

Some twenty years earlier, such a libretto would have been set as a "grand-opéra" featuring choruses, ballet, colorful historical pageants, great love duets and full-hearted lyrical solos. Such components can indeed be found in *Chénier,* but the format is different. The novelty of Giordano's opera consists in the subordination of all those ingredients to the tense rhythm of the action, in the predominance of the situation over the musical form. Giordano's orchestra gives the plot impelling energy and dramatic cohesion. A musical continuum enfolds each "tableau," tightening the frivolous amusements of the aristocrats and the lament of tattered peasants, the grand gestures of Chénier and Gérard and the sneering interjections of the Parisian mob, vocal emphasis and revolutionary songs. Chénier's splendid "Improvviso" in act I, "Un dì all'azzurro spazio" ("One day I gazed at the blue sky"), exemplifies the dynamic nature of most of the vocal pieces in the opera. It is not simply an entry song for the tenor to introduce his character; it gradually upsets the aristocrats with its reference to social inequality and prepares the arrival of the peasants whose chorus spoils a graceful gavotte.

In his next opera, *Fedora,* Giordano had to deal with a murder case set in an exotic environment. The unusual subject stimulated his imagination to explore new ways of transposing the characters and situations of a modern play onto the operatic stage. The solution he adopted was to write a musical commentary which supports the long dialogue sections of the libretto and keeps lyrical expansion at a minimum level. This is particularly evident in act I where, in just over twenty minutes of performing time, a wounded man is brought in, a police interrogation is conducted, the fruitless search of a suspect takes place, and the wounded man dies.

Of the composer's remaining works, *Siberia* was particularly successful for some time in Italy and abroad. After *Fedora,* Giordano chose a second Russian story set in St. Petersburg and featuring aristocrats and officers. The local color was partly due to Illica's own readings and partly derived from the photographs and newspaper reports of Luigi Barzini. Illica's libretto concentrates on the courtisan Stephana, whose genuine passion for a young officer, Vassili, gives her the strength to redeem herself. Vassili fights and wounds her former lover, Prince Alexis, and is arrested and deported to Siberia where Stephana joins him to share a life of misery and hard labor. As they try to escape from the prison camp, the woman is shot by the guards. The second act, set at the frontier between Russia and Siberia, contains highly suggestive music (incorporating the song of the Volga boatmen) and a passionate duet between Stephana and Vassili.

In 1905, during a short season organized by the publisher E. Sonzogno at the Thèâtre Sarah Bernhardt in Paris, *Andrea Chénier, Fedora* and *Siberia* were presented with other operas by Mascagni, Leoncavallo and Cilèa. *Siberia* received the best reviews from French critics, and composers like Bruneau and Fauré praised unreservedly its second act. The opera, however, has not survived, nor has the musical comedy *Madame Sans-Gêne* (from a well-known play by Sardou and Moreau) or *La cena delle beffe* (*The mockery supper*), a decadent drama turned into a libretto by its own author, the D'Annunzian playwright Sem Benelli.

Although Giordano tried to update his harmonic language in his last two operas, he was confined to being a survivor in the twentieth century. His distinctive contribution to late nineteenth-century musical dramaturgy was to consist only of the romantic *Chénier* and the gripping *Fedora.*—MATTEO SANSONE

Glass, Philip

Composer. Born 31 January 1937, in Baltimore. Married: 1) JoAnne Akalaitis, actress (divorced), 2) Luba Burtyk, doctor, 1980. Studied flute at the Peabody Conservatory; studied piano at the University of Chicago, 1952-56; studied composition with Persichetti at Juilliard (M.A., 1962); in Paris on a Fulbright grant, 1964; studied counterpoint with Nadia Boulanger; met and studied with Ravi Shankar, 1965; travel in Morocco and across Asia; returned to New York, 1967; co-founded the recording company Chatham Square Productions; organized the Glass Ensemble, 1968; eight European tours, 1969-75; in India, 1970, 1973; Rockefeller Foundation grant, 1978; recording contract with CBS records, 1982; Musical America Musician of the Year, 1985.

Operas *Einstein on the Beach* (with Robert Wilson), Glass, 1975, France, Avignon, 25 July 1976; *The Panther* (madrigal opera), 1980; *Satyagraha*, C. DeJong (after *Bhagavad Gita*), 1980, Rotterdam, 5 September 1980; *The Photographer* (chamber opera), 1982, Amsterdam, June 1982; *Akhnaten*, Glass and others, 1983, Stuttgart, 24 March 1984; *The Juniper Tree* (with R. Moran), A. Yorinks (after Grimm), 1986; *The Making of the Representative for Planet 8*, Lessing, 1987; *The Fall of the House of Usher*, A. Yorinks (after Poe), 1988; *1000 Airplanes on the Roof*, Hwang, 1988, Vienna, July 1988; *The Voyage*, Hwang, 1991-92, New York, 1992.

Opera is almost by definition a multi-faceted art form composed and produced on a grand scale, and the concept of Minimalism seems ill-suited to it. But so-called Minimalism in music is just a technical term that has to do not with a work's substance but merely with its materials; its prominent features are relatively static harmony and extended repetition of relatively short, but not necessarily simple, melodic-rhythmic figures. Musical Minimalism can yield results that are extraordinarily complex; it can, as in the case of the operas of Philip Glass, be writ large.

Glass's involvement with music in theatrical contexts dates back to the mid 1960s, when he regularly produced incidental music for the avant-garde New York acting company called Mabou Mines. The first work he opted to call an opera, however, was the 1976 work *Einstein on the Beach,* a curiously iconoclastic "portrait" of the scientist that lasts some five hours and whose high-decibel, high-speed instrumental music—played for the most part on synthesizers and electronic organs—is offset by very little singing. Vocal elements in *Einstein on the Beach* are many, but for the most part they take the form of narrations or rhythmic choral recitations of numbers and solfege syllables.

Glass's second major opera, the 1980 work *Satyagraha,* stands in marked contrast to *Einstein on the Beach,* as does the 1984 *Akhnaten* and subsequent works. In these later examples, Glass retains many of his trademark chord progressions and rhythmic patterns, but he varies their rate of flow, and—using the full resources of the conventional orchestra—he softens both their textures and their colors. Musical Minimalism in the later operas is confined largely to accompaniments over which are set lyric lines of often rhapsodic character.

Like *Einstein on the Beach, Satyagraha* and *Akhnaten* are "portrait" operas, the one focusing on Mohandas K. Gandhi and the other on the ancient Egyptian pharaoh named in the title. Neither work, however, features a traditional story-line; they are considerably less abstract in their representations than is *Einstein on the Beach,* but both consist only of isolated scenes from their protagonist's lives, arranged in an order other than chronological. Their texts, too, are deliberately cryptic; *Satyagraha's* is in Sanskrit, and *Akhnaten's* is in a variety of archaic languages, and both works have had productions in which translations—at the composer's request—have not been made available to the audience.

Along with operas built of shuffled vignettes, Glass has written a number of operas in traditional narrative format. These are viable works, dynamic and well crafted. On the whole, though, Glass's skills at storytelling, exemplified in such works as the *The Juniper Tree* (1985) and *The Fall of the House of Usher* (1988), seem not so great as his ability to conjure up vague yet potent images of his heroes.—JAMES WIERZBICKI

Glossop, Peter

Baritone. Born 6 July 1928, in Sheffield. Studied with Joseph Hislop, Leonard Mosley, and Eva Rich. Joined Sadler's Wells Opera Chorus, but assumed leading roles and sang with company until 1962; Covent Garden debut as Demetrius in A Midsummer Night's Dream, *1961; Teatro alla Scala debut as Rigoletto, 1964-65; Metropolitan Opera debut in* Rigoletto, *1967; sang under Karajan at Salzburg, 1970-72; also has appeared in Vienna, Salzburg, San Francisco, and Buenos Aires.*

Peter Glossop began singing with his local Amateur Operatic Society in Sheffield before joining the Sadler's Wells Opera company in London as a member of the chorus. His talent was soon recognised and he began to sing the principal baritone roles, including Rigoletto, Count di Luna (*Il trovatore*), Gerard (*Andrea Chénier*), Scarpia (*Tosca*) and Eugene Onegin. In his *The Grand Tradition* (1974), J.B. Steane recalls, "I remember a principal tenor of Sadler's Wells at this time telling me how he would leave the stage during *Pagliacci,* passing through the chorus and always hearing a voice that would raise goose-pimples on his skin as he heard it. The voice was Glossop's."

As his career developed, Glossop worked principally at Covent Garden, and his international standing became considerable. In 1961 he won the first prize in the International Competition for Young Singers in Sofia, Bulgaria, his performance of the Count di Luna making a particularly strong impression. Later that year he made his Covent Garden debut, singing the role of Demetrius in Britten's *A Midsummer Night's Dream,* and the following year he confirmed his special affinity with the baritone roles of Verdi with a highly praised performance as Renato in *Un ballo in maschera.* An international career soon followed, with appearances from 1964 at the Teatro alla Scala, Milan, and other Italian houses, as well as in the United States and Canada. It was as Rigoletto that he made his debut at the Metropolitan Opera in New York in 1967, and this had been the role in which he had first appeared at La Scala three years before. In 1968 he appeared at the Vienna Staatsoper, and he sang Iago in the performances of *Otello* conducted by Karajan at the 1970 Salzburg Festival, an achievement preserved on an acclaimed recording.

These successes not only represent an outstanding personal achievement, but also played a significant part in establishing a new international recognition for British singers generally. Glossop was especially identified with Verdi through a wide range of different characters portrayed with the utmost commitment, including Renato, Rodrigo (*Don Carlo*), Iago, Di Luna, Germont (*La traviata*) and Simon Boccanegra. While not as extensive as his Verdi roles, Glossop's association with the operas of Benjamin Britten will surely rank as equally important. This judgment stems particularly from his outstanding recording of the title role in *Billy Budd*, under the direction of the composer, in which Glossop's extrovert style seems ideally suited to the part. This, together with his fine Iago recorded for Karajan, makes one regret the lack of major recordings, for at his peak in the 1960s and early 70s, Glossop's sensitive musicianship and his richly colored tone made him an artist of the highest calibre.—TERRY BARFOOT

Gluck, Alma

Soprano. Born Reba Fiersohn, 11 May 1884, in Bucharest. Died 27 October 1938, in New York. Married Bernard Gluck, 1902 (divorced 1912; one daughter, the author Marcia Davenport); married violinist Efrem Zimbalist (one son). Studied with Arturo Buzzi-Peccia, New York, and then with Jean de Reszke and Marcella Sembrich; debut as Sophie in Werther *at the Metropolitan Opera, 1909; remained at Metropolitan Opera until 1912; after 1913 sang only in concert.*

For American record buyers, soprano Alma Gluck was the female Caruso. Not that their voices or styles were in any way similar—Gluck's airy lyricism and delicate sense of concert deportment could not have resembled less that most passionate and Italianate of tenors! What they did share was commercial success unparalleled among classical musicians of the time. Actually Gluck's recording of "Carry me back to old Virginny" was the first RCA Victor Red Seal record to sell one million copies, and she was able to live quite lavishly on her royalties alone: something that could be said about no opera singer before her and very few since.

So today it comes as no surprise that Gluck is remembered almost exclusively as a recital and recording artist, and it seems difficult to grasp that she did, in fact, have a rather substantial career at the Metropolitan Opera, where she performed some of the standard operatic repertoire—Violetta in *La traviata*, Mimì in *La bohème* among others—many times with the aforementioned Enrico Caruso. And it is true that Gluck's "operatic years" were short (after 1918 she returned to the Metropolitan only to sing in concert) and her recordings document few of her roles.

Listening to these records today, Gluck's apparent choice—to veer away from the standard opera singer fare and concentrate instead on song, with only occasional forays into operatic music—seems wise. Not that she lacked anything in the way of appropriate vocal equipment; quite the contrary, for she was an uncommonly accomplished lyric soprano with a purity and tonal bloom that were special even during the years in which she performed, that much discussed and lamented golden age. She was even a pupil of the great Marcella Sembrich, who passed on to Gluck much of her breathtaking sense of line and perfect musical attack—but not her own glamour and affinity for the stage, for Gluck simply lacked an inclination for the theatre, the kind of natural temperament we associate with opera singers.

Her very few records of operatic music from what we think of as the central repertoire (little of it was central to her) are impressively sung, thoughtfully conceived and characterized, and have a graceful and fluent sense of style—but there is always a sense of the recital hall about them and the feeling that the music is removed from a dramatic context. A good example is her performance of Musetta's little waltz song from *La bohème*. This seems an odd choice for her, as Mimì was the role she usually performed and was the one that would seem to fit better her unaffectedness and gift for pathos. Sure enough, the lovely and poised singing is marvelous in its way, but so lacking in the seductiveness which underlies this aria that we almost do not recognize it. Even stranger is her performance of the "Mira O Norma" duet, where she very surprisingly sings Adalgisa to the Norma of contralto Louise Homer. The voices are as well matched and the singing as precise and fluid as we would wish, but we smile at the reverence and decorum of the two artists—it sounds more like Mendelssohn than Bellini.

Gluck is much better in her records of more out-of-the-way operatic music. There is a superb performance of Ljuba's aria from Rimsky-Korsakov's *The Tsar's Bride,* perfect in its intonation and sweetness of tone. Her performance of "Rossignols amoureux" from Rameau's *Hippolyte et Aricie* too is justly celebrated for these qualities as well as the elegant phrasing we associate with a true musician. Gluck also recorded "Le bonheur est chose légère" from Saint-Saëns *Le timbre d'argent,* this one with her husband, the famous violinist Efrem Zimbalist, and no greater praise can be offered than to say that their instruments are managed with equal suavity.

All three of these examples of music which was seldom heard in Gluck's day, and in particular was rarely performed by an artist of her popular fame. It speaks well for her taste and musicality, and is reassuring in the face of her overwhelming discography of sentimental song, much of it less than first rate. But even in this repertoire Gluck's artistry is exquisite. Michael Arne's rather silly "Lass with the delicate air," for example, is a thing of real charm in Gluck's record, filled with delicious rhythmic play and delivered with a bewitching smile in the tone. And to bring us full circle, there is again that famous "Carry me back to old Virginny." In lesser hands such a piece could easily turn maudlin; Gluck invests it with all the scrupulous musicianship and discernment that she offers in "great music," with the result that even this trifle becomes something affecting and treasurable. It is a wonderful example of

Alma Gluck in *Pagliacci*

how to sing a parlor song—and as good an example as any of the refined art of Alma Gluck.—DAVID ANTHONY FOX

Gluck, Christoph Willibald Ritter von

Composer. Born 2 July 1714, in Erasbach. Died 15 November 1787, in Vienna. Married: Marianna Pergin, 1750. In Prague, 1732; chamber musician to Prince Lobkowitz in Vienna, 1736; taken to Milan by Prince Melzi, 1737, where he met and worked with Sammartini; successful production of his first opera, Artaserse, *to a libretto by Metastasio, 1741; commissioned to write two operas for the King's Theatre in the Haymarket in London, 1745; met Handel in London; conducted Mingotti's opera company in Hamburg, Leipzig, and Dresden, 1746-47; in Vienna, 1750, where many of his operas were premiered; statement of the "reform" of opera in the preface to* Alceste, *1767 [published 1769]; in Paris, 1773, where he produced many successful operas; returned to Vienna, 1779. Gluck taught singing and harpsichord to Marie Antoinette.*

Operas *Artaserse,* Metastasio, Milan, Regio Ducal, 26 December 1741; *Demetrio,* Metastasio, Venice, San Samuele, 2 May 1742; *Demofoonte,* Metastasio, Milan, Regio Ducal, 6 January 1743; *Il Tigrane,* Francesco Silvani (after Goldoni, *La virtù trionfante dell' amore e dell' odio*), Crema, 26 September 1743; *La Sofonisba,* Francesco Silvani, with arias by Metastasio, Milan, Regio Ducal, 18 January 1744; *Ipermestra,* Metastasio, Venice, San Giovanni Grisostomo, 21 November 1744; *Poro,* after Metastasio, *Alessandro nell' Indie,* Turin, Regio, 26 December 1744; *Ippolito,* Gioseffo Gorino Corio, Milan, Regio Ducal, 31 January 1745; *La caduta de' giganti,* Francesco Vanneschi, London, King's Theatre in the Haymarket, 7 January 1746; *Artamene,* Vanneschi (after Bartolomeo Vitturi), London, King's Theatre in the Haymarket, 4 March 1746; *Le nozze d'Ercole e d' Ebe,* Pillnitz [near Dresden], 29 June 1747; *La Semiramide riconosciuta,* Metastasio, Vienna, Burgtheater, 14 May 1748; *La contesa de' numi,* Metastasio, Copenhagen, Charlottenborg Castle, 9 April 1749; *Ezio,* Metastasio, Prague, carnival 1750; revised, Vienna, Burgtheater, 26 December 1763; *Issipile,* Metastasio, Prague, carnival 1752; *La clemenza di Tito,* Metastasio, Naples, San Carlo, 4 November 1752; *Le cinesi,* Metastasio, Schlosshof [near Vienna], 24 September 1754; *Les amours champestres,* Schönbrunn, 1755; *La danza,* Metastasio, Laxenburg [near Vienna], 5 May 1755; *L'innocenza giustificata,* Giacomo Durazzo, with arias by Metastasio, Vienna, Burgtheater, 8 December 1755 revised as *La Vestale,* Vienna, Burgtheater, summer 1768; *Antigono,* Metastasio, Rome, Torre Argentina, 9 February 1756; *Il rè pastore,* Metastasio, Vienna, Burgtheater, 8 December 1756; *La fausse esclave,* Louis Anseaume and Marcouville, Vienna, Burgtheater, 8 January 1758; *L'île de Merlin, ou Le monde renversé,* Louis Anseaume (after Le Sage and D'Orneval), Vienna, Schönbrunn, 3 October 1758; *La Cythère assiégée,* Charles-Simon Favart, Vienna, Burgtheater, spring 1759; revised, Paris, Académie Royale, 1 August 1775; *Le diable à quatre, ou La double métamorphose,* Jean Michael Sedaine, Laxenburg (Vienna), 28 May 1759; *L'arbre enchanté, ou Le tuteur dupé,* Pierre-Louis Moline (after J. Vadé), Vienna, Schönbrunn, 3 October 1759; revised Versailles, 27 February 1775; *L'ivrogne corrigé* [*Der bekehrte Trunkenbold*], Louis Anseaume and L. de Sarterre, Vienna, Burgtheater, April 1760; *Tetide,* Gianambrosio Migliavacca, Vienna, Hofburg 10 October 1760; *Le cadi dupé,* Pierre René Le Monnier, Vienna, Burgtheater, 9 December 1761; *Arianna* (pasticcio), Gianambrosio Migliavacca, Laxenburg, 27 May 1762; *Orfeo ed Euridice,* Ranieri Calzabigi,

Vienna, Burgtheater, 5 October 1762; revised as *Orphée et Eurydice,* Pierre-Louis Moline (translated and adapted from Calzabigi), Paris, Académie Royale, 2 August 1774; *Il trionfo di Clelia,* Metastasio, Bologna, Comunale, 14 May 1763; *La rencontre imprévue,* L.H. Dancourt (after Le Sage and d'Orneval, *Les pélerins de la Mecque*), Vienna, Burgtheater, 7 January 1764; *Il Parnaso confuso,* Metastasio, Vienna, Schönbrunn, 24 January 1765; *Il Telemaco ossia L'isola di Circe,* Marco Coltellini (after Carlo Sigismondo Capece), Vienna, Burgtheater, 30 January 1765; *La corona,* Metastasio, for the emperor's name day, 4 October 1765 [not performed]; *Il prologo,* Lorenzo Ottavio del Rosso, Florence, Teatro della Pergola, 22 February 1767; *Alceste,* Ranieri Calzabigi, Vienna, Burgtheater, 26 December 1767; revised, François Louis Grand Lebland du Roullet (translation and revision of Calzabigi), Paris, Académie Royale, 23 April 1776; *Le feste d'Apollo,* Carlo Innocenzio Frugoni and Ranieri Calzabigi, Parma, Corte, 24 August 1769; *Paride ed Elena,* Ranieri Calzabigi, Vienna, Burgtheater, 3 November 1770; *Iphigénie en Aulide,* François Louis Grand Lebland du Roullet (after Racine), Paris, Académie Royale, 19 April 1774; *Armide,* Philippe Quinault, Paris, Académie Royale, 23 September 1777; *Iphigénie en Tauride,* Nicolas-François Guillard and François Louis Grand Lebland du Roullet (after Euripides), Paris, Académie Royale, 18 May 1779; revised in German, translated by J.B. von Alxinger and Gluck), Vienna, Burgtheater, 23 October 1781; *Écho et Narcisse,* L.T. von Tshoudi, Paris, Académie Royale, 24 September 1779

Gluck is certain of a place in any history of music. The nature of his achievements ensures that no account of opera in the eighteenth century can ignore his unique contribution: after Gluck, opera was a changed artform.

Gluck's response to his environment was influenced by a climate of thought affecting the whole of eighteenth-century Europe. Gluck translated the Enlightenment into music. He addressed many interests of that movement in the course of his life: neo-classicism was integral to his concept of opera, sensibility informed his redefinition of the aria, and the imitation of nature was the goal of each of his reforms, which also tended deliberately and explicitly towards a new internationalism in music, eliminating "the ridiculous distinctions" between national styles, to create "music belonging to all nations" (letter, 1 February 1773).

Gluck is always identified as a reformer, though his reputation credits him with more initiative than the facts substantiate. His apparent satisfaction with traditional forms of opera for the first 48 years of his life does nothing to strengthen his revisionist image. It might be truer to say that he attracted reforming spirits to him, by his readiness to follow where they led. Yet other composers had the same opportunities to collaborate with the reformers, and only Gluck took up the challenge. His association with the choreographer Angiolini led to radical changes in the ballet: *Don Juan* showed how natural gesture and acting could replace a more abstract, geometric approach to dance. Friendship with the poet Klopstock led him to devise a new declamatory style for the German language: his settings of eight of Klopstock's *Odes* played a part in the birth of the German art-song, the Lied. Prompted by the theater director Giacomo Durazzo, he discovered he had a genius for comedy: some ten French comic operas resulted. He is associated with two distinct reforms of serious opera, and in both cases the impetus came from a librettist. In Vienna, Ranieri Calzabigi must take the credit (and he did) for much that was new in the three operas, *Orfeo, Alceste* and *Paride ed Elena,* through which Gluck breathed new life into the old *opera seria.* And in Paris, François Louis Grand Lebland du Roullet, the librettist of *Iphigénie en Aulide,* was responsible for strengthening the tired conventions of French opera by blending the lyrical skills Gluck learned in Italy and Austria with the native tradition, although the finest fruits of this reform were not seen until *Iphigénie en Tauride,* a collaboration with yet another librettist, Guillard.

There is a unity of concept in all these developments which can only be explained by attributing a crucial, if selfless, role to Gluck. In each genre that he renewed, everything was to be subordinated to "simplicity, truth and nature" (*Alceste* preface). For opera this meant the smoothly flowing presentation of the drama, with as much continuity between the disparate elements as an eighteenth-century musician could conceive. The overture, earlier regarded as a detachable extra, at best an irrelevance to the opera which was to follow, at worst, disconcertingly inappropriate in mood, became incorporated into the drama. Gluck required the overture to "apprise the spectators of the nature of the action which is to be represented," to form a psycho-

Christoph Willibald Ritter von Gluck, portrait by Joseph Duplessis, 1775

logical or pictorial preparation, continuous with the first scene, as in *Iphigénie en Aulide,* where the overture begins with a taut Andante of searing suspensions whose meaning is revealed when it returns at the beginning of the first scene to accompany a recitative in which the suspensions seem to crush Agamemnon between the millstones of kingship and conscience. Gluck's reform of the overture was one of his most widely influential acts: few composers of serious operas ignored his lead. Beethoven's struggle through four versions to find the right prelude to *Fidelio* shows the same concerns, and his overtures to *Coriolan* and *Egmont* are links in a chain which led directly from Gluck to the symphonic poem.

In the interest of continuity, Gluck also sought to diminish the differences between aria and recitative. He often substituted a strophic or through-composed air for the prevalent da capo aria form (there are no da capo arias in *Orfeo*). Nevertheless, Gluck understood singers: his anxiety to tame the worst excesses of the virtuosi, ever eager to "display the agility of a fine voice," did not hinder his telling use of vocal registers to enhance dramatic expression. Just when, in *Alceste,* it is most difficult and most necessary for the audience to believe in Admetus's capacity for feeling, Gluck wrote one of his finest arias, "Nò crudel, non posso vivere," capturing almost by pitch changes alone both the king's passion and his enforced passivity in the face of his wife's sacrifice. Gluck is rarely given credit for his mastery of lyrical styles, but he possessed a wide melodic range, from the opulent "O malheureuse Iphigénie" (*Iphigénie en Tauride*) to the intimate, lied-like "Chiamo il mio ben così" (*Orfeo*). Recitative in the reform operas is accompanied by the orchestra, and often flowers into an expressive arioso which can hardly be distinguished from the short airs. "Che puro ciel" (*Orfeo*) shows how musically substantial a medium Gluck made the *accompagnato,* while Iphigenia's dream-narration, "Cette nuit j'ai revu le palais de mon père," (*Tauride*) demonstrates the expressive force of his style.

The orchestra plays an increasingly important role throughout the reform operas. Some of Gluck's moments of greatest tension are created with a few bars of instrumental music, dropped into an air or ensemble. These passages create an opportunity for the protagonists to act— always a priority with Gluck—but they also obviate the need for gesture, by matching

341

heightened emotions with graphically expressive music. Such an instance is created in the trio "Je pourrais du Tyran" in *Tauride,* where the priestess's indecision (as she hesitates between two captives, which one is to live and which to die) is marvellously painted in two brief orchestral interpolations. The celebrated portrayal of Orestes haunted by the Furies, in the same opera, is only one among many telling uses of the orchestra to reveal to the audience truths of which the character on stage is ignorant. A further remarkable example is the oracle scene in *Alceste,* which so impressed the eleven-year-old Mozart, watching the first production, that the haunting trombone chords reappear in the ghostly Commendatore's music in *Don Giovanni.*

The lavish choral writing in Gluck's first reform opera came about by accident. *Orfeo* is not an *opera seria* but a *festa teatrale,* a court entertainment in which the chorus traditionally played a substantial role. Seeing the impact of the choruses of mourning shepherds, dancing furies and blessed spirits in this work, Gluck decided to enhance the chorus role in his serious operas, and so in *Alceste* the chorus becomes almost the most important character—the people for whom the king must live, and for whom the queen must die. When Gluck revised this opera for Paris, he augmented their role further. Persuading his librettist to add more choruses to the last act, Gluck urged Du Roullet, "The piece cannot finish before these poor people have been consoled" (letter, 2 December 1775). Gluck's choruses are never passive bystanders. All are strongly characterized—frightened Thessalonians in *Alceste,* angry Greeks in *Aulide*—and often contrasted: Phrygians and Spartans in *Paride,* priestesses and barbarians in *Tauride.* Gluck required his chorus, like all his cast, to act. Although the chorus had always played a substantial role in French opera, Gluck found his Parisian choir expecting to stand motionless at each side of the stage, men with folded arms, the women carrying fans. Teaching these singers to act was by no means the least of his opera reforms.

Shortly after his death, Gluck was identified as one who "belonged to no school and who founded no tradition" (*Allgemeine musikalische Zeitung,* 1804). His strong individual personality isolated him from his contemporaries, and though many of his achievements were imitated by his immediate successors, Mozart, Spontini, and Cherubini, his influence was perhaps even stronger on his more distant heirs, Berlioz and Wagner. Gluck was accused by a contemporary, perhaps accurately, of devising his unique style in order to hide shortcomings in his technique. His harmonic and melodic vocabulary was limited by the times in which he lived. He is one of the "lost generation" of composers (C.P.E. Bach and Jommelli share the year of his birth, and Pergolesi, Wagenseil and Stamitz were close contemporaries) who seem never quite to have achieved their full potential as a result of living through the great stylistic upheaval of the middle decades of the century. Gluck rose above this limitation by harmonizing his talents and his aims. In an age dedicated to dismantling the complexities of the late baroque, Gluck advocated simplicity and produced his best work with direct melodies and spare textures: "Che farò" was for many years the only song from early opera to capture the public's hearts, while his ravishing flute solo, "Dance of the Blessed Spirits" has never been out of favor.—PATRICIA HOWARD

Gobbi, Tito

Baritone. Born 24 October 1913, in Bassano del Grappa, Italy. Died 5 March 1984, in Rome. Studied law at Padua University, then studied singing with Giulio Crimi in Rome; debut as Rodolfo in La sonnambula, *Gubbio, 1935; appeared as Germont in* La traviata *at the Teatro Adriano in Rome, 1937; debut at Teatro alla Scala as Belcore in* L'elisir d'amore,

1942; American debut in San Francisco, 1948; appeared frequently in Chicago, 1954-73; Covent Garden debut, 1955; debut at Metropolitan Opera as Scarpia, 1956; guest in most leading opera houses; also appeared in films, especially early in his career.

Even after his death, Tito Gobbi remains by common consent the great Italian singing actor of our age—in many ways the successor to such singers as Scotti, De Luca, and Stabile. Gobbi, though, was not merely the brilliant student of past traditions, but an authentic creator in a large number of styles, from Monteverdi to Alban Berg. To consider for a moment only the fringes of his repertory, Gobbi's Wozzeck (in Italian) was a creation of astonishing bitterness, his controversial Don Giovanni was a figure of alienating misanthropy, and his recording of Orfeo's "Rosa del ciel," though it might contradict current ideas of seventeenth-century singing practice, showed a fearless conviction that indeed qualified the character for myth.

Gobbi's creative method combined the motivational scrutiny of Stanislavsky with the inventive sweep of the great actors of the previous century—the century in which most of the baritone's major roles were created. In addition to intuition and intelligence, he brought to opera a superbly responsive presence, as quick in *Barbiere* as it was grand in *Simon Boccanegra;* a handsome and expressive face; a painstaking genius in makeup; and a vocal technique which preserved his very individual sound over a long career and yet allowed him maximum capacity for emotional coloring. His Figaro and Rigoletto, filmed in the 1940s, reflect all of this. The other singers (Tagliavini and Sinimberghi among them) are dramatically earnest and a little embarrassing, however well they may sing. Gobbi is dazzlingly quick, attractive, and amused in the Rossini, and at once theatrically extravagant and deeply touching in a quite modern sense in the Verdi. He revives some of the grand dramatic rituals of Verdi's time with exhilarating conviction; there is a legato of gesture and style in his performance (he writes of this element in his autobiography), a sense of histrionic proportion that leads us, if we will allow it, to the values of the theatre for which Verdi composed. Such a style contradicts most of the commonplaces about film acting, but it presents to us some truths about the profundity of the Italian operatic genre at its worthiest.

Gobbi began on the operatic stage in the late 1930s and made his last recordings (including a fine *Gianni Schicchi*) in 1977. His earliest records show a lyric tone of amazing beauty and vitality, a remarkable legato style, and already a masterly dramatic command. For intimate nobility, his 1942 recording of Roderigo's farewell and death (*Don Carlo*) is equalled only by his own later performance (1955) in the complete set. His 1950 Credo (*Otello*) has a dead vitality of tone astonishingly apt for the music, and his "Era la notte" of 1948 is, as seldom in other performances, ravishingly insinuating. Throughout his career the voice remained uniquely expressive and steady, though the top was sometimes dry. Despite a basic sound that was not always ideally roomy in the big Verdi roles for which his theatrical genius and musicianship fitted him so beautifully, his Rigoletto, Simon Boccanegra, Nabucco, and Scarpia, to name only a few, are still among the definitive interpretations on records, and have been analyzed as such by many critics.

A fascinating instance of Gobbi's ability to immortalize even a minor moment is his less famous performance of the smitten stage manager Michonnet's ecstatic description of the actress Adriana Lecouvreur's opening scene in Racine's *Bajazet*. As he watches her from the wings, Michonnet expresses his hidden feelings quite unaware that he is in fact speaking aloud. The intimacy, the jealousy, the hesitancy, the forthrightness, the musing frustration are all there in

Gobbi's remarkably subtle realization of Cilea's touching passage. It is as if Gobbi (and this is quite possible) took as guidelines for his own work Michonnet's reverent words about Adriana's performance: "What charm! What tone! What simplicity! How profound and yet how human!" And finally, as he says, "The truth itself!"—LONDON GREEN

Gomes, Antonio Carlos

Composer. Born 11 July 1836, in Campinas, Brazil. Died 16 September 1896, in Pará (Belém). Studied with his father, and then at the Conservatory of Rio de Janeiro; granted a stipend by Emperor Don Pedro II for study in Milan; productions of his operas in Italy, 1867-72; returned to Rio de Janeiro, 1872; wrote the hymn "Il saluto del Brasile" for the centenary of American independence, 1876; cantata Colombo for the Columbus Festival, 1892; director of the new conservatory at Pará, 1895.

Operas *A noite do castelo,* A.J. Fernandes dos Reis, Rio de Janeiro, 4 September 1861; *Joana de Flandres,* S. de Mendonça, Rio de Janeiro, 15 September 1863; *Il Guarany,* A. Scalvini and C. d'Ormeville (after Jose de Alencar, *O Guarani*), Milan, Teatro alla Scala, 19 March 1870; *Fosca,* A. Ghislanzoni, Milan, Teatro alla Scala, 16 February 1873; revised, 1878; *Salvator Rosa,* A. Ghislanzoni, Genoa, 21 March 1874; *Maria Tudor,* E. Praga (after Hugo), Milan, 27 March 1879; *Lo schiavo,* R. Paravicini (after Taunay), Rio de Janeiro, 27 September 1889; *Condor,* M. Canti, Milan, Teatro alla Scala, 21 February 1891.

Born into a family which contained the town bandmaster (his father), the leader of the opera house orchestra (his brother), and the leading female singer (an aunt), Gomes seems to have been destined for a career in music. At the Conservatory in Rio de Janeiro, his work attracted the attention of the director of the Opera Nacional de Lirica, Jose Amat, who entrusted him with a libretto based on a popular Portuguese gothic horror poem, *A noite do Castel* (1860). The music for *A noite,* like that of its successor, *Joanna de Flandres* (1863), reflects what a talented amateur composer had been able to learn not so much from his teachers as from the operas he had been able to hear, those of Bellini, Rossini, and early Donizetti. Though derivative, his scores demonstrated an inventiveness and persona appropriation of the already outmoded form which garnered him a government scholarship to the Milan Conservatory.

Gomes was a passionate listener; on his trip to Milan he stopped off in Paris, where hearing the operas of Meyerbeer and of the young Bizet made an indelible mark on his approach to orchestration. His keen ear is probably also responsible for the success of his first works for the Italian stage, not operas but musical comedies ("reviews" would be closer to the mark) set in Milanese dialect. As a liberal and patriotic Brazilian, his choice of an opera topic based on a novel by his countryman, Jose de Alencar, *O Guarani,* which had just appeared in Italian translation, constitutes an eminently just historical accident, as he first read it in Italian translation in Milan. Perhaps the fact that one of his grandmothers had been a fullblooded Guarani indian assisted Gomes in his choice, but Alencar's embodiment of the cutting-edge intellectual preoccupation of the time, *indianismo,* with its idealized combination of Rousseau's noble savage and Fenimore Cooper's canny (*North* American) native possessed its own appeal.

Il Guarany reveals how much Gomes had learned of contemporary Italian and French opera since his arrival in Europe. The orchestration owes much to Meyerbeer's example, the structure to Verdi's middle-period operas, which had not yet appeared in Brazil prior to Gomes's departure. Above all he demonstrated an individual gift for melody which, unlike that of his Italian contemporaries, could not be mistaken for Verdi on a bad day. The plot of *Il Guarany*, with its enslaved natives versus imperialist Europeans, owed not a little to Meyerbeer's posthumous masterpiece, *L'Africaine*, but Gomes, following Alencar, introduced a shocking variation. For the first time the theme of love between white and dark skinned people involved not the acceptable European model of white male/native female, but the reverse. Perhaps the Meyerbeerian structure and Verdian sweep of the act I duet between the Indian Pery and the Portuguese noblewoman Cecilia won the sympathy of an audience which might otherwise have rejected the opera's central love interest out of hand.

Having heard the opera in Ferrara, Verdi called Gomes "a true musical genius." Boito, not yet the great man's librettist, publically expressed the opinion that Gomes might be Verdi's heir apparent. The Brazilian's next two operas, *Fosca* (1873) and *Salvator Rosa* (1874) confirmed the possibility. *Fosca* is Gomes's most contemporary Italianate, Verdian score, sublimating his obvious infatuation with Meyerbeer's idea of using and abandoning a plethora of melodic inventions as the dramatic emphasis of the text is shifted, to a remarkable understanding of the development of aria and ensemble themes that Verdi had begun to incorporate into his scores following his conquest of French style in *Don Carlos*. In imitation of the latter, Gomes included a few obvious *Leitmotiven* (leading themes) in *Fosca*, for which he was immediately accused of "Wagnerismo" by conservative operagoers. This controversy ruined the chances of *Fosca*, perhaps Gomes's most viable score in retrospect, to enter the standard repertoire.

Obviously in response to the criticism of his previous opera, Gomes retreated to the safer ground of middle-Verdi/late-Donizetti for his next work, *Salvator Rosa*, that of uncomplicated melody and predictable development. At the time, his decision proved financially beneficial; the opera remained his most popular in Italy for three decades. *Maria Tudor* (1879) shows him betwixt and between. He attempted the popular approach of *Salvator Rosa* but could no longer sublimate his particular genius to the exigencies of popular taste. A return visit to Brazil in 1880 put him again in touch with the most significant liberal movements of his homeland, specifically the struggle to become the last major power to outlaw slavery. He accepted a libretto from the Vicomte de Taunay, a leading abolitionist, dealing with the origin of the odious institution in the early 1600s, *Lo Schiavo*.

Though it became the first of Gomes's mature operas to have its first performance in his native Brazil, by the time he had composed it the subject had become passé; Brazil had become a republic and abolished slavery. Its sophisticated orchestration, especially the prelude to act IV, depicting dawn over Guanabara Bay, and Gomes's return to the Meyerbeerian model of orchestra at the service of dramatic exigency, produced his most personal lyric effusion. Its success was immediate but transitory on European stages.

In the interim, Wagner had conquered Italy and the indigenous response of verismo had been begun by Catalani and Puccini. Gomes tried to respond to the musical demands of the new wave in *Condor* (1891), but could not successfully meld his particular genius to the task. His last stage work, *Colombo*, a scenic cantata commissioned for the four-hundredth anniversary of the discovery of the New World, showed him still in possession of the ability to write effectively for voice and chorus, but he died, as head of the Belém Conservatory, a few months later.

Though still performed in Brazil, as much as a civic duty as otherwise, Gomes's operas have been singularly overlooked in the continuing investigation of forgotten operas which has resulted in our reacquaintance with significant music by Rossini, Donizetti, and Meyerbeer. Even the centennial revival of works by his less-gifted contemporary Mercadante has not focussed much interest in the Brazilian master's operas. His dramatic sensibility, his thoroughly professional and often astonishing orchestration, and his considerable melodic gifts have not yet occasioned a merited reappraisal by opera companies or critics.—WILLIAM J. COLLINS

Gorr, Rita

Mezzo-soprano. Born Marguerite Geirnaert, 18 February 1926, in Zelzaete, Belgium. Studied in Ghent and Brussels; debut as Fricka in Die Walküre, *Antwerp, 1949; sang in Strasbourg Opera, 1949-52; debut at Paris Opéra and Opéra-Comique, 1952; debut at Bayreuth, 1958; appeared at Covent Garden as Amneris in* Aïda, *1959, and sang there regularly until 1971; Teatro alla Scala debut as Kundry, 1960; Metropolitan Opera debut as Amneris in* Aïda, *1962.*

One of the casualties of operatic style in recent times has been the grand tradition of French singing. At the turn of the century, many marvelous artists kept French operas in the core repertoire of every international house; today, the native French-speaking opera singer of distinction has all but disappeared. The 1950s and 60s saw the last wave of the tradition, as a small but significant group of fine French and Francophone singers—including sopranos Régine Crespin and Mady Mesplé, tenor Alain Vanzo, and baritones Michel Dens, Gabriel Bacquier and Gérard Souzay—gave opera audiences a last, glorious "Indian summer" before the current chill set in.

There was no finer artist in this rarified group than Belgian mezzo-soprano Rita Gorr, who used her prodigious resources to illuminate a variety of music. To French opera from Gluck to Massenet she brought a velvety timbre and nobility of phrase that placed her as the successor to such legendary interpreters as Félia Litvinne and Alice Raveau. In the operas of Verdi and Mascagni's *Cavalleria rusticana,* Gorr could provide an Italianate bite and theatricality which were the equal of those to the manner born. And her singing of Wagnerian roles was similarly idiomatic: Gorr's plangent voice and telling sensitivity to words share something of the style and sound of Christa Ludwig.

Like Ludwig's, Gorr's was an unusually large vocal range, and her skills as a colorist allowed her to sound comfortable in contralto, mezzo-soprano, and even some soprano roles. As Orphée, for example, the richness and dark glow of Gorr's tone sound like that of a natural alto; so it may surprise us that, as Amneris, the voice has brightness and a good deal of thrust at the top. The role of Cherubini's Medée (which Gorr sang both on record and in the theater) lies rather high for her, but we sense the strain only in a few isolated passages; for the most part the music is splendidly and easily sung, and her grandeur of scale and commitment are stamped with greatness.

It is these latter qualities, even more than the voice itself, which are the hallmarks of Gorr's artistic mien. French roles in the "classical" style (like Medée, Didon, and Orphée) are notoriously difficult to bring off, for they require a careful balance: if an artist goes too far in one direction, the character becomes almost comically overwrought, while if she goes too far in the other direction the result is a performance that is lifeless and merely statuesque. Gorr's portrayals always found the ideal blend of humanity and heroic size, and her superbly clear enunciation of the language was a particular joy. In recent years, Jessye Norman has brought to a similar repertoire something resembling Gorr's artistry and finesse, but—perhaps inevitably—the younger American singer cannot achieve the natural and idiomatic sense of style of her predecessor.

Records provide a reasonable sampling of Gorr's career, though we might wish for more and particularly for a better representation of her French roles. Her fiery Amneris (with Georg Solti) may be the finest performance of the part on record. The RCA recording of *Lohengrin* finds Gorr sadly out of form as Ortrud (one of her finest parts in the theater), but her recording of Fricka in *Die Walküre* (with Eric Leinsdorf) is a worthy souvenir of her Wagner. Perhaps best of all is her Dalila (with Georges Prêtre), where she is partnered by the stentorian Samson of Jon Vickers. Here is Gorr's voice at its lushest and most sensual, and the crystalline diction is unmistakably that of a native speaker. It is a performance which will not be rivaled—and a style which may not be heard again—in our time.—DAVID ANTHONY FOX

Gounod, Charles François

Composer. Born 17 June 1818, in St. Cloud. Died 17 October 1893, in Paris. Studied piano with his mother; studied with Halévy, Lesueur, and Paër at the Paris Conservatory, beginning 1835; second Prix de Rome for his cantata Marie Stuart et Rizzio, *1837; Grand Prix de Rome for his cantata* Fernand, *1839; studied sacred music in Rome, and composed a Mass for 3 voices and orchestra; his Requiem performed in Vienna, 1842; precentor and organist of the Missions Etrangères; studied theology for two years; conducted the choral society Orphéon, 1852-60; first successful opera,* Faust, *1859; organized Gounod's Choir in London, 1870; returned to Paris, 1874, and primarily composed sacred music.*

Operas *Sapho,* Emile Augier, 1850, Paris, Opéra, 16 April 1851; revised, Paris, Opéra, 2 April 1884; *La nonne sanglante,* Eugène Scribe and Germain Delavigne (after Matthew Gregory Lewis, *The Monk*), 1852-54, Paris, Opéra, 18 October 1854; *Le médecin malgré lui,* Jules Barbier and Michael Carré (after Molière), 1857, Paris, Théâtre-Lyrique, 15 January 1858; *Faust,* Jules Barbier and Michel Carré (after Goethe), 1852-59, Paris, Théâtre-Lyrique, 19 March 1859; revised to include recitatives, Strasbourg, April 1860, and ballet, Paris, Opéra, 3 March 1869; *Philémon et Baucis,* Jules Barbier and Michel Carré, 1859, Paris, Théâtre-Lyrique, 18 February 1860; revised, Paris, Opéra-Comique, 16 May 1876; *La colombe,* Jules Barbier and Michel Carré (after La Fontaine, *Le faucon*), 1859, Baden-Baden, 3 August 1860; *La reine de Saba,* Jules Barbier and Michel Carré (after Gérard de Nerval), 1861, Paris, Opéra, 29 February 1862; *Mireille,* Michel Carré (after Frédéric Mistral, *Mirèio*), 1863, Paris, Théâtre-Lyrique, 19 March 1864; revised, performed 15 December 1864; restored, Henri Büsser, Paris, Opéra-Comique, 6 June 1939; *Roméo et Juliette,* Jules Barbier and Michel Carré (after Shakespeare), 1864, Paris, Théâtre-Lyrique, 27 April 1867; revised to include ballet, Paris, Opéra, 28 November 1888; *George Dandin,* after Molière, 1873 [unfinished]; *Cinq—Mars,* Louis Gallet and Paul Poirson (after a novel by Alfred de Vigny), 1876-77, Paris, Opéra-Comique, 5 April 1877; revised as grand opera, Lyon, 1 December 1877; *Polyeucte,* Jules Barbier and Michel Carré (after Corneille), 1870-78, Paris, Opéra, 7 October 1878; *Le* *tribut de Zamora,* Adolphe Philippe d'Ennery and Jules Brésil, 1878-80, Paris, Opéra, 1 April 1881;

Maître Pierre, Louis Gallet (on the subject of Abelard and Héloise), 1877 [unfinished].

Faust is so much taken for granted that its vast popularity has made it overfamiliar. Yet it is a landmark in the history of French music. In spite of the obvious flaws—the trivial libretto compared to the profundity of Goethe's original, the blaring soldiers' chorus—*Faust* explains Debussy's remark that Gounod represents an important phase in the evolution of French sensibility. It replaced the traditional pomposity of grand opera with a more poetic and intimate approach. Gounod introduced a technique of conversational exchange rather than declamation. True feeling took over from rant, and proportion was restored. The play of emotion was controlled with a subtle touch. The music suggests perpetual nuance.

The triumph of *Faust,* however, contained a danger. Its overwhelming success often led Gounod to emphasize in his later works those very elements in it which are weakest: the showy and the grandiose. These came to the fore in *Polyeucte,* a lofty "fresco" (Gounod's own word) about an early Christian martyr; in *La reine de Saba,* an epic featuring the Queen of Sheba; in *Cinq-Mars,* an historical piece taken from Vigny's novel about a conspiracy against Cardinal Richelieu; and in *Le tribut de Zamora,* an improbable melodrama with a heroine who is, in turn, a bloodthirsty madwoman, a fiercely devoted mother, and in the end a determined murderess. To these operas, which represent Gounod's weaker side, must be added *La nonne sanglante,* an early work based on Matthew Lewis's Gothic thriller *The Monk,* where the ambitious young composer, in vain as it turned out, tried for success by collaborating on the nineteenth-century equivalent of a modern horror film.

The first glimmer of his true originality shines through in *Sapho.* It is bathed in a Hellenic radiance and that pastoral simplicity which thirteen years later characterised *Mireille.* When he turned to Molière for *Le médecin malgré lui* he found the perfect vehicle for his delicate wit, humor and tenderness. The score abounds in clever orchestral detail and exquisite vocal writing which impressed Diaghilev, who revived it sumptuously with recitatives by Erik Satie and Debussy (who chose it as his favorite Gounod opera). Equally light of touch are *Philémon et Baucis* and *La colombe,* which Diaghilev also revived in the 1920s.

Among Gounod's finest achievements must be counted *Mireille.* Its faults—the heroine's rather too edifying death scene and an occasional over-emphasis on melodrama—are far outweighed by the idyllic portrait Gounod draws of the womanly Mireille and by the skillfully blended chiaroscuro in the picture he gives of her native Provence. The music is filled with sunshine, although Gounod has caught as well the tragedy that broods under the bright coloring of the Provençal countryside.

Juliet was another heroine who inspired some of Gounod's best writing. The score of *Roméo et Juliette* flows with a naturalness of speech and a sharpness of youthful feeling that evokes a moving and innocent beauty. The three simple bars accompanying Juliet's "C'est le doux rossignol de l'amour" ("It is the sweet nightingale of love") carry the poignant touch of genius. "Melody alone counts in music," Gounod once said. "Melody, always melody, that is the sole, the unique secret of our art," and clear, flowing, spontaneous melody is characteristic of

Gounod at his best.—JAMES HARDING

Grisi, Giulia

Soprano. Born 22 May 1811, in Milan. Died 29 November 1869, in Berlin. Studied with her sister, the mezzo-soprano Giuditta Grisi, and with Filippo Celli and Pietro Guglielmi; also studied with Marliani in Milan and with Giacomelli in Bologna; debut as Emma in Rossini's Zelmira, Bologna, 1828; created role of Adalgisa in Norma, Milan, 1831; sang in Milan until 1832; Paris debut as Semiramide, 1832; London debut in Rossini's La gazza ladra, 1834; lived with the tenor Mario from c. 1842; toured the U.S. with him in 1854.

Posterity has been extremely unkind to Giulia Grisi. During her lifetime she was universally regarded as the reigning Italian prima donna of the mid-nineteenth century. But no single biography has been devoted exclusively to her, although one book on Grisi and Mario is available and another is in preparation. Worse, a number of historians have stated that she gained most of her fame by imitating her predecessors (most notably Giuditta Pasta). Worse still, she reportedly waged a petty and malicious campaign against her arch-rival, Pauline Viardot, using her companion of many years, the tenor Mario, as her key weapon.

That there was a serious rivalry between Grisi and Viardot cannot be doubted, but the blame should be shared equally by the two prima donnas, not placed entirely on Grisi's shoulders. Viardot remembered, with lasting resentment, that Grisi had replaced Viardot's half sister Maria Malibran in both Paris and London while the latter was still in her prime. The war between the prima donnas started due to a reappearance by Viardot at Covent Garden in *La sonnambula* in 1848. Mario canceled due to illness and a substitute had to be found. Viardot took this as a personal insult, claiming that the illness was feigned, and a plot on Grisi's part. The *Musical World,* a contemporary London periodical stated that Mario was truly sick, and had made every effort to sing. Later that year, Viardot was scheduled to sing Valentine in *Les Huguenots* for her benefit, and Mario again had to cancel due to illness. Grisi offered to sing *Norma* in Viardot's honor; Viardot agreed to *Norma,* but insisted that she sing the title role, leaving Grisi to sing Adalgisa. They finally found a substitute tenor for Mario, the famous Gustave Roger who was to create Jean in *Le prophète* a year later. The opera was a huge success, although Roger sang in French. Again, there is substantive evidence that Mario was truly ill.

Things came to a head in 1850, when on hearing Pasta in scenes from *Anna Bolena,* Viardot said "Now I know where Grisi got all her greatness." Even though this remark was not widely publicized at the time, it must have spread fuel on the fire. Then, once more, in 1852 Mario cancelled an appearance in *La Juive* when Viardot was singing. Again, Grisi was blamed, although Mario's illness was confirmed by a review of the second performance, two nights later. Then, finally, when in 1852 Viardot was not engaged at Covent Garden, Grisi took over the role of Fidès. Instead of being credited by historians for being a good trooper and singing a role which lay too low for her voice so that the show could go on, she was criticized for daring to take on one of her rival's roles.

The charge that Grisi's talent was primarily that of an imitator also deserves brief comment, even when one realizes that it originated with a rival jealous of her success. An examination of numerous contemporary reviews of her in *Norma* reveals no suggestion of any plagiarism. Yet, Viardot's accusation that Grisi plagiarized was taken up years later by Chorley, a great admirer of Viardot's, and even printed in Grisi's obituary in the *Musical World.* The latter is easily explained—Grisi's death was a sudden one; the editors of *Musical World* had a deadline to meet, and it is unlikely that they would have had the time to check the facts, even in the backfiles of their own magazine.

To put it in as few words as possible, Grisi had everything. According to Chorley, "She was known for her great beauty, although she was never known to be a coquette on stage. Her soprano voice was rich, sweet, equal throughout its compass of two octaves (from C to C) without a break, or a note which had to be managed. Nor has any woman ever more thoroughly commanded every gradation of force than she, being capable of any required violence or of any desired delicacy."

Her best role was Norma, and while it had to be modeled to some extent on Pasta's, it was regarded (even by Chorley) as an improvement because of its greater animal passion. She was so ferocious in the part that many tenors took her violence personally. Her acting ability was compared favorably to that of great dramatic actresses such as Sarah Siddons.

Grisi also was famous for her Lucrezia Borgia, Donna Anna and Anna Bolena. She created a number of major *bel canto* roles, including among others, Adalgisa in *Norma,* Elvira in *I Puritani* and Norina in *Don Pasquale.* Oddly, none of these were destined to be among her favorites. In its early years, Adalgisa was usually sung by lesser sopranos, although it eventually became the province of great mezzos and contraltos. Elvira was frequently taken over by Fanny Persiani, while *Don Pasquale* was not fully a repertory work in those years. Important as these were, they probably were less so than the roles created by Pasta.

How important, then, was Grisi? That she learned from Pasta, Malibran, and others is certainly to her credit—she would have been foolish not to do so. That she was little more than an imitator, as some historians suggest, is totally untrue. Assertions that she attempted to fight off challenges from rivals, whether to her or to Mario, are probably partially true, and, if so, are understandable. That she was neurotic, or even fanatical is difficult to believe, although it makes a good story. She accepted Persiani into the *vieille garde,* and even sang Elisetta in Cimarosa's *Matrimonio segreto* while Persiani sang the much more important role of Carolina. Nor is there any record of Grisi or Mario making trouble for his most serious rival, Enrico Tamberlick.

The question of Grisi's importance can best be answered by remembering that she reigned supreme in Paris for 18 seasons, and in London for close to 20, withstanding challenges from Lind, Sontag, Frezzolini, Barbieri-Nini and others in opera seria, although Lind did do better in the light repertory. Only Viardot was able to rival her successfully in some roles and in some seasons, but a comparison of the two careers shows that Grisi's was much more distinguished. This record of supremacy by a single singer in cities of such importance has been equaled in later years only by the likes of Patti and Melba in London, Tamberlick and Battistini in St Petersburg, and Caruso in New York.

Grisi's place in history is secure as the second in a line of great dramatic coloratura sopranos starting with Giuditta Pasta, continuing with Teresa Tietjens and Rosa Ponselle and culminating with Maria Callas, Joan Sutherland and Montserrat Caballé.—TOM KAUFMAN

Gruberova, Edita

Soprano. Born 23 December 1946. Studied music in Prague and Vienna; debut with the Slovak National Theater in Bratislava, 1968; appeared at Vienna State Opera, 1972; has

also appeared at Bayreuth, Hamburg State Opera, Frankfurt Opera, the Bavarian State Opera in Munich, and other major opera houses.

After making her debut at the Slovak National Theater in Bratislava in 1968, Edita Gruberova quickly emerged as one of Europe's leading coloratura sopranos. Her career has developed, for the most part, in central Europe; Salzburg, Vienna and Munich have witnessed many of her triumphs. Her appearances in the United States and Great Britain have been relatively rare. Like Rita Streich, a soprano whose voice Gruberova's resembles somewhat, her repertory is dominated by operas in German; again like Streich, Gruberova specializes in the music of Mozart and Richard Strauss. Gruberova's voice has remarkable dexterity. Her tessitura is high; her lower notes are comparatively weak. When she sings *piano* her voice can be beautiful; in *forte* passages a shrillness, a kind of acid quality often mars her singing.

One of Gruberova's best Mozart roles is the Queen of the Night in *Die Zauberflöte*. In Munich in 1978 Gruberova's Queen was praised (in *Opera*) for her "glittering coloratura cascades"; in Salzburg the following year Gruberova won applause (again in *Opera*), for the "glittering menace" of her portrayal. Among her other Mozart roles is Constanze in *Die Entführung aus dem Serail*. She has also sung and recorded many of Mozart's concert arias.

Some of Gruberova's best qualities can be admired in her portrayal of Marcellina in Paer's *Leonora* (recorded under Peter Maag in 1979). Gruberova executes delicate melismas and tosses off high notes lightly and beautifully in her first aria, "Fedele, mio diletto." Her performance of the aria "Corri, corri" is just as fine: she sings the aria's teasing, playful coloratura with admirable gracefulness.

Less successful is Gruberova's performance of the aria "No, che non sei capace," written by Mozart in 1783 for insertion in Anfossi's opera *Il curioso indiscreto*. Gruberova is to be thanked for bringing this rarely sung aria to the attention of music-lovers in a recording conducted by Leopold Hager (1983); but her performance does not show the music at its best. The voice is often shrill and unpleasant to the ear. The high notes, when sung lightly, are beautiful; but Gruberova executes the climactic coloratura, so reminiscent of the Queen of the Night, with a heavy hand, singing *legato* and *forte* passages that Mozart surely wanted to be sung with a light *staccato*.

Gruberova has won much praise for her many portrayals of Zerbinetta in Strauss's *Ariadne auf Naxos,* a role that she has sung in Salzburg, Vienna and New York, among other cities. A recording made under Solti in 1977 shows why Gruberova has been so successful as Zerbinetta. Her performance of the great aria "Grossmächtige Prinzessin" reveals a voice fuller and richer than those of Streich and Grist, two earlier specialists in this role. At the same time one sometimes misses the dexterity and lightness that Streich and Grist could bring to the coloratura passages. But sometimes Gruberova's coloratura is undeniably beautiful: she does the long cadenza with extraordinary delicacy and charm.—JOHN A. RICE

Gruenberg, Louis

Composer. Born 3 August 1884, near Brest Litovsk. Died 19 June 1964, in Los Angeles. Studied piano with Adele Margulies in New York; studied piano and composition with Busoni in Berlin; debut as a pianist with the Berlin Philharmonic, 1912; took courses at

the Vienna conservatory, and tutored there; returned to United States, 1919; organizer and active member of the League of Composers from 1923; taught composition at the Chicago Music College, 1933-36; settled in Santa Monica, California.

Operas   *Signor Formica,* Gruenberg (after E.T.A. Hoffmann), 1912; *The Witch of Brocken* (children's opera), E.F. Malkowski (translated by L. Vandevere), 1912; *Piccadillymädel* (operetta), 1913; *The Bride of the Gods,* Busoni (after the ancient Hindu epic, *Mahabharata,* translated by C.H. Meltzer), 1913; *The Dumb Wife* (chamber opera), after A. France, 1922-23; *Hallo! Tommy!* (operetta), L. Herzer, 1920s [composed under the pseudonym George Edwards]; *Lady X* (operetta), L. Herzer. c. 1927 [published under the pseudonym George Edwards]; *Jack and the Beanstalk,* J. Erskine, 20 November 1931; *The Emperor Jones,* Gruenberg and K. de Jaffa (after Eugene O'Neill), 1930-31, New York, Metropolitan Opera, January 1932; *Green Mansions* (radio opera), after W.H. Hudson, 1937, Columbia Broadcasting System, 17 October 1937; *Helena's Husband,* P. Moeller, 1938; *Volpone,* Gruenberg (after Ben Jonson), 1949; revised, 1963; *One Night of Cleopatra,* Gruenberg (after T. Gautier); *The Miracle of Flanders* [legend with narrator, actors, music], Gruenberg (after Balzac), 1954; *The Delicate King,* Gruenberg (after Dumas), 1955; *Antony and Cleopatra,* Gruenberg (after Shakespeare), 1955; revised 1958, 1961.

Louis Gruenberg started his career as a concert pianist and composer under the guidance of Ferruccio Busoni. This great composer-teacher was an important influence on Gruenberg, and their association continued from 1908 until Busoni's death in 1924. Busoni encouraged Gruenberg to experiment in his compositions and search for new means of expression. Eventually Gruenberg evolved a musical style based on melodic and rhythmic traits of Black spirituals and the popular jazz of the 1920s. Although Gruenberg's jazz style characterized only one group of his compositions, the popularity of these jazz-influenced works made him known as an important innovator of jazz.

Gruenberg's first operas were *The Witch of Brocken* and *The Bride of the Gods. The Witch of Brocken* was a children's opera completed in 1912. *The Bride of the Gods,* composed in 1913, used a libretto written by Busoni. Adapted from the ancient Hindu epic, the *Mahabharata,* Gruenberg was never satisfied with the work and the opera remains unperformed. In 1922 Gruenberg completed *The Dumb Wife,* a chamber opera in two acts. The work was based on Anatole France's play *The Man Who Married a Dumb Wife.* Regrettably Gruenberg wrote the opera before securing permission to use the play, and the work was not performed. Gruenberg did not complete his next opera until 1930. In the intervening years he devoted most of his efforts towards writing chamber and symphonic music, and it was during this time that his reputation as a jazz composer was established.

In 1930 Gruenberg received a commission from the Juilliard School to write an opera which could be performed by students as part of the celebration for Juilliard's new music building. The result was the opera *Jack and the Beanstalk.* This well-known fairy tale was suggested by John Erskine who was also the librettist. Erskine, a writer and musician, was the president of the Juilliard School. The premiere was given on 20 November 1931, and the opera proved so successful that it was moved to a theater on Broadway, where it continued to play for two additional weeks. The opera is in a lyrical, tonal style well suited to young singers. In his review in *Modern Music,* Randall Thompson wrote "The music bubbles and shimmers. . . . That he wrote an opera practicable for such performers, without once writing down to them, is greatly to his credit."

While working on *Jack and the Beanstalk,* Gruenberg also began composing his most important opera, *The Emperor Jones.* After a lengthy period in which he sought permission from Eugene O'Neill to use his play, Gruenberg finally received approval and began the work in 1930. The opera was completed in 1931. After the premiere in January 1932 by the Metropolitan Opera Company, Giulio Gatti-Casazza, the Metropolitan's director, hailed the work as "an American achievement."

Gruenberg's next opera was *Helena's Husband* which was based on the play by Philip Moeller. Like the earlier opera *The Bride of the Gods,* Gruenberg was not satisfied with the work. Although it was completed in 1938, he never sought to have it performed. In 1937 Gruenberg received a commission from the Columbia Broadcasting Company to write a radio opera. For this unusual medium Gruenberg chose William Hudson's novel *Green Mansions.* Since the work was to be a non-visual opera, Gruenberg experimented with the technology available at that time to achieve a jungle atmosphere. Microphone amplification was used to increase the volume of sound for selected instruments, and phonograph records were used for the jungle sounds. The jungle girl's voice was represented by a musical saw. Although the 17 October 1937 broadcast was the only performance the opera received, it was given praise for its interesting innovations.

Just before the performance of *Green Mansions,* Gruenberg moved to California, where he began a career in film composition. During this period, in which he completed ten film scores, Gruenberg did not complete any more operas until he left the film industry in 1950. In this last period of his life, Gruenberg returned to opera and completed two large and three chamber operas. The large scale operas were *Volpone* (1949) after Ben Jonson and *Antony and Cleopatra* (1961) after Shakespeare. Both operas consist of three acts, and demand large casts and orchestras. Gruenberg's chamber operas were intended for television performance. These works are *One Night of Cleopatra* (after Gautier), *The Miracle of Flanders* (after Balzac) and *The Delicate King* (after Dumas). To most opera companies these later works are unknown, and when Gruenberg died in 1964 he was largely forgotten by his musical colleagues.

Gruenberg remains known for his operatic works primarily through the significance of *The Emperor Jones.* This opera was recognized after its first performance as the most important American opera up to that time. Unfortunately, the work has been neglected for many years, and it is difficult to appreciate its earlier importance. All of Gruenberg's operas written after 1950 remain in manuscript. An examination of these works reveals a mature, well-crafted musical style. It is hoped that future opera companies will take an interest in Gruenberg's works, and that his unperformed operas and a revival of his earlier works will find their way into the operatic repertoire.—ROBERT F. NISBETT

Gueden, Hilde

Soprano. Born 15 September 1917, in Vienna. Died 17 September 1988, in Vienna. Studied with Wetzelsberger at Vienna Conservatory; operetta debut in Stolz's Servus servus, *Vienna, 1939; opera debut as Cherubino in* Le nozze di Figaro *in Zurich, 1939-41; at Bavarian Staatsoper in Munich, 1941-42; Rome, 1942-46; appeared at Salzburg as Zerlina, 1946; associated with Vienna Staatsoper until 1972; Covent Garden, 1947; debut at Metropolitan Opera as Gilda, 1951; made an Austrian Kammersängerin, 1951.*

The light lyric soprano may be the least memorable of all operatic voices. Even very good ones are not, for the most part, in short supply; even during periods when audiences and critics lament the paucity of great voices there seems to be a virtual plethora of talented artists of this vocal type. Moreover, it is a voice type which, while pleasing, is not often especially distinctive, and many excellent lyric sopranos sound much alike. So it follows that only a small number of these singers have ever achieved genuine star status, and those who have offered something quite special and distinctive in addition to their voices.

Hilde Gueden is one of that select company. No doubt her exceptional physical beauty had something to do with it—blond, slender and graceful, her loveliness was heightened by a slightly exotic, Eastern European quality that gave her stage presence a particular glamour. There was an exotic touch of "spice" in Gueden's creamy voice as well, lending it personality and allure.

Had she not possessed these very individual qualities, Gueden's career might have been rather less distinguished than it was, for she was a great charmeuse rather than one of the most accomplished of vocalists. Her intonation was not always true, and sustained notes often flattened into an unattractive whine, an inclination which became more exaggerated as she grew older. This plagues certain critical passages in Gueden's several recorded performances as Sophie in *Der Rosenkavalier,* though much of the singing is lovely. Equally troublesome is her sloppiness and imprecision which emerges specifically as rhythmic laziness, a tendency to sing behind the beat. This lack of energetic thrust and alertness compromises some of Gueden's Mozart singing, where her individual tone otherwise gives much pleasure. A characteristic example is her recording of the motet "Exsultate, Jubilate." The slow middle section is handled with skill and caresses the ear just as it should—but both the outer movements make considerable demands on her coloratura singing, and she seems barely able to keep up with conductor Alberto Erede's rather moderate tempo.

Elsewhere in Gueden's performances of Mozart this tendency is less troubling. As Susanna in *Le nozze di Figaro,* there is less need for virtuoso vocalism and more for real personal charm, and here she is often marvelous. Even the tendency to lag behind the beat pays a certain dividend, as in the climactic aria "Deh vieni, non tardar," where she achieves just the right quality of dreamy rapture, which eludes many fine singers of this role. It is no surprise, particularly with her good looks and formidable skills as an actress, that Gueden became such a favorite in this part—and in the similar roles of Pamina in *Die Zauberflöte* and Zerlina in *Don Giovanni.*

Still it is in the light music of Johann Strauss and Franz Lehár that Hilde Gueden is at her best. Here too the lazy, dreamy quality is beguiling and even the coloratura passages seem to work well for her. Many records preserve memorable examples of Gueden in songs and arias as well as complete operettas. Especially noteworthy are her performances as Rosalinde in *Die Fledermaus,* where her touch of Eastern European panache is just right, and her humor and vivacity fairly leap off the turntable. She may be the best exponent of this delectable part on record.—DAVID ANTHONY FOX

Guillaume Tell [William Tell]

Composer: *Gioachino Rossini.*

Librettists: *E. de Jouy, H.-L.-F. Bis, et al. (after Schiller).*

First Performance: *Paris, Opéra, 3 August 1829.*

Roles: *Guillaume Tell (baritone); Arnold (tenor); Mathilde (soprano); Melcthal (bass); Jemmy (mezzo-soprano); Hedwig (contralto); Walter Furst (bass); Ruedi (tenor); Leuthold (bass); Gesler (bass); Rudolph (tenor); A Hunter (tenor or baritone); chorus (SSATTBB).*

Guillaume Tell was the last opera of Rossini, but it was the first of a proposed series of works by the composer for the Opéra in Paris. Although Rossini previously had written three other French operas, and strains of their influence may be traced in *Guillaume Tell,* the latter work is one of immeasurably greater genius. It exceeds in scope and power the earlier French works and in fundamental style the Italian works upon which Rossini's lasting fame rests. *Guillaume Tell* is one of the first examples of what came to be known as *grand opéra,* a genre whose other early examples are Auber's *La muette de Portici* (1828), Halévy's *La juive* (1830), and Meyerbeer's *Robert le diable* (1831) and *Les Huguenots* (1836).

Popular from the outset, *Guillaume Tell* quickly surpassed the box-office receipts of its major competitor, *La muette de Portici.* However, it soon suffered drastic cuts, and in two years its five acts characteristic of French grand opera were reduced to three. Ultimately, *Guillaume Tell* endured the indignity of reaching the public in the form of act II alone. Nevertheless, it was an important part of the repertory of the Opéra in Paris throughout the nineteenth century and had received 648 performances there by the end of 1880. Its popularity stemmed from several sources: its libretto, local color, orchestration, and, of course, Rossini's inimitable grasp of musico-dramatic principles.

The plot is loosely based upon the well-known medieval legend of the Swiss patriot, the chronicles of whose exploits have attracted generations of poets. Friedrich von Schiller's play of 1804 furnished the basis of the adaptation by Etienne de Jouy, Hippolyte Bis, and others, who made substantial alterations in Schiller's structure, primarily pruning and simplifying it. The central threads of the plot are: 1) the personal opposition of the opera's namesake to the oppressive Hapsburg governor, Gesler, and ultimately the latter's death at Tell's hands; 2) the complications arising from the liaison between the lovers Arnold, son of Melcthal, the peasant conspirator, and Mathilde, daughter of whom else but the tyrannical Gesler; and 3) the triumph of Arnold and his compatriots in rousing the peasants to successful revolution.

These themes of patriotism and liberation from tyranny appealed immensely to the French audiences of the time. The beginning of the revolution of 1830 in Belgium has been attributed in some respects to the riotous audience's reaction at the premiere of Auber's stormy *La muette de Portici.* Always responsive to the times, Rossini had exploited elements of these themes in his previous Parisian works, *Le siège de Corinthe* and *Moïse et Pharaon.*

Among the defining attributes of the Romantic movement of the early nineteenth century is the infusion of the power and picturesque qualities of nature into art. Along with this came an increasing interest in local color—that is, the unique qualities of specific cultures and locales. Clearly, the Swiss peasantry and spectacular scenery of their cantons of Schwyz, Uri, and Unterwalden provided ample resources for exploitation by Rossini. Exotic atmospheres and unusual settings were common in French opera in the early nineteenth century, but few composers exceeded Rossini in successfully melding these elements into the music itself. The famous *ranz des vaches* (song of the Swiss herdsmen) played by the English horn in the overture; the choruses of hunters, wedding celebrants, and conspirators; and the fisherman's song are all informed by atmosphere and characterization adroitly shaped by instrumentation and orchestra-

OPERA

tion. Rossini previously had shown this kind of mastery in other works, notably *La donna del lago*. Edward Dannreuther (*The Oxford History of Music,* 1905) contends that "Local color so perfect was not again seen or heard in opera till 1875, when Bizet's *Carmen* was produced." Bizet's fondness for act II of *Tell* is well documented.

Today, among the least recognized of the important attributes of *Guillaume Tell* is the fine orchestration that most know only from the overture, but which in fact is excelled easily by many sections of the opera itself. Rossini's contemporaries acknowledged the genius of his orchestration, despite the infamous criticism of his brass and percussion "noisiness." Later, the great French scholar, Arthur Pougin (*Musiciens du XIXe siècle,* 1911) observes that "it is finally to Rossini that is owed the innovation and richness of the splendors of the modern dramatic orchestra. Who knows if Wagner's orchestra, that admirable orchestra to which unfortunately everything is sacrificed, would exist today without the advent of Rossini?" The score of *Guillaume Tell* is a model of imagination and mastery in orchestration, but special mention may be made of the writing for horns and for violoncellos.

A horn player himself, Rossini chose that instrument as the key element in the creation of local color. The depiction of the bucolic atmosphere of the Swiss countryside, the virtuoso paean of the hunting chorus, and the antiphonal, on-stage horn calls that rally the Swiss peasants—all contribute to the establishment of the horn as the central instrument of the opera.

The sub-divided solo violoncellos of the opening of the overture portend their creative use in most of the opera. Perhaps most striking, and yet typical, is their aspiring sixteenth-note passage that sets the tone of the aria of the famous archery scene, "Sois immobile" ("Be still").

The florid arias and dazzling set pieces well-known to lovers of Rossini's Italian operas do not dominate his last work for the stage, although the arias are demanding—especially those of the tenor, Melcthal. Rather, we find that a superb coordination of ensembles, choruses, dances, evocative instrumental sections, and solos and duets informed by dramatic lyricism carry the whole in a marvelous unity of expression. Striking scenes abound, but perhaps the most arresting is the entirety of the second act, where Rossini carefully builds to a smashing climax, with soloists, chorus, and orchestra all propelling the drama forward.

Guillaume Tell is Rossini's neglected masterpiece of early French romantic opera. Although it was popular during the nineteenth century, it did not enjoy unqualified success. Today, performances of it are rare, but the meritorious qualities of *Guillaume Tell* easily outstrip the hindrances imposed by a libretto that is occasionally awkward. The ever-popular overture, enduring though it may be, is only a presage of far richer treasures in the opera proper.—WILLIAM E. RUNYAN

Hamlet

Composer: *Ambroise Thomas.*

Librettists: *J. Barbier and M. Carré (after Shakespeare).*

First Performance: *Paris, Opéra, 9 March 1868.*

Roles: *Hamlet (baritone); Claudius (bass); Ophelia (soprano); Gertrude (mezzo-soprano); Laertes (tenor); Horatio (bass); Polonius (bass); Marcellus (tenor); Ghost (bass); Two Gravediggers (baritone, tenor); Players in the Pantomime: King, Queen, Villain; chorus (SSTTBB).*

Premiering at the Paris Opéra shortly after his highly successful *Mignon,* Ambroise Thomas's *Hamlet* consolidated its composer's stature in French music and propelled him into the Directorship of the Conservatoire when the position became vacant several years later.

Shakespeare's play had been set as an opera by at least nine composers before Thomas, and was to receive another five attempts afterwards. None has approached Thomas's in initial popularity (no doubt prompted by a nationalist French desire to compete operatically with Wagner and especially Verdi) or in longevity. Despite some major flaws (especially the ending), inventions, omissions, and differences, Thomas's *Hamlet* resembles Shakespeare's more often than not, and maintains a remarkable measure of the original's introspection and intensity.

In the first scene of the opera's act I, Claudius's and Gertrude's nuptials are celebrated at the Danish court. Hamlet expresses displeasure at his mother's hasty remarriage, and then pledges his love to Ophelia. Her brother Laertes announces his departure on a diplomatic mission, after which Marcellus and Horatio report to Hamlet their sighting of his father's ghost. The second scene takes place on the palace esplanade, where Hamlet encounters the ghost. During this interview the ghost demands that Hamlet avenge his death, but take pity upon Gertrude.

The first scene of act II is set in the palace gardens, where Ophelia is musing over Hamlet's inattention and seeming hostility. Gertrude attempts to console her, and agrees, along with

Claudius, to Hamlet's suggestion that a troupe of actors perform at the palace. Hamlet meets with the players, and instructs them to present "The Murder of Gonzago" that evening. Scene two is the performance, in the course of which Claudius explodes in anger and stalks from the hall. Hamlet feigns insanity and accuses Claudius before the assembled court.

In act III, Hamlet is discovered alone in his mother's bedchamber (where he sings the "To be or not to be" aria). He forgoes an opportunity to strike Claudius, but overhears him with Polonius, Ophelia's father, implicating himself in the murder of the former king. Hamlet confronts and threatens Gertrude, during which the ghost reappears and reminds him to spare his mother. Since the ghost is visible only to Hamlet, Gertrude is convinced of her son's madness.

Act IV begins with an extended ballet. Set before a lake, the dance celebrates the "festival of spring." At its conclusion, Ophelia wanders in for her well-known mad scene. After recalling Hamlet's broken promises of love, the deranged heroine drowns herself in the lake.

The final act takes place in a cemetery, where two gravediggers are preparing a tomb. Hamlet meets Laertes, who holds the hero responsible for his sister's suicide. As the two men cross swords, their duel is interrupted by an approaching cortège, and Hamlet first learns of Ophelia's death. Hamlet tries to stab himself, and the ghost appears again, this time visible to all. Finally Hamlet hesitates no longer, kills Claudius, and orders Gertrude to a nunnery. Hamlet is proclaimed the new king.

In addition to Ophelia's famous mad scene from act IV, several other musical items deserve mention. The love-duet between Hamlet and Ophelia in act I, "Doute de la lumière," must rank among the finest examples of the genre. As a substitute for Hamlet's "instructions to the players" found in the original, the opera presents Hamlet's drinking song "Ô vin, dissipe la tristesse." And Thomas sets Hamlet's monologue ("Être ou ne pas être") with surprising effectiveness and sensitivity. Touches of innovative orchestration are evident throughout the opera, including the use of both alto and baritone saxophones, and the bass saxhorn to emphasize the darker tone colors.

Although *Hamlet* is sometimes performed with an ending that approximates Shakespeare's, Thomas's original conclusion is very much in keeping with the relatively non-violent conventions of early French opéra-lyrique. Given the abundant strengths of the score and a generally valid libretto by Carré and Barbier, it is regrettable that the "happy ending" has so compromised the work's reputation.—MORTON ACHTER

Handel, George Frideric

Composer. Born 23 February 1685, in Halle. Died 14 April 1759, in London. Studied harpsichord, organ and composition with Wilhelm Zachau, organist of the Liebfrauenkirche in Halle; entered the University of Halle, 1702; in Hamburg, 1703, where he was hired as a violinist by Reinhard Keiser for the Hamburg Opera orchestra; met Mattheson in Hamburg; first opera Almira, *produced at the Hamburg Opera, 1705; traveled to Italy, where he lived and worked in Florence, Rome (under the patronage of the Marquis Francesco Ruspoli), Naples, and Venice; first Italian opera* Rodrigo, *1709; succeeded Agostino Steffani as Kapellmeister to the Elector of Hannover, 1710; visited England, and produced his opera* Rinaldo *at the Queen's Theatre in the Haymarket, London, 1711; began permanent residence in England, 1714; composer in residence to the Duke of Chandos, 1717-19; composer and master of the orchestra for the Royal Academy of Music, an Italian opera company established in London at the King's Theatre in the Haymarket, 1719-28; became a naturalized British subject, 1727; second Royal Academy, 1728-1733; honorary doctorate, Oxford University, 1733; Handel continued to compose Italian operas in London until 1741; oratorios Deborah and Athalia, 1733; ode Alexander's Feast, 1736; Handel increasingly composed oratorios from 1737-1752. Handel's circle included the poets and writers Rolli, Haym, Gay, Pope, Jennings, and the composers Mattheson, Telemann, G. Bononcini, Ariosti, and the Scarlattis.*

Operas *Der in Krohnen erlangte Glücks-Wechsel oder Almira, Königin von Castilien [Almira],* F.C. Feustking (after G. Pancieri), Hamburg, Theater am Gänsemarkt, 8 January 1705; *Die durch Blut und Mord erlangte Liebe [Nero],* F.C. Feustking, Hamburg, Theater am Gänsemarkt, 25 February 1705; *Vincer se stesso è la maggior vittoria [Rodrigo],* after F. Silvani, *Il duello d'Amore e di Vendetta,* Florence, Cocomero, November c. 1707; *Der beglückte Florindo; Die verwandelte Daphne,* H. Hinsch, Hamburg, Theater am Gänsemarkt, January 1708; *Agrippina,* V. Grimani, Venice, San Giovanni Grisostomo, c. January 1709; *Rinaldo,* Giacomo Rossi (after a scenario by A. Hill based on Tasso, *La Gerusalemme liberata*), London, Queen's Theatre in the Haymarket, 24 February 1711; revised 1717, 1731; *Il pastor fido,* Giacomo Rossi (after B. Guarini), London, Queen's Theatre in the Haymarket, 22 November 1712; revised 18 May 1734, 9 November 1734; *Teseo,* Nicola F. Haym (after P. Quinault, *Thésée*), London, Queen's Theatre in the Haymarket, 10 January 1713; *Silla,* Giacomo Rossi, London, Burlington House?, 2 June 1713; *Amadigi di Gaula,* Nicola F. Haym (after A.H. de la Motte, *Amadis de Grèce*), London, King's Theatre in the Haymarket, 25 May 1715; revised 16 February 1716, 16 February 1717; *Radamisto,* Nicola F. Haym (after D. Lalli, *L'amor tirannico, o Zenobia,* Florence, 1712), London, King's Theatre in the Haymarket, 27 April 1720; revised 28 December 1720, January-February 1728; *Muzio Scevola* (with F. Amadei and G. Bononcini), Paolo A. Rolli (after S. Stampiglia, Venice, 1710), London, King's Theatre in the Haymarket, 15 April 1721; revised 7 November 1722; *Floridante,* Paolo A. Rolli (after Silvani, *La costanza in trionfo,* Livorno, 1706), London, King's Theatre in the Haymarket, 9 December 1721; revised 4 December 1722, 29 April 1727; *Ottone, Rè di Germania,* Nicola F. Haym (after S.B. Pallavicino, *Teofane*), London, King's Theatre in the Haymarket, 12 January 1723; revised 8 February 1726, 13 November 1733; *Flavio, Rè di Longobardi,* Nicola F. Haym (after M. Noris, *Flavio Cuniberto,* Rome, 1696), London, King's Theatre in the Haymarket, 14 May 1723; revised 18 April 1732; *Giulio Cesare in Egitto,* Nicola F. Haym (after G.F. Bussani), London, King's Theatre in the Haymarket, 20 February 1724; revised 2 January 1725, 17 January 1730; *Tamerlano,* Nicola F. Haym (after A. Piovene, *Il Bajazet,* 1710, and as revised for 1719, based on J. Pradon, *Tamerlan, ou La mort de Bajazet*), London, King's Theatre in the Haymarket, 31 October 1724; revised 13 November 1731; *Rodelinda, Regina de' Longobardi,* Nicola F. Haym (after A. Salvi, based on P. Corneille, *Pertharite*), London, King's Theatre in the Haymarket, 13 February 1725; revised 18 December 1725, 4 May 1731; *Scipione,* Paolo A. Rolli (after A. Salvi), London, King's Theatre in the Haymarket, 12 March 1726; revised 3 November 1730; *Alessandro,* Paolo A. Rolli (after O. Mauro, *La superbia d'Alessandro*), London, King's Theatre in the Haymarket, 5 May 1726; 25 November 1732; as *Rossane,* 1743, 1744, 1748; *Admeto, Rè di Tessaglia* (after O. Mauro, *L' Antigona delusa da Alceste,* based on A. Aureli), London, King's Theatre in the Haymarket, 31 January 1727; revised 25 May 1728, 7 December 1731; *Riccardo Primo, Rè d'Inghilterra,* Paolo A. Rolli (after F. Briani, *Isacio tiranno*), London, King's Theatre in the Haymarket, 11 November 1727; *Genserico*

h

≡≡OPERA

[unfinished; music used in *Siroe* and *Tolomeo*]; *Siroe, Rè di Persia,* Nicola F. Haym (after Metastasio, Naples, 1727), London, King's Theatre in the Haymarket, 17 February 1728; *Tolomeo, Rè di Egitto,* Nicola F. Haym (after C.S. Capece, *Tolomeo et Alessandro*), London, King's Theatre in the Haymarket, 30 April 1728; revised 19 May 1730, 2 January 1733; *Lotario,* after A. Salvi, *Adelaide* (Venice, 1729), London, King's Theatre in the Haymarket, 2 December, 1729; *Partenope,* after S. Stampiglia (Venice, 1707), London, King's Theatre in the Haymarket, 24 February 1730; revised 12 December 1730, Covent Garden, 29 January 1737; *Poro, Rè dell'Indie,* after Metastasio, *Alessandro nell'Indie,* London, King's Theatre in the Haymarket, 2 February 1731; revised 23 November 1731, 8 December 1736; *Tito,* after Racine, *Bérénice* [unfinished; some music used in *Ezio*]; *Ezio,* after Metastasio, London, King's Theatre in the Haymarket, 15 January 1732; *Sosarme, Rè di Media,* after A. Salvi, *Dionisio, Rè di Portogallo,* London, King's Theatre in the Haymarket, 15 February 1732; revised 27 April 1734; *Orlando,* after C.S. Capece (based on Ariosto, *Orlando furioso*), London, King's Theatre in the Haymarket, 27 January 1733; *Arianna in Creta,* after P. Pariati, *Arianna e Teseo* (Naples, 1721; Rome, 1729), London, King's Theatre in the Haymarket, 26 January 1734; revised, Covent Garden, 27 November 1734; *Oreste* (pasticcio), after G. Barlocci, London, Covent Garden, 18 December 1734; *Ariodante,* after A. Salvi, *Ginevra, Principessa di Scozia* (based on Ariosto, *Orlando furioso*), London, Covent Garden, 8 January 1735; revised 5 May 1736; *Alcina,* after *L'isola di Alcina* (1728, based on Ariosto, *Orlando furioso*), London, Covent Garden, 16 April 1735; revised 6 November 1736; *Atalanta,* after B. Valeriano, *La caccia in Etolia,* London, Covent Garden, 12 May 1736; *Arminio,* after A. Salvi, London, Covent Garden, 12 January 1737; *Giustino,* after Pariati (Rome, 1724; based on N. Beregan), London, Covent Garden, 16 February 1737; *Berenice,* after A. Salvi, London, Covent Garden, 18 May 1737; *Faramondo,* after Zeno (Rome, 1720), London, King's Theatre in the Haymarket, 3 January 1738; *Alessandro Severo* (pasticcio), after Zeno (Milan, 1723), London, King's Theatre in the Haymarket, 25 February 1738; *Serse,* after S. Stampiglia (Rome, 1694; based on N. Minato), London, King's Theatre in the Haymarket, 15 April 1738; *Imeneo,* after S. Stampiglia, London, Lincoln's Inn Fields, 22 November 1740; revised for concert performance, Dublin, New Music Hall, 24 March 1742; *Deidamia,* Paolo A. Rolli, London, Lincoln's Inn Fields, 10 January 1741.

Perhaps best known today for his English oratorios (especially *Messiah*) and orchestral music (such as *Water Music*), George Frideric Handel was primarily a man of the theater. Between 1705 and 1741, Handel composed and, with the exception of three, produced forty-two operas. He also produced eleven *pasticcio* operas (in effect, "casserole" operas created by arranging old music): three using his own music and eight using the music of contemporary composers. Furthermore, Handel's twenty-four oratorios are surely dramatic works, even if they are not theatrical. As opposed to the operas, many contain elaborate choruses, having contemplative or reflective, rather than dramatic, functions. However, Handel regularly contin-ued to write stage directions in his dramatic oratorio manuscripts, and certainly his secular oratorios, *Semele* (1744) and *Hercules* (1745), as well as the apocryphal *Susanna* (1749), were seen as directly competitive with contemporary opera.

Whereas Handel's oratorio texts were frequently newly written for the composer in close collaboration with his librettist (such as *Judas Maccabaeus* and *Jephtha* by Thomas Morell), Handel's operas are mostly adaptations of older librettos. The adaptors of his opera texts are not always known, but two of his collaborators stand out, Nicola Haym and Paolo Rolli. Rolli's work illustrates a greater poetic artistry, but Haym, although a rougher poet, forged dramatic scenes

h

OPERA

that awakened Handel's creative powers. Many of Handel's greatest operas had librettos adapted by Haym, including *Radamisto* (1720), *Ottone* (1723), *Giulio Cesare* (1724), *Tamerlano* (1724), and *Rodelinda* (1725).

It is not known what role Handel played in the choice and adaptation of his opera librettos, although what evidence exists suggests that the composer was intimately involved at every stage. First, there is testimony from Handel's oratorio librettists. Second, many of the operas whose librettos were adapted for him are among those Handel had earlier heard performed. For example, *Radamisto, Tamerlano, Sosarme* (1732), *Ariodante* (1735), and *Berenice* (1737) are based on operas the composer probably heard in Florence between 1706 and 1709. *Ottone* is adapted from an opera Handel certainly heard in Dresden in 1719, *Partenope* (1730) from an opera the composer most likely heard in Venice in 1708, and *Lotario* (1729) from an opera Handel had heard in Venice in 1729.

Handel's librettos are typified by the style of construction and composition known as *opera seria* ("serious opera"). In content, these librettos are distinguished by a lack of comic characters and by a high moral tone illustrating characters coming to grips with their own inadequacies, balancing their positions, responsibilities, and duties against their illegitimate (frequently sexual, but sometimes war-like) desires, and, in the case of Handel's librettos especially, acting within the bonds of familial (parental, fraternal, or marital) devotion. In structure, they illustrate a rigid design in which individual scenes generally begin with recitative (typified by blank, or unrhymed, verse of varying lengths) and conclude with a solo aria (in rhymed verse with regular, and generally shorter, line lengths). Individual scenes were defined at their ends by the exit of the character who had sung the aria; frequently, scene beginnings were marked by the entrance of a new character. Within a single scenic backdrop, a number of these scenes would be grouped together by a linked chain of entrances and exits, referred to as the *liaison de scènes* ("tying together of scenes"), so that the stage was never bare of actors except at the change of backdrop.

Musically, these structures elicited a similar rigidity. The recitative text was generally set in *recitativo semplice* ("simple recitative"), with the singers performing (reciting) in a musically heightened speech style, supported only by punctuating chords played by harpsichord and cello. The arias were in *da capo* ("from-the-beginning") form, in which two distinct sections of music were followed by a repeat of the first with elaborate ornamentation added. Ensembles and choruses were very rare. In Handel's operas, this structure became a strong framework of expectation against which the slightest changes had extraordinary dramatic effect.

Handel's operatic career falls into discrete periods defined both by geography and venue and by the structure and content of the librettos. The pre-London operas, composed between 1704 and 1709 for performance in Hamburg, Florence, and Venice, all display a somewhat antiquated style. Both *Almira* (1705), Handel's only surviving opera from Germany, and *Agrippina* (1709), Handel's only opera for Venice, contain comic servant characters, a throwback to the seventeenth century tradition. Furthermore, the surviving librettos from Germany all indicate a dependence on pageantry and ballet that derives from the French tradition. Handel's early English operas (1711-1715), on the other hand, display a style that combines the Italian operatic tradition with the English tradition of dramatic opera, in which there was a heavy reliance on the supernatural and extravagent scenery. *Rinaldo* (1711), *Silla* (1713), and *Teseo* (1713) all include flying dragons and furies; *Rinaldo, Teseo,* and *Amadigi* (1715) all have important roles for sorceresses.

With the opening of the Royal Academy of Music in 1720, Handel can be said to have achieved his mature style. Although this Academy failed financially in 1728, Handel quickly regrouped his forces and reopened the so-called second Academy in the 1729-1730 season. Handel's three operas based on earlier librettos by Pietro Metastasio all derive from late in the first Academy period or early in the second Academy period: *Siroe* (1728), *Poro* (1731), and *Ezio* (1732), but all the operas from this period, especially from *Radamisto* (1720) to *Ezio* reflect the growing trend toward reform style. Arias generally occur at the ends of scenes, after which the singer exits, a structure that is known as the "exit convention," and arias are longer, so that these operas contain approximately thirty or fewer arias, or only about half the number in *Almira*. With the exception of the first Academy's *Admeto* (1727), in which act II opens with Ercole (Hercules) rescuing Alceste from Hell, they lack magical, mythological, and legendary elements, and, at least partially due to that, there are no spectacular stage effects. The librettos are historical and political, and they tend to emphasize parental, sibling, and marital relationships. Mutual concern and respect between parents and children, for example, are especially important to *Radamisto, Giulio Cesare,* and *Tamerlano.*

Beginning with his last opera for the second Academy, *Orlando* (1732), and extending to 1736, Handel returned to the magic, mythological, and legendary operas of the early English period. In part this reflects the intense competition Handel faced during these years from rival companies. In March of 1732 a new company under the direction of Thomas Arne (father of the composer) began producing English operas; in May of that year they produced Handel's *Acis and Galatea*. In autumn of 1733 a rival Italian opera company opened its doors, forcing Handel for the first time out of the Haymarket Theatre. This company not only stole most of Handel's singers and his librettist Rolli, but in 1734, they produced Handel's *Ottone*. Despite the intense competition that sometimes pitted Handel against himself, or perhaps because of it, Handel composed some of his most spectacular scores, including the trilogy of operas based on Ariosto's *Orlando furioso: Orlando, Ariodante* (1734) and *Alcina* (1735). The mad scenes for Orlando exist totally outside the *da capo* tradition and thus define musically the hero's unbalanced state. In *Ariodante* Handel used a full chorus for the first time since *Amadigi,* and for the first time perhaps since his earliest German operas, he had the availability of a ballet troupe. *Ariodante* and *Alcina* are notable for their extended ballets.

After 1736, Handel's last seven operas revert somewhat to the heroic and historical type of libretto. Although the rival companies remained open, by 1736 Handel's superiority was manifest. Perhaps not surprisingly, after the intensely competitive period of 1732 to 1736, there is initially a drop in quality. Handel's last three operas, however, can be set apart from the vast majority of his operas in that they contain decidedly comic characters and situations. The Argument for *Serse* (*Xerxes,* 1738) specifically mentions that "the basis of the story" resides partially in "some imbicilities," and the cast list describes Serse's servant, Elviro, as "a facetious Fellow." Many commentators have described these comic elements as pre-Mozartean, but they look backward more clearly than they look forward. Not only are they reminiscent of Handel's earliest surviving operas, *Almira* and *Agrippina,* but the source libretto for *Serse* derives from 1694.

Throughout his career, Handel created his operatic roles for specific singers whose special abilities strongly influenced the musical characterizations of their roles. Margherita Durastanti was the only soloist regularly employed by the Marquis Ruspoli in Rome, where Handel resided for much of 1707 and 1708. Handel not only wrote many cantatas for her, but he also created for her the role of Santa Maria Maddalena (Mary Magdalene) in *La resurrezione* (*The Resurrection,*

1708) and the title role of *Agrippina* (Venice, 1709). She specialized in parts for strong women (Armida, Agrippina) and "pants roles" (male roles played by a woman). The title male role of *Radamisto* was first performed by her in London, 1720, but the castrato Senesino replaced her at the second set of *Radamisto* performances, after which Handel composed his most famous heroic roles for this singer, including the title roles in *Giulio Cesare, Ottone, Alessandro,* and *Orlando.* For the soprano Francesca Cuzzoni, Handel created, among many others, the role of Cleopatra in *Giulio Cesare,* including the arias "V'adoro pupille" ("Beloved eyes") and "Piangerò" ("I shall weep"). After the arrival of soprano Faustina Bordoni, Handel wrote five operas (*Alessandro* to *Tolomeo*) that balanced distinct roles for both women, Faustina playing the coquette against Cuzzoni's favored pathetic style. For the tenor Francesco Borosini, Handel rewrote the title role of *Tamerlano* to include an extended death scene freed from the constraints of the *da capo* and typical scenic construction. The bass singer Giuseppe Boschi, like Durastanti, performed for Handel in Italy (including the role of Narciso in *Agrippina*) and followed him to London, where he sang Argante in *Rinaldo.* During the Royal Academy, thirteen more, mostly villanous, roles were created for him, leading to the contemporary quip "And Boschi-like be always in a rage." Even during the 1730s, Handel's operas were based largely on the concept of a repertoire company. After Senesino moved into the Opera of Nobility, he was replaced by the castrato Carestini. Soprano Anna Strada was the one singer who stayed with Handel throughout this competitive period, and for her he created thirteen roles, including the title roles of *Arianna, Alcina,* and *Atalanta* (1736).

Handel frequently reused his own music in different contexts, and he borrowed from other composers as well. Sometimes he was able to transform this pre-existent material, often with the simplest changes; other times he transferred music by himself or others unchanged, but even then the change of context seems to change the nature of the music. In some cases Handel borrows ideas from earlier settings of the librettos he uses. For example, some of Bajazet's music in *Tamerlano,* including the opening aria "Forte e lieto" ("Bravely and happily"), derives from Gasparini's setting of the same texts. Similarly the famous Larghetto of *Serse,* "Ombra mai fu" ("Never was there shade more soothing"; often referred to as "Handel's Largo") is based on Bononcini's setting. Three of Handel's earlier operas, *Agrippina, Rinaldo,* and *Il pastor fido,* are so heavily dependent on his earlier music that they could be called *pasticcio* operas. Thus the famous aria "Lascia ch'io pianga" ("Leave me to weep") from *Rinaldo* (London), had earlier been heard as "Lascia la spina" ("Leave the thorns") in *Il trionfo del tempo* (*The Triumph of Time;* 1707, Rome) and as a Sarabande in *Almira* (Hamburg). In this and many other cases, however, the borrowings seem to be Handel's way of preserving his music in an age when composers could not assume their music would be heard more than once within their own lifetimes, much less saved for posterity.—ELLEN T. HARRIS

Hänsel und Gretel

Composer: *Engelbert Humperdinck.*

Librettist: *Adelheid Wette (after the tale by the Brothers Grimm).*

First Performance: *Weimar, Court Theater, 23 December 1893.*

Roles: *Gretel (soprano); Hänsel (mezzo-soprano); Gertrud (mezzo-soprano); Peter (baritone); Witch (mezzo-soprano); Sandman (soprano); Dew Fairy (soprano); chorus (children, SA).*

Hänsel und Gretel

The very title of *Hänsel und Gretel* informs us that it tells a homely tale of old Germany rather than one of gods or heroes. It took some time to develop into a fully-fledged opera, however, for it grew from music that Humperdinck composed for his two young nieces Isolde and Gudrun, who had a home-made puppet theater at their house in Cologne and liked to stage little domestic performances of plays devised by their mother Adelheid Wette. One of these plays was based on the Grimm Brothers' fairy tale of two children who are captured by a wicked witch but outwit her and escape, and besides the immediate family a number of local friends and musicians saw it and were delighted by the story and by Humperdinck's music, not least the lilting dance song "Brother, will you dance with me?" which now comes early in act I. Eventually Frau Wette and her brother the composer turned *Hänsel und Gretel* into the Singspiel or music drama that had its first performance under Richard Strauss at Weimar at Christmastide 1893 and soon won fame elsewhere in Germany and in other centers such as London and New York.

Although usually performed with adult singers, and with a mezzo-soprano singing the role of the young boy Hänsel, the opera is of course about children and to be enjoyed by them. It has therefore to be simple in its appeal but at the same time varied and subtle enough musically and dramatically, so as not to bore audiences of any age in the course of its three acts. Humperdinck and his sister (who supplied the libretto) succeeded remarkably well, and the composer's direct musical language allowed him to include a few traditional children's songs and folksongs without disturbing the overall style. A good production of *Hänsel und Gretel* avoids sentimentality and *kitsch*. Indeed, a German critic has called it "a true German folk opera . . . that awakens, especially in children, affection and at least a little understanding of the art sacred to the Muses, that of Music."

The story is set in medieval Germany, where at the start of act I the two children are alone working at household tasks in the hut of their parents, the broom-maker Peter and his wife Gertrud. But they forget their work and start playing, and when their mother returns she scolds them for idleness. In her anger she accidentally knocks over a jug of precious milk, and so she sends them out into the nearby forest to gather strawberries for supper. When Peter returns unexpectedly laden with provisions, it is too late to recall the children, and he tells her of the danger of the witch of the Ilsenstein who catches children and turns them into gingerbread. The parents rush out in search of their children.

Act II commences with a not-too-scary orchestral "Witch's Ride" and the curtain rises to find the children in the forest with their basket filled. Unfortunately they now start to play and to eat the fruit, and realize too late, and with dismay, that it is getting dark and they can no longer find their way home. When the Sandman appears before them they sing an evening prayer (a touching duet) and fall asleep, protected by fourteen angels from heaven. But when act III begins with their awakening at morning by the Dew Fairy, they espy a little house made entirely of gingerbread and other cookies. Hänsel plucks up courage to break off and eat a piece, but now the witch whose house it is (whose name is Rosina Leckermaul) captures both children and places a spell on them with her wand which prevents them from running away, her idea being to bake them both for gingerbread, just as she has done with others who have got into her clutches. But by a stratagem, the resourceful Gretel persuades the witch to show her how to get into the oven to inspect its contents, and then with great daring she and her brother manage to push their captor inside and to shut the door on her. The oven soon explodes, and by using the witch's wand the children restore to life all the gingerbread children that the witch had previously turned into biscuits, while she herself has been transformed once and for all into a big cake.

The children's parents now appear and everyone sings a joyful song of thanksgiving.
—CHRISTOPHER HEADINGTON

Die Harmonie der Welt [The Harmony of the World]

Composer: *Paul Hindemith.*

Librettist: *Paul Hindemith.*

First Performance: *Munich, Prinzregententheater, 11 August 1957,*

Roles: *(doubled as indicated): Rudolf II/Ferdinand II/Sol (bass); Johannes Kepler/Earth (baritone); Wallenstein/Jupiter (tenor); Ulrich/Soldier/Mars (tenor); Daniel Hizler/ Parson/Mercury (bass); Tansur/Saturn (bass); Baron Starhemberg (baritone); Christoph (tenor); Susanna/Venus (soprano); Katharina/Luna (contralto); Little Susanna (soprano); Bailiff (baritone); Solicitor (baritone); Four Women (two sopranos, two contraltos); Three Assassins (tenor, two basses); chorus.*

Die Harmonie der Welt is Hindemith's last large-scale opera forming a thematic trilogy with the earlier *Cardillac* (1926) and *Mathis der Maler* (1933-35). The principal work of Hindemith's last period (1955-63), it reflects his artistic, philosophical, and artistic credo and can be construed as his musical autobiography. It is a unique and neglected work yet to be staged outside Germany and Austria.

For many years Hindemith was preoccupied with the nature of the creative artist, be it a goldsmith (Cardillac), a painter (Mathis), or a scientist (Kepler). Therefore (as in the case of *Mathis*), he felt it necessary to write his own libretto for *Die Harmonie der Welt,* employing unusual rhyme schemes and occasional archaic German words. The opera's title is taken from the astronomer Johannes Kepler's magnum opus *Harmonices Mundi* (1619) in which Kepler propounded the three laws of planetary motion and speculated upon the actual sounds emitted by the orbiting planets. Hindemith strongly identified with Kepler, the opera's central figure, because both of them believed they had discovered universal laws in their respective disciplines and were devoted to the belief that the harmony of the universe existed and could be made manifest to the intellect of mankind. In addition, Hindemith drew a number of parallels between the circumstances of their lives.

During a long gestation period (1939-57), Hindemith composed a series of sonatas as preparatory exercises, as well as the symphony *Die Harmonie der Welt* (1951), whose three movements were later incorporated into the opera. The final movement, *Musica Mundana,* meaning "the music of the spheres," with vocal parts superimposed, became the opera's final scene. The work is comprised of tableaux, which chronologically depict important events in or surrounding the life of Kepler. It begins in 1608, shortly after the appearance of Halley's comet (used as a symbol of destruction), and ends in 1630, the year of Kepler's death. There is no dramatic progression from scene to scene or character development as such; rather, the opera builds to the final scene in which Hindemith unfolds his vision of the harmony of the world. During the opera a gallery of Kepler's associates and relatives is presented, all of whom have their symbolic meaning in this essentially allegorical work. These characters either impede or assist the steadfast Kepler in his quest to find union with the universal harmony. Those detrimental to Kepler's search are General Wallenstein, the famous military commander during

365

the Thirty Years War (1618-48), which serves as a backdrop to the opera; Tansur, a charlatan and Wallenstein's recruiter; Emperors Rudolf II and Ferdinand II, Kepler's wayward patrons; Pastor Hizler, who denies Kepler the holy sacrament; Ulrich, his ambitious assistant; and his mother Katharina, accused of witchcraft. Only the two Susannas—his second wife and his little daughter—are completely inspirational figures for Kepler.

Each character is associated with the astrological meaning of the sun, moon, and six planets known in Kepler's time. Occasionally there are glimpses of their pure essence but more often they display their negative, lesser selves in opposition to such qualities as love, service, humility, and faith. This polarization was symbolized in part by the juxtaposition of "leit" tonalities a tritone apart, e.g., C and F sharp. For example, the tonality of E stands for the Harmony while the tonality of B flat represents Chaos, all those forces exerted by the imperfection of human nature. This polarity is also highlighted by Hindemith's use of dual scenes in which two distinct events are both alternately and simultaneously presented.

All the obstructions to Kepler's desired union with the Harmony are removed at his death. This opens the door for the purification of not only Kepler but also all the other flawed characters in a kind of heavenly purgatorial world that leads to the source of the Harmony. This final scene of *Musica Mundana* is in the form of a passacaglia, with the constant repetition of its theme symbolizing the constancy of the heavenly world. During the twenty-two variations, each character, transformed into a member of the solar system, repents his errors and expresses his higher self. The final E-major chord is much more than a conventional ending for Hindemith: it is the harmonious portal which leads to the ultimate Harmony.

Hindemith's overriding theme is that the life of humanity on earth cannot be resolved by efforts of will. Rather than ever being reconciled, the polarization of positive versus negative attributes in man must be transcended and resolved in an afterlife state. Hindemith's rather pessimistic view of life on earth and his optimistic view of an afterlife point to the inspiration he found in Catholicism.—JAMES D'ANGELO

Haydn, Franz Joseph

Born 31 March 1732? (baptized 1 April 1732), in Robrau. Died 31 May 1809, in Vienna. Married: Maria Anna Keller, 26 November 1760. Studied with his paternal cousin Johann Mathias Franck in Hainburg; soprano in the choir of St Stephen's Cathedral in Vienna under the direction of Karl Georg Reutter, 1740; became a music tutor to a private family on the recommendation of Pietro Metastasio; accompanied students of Nicola Antonio Porpora in exchange for composition lessons; harpsichordist and singing teacher to Countess Thun, 1751; Kapellmeister to Count Ferdinand Maximilian von Morzin at his estate in Lukavec, 1759; second Kapellmeister at the Esterházy estate in Eisenstadt, 1761; first Kapellmeister at Esterháza, 1766; elected a member of the Modena Philharmonic Society, 1780; received a gold medal from Prince Henry of Prussia, 1784; commissioned to write The Seven Last Words *for the Cathedral of Cádiz, 1785; given a diamond ring by King Friedrich Wilhelm II, 1787; took up permanent residence in Vienna, 1790; in London at the invitation of Johann Peter Salomon, 1791; honorary Mus.D. from Oxford University, 1791; met Beethoven in Bonn, 1792, and accepted him as a student; in London, 1794; became Kapellmeister once again to the Esterházy family; composition of*

h

OPERA

sacred works, including 6 masses, 1796-1802; composition of The Creation, *1796-98; composition of* The Seasons, *1799-1801; due to illness, resigned as Kapellmeister at Esterháza, 1802.*

Operas *Der krumme Teufel* (Singspiel), J. Kurz, 1751?, Vienna, 29 May 1753 [lost]; *Der neue krumme Teufel* (Singspiel), J. Kurz, c. 1758? [lost]; *Acide* (festa teatrale), G.A. Migliavacca, 1762, Eisenstadt, 11 January 1763; revised 1773; *La Marchesa Nespola*, 1763 [fragmentary]; [opera buffa or Italian comedy], 1762? [an aria and recitative survive]; *Il dottore*, c. 1761-65? [lost]; *La vedova*, c. 1761-65? [lost]; *Il scanarello*, c. 1761-65? [lost]; *La canterina* (intermezzo), G. Palomba (after the intermezzo *La canterina* in Niccolo Piccinni, *Origille*), 1760; *Lo speziale* (*Der Apotheker*), C. Goldoni, 1768, Esterháza, fall 1768; *Le pescatrici* (*Die Fischerinnen*), C. Goldoni, 1769, Esterháza, 16, 18 September 1770; *L'infedeltà delusa, (Liebe macht erfinderisch, Untreue lohnt sich nicht)*, M. Coltellini, 1773, Esterháza, 26 July 1773; *Philemon und Baucis oder Jupiters Reise auf die Erde* (Singspiel/marionette opera), G.K. Pfeffel, 1773; revised, Esterháza, 2 September 1773; *Hexenschabbas* (marionette opera), 1773? [lost]; *L'incontro improvviso* (*Die unverhoffte Zusammenkunft, Unverhofftes Begegnen*), K. Friebert (after Dancourt, *La rencontre imprévue*), 1775, Esterháza, 29 August 1775; *Dido* (Singspiel/marionette opera), Bader, 1776?-78, Esterháza, March 1776, fall 1778; *Opéra comique vom abgebrannten Haus*, c. 1773-79 [lost; may be identical to either *Hexenschabbas* or *Die bestrafte Rachbegierde*]; *Die Feuersbrunst?* (Singspiel/marionette opera), 1775?-78; *Genovefens vierter Theil*, 1777; *Il mondo della luna* (*Die Welt auf dem Monde*), C. Goldoni, 1777, Esterháza, 3 August 1777; *Die bestrafte Rachbegierde* (Singspiel/marionette opera), Bader, 1779?, Esterháza, 1779; *La vera costanza*, F. Puttini, 1778?-79, Esterháza, 25 April 1779; revised as *Der flatterhafte Liebhaber* (*Der Sieg der Beständigkeit, Die wahre Beständigkeit, List und Liebe, Laurette*), P.U. Dubuisson, 1785; *L'isola disabitata* (*Die wüste Insel*) (azione teatral), Metastasio, 1779, Esterháza, 6 December 1779; finale revised, 1802; *La fedeltà premiata* (*Die belohnte Treue*), after G. Lorenzi, *L'infedeltà fedele*, 1780, Esterháza, 25 February 1781; *Orlando paladino* (*Der Ritter Roland*), C.F. Badini, N. Porta (after Ariosto), 1782, Esterháza, 6 December 1782; *Armida*, 1783, Esterháza, 26 February 1784; *L'anima del filosofo ossia Orfeo ed Euridice*, C.F. Badini, 1791.

Haydn's production of operas spans the majority of his working life. His earliest German *Singspiele* were written before he began working for Prince Esterházy, while his last Italian opera was written (but never performed) in 1791 during his first sojourn in London. *Philemon und Baucis* is the only fully-authenticated complete German *Singspiel* that has survived; the remainder are either of doubtful authenticity or lost. By contrast, all but the very earliest Italian-language works survive complete. The German-language works are all comic; some of them were written for the marionette theater at Eszterháza, which was capable of spectacular scenic effects. The storm at the beginning of *Philemon und Baucis* is only one small example of this phenomenon. The Italian-language works range from relatively short, completely comic intermezzi like *La canterina,* through comic operas with serious or sentimental characters, to fully-fledged examples of *opera seria.* Over the course of Haydn's career, there is a general progression from the former type of opera to the latter; this may be largely connected to changes in Prince Nicholas Esterházy's taste.

With the exception of the earliest *Singspiele,* and the late *L'anima del filosofo,* Haydn's operas were written in the limited but significant social context of the Esterházy court. Before 1776, Prince Nicholas commissioned Haydn to write operas for particular celebratory occasions, and there were few if any other operas performed during these years. *Lo speziale* was written for the opening of the Esterháza opera house in 1768, for example, and *L'infedeltà delusa* was written to celebrate the visit of the Empress Maria Theresia to Esterháza. From 1776 until 1790, operas were a major part of the regular season of entertainment, and Haydn's took their place alongside works by Anfossi, Cimarosa, Righini, Paisiello, Piccinni, Sarti, Salieri and other successful Italian opera composers. Haydn rearranged, rehearsed, and directed multiple performances of these works, and clearly knew them all intimately. Even before this immersion, however, Haydn's proximity to poet laureate Metastasio and his lessons with the older Italian operatic master Porpora suggest that he was well acquainted with the tradition of Italian opera, both serious and comic. It is therefore relevant and important to see his own operas in this context.

All of Haydn's libretti had been set previously by other composers. Three (see works list) are texts by Goldoni set by several composers before him. The majority of his remaining operas are resettings of libretti with connections to Vienna; *L'incontro improvviso* is a resetting of Gluck's *La rencontre imprévue,* given in Vienna numerous times in the 1760s. A group of works performed in Vienna in 1777 resurface in settings by Haydn over the next 7 years. These include *L'isola disabitata* (Haydn, 1779), a much-set short work by Metastasio, performed in Vienna as a benefit for the singer Metilde Bologna in a setting by Luigi Bologna (Madame Bologna became one of the leading singers at Esterháza from 1781-1790); Puttini's *La vera costanza,* set by Pasquale Anfossi; Badini's *Orlando paladino,* reworked by Nunziato Porta (Esterháza house librettist from 1781) and set by Guglielmi with possible additions by Anfossi; and the much-beloved story of Armida, in a version by Giovanni Bertati and Johann Gottlieb Naumann (Haydn did not in fact set this version of *Armida,* but a variant of it). The origins of the libretto of *L'infedeltà delusa* are not so clear; however, a work of the same title was performed by a company of noble young ladies in the garden of the Imperial Palace in Vienna in 1765, and this may shed new light on the choice of this libretto for Maria Theresia's visit to Esterháza in 1773. Of Haydn's later operas for Esterháza, only *La fedeltà premiata* bears no relation to Vienna; this is a reworking of a text by Giambattista Lorenzi, set first by Cimarosa as *L'infedeltà fedele* (Naples, 1779).

In addition to having clear connections to the Viennese repertory, the operas Haydn composed after 1776 also reflect trends within the Esterháza repertory itself, and often have clear similarities to at least one other work premiered in the same season. For example, the sentimental comedy *La vera costanza* (1779) has much in common with Anfossi's *L'incognita perseguitata* (1779), or the same composer's *La finta giardiniera* (1780). The "dramma eroicomico" *Orlando paladino* (1782) has clear connections with Traëtta's *Il cavaliere errante* (1782). Like *Orlando paladino, Armida* (1784) reflects a growing interest in heroic subject matter and in *opera seria;* Sarti's *Giulio Sabino* was the first opera seria performed at Esterháza, in 1783. *Armida* also connects thematically with Luigi Bologna's *L'isola di Calipso abbandonata* (1784).

It has frequently been noted about Haydn's operas that they are "insufficiently dramatic"—that despite their undoubted musical value, they fail to articulate and flesh out their texts. There is little evidence that Haydn badgered his librettists with the insistence and intensity of a Mozart, and it is true that the relatively relentless alternation of recitative and aria seems "undramatic" to modern taste. On the other hand, within the constraints of the genre as Haydn knew it in the late 1770s and early 1780s (before Mozart had started on *The Marriage of Figaro*), there is much to value in his operas.

Haydn's music is invariably beautiful, and on occasion this beauty is put to impressive dramatic effect. For example, in the first act finale of *Il mondo della luna,* where the dupe Buonafede believes himself to be going to the moon and his daughter and maid believe he is dying, the orchestral music weaves a web around the broken utterances of the characters, and gives emotional plausibility to a superficially trivial situation in a manner which directly anticipates Mozart's *Così fan tutte.* Haydn is also to be valued for his ability to embody a dramatic or psychological situation in music. For example, when the blustering Rodomonte arrives on the scene in act II of *Orlando paladino,* Haydn writes an aria with a single thematic idea which vividly encapsulates the inarticulate and apparently pointless fury of this character. In the first-act finale of the same opera, a sudden modulation from B-flat major to B major, accompanied by a change in tempo and meter, brings home to the audience the affective distance between the world dominated by Rodomonte's pursuit of the princess Angelica, and the world shaped by Angelica's own thoughts and emotions.

In general, Haydn's shaping and deployment of musical form in his arias vividly projects both character and situation. Haydn's well-known propensity for word-painting is also present in his operas, particularly where nature images are invoked. A few of the many examples include the *Sturm und Drang* beginning to *Philemon und Baucis,* the ideal garden imagined by Buonafede in *Il mondo della luna,* or Rinaldo's final temptation in *Armida.*

Haydn's operas did not achieve the contemporary pan-European success of Paisiello's or Cimarosa's; nevertheless, the later works (from *La vera costanza* on) all enjoyed modest success in German-speaking countries (mostly in German translation). *La vera costanza* was performed, much altered, in Paris in 1791 as *Laurette,* and *Armida* was given in Turin in 1804. All of Haydn's operas were consigned to oblivion through the nineteenth century and well into the twentieth, with the exception of *Lo speziale,* which had some modest success in a one-act German-language version. There have been modern revivals of all the Italian operas, of *Philemon und Baucis* and of the unauthenticated *Die Feuersbrunst;* most have been commercially recorded.—MARY HUNTER

Hempel, Frieda

Soprano. Born 26 June 1885, in Leipzig. Died 7 October 1955, in Berlin. Married William B. Kahn, 1918 (divorced 1926). Studied piano at Leipzig Conservatory; studied voice with Selma Nicklass-Kempner in Berlin at Stern Conservatory, 1902-05; debut as Frau Fluth in Die lustigen Weiber von Windsor, *Berlin, 1905; sang at Schwerin, 1905-07; Covent Garden debut as Mozart's Bastienne and Humperdinck's Gretel, 1907; in Berlin, 1907-12; Metropolitan Opera debut as Queen in* Les Huguenots, *1912.*

Frieda Hempel made a brilliant Berlin Opera debut in 1905 as Frau Fluth in Nicolai's *Die lustigen Weiber von Windsor;* she stayed there for five years, winning special acclaim in Mozart operas. In 1911, Richard Strauss offered Hempel her choice of the three leading women's roles in *Der Rosenkavalier* for its Berlin premiere. She chose that of the Marschallin. Strauss was delighted with her lyric voice and gracious interpretation. The following year he wanted her to create Zerbinetta in the Stuttgart launching of *Ariadne auf Naxos,* and composed with her in mind probably the most difficult bravura coloratura aria ever written, "Als ein Gott kam jeder gegangen." Gatti-Casazza, however, had been trying to persuade Hempel to join the Metropolitan Opera. His terms proved irresistible and Hempel accepted—much to Strauss's chagrin, for he knew of no other soprano capable of singing the aria and was forced to simplify it to the form now in the printed score.

On 27 December 1912, Hempel made her Metropolitan Opera debut as Marguerite de Valois in *Les Huguenots,* and the critics commended her voice's agility and ease. Of her Rosina in *Il barbiere di Siviglia* W.J. Henderson wrote that her facility in coloratura had not been surpassed "within the memory of the present generation." There followed her triumphant Queen of the Night, a role in which European critics had ranked her as the greatest exponent since Ilma di Murska. At Richard Strauss's request, she was the first to sing the Marschallin in America (9 December 1913) and in England (4 June 1914).

In the seven seasons spent singing for Gatti-Casazza, Hempel gave some 150 perform-ances of seventeen leading parts. In 1915 Richard Aldrich wrote of her Rosina, "not for a good while has so pure and vibrant a soprano voice delivered the florid measures with so great ease and certainty." Then suddenly in 1919 she left the Metropolitan. No official reason was given for this, causing rumours to spread that Gatti-Casazza wanted Galli-Curci to join his company and that she had accepted conditional on Hempel's being jettisoned. Some thought that having given her best years to the opera public and made her name, she, like other prima donnas before and since, thought it wise to switch to the less arduous work of the concert platform and thus preserve her vocal skills for as long as possible.

Much profitable publicity was gained for Hempel through being selected to impersonate Jenny Lind at the Centennial Concert held in Carnegie Hall on 6 October 1920, when she sang the same program that the Swedish Nightingale had at her American debut in 1850. Opening with "Casta diva" from Bellini's *Norma,* Hempel enchanted her audience and, as a result, an enterprising impresario then arranged for her to repeat the program in costume at all the places Jenny had visited during her historic tour of 1850-51. Over the next decade Hempel gave some 300 such concerts in the United States and the British Isles. Actually she hardly resembled Lind.

Quite apart from these popular programs, Frieda Hempel held more serious recitals selecting what was then regarded as "advanced" music—songs by Brahms, Wolf, Mozart, Schubert and Schumann. It had been becoming increasingly difficult for her to reach high notes and this change made it possible for her to retire gracefully from attempting to compete with younger sopranos in opera houses. After her first recital on 5 January 1921, Richard Aldrich declared in the *New York Times* next day: "Her voice has rarely sounded more beautiful in its rounded smoothness, its color, its equality throughout its range." Hempel's finest achievement in this concert was her singing of the recitative and aria "Non mi dir" from *Don Giovanni.* "Here was the true Mozart style in as near perfection as it is now to be heard; a limpid and translucent delivery of the melody in the most equable tones, in artistic and well-considered phrasings; and, in the few measures at the end, in finished coloratura."

From then on, Hempel appeared nearly every season at Carnegie Hall or the New York Town Hall, giving at the latter her last recital on 7 November 1951. In Britain, besides touring, she sang at both the Queen's Hall and the Royal Albert Hall. Gerald Moore in *Am I Too Loud?* wrote that she asked him, as she did others, to omit the preludes to Wolf's "Er ist's" and "Ich hab' in Penna" because it made a better effect for her, and at the end just to play on for a chord when the voice part ends, saying that if he went on longer it might spoil her applause. Moore, however, would not give in to her.

Frieda Hempel's voice was a naturally brilliant soprano extending at least to the F *in alt* at the start of her career. It was animated and vibrant. Michael Scott in *The Record of Singing* compares her first recordings for Odeon in 1906 with the later series completed for H.M.V. and Victor. In the former, mostly in German, he finds the style "very provincial" with too elaborate ornamentation, but the top clearly more responsive. By 1911, in Adam's variations, Scott regards the passage work as fluent and the staccati as dazzlingly effective but points out that sometimes the "squeezed out" head notes fail to hit the mark and the intonation is occasionally sharp or flat. His final judgment is that while her voice is musical and often attractive it misses having the distinctive character that would place her among the great singers of her era.

The Record Collector for August 1955 contains a detailed discography of Frieda Hempel's art. Asked what were the best, George T. Keating chose: *Traviata* (Victor 88471), *Puritani* (Victor 87179 and 88470), *Bohème* (Gram. 053327), *Die Stumme von Portici* (Odeon 76904/5), *Huguenots* (Victor 88382, Gram. 033125), the Adam *Variations* (Victor 88404, Gram. 033114), *Die Zauberflöte* (Gram. 053260 and 043185) and *Robert le diable* (Gram. 033165). He especially recommended listening to Elvira's exacting aria and recitative from Auber's *Die Stumme von Portici* because it was a fine example of Hempel's technique and artistry in 1910.—CHARLES NEILSON GATTEY

Hindemith, Paul

Composer. Born 16 November 1895, in Hanau, near Frankfurt. Died 28 December 1963, in Frankfurt. Married: Gertrud Rottenberg (daughter of the conductor Ludwig Rottenberg). Studied violin with A. Rebner and composition with Arnold Mendelssohn and Sekles at the Hochschule für Musik in Frankfurt; concertmaster of the orchestra of the Frankfurt Opera House, 1915-23; violist with the Amar String Quartet, 1922-29; participated in the contemporary music concerts at Donaueschingen and Baden-Baden; instructor of composition at the Berlin Hochschule für Musik, 1927; problems in Germany with the Nazis; three visits to Ankara, Turkey, beginning in 1934, where he helped organize the curriculum of the Ankara Conservatory; first American appearance with his unaccompanied viola sonata at the Library of Congress, 1937; in Switzerland briefly, then emigrated to the United States; instructor at the Berkshire Music Center in Tanglewood, summer 1940; professor at Yale University, 1940-53; became an American citizen, 1946; elected a member of the National Institute of Arts and Letters; conducting engagements in Europe, 1947-49; appointed Charles Eliot Norton Lecturer at Harvard University, 1950-51; taught at the University of Zurich, 1953; received the Sibelius Award, 1954; guest conducting appearances in the United States, 1959-61.

Operas *Mörder, Hoffnung der Frauen*, Kokoschka, 1919, Stuttgart, Landestheater, 4 June 1921; *Das Nusch-Nuschi* (marionette opera), Franz Blei, 1920, Stuttgart, Landestheater, 4 June 1921; *Sancta Susanna*, Stramm, 1921, Frankfurt, Opernhaus, 26 March 1922; *Cardillac, Ferdinand Lion* (after Hoffmann, *Das Fräulein von Scuderi*), 1926, Dresden, Staatsoper, 9 November 1926; Hindemith (after Lion), 1952, Zurich, Stadttheater, 20 June 1952; *Hin und zurück* (sketch), Marcellus Schiffer, 1927, Baden-Baden, 15 July 1927; *Neues vom Tage*, Marcellus Schiffer, 1928-29, Berlin, Kroll, 8 June 1929; revised 1953; *Lehrstück*, Brecht, 1929; *Mathis der Maler*, Hindemith, 1934-35, Zurich, Stadttheater, 28

May 1938; *Die Harmonie der Welt,* Hindemith, 1956-57, Munich, Prinzregententheater, 11 August 1957; *The Long Christmas Dinner,* Thornton Wilder, 1960, Mannheim, Nationaltheater, 17 December 1961.

Hindemith's connection with the operatic world began early in his career when, at nineteen, he became a violinist with the Frankfurt Opera (1915-1923). During this period his earliest operas emerged—a set of three one-act operas. These works attracted attention to Hindemith's music but also earned him the reputation of a radical. All the libretti are provocative and sensational, products of high German expressionism.

Mörder, Hoffnung der Frauen (*Murderers, the Hope of Women*) (1919) revolves around the sexual conflicts which flare up between men and women. Despite the feverish expressionism of Oscar Kokoschka's autobiographical libretto, Hindemith resisted the temptation to employ heavy-handed polyphonic writing. Nonetheless the work suffers from an inconsistency between the derivative music (Wagner, Strauss and Puccini) and Kokoschka's obscure text.

Das Nusch-Nuschi (1920), intended to be acted by Burmese marionettes, reflects Hindemith's intent to curb the excesses of late German romanticism. The text by Franz Blei is a blend of whimsy, moderate eroticism and general absurdity. The central figures of this oriental story are a lustful, drunken field marshall, accused of seducing the emperor's four wives, and a strange creature, half-rat and half-alligator (Nusch-Nuschi) who frightens the soldier into submission. Dancing plays a large role in this opera and hence Hindemith's rhythmic style is much stronger than in the other one-act operas. Throughout Hindemith derides late nineteenth century music and romantic dance music by his use of stinging chords and unexpected accents in the manner of Bartok and Stravinsky. He satirizes nineteenth century musical practice by composing a choral fugue that fails to follow the "rules" and by quoting a passage from Wagner's *Tristan und Isolde* whose accompaniment is purposely marred by a persistent wrong note in the bass.

By far the most controversial and explicitly erotic of these one-act operas is *Sancta Susanna* (1921) with text by August Stramm. Its theme is the triumph of Eros over inhibited religious training. A young nun, aroused by a spring evening, a glimpse of peasant love and the sexual experiences of another nun, frenetically strips off her garments and embraces the altar crucifix; at the opera's climax she tears the loin cloth from the Christ figure. Although the opera is tightly controlled and dramatically and stylistically more integrated than his previous operas, it still reveals Hindemith searching for his own language in this experimental period. Undoubtedly these works served as vehicles for his powerful, youthful emotions under the guise of expressionism. Eventually he saw them as such and disowned them. However, the Nazis cited these works in their case against Hindemith as a decadent artist.

Hindemith's first full-length opera *Cardillac* (1926) is based upon a short story by E.T.A. Hoffmann, *Das Fräulein von Scuderi* and adapted by Ferdinand Lion. The librettist made substantial alterations emphasizing the action and even dispensing with the Fräulein of the title. Lion created precise situations of mood that complemented the Baroque forms Hindemith favored, such as the passacaglia. This approach parallels the construction of Berg's *Wozzeck* (1925), based also on classical forms. However, Hindemith's procedures are far more evident, and his application of strict forms to such a dramatic text establishes *Cardillac* as a significant twentieth century opera.

The subject of *Cardillac*—the nature of the artist—was to preoccupy Hindemith for many years, later giving rise to *Mathis der Maler* and *Die Harmonie der Welt*. Cardillac is a goldsmith so attached to his handiwork and indifferent to human relationships and social values that he is compelled to kill his customers and retrieve their purchases. Throughout the opera no moral judgment is passed on Cardillac. Hindemith holds to a consistent objectivity, putting his neo-Baroque style to wonderful dramatic effect as a counterbalance to the dark expressionistic subject. Hindemith eventually decided the libretto was unsatisfactory, and in 1952 wrote an entirely new libretto that is closer to the original play, but cannot be considered an improvement on Lion's text. Because of the textual changes and the retention of the original music with new overlaid vocal parts, the strength and directness of the original are undermined and the character of Cardillac substantially weakened.

After *Cardillac* Hindemith returned to the character of the earlier one-act operas and produced two works on comic themes. The brief chamber opera *Hin und zurück* (*There and Back*) (1927) is a charming miniature, far lighter than most of Hindemith's output and considerably less contrapuntal. The opera's action, written by Marcellus Schiffer, progresses to its central climax in which a jealous husband shoots his wife. Then, through an intervening *deus ex machina,* the action is exactly reversed. This structure undoubtedly intrigued Hindemith who, instead of composing exact retrograde music, reversed the sequence of sections. In *Neues vom Tage* (*News of the Day*) (1929) with a libretto by Schiffer, Hindemith satirizes divorce, journalism, show business and opera itself. This full-length piece revolves around a couple who file for divorce, become celebrities and in the end are not allowed a reconciliation by their public. The opera was only partially successful because Hindemith's highly contrapuntal music stifled the quite simple and high-spirited plot. Also, even though Hindemith possessed a great sense of humor, he lacked the bite necessary to create real satire. In 1953, in another act of repentance, Hindemith revised *Neues vom Tage* making substantial alterations to the music and allowing the couple to save their marriage.

Neues vom Tage was the last work of Hindemith's first creative period. All of these early operas were, in Hindemith's view, the sins of his youth. In 1923 he had momentarily glimpsed his true path in relation to his song cycle *Das Marienleben*. Certainly the subject—the life of the Virgin Mary—was in stark contrast to his operas at that time. Hindemith observed that "the strong impression which the first performance made on the audience . . . made me aware for the first time in my musical existence of the ethical qualities of music and the moral obligations of the composer." This outlook, combined with Hindemith's growing interest in German folk song, produced a new idiom, first heard in the *Konzertmusik* works (1930), that was characterized by strong tonality, clear linear writing and a broad lyricism.

The opera *Mathis der Maler* (1934-35), based upon the life of the painter Matthias Grünewald (1480?-1528?), marks the culmination of this spiritual metamorphosis in Hindemith. In contemplating the life of Grünewald, Hindemith discovered his true nature, seeing parallels between himself and Grünewald as estranged, dedicated artists caught up in an unsettling political world. Such a text demanded that Hindemith write his own libretto.

The backdrop for Hindemith's undertaking was the rising Nazi regime which, by the end of 1934, had effectively banned performances of his music including the *Mathis* opera. The conductor Wilhelm Furtwangler, who pleaded Hindemith's case in a leading German newspaper, presented the premiere of the symphony *Mathis der Maler,* the movements of which were later incorporated into the opera. It was not until 1938 that *Mathis* was staged in Zurich.

373

Despite the parallels drawn between the political environment of Grünewald's time and Nazi doctrine, the deeper issue for Hindemith was the role of the creative artist and the purpose for which his works are created. In the end St Paul tells Mathis that he can serve God best by cultivating his gifts with humility and reverence. Thereupon Mathis unlocks his blocked creative force, paints a stream of great works and, completely drained, resigns himself to death.

Structurally *Mathis* represents a major departure from the strict self-contained forms of *Cardillac*. Hindemith often employs the conventional aria, ensemble and chorus while varying the degrees of musical tension. There are some set musical forms that never intrude upon the action. Overall he put aside much of his neo-Baroque style and found his classical and romantic heritage. This was especially revealed in his new harmonic language with its tonal and often triadic harmony, postulated by Hindemith in his music theory text *The Craft of Musical Composition* (written 1934-36; published 1937).

By 1937 Hindemith had already conceived another opera in the mold of *Mathis*. He had come particularly under the influence of the astronomer/mystic Johannes Kepler (1571-1630) and the early music theorist, Boethius (d. 524), who had described three levels of music—*musica instrumentalis, musica humana* and *musica mundana* or "the music of the spheres." Kepler believed that he had scientifically uncovered these celestial harmonies which he delineated in his *Harmonices Mundi* (1619). It was this work that inspired Hindemith to compose the opera *Die Harmonie der Welt* (*The Harmony of the World*), for he was convinced that in his own musical theory he had found laws that related *musica mundana* to the actual sounds of instruments and voices (*musica instrumentalis*) and the music sounding between two souls (*musica humana*).

After a long gestation period during which he composed the symphony *Die Harmonie der Welt* (1951) (later incorporated into the opera), Hindemith finally undertook the work in 1956, completing it in 1957. Again Hindemith wrote his own libretto so as to use the figure of Kepler as an alter ego and the other characters as his mouthpieces. *Die Harmonie der Welt* is a complete reflection of his artistic, philosophical and religious credo and is, in effect, a musical autobiography. It is a unique work in which episodes of the scientist's life are presented in tableaux form, each dramatic in itself but without cumulative tension. Underpinning the work is not only the whole of Hindemith's music theory, but also a vast network of tonality symbolism. In the final scene the characters, transformed into the solar system and purged of their errors, find their redemption in the postulated World Harmony. This was to have been Hindemith's greatest work, but in the view of most critics it was simply a noble effort. It has yet to be seen outside of Germany and Austria.

Three years before his death Hindemith embarked upon his last opera, *The Long Christmas Dinner* (1960) with a libretto by Thornton Wilder. It is a one-act chamber opera lasting only an hour. Its subjects, death and the passage to an afterlife, are recurring themes in Hindemith's vocal works. In this respect there is a link between the finale of *Die Harmonie der Welt* and *The Long Christmas Dinner*. Both are concerned with endless death and rebirth, an infinite world without beginning or end; both reflect Hindemith's essentially Roman Catholic perspective. The simple plot of *The Long Christmas Dinner* focuses on a family gathered round a table at Christmas. Three generations come and go, their conversation revealing the passage of time. Their births and deaths are represented by two portals at stage right and left. The opera ends with a certainty that this sequence of events will continue without change. Hindemith's music is seamless and unobtrusively complements the text. The opera contains some of his most delicate, transparent music including a sextet harmonized exclusively in triads. In no other work of his late period did the triad play such an important role.

Hindemith's operatic music, like much of his vocal and instrumental music, is currently out of fashion principally because it does not conform to contemporary musical values. His was a music of synthesis, retaining the values of past musical epochs in conjunction with his own twentieth century musical language. His last three operas, with their spiritual and metaphysical themes, are especially at odds with the typical psychological plots of most contemporary operas. —JAMES D'ANGELO

Hines, Jerome Albert Link

Bass. Born Jerome Heinz, 8 November 1921, in Los Angeles. Married singer Lucia Evangelista. Studied with Gennaro Curci in Los Angeles, and later with Samuel Margolis in New York; opera debut as Monterone in Rigoletto, *San Francisco, 1941; employed as chemist during the war; Metropolitan Opera debut as the Sergeant in* Boris Godunov, *1946; appeared at Edinburgh as Nick Shadow in* The Rake's Progress, *1953; appeared in Munich as Don Giovanni, 1954; sang the role of Boris Godunov at the Bol'shoy, Moscow, 1962; composed the opera* I Am the Way.

Standing as perhaps America's only truly great bass of the second half of this century, Jerome Hines has brought numerous distinctions to the art of singing. His early life was consumed with the study of science—an undergraduate degree in chemistry with a minor in mathematics from the University of California in Los Angeles confirms the fact that his approach to life and singing has been, in one sense, an analytical one. In fact, he was successful in developing a non-toxic, special-effects solution to be used as Méphistophélès' youth potion in the opera *Faust*. This development has eliminated a physical danger encountered by the character playing the role of Faust in Metropolitan Opera productions. His interest in vocal techniques led to the publication in 1982 of a book entitled *Great Singers on Great Singing*. The book is a compendium of comments on the production of vocal tone, acquired from interviews with well-known singers, one speech therapist, and a medical doctor.

His almost clinical approach to developing the various operatic roles he has portrayed throughout the years has involved extensive score study on his part and scheduled conferences with psychiatrists regarding character analysis of the roles he is preparing. For example, his portrayal of Boris Godunov has shown a remarkable evolution through the years as he has pursued an intensive character probe. His interest in hypnotism has allowed him an amateur exploration of the benefits this method of introspection and relaxation can give to singing. During the breaks between the acts of an opera he is performing, he frequently practices self-hypnotism in an effort to completely withdraw from the pressures at hand.

A totally American-taught singer, Hines took lessons for years from Gennaro Curci who recognized early the potential in his young pupil. After Curci's death in 1955, Hines received coaching from both Samuel Margolis and Rocco Pandiscio. His professional stage debut came after his first year in college when he sang Bill Bobstay in *H.M.S. Pinafore* for the Los Angeles Civic Light Opera Association. It was for this performance that he changed the spelling of his last name from Heinz to Hines. His debut for the San Francisco Opera came in 1941 as Biterolf in

Wagner's *Tannhäuser*. Performances of Ramfis in Verdi's *Aida* for the San Carlo Opera, Méphistophélès in Gounod's *Faust* for the New Orleans Opera, Osmin in Mozart's *Die Entführung aus dem Serail* for the Central City, Colorado, Opera preceded his debut with the Metropolitan Opera in March 1946. Upon winning the $1000 Caruso Award for that year, he was assured a Metropolitan contract and was awarded it the day after his audition. His debut as the Sergeant in *Boris Godunov,* although a brief role, afforded him immediate recognition from the critics.

He has achieved many firsts at the Metropolitan Opera. He was the first American-born bass to sing the title role in *Boris Godunov* and the roles of Philip II in *Don Carlos* and Wotan in *Die Walküre* and *Das Rheingold.* By composing the opera *I Am the Way,* a work based upon the life of Jesus and staged at the Metropolitan Opera in 1968, he became the first composer to write for himself an opera that has been produced at the Metropolitan. The popularity of the work is evidenced by its being given over fifty times following the initial performance in 1956.

Internationally, Hines distinguished himself by being the first American-born bass to sing the role of Philip II (*Don Carlos*) in Buenos Aires and Palermo. The same distinction was awarded him for portrayals of Gurnemanz in *Parsifal,* King Mark in *Tristan and Isolde,* and Wotan in *Die Walküre* in Bayreuth at the Wagner Festival. These appearances came after his establishment as a singer of international repute through performances at Glyndebourne, Edinburgh, Munich, and Milan. His greatest international triumph, however, came with his 1962 performance of the title role in *Boris Godunov* at the Bolshoi in Moscow and other Soviet cities. He was the first American to sing the role in that country in Russian. This conquest came at the height of the Cuban missile crisis when the political climate between the United States and Russia was especially tenuous. Premier Nikita Khrushchev, who was in the audience on the evening of his debut, joined others in giving him a standing ovation.

Hines has been an imposing figure on the stage in several ways. His towering height (over 6 feet 6 inches) has served him best, according to most critics, in the role of Boris. He has also been a physical stalwart of the Metropolitan Opera by setting a record for longevity of an American-born singer interpreting leading roles. This feat has not been attained without criticism, however. It appeared in the mid-1970s that his voice had literally been spent as a result of the arduous schedules he was forced to assume because he was, at times, the only bass performing leading roles at the Metropolitan Opera. Another result of this relentless schedule was his failure to have sufficient time to have adequate exposure on the international scene either through performances or recordings. The wear and tear did not go unnoticed by either the critics or the audiences, and the deterioration was openly criticized in the 1970s. In addition, the onset of a severe bout with osteoarthritis threatened to shorten his career even further. In recent years, however, he has undertaken an exhaustive physical fitness and nutrition program with surprisingly good results. Apparently his singing voice had a noticeable rejuvenation that has allowed him to enjoy further productive years.—ROSE MARY OWENS

Horne, Marilyn

Mezzo-soprano. Born 16 January 1934, in Bradford, Pennsylvania. Married conductor Henry Lewis in 1960 (separated 1976; one daughter). Studied with William Vennard at the University of Southern California in Los Angeles and attended Lotte Lehmann's master

classes; debut as Hata in The Bartered Bride, *Los Angeles, 1954; appeared as Giulietta at Gelsenkirchen Opera, 1957, where she remained until 1960; Covent Garden debut as Marie in* Wozzeck, *1965; appeared at the Teatro alla Scala as Neocles in* Le siège de Corinthe, *1969; Metropolitan Opera debut as Adalgisa in* Norma, *1970, where she remains a principal singer.*

It is commonplace to attribute the "rediscovery" of the bel canto operas of Donizetti and Bellini first to Maria Callas and later to Joan Sutherland, but Marilyn Horne has been equally inspirational in the more recent revival of interest in the huge and, until recently, generally neglected output of Rossini.

Marilyn Horne's first performances in Los Angeles were largely unheralded—a minor role in Smetana's *The Bartered Bride* and, more significantly, Rossini's *Cenerentola* for Carl Ebert. Her 'galley years' were spent with the small opera company of Gelsenkirchen where she mostly sang soprano territory—Mimì, Minnie in *La fanciulla del West,* Amelia in *Simon Boccanegra* and Tatiana in *Eugene Onegin.* In 1960 she began a long association with the San Francisco Opera by performing Marie in Berg's *Wozzeck.*

Throughout a lengthy career Horne has been attracted to a wide range of musical genres. Her first recording assignment was to dub the voice of Dorothy Dandridge in *Carmen Jones.* Her French repertoire includes Fidès in *Le prophète* and Thomas' *Mignon,* as well as Carmen. Her Verdi roles include Amneris (*Aïda*), Azucena (*Il trovatore*) and Eboli (*Don Carlos*). She has sung many of the Handel operas and several of Mahler's song cycles. Early in her career she recorded an astonishing two LP tribute to Malibran and Viardot. This includes pieces from no less than five operas by Rossini, one of which is an aria of Semiramide's, and Horne has subsequently become an outstanding Arsace in the same opera.

Despite this catholicity of repertoire Horne's international career has been increasingly identified with early nineteenth-century Italian opera and above all with Rossini. Given her superb mezzo voice and professional status, it is hardly surprising that the world's opera houses have continued to press her to sing the basic repertoire. Andrew Porter found her Amneris in *Aïda* at the Metropolitan "curiously unimpressive," which did not deter Salzburg and Karajan from asking her to undertake the same role some months later. Although recognizing the pressure that singing Verdi roles placed on her voice—"I don't want to fight to be heard over the orchestra"—Horne could not resist, but in her own words "it was one of my monumental failures".

In 1961 Horne appeared in Bellini's *Beatrice di Tenda* at New York Town Hall. Sutherland sang the title role and a great operatic partnership was inaugurated. They sang *Norma* together in Vancouver in 1963 and at Covent Garden in 1967 and *Semiramide* in Boston in 1964. In 1969 Horne scored a sensational success at the Teatro alla Scala in Rossini's *Le siège de Corinthe.* The final, belated accolade of success for an American singer came with her first appearance at the Metropolitan in 1970 in *Norma,* again with Sutherland in the title role.

Horne's autobiography suggests an element of "hit and miss" about her training but there can be no doubt of her intense commitment to work. By 1990 she had been singing for three and a half decades. Almost imperceptibly, the career has become ever more dominated by the florid mezzo roles of Rossini. It is here that Horne's incredible technique—replete with runs and roulades, unrivalled in modern times—has come into its own. Andrew Porter's reaction has been

h

OPERA

very different from that quoted previously—"When Miss Horne sings, Rossini's florid writing doesn't sound automatic, and not only because it is embellished and made even more florid: piquant unpredictability enlivens both the musical text and her delivery of it." Many of Horne's greatest performances of Rossini have been in concert versions and Porter makes a tactful reference to Horne's physique and the nature of the "breeches" roles she frequently undertakes—"Her concert presence is warm and winning. She seems far more attractive, far more dramatic, more of a character, than when in boots and plumed helmet; she stomps around and gesticulates on the stage." In 1978 Porter thought her "a vocally brilliant Tancred, singing the music with matchless energy, accuracy and bravura." By 1983 he felt she had added "a new command of the words and of the mood."

Horne's recorded legacy encompasses her range of musical interests, even if not all equally successfully. Thus there is a fine recital of Handel arias and some delicious performances of American songs; in contrast she never seems to "get inside" the Mahler song cycles. There is much fascinating French material: pride of place goes to her Fidès in *Le prophète*. This is one of the glories of the nineteenth-century contralto repertoire; at times the quality of Horne's voice is almost cello-like. In contrast she does not really project as Azucena in *Il trovatore*. Otherwise the legacy of collaboration with Sutherland is superb; Horne features as Adalgisa in *Norma,* Maffeo Orsini in *Lucrezia Borgia* and Arsace in *Semiramide.*

Pride of place has to go to Rossini. Oddly her Rosina in *Il barbiere di Siviglia* seems uninspired compared to some others, but her Isabella in *L'italiana in Algeri* offers bravura singing hardly otherwise encountered on records. The whole is a tour de force. Her Arsace and Tancred are almost as impressive and there is a magnificent recital of pieces from *Donna del lago* and *Le siège de Corinthe.* As with other modern singers, much of Horne's career has been preserved by radio and television and this is true for her performances in the Rossini festivals in Pesaro. In the revival of *Bianca e Falliero,* she sets a new standard of controlled virtuoso singing. We may speculate as to whether Rossini himself ever heard the quality of florid singing required for such roles; in our time this particular art has been rediscovered by Marilyn Horne.—STANLEY HENIG

Hotter, Hans

Bass-baritone. Born 19 January 1909, in Offenbach am Main. Married Helga Fischer, 1936 (one son, one daughter). Studied with Matthäus Roemer in Munich; worked as organist and choirmaster; debut at Troppau, 1930; has appeared in Breslau (1931), Prague (1932-34), Hamburg (1934-35), and Munich (1937-72); Metropolitan debut as the Dutchman in Der fliegende Holländer, 1950, where he appeared until 1954; produced a Ring cycle at Covent Garden, 1961-62; retired from stage in 1972; became a member of the Vienna Hochschule für Musik, 1977; created the Kommandant in Strauss's Friedenstag, Olivier in Capriccio, and Jupiter in Die Liebe der Danaë.

For many, the voice of German bass-baritone Hans Hotter *is* the voice of Wotan. Even those who never saw him in the theater, where he virtually owned the role in the two decades following World War II, came through recordings to identify Hotter's as the true voice of Wagner's anguished god—perhaps these at-home listeners most of all, given the universal currency of the famous Solti performances, which feature Hotter as the *Walküre* Wotan and the Wanderer. That Hotter is so richly satisfying on these records, despite being undeniably past his vocal prime, is a testament to his intelligence and long experience in the role, experience provided through a long career of a kind well-nigh vanished from today's opera scene.

Hotter's early musical inclinations led him to study as an organist and choirmaster; his initial vocal studies arose from the conviction that knowing something about singing would be useful to him as a conductor. It was soon apparent, however, that his future lay on the opera stage. He made his debut at Troppau in 1930, and stayed there three seasons absorbing a wide variety of repertoire. Seasons at Breslau and Prague followed, where among the roles he essayed were Escamillo, Iago, Falstaff, Boris, and, in 1938, his first *Das Rheingold* Wotan. The milieu in which Hotter moved in the first part of his career was extraordinary. Among the conductors he worked with were Furtwängler, Knappertsbusch, Karajan, Kleiber, and Clemens Krauss (who led Hotter in the premieres of Strauss' *Friedenstag* and *Capriccio*); among his role models in the repertoire he would make his own were Friedrich Schorr, Wilhelm Rode, and Rudolf Bockelmann. A comparable school for Wagnerians would be impossible to assemble today. Though soon established as one of Germany's leading singers, Hotter's international career did not begin until after the war, when he visited London with the Vienna State Opera in 1947. His New York Metropolitan debut came in 1950, and by this time the world encountered in Hotter a fully mature artist at the peak of his vocal powers.

Hotter combined a Lieder singer's sensitivity to words and colors with a voice large enough to sing in the biggest houses over Wagnerian orchestras. His voice was instantly recognizable, very dark in color, and projected with a uniquely warm resonance, equally effective in conveying paternal love or godly wrath. One might expect a voice like Hotter's to be prone to muddiness, and though it was not always ideally focused, the basic quality and color were rarely compromised. Despite occasional unsteadiness, distortion rarely crept in, owing most likely to the primacy of the word in Hotter's traversal of even the most vocally demanding operatic literature. His care in communicating the text tends to ensure natural, unexaggerated vocalism.

It is a sad fact that while there are many Hotter recordings, too few of them caught him in his absolute prime, and some of his greatest roles are documented only in piecemeal fashion, if at all. Would that, in the Fifties, some enterprising company had recorded his Hans Sachs or Dutchman, let alone his Cardinal Borromeo in Pfitzner's *Palestrina*. Remarkable documents remain: of course the Solti *Der Ring des Nibelungen* with Hotter's vocally aged but peerlessly expressive Wotan, but also a 1957 record of the duet "Wie aus der Ferne" from *Der fliegende Holländer* with Birgit Nilsson, which for sheer vocal beauty combined with vivid character projection stands among his most memorable achievements; a 1976 Viennese studio recording of *Lulu,* Hotter as a Schigolch comic and sinister, with a core of toughness appropriate for the principal survivor of Berg's *femme fatale;* and, remarkably enough, a *Guerrelieder* recorded in New York in 1991, with Hotter in his eighties giving a mesmerizing account of the narration, the voice still unmistakable, the authority unquestioned. Hearing Hotter, one is reminded afresh that opera, even the rarified world of Wagnerian music-drama, depends on the incantatory power of the human voice. Hotter was a master singer and a master enchanter.—MICHAEL KOTZE

Hugh the Drover; or, Love in the Stocks

Composer: *Ralph Vaughan Williams.*

Librettist: *H. Child.*

First Performance: *London, His Majesty's, 14 July 1924; revised, 1956.*

Roles: *Hugh (tenor); Mary (soprano); John (bass-baritone); Susan (soprano); Nancy (contralto); William (tenor); Robert (bass); Aunt Jane (contralto); The Turnkey (tenor); The Constable (bass); A Fool (baritone); An Innkeeper (bass); A Sergeant (baritone); chorus.*

Set in the small town of Cotsall in the west of England during the Napoleonic Wars, *Hugh the Drover* deals with the love of Mary, the daughter of the town constable, betrothed to John the town butcher, at her father's behest. Mary falls in love with the mysterious Hugh, a drover who roams the country rounding up horses for the army. All he can offer her is a roving life of probable hardship, but at least she will be free, rather than having to endure caged comfort with John. A prize fight is set up with a prize of £20 for any man who can beat John. Hugh sees his chance, stakes £50 on the result, and challenges John to add Mary's hand in marriage to the bet. Hugh wins; but John instantly accuses him of being a French spy; how else could he have come by as large a sum as £50? The crowd turns against Hugh; he is arrested and put in the stocks.

In act II, on May Day, Mary brings the key to the stocks and is about to release Hugh so that they can elope together, but they are interrupted by the May revelers. She gets into the stocks beside Hugh. Finding his daughter missing, the constable arouses the townspeople. The lovers are discovered. Mary refuses to abandon Hugh, and her father disowns her. A troop of soldiers arrives to take the "spy" away. The sergeant in charge of the detachment recognizes Hugh as a man who once saved his life; and instead of arresting Hugh, the soldiers conscript John. Mary hesitates to go off with Hugh, but he wins her over. The lovers bid the townsfolk farewell and go off together.

Hugh the Drover is a conscious attempt to write a kind of English equivalent of Smetana's *Bartered Bride;* but for all its sturdy tunefulness and defiantly "English" idiom, it does not quite manage to do so. This is at least as much Vaughan Williams' fault as that of his librettist Harold Child. There is much fine music in the score: Hugh's stirring ballad "Horse Hooves" in act I and the love music are certainly full-blooded and finely characterized; but the "villain," John, never really comes to life; and the two main figures, though credible as romantic symbols of true love and the desire to challenge the unknown, are not three-dimensional creatures of flesh and blood. The musical construction is straightforward, the scoring effective, and the musical idiom bracing, drawing its sometimes Puccinesque soaring melodic line from the contours of English folksong, and basing its harmonic procedures on the modal implications of the tunes. Dramatically, the work suffers from Vaughan Williams' inexperience in welding the constituent parts of the action into a coherent whole, an example of which is the prize-fight in the finale of the first act (Vaughan Williams' starting point for the plot of the opera), which never really quite gels, though the tension is skillfully built up in the individual sections. Nonetheless, the work is easy on the ear and shows a distinct sense of the theater, which was to be more fully realized in *Sir John in Love* and especially in *Riders to the Sea.*—JAMES DAY

Les Huguenots [The Huguenots]

Composer: *Giacomo Meyerbeer.*

Librettists: *Eugène Scribe and Émile Deschamps.*

First Performance: *Paris, Opéra, 29 February 1836.*

Roles: *Marguerite de Valois (soprano); Valentine (soprano); Raoul de Nangis (tenor); Comte de Nevers (baritone); Comte de St Bris (baritone or bass-baritone); Marcel (bass);*

h

OPERA

Urbain (mezzo-soprano or contralto); Catholic Noblemen (tenors, basses, baritones); Page of Nevers (soprano); Ladies of Honor (sopranos, mezzo-soprano); Huguenot Soldiers (tenor, bass); Archer (tenor); Three Monks (tenors, bass); Two Gypsies (sopranos); chorus (SSAATTBB).

Les Huguenots ensued from the second collaboration between Meyerbeer and the chief librettist of French grand opera, Eugène Scribe. Its premiere came more than four years after that of Meyerbeer's extraordinarily successful *Robert le diable* (1831). The earlier work was a triumph of orchestral innovation and imagination, spectacular staging, and lurid drama. With *Robert* Meyerbeer had taken full advantage of the popular achievement of Auber's *La muette de Portici* (1827) and Rossini's *Guillaume Tell* (1828). These three earlier works collectively defined French grand opera, but as a genre whose mature realization was reached only in *Les Huguenots*. In the creation of *Les Huguenots* Meyerbeer labored with the same unhurried care and attention to detail that had characterized his work on the earlier opera. He has suffered more than the usual criticism accorded those who garner popular success, but whose works are not of transcendent quality. Nonetheless, one cannot accuse him of quickly-wrought hackwork, for he typically labored long, constantly revising in an era when composers of opera were not known for that.

The work's libretto is based upon the St Bartholomew's massacre of the Huguenots by the Catholics in 1572 and revolves around related events in Touraine and Paris. Religious strife between Protestants and Catholics drives the action, complicated, of course, by the love between Raoul, a prominent Huguenot, and Valentine, daughter of the Conte de St Bris, a leader of the Catholics. Queen Marguerite de Valois envisions Valentine as agent for making peace between the two factions by arranging her marriage to Raoul. Unfortunately, Valentine is the fiancée of the Count de Nevers, one of the Catholic leaders. Marcel, rough-hewn old retainer of Raoul, and Urbain, page to the Queen, round out the list of principals.

The on again, off again, relationship between Raoul and Valentine ultimately leads to the marriage of Valentine and Nevers—despite her continuing love for Raoul—all played against a background of imminent bloodshed between the factions. Raoul's visit to newly-wed Valentine's home to try to relight their mutual fire results in his entanglement in the launching of the Catholic plot to slay all Huguenots. Noble husband Nevers virtuously demurs participation and is turned upon by his coreligionists. Bloodshed begins, and Raoul flees knowing of Valentine's continuing love for him. As the massacre proceeds, Raoul and Marcel take refuge in a churchyard, joined by Valentine, whose husband has already perished. Valentine declares allegiance to the Huguenots and all are slain by vengeful Catholics, led by St Bris, who thus orders the murder of his own daughter in ironic error.

The immediate success of *Les Huguenots,* while not quite approaching that of *Robert le diable,* was considerable and the opera soon became Meyerbeer's most important and influential work. By 1880 it had been performed 693 times at the Paris Opéra alone, not to speak of myriad performances the world over. Of the earlier examples of French grand opera, only *Les Huguenots* enjoys many revivals in the twentieth century. Critics generally view it as Meyerbeer's first work that was essentially non-derivative: *Il crociato in Egitto* was considered Italianate, almost Rossinian, and *Robert le diable* possessed more than a few attributes of German romanticism, specifically those of Carl Maria von Weber. But in *Les Huguenots,* Meyerbeer reached the definition of his personal style that, for better or worse, has come to be his cachet.

The characteristic elements of grand opera are present, of course: 1) a structure of five acts of increasing tension which generates a lengthy work; 2) a libretto based upon relatively recent historical incident; 3) important ballet and choral scenes; 4) lavish, spectacular staging; and 5) vivid, colorful orchestration. But in Meyerbeer's hands these elements are executed with an intuitive adroitness and flair that transcend their easy imitation by others. His gift for innovative instrumentation and orchestration, for composing broad, appealing melodies, and for the creation of entertaining drama that moves at a smooth and tightly-constructed pace, all contributed to the immense popularity of *Les Huguenots* with the opera-going public. Critics and scholars have often been ruthless in their analyses of Meyerbeer's creation, but they have not deterred its popularity, especially during the nineteenth century.

Les Huguenots requires exceptional solo voices, and not just a few. There are seven major roles, and all demand singers of world-class ability who have a mastery of *bel canto* technique, as well as an understanding of the nineteenth-century French school. These impressive standards make revivals problematic; perhaps the heyday of performances of *Les Huguenots* during this century was reached early on, at the Metropolitan Opera. The work was a staple of the Metropolitan's repertoire, and performances there were known as "nights of the seven stars." From Marcel's colorful "Piff, paff" account of his wars with the Catholics, accompanied only by piccolo, low instruments, and percussion, to the well-known "Romance" of Raoul, with its extensive part for solo viola d'amore, the arias of *Les Huguenots* are appealing. They succeed because they achieve a memorable quality wrought by a combination of an innate understanding of the *bel canto* voice, a rare ear for orchestra color, and a flair for dramatic insight. Many of the major arias have achieved lives of their own in recital programs, as representatives of the best aspects of the nineteenth-century French school.

It is not upon the coattails of the arias taken alone that the success of the opera rides. Rather, its achievement stems also from their apt juxtaposition with solo ensembles and extraordinarily effective writing for chorus, all placed within a context of scene complexes that drive to forceful, entertaining dénouements.

The young Wagner saw *Les Huguenots* in Paris and praised it effusively, especially its orchestral treatment and staging. It should be more widely acknowledged that he, as well as Berlioz, was immensely influenced by *Les Huguenots*'s example. The evidence clearly is present not only in the straightforward admiration expressed in their own essays, but also in their musical works. Their artistic achievement, as well as that of Verdi, Bizet, and others, owes much to Meyerbeer, whatever his commercial success at pleasing the operatic bourgeoisie.
—WILLIAM E. RUNYAN

Humperdinck, Engelbert

Composer. Born 1 September 1854, in Siegburg, near Bonn. Died 27 September 1921, in Neustrelitz. Studied architecture in Cologne; studied with Ferdinand Hiller, Friedrich Gernsheim, and Gustav Jensen, piano with Seiss and Mertke, and cello with Rensberg and Ehlert at the Cologne Conservatory; Mozart Prize of Frankfurt, 1876; studied with Franz Lachner and Rheinberger in Munich; Mendelssohn Prize for the chorus Die Wallfahrt nach Kevelaar, *1879; Meyerbeer Prize of Berlin, 1881, and travel to France and Italy; met Wagner in Italy, who invited him to Bayreuth, where Humperdinck assisted in the preparation of the score of* Parsifal *for performance and publication; later taught Siegfried Wagner (Wagner's son); professor at the Conservatory in Barcelona, 1885-87; taught in Cologne; hired by the publishing firm Schott in Mainz; professor at the Hochschule für Musik in Frankfurt and music critic for the* Frankfurter Zeitung, *1890;* Hänsel und Gretel *enormously successful, 1893; retired to Boppard on the Rhine to devote himself exclusively to composition, 1896; director of the Akademische Meisterschule in Berlin, 1900.*

Operas *Hänsel und Gretel,* Adelheid Wette (after the tale by the brothers Grimm), Weimar, Court Theater, 23 December 1893; *Die sieben Geislein,* Adelheid Wette (after the brothers Grimm), Berlin, Schiller Theater, 19 December 1895; *Königskinder* (incidental music for the melodrama), Ernst Rosmer [Elsa Bernstein-Porges], Munich, Court Theater, 23 January 1897; revised as an opera, New York, Metropolitan Opera, 28 December 1910; *Dornröschen,* E. Ebeling and B. Filhès (after Perrault), Frankfurt am Main, Municipal Theater, 12 November 1902; *Die Heirat wider Willen,* Hedwig Humperdinck (after Dumas, *Les demoiselles de Saint-Cyr,* Berlin, Royal Opera, 14 April 1905; *Bübchens Weihnachtstraum* (melodramatisches Krippenspiel), G. Falke, Berlin, 30 December 1906; *Die Marketenderin,* Robert Misch, Cologne, Municipal Theater, 10 May 1914; *Gaudeamus: Szenen aus dem deutschen Studentenleben,* Robert Misch, Darmstadt, Provincial Theater, 18 March 1919.

It is above all for his "children's fairy tale" *Hänsel und Gretel* that Humperdinck holds his place in the repertory, while in second place comes his *Königskinder,* which has a young prince as its hero but is also set in an old German forest with its wicked witch. Of his other stage works, four more are also called fairy tales or children's pieces, and it is clear that the nature of his genius led him towards the world of childhood and children's tales to an extent that is unique in opera, although Ravel and Britten also wrote pieces in the same genre.

In fact, *Hänsel und Gretel* is usually performed to adult audiences by adult singers, and the role of the young lad Hänsel is designated as for a mezzo soprano although it has sometimes been sung by a boy treble. Nevertheless, the genesis of *Hänsel und Gretel* was in the right surroundings, for it began to take shape in a children's nursery in which two young girls with good voices liked to sing verses written by their mother Adelheid Wette and set to music by their "uncle Entepent"—who was Engelbert Humperdinck himself. He was then in his thirties, and, as well as teaching music in the Cologne Conservatory, he had a firm association with the musical stage and had assisted Wagner at Bayreuth. Most of his compositions had been for voices, but he had also written incidental music for the theater, and little by little one particular nursery song inspired by the Grimm brothers' fairy tale of the two children turned itself into a *Singspiel* or German opera with a libretto by Adelheid herself, the idea for this having been put forward by her husband Dr. Hermann Wette. Another enthusiastic supporter of the project was the composer Hugo Wolf.

Engelbert Humperdinck, 1912

Richard Strauss conducted the première of *Hänsel und Gretel* in 1893 at Weimar and in a letter to the composer he called the new work "a masterpiece of the first water . . . you have bestowed upon our fellow citizens a work that they hardly deserve, though one hopes that very soon they will be worthy of it." Its immense success came when Humperdinck was forty, and he followed it with nine more stage works of which the earliest version of *Königskinder* was the third, though he later reshaped it considerably. It was always the world of childhood which inspired this genial and melodious composer to give of his best, as in his *Bübchens Weihnachtstraum* of 1906—with its title meaning "Baby boy's Christmas Dream" and its designation as a "musical crib play"—and the pantomime *Das Mirakel* (*The Miracle*), which had its premiere in London five years later.

Later in life, Humperdinck was laid low by ill-health, and he may have been discouraged by the feeling that contemporary music had moved in a way that had left him behind. Nevertheless, the warmth and freshness of his musical inspiration, expressed above all in attractive and memorable themes, together with the unobtrusive but impressive skill with which he constructed his "children's music dramas" (he had learned much from Wagner) won the lasting affection and admiration not only of ordinary operagoers but also of such conductors as Levi, Mahler, Weingartner and Karajan, all of whom performed *Hänsel und Gretel* in the secure knowledge that it would find a ready response with audiences of all ages. This work also helped to show composers and librettists at the turn of the century another way forward for opera besides Wagnerian music drama and Italian *verismo.*—CHRISTOPHER HEADINGTON

Idomeneo, Rè di Creta

Composer: *Wolfgang Amadeus Mozart.*

Librettist: *Giambattista Varesco (after Danchet,* Idomenée*).*

First Performance: *Munich, Hoftheather, 29 January 1781.*

Roles: *Ilia (soprano); Electra (soprano); Idamante (soprano, later tenor); Idomeneo (tenor); Arbaces (baritone); High Priest (tenor); Voice of Neptune (bass); chorus (SSAATB).*

The original tale of Idomeneo (Idomeneus) described how the shipwrecked Cretan general, upon his return from the ten-year siege at Troy, vowed to Neptune (Poseidon) to sacrifice the first human he might encounter upon his hoped-for return to the Cretan shore. This human turned out to be Idomeneo's (nameless) son. The popularity of this myth derived not from Homer's tale of the Trojan War, in which Idomeneo plays a distinguished role, but from Virgil and early medieval Latin sources, including the Trojan saga of Diktys. The myth received little artistic attention thereafter, however, until Crébillon's drama (1705) and Danchet's five-act libretto which was set to music by André Campra and produced at the Paris Opéra in 1712. Abbé Giambattista Varesco adapted Danchet's libretto and rendered the tale in Italian, reducing it to three acts, for Mozart late in 1780.

To the ancient myth eighteenth-century taste necessarily applied additional dramatic layers. Idomeneo's son, given the name Idamante, falls in love with Ilia, a Trojan princess kept in Crete as a hostage. Their romance irks the fiery daughter of Agamemnon, Electra, who has fled to Crete after the notorious Argive patricide. Varesco and Mozart have given each of these roles a vivid characterization, most memorable in the guilt-ridden fear ever apparent in Idomeneo and the relentless jealousy of Electra. They also provided a *deus ex machina* substitution for Idomeneo's avowed sacrifice, which he spends the entire opera carefully averting.

Commissioned by Karl Theodor, Elector of Bavaria, for the Munich carnival in 1781, *Idomeneo* has become universally recognized as Mozart's first great opera. In applying his natural dramatic sense to the *opera seria* form, Mozart replaced the popular *da capo* exit arias with carefully engineered musical bridges connecting aria, recitativo accompagnato, recitativo secco, smaller ensemble, and chorus. By allowing almost nothing (including applause) to interrupt the dramatic tension, Mozart could develop his graceful if determined fix on the drama at hand and establish greater musical consistency. The emotion Mozart sensed in the libretto he recreated either in the vocal score or in the instrumental accompaniment. Except for the advisor Arbaces, who does not seem to belong to this opera, very few of the numbers are irrelevant to the drama. With such Gluckian control of the drama itself, Mozart immediately demonstrated his early mastery—the dress rehearsal was held on his twenty-fifth birthday—of large dramatic form. It must be said, however, that Mozart himself interrupted his own dramatic unity by the additions he composed for the 1786 Vienna production of the same opera, which was the occasion for which he also recast the soprano Idamante as a tenor.

Besides its musical importance, Mozart's *Idomeneo* is of great biographical importance as well because of the many extant letters exchanged between Wolfgang and Leopold Mozart during the late fall and winter of 1780-81, when Wolfgang was in Munich working on *Idomeneo* and Leopold remained in Salzburg. Among a number of interesting episodes described in the letters, one reveals to us Mozart's great disappointment in having the aging tenor Anton Raaff sing the role of Idomeneo. Mozart, although at times insulting, also showed sensitivity in his description of Raaff's abilities and condition. The modern reader is then all the more impressed with how able and determined Mozart was as composer to tailor the part to Raaff's artistic temperament, his personal vanity, his limited acting style and failing vocal ability. Because Varesco himself had remained in Salzburg as well and Mozart had therefore to communicate with him through Leopold, we learn much about what kinds of textual alterations Mozart required or permitted during the early stages of an operatic production.

Despite the success of the Munich *Idomeneo*, this was to be Mozart's last attempt at composing an *opera seria* until he penned *La clemenza di Tito* in the last year of his life. Subsequent productions were limited. Of recent note have been the reconstruction by Richard Strauss and Lothar Wallerstein in 1931, Fritz Busch's revival at Glyndebourne in 1951, and the Metropolitan Opera and television premiere of 1982.—JON SOLOMON

L'incoronazione di Poppea [The Coronation of Poppea]

Composer: *Claudio Monteverdi.*

Librettist: *G.F. Busenello.*

First Performance: *Venice, 1642.*

Roles: *Poppea (mezzo-soprano); Nero (tenor); Ottavia (mezzo-soprano or soprano); Ottone (baritone); Seneca (bass); Drusilla (soprano); Arnalta (contralto); Valetto (soprano); Damigella (soprano); Two Soldiers (tenor); Pallas (soprano); Mercury (tenor); Nutrice (contralto); Amore (soprano); Liberto (tenor); Lictor (bass); chorus (SATTBB).*

There can be no discussion of Monteverdi's *L'incoronazione di Poppea* without mention of the editions according to which it is usually performed. These offer a choice between a somewhat free interpretation of the sources by Raymond Leppard (1962) and a more accurate and scholarly one by Alan Curtis (1967). The former is much cut, the scoring lush and romantic, while the latter provides the full and complete text with lighter scoring typical of the operatic scene in the early 17th century.

An understanding of the original sources is also of importance, in that the Venice manuscript (1646) is not even partly an autograph, and shows signs of having been cut, transposed, and in other ways spoiled. The Naples manuscript is more reliable and complete, containing newly composed material to enlarge the role of Ottavia and give the stage machinery a chance to shine. Both scores derive from a lost autograph.

A copy of the libretto at Treviso, first studied from a scholarly point of view in 1902, shows that Monteverdi followed the libretto very carefully, so that the legend about his having changed the ending and written his own verse for the final duet can be disregarded.

The opera begins with a prologue in which Fortune, Virtue, and Love sing of their influence on human affairs, Love being predominant. Act I, set in first-century Rome, introduces the Emperor Nero who, infatuated with the courtesan Poppea, is intent upon making her his empress. Ottavia, the reigning empress, both jealous and vindictive, is no more moved by the philosopher Seneca's advice than is Nero. A nobleman, Ottone, still in love with Poppea, finds his way to her room blocked by guards. He tries to console himself with Drusilla, a court lady.

In act II we see Seneca go to his death, mourned by his disciples. Poppea's murder is planned by Ottone and Ottavia, with Drusilla's assistance. But as Ottone lingers over the sleeping woman, Love (Amore) appears and foils his attempt. As light relief, we witness the first intimations of love between a page and a lady-in-waiting. Nero and his friend Lucan, a poet, sing a duet in celebration of Seneca's death and Poppea's beauty. Act III sees the banishment of the conspirators, with Ottavia's farewell to the city, while the old nurse Arnalta is raised to the status of confidante to the empress. The final scene consists of Nero and Poppea's radiant love-duet.

L'incoronazione di Poppea has gone down in history as perhaps the first example of a plot in which evil triumphs over good, resulting from a procession of suicide, attempted murder, banishment, and exile. Such a story displays the triumph of power and vaulting ambition, the harshness and corruption of politics, and the venalities of court life, all of which Monteverdi knew well, notably in Cremona, Mantua, and Venice, where he was exposed to the machinery of corruption and the chicanery of musical life. His letters reveal his sufferings, and his music in *L'incoronazione di Poppea* shows him rising above those lowly intrigues. He has left us a musical legacy purified of evil, although he is perfectly capable of representing it.

There are wonderful moments in the character portrayals, notably in Nero's overbearing manner and his all-consuming pride; in Seneca's quiet stoicism and his acceptance of the folly of those set to govern over us; in Ottone's duplicity, transformed "not from Ottone into Drusilla but from a man into a serpent." All these traits are revealed in music that, in the original, relies not on instrumental coloring so much as refinement of melodic expression, vitality of rhythm, and expert word-painting.

Other felicities include the luscious ariosos given to Poppea, whose music certainly reflects her sensuality; the touching pronouncements of the repudiated Ottavia; the helplessness of Drusilla, caught in a plot of increasing complexity; and the superficially amusing yet basically serious attitude of Arnalta, whose change of station shows her to be a changed personality. Monteverdi also deals with his lesser figures in a masterly manner, especially the conversations between the Praetorian Guards and the naive but moving encounter of the page and the lady-in-waiting.

i

OPERA

His grasp of musical style is such that he is never at a loss for a situation or a character, and when certain events central to the story are raised aloft by the librettist, Busenello, it is as if the musician followed the lighted flame and used its beckoning glimmer to inspire his musical thought. It is never less than intense, so that even in a mutilated or cut version we are bound to experience a feeling of illumination, even incandescence. Within a year of its production, Monteverdi was dead, and the first great chapter in the history of opera had come to an end.—DENIS STEVENS

Intermezzo

Composer: *Richard Strauss.*

Librettist: *Richard Strauss.*

First Performance: *Dresden, Staatsoper, 4 November 1924.*

Roles: *Christine Storch (soprano); Robert Storch (baritone); Baron Lummer (tenor); Anna (soprano); Notary (baritone); Notary's Wife (soprano); Conductor Stroh (tenor); Businessman (baritone); Judge (baritone); Singer (bass); Little Franzl (speaking part); Resi (speaking part); Therese (speaking part); Marie (speaking part); Cook (speaking part).*

In 1919 Strauss completed the composition of *Die Frau ohne Schatten.* That enormous and symbolically laden work had taken its toll on the composer both in terms of sheer length and emotional weight, and he longed for the lightness of comic spoofery as an antidote. This urge took form presently with the ballet *Schlagobers,* but found its ultimate outlet in *Intermezzo.*

An autobiographical penchant had long played a significant role in Strauss's music, including *Feuersnot* as well as the better known allusions of *Ein Heldenleben* and *Sinfonia domestica.* Thus an episode from his own personal life seemed an ideal topic for an opera, especially dealing as it did with his marriage to a rather notorious termagant of an ex-prima donna, Pauline de Ahna. Strauss in fact loved his wife very much, and in retrospect it would seem that her tantrums and nagging (along with other more positive qualities) fulfilled a deep need in the composer's psyche. In any case theirs was a lengthy and happy union by all accounts. *Die Frau ohne Schatten* had also dealt with marriage, and thus *Intermezzo* stands in relationship to the monumental earlier work comparable to that of a satyr play, and Strauss even allows the two operas to share one all-important musical idea.

It was predictable, given his intellectual aloofness and distaste for Frau Strauss, that long-time collaborator Hugo von Hofmannsthal found the concept vulgar and refused to participate in the new project. After some false starts with critic and author Hermann Bahr, Strauss was finally convinced to write the text himself, a logical decision since he was, after all, a participant in the events to be related and wanted the words to reflect ordinary conversation and avoid all hints of poetry.

Thus we are in the household of famous conductor and composer Robert Storch and his wife, the rather notorious termagant of an ex-prima donna, Christine. In brief, the plot conflates two episodes. Robert leaves home for Vienna, where he has some concert engagements. In his absence Christine almost accidentally develops an innocent relationship with a featherbrained young man, one Baron Lummer, who takes her dancing but bores her with his vapidity. He finally ruins whatever friendship they might have had by asking her for a considerable sum of money, a request she rightfully refuses to consider. More serious and central to the story is the saga of Mieze Maier. This young lady of dubious reputation (who never appears on stage) sends a letter to the composer which addresses him affectionately ("Lieber Schatz"), asks for some opera tickets and closes with "meet me afterwards in the bar as usual." Christine opens the letter, suspects the worst, and immediately files for divorce. Robert, severely disadvantaged by being out of town, finally unscrambles the situation. He learns that Mieze had confused him with another conductor with a similar last name, and returns home to mollify Christine and revel in a happy ending, his marriage back on track.

The charm of the work, however, lies not in its slender plot but in the wonderfully witty repartee with which Strauss characterized all of the roles, especially the endless chatterbox banter and tantrums of the wife. Written in two acts, the opera's many brief scenes are linked with evocative interludes, virtually the only places where Strauss allows the orchestra to have its head. This is the direct result of those experiments in the conversational style which he deployed in the recently completed prologue to *Ariadne auf Naxos*. Deeming his efforts at textual clarity and effortless passage from speech through recitative to arioso to have been successful, he devotes virtually all of *Intermezzo* to the newly minted technique, allowing the voices to blossom into cantilena only at a few emotionally crucial finales.

Following the lead of Gluck in *Alceste,* Strauss wrote a foreword to the opera which is printed in the *Intermezzo* piano score and is an important statement on his theories of word-setting and indeed operatic composition and performance in general. Thus a harmless and trenchant comedy of manners becomes simultaneously yet unobtrusively a professional tract. *Intermezzo* is probably too specialized to enter the standard repertoire, and there are still those who find the autobiographical element distasteful. Nonetheless it remains an important work in Strauss' operatic canon and will undoubtedly continue to delight and reward the conoisseur.—DENNIS WAKELING

Iolanta

Composer: *Piotr Ilyich Tchaikovsky.*
Librettist: *M. Tchaikovsky (after V. Zotov's translation of H. Hertz's King René's Daughter).*
First Performance: *St Petersburg, Mariinsky, 18 December 1892.*
Roles: *Iolanta (soprano); King René (bass); Count Vaudémont (tenor); Duke Robert (baritone); Bertram (bass); Martha (contralto); Brigitta (soprano); Laura (mezzo-soprano); Ibn-Hakia (baritone); Almerik (tenor); chorus (SATB).*

Both Tchaikovsky's ballet *The Nutcracker* and the opera *Iolanta* belong to the last years of the composer's life. When the ballet and the opera were performed together on 18 December 1892, it was the opera that was successful, not the ballet, though subsequent years have reversed this verdict.

Following the introductory orchestral prelude, marked *piano espressivo,* which may well be suggestive of Iolanta's blindness, the opera opens in a luxurious garden. To a background of four musicians, Princess Iolanta gropes for fruit, which, assisted by her friends Brigitta, Martha, and Laura, she plucks and puts into baskets. Although she is blind, her father, King René, has forbidden anyone to discuss the fact. Iolanta, though unaware of her handicap, realizes instinctively that she is different from other people. She wonders how her friends know she is crying if they do not touch her eyes. She is sad at heart and in an arioso reflects on her former happiness. In the following scene, the sound of hunting horns is heard, announcing the imminent arrival of the king. A discussion between Almerik, the king's armor-bearer, and Bertram, keeper of the castle, discloses that King René is bringing with him a famous Moorish doctor and that Iolanta is engaged to Robert, Duke of Burgundy. The king, wanting to conceal Iolanta's blindness, keeps her isolated in the remote castle where they are now staying.

Another fanfare announces the entry of the king and the Moorish doctor, Ibn-Hakia, who has been summoned as the last hope of curing the princess. The doctor goes to look at the sleeping Iolanta and in his absence René, in a poignant aria, prays to the Lord, asking why he and his daughter have been so punished, and calls for divine assistance. When Ibn-Hakia returns, he tells the king that Iolanta must be made aware of her condition and that only her will-power can save her. But René will not even consider this, and both depart.

Now through the forest appear Robert, Duke of Burgundy, and his friend Count Vaudémont. Vaudémont cannot believe his eyes at the beauty of the garden, which they have come across by accident. Robert, though betrothed to Iolanta, whom he has never seen, wishes to break his engagement, having fallen in love with Mathilde. Both come across the sleeping Iolanta, whose beauty immediately captivates Vaudémont, But Robert, alarmed by the whole business and fearing sorcery, wishes to leave. The sound of their voices wakes Iolanta. Vaudémont begins to talk to her, and while the princess goes to fetch wine, Robert departs to find his retinue. The following duet between Iolanta and Vaudémont, which reveals the growing warmth of their affection, is the highlight of the whole opera, especially the moment when Vaudémont asks for a red rose and is given a white one. When this action is repeated, he suddenly realizes that she is blind. His stunned silence disturbs Iolanta, but Vaudémont reassures her, explaining to her the meaning of light, the first-born gift of the Creator. Iolanta replies in ecstatic terms.

Their reverie is interrupted by the sudden arrival of the king, Ibn-Hakia, and their entourage. The king is alarmed to find his daughter talking to a strange knight and even more so when he discovers that he has told her about the concept of light. René wishes to put Vaudémont to death, but Ibn-Hakia sees the event as reason for hope. René agrees to Ibn-Hakia attempting to cure Iolanta, but tells the knight that if the treatment is unsuccessful, he will forfeit his life. Iolanta, aghast, expresses her love for Vaudémont, and their duet, reintroducing earlier material, forms another climactic moment. Iolanta and the doctor depart, and the king admits to the knight that the threat of death was a ploy to stir Iolanta to action. Robert, Duke of Burgundy, returns and explains all the circumstances to the king, who agrees to release him from his bond, thus enabling Vaudémont to marry Iolanta. To a great chord of C major comes the news that Iolanta has regained her sight. The opera ends with a big ensemble, in which all give thanks to Heaven.

It is surprising that *Iolanta* is not more frequently performed, since it contains many attractive numbers—Iolanta's arioso, René's supplicatory aria, Ibn-Hakia's aria, Robert's aria in praise of Mathilde, as well as the impressive duet between Iolanta and Vaudémont. The scene between René and the doctor in the first part of the work is highly dramatic, and the use of the women's chorus in the opening scene in the garden is charming in its skillful part-writing and novel timbres. The orchestration is effective throughout, the texture unified by a number of recurrent themes.—GERALD SEAMAN

Iphigénie en Tauride

Composer: *Christoph Willibald von Gluck.*

Librettists: *Nicolas-François Guillard and François-Louis Grand Lebland du Roullet (after Euripides).*

First Performance: *Paris, Académie Royale, 18 May 1779; revised in German, translated by J.B. von Alxinger and Gluck, Vienna, Burgtheater, 23 October 1781.*

Roles: *Iphigenia (soprano); Pylades (tenor); Orestes (baritone); Thoas (bass or baritone); Diana (soprano); Greek Woman (soprano); Two priestesses (sopranos); Minister of the Sanctuary (bass); A Scyth (baritone); chorus (SATTB).*

The operatic aims of Christoph Willibald von Gluck are perhaps most effectively realized in *Iphigénie en Tauride,* an impressive work of musical and dramatic power, which is important in the history of opera as well as a significant achievement in its own right. In an open letter published in the *Journal de Paris* two years before the premiere of 1779, Gluck had avowed his desire to revitalize the drama through a search for strong expression and the interconnection of all parts of his works. He accomplished these goals in *Iphigénie en Tauride* by means of vivid dramatic characterizations, fluid musical structures, and a balance between vocal and instrumental components that integrated dance and chorus within a cohesive entity.

The libretto, written by Nicolas-François Guillard on a drama by Euripides, involves a decision by the Greek Iphigenia, who had been brought to the island of Tauris to serve as high priestess to the goddess Diana. King Thoas, barbaric ruler of the Scythians, has decreed that the oracles can be appeased and his life saved only if all strangers to the island are killed. Iphigenia and her priestesses are to carry out these sacrifices. The storm opening the lyric tragedy brings to Tauris two Greek friends, Orestes and Pylades. Both must be killed, but Iphigenia risks Thoas' wrath by determining to spare the life of one. Feeling a tender sentiment toward Orestes, who reminds Iphigenia of her brother, she resolves that Pylades be sacrificed and Orestes be saved to carry a message to her sister in Mycenae.

Orestes has been tormented by guilt and pursued by the Eumenides for having avenged the murder of his father, King Agamemnon, by killing his mother, Clytemnestra. Believing that he must expiate his crime, Orestes urges Pylades to exchange places and let him die, but Pylades refuses and expresses heroic acceptance of the destiny enabling his friend to live. Orestes then implores Iphigenia to reconsider and sacrifice him instead of Pylades; with the greatest reluctance, she accedes. As Orestes is being prepared for the sacrifice, he names his sister, Iphigenia. A joyful recognition scene ensues. King Thoas angrily tries to destroy both Orestes and Iphigenia but is killed by Pylades, who arrives with soldiers from Greece in time to rescue Orestes. The goddess Diana assures Orestes that remorse has assuaged his guilt; he is to reign in Mycenae with Iphigenia restored to her homeland. The final chorus celebrates the return of peace.

Gluck responded with varied musical means to the striking situations, images, and universal themes. A French late-eighteenth-century perspective on ancient Greece produced an emphasis on the conflict between Iphigenia's duty and her human response to nature and individual feeling. Gluck and Guillard intensified the drama between sister, brother, and friend by delineating bonds of family love, friendship, courage, and heroic rescue set against the strife between Scythian and Greek civilizations. Gluck's techniques include the use of unadorned arias, shorter expressive ariosos, dramatically motivated accompanied recitatives, choruses heightening contrast and mood, ballets in the new style that advance rather than impede action, and active orchestral passages that provide a sense of musical continuity.

Concentrated exchanges occur between the three main figures in the second and third acts of the four-act work. The characterization of Orestes is especially successful because the dramatic element of his obsessive guilt has its parallel in Gluck's desire to achieve musical unity through the reiteration of short rhythmic figures that build in intensity. Thus, for example, an inexorable sense of momentum is attained in the first aria of act II, in which Orestes sings in allegro tempo of the gods who pursue him, while oboes, clarinets, horns, trumpets, and timpani reinforce his vocal line with persistent motives as bassoons and strings play vigorous scale-like passages. The next scene has been noted for the psychological insight revealed by Gluck in setting accented orchestral syncopations that reveal the troubled disorientation of Orestes as he sings of calm returning to his heart. There follow a dramatic chorus and ballet-pantomime of terror by the Eumenides punctuated by the cries of Orestes and an intense dialogue in recitative during which Iphigenia hears of her family's fate from Orestes. In the final scene, Iphigenia instructs her priestesses to combine laments for their fallen king with her expression of private grief; their plaintive lines are supported by sustained dissonances in the oboes.

Act III celebrates friendship. Its third scene includes an unusual ensemble between Iphigenia and the two men. Her noble decision to spare one of the victims is set to music whose tempo, rhythmic patterns, instrumentation, and dynamics differ substantially from those in the harmonious accord of the unselfish friends. Three times they exchange statements and responses until the moment when Iphigenia's fateful choice leads the flowing lines to merge into a recitative, an orchestral passage expressive of her despair, and Orestes' anguished solo phrase on learning that it is Pylades who is to be sacrificed.

The duet in C minor between Orestes and Pylades in the next scene is an impassioned dialogue whose first part stresses the intensity felt by each in attempting to convince the other through brief overlapping phrases that accumulate power by means of their sequential repetition in an insistent increase in volume. It is musically stirring and it also serves the crucial dramatic function of lending additional stature to the figure of Pylades, whose steadfast heroism emerges. When later he finds himself free to live, his resolute determination to save Orestes is fully credible. The paean to *amitié,* friendship, in C major with which Pylades closes the act sustains the weight of its position as an effective culmination.

Iphigénie en Tauride balances dramatic expression through truthful characterization with musical concision through deftly conceived structures. Its majestic sweep and energetic vigor admirably convey the new dramatic musical style for which Gluck became renowned.—ORA FRISHBERG SALOMAN

j OPERA

Janáček, Leoš

Composer. Born 3 July 1854, in Hukvaldy, Moravia. Died 12 August 1928, in Ostrava. Sang in the choir of the Augustine monastery in Brno; studied at the Brno Teacher's Training College, 1872-74; studied organ with Skubersky at the Organ School in Prague, 1874-75; studied composition with L. Grill at the Leipzig Conservatory and with Franz Krenn at the Vienna Conservatory, 1879-80; conductor of the Czech Philharmonic, 1881-88; taught at the Conservatory of Brno, 1919-1925. Janáček was very interested in Russian literature and music, and visited Russia three times.

Operas *Šárka*, Julius Zeyer, 1887-88, Brno, National Theater, 11 November 1925; revised 1918-19 (act III orchestrated by O. Chlubna), 1924-25; *The Beginning of a Romance* [*Počátek románu*], Jaroslav Tichý (after a story by Gabriela Preissová), 1891, Brno, National Theater, 10 February 1894; *Jenůfa* [*Její pastorkyňa*], Janáček (after a play by Gabriela Preissová), 1894-1903, Brno, National Theater, 21 January 1904; revised before 1908; *Fate* [*Osud*], Fedora Bartošová and Janáček, 1903-05 (revised 1906-07), radio broadcast from Brno, 1 September 1934; staged, Brno, National Theater, 25 October 1958; *Mr. Brouček's Excursion to the Moon* [*Výlet pana Broučka do měsíce*], Janáček, Viktor Dyk, F.G. Gellner and F.S. Procházka (after a satire by Svatopluk Čech), 1908-17, Prague, National Theater, 23 April 1920; *Mr. Brouček's Excursion to the 15th Century* [*Výlet pana Broučka do XV. století*], Frantisek S. Procházka (after a satire by Svatopluk Čech), 1917, Prague, National Theater, 23 April 1920; *Katia Kabanová*, Janáček (after A.N. Ostrovsky, *The Storm*, translated by Vincenc Červinka), 1919-21, Brno, National Theater, 23 November 1921; *The Cunning Little Vixen* [*Příhody Lišky Bystroušky*], Janáček (after Rudolf Těsnohlídek), 1921-23, Brno, National Theater, 6 November 1924; *The Makropoulos Case* [*Věc Makropulos*], Janáček (after a play by Karel Čapek), 1923-25, Brno, National Theater, 18 December 1926; *From the House of the Dead* [*Z mrtvého domu*], Janáček (after Dostoyevsky), 1927-28; revised and reorchestrated by O. Chlubna and B. Bakala, Brno, National Theater, 12 April 1930.

Europe of the mid-nineteenth century was experiencing the consequences of tidal changes that had started about one hundred years before, first as a philosophical movement, and then as a social and military upheaval. Janácek was born (1854) into the time of the mass man, the industrial revolution, and, paradoxically, the growing importance of the individual.

Shaped by his own excitable nature and the rapid, destabilizing changes in European society, Janácek developed his brilliant gifts to the point that, unlike other musicians, he almost seemed to be an active participant in the changes taking place around him. It might be noted that this is exactly the function of all successful artists, to reflect and intensify the world in which they live, but with many artists this role seems more subconscious than deliberate. With Janácek, the impression is that he spent much of his life and creativity involving himself in his surroundings, and although this aspect of Janácek's work could be illustrated with any of his most significant works, it becomes most apparent when we turn to his operas.

Jenůfa, Janácek's first real success, was first performed in Brno in 1904. While *Jenůfa* was favorably received by many, however, it also shocked some of those who first heard it. On the surface, *Jenůfa* is directly related to the operas of Smetana, Dvořák, and Fibich: it deals with the people and their problems in a small-town, rural setting. But where the work of the earlier masters generally idealizes this lifestyle, Janácek's opera is about the churning conflicts these people really experience.

Jenůfa is about two men in love with the title character, and the conflicts which result. The music is extremely dramatic and quite unforgettably original. Its originality resides in Janácek's treatment of melodic motifs. These are constantly repeated at different pitch levels, and a kind of dissolution by diminution of the material occurs, both metrically and melodically. Janácek creates a musical fabric at once high-strung and exceptionally dramatic. It is difficult to describe, but once experienced, it is not easily forgotten. Its power is obvious, and, listened to carefully, its melodic content is compelling.

Part of this strange score's sound, as well as that of all of Janácek's later scores, is due to his principles of word-setting. As is well known by now, Janácek attempted to notate the natural sound of speech as it was spoken rather than sung. This is a matter of accents, speed, pitch of voice, and speech idiosyncrasies. Janácek was convinced that the usual practice of creating flowing musical lines was wrong. He advocated, rather, that music should mirror, yet heighten the sound and emotion of actual speech. Thus, in *Jenůfa,* it is the interaction of the main characters and their rapid-fire speech which Janácek's music heightens with startling success, and it is the extremely flexible treatment of that musical fabric which sets Janácek's efforts in stark contrast to anyone else's, until the later non-tonal composers of the twentieth century. Later composers had similar ideas, but without the verbal rationale that is so integral to Janácek's work.

Jenůfa also illustrates some other aspects of Janácek's methods. His orchestra is capable of the most brilliant effects, but they are not at all the same as, for example, Wagner's orchestral sonorities. Wagner usually creates orchestral effects of rich opulence by blending his instrumental colors, while Janácek's effects are created more by the brilliance of primary colors played against each other, and by using the extreme registers of instruments. Thus, despite the hyperactivity of the sonorities, there is a prevailing orchestral clarity. Also, voices have little trouble riding over this kind of sound.

As for Janáček's vocal writing, he rarely asks for sustained sound, but rather for an extreme intensity of utterance. If, as happens in the roles of Laca or Kostelnicka, the tessitura is mostly high, there are difficulties, but the relative absence of sustained (and slow) singing mitigates those difficulties. What is exceedingly demanding for the singers is the psychological element. As an extrapolation of the word-setting practices described above, Janáček managed to write music to the texts which sharply mirrored the mental state as well as the personality-types represented. Slimy characters have jagged chromatic music, and madmen have music which is harmonically deranged. Janáček's operas make it imperative for singers to be first rate actors, capable of seeing the verbally realistic elements in the composer's music. Here, the first need is not vocal beauty, but skillful musical-dramatic declamation of naturalistic intensity.

Jenůfa, the only opera so far mentioned, is Janáček's first successful effort to carry out his word-centered theories. He was to follow these principles throughout his later operas, but they were to be more varied and reflective of wider varieties of moods. Thus, in *Katia Kabanova* we see a set of dramatic circumstances similar to *Jenůfa,* but Janáček creates a score of inward, quiet isolation. Katia's tragic situation elicits music of compassion, but Kabanichka, Katia's mother-in-law, visits a kind of casual cruelty on both her son and Katia which is chillingly caught by Janáček's muted but loudly played brass. It should be said that *Katia Kabanova* is perhaps Janáček's most intimate, romantic opera. A product of 1919, it might have heralded a new direction in Janáček's work. In fact, it did not, for in *The Cunning Little Vixen, The Makropulous Case,* and finally, *From the House of the Dead,* there are more violent ways of looking at the tragedy of human existence, as well as its frequent humor and even whimsy.

From the House of the Dead is Janáček's last work, and considering its date of composition, it is often seen as ominously prophetic of the world we were about to enter at that time. In point of fact, however, it derives its libretto directly from the two-volume novel of the same name by F. Dostoyevsky, and that novel reports on circumstances that were common in the nineteenth century. Set in a prison camp, it describes, through the narrations of four people, what brought them to their captivity, and what that life is like. Everyone except one political prisoner has committed a serious crime, but their punishments are seen as crimes of infinitely greater proportions. That is the main point, perhaps, of Dostoyevsky's masterpiece. What is prophetic about Janáček's opera is the ferocity, the brutality of his setting, which smacks of the twentieth century as we have come to know it. He views the cruelty of the camp as something to be depicted in very harsh sounds. His orchestra rages in anger at the inhuman treatment accorded the prisoners by the guard, or it wails in horror at the way the inmates torment each other. It is this raw vividness which, with the aid of hindsight, is so descriptive of what was to happen in Europe fifteen years later. Since the composer died in 1928, he could have had little idea of the future, but his score is so disturbing that it is difficult *not* to think of 1942.

Janáček's art seems to be more a part of his time than is often the case with opera composers. It is a fact that all of the operas discussed here, as well as those not mentioned, constitute some form of social criticism (even the *Vixen*), and it is a measure of Janáček's mastery that they are all effective as social criticism and musical drama. As such, the more we know his operas the more we recognize them as part of the twentieth century's finest artistic products.—HARRIS CROHN

Janowitz, Gundula

Soprano. Born 2 August 1937, in Berlin. Studied at Graz Conservatory with Herbert Thöny; debut as Barbarina in Le nozze di Figaro, *Vienna Staatsoper, 1959; appeared at Bayreuth, 1960-63; member of Frankfurt Opera, 1963-66; Metropolitan Opera debut as Sieglinde, 1967; sang Countess in* Le nozze di Figaro *at reopening of Paris Opéra, 1973; Covent Garden debut as Donna Anna in* Don Giovanni, *1976; became director of Graz Opera, 1990.*

The Berlin-born soprano Gundula Janowitz won a student contract at the Vienna State Opera on finishing her studies at the Graz Conservatory in 1959 at the age of twenty-two, and within two years she had appeared not only in Vienna but Bayreuth, Aix-en-Provence and Glyndebourne. She quickly came under the notice of Herbert von Karajan, who became a major influence in her career; under his guidance she made her mark as Marzelline, Agathe and, at the age of twenty-seven, the Empress in a new Staatsoper production of Strauss's *Die Frau ohne Schatten*.

Although her career took her to the major European houses as well as to America and elsewhere, she divided her time principally between Berlin and Vienna, singing a variety of roles which included not only the Mozart and Strauss for which she became celebrated but Micaela, Fidelio and a number of Verdi roles such as Aïda, Amelia and Odabella in *Atilla*. First attracting attention as Pamina, she progressed through all the major female roles in *Le nozze di Figaro* to achieve a Susanna, Cherubino and Countess of great distinction, to major roles in other Mozart operas, including Donna Anna in *Don Giovanni,* Ilia in *Idomeneo,* and Fiordiligi in *Così fan tutte* as well as mastering a large number of the concert arias. Purity of tone, cleanness of line and aristocratic phrasing were her great gifts in this repertoire, qualities which she brought also to her Wagner and Strauss roles.

An example of the pure "white" soprano tone associated with central European sopranos such as Tiana Lemnitz and the early Schwarzkopf, her voice had a tight vibrato, making it almost instrumental—and very beautiful—in its texture. Janowitz, recognizing these qualities in her own voice and exploiting them with great intelligence and sensitivity, rarely attempted to push it beyond the bounds nature provided it with. Consequently she sang only the lighter Wagner roles—Eva, Elsa and Elizabeth—until Karajan persuaded her to sing (a very successful) Sieglinde for his Salzburg *Ring* in 1967, the role in which she made her debut at the Metropolitan Opera. Her Wagner was fascinating in its rare combination of purity of tone (rarely distorted) and brilliance in the climaxes.

Her performances were sometimes described as cool, some critics tending (as with Birgit Nilsson) to mistake the narrow, brilliant column of tone—J.B. Steane describes it as a "pure 'tube' of sound"—for a personality trait which translated onstage into a dramatic deficiency. But Janowitz, though a very controlled artist, was accurate in describing herself in an interview as *"ein ganz, ganz, normal Mensch,"* ("a very, very usual kind of person"). Her normality was the opposite of flamboyance but did not inhibit, as many of her records will testify, her warmth and communicative power.

Her greatest achievements were perhaps in Strauss, beginning with her interpretation of the Four Last Songs with Karajan and running through her Marschallin, Arabella and, perhaps most of all, her Ariadne. Her recording of this opera with Rudolph Kempe is exquisite from first to last. "Ein Schonës war" becomes almost a dialogue between the instrumental quality—which paradoxically emphasizes the humanity—of her tone and the instruments of the orchestra; the solo violin at the repeat of "Und ging im Licht" is an uncannily beautiful echo of the voice. The elegiac lament for a lost world of love is profoundly moving. So also with "Es gibt ein Reich," superbly shaped both in terms of sound and emotion, rising to the climatic B flat at "Du nimm es von mir."

Janowitz always devoted a large portion of her time to concert activity with orchestra and in recital, achieving real distinction in both. She retired from the opera stage in the spring of 1990 to assume the directorship of the Opera at Graz, where she grew up and pursued her musical studies, while planning to continue with her concert career.—PETER DYSON

Janssen, Herbert

Baritone. Born 22 September 1892, in Cologne. Died 3 June 1965, in New York. Studied in Cologne, then with Oskar Daniel in Berlin; debut in Schreker's Der Schatzgräber, *Berlin State Opera, 1922; remained on Berlin State Opera's roster until 1938; appeared regularly at Covent Garden, 1926-39, and at Bayreuth, 1930-37; Metropolitan Opera touring debut as Wotan, Philadelphia, 1939; New York debut as Wolfram, Metropolitan Opera, 1939; remained on the Met's roster until 1952; became American citizen, 1946.*

Herbert Janssen was perhaps the most cherishable of German baritones in the interwar years: on stage his performances had a nobility and mastery that distinguished them in whatever company, and on records his voice possesses an entirely personal timbre, warm and gently resonant, giving it an inherent depth of character beyond that of his many gifted contemporaries.

In the 1940s when he appeared at the Metropolitan Opera and based his career in the United States, the velvet was beginning to wear thin and the steadiness was not the reliable absolute known previously to audiences at Covent Garden. At his New York house debut in 1939 his voice was considered beautiful and his performance exemplary; but that was as Wolfram, one of the lighter, more lyrical Wagnerian roles, and when he came later to undertake Wotan and Hans Sachs the sheer power was lacking. Off-the-air recordings show something of the deterioration. In 1941 a *Fidelio* conducted by Bruno Walter finds him in his element, portraying the benevolent authority of Don Fernando, but when three years later he was cast as Don Pizarro in a broadcast performance under Toscanini it is not simply in response to the villainy of the character that his voice has lost its attractiveness; by 1949 when he sang Jokanaan to Ljuba Welitsch's Salome, however admirable the performance in some ways, it is no longer identifiable as the voice we remember from the previous decade.

In his best years, roughly from 1925 to 1940, Janssen won not only the admiration of the public but also the respect of the critics to a degree which was probably unique in London. From 1926 onwards he returned for every summer season at Covent Garden, and year after year the characteristic touches came to be held in deeper affection and the art itself grew in mastery till it was recognized as the most consummate of its kind that was then to be found on the lyric stage. "Turning that fine jeweller's art of his upon the music of Kurwenal", as Ernest Newman said, he provided what everyone came to see as the classic portrayal. At first it had seemed a curious piece of casting, that this particularly sensitive, subtle singer with the soft grain in his voice should be chosen for the bluff Kurwenal, but he deepened people's perception of the part, so that he made of it the moving tragedy of a generous faithful soul whose dying words "Schilt mich nicht, dass der Treue auch mit kommt" remained in the mind almost to rank with the more famous love-death that was to follow. As Telramund in *Lohengrin* he would darken his tone, said the *Daily Telegraph's* critic, "yet without ever producing an ugly sound." As the Dutchman, wrote Newman, he presented "one of the truly great things of the operatic stage today; here is a sufferer who carries on his shoulders not only his own but the whole world's woe." To Walter Legge, Janssen's Gunther in *Götterdämmerung* was the most consummate achievement before the public. Even when he sang a secondary role such as the Speaker in *Die Zauberflöte* it registered as "a noble piece of work" (Newman), and his Kothner in *Die Meistersinger* was a masterpiece of comical self-importance.

The voice itself and the way he produced it remain a subject of some fascination. On records the tone often seems to be so gentle that one wonders how well it carried. A reminiscence on the part of one of those stalwart British singers often brought in to the international seasons to fill a suitably inconspicuous gap tells how his colleague on stage asked *sotto voce* who was that singing just now. "Herbert Janssen." "Well, I don't think much of him." "Right," said the other, "you go down there to the back of the stalls and see what you think from there"—which he did, only to hear the most perfect projection of sound, and a remarkable growth of power in the process. The critic of the *Daily Telegraph* made a similar observation in 1930: "his *mezza voce* is quite remarkable for its carrying power."

To listeners in the present day he is no more than a voice on records, a Wagnerian singer with the smoothness and technique of one who (as he said) would practice the aria "Il balen" from *Il trovatore* every day for one whole year, and a Lieder singer belonging to a sensitive but less analytical school than that of the post-war generation. Nobody hearing him sing Wolfram's music in *Tannhäuser*, Schumann's *Die Lotosblume*, Strauss's *Zueignung* or the *Harfenspielerlieder* of Wolf is likely to miss the special quality of his voice; and, once lodged in the mind, it quickly becomes a treasured possession.—J.B. STEANE

Jenůfa [Její pastorkyňa]

Composer: *Leoš Janáček.*

Librettist: *Leoš Janáček (after a play by Gabriela Preissová).*

First Performance: *Brno, National Theater, 21 January 1904.*

Roles: *Grandmother Buryja (contralto); Laca (tenor); Števa (tenor); Kostelnička (soprano); Jenůfa (soprano); Old Foreman (baritone); Mayor (bass); His Wife (mezzo-soprano); Karolka (mezzo-soprano); Maid (mezzo-soprano); Barena (soprano); Jano (soprano); Aunt (contralto); chorus (SATTBB).*

Gabriela Preissová's play *Her Foster-Daughter* (1890) was widely attacked, since it undermined the Prague nationalists' idealized picture of peasant life. But Preissová's uncompromising realism, her personal knowledge of the character of Moravian Slovakia, and her use of his own native dialect appealed powerfully to Janáček; this text liberated his musical imagination, and enabled him to create his first masterpiece—the opera which is known outside Czechoslovakia as *Jenůfa*.

At the opening of act I, we find Jenůfa pregnant by Števa, the feckless heir to an isolated mill in the mountains of Moravia. If he is conscripted into the army, her predicament will be discovered, and she will be disgraced; if not, she hopes to marry him. Števa returns from the recruiting board, unconscripted but also drunk; Jenůfa's foster-mother, the Kostelnička or sextoness of the village, forbids them to marry unless he can stay sober for a year. Števa's half-brother Laca loves Jenůfa deeply, and is bitterly jealous of her affection for Števa, who admires her only for her good looks. Laca destroys Jenůfa's beauty, slashing her cheek with his knife.

By the opening of act II, Jenůfa has secretly given birth to her child, a boy. The Kostelnička is tormented by its existence. She tries to persuade Števa to marry Jenůfa, but fails. Laca is full of remorse, and wants to marry Jenůfa. The baby would be the only obstacle to this marriage; the Kostelnička murders it by throwing it into the freezing river, lies to Jenůfa that it died when she was sick with fever, and brings the couple together.

In act III, on the morning of Jenůfa's wedding day, the baby's body is discovered under the ice. To prevent the villagers from stoning Jenůfa to death, the Kostelnička confesses. After a moment of initial revulsion, Jenůfa forgives her, and gives her the strength to accept her punishment. Left alone with Laca, Jenůfa gives him his freedom; but he insists that they should remain together.

Preissová evokes two themes which became fundamental to Janáček's operatic output; the eternal pattern of life, death and renewal, and the ideal of a morality and spiritual growth which are based on self-knowledge and harmony with nature. In the final outcome three people rise; Jenůfa and Laca to a mature, adult understanding of themselves and others, and the Kostelnička to a true humility in which she can accept the outside world's verdict on her crime. Community standards—in particular those of traditional religious morality—are shown to be useless; the forgiveness and love which resolve the action spread outwards from Jenůfa, who has gained her strength from a hard-won harmony with nature.

Jenůfa obliged Janáček to free himself from traditional ways of setting words to music, and to forge a new operatic style. The composer had to devise an idiom in which he could set the prose text direct, in which the realism of the text would not be marred by excesses of false emotion, and in which Janáček's own visionary portrait of spiritual growth could be convincingly displayed.

In *Jenůfa,* short but intense motifs in the orchestra dominate each successive section of the score. They are repeated as long as is required to illuminate their particular part of the action, and are not usually heard again. There are no arias; there is one traditional ensemble, a quartet with chorus in act I, but otherwise the prose text is set direct, without formal structures. The vocal style is a richly expressive arioso which, for clarity, avoids melisma. Vocal phrases are often repeated, partly to accent the nervous brooding exhibited by many of the characters in this story, and partly because in this opera Janáček had not yet perfected the difficult mesh between the dramatic timing and the musical timing of his action.

In *Jenůfa* Janáček established new standards for opera, in the depth and detail with which the orchestra can illuminate human psychology in action. (Richard Strauss made a corresponding advance, using a symbolist text, at exactly the same time. Both *Salome* and *Jenůfa* were completed in 1903.) The power of Preissová's plot, the strength of the dramatic structure, and the truthfulness, insight and emotional range of Janáček's musical response ensure that a committed performance of this opera is a shattering experience for the audience.

Because of the novelty of the idiom, and certain antagonisms which Janáček's forthrightness had created in Prague, *Jenůfa* was not heard outside his home town of Brno until 1916, and then only in a reorchestration which for many years blurred the stark outlines of the score and romanticized the sound. Charles Mackerras' 1983 Decca recording reverts to the original orchestration, which is also increasingly heard in live performances.

The great success of *Jenůfa* in Prague in 1916, and then in Vienna in 1918, led to its subsequent adoption throughout central Europe. In the English-speaking world recognition took longer (the first British performance was in 1956), but *Jenůfa* now occupies a central place in the twentieth-century repertoire.—MICHAEL EWANS

Jeritza, Maria

Soprano. Born Marie Jedlizka, 6 October 1887, in Brno. Died 10 July 1982, in Orange, New Jersey. Married Baron von Popper. Studied in Brno, with Auspitz in Prague, and later with Sembrich in New York; debut as Elsa in Lohengrin, *Olomouc, 1910; Vienna debut as Elisabeth, Volksoper, 1911; first appeared with Vienna Court Opera in Oberleitner's* Aphrodite, *1912; appeared at Covent Garden, 1925 and 1926; Metropolitan Opera debut as Marietta in Korngold's* Die tote Stadt, *1921, and appeared at Metropolitan Opera until 1932; created Ariadne in both versions of* Ariadne auf Naxos; *created the Empress in* Die Frau ohne Schatten.

The Moravian soprano Maria Jeritza was possessed of all possible attributes to become a successful prima donna: an impressive, well-produced and luxurious voice; exceptional personal beauty and presence; and steadfast devotion to her art. Details of her personal life remain elusive (except that she married three times) and her autobiography goes no further than 1929, omitting many details about herself and her colleagues that one would like to have known. It tends to stress her puritanical diet and blameless early nights in pursuit of her all-important career.

Jeritza came up the hard way through a provincial opera chorus and her official debut was as Elsa in *Lohengrin* in the provincial opera house at Olomouc, north of Brno, where she was born. She then joined the Vienna Volksoper, a thorough training-ground for promotion. While singing Rosalinde in a performance of *Die Fledermaus* before the Emperor Franz Josef in 1912, her personality and physical appearance appealed to him so much that he arranged for her immediate transfer to his Hofoper in Vienna, where she remained until 1935, soon receiving a far higher salary than any other singer there.

Jeritza's spectacular successes included the Empress in *Die Frau ohne Schatten,* Giorgetta in *Il tabarro,* Minnie in *La Fanciulla del West* and Violanta. She was also a famous Thaïs, Jenůfa, Salome, Fedora and Carmen, and her Wagner roles were Senta, Elsa, Elisabeth and Sieglinde. The wide range of her roles indicates her vocal capabilities and how much she was valued as a prima donna. She was known for her temperament and autocratic treatment of possible rivals (notably Lotte Lehmann in Vienna). Strauss and Hofmannsthal engaged her to sing *Ariadne* but failed to obtain her services in Dresden for an opera for which she would have been eminently qualified—*Die ägyptische Helena*—but she finally sang it in Vienna. Strauss paid her the huge compliment of dedicating one of his *Four Last Songs* to her, too late for her to be able to sing it.

Eyewitnesses have described Jeritza's zany sense of humor, usually unexpected and therefore breathtaking when it happened on stage. Her glorious presence as Elisabeth on her first entrance in *Tannhäuser*, as Turandot going up and down the staircase, and as Tosca singing "Vissi d'arte" lying flat on the stage were three show-stoppers. As Minnie, she rode a horse and gamboled among the cowboys; as Carmen she smoked a cigarette and danced on a table. She was also entirely at home in operetta.

Jeritza's voice on gramophone records seems impaired by the uninteresting, sterile atmosphere of recording studios which minimized her gift for effective dramatic characterization. One exception is Ariadne's monologue, beautifully sung in its coolness and assurance, giving some idea of how it must have sounded in performance. All the same, as time went on, an initial fault in training produced increasingly obvious scooping in phrases, but even the critical reviewer of her Met *Tosca* had to admit that she "scooped to conquer." This *Tosca* was the second of her appearances at the Metropolitan Opera, the first having been Marietta in Korngold's *Die tote Stadt*, also receiving its first appearance in that house.

She remained at the Metropolitan Opera until 1932, finally taking up American residence. Her offstage entourage was always large, and even at the age of ninety, Jeritza continued to hold court at her estate in New Jersey. It was not until after her death that among her effects was found the manuscript of the very last song by Richard Strauss called "Malven," which had never been heard. The glamour and mystery surrounding one of the last great prima donnas accompanied her to the grave.—ALAN JEFFERSON

Jerusalem, Siegfried

Tenor. Born 17 April 1940, in Oberhausen. Studied in Essen, and in 1961 began his career as a bassoonist; member of Stuttgart Radio Orchestra, 1972-77; studied singing in Stuttgart with Hertha Kalcher; sang in Stuttgart, Aachen and Hamburg; Bayreuth debut as Froh, 1977; Metropolitan Opera debut as Lohengrin, 1980; London Coliseum debut as Parsifal, 1986; Covent Garden debut as Erik, 1986.

During the 1970s and 1980s Siegfried Jerusalem established a well earned reputation as a fine heroic tenor, especially effective in the operas of Richard Wagner. Among his best Wagner roles are those of Siegmund in *Die Walküre*, Siegfried and Parsifal. Jerusalem has not traveled as much as many leading opera singers: he has given most of his performances in the German-speaking parts of Europe, winning equal applause in the major opera houses of Germany (including Bayreuth), Austria (including Salzburg), and Switzerland.

Parsifal was one of the first Wagner roles that Jerusalem mastered. He won applause for his portrayal of Parsifal in Vienna in 1979; in the same year he brought the role to Salzburg, where critics applauded both his good looks and his beautiful, expressive voice. When Jerusalem performed Siegmund in Zurich in 1988 his singing was loudly applauded, but his acting did not receive unanimous approval; one critic described him as "a bit clod-footed." He triumphed as the young Siegfried at Bayreuth a few months later, winning praise for his fine musicianship and beautiful tone.

One can hear the strengths of Jerusalem's voice in his portrayal of Siegmund in *Die Walküre*, recorded under Marek Janowski in 1981. Jerusalem's Siegmund has a clear, manly voice, firm and strong. A slight vibrato gives the voice richness without affecting its accuracy of pitch. He pronounces the words distinctly, thereby enhancing the vividness of his characterization. His voice can be sweetly lyrical, but he can also express anger and violence. For example, in the soliloquy beginning "Ein Schwert verhiess mir der Vater," Jerusalem sings the words "ein Weib" (a woman) with a warmth and gentleness that communicate his feelings with great immediacy. He sings out "Wälse! Wälse!" with resounding power, as his voice conveys his excitement and anticipation. Jerusalem brings a distinctly darker tone to his voice as he sings the words "nächtiges Dunkel" (darkness of night).

Jerusalem has not limited his performances to Wagner's operas. His portrayal of Florestano in Paer's *Leonora* (recorded under Peter Maag in 1979), shows another side of Jerusalem's artistic personality. This is a fine, virile performance, proving that Jerusalem has a real talent and flair for Italian opera, and making a good case for the dramatic potential of Paer's rarely performed opera. Alone in the dungeon at the beginning of Act II, Jerusalem's Florestano sings the recitative "Ciel! che profonda oscurità tirrana" with intense feeling. In the big aria "Dolce oggetto del mio amore," we can admire Jerusalem's beautiful, rich tone. Lyrical lines, when not too high, he sings with grace and warmth. Yet the performance has weaknesses. Jerusalem does not seem to be completely in control of his high notes, and he cannot master the coloratura near the end of the aria, which seems to demand a light, Rossini-type tenor rather than a *Heldentenor*. But the performance is such as to make us wish that he devoted more of his artistic energy to Italian opera.—JOHN A. RICE

Johnson, Edward

Tenor. Born 22 August 1878, in Guelph, Ontario. Died 20 April 1959, in Guelph, Ontario. Married Viscountess Beatrice d'Arneiro, 1909. Attended University of Toronto, then studied singing with Mme von Feilitsch; sang on Broadway in Oscar Straus's Walzertraum, *1908; studied in Florence with Vincenzo Lombardi, 1909; opera debut under the name Edoardo Di Giovanni as Andrea Chénier at the Teatro Verdi, Padua, 1912; Teatro all Scala debut as Parsifal, 1914; sang in Chicago, 1919-22; Metropolitan Opera debut as Avito in* Amore di tre re, *1922; last Metropolitan Opera performance, 1935; served as general manager of the Metropolitan Opera until 1950.*

In the realm of opera, the name of Edward Johnson is most immediately associated with his role as general manager of the Metropolitan Opera, a position which he held from 1935 until his retirement in 1950. This administrative post was, however, only the final consummation of a long career in opera as a dramatic tenor in Italy, Chicago, and finally in New York at the Metropolitan Opera itself.

Using the stage name Edoardo Di Giovanni (a direct Italian translation of his real name), Johnson made his operatic debut at Padua in 1912, in a production of Giordano's *Andrea Chénier*. Several important Italian appearances followed, including his debut at the Teatro alla Scala in 1914, for which he sang the title role in Wagner's *Parsifal* in the first Italian production of the opera. For five seasons he was principal tenor of Teatro alla Scala, and toured with the company to Latin America and Spain. During this time he created several leading tenor roles and in 1919 he sang in the premieres of two Puccini operas (*Gianni Schicchi* and *Il tabarro*) at the request of the composer. The same year, he first sang Pelléas in the Rome production of

Debussy's *Pelléas et Mélisande,* a role with which he was to be particularly associated in his later career.

Throughout this Italian period, critical reaction to Johnson's singing was consistently laudatory. In particular, he was acclaimed for the intensity of his dramatic interpretations of operatic roles and for the intelligence and skill with which he used his voice. Recordings from this period illustrate his fine sense of control. Although Johnson was billed as a dramatic tenor, his voice was not particularly heavy; his ease in the upper registers was often noted, especially in his early years.

After the death of his wife in 1919, Johnson—resuming the anglicized spelling of his name—returned to the United States. He had earlier established a strong reputation in North America as a singer of oratorio, both in his native Ontario and later in New York where he had also starred in operetta (his performance in Oscar Straus's *Walzertraum* in 1908 had been highly acclaimed). On his return, however, he sang only opera, first with the Chicago Opera for three years, then with the Metropolitan Opera, where he made his debut in 1922 as Avito in Montemezzi's *L'amore di tre re.* Richard Aldrich, reviewing the performance in the *New York Times* (17 November 1922), commented both on the "warm tenor quality" of Johnson's singing and on his intelligence and musical understanding, observing that "here is a tenor who is something more than a voice, who is an artistic personality." This natural artistic presence continued to serve Johnson well for the next twelve seasons, during which time he was one of the most popular tenors at the Met. While he sang a large number of contrasting roles, he was most celebrated for his portrayal of Pelléas, Roméo (Gounod's *Roméo et Juliette*), Sadko (Rimsky-Korsakov's *Sadko*), and especially for the title role that he created in the Deems Taylor opera, *Peter Ibbetson* (1931). Many of his greatest successes were in performances with the Spanish soprano, Lucrezia Bori.

Johnson's tenure as general manager of the Met was clouded by several problems, largely resulting from the economic pressures of the late 1930s and the war years. The most significant change that he oversaw was the gradual shift from acclaimed European stars to native American talent. Under his leadership, the Met became more genuinely a North American company.

Even upon retirement in 1950, Johnson continued to be involved with music. He returned to Canada, where he helped to establish the Edward Johnson Music Foundation, which sponsors the annual Guelph Spring Festival in Ontario. In 1962, the University of Toronto honoured his memory by the posthumous dedication of its new music building and library, the Edward Johnson Building.—JOAN BACKUS

La jolie fille de Perth [The Fair Maid of Perth]

Composer: *Georges Bizet.*

Librettists: *Jules-Henry Vernoy de Saint-Georges and Jules Adenis (after Walter Scott).*

First Performance: *Paris, Théâtre-Lyrique, 26 December 1867.*

Roles: *Catherine (soprano); Mab (soprano); Henry Smith (tenor); Le Duc de Rothsay (baritone or tenor); Ralph (bass or baritone); Simon Glover (bass); Le Majordome, Guyot (bass).*

Despite a promising start, *La jolie fille de Perth* has never attained a secure place in the repertory, unlike Bizet's previous opera *Les pêcheurs de perles* (1863). It will probably remain a work that is revived only occasionally, even though the score has improved upon many of the weaknesses of its predecessor. It has a strong second act and a substantial number of fine pieces in the first and third acts; however, its overall impact onstage is greatly weakened by a hackneyed final act and a libretto that is probably the worst Bizet ever set. Shortly after receiving his text, even Bizet had to admit to a friend, "I am not using the words to compose; I wouldn't find a note!"

In July 1866 Bizet signed a contract with Carvalho, director of the Théâtre-Lyrique, and despite many obligations to various publishers, he finished and delivered his score by 29 December. Budget and casting problems delayed the production. Finally, after the successful dress rehearsal in September 1867, the premiere was unexpectedly postponed until later in the season when a more sophisticated public would have returned to the city. Following the opening night in December, most critics were fairly positive, but both Ernest Reyer (*Le journal des débats*) and Johannès Weber (*Le temps*) pointed out the eclectic style and concessions made for the public and the prima donna. To the latter Bizet confessed: "All my concessions failed! . . . I am delighted with that! The school of oom-pahs, trills and falsehood is dead, quite dead. Let us bury it without tears, without regrets, without emotion and . . . onward!" By February 1868, however, when Bizet saw the possibility of a success evaporating and the run of eighteen performances coming to a close, he described himself to his friend Galabert as sick, discouraged, and worn down by work.

Only the title and some of the characters' names come from the Sir Walter Scott novel, but the convoluted plot depends much more on clichés that had succeeded in other libretti. As arbitrarily strung together here, they create stereotypical characters devoid of believable motivation. The first act involves the protagonists in jealousy and argument. Scarcely have the coquettish Catherine and Henry Smith, an armorer, pledged their love but the lecherous Duke of Rothsay arrives to invite Catherine to that evening's masked carnival celebration. Smith becomes jealous of what he perceives as Catherine's flirtation and starts to attack the duke. Mab, the gypsy queen, prevents disaster, and it is then Catherine's turn to be jealous, for she incorrectly assumes that Mab is Smith's mistress. Act II is driven by disguise and further misunderstanding. Smith serenades his betrothed in the hope that she has forgiven him, but leaves, discouraged, for a nearby tavern when she does not reply. Mab, a former conquest of the duke's, disguises herself as Catherine. Despite his sherry-induced stupor, lovesick Ralph, the apprentice of Simon Glover, notices "Catherine" stepping into the duke's litter and rouses himself to warn Smith. However, before Ralph himself can stumble offstage, the real Catherine appears at her window singing part of Smith's serenade. The third act features an ironic seduction scene in which Mab in disguise hears the duke use some of the same lines to woo "Catherine" that he had earlier used with her. It closes with a public confrontation between the furious Smith and a bewildered Catherine. For the final act, the librettists contrive to include both a mad scene and a reconciliation. Ralph tries to convince Smith of Catherine's innocence, but Smith challenges him to a duel. In the following duet Smith explains to Catherine that his death will restore her honor. She snaps from the stress and may thus sing a fashionably ornate ballade. It is Mab who dreams up the device to restore her reason. Once again the gypsy queen dresses up as Catherine, and once again Smith sings his serenade. Catherine's sanity miraculously returns as she protests that he is singing to the wrong person. The duke never appears in this act, but Mab reports that it is he who has stopped the duel. To conclude, all praise love and Saint Valentine.

OPERA

Like the plot itself, much of the score comes close to the *opéra comique* style of the 1850s and 60s, although Catherine's music, largely unsuccessful, regularly incorporates Italianate coloratura. Bizet's gift for orchestration is immediately demonstrated in a lyrically elegant prelude. Act I also contains a strong series of ensembles, beginning with a tender duo for the young lovers that shows some similarities to the Micaela-Don José duet in *Carmen*. It is followed by a dramatically effective trio in which Smith's rising anger, underlined by the banging of his anvil, alternates with the suave, wooing tune of the duke (here presented in three of the half dozen uses scattered through the opera and imaginatively scored). The succeeding quartet is effective, but reminiscent of Auber. In this score Bizet has not only created some dramatically effective numbers but has also found his own voice at times. A striking example appears in act III, where a small instrumental group plus harp plays a minuet backstage while the duke makes his practiced advances on the false Catherine. (Since *La jolie fille* was largely forgotten by 1880, Guiraud felt free to borrow the charming minuet for the second *Arlésienne* suite.)

More often than elsewhere in *La jolie fille* Bizet's distinctive sound appears in act II. The main theme for the opening chorus features his characteristic woodwinds—dark bassoons that are then joined by higher pitched winds; then the men of the watch sing a square march tune with full orchestra until they scatter in fear at the slightest noise. Though the harmonies are not as piquant as the "Danse bohème" in *Carmen,* a delightful gypsy dance features a great crescendo (starting from *ppp* for flute and harp alone) and acceleration that eventually doubles the pulse. The two finest solos of the opera follow one another near the end of this act. The opening of Smith's serenade is Italianate and memorable, borrowed in part from Bizet's earlier *Don Procopio*. Still more original is Ralph's drunken air, where accents on weak beats create a lurching rhythm and dark bassoons, brass, and low strings underline his maudlin and tragic self-pity.

The score contains fine pieces of every type. The climactic finale of act III even begins to develop a true pathetic and dramatic power that forecasts the equivalent scene in *Carmen*. Yet both score and libretto fall flat in act IV, where only the Saint Valentine's chorus has a fresh, Gounod-like charm. If it did not limp to a close, *La jolie fille de Perth* would have to be ranked one of the finest works of its decade.—LESLEY A. WRIGHT

Jones, Gwyneth

Soprano. Born 7 November 1936, in Pontnewyndd, Wales. Married Till Haberfeld (one daughter). Studied as mezzo-soprano at Royal College of Music with Ruth Parker; at Accademia Chigiana, Siena; in Zurich; and with Maria Carpi in Geneva; debut as Gluck's Orfeo, Zurich, 1962; at Covent Garden since 1963; moved to soprano roles; Vienna debut as Fidelio, 1966; Bayreuth debut, 1966; Metropolitan Opera debut as Sieglinde, 1972.

As with the soprano Leonie Rysanek and a few others, Gwyneth Jones may be characterized as an erratic singer who, when at her best, provides the audience with thrilling vocalism and a powerful theatrical experience. Jones went through a severe vocal crisis in the early 1970s, a period when, unfortunately, she was involved in many recordings of complete operas. That many of these recordings produced results that are unacceptable as pure singing cannot be denied. Her Ortrud under Kubelik, which Charles Osborne termed "a pain in the ears," was perhaps the nadir. There are, however, fine performances from this period, such as a strongly characterized Medea even against the touchstone of Maria Callas, a gorgeously sung "D'amor sull'ali rosee," and a touching portrayal of Desdemona under the languorous baton of Barbirolli. Much less successful are an Octavian under Bernstein with Christa Ludwig as the Marschallin (a role that Jones later successfully undertook), a Salome, partly live from Hamburg under Böhm, and a Kundry from Bayreuth with Boulez. This is a "theatrical" performance in every sense of the word, full of groans, shrieks, and maniacal laughter.

The voice is naturally beautiful, as shown by some of her fine Verdi singing and by a 1969 *Fidelio* with Böhm, although in this role she lacks total control of her large instrument. Yet it is a very feminine voice, which goes a long way in projecting the dramatic and emotional situation in Beethoven's opera. Also with Böhm there is a Senta with Thomas Stewart as the Dutchman. Here she is once again the embodiment of femininity; she engages in lovely soft singing but in the grand, emotional moments it is a bumpy ride.

Jones began her studies as a mezzo-soprano, but Nello Santi in Zurich convinced her to essay the soprano roles. She developed into a true lirico-spinto, taking on Verdi roles at Covent Garden. Her first Wagnerian role in London, Sieglinde in 1965, provoked comparison with Lotte Lehmann and from 1966 she was a regular singer at Vienna and at Bayreuth. The assumption of a taxing schedule, along with intense emotional onstage involvement, took a heavy toll on the production of the voice, causing it, for example, to develop a beat. After her initial Sieglinde at Covent Garden she began to sing regularly at Bayreuth, not only Sieglinde but Eva, Kundry, both

Gwyneth Jones in *Die Walküre,* Bayreuth, 1976

Venus and Elisabeth in *Tannhäuser,* and eventually (in 1976) Brünnhilde. She performed all three Wagner Brünnhildes at Bayreuth in the internationally-televised *Ring* cycle in Patrice Chéreau's controversial production conducted by Boulez.

Although the vocal crisis has been largely surmounted, a Jones night in the theater is never predictable, ranging from squally, unpleasant singing to thrilling theater. Despite any vocal problems, she continued to be in constant demand and has now been in the international spotlight for a quarter of a century and has amassed an extremely diverse repertoire. Recent undertakings have included Poulenc's *La voix humaine* for the Théâtre du Chatelet and a series of Turandots in various venues. For counsel in performing this role she went to Dame Eva Turner, an illustrious Turandot of the past. There is no doubt that a Turandot must have power and volume; the secret to those things seemed to be what Jones was most interested in garnering from Turner. As Jones explains: "It was like getting it from the horse's mouth, and she gave me a wonderful *attacca,* having the voice in front of the mask, the necessary cutting edge, so it comes out like knives." One has to speculate that perhaps an interest in volume has not helped any vocal problems Jones had developed; that she purposely chose volume over steadiness.

Yet, as with Rysanek, she is a mesmerizing, supreme singing-actress and one for whom the opera world should be most grateful. She explains that the emotion in performing a role "comes from the inside and from the face and the eyes, which are the most important thing about your interpretation. With your eyes you can transmit thoughts to the public." From the evidence of her stage performances and the several opera films she has participated in—*The Ring, Tannhäuser, Der Rosenkavalier*—Jones' contribution to opera over a quarter of a century has been a very special one, greatly contributing to the exultation and magic of the genre.—STEPHEN A. WILLIER

Jurinac, Sena

Soprano. Born Srebrenka Jurinac, 24 October, 1921, in Travnik, Yugoslavia. Married the baritone Sesto Bruscantini, 1953 (divorced 1957); married Josef Lederle, 1965. Studied with Milka Kostrenčić in Zagreb; debut as Mimì, Zagreb, 1942; Vienna Staatsoper debut as Cherubino, 1945; Salzburg debut as Dorabella, 1947; Teatro alla Scala debut as Cherubino, 1948; at Glyndebourne as Dorabella, 1949; in Chicago as Desdemona, 1963.

Sena Jurinac first came to international prominence as one of several fine Mozart sopranos championed by Herbert von Karajan. Amid this very select and excellent company—including Elisabeth Schwarzkopf, Irmgard Seefried, Lisa Della Casa and Hilde Gueden—Jurinac's distinction is obvious, for she is also successful and idiomatic in the heavier Italian repertoire of Verdi and Puccini. It is surprisingly rare for a soprano to demonstrate equal skills in these very different arenas, and Jurinac achieves special status through exceptional resources. Hers was certainly one of the most beautiful voices of her time, combining a creamy tonal richness and perfect legato line that is intrinsic to all great Mozart voices with a power and size that sets her quite apart. The color too is unusual, darker than that of her silvery-toned colleagues, and yet shaded with great delicacy and femininity, so that as Butterfly, for example, she combined the necessary stamina and force with a marvelously girlish frailty that was unique and memorable.

Jurinac was also a naturally gifted actress with an affinity for an audience, the kind of charisma with which it seems a stage personality must be born. Seefried had it too, and shared with Jurinac a similar sense of fragility and charm. But where Seefried's persona seemed rooted in a childlike sense of joy, Jurinac was, by contrast, immediately identified with pathos and tragedy. Though she sang a number of comic roles with considerable success—Fiordiligi in *Così fan tutte* is one good example among many—one always sensed the underlying sadness of the character. In parts which were themselves of a more serious and pensive nature—Butterfly and Tosca or Donna Anna and Ilia in *Idomeneo*—Jurinac could create a heartbreaking sense of theater; yet this vulnerability was never achieved at the expense of a shining, well-nourished tone.

There are many recorded examples of Jurinac in Mozart which support her fine reputation. She appears as Ilia in highlights of *Idomeneo* under Fritz Busch as well as in a complete performance with John Pritchard, and surely the role has never been better sung or more elegantly and movingly interpreted. As Fiordiligi the competition is stiffer (including her colleagues Schwarzkopf and Della Casa), here the voice per se is wonderfully rich, but with its size and thrust comes a certain awkwardness; she is not entirely up to the florid passages of the role. Better are her Donna Anna and Elvira and her Countess in *Le nozze di Figaro,* all of which display her gracious sense of style and show off the voice at its lustrous best.

Like many other fine Mozarteans, Jurinac was also highly regarded in the operas of Richard Strauss. She made something of a specialty of the roles of Octavian in *Der Rosenkavalier* and the Composer in *Ariadne auf Naxos,* as did Seefried. Comparing the two singers, particularly in the latter role, does not entirely flatter Jurinac, who is less impassioned and imaginative than her colleague, but on her own terms she is noble and involving. The generous, radiant tone is a constant source of pleasure. On records she is probably best heard in Strauss's *Vier letzte Lieder,* where the sultry tone makes us more than usually aware of the grandeur and scope of these songs, and her superbly steady line is especially welcome.

Regrettably, Jurinac committed few of her Italian roles to disc, perhaps because quite a few formidable Italianate sopranos—including Callas and Tebaldi—were also kept busy in the recording studios. Still, the loss is ours, as a broadcast performance of *Don Carlos* under Herbert von Karajan amply illustrates. Here Jurinac is the Elisabetta of one's dreams; no soprano before or since has launched the last act scena "Tu che le vanità" with such perfectly poised attack and incandescent tone. We may lament that there are not more such unforgettable souvenirs, but we may also rejoice in what we have—a significant legacy of a unique and thrilling artist.
—DAVID ANTHONY FOX

k OPERA

Katia Kabanová

Composer: *Leoš Janáček.*

Librettist: *Leoš Janáček (after A.N. Ostrovsky, "The Thunderstorm," translated by Vincenc Červinka).*

First Performance: *Brno, National Theater, 23 November 1921.*

Roles: *Katia (soprano); Kabanicha (contralto); Boris (tenor); Dikoj (bass); Varvara (soprano); Váňa Kudrjáš (tenor); Tichon (tenor); Glasha (mezzo-soprano); Feklusha (mezzo-soprano); Kudrjáš (baritone); chorus (SATB).*

After *Jenůfa,* the best-known, most frequently performed, and most dramatically successful of Leoš Janáček's nine operas, *Katia Kabanová* is only one of four major works the composer wrote in response to Russian literature. These include the 1918 orchestral rhapsody *Taras Bulba* (after Gogol), the 1923 String Quartet No. 1, "Kreutzer Sonata" (after Tolstoy) and two operas: *Katia Kabanová,* from a play by Alexander Ostrovsky, and *From the House of the Dead,* based on Fyodor Dostoevsky's prison memoirs, *The House of the Dead.* Like most Czechs of his generation, Janáček looked to Russia and Russian culture as positive nationalistic alternatives to the non-Slavic Austrian civilization that had oppressed Bohemia for centuries. Even more important, the composer found in Russian literature the same passionate concern for the large spiritual questions that so deeply disturbed him, especially the relationship between sin and virtue, guilt and innocence, sexuality and fidelity.

Janáček himself wrote the libretto for *Katia,* using Vincenc Červinka's Czech translation of Ostrovsky's powerful 1859 play, "The Thunderstorm." The prolific author of 50 plays, Ostrovsky (1823-86) almost single-handedly created a modern professional theater in Russia. The gloomy and powerful "Thunderstorm," describing the hopeless struggle between enlightenment and ignorance in a remote, backward, and repressive merchant town on the Volga in the 1850s—on the eve of the emancipation of the serfs—has achieved the greatest popular success both in Russia and elsewhere.

Katia Kabanová contains three acts, each with two scenes. In act I, scene i, we meet all the main characters as they gather in a park on the steep Volga riverbank: Dikoj, a rich and brutal merchant; his nephew Boris; the domineering and shrewish merchant's widow Kabanicha; her timid son Tichon; his wife, the naively pious and spiritually vulnerable Katia; her friend Varvara; and Varvara's boyfriend Váňa Kudrjáš. Dikoj and Kabanicha abuse the others for their supposed disrespect. In the following scene, Katia shares her ecstatic visions with Varvara before Kabanicha bullies Tichon, about to leave on a business trip, into extracting a pledge of fidelity from his humiliated wife. In act II, Varvara persuades Katia to overcome her hesitation and meet secretly in the garden with Boris, with whom she has become infatuated. The two couples enjoy a romantic nocturnal interlude. In act III, Tichon returns as a thunderstorm breaks over the town, and the overwrought Katia makes an unprovoked hysterical public confession of her adultery. The opera's final scene brings Katia and Boris together for a final reunion, followed by her farewell lament. Katia then throws herself in the Volga, unable to live with her guilt and shame.

Katia's "natural" personality, expressed through her love for birds and flowers and, ultimately, by her merging, rather like a doomed water sprite, with the eternal stream of the Volga, exercised a strong appeal over the pantheistic Janáček. (In *Jenůfa*, too, nature is an important agent: the ice conceals, and then the spring thaw reveals, the body of Jenůfa's illegitimate baby.) In a letter to Kamila Stoesslová, the composer described the genesis of *Katia Kabanová.* "It was in the sunshine of summer. The sun-warmed slope of the hill where the flowers wilted. That was when the first thoughts about poor Katia Kabanová and her great love came to my mind. She calls to the flowers, she calls to the birds—flowers to bow down to her, birds to sing for her the last song of love. My Katia grows in you, in Kamila! This will be the most gentle and tender of my works." In 1928, the year he died, Janáček formally dedicated the opera to Kamila, with whom he seems to have had nothing more than a platonic relationship.

Like Musorgsky—whom he greatly admired—and Prokofiev, Janáček welcomed the challenge of prose texts, believing they could be dramatized more easily and effectively. Also like them, he attempted to find a kind of musical "intonation" or "phrase" for each character or idea. Usually, this is a very short motif—no more than three or four measures—that goes through endless harmonic, metrical, and dynamic changes, in an extended theme-and-variations process. Two examples from *Katia* are the ominous "fate" theme, heavy with timpani, that sounds first in the overture's fifth measure; and the lighter, "trivial" Russian theme associated primarily with Katia's cowardly husband Tichon. Later, in the magnificent garden scene (act II, scene ii), Janáček makes superb use of Russian-style folk melodies to characterize Varvara and Kudrjáš, the carefree, if morally inferior, counterparts to Katia and Boris. The opera succeeds brilliantly at conveying in musical terms the growing atmosphere of doom and tragedy that finally suffocates the ethereal title character.

Two musical worlds coexist in *Katia Kabanová:* Katia's, and that of the "kingdom of darkness." Katia's vocal line is frequently accompanied by flute or clarinet, producing a light, open, airy texture in contrast to the heavier, lower music associated with Dikoj and Kabanicha. First stated in the overture, her simple, soaring lyrical theme appears in small stuttering bits until its complete unfolding at Katia's first appearance. Boris, on the other hand, sings mundane, unimaginative phrases, including his act I solo, which demonstrate his lack of complexity and romantic depth. Because they have no souls to express, Kabanicha and Dikoj do not receive defined themes; Dikoj's blustering line comes the closest to actual speech, since his prosaic and

destructive personality lacks spirituality and love.

From start to finish, both onstage and off, Katia, fragile and fascinating, dominates the action. One of the most rewarding and completely realized soprano roles created in the twentieth century, she recalls (in her hopeless love, passionate nature, and riverbank suicide) the heroine of Janáček's favorite Tchaikovsky opera, *The Queen of Spades*. Another operatic suicide, the hara-kiri of Puccini's Madama Butterfly, who is incapable, like Katia, of reconciling her ecstatic visions and romantic delusions with oppressive social realities, also influenced Janáček here. A wise and universal empathy propels *Katia Kabanová* on its dark and doomed course, dispensing pain and compassion, celebrating Katia's spiritual beauty even as it mourns her inevitable destruction at the hands of savage small-town Philistines.—HARLOW ROBINSON

Khovanshchina [The Khovansky Plot]

Composer: *Modest Musorgsky [completed and orchestrated by Rimsky-Korsakov; later re-worked by Ravel, Stravinsky, and Shostakovich].*

Librettist: *Modest Musorgsky.*

First Performance: *St Petersburg, 21 February 1886.*

Roles: *Ivan Khovansky (bass); Marfa (contralto); Andrei Khovansky (tenor); Vassily Golitsyn (tenor); Dosifei (bass); Shaklovity (baritone); Emma (soprano); Scrivener (tenor); Susanna (soprano); Varsonofiev (baritone); Kuzka (tenor); Streshniev (tenor); Three Streltsy (basses, tenor); chorus (SSAATTBB).*

Already in 1872, while he was still completing *Boris Godunov,* Musorgsky began gathering materials for his historical opera on the political problems associated with the reign of Peter the Great. Philosophically, this period (the 1680s) is dominated by the friction between Peter's modernist orientation and the conservative beliefs of "old" Russia. It was just this turbulence that so fascinated Musorgsky and his friend Vladimir Stasov, whom Musorgsky credited with introducing the idea of this opera to him. He worked on the music for *Khovanshchina* from 1873 until his death, leaving a fairly complete piano-vocal score but with most of the orchestration still to be done. Rimsky-Korsakov, Ravel, and Stravinsky all worked at completing this opera, but it is in the 1959 Shostakovich scoring that the work is currently best known.

The opera begins with a strikingly visual orchestral prelude, "Dawn on the Moscow River," then moves to St Basil's Square, on the morning after a bloody raid by a quasi-police force called the Streltsy, led by Ivan Khovansky. He and his son Andrei would like to depose Peter, perhaps using an alliance of the Streltsy and the Old Believers, a religious sect, to achieve this end. Shaklovity, a boyar prince, informs the tsar of the impending treachery, while the leader of the Old Believers, Dosifei, warns of the troubles that undoubtedly lie in the future for Russia's people. This first act forms the basis against which subsequent scenes may be understood in relation to the opera's central conflicts.

Other characters who give shape to these conflicts are Marfa, an Old Believer, a fortune teller, and also Andrei Khovansky's former lover; and Golitsyn, a prince trying to bring the various elements of society together to achieve Peter's modernization. As the opera concludes, the Streltsy have been threatened with execution, and the Old Believers, also facing certain persecution and death, gather themselves, Marfa and Andrei included, into their hermitage for the ritualistic cleansing of self-immolation.

k

OPERA

411

The interwoven political, religious, and social conflicts that lie at the heart of *Khovanshchina,* while certainly suggestive of grand opera, gave Musorgsky great difficulties in plot organization. The resultant libretto is more like a sequence of excerpts from a larger story, as it were, than a logical unfolding of a compelling drama. While Marfa, who embodies many of the opera's conflicts, is perhaps the most interesting character, it is really the Russian people who are central in this opera. Elements of action and character development play a distinctly secondary role.

As a giant canvas depicting the Russian psyche during this important historical period, the work is a significant accomplishment. As an opera, it is most certainly flawed, in part because of Musorgsky's problems with the libretto, in part because he was unable to complete the work. It nonetheless contains moments of great musical portraiture, including the prelude, Shaklovity's prayer for his country in act III, and the final chorus of Old Believers. While *Boris Godunov* may be the greater work of art, *Khovanshchina* makes a most important contribution to our fuller understanding of Musorgsky's aesthetic and cultural identity.—ROY J. GUENTHER

King, James

Tenor. Born 22 May 1925, in Dodge City, Kansas. Studied at University of Kansas City as a baritone; trained as a tenor with Singher in New York; also studied with Max Lorenz; European debut as Cavaradossi at Teatro della Pergola, Florence, 1961; joined Deutsche Oper, Berlin, 1962; appeared as Achilles in Iphigénie en Aulide *at Salzburg, 1962; Bacchus in* Ariadne auf Naxos, *Vienna, 1963; appeared at Bayreuth as Siegmund, 1965; London, 1966; debut at Metropolitan opera as Florestan, 1966; has taught at Indiana University from 1984.*

In these post-Melchior decades in which opera has lacked true heldentenors, opera audiences have had to make do with lyric tenors who have pushed themselves to the limit in attempting to cope with dramatic roles. There has been, however, a small number of singers who have been able to fill the gap, despite vocal endowments smaller than the ideal. James King is one of these: possessor of a dependable, potentially exciting voice, with sufficient stamina and power to sustain the longer, more dramatic roles without collapse. In hindsight, given the current state of dramatic tenor singing, it appears that the quality of his singing may have been underestimated over the course of his long career.

King's proficiency in the Wagnerian roles derives in part from his possession of a baritonal quality in his lower notes, a characteristic found in most successful—that is, long-lived— Wagnerian tenors; like many such tenors, King began singing as a baritone before the start of his professional career. He moved on to tenor roles when he was thirty-one; however, he was advised to restrict himself to high Italian roles for as long as possible before moving on to the heavier dramatic parts.

As his career progressed, King moved to the heroic repertoire from lyric and spinto Italian roles. He has made a specialty of the taxing, usually thankless tenor roles of the Richard Strauss operas, such as Bacchus in *Ariadne auf Naxos,* Apollo in *Daphne,* the Emperor in *Die Frau ohne Schatten,* and Aegisth in *Elektra,* and the lighter Wagnerian repertoire, most notably Walther in *Die Meistersinger von Nürnberg,* Parsifal, and Lohengrin. The possessor of a voice with a distinctive, immediately recognizable timbre and, at least in his earlier years, an easy top, he lacks only an exceptionally beautiful tone.

Aside from his core repertoire of Wagner and Strauss, King has sung a limited number of Italian roles, notably Calaf in Puccini's *Turandot,* Cavaradossi in Puccini's *Tosca,* Des Grieux in Puccini's *Manon Lescaut,* Verdi's Don Carlos, and Canio in Leoncavallo's *I pagliacci.* After an early performance in Gluck's *Iphigénie en Aulide,* he has sung few French roles, including Samson in Saint-Saëns's *Samson et Dalila* and Cherubini's Anacréon.

After his debut at the Teatro della Pergola in Florence (as Cavaradossi) in 1961, King has sung in Berlin (beginning with the Emperor in *Die Frau ohne Schatten*), Salzburg, Bayreuth (first as Siegmund in *Die Walküre*), La Scala, Paris (as Calaf), and Covent Garden (as the Emperor).

In Vienna King made his debut as Bacchus in 1963. For the Vienna Festival in 1964, Strauss's centennial year, he sang Apollo, an especially high-lying role, and one that he had to learn within three months of another difficult Strauss role, the Emperor.

King has appeared at the Metropolitan Opera since 1966, beginning in the last season held at the old house, singing such roles as Bacchus, Don José in Bizet's *Carmen,* Aegisth, Florestan in Beethoven's *Fidelio,* Erik in Wagner's *Der fliegende Holländer,* the Emperor, Lohengrin, Walther, Cavaradossi, Calaf, Siegmund in Wagner's *Die Walküre,* Captain Vere in Britten's *Billy Budd,* and the Drum Major in Berg's *Wozzeck.*

In San Francisco King added Verdi's Otello to his repertoire, but this venture into the heaviest end of the operatic spectrum was not fully successful, his voice being rather too light for the role. In recent years he has sung a number of character roles, most notably Aegisth. Despite his many years of singing, his voice has remained remarkably fresh and has retained its basic quality.

King's voice has been described as burly, honest, virile, and accurate. It contains a touch of metal, useful in his chosen repertoire. It is not an ingratiating, beguiling sound, nor is it an especially heroic one, although it can take on heroic proportions at times. His high notes occasionally bely some strain. He can sing softly, not a common trait among dramatic tenors, but he is not an elegant, stylish singer. Yet, within its limits, it is a reliable, strong, sometimes thrilling voice. Interpretively, King lacks the ability to phrase with subtlety—his phrasing is somewhat wooden—and acting is not his strongest area.

King's recordings of complete operas, not including those derived from stage perform- ances, include Mozart's *Die Zauberflöte* (as one of the Armed Men, 1965, under Böhm), Siegmund (1966, under Solti), Strauss's *Salome* (as Narraboth, 1968, under Leinsdorf), *Ariadne auf Naxos* (as Bacchus, 1968, under Kempe), *Fidelio* (as Florestan, 1969, under Böhm), *Lohengrin* (1971, under Kubelik), *Samson et Dalila* (as Samson, 1973, under Patané), Berlioz's *La damnation de Faust* (as Brander, 1980, under Solti), and Schmidt's *Notre Dame* (as Phoebus, 1988, under Perick).—MICHAEL SIMS

Kipnis, Alexander

Bass. Born 13 February 1891, in Zhitomir, Ukraine. Died 14 May 1978, in Westport, Connecticut. Father of the harpsichordist Igor Kipnis. Studied conducting at Warsaw until 1912 and then served as a bandmaster in Russian army; studied voice with Ernst

Grenzebach at Klindworth-Scharwenka Conservatory, in Berlin; opera debut in Hamburg, 1915/16; at Wiesbaden, 1917-22; leading bass in Berlin Charlottenburg (later Städtische) Oper, 1919-29, and the Staatsoper, 1930-35; in Vienna to 1938; United States debut as Pogner in Die Meistersinger von Nürnberg, *Baltimore, 1923; in Chicago, 1923-32; appeared at Covent Garden, 1927, 1929, and 1933-35; appeared at Bayreuth, 1927, 1930, and 1933; Glyndebourne, 1936; Salzburg, 1937; Metropolitan Opera debut as Gurnemanz, 1940, and remained there until his retirement in 1946; taught singing in New York.*

Alexander Kipnis is a prime example of the artist-musician who had everything: the respect and admiration of audiences, critics, and his peers. His large recorded legacy contains many performances of arias and Lieder that are unsurpassed, only a few that are unremarkable, and almost no failures. This appraisal could equally describe his career, which was on the very highest plane. Although some engagements were of routine quality, there was never a failure.

Kipnis was to a large degree both a victim and a representative of his background. As a Russian Jew who matured at the beginning of World War I he had gravitated to Germany for his musical schooling and apprenticeship. Throughout his career he dabbled in Russian repertoire, but he was never considered a Russian singer in style, vocal quality, or instinct. He was, in fact, the finest German-style bass of his epoch. The smooth voice, spacious phrasing, and sheer vocal resource, however, were a marked departure from the accepted German bass school of his time, which emphasized cavernous black sound at the bottom and "barking" the upper register with disregard for pitch. Instead of black sound Kipnis produced a deep rich velvety sound, never "barked" the upper register, and was scrupulous in matters of pitch. This vocal culture enabled him to sing the big Italian roles with extraordinary smoothness.

In many ways Kipnis was a performing nomad; there was no central theater where he was a dominating force. Instead his career was marked by steady engagements of high quality and prestigious guest appearances. Other than an ongoing but sporadic association with Berlin, at least up to 1935, his closest operatic associations were a decade at the Chicago Opera (1923-1932) and seven seasons at the Metropolitan Opera (1940-1946). The American phase of his activities is important both artistically and personally. In Chicago he evolved from a utility artist to a genuine star. By the time he came to the Metropolitan he was nearing the end of his career, and he specialized in the Wagner bass parts.

In Chicago in 1925 he married the daughter of the distinguished composer-pianist Heniot Levy. This helped firm up his American ties, and he later became an American citizen.

His periodic visits to Berlin would see him featured in Wagner casts that were the best of his time; in a 1929 Furtwängler production of *Tristan und Isolde,* for example, he played King Marke in a cast that featured Leider, Onegin, Melchior and Schorr. In his wanderings as a guest artist a drop-in performance in Oslo in 1932 introduced him to the then completely unknown Kirsten Flagstad, who deeply impressed him. He immediately spread the word about her unique voice, thus helping lay the groundwork for her fateful encounter two years later with Gatti-Casazza of the Metropolitan.

His recorded legacy is mostly of the highest calibre. Mozart arias of Sarastro, Osmin, and Bartolo are virtually definitive; his Wotan Farewell noteworthy; and his Parsifal Good Friday Spell from Bayreuth under Siegfried Wagner unsurpassed to this day. His *Simon Boccanegra* aria is a lesson in classically broad phrasing and vocal control. There are hardly any of his recordings that are not definitive or at least so good as to be almost definitive. The one drawback is the lack of an overriding vocal personality such as distinguishes Chaliapin and Pinza. Kipnis is ultimately a textbook study of correct and musical rather than inspiring singing. His artistry thus reflects his career: prestigious in the extreme, but ultimately not as unique or impressive as the handful of other great bassos of the century.—CHARLES B. MINTZER

Kollo, René

Tenor. Born 20 November 1937, in Berlin. Studied with Elsa Varena, Berlin. Debut in triple bill of Oedipus Rex, Mavra, *and* Renard, *Brunswick, 1965, where he remained until 1967; at Düsseldorf, 1967-71; Bayreuth debut as Steersman in* Tristan und Isolde, *1969; Metropolitan Opera debut as Lohengrin, 1976; Covent Garden debut as Siegmund, 1976; sang both Siegfrieds in San Francisco, 1985.*

René Kollo began his career as a successful pop singer, but in 1958 he began to study voice with Elsa Verena in Berlin. In 1965 he signed a beginner's contract with the Braunschweig Opera where he made his debut in *Oedipus Rex.* Two years later he joined the German Opera on the Rhine in Düsseldorf where he sang a number of lyric tenor roles including Froh, Eisenstein, Titus, Pinkerton, and the Steuermann (*Tristan und Isolde*). It was with the latter part that he made his Bayreuth debut in 1969. Since then he has been one of the most important tenors on the Bayreuth festival rosters. His leading roles there included Erik (1970), Lohengrin (1971), Stolzing (1973), Parsifal (1975), the Young Siegfried (1976), and Tristan (1981). For such major tenor roles, René Kollo's voice was somewhat light, but he was so believable a stage figure and such an intelligent and musical singer that during the 1970s and 80s his successes in Bayreuth were overwhelming. In 1974 René Kollo sang in both the Salzburg Easter Festival (Stolzing) and the summer performances of *Die Zauberflöte* (Tamino). Covent Garden heard his Siegmund in 1976, and Max in *Der Freischütz* and Lohengrin a year later. In 1968 Kollo made his Munich debut as Lohengrin and followed that the next year with Stolzing. In 1981 Lohengrin was his introduction to the Teatro alla Scala, as it had been in 1976 at New York's Metropolitan Opera. In 1984 he sang Stolzing in the first performance at the newly renovated opera house in Zurich. Tristan was his debut role at the Paris Opéra during the 1985 season.

Side by side with his Wagnerian tenor roles, Kollo also sang a number of lyric parts including Lensky (*Eugene Onegin*), Matteo (*Arabella*), Vladimir (*Prince Igor*), Laca in *Jenufa* and the dramatic roles of Hermann in *Pique Dame* and Otello in Frankfurt (1988). In 1990 he sang Siegfried in the San Francisco *Der Ring des Nibelungen,* Stolzing in the Munich Festival's *Die Meistersinger von Nürnberg* and Tannhäuser in Hamburg.

René Kollo has continued with the family tradition of operetta and has appeared in countless television programs in that genre. His recordings for major European labels are also extensive. They include HMV-Electrola (*Die Meistersinger von Nürnberg* and *Lohengrin*), DGG (*Die Lustige Witwe, Fidelio,* and *Tristan und Isolde*), Eurodisc (*The Bartered Bride* and Siegfried in the complete *Ring*), CBS (operetta arias, Stravinsky's *Oedipus Rex*) and Decca (*The Magic Flute,* Stolzing in *Die Meistersinger von Nürnberg, Tannhäuser, Parsifal, Der fliegende Holländer, Ariadne auf Naxos,* and *Freischütz*), and RCA (*Die tote Stadt* by Korngold).—SUZANNE SUMMERVILLE

Korngold, Erich Wolfgang

Composer. Born 29 May 1897, in Brno, Czechoslovakia. Died 29 November 1957, in Hollywood. Early music education with his father, Julius Korngold, a music critic; studied with Fuchs, Zemlinsky, and Grädener in Vienna; published compositions, 1909; public success in Vienna, Leipzig, Berlin, and Munich, 1910-20; collaborated with the film director Max Reinhardt beginning in 1929; taught at the Vienna Academy of Music, 1930-34; in Hollywood arranging Mendelssohn's A Midsummer Night's Dream *for the Reinhardt film of Shakespeare's play, 1934; numerous film scores; conducted at the New York Opera Company, 1942 and 1944; American citizen, 1943; lived in the United States and Europe after 1945.*

Operas *Der Ring des Polykrates*, after Heinrich Teweles, Munich, 28 March 1916; *Violanta*, Hans Müller, Munich, 28 March 1916; *Die tote Stadt*, Paul Schott [=E.W. and J. Korngold] (after Georges Rodenbach, *Bruges la morte*), Hamburg and Cologne, 4 December 1920; *Das Wunder der Heliane*, Hans Müller (after Hans Kaltneker), Hamburg, 10 October 1927; *Die Kathrin*, E. Decsey, Stockholm, 7 October 1939; *The Silent Serenade*, E.W. Korngold and H. Reisfeld, 1946.

Gustav Mahler called Erich Korngold a genius; Richard Strauss wrote upon hearing the fourteen year-old's *Schauspiel-Ouverture* that "Such mastery fills me with awe and fear"; and Giacomo Puccini noted that "he has so much talent, he could easily give us half and still have enough left for himself." Throughout Korngold's career, Europe's most prominent conductors and musicians, including Bruno Walter, Arthur Nikisch, Artur Schnabel, Jasha Heifetz, and Maria Jeritza premiered his works. Yet despite extraordinary public success, Korngold's operas have not attained the level of interest and critical enthusiasm which sustain great masterpieces. Even with the recent resurgence of Neo-Romantic compositional idioms and the fact that critics no longer dismiss Korngold outright because of his Hollywood film scores, revivals of his most successful early works, *Violanta* and *Die tote Stadt,* have often met with lukewarm and often hostile reviews.

Korngold's defenders claim that his voice is bold, expressive and original. Brendan Carroll, Korngold's most recent biographer, writes: "He composed in a densely chromatic style, which is the logical extension of the post-Wagnerian school, beyond Richard Strauss and Franz Schreker, but not into the territory explored by the serialists. His musical language is idiosyncratic and receives its impetus from his frenetic rhythms. The combination of these elements, deployed on a large orchestra with brilliant technique, and coupled with an exceptional melodic gift, identifies his artistic uniqueness." (Carroll, 1984) Many critics view Korngold's operas as an alternative to the atonal vocal works of Schoenberg, Berg, and Webern. In reviewing Korngold's first mature and best known opera *Die tote Stadt,* Ann Lingg cites the "colorful yet lucid [orchestration], with full sonorities, telling leitmotifs, uncanny musical characterization and bold harmonies that never manage to offend the ear. Above all, Korngold was a master of melody, untouched by the Viennese School's new fad for atonality." Lingg also finds that the opera's positive outlook announces "the triumph of life over death, the fallacy of living in the past." Winthrop Sargeant concurs that "[Korngold wrote] rich, melodious music that communicated something to his listeners. . . . [*Die tote Stadt*] has been clothed by Korngold in the most ravishing score—music of the effulgent and vocally knowing sort that Strauss wrote—but . . . is quite original and extremely beautiful, and the pre-Schoenberg Viennese idiom is employed in a manner all Korngold's own."

While acknowledging the colorful nature of Korngold's scores, other critics have questioned the relationship of the music to the drama. William Ashbrook writes that in *Die tote Stadt,* "the composer, for all his cleverness, is rarely able to invoke visually credible atmosphere through his music alone. The score is crammed chockablock with 'effects', but they do not add up to much." At the 1975 revival of this same work, Patrick J. Smith commented more harshly: "[One hears] lushly orchestrated seas of velveteen with every emotion made shamelessly obvious. . . . [though] Korngold's orchestrational ear was sound enough, if not particularly inspired . . . [h]is extremely limited inventional ability . . . tells more heavily with each passing moment."

Erich Korngold, 1916

In a review of the 1975 recording, Royal Brown also found fault with Korngold's decision to rework portions of Rodenbach's original novel—the protagonist's murder of his lover—as a dream sequence: "[E]ither you work within the limits of a certain domain envisaged by an author or you turn to a different writer; by tacking a happy ending onto Rodenbach's lugubrious vision, and by applying a nicely Germanic, logical distinction between "real" life and dream to a work that assumes an ambiguity between the two, the libretto very simply emasculates the work's narrative as well as its thematic impact." Andrew Porter, dismissing the music as "tawdry—Strauss and Puccini, plus dashes of Mahler and Debussy, served in syrup," also found fault with the dramaturgy: "So it *is* a pretty tale after all; the eroticism and violence are spices, not substance."—DAVID PACUN

Kraus, Alfredo

Tenor. Born 24 November 1927, in Las Palmas, Canary Islands. Studied in Barcelona with Gali Markoff, in Valencia with Francisco Andres, and in Milan with Mercedes Llopart; debut as Duke in Rigoletto, *Cairo, 1956; European debut as Cavaradossi, 1956; Covent Garden debut as Edgardo in* Lucia di Lammermoor, *1959; Teatro alla Scala debut as Elvino in* La sonnambula, *1960; in Chicago as Nemorino in* L'elisir d'amore, *1962, and has returned regularly; Metropolitan Opera debut as the Duke,* Rigoletto *1966.*

Alfredo Kraus is an aristocrat among modern tenors, never forcing his voice or singing roles too big for him. The result is that to an amazing degree he sounds as fresh as he did twenty-five years ago. His timbre and style have little in common with most other post-war tenors such as Del Monaco, Di Stefano, Corelli, or Domingo; instead, critics are forced to make comparisons with tenors of a much earlier age—Tito Schipa and Fernando De Lucia—although not always to Kraus's advantage. Kraus himself reverts to this earlier period in naming his own models. His idol is Schipa, "an artist because of his limitations," and he also admires Aureliano Pertile.

Not only does Kraus never damage his voice by venturing outside of a somewhat circumscribed range of roles, but he also limits himself to roughly fifty performances a year. He will not perform operas like *La bohème* or *Tosca* because of the thick orchestration; rather, his great successes are Don Ottavio, Count Almaviva, Alfredo, the Duke of Mantua, Massenet's Des Grieux, and Werther. The voice itself is not of the warm, melting variety of a Di Stefano or a Gigli, but is bright, penetrating, dry, and somewhat thin. The remarkable aspect of his artistry lies in the elegant manner in which he phrases and shapes a musical line. Another facet of his artistry is the great upward range of the voice, up to a high D; in this regard he has been compared to Giacomo Lauri-Volpi, a famous high-note tenor of the past. These high notes are a great asset in works such as *La favorita* by Donizetti and Bellini's *I Puritani*. Kraus worked with Tullio Serafin, a conductor who was very knowledgeable about the human voice, on the role of Arturo in *I Puritani* and sang it untransposed for twenty years. Furthermore, Kraus's stage presence is elegant; he is a matinee idol in his native Spain and Rodolfo Celletti has written that "It is difficult to imagine Kraus portraying a character who does not wear sumptuous costumes and whose language is not noble and in a certain sense idealized, because the smooth gentleness of his singing, the elegance of his phrasing and his good stage looks make Kraus the only *grand seigneur* tenor of our time."

Kraus' vocal longevity may also be attributed in part to the fact that his career began fairly late in life; he is the antithesis of the over-achiever singer who burns himself out in a few thrilling seasons or the superstar tenors such as Domingo and Pavarotti. Kraus was in his late twenties when he came to the stage in Turin as Alfredo Germont after study with Mercedes Llopart in Milan. He sang Alfredo also in the famous 1958 "Lisbon Traviata" with Maria Callas, a performance that has for some time been available in recorded form and which shows Kraus as a perfect Alfredo, vocally and dramatically youthful, passionate and impetuous. He has recorded extensively, not only his most celebrated roles, but others as well. These include Ferrando in *Così fan tutte;* Gennaro in *Lucrezia Borgia* with Caballé and Verrett; Des Grieux to Cotrubas' Manon, Edgardo to Gruberova's Lucia di Lammermoor, and a number of recordings with Beverly Sills: the Duke of Mantua, Almaviva, and Ernesto in *Don Pasquale* among them.

Alfredo Kraus as Gennaro in *Lucrezia Borgia*, Royal Opera, London, 1980

Although he is equally renowned in the Italian and French repertoires, it is to the latter that Kraus, with his particular qualities of voice—the color, the lack of portamento, the scrupulous observance of rhythmic values—is suited. If his voice does not possess the heft or the velvet for many Italian roles, it must be borne in mind that the qualities that make for an ideal French singer are rather more rare. Thus Kraus is a connoisseur's singer, yet a *tenore di grazia* who pleases critics and public alike. At a 1975 performance of *La favorite* in Carnegie Hall, with Eve Queler, Andrew Porter reported that Kraus's "Spirto gentil" elicited "the longest mid-scene ovation I have ever heard any singer receive anywhere," and went on to say that Kraus had "no inhibitions about accepting applause," that "in this repertory he is peerless," exhibiting a "finer-drawn distinction of style than Pavarotti."—STEPHEN WILLIER

Król Roger [King Roger]

Composer: *Karol Szymanowski.*

Librettists: *Karol Szymanowski and J. Iwaszkiewicz.*

First Performance: *Warsaw, 19 June 1926.*

Roles: *King Roger (baritone); Roxana (soprano); Edrisi (tenor); The Shepherd (tenor); Archbishop (bass); Diakonissa (contralto); chorus.*

Król Roger, to a libretto by Jarosław Iwaszkiewicz (modified by the composer), is often considered to be Szymanowski's masterpiece. Ostensibly it concerns the conflict between the Christian church in medieval Sicily and a pagan creed of beauty and pleasure proclaimed by a young shepherd-prophet. Queen Roxana is seduced by the allurements of the shepherd and his faith and leaves with him and his followers. King Roger eventually follows the shepherd as a pilgrim, but in the end stands alone. This provides the framework for a Nietzschean reworking of Euripides' *Bacchae,* which Szymanowski knew in Zieliński's Russian translation, where Roger (Pentheus) emerges "strong enough for freedom," having "overcome" the enriching but dangerous Dionysian forces within himself.

The ending (in which Roger alone resists the Shepherd's influence) marked a crucial modification by Szymanowski himself of the original version of the libretto (where Roger followed the shepherd as a disciple). The change was symptomatic of a change in Szymanowski's attitude to the hedonistic private world inhabited by his earlier music. In *Król Roger* that private world is symbolized above all by the "Bacchic singing and dancing" of the second act, built as it is around two extended set numbers: Roxana's aria, in which she pleads for clemency for the shepherd, and the ritual dance of the shepherd's followers. Yet the seductions of this second act are given distance and perspective by means of a gentle stylistic counterpoint arising naturally out of specific stylizations of Byzantine, Arabic, and Hellenic elements in the opera.

It is possible in fact to view the three acts as vast static *tableaux*—Byzantine, Oriental, and Hellenic respectively—in a way which suggests oratorio as much as opera. The first act stylizes the Byzantine religious-cultural world. Its first formal unit presents the deliberate archaisms of a solemn mass, while its second is the shepherd's *apologia*. The motivic links between these two units help to clarify the symbolic meaning of the opera and of its *dramatis personae*. It is apparent already that the conflict between medieval scholasticism and the Dionysian cult of self-abandoning beauty is an externalization of opposing forces within Roger himself. Much of the opera works on this symbolic level. Edrisi, the Arabian advisor, might be viewed as a symbol of rationality, for instance, and Roxana as an embodiment of the allurements of love.

The second act is an Oriental (Arabic-Indian) tableau whose sumptuous orchestral impressionism (recalling the Ravel of *Daphnis et Chloë*) and Oriental stylizations are in sharp contrast to the archaisms of the first act. Here the attractions of Dionysus are presented without dilution in a musical language which recalls—often in close detail—the most opulent of

419

Szymanowski's middle-period works. In act III the symbolism of the opera becomes explicit. Here, in the ruins of a Greek temple, the shepherd appears to Roger as Dionysus and the King makes a sacrifice to him, no longer suppressing the Dionysian within himself. At the end, recognizing that the "dream is over . . . the beautiful illusion passed," Roger sings a hymn to the rising sun and his vocal line achieves a strength and dignity which had formerly eluded it. He stands alone, enriched and transformed by the truths of Dionysus but no slave to them, a powerful symbol of modern Nietzschean man.—JIM SAMSON

L
OPERA

The Lady Macbeth of Mtsensk District
[Ledi Makbet Mtsenskogo uezda]

Composer: *Dmitri Shostakovich.*

Librettist: *A. Preis (after Leskov).*

First Performance: *Leningrad, 22 January 1934; revised as Katerina Izmailova,* Moscow, 8 January 1963.

Roles: *Katerina Izmailova (soprano); Sergei (tenor); Boris Timofeevich Izmailov (bass); Zinovi Borisovich Izmailov (tenor); Aksinya (soprano); Village Drunk (tenor); Sonetka (contralto); Police Inspector (bass); Priest (bass); several bit parts; chorus (SAATBB).*

The finest and most significant Russian opera since Tchaikovsky's *Queen of Spades, The Lady Macbeth of Mtsensk District* (to give it its full translation) is also a link in the chain of victim-hero operas from Berg's *Wozzeck* to Britten's *Peter Grimes* and beyond (Britten heard a concert performance conducted by Albert Coates in 1936 and described it as "A most moving and exciting work of a real and inspired genius"). The target of an unsigned *Pravda* article, "Chaos instead of music" (28 January 1936), and attacked by influential Western critics for its passages of banality and emotional excess, *Lady Macbeth* languished until the early 1960s, when Shostakovich's revision, entitled *Katerina Izmailova,* sparked new interest. Rostropovich's 1979 recording of the original version was a landmark. In line with Shostakovich's increasingly high critical standing in the 1980s, *Lady Macbeth* has come to be recognized as one of the pinnacles of twentieth-century opera.

Katerina Lvovna Izmailova, wife of the merchant Zinovi Borisovich Izmailov, is childless, bored, and sexually frustrated. During her husband's absence on business she is seduced by Sergei, a recently hired worker on the estate. At the beginning of act II, Zinovi's father, Boris Timofeevich, catches Sergei emerging from Katerina's bedroom and brutally flogs him in front of her. Katerina laces Boris's supper with rat poison, and he dies in agony. For some days Katerina and Sergei continue their affair, she haunted by the ghost of Boris Timofeevich. Zinovi returns and confronts her with her infidelity; she calls Sergei from hiding, and they strangle Zinovi and

421

hide his body in a cellar. In act III a peasant in search of vodka stumbles on the body and rushes off to the police station. The police are bored and angry with Katerina for failing to invite them to her wedding with Sergei; they taunt a local teacher suspected of "nihilism." Overjoyed at the peasant's news, they hurry to the wedding feast and arrest the newlyweds. Act IV sees the couple in a chain-gang marching through Siberia. Sergei has transfered his affections to a pretty convict-girl, Sonetka. He tricks Katerina into giving him her stockings, which he promptly passes to his new girl-friend. In utter despair Katerina throws herself and Sonetka into the lake. Both drown. The convicts sing a final lament for the cruelty of their captivity.

Just as Britten was to alter the original character of Peter Grimes, so Shostakovich and his co-librettist Alexander Preis set out to justify and excuse Katerina (the precise division of their labors on the text is not known). In Leskov's original short story, Katerina is a morally reprehensible character, who, in addition to the crimes seen in the opera, suffocates her young nephew, a co-heir to her late husband's estate. Shostakovich and Preis greatly increase the oppressiveness of her environment, in particular the domineering and lecherous character of her father-in-law. Thus the relevance of Shakespeare's Lady Macbeth is decreased, and the drama develops close parallels to Ostrovsky's *The Storm,* from which Janáček took the story of *Katia Kabanová* (there is no evidence to suggest that Shostakovich knew this opera, however). The scene in the police station—an addition to the original story—is modeled on the writings of the nineteenth-century satirist Saltykov-Shchedrin.

It is impossible to separate out the three strands of Shostakovich's dramatic intentions. These are his own inner drives, reinforced by his stormy courtship with Nina Varzar whom he married in May 1932; his awareness of and commentary on social-political developments at a time of mass collectivization, show trials, and State terrorism; and his attempt to take official artistic doctrines into account (these were not properly formalized until 1934 and even then remained vaguely defined). At the present time, however, there is a strong tendency in Western productions and commentaries to emphasize the element of denunciation of the Stalin regime. In any case, the unusual vacillation of dramatic tone from introspection to brutality, burlesque comedy to hard-hitting tragedy, partly reflected in Shostakovich's own references to the genre of "tragedy-satire," has come to be regarded as a source of strength rather than an artistic miscalculation.

The musical language of *Lady Macbeth* reflects the full range of the young Shostakovich's eclectic enthusiasms—from the modal harmonic style of Musorgsky, through the lyricism of Mahler and the stylizations of Stravinsky, to the atonal-modernist trends of the 1920s as exemplified by Berg's *Wozzeck* and Krenek's *Der Sprung über den Schatten*. Katerina's boredom, Zinovi's ineffectuality, and the three scenes of obsessive brutality, are all memorably expressed in musical terms. In the interlude following the poisoning of Boris, Shostakovich rises to the dramatic challenge with the first of his great tragedy-absorbing passacaglias (again suggesting the influence of Berg).

In 1956, with the Khrushchev "Thaw" well under way, Shostakovich began revising the opera, which eventually appeared six years later as *Katerina Izmailova*. Here the excesses of the original are much toned down, vocal tessitura is less extreme, and there are newly composed, less "radical" entr'actes between scenes i and ii and scenes vii and viii. It should be noted, incidentally, that the version of *Lady Macbeth* to which the *Pravda* article took exception, and which was found shocking by many Western critics as well, had already had many of its most blatant excesses removed—notably the trombone glissandi at the height of the seduction scene. Again it is impossible to determine the role of self-criticism or imposed censorship in these changes. The composer's son, as well as many of his artistic associates now in the West and the majority of commentators outside the former Soviet Union, are united in preferring the original version and in considering the revisions to have been forced on the composer against his will.—DAVID FANNING

Lakmé

Composer: *Léo Delibes.*

Librettists: *Edmond Gondinet and Philippe Gille (based on Gondinet's play* Le marriage de Loti*).*

First Performance: *Paris, Opéra-Comique, 14 April 1883.*

Roles: *Lakmé (soprano); Gérald (tenor); Nilakantha (bass); Frédéric (baritone); Hadji (tenor); Ellen (soprano); Rose (soprano); Mrs. Benson (mezzo-soprano); Mallika (mezzo-soprano); chorus (SSTTBB).*

To describe Léo Delibes as a one-opera composer would be an oversimplification. His *Le roi l'a dit* (*The King Has Commanded it*) is a decent production and still is sporadically performed. Yet within the realm of opera (as contrasted with ballet where he made a much greater impact), most people associate him only with the colorful oriental-motif masterpiece, *Lakmé*.

The tale takes place in mid-nineteenth century India. Two English officers with French names, Frédéric and Gérald, are intrigued by the attractive garden and mysterious temple of the foreigner-hating Brahmin priest, Nilakantha. They penetrate the fence surrounding the complex. Gérald is soon infatuated with the beauty and charm of Lakmé, Nilakantha's daughter, and the romantic interest is reciprocated. When Lakmé's father returns, Gérald leaves and almost manages to avoid detection by the fanatical Brahmin. But Nilakantha is aware that the sacred Hindu ground has been violated and vows vengeance as soon as he discovers the identity of the infidel. He cleverly arranges for Lakmé to sing in the town where the British soldiers are stationed, hoping that either Lakmé or the foreigner will in some way tip their hand. The ploy works, and angry Nilakantha stabs Gérald, but not seriously. Gérald awakes in Lakmé's hut in the forest, where Lakmé has had her lover transported. Gérald's fellow officer Frédéric finds Gérald, and Frédéric convinces his colleague to return to the garrison. When Lakmé realizes that Gérald is having trouble deciding between duty and his love for her, she makes the decision for him and poisons herself. After Lakmé has died, Nilakantha comes upon the scene, but his hatred is quickly dissipated when he finds that his daughter has gone to her celestial reward.

Delibes managed to capture the flavor of the Orient about as well as any western composer. Ironically, this successful reflection of the culture of India was also a major factor in *Lakmé's* substantial decline in public favor by the mid-twentieth century. Asian themes were in vogue at the time Delibes wrote *Lakmé,* and when the vogue inevitably faded, the popularity of the opera correspondingly followed suit.

In spite of the limitations of the plot and the changing tastes of audiences, *Lakmé* continues to live on fairly strongly, and in recent years appears to be regaining a degree of the prominence it enjoyed in the late nineteenth and early twentieth century. Delibes' fine and at times quite brilliant score keeps *Lakmé* a persistent player in the repertory game. The legendary "Bell Song" ("Où va la jeune Hindoue?" or, "Where Does the Young Hindu Woman Go?") from act II is clearly the most famous portion of the music, but although sparkling and exciting it is not necessarily the best number. The Bell Song's renown owes as much to the demanding technical requirements of an agile, high soprano voice and to audience amazement at its execution as to its inherent beauty.

The Bell Song has tended to overwhelm other good sections, especially the excellent barcarolle "Dôme épais, le jasmin" ("Jasmine, the Dense Canopy") and the superlative aria "Fantaisie aux divins mensonges"

Lily Pons as Lakmé

("Fantasy of the Divine Lies") in the first act. Furthermore, the act II ballet scene which precedes the Bell Song is colorful, vibrant, and quite well crafted, and there are additional high points throughout the production. *Lakmé* should be remembered and cherished for the innovative Bell Song, but the rest of the opera also deserves a comparable level of attention. *Lakmé* overall is a definite jewel of the lighter operatic muse, but it doesn't pretend to rival the more serious and substantial works of major masters like Wagner, Verdi, and Mozart.—WILLIAM E. STUDWELL

Lauri-Volpi, Giacomo

Tenor. Born 11 December 1892, in Lanuvio, near Rome. Died 17 March 1979, in Valencia, Spain. Studied at Accademia di Santa Cecilia in Rome with Antonio Cotogni, and later with Enrico Rosati; debut as Arturo in I Puritani, Viterbo, 1919, using the name Giacomo Rubini; sang Massenet's Des Grieux under his own name, Rome, 1920; Teatro alla Scala debut as Duke of Mantua in Rigoletto, 1922, and sang regularly there in the 1930s and 1940s; at Metropolitan Opera, 1923-33; appeared at Covent Garden, 1925, 1936; also sang at Paris Opera and the Teatro Colon; continued to sing in public until 1959, and sang at the Teatro Liceo, Barcelona in 1972.

After the death of Caruso in 1921, there were several exceptionally gifted tenors who might have assumed his mantle. Gigli was at the outset of a brilliant career and could rival Caruso for lyrical excellence but could not achieve the robust power of the great Neapolitan. Pertile could match Caruso's intensity and his excellent musicality but perhaps not his beauty of tone. Martinelli possessed nearly all of Caruso's qualities but his voice was of sterling silver rather than gold.

Not two years before Caruso's demise, the young Roman Giacomo Lauri-Volpi was beginning his career. In many respects Lauri-Volpi possessed much of the prodigious talent that made Caruso great; a voice of ravishing beauty, particularly in a honeyed mezza-voce (half-voice), Caruso's clarity of enunciation, nobility of manner, elegance of style and superb musicality. But, he was also gifted with a magnificent upper register for which Caruso was never renowned, particularly later in the latter's career. Lauri-Volpi shared with Caruso much of the standard tenor repertoire but was also able to sing the high tenor roles such as in *I Puritani* and *Guillome Tell* that were never Caruso's.

Lauri-Volpi's career was a major one: he sang in all the important theaters of the world and, owing to the excellence of his

Giacomo Lauri-Volpi (Culver Pictures)

425

technique, sang well into his sixties. His early career was confined to the more lyric roles such as Rodolfo (*La bohème*), Des Grieux (*Manon*), Arturo (*I Puritani*) and roles which he soon dropped from his repertoire, such as Almaviva (*Il barbiere di Siviglia*). As his career progressed, he increasingly assumed more dramatic roles, which suited the more robust quality of the voice, such as Manrico (*Il trovatore*) and Radames (*Aida*). He continued to sing these roles until the end of his career, when he could still create a sensation with his top C, for which the public largely forgave the by-then worn quality of the remainder of the voice.

Lauri-Volpi recorded extensively and, on records, his career can be nicely divided into early, middle and late periods. Few tenors have made both acoustic 78s and stereo LPs, though his late records can be difficult listening and are for his real admirers only. The early acoustic records for Fonotipia already show a surprising degree of artistry, considering they were made only shortly after his debut. The voice is somewhat dark, with a flickering vibrato as recorded (which may have been exaggerated by the close proximity of the recording horn), and is employed with skill and all the graces of the bel canto school. The thrilling quality of the high notes is already evident. Just occasionally, the relative immaturity of the artist is betrayed by exaggeration of the vocal line for effect.

Lauri-Volpi's voice was probably at its finest in the late twenties and thirties when he recorded, regrettably little, for Victor. Here, the voice is at its loveliest, the artistry at its most mature and his interpretations at their most satisfying. Later HMV recordings, from the forties, show somewhat of a loosening of the tonal quality, but this is compensated for by a more robust approach and a nobility of utterance in the heavier roles he had by then assumed, such as Otello. At the end of his career he participated in several complete operas, for Italian Radio and Cetra. Though the voice is undeniably worn, the artistry is that of the seasoned artist and the high notes still ring with a brilliance and quality worthy of a tenor half his age.

A deeply religious and cultured man, Lauri-Volpi wrote numerous articles for newspapers and magazines and several books. One, *Voci Parallele,* is a book of critical and comparative analyses of fellow singers, many of whom he had known personally. He was renowned as a singer but definitely not for his modesty, for, in this book, Lauri-Volpi suggests singers that he would consider *voci isolati* (unique voices), the first of them: Giacomo Lauri-Volpi.—LARRY LUSTIG

Lear, Evelyn

Soprano. Born Evelyn Shulman, 8 January 1926, in Brooklyn. Married: 1) Dr. Walter Lear, 1943 (two daughters); 2) baritone Thomas Stewart, 1955. Studied piano and horn, then had vocal training with John Yard in Washington, D.C., with Sergius Kagen at Juilliard, and with Maria Ivogün in Berlin; debut as Composer in Ariadne auf Naxos, *Berlin Städtische Oper, 1957; sang Cherubino in Salzburg, 1962-64; Covent Garden debut as Donna Elvira, 1965; Metropolitan Opera debut in premiere of* Mourning Becomes Electra, *1967; farewell performance at Metropolitan Opera as Marschallin, 1985; created Jeanne in Egk's* Die Verlobung in San Domingo, *title role in Klebe's* Alkmene, *Irma Arkadina in Pasatieri's* The Seagull, *and Magda in Ward's* Minutes to Midnight.

The key words for Evelyn Lear's extraordinary vocal career are versatility and flexibility. Her instinctive feeling for stage characterization made it possible for her to traverse the whole range of roles in the repertoire she loved most, Mozart and Richard Strauss, despite her dedication to 20th-century opera as Berg's Marie and Lulu and in seven other roles she created in operas by Kelterborn, Klebe, Egk, Levy, Pasatieri, Ward and others. Her vocal agility first made her right for Despina and Zerlina, the bright forward-placement of her tone creating an ideal Sophie. But after joining the West Berlin Opera ensemble her voice developed a rich breadth of tone enabling her to move at ease among *spinto,* heavier lyric and outright mezzo-soprano roles, even essaying several dramatic soprano roles on record, though never on stage.

Among Evelyn Lear's 33 recordings are excerpts from Nicolai's *Merry Wives of Windsor, Un ballo in maschera, Nabucco, Eugene Onegin, Der fliegende Holländer, Jonny spielt auf,* complete recordings of *Boris Godunov, Der Rosenkavalier, Le nozze di Figaro, Die Zauberflöte, Wozzeck, Lulu, Die Gezeichneten* (Schreker), the c minor Mass (Mozart), St. John Passion (J.S. Bach), Te Deum (Nicolai), Glagolithic Mass (Janáček), Klagende Lied (Mahler), Stabat Mater (Pergolesi), songs by Richard Strauss, Hugo Wolf, Stravinsky, Schumann, Weill, Blitzstein, Bernstein and Sondheim together with five duet recordings with her husband. In 1974 Evelyn Lear starred together with Paul Newman, Joel Grey and Burt Lancaster in the Robert Altman film "Buffalo Bill and the Indians."

She is one of few sopranos to have sung Sophie, Octavian *and* the Marschallin in *Der Rosenkavalier,* Despina *and* Fiordiligi in *Così fan tutte,* Cherubino *and* the Countess in *Figaro,* Lulu *and* Geschwitz in *Lulu,* Zerbinetta *and* the Composer in *Ariadne auf Naxos,* the Countess *and* Clairon in *Capriccio,* and Micaela *and* Carmen. An untiring seeker of perfection, her meticulous preparation of her roles and her Lieder programs meant that every aspect of interpretation—phrasing, language (for which she possessed instinctive feeling, making every word count), breath control, dynamics and the always tasteful use of expressive devices such as portamento and vocal coloration—underwent a conscious process of selection and control but without ever leading to interpretative coldness, as the grand cantilenas she could always call upon demonstrated. Perhaps because her innate musicianship first showed itself on the French horn (breath control) and the piano (in an emergency she taught herself the role of Micaela in two days) she became that rarity among singers, a vocalist who was first and foremost a musician.—JAMES HELME SUTCLIFFE

Lehmann, Lilli

Soprano. Born 24 November 1848, in Würzburg. Died 17 May 1929, in Berlin. Studied with mother Marie Loewe in Prague; debut as first boy and Pamina in Die Zauberflöte in Prague, 1865; sang in Danzig (1868), in Leipzig (1869), and the Berlin Court Opera (1869), in each case first appearing as Marguerite de Valois in Les Huguenots; principal singer in Berlin until 1885; appeared in the first Bayreuth Ring as Woglinde, Helmwige, and the Forest Bird, 1876; Vienna debut, 1882; moved into dramatic roles after 1884; London debut at Her Majesty's Theatre as Violetta, 1880; Metropolitan Opera debut as Carmen, 1885; returned to Berlin in 1891; pupils include Farrar, Fremstad, Kurt, and Lubin.

No singer has been more respected and indeed more feared than Lilli Lehmann, whose technique, industry, musicianship, and executive authority made her one of the most daunting artists of her day. Her performances, and indeed her life, exemplified impassioned discipline, and her recordings, made as she approached sixty, reflect the praise of her colleagues precisely. She debuted at sixteen, and after almost a decade as Berlin's leading coloratura, went to Bayreuth in 1876, most importantly as Siegfried's charming Woodbird—and thereafter fought to remodel herself as a dramatic soprano. "One grows weary of singing nothing but princesses for fifteen years," she remarked, and gradually added Elsa, Elisabeth, Sieglinde, Isolde, Brünnhilde, Ortrud, Norma, Donna Anna, and Leonore (*Fidelio*) to her repertoire. After years of glory in these and similar roles at the Metropolitan and elsewhere, she returned in triumph to Bayreuth as Brünnhilde in 1896. Even after the turn of the century she continued to sing in opera and then in concert for two decades. Inevitably, she also taught, and was both demanding and caustic. "With her," said Geraldine Farrar, "Will was Power," and the nevertheless grateful Germaine Lubin called her Salzburg classes "veritable killers." Lehmann herself practised constantly, testing her voice sometimes for nearly an hour with a slow two-octave scale for faults of breath, attack, and dynamic control, and in rehearsals singing at full voice. Volume alone was not her goal: "One need not roar," she commented, finding that "one could sing well even with a little voice if the sound were noble."

Farrar thought that Lehmann combined the best of both the French and the Italian methods, and such a union of projection from the masque and diaphragmatic control is what emerges from Lehmann's records, made in 1906-07. It was a voice of modest size for Wagner, still absolutely steady, and glittering if occasionally pinched at the top, though by then a little pallid and worn in the middle. The legato technique of her coloratura days met with her dramatic thrust to produce a Norma of tragic command and a Lieder singer of lyric compulsion. With age and constricted recording to contend with, she relied on an iron control and support to send her triumphantly through the terrors of both Mozart ("Martern aller arten," for example) and Wagner ("Du bist der Lenz").

Of Lehmann's dramatic range it is more difficult to speak comprehensively. Critics (Hanslick, Krehbiel, Henderson), singers (Farrar, Calvé, Fremstad), and entrepreneurs and conductors (Mapleson, Walter Damrosch) all wrote of her noble and electrifying qualities as an actress, though others thought she lacked charm. Certainly Donna Anna's "Or sai, chi l'onore" and its recitativo, describing an attempted rape, have never been sung with such a sense of outrage; there is nothing of touching vulnerability in her delivery. Norma's "Casta diva" is splendidly articulated in her recording, but hardly visionary, although it certainly may have been so in the ambience of an opera house. One hears the same bright edge and foursquare approach in her excerpts from *La traviata,* doggedly accurate, and "Du bist der Lenz," fresh and intense but not really affectionate. This cannot be the whole story, however. In writing about performance, she often stresses the necessity of "life-giving style"—the real projection and not simply the indication of feeling, and the mingling of personal responses with those of the character in interpretation. To imagine her artistic aims in terms of recent singers, one might think of the technical mastery of the young Joan Sutherland wedded to the focused intensity of someone like Hildegard Behrens, in roles stretching from the Queen of the Night to Isolde.

Lehmann's extraordinary qualities become clearer in comparison with the work of other German sopranos of the time. Most of her exact contemporaries, in fact, had lost their voices and retired when she came to make records. What we can hear is largely the work of a somewhat younger generation recording at the same period: Sophie Sedlmair, Thila Plaichinger, Anna Bahr-Mildenburg, Lucie Weidt and others. Bahr-Mildenburg (in her one extant record) has fine attack and reliable pitch, and Weidt some of Lehmann's sculptural sense, but none of them demonstrates her combination of sovereign authority in phrasing Mozart *and* Wagner, finish, lyricism, patrician utterance—and longevity. Perhaps her most moving and representative record is of Leonore's "Abscheulicher!" Its noble outrage and impassioned faith were touchstones of Lehmann's philosophy as well as her art. The voice, technique, and dramatic range, expanded throughout a lifetime of devoted study and performance, are here tested to the limit and emerge victorious. That was her way.—LONDON GREEN

Lehmann, Lotte

Soprano. Born 27 February 1888, in Perleberg, Germany. Died 26 August 1976, in Santa Barbara, California. Married Otto Krause in 1926 (died 1939). Studied at Berlin Hochschule für Musik in 1904 and under Mathilde Mallinger, 1908-9; debut as Second Boy in Die Zauberflöte, *Hamburg, 1910; London Drury Lane debut as Sophie in* Der Rosenkavalier, *1914; in Vienna 1916-37, where she created the Composer in the revised version of* Ariadne auf Naxos, *the Dyer's Wife in* Die Frau ohne Schatten, *and Christine in* Intermezzo; *Covent Garden debut as the Marschallin, 1924; appeared in Buenos Aires, 1922; in Paris, 1928-34; in Chicago, 1930-37; appeared at Salzburg 1926-37; Metropolitan Opera debut as Sieglinde, 1934, and sang there twelve seasons until 1946; gave recitals until 1951; taught in Santa Barbara.*

Lotte Lehmann was able to achieve astonishing vocal and physical effects on both the stage and the concert platform by relying on her personality and sweetness of delivery rather than on a naturally beautiful appearance, which she lacked. She came from a humdrum background in North Germany where her father, a civil servant, forbade his only daughter to become a professional singer. Her determination and sheer persuasiveness overcame this obstacle, though female professors insisted that she had no vocal talent. At last she managed to find her ideal teacher in Mathilde Mallinger (Wagner's first Eva), and was then "taken up" by a rich German family who helped smooth out some of her gauche manners and assisted her in obtaining her first contract with the Hamburg Opera in 1910.

Hard work, a cheerful spirit and constant pestering of the management gained her several small roles until, in 1912, a fortunate break gave her the opportunity to sing Elsa in *Lohengrin* under the savage tuition and the baton of Hamburg's young conductor, Otto Klemperer. From then on she rose in the ranks of the Hamburg company, eventually singing 56 different roles there before reluctantly leaving to join the Vienna Court Opera at the end of 1916.

At first Lehmann was a fish out of water in the elegant Habsburg capital and center of operatic Europe; although she had several interesting roles to sing with the most dazzling partners, nobody took much notice of her. Within a mere two months, partly due to the negligence at rehearsals of the great Marie Gutheil-Schoder, Lehmann was suddenly given the important new role of the Young Composer at the premiere of Richard Strauss's revised version of *Ariadne auf Naxos*. Her success was immediate, and she remained a member of the Vienna Opera until 1938, becoming Viennese herself in the process.

Her special relationship with Strauss gave her several more characters to create for him in his operas, but all the time she felt herself to be in the shadow of other sopranos more famous, certainly more beautiful and generally with more powerful political connections. As a result Lehmann assumed a sullen and defensive attitude, so that her relationships with some of her female colleagues deteriorated as she became acknowledged as the finest portrayer of certain roles, including the Marschallin in *Der Rosenkavalier,* Leonore in *Fidelio,* Sieglinde in *Die Walküre,* Eva in *Die Meistersinger* and as Massenet's Manon.

Although she completed her training with Mallinger, Lehmann had never perfected her technique due to her unhappiness with several previous teachers. Breath control was always difficult, although this mattered little when the performance was so thoroughly prepared and backed by a personality radiating charm, warmth and goodness through every note. The top of the voice was a little deficient in body, which makes it all the more amazing that Lehmann sang the first Vienna Turandot and eight more performances of it in the 1926-27 season. Although vocal deterioration is evident from her gramophone records of the following years, Lehmann was always game to take on a difficult role and conquer it, making it unmistakably her own creation.

Lehmann was a welcome visitor to many European cities, especially London and Paris, as well as South America and Chicago, though she did not arrive at the Metropolitan Opera until 1934, as a triumphant Sieglinde. There Lehmann was again confronted by competition from other sopranos and bore grudges against "unfair" casting. Initially in Hamburg her imagined antagonist had been Elisabeth Schumann, but that was soon put right; in Vienna her rival was Maria Jeritza, who really behaved obnoxiously towards her; upon Jeritza's departure, the bête-noire became Viorica Ursuleac. At the Met the enemy was Flagstad. Each of these voices offered such different timbres, coloring and dramatic qualities that they should have been considered alternatives rather than rivals, but Lehmann failed to understand this.

America was to become her home when she settled in California in 1939, away from both Nazi and professional enemies in Vienna. When engagements dwindled and then stopped altogether, she concentrated on her concert career, something which she had allowed to mature since the First World War and which had grown to a peak at Salzburg Festivals in the 1930s with Bruno Walter as her accompanist. Her concert repertoire was extensive and not exclusively German. She was always able to establish great *rapport* with her audiences in the concert hall, where she had learned to mould her projection and delivery to suit her varied and often humorous repertoire.

Despite vocal shortcomings from the beginning of her career, Lehmann's voice was long-lived. She was obliged to enter the last phase of her long and varied career as vocal teacher in Santa Barbara where she reveled in a life among dedicated young people, communicating to them the lessons which she had learned so painfully, urging them to grasp the wisdom of her experience.

Lehmann was greatly beloved by Arturo Toscanini, Bruno Walter, Otto Klemperer and Franz Schalk. She had a string of lovers and one husband (for a short time) but no children. She was an avid letter-writer, an author and novelist; she painted, potted and drew many penetrating sketches and caricatures.

Much of Lehmann's vocal output is preserved on records (455 sides of 78s) which are nearly all transfered to CD. They include much of the Marschallin's role in *Der Rosenkavalier* and Sieglinde in its entirety. In addition, many pictorial and vocal proofs of her art remain at a time when those who knew and heard her perform gradually disappear.—ALAN JEFFERSON

Leider, Frida

Soprano. Born 4 April 1888, in Berlin. Died 4 June 1975, in Berlin. Married violinist Rudolf Deman. Studied with Otto Schwarz; debut as Venus in Tannhäuser, *Halle, 1915; in Rostock, 1916-18; in Königsberg, 1918-19; at Hamburg State Opera, 1919-23; at Berlin State Opera, 1923-40; appeared at Covent Garden, 1924-38; appeared at Bayreuth, 1928-38; Chicago debut as Brünnhilde in* Die Walküre, *1928; Paris Opéra, 1930-32; Metropolitan Opera debut in* Tristan und Isolde, *1933; after World War II she had a vocal studio at the Berlin State Opera until 1952; at Berlin Hochschule, 1948-58.*

Frida Leider's obituary in a Berlin publication stated, "In the early morning hours of 4 June 1975, the Berlin Kammersängerin Professor Frida Leider, honorary member of the Deutsche Oper Berlin, died. She was one of the most important personalities in the music history of the first half of our century. Without her the Wagner repertoire during these years would not have been possible. Seldom has the fusion of text and music, seldom the art of phrasing and dramatic expression celebrated such triumphs as in the years that this great soprano was gracing our opera stages."

Frida Leider was born in Berlin. She studied voice with Otto Schwarz while supporting herself by working as a clerk in the Berliner Bank. In 1915 she made her debut in Halle as Venus in *Tannhäuser*. From 1916 to 1918 Leider was engaged by the City Opera in Rostock. In 1918-19 she sang in Königsberg and then joined the roster of singers at the Hamburg State Opera for the seasons 1919 through 1923. In 1924 Leider was engaged by the Berlin State Opera and soon celebrated the first of her many operatic triumphs.

Her guest appearances included performances in Milan's Teatro alla Scala, in Paris, Vienna, Munich, and Stuttgart, as well as in Stockholm, Amsterdam, and Brussels. Covent Garden invited her as a guest every year from 1924 through 1938. For ten years, between 1928-1938, Frida Leider was one of the greatest stars of the Bayreuth Festival. Her performances of the three Brünnhildes and Isolde led to her being considered the most important German Wagnerian soprano of her generation. She did not neglect other important roles for dramatic soprano. Frida Leider was also highly praised for her interpretations of Fidelio, the Marschallin in *Rosenkavalier,* Donna Anna, and Gluck's Armide.

Brünnhilde in *Walküre* was her debut role in Chicago during the 1928 season. Because the rivalry between the Metropolitan Opera and the Chicago Opera was so bitter, both companies had agreed not to raid one another's roster. This delayed Leider's Metropolitan career until January 16, 1933, when she appeared in a glorious performance of *Tristan und Isolde.* Her close friend Lauritz Melchior sang Tristan and contralto Maria Olczewska made her Metropolitan debut as Brangäne. All shared equally in the critical acclaim. Leider was praised for her "deep and enlarging tenderness, richness of feeling, poetry of imagination." Another critic described the performance as surpassing "any that memory can recall" since before the war and a third rejoiced with the words "At last a cast!"

The rise of the Nazi Party to power in Berlin made the last years of Leider's career very difficult. Her husband, Rudolf Deman, was Jewish. Deman, concertmaster of the Berlin State Opera, was forced to flee to Switzerland. Leider chose to remain with her husband and her career at the Berlin State Opera ended in 1940. It was through the financial generosity of Lauritz Melchior that the couple was able to exist in exile.

After World War II Leider sang only a few concerts. She became a stage director at the Berlin State Opera and began to teach. From 1945 to 1952 she directed the company's voice studio, and in 1948 Frida Leider accepted a professorship at the Berlin Hochschule für Musik, where she remained until her retirement in 1958.

On her eightieth birthday, Lauritz Melchior composed this tribute to his longtime colleague and friend: "I think there has never been a more sincere artist, and the greatness of her heart that you hear on the recordings is only a small percentage of what you heard when you saw her and heard her on the stage. As she filled her parts absolutely, she also made her partners do their very best, and through that made the performances something very special."

Frida Leider was the recipient of the German Service Cross, First Class. Her memoirs, *Das war mein Teil,* were published in Berlin in 1959.—SUZANNE SUMMERVILLE

Leoncavallo, Ruggero

Composer. Born 23 April 1857, in Naples. Died 9 August 1919, in Montecatini. Studied piano with B. Cesi and composition with M. Ruta and L. Rossi at the Naples Conservatory; read Italian at Bologna University. Pianist in Egypt, 1879; accompanist and song-writer in cafés in Paris, 1882-88; project to compose a trilogy on the Italian Renaissance entitled Crepusculum *inspired by his study of Wagner, 1878-88; in Milan,* Pagliacci *composed and sold to the publisher Sonzogno, and achieved international success; first part of his trilogy* Crepusculum *entitled* I Medici, *unsuccessful; commissioned by Emperor Wilhelm II of Germany to compose* Der Roland von Berlin *for Berlin, 1904; United States and Canada tour, 1906; in London, 1912; conducting in San Francisco, 1913; continued composing opera and operetta in Italy until his death.*

Operas *Tommaso Chatterton,* Leoncavallo (after A. de Vigny), c. 1876, Rome, Nazionale, 10 March 1896; revised, Rome, Torre Argentina, 10 March 1896; revised Nice, 7 April 1905; *Pagliacci,* Leoncavallo, Milan, Teatro dal Verme, 21 May 1892; *Crepusculum: I Medici,* Leoncavallo, Milan, Teatro dal Verme, 9 November 1893; *La bohème,* Leoncavallo (after Henri Murger), Venice, Teatro La Fenice, 6 May 1897; revised as *Mimì Pinson,* Palermo, Massimo, 14 April 1913; *Zazà,* Leoncavallo (after P. Berton and C. Simon), Milan, Lirico, 10 November 1900; *Der Roland von Berlin,* Leoncavallo (after Willibald Alexis; German translation by G. Droescher), Berlin, Royal Opera, 13 December 1904; *La jeunesse de Figaro* (operetta), after Sardou, *Les premières de Figaro,* United States, 1906; *Maia,* A. Nessi (after Paul de Choudens), Rome, Costanzi, 15 January 1910; *Malbrouck* (fantasia comica medioevale), A. Nessi, Rome, Nazionale, 19 January 1910; *Zingari,* E. Cavacchioli and G. Emanuel (after Pushkin), London, Hippodrome, 16 September 1912; *La reginetta delle rose* (operetta), G. Forzano, Rome, Costanzi, 24 June 1912; *Are you there?* (farce), A. de Courville and E. Wallace, London, Prince of Wales, 1 November 1913; *Ave Maria,* L. Illica and E. Cavacchioli, 1915 [unfinished]; *La candidata* (operetta), G. Forzano, Rome, Nazionale, 6 February 1915; *Goffredo Mameli* (operetta), G. Belvederi, Genoa, Carlo Felice, 27 April 1916; *Prestami tua moglie* (operetta), E. Corradi, Montecatini, Casino, 2 September 1916; *Edipo re,* G. Forzano (after Sophocles) [unfinished; completed by G. Pennacchio, Chicago, Opera, 13 December

1920]; *A chi la giarrettiera?* (operetta), Rome, Adriano, 16 October 1919 [posthumous]; *Il primo bacio* (operetta), L. Bonelli, Montecatini, Salone di Cura, 29 April 1923 [posthumous]; *La maschera nuda* (operetta), L. Bonelli and F. Paolieri, Naples, Politeama, 26 June 1925 [unfinished; completed by S. Allegri]; *Prometeo* [unfinished]; *Tormenta,* G. Belvederi [unfinished].

Leoncavallo has been more easily vilified than praised, though it has often been stressed that he had a good literary education and a wide cultural background. He was the only composer of the young Italian school who could write his own librettos, but he was musically less gifted than his colleagues. Before 1892 (the year of *Pagliacci*), one opera could testify to Leoncavallo's cultural ambitions and genuine tastes, and that was *I Medici,* the first part of an "Epic Poem in the form of an Historical Trilogy" on the Italian Renaissance which the composer called *Crepusculum* (*Twilight*) in emulation of Wagner's *Götterdämmerung*. This large-scale project was conceived during Leoncavallo's stay in Bologna (the Wagnerian stronghold in Italy), and was to include *Gerolamo Savonarola* and *Cesare Borgia,* which were never written. The young composer put in a lot of work researching Lorenzo de' Medici, Poliziano, Savonarola and the Borgias, and the libretto of *I Medici* is meticulously annotated with literary and historical references. However, the opera failed hopelessly because of the pretentiousness of the text and the grandiloquence and lack of originality of the music. It could only be performed after the composer achieved sudden popularity with *Pagliacci,* just as the youthful, romantic *Chatterton,* which did not reach the stage until 1896.

Three operas best exemplify Leoncavallo's skills as a librettist and musician: *Pagliacci* (*Clowns*), *La bohème* and *Zazà,* all of them composed in the heyday of *verismo*. His reputation, however, rests entirely on *Pagliacci,* the only opera in which his literary abilities were effectively matched by his musical talent.

Leoncavallo was a master in creating stylistic pastiche. The subject matter selected for his operas enabled him to contrive situations which justified the use of different linguistic registers and compositional styles. His creative limits made him turn to the relics of the dismantled romantic melodrama no less than to the fashionable light music of his time. With the sensibility of an operetta composer, Leoncavallo pieced together agitated duets, impassioned romanzas, drawing-room melodies, music-hall songs, waltzes and marches. Wagnerian reminiscences and borrowings from other major composers were interwoven with violent vocal outbursts in the new veristic fashion. The stylistic pastiche is a common feature of *Pagliacci, La bohème* and *Zazà*. In the most popular of the three operas it yields appreciable results.

It was the success of Mascagni's *Cavalleria rusticana* (*Rustic Chivalry*) that prompted Leoncavallo to turn to a naturalistic subject. As early as 1893, *Cavalleria* and *Pagliacci* were paired in a production at the Metropolitan Opera of New York and have since been identified by audiences and critics as the archetypes of *verismo*. In the case of *Pagliacci* the term covers two aspects that are only latent in Mascagni's opera: sensationalism and violence. The subtle use of the device of the play-within-the-play in Leoncavallo's libretto adds an intellectual, estranging dimension to the dramatization of a crime of passion. As for the music, the rococo style adopted for the *commedia dell'arte* farce in act II cleverly differentiates the stereotyped acting of the clowns from their violent exchanges in real life.

In *La bohème,* the larger, four-act structure of the "lyric comedy" shows up all the seams and threads of the pastiche and betrays the composer's lack of sustained inspiration and formal control. Clearly, Leoncavallo's clattering music does not stand comparison with Puccini's setting of the same subject. Yet it is only fair to acknowledge Leoncavallo's single-handed efforts in extracting a dramatic action from Murger's novel *Scenes of Bohemian Life*. His libretto makes a detailed and faithful use of the narrative material and respects Murger's own characterization of the bohemians. No fewer than six poems by Murger and Musset are used as texts for songs. Leoncavallo keeps the emphasis on the bohemians as a group and sets his first act *inside* the Café Momus on Christmas eve. All the characters of the source are included: Rodolfo, Marcello, Schaunard, Colline, Mimi, Musette, Eufemia (Schaunard's mistress) and the philosopher Barbemuche who volunteers to settle the huge bill of the bohemians' dinner party. The same group is featured in act II, set in a courtyard of Rue de la Bruyère on 15th April, when insolvent tenants are evicted. Musette's furniture has been moved out of her rented flat and assembled in the courtyard of the building. The bohemians organize a lively party during which Barbemuche's disciple, Viscount Paolo, succeeds in convincing Mimi to run away with him abandoning Rodolfo for a life of luxury and comfort. The separation between the two bohemians is thus more clearly motivated than in Puccini's opera (an early draft of the Illica-Giacosa libretto included a "Courtyard act" which was later deleted). The only weak part of Leoncavallo's version is act III, featuring Marcello's garret, almost a duplicate of Rodolfo's similar dwelling. The events of the act are inessential: a starving Musette decides to leave her penniless lover just when the elegant and healthy Mimi reappears to attempt a reconciliation with Rodolfo. In act IV, Mimi returns once more and dies in Rodolfo's cold garret on Christmas eve, remembering the happy time at the Café Momus the year before.

The problem with *La bohème* is that Leoncavallo cannot devise a suitable musical medium for the lively conversations of his characters, nor can he strike the right balance between humor and sentiment. The dialogues are often accompanied by perfunctory dance rhythms; Mimi's and Musette's songs are trivial operetta numbers while Marcello's and Rodolfo's romanzas (acts III and IV) exude pathos and emphasis. Sometimes the adoption of a different style has a clear parodic purpose, as in Schaunard's Rossinian cantata "The influence of blue on the arts" (act II) or in some Verdian choral passages, but the overall impression the opera makes is one of inadequacy and artistic insincerity.

No stylistic evolution is noticeable in *Zazà*, Leoncavallo's contribution to the gallery of *fin-de-siècle* great female roles (*Fedora, Tosca, Adriana Lecouvreur*). The choice of a contemporary French play centered on a music-hall singing actress evidences once more his adhesion to *verismo*. *Zazà* tries to mix opera with operetta. The device of the theater-within-the-theater, already used in *Pagliacci*, is now employed to present the backstage of a provincial music-hall. The cabaret numbers being performed on the front stage are part of the action (act I). That is the starting point of the love affair between Zazà, the local star, and a married man, Milio Dufresne. When Zazà finds out that he loves his wife and daughter more than her, she sends him away and weeps her heart out.

The cabaret songs seem to have a contagious effect on the music of the opera. Insincerity and vulgarity remain its dominant characteristics. Act III contains few enjoyable moments of subdued, expressive singing. The scene is set in Dufresne's bourgeois drawing-room in Paris. Zazà, disguising her identity, is there with her maid Natalia to find out about her lover's family. While Milio and his wife are away, she talks to their little daughter Totò, a spoken role. The girl plays Cherubini's *Ave Maria* on the piano and Zazà pours out her misery to Natalia. The idea of an emotional solo against the musical background of a piano piece was not new (Giordano had already used it in *Fedora*), but it retains its efficacy in *Zazà*.

In his later years, Leoncavallo drifted towards operetta or accepted texts prepared by third-rate dramatists like G. Forzano. In any case, these productions add nothing to the three operas of his best creative period.—MATTEO SANSONE

Licht: Die sieben Tage der Woche [Light: The Seven Days of the Week]

Composer: *Karlheinz Stockhausen.*

First Performance: Der Jahreslauf *(scene from* Dienstag aus Licht*), 1977;* Donnerstag aus Licht, *Milan, 1981;* Samstag aus Licht, *Milan, 1984;* Montag aus Licht, *Milan, 1988.*

Roles: *Michael (tenor); Eve (soprano); Lucifer (bass); chorus.*

Since 1977 Stockhausen has been wholly engaged on a cycle of seven operas, *Licht,* one for each day of the week, of which *Donnerstag, Samstag,* and *Montag aus Licht* have been completed, and the fourth, *Dienstag aus Licht,* is due for completion in 1991. Not only the week-long architecture of the entire cycle, but the essential lineaments of each opera, its dramatis personae, scenic divisions, temperament, actions, and musical textures are all derived from an initial three-line musical formula embodying in ornamental form the germ-cells of specific melodic, rhythmic, and harmonic functions. These three strands of counterpoint are identified with mythic characters, a secular trinity, expressing three aspects of ideal humanity, approximately equivalent to the valiant knight (Michael), the eternal woman (Eve), and the wise man (or mad scientist) and anti-hero (Lucifer). Their roles and actions on stage are almost wholly symbolic, though alluding at times to events in the composer's life and his experiences with the public. This autobiographical dimension is most evident perhaps in the heroic imagery of *Donnerstag aus Licht,* in which Michael's getting of wisdom is clearly modelled on the turns and trials of the composer's life history. In *Samstag aus Licht* the character of Lucifer takes center stage, though the dramatic point has more to do with Lucifer as a representation of existential fear and how that fear is conquered: it leads the composer to some of his most brilliant scenic and musical inventions. *Montag aus Licht* is an opera in celebration of woman, motherhood, nature, and childhood; its imagery is fertile, green, and childlike, even hinting at the tonal kitsch of Disney or the Humperdinck *Hänsel und Gretel* Stockhausen directed for the Blecher town operetta society as a youth in the shell-shocked years after the end of World War II.

Stockhausen's approach to opera remains true to his abstract convictions while at the same time creating a compelling and often magical theatre. If his definition of opera seems to owe more perhaps to Berio and Kagel than Donizetti, his ideas for the stage are not lacking in references to more distant twentieth-century models, such as Kandinsky's dream for a series of operas based on colors, Piscator's theory of staging, and the concrete poetry of Hugo Ball. The imagery of *Licht* also reaches beyond European tradition to non-Western theatrical and musical rituals encountered by the composer in Japan, Bali, the African and Indian subcontinents, and Latin America. These older traditions provide a repertoire of dramatic or scenic templates for actions and processes essentially musical in inspiration. Rather than starting with an idea or libretto and finding the music to go with it, Stockhausen's visual and choreographic inventions, not to mention his libretti, are invented to fit the requirements of an existing musical formula, which is why so much of what happens seems mysterious at first encounter. The principle of the hidden agenda in music drama is ancient and honourable, and in Stockhausen's hands offers a rationale for wilfully unexpected results, intensities of experience and extraordinary audience reactions.—ROBIN MACONIE

Ligeti, György

Composer. Born 28 May 1923, in Dicsöszentmartin, Transylvania. Studied composition with Sándor Veress and Ferenc Farkas at the Budapest Music Academy, 1945-49; instructor at the Budapest Music Academy, 1950-56; worked in the Studio for Electronic Music in Cologne, 1957-59; in Vienna, 1959-69; in Berlin, 1969-73; lectured at the International Courses for New Music in Darmstadt; guest professor of composition at the Musical High School in Stockholm, 1961; lectured in Spain, the Netherlands, Germany, Finland, and at Tanglewood; composer-in residence at Stanford University, 1972; professor of composition, Hochschule für Musik, Hamburg, 1973.

Operas *Aventures*, Ligeti, 1962; arranged as a chamber opera, 1966; *Nouvelles aventures*, Ligeti, 1962-65; arranged as a chamber opera, 1966; *Le grand macabre*, M. Meschke (after Ghelderode), Stockholm, Royal Opera, 12 April 1978; *Rondeau*, 1976, Stuttgart, 26 February 1977.

Ligeti is generally recognized as one of the most gifted composers to have emerged since the Second World War. While he is generally thought of as a radical member of the avant-garde, his compositions vary widely in style, from jokes to highly sophisticated pieces in the mainstream tradition.

The major change in Ligeti's compositional style can be directly related to his leaving his native Hungary in 1956. Up to that point the most important influence was Bartók, and Ligeti's education had included a period of research into Romanian folk music. Most of Ligeti's pre-1956 pieces continue Bartók's project of linking folk music with the concert hall, and show a thorough grasp of the traditional means of musical construction. However, any exploration of radically new compositional styles was strongly discouraged within Hungary at that time.

Ligeti's move to Austria in 1956 was into a new world, where the avant-garde was attempting to forge a new musical language. Ligeti was given the opportunity to work in the electronic studio of the West German Radio in Cologne, and he later described his study of the most fundamental elements of music as showing him the way to realize some of the sound worlds he had previously only been able to imagine.

Only two purely electronic pieces resulted from this work, *Glissandi* and *Articulation,* but this new way of hearing and analyzing sound led to the orchestral works *Apparitions* and *Atmospheres.* The principal characteristic of these pieces is the use of clusters of sound rather than individual pitches. The composer uses these to create shapes and lines by varying the dynamic levels, the size of the cluster, the registers, and the instrumentation. The effects which Ligeti achieves with this compositional technique range from a directionless soft fading in and out of colors to an aggressive play of contrasts. Further, Ligeti realized that one could make the surface texture of the music more lively by restricting the pitches used to the same narrow band, but giving each individual part many notes, played very fast. If each part has a different rhythm and pitch pattern, the ear can hear the music in two ways, following either the overall movement of the bands of sound or the texture in an attempt to follow the maze of lines that fill in the area.

This technique of creating a broad, general effect by a proliferation of lines Ligeti termed "micropolyphony." The use of the technique is Ligeti's most individual characteristic, and it appears in many of his works, including works with voices, such as the *Requiem* and *Lux aeterna*, and sections of his opera *Le grand macabre*.

A different side of Ligeti is seen in the two works *Aventures* and *Nouvelle aventures,* written in the early sixties. Originally concert works, they were later transferred to the stage as chamber operas. They are scored for one male and two female singers, with a chamber orchestra of seven players, and together last a little over half an hour. The works pivot on the fact that the text is, in linguistic terms, completely meaningless, being a collection of vocal sounds and fragments of words. Ligeti shows us that this is no impediment to communication, as the combination of musical references and inflection—cries, laughter, sighs, and so on—make the thoughts and emotions of the singers perfectly transparent. Ligeti incorporates a huge number of sound effects in the instrumental parts, again exploring the boundary between conventional meaning and onomatopoeia. The pieces are truly grotesque, initially very funny, but by reducing emotion to its absurd appearance, somewhat sinister.

The most extreme example of Ligeti's humor is surely his *Poème symphonique,* scored for a hundred metronomes. Each of the metronomes is set to a different tempo, and they are released simultaneously. At the start of the piece there is a great cloud of ticking, which gradually thins out as the mechanisms run down, first forming a regular rhythmic pattern, and then reducing to a solitary pulse.

Alongside these exploratory works Ligeti has written a series of pieces appealing to more traditional aesthetic values. Each successive piece shows an increase in scope and assurance. One would expect that it is on these works that Ligeti's reputation will eventually rest, provided they are not overshadowed by the sensationalism of his other styles. The piano concerto, first heard in its complete version in 1988, will surely take its place in the repertoire alongside the cello concerto of 1966, and the concerto for flute and oboe of 1972. Ligeti has also made a substantial contribution to the literature of chamber music with the trio for violin, horn and piano of 1982, and to that of the piano with the duets *Monument, Selbstporträt, Bewegung* of 1976, and the solo *Etudes* of 1985.

Given Ligeti's growing musical powers and his understanding of the voice which his choral music demonstrates, it is to be hoped that *Le grand macabre* will not be Ligeti's ultimate statement in the operatic medium. Much of Ligeti's music of the 1980s shows us that large scale forms constructed with a unified musical language are possible, and one cannot help hoping that this language, beyond irony, will be used to connect the abstract world of instrumental music with the social world of music theater.—ROBIN HARTWELL

Lind, Jenny

Soprano. Born 6 October 1820, in Stockholm. Died 2 November 1887, in Malvern Hills, Shropshire. Married: Otto Goldschmidt, 1852 (2 sons, 1 daughter). First stage appearance at age 10; formal opera debut as Agathe in Der Freischütz, *Royal Opera, Stockholm, 1838; became regular member of Swedish Academy of Music, 1840; brief retirement, 1841-42, when she went to study with Manuel Garcia in Paris; returned to Stockholm and sang* Norma, *1842; appeared at Leipzig Gewandhaus, 1845; Vienna debut as Norma at Theater an der Wien, 1846; gave her New York debut in 1850; settled in England in 1858; appeared in oratorio and concert performances until she retired in 1883.*

Jenny Lind studied first in Stockholm where she made her debut as Agathe in *Der Freischütz* in 1838. Puritanically, she refused to wear make-up when acting. Becoming unable to control sustained notes in the upper register without difficulty, she went to Paris to study with Manuel Garcia in 1841. He discovered that she had been taught an unsound way of breathing; to have continued singing in this way would have permanently destroyed her voice. She wrote to a friend: "I have had to begin again from the beginning." Garcia kept stressing his axiom that a singer should always keep something back. After a year she returned to Stockholm's Royal Opera to take the title role in Bellini's *Norma*. Critics were astonished by the improvement in her voice, which now ranged from B below the stave to C on the fourth line above it—two and three-quarter octaves. It had gained depth of tone and clarity and was capable of easily adapting itself to all shades of expression. In her shake, scales, *legato* and *staccato* passages, she employed such ornaments only when in harmony with the music's inner meaning.

In 1844, Lind made her Berlin Opera debut also as Norma. The first to play the Druid priestess, Pasta, had done so with fire and little tenderness. "Pasta presents a Norma *before* whom, our artist (Lind) a Norma *with* whom we tremble," wrote critic Ludwig Rellstab.

For her last role of the season, Jenny chose Amina in *La sonnambula,* for which her gentleness and crystal-pure voice were ideal. When she later sang the part in Vienna, the audience clamored for an encore of the rondo finale, so she went down to the footlights and pleaded: "May I first have five minutes to drink some lemonade?" This engaging lack of sophistication delighted the Viennese.

Jenny Lind made her London debut at Her Majesty's on 4 May 1847 as Alice in Meyerbeer's *Robert le diable* sung in Italian, chosen, as she confided to manager Lumley, because making her first appearance in a crowd would enable her to overcome any nervousness before she sang solo. He wrote of the first night that "the struggle for entrance was violent beyond precedent—so violent indeed, that the phrase 'a Jenny Lind crush' became a proverbial expression." *The Times* reported "torn dresses and evening coats reduced to rags; ladies fainting in the pressure and even gentlemen carried out senseless."

In the following year, the Swedish Nightingale made her London debut as Lucia. *The Times* wrote that in the second and third acts she brought out the distress and madness of the character with a force hitherto unknown. "The eye, glaring and vacant, appeared absorbed by fantasies, and blind to all external objects. The passions by which she is supposed to be influenced, while in this painful situation, are of the most varied kind; but she never for a moment lost sight of the insanity. At the conclusion, instead of running off the stage in the usual fashion, she fell senseless, which brought the situation to a more pointed conclusion."

On 29 July, Jenny's Elvira in Bellini's *I puritani* was the last new role in which she was seen on the operatic stage. The cadenza she composed for the opening movement of "Qui la voce" was one of the most brilliant and original of the passages of *fioritura* with which it was her practice to ornament the Italian arias she liked best. Arthur Coleridge in his *Musical Recollections* wrote: "She showered her trills and roulades like sparkling diamonds all over the place. It was the first time and the last, with the single exception of Rachel, that I have seen such unmistakable genius on the stage."

Brainwashed by associates who regarded the stage as a sort of ante-room to hell, Lind now announced that she would only sing in concerts in future. At Exeter Hall on 15 December, she sang with dramatic power the soprano part in Mendelssonn's last work, *Elijah,* which he had written with her in mind.

Probably it was as well that Jenny Lind retired from opera when she did. The critic H.F. Chorley thought that her repertory was so limited that it must have "exposed her on every side to comparisons should she have remained on the stage till enthusiasm cooled, as it must inevitably have done." She now played a new role, one of some importance in social history. Phineas T. Barnum was then the world's leading showman. While catering for the crude tastes of the masses had brought him immense wealth, his secret ambition was to make the American public acquire an appetite for culture and

Jenny Lind as Amina in *La sonnambula,* **1848**

he regarded the "Swedish Nightingale" as the perfect vehicle for achieving this. In the negotiations that followed, Jenny Lind proved an astute businesswoman, conducting them entirely on her own.

Lind's farewell English concerts were a series of frenzied triumphs. At her final one in Liverpool, she gave *Messiah,* for the singing of which she was to rank supreme for the rest of her days. She held ninety-three concerts in America before falling out with Barnum and continuing to tour on her own with a new accompanist, Otto Goldschmidt, whom she married. But the public was tiring of programmes that were always the same and her husband proved a dull pianist. On 24 May 1852, nearly five months after arriving in New York, Lind gave her farewell concert at Castle Gardens; profits amounted to barely half of what they totalled at her debut. Barnum went to see her afterwards in her dressing-room. She told him she would never sing in public again. "Your voice is a God-given gift," he returned. "You must never cease using it." This appeal to her religious feelings succeeded and she relented, saying that she would continue so long as her voice lasted, but it would be mostly for charity as she now had all the money which she would ever need.

In 1862 Chorley wrote a perceptive estimation of Jenny Lind's talents: "It can now, without treason, be recorded that her voice was a soprano, two octaves in compass—from D to D—having a possible higher note or two available on rare occasions, and that the lower half and the upper one were of two distinct qualities. The former was not strong—veiled, if not husky, and apt to be out of tune. The latter was rich, brilliant and powerful—finest in its highest portions. . . . she could turn her 'very long breath' to account in every gradation of tone; and thus, by subduing her upper notes, and giving out her lower ones with great care, could conceal the disproportions of her organ."—CHARLES NEILSON GATTEY

Lohengrin

Composer: *Richard Wagner.*
Librettist: *Richard Wagner.*

Lohengrin

First Performance: *Weimar, Hoftheater, 28 August 1850.*

Roles: *Lohengrin (tenor); Henry I [Henry the Fowler] (bass); Frederick, Count Telramund (baritone); Elsa (soprano); Ortrud (soprano or mezzo-soprano); Royal Herald (baritone); Gottfried (mute); Four Nobles of Brabant (tenors, basses); Four Pages (sopranos, altos); Eight Ladies (sopranos, altos); chorus (SSAATTBB).*

Henry the Fowler, the tenth-century king of the Germans, comes to Brabant to gather forces for the defense of his states against the Hungarians and finds the northern duchy torn by dissent. Gottfried, the boy heir to the throne, has disappeared, and Count Telramund has accused the boy's older sister, Elsa, of murdering him. Elsa, called to court, says that she will be vindicated by a knight in shining armor, who has appeared to her in a dream. A summons is issued to the four winds, and the knight materializes, sailing up the Scheldt in a boat drawn by a swan. He will champion Elsa's cause if she will never ask his name. She consents, and the shining knight defeats Telramund in combat, but spares his life.

Telramund's pagan wife Ortrud plans revenge: as Elsa is about to marry her champion, she and Telramund interrupt the procession to tempt Elsa with doubts about the knight's origin. When the newlyweds are alone in their bedchamber, Elsa asks her husband the forbidden question, and at that moment Telramund enters with a drawn sword. The knight slays his assailant, and then says he must now leave Elsa forever; he will never, as the king had hoped, lead the combined German-Brabantian forces; his name is Lohengrin, and he must return to his

***Lohengrin*, production by Herbert von Karajan, 1976**

father Parsifal, king of the Holy Grail. The swan boat reappears, and Ortrud in triumph recognizes, from the pendant around its neck, that the swan is the long-lost Gottfried, whom she had made disappear. Lohengrin kneels in prayer, and the swan sinks into the waves and rises again, now as Gottfried, ready to lead the pan-German crusade in Lohengrin's stead. Ortrud cries out in defeat, and Elsa, as she sees her husband fade from view, falls lifeless.

Lohengrin is the last opera Wagner wrote before the six-year silence from which the new musical world of the *Ring* emerged. It is also the last and greatest Romantic opera—if Romantic means visionary, lyrical, steeped in the folktales of the Middle Ages and, above all, German. Wagner was, at the time of the premiere, a political exile in Switzerland, and his still-active hopes for a united Germany are clearly part of the opera's texture. In many respects Lohengrin is, like Tannhäuser before him, a figure for the composer himself.

In *Lohengrin* Wagner's musical powers reach new heights, and he was never to surpass the orchestral coloring of the famous prelude, where soft divided strings in the traditionally "bright" key of A major suggest what Thomas Mann has called "a silvery blue beauty." The score still features traditional arias, duets, choruses and ensembles, but each act builds with a new and impressive architectonic sense, and increasingly the orchestra comments on the action with leitmotifs in the manner that will eventually pervade the *Ring*.

The mythic aspects of *Lohengrin* have not always been properly appreciated, and Elsa in particular has been maligned as a weak character, though Wagner himself told us to think of her as "the unconscious, the intuitive ... the feminine, hitherto not understood by me, now understood at last." (He was already moving on to Brünnhilde, the questioning, intuitive, saving woman of the *Ring*.) Elsa breaking an imposed taboo is not just an anticipation of Brünnhilde disobeying her father, but one of a whole pattern of mythic heroines who give way to curiosity and bring immediate tragedy but also hope for the future, even the promise of a world savior. Brünnhilde's disobedience brings, eventually, Siegfried, as in other mythologies Pandora's disobedience brings Elpis, Semele's Dionysus, Psyche's Eros, and Eve's (as the Church sings in her liturgy) the redeeming Jesus. These taboo-breaking myths describe a great evolutionary moment in prehistory, when the human race passed from unconsciousness to the much more problematic state of consciousness. ("You will be like gods," the tempter said to Eve.) Woman precipitates this, not because she is weaker, but because she is more intuitive. Elsa's questioning means the loss of Lohengrin, but restores Gottfried, the Grail-sent hope for the future, hidden for a time under a figure our mythologists would call a transcendence symbol—the swan.

Lohengrin is an astonishing work for anyone with ears for the pre-Raphaelite beauty and brassy glory of its music, and with the insight to see deeply into its text. Baudelaire, astonished, wrote that *Lohengrin* held him suspended "in an ecstasy compounded of joy and insight."—M. OWEN LEE

I Lombardi alla prima crociata [The Lombards at the First Crusade]

Composer: *Giuseppe Verdi.*

Librettist: *Temistocle Solera (after Tommaso Grossi).*

First Performance: *Milan, Teatro alla Scala, 11 February 1843; revised as* Jérusalem, *libretto by Gustave Vaëz and Alphonse Royer, Paris, Opéra, 26 November 1847.*

441

I Lombardi alla prima crociata

Roles: *Arvino (tenor); Pagano (bass); Viclinda (soprano); Giselda (soprano); Oronte (tenor); Pirro (bass); Prior of Milan (tenor); Acciano (bass); Sofia (soprano); chorus (SATB).*

I Lombardi alla prima crociata, Giuseppe Verdi's fourth opera, was premiered at the Teatro alla Scala on 11 February 1843. The librettist Temistocle Solera based the work on Tommaso Grossi's novel-poem of the same name from 1826. The action takes place at the end of the eleventh century. Act I is subtitled "The Vendetta." Two brothers, Pagano and Arvino, both love Viclinda. She chooses Arvino; on their wedding day Pagano tries to kill his brother. Pagano is exiled but many years later returns to Milan dressed as a penitent; he is reconciled with his brother, with Viclinda, and with their daughter, Giselda. Pagano still seeks revenge, however. Thinking to attack his brother, he mistakenly kills his father; Pagano tries unsuccessfully to kill himself in remorse and is once again exiled. In act II, "The Man in the Cave," Oronte, the son of Acciano, the tyrant of Antioch, is in love with one of the Christian prisoners, Giselda. Pagano has become a hermit. His former follower, Pirro, comes to him offering to betray Antioch, which action allows the crusading Lombards, led by Arvino, to capture Antioch. Giselda, in the harem, learns that both Acciano and Oronte have been killed. When the Lombards enter she curses the god who allowed this war; incensed at this, her father tries to kill her. Pagano, unrecognized, saves her, pleading that she is only "a poor mad girl." Act III, "The Conversion," takes place in the valley of Jehoshaphat outside Jerusalem. Oronte, in fact alive although critically wounded, disguised as a crusader, meets Giselda before he dies in her arms. In act IV, "The Holy Sepulchre," Giselda and her father are now reconciled. She has a vision of Oronte among the angels. In the battle for Jerusalem, Pagano is mortally wounded. He discloses his identity as he lies dying in Arvino's tent. He is forgiven; Arvino carries him to the entrance of the tent, where the two brothers regard the flags of the crusaders flying on the conquered city.

I Lombardi was Verdi's first opera after the extremely popular *Nabucco* of 1842. Because of the current political situation in Italy, *I Lombardi,* with its Lombards (seen allegorically as the Italians) pitted against the Saracens (the Austrian oppressors), caused even greater furor at its premiere than had *Nabucco*. One reads of stampedes in the theater and of frenzied applause and many demands for encores. Arvino's outcry in the final act calling the Lombards to battle, "La santa terra oggi nostra sarà" (The Holy Land will today be ours!) caused the audience to go wild; many shouted "Si! guerra, guerra!" (Yes, war!) along with the chorus. The opera was performed a total of twenty-seven times before the end of the season. It was the right subject at the right time to stir such feelings, and some of the credit must also go to Verdi's rousing, full-blooded tunes. Yet *I Lombardi* is not on an artistic level with *Nabucco;* it is much more of a patchwork, and many of its effects are blatantly crude and banal. The critics recognized this immediately; some noted that Verdi's writing was unvocal and potentially damaging to good singing, and a correspondent of *France musicale* stated that "Nothing could be poorer than this work from the technical point of view. Counterpoint is inexcusably neglected and the deafening noise of the brass instruments and the big drum does not suffice to hide the emptiness of the orchestration."

Although *I Lombardi* does contain a great deal of town-band music (reflecting Verdi's earlier musical experiences), much of the music fits and even heightens the situation. The chorus "O Signore dal tetto natio" aroused great enthusiasm and for a time threatened to displace "Va, pensiero" from *Nabucco* in the public's affection as a sort of unofficial national hymn. Giselda's "Salve Maria," a lovely piece the elements of which are found almost half a century later in Desdemona's "Ave Maria," was much admired by Rossini. Of much poorer quality was Solera's

l ≣OPERA

libretto, muddled and perfunctory. Francis Toye went so far as to state that "It may be doubted whether the annals of opera contain a more uncouth libretto than this." In all fairness, it was an almost impossible task to fashion an intelligible libretto from Grossi's novel-epic because much of the complicated action, which takes place over a long span of time, is told out of sequence. In addition, there are too many secondary characters for the operatic stage. The resulting opera presents certain difficulties in staging: it requires eleven scenes, a number of them calling for a high degree of spectacle, two star tenors of quite different vocal weight, not to mention the ubiquitous town-band.

Even though *I Lombardi* was written against the backdrop of a volatile political situation, it was the Church rather than the political authorities that caused Verdi censorship problems. The Archbishop of Milan thought it sacrilegious in its onstage depiction of baptism, its biblical setting in the Holy Land, and in its incense and banners. This was Verdi's first major battle with censorship but it ended with him only being obliged to change Giselda's "Ave Maria" to "Salve Maria." In the manuscript one can see the addition of the "S" and the "1" in Verdi's own hand.

The success of *I Lombardi* was not repeated when it was staged in Venice later in 1843. Verdi, writing to the Countess Giuseppina Appioni, called the performance there *"un gran fiasco,* one of those fiascos that may truly be called classic." In 1847 the work was re-fashioned by Verdi as *Jérusalem* for Paris. It was his first attempt, carried through with *Les vêpres siciliennes,* the 1865 revision of *Macbeth,* and *Don Carlos,* to conquer the French capital. The librettists, Royer and Vaëz, abolished the crusades, transformed Milan into Toulouse, turning Italians into Frenchmen. Verdi added the obligatory ballet music, made many changes throughout, and even replaced some numbers with new ones. The effect of *Jérusalem* is not as immediate and vital as that of *I Lombardi.* Julian Budden sums up the Italian work thus: "If *I Lombardi* is a very imperfect work of art, it is nevertheless a rich compost-heap which fertilized the soil of many a later [Verdi] opera."—STEPHEN WILLIER

London, George

Bass-baritone. Born George Burnstein, 5 May 1919, in Montreal. Died 23 March 1985, in Armonk, New York. Studied in Los Angeles with Richard Lert, voice with Hugo Strelitzer and Nathan Stewart; debut (as George Burnstein) as Dr. Grenvil in La traviata, *Hollywood Bowl; then studied in New York with Enrico Rosati and Paola Novikova; sang Monterone with San Francisco Opera, 1943; toured in 1947 with Frances Yeend and Paola Novikova; appeared as Amonasro at Vienna, 1949; in Edinburgh as Figaro, 1950; sang Amfortas at Bayreuth, 1951; Metropolitan opera debut as Amonasro, 1951, and sang with that company until 1966; appeared at Salzburg, 1952; at Teatro alla Scala as Don Pizarro in* Fidelio, *1952; at Buenos Aires and Paris Opéra; suffered paralysis of vocal cords, 1967, but continued to work in arts management; artistic administrator of John F. Kennedy Center for the Performing Arts, Washington, D.C., 1968-71; executive director of National Opera Institute, 1971-77; staged* Ring *cycle in Seattle, 1975; directed Opera Society of Washington, 1975-77.*

Devotees of George London's vocal art value him not because his bass-baritone was a perfect voice used perfectly but because of the rare dramatic power and vocal conviction he

George London as Amfortas in Wagner's *Parsifal*, Bayreuth, 1951

conveyed at his best, especially onstage. Indeed J.B. Steane, remarking that London's singing is not flattered by recording, compares the interpretation of London and two other modern singers of Wotan's Farewell against the versions made by earlier singers Friedrich Schorr and Alexander Kipnis and finds all the moderns, including London, wanting. Smoothness of vocal emission and firmness of vocal control among Wagner baritones are something that, in Steane's view, had vanished at the time he was writing. Nevertheless, it is only fair to say, as indeed Steane himself does, that recording can only capture part of George London's dramatic excitement and not at all his dark, brooding theatrical presence.

Born in Canada, London's training and early career were in North America; his international career began with an Amonasro in Vienna in 1949. This was soon followed by Glyndebourne, Bayreuth, the Metropolitan Opera in 1951, and, among other notable milestones, the Bolshoi in 1960 as the first non-Russian to sing Boris Godunov there. Early in his career he began concentrating on the Wagner repertoire; an important phase in his development was his extensive collaboration with Wieland Wagner during the fifties and sixties which culminated in *Der Ring des Nibelungen* at Bayreuth and other centers, such as Cologne, in 1962. Perhaps his most memorable achievement with Wieland was his playing of Amfortas, an almost unbearably intense portrayal. He was also a notable Dutchman and Hans Sachs. His reputation as a leading Wagnerian made it natural that in the first complete recording of the *Der Ring des Nibelungen* in the late fifties and early sixties he was invited to assume the *Das Rheingold* Wotan under Solti and *Die Walküre* Wotan under Leinsdorf.

His achievements outside the Wagner repertoire were also distinguished. His Scarpia, the Count in *Le nozze di Figaro,* Don Giovanni, Mephistopheles (Gounod), Escamillo, and the villains in *Les Contes d'Hoffman* were among his successful stage assumptions and he has left recordings of these, in whole or in part. But one of his most exciting and moving recorded performances is to be found in the brief aria, "Standin' in the need of prayer" from Louis Gruenberg's *Emperor Jones,* a Lawrence Tibbett vehicle in the thirties at the Met. The fear, supplication, and above all the hallucinatory quality of the scene make it the most intense memorial he has left of his art. George London was forced into premature retirement while still in his prime (1967) for medical reasons. He pursued a career in arts administration until ill health gradually forced withdrawal from all activity; he died in 1985.—PETER DYSON

Lorengar, Pilar

Soprano. Born Pilar Lorenza Garcia, 16 January 1928, in Saragossa, Spain. Studied with Angeles Ottein in Madrid and later with Carl Ebert and Martha Klust in Berlin; debut in Zarzuelas, Madrid, 1949; concert debut, 1952; opera debut as Cherubino in Aix-en-Provence, 1955; New York concert debut as Rosario in Goyescas, *1955; Covent Garden debut as Violetta, 1955; appeared as Pamina at Buenos Aires, 1958; sang in Berlin from the late 1950s to the late 1980s; appeared at Glyndebourne, 1956-60; Salzburg, 1961-64; Metropolitan Opera debut as Donna Elvira, 1966, and sang there for twelve seasons; inaugurated the Deutsche Oper, 1961, and named Kammersängerin, 1963.*

During a career that stretched from the mid 1950s to the mid 1980s the Spanish soprano Pilar Lorengar sang a wide variety of roles in some of the world's leading opera houses. Her voice and stage *persona* evolved over the course of her career. A youthful Cherubino (Mozart's *Le nozze di Figaro*) grew gradually into a Countess. A specialist in Mozart expanded her repertory to Weber and Wagner, to Verdi and Puccini.

Lorengar's portrayal of Cherubino at the summer festival at Aix-en-Provence in the mid-1950s is among the many fine performances that established her international reputation. Her looks were not quite right; *Opera* called her "the most unboylike page imaginable, discarding the usual periwig in favor of a feminine hair-style which even the text of 'Non più andrai' could hardly justify." Recorded under Hans Rosbaud, Lorengar's Cherubino has a bright, pretty voice. In her aria "Non so più cosa son, cosa faccio" Lorengar projects a vivacious, fresh stage personality. Her clear enunciation of the words infuses the music with an infectious liveliness. Less successful, perhaps, is Lorengar's lyrical rendition of "Voi che sapete." The slower tempo and sustained notes here make Lorengar's wide vibrato more apparent than in "Non so più cosa son." The vibrato gives the voice a somewhat overripe quality that seems out of character. The clarity of enunciation that one can admire in "Non so più cosa son" is not so apparent here. Lorengar sacrifices words in the interests of smoothness of line; the result, however beautiful from a purely musical point of view, is a weakening of dramatic force and vividness of characterization.

A more mature Lorengar with a wider repertory won success later in her career. Her voice grew: a critic in *Opera* praised her performance in the title role of *Jenůfa* in Berlin (1976): "her once rather limited lyric soprano has grown surprisingly in volume and power while still retaining its perfection of tonal beauty and resonance in the upper register." Lorengar was loudly applauded for her subtle acting and pure voice when she portrayed Elisabetta (Verdi's *Don Carlos*) in Chicago in 1972. As Agathe in Weber's *Der Freischütz*, as Eva in Wagner's *Die Meistersinger*, and as the Countess in Mozart's *Figaro* at the Metropolitan Opera in New York, Lorengar was praised by listeners and critics alike.

Lorengar has sung successfully in light opera, including the zarzuelas of her native land. In Rafael Millan's *La dogaresa,* as recorded under Ataulfo Argento, one can hear Lorengar the zarzuela singer. Hers is a voice consistently pleasant to listen to. She delivers the aria "Ya muerto esta" with bright, clearly focused singing; but there is something impersonal, detached, about her performance. One misses in the aria "Las flores de mil colores," for example, a sense of the character's personality and emotional state. A listener with no knowledge of Spanish and no translation at hand might have difficulty in understanding what Lorengar's character is feeling.—JOHN A. RICE

Lorenz, Max

Tenor. Born 17 May 1901, in Düsseldorf. Died 11 January 1975, in Salzburg. Studied in Berlin; debut as Walther von der Vogelweide in Tannhäuser; *appeared at Berlin State Opera, 1931-44, where he was a member, 1933-37; at Vienna State Opera from 1937; appeared at Covent Garden, 1934, 1937; at Bayreuth, 1933, 1952; Metropolitan Opera debut as Walther von Stolzing in* Die Meistersinger, *and sang eleven roles there.*

A supremely important and true heldentenor, Max Lorenz was perhaps the only artist in that category to rival the exploits of his Wagnerian colleague, Lauritz Melchior. While he also sang the same repertoire as Melchior, Lorenz' voice was naturally pitched a bit higher, allowing him to sing Walther in *Die Meistersinger,* a role which Melchior preferred not to attempt. Lorenz also sang Rienzi, Erik and Loge: the complete Wagnerian panoply.

Lorenz, too, ventured (or was given the opportunities to venture) into repertoires other than Wagner. He sang in the Strauss operas, *Salome* (Herod was his final performance, Vienna, 1962), *Elektra, Die äegyptische Helene, Die Frau ohne Schatten* and *Ariadne.* He even sang the Italian tenor in *Rosenkavalier.* He was a famous Otello (often compared favorably to Leo Slezak), and also sang Manrico, Alvaro, Riccardo, and Radames. He sang the Calif and Des Grieux in the Puccini operas, and a wide variety of other roles, from Offenbach to Irving Berlin (Buffalo Bill in *Annie Get Your Gun),* including Florestan, Don José, and Pfitzner's Palestrina. He sang the Idamantes of Mozart and Gluck's Achilles, Berg's Drum Major and Pedro in *Tiefland,* Mussorgsky's False Dimitri and Weber's Max.

Max Lorenz appeared in several world premieres, among them Josef K. in von Einem's *Der Prozess,* and some of his last appearances were as Teresias in *Alcestiad* by the American composer Louise Talma in Frankfurt a. Main 1962. His repertoire included some 50 roles.

He was born in Düsseldorf in 1901 and made his stage debut in Dresden, 1927. He appeared in the major houses throughout Europe, was a regular at the Bayreuth and Salzburg Festivals, sang at Covent Garden, appeared at the Metropolitan Opera before the War (and returned after), and performed in South America. Berlin was his first artistic home, then Vienna. After his retirement from the stage, he taught at the Mozarteum in Salzburg and privately in Salzburg and Munich. He died in January 1975, in Salzburg. A memorial was held 10 days later at the Vienna State Opera before his interment in Vienna's Central Cemetery.

Max Lorenz is represented today by a myriad of recordings, many from live performances. There is an especially exciting *Tristan und Isolde* from Berlin, 1942, conducted by Robert Heger, among other *Tristan* live recordings; the *Götterdämmerung* Siegfried with Furtwängler from Milan; innumerable *Walküre* act I, scene III's; excerpts from *Tannhäuser,* led by Heger, 1943; a complete *Ariadne auf Naxos* conducted by Böhm; Bayreuth performance excerpts; a *Salome;* some singer portrait collections; and much else.

An always exciting singer, refined musically, and extremely versatile, Max Lorenz' 35-year professional career was a rewarding one for audiences everywhere.—BERT WECHSLER

Louise

Composer: *Gustave Charpentier.*

Librettist: *Gustave Charpentier [and Saint Pol-Roux].*

First Performance: *Paris, Opéra-Comique, 2 February 1900.*

Roles: *Louise (soprano); Julien (tenor); The Mother (mezzo-soprano); The Father (baritone); Irma (soprano); Camille (soprano); Gertrude (mezzo-soprano); Errand Girl (soprano); Elise (soprano); Blanche (soprano); Suzanne (mezzo-soprano); Streetwalker (mezzo-soprano); Young Ragpicker (mezzo-soprano); Forewoman (mezzo-soprano); Milk Woman (soprano); Newspaper Girl (soprano); Coal Gatherer (Mezzo-soprano); Marguerite (soprano); Madeleine (mezzo-soprano); Dancer (mute); Noctambulist (tenor); Ragman (bass); Old Bohemian (baritone); Song Writer (baritone); Junkman (bass); Painter (bass); Two Philosophers (tenor, bass); Young Poet (baritone); Student (tenor); Two Policemen (baritones); Street Arab (soprano); Sculptor (baritone); Old Clothes Man (tenor); Apprentice (baritone); King of Fools (tenor); chorus (SATB) [many of the bit parts may be doubled].*

One day at the Paris Conservatory Charpentier's teacher Jules Massenet is supposed to have said to him: "Don't try to surprise people with cleverness. Give your temperament a chance. Go to Montmartre, look at some pretty girl, and let your heart say what it feels." Charpentier took his advice. There was, in fact, a real-life Louise, a working girl with shining eyes and black hair, who longed to be free. He never forgot her and always spoke of her in later years with respectful emotion. In the opera she is wooed by the poet Julien, who lives next door and who tries to persuade her to elope with him if her parents do not agree to their marriage. Her mother disapproves of a young man whom she, a respectable working-class woman, regards as a good-for-nothing Bohemian, although Louise's father, work-worn and weary, is more tolerant. A bitter quarrel between mother and daughter ends with the father trying to calm Louise and telling her that she must forget Julien. In act II Julien continues the siege by following her to her work as a seamstress. At last she agrees to go off with him, and by act III they are living in a hill-top Montmartre cottage overlooking the bright lights of Paris. Bohemian friends arrive and crown Louise "The Muse of Montmartre." The festivities are interrupted by the entry of Louise's mother, who reports that her father is desperately ill: will she try to save his life by giving him the joy of seeing her again? She does so, but the affectionate reunion ends in anger when she refuses his plea to give up Julien. She escapes, leaving him to curse the city of Paris for robbing him of his beloved daughter.

Although Charpentier is credited with the libretto of *Louise,* and certainly provided the words for the first act, his anonymous collaborator who pulled the whole thing into shape was a friend of his youth, the symbolist poet Saint-Pol-Roux. The original concept and the music, however, are entirely his own. The story line is clear and succinct, and the four main characters are vividly depicted. Charpentier follows Massenet in the cut and shape of his melodies and in his handling of the words. Note, for example, his unconventional prosody in Louise's famous aria "Depuis le jour," in which she recalls the first time she gave herself to Julien. He also draws, very successfully, on the *verismo* of Puccini to create a wholly realistic picture of Paris and its working people. Another device he adopts is the Wagnerian *leitmotif,* as in the leaping theme that introduces the opera and often recurs as a symbol of the passion between Julien and Louise. It is possible to argue that the main character of the opera is Paris itself. By weaving genuine street cries into his score and by his cunning depiction of the "petits gens" of the capital—especially in act II when he shows the city awakening at dawn and in the "Muse de Montmartre" episode of act III—Charpentier evokes an unforgettable impression of the greedy Paris which deprives Louise's father of his daughter. If *Louise* is an ardent plea for free love and for the right of every person to absolute liberty, it is also a wonderfully graphic re-creation of the atmosphere and personality of a great city.—JAMES HARDING

The Love for Three Oranges [Lyubov'k tryom apel'sinam]

Composer: *Sergei Prokofiev.*

Librettist: *Sergei Prokofiev (after Gozzi).*

First Performance: *Chicago, Auditorium Theater, 30 December 1921.*

Roles: *The Prince (tenor); Fata Morgana (soprano); Truffaldino (tenor); Leandro (baritone); King of Clubs (bass); Princess Clarissa (contralto); Pantalon (baritone); Celio (bass); Ninetta (soprano); Smeraldina (mezzo-soprano); Cleonte (bass); Linetta (contralto); Nicoletta (mezzo-soprano); Farfarello (bass); Master of Ceremonies (tenor); Herald (bass); Ten Reasonable Spectators (five tenors, five basses); chorus (SSAATTTTTBBBBBB).*

Prokofiev picked the subject for his second mature opera while still at work on *The Gambler*. In the artistic ferment of revolutionary Russia, the controversial theater director Vsevolod Meyerhold found a kindred spirit in the eighteenth-century Italian playwright Carlo Gozzi. Gozzi's concept of "abstract" theater owed a considerable debt to the improvisatory and stylized traditions of *commedia dell'arte*. Among advanced circles, Gozzi's *The Love for Three Oranges* was sufficiently well known to be adopted as the title of an avant-garde magazine: it would have been familiar to the composer even before Meyerhold recommended it as ideal opera material.

The starting point of its central fairy-tale is the melancholia of a young prince, son of the King of Clubs. He will be cured, if only he can be made to laugh. Two wicked conspirators, the Prime Minister Leandro and the king's niece Clarissa, set out to ensure that he never recovers. The jester Truffaldino is summoned to organize festivities to amuse the prince, but all his efforts fail until Fata Morgana, Leandro's witch-protectress who is present in disguise, totters over in undignified fashion. Enraged by the prince's hysterical laughter, she curses him with a consuming love for three oranges which he must pursue to the ends of the earth. After various adventures, the oranges are successfully retrieved from under the nose of sorceress Creonta's enormous cook (amusingly cast as a *basso profondo*). One of the oranges contains the Princess Ninetta, with whom the Prince falls in love and eventually marries. There are hazards still to be overcome (Ninetta, for example, is promptly turned into a rat) but all complications are resolved in the end. In addition to the real personages of the story, we are privy to a world of magic: the ineffectual Celio (Tchelio), sorcerer to the king, set against a number of obstructive demons. A third ingredient, a sort of disparaging commentary, is provided by the chorus. Its various pressure-groups comment, criticize and disrupt—"a critical 'conscience' for composer and audience," suggests Donald Mitchell (*Tempo,* Autumn 1956).

The conceit of a play within a play whose spectators interfere with the inner action whenever so disposed had obvious appeal for Prokofiev. He could suggest serious morals without explicitly committing himself, and make fun of them (and anything else) at the same time. While the score abounds with his usual sly turns of wit and deceptive harmonic quirks, the scheme does have its disadvantages. The emphasis on dramatic *non sequitur* and the slender opportunities for characterization impose heavy demands on purely musical invention. With everyone singing in much the same idiom and differences between the fabulous and the earthy effectively ironed out, there can be little contrast of light and shade. At his best, notably in act III, where his heroine *and* his lyrical powers put in a belated appearance, Prokofiev manages to avoid the barren patches. The text maintains a farcical tone throughout, and the humor *is* sometimes a trifle unsubtle, as when the bass trombone produces a not unrealistic fart on behalf of the fanfaring stage trumpeter.

For Israel Nestyev, Prokofiev's Soviet biographer, *The Love for Three Oranges* is "a work of limited appeal" that offers further evidence of nihilism in its "rejection of the principles of classical operatic form." The opera may not be a flawless masterpiece; yet the structural problems which remain unsolved were created by the composer's scarcely unprecedented attempt to devise a dramatic form appropriate to the subject matter. He closely follows the text and spirit of Gozzi's play, and the result is a kaleidoscopic theatrical extravaganza rather than convincing drama or even conventional comedy. Some very familiar music accompanies the many dances, processions, and pantomimes: Prokofiev drew upon these sections for his orchestral suite of 1924, which includes the celebrated *March*. Most of what is sung, in his typical

The English National Opera production of *The Love for Three Oranges*, 1990

declamatory style, is too closely allied to the stage action (and to individual sight-gags) to survive outside the theater. As for hidden meanings, Prokofiev himself was insistent: "All I tried to do was write an amusing opera." It succeeds best if translated into the language of the audience and played very much for laughs.

Like most of Prokofiev's operas, *The Love for Three Oranges* had a lengthy gestation period, and it was not until after the success of his concerts in Chicago in December 1918 that Prokofiev returned to the project, prompted by an offer of production from Chicago Opera. Despite unseemly postponements and wrangles over financial compensation, the work finally reached the stage in December 1921. That initial Chicago production was followed by stagings worldwide: at New York (1922), Cologne (1925), Berlin (1926) and Leningrad (1927). And although the work was not introduced to British audiences until the Edinburgh Festival of 1962 (courtesy of Belgrade Opera), it has since been given at Sadler's Wells Theatre (1963), in a BBC television production, at Glyndebourne (1982), and (most sensationally) in the Richard Jones production, originally staged by Opera North in 1988, which grafted on a further level of audience participation through the use of "scratch-and-sniff" cards impregnated with "microfragrances"!—DAVID GUTMAN

Lucia di Lammermoor

Composer: *Gaetano Donizetti.*

Librettist: *S. Cammarano (after Sir Walter Scott, The Bride of Lammermoor).*

First Performance: *Naples, San Carlo, 26 September 1835; revised 1839.*

Roles: *Lucia (soprano); Edgardo (tenor); Enrico Ashton (baritone); Alisa (mezzo-soprano); Normanno (tenor); Arturo Bucklaw (tenor); Raimondo Bidebent (bass); chorus (SSTTBB).*

Lucia di Lammermoor demonstrates how listening habits were changing in the Italy of the 1830s. Audiences who once only paid attention to choice plums in the score, who moved into their seats to hear a big aria by this or that *prima donna* and then went out again to chat or eat ices leaving the *hoi polloi* to the recitatives and the *comprimari,* now, it seems, could sit through a whole act with a musical logic intact from start to finish. In this unflinchingly romantic opera Donizetti held to a consistent orchestral coloring from the prologue onwards, with the sometimes athletic vocal line only underlining the mood, never fighting against it, as had been the norm.

Lucia di Lammermoor is set at Ravenswood Castle, whose true owners have been ousted by the Ashton family. The sole remaining heir of the former, Edgar (Edgardo), has, however, fallen in love with Lucy Ashton (Lucia) to the dismay of her brother Henry (Enrico), who wishes her to make a political marriage to boost his fortunes. He forges a letter from Edgardo, persuading the deceived Lucia into a reluctant marriage with Arthur Bucklaw (Arturo). At the marriage ceremony, Edgardo bursts into the castle, cursing Lucia for her faithlessness. During the celebrations which follow, however, Lucia emerges from the bridal chamber drenched in blood. She has stabbed Arturo and before the horrified guests enacts the wedding with Edgardo which should have taken place, singing crazily of love, ghosts, altars, and marital bliss, at the end of which she collapses. Edgardo, who has been bitterly watching the illuminated castle, is told of Lucia's death and falls on his sword in order to join her in heaven.

A few unconventional twists of plot notwithstanding, *Lucia di Lammermoor* cannot really be considered a radical score. It thrives on its stream of celestial melodies and on the passionate conviction which suffuses the tragic tale. At the first performance the great opera house in Naples resounded with sobs and tears; never before had Donizetti managed to encapsulate despair so fervently and with an ecstatic coloring surpassing mere charm. Various of the pieces were immediately enrolled in the musical pantheon, including the celebrated sextet "Chi mi frena in tal momento," Lucia's mad scene, and Edgardo's elegiac "Tu che a Dio spiegasti l'ali," its dying reprise given to the cello, which replaces the expiring hero's voice with an echo of his lament.

The score is a puzzle. The composer's autograph shows that he wrote it for singers very different from those who actually sang at the premiere. *Lucia* took quite a long time to come to the stage, and in the interim Donizetti got a different roster of artists. Even the instrumentation presents some problems unanswerable today. Did Donizetti really intend the heroine's mad scene to be accompanied by a glass harmonica? How could anyone have heard it beyond the first rows of stalls? No one really knows who wrote the celebrated cadenza for flute in the mad scene which urges her higher and higher, matching her note for note. It is not in the original score, though Donizetti would certainly have expected the soprano to interpolate a cadenza of her own. Even more astonishingly, the composer sanctioned alternatives in the choice of arias which, on the surface at least, diminish the effect of this fabled score. One of these arias he later incorporated in a French version of the opera (1839). To be precise, he allowed Fanny Tacchinardi-Persiani, who was the first Lucia, to replace her magical "Regnava nel silenzio" with the all-purpose "Perchè non ho del vento," an *aria di sortita* she had sung in *Rosmonda d'Inghilterra* (1834).—ALEXANDER WEATHERSON

Lucrezia Borgia

Composer: *Gaetano Donizetti.*

Librettist: *Felice Romani (after Hugo).*

First Performance: *Milan, Teatro alla Scala, 26 December 1833.*

Roles: *Lucrezia Borgia (soprano); Alfonso d'Este (bass); Gennaro (tenor); Maffio Orsini (contralto); Jeppo Liverotto (tenor); Don Apostolo Gazella (bass); Ascanio Petrucci (bass); Oloferno Vitellozzo (tenor); Gubetta (bass); Rustighello (tenor); Astolfo (bass); chorus (SATB).*

Even in Italy Lucrezia Borgia was a scandalous subject. In choosing it for an opera Donizetti was looking for change, even confrontation. From the start it was clear that the composer was planning a *coup,* dusting off the accepted routines of a score in numbers in favor of speed, a vast cast, a romantic gallimaufry of poisonings and *grand-guignol.* There was to be no love interest as such; Lucrezia was an anti-heroine, a thoroughly disreputable virago, the precursor of a whole succession of barnstorming Verdian sopranos whose violence and vehemence would be expressed with the same kind of energy, the same kind of leaping vocal lines.

The opera's layout was novel, a *prologo*—a flashback of sorts—followed by two acts set in Ferrara. There was to be only one concerted *finale,* and that was to the prologue. Both acts were to end with a vocal stint mostly on the part of the *prima donna*. It was to be a bold opera, fit to bring instant fame, had not all sorts of obstacles arisen (censorship, singers' protests, complaints from the Borgia descendents and a lawsuit from Victor Hugo amongst them). The *prologo* is set in Venice; a young soldier, Gennaro, sleeping peacefully in a doorway, awakes to find a splendidly-dressed woman bending over him. Astonished, he pours out his troubles, his unknown parentage, his unhappy upbringing, but when his friends return they begin insulting the lady. Gennaro is amazed: who is it, he asks? It's *La Borgia* they say, and snatch off her mask. Gennaro stares in fascinated bewilderment.

In Ferrara, the Duke (who has secretly witnessed his wife's encounter with the young man), determines to punish her "infidelity." When she comes to complain that her coat of arms has been desecrated (BORGIA has been altered to read ORGIA), he agrees that the culprit should be punished, but then triumphantly leads in Gennaro, who admits his guilt.

The Duchess is shaken. She pleads for Gennaro's release, but when this proves unsuccessful she threatens Alfonso, who remains unmoved and obliges her to administer a cup of poisoned wine to the witless youth. As soon as the Duke's back is turned, however, Lucrezia forces Gennaro to swallow an antidote and pushes him out through a secret panel. That evening there is a party at the Princess Negroni's palace. Gennaro's friends carouse joyfully, not much disturbed by the singing of a *miserere* in a nearby chapel. But when they try to leave they find the room locked, one door opening to admit the Duchess Lucrezia who has poisoned their wine in return for their insults in Venice. To her horror Gennaro is amongst them. This time he refuses to drink the antidote and attempts to stab her. In desperation she reveals that she is the mother he has so longed to find, and in agony Gennaro dies in her arms. At her cries Alfonso and all the courtiers rush in as Lucrezia, in a final elegy of despair and self-reproach, falls in extremis on the body of the son.

For this regrettable travesty of history (the real Lucrezia—whatever her despised dynasty—was noted for her piety), the composer supplied a stream of compelling music. Never before had he achieved quite such a momentum, nor such supreme flexibility. The superb trio which ends act I is a miracle of inventive variety, blending *cantilena* with *arioso,* declamation and vivid exchanges which look forward to Verdi and even beyond. It had everything that would focus Italian opera to come—a whispered colloquy *à la Macbeth,* innocence, insolence, insinuation, treachery, arrogance, heartbreak, and a devastating *stretta* which brought audiences to their feet. Perhaps most astonishingly, the opera preserved the expected contours perfectly intact. Certain of the *arie* became celebrated; Orsini's *brindisi* "Il segreto per esser felici" soon became staple diet for booming contraltos, with the ironical *miserere* that bisects it presaging *Il trovatore.*

As an operatic monster, this impure Lucrezia succeeded in capping the maternal anguish of Norma. Like Norma, she provided a vocal storehouse for several generations of great sopranos, most notably for Giulia Grisi and Thérèse Tietjens, both of whom made it the role for their final appearance on the stage, the latter making her final collapse on the body of her son her own final collapse.

There have been disputes about the florid ending to this opera. Donizetti himself, true perhaps to the radical intentions behind the whole score, tried to dispense with the *cabaletta finale* and in 1840 supplied a new finale to replace it in which the curtain falls directly after Gennaro's death. But this, though theatrically viable, is an anti-climax, and *Lucrezia Borgia* has never thrived with this revised ending.—ALEXANDER WEATHERSON

Ludwig, Christa

Mezzo-soprano and soprano. Married: 1) baritone Walter Berry, 1957 (divorced 1970; one son); 2) actor and stage director Paul-Emile Deiber, 1972. Studied with her mother, Eugenia Besalla, and with Hüni-Mihaček in Frankfurt; debut as Orlovsky in Die Fledermaus, *Frankfurt, 1946; in Salzburg from 1954; member of Vienna Staatsoper from 1955; Metropolitan Opera debut as Cherubino, 1959; at Metropolitan Opera for ten seasons; appeared at Bayreuth, 1966-67; Covent Garden debut as Amneris, 1969; created Claire Zachanassian in* Der Besuch der alten Dame, *1971; received the Golden Ring, 1980; became honorary member of Vienna Staatsoper, 1981.*

Christa Ludwig arguably possesses the most prodigious natural talent of our time. In years to come her powerful, radiant voice will be mentioned alongside those of Kirsten Flagstad and Rosa Ponselle. With such extraordinary resources her reputation would have been assured as a vocalist—but for Ludwig, the sound is never an end in itself. She brings to all of her roles potent insights and imagination. Ludwig is no mere virtuosa but one of the consistently thrilling artists of our time.

The sovereign technique which allows Ludwig such mastery is the happy alliance of a beautiful instrument with fastidious training. Ludwig's only teacher was her mother, and she has often described the detailed process by which the two of them quite literally "built" her voice, note by note, upon the solid foundation of proper breath support. This meticulous preparation has paid handsome dividends. Ludwig's lustrous mezzo-soprano—from the deep contralto of her lower notes to the gleaming soprano top tones—is a seamless whole, absolutely integrated in color. Her legato line is rock solid, yet she can cope with florid music with a nimbleness and ease that today we expect only from lighter voices. Her thorough schooling has also paid off with career longevity; she continues to perform some of the most rigorous roles in opera with a freshness that would honor a singer half her age.

Her vocal command has allowed Ludwig to explore successfully an astonishingly broad repertoire. Although we do not associate her with the coloratura roles of Rossini, she made her debut as Angelina in *La cenerentola* and also sang in *Il barbiere di Siviglia:* a recording of Rosina's "Una voce poco fa," extensively decorated, is not entirely idiomatic but more than compensates through the skill of her fioratura and the palpable charm of her personality. She was a memorable Carmen and has sung Verdi's Amneris (*Aida*) and Eboli (*Don Carlos*) with distinction. For several years she focused on soprano roles, performing Verdi's Lady Macbeth and Strauss's Ariadne, the Marschallin (*Der Rovenkavalier*) and the Dyer's Wife. She even ventured—in concert—the Immolation Scene from *Götterdämmerung,* though Ludwig abandoned plans to sing Brünnhilde on the stage and decided to return to the mezzo-soprano repertoire. The choice was probably a wise one, but on records at least the higher roles appear completely comfortable for her—unlike so many mezzos who attempt this transition, Ludwig sounds like a real soprano. Also unlike many others, she managed the return to her original repertoire unscathed. Among Ludwig's excursions into the soprano repertoire there has been at least one major contribution: on records and in the theater she was the greatest Leonore in *Fidelio* of our time.

Ludwig's central recorded repertoire includes Octavian in *Der Rosenkavalier,* Dorabella in *Così fan tutte,* and in the mezzo soprano roles of Wagner, in which she has few if any equals. As Octavian, Ludwig is able to vividly characterize the boy's youthful brashness, yet at the same time her voice remains rich and vibrant, coping easily with the high tessitura and dense Strauss orchestration. She recorded Dorabella twice. In her early performance for Decca the singing is poised but a trifle anonymous, not yet the detailed reading it was to become. By her second recording for EMI, Ludwig is superbly humorous and feminine, marvelously knowing yet innocent. Her Fiordiligi here is the incomparable Schwarzkopf, and no two singers on records work together with more aplomb—the silvery sheen of Schwarzkopf's soprano is the perfect complement to Ludwig's warmer mezzo, and for once the two really do seem like sisters. It is no wonder that this pairing was, for several seasons, one of the glories of the Salzburg festival.

In the major Wagner roles—Kundry, Ortrud, Venus, Brangäne, and Fricka and Waltraute in *Der Ring des Nibelungen*—Ludwig was equally if differently impressive. Here the demands are less for personal charm than unflagging reserves of power, and the magisterial solidity of Ludwig's tone and the glow of her upper register are peerless. In this music we recognize that she is the fitting successor to the great Margaret Matzenauer. No doubt generations to come will wonder who is the fitting successor to the great Christa Ludwig.—DAVID ANTHONY FOX

Luisa Miller

Composer: *Giuseppe Verdi.*

Librettist: *Salvadore Cammarano (after Schiller, Kabale und Liebe).*

First Performance: *Naples, San Carlo, 8 December 1849.*

Roles: *Luisa (soprano); Rodolfo (tenor); Miller (baritone); Count Walther (bass); Wurm (bass); Federica (contralto); Laura (mezzo-soprano); A Peasant (tenor); chorus (SSTTBB).*

Luisa Miller has long been considered the all-important gateway to middle Verdi, especially in the intimacy of expression employed by the composer in the opera's third act. It represents the second time that Verdi conscientiously tried to come to grips with a drama by Schiller. The first, *I masnadieri* of 1847 (based on *Die Räuber*) was hampered by a text which, while relatively faithful to its parent play, was written by an intellectual friend who for all his scholarly accomplishments was a theatrical amateur. With his new work Verdi had learned better than to repeat that mistake, and instead collaborated with the most respected and established professional librettist in Italy, Salvatore Cammarano.

Kabale und Liebe (Intrigue and Love) is a play of social consciousness, pitting an innocent lower-middle-class girl against the evil machinations of a basically corrupt upper-crust society. While it is true that Cammarano was almost too slick for his own good when he ruthlessly cut out characters and scenes which either did not lend themselves to the standard dos and don'ts (the "Convenienze") of mid-century Italian opera or would have trouble getting past the censorship, still he presented Verdi with a text which elicited the most poetic and intimate music yet to issue from the composer's pen: a vital landmark on the road to the bourgeois apotheosis of *La traviata.* Indeed the correspondence between musician and poet as *Luisa Miller* was thrashed out of *Kabale und Liebe* makes fascinating reading for the insights it sheds on the artistic process.

In a Tyrolean village in the early seventeenth century lives a retired soldier named Miller and his only child, a daughter named Luisa. She has fallen in love, and her love is returned by a young man whom she knows as "Carlo" but who is actually Rodolfo, son of the local aristocrat Count Walther, who lives in the castle on the hill. Walther's steward, Wurm, also desires Luisa and threatens revenge when Miller refuses her hand to him. Meanwhile Count Walther, anxious to break up his son's romance with a lower-class girl, insists that he instead marry Federica, Duchess of Ostheim. Rodolfo refuses and has gone to Miller's cottage to claim Luisa when his father storms in with a group of soldiers. The count accuses Luisa of being a whore and is about to have both Millers thrown into prison when his son compels him to retreat by threatening to reveal to the world his father's guilty secret; namely, that he and Wurm had murdered the previous count in order to secure the succession.

In act II, however, Miller has been arrested after all and is threatened by torture and death. Wurm comes to Luisa, and as price for her father's life he forces her to write a letter of "confession," which he dictates. The letter states that she desires Wurm rather than Rodolfo, whom she pretended to love merely for the sake of his fortune. When the heartbroken Rodolfo reads the false letter, he threatens Wurm with a duel, which the latter manages to evade. In the final act we return to the Miller cottage. Luisa is contemplating suicide, but her father's pleading causes her to relent, and the two of them decide to leave the village forever in the morning, even if they must become beggars. When Miller retires for the night, Rodolfo appears and secretly pours poison into a glass of wine which he forces Luisa to share with him. Told by Rodolfo that she soon will die, Luisa is freed from her unholy vow to Wurm and reveals the terms of his fatal bargain, to the despair of Rodolfo. The girl dies in her lover's arms as her hapless father looks on. Wurm, Count Walther and the villagers rush in to witness as Rodolfo, with his dying breath, stabs Wurm to the heart, leaving both fathers alone with their grief.

The loving father-daughter relationship and its centrality to Verdi's output (*Rigoletto, Simon Boccanegra, Aida,* etc.) has long been a topic of comment, as has, to a slightly lesser degree, that of father-son animosity (*Vêpres siciliennes, Don Carlos*). However, only in *Luisa Miller* do both themes appear in the same work, and indeed in many ways the polarity between the two fathers is one of the greatest strengths of this piece. It also has a well deserved reputation as a tenor's opera, inasmuch as Rodolfo's role takes extraordinary vocal stamina for its low-lying stentorian passages, yet must dominate equally in the many lyric moments, most particularly the famous aria "Quando le sere al placido" in act II. Luisa for her part must negotiate some awkward shifts from Bellini-esque ingenue in act I through typical early Verdian heroine with grandiose aria and cabaletta in act II on to the bona fide suffering and three-dimensionally characterized girl of the magnificent final act. Attention should also be drawn to the overture, arguably Verdi's finest structural achievement in that form. Amazingly, it is couched as a monothematic sonata movement, a format it shares with that which Mozart wrote for *Così fan tutte* but is otherwise quite rare in the operatic literature.—DENNIS WAKELING

Lully, Jean-Baptiste

Composer. Born Giovanni Battista Lulli, 28 November 1632, in Florence. Died 22 March 1687, in Paris. Married: Madeleine Lambert, daughter of the musician Michael Lambert, 1662. Studied the elements of music with a Franciscan monk; taken by the Chevalier de Guise to Paris to become page to Mlle de Montpensier, 1646; position in the private band of Mlle de Montpensier; in the service of Louis XIV as a ballet dancer and composer, 1652; studied harpsichord and composition with Nicolas Métru, organist of St Nicholas-des-

Champs, and François Roberday, organist at the Eglise des Petits-Pères; member of "les 24 violons du roi"; organized "les petits violons"; composer to the king, 1653; Surintendant de la Musique, 1661; composed music for comic ballets by Molière, 1663-71; acquired control of the Académie Royale de Musique, 1672; composed French operas from 1672, primarily with the librettist Quinault.

Operas *Les fêtes de l'Amour et de Bacchus* (pastorale-pastiche), Philippe Quinault, Molière and Lully, Paris, Jeu de paume de Béquet, 15? November 1672. *Cadmus et Hermione,* Philippe Quinault (after Ovid, *Metamorphoses*), Paris, Jeu de paume de Béquet, 27 April 1673; *Alceste, ou Le triomphe d'Alcide,* Philippe Quinault (after Euripides, *Alcestis*), Paris, Opéra, 19 January 1674; *Thésée,* Philippe Quinault (after Ovid, *Metamorphoses*), Saint-Germain, 11 January 1675; *Atys,* Philippe Quinault (after Ovid, *Fasti*), Saint-Germain, 10 January 1676; *Isis,* Philippe Quinault (after Ovid, *Metamorphoses*), Saint-Germain, 5 January 1677; *Psyché,* Thomas Corneille (after Apuleius, *The Golden Ass*), Paris, Opéra, 19 April 1678; *Bellérophon,* Thomas Corneille and Bernard le Bovier de Fontenelle (after Hesiod, *Theogeny*), Paris, Opéra, 31 January 1679; *Proserpine,* Philippe Quinault (after Ovid, *Metamorphoses*), Saint-Germain, 3 February 1680; *Persée,* Philippe Quinault (after Ovid, *Metamorphoses*), Paris, Opéra, 17 or 18 April 1682; *Phaëton,* Philippe Quinault (after Ovid, *Metamorphoses*), Versailles, 6 January 1683; *Amadis,* Philippe Quinault (after Montalvo, adapted by Herberay des Essarts, *Amadis de Gaule*), Paris, Opéra, 18 January 1684; *Roland,* Philippe Quinault, Versailles, 18 January 1685; *Armide,* Philippe Quinault (after Tasso, *Gerusalemme liberata*), Paris, Opéra, 15 February 1686; *Acis et Galatée* (pastorale héroïque), Jean Galbert de Campistron (after Ovid, *Metamorphoses*), Anet, 6 September 1686; Paris; *Achille et Polyxène,* Jean Galbert de Campistron (after Homer, *Iliad*), Paris, Opéra, 7 November 1687.

The leading figure in the musical court of Louis XIV, and the most influential musical figure in French culture in the seventeenth and eighteenth centuries, Giovanni Battista Lulli was born Italian, the son of a miller. He was thirteen years old when he arrived in France in March of 1646 to enter the service of Mlle de Montpensier, who had Lully brought to the household so that she would have someone with whom to practise her Italian. He worked as a musician/page (*garçon de chambre*) until he was 20, developing his musical skills as a guitarist, a violinist and a dancer all to a high level during this time.

His presence in Mlle de Montpensier's court at the Tuileries exposed Lully to the richness of the developing musical and cultural scene that surrounded the French court. Lully became a friend, and possibly a pupil, of the royal court composer, Italian violinist Lazzarini, and managed to attract the attention of the young Louis XIV through his exceptional skill as a dancer and mime. Managing to avoid any personal setback with the defeat of the Fronde, despite his employer's role in it, Lully secured his release from Mlle de Montpensier and returned to Paris in 1652.

When Mazarin died, in March of 1661, Italian music lost its most powerful advocate in France, but Lully's career continued to advance. Appointed director of music and composer for the royal household in May of that year, Lully then received his naturalization papers from Louis XIV the following December. In July of 1662 Lully married Madeleine, the daughter of Michel Lambert, chief musician for the royal family. The signatures of Louis XIV, the queen, and Colbert testify to Lully's expanding power in the musical scene at the French royal court. During these important times Lully not only changed the spelling of his name in the formal documents, he also erased his humble origins, declaring himself "Jean-Baptiste de Lully, esquire, son of 'Laurent de Lully,' Florentine gentleman.''

After his admittance to the king's string orchestra, the *Vingt-quatre violons,* Lully secured Louis's permission to establish a new string ensemble, the *Petits violons.* Between 1656 and 1664 Lully developed this group to an exceptionally high level of performing precision, and thus attracted the musical attention of the royal court and of Europe. This achievement strengthened Lully's growing position in Louis XIV's centralized regime.

Lully's career as a composer proceeded in a rather orderly fashion from the preparation of court ballets (1655-1672) to *comédie-ballets* (1663-1671) and then to operas (1673-1687). Lully possessed a gift for comedy, which he utilized in his ballets and in the subsequent collaborations with Molière and Corneille. In these collaborations with the great playwrights, the composer skillfully exploited Louis XIV's great interest in dancing to further his own career—the *Gazzette de France* in 1670 even described *Le bourgeois gentilhomme* as a "ballet accompanied by a comedy.'' In the later part of his career, however, Lully eschewed comedy in favor of epic drama in his operas.

The establishment of the French opera academies under a patent secured by Pierre Perrin in 1669 initially drew criticism from Lully, who then considered the French language inappropriate for large stage works. But the success of Perrin's *Pomone* in 1671 must have altered Lully's opinion, for when Perrin was incarcerated for debts, Lully quickly turned the situation to his own advantage, buying Perrin's privilege by offering him enough to pay off his creditors in addition to a pension for life. The royal privilege Lully obtained in 1672 gave him and his heirs the sole right to establish a royal academy of music. With that privilege, opera, defined as any work that was sung throughout, could only be performed with Lully's permission. So powerful did Lully become that subsequent legislation forbade more than two singers and six instrumentalists from appearing in productions independent of the newly established Royal Academy of Music.

Lully then secured a theater, the Jeu de paume de Béquet near the Luxembourg gardens, a stage machinist and architect, Carlo Vigarani, and a librettist, Philippe Quinault, with whom Lully had already worked in the ballets *La grotte de Versailles* (1668) and *Psyché* (1671). In this theater Lully's first operas were performed: *Les fêtes de l'Amour et de Bacchus,* a *pastorale-pastiche,* and *Cadmus et Hermione,* the first *tragédie-lyrique.* With this last work, what became known as French opera was born.

Lully and other composers preferred the term *tragédie en musique,* but the term *tragédie-lyrique* came into vogue and remained common until the time of the revolution. Lully's *tragédies-lyriques* were collaborations between the composer Lully, the librettist Quinault (who prepared 11 such works for Lully), and the French Academy, which held approval authority over the libretti. Lully's *Cadmus et Hermione* provided the model for the genre, which included a prologue followed by five acts, and the Lullian model became the standard for subsequent composers, including Campra, Rameau, and Gluck in his reform operas.

The subject matter of Lully's *tragédies-lyriques* came either from mythology (*Cadmus et Hermione, Alceste, Isis, Atys, Persée, Proserpine, Thésée* and *Phaëton*) or from tales of chivalry (*Amadis, Armide,* and *Roland*). Lully's prologues are usually separated distinctly from the subject material of the main action, and they generally pay homage to Louis XIV and his "heroic'' achievements in war.

Lully's output of Latin sacred music is much smaller than that of his stage works, but because he composed sacred motets throughout his career, these works bear special significance to Lully's development as a composer. As early as 1664 he composed the *grand motet Miserere*. Other works followed for specific occasions: the *Plaude laetare Gallia* for the birth of the Dauphin in 1668, and the *Te Deum* of 1677 for the baptism of Lully's eldest son, for whom the king had agreed to serve as godfather. The last dated sacred work is the *Exaudiat te, Domine* of 1685, but two other motets, *Notus in Judaea* and *Quare fremuerunt gentes,* probably also came from Lully's last years. Fourteen *petits motets* are also credited to Lully.

On January 8, 1687, Lully struck his foot with a staff used to beat musical time while conducting 150 musicians in a performance of his *Te Deum*. The wound abscessed, but Lully refused to have a toe amputated, and he died of complications on the following March 22. He was interred according to his wishes in a private chapel at the church of the Petits-Pères, today Notre-Dame-des-Victoires, near the Bibliothèque Nationale.

Modern audiences tend to overlook Lully's importance in the history of western music. This remarkable figure stands alone in several respects: (1) he was the most influential individual composer of his era, for as the Italian and French styles came to dominate Europe from the late seventeenth through the eighteenth centuries, Lully alone personified a style that became the fashion in courts from England to Germany to Sweden and farther east; (2) he was an extraordinary administrator and businessman. Neal Zaslaw has pointed out that Lully was the only person who, during three centuries of the existence of the Paris Opéra, managed to make rather than to lose money. Lully built a personal fortune, at his death valued at more than P800,000 (at a time when the average court musician earned approximately P1500 annually). His wealth probably exceeded that of any musician of his time or before him. During his career he built several grand residences in Paris and in the surrounding communities in the direction of Versailles.

Lully jealously guarded the originals of his compositions, and the history of their existence after his death remains a subject of inquiry. None is known to have survived. Henri Prunières identified a fragment of manuscript from an unknown work and proposed it as a Lully autograph, but this identification has not been widely accepted by scholars. This absence of originals has made the preparation of a collected works difficult, and thus Lully remains one of the most important major figures in the history of western music for whom a collected edition has never been completed. The project, suspended with the outbreak of World War II, was recently resumed by an international team of scholars in a *New Collected Works* under the general editorship of Carl Schmidt.

The style that Lully developed in his decidedly French works separates itself sharply from Italian music in the mid to late seventeenth century. As a result, debate over the virtues of the two styles, French and Italian, developed and continued in various forms for more than a century. The crispness of rhythm appropriate to the French dance style, and the French classical requirement for clarity of declamation of text precluded the employment of the dense counterpoint found in Italian, and most particularly in German, Baroque music. The aesthetic values of proportion in time and balance in melodic contour came to the fore in French music, while the art of counterpoint was much less developed. As a result, canon and fugue are rare in Lully's music. Thus, Lully's music suffered in the assessment of later audiences who were captivated by eighteenth century counterpoint, the Italian Baroque style, and the German music it inspired. Only with the surge of interest in period instruments in the later twentieth century and with the renaissance of seventeenth- and eighteenth-century performance practices has Lully's music begun to find acceptance with modern audiences and critics. An important advancement occurred in 1987 with a critically acclaimed production of *Atys* at the Paris Opéra under the direction of William Christy and using period instruments, historically informed choreography, costumes and sets. The technology of film, video, and the faithfulness of digital sound reproduction lends promise to the hope that in the future Lully's achievements will be more widely understood and appreciated.—JOHN HAJDU HEYER

Lulu

Composer: *Alban Berg.*

Librettist: *Alban Berg (after Frank Wedekind's* Erdgeist *and* Die Büchse der Pandora*).*

First Performance: *Zurich, Stadttheater, 2 June 1937; first complete performance, Paris, Opéra, 24 February 1979.*

Roles: *Lulu (soprano); Dr. Schön (baritone); Countess Geschwitz (mezzo-soprano); Alwa (baritone); Painter (tenor); Schigolch (bass); Rodrigo (doubles with Animal Trainer, bass); Schoolboy (doubles with Wardrobe Mistress, contralto); Theater Manager (bass); Prince (tenor); Servant (tenor); Dr. Goll (speaking part); Jack the Ripper (mute).*

Wedekind's Lulu plays liberated Alban Berg from the rigid moral atmosphere of Vienna in the first decade of the twentieth century. On first reading them he proclaimed that "sensuality is not a weakness, does not mean a surrender to one's own will. Rather it is an immense strength that lies in us—the pivot of all being and thinking."

In the prologue to Berg's *Lulu,* an Animal Tamer presents the principal characters as animals. Lulu, the snake, embodies "the fundamental nature of womankind." She is desired by all the men in the first half of the opera (and truly loved only by the lesbian Countess Geschwitz, whose affection she does not reciprocate). She causes the death of two successive husbands when they discover her infidelity; and her marriage to the only man she ever loved, the wealthy newspaper editor Dr. Schön, ends when he presses her to kill herself, and she shoots him instead.

In the second half of the opera Lulu escapes from prison through the Countess' self-sacrifice. She flees Germany with her new lover, Schön's son Alwa. Blackmailers force her to abandon a luxurious life in Parisian high society; she then becomes a London prostitute and dies at the hands of her third client, Jack the Ripper.

Wedekind's Lulu is the victim of men who cannot accept her sensuality and her honesty. They imprint upon her their own images of the ideal of feminine conduct (a point neatly symbolized by the new name which each of her lovers bestows upon her). By contrast, Lulu herself has an absolute integrity, a determination not to prostitute her sexuality or to compromise her love. This is why her descent into prostitution is so powerful an image; and her death at the hands of Jack the Ripper embodies the revenge of men on a female sensuality which is beyond male control.

The Lulu plays are a critique of contemporary German society, in particular of the tension between its monetary bases and the human feelings which mercantilism stifles. Berg responds to the strange mixture in Wedekind's texts of satire, farce, and tragedy with a music which can shift

459

its perspective from moment to moment. In some parts of the opera, the music is of a Wagnerian or Mahlerian intensity; Berg demands a total involvement when he pours out his compassion for the tragedy of suffering humanity. Elsewhere, the composer offers a detached commentary, sardonic, ironic, and parodistic—a music which is essentially of its time, and frequently reflects the European mania for jazz in the twenties and thirties.

The most remarkable feature of *Lulu* is what Douglas Jarman has termed Berg's "extraordinary combination of technical calculation and emotional spontaneity." A score which unleashes some of the most tumultuous and passionate music of the twentieth century is also rigorously through-composed—clearly divided into formal numbers, and precisely controlled by Berg's intricate development of the twelve-tone technique.

Each act includes a form from instrumental music, which gives unity to the incidents which surround it. Act I is dominated by a sonata devoted to Dr. Schön's unsuccessful struggle for freedom from Lulu, act II by a rondo which symbolizes Alwa's constant reversion to his passion for her, and act III by a theme and variations which evoke and chronicle the final descent of Lulu to her death.

Berg's compression of Wedekind's lengthy text is based on one basic structural principle. Lulu rises through the early scenes to the apex of her power and influence, when she has achieved her ambition and is married to Dr. Schön. Then, after his death, she plunges inexorably towards her destruction. Berg sees her murder of Schön as the center point of his narrative, places it at the middle of the second of three acts, and enforces its centrality, firstly by constructing the film-interlude between the two scenes of act II as a palindrome, so that at the center point of the opera the music seems almost to be in equipoise; and secondly by the use of musical recapitulation, so that the second half of the opera seems almost to be a nightmarish reenactment of the events of the first.

Berg adapted the final scene of Wedekind's play, so that by extensive musical recapitulations, and by the doubling of parts on stage, Lulu's three clients reembody the three men whose deaths she caused in the first half of the opera. The third and last is Jack; there is hideous irony in the disjunction between text and music, as she haggles with him over the price for her favors to the most powerful presentation yet of the tragic music for her tortured affair with Dr. Schön. Here, sexual need is seen simply as a lethal torment, for both men and women. But in his setting of the Countess' final, dying words Berg presents a counterbalancing image of the transcendent nobility and beauty of a love which can be fulfilled only in heaven.

Berg died before finishing the orchestration of act III. After initial enthusiasm, his widow banned completion of the opera, and *Lulu* had to be performed from 1937 to 1979 as a two-act torso. But Berg's publishers secretly commissioned from Friedrich Cerha an orchestration of the passages which Berg had left incomplete. Helene Berg died in 1976, and the opera was first performed in its entirety in Paris in February 1979. The completion allows us to appreciate, at last, Berg's symmetrical conception of the opera. And the London scene is an overwhelming finale, although the Paris scene is a disappointment. Berg's extraordinarily dense vocal ensembles in the Paris scene make comprehension difficult, even of crucial material; and the level of musical inspiration is lower than elsewhere. Despite this, *Lulu* is unquestionably one of the greatest operas of the twentieth century.—MICHAEL EVANS

Die Lustigen Weiber von Windsor [The Merry Wives of Windsor]

Composer: *Otto Nicolai.*

Librettist: *S.H. Mosenthal (after Shakespeare, The Merry Wives of Windsor).*

First Performance: *Berlin, Hofoper, 9 March 1849.*

Roles: *Sir John Falstaff (bass); Mr. Ford/Herr Fluth (baritone); Mr. Page/Herr Reich (bass); Fenton (tenor); Mistress Ford/Frau Fluth (soprano); Mistress Page/Frau Reich (mezzo-soprano); Anne Page (soprano); Slender Spärlich (tenor); Dr. Caius (bass); chorus (SATB).*

Nicolai's classic operatic treatment of Shakespeare's *Merry Wives of Windsor* was the culmination of a brief career theretofore devoted to Italian opera, in addition to smaller forms (*Lieder,* sacred music, part-songs, and miscellaneous instrumental music). Nicolai had aspired to the composition of a German opera ever since leaving Italy for Vienna in 1842. But difficulties in finding a suitable libretto, periods of bad health, and lack of co-operation from the Viennese Court Theater administration delayed the completion of the work by several years, by which time the composer had moved to Berlin.

The opera begins with Shakespeare's second act, as Mistresses Page (Reich) and Ford (Fluth) compare the identical letters they have received from the rotund and currently impecunious old knight, John Falstaff. To punish him for his presumption and Mr. Ford for his habitual jealousy, the wives arrange an assignation between Sir John and Mistress Ford, intending that her husband should discover them. When Ford does arrive, posse in tow, Falstaff is quickly packed into a large laundry basket and unceremoniously deposited in the river while Ford and the others search the house in vain (finale, act I). Ford remains determined to catch the suspected intruder, and disguised as "Master Brook" ("Sir Bach") he enlists Falstaff as a surrogate lover to pry loose for him the rigid scruples of his beloved Mistress Ford, thus to verify her infidelity and the knight's guilt. In the meantime Squire Slender (Junker Spärlich) and the French physician Dr. Caius are in competition with the impoverished young Fenton for the hand of Anne, daughter of the wealthy Mr. Page (Herr "Reich," i.e. rich). Fenton serenades her ("Horch, die Lerche singt im Hain") while his rivals look on angrily, in hiding. In the finale to act II, Falstaff is again spirited out of the house, this time in the guise of the "fat old woman from Brainford," but not without receiving a beating from Mr. Ford, who takes Falstaff for a fortune-teller and swindler. After Ford is let in on the merry wives' pranks, Mistress Page sings a ballad about Herne's Oak and together they plot their final act of revenge against Falstaff, to lure him into a mock fairy ritual in Windsor Forest. The elder Pages each set a plan to ensure the secret betrothal of Anne to their suitor of choice (Slender for Mr. Page, Caius for his wife). But Anne determines to foil them by plighting her troth to Fenton first (the aria, "Wohl denn!, gefaßt ist der Entschluß"). As the moon rises on Windsor Forest in the final scene, Falstaff appears, adorned with stag horns, for his third attempted rendezvous. After a brief trio Mistresses Page and Ford suddenly flee, as the elfin pantomime begins. Falstaff is discovered, duly pinched and pummeled, and finally disabused of the masquerade. In the confusion of disguise, Slender and Caius find they have been wedded to one another, while Anne has been joined with Fenton.

The use of spoken dialogue, according to the convention of German comic opera, enables Nicolai and his librettist, S.H. Mosenthal, to preserve more details of Shakespeare's comedy than are found in the Verdi-Boito version (the role of Anne's third suitor, Slender, or Falstaff's second misadventure at Ford's house, for example). But conversely, Mosenthal's libretto cannot match the elegant economy of Boito's, and the act-II finale of Nicolai's opera (Falstaff's escape as the "fat woman of Brainford") seems redundant in terms of operatic dramaturgy, which cannot support the episodic density of incident characteristic of the spoken comedy. The frequency of dialogue scenes, on the other hand, is considerably curtailed in comparison with other German and French comic opera of the period, perhaps making its continued presence at all only more awkward. Act II, for instance, is only twice interrupted by dialogue. A rather long *secco* style recitative between Ford (as "Brook") and Falstaff introduces a continuous series of small, well-wrought musical numbers structured around Fenton's serenade to Anne in the garden. This well-known *Romanze,* "Horch, die Lerche singt im Hain," demonstrates Nicolai's experience as a composer of *Lieder* and his expertise as orchestrator.

Nicolai seized the lyric opportunities implicit in the originally rather subordinate love-intrigue of Anne and Fenton, as Verdi and Boito did in turn. Also like Verdi, he made the most of the romantic-fantastic atmosphere suggested by the nocturnal scene in Windsor Forest. This final scene, which provides much of the thematic material for the popular overture, is a good example of the blending of lyrical mood-painting (the "moonrise" with its shimmering sustained strings supporting a gradually rising line passed between woodwinds and brass) with the folk-like popular tunefulness of Lortzing or Flotow (the trio between Falstaff and the two wives). The essential quality of Nicolai's opera lies in this happy synthesis of brusque, earthy idiom of the German comic opera tradition with the more elevated manner of Mendelssohn's music to *A Midsummer Night's Dream* and with an easy control of the large-scale ensemble tableau of Italian opera (e.g., finale to act I, "Ich kam, ein Wild zu jagen, und finde keine Spur").—THOMAS S. GREY

Macbeth

Composer: *Giuseppe Verdi.*

Librettists: *Francesco Maria Piave and Andrea Maffei (after Shakespeare).*

First Performance: *Florence, Teatro della Pergola, 14 March 1847; revised, Piave, French translation by Charles Nuitter and A. Beaumont, Paris, Théâtre-Lyrique, 21 April 1865.*

Roles: *Lady Macbeth (soprano); Macbeth (baritone); Macduff (tenor); Banquo (bass); Lady-in-Waiting (mezzo-soprano); Malcolm (tenor); Doctor (bass); Servant (bass); Murderer (bass); Herald (bass); Apparitions (sopranos, bass); Hecate (dancer); Duncan (mute); Fleance (mute); chorus (SSAATTBB).*

Macbeth is the first of three operas which Verdi drew from works by Shakespeare, the dramatist he most admired. There are two main versions of the work, one written for the 1847 carnival season in Florence, and a substantial revision for the 1865 season at the Théâtre-Lyrique in Paris. Although the earlier version was more successful with audiences than the revision, it is nonetheless the revised version that is heard today.

Verdi drew closely on the Shakespearean source for his plot, which he sketched in prose before turning the versification over to his librettist Piave, as was his usual practice. In act I, Macbeth and Banquo come across a band of witches, who prophesy that Macbeth will be Thane of Cawdor and King of Scotland, and that Banquo will be the father of future kings. The first prophecy is shortly thereafter proven, when messengers arrive to hail Macbeth as Thane of Cawdor, leaving him in turn to wonder about the truth of the other predictions. When Lady Macbeth hears of these events, and of King Duncan's intended visit to their castle, she decides Duncan must be murdered to fulfill the prophecy, and, convincing her more reluctant husband, they kill him in his sleep. In act II, King Macbeth broods over the predicted reign of Banquo's sons, and decides to hire an assassin to kill Banquo and his son Fleance, but Fleance escapes. At a banquet in the closing scene of the act, Macbeth learns of the escape, and is terrified by the ghost of Banquo, leading the guests to suspect his guilt—including Macduff, who decides to flee to England and gather support against Macbeth. In act III, Macbeth returns to the witches, and frightening apparitions appear from their cauldron to give him mysterious advice: to beware of Macduff, that "none of woman born" shall harm him, and that he need fear not until Birnam Wood advances. After the apparitions and witches vanish, he and Lady Macbeth decide that Banquo's son and Macduff's family must also die. Act IV begins as Macduff, along with the other Scottish refugees in England, mourns the death of his wife and children, and prepares for battle with the English army of Malcolm, now heir to the Scottish throne; they arm themselves with boughs of Birnam Wood for camouflage. Back in Scotland, Lady Macbeth is seen in her tormented nightly trance, trying to wash off the blood she imagines she sees on her hands. This is followed by a brooding scene in which Macbeth learns of his wife's death and of the advancing of Birnam Wood. In the final scene Macbeth is confronted and killed in battle by Macduff (who was not of woman born, but ripped from the womb), and Malcolm is joyously declared the new King of Scotland.

Notwithstanding his love for Shakespeare, Verdi's reason for choosing *Macbeth* as an operatic subject initially had little to do with the drama. The idea was proposed to him, along with two others, by the Florentine theater manager Lanari during contract negotiations; and it was the absence of a good romantic tenor on the one hand and the availability of a fine baritone on the other (more suited to the dark, non-romantic role of Macbeth), that determined Verdi's choice. However, after the initial, singer-related strategies, Verdi became deeply involved with the dramatic aspects of the project, so much so that Julian Budden, for instance, considers *Macbeth* to contain the composer's first "glimpses of a new freedom," as distinct from his earlier "years in the galley," in which Verdi primarily labored to please audiences, singers, and managers, rather than to fulfill his own dramatic conceptions. Although the many closed set-piece forms, especially the conventional cavatinas and cabalettas, seem to belie this new dramatic emphasis, Verdi's letters to his librettist Piave and to the lead singers tell a different story. For example, with Piave he insisted on a new approach of "FEW WORDS . . . FEW WORDS . . . CONCISE STYLE," and from the singers he demanded a departure from *bel canto,* suggesting to Varesi that he must sing the crucial murder duet with Lady Macbeth in act I "in a hollow voice such as will inspire terror," and to the soprano Barbieri-Nini that her singing in the sleepwalking scene must be "sotto voce and in such a way as to arouse terror and pity." Another forward-looking aspect of the 1847 version was Verdi's increasingly dramatic use of the orchestra, as seen for example in the evocative accompanimental pattern to the sleepwalking scene, made up of chromatically shuddering muted strings and sighing English horn.

Besides attempting (unsuccessfully) to answer the French tastes for ballet and general scenic grandeur, Verdi's revisions for the later Théâtre-Lyrique production reveal his stylistic evolution between 1847 and 1865, a period of striking experimentation in his operatic career. The result is a mixture of styles, with the early, crudely energetic music of the witches, the banquet scene, and the on-stage *banda* music for King Duncan's entry, for example, standing adjacent to scenes composed in the far more subtle, flexible style of melody and harmony which characterizes Verdi's late middle-period approach. The mixture is sometimes disconcerting and disturbing to the successful rhythm of dramatic flow present in the original version, but modern audiences would probably still be loathe to give up the special beauties of the revised score, such as Lady Macbeth's act II aria "La luce langue" ("The light fades," replacing the conventional cabaletta of the earlier version), the act IV Exiles' Chorus, and the revised act III apparition scene.—CLAIRE DETELS

MacNeil, Cornell

Baritone. Born 24 September 1922, in Minneapolis. Married: 1) Margaret Gavan, 1947 (two sons, three daughters, divorced 1972); 2) Tania Rudensky, 1972. Studied with Friedrich Schorr at the Hartt School of Music in Hartford, Connecticut; opera debut in Menotti's The Consul, *on Broadway, 1950; New York City Opera debut as Germont in* La traviata, *1953, and sang there until 1956; appeared at San Francisco as Escamillo, 1955; appeared at Chicago as Puccini's Lescaut, 1957; Teatro alla Scala debut as Carlo in* Ernani, *1959; Metropolitan Opera debut as Rigoletto, 1959; became president of American Guild of Musical Artists, 1971.*

Cornell MacNeil was a natural singer from his earliest youth. He studied at the Hartt School of Music in Hartford, Connecticut with Friedrich Schorr. In 1945, he became a regular member of the glee club at Radio City Music Hall in New York City and joined the summer stock company at the Paper Mill Playhouse in Millburn, New Jersey. During this time he auditioned for Broadway parts. In 1947, he landed a small role in Victor Herbert's *Sweethearts* and understudied the juvenile lead in the long running musical *Where's Charley?,* which opened October 1948. MacNeil received his first major operatic opportunity when composer Menotti offered him the role of John Sorel in his musical drama *The Consul,* which opened in 1950 at the Ethel Barrymore Theatre on Broadway. It ran for 269 performances. The opera, which won the Pulitzer Prize for music and the Drama Critics Circle Award as Best Musical, also earned praise for MacNeil. Olin Downes of the *New York Times* (17 March 1950) commended the young MacNeil for his "excellent" singing and the "appropriate pathos and simplicity" of his acting. MacNeil also impressed Menotti with his natural talent, and following Menotti's advice, MacNeil retired from the Broadway stage to prepare seriously for an operatic career. From 1953-56, after a successful debut, MacNeil sang a variety of roles while on the roster of the New York City Opera. After 1959 he traveled extensively, making guest appearances and debuts in San Francisco, Chicago, Caracas, Mexico City and Central City, Colorado.

MacNeil established himself internationally by singing two important debuts substituting for ailing singers. In March 1959, while performing in California, MacNeil received an urgent request from the Teatro alla Scala offering him a debut performance as Charles V in Verdi's *Ernani;* shortly after his warm reception in Italy, he received another urgent call from the Metropolitan Opera, to substitute for Robert Merrill in the title role of Verdi's *Rigoletto.* Both these substitutions served to establish MacNeil as a remarkably adaptable and versatile performer, with an almost instantaneous reputation nationally and internationally. He has also sung with great success in many houses throughout Europe including Covent Garden, the Vienna Staatsoper and the Paris Opéra. MacNeil would sing one more important premiere performance, *Nabucco,* again substituting for another singer, this time Leonard Warren. The Metropolitan Opera premiere in October 1960 was originally intended for Warren, but MacNeil was called on to fill the unexpected hole left by Warren's sudden death in March 1960.

MacNeil is a true Verdi baritone, who has been hailed throughout his career for his vocal consistency and his naturally produced sound. During his tenure at the Metropolitan Opera, MacNeil has shown himself to be well-rounded by presenting a truly broad spectrum of Verdi roles. His Verdi roles for the Metropolitan Opera have included Amonasro in *Aida,* Macbeth, the Count di Luna in *Il trovatore,* Simon Boccanegra, Iago in *Otello,* Guido di Monteforte in *I vespri siciliani* and Sir John Falstaff. He has presented himself equally well in non-Verdi literature and has offered such roles as the Baron Scarpia in Puccini's *Tosca* and Barnaba in Ponchielli's *La Gioconda*. He has also won recognition as a Wagnerian baritone with performances of the Dutchman in Wagner's *Der fliegende Holländer*.

His successes can be monitored by the many newspaper accounts which have recorded his premieres and performances. For the most part, he has always been received warmly and with high critical regard. Early in MacNeil's career, Paul Henry Lang of the *New York Herald Tribune* (25 October 1960) described his voice as "warm, with good color and carrying power" and although Lang mentioned some "slightly uncertain spots in the middle," he thought that MacNeil "sang well" and possessed the necessary "temperament." Winthrop Sargeant of the *New Yorker* (26 February 1966) assessed MacNeil as "one of the truly great Rigoletto's, with a voice of immense size and a fine grasp of character." Richard Freed of the *New York Times* (16 February 1966) proclaimed that MacNeil's Amonasro "reconfirmed" MacNeil as "the great Verdi baritone of this decade" and further that MacNeil's "characterizations seem to grow in subtlety and power from season to season."

No stranger to the American public, MacNeil has been seen many times on live telecasts from the Metropolitan Opera including: Verdi's *Rigoletto, Otello* and *La traviata;* Puccini's *Tosca* and *Il trittico,* and Kurt Weill's *Mahogonny*. He portrayed the elder Germont in Zeffirelli's film version of *La traviata* with Teresa Stratas and Placido Domingo, and can be seen in several "From the Met" video productions including a spectacular performance of the Baron Scarpia in Puccini's *Tosca* with Hildegard Behrens. His opera recording *La traviata* won him an American Grammy Award in 1984 for the Best Opera Recording.

Throughout his career, MacNeil has been committed to improving the life and working conditions of the artists and technicians connected with professional opera. This commitment culminated in his becoming the president of the American Guild of Musical Artists in 1971. In this capacity MacNeil was responsible for the contract negotiations between the on-stage performers and the management of the Metropolitan Opera. Robert Jones of the *New York Sunday News* (21 September 1975) suggests that MacNeil may well be best remembered for his "work as a musical political figure."—PATRICIA ROBERTSON

Madama Butterfly

Composer: *Giacomo Puccini.*

Librettists: *Giuseppe Giacosa and Luigi Illica (after the drama by David Belasco based on the story by John Luther Long).*

First Performance: *Milan, Teatro alla Scala 17 February 1904; revised, Brescia, Grande, 28 May 1904; revised, London, Covent Garden, 10 July 1905; revised, Paris, Opéra-Comique, 28 December 1906.*

Roles: *Cio-Cio-San (soprano); Lt B.F. Pinkerton (tenor); Sharpless (baritone); Suzuki (mezzo-soprano); Kate Pinkerton (mezzo-soprano); Goro (tenor); Prince Yamadori (baritone); The Bonze (bass); The Imperial Commissioner (bass); The Official Registrar (baritone); Yakuside (baritone); Cio-Cio-San's Mother (mezzo-soprano); Aunt (mezzo-soprano); Cousin (soprano); Trouble (mute); chorus (SSATT).*

Most likely due to the organized opposition of the dreaded Teatro alla Scala claque, Puccini's sixth opera, *Madama Butterfly,* was a fiasco in its 1904 Milan premiere, a failure so terrible that the composer withdrew the work and returned the royalties after the very first night. However, following some cuts in the originally lengthy act I, the addition of an intermission between what had been scenes i and ii of act II, and the removal three months later to the more intimate Teatro Grande at Brescia, the opera quickly became one of the most widely performed works in the repertory. Indeed, it is perhaps the most modern work in terms of harmonic style to achieve such popularity.

The dramatic source of *Madama Butterfly* was the American David Belasco's one-act play (itself adapted for the stage from an 1898 magazine story by John Luther Long) about a geisha girl (Butterfly) who marries and is abandoned by an American sailor. After admiring the play and securing the rights from Belasco during a trip to London in the summer of 1900, Puccini set quickly to work with his practiced team of librettists Luigi Illica and Giuseppe Giacosa (writers of *La bohème* and *Tosca*), focusing the story more directly on the title figure by enlarging on the tragic dimension of her character, in particular the dishonor and impoverishment of her family following her father's suicide (before the onset of the story), the passionate sincerity of her love for the American sailor and her desperate, doomed attempt to gain acceptance into his culture. Thus in act I, Madama Butterfly, or Cio-Cio-San, marries the American sailor, Lieutenant Benjamin Franklin Pinkerton; she for love (and to escape her life as a geisha girl) and he for amusement while he waits to find a "real" American wife. In doing so she renounces her religion and in turn brings the renunciation of her priestly uncle the Bonze and her family back on herself; but her love for Pinkerton and their rapturous wedding night overshadows the rest.

In act II, set three years later, Cio-Cio-San is patiently awaiting Pinkerton's return, despite everyone else's certainty that she has been abandoned. When the American ambassador Sharpless hints of Pinkerton's abandonment, she responds by showing him her son by Pinkerton, and he agrees to contact Pinkerton for her. When Pinkerton's ship suddenly appears in the harbor, the enraptured Cio-Cio-San and her maid Suzuki cover the house with flowers and hold a vigil for Pinkerton. In fact, Pinkerton has returned, but he has come with his American wife Kate, not to join Cio-Cio-San but to take the son away to America, as Kate explains in act III. Cio-Cio-San stoically agrees to the plan, but insists that Pinkerton come in person; then she prepares a ritualized death scene in imitation of her father's suicide, first saying good-bye to her son, blindfolding him, and stabbing herself with her father's hara-kiri knife, just as Pinkerton finally arrives.

Although initially criticized as derivative, *Madama Butterfly* stands apart from Puccini's earlier works in several respects. First there is the fully tragic dimension of the heroine. Cio-Cio-San is not just one of the passive "victim-women" that Puccini supposedly featured throughout his career (a clichéd supposition which does not account for the majority of his heroines); she is a brave woman who has made a fatal mistake, and whose discovery and accompanying reaction to that mistake work well to evoke the definitively tragic mixture of fear and pity.

Second, Puccini's use of motivic and thematic recurrence to depict the main characters, ideas, and events in the drama is more psychologically acute and thorough-going than in any of his other works. That is to say, where Puccini had been content to repeat a good tune for its own sake in his earlier operas, all of the reprises in *Madama Butterfly* are psychologically revealing. For example, the main theme of Cio-Cio-San's late second-act aria—where she had explained to Sharpless that she would rather die than return to the geisha life—returns at the end of the

m

OPERA

opera as an orchestral accompaniment to her suicide, thus conveying a strong message to Pinkerton and the other persecutors that she will dance no more for their pleasure. Recurrences and transformations of other prominent themes and motives are also used to careful psychological effect, comparable to the leitmotivic usage of Wagner.

Other special features of *Madama Butterfly* include Puccini's use of authentic Japanese songs and other exotic details of style, such as whole tone and pentatonic harmonies, heterophonic textures and use of various gongs, bells, and other oriental-sounding percussion instruments. These exotic aspects of *Madama Butterfly* have sometimes been criticized as superficial, or merely indicative of the contemporary fad for the Orient, but they are actually very convincingly absorbed into Puccini's native Italian style, as demonstrated in the beauty and lyricism of the act-I love duet, among other scenes. Considered in their total effect, it is the above-mentioned unique features rather than the supposed sentimentality of the story which account for the longevity—following the initial fiasco—of this opera's extraordinary appeal.—CLAIRE DETELS

Mahagonny

Composer: *Kurt Weill.*

Librettist: *B. Brecht.*

First Performance: *Baden-Baden, 17 July 1927; revised as* Aufstieg und Fall der Stadt Mahagonny, *first performed Leipzig, Neues Theater, 9 March 1930.*

Roles: *Leocadia Begbick (contralto or mezzo-soprano); Fatty (tenor); Trinity Moses (baritone); Jenny (soprano); Jim Mahoney (tenor); Jack (tenor); Billy Bankbook (baritone); Alaska Wolf Joe (bass); Toby Higgins (tenor); chorus (SATB).*

In the summer of 1927 the Baden-Baden chamber music festival presented, together with premieres of serious works, a "Songspiel" as its authors Bertolt Brecht and Kurt Weill called it: in effect, a cross between a scenic cantata and cabaret-style skit. Entitled *Mahagonny,* the invented name for a symbolic American city that succumbs to corruption, the work used dance and popular music idioms of the day as the basis for a staged setting of satirical poems from Brecht's *Die Hauspostille* (*Domestic Breviary*). Brecht and Weill, encouraged by the rather scandalous success of their little piece, later that year agreed to incorporate it into what turned out to be their only joint full-blown opera, now entitled *Aufstieg und Fall der Stadt Mahagonny* (*Rise and Fall of the City of Mahagonny*). Interrupted by other undertakings, most notably their *Die Dreigroschenoper* (*The Threepenny Opera*), the opera was finally given its premiere in Leipzig on March 9th, 1930, to a stormy reception whipped up by political demonstrations.

The subject of the opera is the history of the city of Mahagonny itself: from its founding and development to its disintegration, after several crises, and final downfall. The people of this city, common adventurers, criminals and prostitutes, are reduced to types representing modern, capitalist society, shown with all its insatiable greed, lust for pleasure, and supreme regard for money. Four men arrive in the city, flush with earnings from lumberjacking in Alaska, and determined to enjoy every penny's worth to the hilt. Soon, however, they become bored and disillusioned. A hurricane almost destroys the city, and Jim, their leader, is led to nihilism: absolute self-indulgence is now all that matters. Anarchy descends on Mahagonny. In the end

Jim cannot pay for his pleasures and is condemned to death. After his execution, further catastrophes are followed by the city's destruction.

The opera is constructed according to Brecht's principles of epic theater, with which Weill at the time found himself in sympathy, seeing in them a means by which he could realize a neoclassical ambition to revive the old number opera while also injecting the genre with a modern approach and socially relevant content. Thus music, text, and staging do not fuse or reciprocally illustrate each other, but rather interact as independent forces to create a series of what Weill called "morality pictures of our time." The opera's twenty-one scenes, separated by spoken narrative and projected inscriptions, use music to comment on, and even take issue with, the text and stage action. Techniques of parody and caricature include musical quotation and allusions to already familiar idioms. Such popular styles of the day as tango, fox-trot, and shimmy, cast in dance-band instrumentation, appear in distorted form to point an accusing finger at the perversion of a world ruled by consumption. These mix with sections worked in "serious" operatic style, but made subject to a disjointedness which serves, similarly, a morally critical purpose. That is, Weill's constant interruption of expectations for formal continuity and closure, principally through a cleverly altered harmony but also through having a meter and rhythm that do not support the harmony as they should, has the effect of shocks that rupture any illusion of aesthetic unity. Through the gaps in the form we are shown reality, or, as Weill himself put it, "the state of things in their most crass form and without varnish." By detaching itself and refusing emotional support, the music does more, however, than merely report on what happens in the play; rather it is made to speak out, often with an expression of protest all of its own, against what are shown on stage as the evils inherent in the breakdown of humanity.

The *Mahagonny* opera must be viewed as a topical work in that it was concerned to illuminate, through an imaginative, perhaps even surrealistic treatment of character and situation, the social malaise which Brecht saw to be overtaking his own age. Weill may have lacked the political convictions of his collaborator, but he was possessed of a comparable social conscience and consciousness, such as would produce for this opera as well as other joint stage works of the period music of a peculiarly searching, critical, and perhaps even revolutionary quality. It is precisely this quality that explains the opera's troubled career in the few years before it fell victim to the Nazi regime. After the Leipzig premiere a series of revisions and cuts were forced on it by nervous producers; in particular the versions for Berlin and Vienna in 1931 and 1932 respectively, by reducing the work merely to its most striking numbers, robbed it of much of its operatic character. Revivals beginning in Germany (Darmstadt, 1957), followed by those in Britain, Canada, and America, while they have restored the authentic version, have struggled (not always successfully) to give a convincing interpretation of a score strung between the poles of the artful and the almost crudely subversive.—ALAN LESSEM

The Maid of Orleans [Orleanskaya deva]

Composer: *Piotr Ilyich Tchaikovsky.*

Librettist: *Piotr Ilyich Tchaikovsky (after Zhukovsky's translation of Schiller, Die Jungfrau von Orleans).*

First Performance: *St Petersburg, Mariinsky, 25 February 1881; revised, 1882.*

While browsing through his sister Alexandra's library one day, Tchaikovsky came across a copy of Schiller's drama, *Die Jungfrau von Orleans,* translated into Russian by Zhukovsky. In *Die Jungfrau,* Friedrich von Schiller, the leading German poet, playwright, and essayist of the latter eighteenth century, had reworked the facts about Joan of Arc into a heroic tale of good and evil. With the French arrayed against the English, Joan appears in the form of divine intervention as a savior for the French. No longer merely a stolid peasant girl, Schiller's Joan is an eloquent, elegant beauty who becomes involved in a fictional love affair with one of the enemy. Joan atones for this sin by her death on the battlefield rather than at the stake. Schiller's dramatization is thus a story of innocence, sin, guilt, and redemption.

Tchaikovsky, casting about for a new opera subject after *Eugene Onegin,* seized upon this famous historical tale. The subject itself, Tchaikovsky's treatment of it, and hints in his correspondence suggest that he was hoping to break into the world of international opera. It was Tchaikovsky's first opera from a non-Russian literary source, with a subject quite different from opera plots by Tchaikovsky's contemporaries. With its extensive use of a chorus, and the interpolation of a long ballet for the dwarves and pages, it exhibits the influence of the highly successful French grand opera style. "I do not think *The Maid of Orleans* the finest, or the most emotional, of my works, but it seems to me to be the one most likely to make my name popular," he wrote to his patron Madame von Meck. His hope, however, was not to be realized.

Fired by the subject, Tchaikovsky worked quickly. He planned a special trip to Paris to collect literary sources, but he was so eager to get started that he began to put together his own text from Zhukovsky's translation, and von Meck sent him a copy of Henri Wallon's *Jeanne d'Arc.* Even after the trip to Paris, he continued to work without a libretto or even a completely worked-out scenario. Each evening he would work on the text for the following day's music.

He followed up on plans to investigate other settings of the story of Joan of Arc, examining Auguste Mermet's opera *Jeanne d'Arc* and Verdi's *Giovanna d'Arco,* as well as a number of other literary sources. When he looked at Mermet's libretto, however, he was unimpressed. "In the end I have come to the conclusion that Schiller's tragedy, although it is not consistent with historical accuracy, still outstrips all other artistic presentations of *Joan* in its depth of psychological truth," he wrote to von Meck.

The opera opens with Joan at home on the farm with her father Thibault, when news arrives of the approach of the English army. Joan, overhearing this, suddenly speaks out and begins to prophesy. The time has come for action, and she bids farewell to her home. Act II finds Joan with king-to-be Charles VII in despair over the war situation approaching Orleans. Joan convinces everyone that she is sent from God by identifying the hidden Charles immediately and revealing his private prayers.

In act III Joan meets Lionel in battle, vanquishing him but hesitating to kill him when she catches sight of his face. In a peculiar emotional reversal, the two fall in love. Lionel refuses to flee, joining the French cause. But at the coronation, Thibault accuses his daughter of consorting with the devil rather than God. When challenged, she is overcome with guilt over her encounter with Lionel, and she cannot defend herself. In act IV, when Lionel pursues her to comfort her, she flees, but then yields to their mutual passion in a love scene. The English approach, but Joan refuses to escape. Lionel is killed trying to defend her. In the final scene, a chorus of angels sing support as Joan is led to her death at the stake.

When Tchaikovsky took up the strands of this drama, he was inspired by the image Schiller had woven of a noble girl trapped by fate, divinely inspired but susceptible to human love. Tchaikovsky's libretto was a Russified adaptation of Schiller's remaking of the historical Joan of Arc. The result is a hodgepodge of the Schiller version and Tchaikovsky's other sources, with a more historically accurate version of Joan's death at the stake tacked on at the end. However, Tchaikovsky's most notable embellishments involve the treatment of the love affair between Joan and Lionel. Schiller's Joan felt an involuntary attraction to the knight, though she fought against it and rejected his advances. Tchaikovsky, however, aggrandized the love affair, allowing Joan to wallow in and agonize over her feelings.

Much of the music in the opera is uninspiring, as if Tchaikovsky had watered down his style for an international audience. "I am glad to know that *The Maid of Orleans* is free from the faults of my earlier pseudo-opera style," he wrote to von Meck, "in which I wearied my listeners with a superfluity of details, and made my harmony too complicated, so that there was no moderation in my orchestral effects. . . . Opera style should be broad, simple, and decorative." But by and large, the music consists of discouragingly long stretches of eminently forgettable music and insipid dialogue, interspersed with stirring instrumental numbers and occasional moments of great beauty, such as Joan's farewell to the scenes of her childhood in act I.

Though the two works are not without interest, neither Schiller's play nor Tchaikovsky's opera are held in universally high esteem today. Ultimately *The Maid of Orleans* is most interesting for its revelations about Tchaikovsky's operatic technique, his interest in the successful tradition of French grand opera, and for his ongoing efforts to achieve a major operatic success.—ELIZABETH W. PATTON

The Makropoulos Case [Věc Makropoulos]

Composer: *Leoš Janáček.*

Librettist: *Leoš Janáček (after a play by Karel Čapek).*

First Performance: *Brno, National Theater, 18 December 1926.*

Roles: *Emilia Marty (soprano); Albert Gregor (tenor); Jaroslav Prus (baritone); Vitek (tenor); Kolenaty (baritone); Janek (tenor); Krista (mezzo-soprano); Hauk-Sendorf (tenor); Stagehand (bass); Servants (contraltos); chorus (TTBB).*

In act I we are in the law offices of Dr. Kolenaty, whose assistant, Vitek, is working on a case of inheritance. This process has been, off and on, in the courts for about 100 years with no legal resolution, owing to the fact that a will said to have existed has never been found despite massive searches. The would-be inheritor is one Albert Gregor.

In the midst of the legal discussions between Vitek and Albert Gregor, Krista, Vitek's daughter, enters. She has just heard the great opera singer, Emilia Marty, the night before and is still in a trance. An opera student herself, she is inspired to work harder after hearing the great singer. They are interrupted by the entrance of Dr. Kolenaty and the great Marty herself. Everyone is fascinated by her beauty and her cold personality, while she, in turn, seems interested only in the Gregor case. She has come to Dr. Kolenaty for a complete history of it. Kolenaty obliges with a didactic recital of the facts of the case. Emilia interrupts him with supposed facts about the people involved from generations ago. Dr. Kolenaty and Albert Gregor

471

are puzzled and irritated by her remarks, since they refer to things that she couldn't know, but still, they aren't quite sure what to make of her. She speaks as if she knew the founder of the family, Ferdinand Prus; in fact she uses his nickname, Pepi. She also knows that he had a son; she says that the mother was one Elliana MacGregor, a famous opera singer. Due to the son's illegitimacy, he was given the last name of MacGregor, or perhaps just Gregor.

Ferdinand Prus, it seems, left a will but nobody seems to know its whereabouts or whether, in fact, it really ever existed. But Marty knows, she says. It is to be found in a desk located in the Prus house. Marty urges Dr. Kolenaty to break into that house to retrieve old "Pepi's" papers and the will; he flatly refuses. He thinks Marty is mad. But Albert, believing her, forces Dr. Kolenaty to burglarize the house. While he is gone, Albert and Emilia talk. He becomes infatuated with the mysterious woman, but Emilia rejects his advances, treats him rudely, and angers him by her harsh rejection. Suddenly, Dr. Kolenaty returns, and, stunningly, has the papers in his hand, including the will, which clinches the case for Albert Gregor.

The remainder of the plot is taken up with identifying the person of Emilia Marty. Pressed for an explanation, Emilia relates that when she was a young girl her father, Dr. Makropoulos, was asked by Emperor Rudolf for a medication to postpone aging and death. When Makropoulos developed the drug, the emperor demanded that it be tested on someone, so Dr. Makropoulos' own daughter, Elena, was chosen for the job. Elena suffered but recovered, and the drug was eventually proven successful, for Elena was to live much past the normal human life span. Through the years she moved around, with each move taking a new name, but always with the

initials E.M. At various times she was known as Elliana MacGregor (from Ireland!), Elena Makropoulos, Eugenia Montez, and now Emilia Marty. Now 342 years old, she has experienced everything and has become embittered by the very process of life. To her there is no good, no evil, nothing moral or immoral any more. She has come to see all life as insubstantial, and has lost all capacity to feel anything. She rejects the chance to live longer by using the parchment with its drug prescription, which Prus has found among the papers of Ellian MacGregor. Emilia slowly falls into a stupor and then death. Before dying, she hands the parchment to Krista, who, after a moment's thought, burns it.

The Makropoulos Case, one of Janáček's most important operas, is also one of his most problematic. The first difficulty is the nature of the text. The libretto is taken directly from a play by Czechoslovakia's great playwright, Karel Čapek. Čapek's play was contemporary, with idiomatic language and very little of a poetic nature. Janáček remains

Anja Silja in *The Makropoulos Case,* Stuttgart Opera, 1970

faithful to Čapek's language. Thus, people order taxis, answer telephones, and speak the language of normal conversation.

Many years before, Janáček was engaged in researching the "music" of every day speech. He believed that speech was the major clue to a person's emotional life and identity, so he traveled over much of Eastern Europe transcribing into pitches what he heard people say in their normal conversations. How fast did they talk, how slow, how high, how low, when did they stutter, when did they hesitate? These and many other characteristics were of critical importance to the composer. He was particularly interested in the changes wrought in speech patterns under the pressure of emotional stress. To Janáček, this was the "music" hidden in speech and it came to be more and more of a controlling factor in his compositions. It is the extreme of this method that one encounters in *The Makropoulos Case,* and it is perfectly suited to the language found there. It isn't valid to criticize Janáček for the absence of long line melodies as he was striving for the exact opposite, the melodic cell, always reflective of mind states, of the emotional temperature so to speak. It is an art of considerable subtlety, and its effect on the listener is likely to be variable. In a sense, it takes a gifted listener to make sense of Janáček's jagged, naturalistic rhythms, and his telegraphic melodic style.

Similarly, Janáček's orchestra lacks a conventionally beautiful sound. One's ears are constantly directed from one choir to another, as if one is hearing an extraordinary conversation about the stage action. As a fitfully convinced admirer of Wagner, Janáček assigns the orchestra a similar function assigned to it by the earlier master, but the leitmotif technique is not exactly what Janáček uses here. The orchestra acts as a commentary to the stage, but its musical material is often quite different from that of the voices. Despite its close mirroring of the stage events, it remains motivically separated from the action to a remarkable degree.

As for the harmonic language, *Makropoulos* is a thoroughly tonal score, but the tonal focus shifts very quickly, and the sense of incessant movement to new tonal centers can make one feel that it veers from conventional tonal thinking into pan-tonality.

Finally, one must ask whether Janáček's methods "work" for the listener. This is not difficult music to follow, but it requires an agile mind, and a developed ear to respond to its real nature. The number of such listeners seems to be growing rapidly.—HARRIS CROHN

Malfitano, Catherine

Soprano. Born 18 April 1948 in New York City. Married opera administrator Stephen J. Holowid, 1977; daughter Daphne Rose born 1986; studied voice with her father, Joseph Malfitano, a violinist in the Metropolitan Opera Orchestra, and with conductor Henry Lewis; received bachelor of arts degree from Manhattan School of Music, 1971; diverse repertoire encompasses more than 60 roles in both lyric and dramatic repertory; sang principal roles in a series of world premieres, including Susa's Transformations *(Minnesota Opera, 1973),* Floyd's Bilby's Doll *(Houston Grand Opera, 1976),* Pasatieri's Washington Square *(Michigan Opera Theatre, 1976) and Bolcom's* McTeague *(Lyric Opera of Chicago, 1992); professional debut at Central City Opera as Nannetta, 1972; European debut as Susanna at Holland Festival, 1974; Chicago debut as Susanna at Lyric Opera of Chicago; New York debut as Gretel at the Metropolitan Opera, 1979; has made videos of*

Stiffelio, Salome, La celemenza di Tito *and* Tosca, *and recordings of* Salome, L'incoronazione di Poppea, Romeo et Juliette *and Rossini's* Stabat Mater.

Catherine Malfitano is a versatile soprano unafraid to take chances. The range of roles she has essayed onstage, most of them widely praised, would seem to have little in common outside of being composed for the soprano voice.

Malfitano began her career singing lyric roles like Verdi's Nanetta and Mozart's Susanna, moving on to roles mixing dramatic and lyric elements (like Verdi's Violetta, which she sang for the first time for Michigan Opera Theatre in 1978). In recent years she has tackled even heavier roles, garnering favorable notices for her portrayal of the title role in Luc Bondy's controversial 1992 production of Richard Strauss' *Salome* at the Salzburg Festival, which she subsequently sang at Covent Garden and the Metropolitan Opera.

Throughout her career Malfitano has championed contemporary composers in the most direct way possible: by singing in their operas. Her portrayal of Catherine Sloper in Thomas Pasatieri's *Washington Square*, commissioned by the Michigan Opera Theatre and premiered there in 1976, was consistently riveting, even though the opera was not. Likewise, one of the strongest elements of William Bolcom's *McTeague*, commissioned by the Lyric Opera of Chicago and premiered there in 1992, was her portrayal of Trina Sieppe, the avaricious wife of the title character.

Onstage, Malfitano is a consummate singing actress in the Callas mold. Like Callas, she is not afraid to let her voice turn harsh to make a dramatic point. Like Callas, she was heavy for a time, but has transformed herself into a lean vocal machine. Some observers say that, again like Callas, she has paid a price for the uncompromising way she approaches her art. Most critics describing her voice mention its penetrating, steely, laser-like quality; some claim she is pushing it dangerously beyond its natural limits. To date, though, it continues to sound healthy and vigorous.

Few fail to fall under the spell of Malfitano's dramatic portrayals. As the end of the century approaches—and as she nears her own half-century mark—she continues to perform with a durable artistic integrity that is extremely rare and highly praiseworthy in an age when so many singers sound like their voices and gestures have been pre-recorded.—JOHN GUINN

Malibran, Maria Felicità

Mezzo-soprano. Born 24 March 1808, in Paris. Died 23 September 1836, in Manchester. Married: 1) merchant François Eugène Malibran, 1826 (divorced 1835); 2) violinist Charles de Bériot, 1836 (one son). Studied with her father, the tenor Manuel Garcia, and with Panseron and Herold in Naples; first appeared on stage at age six in Paer's Agnese, *Naples, 1814; London debut as Rosina in* Il barbiere di Siviglia, *1825; in New York with her father, 1825-26; returned to Europe in 1827; Paris debut in* Semiramide, *1828; sang in Paris and London, 1829-32, then went to Italy; sang Bellini's Romeo in* I Capuleti ed i Montecchi, *Bologna, 1832; sang in* La sonnambula, *Naples, 1833; Teatro alla Scala debut as Norma, 1834.*

As the daughter of a great tenor, Maria Malibran (née Garcia) grew up in the theater and appeared onstage with her father whenever the plot called for a child. The earliest recorded mention of these instances was in Italy, during Garcia's engagements there 1811-16, when she appeared in Mayr's *Medea in Corinto* and Paer's *Agnese*. Legend says that in the latter, during a memory lapse by the soprano, little Maria delighted the audience by singing the melody herself. As she matured, her father devoted his considerable energies to training her voice, which at first seemed unpromising.

While in Italy, Garcia had refined his art under the great Italian masters, especially Giovanni Ansani, and was thus able to pass this knowledge to his daughter. In addition, he was very impressed with the art of Giuditta Pasta, his constant partner onstage in Paris and London. Pasta's ability to extend her upper and lower registers into the middle range enabled her to bring an unaccustomed drama to the music; she could sing a given note or passage in the lightness and sweetness of her head voice, or in the power and richness of her chest tones depending on the demands of the music or the dramatic situation. This was the ability that Garcia sought to give his daughter, and Maria's success in achieving it was one of the qualities that would establish her as the greatest singer of the age.

This period of Maria's life was not a happy one. Garcia was a brutal parent, merciless in his demands; in her later life Maria would remark that she learned how to sing through tears during her father's lessons.

In 1825, Garcia determined that his seventeen year old daughter, if not a finished artist, was at least marketable, and during a casting crisis at the King's Theatre in London he contracted her to that theater's desperate manager, John Ebers, at an absurdly high fee. Thus she made her formal operatic debut in June 1825 as Rosina, opposite her father's Almaviva in Rossini's *Il barbiere di Siviglia*. Despite the circumstances of this appearance, she succeeded in winning both public and critical approval and soon sang in the first London production of Meyerbeer's *Il Crociato in Egitto*. Subsequent performances in the English musical festivals that summer were less successful however, as both the inadequacies of her art and her status as a beginner became more apparent.

At this time, Manuel Garcia, now fifty years old and in vocal decline, accepted an engagement in the Americas. Assembling a troop largely consisting of his family, he arrived in New York in November 1825 and presented the first Italian Opera heard in the New World. In that less cultured land, before less demanding audiences, Maria Garcia spent two years perfecting her art and establishing herself as America's first prima donna. There too she escaped her father's unbearable cruelty by marrying Eugène Malibran, a French businessman three times her age. In the fall of 1826 the Garcia troop departed for Mexico and Maria Malibran retired from the stage, but within weeks her husband's business affairs suffered reversals that demanded her return to the theater at the highest fees possible, and by the autumn of 1827 his problems were such that the couple agreed that she should return to Paris where she could earn even more money.

Arriving in Paris in November 1827, Maria sought out family and friends, particularly the Countess Merlin and Rossini, who quickly presented her in the best salons before the musical *cognoscenti*. Then in January 1828 she appeared at the Académie Royale de Musique as Semiramide. Her success was immense. From this time until her death her career moved with a power hitherto unknown in the opera world. "She set the world on fire," wrote a contemporary, and such was the public hysteria in England, France, Italy, wherever she sang, that those words hardly seem overstated. Theaters in which she sang reported their highest gross receipts ever; drawings of her and incidents in her life were sold to an avid public; her arrival in Venice stopped the city for hours, and before she left a theater had been renamed for her. After her La Scala debut the audience unhitched her carriage and drew her home. Even governments in those revolutionary times trembled before her emotional control of crowds. At the premier of Persiani's *Ines de Castro,* which was written for her, the applause "rivalled Vesuvius's most violent eruptions" and people were carried fainting from the theater. All but deified, Maria Malibran redefined fame.

It would seem that everyone who attended a Malibran performance and who could hold a pen attempted to describe the indescribable. Her voice was "not exactly beautiful" (although many, including Chopin, disagreed), nor was it perfect, particularly in the middle register, which could be unfocused, even hollow, in sound. But its range was a remarkable three octaves, from low D to high D (sometimes E), and its quality, that of a rich contralto with a soprano register superadded, was distinguished by a strange and exciting timbre. The soprano register possessed a liquid sweetness; her contralto notes were richer, with a singular power and smoothness. The middle voice could be sung in either the brilliance of her soprano register or the rich power of her chest tones, which she used frequently and with more force than any singer before her. In addition, she executed the most difficult coloratura passages and embellishments as brilliantly as any singer before the public: her arpeggios and trills were astonishing, her ability to embellish and improvise apparently limitless. She was particularly adept at immense leaps of two and even three octaves, which she used to avoid the weakness between the mezzo and soprano registers. Her use of ornamentation for dramatic effect (as opposed to mere vocal display) was considered unique. That her voice was "unrivalled for compass, volume, and richness," might be ascertained from those legendary evenings when she sang both *Fidelio* and *Sonnambula* in sequence.

Malibran's vocal abilities were matched by a dramatic aptitude quite new to the operatic stage. Equally adept at both drama and comedy, she brought an unaccustomed naturalness, an emotional realism to her roles, eschewing the stock gestures then in currency. Giuditta Pasta, her only rival, was the perfection of the classic style, her "walk of terrible grandeur," the noble gestures, every movement accomplished with the full awareness that she was acting before an audience. In contrast, Malibran "forgot to find herself before a public," and varied her performances according to her mood, just as she could vary her musical embellishments according to her audience or inspiration. Furthermore, her very feminine appearance and appealing features immediately captured audience sympathy; visually she was always in character. Chorley tells us that although "not handsome, she was better than beautiful," that she possessed "great mobility of expression in her features," and that her style of dress indicated the character of a woman "thoroughly, fearlessly original." Acute swings of mood—her letters range from profound depression to the gayest hilarity—indicate both a manic-depressive temperament and an emotional range clearly mirrored in an art producing such a powerful impression that "few among her contemporaries could go home and sit in cool judgement upon one who, while she was before them, carried them as she pleased to the extremities of grave or gay."

Unfortunately, those same qualities would prove highly self-destructive. The impresario Alfred Bunn, who presented her in London, had long foreseen the inevitable outcome of such a life, the fate of one who would sing two operas on the same evening and rush off to the salons (where socialites would pay anything for a song from the throat of La Malibran), and even then dash off to town for further diversion. Bunn wrote, "The powerful and conflicting elements in her composition were gifts indeed, but of a very fatal nature—the mind was far too great for the body, and it did not require any wonderful gift of prophecy to foresee that, in their contention, the triumph would be but short, however brilliant and decisive."

In 1829, Maria fell in love with the Belgian violinist Charles de Bériot. As a citizen of Catholic France, she could not divorce Eugène, still an ocean away and with whom she had become thoroughly disgusted. In desperation, she wrote to General Lafayette, whom she had met only once but who was only too glad to help the famous and charming Maria Malibran. For years he tried, futiley, to push a divorce law through Parliament, but ultimately her lawyers had the marriage annulled under logic so flimsy that one suspects bribery or other political manipulation, and she married Charles. Meanwhile, she had given birth to their son, Charles Wilfred, who was, of course, illegitimate in a hypocritical age that did not accept such social transgressions gracefully and from which she suffered greatly.

In the spring of 1836 she was thrown from a horse and suffered cranial injuries (probably a severe concussion). Refusing to slow the pace of her career, she continued singing but died under the most dramatic of circumstances in Manchester during a music festival that September. She was twenty-eight years old. Her youthful demise sealed the immortality of her legend, and she remains one of the most famous and intriguing singers in musical history. After her final performances in Naples, 1835, a critic wrote: "And when we live in memories, recalling how nature and art lavished on you their utmost powers, we will have those memories with which to embitter the youth of our children." She must have been phenomenal.—HOWARD BUSHNELL

Manon

Composer: *Jules Massenet.*

Librettists: *Henri Meilhac and Philippe Gille (after Prévost).*

First Performance: *Paris, Opéra-Comique, 19 January 1884.*

Roles: *Manon (soprano); Des Grieux (tenor); Lescaut (baritone); Count des Grieux (bass); Guillot de Morfontaine (tenor); De Brétigny (baritone); Pousette (soprano); Javotte (soprano or mezzo-soprano); Rosette (soprano or mezzo-soprano); chorus (SATB).*

Like the Parisian gentlemen in Prévost's *Manon Lescaut,* Massenet found Manon irresistible. Most of his twenty-nine existing operas feature women characters, but Manon surpasses them all in unrestrained seductiveness. Aristocrats vie for her regard. At the sight of her, old men wish themselves young. All of sixteen, Manon lives only by the moment. Her appetite for pleasure is outrageous, her behavior scandalous; yet men indulge her excessive whims to the limit.

We first see her stepping from a coach outside an inn at Amiens where her cousin Lescaut, a soldier, inveterate gambler, and guardian of the family honor, awaits her. Guillot, a Minister of France, makes an unsuccessful pass at her, but confident in the power of his wealth and position, he hires a carriage for the two of them. Moments later the young Chevalier des Grieux sets his eyes on Manon and immediately falls in love with her. Forgetting both Lescaut and the convent she is bound for, she succumbs to Des Grieux's ardent advances, and departs with him to Paris in Guillot's carriage.

The lovers live together contentedly until Lescaut and De Brétigny, a nobleman infatuated with Manon, track them down. While Des Grieux tries to convince Lescaut that he truly loves Manon, De Brétigny secretly informs the covetous girl that Des Grieux's father, the Count des Grieux, will end his son's illicit affair by having the chevalier abducted that very day. De Brétigny promises to shower Manon with wealth if she will live with him instead and not reveal the count's plot to Des Grieux. The temptation of luxury proves too much for Manon, who bids a wistful farewell to their love nest. A knock from outside the apartment brings Des Grieux to the door. There are sounds of a struggle; Des Grieux does not return.

Manon appears lavishly dressed at a festival in the Cours la Reine. She overhears De Brétigny and the count discussing Des Grieux, who soon will be ordained an abbé of the Church, having "forgotten" his former love. This so distresses Manon that she hardly notices the ballet Guillot has engaged to impress her, and she hurries off to St Sulpice where Des Grieux has just delivered a sermon. After a few minutes alone with him, Manon wins him back.

Short of money, Des Grieux, accompanied by Manon, tries his luck at gambling in the Hotel Transylvania. Among the players is Guillot, who challenges Des Grieux to a game of chance and loses so badly that he accuses his young rival of cheating. Bent on vengeance, he has both Des Grieux and Manon arrested. The chevalier is soon released thanks to the count's influence, but Manon is imprisoned and later deported as a woman of ill repute. Lescaut and Des Grieux attempt to rescue her from a corps of prisoners taken under guard to Le Havre, but the plan fails. A bribe, however, procures the lovers brief privacy. Des Grieux talks of escape to a new life, but Manon is too ill to dream. Recalling their past happiness, she dies murmuring, "And so ends the story of Manon Lescaut."

Reconciling this melodramatic plot with the pleasantries of *opéra comique* required ingenuity. To accommodate the popular genre, Massenet strewed the score with affable tunes and diverting choruses; but he fused the patchwork of arias and ensembles with recitative and spoken dialogue by making every note of the accompaniment dramatically adroit and evocative, and by devising frequent orchestral allusions to representative themes. The abundance of blithesome music does not afford perfunctory entertainment, but evokes the gaiety of Paris to offset Manon's amorous vicissitudes. Pleasures and agonies intensify against a background of frivolity. The score, in fact, enchants more advantageously than it emotes, for its most impassioned music is unabashedly sentimental. Massenet found passage from pathos to bathos the easiest of modulations. In *Manon,* there seems no clear boundary between them. Without large doses of *joie de vivre* to buoy it up, the work would sink into the maudlin ooze that imbues so many forgotten operas.

For more than a century *Manon* has held its place in the standard repertoire. During the composer's lifetime, the opera received over 700 performances at the Opéra-Comique alone. Massenet made musical portraiture in French opera a finer art by endowing Manon with inexhaustible fascination. Charpentier, Debussy, and Poulenc learned from him the subtle meanings couched in melodic inflection. With *Manon, opéra comique* became music theater *à la française,* but it preserved the best qualities of popular French opera in the 1880s. Audiences found it affecting and entertaining, and singers relished its fluent lyricism and virtuosic luster. Five of its arias remain perennial favorites from the French repertoire. Like *Carmen* and *Les contes d'Hoffmann, Manon* triumphs over banality. Massenet later courted many women characters, among them, Esclarmonde, Thaïs, Sapho, and Cléopâtre, and gave each something of Manon's illusive charm, but he reserved for her alone the blend of puissance and finesse that makes a cynosure of a brief flame.—JAMES ALLEN FELDMAN

Manon Lescaut

Composer: *Giacomo Puccini.*

Librettists: *Ruggero Leoncavallo, Marco Praga, Domenico Olivia, Luigi Illica, and Giuseppe Giacosa (after Prévost).*

First Performance: *Turin, Regio, 1 February 1893.*

Roles: *Manon Lescaut (soprano); Lescaut (baritone); Chevalier des Grieux (tenor); Geronte di Ravoir (baritone); Edmondo (tenor); Singer (soprano or mezzo-soprano); Music Master (tenor); Naval Captain (bass); Sergeant (bass); Lamplighter (tenor); chorus (SATTBB).*

Manon Lescaut was the first major success of Puccini's career, achieved after nine years of generous subsidy by publisher Giulio Ricordi, who had seen in the young composer of *Le villi* (1884) the most likely successor to the fame and riches of Giuseppe Verdi. Puccini had taken a dangerous chance by choosing for his subject the well-known story by Abbé Antoine Prévost (*L'histoire du Chevalier des Grieux et de Manon Lescaut,* 1731), given the successful Paris premiere of a setting, *Manon,* by Jules Massenet only nine years previously, not to mention other nineteenth-century musical settings by Balfe, Halévy, and Auber. However, Puccini's conception, maintained through six different librettists (including himself), was considerably different from that of Massenet and of Prévost, both in his more somber choice of scene and plot incident—excluding, for example, any scene of the blissful if poor lovers living together in Paris—and in his treatment of the title character, by tradition a classic *femme fatale,* but in Puccini's eyes a helpless and mainly sympathetic figure who is herself the victim of greed, repression, and deceit.

In act I the young Chevalier des Grieux encounters Manon at an inn where she is staying *en route* to the nunnery her father is forcing her to enter; Des Grieux instantly falls in love and by the end of the act has convinced her to run away with him, a plan which in turn foils her brother's plan to sell her to the rich elderly Parisian, Geronte di Ravoir. In act II, Manon is nonetheless living a pampered, stilted existence with Geronte, having left Des Grieux at her brother's urging when the money ran short. When Des Grieux returns, she defies Geronte and leaves with her lover, but to the latter's despair she insists on returning to take the old man's jewels with her, and she is arrested in the process. In act III, Des Grieux and Lescaut follow Manon to Le Havre, the debarkation point to Louisiana for "fallen women," and attempt a rescue to no avail, but the captain does agree to allow the love-torn Des Grieux to accompany Manon to Louisiana. In act IV, Manon dies poverty-stricken, exhausted, and hopeless on a desolate wilderness plain, in the arms of Des Grieux.

In his sympathetic treatment of Manon as well as of later heroines, Puccini showed himself to be strikingly out of step with the disturbing, frequently demonic treatments of women by contemporary artists and writers such as Klimt, Wilde, d'Annunzio, Verga, and Louÿs, to mention a few. This is an important aspect of Puccini's success in his time as well as our own, and one that has often escaped notice, or if noticed, has evoked criticisms of excessive sentimentality or even sado-masochistic neurosis (as in Mosco Carner's *Puccini: A Critical Biography*). In addition, other aspects of Puccini's mature style, such as his colorful use of harmony and orchestration, his lyrical, languid vocal writing, his fluid, post-Wagnerian formal mixture of vocal set pieces and continuous orchestral melody, and his keen sense of theater are also fully in place in *Manon Lescaut,* with the possible exception of Manon's plodding, pathetic final scene and aria "Sola, perduta, abbandonata" ("Alone, lost, abandoned"), which Puccini considered cutting as late as the 1922 Vienna production.

Fortunately for the young composer—whose career and future support from Ricordi were on the line—*Manon Lescaut* was a huge success in its premiere performance at the Teatro Regio in Turin (eight days before the Teatro alla Scala premiere of Verdi's *Falstaff*): Puccini was called for twenty-five bows between acts. Within the year, the opera had been performed all over Italy and in such far-away locales as Buenos Aires, Rio de Janeiro, St Petersburg, Madrid, and Hamburg (in German translation), traveling faster and further than Massenet's *Manon* or any of Puccini's later operas. This popular success and the accompanying critical opinion served to establish Puccini's primacy within the world of Italian opera until his death in 1924 and even afterward. As George Bernard Shaw put it in his review of the Covent Garden premiere of *Manon Lescaut* on 14 May 1894, "Puccini looks to me more like the heir of Verdi than any other of his rivals." *Manon Lescaut* remains a solid part of the operatic repertory today, if less often performed than the perennial Puccini favorites *La bohème, Tosca* and *Madama Butterfly,* and, as it turns out, Massenet's *Manon.*—CLAIRE DETELS

Maria Stuarda [Mary Stuart]

Composer: *Gaetano Donizetti.*

Librettist: *G. Bardari (after Schiller).*

First Performance: *Milan, Teatro alla Scala, 30 December 1835.*

Roles: *Maria (soprano); Elisabetta (mezzo-soprano or soprano); Leicester (tenor); Talbot (bass); Cecil (baritone); Anna (contralto); chorus (SATTB).*

Donizetti's *Maria Stuarda,* based on the final days of Mary Stuart and exhibiting the *primo ottocento* fascination for English historical subjects, was heard for the last time during the nineteenth century in 1865 in Naples; it was not revived until 1958, in Bergamo. The historically inaccurate libretto was fashioned by the obscure Giuseppe Bardari after Schiller, after Donizetti found the much sought-after librettist, Felice Romani, to be unavailable. At the opening of act I a tournament is being held for the French ambassador, who has come to England on behalf of the King of France to ask for Queen Elizabeth's hand in marriage. The queen, however, is in love with the Earl of Leicester. Talbot pleads with Elizabeth for mercy for Mary Stuart, while Cecil wants Mary to be executed. Elizabeth is inclined towards vengeance if Mary is indeed a rival for Leicester. When Leicester enters, Elizabeth gives him a ring, asking him to tell the French ambassador that she accepts the proposal tentatively. Leicester appears unmoved. Talbot gives Leicester a letter and a picture sent by Mary from Fotheringay Castle and Leicester rejoices, vowing either to free her or die with her. Leicester encounters Elizabeth and is obliged to give her the letter from Mary asking Elizabeth to meet her. Upon being questioned by the queen, Leicester denies his love for Mary, although he describes her physical beauty in passionate terms. Elizabeth agrees to the meeting with Mary.

In act II Mary is enjoying the grounds at Fotheringay while lamenting her enforced exile from her beloved France. When Elizabeth arrives she is initially reluctant to speak to Mary. The latter kneels at Elizabeth's feet, begging her forgiveness, but Elizabeth's behavior repulses her. Mary, able to bear no more, insults the queen with the words "Vil bastarda." This meeting between the two queens never actually occurred in history. Mary is arrested and told by Elizabeth to prepare for death. In act III, scene i, Elizabeth signs Mary's death warrant and tells Leicester that he must witness the execution. In scene ii Mary's friends gather in a room next to the execution chamber, expressing repulsion at the sight of the instruments of execution. Mary enters and asks them to pray. As the cannon shots are fired she goes to her death.

Even though there are two queens and two soprano roles in Donizetti's opera, Mary Stuart is clearly the heroine and the character with whom one identifies emotionally. Schiller wrote that a tragic heroine is one who becomes transfigured through suffering; this is a drama that moves swiftly and inexorably to its fatal conclusion, Mary's death. Donizetti differentiates musically between the two queens, Elizabeth being given melodic lines of emphatic declamation in contrast to Mary's floating, limpid legato *cantilene*. A number of stylistic features heighten the tension and help achieve the ultimate catharsis. In the fictional confrontation scene, the "Dialogo delle due regine," the orchestration is telling, especially the use of the regal, foreboding trombone at certain points. This scene is a good illustration of the polarities on which the opera is built: with the difference in their musical material Mary is portrayed as a feminine figure and Elizabeth, with her great power and dominant personality, as masculine. There is also a suggestion of good pitted against evil and a display of chiaroscuro effects. In the corresponding scene of the play, Schiller specifies a moment of "general silence" as the two queens confront each other. This concept is especially apt for musical portrayal, and Donizetti provides a sparse accompaniment (mainly pizzicato strings) and extensive use of rests, as if time were suspended.

The prison motif is prominent in *Maria Stuarda*. At the beginning of act II Mary is incarcerated as she sings nostalgically of France. Following this *scena ed aria* is a duet with Leicester, in which much of Mary's character is revealed. Schiller had made Leicester Mary's lover, another detail contrary to history that became part of Bardari's libretto. In the opera, then, the love triangle propels the plot, and Mary is portrayed as a typical suffering Romantic heroine. Her roots are in the sentimental, pathetic figures found in gothic fiction and in *opera semiseria* earlier in the century.

After the fateful encounter with Elizabeth that seals Mary's fate, Mary is featured in a scene in which she confesses to Talbot; her suffering is reflected in the prominence of minor seconds in the orchestra, both in the prelude and in the accompaniment to her opening recitative. Mary then requests all her gathered friends to join her in a prayer forgiving all of those who have harmed her; it is a sublimely transcendent operatic scene. In the orchestral prelude to this prayer scene the character's emotions are most clearly portrayed: the key is E minor and the music is in the "horror" style of Weber's *Der Freischütz* and certain parts of *Fidelio* and *Don Giovanni,* full of ominous iterations and thudding figures. The chorus adds to the unsettled mood with a broadly elegiac melody ending in E major. The chorus then provides the musical underpinning for Mary's prayer, making it assume a broader meaning: Mary's personal plight stands for the plight of beleaguered Scotland. The mixture of personal and political sentiments becomes more explicit in Mary's final cavatina and cabaletta. The former begins in F minor, modulates to D-flat major, returns to F minor, and then goes to the parallel major in the Coda. The general effect is celestial and one of apotheosis in the F-major section of the Coda. Mary's solo vocal line ascends to high

A and B-flat, pianissimo, hovering high above the chorus, often with long-held notes. The sentiment of the text is that Mary's blood will cancel all her sins.

The autograph manuscript of Donizetti's *Maria Stuarda* is lost. The opera was prohibited in Naples before it was ever performed; the music had to be adapted to a new subject, *Buondelmonte*. The score was first performed as *Maria Stuarda* in Milan with Maria Malibran in 1835. Although there is no original text there are several secondary ones, including at least four non-autograph manuscript scores and many vocal scores published around the time that Malibran assumed the role.—STEPHEN WILLIER

Martha, oder, Der Markt zu Richmond
[Martha or, The Richmond Fair]

Composer: *Friedrich von Flotow.*

Librettist: *F.W. Riese (after the ballet, Lady Herriette).*

First Performance: *Vienna, Kärntnertor, 25 November 1847.*

Roles: *Lady Harriet (soprano); Nancy (mezzo-soprano); Lionel (tenor); Plunkett (baritone or bass); Lord Tristan of Mickleford (bass); Sheriff (bass); chorus (SATB).*

Martha, Flotow's most successful opera and virtually the only music of his which has survived into the late twentieth century, originated in a collaborative ballet, *Lady Harriet, or the Servant of Greenwich* (1844) for which Flotow wrote the music of the first act. Three years later, the Berlin journalist Friederich Wilhelm Riese, who had provided the libretto for Flotow's first international success, *Alessandro Stradella* (1844), supplied words to the music of act I of *Lady Harriet* and added another three acts based on the ballet's story. The result, *Martha,* became one of the most popular operas of the nineteenth century, which survives through a few complete recordings and an ever-decreasing number of actual performances, even in the last stronghold of its success, provincial Germany.

The story Riese adapted is simple. Lady Harriet, on a whim, decides to disguise herself as a servant (calling herself Martha) to be auctioned for a year's employment at the Richmond Fair. Her services are won by a young farmer, Lionel, who immediately falls in love with her. She is likewise attracted, but realizing the impossible difference in their stations, she sneaks away before her caprice can cause further harm. Heartbroken at her disappearance, Lionel is driven into madness when he sees Martha among Queen Anne's retinue, dressed in finery. He gives his foster brother Plunkett a ring which reveals that Lionel is of noble birth, hidden among the peasantry as a baby because of political strife. Lady Harriet arranges a reprise of the Fair to restore him to sanity. Thus, all can end happily, with the lovers (including Plunkett and Lady Harriet's maid Nancy) reunited.

Ironically, neither of the two arias by which *Martha* is best remembered was composed for it. Lionel's lament, "Ach so fromm" (better known in its Italian translation "M'appari tutt'amor") originally appeared in Flotow's *L'âme en peine* (1846), while Lady Harriet's *"letzte Rose"* is none other than the traditional Irish melody of Thomas Moore's poem "The Last Rose of Summer," used as a leitmotif for Lionel's love of "Martha" both in the overture and throughout the opera. It is also noteworthy that these are the only numbers in the original score for one solo voice. Plunkett has the only other aria, a drinking song, but he shares it with the chorus (for later productions in Italian theaters Flotow added arias for Plunkett and Nancy).

Otherwise the opera is a succession of duets, trios, quartets, and concerted numbers, a fact that may explain why Flotow is at his most inventive in this score, reflecting the unsophisticated emotions of the characters with wit and a perfect sense of architecture. Act II provides the best example, opening with an animated quartet in which Lionel and Plunkett express their excitement at getting their new bondmaidens home, while the women grow more and more upset at the situation Lady Harriet's caprice has gotten them into. After an extremely brief recitative (in the 246 pages of the piano score, there are only about ten of recitative) in which Martha and Nancy refuse to do any menial work, Lionel begins another quartet at a reflective tempo, wondering at both the beauty and impertinence of his new acquisition. As Plunkett intrudes to instruct the women in sewing, the tempo reproduces that of the spinning wheel, then relaxes again in a duet for Lionel and Lady Harriet that culminates in her singing, at his request, "The Last Rose of Summer," in whose reprise he joins. Finally, in another quartet in which the four characters say good night, the music's accents follow those of a slowly-tolling clock. The terzettino/duet which actually concludes the act (and must, to get Lady Harriet and Nancy out of their rustic surroundings) is commendably brief, the "Gute Nacht" quartet being the true musico-dramatic conclusion of the act.

The high point, both musically and dramatically, is the ensemble "Mag der Himmel euch vergeben" which closes act III. To a sweeping melody first heard at the conclusion of the overture, Lionel berates Lady Harriet for her deception. While he recapitulates the main theme, first Nancy and Plunkett, then Lady Harriet react in sympathetic counterpoint, all to be swept up in the final statement of the theme in which the chorus joins, investing it with genuine pathos.

Though Flotow's career would not depend, while he lived, on *Martha*'s success, posterity has chosen it as his only work worthy of retention. Its wistful charm, sure-handed dramatic development, and lyric inventiveness, and the genius of the "Ach so fromm" melody, merit for its composer at least that small measure of remembrance.—WILLIAM J. COLLINS

Martinu, Bohuslav

Composer. Born 8 December 1890, in Polička. Died 28 August 1959, in Liestal, near Basel, Switzerland. Studied violin at home in his youth; enrolled in the Prague Conservatory, 1907-09; entered the Prague Organ School, but was dismissed, 1910; played second violin in the Czech Philharmonic in Prague, 1913-14; in Polička, 1914-18; reentered the Prague Conservatory, studied with Suk; private lessons with Albert Roussel in Paris, 1923; performances of his works at the festivals of the International Society for Contemporary Music; Elizabeth Sprague Coolidge Award for his String Sextet, 1932; in Portugal, 1940; in the United States, 1941; visiting professor at Princeton University, 1948-51; in Switzerland, 1957-59.

Operas   *The Soldier and the Dancer* [*Voják a tanečnice*]. J.L. Budin (after Plautus, *Pseudolus*), 1926-27, Brno, 5 May 1928; *Les larmes du couteau*, Ribemont-Dessaignes, 1928; Brno, 1968 [posthumous performance]; *Les vicissitudes de la vie*, Ribemont-Dessaignes, 1928 [unfinished]; *Les trois souhaits*. Martinů, Ilja Ehrenburg and Ribemont-Dessaignes, 1929; *The Miracle of Our Lady* [*Hry o Marii*].

Martinů and Henri Ghéon, 1933, Brno, 1934; *The Voice of the Forest* [*Hlas lesa*] (radio opera), 1935, Czech Radio, 6 October 1936; *The Suburban Theater* [*Divadlo za bránou*], Martinů, 1935, Brno, 1936; *Comedy on the Bridge* [*Veselohra na mostě*] (radio opera), after Václav Klicpera, 1935, Czech Radio, 18 March 1937; revised c. 1950; *Alexandre bis*, André Wormser, 1937, Mannheim, 18 February 1964 [posthumous production]; *Julietta, or The Key to Dreams*, Georges Neveux, 1936-37, Prague, 1938; *What Men Live By* [*Čím člověk žije*] (television opera), Martinů (after Tolstoy), 1952, New York, 1953; *The Marriage* [*Ženitba*] (television opera), Martinů (after Gogol), 1952, New York, 11 February 1953; *La plainte contre inconnu*, 1953 [unfinished]; *Mirandolina*, 1954, Prague, 17 May 1959; *Ariadne*, Georges Neveux, 1958, Gelsenkirchen, West Germany, 2 March 1961; *The Greek Passion* [*Recké pasije*], after Nikos Kazantzakis, *Christ Recrucified*, 1955-59, Zurich, 9 June 1961.

Bohuslav Martinů's musical talents did not blossom in his conventional studies, for the Prague Conservatory found him incompetent in every subject except his ability to teach, and he was even expelled from the Organ School on grounds of "incorrigible negligence." Such was the unlikely background of one of the most prolific of composers; in fact, Martinů went on to write approximately four hundred compositions.

Although born in Bohemia, Martinů spent nearly all of his career in distant lands including Paris, the United States, Switzerland and Italy. He completed fourteen operas, all of them composed after he had left his homeland, and both musically and dramatically they represent a wide range of styles.

Martinů was much influenced by artistic developments in Paris during the 1920s. His first opera, *The Soldier and the Dancer,* was a comedy after Plautus's *Pseudolus* in which the composer attempted to emulate the wit of Offenbach by incorporating contemporary dances into the music. A jazz influence pervades *The Tears of the Knife,* a twenty-minute piece with surrealist imagery. More substantial altogether is his third opera, *Les trois souhaits*. This work reveals an interest in film, with the inner thoughts of the characters on stage portrayed on a screen behind them. The music reflects this complexity of thought, mixing elements of jazz with speech-song and advanced harmonies, and as in Stravinsky's *Oedipus Rex* a chorus comments on the action.

During the 1930s, Martinů's operas were more closely linked with his native Czechoslovakia. *The Miracle of Our Lady, or The Plays of Mary* is a cycle of four mystery plays based upon a tradition dating from twelfth century Prague. The chief consideration was not religious, however, since the composer chose them "because they are well suited to my music, that is treating them in folk style . . . This work is a return to the old theatre, and that is the theatre I was looking for. It has been conceived, not in a religious sense, but in a folk or popular way." There are four sections, the shorter items preceding the longer ones. The longest and most complex story is that of Sister Pasqualina, which is set to music of great expressiveness, and on a scale which brings the whole work to a powerful conclusion.

In 1935, Martinů composed two short operas for Radio Prague. The tuneful and lively *The Voice of the Forest* is based on the tale of a kidnapped hunter rescued by his wife, while in *The Comedy on the Bridge,* the basis of the story is an eighteenth-century play by Václav Klicpera. This brilliant comedy deals with the absurdities of war, its music characterizing the dramatic situation by means of elements such as fanfare figures and clashing harmonies. Another folk theme is treated in *The Suburban Theater,* namely, the entertainment given by traveling players at a fair. Accordingly, the scenes move along quickly and the musical language is simplified; the earlier part of the work is purely balletic. Here, the style is that of the commedia dell' arte, whereas in *Alexandra bis,* the single act adopts an *opera buffa* approach.

Both chronologically and musically, *Juliette* is the central composition in Martinů's output. Adapted from a play by Georges Neveux, *Juliette* deals with the relationship between reality, dreams and memory. Juliette is the idealized woman in the eyes of Michel, but he is the only character to possess a memory. He cannot therefore be sure if she is real, and the emotional intensity generated by the plot is enhanced by the arioso style and rich textures of the music, much of which achieves a truly haunting quality.

Martinů was blacklisted by the Nazis and in 1940 left Europe for the United States, where he turned to the one major genre he had not hitherto attempted, the symphony. After a gap of approximately fourteen years, the successful New York revival of *The Comedy on the Bridge* rekindled his enthusiasm for opera, and in 1953 he completed an adaptation of Tolstoy's *Tales for the People. What Men Live By* was intended to be a television opera, with chamber dimensions and a cast of seven. It was soon followed by *The Marriage,* in which Gogol's story is treated in a classical manner, using recitatives, arias, dances and ensembles.

The comedy *Mirandolina* is an altogether more striking achievement. Martinů described it as "a light, uncomplicated thing, with something of Goldoni," and its plot concerns the battle between the sexes, the hostess of the title reveling in the power she has over her guests. The leading soprano role has an exciting coloratura which skillfully enhances the characterization, while the interludes add considerable atmosphere.

In *Ariadne,* the inspiration was once again a play by Neveux, but Martinů had already made up his mind to write a chamber opera for Maria Callas, whose voice had so impressed him in broadcasts. She never sang the role, however, which seems a pity since its lyricism and wide vocal range would have been well suited to her artistry.

Martinů's final opera, *The Greek Passion,* is a tragedy based upon Nikos Kazantzakis's novel *Christ Recrucified.* The theme of the play within the play is used again, for in this story the actors of the village passion play take on the exact nature of their roles when they find that a group of refugees have arrived seeking help. At the end the refugees depart and continue their search for a new home. The music is atmospheric and dramatic, linking a series of short scenes and building a cumulative effect, and Martinů related its style to the hymns and chants of the Greek Orthodox Church.

The operas of Martinů cover many topics and styles, for like Stravinsky he had the ability to adopt different approaches and yet remain recognizably himself. His most significant operatic achievements are probably *The Miracle of Our Lady, Juliette* and *The Greek Passion,* but all his music is thoroughly worthy of our attention.—TERRY BARFOOT

Martón, Eva

Soprano. Born Eva Heinrich, 18 June 1943, in Budapest. Studied with Endre Rosler and Jeno Sipos at the Franz Liszt Academy in Budapest; debut as Queen of Shemakhan in Le coq d'or, *Budapest, 1968; member of Budapest State opera, 1968-72; sang in Frankfurt, 1972-77; Vienna debut, 1973; appeared in Munich as Donna Anna, 1974; in Hamburg as the Empress in* Die Frau ohne Schatten, *1977; at Teatro alla Scala as Leonora in* Il trovatore, *1978; Metropolitan Opera debut as Eva in* Die Meistersinger von Nürnberg, *1976; appeared in* Ring *at San Francisco, 1985.*

In the decade of the 1980s there were very few sopranos who could match the dramatic soprano from Hungary, Eva Martón, in power and attack, or who could expand the top notes so remarkably. These traits have served her well in such roles as Turandot, the Empress in Strauss's *Die Frau ohne Schatten* and *Elektra,* the last a role she has recently recorded under Sawallisch. She has performed this role onstage in very different productions under Abbado (in Vienna and Salzburg) and Navarro. Her assessment of Elektra is that "It's dangerous for the voice. I don't want to sing it too often, unlike Turandot, which suits me ideally. On record it's different." In Munich with Sawallisch, whom she greatly admires, Martón has sung Donna Anna (1974), the title role in Strauss's *Die ägyptische Helena* in 1981, and Ariadne, the last also at the Teatro alla Scala. She sang under Sawallisch in Ponnelle's production of *Die Frau ohne Schatten,* "one of the favorite stagings of my career." Not since Leonie Rysanek has there been a soprano equipped to project in such a dazzling manner the Empress's cruel tessitura. This role she has also performed in Hamburg with Dohnányi, at the Metropolitan Opera and the Teatro Colón in Buenos Aires with Birgit Nilsson as the Dyer's Wife, and at the Lyric Opera of Chicago. Although her repertoire is extensive and varied, she has made a specialty of Strauss roles. In addition to the above, there was a Salome with Janowski at the Metropolitan Opera that prompted Martin Mayer to declare that "If the title role is sung as splendidly as Martón sang it, you could set *Salome* as a tale of Martians on Mars and nobody would mind." A recording on CBS of the final scene from a live performance of *Salome* with the Toronto Symphony under Davis is less splendidly sung, catching most of Martón's more blatant faults, such as a tendency to wobble when attempting to sing softly and a certain fuzziness of timbre producing an unfocused pitch.

Martón has also appeared extensively in the operas of Wagner. Her early roles in Budapest included the Third Norn in *Die Götterdämmerung* and Elsa in *Lohengrin.* In 1977 she made her debut at Bayreuth, singing both Venus and Elisabeth in *Tannhäuser.* Her Elisabeth was subsequently brought to Geneva. Martón's first attempt at Brünnhilde was in San Francisco in 1984 in the Lehnhoff-Conklin *Ring* cycle; she had a notable success there in the *Götterdämmerung* Brünnhilde in 1985, of which Robert Jacobson noted that she "does not command the steely laser quality of a Nilsson . . . but suggests more the depth, roundness, and radiance of a Varnay or a Leider." He described her act I duet with René Kollo as Siegfried as "spectacular in its all-encompassing voluminousness, color and caloric content." She is currently recording the role in the complete Ring cycle under Bernard Haitink. Since her early years in Budapest she has made a great success in a number of houses with her Elsa and has even sung Ortrud at the Metropolitan to great acclaim. Her great ambition is to sing Isolde; she has recorded the *Liebestod,* sung a bit too grandly, negating the opening words of the text, "Mild und leise" (gently and softly).

Martón has by no means limited herself to German roles, although she is better suited to them than to most of the Italian roles she has undertaken. Her career began at the National Theater in Budapest with small parts such as the "Celestial Voice" in Verdi's *Don Carlos* and Kate Pinkerton in *Madama Butterfly;* her debut there, in 1968, was as a coloratura in the role of the Queen of Shemakha in Rimsky-Korsakov's *Le coq d'or.* She quickly progressed to the Countess Almaviva in *Le nozze di Figaro* and *Manon Lescaut,* among others.

Mártón grew up singing the main roles in children's operas and in children's choirs. She loved to play the piano and still performs jazz when she has the spare time. At the Franz Liszt Academy she studied with Endre Rösler and left Hungary in 1972 to begin her career in the West in Frankfurt two years later, eventually settling in Hamburg where she makes her home today. In 1984 she was allowed back into Hungary because she held a German passport.

In the Italian repertoire Mártón makes a fine Turandot, for her voice, when at its best (she is often uneven), is big, gleaming, and under firm control. She made her Covent Garden debut in this role in 1987 and can be heard performing it under Maazel in a live recording from Vienna with Carreras as Calaf. Mártón is very solid—she has power, attack, intensity and stamina—but she does not have a true Italianate sound. This is permissible and even desirable for Turandot but a serious fault when she undertakes a role such as Leonora in Verdi's *Il trovatore,* which she has sung in a telecast from the Metropolitan and at La Scala in 1978 under Mehta. Of her 1980 Aida at the Baths of Caracalla (her first Aida in Italy), Lanfranco Rasponi wrote that "Despite a lack of involvement and a rather routine stage presence, she possesses the vocal resources needed for the assignment. The instrument is strong, the pianissimos are well supported." Other Italian roles she has sung with varying degrees of success include Maddalena in *Andrea Chénier,* the title role in Ponchielli's *La Gioconda,* and Puccini's Tosca. Mártón has recorded a recital disc of Puccini arias ranging from Musetta's Waltz to Turandot's "In questa reggia." In this album the tone is somewhat creamier than in many of her Italian endeavors. She claims a special affinity for the music of Puccini and has plans to add Minnie in *La fanciulla del West* at the Metropolitan with Domingo as Dick Johnson. Future plans also include a recording of Leonore in Beethoven's *Fidelio* under Colin Davis, but no plans to sing in a staged production of that opera. She has also recorded Bartók's *Bluebeard's Castle,* an opera learned in her early days, in Hungarian with Samuel Ramey, *Fedora* with Carreras, *La Gioconda,* Catalani's *La Wally,* d'Albert's *Tiefland* with Kollo under Janowski, and act I of *Die Walküre* (from a live concert performance) with Peter Hofmann, Marti Talvela and the New York Philharmonic under Mehta.—STEPHEN WILLIER

Mascagni, Pietro

Composer. Born 7 December 1863, in Livorno. Died 2 August 1945, in Rome. Studied privately with Alfredo Soffredini in Livorno; studied with Ponchielli and Saladino at the Milan Conservatory, 1882, but dismissed from the conservatory in 1884; conductor of the municipal band of Cerignola, 1885; won first prize in the competition sponsored by the publisher Sonzogno for his one-act opera Cavalleria rusticana, *1890; knight of the Crown of Italy, 1890; director of the Rossini Conservatory in Pesaro, 1895-1902; conducted the premiere of his opera* Le maschere *in Rome, 1901, which was premiered simultaneously in Milan, Turin, Genoa, Venice, and Verona; United States tour, 1902; South American tour, 1911; member of the Italian Academy, 1929; supporter of the fascist regime in Italy during the Second World War.*

Operas *Pinotta,* G. Targioni-Tozzetti, c. 1880, San Remo, Casino, 23 March 1932; *Il re a Napoli* (operetta), Cremona, Municipale; *Guglielmo Ratcliff,* A. Maffei (after Heine), c. 1885, Milan, Teatro alla Scala, 16 February 1895; *Cavalleria rusticana,* G. Targioni-Tozzetti and G. Menasci (after Verga), Rome, Costanzi, 17 May 1890; *L' amico Fritz,* P. Suardon [= N. Daspuro] (after Erckmann-Chatrian), Rome, Costanzi, 31 October 1891; *I Rantzau,* G. Targioni-Tozzetti and G. Menasci (after Erckmann-

Chatrian), Florence, Teatro della Pergola, Florence, 10 November 1892; *Silvano,* G. Targioni-Tozzetti, Milan, Teatro alla Scala, 25 March 1895; *Zanetto,* G. Targioni-Tozzetti and G. Menasci (after Coppée), Pesaro, Liceo Musicale, 2 March 1896; *Iris,* L. Illica, Rome, Costanzi, 22 November 1898; revised, Milan, Teatro alla Scala, 19 January 1899; *Le maschere,* L. Illica, simultaneous premiere in Rome, Costanzi; Milan, Teatro alla Scala; Turin, Regio; Genoa, Carlo Felice; Venice, La Fenice; Verona, Filarmonica; 17 January 1901; *Amica,* P. Verel [= de Choudens], Monte Carlo, 16 March 1905; *Isabeau,* L. Illica (after Lady Godiva legend), Buenos Aires, Coliseo, 2 June 1911; *Parisina,* G. D'Annunzio, Milan, Teatro alla Scala, 15 December 1913; *Lodoletta,* G. Forzano (after Ouida), Rome, Costanzi, 30 April 1917; *Sì* (operetta), C. Lombardo and A. Franci, Rome, Quirino, 13 December 1919; *Il piccolo Marat,* G. Forzano and G. Targioni-Tozzetti, Rome, Costanzi, 2 May 1921; *Nerone,* Milan, G. Targioni-Tozzetti (after Cossa), Milan, Teatro alla Scala, 16 January 1935.

One hundred years since the sensational premiere of *Cavalleria rusticana,* Pietro Mascagni still owes his international reputation to that Sicilian story of love, jealousy and revenge, and any critical assessment of his work only credits him with being the initiator of operatic *verismo.* Yet Mascagni's sixteen operas covering a wide range of genres from romantic tragedy, veristic scenes, bourgeois idyll and symbolic music drama to Goldonian comedy and operetta and containing pages of inspired, imaginative music, should have elicited more critical attention or at least suggested caution before dismissing Mascagni as a negligible figure within the Young Italian School.

Cavalleria was undoubtedly the best libretto Mascagni ever set in his career. No innovative intentions were behind his choice of a veristic subject. The source was a play by the Sicilian writer Giovanni Verga, which had already enjoyed the favor of the public and had a one-act format as required by the contest sponsored by the publisher Sonzogno for which the opera was intended. The operatic adaptation mostly preserved the vividness of dialogue and the quick pace of the action, but it distorted the social peculiarities of the story and capitalized on the "exotic" color of its setting.

With his coarse-grained, fresh, impassioned music Mascagni was able to delineate flesh-and-blood characters and give them a musical idiom consistent with their "rustic" nature. On the other hand, the inclusion of idyllic choruses, religious hymns, a serenade in Sicilian dialect, and a drinking song gave the opera a convenient balance between novelty and tradition that secured its initial and subsequently undiminished popularity.

The success of *Cavalleria* resulted in the adoption of the term *verismo* to define both the subject and the stylistic solutions devised by Mascagni to set Verga's story. The opera became the prototype of a new genre—operatic *verismo*—and, in the 1890s, a number of *Cavalleria* imitations flooded the opera houses to meet the demand for working-class tragedies: Giordano's *Mala vita,* Leoncavallo's *Pagliacci,* Massenet's *La navarraise,* and D'Albert's *Tiefland* are relevant examples to which Mascagni's own mediocre *Silvano* can be added.

When the whole of Mascagni's production is surveyed, however, it soon becomes clear how misrepresented he is under the label of *verismo.* The very next opera after *Cavalleria, L'amico Fritz,* baffled Mascagni's admirers for its definitely *un*veristic nature. The gentle idyll by Erckmann-Chatrian may have been a tenuous story to turn into a three-act "lyric comedy," but Mascagni took great care in shaping its pastoral setting and the three main characters, particularly the graceful Suzel, whose naive charm wins the bachelor Fritz over to marriage.

Apart from some occasional lapses into his earlier *Cavalleria*-style, Mascagni's orchestra in *Fritz* sounds more refined, more elegant. The opera is full of tenderness, and the vocal part of Suzel contains exquisite melodies of Puccinian delicacy, such as the romanza "Son pochi fiori" (act I), the passionate lament "Non mi resta altro che il pianto" (act III). No less charming are the celebrated "Cherry Duet" (act II) between Suzel and Fritz, and the off-stage choruses for which Mascagni used two Alsatian folk-songs.

Even further away from *verismo* in terms of the subject and the musico-dramatic structures, is the four-act romantic tragedy *Guglielmo Ratcliff,* with its ghosts and bleak Scottish landscape. Although it was first performed in 1895, the opera had been a pet project of the composer since about 1885. Whereas the choice of *Cavalleria* was dictated by sheer expediency, the setting of the almost integral translation of Heine's gloomy

Pietro Mascagni

tragedy was resumed with youthful zeal and earnest effort once Mascagni had achieved success. However, the unremarkable music and the length and frequency of the narrative monologues have doomed the opera to oblivion save for a Massenetian intermezzo (act III, 3) known as "Ratcliff's Dream."

The 1890s were the most prolific years in Mascagni's career. During this period, Mascagni composed no fewer than eight operas, each apparently marking the adherence to a different cultural trend, and demonstrating the composer's eclecticism. These works include one more Erckmann-Chatrian story (the unexciting and modest *I Rantzau*), *Silvano*, *Zanetto* (a one-act opera, set in Renaissance Florence and based on a play by the Parnassian poet François Coppée), the decadent *Iris,* and a revival of the commedia dell'arte masks with *Le maschere.*

One common feature is noticeable in these and in Mascagni's later operas; although they may well contain finer music than *Cavalleria,* their overall theatrical effectiveness is hindered by some intrinsic fault of the librettos. Mascagni lacks self-criticism and Puccini's unerring sense of the theater. It was not for him to pester his librettists and require extensive alterations and readjustments as his more perceptive colleague did. Mascagni may have occasionally complained, but the librettist had the last word. This was the case with the highly skilled and much sought-after librettist Luigi Illica, who wrote the librettos of *Iris, Le maschere* and *Isabeau.*

Iris exemplifies Mascagni's most advanced stage of artistic development. A Japanese legend is dramatized in the first two acts. Osaka, a lustful nobleman, sets his eyes on the ingenuous and beautiful Iris and engages Kyoto, the owner of a geisha house, to abduct the girl. Once in Kyoto's luxurious place, Iris does not respond to Osaka's passionate advances and is therefore put on public display. When her blind father curses her, flinging mud in her face, Iris, in despair, throws herself down a dark pit. The opera might come to an end on this gruesome event. Instead, act III shows the dying girl at dawn on the bank of an open sewer. Some ragpickers are attracted by her glittering attire. Iris dies as the sun rises and the horrid place is engulfed by flowers. After Baudelaire, Illica had read Maeterlinck, and a veil of symbolism is laid on people and events. The fashionable orientalism of the setting adds color to the decadent

OPERA

ingredients of the story, which include Osaka's eroticism, Kyoto's sadism, and Iris's passive, dreamy nature.

Stimulated by this material, Mascagni produces a sparkling score characterized by sophisticated harmonies and polychrome orchestration. A highly sensitive idiom is devised for Iris's nightmares and lyrical outbursts, such as in her dream monologue in act I, "Ho fatto un triste sogno," and the act II aria "Un dì (ero piccina)".

Despite Illica's pretentious text and its dramatic shortcomings, *Iris* has generally received a favorable critical response, to the point that some claim *Iris* to be an anticipation of Puccini's *Butterfly* and *Turandot*. The opera marks Mascagni's approach to *fin-de-siècle* aestheticism, and, through the later *Isabeau* (Illica's adaptation of the Lady Godiva legend), leads to the "lyric tragedy" *Parisina* (1913), expressly written by Gabriele D'Annunzio for the composer.

Later, in *Il piccolo Marat*, Mascagni returned to his early *verismo* style with no appreciable results. Both this opera and his last, *Nerone*, do not add much to the composer's artistic achievement.—MATTEO SANSONE

Massenet, Jules

Composer. Born 12 May 1842, in Montaud, near St-Etienne, Loire. Died 13 August 1912, in Paris. Married: Constance de Sainte-Marie, 1866 (one daughter). Studied piano with Laurent, harmony with Reber, and composition with Savard and Ambroise Thomas at the Paris Conservatory, 1851; first prize for piano and fugue at the Paris Conservatory, 1859; Grand Prix de Rome for his cantata, David Rizzio, 1863; professor of composition at the Paris Conservatory, 1878; member of the Académie des Beaux-Arts, 1878. Massenet's students included Alfred Bruneau, Gabriel Pierné, Charles Koechlin, Reynaldo Hahn, Florent Schmitt, Henri Rabaud, and Gustave Charpentier.

Operas *Esmeralda,* after Hugo, c. 1865; *La coupe du roi de Thulé,* L. Gallet, c. 1866; *La grand'tante,* Jules Adénis and Charles Grandvallet, Paris, Opéra-Comique, 3 April 1867; *Manfred,* after Byron, c. 1869 [unfinished]; *Méduse,* M. Carré, 1870 [unfinished]; *Don César de Bazan,* Adolphe Philippe d'Ennery, P.E. Pinel Dumanoir and Jules Chantepie (after Hugo, *Ruy Blas*), Paris, Opéra-Comique, 30 November 1872; *L'adorable bel'-boul',* Louis Gallet, Paris, Cercle des Mirlitons, 17 April 1874; *Les templiers* [unfinished]; *Bérengère et Anatole,* Henri Meilhac and Paul Poirson, Paris, Cercle de l'Union Artistique, February 1876; *Le roi de Lahore,* Louis Gallet, Paris, Opéra, 27 April 1877 [act III based on act II of *La coupe du roi de Thulé*]; *Robert de France,* c. 1880; *Les Girondins,* 1881; *Hérodiade,* Paul Milliet and Henri Grémont [=Georges Hartmann] and Zamadini (after Flaubert), Brussels, Théâtre de la Monnaie, 19 December 1881; *Manon,* Henri Meilhac and Philippe Gille (after Prévost), Paris, Opéra-Comique, 19 January 1884; *Le Cid,* Adolphe Philippe d'Ennery, Louis Gallet, and Edouard Blau (after Corneille), Paris, Opéra, 30 November 1885; *Esclarmonde,* Alfred Blau and Louis de Gramont, Paris, Opéra-Comique, 14 May 1889; *Le mage,* Jean Richepin, Paris, Opéra, 16 March 1891; *Werther,* Edouard Blau, Paul Milliet, and Georges Hartmann (after Goethe) [libretto translated into German by Max Kalbeck], Vienna, Court Opera, 16 February 1892; *Thaïs,* Louis Gallet (after Anatole France), Paris, Opéra, 16 March 1894; *Le portrait de Manon,* Georges Boyer, Paris, Opéra-Comique, 8 May 1894; *La navarraise,* Jules Claretie and Henri Cain, London, Covent Garden, 20 June 1894; *Sapho,* Henri Cain and Arthur Bernède (after Daudet), Paris, Opéra-Comique, 27 November 1897; *Cendrillon,* Henri Cain (after Perrault), Paris, Opéra-Comique, 24 May 1899; *Grisélidis,* Paul Armand Silvestre and Eugène Morand, Paris, Opéra-Comique, 20 November 1901; *Amadis,* Jules Claretie, c. 1902, Monte Carlo, Opéra, 1 April 1922 [posthumous]; *Le jongleur de Notre Dame,* Maurice Léna, Monte Carlo, 18 February 1902; *Chérubin,* Francis de Croisset and Henri Cain, Monte Carlo, Opéra, 14 February 1905; *Ariane,* Catulle Mendès, Paris, Opéra, 31 October 1906; *Thérèse,* Jules Claretie, Monte Carlo, Opéra, 7 February 1907; *Bacchus,* Catulle Mendès, Paris, Opéra, 5 May 1909; *Don Quichotte,* Henri Cain (after Jacques Le Lorrain, *Le chevalier de la longue figure*), Monte Carlo, Opéra, 19 February 1910; *Roma,* Henri Cain (after Dominique Alexandre Parodi, *Rome vaincue*), Monte Carlo, Opéra, 17 February 1912; *Panurge,* Georges Spitzmüller and Maurice Boukay (after Rabelais), Paris, Théâtre de la Gaîté, 25 April 1913 [posthumous]; *Cléopâtre,* Louis Payen [=Albert Liénard], Monte Carlo, Opéra, 23 February 1914 [posthumous].

In his time, Massenet was the most popular of all French composers for the stage. He owed his success to a brilliant sense of theater, a sharp awareness of prevailing fashions and an inexhaustible capacity for hard work.

Some of the qualities Massenet was to display in his triumphant career are clearly discernible in his first important opera, *Don César de Bazan* (1872). Although it bears traces of haste and clumsiness, it has a neat touch of Spanish local color, and the rhythms are handled to full theatrical effect. The stageworthy quality of the opera is what strikes one most, even in this early work. Here Massenet shows evidence of a remarkable gift for the theater despite the nature of the music, which today sounds conventional and often faded. Massenet knew instinctively how to create emotion by means of dramatic illusion; his natural talent, formed and instructed by years of humble work in the orchestra pit had begun to flower rewardingly.

Massenet's next important opera, *Le roi de Lahore* (1877), proved that he knew what the public of the Paris Opéra wanted: color, spectacle, exotic scenery, and all the grandiose delights which Meyerbeer had given them in profusion. Set in ancient India, *Le roi de Lahore* is modeled on Bizet's *Les pêcheurs de perles,* and makes clever use of pseudo-oriental harmonies. The third act is set in a Hindu paradise which, needless to say, gave excellent opportunities for the ballet without which no Parisian opera production would have been complete. The formula was impeccable.

Le roi de Lahore was a turning point in Massenet's career. It won rapturous acclaim and soon established itself in the repertory, not only at home but throughout the rest of Europe. The same exoticism marks *Hérodiade* (1881), which is inspired by one of Flaubert's *Trois contes*. In Salomé we see the emergence of what was to become known as a typical Massenet heroine: the suave seductress, langorous and tempting. With her aria "Il est doux, il est bon," Massenet demonstrates his mature and most characteristic style. Rather like the Symbolist poets of the time, he breaks up the conventional rhythm of a line, shifts the accent and introduces enjambements (lines running over into the next one) which enable him to extend the melodic line in a novel way. There are links here with Debussy's *Enfant prodigue* and a forward glance at the unrealities of *Pelléas et Mélisande*.

If this style was not entirely suited to the torrid Eastern setting for which it was intended, it came fully into its own with *Manon* (1884). Prévost's short novel, a "passionate and beautiful romance" as Lytton Strachey called it, gave Massenet the chance of a lifetime. His mellifluous and

Jules Massenet

caressing style fitted the eighteenth-century atmosphere of *Manon* to perfection. A setting of dainty boudoirs and rococo gambling rooms, an ambience of flowered waistcoats, silver shoe-buckles and swaying panniers, and above all a heroine of ravishing charm, were the elements that moved Massenet to write his masterpiece. Although there is a hint of Wagnerian techniques in his use of motifs associated with various characters, Massenet's handling of the material is wholly original. Manon herself is the best-known character in the gallery of operatic women that Massenet depicted. Like her creator, she has the art of wooing an audience, of captivating them with a seductive charm expressed in luscious melodies and ripe orchestration. While the opera belongs to Manon with her scintillating roulades and dizzying *ports de voix,* Massenet is careful nonetheless to give the men some fine opportunities. The score is unfailingly inventive and is embellished with many delicious pages of minuet, gavotte and ballet which add splendor to the production numbers.

The three operas which succeeded Massenet's greatest triumph are exercises on a more ambitious scale. *Le Cid* (1885), based on the Spanish epic, was hampered by a poor libretto and Massenet's inability to encompass the heroic gesture. *Esclarmonde* (1889) proved more congenial with its evocation of medieval sorcery, enchanted gardens, magic palaces and mystic chivalry. The style is bewilderingly eclectic and has decided echoes of Wagnerian pomp (the processional march in act 2, for example), not to mention hints of Gounod, Meyerbeer and Verdi. Massenet always maintained that *Esclarmonde* was his favorite opera—but that was only because he wrote it for his protégée, the American singer Sybil Sanderson, with whom he was infatuated at the time.

After *Le Mage* (1891), an overblown failure, Massenet returned to his best form with *Werther* (1892). In this version of Goethe's sentimental novel, the acts are conceived as unities rather than as a series of individual numbers, and the orchestral texture is rich in Wagnerian sonorities. Massenet knew which way the wind was blowing and shared with Puccini a flair for adapting whatever suited him best in the work of contemporaries and assimilating it into his own formulas. Yet he was very much more than just a snapper-up of other people's good ideas. *Werther* contains some of his most individual features: the naïf little melody of the short prelude which recurs from time to time, the innocent lyricism, and the exquisite simplicity of the famous moonlight scene where both Werther and Charlotte realize the impossibility of their love. As in *Manon,* the composer breaks up the line of verse and varies it with displaced accents to create a more fluid effect. Charlotte, another of his great heroines, is drawn in rather greater depth than he had attempted before, and she has a self-denial and a nobility that are foreign to his other women. Taken on its own terms, *Werther* is an artistic success. The sequences are shaped with perfect balance, climaxes are developed with sureness, and the variety of mood and action is wonderfully maintained. It is one of the most obvious examples of the freshness, the command of the stage, and the grateful writing for voice and orchestra that characterize Massenet at his best. It also shows how he could husband his gifts to the utmost and use them so as to achieve theatrical effect in every bar he wrote.

After *Werther,* Massenet composed a series of elegant variations on a theme he had made particularly his own. *Thaïs* (1894) offers yet another portrait of a temptress, in this case the beautiful Egyptian courtesan who brings about the downfall of a holy man and herself aspires to sainthood. The limpid irony of Anatole France's novel from which the opera is taken, whereby the saint becomes a sinner and the sinner turns into a saint, is blunted by adaptation for the stage, which calls for sharp dramatic contrast and the broad strokes which are necessary in the theater. Massenet's solution is to compress and simplify, as in the famous aria where Thaïs looks in the mirror and decides that, despite her luxurious life, she does not know the meaning of true happiness. Her only solace is her beauty, and that, too, she knows will fade. The melodic line rises, falls, then leaps again in a typically Massenetic way as she pleads with the goddess Venus to halt the passage of time. Another instance of compression is the interlude entitled *Méditation* for solo violin and orchestra, hackneyed now, but, if heard with fresh ears, an ingenious solution to the problem of showing the courtesan's dilemma as she wavers between thoughts of conversion and of carrying on her old sinful life. Within a very short space of time Massenet had to depict an event which France, in the leisurely pages of his novel, could describe with ample and convincing detail. From the point of view of characterization, Thaïs differs little, it must be admitted, from all the other heroines in Massenet's collection. Yet the music she has to sing is so ingratiating, the orchestration so inventive and flexible, that the charm of the opera still acts on a receptive audience. A few months after its premiere came the first performance of Debussy's *Prélude à l'après-midi d'un faune,* where the fluid line developed still further the direction Massenet had taken with his supple phrasing and broken rhythms. It is worth noting that Poulenc once remarked that he could never hear the second of Debussy's *Chansons de Bilitis* (1897) without thinking of the mirror aria in *Thaïs.*

La navarraise (1894), a piece of Spanish blood and thunder and doubtlessly the noisiest opera Massenet ever wrote, presents a heroine of Carmen-like intensity. It also shows the influence of the Italian *verismo* composers. Another passionate heroine is *Sapho* (1897), based on Alphonse Daudet's best-selling novel. This anguished account of how a vulnerable youth falls victim to his passion and is destroyed by it portrays the woman as the dominant partner and the man as the helpless object of her calculation. In some ways the opera is *Manon* brought up to date, and there are distinct parallels between each of the five acts of the two operas so far as action and plot are concerned. Like Manon, Sapho dominates the opera, although it is undeniably late nineteenth century with its Bohemian artists' studios and assignations in suburban taverns. Some of the music owes a debt to Tchaikovsky, whose influence was already apparent in *Werther,* and one of the big love arias carries an echo of *Eugène Onegin.*

By the nineteen hundreds, Massenet's star had begun to wane. Of the nine operas Massenet was to write in his last decade, only *Thérèse* (1907), a romance of the French Revolution, and *Don Quichotte* (1910), a moving portrayal of Cervantes's old hero, showed flashes of the old brilliance. Taken as a whole, however, the substantial body of work he left proves that he is too complex a figure to be pigeon-holed merely as a writer of pretty tunes. Even in his minor operas there is usually some neat piece of invention or some clever technical device to be admired. He worked his talent with infinite care and made it yield up all that could be harvested.

The operas leading up to *Manon* show Massenet perfecting the unique style for which he became famous. *Werther* represents a new departure and demonstrates how he could adapt his gifts so that he moved with complete naturalness from the eighteenth century of Fragonard to early German romanticism.—JAMES HARDING

Mathis der Maler [Mathias the Painter]

Composer: *Paul Hindemith.*

Librettist: *Paul Hindemith.*

First Performance: *Zurich, Stadttheater, 28 May 1938.*

Roles: *Mathis/St Anthony (baritone); Albrecht von Brandenburg/St Paul (tenor); Lorenz von Pommersfelden/Wealth (bass); Wolfgang Capito/Scholar (tenor); Ursula/ Martyr (soprano); Regina (soprano); Riedinger (bass); Hans Schwalb/Knight (tenor); Countess von Helfenstein/Luxury (contralto); Truchsess von Waldburg (bass); Sylvester von Schaumberg (tenor); Piper (tenor); Count von Helfenstein (mute); chorus (SSAATTBB).*

Mathis der Maler is a historical romance, a musically and dramatically vital stage piece which Hindemith himself came to regard as his masterpiece and which is generally taken to be the central work in his career.

The opera is unusual among Hindemith's compositions in that it has a strong autobiographical element. Having embraced a concept of music, loosely gathered under the term *Gebrauchsmusik,* which emphasized music's social functions rather than its aesthetic autonomy, Hindemith wrote the libretto as his first major literary effort and composed the music at a time when his personal circumstances were becoming unsettled and the political environment threatening. He was routinely denounced in the Nazi press as a "bolshevik atonalist" and had strong, longstanding personal and professional ties to Jewish musicians. Though suspect, his work was not officially banned until 1936. The premiere of the *Mathis* Symphony in 1934 met with great success, but the opera could not be produced, the particularly offending item being its book-burning scene.

Mathis describes a cycle of self-doubt, struggle, and final personal solution to the problem of the artist's role in society. The parallel between the opera's setting (Germany during the Peasants' Revolt, circa 1525) and the contemporary situation is hard to miss, as is the fact that the artistic personality ascribed to the principal character, the painter Mathias Grünewald, is Hindemith's own. Likewise, the central problem for both artists is the same: how can one justify creating art that is not politically engaged in a time of dangerous political uncertainty? Or, more basically, how can one continue to create art at all? In an apotheosis following a series of painful visions, Mathis's artistry is returned to him in the form of a "mission" to perfect an art that presents suffering but which is transformed by a moral power transcending its outward appearance.

Thus, the core of the plot is that the artist who cannot nurture his own creative abilities remains politically and socially impotent, no matter how much he uses activism in an attempt to quiet his conscience. This message, timely enough in 1935, was criticized after the end of World War II for an apparent capitulation to established power and lack of political forcefulness, but in more recent years its surprisingly complex parable of the artist in the world has received good productions and more positive press.

The music achieves a remarkable synthesis of stylistic and technical elements of Hindemith's stylistically varied music from the 1920s, as it shows the clearest evidence of his rediscovery of historical musics. The prevailing "modernist" style of the 1920s was characterized by great emphasis on melody and rhythm and, by extension, on counterpoint. Such music could also be indifferent (deliberately so) in motivic development and harmony, these being the two features of composition most deeply associated with the Romantic composers. In *Mathis,* however, Hindemith made his peace with the nineteenth century—he was once again willing to draw into his music motivic development and directed harmonic progression when they suited his purposes. This synthesis or, one might say, rounding out of his compositional tools and the careful planning exhibited on smaller and larger scales gave more substance to the modish "linear counterpoint" style, but simultaneously infused traditional romantic techniques with new vitality and movement. The manner achieved here remained characteristic of all his later work. In the course of achieving this personal solution to the Romantic-Modernist polarity, Hindemith exploited the most thorough-going historicism of any composer in this century. In the end, like *Mathis,* he came to see the need for this dialogue with history in moral terms.

As an example of this hard-won but fundamentally positive orientation toward both a contemporary musical aesthetic and the preservation of tradition, we may cite the opera's sixth tableau, which begins with an intense, dissonant orchestral recitative that has been (erroneously) described as twelve-tone. Both the second and third main divisions of the tableau are inspired by an altarpiece panel. At the climactic point of "The Temptation of Saint Anthony," also the high climax of the entire opera, a chorus of demons and a quintet of soloists pursue Mathis, who in his dream has been transmuted into St Anthony. To the text "Ubi eras bone Jesu . . .?" ["Where were you, good Jesus?"], which, incidentally, appears on a small piece of paper in a corner of the panel, Mathis sings a newly composed, typically Hindemithian melody—chromatic in its overall plan, but built out of diatonic cells of varying size and emphasizing the intervals of the major second and perfect fourth. At the same time, the upper winds accompany one of the quintet, Ursula, as she sings, to a new text, the melody of the sequence "Lauda Sion Salvatorem." Ursula (a character also based on a historical personage) had appeared earlier in the Temptation in three guises—beggar, seductress, and finally martyr. She appears here as the latter, and clearly the symbolism of the melody she sings is that of rising above chaos, holding out the hope of salvation or of healing, a process which takes place for Mathis/St Anthony in the third main section of the tableau, built around the scene depicted in the panel opposing the Temptation, The Visit of St Anthony to St Paul the Eremite. Their final "Alleluia" has become well-known as the dramatic ending of the *Mathis* Symphony.

Like Hindemith's other full-length operas, *Mathis* is an effective stage piece with several dramatic group scenes and ample opportunities for the singers to develop characterizations. It is, on the other hand, rather long and makes particularly heavy demands on the lead baritone part; a successful German production in 1979 changed some sections to dialogue.—DAVID NEUMEYER

Mathis, Edith

Soprano. Born 11 February 1938, in Lucerne, Switzerland. Studied at Lucerne Conservatory; debut as boy in Die Zauberflöte, *Lucerne, 1956; engaged at Cologne Opera, 1959-62; member of Hamburg Staatsoper, 1960-75; has also appeared at Deutsche Oper,*

Berlin; Metropolitan Opera debut as Pamina, 1970; appearances at Salzburg and Glyndebourne.

Like her contemporary Mirella Freni, Edith Mathis has evolved over the course of a long and successful career from a light soprano (during the 1960s) to a more dramatic soprano. The maturing of Mathis's voice during the 1970s resulted in some miscasting and some flawed performances, but it also gave opera-goers a chance to hear Mathis give some memorable performances of works that she would not have been able to sing earlier.

During the first phase of her career, in the 1960s, Mathis won much applause for her Mozart singing: Cherubino, Susanna and Pamina were among her best roles. Outside of the Mozart operas she was successful also as Ännchen (Weber's *Der Freischütz*) and Sophie (Strauss's *Rosenkavalier*), roles in which Mathis could put to good use not only her light, pure soprano voice, but also her youthful wit and playfulness. Her portrayal of Marzelline (Beethoven's *Fidelio*) as recorded under Karl Böhm is a good example of her singing in the 1960s. In the opening duet with Jaquino we hear Marzelline as a young, innocent girl, cheerful and good-hearted. But Mathis's singing leaves some things to be desired. The way that Peter Schreier, as Jaquino, vividly enunciates his words makes one miss such enunciation when Mathis sings. And one can hear in Mathis's voice, even in this relatively early recording, a wide vibrato that sometimes obscures the pitch.

Some of her later performances were not so successful. In a recording of Mozart's *Zaide* under Bernhard Klee (1975) the big, full-bodied sound of the older Mathis seems out of place. Although she sings the beautiful aria "Ruhe sanft" with great feeling, one misses the purity that Stich-Randall or Margaret Price (or Mathis ten years earlier) could have brought to this music. When she sang Sophie at Covent Garden in 1975 she won praise for her acting; but one critic also noted that her voice "is now a trifle heavy for the part."

Trying to sound and act younger than she was, Mathis sometimes gave portrayals that sounded forced. She was criticized as "overly pert" in her portrayal of Susanna (Mozart's *Le nozze di Figaro*) in Paris in 1975. Her performance of Ännchen in a recording of Weber's *Der Freischütz* under Carlos Kleiber (1973), admirable in many ways, suffers from the same problem. Agathe's "young relative," with her heavy vibrato, sounds older than Agathe herself. Ännchen's light-hearted attempts to cheer up Agathe are pleasing to listen to, but dramatically unconvincing (and made more so by the unfortunate use, in this recording, of non-singing actors to perform the spoken dialogue).

Mathis's portrayals of another young woman, Pamina in *Die Zauberflöte,* have been consistently satisfying, even as the singer grew older. Her performance of the role as recorded under Karajan (c. 1980) has been hailed by Rodney Milnes as "a classic interpretation." Among other roles in which Mathis has won much applause are those of Mistress Ford in Nicolai's *Die lustigen Weiber von Windsor* (a role that she has recorded) and Mélisande in Debussy's *Pelléas and Mélisande.*—JOHN A. RICE

McCormack, John

Tenor. Born 14 June 1884, in Athlone, Ireland. Died 16 September 1945, in Dublin. Married: Lily Foley. Studied with Vincent O'Brien in Dublin and with Vincenzo Sabatini

in Milan; stage debut as Beppe in L'amico Fritz, *Savona, 1906; Covent Garden debut as Turiddu, 1907, and sang there regularly until 1914; in Naples, 1909; Manhattan Opera debut as Alfredo, 1909; Metropolitan Opera debut in the same role, 1910; spent World War I in the United States and became a United States citizen in 1917, then returned to England; appeared in Monte Carlo, 1921 and 1923; gave recitals after retiring from stage.*

John McCormack, an extremely popular and beloved recitalist, had a somewhat limited but very distinguished operatic career that began in Italy in 1906. He was barely past thirty years of age when his voice began to lose the fresh silvery quality of its youth and the high notes became problematic. Yet until the very end of his long life, and even in the last recordings where the tone is no longer rounded and the legato and portamento no longer melting, McCormack's impeccable diction and magical interpretations must be admired. It was principally in the realm of Irish ballads and songs, sung in English, that McCormack made his greatest impact.

In 1904 when McCormack was twenty years old, he heard Enrico Caruso sing at Covent Garden, which made an overwhelming impression on him. Even though McCormack wisely never attempted to imitate Caruso's vocal production, the experience left him with the resolve to become an Italian tenor. McCormack made some unsuccessful recordings in 1904 but then went to study with Vincenzo Sabatini in Italy, where he quickly mastered the Italian language and the core of his Italian operatic repertoire. In 1907 he debuted as Tur-iddu at Covent Garden, performing some fifteen roles there until World War I. In 1911 he toured Australia with Melba; their vocal timbres and even scales matched perfectly. He had already made his Metropolitan Opera debut in 1910 with Melba in *La traviata* and was especially popular with the large Irish population in New York City, but also with the public in general; in 1918 he sang in the Hippodrome for an audience of more than 7,000. McCormack's last opera performances were in Monte Carlo in the early 1920s; for the subsequent twenty years of his career he sang concerts, continued to make recordings, many of which sold at least 100,000 copies, and starred in a film, *Song of My Heart,* in 1929.

McCormack's voice was not large, but rather a nasal-sounding, lyrical, unforced, high tenor that, being well-placed, could fill vast spaces. He sang with a strong Irish brogue. Part of McCormack's magic was that he could make something spellbinding of the simplest material. Among his many charming recordings, the collector's items are pieces by Mozart and Handel. His "Il mio tesoro" from *Don Giovanni* set a standard that no subsequent tenor has been able to match on record. As with many other recorded selections (e.g., "Spirto gentil" from Donizetti's *La favorita,* in which he takes the first four phrases all in one breath), McCormack's breath control in "Il mio tesoro" is astonishing—a prime reason that his version stands above the rest. Also noteworthy is the seamless scale in which each note of the runs is quite distinct; and with all of the considerable demands of the aria, the lovely quality of sound of the voice never suffers. One of his best Handel recordings is "Come, my beloved" (original "Care selve") from *Atalanta,* for the above reasons; another is "Oh Sleep, Why Dost Thou Leave Me" from *Semele,* in which he sings a miraculous phrase on one breath on the rising line of the word "wandering."

Other noteworthy opera recordings by McCormack include "Una furtiva lagrima" from Donizetti's *L'elisir d'amore,* showing fine *bel canto* style and in general comparing favorably with Caruso's rendition. A typical McCormack feature is obvious here, however—the lack of dramatic tension on "m'ama," for example, and the stiffness of the cadenza. Similarly, the cadenza in Edgardo's final scene from *Lucia di Lammermoor,* "Fra poco a me ricovero," is too metrically strict in what is otherwise a stunning performance, complete with exemplary diction, sensitive phrasing, gorgeous, unrestrained outpouring of tone in the highest tessitura, and correct application of tempo rubato. The aria from act II of Donizetti's *La fille du régiment* is sung in Italian by McCormack as "Per viver vicino." Here he displays a model *messa di voce*, fine use of head voice and a well-controlled, beautiful tone throughout. As an interpreter of the music of Donizetti, McCormack is ideal among recorded tenors.

There exist a number of selections by McCormack from Verdi's *La traviata*, including a "De' miei bollenti spiriti" from 1910 with a long-held "Vivo" and an excellent cadenza; there is also a "Parigi, o cara" with Lucrezia Bori from 1914. The duet is very graceful, the voices blend together beautifully, yet McCormack cannot disguise his Irish accent and he does something no native Italian would do, dividing "Parigi" from "o cara."

For all his great storytelling ability, McCormack was no actor, and the operatic stage was not his natural milieu. As a recitalist he became, along with Ernestine Schumann-Heink, the first vocal "superstar"; with concerts and recordings he earned as much as a million dollars during certain years. There were a few faults. He never securely possessed the top notes above a B-flat and they soon disappeared; the Irish brogue, especially on the vowel "ee," could in later years be grating; and he was often harshly criticized for the popular quality of much of the material he presented in recital. Yet for vocal sweetness, prodigious breath control, crystal clear diction, exemplary legato and phrasing, and immediacy of communication to vast groups of people, McCormack had no peers. He is one of the most magical and enchanting singers on record.—STEPHEN WILLIER

McIntyre, (Sir) Donald (Conroy)

Bass-baritone. Born 22 October 1934, in Auckland, New Zealand. Studied at Guildhall School of Music, London; debut as Zaccaria in Nabucco, with Welsh National Opera, Cardiff, 1959; sang with Sadlers Wells Opera, 1960-67; Bayreuth debut as Telramund, 1967, and appeared there regularly until 1988; Metropolitan Opera debut as Wotan in Das Rheingold, 1975; became Officer of Order of British Empire, 1977; Commander of Order of British Empire, 1985, knighted, 1992.

At the outset of his career, Donald McIntyre scored important successes in two Wagnerian roles: the Dutchman in *Der fliegende Holländer* for Sadlers Wells in 1965, and Hunding in *Die Walküre* for Scottish Opera in 1966. These successes were prophetic. McIntyre's impressive physical presence, allied to a solid dark bass-baritone voice, firmly focussed and with unusual freedom in the upper register, proved ideally suited to Wagner. Invited to audition for Bayreuth in 1967, for the minor role of the Herald in *Lohengrin,* he gained instead the much larger part of the villainous Telramund. Critic Richard Law, hearing him repeat the role the following year, wrote in *Opera* (Autumn 1968), "He combines the weight of voice with total mastery of the innumerable cruelly high notes in the part, and he should be part of the Bayreuth scene for a long time to come." In fact, McIntyre was to appear regularly at the Bayreuth Festival until 1988, a record surpassed by few other singers and one which places him firmly as one of the leading Wagnerians of his generation.

The range of his Bayreuth repertoire is impressive: apart from Telramund, he has sung the Dutchman (1969-71, 1981), Klingsor in *Parsifal* (1968, 1970, 1972), Amfortas in *Parsifal* (1981, 1987-88), Kurwenal in *Tristan und Isolde* (1974), Wanderer in *Siegfried* (1973-80) and Wotan in *Der Ring des Nibelungen* (1975-80). It is for the dual role of Wanderer/Wotan in Patrice Chéreau's controversial production of the *Ring* cycle that he will probably be most remembered.

Although McIntyre's voice has generally been described as a bass-baritone, he tends to reject categorization by vocal range, basing his approach to a role on what he can get out of it rather than on whether he exactly matches how it has been classified. This pragmatism has allowed him to encompass the extremes of Sarastro and Scarpia. He has recently expanded his repertoire by accepting the challenge of more contemporary roles—most notably Balstrode in *Peter Grimes,* the title role in Hindemith's *Cardillac,* the Doctor in *Wozzeck* and Prospero in Berio's *Un re in ascolto.*

McIntyre's concern has always been to keep his interpretations fresh and adventurous. He no longer sings Wotan because he feels he has exhausted the possibilities of the role. Instead, he has shifted his attention to perhaps the most complex of all Wagnerian creations, Hans Sachs in *Die Meistersinger von Nürnberg*. His Sachs is, characteristically, a powerful and charismatic figure in the vigorous prime of life. This reading gives a unique poignancy to his actions in the opera and is another example of the individuality with which McIntyre has always approached his art.

Considering his reputation, McIntyre has been poorly treated by recording companies. Relatively few of his major roles are represented on disc. However, his portrayals of the Wanderer and Wotan in the Chéreau *Ring* cycle and of Hans Sachs in the 1988 Hampe production of *Die Meistersinger* for Australian Opera, have been preserved on video. They confirm the qualities on which his reputation is based: a dark, well-focussed voice with a dramatic edge to its timbre, an imaginative insight into character, and a commanding stage personality.—ADRIENNE SIMPSON

Médée [Medea]

Composer: *Luigi Cherubini.*

Librettist: *François Benôit Hoffman (after Euripides).*

First performance: *Paris, Théâtre Feydeau, 13 March 1797.*

Roles: *Jason (tenor); Médée (soprano); Néris (mezzo-soprano); Créon (bass); Dircé (soprano); First Maidservant (soprano); Second Maidservant (mezzo-soprano).*

In act I of Cherubini's *Médée*, Dircé is fearful of marrying Jason but is convinced by her attendants that Médée is no longer a threat. Créon promises Jason protection for his sons, and Jason presents the Golden Fleece to Dircé during the March of the Argonauts. As the Corinthians are invoking Hymen to bless the marriage, Médée enters. Créon orders her to depart immediately, and the act ends with a prolonged duet between Médée and Jason during which both deplore the fatal influence of the Golden Fleece.

During act II, Médée convinces Créon to allow her to remain one day to have time to bid farewell to her children. She uses the time to have her children give a poisoned robe, crown, and jewels as presents to Dircé. The final act is preceded by an orchestral interlude depicting the storm raging both in nature and in Médée's heart. She curses her maternal weakness and, aided by cries from the palace, where Dircé is consumed by the flames of Médée's presents, drags the children into the temple to murder them. Jason rushes in with the people of Corinth, but too late. Médée, wielding her knife and surrounded by the three Eumenides, appears in the temple's doorway. She prophesies that Jason will wander homeless for the rest of his life and will meet her in Hades. Médée rises into the air, the temple bursts into flames and the people flee terror-stricken as the curtain falls.

Although receiving critical approval, *Médée* enjoyed only a *succès d'estime,* disappearing after twenty performances. Paris did not see another production until the mid-twentieth century. However, the Germans were taken with the work, performing it on numerous occasions throughout the nineteenth century. Mme Margarite Luise Schick (1773-1809) was Médée in the first Berlin production on 17 April 1800, for which the *Allgemeine musikalische Zeitung* published an extensive analysis, and it was still performed there in 1880. Franz Lachner (1803-1890) set the spoken dialogue to a Wagnerian-style recitative for an 1855 Frankfurt production. This became the opera's standard form until the 1980s. Vienna was introduced to *Médée* in 1803 and it would appear that performances in 1809 were the occasion for Cherubini to make extensive cuts of about 500 bars which were supposedly incorporated into a Peters' published edition. It was revived again in 1812 for Mlle Pauline Anna Milder-Hauptmann (1785-1839) and was still in repertory in 1871.

The destiny of *Médée* in England and Italy was less fortunate. It was presented in London at Her Majesty's, Haymarket on 6 June 1865 with Mlle Thérèse Cathline Johanna Alexandra Tietjens (1831-1877) as Médée and recitatives by Luigi Arditi (1822-1903). It was repeated on 30 December 1870 at Covent Garden. In Italy, it was not staged until 30 December 1909 at the Teatro alla Scala, Milan in a translation by Carlo Zangarini, of which the edited version has been the standard Italian form of the score used until recently. The reception was mediocre, and it was not redone until the 16th Maggio musicale fiorentino in 1953, when Maria Callas (1923-1977) sang the title role and assured the opera's renewed success in the 20th century. The original French version, with reduced spoken dialogue, was mounted at Buxton Festival on 28 July 1984. Covent Garden presented the original version with nearly complete spoken dialogue on 6 November 1989.

Médée represents the culmination of Cherubini's work in the *opéra comique* genre. Although his *Les deux journées* of 1800 was more popular, *Médée* is far more innovative and extends the techniques of this genre to their limits. In many places, the music for an ensemble number or an aria continues into the dialogue and appears to stop only because some spoken words are required in order for the work to remain an *opéra comique.* In his use of form, Cherubini expresses himself as a classical musician; it is this quality which has been missed by audiences since the recitatives of Lachner were added in the mid-19th century. Only a revival of the complete opera without any musical excisions and with all the spoken dialogue will allow contemporary listeners to appreciate the symphonic proportions of the music and emotions of this work.

In its unmitigated horror, this opera has few equals. Its savage fury ties it closely to its Greek ancestry. Hoffman took one sentiment (revenge) and one action (murder) and expanded them into three hours of unrestrained emotion such as the French lyric stage had never seen. He provided excellent characterizations with which Cherubini could work, portraying the two main protagonists in depth. Because of the spoken dialogue, *Médée* is classed as an *opéra comique,* although the first edition labels it simply *opéra*. There are no comic interludes, and the majority of the musical numbers are ensembles (9 to 3 arias). In fact, the music of *Médée* foreshadows French or German Grand Opera of the mid-nineteenth century, and one has to wait until Bizet's *Carmen* to find a continuation of *Médée's* style and form. As Brahms said: "This *Médée* is the work we musicians recognize among ourselves as the highest peak of dramatic music."—STEPHEN C. WILLIS

The Medium

Composer: *Gian Carlo Menotti.*

Librettist: *Gian Carlo Menotti.*

First Performance: *New York, 8 May 1946.*

Roles: *Madame Flora, or Baba (contralto); Monica (soprano); Toby (mute); Mrs. Gobineau (soprano); Mr. Gobineau (baritone); Mrs. Nolan (mezzo-soprano).*

For a chamber opera lasting less than an hour, *The Medium* boasts an impressive list of credits. Composed for five singers, a tacit actor, and an orchestra of fourteen instruments, it is the first twentieth-century chamber opera to achieve international acclaim, advancing Menotti to the front rank of celebrity. It ran for two hundred and eleven performances on Broadway during the 1947-48 season at the Ethel Barrymore Theatre, and was filmed in 1950 under Menotti's direction by Scalera Studios in Rome. Artfully conceived both as music and theater, it has won the esteem of most critics and earned a secure place in the contemporary operatic repertoire.

Though manifestly a ghost story, *The Medium* harbors themes and poses questions worthy of ancient Greek drama. The action takes place in the contemporary parlor of Madame Flora (called Baba by her fanciful adolescent daughter Monica), a spiritualist who shams seances for her credulous clients. In the flat with Baba and her daughter lives Toby, a mute gypsy boy, whom the medium has taken in and incessantly abuses. Infatuated with Monica, he readily joins in her games of childish fantasy, sometimes arraying himself like an ancient king in Baba's finery.

As the opera begins, Baba interrupts one of the children's games and crossly tells them to get ready for a seance. The clients are Mr. and Mrs. Gobineau, whose infant son drowned in their garden fountain, and Mrs. Nolan, who comes for the first time to communicate with her daughter, a girl about Monica's age. Monica impersonates the spirits while Toby manages the ghostly effects. They convince Mrs. Nolan so completely that she becomes hysterical and must be calmed. As Monica imitates the laughing voice of the Gobineau's little boy, Baba suddenly wakes from her trance. She has felt a cold hand on her throat. "Who touched me?" she cries out, but the clients can tell her nothing and depart asking, "Why be afraid of the dead?" Terrified, Baba insists that Toby is at the bottom of this omen from the spirit world, and she wildly interrogates him. Monica intercedes, soothing Baba with the "Ballad of the Black Swan," but Baba hears the voice of Mrs. Nolan's daughter and sends Toby on a fruitless search through the flat. As Monica resumes the song, Baba chants in a low voice over her rosary.

In act II, we see Toby performing a puppet show for Monica. The girl responds by singing him a gay waltz, then casts Toby and herself in a fairy tale about love, giving the mute boy her own voice. Baba comes in drunk and disheveled and accosts Toby. Certain of his duplicity, she tries to coax him, then to bribe him into telling what he knows, but the frightened boy reveals nothing. Finally Baba asks him if he would like to marry Monica, but even this desperate offer

501

fails to penetrate Toby's enigmatic stare. Exasperated, Baba whips him until the doorbell distracts her. The Gobineaus and Mrs. Nolan have arrived, expecting a seance. The guilt-ridden Baba admits to fraud and exposes all her tricks of ghostmanship, but the bereaved clients ignore her confession and implore her to conduct the seance. In despair, Baba orders them from the house; then, despite Monica's protests, she turns out Toby "before it is too late!" After locking Monica in her room, Baba ponders her unwonted fear, finally breaking into deranged laughter. Sick and exhausted, she falls into a drunken stupor. As she sleeps, Toby steals back into the flat to see Monica. While he rummages for his belongings, a trunk lid falls, waking Baba. Toby runs behind the white curtain of the puppet theater. Screaming, "Who's there?" Baba seizes a pistol from a drawer, sees the curtain move, and fires at it. Blood trickles down the white cloth, and the boy falls to the floor with the curtain wrapped about him. "I've killed the ghost!" Baba proclaims. She unlocks Monica's door. In a stifled voice, the horror-stricken girl calls for help, and rushes from the flat. Peering into Toby's vacant eyes, wide open in death, Baba whispers, "Was it you?"

Menotti himself interprets *The Medium* as "a play of ideas. . . . the tragedy of a woman caught between . . . a world of reality, which she cannot wholly comprehend, and a supernatural world, in which she cannot believe." Baba, he explains, represents Doubt, Monica Love, the three clients Faith, and Toby the Unknown. Like many artists discussing their work, Menotti has opened the door but not invited us in. The real and supernatural worlds compete within the medium herself. She is Madame Flora the spiritualist and Baba the mother. Youthful, compassionate, and innocent, Monica is everything her decrepit mother is not or no longer can be. Both contrive illusions, but Monica's are puerile while Baba's are devious. Toby serves as Baba's son, though the drama presents him as a foundling, making him a natural prey to Baba's assaults and preserving his romance with Monica from incest. He personifies the mystery of ripening sexuality. Forever mute, he keeps his secrets.

The score of *The Medium* is ingeniously eclectic, containing arias, ensembles, recitatives, a freely composed dramatic monologue, and orchestral music to support the wordless movement. The musical style shifts from one segment to the next. Gentle harmonies intersperse with peppery ones, homophonic texture with counterpoint, straightforward rhythms with complex syncopations, and diatonic melodies with chromatically contorted ones of dubious tonality. Menotti liberally employs whatever suits the thought, the word, and the action.—JAMES ALLEN FELDMAN

Mefistofele [Mephistopheles]

Composer: *Arrigo Boito.*

Librettist: *Arrigo Boito (after Goethe, Faust).*

First Performance: *Milan, Teatro alla Scala, 5 March 1868.*

Roles: *Mefistofele (bass); Faust (tenor); Margherita (soprano); Marta (contralto); Wagner (tenor); Elena (soprano); Pantalis (contralto); Nereo (tenor); chorus (SATB).*

Mefistofele is the best-known composition by Arrigo Boito, whose fame largely resides in the fact that he was the librettist for Verdi's *Otello* and *Falstaff*. Although it has now gained a foothold in the standard repertory, *Mefistofele*'s popular success has been achieved through a lengthy and incremental process. Boito had to revise (and greatly shorten) the opera several times before audiences discovered the intrinsic beauty and majesty of the opera's text and music.

The literary-minded Boito attempted to fashion a libretto that would remain true to Goethe's *Faust*. Of necessity, Boito had to condense and excise considerable portions of his model. The opera begins with the "Prologue in Heaven," in which Mefistofele and God (in the form of the Mystic Chorus and Celestial Host) make the wager concerning Faust's soul. Act I, scene i is set on Easter Sunday in the city of Frankfurt-am-Main (incidentally, Goethe's birthplace). Townspeople and students are celebrating the Paschal festivities. Faust comments on the change of seasons to his assistant, Wagner. They notice a grey friar approaching whom Faust views with apprehension. Scene ii is set at night in Faust's laboratory. The grey friar enters, reveals himself to be Mefistofele, and he and Faust sign a pact in which the latter agrees to a forfeiture of his soul if he ever says to the fleeting moment "Arrestati, sei bello!" ("Linger yet, thou art so fair!"). Act II, scene i is set in Marta's garden, in which the two couples (Faust-Margherita and Mefistofele-Marta) promenade. Faust and Margherita fall in love, and Faust gives Margherita a potion to make her mother fall asleep so that the two lovers may effect an illicit assignation. Scene ii is the "Witches' Sabbath," but even in this phantasmagorical setting Faust is unable to think of anyone or anything but Margherita. Act III concerns itself with the imprisonment and death of Margherita, who has murdered her mother and the child that she bore to Faust. The delirious Margherita refuses the intercession offered by Faust, she prays to God for forgiveness, and ascends to Heaven at her death. Act IV is the "Classical Sabbath" in which Faust and Helen of Troy (the idealized counterpart to the quotidian Margherita) are introduced and fall in love. As is revealed later, the Helen episode is merely a dream. The epilogue is set once again in Faust's laboratory. Faust admits to world weariness, a dissatisfaction with both the real (Margherita) and the ideal (Helen). Mefistofele fails in his final attempt to entice Faust into sinful ways. Faust opens a Bible and prays to God for forgiveness, then asks for the fleeting moment to linger, falls dead, and ascends to Heaven much to the consternation of Mefistofele.

Although Boito's version is the most faithful of all Faust operas to Goethe's *Faust,* only a very few sections of Goethe's drama are actually utilized. These include from Part I: "Prologue in Heaven," "Outside the City Gate," "Study [from line 1322 ff.]," "Garden," "Walpurgis Night," and "Dungeon"; and from Part II: "Classical Walpurgis Night [of act III]," the Helen of Troy sections of act III, and a transformed version of act V. As the title of the opera indicates, Boito's main preoccupation is with the nature of evil rather than the potential of man to evolve and eventually possess a higher moral consciousness, as is the case with Goethe's *Faust*.

Some of Boito's alterations of Goethe's text may result from the necessities of adhering to the theatrical conventions of the day, catering to Italian taste, and avoiding problems with Italian censors. For example, in the "Prologue to Heaven," Mefistofele speaks to the Mystic Chorus rather than to God directly, as he does in Goethe's *Faust*. Additionally, Faust's salvation scene is significantly altered by Boito. Faust is saved not through the intercession of the "Eternal-Feminine" nor because of ceaseless striving after unobtainable goals, but because of his prayer for salvation.

In order to conform more closely with Christian theology, Boito has Faust's moment of supreme bliss come precisely at the point of spiritual reconciliation. Goethe's Faust, in contrast, never makes a sign of atonement. Boito's libretto minimizes the Goethean concept of *verweile doch, du bist so schön* (stay, thou art so fair) and, by extension, mitigates the necessity and logic of the wager between Mefistofele and God. In *Mefistofele* the wager is rendered moot by Faust's prayer for salvation.

m

OPERA

The music of *Mefistofele* displays Boito's concern for harmonic structure and thematic organization. Even though Boito was forced to make severe cuts in the original version of the opera, its extant form reveals considerable musical unity. This is extremely important because the unifying structure of the music is essential to the realization of the tight organic structure with which Goethe held together the seemingly disparate and disjointed sections of his text. The unifying structure of *Mefistofele* is realized most effectively by Boito in his careful and consistent selection of tonalities. Flat keys are used for those sections of the opera dealing with movement, action, and reflection, whereas, sharp keys are reserved for moments of resolution and transcendence.

Boito emphasizes the paradoxical nature of Mefistofele in a number of ways. When Mefistofele first appears before the Celestial Host, his intoned style of declamation is a parody of the psalm tone-like recitation of the Celestial Host. Also, Mefistofele grotesquely parodies Faust's arias. The well-known aria "Dai campi" in F major sung by Faust reappears, transmogrified into F minor, when Mefistofele makes his first appearance before Faust ("Son lo spirito"). Boito's use of the same musical material for different sections of the text with entirely contrasting literary connotations should not be considered infelicitous, but is rather the result of the composer's awareness of Goethe's preference for strophic over through-composed musical settings. Like Goethe, Boito employed a wide variety of technical devices and quotations to enhance his score. For instance, the beginning open 5th harmonies of the "Witches' Sabbath" are clearly and deliberately reminiscent of Franz Liszt's *Mephisto Waltz*.

In sum, *Mefistofele* is an opera of the highest literary and musical quality that is deserving of wider recognition and performance. Boito has successfully transfered Goethe's general conception of the Faust legend (if not in every detail) from spoken drama to the operatic stage, a feat seldom accomplished in the history of opera. Additionally, *Mefistofele* is one of those extremely rare operas in which the text of the libretto is both subtle and substantial, an equal partner to its accompanying music.—WILLIAM E. GRIM

Die Meistersinger von Nürnberg [The Mastersingers of Nuremburg]

Composer: *Richard Wagner.*

Librettist: *Richard Wagner.*

First Performance: *Munich, Königliches Hof- und Nationaltheater, 21 June 1868.*

Roles: *Eva (soprano); Walther (tenor); Hans Sachs (bass); Magdalena (soprano or mezzo-soprano); David (tenor); Beckmesser (bass); Pogner (bass); Kothner (bass); Vogelgesang (tenor); Nachtigall (bass); Zorn (tenor); Eisslinger (tenor); Moser (tenor); Ortel (bass); Schwarz (bass); Foltz (bass); A Nightwatchman (bass); chorus (SSSSAAATTTTTTBBBB).*

Wagner wrote the libretto of *Die Meistersinger von Nürnberg* in 1845, but it was sixteen years before the work came to fruition. This, Wagner's only comic opera, dealt with an historical rather than a mythical subject. Wagner based his libretto on the life of Hans Sachs (1496-1576), cobbler, poet, composer, and a member of the Mastersingers' Guild. He also borrowed the names of various other sixteenth-century personages and added in an imaginary character, the knight Walther von Stolzing, who is portrayed as a musical innovator, like Wagner himself.

Wagner did not scorn the guild's ideals and even quoted some of the original music, but he did convey his disapproval of the guild's inflexible nature. Sachs is portrayed more as a philosopher than as a writer, willing to incorporate Walther's new and disturbing artistic concepts within the traditional, "regulated" style. To emphasize the conflict between innovation and tradition, Wagner introduced Beckmesser, a master of the guild and die-hard representative of the Mastersingers' set manner of writing.

Act I opens in St Katherine's church, Nuremberg, with a chorale in which a full organ interrupts the overture. The chorale, apart from the orchestral interpolations between phrases, is written in pure Baroque style. Eva, her nurse Magdalena, Walther, and David (Sachs' apprentice) quickly establish themselves as real people, quite unlike the mythical personages of Wagner's other works. Walther, who is unfamiliar with the Mastersingers' craft, learns of a forthcoming song contest, and David explains to him some of the guild's regulations. The twelve masters enter. Pogner, the goldsmith, announces that his daughter Eva is to marry the winner of the contest. Walther, wishing to take part in the competition, asks to become a mastersinger. One of the mastersingers recites the guild's regulations, after which Walther sings a trial song for acceptance. This, however, is quickly rejected as breaking the masters' rules. All are outraged except Sachs, and Walther is disqualified.

The second act is set in a narrow street. It is late, and David closes Sachs' shop. Eva is alarmed to learn that if she were to reject the winner of the contest she would remain perpetually a spinster. Sachs, now alone, reflects on Walther's trial song. But when Eva arrives he warns her

Die Meistersinger von Nürnberg, **production by Wieland Wagner, 1956**

that Beckmesser intends to enter the contest. Eva secretly meets Walther outside Sachs' house, and the two plan to elope. Their expression of love is interrupted by the nightwatchman's horn, and they hide as Beckmesser appears and prepares to serenade Eva. Sachs, singing noisily over his work, interrupts Beckmesser's song. He agrees to be silent only if he is allowed to mark the serenade, using his shoemaker's hammer to record any errors, but the song is so clumsy and the hammering becomes so noisy that David is awakened. He notices that Beckmesser is serenading not Eva but Magdalena (to whom he is betrothed), and he attacks him. In the general brawl that follows, Walther and Eva try to escape, but Sachs hands Eva over to Pogner, mistaking her for Magdalena, and pulls Walther into his shop. Only when the nightwatchman's horn is heard does the tumult die away.

The long third act opens in Sachs' workshop as the cobbler reflects on attitudes towards tradition and innovation. When Walther appears and delivers a new song revealed to him in a dream, Sachs tries to adapt it slightly to a style more acceptable to the masters' requirements. After their departure, Beckmesser arrives. Finding the text of Walther's song in Sachs' handwriting, he pockets it, thinking he will be sure to win the contest. When Sachs realizes what Beckmesser has done, he allows him to keep the song and promises not to claim to be its author. In order to see Walther again, Eva uses the pretext of an ill-fitting shoe to enter Sachs' shop. Her words, as she explains the problem to Sachs, express her adoration for Walther, at which point Wagner introduces a musical quotation from *Tristan und Isolde*. In his happiness, Walther improvises the remaining stanza of his song and with David and Magdalena, they join together in a joyous quintet.

The scene moves to a meadow outside Nuremberg, where a large crowd has assembled. After the ceremonial entry of the masters, Sachs explains the terms of the contest. Beckmesser, with his lute, begins his song on the stolen sketch, but his memory fails: the words, becoming ludicrously garbled, provoke the onlookers first to astonishment and then ridicule. Beckmesser horrifies them by claiming that the text is by Sachs but Sachs disclaims responsibility and introduces the true composer. As Walther renders his Prize Song, all are amazed at its beauty. Despite his disqualification, Walther is declared the winner. He nevertheless impetuously refuses the golden chain of honor until Sachs, in a homily on German art, persuades him to accept it. As the opera ends, the people pay homage to Sachs.

The sheer size of *Die Meistersinger,* with its seventeen roles, a chorus of apprentices, three male choruses and the large full chorus, at once limits the possibilities of performance. Although, strangely enough, the orchestra is smaller than that of any of Wagner's other works, the instrumentation is weighty; the string players, for example, seldom stop playing throughout the entire opera.

Wagner uses pure melody to heighten the human dimensions of the story. Leitmotives draw the work together. The motives are associated more with emotions, places, and times (joy, Nuremberg, and midsummer day) than with people or objects, and are usually given to the orchestra rather than to the singers. Wagner's contrapuntal ingenuity in combining them first becomes evident in the overture, where three different motives appear at once.

The text of *Die Meistersinger,* unlike those of Wagner's other works, is written in rhyming verse. Its musical style is more diatonic than *Tristan und Isolde,* giving the work a certain solidity appropriate to its subject. Chromaticism is mostly associated with Walther's music—appropriately, perhaps, in view of the role's autobiographical associations.

Die Meistersinger appears as a hymn to German art, yet Wagner seems to have had some doubts over this in Sachs' final monologue, included only at his wife Cosima's insistence. Yet the opera's greatness, transcending national boundaries, comes from its richness in characterization and from the diversity, not only in the story and music, but in the essential relationship between characters.—ALAN LAING

Melba, Nellie

Soprano. Born Helen Porter Mitchell, 19 May 1861, in Richmond, Australia. Died 23 February 1931, in Sydney. Married: Charles Armstrong, 1882 (one son; divorced 1900). Studied with Mary Ellen Christian at Presbyterian Ladies College and Pietro Cecchi in Melbourne; gave concerts in Melbourne, from which her stage name derives; studied in Paris with Mathilde Marchesi, 1886-87; debut as Gilda in Brussels at Théâtre de la Monnaie, 1887; sang regularly at Covent Garden, where she first appeared as Lucia, from 1888 to 1926; Paris Opéra debut as Ophélie, 1889; appeared in Monte Carlo and St Petersburg, 1890-91; Teatro alla Scala debut as Lucia, 1893; Metropolitan Opera debut in same role, 1893; formal farewell concert at Covent Garden, 1926; teacher at Albert Street Conservatorium, Melbourne, from 1915.

"She [was] 32 when she came to the Metropolitan" wrote W.J. Henderson. "The voice was in the plenitude of its glory and it was quickly accepted as one of the great voices of operatic history. The quality of musical tone cannot be adequately described. No words can convey to a music lover who did not hear Melba any idea of the sounds with which she ravished all ears. . . . On the evening of her debut at the Metropolitan she sang in the cadenza of the mad scene a prodigiously long crescendo trill which was not merely astonishing, but also beautiful. Her stacatti were as firm, as well placed, and as musical as if they had been played on a piano. Her catilena was flawless in smoothness and purity. She phrased with elegance and sound musicianship as well as with consideration for the import of the text. In short, her technic was such as to bring out completely the whole beauty of her voice and to enhance her delivery with all the graces of vocal art."

Henderson was not by any means alone in his praise of the Melba technique. Writing in 1958, voice teacher J.H. Duval said: "Galli-Curci had some splendid vocal effects, as had Sembrich, but . . . whoever has heard [Melba's] marvelous crescendo on the trill in the Mad Scene in *Lucia* will remain unmoved by any vocal feat that has been performed since. It began pianissimo. It grew steadily stronger and stronger, more and more intense, and at last . . . that vast auditorium which is the Metropolitan Opera House of New York just vibrated with its wonderful fortissimo of crystalline purity. . . ."

Mary Garden's words about Melba's voice are famous but worth repeating: "I have no hesitation in declaring that Melba had the most phenomenal effect on me of any singer I have ever heard. I went once to Covent Garden to hear her do Mimi in *La bohème*. . . . Melba didn't impersonate the role at all—she never did that—but my God, how she sang it! You know, the last note for the first act of *La bohème*. . . is a high C, and Mimi sings it when she walks out the door with Rodolfo. She closes the door and then takes the note. The way Melba sang that high C was the strangest and weirdest thing I have ever experienced in my life. The note came floating over the auditorium of Covent Garden: it left Melba's throat, it left Melba's body, it left everything, and came over like a star and passed us in our box, and went out into the infinite. I have never heard anything like it in my life, not from any other singer, ever. It just rolled over the hall . . . My God, how beautiful it was! . . . That note of Melba's was just like a ball of light. It wasn't attached to anything at all—it was *out* of everything."

To those who know the Melba voice only from commercial phonograph records, it has always been difficult to understand how she could have had any success as Aïda. She first sang the part at Covent Garden 4 November 1892, "displaying greater energy as an actress than ever before, and displaying faultless vocalization." Hurst stated that as Aida "her performance was so fine as to excite the highest admiration, for she threw aside her usual reserve to sing with passionate emotion, and easily dominated the great *ensemble* in the second act without apparent effort or loss of quality."

Of Melba's attempt to add the *Siegfried* Brünnhilde to her repertory in New York in 1896 much has been written. Most critics found her performance remarkable. In spite of the fact that, as one critic wrote, "her voice had the ring of true passion," all gave a word of warning that the attempt was "more potent than wise." Krehbiel wrote that "the music of the part does not lie well in her voice, and if she continues to sing it, it is much to be feared there will soon be an end to the charm which the voice discloses when employed in its legitimate sphere. The world can ill afford to loose a Melba, even if it should gain a Brünnhilde." But Nellie Melba needed no warning from others. In her typical frank style, she told her manager: "Tell the critics I am never going to do that again. It is beyond me. I have been a fool!" Melba knew her limitations. In 1914 she wrote, "I have never continued roles that proved unsuited to me," and in giving advice to young singers she maintained that she "always drew on the interest, never the principal." One experience taught her that Brünnhilde was "off limits," and as it became the fashion to sing Elsa and Elisabeth in German rather than French or Italian, she dropped those roles, as well as Aida.

Melba was unfortunate in that two operas written for her, Bemberg's *Elaine* and Saint-Saëns' *Hélène,* did not prove to be lasting works. She created Mascagni's *I Rantzau,* and while she created Nedda in Leoncavallo's *Pagliacci* in both London and New York at the composer's request, she did not attempt to maintain the role in her repertory. She can be credited, perhaps self-servingly, with recognizing Puccini's *La bohème* as a masterpiece, making it a point to study the opera with the composer. She virtually introduced the opera to the United States when touring with her own company, and she applied pressure to the managements of Covent Garden and the Metropolitan to include the work, promising to allow them to "give the public their money's worth" by supplementing each performance with a "free" mad scene from *Lucia* or *Hamlet* after Mimi expired, a practice which was actually carried on in both houses until the public indicated that the opera could stand on its own.

Melba's first commercial recordings were made in 1904, when she was forty-three years of age, and she continued to record into the beginning of the electrical recording era. Her farewell at Covent Garden in June 1926 was partially recorded, and her last records were made in December of that year. While there is no doubt that some of the bloom of youth had passed, some of her recordings are quite remarkable. Many of them are important documents, including material studied with Thomas, Gounod, Massenet, Verdi, and Puccini or songs written for her and often accompanied by composers such as Landon Ronald and Herman Bemberg. Recording technicians recognized the size and power of the Melba voice, and she was placed well back from the receiving horn, so that many of her recordings give the impression that she owned a small voice; as we have seen from quotations from critics who heard her, this was certainly not the case. We are fortunate that she left us some remarkable evidence of at least a part of one of the most remarkable careers which spanned the nineteenth and twentieth centuries.—WILLIAM R. MORAN

Melchior, Lauritz

Tenor. Born 20 March 1890, in Copenhagen. Died 18 March 1973, in Santa Monica, California. Studied as a baritone with Paul Bang at Copenhagen Royal Opera School; debut as Silvio in I pagliacci, *Copenhagen, 1913; sang as baritone for several seasons, then studied with Vilhelm Herold; second debut as tenor in* Tannhäuser, *Copenhagen, 1918; went to London in 1921 to study with Beigel; studied with Grenzebach in Berlin and Bahr-Mildenburg in Munich; appeared as Siegmund at Covent Garden, 1924, and returned regularly 1926-39; Bayreuth debut as Parsifal, 1924, and sang there until 1931; appeared in Hamburg (1928), Barcelona (1929), and Buenos Aires (1931-43); at Metropolitan Opera 1926-50, where he first appeared as Tannhäuser; after retiring in 1950 Melchior continued to work in film and operetta.*

It is the fate of all modern aspirants to the title of heldentenor to be compared to Danish tenor Lauritz Melchior. Melchior reigned as the king of Wagnerian tenors throughout his career, from the time he switched from singing baritone roles (which he sang from 1913 to 1918) until his farewell performance as Lohengrin at the Metropolitan Opera in 1950. After a hiatus of a decade, he made his final operatic appearance in 1960, when he was seventy, and his influence continues to the present thanks to his numerous recordings. Melchior's fame spread far beyond the opera house. He was the first male singer to be heard on radio, in an experimental broadcast from Chelmsford, England, in July 1920; his appearances in Hollywood films of the 1940s and 1950s, as both singer and comedian, helped popularize opera for the American public and reshape its image of opera singers.

Although Melchior's fame rests on his assumptions of the heavier roles in the tenor repertoire, he essayed several baritone roles (including di Luna in Verdi's *Il trovatore,* Giorgio Germont in Verdi's *La traviata,* and Silvio in Leoncavallo's *I pagliacci,* the role of his professional operatic debut in Copenhagen in 1913). After an audition before Wagner's son Siegfried, made possible by the Wagnerian soprano Anna Bahr-Mildenberg, Melchior first appeared at Bayreuth in 1924,

Lauritz Melchior as Siegfried

where he was heard as Siegmund and Parsifal. His Metropolitan Opera debut came in 1926 as Tannhäuser; the performance was not completely successful, partly because the role lay too high for him at the time. By the 1930s he had become the company's leading Siegmund, Siegfried, and Tristan, and he remained at the Metropolitan Opera until 1950, singing only Wagnerian roles there.

Physically imposing, Melchior possessed a voice that can be characterized as brilliant and enormously powerful, yet with the potential to be sweet and gentle. His singing had stamina, intensity, and enthusiasm; his sense of humor is apparent despite the heroic nature of the sound. Possibly because of his baritonal beginnings, his voice had a basic darkness; his secure technical foundation allowed him to master the difficult transitional vocal passage between E and F that are essential in the Wagnerian roles, and there is no discernible break between the registers.

What separates Melchior from virtually all other Wagnerian tenors is that he possessed a combination of full, firm, steady tone, brilliant high notes, the ability to maintain a lyrical quality even during the most strenuous passages sung over the heaviest orchestration, a liquid legato, excellent diction, and the skill to produce soft, caressing tones. His singing was remarkably consistent throughout his career, as attested to by his many recordings, including a recording of act I of *Die Walküre* made as late as 1960, and this consistency is a tribute to the soundness of his technique. The basic sound of the voice was maintained over the years, although it darkened somewhat as he got older, but without any loss of brilliance; his interpretive ability developed, gaining in subtlety as his career progressed.

In addition to his Wagnerian roles of Lohengrin, Parsifal, Siegfried, Siegmund, Tristan, and Tannhäuser, Melchior scored successes as Verdi's Otello, Canio in Leoncavallo's *I pagliacci,* Turiddu in Mascagni's *Cavalleria rusticana,* Florestan in Beethoven's *Fidelio,* Radamès in Verdi's *Aida,* John of Leyden in Meyerbeer's *Le Prophète,* and Samson in Saint-Saëns's *Samson et Dalila,* but he performed these roles relatively infrequently.

During his career, Melchior was criticized for several nonvocal failings: his appearance (early critics found the combination of unflattering costumes and Melchior's bulk laughable), his dramatic shortcomings, some rhythmic inaccuracy (especially a tendency to rush ahead of the beat and some sloppiness over note values), and a lack of discipline (he reportedly would leave the stage whenever his character had nothing to do but stand around, and he is said to have been liable to stay at card games in the wings until the last possible moment). His dismissal by Rudolf Bing from the Metropolitan Opera in 1950 apparently was precipitated by this kind of behavior; the intolerant Bing, in one of his first acts as general manager, thereby prevented Melchior from celebrating his twenty-fifth anniversary with the company.

His reputed rhythmic inaccuracy is little substantiated by his recordings, of which there is a vast number, beginning with several baritone arias in the period before he switched to tenor roles, and including most of his major roles. He was a prolific recording artist, making approximately 300 records between 1913 and 1954. His contribution as Siegmund in a recording of act I of *Die Walküre* made in 1935, with Bruno Walter conducting, Lotte Lehmann as Sieglinde, and Emanuel List as Hunding, helped make it one of the greatest of all opera recordings.

—MICHAEL SIMS

Menotti, Gian Carlo

Composer. Born 7 July 1911, in Cadegliano, Italy. Basic music instruction from his mother: first opera attempt, The Death of Pierrot, *composed at the age of ten; studied at the Milan Conservatory, 1923-27; in the United States, 1927; studied with Rosario Scalero at the Curtis Institute, 1927-33; taught composition at the Curtis Institute, 1941-58; Guggenheim fellowships, 1946-47; Pulitzer Prize and Drama Critics' Circle award for* The Consul, *1950; Drama Critics' Circle Award and Music Critics' Circle Award for* The Saint of Bleecker Street, *1954, and Pulitzer Prize, 1955;* The Unicorn, the Gorgon and the Manticore *commissioned by the Elizabeth Sprague Coolidge Foundation, 1956;* Maria Golovin *composed for the International Exposition at Brussels, 1958; organized the Festival of Two Worlds, Spoleto, Italy, 1958, and Charleston, South Carolina, 1977; settled in Scotland, 1974. Menotti was the librettist for Samuel Barber's* Vanessa *(1958),* A Hand of Bridge *(1959), and the libretto revisions of* Anthony and Cleopatra *(1975; original libretto by Zeffirelli, 1966).*

Operas *Amelia al ballo,* 1936, Philadelphia, 1 April 1937; *The Old Maid and the Thief* (radio opera), 1939, National Broadcasting Company, 22 April 1939; stage premiere, Philadelphia, 11 February 1941; *The Island God,* 1942, New York, Metropolitan Opera, 20 February 1942; *The Medium,* 1945, New York, 8 May 1946; *The Telephone,* 1946, New York, 18 February 1947; *The Consul,* 1949, Philadelphia, 1 March 1950; *Amahl and the Night Visitors* (television opera), 1951, National Broadcasting Company, 24 December 1951; stage premiere, Bloomington, Indiana, 21 February 1952; *The Saint of Bleecker Street,* 1954, New York, 27 December 1954; *Maria Golovin,* 1958, Brussels, 20 August 1958; *The Labyrinth* (television opera), 1963, National Broadcasting Company, 3 March 1963; *Le dernier sauvage,* 1963, Paris, Opéra-Comique, 21 October 1963; *Martin's Lie* (children's church opera), 1964, Bristol, England, 3 June 1964; *Help, Help, the Globolinks!,* 1968, Hamburg, Staatsoper, 21 December 1968; *The Most Important Man,* 1971, New York, 12 March 1971; *Tamu-Tamu,* 1973, Chicago, 5 September 1973; *The Egg* (children's church opera), 1976, Washington, District of Columbia, 17 June 1976; *The Hero,* 1976, Philadelphia, 1 June 1976; *The Trial of the Gypsy* (children's opera), 1978, New York, 24 May 1978; *Chip and his Dog* (children's opera), 1979, Guelph, Canada, 5 May 1979; *La loca,* 1979, San Diego, 3 June 1979; *A Bride from Pluto,* 1982, New York, 14 April 1982; *The Boy who Grew too Fast* (children's opera), 1982, Wilmington, Delaware, 24 September 1982; *Goya,* 1986, Washington, Kennedy Center for the Performing Arts, 15 November 1986.

Menotti is Italian by birth and also by citizenship, but, because from the age of sixteen he has studied, written, and premiered his music so extensively in the United States, even *The New Grove Dictionary of Music and Musicians* classifies him as an American composer. He is really an internationalist, "a man of two worlds," and the sad fact is that the two countries most integral to his life have been the most hostile to his talent, leading him to the refuge and solitude of a manor house in Scotland, which he acquired in 1974. "Italy created me; America nourished me; and Scotland will bury me," he has said; "I've chosen to live here, so that I could be completely cut off from my past . . . to take stock . . . [and] time for reflection."

When Gian Carlo Menotti accepted the scholarship at the Curtis Institute to study composition with Rosario Scalero, he could speak no English, but he tutored himself in this adopted language by going to the movies four times a week. Shortly after his graduation with honors from Curtis, he spent the winter in Vienna with his close friend, Samuel Barber, and while there began writing his first opera, *Amelia al ballo*. The Curtis years with Scalero had been steeped in contrapuntal studies, and although Menotti wrote two operas before the age of ten, he had come to regard opera as an inferior art form, not expecting the genre to dominate his life's work. He has dubbed *Amelia* "the beginning of my end!"

Amelia al ballo was an instant success; the premiere in Philadelphia was followed by a Metropolitan Opera performance the following March, and the opera was retained in the Met's repertoire for the next season. During the next decade, fame burst upon the young composer. The National Broadcasting Company commissioned an opera written especially for radio, and Menotti produced *The Old Maid and the Thief*, another one-act *opera buffa*, with high-spirited farce, lyric arias, and his first attempt at writing an English libretto.

After beginning his career with two works acclaimed by audiences and critics alike, Menotti's next opera, *The Island God*, commissioned by the Metropolitan Opera, was removed from the repertoire after only four performances and withdrawn from circulation by the composer, except for some concert editions of the orchestral episodes. Menotti quickly recognized that he was out of his element in attempting "a subject too heroic for my kind of music." It was a depressing setback, nonetheless, and he sought refuge in "Capricorn," the house in Mt. Kisco, New York that he and Barber had just acquired through their patron, Mary Louise Bok (now Mrs. Efrem Zimbalist). The house was a sprawling affair that provided separate work areas with ample seclusion and no interruptions. For the next four years, Menotti abandoned writing opera to concentrate on other musical forms, including a piano concerto, a commissioned ballet score, and an orchestral suite from the latter that became popular at concerts.

Meanwhile, Menotti was appointed in 1941 to the composition department at the Curtis Institute to teach a new course on "dramatic forms," and retained a teaching post there for the next seventeen years. Curtis awarded him an honorary bachelor of music degree in 1945, the same year that he won grants from the American Academy of Arts and Sciences and the National Institute of Arts. The following year, with a Guggenheim Fellowship and a grant from the Alice M. Ditson Fund of Columbia University, he began work on a new tragic opera more economic and modest in scope than *The Island God*. It was *The Medium*, a two-act chamber opera with its story "of a person caught between two worlds, the world of reality which she cannot wholly comprehend, and the supernatural world which she cannot believe," that set forth for the first time the fundamental elements that have become the mark of identity for Menotti as a composer. With its macabre text (written by the composer), the mixture of odd characters who evoke such strong feelings from the audience, and what Cocteau described as "a vocal style which elevates the ordinary and every-day into lyric drama," Menotti brought opera in America down from the heights to the level of the masses, and established it as a popular art form. *The Medium*, after its Columbia premiere, had a seven-month run the following year on Broadway, paired with *The Telephone*, an introductory one-act comedy for two actors.

The two works were lauded for their straightforward sincerity: the quality of *verismo* that led critics immediately to compare Menotti with Puccini, Rimsky-Korsakov, Ravel, and others. Critics and fellow composers stated then and have persisted in claiming that Menotti's work is all derivative; as one said, "Menotti has never written an original note in his life, and yet every note immediately has the signature of Menotti. . . . his music lasts." Menotti freely admits his debt to other composers, albeit a different list: Schubert ("I adore his simplicity, . . . the way he can communicate, can create something out of the most simple means . . ."); Monteverdi madrigals; Mussorgsky, Puccini, and Debussy ("Only in [their works] did I find admirable examples of what I myself was looking for"); and Stravinsky (". . . an indispensable item . . . He is like electricity: whether you approve of it or not, you can no longer do without it"). He is also grateful to Wolf-Ferrari, whose music he did not admire, for an early word of timely advice on writing opera: ". . . the orchestra and the voice must be knitted together like the cogs in two wheels . . . the accents of either . . . must never meet, otherwise they will destroy each other."

Within the next few years, *The Medium* was given more than a thousand performances in Europe and America, was recorded, made into a motion picture, and taken to Europe on a State Department tour.

Broadway continued to produce popular operas by Menotti: his first full-length opera, *The Consul* (1949), premiered in 1950 and won the Pulitzer Prize, as well as the Drama Critics Award. As with *The Medium,* the dramatic tension and use of orchestral dissonance to heighten moments of emotional impact were well knit with contrasts of stark drama and tender lyricism, and *The Consul* was a sensation. The following year it was produced in London, Munich, Hamburg, Berlin, Zurich, Vienna, and even in Milan (the first American opera to be produced at the Teatro alla Scala). *The Consul* was acclaimed everywhere but in Italy, where left-wing demonstrations denounced it for its anti-communist stance, while others saw Menotti's American residency as an unpatriotic act.

The composer has cited *The Consul* as an example of his insistence on the unified whole of words, music and action: ". . . a good opera must be a happy marriage in which the music is the asserting husband, and the words the accepting wife." In his view, the music must shape the libretto: Menotti claims that some of the best literary phrases of his original text ended up on the cutting-floor to accommodate the music.

In Menotti's next opera, *Amahl and the Night Visitors, verismo* was replaced by the composer's love of folklore and his childhood absorption with puppet theater. There followed *The Saint of Bleecker Street,* set in New York City's Italian quarter, the composer's first opera with an American setting. When asked about his religious beliefs, Menotti said, "I definitely am not a religious man . . . [but it] is undeniable that the intense and incandescent faith which nourished my childhood and my adolescence has seared my soul forever. . . . [The loss of my faith] has left me uneasy . . . And it is this very duality in my character, this inner conflict, which I have tried to express in some of my operas. . . ." *The Saint of Bleecker Street* garnered for Menotti his second Pulitzer Prize, the Drama Critics and also the Music Critics Circle awards.

The lukewarm reception accorded *Maria Golovin,* commissioned as the American contribution to the 1958 Brussels Exposition, presaged a downward slant with his critical reviewers in Menotti's success as an opera composer. As Harold Schonberg pointed out, the 1930s and 40s hailed Menotti as a new hero of opera; his directness and romantic lyricism delighted the "aging lot" of critics "whose roots were in the nineteenth century. . . ." But after World War II, musical criticism was increasingly in the hands of a young generation weary of romanticism and eager for dissonance, serialism, and all other aspects of "the new speech," including the electronic medium. Menotti's works were still performed, but he was suddenly dismissed as old-fashioned, "hopelessly naïve," and not to be taken seriously. Many composers adapted their musical idioms to the new tastes, but Menotti refused: "Music history will place me somewhere," he said, "but that is no concern of mine." He would not forsake the cultivation of "the evocative power of melody," the fascinating problem of the *parlar cantando,* nor the gathering of melody "without harming or soiling its purity." He felt that many of the new breed of composers were confusing "the discoverer of a hidden natural force [with] the inventor of a fascinating and even at times useful gadget." He could not fathom why "modern" should be equated only with dissonance and nervousness, when consonance and serenity also had their place. Like Gottfried von Einem, he was dismayed at the idea of attempting to present the new and radical without a backdrop of the familiar, in the interest of form and coherence.

The 1960s were discouraging times for Menotti as a composer, compounded by the increasing demands of his role as founder of the Spoleto Festival of Two Worlds. *The Last Savage,* commissioned for Paris, was written with an Italian libretto (his first since *Amelia*), for translation into French and, later, English. It was dismissed by the critics, one of whom called it "a fiasco of American drivel." Americans objected to its French *opéra buffe* structure, with set numbers, arias, and duets. For the next seven years Menotti abandoned large forms and concentrated on chamber works. Vocal compositions in this period included a dramatic cantata and two one-act operas commissioned for television: *The Labyrinth,* which was so carefully designed for television's unique attributes that it is confined to that medium; and *Martin's Lie,* a medieval tale written for the Bath Festival in England.

The 1970s did not improve the critics' view of Menotti as a composer. *The Most Important Man,* his first full-length opera in almost a decade, was viciously denounced by the critics, who insisted that he was only repeating himself. *Amelia at the Ball* was called "maudlin," and a New York revival of *The Consul* brought cries of "overtheatrical," which Menotti retorted was rather like accusing music of being "too musical." The composer was distressed by the vituperative quality of the criticism, which extended to any work that left his pen, including a magnificent cycle of songs commissioned by Elisabeth Schwarzkopf, called *Canti Della Lontananza.* The trouble lay not in the songs but in an unfortunate mismatch of music and musician; the critics were adamant in their conviction that only the composer was at fault. In a wonderful mix of drama and lyricism with touches of whimsy, Menotti's seven poems are a dramatic *scena* for soprano, and rank among the finest vocal writing of the century.

Menotti's one-act opera for children, *Help! Help! The Globolinks!,* was, in Harold Schonberg's opinion, the composer's polemic response to his critics. Written as a companion piece for a performance of *Amahl* in Hamburg, this fanciful tale of children threatened by extra-terrestrial creatures who "speak" in electronic sounds, was the first of several works for children, including *Chip and His Dog,* created for his adopted son, Francis Phelan, who now bears his name. The three mature "late" operas, all from the 1970s, were written for specific occasions and had the customarily uncertain response from the critics. *Tamu-Tamu, The Hero,* and *Juana la Loca* remain unpublished—principally because they were created for a specific audience, and would not have wide appeal. There are a host of Menotti works, including non-musical plays, which are not in print because they await revision and polishing, a task the composer confesses to avoiding.

The heavy commitment to the two Spoleto Festivals in Italy and the USA has taken its toll on Menotti's scores, but there is also his reluctance to "seal in" a work as a totally finished product: ". . . the agonizing process of freezing on the written page the fluctuations of my thoughts. . . ." He has a horror of the "frozen music" of recordings, which tend to be labelled definitive by the public regarding tempo and interpretation. Both, says Menotti, must be "necessarily fluid according to temperament and mood and change as people change in an ever-changing world. . . . I don't think a definitive recording of my music exists."

Gian Carlo Menotti remains a figure of controversy, refusing to alter his basic philosophy regarding opera, wherein drama means strong texts allied closely to music and action in a "unified whole"; where there is little or no "gratuitous lyricism" and the vocal arias are actively essential to the drama; where a conscious attempt is made to keep the elements taut, the speech coherent and comprehensible, and the ingredients lean and spare. The critics still tend to dismiss him, but the number of performances, translated into more than 20 languages, increases annually. To Wiley Hitchcock's summation of Menotti's achievement in combining "the theatrical sense of a popular playwright and a Pucciniesque musical vocabulary with an Italianate love of liquid language and . . . characters as real human beings," Ned Rorem adds: "Whether you like his music or not, the fact exists that due to Menotti, and only Menotti, the whole point of view of contemporary opera in America, and perhaps in the world, is different from what it would have been had he not existed."—JEAN C. SLOOP

Merrill, Robert

Baritone. Born 4 June 1917, in Brooklyn. Married: Roberta Peters (divorced). Studied with his mother Lillian Miller Merril and with Samuel Margolis and Angelo Conarutto; debut as Amonasro, Trenton, 1944; Metropolitan Opera debut as Germont, 1945, and appeared there for thirty seasons; appeared in San Francisco, 1957; in Chicago, 1960; appeared in Venice as Germont, 1961; Covent Garden debut in same role, 1967.

Gifted with a powerful, resonant and biting voice, Robert Merrill frequently sang as if by rote, failing to communicate rhythmic pulse, much less musical ebb and flow, or feeling for drama in music. For him the basic unit of utterance was the note, not the phrase. The notes themselves stayed more or less at the same volume and thus lacked dynamic direction. As a result he couldn't prepare emphases with crescendos. This, combined with his tendency to treat legato passages as if they were declamation and to substitute bluster and cliched snarls for emotional substance, caused much of the music he sang to sound jagged. Nevertheless, his legato was excellent, for he was able to join notes together seamlessly (unlike many Americans who habitually disrupt legato passages with sudden, quick diminuendos before the consonants d and t).

On records from the forties and early fifties Merrill often sings marginally under pitch, and in Italian arias he is boring. In "Cortigiani," whenever he musters some feeling, as at the words "Marullo, signore," he fails to sustain it. Elsewhere, he has episodes where he interprets or is animated—but they usually don't last. A notable exception is Thaïs's death scene, with Dorothy Kirsten, recorded in 1947, where he sings with passion. Merrill's most successful early recordings are of light songs in English, in which he sounds fully at home with words and music. His best, "The Green Eyed Dragon," was made around 1949 (but it pales in comparison with John Charles Thomas's rendition). When Merrill does vary his sound here, as in another song, "Shadrack," it is with inflections seemingly borrowed from Lawrence Tibbett. Merrill recorded a number of duets with Jussi Björling—and it is to Björling that you end up paying attention.

By 1963, when Merrill recorded Ford's monolog from *Falstaff*, the voice had become bass tinged to the point that it was a dramatic baritone, suitable for heavy Verdi roles. By then, too, he had stopped sounding like an outsider to Italian opera and was not only vocally but also emotionally powerful throughout such selections as "Urna fatale."

As an actor on stage Merrill was wooden and lacked spontaneity. As the Toreador he had no pizzazz. As an actor with the voice, even at his best he didn't have Leonard Warren's or Giuseppe De Luca's ability to underscore the meaning of words, while as a vocal personality he lacked the latter's warmth and humanity. Merrill's diction was better than Warren's, who, however, had a beautiful pianissimo.

What enabled Merrill to become—and remain—a star? Particularly in the middle voice he had an imposing sound uncharacteristic of American baritones. Performing light music in concert and on radio, television and film made him famous throughout the U.S. (although he never achieved international stardom).

Merrill's opera career was based at the Met, where loudness counts for much. In the fifties he was in Warren's shadow. By the early seventies Sherrill Milnes got most of the great assignments. Merrill was, however, the leading American baritone of the sixties.—STEFAN ZUCKER

Messiaen, Olivier

Composer. Born 10 December 1908, in Avignon. Died 28 April 1992, in Paris. Married: 1) the violinist Claire Delbos (died 1959), 1936 (one son); 2) the pianist Yvonne Loriod, 1962. Studied organ, improvisation, and composition with Jean and Noël Gallon, Marcel Dupré, Maurice Emmanuel, and Paul Dukas at the Paris Conservatory, 1919-30; organist at Trinity church in Montmartre, Paris, 1930; teacher at the Ecole Normale de Musique and at the Schola Cantorum, 1930; also organized a group with André Jolivet, Ives Baudrier, and Daniel-Lesur called La Jeune France, 1936; in the French army, 1939; taken prisoner, and spent two years in a German prison camp in Görlitz, Silesia, where he composed his Quatuor pour la fin du temps (Quartet for the End of Time); *returned to France, 1942, and reassumed his position as organist at Trinity; on the faculty of the Paris Conservatory; taught at the Berkshire Music Center in Tanglewood, 1948, and at Darmstadt, 1950-53. Messiaen is a Grand Officier de la Légion d'Honneur, a member of the Institut de France, the Bavarian Academy of the Fine Arts, the Santa Cecilia Academy in Rome, and the American Academy of Arts and Letters. Messiaen's pupils include Boulez, Martinet, Stockhausen, and Xenakis.*

Operas *St François d'Assise,* Messiaen (after the anonymous 14th century *Fioretti* and *Contemplations of the Stigmata*), 1975-1983, Paris, Opéra, 28 November 1983.

Messiaen was strongly influenced in his upbringing by the literary background of his parents. His mother was a poet (Messiaen was later to set some of her poetry to music) and his father translated the whole of Shakespeare into French. During his formative years, he obtained the scores of a variety of operas, including Debussy's *Pelléas et Mélisande*. Although, no doubt because of these early influences, there is a strong sense of theater running through much of his music, it was not until 1975 that he commenced work on his only stage work, the opera *St François d'Assise*. He entered the National Conservatoire de la Musique in Paris in 1919 to study a wide range of subjects: piano, organ, composition, harmony, history of music and percussion.

Although he no doubt received some stimulus from the French organ school of composers, his own work for organ followed a very individual path and ultimately was to form only a small (and not the most important) part of his total output. He left the Conservatory in 1930, and was appointed organist at the church of the Sainte Trinité, Montmartre in 1931, a post which he still holds.

From the time of Messiaen's earliest compositions, one of the most important features of his music has been a highly developed sense of correlation between color and musical sound. Others have often claimed a rather simplistic relationship between color and specific keys, or even individual pitches, but with Messiaen, the phenomenon is much more complex. He rarely speaks of individual colors in connection with passages in his music; rather, whole combinations of colors set up by modal, harmonic, timbral and even rhythmic factors are present in his music. Connected with the sense of color in music is his predilection for his *Modes of Limited Transposition*. These are artificial modes of his own invention, from which he derives characteristic streams of harmonies or "color chords." A particular feature of his early work, Messiaen became less dependent on these modes as his musical language developed.

An equally important, but slightly less all-pervading influence on Messiaen's music is his own religious convictions. It might seem odd that, as a Catholic, he has published no works for liturgical use other than the short motet, *O Sacrum Convivium!* He has preferred to write works of a meditative nature either for the organ, for use during services, or for the concert hall. It has been his aim in these works to express, as he puts it, theological truths, rather than to write mystical works (although he occasionally borders on mysticism in some movements). Because of their ritual nature, some works, such as *Trois petites liturgies de la présence divine,* approach a liturgical act within the context of the concert hall.

Also dating from his student days is his interest in exotic rhythm. His teachers at the Conservatory had stimulated his interest in Greek rhythms, an interest which he extended himself to Indian rhythms on his discovery of the table of deçi-tâlas published in Lavignac's *Encyclopédie de la Musique et Dictionnaire de la Conservatoire,* published in 1924 by Delagrave. Although he did not apply these rhythms to his own music until *La Nativité du Seigneur* for organ (written in 1935), the principles involved had a profound influence on the rhythmic shape of his music from that time onwards. Also dating from his student days was his interest in birdsong and his first attempts at notating it. In his early works there are occasional references to *style oiseaux,* but it was not until 1940 in *Quatuor pour la fin du temps* that he actually names birdsongs in the score. From that time on, birdsong plays an increasingly important role in his music, culminating in 1953 with *Réveil des oiseaux* for piano and orchestra, which is based entirely on birdsong. Birdsong subsequently remained a prominent feature of his music, and in 1958 he completed one of his most important piano works, *Catalogue d'oiseaux.* Prior to the composition of this work, he visited various parts of France, collecting birdsong. The work is in the nature of a documentary, painting a picture of specific regions and particular birds associated with those regions.

From his first published work in 1928 until 1956, Messiaen's musical language shows changes of emphasis from an early style, which is heavily based on the modes of limited transposition and Greek meters, through the incorporation of Indian rhythms into his music from 1935, to the crowning and most rhythmically complex work of this period, the *Turangalîla-symphonie* (1946-48). Following this, he experimented with serial methods involving the serialization of duration, intensity and timbre as well as pitch, but turned to works relying mainly

517

on birdsong for their material from 1953. In *Catalogue d'oiseaux* and subsequent works, especially from the oratorio *La Transfiguration de Notre Seigneur Jésus-Christ* (1963-69), he returns, in part, to an earlier musical language involving the modes of limited transposition and Indian and Greek rhythms. This does not represent a return, however, to an earlier style, but a more integrated musical language, drawing from all periods of his working career.

A distinctly theatrical element is discernible in many of his larger works, such as the *Turangalîla-symphonie*. This is the central work in a trilogy in which he turns away from specifically Christian symbols to those of Hindu, Inca and Peruvian religions. He also draws on the Celtic myth of Tristan and Isolde, to exploit the same symbolism of the love-death which is the basis of Wagner's music-drama. In this work, the music is imbued with a sense of theatrical ritual which renders it complete in itself, without the need for a visual element. It is important to the surrealistic nature of the work and the experience which it arouses that the concepts behind such movements as the sixth, *Jardin du sommeil d'amour* and the seventh, *Turangalîla II,* should remain in the imagination of the listener. In the first of these we are asked to imagine the lovers sleeping in a garden full of exotic flowers, and the second is associated with pain and death as exemplified in Edgar Allan Poe's *The Pit and the Pendulum*. Even if it were feasible to represent these extra-musical elements theatrically, it would not add to, and might even detract from the music. As the imagination is often an important factor in listening to Messiaen's music, it is not surprising that it took him so long, and even then unwillingly, to embark on an actual opera, and that visually the result should consist of a series of static tableaux rather than a dynamically developing drama which we would normally associate with the medium.
ROBERT SHERLAW-JOHNSON

Meyerbeer, Giacomo

Composer. Born Jakob Liebmann Beer, 5 September 1791, in Vogelsdorf, near Berlin. Died 2 May 1864, in Paris. Married: Minna Mosson, 25 May 1826 (two children who died in infancy). Studied piano with Lauska, and briefly with Clementi, who was a guest at his house in Berlin; studied theory with Zelter and Anselm Weber; studied with the Abbé Vogler (a fellow student was Carl Maria von Weber) at Darmstadt, 1810-12; opera productions in Munich, Stuttgart, and Vienna, 1812-14; opera productions in Venice, Padua, Turin, 1815-24; collaboration with Eugène Scribe began, 1827; Chevalier of the Légion d'Honneur; member of the French Institut, 1834; Generalmusikdirektor to King Friedrich Wilhelm IV, Berlin, 1842; in England, 1862. Meyerbeer was friends with and was advised by Antonio Salieri, and assisted the young Wagner both artistically (he conducted the Berlin performances of Rienzi*) and financially.*

Operas *Jephtas Gelübde,* Alois Schreiber, Munich, Court, 23 December 1812; *Wirth und Gast, oder Aus Scherz Ernst (Die beyden Kalifen, Alimelek),* Johann Gottfried Wohlbrück, Stuttgart, 6 January 1813; *Das Brandenburger Tor,* Emanuel Veith, written for Berlin, 1814 [not performed]; *Romilda e Costanza,* G. Rossi, Padua, Nuovo, 19 July 1817; *Semiramide riconosciuta,* G. Rossi (after Metastasio), Turin, Regio, March 1819; *Emma di Resburgo (Emma di Leicester),* G. Rossi, Venice, San Benedetto, 26 June 1819; *Margherita d'Anjou,* Felice Romani (after René Charles Guilbert de Pixérécourt), Milan, Teatro alla Scala, 14 November 1820; revised Paris, 1826; *L'Almanzore,* G. Rossi, intended for Rome,

Torre Argentina, carnival 1821 [unfinished]; *L'esule di Granata,* Felice Romani, Milan, Teatro alla Scala, 12 March 1821; *Il crociato in Egitto,* G. Rossi, Venice, La Fenice, 7 March 1824; revised Paris, 1826; *Robert le diable,* Eugène Scribe and G. Delavigne, Paris, Opéra, 21 November 1831; *Les Huguenots,* Eugène Scribe and Émile Deschamps, Paris, Opéra, 29 February 1836; *Ein Feldlager in Schlesien (Vielka),* Eugène Scribe, Ludwig Rellstab, and C. Birch-Pfeiffer, Berlin, Court, 7 December 1844; *Le prophète,* Eugène Scribe, Paris, Opéra, 16 April 1849; *L'étoile du nord,* Eugène Scribe (partially after his ballet, *La cantinière*), Paris, Opéra-Comique, 16 February 1854; music based on *Ein Feldlager in Schlesien. Le pardon de Ploërmel* (*Le chercheur du trésor, Dinorah, oder Die Wallfahrt nach Ploërmel*), Jules Barbier and Michel Carré, Paris, Opéra-Comique, 4 April 1859; *L'Africaine* (*Vasco de Gama*), Eugène Scribe and F.J. Fétis, Paris, Opéra, 28 April 1865 [posthumous; final revisions by Fétis].

Blessed with an independent income and a natural facility for both music and languages, Meyerbeer was, from the beginning, free to practice his art when and wherever he chose. As a pupil of the Abbé Vogler in Darmstadt, and befriended by Vogler's most successful pupil, Carl Maria von Weber, Meyerbeer naturally gravitated to vocal music. Of his German student compositions, few have survived and none have been revived. Henri de Curzon describes them as overly complex, confused, and scholastic. Though the descriptions are abstract, they point to a natural tendency, even as a student, to impose on the vocal art a sophisticated orchestration, a trait which would distinguish his mature work.

A meeting with Antonio Salieri in Vienna led to Meyerbeer's departure for Italy, to study the methods of writing for the human voice. The immediate success of his operas written to Italian texts testifies to his ability to learn quickly, but the libretti to which he set his music did not overly please him. In an 1823 letter to the basso Prosper Levasseur, he expressed the wish to go to Paris; there alone did he feel he could find texts to satisfy his dramatic sensibilities.

In Italy, and later in Paris itself, he could not avoid comparison of his music with Rossini's. Certainly there is a formal similarity of approach, one he shares with his Italian contemporaries, but this is a matter of the style of the time, not of imitation. The Italian operas also reveal that Meyerbeer could write a fully-developed aria or ensemble, a fact that would always be evident in his French operas as well, despite criticism that he indulged in rhythmic complexity because he lacked the ability to develop a melody except at the most banal level.

His most popular Italian work, *Il crociato in Egitto,* has its Rossinian moments, notably the opening chorus and Armando's "Oh, come rapida," but also looks forward to the

Giacomo Meyerbeer

French operas, especially in his use of the brass band not only to accompany the crusaders into battle, but to replace the pit orchestra for a lyrical aria by Adriano.

In Paris a new spirit of historicism had begun to invade the dramatic arts. The success of Auber's *La muette de Portici* and Rossini's *Guillaume Tell* at the Opéra and the plays of Victor Hugo and Alexandre Dumas heralded a new approach to historical drama; romantic protagonists might remain in the persons of lovers, but the treatment of history as a complex web of sociopolitical forces rather than as a contrived excuse for a tragico-romantic denouement reflected a new, more realistic approach to drama, both legitimate and lyric.

Meyerbeer's arrival in Paris fortunately coincided with the ascendance of Eugene Scribe, librettist of *La muette de Portici,* as practitioner of the new romantic realism. Together they assembled what would become known as "grand opera." At its zenith, it consisted (almost always with variations, to be sure) of a love story set against a background of political and/or religious strife centered around a specific post-medieval historical event. The *mise-en-scène* sought to reflect the historical period and recognizable locales. At least one scene ought to provide a legitimate excuse for an extended ballet, usually but not exclusively in the third of five acts. The chorus played a prominent part in the drama, and original orchestral effects were looked forward to with as much anticipation as the contributions of the vocalists (this in spite of the myth that, like the Italian opera it replaced, grand opera displayed only spectacular vocalism and equally spectacular scenery). The ideal was that of a collaboration between composer, librettist, designer, conductor, chorus master and ballet master to produce a unified work, an ideal Richard Wagner would also embrace, with the one significant difference that he himself would be all the collaborators.

Meyerbeer and Scribe's first joint effort, *Robert le diable,* though it lacked historical specificity, combined the other elements of grand opera with an effectiveness and popularity which established its format as the measure for all subsequent works, a measure which stood for almost half a century in Paris. The excitement following *Robert's* premiere has few parallels in music history; at the center lay Meyerbeer's score, whose originality and dramatic effectiveness Hector Berlioz both praised and emulated.

The most perfect (not necessarily the best) grand opera Meyerbeer composed was *Les Huguenots,* which portrayed the love of a Protestant nobleman for a Catholic lady-in-waiting on the eve of the infamous massacre of Huguenots by the Catholic nobility on St Bartholomew's Day, 1572. Meyerbeer displayed significant advances in his use of the chorus as protagonists representing the fanaticism of both religious camps, whereas in *Robert* the chorus had played a passive role as knights and ladies offering appropriate but anonymous commentary on the events of the plot. Also in *Les Huguenots,* the composer continues the move, begun in *Robert,* away from traditionally-constructed arias, replacing them with extended ariosos such as Raoul's "Plus blanche que la blanche herminée" and Nevers's "Noble dame." Meyerbeer includes a conventional aria/cabaletta (the queen's "O beau pays de la Touraine"), and a conventionally constructed duet (such as that for the queen and Raoul), but prefers a more shifting structure, displaying a succession of themes. None of these themes is developed to the conventional extent; instead, they reflect subtle changes in the dynamics of the drama, as is the case in the long act III duet for Marcel and Valentine, and the justly-famous "Tu l'a dit" for Raoul and Valentine in act IV.

Following his return to Germany to compose the Singspiel *Ein Feldlager in Schlesien,* Meyerbeer returned to Paris to collaborate again with Scribe on *Le prophète.* In this opera, the obligatory love relationship (that of Jean for Berthe) is almost completely overshadowed by the love of mother for son (of the rejected Fidès for Jean the Prophet). Unfortunately, the plot also illustrates Scribe's increasing tendency to warp history in order to create a good story. The historical John of Leyden was a hypocritical voluptuary who used fundamentalist religion as a base for power and sexual license, and who was eventually captured and executed for his crimes. Scribe's protagonist is a dreamer prodded into action by the kidnapping of his fiancée.

Meyerbeer always tried to write for particular singers. The thirty years which elapsed between his first efforts to write *L'Africaine* and its final posthumous production resulted from the loss of his intended heroine, Cornélie Falcon, to irrevocable vocal decline, and the lack of a successor of her stature. Similarly, the availability of Pauline Viardot contributed much to Meyerbeer's treatment of the central character of *Le prophète:* Fidès three scenes overshadow even Jean's admittedly effective ariosos, the mad scene for Berthe, and the spectacular coronation scene at Münster Cathedral.

Having secured his place as the leading composer of grand opera, Meyerbeer turned to the quite different demands of the opéra-comique, where three acts rather than five, traditionally melodic arias and ensembles separated by spoken dialogue, and less complex plot and orchestral texture were the rule. Scribe adapted the libretto he had provided for translation as *Ein Feldlager in Schlesien* to a plot already set to music by Lortzing and Donizetti, that of Tsar Peter the Great's masquerading as a simple shipbuilder in Holland. The score seems to have been ignored by those who maintain that Meyerbeer could not write developed melodies; here they abound, especially in the music for the two soprano leads, with the orchestra reduced to accompaniment level.

For his second outing at the Opéra-Comique, Meyerbeer chose a Breton legend, *Le pardon de Plöermel* (better known under its Italian-language title, *Dinorah*), restricting much of his orchestral mastery to the overture, this one twenty minutes long and with an off-stage chorus. His arias, especially Dinorah's "Ombre légère," Höel's "Ah, mon remords," and the huntsman's aria beginning act III, show him still able to write effective traditional melody. No amount of sympathy with the different expectations and requirements of the mid-nineteenth century stage, however, can help to justify the opera's central drama, that of a peasant girl driven insane by the loss of her pet goat.

With the advent of the German soprano Marie Saxe, Meyerbeer turned again to the long-neglected *L'Africaine,* which owes its title to an earlier version of the libretto which had neither Vasco da Gama nor Hindu temples in its makeup. Meyerbeer's death before the opera went into rehearsal deprived the world of a definitive version, leaving its four and a half hours of music to be cut down by the Belgian musicologist Fétis. Even so, the score shows Meyerbeer at his most effective. The arias especially demonstrate a maturity of approach. Vasco's justly famous "O paradis" and Selika's "Sur mes genoux" strike a highly original balance between the traditional aria and the Meyerbeerian arioso. The argument between the liberal and conservative factions of the Grand Council, with the chorus of inquisitors injecting sinister asides, revives his mastery of the chorus-as-protagonist, and the opera's culmination, Selika's hallucinatory death scene, builds on the symphonic model of Fidès's "O prêtres de Baal" (and on the great "Adieu, fiere cité" from Berlioz' *Les Troyens,* which "O prêtres" influenced) to form a fitting finale to the career of the most influential musician of his time.—WILLIAM J. COLLINS

OPERA

A Midsummer Night's Dream

Composer: *Benjamin Britten.*

Librettists: *Benjamin Britten and Peter Pears (after Shakespeare).*

First Performance: *Aldeburgh, Jubilee Hall, 11 June 1960.*

Roles: *Oberon (counter tenor or contralto); Titania (soprano); Hippolita (contralto); Theseus (bass); Lysander (tenor); Demetrius (baritone); Hermia (mezzo-soprano); Helena (soprano); Bottom/Pyramus (bass-baritone); Puck (speaking part); Quince (bass); Flute (tenor); Snug (bass); Snout (tenor); Starveling (baritone); Peaseblossom, Cobweb, Mustardseed, Moth (treble).*

Benjamin Britten, England's foremost opera composer, was blessed and cursed with an exceptionally keen ear for music. He could perceive and conceive sonic intricacies abstruse to general audiences and overweening critics. Always intending to communicate his art, he could not understand why his operas, esteemed by many, endeared so few. *A Midsummer Night's Dream* glimmers more than glitters with musical delights. To Shakespeare's natural and supernatural colorations, Britten adds one unnatural tone, the countertenor voice of Oberon. Children play the fairies attending Titania, a coloratura soprano. A boy-acrobat speaks Puck. The Rustics must modulate their voices to suit each line, especially Bottom when he wears the ass's head. A harpsichord, celesta, two harps, two recorders, and an array of percussion instruments augment the chamber orchestra. Indeed, the score is a veritable textbook on fanciful orchestration. Mutes, harmonics, glissandos, flutter-tonguing, and other effects embellish a profusion of textures, most of them lean. Like Debussy, Britten shifts the color scheme every few measures with inexhaustible invention, rarely reverting to the mixture as before. But the magic is subtle, elusive, ephemeral. There is no looking back, no dwelling place for thought, as if the listener were pursuing Puck himself.

To adapt the play as an opera of two and a quarter hours, Britten and Peter Pears omitted about half the lines and shuffled those retained, combining and redisposing entire scenes. Shakespeare's words, however, remain unchanged, with a single line invented to restore a link in the plot imparted in the deleted first scene. Although it transplants some events in the play, the opera tightens the action and faithfully presents the three entangled stories, while giving Theseus and Hippolita less to do.

Britten composed the work in only seven months to celebrate the 1960 reconstruction of Jubilee Hall, at the time the main concert facility of the Aldeburgh Festival. It was the eleventh of his sixteen operas, if we include his adaptation of *The Beggar's Opera*. Appropriately festive and jubilant, *A Midsummer Night's Dream* eschews psychological portrayal, evoking instead an ethereal enchantment quite unlike the stuff Britten's other operas are made of. He might have subtitled it "Love the Magician," as Falla called his ballet, for Love is the guiding and confounding power behind the drama and its music. When passion subverts reason, volatility prevails. Recondite wishes emerge as in a dream, and in one night matches can be broken and remade by Puck's intrigues. Pyramus and Thisbe, farcically played by Bottom and Flute, die for Love's absurdity, mistaking it for Love's sorrow.

The characters, as Britten portrays them musically, are like enameled dolls, burnished but depthless, intoning measured lines with cold luster. We observe them from a distance by their own nocturnal light. Most substantial of the lovers is Helena, at first breathlessly pursuing Demetrius, later incredulous and indignant when her beloved and Lysander as well dote upon her. Among the Rustics, Bottom is easily the most ponderable and opaque. Too ebullient to know he plays the fool, he oversteps the boundaries of comedy as good clowns must. The rarefied and translucent realm of fairies cannot confine him. His angular declamations and immodest conduct immunizes him to the spell of the wood. Musically he is a lost character who seems to have stumbled into the wrong opera.

Like the play, Britten's music hinges on contrasts. Diatonic lines deflect to new modalities in mid-phrase. Modulatory legerdemain summarily shifts the tonal floor under our feet without a jog. Orthodox harmonies bear eccentric dissonances or fall together in solecistic clinches. Alien meters invade the iambic symmetry. Vocal and orchestral lines diverge and meet again in a network of interlacing streams. The score is a tour de force of circuitry behind an illusion.—JAMES ALLEN FELDMAN

Mignon

Composer: *Ambroise Thomas.*
Librettists: *J. Barbier and M. Carré (after Goethe, Wilhelm Meister).*
First Performance: *Paris, Opéra-Comique, Salle Favart, 17 November 1866.*
Roles: *Mignon (soprano or mezzo-soprano); Philine (soprano); Wilhelm Meister (tenor); Lothario (bass); Frederick (tenor); Laerte (tenor); Giarno (bass); chorus (SATB).*

Mignon, along with *Carmen* and *Faust,* has to be considered one of the most successful French operas ever composed. Premiered at the Opéra-Comique in 1866, it received its 1000th performance there in 1894 and eventually surpassed 2000. Translated into nearly twenty languages, *Mignon* did much to secure Thomas's reputation (along with *Hamlet,* 1868) as the leading composer of French opera and his appointment as Director of the Paris Conservatory five years later.

Based upon characters and selected situations from the first part of Goethe's *Wilhelm Meister,* the libretto by Carré and Barbier (who also provided for Gounod's *Faust*) was first offered to Meyerbeer and then to Gounod. Essentially a romantic triangle among Goethe's titular hero, the mysterious child/woman Mignon, and the extroverted actress Philine, the libretto bears little resemblance to the novel. In act I of the opera, a band of gypsies is entertaining the townspeople in the courtyard of an eighteenth-century German inn. When one of them, Mignon, refuses to dance as ordered, she is first shielded by Lothario, an old and partially-demented harper seeking his long-lost daughter, and then rescued by Wilhelm, a student. All this has been observed by Philine and Laerte, unemployed actors also staying at the inn. Wilhelm purchases Mignon's freedom from the gypsies. A letter borne by Frederick, Philine's Cherubino-like admirer, invites the acting troupe to perform at his uncle's castle. Wilhelm agrees to join the company, with Mignon in tow.

Act II contains two scenes, the first of which takes place at the castle in the bedroom assigned to Philine. Wilhelm, infatuated with the actress, seems not to notice that Mignon, serving as his page, is jealous. Philine prepares to perform as Titania in *A Midsummer Night's Dream.* Scene ii is set in a park outside the castle, where Mignon contemplates suicide because of Wilhelm's inattention. The heroine is consoled by Lothario, who hears her rhetorical wish that the theater in which Philine is performing be engulfed in flames. The play completed, Philine enters in triumph. She sends Mignon back into the theater on an errand, after which the building suddenly bursts into flames. Wilhelm dramatically rescues Mignon again.

In order to convalesce from the fire, Mignon is brought to an Italian palace for act III. Wilhelm finally assures her of his love. Now Lothario appears dressed as a nobleman, in possession of both his sanity and his ancestral home. Childhood mementos convince all that Mignon is really Lothario's lost daughter, Sperata, and rejoicing ensues.

Thus ends *Mignon* as it is ordinarily presented today, but this is not what the opening night audience witnessed. In fact, four different conclusions to the opera have been performed at one time or another. At the opera's premiere, the action continued with Philine's voice heard off-stage, causing Mignon to run out in fright. Act III had a second scene, set in the Italian countryside. After a brief ballet, Philine offers her hand in friendship to Mignon, claims Frederick as her husband, and even more rejoicing ensues. The next version of the ending, substituted soon after the premiere, omits act III's additional scene and the ballet but is essentially similar to the original. Version three, intended for German audiences, has Mignon die (as in Goethe's novel) in Wilhelm's arms after confronting Philine. The fourth version has the standard denouement, described in the synopsis above.

The opera contains some of Thomas's most memorable music, including a brilliantly scored overture and several highly effective arias. Among the best known are Mignon's gentle "Connais-tu le pays," a remarkably faithful adaptation of Goethe's "Kennst du das Land," and Philine's treacherous "Je suis Titania" from act II, surely one of the most demanding arias in the coloratura repertory. Frederick's "Me voici dans son boudoir," sometimes referred to as the gavotte from *Mignon,* is also notable.

Conceived originally as an opéra-comique, that is, with spoken dialogue, Thomas composed recitatives in 1868 for a production in Germany. It is in this latter form that the work is nearly always performed today.—MORTON ACHTER

Milanov, Zinka

Soprano. Born Mira Zinka Teresa Kunç, 17 May 1906, in Zagreb, Croatia. Died 30 May 1989, in New York. Married: 1) theater director Predrag Milanov, 1937 (divorced); 2) General Ljubomir Ilic, 1947. Studied at Zagreb Academy and with Milka Ternina, Maria Kostrenćić and Fernando Carpi (in Prague); debut at Ljubljana Opera as Leonora in Il trovatore, 1927; appeared at Zagreb Opera, 1928-35; began association with Toscanini in Verdi's Requiem at Salzburg, 1937; Metropolitan Opera debut as Leonora, 1937; Teatro alla Scala debut as Tosca, 1950; farewell performance at Metropolitan opera as Maddalena in Andrea Chénier, 1966.

Zinka Milanov towered over her generation of singers not as an innovator but as a standard-bearer. She stretched no boundaries; unlike so many artists of her time, she did not "reinterpret" a composer's intentions by filtering them through a raft of vocal shortcomings in the ostensible search for some elusive dramatic truth. She *did* become the very last singer of her type to realize every aspect of her potential and to maintain it in the heaviest Italian repertory throughout an unusually long career.

Milanov dedicated her life to what she considered the highest calling: serving an ideal of beauty that defined the reason for the very existence of the singer of opera. Her devotion to maintaining and perpetuating the vocal standards of her greatest predecessors (Rosa Ponselle, to whose place she succeeded at the Metropolitan Opera, was emphatically an admirer) produced "singing of a school already severely in decline, and it demanded attention," wrote Alan Blyth. Though she fell short of her self-set goal often enough, Milanov nonetheless fulfilled her destiny to a degree that made her, among her colleagues, the most esteemed of all singers.

Her majestic, larger-than-life stage persona seemed a throwback to an earlier era ("grand manner," it was called, and for no other singer was the designation invoked as often), but she had the goods to go with it: "To an age of somewhat dislocated musical values, Zinka Milanov stands as a kind of magnetic pole of old-fashioned musical virtue," was Irving Kolodin's 1953 assessment.

That "dislocation" had developed through the gradual abdication of critical responsibility to stress the importance of healthy vocalism vis-a-vis the presentation of dramatic values, until the two had become almost mutually exclusive. Milanov's priorities were clearly vocal, and hers was an instrument before which all other considerations paled. The sound was silver with a vein of amber, round and opulent, and all of a piece from top to bottom. Its hues ranged securely from brilliant to mellow, from honeyed and silky to dark and vibrant. Because of the prodigal size of her voice, Milanov could dominate any ensemble easily and impressively. But unlike other big voices, hers could be graded to the most refined and delicate of floated sounds, not just in midrange but to the very top of the compass. This extraordinary *pianissimo* seemed detached in

space, not emanating from the stage at all but hovering directly at the listener's ear in any location inside the opera house. Milanov's finely spun legato, sense of phrasing, and feel for vocal color created a tone and line that conveyed all that was meaningful about her roles. Her emotional projection was "direct, deeply felt, infinitely touching," wrote John Ardoin. Olin Downes praised her "nobility of expression and complete mastery of every phase of the singer's art."

In the early years of her career, the going was indeed rough. Milanov sang constantly in Yugoslavia, in an extraordinary variety of roles, for very little money, and went as a guest artist to Germany, Bulgaria, and Czechoslovakia, often just for one-off performances with long train rides on the days she had to sing. Though she is remembered as a statuesque stand-pat diva who sang "old" music, she began as quite the vocal firebrand, and a good bit of her repertory was new by operatic standards. As one of her country's pioneer Turandots (1929),

Zinka Milanov (Culver Pictures)

for instance, she introduced a role barely three years past its premiere; and she sang in several other operas written in her own lifetime.

An *Aïda* in Vienna in 1936 under Bruno Walter turned the tide; he loved her, and sent her to Toscanini, who engaged her at once for his 1937 performances of Verdi's Requiem at Salzburg. (Contrary to legend, she had already been invited to the Metropolitan *before* her spectacular success with Toscanini.) She was principal soprano in New York until the gala performance that closed the old Metropolitan Opera House, 16 April 1966, just prior to which she was granted a formal farewell. Though she made several historically important recordings, she did not commit a complete role to disc until her twenty-fifth year onstage. In any case, hers was a massive voice requiring the surrounding space of the theater to be heard to full advantage. Thus, generations that did not witness her in the house can never know the impact of her presence and her prime sound, the reasons for the tremendous extent of her influence.

As soon as Milanov retired, younger colleagues—Christa Ludwig, Régine Crespin, Grace Bumbry, Sandor Konya, Anna Moffo, Elinor Ross, Rosalind Elias, Walter Berry, and many others—flocked to her for lessons, all seeking the secrets that had made her singing so special, not to mention so healthy and durable. The root of their interest was summarized by Ludwig: "Zinka Milanov—this voice is really *the* voice of our century and not surpassed by other wonderful artists."

The international outpouring of analysis at the time of Milanov's death elucidated the source of her supereminent stature and made clear at just what point vocal history had taken the wrong turn: "It is a tragedy for operatic singing," wrote Hugh Canning, "that Callas rather than Milanov became the postwar icon," and Blyth recognized that American opera lovers, in particular, would rank Milanov as the "foremost of all *lirico-spinto* sopranos of the past fifty years." In so doing, a still grateful public simply seconds Rudolf Bing's valuation on the soprano's last night, when he acclaimed Milanov as "a supremely great singer."—BRUCE BURROUGHS

Milhaud, Darius

Composer. Born 4 September 1892, in Aix-en-Provence. Died 22 June 1974, in Geneva. Married: Madeleine Milhaud (his cousin), 1926 (one son). Studied violin with Berthelier and counterpoint with Gédalge at the Paris Conservatory, beginning 1909; secretary to the French Minister in Brazil, Paul Claudel, 1917-18; returned to Paris, 1918; active in French music circles until the outbreak of World War II; conducted and performed (as pianist) his own compositions and lectured at Harvard, Princeton, and Vassar during trips to the United States in 1922 and 1926; traveled and performed in Italy, Holland, Germany, Austria, Poland, and Russia, 1922-26; lived in the United States and taught at Mills College (Oakland, California), 1940-71; professor at the Paris Conservatory, 1947, and spent alternate years at the conservatory and Mills; settled in Geneva, 1971. Milhaud was one of "Les Six" that included Auric, Durey, Honegger, Poulenc, and Tailleferre; his circle included Erik Satie and Jean Cocteau; his pupils include Gilbert Amy, Elinor Armer, Dave and Howard Brubeck, Richard Felciano, Betsy Jolas, Leland Smith, and Morton Subotnick.

Operas *La brebis égarée,* Francis Jammes, 1910-14, Paris, Opéra-Comique, 10 December 1923; *Les euménides* (last work in the three-part cycle, *L'Orestie*), Paul Claudel (after Aeschylus), 1917-22, Berlin, Berlin Opera, 18 November 1949; *Les malheurs d'Orphée,* Armand Lunel, 1924, Brussels, Théâtre de la Monnaie, 7 May 1926; *Esther de Carpentras,* Armand Lunel, 1925-26, Paris, Opéra-Comique, 3 February 1938; *Le pauvre matelot,* Jean Cocteau, 1926, Paris, Opéra-Comique, 16 December 1927; *Trois opéras-minutes,* Henri Hoppenot, 1927, 1) *L'enlèvement d'Europe,* Baden-Baden, 17 July 1927; 2) *L'abandon d'Ariane* and 3) *La délivrence de Thésée,* Wiesbaden, 20 April 1928; *Christophe Colomb,* Paul Claudel, Berlin, State Opera, 5 May 1930; *Maximilien,* R.S. Hoffman, translated by Armand Lunel (after Franz Werfel), 1930-31, Paris, Opéra, 5 January 1932; *Medée,* Madeleine Milhaud (after Euripides), 1938, Antwerp, Flemish Opera, 7 October 1939; *Bolivar,* Madeleine Milhaud (after Jules Supervielle), 1943, Paris, Opéra, 12 May 1950; *David,* Armand Lunel, 1952-53, Jerusalem (King David Festival), 1 June 1954; *Fiesta,* Boris Vian, 1958, Berlin, Städtische Opera, 3 October 1958; *La mère coupable,* Madeleine Milhaud (after Beaumarchais), 1964-65, Geneva, Grand Théâtre, 13 June 1965; *Saint Louis, roi de France* (opera-oratorio), Paul Claudel and Henri Doublier, 1970-71, Rome, Radio Audizioni Italiana, 18 March 1972.

Mention the name Darius Milhaud to most musicians and they will call to mind his huge output of scores (four hundred and forty-three opus numbers) but will probably not classify him as primarily an opera composer. Nevertheless, it is the contention of Milhaud's biographer, Paul Collaer, that the essence of this composer's style is dramatic and that the operas stand like pillars marking the path of his total musical journey. In fact, the first of his sixteen operas, *La brebis égarée* (*The Lost Lamb*), was begun when he was only eighteen years old, and the final one, an opera-oratorio commissioned by the French government to commemorate the seven-hundreth anniversary of King Louis IX's demise, was completed shortly before his own death.

Milhaud was catapulted into the conscience of the musical world in the 1920s when, as one of the group of "enfants terribles" of post-war Paris, his compositions elicited hoots and howls from the listening public and outraged invective from the press. Several composers, quite arbitrarily dubbed "Les Six" by a music critic, took up Erik Satie's battle cry, "Down with Wagner," and Milhaud, as the most prolific of the group, became a standard-bearer in the revolt against all that was pompous, obtuse and cloying in late nineteenth-century music. In Milhaud's operas, this revolt manifested itself in his insistence on meticulous matching of every element of the musical score to the expressive requirements of the text.

In his study of Milhaud's operas, Jeremy Drake divides the works into three periods. The first two operas, *La brebis égarée* and *Les euménides,* stand somewhat apart from this classification, and *Christophe Colomb* occupies a transitional position between the first and second periods. Drake includes *Les malheurs d'Orphée* (*The Misfortunes of Orpheus*), *Esther de Carpentras, Le pauvre matelot,* and the three *Opéras-minutes* in the first period, and *Maximilien, Medée, Bolivar* and *David* in the second, which is characterized by thicker textures, minimal use of groups of solo instruments, less emphasis on counterpoint, and increased motivic development. *Fiesta, La mère coupable,* (*The Guilty Mother*), and *Saint Louis* make up the third period, which marks a return to the contrapuntal constructions that typified the first period. Whereas this classification is useful as a point of departure for examining the different works, close scrutiny will reveal that the stylistic elements that bind the operas together are far stronger than the chronology that separates them.

Melody is certainly the hallmark of Milhaud's operatic style, as it is of all his music. Sometimes the operas contain short, song-like sections, but more often the vocal lines are spun out either against an instrumental background or integrated polyphonically into the instrumental texture itself. The music responds to the nuances of each dramatic situation, and every melodic line has its own shape and symmetry which, far from "setting" the words of the libretto, expresses the mood of the text and, in fact, often subordinates the prosody to the metric pattern of the musical phrase.

Rhythmically, Milhaud uses mostly simple meters that contribute an element of cohesiveness to his flexible and often complex melodic structures. Harmonically, he is well known as the chief protagonist of polytonality and, as the word implies, his style is essentially tonal. His most typical compositional technique is counterpoint, which he applies in a variety of ways. The chamber orchestras of his early operas, such as *Les malheurs d'Orphée* and the *Opéras-minutes,* are perfectly adapted to his polytonal concept of using one instrument (or voice) to a part, each line standing out from the others by virtue of its special timbre. In later works involving full orchestra, his polyphonic structures are frequently festooned over great harmonic blocks, many times supported by powerful ostenati, while unequivocal cadences reaffirm the tonal centers of the music.

Three forces shaped Darius Milhaud as man and as musician, his Jewish faith, the heritage of his native Provence, and French rationality. As a result, his approach to art was both humanistic and fatalistic. Everything, he believed, including inanimate objects, plants, animals and people, is both spectator of and participant in the great eternal drama of mankind presided over by ineluctable fate. The protagonists of the individual operas may be simple people overcome by human passions, like Pierre and Françoise in *La brebis égarée* and the wife in *Le pauvre matelot;* they may be tragic characters, like Medea and Orestes, from Classical antiquity, or historical figures like Columbus and Bolivar. Some of the operas are short (each of the *Opéras-minutes* lasts eight to ten minutes), some provide an evening's entertainment, but every work is exactly as long as the particular dramatic situation demands. Nor does length necessarily equal importance. Writing to a friend about *Les malheurs d'Orphée.* Milhaud said: "It is such a magnificent subject, but I want to make it very human. . . ." The purity of the musical texture, the absolute economy of means should "project a total atmosphere of grandeur."

It is not surprising that Milhaud chose as collaborators people who shared his love of simplicity, his profound spirituality, and his affinity for his Provençal milieu. The poets Francis Jammes and Paul Claudel, his childhood friend Armand Lunel, and his wife Madeleine Milhaud provided most of the librettos. The recognition of Milhaud's world-wide prominence as an opera composer is borne-out by the wide range of cities in which first or second performances of his works have been given, such as Paris, Berlin, Brussels, Geneva, Graz, Rome, Milan, Rio de Janeiro, and Jerusalem. Whereas some of the larger works have received few performances because of the enormous resources required to stage them, the chamber operas are frequently presented, and interest in his entire operatic output never ceases to grow.—JANE HOHFELD GALANTE

Milnes, Sherrill

Baritone. Born 10 January 1935, in Downers Grove, Illinois. Studied at Drake University with Andrew White, at Northwestern University with Hermanus Baer, and with Rosa Ponselle; at Santa Fe, 1960; toured with Boris Goldovsky's Opera Company, with whom he

made his debut as Masetto, 1960; later sang Gérard in Andrea Chénier *in Baltimore, 1961; New York City Opera debut as Valentin in* Faust, *1964; Metropolitan Opera debut in same role, 1965; Covent Garden debut, 1971; created Adam in* Mourning Becomes Electra, *1967.*

Sherrill Milnes's art has improved as his voice has declined—the classic opera-singer syndrome. When he made his New York City Opera debut in 1964, he had the lean bright sound and easily accessible top notes characteristic of American baritones, exemplified by Lawrence Tibbett. But whereas from the start of his career Tibbett sang with imagination and pizzazz, Milnes was lacking in musical sensibility, detailed characterization and depth of feeling until the early eighties. He frequently didn't express words or music with enough intensity. He wasn't tender enough or distraught enough or sufficiently aflame. He did not have enough passion, urgency or emotional tension. He was boring in romantic or contemplative passages, rising to the occasion only when the music turned brilliant or vehement. His phrasing had little dynamic ebb and flow, for he seldom imparted forward motion to upbeats and he rarely tapered the ends of climactic downbeats with diminuendos. He routinely accentuated and held onto the last syllable of a phrase, even where that syllable was on a weak beat that resolved a dissonance. He thus dislocated the phrase's climax, inappropriately transfering it from a point of structural tension to one of structural repose. In addition to throwing music out of kilter, mislocating accents at phrase endings also caused him to stress Italian incorrectly: "amo*re*" instead of "*amo*re." On a recording of *Don Carlo* from 1970, his singing is unresponsive to phrase shape and blighted by random and misplaced accentuations.

To negotiate the *passaggio*—the area of the voice where chest and head resonance abut— Milnes uses a technique called "covering." Older voice manuals make no mention of it. To judge from letters and reviews, covering gradually came into use in the nineteenth century. After World War I most singers—Italians in particular—covered the *passaggio* and sometimes other areas of the voice. Those who resort to covering often dispute when and where to use it. For many singers covering becomes a matter not of interpretive choice but of technical necessity. Milnes heavily covered notes in the area of his *passaggio*—around F. Although a chief benefit of covering is increased security, he often had intonation difficulties there.

On a 1974 aria album his voice rings forth, particularly on high notes—he sings a number of A-flats, A-naturals and even a B-flat, sounding more like a tenor than a baritone (he probably could have negotiated Siegmund with little difficulty). He trills agreeably and in Rodrigo's death scene encompasses in one breath phrases that many others take in two. His account of "Largo al factotum" surpasses most in variety of inflection. But his renditions of scenes from *I puritani, La favorite, Ernani, Don Carlos* and *La gioconda* suffer from predictability, sameness of expression and insufficient emotion. Although his high voice is not displayed to best advantage in the "Credo" from *Otello* or Rance's monologue from *La fanciulla del West,* he becomes more emotionally involved in them than in the generally more tender and introspective selections from the older operas, where among other things his music making lacks *Schwung,* with one downbeat thumped much like another.

In the early eighties Milnes dropped from sight, and rumors began to circulate that he was seriously ill. Returning, he started to sing with shading, nuance and structural awareness, contouring dynamics and lengthening dissonances so that the vocal line mirrored harmonic tension, moving phrases ahead by adding a touch of crescendo. He learned how to do appoggiaturas expressively, preparing them with crescendos and making diminuendos on resolutions, and came to phrase with regard to proportion and balance. Simon Boccanegra in the fall of 1984 was his zenith—memorable for depth of feeling—although by then the voice had begun to lose bloom and power and to sound constricted in the *passaggio*. Unfortunately, because of his vocal decline, many of New York's opera cognoscenti already had become hostile to him, to the point that they failed to recognize his artistic growth.

By the following season, when he reappeared in the role, his vocal problems had increased. By 1986 his sound was less true, thicker and more spread, also still more covered on top, while the *passaggio* was no better than before: most high Es were scooped (slid up to from below), if they ever reached pitch. In *I puritani* he sometimes failed to render dotted rhythms accurately, making short notes too long. His cavatina had little intense tenderness and his duet with the Arturo (Salvatore Fisichella) no ferocity. Yet he did have passion in some passages, for example, "E di morte lo stral." Recently, Milnes has sounded strangulated on such notes as the F-sharp of "delle lagrime *mie*" (*Un ballo in maschera*), the F of "gridan*ò*", the F of "fan*ciu*lli" and the F of "e*ra* voler" (all from *Aida*).

Cornell MacNeil's career paralleled Milnes's. Early on he too was lacking in feeling and characterization. He too developed them—even as his voice declined. The voice itself was bigger. Milnes's sound, particularly in recent years, hasn't seemed quite ample enough for the Met, except on high notes. Still, Milnes was the most prominent American baritone of the seventies and eighties.—STEFAN ZUCKER

Minton, Yvonne

Mezzo-soprano. Born 4 December 1938, in Sydney, New South Wales. Married: William Barclay, 1965; one son, one daughter. Studied with Marjorie Walker at Sydney Conservatory and with Henry Cummings and Joan Cross in London; won Kathleen Ferrier prize and Hertogenbosch Competition in 1961; debut as Britten's Lucretia, London, 1964; at Covent Garden since 1965, where she first appeared as Lola in Cavalleria rusticana; *Cologne debut as Sesto in* La clemenza di Tito, *1969; created Thea in Tippett's* The Knot Garden, *1970; Chicago debut as Octavian, 1970; debut at Metropolitan Opera in 1973 and Paris Opéra in 1976 in same role; made a Commander of Order of the British Empire, 1980.*

Few recent singers can compete with Yvonne Minton in versatility. She won applause for her performances of roles in operas by Mozart and Berg, Wagner and Bartók, Berlioz and Strauss. Her success as Dorabella (Mozart's *Così fan tutte*) hardly prepared opera-goers for her equally successful interpretations of Kundry (Wagner's *Parsifal*) and Waltraute (*Götterdämmerung*). Nor did her triumph as Charlotte (Massenet's *Werther*) prepare listeners for her fine portrayals of Countess Geschwitz (Berg's *Lulu*) and of Judith (Bartók's *Bluebeard's Castle*).

Minton's portrayal of Sesto in Mozart's *La clemenza di Tito* (as recorded under Colin Davis) reveals a big voice marred sometimes, as in the opening duet "Come ti piace, imponi," by a wide vibrato that can obscure the pitch. Elsewhere her voice is less wobbly. In "Parto, ma tu, ben mio" Minton, perhaps inspired by the beautifully in-tune clarinet solo, sings admirably smooth, expressive melodic lines. She sings the great accompanied recitative "Oh dei, che smania è questa" with fire and passion; but to some of the more delicate and sentimental of Sesto's melodies, as in the trio "Se al volto mai ti senti," she brings too much heaviness and richness of voice.

That same richness and heaviness help make Minton a fine Wagner singer. She has won much praise for her many portrayals of Waltraute at Covent Garden, Bayreuth and elsewhere. "Urgent," "impassioned," and "most musical" are among the accolades that critics have awarded Minton for her Wagner singing, often concluding that Minton's Waltraute was the highlight of the entire performance of *Götterdämmerung*.

Minton shares some of her repertory with another leading mezzo-soprano, her younger contemporary Frederica von Stade. They are both first-rate Charlottes in Massenet's *Werther*. Like von Stade, Minton is effective in trouser roles. Early in her career she won praise for her portrayal of Ascanio in Berlioz's *Benvenuto Cellini;* the part was "exquisitely sung," according to one critic. She has sung a "youthful, eager" Octavian in a recording of Strauss's *Rosenkavalier;* she has also sung this latter role at Salzburg and the Metropolitan Opera with great success. And she has won applause for her portrayals of Cherubino (Mozart's *Figaro*), a role that von Stade too has sung to critical acclaim. Minton's voice is a good deal heavier than von Stade's, and this accounts for the difference in their repertories. Unlike von Stade, Minton has rarely ventured into opera of the baroque, classical (Mozart excepted), and early romantic periods. Minton has had little success in the bel canto operas of Rossini, while von Stade has won great applause in Rossini's operas, serious as well as comic. Von Stade, on the other hand, has not found the success achieved by Minton in Wagnerian and twentieth-century opera.—JOHN A. RICE

Moffo, Anna

Soprano. Born 27 June 1932, in Wayne, Pennsylvania. Studied with Giannini-Gregory at the Curtis Institute of Music and in Rome at the Accademia di Santa Cecilia with Luigi Ricci and Mercedes Llopart; debut as Norina in Spoleto, 1955; appeared as Butterfly for Milan television, 1956; Vienna Staatsoper debut, 1958; Salzburg, 1959; American debut as Mimì at Chicago Lyric Opera, 1957; Metropolitan Opera debut as Violetta, 1959; suffered a vocal breakdown in 1974, but resumed her career in 1976.

Anna Moffo was born in Wayne, Pennsylvania, on 27 June 1932, of Italian parentage. She studied at the University of Pennsylvania and the Curtis Institute of Music with Eufemia Giannini-Gregory. She received a Fulbright grant to study voice in Italy and attended Rome's Accademia di Santa Cecilia, where her teachers included Luigi Ricci and Mercedes Llopart. She has received honorary doctorates from Temple University and Ursinus College; and in 1985 she received a Doctor of Humane Letters degree from Nazareth College of Rochester.

After several appearances over Italian radio, she sang the title role of Puccini's *Madama Butterfly* for a Milan television production. She also appeared as Norina in *Don Pasquale* at the Spoleto "Festival of Two Worlds." These two performances established her reputation as a singer in Europe. In 1956 she sang Zerlina at Aix-en-Provence. In 1958 she made her debut at the Vienna Staatsoper and in 1959 she sang at the Salzburg Festival, in Austria.

Meanwhile in 1957, she was engaged by the Chicago Lyric Opera, and sang her American opera debut there as Mimì in *La bohème*. She returned to the United States in 1959 for her

Metropolitan debut as Violetta in Verdi's *La traviata*. Throughout the 1960s and early 1970s Moffo appeared in opera houses around the world including Milan, Vienna, Hamburg, Munich, London, Rome, Chicago, Buenos Aires, as well as performing eighteen major roles at the Metropolitan Opera in New York City. Her roles have included Norina in *Don Pasquale*, Pamina in *Die Zauberflöte*, Gilda in *Rigoletto*, Marguerite in *Faust*, Violetta in *La traviata*, as well as the heroines of *Les contes d'Hoffmann*.

Moffo's varied and successful career has helped to broaden the general appeal of opera. Her work in films and television, as well as her natural beauty, charming stage presence, and considerable dramatic talents have made her a role model for the modern opera singer.

Moffo has not confined herself to the operatic stage, but has made numerous television appearances, including her own Italian television series *The Anna Moffo Show*. She has also been a guest on special segments of *The Caterina Valente Show*, telecast live from Stuttgart, Germany, and on the American premiere of *Buonasera Raffaella* which was beamed live via satellite to forty-six countries on Radiotelevisione Italiana. She has also starred in film versions of *La traviata*, *Lucia di Lammermoor*, *La belle Hélène*, *Die Czardasfürstin* and *La serva padrona*, as well as in fourteen non-operatic feature films.

In the fall of 1984, Video Arts International released a video cassette of *Lucia di Lammermoor* for home viewers. Her performance received glowing praise. *Video Now* (February 1985) called her "vocally radiant, dramatically convincing, and heartbreakingly beautiful as Lucia" and *Opera News* (March 30, 1985) called the video a "satisfying film" and lauded Moffo's "expressive" singing and acting ability.

Noteworthy among her recordings of complete operas, is Puccini's *La bohème* recorded with Maria Callas, recently released on compact disc by EMI. She has also made several recordings of operatic arias which have been well produced and well received. Her recording devoted to Verdi heroines was awarded the Orfée d'Or and her recording of coloratura arias, coached by Tullio Serafin, is probably her best work on record.

Moffo has a soprano quality which defies categorization; she has been critically assessed as a lyric, a coloratura and also a dramatic soprano. The broad range of her musical capabilities has enabled her to perform a broad range of roles rather than specialize in a certain "Fach" or "type." However, the exploitation of her musical and dramatic breadth by unsuitable choices in theater roles and in recordings led to vocal problems in the mid-1970s.

Her long list of honors include the Commendatore of the Order of Merit of the Republic of Italy and Rome's Masquera d'Argento, the prestigious Michelangelo Award and the Golden Rose of Montreux for the television production of *La sonnambula*. Recent additions include Liebe Augustin from the city of Vienna (1984), induction into the Academy of Vocal Arts (Philadelphia) First Hall of Fame for Great American Opera Singers (1985) and the Citation of Merit from the New York Singing Teacher's Association (1986). In 1987 she was given the first annual Voice Award by the Academy of Arts and Culture under the auspices of the American Israel Opera Foundation. In 1990 Moffo received a special award from the Friends of the Staatsoper in Vienna and La Caveja d'Oro for "Artist of the Year" in Milan.—PATRICIA ROBERTSON

Moll, Kurt

Bass. Born 11 April 1938, in Buir, Germany. Studied at Cologne Hochschule für Musik and with Emmy Müller in Krefeld; small roles with Cologne Opera while a student, 1958-61; official debut as Lodovico in Otello, *Cologne, 1961; in Aachen, 1961-63; Mainz, 1964-65; in Wuppertal, 1966-69; joined Hamburg Staatsoper in 1970; sang Fafner at Bayreuth, 1974; sang Marke at the Teatro alla Scala, 1974; appeared as Gurnemanz in* Parsifal *in San Francisco, 1974; Covent Garden debut as Caspar in* Der Freischütz, *1975; Metropolitan Opera debut as Landgrave in* Tannhäuser, *1978; Chicago Lyric Opera debut as Daland, 1983; created the King in Biala's* Der geistefelte Kater.

Kurt Moll's voice encompasses the major bass roles of the German, Italian, Russian, and French repertoires, especially those of Wagner, Mozart, and Richard Strauss. His legato phrasing, which is to a large extent the key to the quality of his singing, may derive in part from his early training as a cellist. Moll's operatic career began in 1959 in small theaters of Germany—Aachen, Wuppertal, Mainz, Cologne—where he gained experience and slowly grew into his roles. He has been careful to remain within his *Fach* (vocal category)—true bass roles—performing roles that avoid the high Es, Fs, and F-sharps required for bass-baritone roles, which he feels would shorten his vocal life. His chief Wagner role is Gurnemanz in *Parsifal*—an extremely long role that the beauty of Moll's voice can make seem short—which he has sung at the Salzburg Easter Festival and at the Metropolitan Opera and which he has recorded under Herbert von Karajan; he has avoided the higher roles of Wotan and Hans Sachs. Musorgsky's *Boris Godunov* has also figured in Moll's career.

Since Moll's Metropolitan debut in 1978 he has sung there, in addition to Gurnemanz, Osmin in Mozart's *Die Entführung aus dem Serail,* Sparafucile in Verdi's *Rigoletto,* Rocco in Beethoven's *Fidelio,* Hermann in Wagner's *Tannhäuser,* Baron Ochs in Richard Strauss's *Der Rosenkavalier,* and Lodovico in Verdi's *Otello.*

A frequent performer at the major opera houses of Europe, Moll has appeared at many European opera festivals; he has portrayed King Marke in Wagner's *Tristan und Isolde* at the 1974 Bayreuth Festival; the King in Verdi's *Aida* and Baron Ochs at the Salzburg Festival; and Pogner in Wagner's *Die Meistersinger,* King Marke in Wagner's *Tristan und Isolde,* the Alcalde in Wolf's *Die Corregidor,* Sarastro in Mozart's *Die Zauberflöte,* and Abul Hassan in Cornelius's *Der Barbier von Bagdad* at the Munich Festival, among many other roles, under the guidance of such directors as Peter Stein, August Everding, Otto Schenk, and Günther Rennert.

Moll's comic roles include a satisfyingly understated, almost noble Baron Ochs—in keeping with Strauss's description of Ochs as coarse and vulgar only on the inside, but outwardly presentable—and an Osmin who never needs to flirt with the flat side of the note for supposedly humorous effect.

Moll's voice has been described by critics as full, round-toned, resonant, richly sonorous, and plush, with a quality that has been called splendor. He conveys a vigorous, lively intelligence and an underlying sense of humor that preempt dullness, although he has been criticized for a certain interpretive blandness. His has been called the most beautiful German bass voice in the world today, and he is known for his human and characterful singing as well as his beautifully formed vocalism.

He has described himself as a "vocal painter, finding new colors in a role, bringing out the emotional chiaroscuro as well as stark blacks and whites" (in an interview in *Opera News,* 12 March 1983).—MICHAEL SIMS

Montemezzi, Italo

Composer. Born 4 August 1875, in Vigasio, near Verona. Died 15 May 1952, in Vigasio. Studied with Saladino and Ferroni at the Milan Conservatory, graduating 1900; in the United States, 1939, where he lived primarily in California; returned to Italy, 1949.

Operas *Bianca,* Z. Strani; *Giovanni Gallurese,* F. d'Angelantonio, Turin, 28 January 1905; *Hellera,* Luigi Illica (after Benjamin Constant, *Adolphe*), Turin, 17 March 1909; *L'amore dei tre re,* after S. Benelli, Milan, Teatro alla Scala, 10 April 1913; *La nave,* G. d'Annunzio, Milan, Teatro alla Scala, 1 November 1918; *La notte di Zoraima,* M. Ghisalberti, Milan, Teatro alla Scala, 31 January 1931; *L'incantesimo,* S. Benelli, National Broadcasting Company, 1943; staged performance, Verona, 1952.

Italo Montemezzi was born and died in Vigasio, near Verona, although from 1939 to 1949 he lived mainly in California. At the time of his death various world-class conductors paid him homage. Eugene Ormandy called him "one of the greatest Italian composers of our epoch"; Leopold Stokowski expressed "immense admiration for his creative powers"; and Bruno Walter noted that Montemezzi's place is "honorable and lasting in the great history of Italian opera." Much of Montemezzi's career was closely allied with that of another great conductor, Tullio Serafin. The two met as composition students at the Milan Conservatory, where Montemezzi took a diploma in 1900 and then taught harmony for a year. During that year he composed his first opera, a one-act work titled *Bianca,* for a prize competition.

Aside from his one year of teaching, Montemezzi was able to live entirely from composition for his entire career. His second opera, *Giovanni Gallurese,* was, like *Bianca,* originally written in one act for a competition; the work did not win Montemezzi the competition and was then recast in three acts to a libretto by d'Angelantonio. Serafin helped to get this work produced in Turin, where it premiered on 28 January 1905. Although Montemezzi and Serafin were apprehensive because they did not consider the chorus to be ready at the dress rehearsal, the opera was a great success and was given seventeen times in one month. In 1924 it was conducted at the Metropolitan Opera by Serafin with Giacomo Lauri-Volpi in the leading tenor role. With *Giovanni Gallurese* the principal features of Montemezzi's operatic style were already established: a dramatic instinct allied with solid craftsmanship; a score that included touches of local color; Wagnerian harmonies; and, in the Italian tradition, a texture that promotes predominance of the voice.

Montemezzi's second professional undertaking was the opera *Hellera,* composed to a three-act libretto by Puccini's librettist, Luigi Illica. Serafin likewise directed the premiere of this work, in addition to the revival at the Rome Opera in 1937. Montemezzi's reputation rests mainly on his next opera, *L'amore dei tre re,* the premiere of which was conducted by Serafin in 1913 and then given the following year at the Metropolitan with Toscanini in the pit. This opera has in fact proven far more popular in the United States than in Italy. It is characterized by a lack of vocal lyricism, even though the orchestral music is very stirring and closely depictive of emotions and events. The work is based on the play of the same name by Sem Benelli, and Montemezzi's vocal writing has obviously been influenced by the sung-play declamation of Debussy's *Pelléas et Mélisande*. The two operas also have a number of elements of plot in common. Writing in *Opera* in June 1982, Patrick Smith deemed Montemezzi's *L'amore dei tre re* "weak-water stuff, expertly put together but sounding like this or that late nineteenth-century composition."

In an *Opera News* article just after Montemezzi's death, Serafin revealed that he considered *La nave,* premiered in 1918, to be the composer's best opera; it was a work that was well received by the critics at the time of its premiere. The libretto is by Gabriele D'Annunzio and the score shows decided Straussian influences. Serafin also notes that *La nave* is both difficult to sing and expensive to stage, for the ship of the title must sink in the last act. The work opened the 1919 Chicago season starring Rosa Raisa. After *La nave* Montemezzi's career entered a long silence, interrupted by a few stage works such as *La notte di Zoraima,* sung by Rosa Ponselle at the Metropolitan under Serafin's baton in 1931, and *L'incantesimo*. Neither of these works shows any advance in Montemezzi's musical language from his earliest works.—STEPHEN WILLIER

Monteverdi, Claudio

Composer. Born 1567 (baptized 15 May), in Cremona. Died 29 November 1643, in Venice. Married: Claudia de Cattaneis (died 10 September 1607), a singer at the Mantuan court, 20 May 1599 (two sons, one daughter who died in infancy). Learned to play the organ, and studied singing and theory with Marc' Antonio Ingegneri, maestro di capella at the Cathedral of Cremona; visited Milan, 1589; viol and violin player at the court of Vincenzo I, Duke of Mantua, by 1592; met Giaches de Wert, maestro di capella at the Mantuan court; accompanied the Duke of Mantua on battles against the Turks in Austria and Hungary, and accompanied him to Flanders in 1599; appointed maestro di capella in Mantua, succeeding Pallavicino, 1601; La favola d'Orfeo *performed for the Accademia degli Invaghiti in Mantua, 1607; membership in the Accademia degli Animori of Cremona, 1607;* L'Arianna *composed to celebrate the marriage of Francesco Gonzaga of Mantua to Margaret of Savoy, 1608; lost his post in Mantua after the death of Vincenzo I, 1612; maestro di capella at San Marco, Venice, 1613; cantata* Il combattimento di Tancredi e Clorinda *performed for the Venetian nobleman Girolamo Mocenigo, 1624; his late operas performed in the then recently opened public theaters of Venice, 1640-42. Monteverdi is buried in the church of the Fratri in Venice.*

Operas *La favola d'Orfeo,* A. Striggio, Mantua, February 1607; *L'Arianna,* O. Rinuccini, Mantua, 28 May 1608; *Le nozze di Tetide,* 1616 [unfinished; lost]; *Andromeda,* E. Marigliani, 1618-20 [unfinished; lost]; *La finta pazza Licori,* G. Strozzi, composed for Mantua, 1927. [lost]; *Gli amori di Diana e di Endimione,* A. Pio, Parma, 1628 [lost]; *Proserpina rapita,* G. Strozzi, Venice, 1630 [music mostly lost]; *Il ritorno d'Ulisse in patria,* G. Badoaro, Venice, 1640; *Le nozze d'Enea con Lavinia,* Venice, 1641 [lost]; *L'incoronazione di Poppea,* G.F. Busenello, Venice, 1642.

Claudio Monteverdi is regarded not only as the first great opera composer, but one of the greatest of all time. That he has attained this stature is testimony to the extraordinary nature of his extant operas. Of his ten operas, the only to survive are his first opera *Orfeo* and a fragment from his second opera *Arianna*—both of which were written for the Mantua court during the early years of the genre—along with *Il ritorno d'Ulisse in patria* and *L'incoronazione di Poppea,* composed during his final years for the public opera theater in Venice. These four works, standing at the two opposite poles of Monteverdi's operatic career, thus necessarily provide only a glimpse into the development and full range of his operatic genius.

Monteverdi is the only seventeenth-century composer whose works have found a permanent position in today's operatic repertoire. This is not entirely surprising; he has received more scholarly attention than any other composer of his century. In addition, inquiry into seventeenth-century opera has tended to focus on the origins of the genre and the humanistic neo-classicizing impulses that inspired its birth. Thus, *Orfeo,* long regarded as the first great opera, has been the subject of intense scrutiny. At a time when much of the opera produced for the Venice stage languished in relative obscurity, Monteverdi's Venetian operas, and in particular *L'incoronazione di Poppea,* were acknowledged as masterworks.

Recent scholarship has long since increased the visibility of Monteverdi's Venetian contemporaries, yet this has only made more apparent the extent to which his latter two operas differ from those of his younger contemporaries writing for the Venetian theater. Monteverdi brought to opera composition his Renaissance heritage and a musical style shaped by decades of madrigal composition. The madrigal books, masterpieces in themselves, were also a sort of laboratory in which Monteverdi developed various rhythmic, tonal, and vocal styles that would accommodate the dramatic requirements of opera. As Eric Chafe has recently shown, Monteverdi also inherited a tonal language based on Renaissance modal-hexachordal thinking, which he transformed into a highly expressive device for the new genre. In a sense, the unique quality of Monteverdi's sound and style results from the application of the most fundamental precepts and principles of Renaissance style to opera—the genre that embodies the Baroque aesthetic.

Monteverdi's *La favola d'Orfeo* was performed in 1607 in Mantua under the auspices of the *Accademia degli Invaghiti.* For his librettist, Monteverdi chose Alessandro Striggio, a diplomat and lawyer in the service of the ruling Gonzaga family of Mantua who, as the son of a composer, also had considerable interest in music and poetry. Monteverdi's and Striggio's *Orfeo* was not the first work of its kind. As numerous scholars have pointed out, *Orfeo* was modeled after an earlier work, *Euridice,* by poet Ottavio Rinuccini and composer Jacopo Peri. Like Rinuccini, Striggio set his libretto within the pastorale tragicomedic world that was popular from other Mantuan and Florentine theatrical entertainments such as Guarini's play *Il pastor fido.* Striggio also followed a similar dramatic structure, organizing his libretto as a prologue followed by five acts or sections, with the first two acts of the two versions roughly analogous in terms of content. Specific resemblances between the two works occur particularly in recitative passages—as in the messenger's revelation of Euridice's death—and it is in those instances that Monteverdi's musical setting demonstrates its greatest debt to Peri's work. Monteverdi also drew upon the theatrical traditions of the Florentine and Mantuan court. Thus, rather than relying so heavily upon the *stile rappresentativo* favored by the Florentine opera pioneers, Monteverdi and Striggio designed *Orfeo* as a composite of various forms and styles for both voices and instruments, enhanced by a wide spectrum of instrumental colors—indicated with great specificity by the composer—and with a greater variety of stage settings that undoubtedly contradicted classical demands for unity of place.

The appearance of the allegorical figure of Music in the prologue provides an important clue as to the actual purpose of this recounting of Orfeo's tale: a demonstration of music's power. In *Orfeo,* however, the ability to wield music's power does not necessarily rest in the hands of this gifted protagonist. Orfeo's songs are no doubt pleasing in times of joy, as in the delightfully simple strophic song "Vi ricorda" or as in the impetuous burst of emotional display of "Rosa del ciel," and his sorrow is movingly expressed in the sharply felt lament "Tu sei morta." Yet Orfeo's most virtuosic musical display and urgent evocation of music's power, "Possente spirto," only temporarily gains him his desired goal and ultimately cannot save him from his human failings. In *Orfeo,* it would seem that Monteverdi proves that the true power of music belongs to the composer. Indeed, the organization of *Orfeo* is by no means determined solely by the flow of the drama. Numerous scholars have noted the symmetrical design in the distribution of the closed forms, as in the patterns of choruses between the nymphs and shepherds in act I. More recently, Eric Chafe has shown the careful and logical way in which tonality is used both in terms of overall organization and in expressing the allegorical meaning of the drama. The dramatic tonal juxtapositions that occur in moments of rapidly shifting emotion—as in the messenger's announcement of Euridice's death—are not only localized effects, but rather can logically be accounted for within a rational tonal system that Monteverdi carefully employed in this work and explored in his contemporaneous madrigal composition.

In his musical characterization of the allegorical, somewhat two-dimensional Orfeo, Monteverdi provides only a glimpse of the psychological depth and human insight that was to mark the characters in his later operas. In the surviving fragment from the opera *Arianna,* written the following year, Monteverdi uses the monodic style to trace the various stages of Arianna's reaction to her abandonment by Theseus. Closely mirroring the intricacies of the text, Monteverdi sensitively evokes Arianna's despair, disbelief, hope, and anger. Yet the entire lament is musically unified by the repetitions of her obsessive cries for death, poignantly set with a striking chromaticism that has since become inseparable from the idea of lament.

In his latter two operas, Monteverdi also succeeds in creating characters with profoundly human depth; nevertheless, these works differ sharply from the earlier operas in musical and rhetorical style as well as in meaning. Undoubtedly, some of this is a result of the cultural and aesthetic climate in which they were produced. No longer employed by the Gonzaga family of Mantua, Monteverdi was now writing for the relatively new and successful public opera theater in Venice. Some of the striking peculiarities of these works thus reflect the intellectual leanings of those involved in Venetian opera production during its early decades. Both of the librettists for Monteverdi's late operas, Giacomo Badoaro and Gian Francesco Busenello, were members of the Accademia degli Incogniti, a group whose libertine and skeptical brand of philosophy was adopted by much of the noble intelligentsia of Venice. Opera librettos were but a small portion of their literary output, yet it is evident that these works reflect in some ways the numerous Incogniti discussions on love, women, virtue, death, and the survival of the flesh. As Ellen Rosand has pointed out, *Il ritorno d' Ulisse,* with its demonstration of the victory of virtuous love, and *L'incoronazione di Poppea,* with its celebration of illicit, passionate love, can be viewed as representing two sides of an Incogniti debate.

Neither the skepticism nor the intellectual leanings of these librettists interfered with Monteverdi's ability to infuse his characters with extraordinary humanity. Notably, among his contemporaries only Monteverdi chose to reshape portions of his librettos so as to alter their musical or dramatic implications. This is particularly evident in *Il ritorno d'Ulisse,* where the librettist Badoaro provided Monteverdi with mostly recitative poetry, with few strophic texts or other explicit indications for lyricism. In Penelope's opening lament, for example, Monteverdi rearranged the text in a manner that was not only more compelling dramatically—capturing

Penelope's shifting moods as she longed for Ulisse's return—but also more musically coherent. Penelope's repeated lyrical plea for Ulisse's safe return, with its haunting melody and surprising tonal shifts, not only provides contrast from the recitative and bestows musical unity on the lengthy monologue, but also appropriately reflects Penelope's obsessive devotion to Ulisse, despite his continued absence. As Rosand has shown in her discussion of Iro, the *parte ridicolo* in *Il ritorno d' Ulisse*—whose expanded role in this libretto was librettist Badoaro's only significant departure from Homer—Monteverdi uses an extreme sort of musical imitation that captures and yet exaggerates the essence of each word, distorting the musical surface so as to realize Iro's amusing but highly disturbing craving for nourishment that precipitates his suicide.

It is precisely this kind of musical imitation, employed with such opposite results in Penelope's lament and Iro's suicide, that Monteverdi used to such advantage in his masterpiece, *L'incoronazione di Poppea.* These characters bear little resemblance to the allegorical Orfeo or the heroically lamentful Arianna. They are complex combinations of conflicting emotions and motivations, yet their depth is made explicit through Monteverdi's musical realizations. The listener may sympathize with the unfortunate predicament of Nero's abandoned wife Ottavia, but it is not solely on account of her murderous actions that she ultimately fails to inspire compassion. In Ottavia's act I monologue, Monteverdi uses a terse, somewhat angular recitative for her denouncement of women's fate and their victimization by men, moving easily into a strained lyricism as she visualizes Nero and Poppea's passion, then briefly employing the *guerriero* style in a futile gesture of anger as she decries Jove's impotence—and her own. The starkness of Ottavia's music is directly in contrast to the seductive, voluptuous nature of Poppea's music. In the first of Nero and Poppea's exquisite duets, for example, Monteverdi empowers Poppea with languid lyric gesture, seductive virtuosity, and tonal control that infuse the spent Nero with new passion and thus extract from him the first of several promises that ultimately lead to her coronation. Above all, it is Poppea's music that urges the listeners to abandon their moral reservations and rejoice with her in the triumph of love over virtue.

The complicated state of the surviving sources as well as some of their notational anomalies, noted most recently by Alan Curtis, have called into question the authorship of portions of *L'incoronazione di Poppea,* including the popular and highly sensuous final duet. Some commentators, however, have argued that the uniformity of features such as text setting, tonal style, melodic writing, and the application of musical devices from the madrigal tradition, still point to Monteverdi's authorship for much of the opera. While it is likely that these questions will never be definitively solved, the unique and subtle musical realizations of the characters throughout this opera would seem at the very least to argue for Monteverdi's guiding spirit in the creation of this masterwork.—WENDY HELLER

Moore, Douglas Stuart

Composer. Born 10 August 1893, in Cutchogue, New York. Died 25 July 1969, in Greenport, Long Island, New York. Studied with D.S. Smith and Horatio Parker at Yale University; B.A., 1915, and Mus. Bac., 1917, from Yale; in the United States Navy, 1917-18; studied with Vincent d'Indy at the Schola Cantorum in Paris; studied organ with Tournemire and composition with Nadia Boulanger in Paris; studied with Ernest Bloch in Cleveland, upon his return to the United States; organist at the Cleveland Museum of Art, 1921-23, and at Adelbert College, Western Reserve University, 1923-25; in Europe on a

Pulitzer traveling scholarship, 1925; on the faculty of Columbia University, 1926; succeeded Daniel Gregory Mason as the head of the Columbia music department, 1940; honorable mention by the New York Music Critic's Circle for his Symphony in A, 1947; Pulitzer Prize for Giants in the Earth, *1951; retired, 1962.*

Operas *Jesse James,* J.M. Brown, 1928 [unfinished]; *White Wings* (chamber opera), Philip Barry, 1935, Hartford, Connecticut, 9 February 1949; *The Headless Horseman* (high-school opera), S.V. Benét (after W. Irving, *A Legend of Sleepy Hollow*), 1936, Bronxville, New York, 4 March 1937; *The Devil and Daniel Webster,* S.V. Benét, 1938, New York, 18 May 1939; *The Emperor's New Clothes* (children's opera), R. Abrashkin (after Hans Christian Andersen), 1948, New York, 19 February 1949; revised 1956; *Giants in the Earth,* Arnold Sundgaard (after O.E. Rølvaag), 1949, New York, 28 March 1951; revised, 1963; *Puss in Boots* (children's operetta), R. Abrashkin (after C. Perrault), 1949, New York, 18 November 1950; *Ballad of Baby Doe* (folk opera), J. Latouche, 1956, Central City, Colorado, 7 July 1958; *Gallantry* ("soap opera"), A. Sundgaard, 1957, New York, 19 March 1958; *The Wings of the Dove,* E. Ayer (after H. James), 1961, New York, 12 October 1961; *The Greenfield Christmas Tree,* A. Sundgaard, 1962, Baltimore, 8 December 1962; *Carry Nation,* W.N. Jayme, 1966, Lawrence, Kansas, 28 April 1966.

Although Douglas Moore wrote a number of songs and purely instrumental pieces, opera was his primary concern. His creative impulses, like those of any successful opera composer, overflowed the confines of the strictly musical. A friend of Moore's, Jack Beeson, who is himself an opera composer, has succinctly described what his longtime colleague aimed for: "Moore's expressive intent was clear and unequivocal from early on: to write for the voice- and stage-dominated musical theater, using subject matter from his country's past."

Moore's sense of the American past might have reached back, through an awareness of his family history, to colonial settlements of the 1640s, but his operatic imagination was chiefly drawn to the time of his youth or, more expansively, to the nineteenth century. Within these limits his dramatic subjects have a considerable range. Sometimes his librettos have a factual basis for their stories (*The Ballad of Baby Doe, Carry Nation*); sometimes they are derived from substantial literary sources (Washington Irving, Henry James, O.E. Rølvaag, Stephen Vincent Benét). Their characters may face hardscrabble pioneer problems (*Giants in the Earth*) or, again, intrigues arising in the European world of deracinated Americans (*The Wings of the Dove*). Where the characters are unsophisticated, the homespun aspects of early American life are occasionally celebrated in an almost patronizing fashion. (Exceptionally, *Gallantry,* a short "soap opera," has not only a contemporary setting but also an openly parodistic tone.)

If Moore's librettos have plots and characters that are designed to be readily understood by audiences, even to be familiar to them, so too the musical layout of his operas builds upon the expectations of the seasoned operagoer. When John Houseman, the earliest director of *The Devil and Daniel Webster,* first heard Moore's score, he thought it "effective, melodious and conventional." This response could not have been unanticipated by so knowledgeable a composer as Moore. In fact, the music in his operas is effective in large part because it is melodious and relies firmly on operatic conventions. Love duets, ensembles of perplexity, mad songs, letter arias, the use of onstage music, and melodrama (as when the characters in *The Devil and Daniel Webster* speak over musical accompaniment)—such are the resources Moore tellingly exploits. By means of well-calculated arrangements of parlando passages, full-scale solo numbers and ensembles, and choruses, he and his librettists rework the standard opera components.

The style of Moore's music fits both his American themes and his traditional approach to operatic drama. One of its wellsprings is American popular and folk music in its broadest sense, including hymn tunes, dances, marches, and sentimental ballads. This gives his melodic writing a strong diatonic, at times even a pentatonic foundation. At the same time, the way in which a dramatic scene will emerge from preparatory parlando moments suggests especially nineteenth century Italian opera. *The Wings of the Dove* in particular seems to adapt Verdian techniques. But Moore seldom attempts elaborate or novel musical procedures, and he makes no extraordinary demands on the performers. Not the Metropolitan Opera House but opera workshops and regional opera companies are his most likely venues. Works with spoken dialogue (e.g., *The Headless Horseman*) are destined for this end.

Moore had been trained by gifted teachers—Horatio Parker, Nadia Boulanger, Vincent d'Indy, and Ernest Bloch—and the very breadth of his education may have helped him to stand apart from the various schools of modern music that flourished during his lifetime. He evidently reacted to modernism with a resistance such as was fairly common in American and English artistic circles of his day. For Moore the goal of being American transcended that of being modern. Yet he made his peace with twentieth-century trends; in 1926, years before his first opera, he wrote that he would "try to combine a reasonable modernity with attention to melody." Although this statement referred to a specific work he then had in mind, it evokes his musical style in general. Perhaps today, when twentieth-century modernism in all the arts is being re-evaluated, Moore's operas, well grounded in musical tradition and faithful to their national origin, deserve renewed respect.—CHRISTOPHER HATCH

Moore, Grace

Soprano. Born 5 December 1898, in Nough, Tennessee. Died 26 January 1947, in airplane crash near Copenhagen. Studied with Marafioti in New York; appeared in musical comedy and operetta in New York, 1921-26; worked with Richard Berthélemy in Antibes; Metropolitan Opera debut as Mimi, 1928, and sang there until 1946; Opéra-Comique debut, 1928; appeared at Covent Garden as Mimi, 1935; her many films include One Night of Love, *1934.*

Although she appeared with other opera companies, New York's Metropolitan Opera was Grace Moore's home. During her career there, which began with a much publicized debut in 1928, until her tragic death in 1947, she had, at one time or another, soprano colleagues Lucrezia Bori, Amelita Galli-Curci, Rosa Ponselle, Elisabeth Rethberg, Claudia Muzio, Kirsten Flagstad, Lily Pons, Helen Traubel, Zinka Milanov, Bidu Sayao, Licia Albanese, Eleanor Steber and her protégé, Dorothy Kirsten, among others. Considering the vocal riches which surrounded her, the fact that an ex-Broadway review headliner such as Moore could not only reach the stage of one of the world's most important opera houses but become one of its reigning stars is almost miraculous. In comparison with some others, her voice was not exceptional, but her charisma was. She could charm an audience into total and complete submission as easily as she could change outfits.

Grace Moore had an effervescence which was almost palpable. With her blond hair and her radiant smile she literally glowed. In addition, she had a voice of good size and texture. By the time she reached her third film and greatest success, *One Night of Love,* she was a very good actress. In Abel Gance's cinematic version of Charpentier's *Louise,* Moore had the good fortune to leave a lasting record of a role which is closely identified with her. Although she is not at her best vocally, she brings Louise to life in an appealing way and captures the essence of a young woman in love with love. Her acting abilities carried over into the opera house, but there she was called "stagey" more often than not—a complaint leveled a generation earlier against Geraldine Farrar. The "stigma" of Hollywood is hard to erase and Moore was thought by some to be too much the celebrity to be taken seriously as a classical artist. It is easy to fall into that trap when dealing with someone who carved out for herself a career which encompassed Broadway, opera, Hollywood, radio, recordings, recitals, concerts and war relief tours, the last of which took up as much of her time and energy as all of the rest combined. The fact that must not be overlooked is that she was a singer long before she was anything else. Her voice was a trained lyric soprano, at first, more suitable for musicals, but eventually through study and determination, an instrument quite capable of performing opera. Her recordings, while not vast, attest to this. Arias from *La bohème, Louise, Manon, Hérodiade* and *Tosca* are very expertly executed in a voice of agreeable timbre and sizeable range. The song literature is, as one would expect, where Moore shines best—not so much in the classic songs of Hahn or Duparc, which are rendered with great respect but little insight or attention to the fine points of French pronunciation, but in the semi-classical songs, especially "One Night of Love," "Ciribiribin," and, particularly "The Dubarry," from a show she starred in while on sabbatical from opera. There is enough evidence that her vocal production was erratic at times, most notably in intonation. In others this would have been a decided handicap, but in Moore it only seems to add to her glamour. "Glamour" is the key word here, for Moore personified it as much as her illustrious contemporaries Gertrude Lawrence and Carol Lombard. In the final analysis, it can be said that Grace Moore became an opera star not because of all she had going for her but in spite of it.—JOHN PENNINO

Morris, James

Bass-baritone. Born 10 January 1947, in Baltimore. Studied with Frank Valentino at Peabody Conservatory, Nicola Moscona and Anton Guadagno; debut as Crespel in Les contes d'Hoffman, *Baltimore Civic Opera, 1968; Metropolitan Opera debut as King in* Aida, *1971, where he sang Don Giovanni in 1975; appeared widely in Europe; appeared as Wotan in* Die Walküre *in San Francisco, 1985.*

"A new super god . . . a Wotan of today and tomorrow," proclaimed the Vienna *Kronen Zeitung* upon the 1984 debut of James Morris at the Vienna State Opera in Wagner's *Die Walküre*—the American bass-baritone's first Wagnerian performance before a German-speaking audience. This and other laudatory reviews in Europe and the Americas have enabled Morris to take his place with such American-born predecessors as Clarence Whitehill, George London, and Jerome Hines among world-class Wagnerian interpreters.

Born in Baltimore, Maryland, on 10 January 1947, James Morris began his vocal studies as a teenager with a local teacher, Forrest Barrett. Upon graduating from high school Morris competed successfully for the first voice scholarship ever awarded by the University of Maryland; but, on the subsequent advice of soprano Rosa Ponselle, he completed his vocal studies at the Peabody Conservatory of Music under the tutelage of former Metropolitan Opera baritone Frank Valentino.

Although Rosa Ponselle is often cited as being Morris' first professional teacher (some sources, in fact, indicate that she came out of retirement in order to teach him), Ponselle in her memoirs (1982) wrote that although she "could hear the promise in [his] voice . . . I didn't feel I could take the responsibility for shaping his talents." After working with Morris in individual and group coaching sessions for a few months, Ponselle, with Valentino's concurrence, referred him to Metropolitan basso Nicola Moscona, with whom Morris studied for three years at Philadelphia's Academy of Vocal Arts. Still, the influence of Rosa Ponselle—to whom Morris was nominally related by marriage, from the maternal side of his family—did exert a lasting influence on his interpretive approach with new roles, instilling in him the necessity of "singing with your heart and emotion," as he expressed it.

Under Ponselle's artistic direction at the Baltimore Civic Opera Company, Morris sang comprimario roles in *La bohème, La forza del destino, Gianni Schicchi, La traviata* and other staples, in time advancing to Ramfis in *Aida,* the villains in *Les contes d'Hoffman,* and eventually to important roles in *Il barbiere di Siviglia, Rigoletto, Tosca,* and *Don Giovanni.* Morris' debut with the Baltimore Opera was as Crespel in *Hoffmann* (1968), which he sang opposite the Antonia of Beverly Sills, who also had coached under Ponselle.

In early November of 1970, at age twenty-three, Morris was given a Metropolitan Opera audition, which resulted in an invitation to join the company's Opera Studio. Morris declined the invitation, preferring instead to compete for a full-fledged contract at some later time. Through Moscona's influence, augmented by that of the Hurok agency (with whom Morris had recently signed as a client), a second Metropolitan audition was arranged; Rudolf Bing, then General Manager, was present. This second audition yielded an offer of a contract—which, when Morris accepted it, made him the youngest male singer ever engaged by the Metropolitan Opera.

After four seasons of singing smaller "character" parts (the Friar in *Don Carlos,* the Marquis in *Forza del destino,* Monterone in *Rigoletto*), Morris' self-described "longing for a real role" was partially satisfied when he was offered Timur in the Metropolitan production of *Turandot* (1974). Lacking many other opportunities for better roles at the Metropolitan, he accepted off-season engagements during the early 1970s with the Houston Grand Opera Company, the Philadelphia Lyric Opera, the Santa Fe Opera, and the Cincinnati Summer Opera. Other appearances in concertized operas produced by the Opera Orchestra of New York (including *Guillaume Tell,* 1972; Donizetti's *Parisina d'Este* and *Lucia,* 1974; and *Semiramide,* 1976) enabled Morris to expand both his repertoire and his ensemble experience.

In 1976, under the aegis of Rosa Ponselle and Tito Capobianco, Morris returned to the Baltimore Opera to create the role of King Alfonso in the world premiere of Pasatieri's *Ines de Castro.* The following year, under the direction of Richard Bonynge, he created the role of Timur in the centenary revival of Massenet's *Le roi de Lahore.* But it was midway through the 1975-76 Metropolitan season that Morris achieved the greatest critical acclaim of his career up to that time: with only a few days' notice he replaced baritone Roger Soyer as Don Giovanni, also singing the role in that season's PBS "Live from the Met" telecast. It became one of the finest achievements of his career.

Having diversified his growing repertoire in challenging French and Italian roles, Morris prepared the role of Wotan in *Die Walküre* with Hans Hotter, generally considered the foremost

Wotan of his time. Morris again returned to the Baltimore Opera for his first Wotan, and then followed it with a highly-praised Dutchman (also prepared under Hotter) at the Houston Grand Opera (1984). Morris' much-acclaimed Vienna State Opera debut as Wotan took place shortly afterward. The following year, when he appeared as Wotan in the San Francisco Opera Company's complete *Ring* cycle, he was judged "the greatest Wotan . . . since Hotter" (Arthur Bloomfield), and "a Wagnerian of the very first rank" (Paul Moor). Subsequent *Ring* performances at the Munich State Opera yielded the same enthusiastic responses from the critics.

Especially with Joan Sutherland, under the baton of Richard Bonynge, James Morris has made a number of well-received opera recordings, including *Maria Stuarda, Roi de Lahore,* Thomas' *Hamlet,* and Gay's *The Beggar's Opera,* all on the Decca/London label. He has also recorded *Così fan tutte* (under Riccardo Muti) and Haydn's *Die Schöpfung* (under Sir Georg Solti) in recent years. In all of his commercial recordings, Morris' pure *basso cantante* sound—dark in color, sonorous, impressively ductile, baritonal in range, and complemented by a profound musicality and artistic sensitivity—has been captured fully for contemporary audiences and, as his career continues at its zenith, for posterity as well.—JAMES A. DRAKE

Mosè in Egitto [Moses in Egypt]

Composer: *Gioachino Rossini.*

Librettist: *A.L. Tottola (after F. Ringhierei, L'Osiride).*

First Performance: *Naples, San Carlo, 5 March 1818; revised as Moïse et Pharaon, Paris, 26 March 1827.*

Roles: *Pharaoh (bass); Amaltea (soprano); Osiris (tenor); Elcia (soprano); Mambre (tenor); Moses (bass); Aaron (tenor); Amenophis (mezzo-soprano).*

Mosè in Egitto is an opera designed to circumvent the ecclesiastical prohibition of opera performances during Lent; thus it has a biblical subject and proclaims itself an *"azione tragico-sacra"* (tragico-sacred action). In terms of plot it is very much a standard operatic love story, set in an exotic place and a remote time, with only the outlines of the Exodus account to get it past the censors.

In a stunning opening, Rossini reduces the overture to the briefest introduction in which the orchestra strikes the pitch "C" three times; on a dark stage the chorus laments in C minor until a change of key to C major signals the end of the plague and the return of light. Although Pharaoh has granted Moses permission to take the Israelites out of Egypt, the crown prince Osiris induces his father to change his mind, for Osiris is secretly married to Elcia, a Hebrew woman, whom he does not want to lose.

A plague of hailstones and fiery rain convinces Pharaoh to let the Israelites go, but again, influenced by his court, he revokes his permission and Moses threatens the death of Osiris and the other Egyptian first-born at God's hand. Although Osiris and Elcia attempted to hide, they have been discovered. Moses and Elcia are brought before Pharaoh and Osiris. Elcia reveals her marriage to Osiris and offers herself in return for her people's freedom. Osiris raises his sword to kill Moses but lightning from heaven strikes him down. In the final act, Moses and the Israelites, after praying for God's help, cross the Red Sea, but the pursuing Egyptian army drowns.

The music Rossini provided for the lovers is no different in style from that of his secular serious operas, but he treats the biblical elements of the story in a more majestic, oratorical way. Large ensembles and choral movements figure prominently, and the music for Moses himself is largely declamatory in nature. His well-known prayer, "Dal tuo stellato soglio" (From your starry throne), was not part of the original version: the staging of the crossing of the Red Sea so amused the audience that Rossini revised the third act the following year, adding this number.

In 1827 Rossini revised the entire opera for Paris, where it was presented on 26 March 1827 as *Moïse et Pharaon, ou Le Passage de la Mer Rouge* (*Moses and Pharaoh, or The Passage through the Red Sea*). The three-act libretto was expanded into the typical French four-act version by Luigi Balocchi and Etienne de Jouy. In addition to providing French texts for the Italian numbers, they created dramatic situations for additional pieces. An entirely new first scene was created in which the Israelites await the return of Moses' brother, who has gone to plead their cause with Pharaoh. Act II begins with the original opening of the plague of darkness. Aménophis (Osiris) is not yet married to Anaï (Elcia), and the queen persuades her son to agree to marry an Assyrian princess. The third act has an extended ballet performed in the Temple of Isis. When the Israelites refuse to worship the goddess, Pharaoh orders them expelled from Egypt. In the last act Aménophis, offering to give up the throne, asks Anaï to marry him, but she refuses to leave her people. Aménophis then joins his father in leading the doomed Egyptian army into the Red Sea.

The new music Rossini composed is admirable, although the added French spectacle weakens the drama. The best music from *Mosè in Egitto* was kept, while some which by then might have been considered old-fashioned was eliminated. Rossini's re-use of pieces from the first version in new dramatic contexts illustrates that his music is not intended to imitate specific emotions. For example, in an aria in *Mosè in Egitto* Elcia pleads with Osiris to marry a princess and allow her to leave with the Israelites; Osiris is killed, and Elcia expresses her grief in the cabaletta. In *Moïse et Pharaon* the aria is sung by Osiris' mother, the queen, who begs him to marry a princess and then in the cabaletta expresses her joy at his capitulation.—PATRICIA BRAUNER

Moses und Aron [Moses and Aaron]

Composer: *Arnold Schoenberg.*

Librettist: *Arnold Schoenberg (based on the Old Testament).*

First Performance: *partial performance [act III was never composed], Darmstadt, 2 July 1951; concert performance of acts I and II, Hamburg, 12 March 1954; staged performance of acts I and II, Zurich, Stadttheater, 6 June 1957.*

Roles: *Moses (bass-baritone); Aron (tenor); Young Maiden (soprano); Female Invalid (contralto); Young Man (tenor); Naked Youth (tenor); Man (baritone); Ephraimite (baritone); Priest (bass); Four Naked Virgins (sopranos, contraltos); Voice from Burning Bush (soprano, boy sopranos, contralto, tenor, baritone, bass); chorus (SSAATTBB).*

Operas are usually concerned with love, in its comic or tragic aspects, or they are about intrigue or revenge; there are also political operas, satires, national epics, magical fantasies. Only Schoenberg could have conceived of writing an opera about the incommunicability of the nature of God. This is the philosophical core of *Moses und Aron;* but since it is a representation of the effect of that incommunicability on ordinary human beings—those wracked with the reality of it, and those unable to grasp it—the opera is also, paradoxically, the most dramatic work Schoenberg ever wrote, and one which has always "communicated" to its audiences with astonishing power.

Of the two acts for which Schoenberg actually composed the music, the first opens with Moses before the Burning Bush, receiving the Word of God. Subsequent scenes establish his relationship with his brother Aron, who eagerly accepts the role of priest and interpreter of Moses' vision in order to bring a finite political good—liberation from the power of Pharaoh—to the people of Israel, although to Moses this is a cheapening of the sacred Idea of God. They attempt to bring God's message to the fickle and sceptical people, who are only convinced when Aron performs three miracles: curing Moses' leprous hand, transforming the rod into a serpent, and turning Nile water into blood (the last symbolizing liberation from Egypt)—all of which further distort the essence of Moses' insight. Encouraged by these signs of a God "more powerful than Pharaoh's gods," the Israelites prepare to follow the brothers on the quest for the Promised Land.

In act II the people are encamped in the desert, alarmed by Moses' long absence on the mountain of revelation. They demand of Aron a new and visible god like those of the surrounding tribes, and he eventually acquiesces in the creation of the Golden Calf. This leads to a huge communal orgy. Moses returns from the mountain bearing the Tables of the Law, and destroys the Calf in fury. But Aron defends himself, claiming the Tables are themselves a symbol, and yet another, the Pillar of Fire, appears to lead the Israelites onward. The music concludes with Moses' anguished monologue: "I too have fashioned an image, false, as an image must be . . . O word, thou word, that I lack!"

Moses und Aron can be seen to develop the dramatic themes of Schoenberg's (unper-formed) stage-play *Der biblische Weg* (The Biblical Way) of 1927. Set in the contemporary world, this concerns an attempt to establish a Jewish homeland in Africa; the protagonist, Max Aruns, embodies within himself the conflicting forces of idealism and compromise that in the opera are separated out into the opposing characters of Moses and his brother. *Moses und Aron* was originally conceived as an oratorio, and goes back to the Book of Exodus and the original search for the Promised Land, which Schoenberg parallels with Moses' endeavour to forge the Israelites into a people dedicated to spiritual truth, to the "Only, infinite, omnipresent, unperceived and inconceivable God." In fact Moses also fails, for while his people are liberated from Egypt, they are not liberated from their craving for the symbols of nationhood. Despite—perhaps even because of—Schoenberg's inability to write the music for the brief, epilogue-like last act, which would have depicted Aron's death and Moses' triumph, the opera as it stands embodies a complete artistic design, which achieves its expressive purpose with unerring theatrical instinct. It is also the largest work Schoenberg ever composed according to the twelve-note method: its enormous variety of music derives from a single note-row (inhabiting the fabric of the opera like the "omnipresent and unperceived" God), and it exemplifies the entire range of his compositional mastery.

The core of the drama is implicit in the title: the contrasting mentalities of the two brothers, the prophet and the priest. All the other characters are merely representative figures from the Israelites, who are embodied *en masse* by the chorus. In a brilliantly effective stroke of operatic pathos, Schoenberg makes Moses—the only one who receives God's word, whose mind can encompass the spiritual reality—literally unable to sing. His part, notated throughout in a halting, uncouth *Sprechstimme* (Speech-song), cuts easily through the densest ensembles, yet it

545

presents a man laboring under an immense interior burden. Moses therefore desperately *needs* Aron to get his message across, in words, which inevitably shackle and limit the force of the underlying idea; and for Aron, a golden-voiced lyric tenor, Schoenberg has composed some of the most seductive vocal lines in twelve-note music.

Indeed, for all the austerity of its philosophical message, *Moses und Aron* is probably the richest of all Schoenberg's works in sheer sonic invention, ranging from the mysterious disembodied glow of the Burning Bush (six solo voices doubled by six solo instruments), through the extreme complexity and layering of the massed choral sections, to the frenzied orgy-music of the Dances Round the Golden Calf—a kind of five-movement dance-symphony which ranks as one of his most staggering orchestral showpieces. Even this, however, is surpassed by the harrowing tragic grandeur of Moses' final monologue, accompanied only by a magnificently elegiac monody in the violins. Here, perhaps, Schoenberg gives us his self-portrait, as a prophet of musical truths which are always obscured through others' fascination with mere technical details: "how it is *done*," as he once wrote, "whereas I have always helped people to see: what it *is!*"—MALCOLM MACDONALD

The Mother of Us All

Composer: *Virgil Thomson.*

Librettist: *Gertrude Stein.*

First Performance: *New York, 7 May 1947.*

Roles: *Susan B. Anthony (soprano); Anne (contralto); Daniel Webster (bass); Constance Fletcher (mezzo-soprano); John Adams (tenor); Jo the Loiterer (tenor); Gertrude S., the Narrator (soprano); Virgil T., the Master of Ceremonies (baritone); Indiana Elliot (contralto); Angel More (soprano); Chris the Citizen (baritone); Andrew Johnson (tenor); Thaddeus Stevens (tenor); Lillian Russell (soprano); Ulysses S. Grant (bass-baritone); Anthony Comstock (bass); Jenny Reefer (mezzo-soprano); Anna Hope (contralto); Herman Atlan (baritone); Donald Gallup (baritone); Gloster Heming (baritone); Isabella Wentworth (mezzo-soprano); Henrietta M. (soprano); Henry B. (bass-baritone); Indiana Elliot's Brother (bass-baritone); Negro Man (speaking); Negro Woman (speaking); chorus (TTAA); chorus (SATB).*

After the scandalous success of their first opera, *Four Saints in Three Acts* in 1934, one might have expected that fellow expatriates in Paris Virgil Thomson and writer Gertrude Stein would continue their fruitful association, bringing forth one unusual and evocative opera after another. However, the two suffered a falling out over financial matters. Thomson continued to compose and write prolifically, but he no longer set Stein's off-beat melodious words. When World War II broke out, Stein remained in Europe, but Thomson returned to the U.S.A. in 1940, where he took up the post of music critic for the *New York Herald Tribune*. The two were not at work on an opera again until 1945, when Thomson returned to Paris for a time. He had a commission for an opera in hand and a deep interest in working on a subject from nineteenth-century American history. Stein leaped at the topic, chose Susan B. Anthony, leader of the women's suffrage movement, for her protagonist, and finished the libretto in March of 1946, just four months before her death.

The Mother of Us All is another Stein fantasy, this time centering on feminism and calling up such figures as John Adams, Daniel Webster, Ulysses S. Grant, and Lillian Russell. Even the characters Virgil Thomson and Gertrude Stein appear as narrators. Lacking a hard-and-fast plot per se, the work explores personalities and issues through boldly-drawn characters and their vivid words. Much of the time these figures do not seem to be speaking or listening to each other. With her usual liberating and liberated abandon, Stein ignores the conventions of chronology and conversation. These larger-than-life characters, even when they engage in stichomythia, often appear isolated and unable to connect emotionally. Speeches are made but communication is rare. Still there is a sense of progression through the scenes which include a political rally, a wedding, and several vignettes of Susan B. Anthony at home with her companion Anne. Quite moving is the final scene, the unveiling in the halls of Congress of a statue of Anthony some years after her death. An epilogue is delivered by the statue itself which sings of Anthony's "long life of effort and strife." The statue is at last left standing alone singing before a slow curtain fall.

Thomson's score is a brilliant nostalgic confusion of musical Americana. Echoing the flavor but never the exact melodies of popular parlor tunes, gospel and folk songs, maudlin ballads, and street bands, among others, Thomson deftly weaves the familiar, the trite, and the conventional in fresh, amusing, and evocative ways. In his autobiography Thomson himself described the harmonies as "plain-as-Dick's-hatband," but plain does not always mean simple or simplistic. Thomson's characteristic attention to instrumental texture and to the delicate interplay between voice and orchestra, and his marvelous ear for declamation and musical meaning shine through luminously here. The score of *The Mother of Us All* is by turns, amusing and poignant, but it is always well-wrought.

The premiere in 1947, with its student orchestra and blend of professional and amateur singers, was not a roaring success, but the work did receive acclaim. The Music Critics' Circle honored it with a special award. In 1949 Thomson arranged a suite for orchestra from *The Mother of Us All* which, brushing aside Stein's animating poetry, lacks the punch and appeal of the original work. This only serves as proof that the union of word and music in the work is miraculously robust, apt, and indissoluble. Thomson and Stein, both violent individualists, were a remarkable duo indeed.—MICHAEL MECKNA

Mozart, Wolfgang Amadeus

Composer. Born 27 January 1756, in Salzburg. Died 5 December 1791, in Vienna. Married: Constanze Weber, 4 August 1782. Studied with his father from a very early age; performed with his sister for the Elector of Bavaria, 17 January 1762, for Emperor Francis I at his palace in Vienna, September 1762, for Louis XV of France and Marie Antoinette, 1 January 1764, and for King George III of England, 1764; studied and performed with Johann Christian Bach in London; composed symphonies for performance in London; visited the Netherlands, Dijon, Lyons, Geneva, Bern, Zurich, Donaueschingen, and Munich on the way back to Salzburg, 1766; in Vienna, 1768, where he studied counterpoint with his father and worked on the opera La finta semplice; *performance of his* Missa solemnis *in C minor for the royal family and court at the consecration of the Waisenhauskirche, 7 December 1768; Konzertmeister to Archbishop Sigismund von Schrattenbach in Salzburg, October, 1769; tour of Italy, 1770; elected to the Accademia*

Filarmonica in Bologna; made a Knight of the Golden Spur by the Pope, 1770; directed performances of his works in Milan, Salzburg, Vienna, and Paris, 1770-78; court organist in Salzburg, 1779; Idomeneo *commissioned by the Elector of Bavaria, 1780; lost his position with the Archbishop in Salzburg, and moved to Vienna, 1781; joined the Masonic Order in Vienna, 1784; string quartets dedicated to Haydn, 1785; succeeded Gluck as Kammermusicus in Vienna, 1787; three last symphonies composed, 1788; performed as soloist in one of his piano concertos for the Elector of Saxony in Dresden, 1789; performed at the court of King Friedrich Wilhelm II, Berlin, 1789; in Frankfurt for the coronation of Emperor Leopold II, 1790; completed the score of* Die Zauberflöte, *1791.*

Operas *Apollo et Hyacinthus* (intermezzo to *Clementia Croesi*), P.F. Widl? Salzburg, University, 13 May 1767; *La finta semplice,* Marco Coltellini (after Goldoni), 1768, written for Vienna, performed Salzburg. Archbishop's palace, 1 May 1769; *Bastien und Bastienne* (Singspiel), Friedrich Wilhelm Weiskern and J.A. Schachtner (after J.J. Rousseau, *Le devin du village,* and C.S. Favart, *Les amours de Bastien et Bastienne*), Dr. F. Anton Mesmer's garden theater, September/October? 1768; *Mitridate, rè di Ponto,* Vittorio Amadeo Cigna-Santi (after Giuseppe Parini and Racine), Milan, Teatro Regio Ducal, 26 December 1770; *Ascanio in Alba* (festa teatrale), Giuseppe Parini, Milan, Teatro Regio Ducal, 17 October 1771; *Il sogno di Scipione* (serenata), Metastasio, Salzburg, Archbishop's palace, c. May 1772; *Lucio Silla,* Giovanni de Gamerra, Milan, Teatro Regio Ducal, 26 December 1772; *La finta giardiniera,* Ranieri Calzabigi? (revised Coltellini), Munich, Assembly Rooms, 13 January 1775; *Il rè pastore,* after Metastasio, Salzburg, Archbishop's palace, 23 April 1775; *Semiramide* (melodrama), O. von Gemmingen [lost or projected]; *Thamos, König von Ägypten* (play with music), T.P. Gebler, Salzburg, 1776-79; *Zaide* (Singspiel), Johann Andreas Schachtner (after F.J. Sebastiani, *Das Serail?*), 1779-80 [unfinished]; *Idomeneo, Rè di Creta,* Giambattista Varesco (after Danchet, *Idoménée*), Munich, Hoftheater, 29 January 1781; *Die Entführung aus dem Serail* (Singspiel), J. Gottlieb Stephanie, Jr (after C.F. Bretzner, *Belmonte und Constanze*), Vienna, Burgtheater, 16 July 1782; *L' oca del Cairo,* Giambattista Varesco, 1783 [unfinished]; *Lo sposo deluso,* Lorenzo Da Ponte?, 1783 [unfinished]; *Der Schauspieldirektor,* J. Gottlieb Stephanie, Jr, 1786, Vienna, Schönbrunn Palace, Orangery, 7 February 1786; *Le nozze di Figaro,* Lorenzo Da Ponte (after Beaumarchais), Vienna, Burgtheater, 1 May 1786; *Il dissoluto punito, ossia Il Don Giovanni,* Lorenzo Da Ponte, Prague, National Theater, 29 October 1787; *Così fan tutte, ossia La scuola degli amanti,* Lorenzo Da Ponte, Vienna, Burgtheater, 26 January 1790; *La clemenza di Tito,* Caterino Mazzolà (after Metastasio), Prague, National Theater, 6 September 1791; *Die Zauberflöte,* Emanuel Schikaneder, Vienna, Theater auf der Wieden, 30 September 1791.

Mozart's career as an opera composer spanned over two decades, from *Apollo et Hyacinthus* in 1767 to *La clemenza di Tito* in 1791. He composed works in most of the major operatic genres of his day—including *opera seria, opera buffa,* and Singspiel—and received commissions from diverse institutions, including the Archbishop's court in Salzburg, the ducal court in Milan, the Electoral court in Munich, the imperial court in Vienna, the Prague National Theater, and the private theater of Emanuel Schikaneder. Throughout his career Mozart demonstrated remarkable mastery of the styles and conventions popular at the time, but he regularly pushed the conventions to fit with new ideas of his own. His later works reveal the confident hand of a master dramatist balancing aria and ensemble, voice and orchestra, sectional form and through-composed rhetoric, melodic inventiveness and motivic development. But his earlier works, too, often demonstrate adaptation rather than wholesale adoption of established styles.

Mozart's first experience in setting dramatic texts to music came in 1765-66 in London and The Hague, where he set some fifteen individual aria texts to music in a typical *opera seria* style. Work on a longer span of opera came in 1767 when Mozart composed *Apollo et Hyacinthus,* a Latin intermezzo performed between the acts of a Latin play. Drawing on a conservative Baroque style in keeping with the Salzburg practice of the period, Mozart demonstrated precocious inventiveness in both the vocal and accompanimental parts.

While spending almost a year in Vienna in 1768 at the age of twelve, Mozart composed his first full-length operas: *La finta semplice* and *Bastien und Bastienne. La finta semplice,* which eventually premiered in Salzburg rather than in Vienna, as first planned, demonstrates Mozart's astute grasp of the *opera buffa* ("comic opera") conventions of the 1760s. The opera is dominated by arias rather than ensemble numbers, and Mozart seized the chance to compose a wide range of different aria types, from short pattering comic pieces for the *buffo* characters to more extended lyrical soliloquies for the more serious characters. Though not especially daring in formal structure (most of the arias follow an ABA'B' or ABA' form), the pieces testify to Mozart's growing repertory of expressive techniques. The Singspiel *Bastien und Bastienne,* which probably premiered at the Viennese home of Dr. Franz Anton Mesmer, shows Mozart grappling with a newer, less defined tradition: that of the Austro-German Singspiel. Mozart's music features simple, though not folk-like, melodies; some use of *buffo*-type patter and mock-*seria* elements, especially for the comic sorcerer, Colas; a direct, flexible, often elegant style of text-setting; and avoidance of strict sectional forms. In all, Mozart combined German, French, and Italian operatic conventions to achieve a musical effect highly suited to the one-act sentimental pastoral.

The operas Mozart composed during his teen years reflect his increasing experience with the broad range of operatic styles across late-eighteenth-century Europe. *Mitridate, rè di Ponto* (1770) and *Lucio Silla* (1772), both composed for the Milanese court, are full-scale *opere serie*. Dominated by extended multi-sectional arias in a typical Baroque *seria* vein, the two operas explore a wealth of highly-charged emotional states. Mozart manages his panoply of stylized expressions and virtuosic solo passages well and even at times adds compelling drama to the otherwise rigid, slow-moving stories.

Contrasting these two full-fledged operas are *Ascanio in Alba* (1771, Milan), *Il sogno di Scipione* (1772, Salzburg), and *Il rè pastore* (1775, Salzburg), all composed for important state occasions (the wedding of Archduke Ferdinand of Austria to Maria Ricciarda Berenice of Modena, the enthronement of Prince-Archbishop Colloredo, and the visit of the Archduke Maximilian Franz, respectively). All three generally adhere to the conventions of *opera seria,* but each exemplifies the adaptations necessary to serve the occasion. In *Ascanio in Alba* choruses and dances come to the fore, while most of the arias are shorter than in conventional *opere serie* and are for the most part built on the more modern ternary (ABA') structure. In *Sogno di Scipione,* dominated almost completely by arias, Mozart turns back to the more old-fashioned, drawn-out *dal segno* form, perhaps in reflection of the more conservative and solemn occasion for which the work was composed. *Il rè pastore,* revealing less pretentious musical expression, features shorter numbers and graceful expression that lend a dignified elegance to the pastoral work. *La finta giardiniera* (1775), which premiered at the electoral court of Munich, was Mozart's only comic work of the 1770s. The libretto gave Mozart occasion to paint a variety of moods in his arias—passion, poignancy, anger, and humor—and to try his hand at two act-ending finales.

In the letters he wrote to his father during his long journey to Munich, Mannheim, and Paris in 1777-79, Mozart frequently voiced a desire to write more operas. He also indulged in increasingly opinionated assessments of works he heard. Some of his most notable comments were occasioned by performances in Mannheim and Munich of innovative German operas and melodramas, including those by Ignaz Holzbauer, Anton Schweitzer, and Georg Benda. So inspired was Mozart by Benda's melodramas that he even started, or at least planned to start, a melodrama of his own, entitled *Semiramide*. The Singspiel *Zaide* (1779-80) and new numbers added to his incidental music for the play *Thamos, König von Ägypten* (1773; revised in 1776-77 and 1779) were composed soon after Mozart returned from his highly stimulating trip and were, in a large part, the products of his grappling with ideas he had encountered. *Zaide* reveals a number of significant developments in his style, including the use of melodrama as a substitute for recitative, a bold mixture of comic and serious conventions, the streamlining and recasting of traditional aria structures, and more daring representation of texts.

Idomeneo, rè di Creta (1781), an *opera seria* commissioned by Munich's Electoral court, built on some of the experiments in *Zaide,* such as shorter and more fluid aria forms, flexible melodic phrasing, and colorful orchestral writing, but also reflected Mozart's maturing concern with the opera as a whole, not as a haphazard conglomerate of scenes and numbers. This concern was evident in the suggestions he made to his librettist, Gianbattista Varesco, about aria and recitative texts that were too long, unrealistic asides that needed elimination, and entire scenes that called for clearer direction. The overall result was an opera marked by careful dramatic pacing, effective juxtapositions of styles and expressions, compelling characterization, and brilliant orchestral and choral writing.

In the decade after *Idomeneo,* up until 1790, Mozart was commissioned to compose only comic operas, the genre of choice among residents of Mozart's new home city, Vienna. He wrote *Die Entführung aus dem Serail* (1782) for the Viennese National Singspiel, the theater for German opera that Emperor Joseph II had set up in 1778 in order to forward the cause of Austrian and German musical drama. Mozart, like many of the other composers writing for the National Singspiel, combined German elements with *opera buffa* gestures. For example, several of the servant characters rely on typical German strophic and rondo forms, while other characters depend on Italian-style lyrical, bravura, or pattering expression. In the same fashion, the second act ends with a long *buffo*-type finale, built of contrasting sections and rising dramatic intensity, but the third act concludes with a traditional German "Rundgesang," in which each character in turn sings one strophe in a verse-refrain number. A success among the Viennese and shortly thereafter in other Austrian and German cities, *Die Entführung* did much to boost Mozart's fame as an opera composer across Europe.

During 1783, rather than wait for further commissions, Mozart pursued two *opera buffa* projects on his own. For *L'oca del Cairo* Mozart solicited the help of the poet Varesco and, as in their previous collaboration, *Idomeneo,* made many suggestions as to the structure of the libretto and the number and types of characters. Mozart finished only a trio and sketched out six other numbers in the first act. Around that same time, he also began work on *Lo sposo deluso,* probably with librettist Lorenzo Da Ponte. Mozart finished only the overture, a trio, and a quartet and sketched out two other numbers before abandoning his work. His reasons for not completing the operas are not clear: perhaps he finally judged the librettos too weak or he was diverted by prospects of concertizing or composing other types of pieces. Whatever the reasons, Mozart never took up these operas again, nor did he express an interest in doing so in any of his surviving letters.

Mozart did not return to dramatic music until 1786, when he provided an overture and four numbers for the one-act "comedy with music" *Der Schauspieldirektor,* performed in the Orangery of the Schönbrunn palace for the visit of the Governor-General of the Austrian Netherlands. The story sets up a competition between two *prime donne,* and their arias, the first two numbers of the piece, reinforce the feud with a juxtaposition of the lyrical and bravura styles. In the trio the two sopranos indulge in fast-paced imitative bickering, while the final "Schlussgesang" allows each of the four main characters a strophe in a verse-refrain number. The satiric vein of the comedy and the small number of musical pieces limited Mozart's opportunity for elaborate musical-dramatic development, but the numbers show fine crafts-manship and a shrewd sense of characterization without caricature.

Mozart's next three operas, *Le nozze di Figaro* (1786, Vienna), *Il dissolute punito, ossia il Don Giovanni* (1787, Prague), and *Così fan tutte* (1790, Vienna), demonstrate his exceptional mastery of the *opera buffa* style and the full extent of his ability to shape the pacing, development, and tone of entire operas and their constituent parts. For all three operas Mozart collaborated with Lorenzo Da Ponte, Poet to the Imperial Theaters, who had a sharp eye for effective stagecraft and a versatile pen for appropriate texts.

Figaro gains much of its power from its characterizations: Da Ponte and Mozart did not rely on operatic stereotypes, but instead depicted characters with uncommon combinations of strengths, weaknesses, and idiosyncrasies. The characters are kept busy with a very intricate *buffo* plot, but the underlying themes of class struggle, social change, and gender ties are touched upon often and with dramatic and musical profundity. The three finales in the opera demonstrate the exceptional versatility and control of Mozart's compositional technique. The second-act finale, the longest, consists of careful alternation between playful action episodes that move the plot forward and more expansive, in places breathtaking, ensemble reflection on those events. In the third-act finale, Mozart relies on the wedding ceremony of Susanna and Figaro to define his musical sections. In the main sections of the finale, the processional march and the dance, he gives the orchestra the main melodic material while the characters interact in a simple melodic style above it. The fourth-act finale demonstrates how Mozart could shape a finale to climax not in loud, uproarious ensemble singing, but in the quiet sincerity of a contrite husband's apology.

The libretto to *Don Giovanni* derives much of its dramatic effect from the continuous battle between those who tolerate and those who condemn the Don's actions. Musically this translates into a struggle between the high moralism represented by the *seria* style (in the numbers for Donna Anna, Don Ottavio, Donna Elvira, and the Commendatore) and the earthy permissiveness embodied in the comic style. The continual juxtaposition of the disparate styles and sentiments is more glaring than in *Figaro,* where the stylistic polarities are not as extreme, and the tightly woven plot holds the numbers more closely together. In *Don Giovanni* Mozart succeeds at times in combining the divergent styles, as in the masterful first-act finale in which three stage orchestras simultaneously play an aristocratic minuet, a middle-class contredanse, and a peasant allemande. But the fundamental irreconcilability of clashing moralities and musical sentiments remains: neither Mozart nor Da Ponte simplistically reconciles them. The

551

opera remains a dramatic testimony to powerful class and gender oppositions fuming in Enlightenment Europe.

Così fan tutte, based on a plot as clever and symmetrical as, if not more so than, *Figaro* or *Don Giovanni,* fails to tap the complex social issues of the period. Da Ponte's libretto contains even more ensemble numbers than the previous two librettos do, but this very emphasis on ensemble numbers leads in the end to characters that do not demonstrate the individuality of the main characters in *Figaro* or *Don Giovanni.* In addition, the characters are often called upon to feign emotions to deceive one another, again decreasing the opportunity for genuine characterization. Musically, *Così* demonstrates a distinctive turn in Mozart's operatic writing in that many of the ensemble numbers are slow and lyrical, not bouncy and comic. He relies on rich orchestral writing and the blending of long lyrical vocal lines in this departure from typical *buffo*-style ensemble writing. In all, the opera, though lacking somewhat in the directness and intensity of *Figaro* and *Don Giovanni,* is charming, elegant, and superbly crafted.

Mozart's final two operas, *La clemenza di Tito* and *Die Zauberflöte,* premiered within twenty-four days of one another in September 1791. *Tito,* commissioned for Prague on the occasion of Leopold II's coronation as King of Bohemia, is based on a Metastasian libretto, updated to include more ensemble numbers and fewer arias. Mozart, who composed most of the opera in eighteen days, reached back to the *opera seria* style he had practiced as a youth. But the frequency of ensemble numbers and Mozart's choice not to indulge in the long-windedness of typical *opere serie* lends a modern air to the work. His setting responds to the solemnity and profundity of the occasion and the libretto but reveals, too, an Enlightened elegance and restraint.

Die Zauberflöte, called a *grosse Oper* (grand opera) by Mozart and his librettist, Emanuel Schikaneder, combined elements of Viennese comedy, German fairy tales, Singspiel, *opera seria, opera buffa,* and the high Baroque polyphonic style. Mozart depicts the major conflict in the drama—that between Sarastro's realm of the Enlightened and the Queen's kingdom of the Night—with two distinctive musical styles: Sarastro and his followers sing in the German Baroque church style, while the Queen and her entourage use an Italianate operatic style, with the Queen relying on the consummate Italianate rhetoric, the coloratura virtuosic style. The two seekers, Tamino and Pamina, who must choose between the two kingdoms, sing in a more earnest lyrical style, while Tamino's comic sidekick, Papageno, offers up folk-like songs with occasional *buffo* flourishes. Though at times this hodgepodge of conventions results in a disparate, episodic drama, it nonetheless communicates a wide gamut and depth of emotion. As in so many of his other operas, in *Die Zauberflöte* Mozart adapted, recombined, and transformed the operatic conventions he inherited in the late eighteenth century to create a distinctive dramatic work. His unfailing instinct for the possibilities of compelling musical drama and his capacity for brilliant technical execution of his ideas distinguish his operas as tributes not only to the richness of operatic styles in the Classical period, but also to Mozart's dramatic and musical genius.—LINDA TYLER

Musorgsky, Modest Petrovich

Composer. Born 21 March 1839, in Karevo, Pskov district, Russia. Died 28 March 1881, in St Petersburg. Studied piano with his mother, then with Anton Herke in St Petersburg; entered the cadet school of the Imperial Guard, 1852, and joined the Guard after

graduation; met Dargomizbsky, Cui, and Balakirev, 1857; clerk at the Ministry of Communications, 1863-67; worked for the Forestry Department, 1869. Musorgsky was one of the "Mighty Handful" of Russian composers that included Dargomizbsky, Rimsky-Korsakov, Cui, and Balakirev; he frequently sought the advice and help of Rimsky-Korsakov and the music critic Stasov in musical matters.

Operas   *Salammbô,* after Flaubert, 1863-66 [unfinished]; *The Marriage [Zhenit'ba],* Musorgsky (after Gogol), 1868, [unfinished]: posthumous production of act I, St Petersburg, Suvorin Theater School, 1 April 1909; *Boris Godunov,* Musorgsky (after Pushkin and Karamzin), 1868-69, Leningrad, 16 February 1928 [posthumous production]: revised 1871-72; further revised, 1873, St Petersburg, Maryinsky Theater, 8 February 1874; *Khovanshchina,* Musorgsky, 1872-80 [unfinished]: completed and orchestrated by Rimsky-Korsakov, St Petersburg, February 21 1886; *Sorochintsy Fair [Sorochinskaya yarmarka],* Musorgsky (after Gogol), 1874-80 [unfinished]: completed by Lyadov, V.G. Karatïgin and others, Moscow, Free Theater, 21 October 1913.

Modest Musorgsky is considered by most musicians and scholars to be the most innovative and imaginative of the group of Russian composers dubbed in its day as the "Moguchaia Kuchka," the "Mighty Handful." Musorgsky's freshness stems first from his intense spiritual kinship with the Russian people, identified by him most keenly in the peasantry—their lives, their feelings, their simplicity, and their language. From this, Musorgsky's fascination with Russian drama and poetry as well as his interest in the history of his native land follow logically, as does the further observation that his most important and most characteristic contributions to Russian music were his vocal works, especially his operas.

This image of Musorgsky's creative foundation pervades his total output, from his early songs (e.g., "Where Art Thou, Little Star") and the orchestral tone poem *Night on Bald Mountain* to his mature song cycles (*The Nursery* and *Sunless*), the piano masterpiece *Pictures at an Exhibition* and his three great operatic efforts (*Boris Godunov, Khovanshchina,* and *The Fair at Sorochintsy,* the latter two completed after his death by other composers). Throughout these works one observes not only an emphasis on things Russian—literary sources and scenes from life—but also Musorgsky's evolving and ever more free empirical approach to the craft of composition. While one might easily cite examples of his crudeness (by traditional standards) in harmony, structure, and the like, one cannot often justly criticize the composer for being unable to give clarity and succinctness to the musical imagery or expressive content he means to convey.

There are two principal characteristics of this clarity. One is melodic style, especially in Musorgsky's vocal music, where he shows the influences of both Glinka and Dargomizhsky as well as of Italian opera. Musorgsky's vocal lines have a rhythmic and intervallic freedom that allows them to follow the natural inflections of the Russian language without losing their inher-

Modest Musorgsky, portrait by Ilja Repin, 1881

ent lyricism. The other is Musorgsky's realistic sense of visual and emotional drama which manifests itself musically in his unique harmonic style, his use of orchestral and vocal color, and in the intensely lyric and often folklike nature of his melodies. It is precisely this trait that gives such power to the psychological development of Czar Boris in *Boris Godunov* and to the pageantry of the coronation scene in the same work, to cite only the most familiar of several such examples.

On balance, Musorgsky's importance, perhaps, should be viewed less for his influence on other composers (although Debussy and Stravinsky must be mentioned in this regard) than for the skillful and determined manner in which he gave a musical voice to aspects of Russian culture and the segments of Russian society where that culture was seen in its purest state. In that sense, Musorgsky was part of an important trend in the arts of his day, following the examples of Pushkin in literature and Glinka in music.—ROY J. GUENTHER

Muzio, Claudia

Soprano. Born 7 February 1889, in Pavia. Died 24 May 1936, in Rome. Studied with Annetta Casaloni in Turin and Viviani in Milan; debut as Massenet's Manon, Arezzo, 1910; Teatro alla Scala debut as Desdemona, 1913-14; appeared at Covent Garden, 1914; also appeared in South America; Metropolitan Opera debut as Tosca, 1916, and remained there until 1922; in Chicago 1922-32, where she first appeared as Aida; Teatro alla Scala, 1926-27.

Sixty years after Claudia Muzio's death, her short career and her strikingly individual voice have given her legendary status. The enigma of Claudia Muzio (1889-1936) remains unsolved by any full-length biography in English. In *Prima Donna*, Rupert Christiansen writes that contemporaries remember her as a reclusive soprano "who never said anything." Writers praise her artistic achievements and portray her as a tragic figure whose recordings resonate with personal sadness. Most people know her voice only through opera and song recordings and her acting ability through dramatic poses in still photographs. Even so, the records and pictures make an impression of freshness, vitality and dramatic presence.

Opera figured strongly in Muzio's background: her father was a stage director at Covent Garden and the Metropolitan, her mother a chorus singer. Her teacher was Annetta Casaloni (the first Maddalena in *Rigoletto*). Through these influences and her natural abilities, Muzio perfected a style of *verismo* singing which never resorted to gasping, sobbing, or noise-making for effect, and which she could adapt to lyric roles. Admirers including Christiansen, Giorgio Gualerzi, and Rodolfo Celletti remark on the purity and subtle shading of her tone which avoided histrionics. Muzio's voice has an instantly recognizable timbre—a great melancholy with the capacity for lightness.

It is a voice of opposing forces, at times personal and small, yet large and flexible enough for her to have been the first Turandot of Buenos Aires. Her vocal negotiations between grand manner and endearing intimacy produced a sound which lent a human warmth to the most taxing of roles. She used opposing styles for dramatic effect, moving from sustained full voiced passages to pianissimi, from brightness of tone to darkness, with galvanizing ease. Some find this movement jarring, some find it a revelation. In either case, her records bear witness to the dramatic intensity of her voice.

Her recorded legacy spans the early acoustic age of 1911 to the later electrical EMI records of 1934-35. Some critics note in her last records a loss of the ease demonstrated in the diamond discs and attribute this to her bad health. However, for this listener, the ease and flexibility of voice are still there in her later efforts, and if I prefer the EMI sides to her Edison recordings it is because of technical sound quality. She was capable of great freshness during the EMI sessions, especially in "Per amor di Gesu," an aria she recorded in 1934 from Licino Refice's *Cecilia,* a mystical opera composed especially for her. The Angel of God beseeches listeners to hear the inspiring story of Cecilia (the patron saint of music). Muzio's voice has all the requisite brightness one might expect of an angel, but also a burnished melancholy which reads as impassioned concern that her listeners should take heed for their salvation. Her voice shimmers at the opening then deepens, and as the Angel describes Cecilia: "O chiara sposa, con socchiuso ciglio/a Dio cantasti: 'Deh! serbami pura!' " ["O radiant bride, with veiled eyes to God you sang 'Ah, keep me pure!' "], Muzio descends to a chest note at "pura" with spine-tingling results— mystical indeed. Celletti describes her technique as the creation of sound which "lit certain words with a sudden flash." She achieved the flash with breath control and the contrast of light and dark sounds.

Just as freshness surfaces in her later records, the mature cast, the dark vocal inflection, of her voice appears in the early recordings, too. In "Ebben ne andro lontano" from Catalani's *La Wally,* recorded in 1920, she has the light timbre to be expected of youth, but also the gravity which portends things to come. From 1921, her recording from Leoncavallo's *Zaza* evinces depth of feeling set against youthful freshness of sound. Gualerzi suggests that Muzio used the contrast of light and dark vocal inflection to cope with divergent styles of opera, enabling her to sing Mascagni as well as Bellini. She judiciously contrasted volume and vocal coloring to bring to dramatic roles (such as Santuzza in *Cavalleria rusticana*) an effervescence which revealed character, and to lyric roles (such as Amina in *La sonnambula*) a dramatic pathos which added character. Her earliest recordings suggest Muzio was aware of the limitations and advantages of her voice and how to use them. Her distinction over typical *verismo* singers was the dimension which her pianissimi and restraint gave to melodramatic roles—without detracting from the drama.

Among her thirty or so EMIs, we find intense dramatic interpretations of arias from *Norma, Il trovatore, La traviata* (a legendary "Teneste la promessa" which many read biographically), and *Mefistofele,* each imprinted with Muzio's distinctive individuality. The palpable tension of "L'altra notte" provides as good an example of the singer's presence as we can get through recordings. Her visually suggestive voice inspires color associations (Christiansen cites brown and purple), but also suggests a persona. The strength of presence she had on stage comes through her voice "made of tears and sighs and restrained inner fire," as the tenor Giacomo Lauri-Volpi remarked. Photographs from roles such as Violetta, Tosca and the *Trovatore* Leonora show a remarkable combination of great dignity and inner fire.

We go to Muzio to hear reliably beautiful dramatic singing which achieves its effect through restraint. The effect of her singing is to endow characters with personality and dimension; she excels in the *verismo* style through a nearly impossible-to-describe form of breath control and vocal coloring, and in the lyric style through well-rounded tone and brightness tempered by melancholy. If her repertoire seems adventurous to modern ears, it is because she was a proponent of the *verismo* style and the music of her time.—TIMOTHY O. GRAY

OPERA *n*

Nabucco [Nabucodonosor]

Composer: *Giuseppe Verdi.*

Librettist: *Temistocle Solera (after the ballet by A. Cortesi, 1838).*

First Performance: *Milan, Teatro alla Scala, 9 March 1842.*

Roles: *Nabucco (baritone); Ismaele (tenor); Zaccaria (bass); Abigaille (soprano); Fenena (soprano or mezzo-soprano); High Priest of Baal (bass); Anna (soprano); Abdallo (tenor); chorus (SSATTBB).*

Nabucco occupies a unique place in the Verdi canon since Verdi himself dated the beginning of his artistic career from its composition, although it was his third opera. After the failure of *Un giorno di regno* and the deaths of his two children and then his wife, he was despondent and could do little musically. The story is well known how Merelli, the director of the Teatro alla Scala, forced the libretto of *Nabucco* onto the unwilling Verdi and how the words, *"Va, pensiero, sull' ali dorate"* ("Fly, O thought, on golden wings") caught his attention. These words, which became the choral lament of the Hebrew people exiled in Babylon, also became the cornerstone of the opera itself; raising the already excited opening night audience to unprecedented pitches of enthusiasm, the chorus went on to provide the dawning political movement toward a united Italy, the Risorgimento, with its battle hymn. The opera was played seventy-five times that year at La Scala alone and soon appeared all over Italy, Europe, and the Americas. Fifty-nine years later, the crowds lining the Milan streets for Verdi's funeral spontaneously broke out into the chorus that was still identified with him in a way none of his other compositions ever came to be. Revived in the 1930s, *Nabucco* has retained an important place in Verdi performances.

The introduction of the chorus to function as a protagonist came from the librettist, Temistocle Solera, who, basing his text on a French play and a ballet mounted at La Scala four years earlier (both called *Nabucodonosor*), emphasized the Old Testament element of Hebrew suffering implicit in the story. The action seems disjointed because it is divided, according to contemporary custom, into four parts each with a title taken from the Book of Jeremiah, four vast static tableaux culminating in bursts of activity. The action, set in 586 B.C. in Jerusalem and Babylon, is essentially a series of power struggles, first between Nabucco, King of Babylon, and the Hebrews; then between Nabucco and his supposed daughter, Abigaille (revealed to be the offspring of slaves), who attempts to usurp the throne. Both of these are complicated by a love triangle of minor musical interest: Nabucco's real daughter, Fenena, at first a hostage of the Hebrews, converts to Judaism and loves Ismaele, nephew of the King of Jerusalem, who returns her love. He is also loved by the jealous Abigaille, who, seizing power in Nabucco's absence, almost succeeds in having the lovers executed. Nabucco himself is ultimately converted to Judaism, as is the defeated Abigaille, who, committing suicide, dies repentant.

Musically the work owes a debt to late Rossini, to *Guillaume Tell, Le siège de Corinth,* and structurally, to *Moïse,* but the musical language is unmistakably new, exhibiting the melodic breadth, vigor and dramatic drive we think of as characteristically Verdian. Structurally Verdi establishes several new directions in which he continued to move throughout his career: his use of the chorus both on its own and in relation to the principals; scoring for particular instruments or combinations to achieve special effects; creating duets and ensembles to express conflicting emotions in musical as well as dramatic terms, indeed, creating real music drama in the sense that the dialectic of the drama is developed in the music as well as in the stage action. Sensitive from the very beginning to the dramatic potential of different voice types, Verdi gives us in Nabucco himself the prototype of the Verdian baritone, the "high" deep masculine voice as the primary locus for expressing conflicting emotions.

Verdi's mastery is quickly demonstrated in the opening scene by the way in which the chorus, intervening in both the aria and cabaletta ("D'Egitto là sui lidi") of the solo bass, Zaccaria, establishes itself as a direct participant in the action. Abigaille's entry ("Prode guerrier"), a fiercely bitter declamation leaping from low B to high C, establishes her as a *persona* and the role as one of the most difficult soprano roles Verdi ever wrote. Her act II recitative (with a spectacular two-octave leap) and aria, ("Anch'io duschuiso un giorno") includes a decorated Bellinian *andante* followed, after the urging of the Babylonians to seize the throne, by a brilliantly exciting cabaletta ("Salgo già del trono aurato"). Act II, scene ii opens with another Verdian touch, an introduction to Zaccaria's prayer ("Tu che sul labbro") scored for six cellos, and moves toward an innovative finale. Beginning as a canonic quartet for Nabucco, Abigaille, Ismaele, and Fenena, gradually joined by the other minor characters and the chorus, it moves into a defiant recitative for Nabucco, who proclaims himself God. The resultant thunderclap leads not into the expected stretta but into a kind of mad scene for the king, a rapidly changing musical and emotional scenario (it points forward to Rigoletto's half-demented vilifications of the courtiers), which ends with Abigaille reasserting the glory of Baal.

The opening scene of act III contains one of the earliest of Verdi's wonderful father-daughter duets. Opening with an allegro dialogue, "Donna, chi sei?" it moves through a middle section full of powerful contrasts in which Nabucco grieves while Abigaille exults in dreams of glory, to the finale where Nabucco is led away as her prisoner. The "Va, pensiero," which now appears, is the emotional center of the opera. Elegiac, melancholic, its leisurely yet grand, sweeping rhythm creates the effect of a thousand voices reaching out to a promised land; the shift from unison to harmony on the words, *"arpe dor,"* is a thrilling master stroke. Act IV is less gripping—the ending especially is a little routine—but the opening contains another fine scene as the distracted Nabucco moves into an oasis of orchestral tranquillity and prayer—a version of the tune we know as "Home Sweet Home"—to the God of the Hebrews (*"Dio di Giuda"*) to save his daughter Fenena.—PETER DYSON

Nesterenko, Evgeny Evgenievich

Bass. Born 8 January 1938, in Moscow. Studied at Leningrad Conservatory under V. Lukanin; debut as Prince Gremin in Eugene Onegin, *Maly Theater in Leningrad, 1963; at Maly Opera 1963-67; at Kirov Opera, 1967-71; joined the Bolshoi Opera, Moscow, 1971; sang Boris on tour at the Teatro alla Scala (1973), the Vienna Staatsoper (1974), and the Metropolitan Opera (1975); Covent Garden debut as Don Basilio, 1978; sang Philippe II in* Don Carlos *at the Teatro alla Scala, 1978; taught at Leningrad Conservatory, 1967-71; chairman of voice department at Moscow Conservatory from 1975; first prize in Tchaikovsky Competition, Moscow, 1970; awarded Lenin Prize in 1982.*

Since his debut as Prince Gremin in Tchaikovsky's *Eugene Onegin* at St Petersberg's Maly Theater in 1963, Russian bass Evgeny Nesterenko has sung at the Bolshoi, Covent Garden, San Francisco, La Scala, Rome, Verona, East Berlin, Savolinna, Nice, Munich, Wiesbaden, Vienna, Buenos Aires, Madrid, Barcelona, Budapest, and Bregenz, in roles including Bluebeard in Bartok's *Bluebeard's Castle,* Mussorgsky's Boris Godunov, Philip II in Verdi's *Don Carlos,* Mephistopheles in Gounod's *Faust,* Ruslan in Glinka's *Ruslan and Ludmila,* Prince Gremin in Tchaikovsky's *Eugene Onegin,* Don Basilio in Rossini's *Il barbiere di Siviglia,* Dosifei and Ivan Khovansky in Mussorgsky's *Khovanschina,* Rossini's Mosè, Colline in Puccini's *La bohème,* Tiresias in Stravinsky's *Oedipus Rex,* Sarastro in Mozart's *Die Zauberflöte,* Arkel in Debussy's *Pélleas et Mélisande,* Salieri in Rimsky-Korsakov's *Mozart and Salieri,* Zaccaria in Verdi's *Nabucco,* Verdi's Attila, Henry VIII in Donizetti's *Anna Bolena,* the Water Sprite in Dvořák's *Rusalka,* Boito's Mefistofele, Konchak in Borodin's *Prince Igor,* and Rachmaninoff's Aleko.

Nesterenko possesses a lyric bass voice that tends to be somewhat lighter than usual for some of the roles of his repertoire, yet can convey their grandeur. A versatile singer with a rich voice, he is an effective and interesting, even idiosyncratic, actor, with an especially expressive face, capable of bringing his characters to life. Possessing a monumental stage presence, he has been hailed for his powerful declamation and sense of character, a highly evocative style, majesty, and physical and vocal stature. While not massive, his voice in its prime was solid and imposing. Colorful, warm, and expressive, it was evenly distributed throughout its range.

Known especially for his work in the Russian repertoire, he has also had notable success in Italian roles, particularly those of Verdi; he was less adept at Rossini. Problems with his pronunciation of French limited his effectiveness in roles in that language (and as seems to be true of many basses, the role of Mephistopheles brought out a tendency to overact). By the late 1980s signs of vocal strain, with concomitant lapses of intonation, an increasingly monochromatic sound, and a reduction in dynamic range began to reduce his vocal and dramatic capabilities. As his voice lost power, he tended toward a more baritonal sound and began to lack some of his former authority.

His appearances in recordings of complete operas include Sobakin in Rimsky-Korsakov's *The Tsar's Bride* under Mansurov (1972), Lanciotti in Rachmaninoff's *Francesca da Rimini* under Ermler (1979), Prince Gremin under Ermler (1980), Ruslan under Simonov (1982); Bluebeard under Ferencsik (1982), Zaccaria under Sinopoli (1983); Ferrando in Verdi's *Il trovatore* under Giulini (1984), and Mephistopheles under Colin Davis (1987).—MICHAEL SIMS

Nicolai, (Carl) Otto (Ehrenfried)

Composer. Born 9 June 1810, in Königsberg. Died 11 May 1849, in Berlin. Studied piano with Zelter in Berlin, 1827; studied with Bernhard Klein at the Royal Institute for Church Music; concert debut in Berlin, 13 April 1833; organist to the embassy chapel in Rome by the German Ambassador, 1834; studied counterpoint with Giuseppe Baini; singing teacher and conductor at the Kärntnertor theater, Vienna, 1837; returned to Italy, 1838; first opera presented in Trieste, 1839; succeeded Kreutzer as court Kapellmeister in Vienna, 1841; conducted the inaugural concert of the Vienna Philharmonic Orchestra, 1842; Kapellmeister of the Royal Opera in Berlin, 1848. Hans Richter began an annual "Nicolai-Konzert" with the Vienna Philharmonic, which over the years has been conducted by such notable conductors as Gustav Mahler, Felix Weingartner, Wilhelm Furtwängler, Karl Böhm, and Claudio Abbado.

Operas *Enrico II (Rosmonda d'Inghilterra)*, Felice Romani, 1836, Trieste, 26 November 1839; *Il templario*, Girolamo Maria Marini (after Scott, *Ivanhoe*), Turin, 11 February 1840; revised as *Der Tempelritter*, translated S. Kapper, Vienna, 20 December 1845; *Gildippe ed Odoardo*, T. Solera, Genoa, 26 December 1840; *Il proscritto*, G. Rossi, Milan, Teatro alla Scala, 13 March 1841; revised as *Die Heimkehr des Verbannten*, translated S. Kapper, 3 February 1846; *Die lustigen Weiber von Windsor*, S.H. Mosenthal (after Shakespeare, *The Merry Wives of Windsor*), Berlin, Hofoper, 9 March 1849.

Like Georges Bizet, Nicolai lived just long enough to witness the production of the one opera on which his posthumous fame would entirely rest (*Die lustigen Weiber von Windsor*, 9 March 1849). If this premiere was on the whole better received than that of *Carmen*, neither composer survived to see the ultimate vindication of his final opera. Whatever Nicolai himself thought to be the merits of *Die lustigen Weiber* (his first comedy and first German opera, after 4 Italian works) its initial reception gave him no reason to believe that it would soon become a staple of the repertory.

As an adolescent Nicolai fled his East Prussian home to escape aggressive and exploitative treatment at the hands of his father, a minor musical figure in Königsberg. Later in Berlin he received instruction from Carl Friedrich Zelter, Goethe's friend and doyen of the musical scene in the Prussian capital. Other teachers included the pianist composer Ludwig Berger and a noted composer of liturgical music and oratorios, Bernhard Klein. Nicolai's training in Berlin was consequently geared toward sacred music, and when he went to Rome in 1834 as chapel organist to the German Embassy, his attention was at first directed to the musical institutions of the Catholic Church and the venerable tradition of Renaissance polyphony (especially as practiced by Palestrina) fostered by Giuseppe Baini and others.

The composition of a ten-voice setting of Psalm 54 in the "strict style" followed by a fantasy for piano and orchestra on themes from Bellini's *Norma* (Op. 25), both in the summer of 1835, is suggestive of the new orientation of the young composer's enthusiasm. This burgeoning interest in the world of Italian opera—despite complaints about poor standards and conditions for performance, so commonly voiced by foreign musicians in Italy—received still stronger symbolic manifestation in memorial compositions in honor of Bellini (a funeral march played as an entracte to *La sonnambula* in Rome, 14 October 1835) and Maria Malibran (Bologna, 1836). After a difficult year as Kapellmeister at the Vienna Court Opera (Kärntnertor theater) in 1837-38 Nicolai returned to Italy, determined to make a career in opera. A work begun for Vienna as *Rosmonda d'Inghilterra* (libretto by Felice Romani) was eventually staged in Trieste as *Enrico II* in 1839. Of three more operas produced in Italy, *Il templario* (Turin, 11 February 1840) and *Il proscritto* (Teatro alla Scala, Milan, 13 March 1841) achieved notable success and were subsequently performed in Vienna and in various German theaters as *Der Tempelritter* and *Die Heimkehr des Verbannten,* respectively. The libretto to *Il proscritto* was acquired in exchange for *Nabucodonosor* (later *Nabucco*), which was turned over to Verdi.

A longer period as Kapellmeister back at the Vienna Court Opera (1841-47) was distinguished by significant contributions to the musical life of the city, including a series of orchestral concerts which marked the establishment of the Vienna Philharmonic as an institution. However, Nicolai was continually frustrated by envy, intrigues, and general ill-will on the part of his colleagues, and the rejection of his nearly completed new opera *Die lustigen Weiber von Windsor* on the grounds of a contractual technicality led Nicolai to resign, assuming a similar post in Berlin. His meticulous musical standards and the expertise he had acquired as conductor were much appreciated during his two years in Berlin, where he also conducted the cathedral choir. *Die lustigen Weiber* finally reached the stage there two months before his early death at the age of 39.

Nicolai was perhaps the last German composer, following Meyerbeer, to undergo an active Italian apprenticeship. Like Meyerbeer, he appreciated the value of this induction into the traditions of the operatic stage and the techniques of vocal writing. Both composers ceased to write in the Italian style upon leaving the country, although both re-arranged their Italian operas for performance abroad, in translation.

Nicolai's Italian operas reflect something of his own mixed attitude toward the genre as he encountered it in the later 1830s. Like many Germans, he admired the quality of the vocal tradition in Italy, but lamented the tendency to sacrifice any serious concern for musical, dramatic, or even scenic matters to a narrow emphasis on the singer's art. He admired what he judged to be the most substantial products of the bel canto repertory, such as Bellini's *La sonnambula* and *Norma,* Donizetti's *Anna Bolena,* and Rossini's *Guillaume Tell* (despite his distaste for the wider influence of Rossinian formulas). In *Il templario* (based on Scott's *Ivanhoe,* which had already served as the basis for operas by Giovanni Pacini and Heinrich Marschner, as well as a Rossini *pasticcio*) Nicolai displays a fluent command of the contemporary Italian idiom, occasionally betraying traces of a German accent. The symphonically conceived overture, for instance, suggests a grafting of the style of Weber and Marschner onto the conventional Italian *sinfonia.* Many of the solo numbers or passages are written in a typically bel canto style, as lyrical or virtuosic displays. But Rebecca's *preghiera* in act III (like Wagner's Elsa, she prays for a champion to come to her defense) is, despite her Jewish faith, clearly indebted to the Protestant chorale tradition, recalling the composer's original training in Berlin.

Given such a synthesis of Italian and German influences, it is no surprise that Nicolai held up Mozart as his musical idol. (Instrumental and vocal works of Mozart figured prominently on the programs of his "Philharmonic Academies" in Vienna.) Certainly the beloved image of Mozart informed Nicolai's ambitions to create a German opera for Vienna after returning there in

1841. Although these ambitions were to be frustrated for some time, they were fittingly realized at last in *Die lustigen Weiber von Windsor*. Perhaps the finest German comic opera since *Die Zauberflöte*, this score combines the spirit of Mozart's operas (especially *Figaro*) with the warm but light-footed "classical" romanticism of Mendelssohn at his best.—THOMAS S. GREY

Nilsson, Birgit

Soprano. Born Märta Birgit Svensson 17 May 1918, in Västra Karups, Sweden. Studied with Joseph Hislop in Stockholm; debut as substitute for role of Agathe in Der Freischütz, *1946; formal debut as Lady Macbeth at Stockholm; with Stockholm Opera, 1947-51; appeared as Elektra in* Idomeneo *at Glyndebourne, 1951; Bayreuth debut as Elsa, 1954, and sang there regularly until 1970; appeared at Covent Garden from 1957; appeared at Teatro alla Scala from 1958, first as Turandot; Metropolitan Opera debut as Isolde, 1959, and sang there until 1982.*

The Swedish soprano Birgit Nilsson dominated the soprano Wagnerian roles after World War II and was considered the Wagnerian soprano of her generation and the heir to Kirsten Flagstad. She made her debut in Stockholm as Agathe in *Der Freischütz* in 1946 and gained international attention as a result of her stellar Elektra in Mozart's *Idomeneo* at Glyndebourne in 1951. In 1954 and 1955 she sang Brünnhilde (in Wagner's *Ring* cycle) and the title role of *Salome* in Munich; thereafter, she was a real superstar.

Nilsson became famous for the power and force of her voice, in addition to her ability to sing wonderfully with portamento; her interpretations also impressed with their insight and drama. She was best known for the main Wagnerian soprano roles: all three Brünnhildes in the Ring cycle, Isolde in *Tristan und Isolde*, Elsa in *Lohengrin*, and both Elisabeth and Venus in *Tannhäuser*. She also sang Mozart with success, Donna Anna in *Don Giovanni* and Elektra being her best Mozart roles. In the Italian repertory, she was best in the title roles of *Turandot, Tosca, Aïda*, and Minnie in *La fanciulla del West*. By the early 1960s Nilsson had created sensations in Milan, Chicago, London, Munich, and New York. She also collaborated in the 60s with Wieland Wagner at Bayreuth for wonderful productions of the *Ring* cycle and *Tristan und Isolde*.

Toward the end of her career, Nilsson sang two Strauss roles with great acclaim: the Dyer's Wife in *Die Frau ohne Schatten* and the title role in *Elektra*. She appeared at all the great opera houses, but was especially familiar at New York's Metropolitan Opera, Milan's Teatro alla Scala, Munich's Bavarian State Opera, and London's Covent Garden.

Nilsson has left a fine recorded legacy, particularly in her fruitful collaboration with the conductor Sir Georg Solti. They recorded a wonderful *Ring* cycle with her as all three Brünnhildes, plus Strauss' *Salome* and *Elektra*. With the conductor Karl Böhm she also recorded an exciting *Ring* cycle plus *Tristan und Isolde* with the tenor Wolfgang Windgassen.
—JOHN LOUIS DIGAETANI

Nixon in China

Composer: *John Adams.*

Librettist: *Alice Goodman.*

First Performance: *Houston, Houston Grand Opera, 22 October 1987.*

Roles: *Chou En-lai (baritone); Richard Nixon (baritone); Henry Kissinger (baritone); Nancy T'ang (mezzo-soprano); Second Secretary to Mao (mezzo-soprano); Third Secretary to Mao (mezzo-soprano); Mao Tse-Tung (tenor); Pat Nixon (soprano); Chiang Ch'ing (soprano); chorus (SATB).*

Nixon in China begins with the arrival of the presidential plane at the Beijing airport. A chorus of troops sings a revolutionary hymn to the sky as the American jet lands. Premier Chou En-lai greets the Nixons and Henry Kissinger. The action continues with the historic meeting and discussions between Richard Nixon and Chairman Mao. The first act closes with a state banquet in the Great Hall of the People.

In the second act, Patricia Nixon visits various Communist showplaces—a medical clinic, a model pig farm, and finally the Ming Tombs. She sings a long, melancholic aria about life in middle class America. Later, Madame Mao (Chiang Ch'ing) entertains the dignitaries with a performance of her revolutionary ballet entitled "The Red Detachment of Women." The three Americans become mesmerized and are drawn into the atrocities portrayed in the ballet. In the midst of the chaos Madame Mao sings her spectacular aria which displays all the revolutionary charismatic fervor of China's first lady.

Made up of only one scene, act III is the shortest act in the opera. Played out in the individual bedrooms, it is a weary sequence of soliloquies interwoven with a double duet. The couples dance a slow fox-trot. They each reminisce about the past—Nixon about his tour of duty in World War II and Madame Mao about the days spent with the young chairman in the caves at Yenan. At the end of the opera, Chou En-lai, who has seemed a peripheral figure up to now, emerges as the opera's philosophical hero. Taking up the thread of the soliloquy, he sings the aria which ends the opera.

The opera is uniquely constructed, in that its structural units decrease proportionally throughout the opera. There are three scenes in the first act (sixty minutes), two scenes in the second act (forty-five minutes) and one scene in the third act (thirty minutes). The dramatic plot parallels the diminishing construction. The first act presents a flurry of events depicting the ceremonial and public nature of the celebrated visit; in the second act the women are seen in closer focus; and in the third act, we see the main characters stripped of their public faces. We peer into their private memories, their lack of comprehension and their fatigue. In an interview with Andrew Porter, reported in *Tempo* (December 1988), Adams stated that one of the things which drew him to this vehicle was the "opportunity" to explore the "uncertain, vulnerable human beings" who stand behind the public figures. He described the diminishing structure as a narrowing of focus, until finally, in the third act, we see the characters in their "psychological and emotional undress."

The premiere of *Nixon in China* on 22 October 1987, by the Houston Grand Opera, took place amid a storm of publicity, which is understandable because the subject matter alone is newsworthy, and must be weighed carefully. Critical response was strongly divided. David

Patrick Sterns reported for *Gramophone* (October 1988) that "the music was either considered so insubstantial as to be boring or so entrancing as to be unforgettable." Among the opera's strong supporters, John Rockwell, critic for the *New York Times* (6 December 1987), held that the opera was "full of charm and wit, and in the end, beauty." Other voices in favor of the Houston production included Michael Walsh of *Time Magazine* (9 November 1987), who praised the "dramatic qualities" and its "theatricality," and John Ardoin, critic for the *Dallas Morning News* (24 October 1987) who hailed the appropriateness of Peter Sellar's staging and praised its suitability as "that sort of simplicity that brings dramatic necessities down to musical essentials." Two months after its Houston premiere, the production traveled to the Brooklyn Academy of Music's *Next Wave Festival* and shortly afterwards to the Kennedy Center in Washington D.C. The production was also mounted with positive response at the Netherlands Opera in Amsterdam (June 1988) and at the Edinburgh Festival (August 1988).

Despite its foundations in minimalism, *Nixon in China* is dramatically moving rather than simply repetitive. Adams has not abandoned the repetition and arpeggiation of minimalism; he simply relegates them to the orchestral accompaniment, and by doing so makes the vocal lines stand out in dramatic relief. This preservation of minimalistic elements in the orchestral scoring allows a freedom of vocal writing previously unseen in minimalistic opera. Furthermore, Adams has a gift for melody and is able to strike an amiable compromise between soaring melody and the rhythmic demands of inflected speech. This melodic sense, along with Alice Goodman's eloquent libretto, allows Adams to mold his characters into melodic types, as demonstrated by a comparison of the melodic writing for the three main Communist characters: Madame Mao sings in a compositional voice that is fiery, the Chairman requires a more sustained vocal style, while Premier Chou En-lai sings always with a seemingly fluid and chant-like line. Many great moments stand out in the score, among them Nixon's breathless act I aria, Chou En-lai's noble lyricism during the State banquet as well as his stunning final aria. The arias of the women also deserve mention. One recording of *Nixon in China* has been made, on the Nonesuch Label, recorded between performances at the Brooklyn Academy of Music in New York City. It features the original cast members and can therefore be considered a good, if not exact, representation of the original performance.—PATRICIA ROBERTSON

Nono, Luigi

Composer. Born 29 January 1924, in Venice. Died 8 May 1990, in Venice. Married: Nuria Schoenberg, daughter of the composer, 1955 (two daughters; divorced). Studied law at the University of Padua, graduated 1946; studied composition with Malipiero at the Benedetto Marcello Conservatory in Venice; studied advanced harmony and counterpoint with Bruno Maderna and Hermann Scherchen; involved in the Italian resistance movement against the Nazis at the end of World War II; electronic music research at the Studio di Fonologia Musicale, 1954-60; teacher, Ferienkurse für Neue Musik, Darmstadt, 1957; elected to the Central Committee of the Italian Communist Party, 1975; three visits to the Soviet Union, 1963, 1973, and 1976.

Operas *Intolleranza 1960* (scenic action), after an idea by A.M. Ripellino (based on texts by Brecht, Eluard, Sartre, and Mayakovsky), Venice, 13 April 1961; revised as *Intolleranza 1970,* new scene after J. Karsunke, Florence, 1974; *Il gran sole carico d'amore (Au grand soleil d'amour chargé)* (scenic action),

Nono, 1972-75, Milan, 4 April 1975; revised, 1977, Milan, 11 February 1978; *Prometeo: Tragedia dell' ascolto,* Cacciari, 1981-85, Venice, 25 September 1984.

Luigi Nono achieved fame and notoriety as much for his compositional techniques as for his political propensities. Like many composers before him, he studied law, the culmination of which was, in his case, a doctoral degree (Padua). Concurrent with his legal preparation, Nono studied musical composition. From 1941-1945, he worked with Gian Francesco Malipiero at the Venice Conservatory; his other principal teachers were Bruno Maderna and Hermann Scherchen. From the latter two in particular, Nono learned the intricacies of twelve-tone and electronic composition, and, indeed, it was this orientation which charted his entire creative career.

Nono's first flush of fame emerged with the *Variazioni Canoniche,* a dodecaphonic work based on a tone row employed in Schoenberg's *Ode to Napoleon.* It was premiered August 27, 1950 under Scherchen's direction at the Darmstadt summer music school. Of the chamber and symphonic works which followed, *Polifonica, Monodia, Ritmica* for flute, clarinet, bass clarinet, saxophone, horn, piano, and percussion (1951) and *Due Espressioni* (1953) are representative. The former was introduced by Scherchen, again at Darmstadt, while the latter was presented first by Hans Rosbaud and the Donaueschingen Festival Orchestra for which it was commissioned. William Steinberg and the Pittsburgh Symphony brought *Due Espressioni* to the United States in 1958. The work established Nono as a colorist and sonorist within the serial sphere.

The twelve-tone approach was extended to the ballet in *Der rote Mantel* (1954), based on the poetry of Garcia Lorca, whose work had a lasting effect on the composer. The melodic contours are, as might be expected, free and seemingly unpredictable; they are, however, systematically determined by means of serial techniques. The *Epitaph for Federico Garcia Lorca,* a homage to the poet, is a three-part composition featuring solo voices, chorus, and orchestra. Bruno Maderna conducted part one at Darmstadt (July 21, 1952) and part three via the Northwest German Radio in Hamburg on February 16, 1953; Hans Rosbaud presented part two at Baden-Baden on December 12, 1952. In the first and third parts, the vocal soloists and chorus have speaking parts (in Spanish) and sometimes utter words penned by Lorca and by Pablo Neruda. The middle part, a concertante for flute and orchestra, reveals an intense emotionality not often encountered in serial works of this type.

Nono's leftist political attitude manifested itself unmistakably in the opera *Intolleranza 1960,* which, when premiered in Venice on April 13, 1961 at the Festival of Contemporary Music, resulted in a riot. Using the opera as a scaffold upon which to build a text which attacked intolerance in general, Nono mounted a musical pulpit to lash out against segregation and Fascism, as well as the atomic bomb. Electronic sounds are introduced within the framework of strict serialism. The composer's membership in the Communist Party in Italy helped to polarize the audience as well as the various pro-Nazi and Fascist demonstrators inside and outside the theater. Interestingly, the American premiere in Boston (1965) resulted in only mild protestation. A State Department reversal of an earlier denial of a visa for the composer resulted in "free" publicity. By now the serial techniques employed (including pointilism) and sequences on magnetic tape no longer had the shock value of earlier forays along these lines.

Nono found himself at the center of another controversy at the first performance of his oratorio *The Representative* (text by Peter Weiss), based on portions of Dante's *Divine Comedy.* The inflammatory text, much more than the Webernian serialism, provoked the audience. The subject matter deals with the trial of Auschwitz guards in Frankfurt in 1965. In this sense, the subject, as well as the music, was both topical and contemporary.

Intolleranza 1960 and *The Representative* firmly clarified Nono's chosen mode of expression. In the opera especially it becomes apparent that the vocal/choral component is the conveyor of the central ideas and thus needs to be understood both figuratively and literally. The orchestral writing moves away from the translucence and subtle expressivity associated with Webern's serialism and toward a massed polychromatic and sometimes static series of layers of sound. Expressionism is therefore linked with agitation-propaganda themes as in the musical theater of the 1920s.

Collectivism emerges in the 1975 opus, *Al gran sole carico d'amore* (a celebration of the Paris commune of 1871). Here, Nono collaborated with the scenographer Borovsky and the director Lyubimov (of Moscow's Taganka Theater), and, ultimately, with the choreographer Jakobson and the conductor Abbado (the work was dedicated to Abbado and Pollini). The libretto contains a curious mix of Marxist quotations and words by forgotten workers punctuated by both instrumental and electronic interjections. Unlike *Intolleranza,* this work possesses self-contained scenes. Of particular interest, because of its break with Nono's past utterances, is the inclusion of a classical ballet which symbolizes the domination of the bourgeoisie.

Luigi Nono, along with Maderna, Dallapiccola, and Berio, is a luminous figure in late twentieth-century Italian art music. He has found a language which, while complex and modeled on the formulations of the Second Viennese School, is nevertheless one well-suited to the polemical messages its creator wished to enunciate.—DAVID Z. KUSHNER

Norma

Composer: *Vincenzo Bellini.*

Librettist: *Felice Romani (after Louis Alexandre Soumet).*

First Performance: *Milan, Teatro alla Scala, 26 December 1831.*

Roles: *Norma (soprano); Adalgisa (mezzo-soprano or soprano); Pollione (tenor); Oroveso (bass); Flavio (tenor); Clotilde (mezzo-soprano); chorus (SSTTBB).*

Vincenzo Bellini's *Norma* transcended the Italian operatic tradition of vocal elegance to reaffirm with Monteverdi, Gluck, and Mozart the supremacy of dramatic representation. By purging bel canto of its affectations while retaining its functional qualities, Bellini imbued *Norma* with trenchant character portrayals and a prodigious emotional intensity without sacrificing melodic beauty or harmonic cordiality. Felice Romani's exceptionally adroit adaptation of Soumet's play (produced in Paris only eight months before the opera's premiere) may well have inspired Bellini to abandon the facile rubric of his early operas. Never before had he confronted so volatile and paradoxical a heroine as Norma. She is the axis and prime agent of a plot incited by human viscousness. Providing her with musical mind and marrow demanded supreme ingenuity of a bel canto composer, but Bellini, like Mozart, both permeated and absorbed his characters. To make Norma musically authentic, he had to transform Italian opera, surpassing even the stylistic advances of Donizetti. Soon French composers followed suit, and Wagner, despite his contempt for Italian opera, praised the intimacy of music and drama achieved by Bellini and savored his vinaceous melodies.

Norma is deeply troubled as the story begins. As high priestess of the Druid temple in Gaul during the Roman occupation (ca. 50 B.C.), she avows chastity, but has borne two children by Pollione, the Roman preconsul who has vanquished her people. Assisted by her confidante Clotilde, Norma has managed to conceal her children from all Gaul, even from her father Oroveso, the Archdruid. Pollione, however, has redirected his passions to Adalgisa, a young virgin of the temple for whom Norma shows maternal fondness. The Druids, eager to revolt against the Roman conquerors, consult Norma, who prophesies disaster should they take up arms. She prays to the goddess Irminsul for peace, a devotion even more personal than collective.

Meeting Pollione secretly in act II, the vulnerable Adalgisa succumbs to his ardor and promises to depart with him for Rome. Without naming her lover, she confides her plans to Norma, who sympathizes knowingly and frees Adalgisa from her vows. A moment later, Pollione enters; Adalgisa addresses him as her lover, Norma addresses him as the father of her children. The mutually astounded women berate Pollione until the temple gong summons Norma to the altar.

In act III, overwrought with shame and obsessed with vengeance, Norma stands over her sleeping children, dagger in hand, but, after some eloquent soul searching, proves herself a kinder mother than Medea. She charges Adalgisa to take the children to their father, who will raise them as Romans. After much remonstration, Adalgisa agrees, hoping that the sight of the children will move Pollione to return to Norma. Softened by the girl's altruism, Norma embraces her rival and the two vow eternal friendship. But Pollione insists on leaving for Rome with Adalgisa. The despairing girl returns in act IV to the temple, and Norma at last calls for war. Pursuing Adalgisa, Pollione is captured and brought before Norma. With magisterial aplomb, the priestess offers to spare his life if he will abandon Adalgisa. When Pollione refuses, Norma threatens to immolate his preferred mistress; she enjoys Pollione's tormented attempts to die in her stead. Then, to Pollione's amazement, Norma turns her moment of retribution into a confession of impiety. Persuading her father to look after the children, she commits herself to death by fire. Loving her in sacrifice more than in sacrilege, Pollione joins her in the flames.

The Romantic excesses of *Norma* accentuate its psychological validity. The agonized priestess compresses and intensifies the pivotal struggles of womanhood. Her lover literally subverts her father and usurps her allegiance. She is biological mother to Pollione's children, vicarious mother to Adalgisa, and spiritual mother to the Druids, but the momentum of vindictiveness makes her maternal burdens almost unbearable, and she nearly adds murder and treason to her offenses before regaining her higher nature. She is both sanctified and profane, conspicuous and clandestine, formidable and benign. She drives those she loves to utmost distress while placating her war-minded people. Her music, best suited for a dramatic soprano, is by turns resounding and mellifluous. It requires unfaltering agility, sustaining power, minute control of dynamics, and a wide spectrum of vocal colors. Remarkably few sopranos have attempted the role, and fewer still have proved equal to its technical and interpretive demands.

Although *Norma* hardly typifies its genre, Bellini preserved the formalities of *opera seria*. For the most part, he clearly distinguishes arias and ensemble from recitatives, cavatinas from cabalettas, and ariosos from all else. The opera begins with a formal overture, and punctuates the end of each number with conclusive harmonies. Arpeggiated and repeated chords abound in the accompaniment, except during recitatives where Bellini braces the vocal lines with discrete chords, or vivifies them with a vocabulary of rhetorical figures that the young Verdi learned well.

The chorus has much to sing, and the orchestra much to play on its own with all its thematic introductions and postludes. Nor does Bellini renounce melodic appeal for dramatic expression; Norma's prayer in act I sets linear beauty and poignant emotion in perfect balance.

In style and substance, *Norma* pointed the way for Verdi. Romani's libretto integrates lyricism and plot, making the visually static arias and ensembles essential to the drama. Everywhere Bellini's music reinforces the thrust of Romani's verse, charting the interplay of characters and confiding their secret musings and inducements. Even the recitatives impart poetic nuances and implicit meanings, as Norma's filicidal monologue affectingly demonstrates. The harmonic current, spurred by accented dissonances, diverted by altered chords, and delayed by circuits and reversals, frequently brings the emotional intensity to a fervid glow. More prospector than reformer, Bellini amplified the language of bel canto to sound the churning of affinities and disengagements. He heard the inner music of opera's most forbearing woman, and enriched the singer's art with her prophetic voice.—JAMES ALLEN FELDMAN

Norman, Jessye

Soprano. Born 15 September 1945, in Augusta, Georgia. Studied with Carolyn Grant at Howard University, Washington, DC, with Alice Duschak at Peabody Conservatory and with Pierre Bernac and Elizabeth Mannion at the University of Michigan; debut as Elisabeth in Tannhäuser, *Deutsche Oper, Berlin, 1969; appeared in Florence as Selika in* L'africaine, *Maggio Musicale, 1971; Teatro alla Scala debut as Aida, 1972; Covent Garden debut as Cassandre in* Les Troyens, *1972; U.S. stage debut with Opera Company of Philadelphia as Jocasta in* Oedipus Rex *and Purcell's Dido; Metropolitan Opera debut as Cassandre, 1983.*

Born into a musical family in Augusta, Georgia, Jessye Norman learned the piano at an early age and first remembers singing in public at age six when she performed "Jesus is Calling" in the key of C. In 1961 she went to study singing with Carolyn Grant at Howard University in Washington, DC. Grant did not attempt to put her voice into a specific category but let her explore a wide range of music. Study with Alice Duschak at Peabody and Pierre Bernac at the University of Michigan followed. As might be expected, Norman has an affinity for songs of all kinds, from the German Lieder of Schubert, Brahms, Mahler, and Schoenberg, to French *mélodies,* Russian songs, spirituals, and the songs of Jerome Kern. Miss Norman performs spirituals, usually at the close of a recital, to "bring music to people who have no interest in classical music on a grand scale but who can approach folk music." With spirituals and the music of composers such as Kern she feels a "Lied-like unity of poem and melody." Norman has recorded copious examples of this wide range of song literature, reflecting her extensive activity in the recital hall.

As an opera singer Norman has had to find her way gradually. Her sumptuous voice, one of the richest and most expressive of recent decades, is in range and timbre a cross between a soprano and a mezzo-soprano and is shown to advantage only in certain repertory. Her operatic debut was as Elisabeth in *Tannhäuser* at the Deutsche Oper, Berlin, in 1969. The three years Norman spent at that house, singing Aida, the Countess, Elsa, and many other roles, brought her only partial success for she did not want to sing standard soprano repertory and was still finding her way. Of the major Verdi soprano roles, for example, Aïda is the only one she cares for: "I've turned down all the Leonoras." She has since sung, at least on disc, a few of the early Verdi heroines, appearing as Medora on the Philips *Il corsaro* set with Caballé and Carreras and on Philips's *Un giorno di regno*. From 1975 to 1980 Norman turned down all opera engagements and gave only Lieder recitals and orchestra concerts. Her statuesque appearance has also been a factor in selecting appropriate roles and it is perhaps significant that her first appearance after her operatic hiatus was in that most static of roles, Strauss's Ariadne. Harold Rosenthal, writing in *Opera* of Norman's Ariadne, which she has subsequently recorded, called her "a prima donna to her fingertips. 'Es gibt ein Reich' was gloriously projected. . . ."

Two standard roles that Norman performed in her Berlin years have been recorded commercially. Her Elsa in *Lohengrin* may be heard on Decca with Domingo in the title role, conducted by Solti. In the recording of her Countess in Mozart's *Le nozze di Figaro,* Norman's spacious voice (she says her voice "can only go *so* quickly" and "needs space in which to resound") conveys dignity, yet Norman's characterization displays the Countess's sense of humor, never letting the listener forget that she is Rosina who was not born with a title. Much more recently Norman has recorded roles in Offenbach's *Les contes d'Hoffmann, Fidelio,* and *Carmen,* operas that she has not performed on stage. She has always kept a long list of roles to be considered, rejecting many but working gradually up to others. One direction she moved towards was to sing more Wagner and Strauss, with Isolde as her ultimate goal. To that end she has sung the three acts of *Tristan und Isolde* on separate nights in concert. Isolde is a part that she is afraid of "using up every ounce of [my] energy in the first act alone." Sieglinde is a character she has been identified with, in a recording of *Die Walküre* from Dresden under Janowski and in the Metropolitan Opera telecast in the summer of 1990. Her Sieglinde has much of the femininity and passion of Lotte Lehmann with more sumptuousness of voice.

In the 1972-73 season at Covent Garden, Norman performed in Berlioz' *Les Troyens* and made her Metropolitan Opera debut as Cassandre in 1983. At the Met she has also sung, in addition to Sieglinde, Didon in *Les Troyens,* Jocasta, Ariadne, Elisabeth, and Mme. Lidoine in Poulenc's *Les dialogues des Carmélites.* Poulenc seems to be a favorite; in addition to his songs Miss Norman has also appeared in *La voix humaine.* In addition to early Verdi works, rarities or unusual repertoire that Norman has sung or recorded include Selika in Meyerbeer's *L'africaine* conducted by Muti at the 1971 Florence May festival, of which a pirate recording exists; a recording of Mozart's *La finta giardiniera;* Faure's *Pénélope* on disc; and, from the late 1970s recordings of seldom-performed operas by Haydn. These include *La vera costanza* (1977) under Dorati with Norman as a dashing Rosina and *Armida* (1979) with Norman in the title role in magnificent voice, ranging in mood from terrifying vengeance to heartfelt pleas. In the French repertoire there is a stunning recorded account of Gluck's French *Alceste* with Gedda in which Norman sings poignantly and, from the Baroque, she has sung Rameau's *Hippolyte et Aricie* at Aix-en-Provence. As a result of her upbringing Norman has an affinity with music of a spiritual nature: she has sung *Messiah,* some Haydn oratorios, and Mahler's Second and Eighth symphonies. She has recorded an affecting *Gurrelieder* of Schoenberg and has performed Shostakovich's Symphony No. 14 with Giulini and the Los Angeles Philharmonic.

Jessye Norman will no doubt continue to explore the possibilities of her unique voice, discarding or rejecting certain roles while at the same time rising to new challenges.

—STEPHEN A. WILLIER

Le nozze di Figaro [The Marriage of Figaro]

Composer: *Wolfgang Amadeus Mozart.*

Librettist: *Lorenzo Da Ponte (after Beaumarchais).*

First Performance: *Vienna, Burgtheater, 1 May 1786.*

Roles: *Figaro (baritone); Count Almaviva (baritone); Countess (soprano); Susanna (soprano); Cherubino (soprano or mezzo-soprano); Marcellina (soprano or mezzo-soprano); Dr. Bartolo (bass); Don Basilio (tenor); Don Curzio (tenor); Antonio (bass); Barbarina (soprano); chorus (SATB).*

Le nozze di Figaro was Mozart's second opera for Vienna, and his first major collaboration with the librettist Lorenzo Da Ponte (1749-1838). The composer had found it hard to establish himself in the imperial city since his arrival in 1781; not surprisingly, he took some time to settle on the subject for his first Italian *opera buffa* for the sophisticated Viennese. After two false starts, he chose a controversial French play by Pierre-Augustin Caron de Beaumarchais (1732-99), *La folle journée ou Le mariage de Figaro* (1784). This, the second of a trilogy about the Spanish barber Figaro, had recently created a scandal across Europe for its political content: the notion of a count getting his come-uppance for his wicked designs on Susanna, the fiancée of his servant, Figaro, at the hands of his wife, the countess, and of his social inferiors was clearly inflammatory. Louis XIV called the play "detestable," while Napoleon claimed it "the revolution in action."

But social satire apart, the play is also a sparkling comedy of manners: the harridan Marcellina and the pedantic lawyer Dr. Bartolo—who are both enlisted to help the count, but who turn against him on the discovery that they are Figaro's parents—plus the fawning music-master, Don Basilio, and the love-sick adolescent, Cherubino, are splendid characters. All this, and its *succès de scandale,* surely made the play attractive for Mozart. It also enabled him to rival Paisiello, whose *Il barbiere di Siviglia* (St Petersburg, 1782), based on Beaumarchais' first Figaro play, had been an outstanding success when performed in Vienna in 1783.

Lorenzo Da Ponte was a good librettist who knew what worked on a stage. He could also write polished verse well suited to music. The account in his *Memoirs* of working with Mozart on *Le nozze di Figaro,* hoodwinking Emperor Joseph II into accepting the project, and engineering that the act III finale should not be cut despite a recent ban on dances within operas, should be read with caution. But Da Ponte and Mozart were certainly at work by mid 1785, and on 11 November Leopold Mozart reported that his son was up to his eyes in the score: "I know the piece: it is a very tiresome play and the translation from the French will certainly have to be altered very freely if it is to be effective as an opera. God grant that the text may be a success. I have no doubt about the music. But there will be a lot of running about and discussions before he gets the libretto so adjusted as to suit his purposes exactly."

Da Ponte had to tone down the more obviously seditious passages of the play, and also focus and simplify the dialogue to accommodate the slower speed of sung rather than spoken delivery. But he did not alter the play as much as one might expect (or as much as the emperor was led to believe); it was too tautly structured to be cut extensively, and much of the libretto simply translates Beaumarchais word for word. Indeed, most of the comic masterstrokes in the opera are thanks to the playwright. And even though the play was reduced from five acts to four, Da Ponte still had to apologize for its length in his preface to the libretto.

569

In deciding which sections of the play would be treated as arias and ensembles, the librettist and composer sometimes took their cue from musical references in the play: for example, Chérubin's *romance* "Mon coursier hors d'haleine" sung to the countess in act II of Beaumarchais' play was transformed into Cherubino's "Voi che sapete." Elsewhere Beaumarchais' episodic organization allowed the choice of sections suitable for extended musical treatment by virtue of their pace, their importance to the overall intrigue, and their possibilities for comic characterization: good examples are provided by the act I trio "Cosa sento! tosto andate" (from act I, scene ix in the play) and by the act II finale. Finally, arias had to be provided for the main members of the cast, if only to meet the demands of the singers, each of whom required at least one show-piece.

These arias also raise further issues. Although some (e.g., Cherubino's "Non so più cosa son, cosa faccio" and Figaro's "Non più andrai farfallone amoroso") translate parallel speeches in the play, elsewhere Da Ponte was forced to halt the action to provide an aria and thus to develop his characters more extensively. Beaumarchais generally maintains a fast pace in the play, reveling more in comic action and witty repartee than in emotional introspection. But Figaro's "Se vuol ballare," the count's "Vedrò mentre io sospiro," Susanna's "Deh vieni, non tardar, o gioia bella," and the countess' "Porgi amor, qualche ristoro" and "Dove sono i bei momenti," take the opera into a different world: the carefully calculated transformation of the countess, whose renewed self-understanding becomes the focal point of the action, is particularly striking. And if the libretto had to delve more deeply into the characters than Beaumarchais might have wished, Mozart's music delves deeper still. For everyone in the opera, what starts out as a rather innocent game becomes (by the middle of act II) an intense, almost frightening, and ultimately revelatory experience.

Mozart renders his characters far more human than their derivation from *commedia dell'arte* stereotypes would suggest. He also found ways of restoring the political elements cut from the libretto: the music for Figaro and Susanna goes beyond what *opera buffa* conventions decreed suitable for the lower classes, and dance patterns, in particular the courtly minuet, allow the servants to challenge their masters in subtle ways. Finally, Mozart develops a musical style that fully meets the demands of comedy. This is especially apparent in the glorious ensembles. Two structural procedures that Mozart was currently developing in his instrumental works come to fruition here: contrapuntal techniques that enable characters to present different points of view simultaneously, and sonata-form organization exploiting the ability of tonality to establish and resolve musical conflicts that mirror the conflicts and resolutions of the action. The best example is the act III sextet, "Riconosci in questo amplesso"—reportedly Mozart's favorite piece in the opera—where the drama of Figaro recovering his long-lost parents is matched perfectly by Mozart's music. Similarly, the magnificent act II finale elaborates a well-founded musical structure of unprecedented length to support the ebb and flow of the action. Perhaps for the first time, Mozart has fully realized the potential of the Classical style. The result is a comic masterpiece.

Although the premiere of *Figaro* was planned for early 1786, it was delayed until 1 May. The performance was not outstanding: it is a difficult score, and anti-Mozart factions in the audience sought to sabotage the event. But it was by no means a disaster: according to Michael Kelly, "At the end of the opera, I thought the audience would never have done applauding and calling for Mozart: almost every piece was encored, which prolonged it nearly to the length of two operas. . . . Never was any thing more complete, than the triumph of Mozart, and his 'Nozze di Figaro,' to which numerous overflowing audiences bore witness." The opera was even more successful in Prague, from where Mozart wrote excitedly on 15 January 1787, "here they talk about nothing but 'Figaro.' Nothing is played, sung or whistled but 'Figaro.' No opera is drawing like 'Figaro.' Nothing, nothing but 'Figaro'." It was revived for Vienna in 1789, when Mozart wrote two substitute arias for Susanna (K577, 579) and made other adjustments to suit his new cast.—TIM CARTER

OPERA 0

Oberon

Composer: *Carl Maria von Weber.*

Librettist: *J.R. Planché (after C.M. Wieland).*

First Performance: *London, Covent Garden, 12 April 1826.*

Roles: *Oberon (tenor); Puck (contralto); Reiza (soprano); Fatima (mezzo-soprano); Huon of Bordeaux (tenor); Sherasmin (baritone); Droll (contralto); First and Second Mermaids (sopranos); Speaking Roles: Titania; Haroun al Rashid; Babekan; Mesru; Almansor; Roschana; Nadine; Abdulla; First and Second Gardeners; Charlemagne; chorus (SATB).*

Set in the thirteenth century and in places as different as Shakespeare's fairyland and Baghdad, *Oberon,* Weber's last opera, was designed for a London production with a libretto in English. But the story is taken mostly from an old French *chanson de geste* called *Huon of Bordeaux.* Unlike that of *Euryanthe,* the music for *Oberon* is interrupted by scenes of spoken dialogue and stage action without music.

Although Oberon, Titania, and Puck all play their part in the opera, Shakespeare and his "wood near Athens" are soon left far behind in act I, as the story takes a variety of new turns. But it resembles *A Midsummer Night's Dream* in that it begins with the King of Fairyland and his Queen at odds. Oberon has vowed not to be reconciled with her until he finds two lovers who shall remain faithful through all temptations and dangers. Soon he regrets his vow, despairing of success, but he then hears of the knight Huon of Bordeaux, who has killed Charlemagne's son in a duel and is to be sent as a punishment to Baghdad to claim the Caliph's daughter as a bride after killing the man who sits at the Caliph's right hand. In a vision, Oberon shows Huon the beautiful Reiza whom he must claim and with whom he at once falls in love. Then he gives the young knight a magic horn and transports him to the Middle East along with his squire Sherasmin. In their first adventure they rescue Prince Babekan from a lion, but it turns out that he is evil and about to be married to Reiza—against her will, as we learn in the final scene of the act, which shows her in Haroun el Rashid's palace with her attendant Fatima. But Reiza too has seen a vision, sent by Oberon, of the knight who will save her from the hated Babekan, and Fatima tells her mistress that she foresees her deliverance. Huon, too, has reaffirmed his chivalrous mission in a big aria earlier in the act.

Act II begins still in the palace, where attendants praise the Caliph, who sits with Babekan beside him. Dancing girls precede Reiza's entrance, but Huon is on hand with his sword, and, after overcoming Babekan and blowing his magic horn to subdue the court, he and Sherasmin, take Reiza and Fatima away. A number of adventures and hardships ensue, which place all four characters in danger, these being Oberon's test of their strength, but the love which binds them (for Sherasmin and Fatima now also love each other) carries them through: among these adventures is the storm at sea and shipwreck, after which Reiza sings her florid and dramatic aria "Ocean, thou mighty monster." Pirates separate the lovers, too, when Reiza is taken into slavery in Tunis, as are Fatima and Sherasmin. But in act III her master, the Emir Almanzor, respects her chastity, and when Huon is guided by Puck to Tunis he is able to rescue her despite being courted by the Emir's wife. This rescue can occur only after greater dangers (Huon is arrested and condemned to be burned alive) and the intervention of Sherasmin armed with the horn of Oberon. To its magical music, all must dance and be reconciled, and Oberon himself appears and tells the lovers that all their prayers are answered, after which he transports them back to Charlemagne's Frankish court. There Huon claims his pardon, and the opera ends with a chorus of thanksgiving.

The music of *Oberon* makes us regret the composer's untimely death in London less than two months after the premiere. The work is remarkable perhaps above all for the orchestral writing, and indeed the magic horn of Oberon, heard in the orchestra in the very first notes of the famous overture, returns as a kind of motto throughout. The music of fairyland, too, occurs not only in act I but also in other places such as the end of act II, where Oberon and Puck and their attendants once again appear. Oberon and Huon are both tenor roles, and each singer has interesting music although that of the heroic young knight is more varied and challenging, while Reiza too has fine solos to sing besides her famous address to the ocean after the shipwreck. Even Sherasmin and Fatima are well characterized vocally, not least in their charming exchanges at the start of act III. Dramatically, we can see parallels in act III not only with Mozart's *Die Entführung aus dem Serail* but also with the same composer's *Die Zauberflöte* in both of which pairs of lovers are held captive and in some way spiritually tested. Because of its spoken scenes and sheer length, the opera is difficult to stage, but as always with the mature Weber we are clearly in the presence of a highly imaginative and often masterly musical mind. After the London production the composer planned to reshape *Oberon* and use more recitative instead of the speech, but unfortunately he did not live to carry out this plan. However, Gustav Mahler later made a carefully arranged performing version.—CHRISTOPHER HEADINGTON

Oedipus Rex

Composer: *Igor Stravinsky.*

Librettist: *J. Cocteau (translated into Latin by J. Danielou).*

First Performance: *concert performance, Paris, Sarah Bernhardt, 30 May 1927; staged performance, Vienna, 23 February 1928; revised, 1948.*

Roles: *Oedipus (tenor); Jocasta (mezzo-soprano); Creon (bass-baritone); Tiresias (bass); Shepherd (tenor); Messenger (bass-baritone); chorus (TTBB).*

In the mid-1920s, Stravinsky, whose career to that point had been devoted primarily to works for the ballet and for the theater, turned to composing the kind of instrumental works that suited his new neo-classical style: the Octet for Winds, the Piano Sonata and Serenade, and the Concerto for Piano and Winds. He returned to the theater with the opera-oratorio *Oedipus Rex* (1927), written partly as a surprise gift to Diaghilev on his twentieth anniversary as ballet and opera impresario. Indeed, since the existence of the work was kept secret from Diaghilev until virtually the last minute, it was initially produced by Diaghilev's Ballets Russes in concert form. In the opinion of many, *Oedipus Rex* has never fully recovered from this inauspicious launching; when plunked in the midst of a program that included a full mounting of *Firebird,* the work seemed especially impenetrable to audience and critics alike. Diaghilev himself regarded the work, according to Stravinsky, as "un cadeau très macabre."

Subsequent stagings have done little to improve upon that first impression, for in composing his opera-oratorio, Stravinsky was experimenting with a theatrical style in which the work would be seen as a "still-life," with stationary characters in masks placed at various heights on an immobile set. By adapting a story the plot of which was well-known, Stravinsky would be free to concentrate on musical dramatization; by having the work sung in Latin, he would be able to distance the emotions from the directness of word-to-word comprehensibility and thus be able to use the text more for its purely phonetic qualities than for the exigencies of exposition and elucidation.

Stravinsky enlisted the aid of librettist Jean Cocteau, whom he had known for over fifteen years and who certainly was no stranger to Diaghilev projects. When Stravinsky informed Cocteau that his verses were to be recast in Latin, the latter must have surely felt the same artistic side-stepping as had occurred ten years earlier, when, as scenarist and putative librettist for *Parade,* his text was jettisoned in favor of a purely balletic approach. Nevertheless, the two authors came up with a compromise scheme in which a narrator, in evening dress and speaking French, would introduce the drama's various scenes, with the bulk of the work sung, by the soloists and male chorus, in Latin. In Cocteau's eyes, the sternness of the musical presentation would be relieved by the Parisian chic of the narration.

The story is taken directly from Sophocles. The people of Thebes implore Oedipus, their king, to save them from the plague. Creon, who has been sent to consult the oracle, returns with the information that for the plague to cease, the murder of King Laius must be avenged, and that the murderer is amongst them. Tiresias, the blind seer, is consulted, but he knows the truth and will not speak. Only when Oedipus impetuously accuses him of the murder does Tiresias reply that the murderer of the king is himself a king.

In the opera's second act, the facts fall into place. Oedipus' wife Jocasta mentions that Laius was killed at a crossroads; the chorus reminds Oedipus that he killed a man at a crossroads; the death of the elderly King Polybus is announced, and it is revealed that he was not the true father of Oedipus, as the latter had thought; Oedipus' lineage is revealed, whereupon he realizes that he has actually killed his father and married his mother (fulfilling an earlier oracle). Jocasta commits suicide, Oedipus gouges out his eyes, and the chorus mourns their fallen leader.

The implacable ostinatos (predominantly of minor thirds) of the chorus' initial appeal to Oedipus set the severe tone of the work's emotional atmosphere, and most of the music of the first act, though superficially forbidding, is nevertheless wonderfully expressive even in the sense of "expressive" to which Stravinsky himself might admit. From Oedipus' proud fioritura, to the blaring C-major of Creon's revelations, to the heart-piercing wind chords of Tiresias' refusal to speak (the 1920s was Stravinsky's "wind decade"), to the brilliant chorus hailing Jocasta at the end of the act, the first half of the drama surges forward with a determination and logic that are always compelling.

The second act is more diffuse and less successful, starting with Jocasta's strangely vampy aria, with its teasing alterations of raised and lowered sevenths. The choral contributions, except for the magnificent conclusion (essentially a tonally altered recapitulation of the work's opening) are far less focused, and in two instances are rather silly: the "Mulier in vestibulo" episodes in the rondo announcing Jocasta's death, and the "Aspikite" fugue ending that section (having the chorus sing a pompous academic fugue at this point is mannerist excess).

Like the contemporaneous German playwright Bertolt Brecht, whose name will be forever linked to his theory of "Verfremdung" ("alienation," as it is often translated; keeping the audience at an emotional distance), Stravinsky so often spoke polemically of music being "powerless to express anything but itself" that audiences and commentators often prejudge his works as cold and uninvolving. There can be little doubt that *Oedipus Rex,* given its elaborate strategems of remoteness, figures among the most austere of Stravinsky's many theater works. But there is as little doubt that Stravinsky's incomparable techniques of word-setting, of orchestrational mastery and refinement, of character portrayal by means of harmonic and tonal delineation are all but lost on this uninvolved public.—GERALD MOSHELL

Offenbach, Jacques

Composer. Born 20 June 1819, in Cologne. Died 5 October 1880, in Paris. Studied cello with Vaslin at the Paris Conservatory, 1833-34; cellist in the orchestra of the Opéra-Comique; conductor at the Théâtre Français, 1850; opened the Théâtre des Bouffes-Parisiens, 1855, and managed it until 1866; operas produced in Ems, Germany, and Vienna; management of the Théâtre de la Gaîté; toured the United States, 1877.

Operas *L'alcôve,* P.P. de Forges and A. de Leuven, Paris, Tour d'Auvergne, 24 April 1847; *Le trésor à Mathurin,* L. Battu, Paris, Salle Herz, May 1853; revised as *Le mariage aux lanternes,* J. Dubois [=M. Carré] and L. Battu, Paris, Bouffes-Parisiens, 10 October 1857; *Pépito,* J. Moinaux, L. Battu, Paris, Variétés, 28 October 1853; *Luc et Lucette,* P.P. de Forges, E.-G. Roche, Paris, Salle Herz, 2 May 1854; *Oyayaie, ou La reine des îles,* J. Moinaux, Paris, Folies-Nouvelles, 26 June 1855; *Entrez, messieurs, mesdames,* F.-J. Méry and J. Servières [=L. Halévy], Paris, Bouffes-Parisiens (at Salle Marigny), 5 July 1855; *Les deux aveugles,* J. Moinaux, Paris, Bouffes-Parisiens (at Salle Marigny), 5 July 1855; *Une nuit blanche,* E. Plouvier, Paris, Bouffes-Parisiens (at Salle Marigny), 5 July 1855; *Le rêve d'une nuit d'été,* E. Tréfeu, Paris, Bouffes-Parisiens (at Salle Marigny), 30 July 1855; *Le violoneux,* E. Mestépès and E. Chevalet, Paris, Bouffes-Parisiens (at Salle Marigny), 31 August 1855; *Madame Papillon,* J. Servières [=L. Halévy], Paris, Bouffes-Parisiens (at Salle Marigny), 3 October 1855; *Paimpol et Périnette,* P.P. de Forges, Paris, Bouffes-Parisiens (at Salle Marigny), 29 October 1855; *Ba-ta-clan,* L. Halévy, Paris, Bouffes-Parisiens, 29 December 1855; *Elodie, ou Le forfait nocturne,* L. Battu and H. Crémieux, Paris, Bouffes-Parisiens, 19 January 1856; *Le postillon en gage,* E. Plouvier and J. Adenis, Paris, Bouffes-Parisiens, 9 February 1856; *Trombalcazar, ou Les criminels dramatiques,* C.D. Dupeuty and E. Bourget, Paris, Bouffes-Parisiens, 3 April 1856; *La rose de Saint-Flour,* M. Carré, Paris, Bouffes-Parisiens (at Salle

Marigny), 12 June 1856; *Les dragées du baptême,* C.D. Dupeuty and E. Bourget, Paris, Bouffes-Parisiens (at Salle Marigny), 18 June 1856; *Le "66",* P.P. de Forges and M. Laurencin [=P.A. Chapelle], Paris, Bouffes-Parisiens (at Salle Marigny), 31 July 1856; *Le savetier et le financier,* Choiseul, Paris, Bouffes-Parisiens, 23 September 1856; *La bonne d'enfants,* E. Bercioux, Paris, Bouffes-Parisiens, 14 October 1856; *Les trois baisers du diable,* E. Mestépès, Paris, Bouffes-Parisiens, 15 January 1857; *Croquefer, ou Le dernier des paladins,* A. Jaime, E. Tréfeu, Paris, 12 February 1857; *Dragonette,* E. Mestépès and A. Jaime, Paris, Bouffes-Parisiens, 30 April 1857; *Vent du soir, ou L'horrible festin,* P. Gille, Paris, Bouffes-Parisiens, 16 May 1857; *Une demoiselle en lôterie,* A. Jaime and H. Crémieux, Paris, Bouffes-Parisiens, 27 July 1857; *Les deux pêcheurs,* C.D. Dupeuty and E. Bourget, Paris, Bouffes-Parisiens, 13 November 1857; *Mesdames de la Halle,* A. Lapointe, Paris, Bouffes-Parisiens, 3 March 1858; *La chatte metamorphosée en femme,* Eugène Scribe and Mélesville, Paris, Bouffes-Parisiens, 19 April 1858; *Orphée aux enfers,* H. Crémieux and L. Halévy, Paris, Bouffes-Parisiens, 21 October 1858; revised, Paris, Théâtre de la Gaîté, 7 February 1874; *Un mari à la porte,* A. Delacour and L. Morand, Paris, Bouffes-Parisiens, 22 June 1859; *Les vivandières de la grande armée,* A. Jaime and P.P. de Forges, Paris, Bouffes-Parisiens, 6 July 1859; *Geneviève de Brabant,* A. Jaime and E. Tréfeu, Paris, Bouffes-Parisiens, 19 November 1859; revised, H. Crémieux, Paris, Menus Plaisirs, 26 December 1867; revised, H. Crémieux, Paris, Théâtre de la Gaîté, 25 February 1875; *Le carnaval des revues,* E. Grangé, P. Gille, L. Halévy, Paris, Bouffes-Parisiens, 10 February 1860; *Daphnis et Chloé,* Clairville [=L.F. Nicolaie], J. Cordier [=E.T. de Vaulabelle], Paris, Bouffes-Parisiens, 27 March 1860; *Barkouf,* Eugène Scribe and H. Boisseaux, Paris, Opéra-Comique, 24 December 1860; revised as *Boule de neige,* Nuitter and E. Tréfeu, Paris, Bouffes-Parisiens, 14 December 1871; *La chanson de Fortunio,* H. Crémieux and L. Halévy, Paris, Bouffes-Parisiens, 5 January 1861; *Le pont des soupirs,* H. Crémieux and L. Halévy, Paris, Bouffes-Parisiens, 23 March 1861; revised, Paris, Variétés, 8 May 1868; *M. Choufleuri restera chez lui le . . .,* Saint-Rémy [=Duc de Morny], E. L'Epine, H. Crémieux, L. Halévy, Présidence du Corps Législatif, 31 May 1861; *Apothicaire et perruquier,* E. Frébault, Paris, Bouffes-Parisiens, 17 October 1861; *Le roman comique,* H. Crémieux and L. Halévy, Paris, Bouffes-Parisiens, 10 December 1861; *Monsieur et Madame Denis,* M. Laurencin [=Chapelle] and M. Delaporte, Paris, Bouffes-Parisiens, 11 January 1862; *Le voyage de MM. Dunanan père et fils,* P. Siraudin and J. Moinaux, Paris, Bouffes-Parisiens, 23 March 1862; *Les bavards (Bavard et bavarde),* Nuitter (after Cervantes, *Los habladores*), Bad Ems, 11 June 1862; *Jacqueline,* P. d'Arcy [=H. Crémieux and L. Halévy], Paris, Bouffes-Parisiens, 14 October 1862; *Il Signor Fagotto,* Nuitter and E. Tréfeu, Bad Ems, 11 July 1863; *Lischen et Fritzchen,* P. Dubois [=P. Boisselot], Bad Ems, 21 July 1863; *L'amour chanteur,* Nuitter and E. L'Epine, Paris, Bouffes-Parisiens, 5 January 1864; *Die Rheinnixen,* A. von Wolzogen (after Nuitter and E. Tréfeu), Vienna, Hofoper, 4 February 1864; *Les géorgiennes,* J. Moinaux, Paris, Palais-Royal, 16 March 1864; *Jeanne qui pleure et Jean qui rit,* Nuitter and E. Tréfeu, Bad Ems, July 1864; *Le fifre enchanté, ou Le soldat magicien,* Nuitter and E. Tréfeu, Bad Ems, 9 July 1864; *La belle Hélène,* H. Meilhac and L. Halévy, Paris, Variétés, 17 December 1864; *Coscoletto, ou Le lazzarone,* Nuitter and E. Tréfeu, Bad Ems, 24 July 1865; *Les refrains des bouffes,* Paris, Bouffes-Parisiens, 21 September 1865; *Les bergers,* H. Crémieux and P. Gille, Paris, Bouffes-Parisiens, 11 December 1865; *Barbe-bleue,* H. Meilhac and L. Halévy, Paris, Variétés, 5 February 1866; *La vie parisienne,* H. Meilhac and L. Halévy, Paris, Palais-Royal, 31 October 1866; *La Grande-Duchesse de Gérolstein,* H. Meilhac and L. Halévy, Paris, Variétés, 12 April 1867; *La permission de dix heures,* Mélesville [=A.H.I. Duveyrier] and P.F.A. Carmouche, Bad Ems, 9 July 1867; *La leçon de chant,* E. Bourget, Bad Ems, August 1867, Folies-Marigny, 17 June 1873; *Robinson Crusoé,* E. Cormon and H.

Crémieux (after Defoe), Paris, Opéra-Comique, 23 November 1867; *Le château à Toto,* H. Meilhac and L. Halévy, Paris, Palais-Royale, 6 May 1868; *L'île de Tulipatan,* H. Chivot and A. Duru, Paris, Bouffes-Parisiens, 30 September 1868; *La périchole,* H. Meilhac and L. Halévy, Paris, Variétés, 6 October 1868; revised, 25 April 1874; *Vert-vert,* H. Meilhac and Nuitter, Paris, Opéra-Comique, 10 March 1869; *La diva,* H. Meilhac and L. Halévy, Paris, Bouffes-Parisiens, 22 March 1869; *La princesse de Trébizonde,* Nuitter and E. Tréfeu, Baden-Baden, 31 July 1869; revised, Paris, Bouffes-Parisiens, 7 December 1869; *Les brigands,* H. Meilhac and L. Halévy, Paris, Variétés, 10 December 1869; *La romance de la rose,* E. Tréfeu and J. Prével, Paris, Bouffes-Parisiens, 11 December 1869; *Mam'zelle Moucheron,* E. Leterrier and A. Vanloo, c. 1870, Paris, Renaissance, 10 May 1881; *Le roi Carotte,* Sardou (after Hoffmann), Paris, Théâtre de la Gaîté, 15 January 1872; *Fantasio,* P. de Musset, Paris, Opéra-Comique, 18 January 1872; *Fleurette, oder Näherin und Trompeter,* J. Hopp and F. Zell [=C. Walzel] (after Pittaud de Forges, M. Laurencin [=P.-A. Chapelle]), Vienna, Carl-Theater, 8 March 1872; *Der schwarze Korsar,* J. Offenbach and R. Genée, Vienna, Theater an der Wien, 21 September 1872; *Les braconniers,* H. Chivot and A. Duru, Paris, Variétés, 29 January 1873; *Pomme d'api,* L. Halévy and W. Busnach, Paris, Renaissance, 4 September 1873; *La jolie parfumeuse,* H. Crémieux and E. Blum, Paris, Renaissance, 29 November 1873; *Bagatelle,* H. Crémieux and E. Blum, Paris, Bouffes-Parisiens, 21 May 1874; *Madame l'archiduc,* H. Meilhac, L. Halévy and A. Millaud, Paris, Bouffes-Parisiens, 31 October 1874; *Whittington,* Nuitter, E. Tréfeu, H.B. Farnie, London, Alhambra, 26 December 1874; *Les hannetons,* E. Grangé and A. Millaud, Paris, Bouffes-Parisiens, 22 April 1875; *La boulangère a des écus,* H. Meilhac and L. Halévy, Paris, Variétés, 19 October 1875; *La créole,* A. Millaud and H. Meilhac, Paris, Bouffes-Parisiens, 3 November 1875; *Le voyage dans la lune,* E. Leterrier, A. Vanloo, and A. Mortier, Paris, Théâtre de la Gaîté, 26 November 1875; *Tarte à la crème,* A. Millaud, Paris, Bouffes-Parisiens, 14 December 1875; *Pierrette et Jacquot,* J. Noriac and P. Gille, Paris, Bouffes-Parisiens, 13 October 1876; *La boîte au lait,* A. Grangé and J. Noriac, Paris, Bouffes-Parisiens, 3 November 1876; *Le docteur Ox,* A. Mortier and P. Gille (after J. Verne), Paris, Variétés, 26 January 1877; *La Foire Saint-Laurent,* H. Crémieux and A. de Saint-Albin, Paris, Folies-Dramatiques, 10 February 1877; *Maître Péronilla,* Nuitter and Ferrier, Paris, Bouffes-Parisiens, 13 March 1878; *Madame Favart,* H. Chivot and A. Duru, Paris, Folies-Dramatiques, 28 December 1878; *La marocaine,* Ferrier and L. Halévy, Paris, Bouffes-Parisiens, 13 January 1879; *La fille du tambour-major,* H. Chivot and A. Duru, Paris, Folies-Dramatiques, 13 December 1879; *Belle Lurette,* E. Blum, E. Blau, R. Toché, Paris, Renaissance, 30 October 1880 [unfinished; completed by Delibes]; *Les contes d'Hoffmann,* J. Barbier, Paris, Opéra-Comique, 10 February 1881 [unfinished; completed by Guiraud].

"There is in Paris a very young celebrity whose existence is, alas, not suspected by the musical world," remarked the Paris paper *Le ménestrel,* shortly after the appearance of a waltz called "Fleurs d'hiver" (Flowers of winter) in 1836. "M. Offenbach regularly composes three waltzes before luncheon, a mazurka after dinner, and four gallops between the two meals." At the age of seventeen, Offenbach had begun to make his name as a composer. Though he went on to write for the theater, he retained both his affinity for dance music and his prolific speed of composition.

Jacques (born Jakob) Offenbach, king of French comic operetta, began his musical career as a cellist. He was determined to pursue his ambition to write for theater, although his antagonistic relationship with the operatic establishment, especially the prestigious Opéra-Comique, meant that the only sources of commissions were closed to him. He finally joined the orchestra of the Opéra-Comique as a cellist, though he soon grew bored with this activity, and escaped to his first theatrical appointment: conductor for the Théâtre-Français. But he wanted to write his own music. Still unable to obtain commissions to write his music for the established theaters, Offenbach in 1855 applied for the necessary government permission to start his own theater, *Les Bouffes-Parisiens*. Success came immediately on opening night with *Les deux aveugles* (The Blind Beggars), among others. With this new-found popularity, Offenbach's career as a professional composer for the theater was launched.

Popular approval did not automatically bring critical acclaim, and critics were often hostile toward the immoral content of the librettos. But Offenbach slowly won more wide-spread approval. By 1857, the company was ready to tour London, with nineteen operettas by Offenbach in their repertoire. Offenbach had already been to London in 1844 as a cello virtuoso, but now he took London by storm with a season of operettas, an example on which Gilbert and Sullivan were to build—and from which they sometimes borrowed heavily. Offenbach's hold on London taste lasted more than twenty years.

Eager to write larger-scale works, Offenbach acquired a new license and used a large cast for the first time with *Mesdames de la Halle* (The Ladies of the Marketplace) in 1858. But the first truly large-scale production was *Orphée aux enfers* (Orpheus in the Underworld). Thereafter there was no turning back, and Offenbach continued to turn out music at an extraordinary pace. Though he wrote other music—songs and miscellaneous instrumental music—Offenbach is remembered for his great bulk of operettas, about 100 works. Many are short one-act pieces, but he worked quickly and constantly. Once, on a bet, he set a libretto in eight days.

Offenbach's fame rests on a mere handful of his works: *Les contes d'Hoffmann* (Tales of Hoffmann), his one relatively serious major opera, plus six comic operettas: *Orphée aux enfers, La belle Hélène* (Fair Helen), *La vie parisienne* (Life in Paris), *Barbe-bleu* (Bluebeard), *La Grande-Duchesse de Gerolstein* (The Grand Duchesse of Gerolstein), and *La Périchole* (The Périchole).

During his lifetime, Offenbach's stature was considerable. He often profited from good relations and good standing at court and in government circles, using his connections to acquire licenses and gain French citizenship, among other things. In 1861, Louis Napoleon awarded him the title "Chevalier de la Légion d'honneur." But Napoleon's empire collapsed after the Franco-Prussian war, and for the rest of his life Offenbach suffered suspicion from both the French and the Germans as a man with potentially divided loyalties. He fell on harder times, and faced continuing hostility from the Republicans seeking scapegoats from the second empire. Late in life, suffering from poor health, he continued to write, producing a few successes, though his masterpiece, *Les contes d'Hoffmann,* was left incomplete upon his death on 5 October 1880.

Offenbach's mature musical style owes much to the tradition of comic opera, with spoken dialogue rather than recitative separating the musical numbers. And Offenbach's love of Mozart shows unmistakably in the skillful part-writing for the larger vocal ensembles, influenced by *Die Zauberflöte* and *Così fan tutte.* Offenbach made effective use of the *opera buffa* patter song, with its breathless one syllable per note, popularized earlier by Rossini ("Largo al Factotum") and later by Gilbert and Sullivan. But perhaps the most striking aspect of Offenbach's musicality is his lyrical flair. Brilliant, memorable melodies scintillate throughout his scores, especially in the solos and duets. Many of the melodies are based on dances; the cancan immortalized by Offenbach is a breathlessly exciting 2/4 dance with the nonstop beat. But the most important characteristic of his music is parody.

Offenbach loved parody and satire. Meyerbeer and serious grand opera were frequent victims of his attentions, with a notable instance in the finale of *Ba-ta-clan,* when the oriental ruler Fé-ni-han decides to die in the noble manner of *Les Huguenots.* He calls on his comrades to join him in the German chorale "Ein' feste Burg," with voices preposterously imitating trumpet fanfares. Meyerbeer maintained a reasonably good humor over the situation, attending the Bouffes regularly, though he always waited until the second night rather than attend the opening.

Offenbach's irreverent imitations brought him popularity with the public, but not all his victims were so forgiving. Richard Wagner, who had come to Paris in 1859, avowed a high-minded pretentiousness that made him an obvious target. Following Wagner's book *Das Kunstwerk der Zukunft* (The Work of Art of the Future), Offenbach lampooned his style with *La symphonie de l'avenir* (The symphony of the future), and again in *Le carnaval des revues* (The Carnival of Revues, 1864). The result was an exchange of invective and a lifelong feud. Wagner retaliated with *Eine Kapitulation* (Capitulation), in which he mercilessly mocked the hapless Parisians suffering during the disastrous Franco-Prussian War, 1870-71.

For a long time Offenbach's work was largely ignored, due partly to a belief that the satire was too topical to be of interest today. But interest has grown since the centenary of his death in 1980. Attempts have been made to write entirely new scripts to accompany Offenbach's music, and recent efforts have also been made to update librettos with modern references. Further, in recent scholarship, an attempt has been made to analyze the social, cultural, and political basis of Offenbach's parody within the context of France's second empire, potentially lending serious theoretical weight to Offenbach's frivolity. The composer did indeed poke fun at contemporary political situations, as in *The Grand Duchesse of Gerolstein*'s mockery of petty duchies, or the question of legitimate rule in *The Brigands,* or the critique of the Paris Commune in *King Carrot.* But Offenbach did not parody war and the military, or satirize court life, with any revolutionary intent.

Offenbach's popularity was undoubtedly connected with the rise of the middle class and the concomitant need for music somewhere between highbrow and vulgar. His work may be thoroughly entrenched in its time, but it can still be enjoyed today in the spirit in which it was intended: delicious entertainment.—ELIZABETH W. PATTON

Opera

Composer: *Luciano Berio.*

Librettists: *Luciano Berio, U. Eco, and F. Colombo.*

First Performance: *Santa Fe, New Mexico, 12 August 1970; revised, 1977.*

Berio intended the title *Opera* to convey the plural of the Latin word *opus* for work rather than *opera* in the traditional sense. Indeed, Berio includes elements of at least three works, or *opera,* within *Opera:* 1) quotations from Striggio's libretto for Monteverdi's *Orfeo;* 2) scenes from *Terminal,* a dramatic work about terminally ill persons in a hospital ward, and also about travelers arriving at a terminal; and 3) the sinking of the Titanic, an event which took place in 1912 and which in 1957 became the basis for Berio's collaboration with Umberto Eco and Furio Colombo in the writing of a *Rappresentazione.* (This latter project was never completed.) In Berio's words, "all three [works within *Opera*] have one subject in common: death. *Opera* is a celebration of ending."

Berio has punctuated *Opera* with three different performances of an Aria, designated as Air I, Air II, and Air III, performed by a Soprano and accompanied on the piano by her vocal coach. The text is sung in English, and based in part on Striggio's libretto for *Orfeo*.

> Now, as the tunes change, now gay, now sad,
> Behold the trav'ler
> For whom, only a short time ago
> Sighs were food and tears were drink.

The opening line is similar to that sung in Italian by La musica (the Spirit of Music) at the end of the Prologue of Monteverdi's *Orfeo,* while the sources for lines three and four are the words sung by the Chorus of Nymphs and Shepherds which comes at the end of act I of *Orfeo*. By adding the line "Behold the trav'ler," Berio included all of the travelers in *Opera:* those on the Titanic, those in *Terminal,* as well as Orfeo himself. Each time the Aria is repeated in *Opera,* the quality of performance improves—as if the Soprano is making progress in her voice lessons. This is in keeping with Berio's idea that various episodes in *Opera* are developmental. Berio comments that: "The structure of the music, the expressive nature of certain elements continue to grow while everything on stage is dying. This contrary motion is one of the basic elements of *Opera. . . .*"

The musical and dramatic elements of Air III provide a smooth transition to Memoria in act III. This is the third of three Memoria in *Opera*. For these episodes, Berio extracted part of the text sung by the Messenger in act II of *Orfeo*. All three episodes (Memoria) are similar to each other in musical and dramatic content. A tritone prevails throughout the melodic setting of this text, which creates a haunting sound in keeping with the devastating news delivered by the messenger.

In act I, the Memoria episode serves as a transition to scene one. This is also the case in act II where Memoria moves directly to scene ii, in which the texture becomes more complicated since all three works of *Opera* are intertwined. Shortly after Berio's musical reference to Stravinsky's *Fireworks,* the choir sustains the diminished triad of scene i (F#, A, C) as a continuous sound block, as some of the instruments alternate pitches of an ascending chromatic scale fragment. This leads the choir to utterances of "addio," which spins off into some vocal alliteration, almost as a warning of a later episode which is entitled "Addio." The reference is to Orfeo's lament at the end of act II.

The tritone which was so evident in scenes i and ii in the Chorus of Spirits, and in Memoria where the Messenger announced death, is also used to characterize the reference to the Westwind in Melodrama. This thread of melodic dissonance is also carried through to Documentario I and II. In Documentario I (act II), a feeling of stasis is created by the repetition of the ascending melodic pattern of the tritone and perfect fourth on the piano which creates a feeling that the dramatic motion as well as the Titanic are standing still. At this point, the actors are mimicing the sounds of the ship's engine. In the second Documentario, the feeling of stasis is even more extreme than that of Documentario I, because of the repeated notes and blocks of sound created by instrumentalists and members of the chorus. In the introductory bars, the marimba and vibraphone share the same tritone E—B flat as if *Opera* is moving to a climax. In fact, this is the point at which Berio frees *Opera* from the influences of the Titanic, *Terminal,* and *Orfeo* and focuses the dramatic and musical action on dead children.

Immediately before the second Documentario, Berio has placed Concerto II (based on his earlier work, *Tempi Concertati* [1958]), which helps to complete Concerto I (act I). In *Opera,* Berio used these episodes as the backdrop for the surviving passengers of the Titanic to introduce themselves to each other. He says that "The episode [Concerto II] continues at the end of the piece, before the scene of the children: we can hear a development of the concerto and of the characters." The musical texture of both of these concertos is characterized by long sustained notes. There are also layers of melodic activity which result in jagged lines. The overall effect is only mildly dissonant because of the blocks of sound. Contrast is achieved by tempo changes.

For the musical labyrinth surrounding the "Non-Story" of *Opera,* Berio succeeded in weaving numerous fragments together in support of the episodic nature of the work. Certain motives appear in the Aria which are transformed in the haunting references to the Westwind in Melodrama, having to do with the Titanic, or to the musical background of the Chorus of Spirits in scene i, and so on. Berio's quotation and elaboration of the most futuristic segment of Stravinsky's *Fireworks* is also revealing, since Berio's compositional style in *Opera* often resembles that of the youthful, forward-looking Stravinsky. The technique is freely atonal, with emphasis on motivic development in the sections that are melodically and contrapuntally oriented. In *Opera,* Berio was always able to support the drama with his musical instincts. By controlling the libretto and the music, he had a clear idea of how to use expressive means to the advantage of *Opera.* Because of the overall sequence of episodes within each act, a certain symmetry is evident in the revised version (1977) of *Opera,* which might not have been apparent in the original version (1970).

It should come as no surprise that Berio himself has suggested that ". . . a discussion of *Opera* would need a book by itself . . ." At the very least, a documentary film ought to be considered as a means of preserving some of the scenes from *Opera* for further study by scholars.—MAUREEN A. CARR

Orfeo ed Euridice [Orpheus and Eurydice]

Composer: *Christoph Willibald von Gluck.*

Librettist: *Ranieri de Calzabigi.*

First Performance: *Vienna, Burgtheater, 5 October 1762; revised as Orphée et Euridice,* Moline (translated and adapted from Calzabigi), Paris, Académie Royale, 2 August 1774.

Roles: *Orfeo (mezzo-soprano); Euridice (soprano); Amor (soprano); Ombra Felice [Happy Spirit] (soprano); chorus (SATB).*

Gluck's *Orfeo* is in fact two operas. The first version, *Orfeo ed Euridice,* was presented in Vienna on 5 October 1762. The principal part was sung by the celebrated Gaetano Guadagni (1725-1792), who was much admired by Handel, having sung the part of Didimus in the premiere of *Theodora.* He was trained by David Garrick. Burney notes that Guadagni as an actor "seems to have had no equal on any stage in Europe; his figure was uncommonly elegant and noble; his countenance replete with beauty, intelligence, and dignity." These characteristics must have made him the ideal Orfeo, for, although with *Orfeo* Gluck consciously set out to reform opera, he did not for this opera abandon the prevailing custom of assigning the leading male role to a castrato.

The opera opens with Orfeo standing by Euridice's tomb, mourning her death. Gluck instructed a later singer to deliver the heart-rending cries for Euridice during the opening chorus "as if he were having his leg sawn off." Amor, the god of love, is moved to tell Orfeo that he may go to Hades to fetch Euridice on condition that he does not look at her until they are back on earth. In act II, Orfeo is repelled by the furies who guard the underworld but he soothes the savage beasts while accompanying himself on the lyre. They let him enter. Orfeo gazes in wonder at the beauty of the Elysian fields. Euridice is restored to him, but she cannot understand his indifference. She pleads with him to look at her, and he eventually does so. She dies once again, at which point Orfeo sings the most famous aria in the piece, "Che farò senza Euridice." Amor again takes pity on Orfeo, and Euridice is restored to him amid general rejoicing.

With *Orfeo,* the forty-eight year old composer of almost three dozen operas set out, aided by his excellent librettist Ranieri de Calzabigi (1714-90), to change the course of opera and to break with the conventions of opera seria. This is best expressed in Gluck's own introduction to *Alceste:* "I resolved to divest it [opera] entirely of all those abuses, introduced into it either by the mistaken vanity of singers or by the too great complaisance of composers, which have so long disfigured Italian opera and made of the most splendid and most beautiful of spectacles the most ridiculous and wearisome." Gluck goes on to mention specifically ornamentation, extended ritornelli, cadenzas, da capo arias. He also notes that the overture should anticipate the nature of the action. Most significantly he adds, "I believed that my greatest labour should be devoted to seeking a beautiful simplicity." Burney attested to the success of Gluck's goals when he wrote that most of the arias in *Orfeo* "are as plain and simple as English ballads."

Calzabigi wrote the libretto of *Orfeo* expressly for Gluck. The convention of six characters (occasionally a few more) was broken by having only three, and two of them fairly small at that. The chorus, traditionally relegated to a minor role and sometimes eliminated altogether, plays a major part, and the opera omits any aria in full da capo form. Secco recitatives are completely abandoned.

The Viennese version is short, direct, and quite stunning. Twelve years later Gluck revised the work for Paris under the title, *Orphée et Euridice.* The title role was rewritten for a high tenor, Joseph Legros (1739-93), who became director of the Concerts Spirituels in Paris, and not only befriended Mozart but commissioned works from him for these concerts. He performed parts in several of Gluck's Paris operas. His was a high tenor voice, which has perhaps militated against the greater use of the Paris version. It is longer and less dramatically concise than its predecessor, but enormously rich in detail. There are noticeable differences in the orchestration between the two versions. The Paris version is more colored than its predecessor. It is worthwhile to compare the two settings of scene ii of act II. It is preceded in the Paris version by the "Air de Furies," which is omitted in the Viennese version, not surprisingly as it is lifted from the final movement of Gluck's 1761 ballet *Don Juan.* Then follows the famous "Dance of the Blessed Spirits" in both scores, but extended in the Paris version by the well-loved middle section in D minor for the solo flute. Euridice's first aria follows. It is a tender piece in F major, hard to give up but missing in the Vienna score. Next is Orfeo's wonderful "Che puro ciel," which is more subtly scored in the earlier version, with the solo flute much more in evidence than in the 1774 version. The remainder of the act is similar in both scores, but subtle differences abound. As might be expected, the Paris version contains considerably more ballet music throughout the opera.

Which version is to be preferred is perhaps a matter of taste, but what is not to be preferred is the uncomfortable mixture of the two, with which innocent audiences have frequently been presented. The origins of the mixture go back to Berlioz's famed version of the opera prepared specially in 1859 for Pauline Viardot-Garcia, and which she sang with outstanding success for almost 150 performances. That text is a retranslation from the French. Since that time the opera in hybrid form has been much favored by contraltos.

In 1936 Alfred Einstein, one of the important Gluck scholars, wrote, "Anyone who wishes to stage *Orfeo ed Euridice* nowadays should not keep wholly to the Vienna or to the Paris version, but will have to attempt to fashion the ideal form of the work out of both." And as recently as 1972 the writer in Kobbe's *Complete Opera Book* stated, "Some reconciliation between the Vienna and the Paris versions has, to this day, to be made for each and every production." With the importance attached nowadays to "authentic" performances, those views are no longer acceptable. Directors and singers must make a choice, for this is not one but two operas, in much the same way as are Strauss's *Ariadne auf Naxos* and Verdi's *Macbeth*. They both have their strengths—the Vienna score, tightness, directness, simplicity; the Paris score, a greater richness, more brilliant (though not necessarily more effective) orchestration, and some additional music.

Handel said that his cook knew more about counterpoint than Gluck! *Orfeo*, in both versions, is sustained by the composer's inventive imagination, subtle scoring, and structural daring, but there is little of that rich musical texture one finds, even as early as 1770, in Mozart's operatic writing. Handel was correct. That is doubtless why Gluck's works, with the exception only of a few of the reform operas, have never held the stage. But *Orfeo* is appropriately accorded an important place in opera for it is not merely a museum piece, but one charged with great beauty, dramatic intensity, and genuine feeling.—LAWRENCE J. DENNIS

Orlando

Composer: *George Frideric Handel.*

Librettist: *after C.S. Capeci (based on Ariosto, Orlando furioso).*

First Performance: *London, King's Theatre in the Haymarket, 27 January 1733.*

Roles: *Orlando (contralto); Angelica (soprano); Medoro (contralto); Dorinda (soprano); Zoroastro (bass).*

Orlando tells the story of Orlando (Roland), the warrior knight, whose love for the Princess Angelica is thwarted by her preference for the Moorish youth Medoro. Although it lacks the memorable arias that make other Handel operas so well-known, the opera is remarkable for its spectacle and for its characterization of Orlando's madness. The libretto is based on Ariosto's epic poem *Orlando furioso* of 1516, as are Handel's operas *Ariodante* (1734) and *Alcina* (1735). In the poem, Orlando's love-sickness causes him to rage uncontrollably; Ariosto writes that he pulls up tall pines at a single pull. Orlando is cured when the knight Astolpho, with St John as his guide, takes the chariot of Elijah to the moon and recovers Orlando's lost senses in a vessel labeled "Orlando's wit."

Handel's libretto, which is based on a libretto from Rome, 1711, by C.S. Capeci, elaborates upon this skeletal story. Capeci's libretto of *La resurrezione* (*The Resurrection*) had been written directly for Handel in 1708, and his *Tolomeo,* also of 1711, formed the basis of Handel's opera of the same name (1728). In 1728, Handel's adaptor had been his regular librettist, Nicola Haym. The adaptor of *Orlando* is not known, but it may be that Haym prepared this libretto before his death in 1729 or that Handel revised it himself. Capeci's libretto adds to Ariosto's story the shepherdess Dorinda, who is in love with Medoro. It also includes a second pair of lovers, Isabella and Zerbino from Ariosto's epic, but these characters are omitted in Handel's version. Handel's version adds the sorcerer Zoroastro, who in the opening scenes urges Orlando to forsake love for duty (which advice Orlando chooses to ignore), and who in the closing scenes restores Orlando to his senses, the "golden vessel" containing his wits arriving in the beak of an eagle.

Orlando marks the first time since the early London operas (1711-1715) that Handel worked with a libretto containing magic, sorcery, and transformations. In fact, comparison with *Rinaldo* (1711), *Teseo* (1713), and *Amadigi* (1715) reveals many similarities to the extent that one might easily conclude the moments of spectacle were devised with the old stage machinery and equipment in mind. To pick but one example, Angelica's magical rescue from Orlando in act II, scene x ("Angelica flies, and Orlando pursues her, on which a large Cloud descending, covers Angelica, and bears her away into the Air, accompanied by four Genij that surround her") closely parallels Almirena's abduction in *Rinaldo,* act I, scene vii ("a black Cloud descends, all fill'd with dreadful Monsters. . . . The Cloud covers Almirena and Armida, and carries 'em up swiftly into the Air, leaving in their place, two frightful Furies . . ."). In Capeci's source libretto, as in Ariosto's poem, Angelica escapes from Orlando simply by putting in her mouth the magic ring that makes her invisible. The visual display in Handel's libretto that is lacking in the source libretto is frequently summoned directly by Zoroastro, a new character in Handel's version. His addition may thus have been less an aid to the story line than an aid to the desired spectacle.

Orlando's madness is depicted musically by playing on the convention of the *da capo* (from the beginning) aria, in which two distinct sections of text and music were invariably followed by a repetition of the first, during which the singer was expected to add ornamentation. An average Handel opera contained thirty such arias separated by simple recitative (sung speech) accompanied only by harpsichord and cello. *Orlando* offers a very different picture.

After the opening scenes with Orlando and Zoroastro, which show Orlando in a magical realm wrestling with his destiny, the scene changes to "A little Wood, interspers'd with the Cots of Shepherds." Almost immediately the music falls into normative patterns. Beginning with Dorinda's aria "Ho un certo rossore" ("I feel a strange confusion"), there follow seven *da capo* arias, including the act-ending trio for Medoro, Angelica and Dorinda, "Consolati, Oh bella" ("Lovely one, be comforted"), one of the rare ensembles in Handel's operas. During this series, only the duet for Angelica and Medoro, "Ritornava al suo bel viso" ("Restored to that fair face") fails to fall into the *da capo* pattern; all the recitatives are simple.

The same regularity of structure obtains throughout most of the second act. Beginning with Dorinda's "Se mi rivolgo al prato" ("If I wander to the meadow"), there are six *da capo* arias separated by simple recitative. At this point, Angelica is borne into the heavens on a cloud, and Orlando goes mad. He begins in recitative, "Ah, stigie larve" ("Ah, Stygian monsters"), accompanied by full orchestra (accompanied recitative) and moves freely through sections more song-like. A very unusual passage of music in 5/8 time (five eighth notes to a bar) marks his belief that he is crossing the River Styx into the underworld. The scene culminates with a rondo (refrains separated by contrasting interludes) in which the last refrain sets a changed text. For Orlando at this point nothing is stable, not even the rondo form, and his loss of mind is equated with the musical loss of the *da capo*. This continues in the third act, where the only non-*da capo* pieces are sung by the demented hero.

The dramatically intense scenes written for Orlando without recourse to the conventional *da capo* form, and the extraordinary visual effects, have made *Orlando* one of Handel's most frequently performed operas in this century. Although it was also admired when it was written—one contemporary writer deemed it "extraordinary fine & magnificent"—it did not prevent the temporary collapse of Handel's operatic venture. *Orlando* was the last opera of Handel's Second Academy.—ELLEN T. HARRIS

Orlando [originally called Orlando finto pazzo]

Composer: *Antonio Vivaldi.*

Librettist: *G.B. Braccioli (after Ariosto, Orlando furioso).*

First Performance: *Venice, Sant' Angelo, fall 1714; revised as Orlando,* first performed Venice, Sant' Angelo, fall 1727.

Roles: *Orlando (mezzo-soprano); Angelica (soprano); Alcina (mezzo-soprano); Bradamante (contralto); Medoro (tenor); Ruggiero (baritone); Astolfo (bass).*

Perhaps the first thing to be said of the 1978 Verona and 1980 Dallas productions of "Vivaldi's" three-act opera *Orlando* (subsequently given in San Francisco in 1989) is that neither one was entirely the handiwork of the celebrated "Red Priest." Then again, the same also could be said of Vivaldi's staging of the work in 1727. There, in addition to composing music especially for the occasion, Vivaldi borrowed from his own 1714 *Orlando finto pazzo,* in turn a reworking of the 1713 *Orlando,* libretto by Grazio Braccioli, music by Giovanni Alberto Ristori, from which he retained a fair portion of Ristori's music (John Walter Hill has argued that almost all the music used by Vivaldi in act II of the 1727 score is Ristori's). In addition, he also may have used numbers from his 1727 *Siroe re di Persia* (Siroes, King of Persia). The 1714 opera bore the title *Orlando finto pazzo;* the 1727 work was called simply *Orlando.* The use of the title *Orlando furioso* for the modern revival of the 1727 opera, an unnecessary change that succeeded only in complicating an already confusing state of affairs, evidently was the inspiration of the editor of the Verona/Dallas score, Claudio Scimone. Nor was this the only change Scimone wrought. The role of Ruggiero, for example, in Vivaldi's day sung by a castrato, was transposed down an octave for the performances in Verona (in Dallas it was taken by a countertenor); the score, particularly act I, was heavily cut, and at least one aria was imported from another Vivaldi work.

Vivaldi based his 1727 opera on Ludovico Ariosto's immensely popular epic poem *Orlando furioso,* an exhilarating mélange treating "Of Dames, of Knights, of armes, of love's delight" (to quote from the opening of John Harington's 1591 English verse translation), but mainly given over to the adventures of the Christian knight Roland (Orlando), nephew of Charlemagne. Begun in 1502 or 1503, Ariosto completed the poem some forty-six cantos later in 1532 when the work was brought out in its third edition. Vivaldi's operatic accounts of the saga necessarily were considerably condensed. Although Braccioli says in the preface to his 1713 libretto that the numerous exploits of the epic roam half the world, he limits his setting to the sorceress Alcina's enchanted island and takes as his main action the love, madness, and recovery of Orlando. But "the loves of Bradamante and Ruggiero, Angelica and Medoro, the various inclinations of Alcina, and diverse passions of Astolfo serve to accompany this action and lead to its end." Amorous machinations therefore abound in the 1727 opera. Orlando loves Angelica, the proud princess of Cathay, who has turned the heads of half of Europe's heroes and whose inconstancy in love has angered the God of Love; as punishment he wills that she fall in love with a completely unsuited person—in the event the lowborn but handsome Saracen warrior Medoro. Angelica first encounters Medoro mortally wounded; she cures him with Oriental potions and the pair retire to a shepherd's hut, are married, and afterwards carve their names in the bark of nearby trees. The two depart, whereupon Orlando comes upon the carved trees, learns of their marriage, and consequently loses his reason. Meanwhile, Alcina, King Arthur's sister, an old woman still craving sensual pleasures, maintains her seductive beauty by her sorcery; the latter she presently works on Ruggiero, another Christian knight. Bradamante, niece of Charlemagne, seeing her beloved Ruggiero under Alcina's spell, seeks help from the enchantress Melissa. Legions of plot twists later, the opera ends with Orlando's recovery of his senses thanks to the intervention of his cousin Astolfo; Alcina's vow of vengeance and loss of magical powers; and the reunion of Bradamante and Ruggiero. Orlando calmly pardons Angelica and Medoro and blesses their marriage.

Before the Verona and Dallas revivals of *Orlando*—the latter evidently the first Vivaldi opera staged in America—the received wisdom was pretty much dependent on the appraisals of mid eighteenth-century critics who cited them as evidence of Vivaldi's supposed inability to keep pace with changing styles. Thus Tartini declared in 1740: "a gullet is not the neck of a violin. Vivaldi, who wanted to practice both genres [i.e., operatic and instrumental writing], always failed to go over in the one, whereas in the other he succeeded very well." And Quantz, in his 1752 treatise *On Playing the Flute,* was of the opinion that after Vivaldi began to write "theatrical vocal pieces [the first in 1713 at age thirty-five], he sank into frivolity and eccentricity both in composition and performance."

While it would be a mistake to hazard, from a single composition, an evaluation of all ninety-four operas Vivaldi claimed—late in his life—to have written, his 1727 *Orlando* nevertheless forcefully disproves Tartini's and Quantz's pronouncements. *Orlando* also explodes one of the "rules" set forth in 1720 by Benetto Marcello in his satirical *Teatro alla moda* when he says that a composer should see to it "that the arias, to the very end of the opera, are alternately lively and pathetic, without regard to the words [of the libretto]." Vivaldi broke with convention and grouped within each of the opera's nine stage settings arias of the same type, the result being an infinitely more trenchant and dramatic whole than that derided by Marcello. Similar emotions—tenderness, vengeance, etc.—thus catch different characters differently. Other dramatic surprises at variance with the "rules" include launching an aria without recitative, halting a number at an unexpected moment, and keeping a character onstage after an apparent "exit aria." (Such innovations are just one reason why the changes introduced by Scimone are to be regretted.) Borrowings from his own work and from the work of others notwithstanding, Vivaldi crafted the 1727 *Orlando* with unusual care, creating a work abounding with energy and beautiful, stirring music. If *Orlando* is in any way representative of Vivaldi's achievement as an operatic composer, it can only be hoped that it will not be long before more of his operas are revived as well.—JAMES PARSONS

Otello

Composer: *Giuseppe Verdi.*

Librettist: *Arrigo Boito (after Shakespeare).*

First Performance: *Milan, Teatro alla Scala, 5 February 1887.*

Roles: *Otello (tenor); Iago (baritone); Desdemona (soprano); Cassio (tenor); Emilia (mezzo-soprano); Roderigo (tenor); Lodovico (bass); Montano (bass); A Herald (bass); chorus (SSATB).*

It was publisher Giulio Ricordi's fondest wish in the late 1870s to bring Giuseppe Verdi out of his post-*Aida* retirement and back to the business of writing new operas. He ultimately accomplished this feat by arranging a collaboration between the composer and the brilliant librettist Arrigo Boito, whose flamboyant, youthful views in the 1860s on the need for operatic reform had once alienated Verdi. They worked together first on a revision of Verdi's much lamented mid-career fiasco, *Simon Boccanegra* (1857), and, beginning almost simultaneously, on a work that fired Verdi's imagination from the beginning: *Otello,* based on the play *Othello* by his most beloved playwright, Shakespeare. The project was secret at first, and Verdi refused to make any promises that the opera would ever be finished or performed; indeed his eventual contract for the 1887 Teatro alla Scala season included stipulations that he could withdraw the work at any time for any reason. The control Verdi thus exercised over the compositional process of *Otello* contrasts strikingly with that of the operas of his early-period "years in the galley" (as he called them); and the results of this control, along with Boito's poetic and scenic input, are intensely dramatic, very much in keeping with Verdi's stated aims for opera throughout his career.

The plot involved some significant changes from the Shakespearean source, including the removal of the play's act I in Venice, and the telescoping of Iago's tempting of Otello to jealousy and destruction into fewer, more melodramatic scenes. To review the main action: act I begins on a stormy night in Cyprus, as the jealous Iago sets up Otello's favored lieutenant Cassio into drinking too much, losing his temper, and wounding a fellow soldier, Montano, in a fight. Iago has his henchman Roderigo sound the alarm, and when Otello, the Moorish commander of the Venetian forces and Governor of Cyprus, arrives, Iago allows him to believe that Cassio is completely at fault. Otello dismisses Cassio from his service, and the act closes with a love scene between Otello and his beautiful wife Desdemona, reminiscing on their early courtship. In act II, Iago advises Cassio to beg Otello's forgiveness through his wife Desdemona, and then encourages Otello to be suspicious of the intimate scene he sees between Desdemona and Cassio (as the latter follows Iago's advice), and of her ensuing intercession on Cassio's behalf. In act III Otello becomes increasingly filled with the jealousy Iago sows in him; he believes that a special handkerchief of Desdemona's which Iago steals and plants on Cassio furnishes the proof of Desdemona's unfaithfulness. In front of the Venetian ambassador—who has come to deliver the orders of Otello's recall to Venice and his replacement by Cassio—Otello strikes and curses Desdemona, and yields to Iago's insistence that Desdemona and Cassio be punished immediately, before the change in command takes effect. Dismissing the crowd, who are then heard in the distance shouting praise to Otello, "Leon di Venezia" ("Lion of Venice"), he collapses in a psychotic rage, leaving Iago to snarl with triumph his ironic line "Ecco il Leone"—"Here's the Lion!" Act IV begins with the frightened Desdemona's Willow Song and prayer, followed quickly by Otello's entrance and the murder. But Otello realizes his mistake when Emilia arrives with the news that Roderigo, dead at Cassio's hand, has revealed Iago's treachery. The opera ends as Otello takes a final kiss from the dead Desdemona and kills himself with his dagger.

Verdi's musical language in *Otello* illustrates his successful late-period merging of the vocally-oriented set piece traditions of Italian opera, with a thematically and harmonically unified approach, more characteristic of the French and German traditions. Thus Iago, for

O

OPERA

instance, communicates his evil act II "Credo" in a traditional aria form, and elsewhere employs the traditional drinking song (act I) and cabaletta form (the closing duet of act II, with Otello); but on the other hand his appearances are just as powerfully characterized by recurring orchestral ideas, such as the ragged brass fanfare and the long, eery woodwind trills of the Credo, and the winding unison melody of "É un idra fosca, livida" ("It's a dark, malign monster," referring to jealousy), which appears again as the prelude to act III to symbolize the working of Iago's poison on Otello's mind. Otello and Desdemona too have powerful solo moments, she in the haunting Willow Song and "Ave Maria" of act IV, and he in the passionate act III arioso "Dio! mi potevi scagliar" ("Heaven! Had it pleased thee to try me") and his death scene in act IV. At the same time, the large-scale tonal and thematic design, as well as deceptive cadences and connecting orchestral interludes, serve to override the separations of these vocally-oriented segments and give coherence, at least subliminally, to the drama.

Probably the most brilliant sections of the opera are the duets and ensembles, for which Verdi combines his new-found command of large-scale tonal and thematic unity with the dissimilar ensemble technique he had developed in the middle period, where dissimilarity in the vocal lines of each of the characters reveals the separate qualities of their personalities and/or situations. Thus for example in the act III ensemble "A terra! si . . . nel livido fango" ("Yea, prostrate I lie in the dust"), Desdemona's high leaps and soothing stepwise descents express her pleas for restored peace and love, and contrast against the more hymn-like sympathies of the crowd, and the speech-like dialogue of Otello and Iago, as they plan to expedite the punishments of Cassio and Desdemona. Meanwhile, symmetries of theme and key provide unity to the scene and link it with the drama of the rest of the act.

Out of his first complete collaboration with the gifted Boito, Verdi received the benefits of some excellent dramatic advice, leading for example to the powerful ironic ending of act III, and a poetic style featuring the very concision and scenic focus that he had long hoped and asked for from other librettists. The powerful concision of such lines as "Ecco il Leone!" and "Ancora un bacio" ("One more kiss") when accompanied with such deft musical imagery as the swelling "Bacio" theme, create the most memorable moments in *Otello*. In addition, Verdi's orchestration of the score is masterfully colorful and dramatic, especially in his unique solo melodic use of muted double basses at Otello's act IV entrance to Desdemona's bedchamber.

The opera was an immense success in its La Scala premiere, and within two years had reached most of the operatic theaters in the world. Verdi received all the adulation that one might expect for a long-missed national hero and theatrical genius; he was carried through the streets and applauded through the night, according to the account in the *Musical Times*. Today *Otello* remains among the most admired works of the operatic literature.—CLAIRE DETELS

Otello, ossia il moro de Venezia [Othello, or The Moor of Venice]

Composer: *Gioachino Rossini.*

Librettist: *F. Berio di Salsa (after Shakespeare).*

First Performance: *Naples, Teatro del Fondo, 4 December 1816.*

Roles: *Otello (tenor); Desdemona (soprano); Rodrigo (tenor); Iago (tenor); Elmiro (bass); Emilia (mezzo-soprano); The Doge (tenor); Gondolier (tenor); chorus (SATB).*

Although the opera is based on Shakespeare's play, it treats its source more freely than Verdi's *Otello*. Rossini's opera plays down the love between Otello and Desdemona, who have no love duet (their only duet is the frantic one leading up to the murder of Desdemona). Desdemona is given a father, Elmiro, who despises Otello and curses his daughter when she tells him of her love for the Moor. The intricate process by which Shakespeare (and Verdi) have Iago gradually enflame Otello's jealousy is much abridged and simplified; Rossini's opera leaves out Cassio (a character crucial to Shakespeare and Verdi) altogether.

But comparisons with Shakespeare and Verdi do little to reveal the real worth of Rossini's *Otello*, a fine example of early nineteenth-century *opera seria*, and a work that can stand securely on its own. Rossini composed the opera for the San Carlo theater in Naples, whose company included three tenors capable of taking leading roles; this led to the casting of not only Otello but also Rodrigo and Iago as tenors (Desdemona's father is the only bass among the principals). Rossini used his plethora of tenors to dramatic purpose. He composed the confrontation between Rodrigo and Otello (in the second-act trio "Ah vieni, nel tuo sangue") as a kind of singing contest between the two rivals: the ensemble begins with Rodrigo and Otello singing, in turn, almost exactly the same music, culminating in a high C and a run of coloratura.

This was not the only place where Rossini left the singers themselves to differentiate their characters. He also did so in the first-act duet for Emilia and Desdemona, "Vorrei che il tuo pensier," where Emilia tries to cheer up Desdemona. The duet lacks the kind of musical characterization with which Weber, in an analogous scene in *Der Freischütz* (composed five years later), distinguished Agathe and Aennchen. But Weber did not surpass the beauty of Rossini's duet, with its delicate intertwining of soprano voices.

Among the many remarkable features of Rossini's drama is its orchestral writing. The plot unfolds at a leisurely pace, interspersed with orchestral passages of considerable length and complexity. Otello's triumphant aria "Ah! sì per voi sento," in act I, is followed by an orchestral postlude that recapitulates the march that accompanied Otello's arrival in Venice; later in act I a long orchestral introduction with beautiful woodwind writing and an elaborate horn solo sets a mood of gentle melancholy for the scene in which Emilia tries to comfort Desdemona. The intensely lyrical clarinet solo in Rodrigo's aria "Che ascolto?" (act II) and the harp solo in Desdemona's Willow Song (act III) are among the instrumental passages that embellish *Otello* and evoke its shifting moods.

Rossini's manipulation of harmonic resources is no less effective. The simple shift from minor to major near the end of each strophe of the Willow Song is rich in pathos. In the trio "Ah vieni, nel tuo sangue," a quiet yet daring modulation after a long, harmonically static passage shows Rossini, with a perfect sense of timing, preparing the audience for an explosion of emotion as the trio ends.—JOHN A. RICE

O

OPERA

OPERA *p*

Pacini, Giovanni

Composer. Born 17 February 1796, in Catania. Died 6 December 1867, in Pescia. Studied with Marchesi and Padre Mattei in Bologna, and with Furlanetto in Venice; composed forty-six operas up to the failure of Carlo di Borgogna, *1835, when he stopped composing operas for a period; established a music school at Viareggio, near Lucca, later moving it to Lucca;* Saffo *a great success, 1840; thirty-one more operas up to 1867. Pacini was a contributor to several musical journals; his brother Emilio Pacini (1810-98) was a well-known librettist.*

Operas *Don Pomponio,* G. Paganini, 1813 [not performed]; *Annetta e Lucindo,* F. Marconi, Milan, S. Radegonda, 17 October 1813; *La ballerina raggiratrice,* G. Palomba, Florence, Teatro della Pergola, spring 1814; *L'ambizione delusa,* G. Palomba, Florence, Teatro della Pergola, spring 1814; *L'escavazione del tesoro,* F. Marconi, Pisa, Ravvivati, 18 December 1814; *Gli sponsali de' silfe,* F. Marconi, Milan, Filodrammatici, carnival 1814-15; *Bettina vedova (Il seguito di Ser Mercantonio),* A. Anelli, Venice, San Moisè, spring 1815; *La Rosina,* G. Palomba, Florence, Teatro della Pergola, summer 1815; *La Chiarina* (?), A. Anelli, Venice, San Benedetto, carnival 1815-16; *L'ingenua,* Marconi, Venice, San Benedetto, 4 May 1816; *Il matromonio per procura,* A. Anelli, Milan, Re, 2 January 1817; *Dalla beffa il disinganno, ossia La poetessa,* A. Anelli, Milan, Re, carnival 1816-17; revised with a new text as *Il carnevale di Milano,* P. Latanza, Milan, Re, 23 February 1817; *Piglia il mondo come viene,* Anelli, Milan, Re, 28 May 1817; *I virtuosi del Teatro* (?), G. Rossi, Milan, Re, 1817; *La bottega di Cafè* (?), G. Foppa, Milan, Re, 1817; *Adelaide e Comingio,* Rossi, Milan, Re, 30 December 1817; *Atala,* A. Peracchi, Padua, Nuovo, June 1818; *Gl'illinesi,* F. Romani, 1818 [not performed]; *Il barone di Dolsheim (Federico Il re di Prussia, Il barone di Felcheim, La colpa emendata dal valore),* F. Romani, Milan, Teatro alla Scala, 23 September 1818; *La sposa fedele,* Rossi, Venice, San Benedetto, 14 January 1819; revised, Milan, Teatro alla Scala, 1 August 1819; *Il falegname di Livonia,* F. Romani, Milan, Teatro alla Scala, 12 April 1819; revised, Florence, Teatro della Pergola, 28 February 1823; *Vallace, o L'eroe scozzese,* F. Romani, Milan, Teatro alla Scala, 14 February 1820; *La sacerdotessa d'Irminsul,* F. Romani, Trieste, Grande, 11 May 1820; *La* *schiava in Bagdad, ossia il papucciajo,* Turin, Carignano, 20 October 1820; *La gioventù di Enrico V (La bella tavernara, ossia L'avventure d'une notte),* G. Tarducci or J. Ferretti (in part after Shakespeare), Rome, Valle, 26 December 1820; *Cesare in Egitto,* J. Feretti, Rome, Torre Argentina, 26 December 1821; *La vestale,* L. Romanelli, Milan, Teatro alla Scala, 6 February 1823; *Temistocle,* P. Anguillesi (after Metastasio), Lucca, Giglio, 23 August 1823; *Isabella ed Enrico,* L. Romanelli, Milan, Teatro alla Scala, 12 June 1824; *Alessandro nell'Indie,* A.L. Tottola (after Metastasio), Naples, San Carlo, 29 September 1824; *Amazilia,* G. Schmidt, Naples, San Carlo, 6 July 1825; revised, Vienna, 20 February 1827; *L'ultimo giorno di Pompei,* A.L. Tottola, Naples, San Carlo, 19 November 1825; *La gelosia corretta,* L. Romanelli, Milan, Teatro alla Scala, 27 March 1826; *Niobe,* A.L. Tottola, Naples, San Carlo, 19 November 1826; *Gli arabi nelle Gallie, ossia Il trionfo della fede,* L. Romanelli (after d'Arlincourt, *Le renégat*), Milan, Teatro alla Scala, 8 March 1827; revised, Paris, Théâtre-Italien, 30 January 1855; *Margherita, regina d'Inghilterra,* A.L. Tottola, Naples, San Carlo, 19 November 1827; *I cavalieri di Valenza,* Rossi, Milan, Teatro alla Scala, 11 June 1828; *I crociati in Tolemaide, ossia Malek-Adel (La morte di Malek-Adel),* C. Bassi, Trieste, Grande, 13 November 1828; *Il talismano, ovvero La terza crociata in Palestina,* G. Barbieri (after Scott), Milan, Teatro alla Scala, 10 June 1829; *I fidanzati, ossia Il contestabile di Chester,* D. Gilardoni (after Scott), Naples, San Carlo, 19 November 1829; *Giovanna d'Arco,* G. Barbieri, Milan, Teatro alla Scala, 14 March 1830; *Il corsaro,* J. Ferretti (after Byron), Rome, Apollo, 15 January 1831; *Il rinnegato portoghese (Gusmano d'Almeida),* L. Romanelli, written for Venice, La Fenice, 1831 [not performed]; *Ivanhoe,* Rossi (after Scott), Venice, La Fenice, 19 March 1832; *Don Giovanni Tenorio, o Il convitato di pietra,* G. Bertati, Viareggio, Casa Belluomini, spring 1832; *Gli elvezi, ovvero Corrado di Tochemburgo,* Rossi, Naples, San Carlo, 12 January 1833; *Fernando duca di Valenza,* P. Pola, Naples, San Carlo, 30 May 1833; *Irene, o L'assedio di Messina,* Rossi?, Naples, San Carlo, 30 November 1833; *Carlo di Borgogna,* Rossi, Venice, La Fenice, 21 February 1835; *La foresta d'Hermanstadt,* Viareggio, 1839 [not performed]; *Furio Camillo,* J. Ferretti, Rome, Apollo, 26 December 1839; *Saffo,* S. Cammarano, Naples, San Carlo, 29 November 1840; *L'uomo del mistero,* D. Andreotti (after Scott), Naples, Nuovo, 9 November 1841; *Il duca d'Alba (Adolpho di Warbel),* G. Peruzzini and F.M. Piave, Venice, La Fenice, 26 February 1842; *La fidanzata corsa,* S. Cammarano (after Mérimée, *Colomba*), Naples, San Carlo, 10 December 1842; *Maria, regina d'Inghilterra,* L. Tarantini, Palermo, Carolino, 11 February 1843; *Medea,* B. Castiglia, Palermo, Carolino, 28 November 1843; *Luisella, ossia La cantatrice del molo [di Napoli],* L. Tarantini, Naples, Nuovo, 13 December 1843; *L'ebrea,* G. Sacchèro, Milan, Teatro alla Scala, 27 February 1844; *Lorenzino de' Medici,* F.M. Piave, Venice, La Fenice, 4 March 1845; revised as *Elisa Velasco,* Rome, Apollo, 3 January 1854; revised as *Rolandino di Torresmondo,* D. Bolognese, Naples, San Carlo, 20 March 1858; *Bondelmonte,* S. Cammarano, Florence, Teatro della Pergola, 18 June 1845; *Stella di Napoli,* S. Cammarano, Naples, San Carlo, 11 December 1845; *La regina di Cipro,* F. Guidi, Turin, Regio, 7 February 1846; *Merope,* S. Cammarano, Naples, San Carlo, 25 November 1847; *Ester d'Engaddi,* F. Guidi, Turin, Regio, 1 February 1848; *Allan Cameron,* F.M. Piave, Venice, La Fenice, 28 March 1848; *Alfrida,* Bertolozzi [not performed]; *Zaffira, o La riconciliazione,* A. de Lauzières, Naples, Nuovo, 15 November 1851; *Malvina di Scozia,* S. Cammarano, Naples, San Carlo, 27 December 1851; *L'assedio di Leida (Elnaya),* F.M. Piave, 1852? [not performed]; *Rodrigo di Valenza,* written for Palermo, Carolino, carnival 1852-53 [not performed]; *Il Cid,* A. de Lauzières, Milan, Teatro all Scala, 12 March 1853; *Lidia di Brabante,* Gaetano, 1853 [not performed]; *Romilda di Provenza,* G. Miccio, Naples, San Carlo, 8 December 1853; *La donna delle isole,* F.M. Piave, written for Venice, La Fenice, carnival 1853-54 [not performed]; *La punizione,* C. Perini, Venice, La Fenice, 8 March 1854, [revision of *Lidia di*

Brabante]; *Margherita Pusterla*, D. Bolognese, Naples, San Carlo, 25 February 1856; *Il saltimbanco*, G. Checchetelli, Rome, Torre Argentina, 24 May 1858; *Lidia di Bruxelles*, G. Cencetti, Bologna, Comunale, 21 October 1858 [revision of *Lidia di Brabante*, 1853]; *Gianni di Nisida*, G. Checchetelli, Rome, Torre Argentina, 29 October 1860; *Il mulattiere di Toledo*, G. Cencetti, Rome, Apollo, 25 May 1861; *Belfagor*, A. Lanari (after Machiavelli), Florence, Teatro della Pergola, 1 December 1861 [composed 1851?]; *Carmelita*, F.M. Piave (after Dumas, *Don Juan de Marana*), written for Milan, Teatro alla Scala, 1863 [not performed]; *Don Diego di Mendoza*, F.M. Piave, Venice, La Fenice, 12 January 1867; *Berta di Varnol*, F.M. Piave, Naples, San Carlo, 6 April 1867; *Nicola de Lapi*, C. Perini, 1855, Florence, Pagliano, 1873 [revision of *Lidia di Brabante*].

With the possible exception of Saverio Mercadante, no nineteenth-century Italian opera composer was as successful in his day, or as forgotten in ours as Giovanni Pacini. Even Mercadante does not really qualify, in that some eight Mercadante operas have had recent revivals; while there have been only two recent revivals of works by Pacini.

During his lifetime, Pacini composed some 73 operas (the exact number is difficult, if not impossible, to establish, because some of the titles listed may have been revisions of earlier works). His first 30 or so operas, composed during the time when Rossini was still in Italy were, not surprisingly, in the Rossini style, but so were everybody else's. Pacini and his contemporaries (Meyerbeer, Bellini, Donizetti and Mercadante) started to modify the nature of Italian opera around 1824. Collectively, they started to create a new style for bel canto opera.

It would be inaccurate to say that each of these composers evolved a style of his own and followed it throughout his career. Instead, they were strongly influenced by one another; with the exception of Meyerbeer's French works, the differences in style between these composers are much less apparent than the similarities. Similarly, the differences in style between operas by different composers dating from the same period (e.g. the early 1840s or the late 1810s) are less significant than the differences between one composer's early and late operas. These composers did, however develop their own trademarks; thus, just as Bellini was best known for his long melodic line, Pacini earned considerable fame by the vigor and variety of his cabalettas.

Early in his career, Pacini became one of the most prominent composers in Italy. His position was greatly enhanced by the success of *Gli arabi nelle Gallie* (Milan, 1827), which eventually reached many of the world's most important stages, and was the first of Pacini's operas to be given in the United States. It was mounted quite frequently in Italy, and in fact it was not until 1830 that Bellini's first success, *Il pirata* (also Milan, 1827) passed *Gli arabi nelle Gallie* in performances at the Teatro alla Scala.

While almost each of Bellini's subsequent works was moderately to highly successful, and Donizetti also had more than his share of triumphs, Pacini was unable to keep up, most of his ensuing operas being failures. He was the first to recognize his defeat and made the following entry in his memoirs: "I began to realize that I must withdraw from the field—Bellini, the divine Bellini has surpassed me." Some years later, he decided to reenter the field, and, after one more setback, enjoyed his greatest success, *Saffo* (Naples, 1840).

After *Saffo*, Pacini entered into another period of great prominence in the early and mid 1840s. Bellini had passed away years ago, Donizetti had left for Paris, and only Mercadante and the young Verdi were important enough to be serious rivals. Mercadante's major successes were already behind him, thus Verdi offered the only important competition, and it was not until 1844 that Verdi eclipsed Pacini with the unparalelled triumph of *Ernani*. (Successful as *Nabucco* was, it was less so than *Saffo*.) It was in these 1840s that Pacini enjoyed his most glorious years, with one hit after another. These included *La fidanzata corsa* (Naples, 1842), *Medea* (Palermo, 1843), *Lorenzino de'Medici* (Venice, 1845) and *Bondelmonte* (Florence, 1845). This was followed by another, and much longer, period of gradual decline, marked only by *Il saltimbanco* (Rome, 1858).

The bel canto revival of recent years has not been particularily kind to Pacini. All of Verdi's output, almost all of Bellini's, most of Rossini's, much of Donizetti's and even eight Mercadante operas have already been revived, but only two of Pacini's: *Saffo* and *Maria, regina d'Inghilterra*. Judging from the revivals and recordings of these works, Pacini's abilities as a melodist do not seem to be far behind those of Donizetti and Bellini, and they clearly surpass those of Mercadante.

Like *Saffo*, *Maria, regina d'Inghilterra* contains many individual pieces of great beauty, especially the closing arias for the two protagonists, Mary Tudor and Riccardo Fenimoore. The latter's prison scene is particularly effective in all of its movements: a melancholy prelude, an elegiac first part sung with great feeling and a striking cabaletta. It is superior to many prison scenes by better known composers. The final scene for the Queen is just as beautiful, in which Pacini first sets the mood and builds tension with a heart-rending funeral march.

If Pacini was less successful than some of his contemporaries, it may be because he was less of an innovator. Just as his early operas were modeled on Rossini, some of his middle period works show the heavy influence of his idol, Vincenzo Bellini, as well as some of Donizetti. His still later operas, none of which has yet been revived, show many influences of Mercadante and even Verdi. Yet there can be little doubt that Pacini contributed to the changes in style away from Rossini, or that he, like Mercadante, exerted an influence on the far greater changes to be eventually made by Verdi.—TOM KAUFMAN

I pagliacci [The Clowns]

Composer: *Ruggero Leoncavallo.*
Librettist: *Ruggero Leoncavallo.*
First Performance: *Milan, Teatro dal Verme, 21 May 1892.*
Roles: *Canio (tenor); Nedda (soprano); Tonio (baritone); Silvio (baritone); Beppe (tenor); chorus (SSTTBB).*

I pagliacci was composed in the wake of the sensational success of Mascagni's *Cavalleria rusticana,* which started a fashion for veristic subjects in the Italian music theater. Leoncavallo wrote both the libretto and the music. By his own admission, he took the subject from an incident that occurred in a Calabrian village where he lived for a few years while his father was posted there as a judge. As a *verismo* opera, *Pagliacci* should, therefore, have the best possible claim to authenticity, since it is based on a true story. However, an examination of the court records of that incident (the murder of a young man by two brothers due to the jealousy over a local woman) shows that most of the opera's plot is pure fiction, to be attributed to Leoncavallo's own imagination or traced back to other sources.

A troupe of strolling players arrives in a village to put on a *commedia dell'arte* show. One of the clowns, Tonio, makes advances to Nedda, the leader's wife, but she is in love with a villager, Silvio. The two lovers agree to run away together after the performance. Their conversation is overheard by Tonio who alerts Canio, Nedda's husband. Canio tries in vain to make her reveal the man's name. The clowns' farce seems to reproduce their real-life situation since Columbine (Nedda) is secretly in love with Harlequin, and Pagliaccio (Canio) demands the name of her lover, which she refuses to give. The enraged clown can no longer keep up the pretence. Mad with jealousy, he stabs Nedda and then Silvio who had rushed to her help.

The village murder on which Leoncavallo claimed to have based his opera is hardly more than a pretext for the Calabrian setting of the plot. The brutal violence of the double murder committed by the white-faced clown in front of his audience is at the same time more sensational and more sophisticated than the rustic challenge and the off-stage fight of *Cavalleria rusticana*. The *verismo* of *Pagliacci* is, in fact, of a different nature from that of Mascagni's archetypal opera.

The characterization of Canio/Pagliaccio is focused on the antitheses of appearance/reality, clown/man. The device of the play-within-a-play with *commedia dell'arte* masks and the Pierrot-like personality of Pagliaccio point to broader cultural influences that should be dated back to the 1880s, the years Leoncavallo spent in Paris trying to make a living as a songwriter. In that period two works were produced which contain similarities with *Pagliacci*: *Tabarin* (1885), an opera in two acts by Émile Pessard based on a comedy by Paul Ferrier, and *La Femme de Tabarin* (1887), a one-act play by the Parnassian poet Catulle Mendès. Both feature the seventeenth-century *commedia dell'arte* clown Tabarin, and both deal with the unfaithfulness of his wife Francisquine. A substantial part of the action in the two pieces consists in the sudden shift from the performance of a light farce to real-life tragedy on the small stage of Tabarin's open-air theater, in front of an audience responding with loud comments to the unusually impressive acting. Pessard's opera, in particular, seems close to the plot of *Pagliacci*, even though it ends with the reconciliation of the clown and his wife.

The 1880s also witnessed a revival of interest in pantomimes centered on the sad and violent Pierrot, a *commedia dell'arte* mask similar to Pagliaccio both in character and costume. In 1883, even the great Sarah Bernhardt donned the white costume of the male mask to perform *Pierrot assassin,* a pantomime by Jean Richepin.

Leoncavallo was well aware of the latest fashions in the French theater while he worked and made friends in Paris. A few years later, when he chose to follow Mascagni's example and wrote a veristic opera, his Parisian recollections were probably more influential than his childhood memories. So the libretto of *Pagliacci* resulted from the skilful blending of a veristic crime of passion with the well-tried device of the play-within-a-play, which allowed the composer a clever differentiation in the musical treatment of the main story and the inset "comedy." This is the opera's best asset besides the strongly emotional numbers such as Canio's "Vesti la giubba" ("Put on the costume").

On the whole, the music of *Pagliacci* exhibits the typical characteristics of the new veristic genre inaugurated by *Cavalleria:* loud and coarse orchestration, sensational effects, hybrid style. Reviewing a Viennese production of the opera in 1893, Eduard Hanslick compared *Pagliacci* with *Cavalleria* and noted that Leoncavallo's music is "less fragmented and disjointed" than Mascagni's, though "his melodic invention can scarcely be praised for its richness and originality."

A distinctive feature of *Pagliacci* is the unnecessary and pretentious prologue where Tonio informs us that the author has tried to portray a "squarcio di vita," a slice of life, that is the naturalistic *tranche de vie:* though we will be seeing "le antiche maschere," the old masks, we are invited to consider that comedians are flesh and blood creatures. A "nest of memories" moved the author to write "with real tears," and "his sobs beat the tempo for him." We shall hear "shouts of rage" and "cynic laughter" from his true-to-life characters. Was this meant to be an aesthetic manifesto of operatic *verismo?* Or was it, rather, a cunning device to reconcile the clown's story with the sordid incident dug out from the composer's childhood memories? Possibly both, but, in the first place, the prologue was to be a reward for the baritone Victor Maurel (the first Tonio) who used his influence on the impresario of the Teatro dal Verme in Milan to have *Pagliacci* premiered there. With this addition, Leoncavallo gave Maurel the opportunity to introduce the opera and conclude it with the spoken line "The comedy is ended" which was eventually appropriated by the tenor.—MATTEO SANSONE

Paisiello, Giovanni

Composer. Born 9 May 1740, in Taranto. Died 5 June 1816, in Naples. Studied with Durante, Cotumacci, and Abos at the Conservatorio di Sant'Onofrio in Naples, 1754-59; taught at the Conservatorio, 1759-63; commissioned to write an opera for the Marsigli-Rossi theater in Bologna as a result of the success of one of his comic intermezzos, 1763; invited to St Petersburg by Empress Catherine II, 1776; maestro di cappella to Ferdinand IV of Naples, 1784-99; maître de chapelle to Napoleon in Paris, 1802-03; various posts of importance under Napoleon's government, but lost them with the restoration of the Bourbons in 1815.

Operas *Il ciarlone,* A. Palomba, Bologna, Marsigli-Rossi, 12 May 1764; *I francesi brillanti,* P. Mililotti, Bologna, Marsigli-Rossi, 24 June 1764; *Madama l'umorista, o Gli stravaganti,* A. Palomba, Modena, Rangoni, 26 January 1765; *I bagni d'Abano,* C. Goldoni, Parma, Ducale, spring 1765; *Demetrio,* Metastasio, Modena, Rangoni, Lent 1765; revised, Tsarskoye Selo, 1779; *Il negligente,* C. Goldoni, Parma, Ducale, 1765; *Le virtuose ridicole,* C. Goldoni, Parma, Ducale, 1765; *Le nozze disturbate,* G. Martinelli, Venice, San Moisè, carnival 1766; *Le finte contesse,* after P. Chiari, *Marchese Villano,* Rome, Valle, February 1766; *La vedova di bel genio,* P. Mililotti, Naples, Nuovo, spring 1766; *L'idolo cinese,* G.B. Lorenzi, Naples, Nuovo, spring 1767; *Lucio Papirio dittatore,* Zeno, Naples, San Carlo, summer 1767; *Il furbo malaccorto,* G.B. Lorenzi, Naples, Nuovo, winter 1767; *Le 'mbroglie de la Bajasse,* P. Mililotti, Naples, Teatro dei Fiorentini, summer 1767; revised as *La serva fatta padrona,* Naples, Teatro dei Fiorentini, summer 1769; *Alceste in Ebuda, ovvero Olimpia,* A. Trabucco, Naples, San Carlo, 20 January 1768; *Festa teatrale in musica (Le nozze di Peleo e Tetide),* G.B. Basso-Bassi, Naples, Royal Palace, 31 May 1768; *La luna abitata,* G.B. Lorenzi, Naples, Nuovo, summer 1768; *La finta maga per vendetta,* G.B. Lorenzi, Naples, Teatro dei Fiorentini, fall? 1768; *L'osteria di Marecchiaro,* F. Cerlone, Naples, Teatro dei Fiorentini, winter 1768; performed with a separate third act, *La Claudia vendicata. Don Chisciotte della Mancia,* G.B. Lorenzi, Naples, Teatro dei Fiorentini, summer 1769; *L'arabo cortese,* P. Mililotti, Naples, Nuovo, winter, 1769; *La Zelmira, o sia La marina del Granatello,* F. Cerlone, Naples, Nuovo, summer 1770; *Le traume per amore,* F. Cerlone, Naples, Nuovo, 7 October 1770; *Annibale in Torino,* J. Durand, Turin, Regio, 16 January 1771; *La somiglianza de' nomi,* P. Mililotti, Naples, Nuovo, spring 1771; *I scherzi d'amore e di fortuna,* F. Cerlone, Naples, Nuovo, summer 1771; *Artaserse,* Metastasio, Modena, Court, 26 December 1771; *Semiramide in villa* (intermezzo), G.

Martinelli?, Rome, Capranica, carnival 1772; *Motezuma*, V.A. Cigna-Santi, Rome, Teatro delle Dame, January 1772; *La Dardanè*, F. Cerlone, Naples, Nuovo, spring 1772; *Gli amanti comici*, G.B. Lorenzi (after his *Don Anchise*), Naples, Nuovo, fall 1772; revised as *Don Anchise Campanone*, Venice, 1773; *L'innocente fortunata*, F. Livigni, Venice, San Moisè, carnival 1773; revised as *La semplice fortunata*, Naples, Nuovo, summer 1773; *Sismano nel Mogol*, G. de Gamerra, Milan, Regio Ducale, carnival 1773; *Il tamburo*, G.B. Lorenzi (after Addison, *The Drummer*), Naples, Nuovo, spring 1773; *Alessandro nel' Indie*, Metastasio, Modena, Court, 26 December 1773; *Andromeda*, V.A. Cigni-Santi, Milan, Regio Ducale, carnival 1774; *Il duello*, G.B. Lorenzi, Naples, Nuovo, spring 1774; revised as *Il duello comico*, Tsarskoye Selo, 1782; *Il credulo deluso*, after C. Goldoni, *Il mondo della luna*, Naples, Nuovo, fall 1774; *La frascatana*, F. Livigni, Venice, San Samuele, fall 1774; *Il divertimento dei numi* (scherzo rappresentativo per musica), G.B. Lorenzi, Naples, Royal Palace, 4 December 1774; performed as *Lo scherzo degli dei Caserta*, 1771, with Gluck, *Orfeo*. *Demofoonte*, Metastasio, Venice, San Benedetto, carnival 1775; *La discordia fortunata*, Abate F.B.A.F., Venice, San Samuele, carnival 1775; *L'amore ingegnoso, o sia La giovane scaltra*, Padua, Obizzi, carnival 1775; *Le astuzie amorose*, F. Cerlone, Naples, Nuovo, spring 1775; *Socrate immaginario*, G.B. Lorenzi, Naples, Nuovo, fall 1775; *Il gran Cid*, R. Pizzi, Florence, Teatro della Pergola, 3 November 1775; *Le due contesse* (intermezzo), G. Petrosellini, Rome, Valle, 3 January 1776; *La disfatta di Dario*, N. Morbilli, Rome, Torre Argentina, carnival 1776; *Dal finto il vero*, S. Zini, Naples, Nuovo, spring 1776; *Nitteti*, Metastasio, St Petersburg, Court, 28 January 1777; *Lucinda ed Armidoro*, M. Coltellini, St Petersburg, fall 1777; *Achille in Sciro*, Metastasio, St Petersburg, Court, 6 February 1778; *Lo sposo burlato*, G. Casti, St Petersburg, Court, 24 July 1778; *Gli astrologi immaginari*, G. Bertati, St Petersburg, Hermitage, 14 February 1779; *Il matrimonio inaspettato (La contadina di spirito)*, Kammeniÿ Ostrov, 1779; *La finta amante*, G. Casti?, Mogilev, Poland, 5 June 1780; *Alcide al bivio*, Metastasio, St Petersburg, Hermitage, 6 December 1780; *La serva padrona* (intermezzo), G.A. Federico, Tsarskoye Selo, 10 September? 1781; *Il barbiere di Siviglia, ovvero la precauzione inutile*, G. Petrosellini (after Beaumarchais), St Petersburg, Court, 26 September 1782; *Il mondo della luna*, Kammeniÿ Ostrov, 1782; *Il re Teodoro in Venezia*, G. Casti, Vienna, Burgtheater, 23 August 1784; *Antigono*, Metastasio, Naples, San Carlo, 12 January 1785; *La grotta di Trofonio*, G. Palomba, Naples, Teatro dei Fiorentini, December 1785; *Olimpiade*, Metastasio, Naples, San Carlo, 20 January 1786; *Le gare generose*, G. Palomba, Naples, Teatro dei Fiorentini, spring 1786 [seperate, untitled third act]; *Pirro*, G. de Gamerra, Naples, San Carlo, 12 January 1787; *La modista raggiratrice*, G.B. Lorenzi, Naples, Teatro dei Fiorentini, fall 1787; *Giunone e Lucina*, C. Sernicola, Naples, San Carlo, 8 September 1787; *Fedra*, L.B. Salvioni, Naples, San Carlo, 1 January 1788; *L'amor contrastato [La molinara]*, G. Palomba, Naples, Teatro dei Fiorentini, carnival 1789; *Catone in Utica*, Metastasio, Naples, San Carlo, 5 February 1789; *Nina, o sia La pazza per amore*, G. Carpani (after B.J. Mersollier, with additions by G.B. Lorenzi), Caserta, Royal Palace, 25 June 1789; revised, Naples, Teatro dei Fiorentini, 1790; *I zingari in fiera*, G. Palomba, Naples, Fondo, 21 November 1789; *Le vane gelosie* (with Silvestro Palma), G.B. Lorenzi, Naples, Teatro dei Fiorentini, spring 1790; *Zenobia in Palmira*, G. Sertor, Naples, San Carlo, 30 May 1790; *Ipermestra*, Metastasio, Padua, Nuovo, June 1791; *La locanda*, G. Toniolo (after Bertati), London, Pantheon, 16 June 1791; *I giuochi d'Agrigento*, A. Pepoli, Venice, La Fenice, 16 May 1792; *Il ritorno d'Idomeneo in Creta*, S. Salsi, Perugia, Teatro del Verzaro, fall 1792; *Elfrida*, R. Calzabigi, Naples, San Carlo, 4 November 1792; *Elvira*, R. Calzabigi, Naples, San Carlo, 12 January 1794; *Didone abbandonata*, Metastasio, Naples, San Carlo, 4 November 1794; *Chi la dura la vince*, S. Zini, Milan, Teatro alla Scala, 9 June 1797; *La Daunia felice* (festa teatrale), Foggia, 26 June 1797; *Andromaca*, G.B.

Lorenzi (after A. Salvi), Naples, San Carlo, 4 November 1797; *L'inganno felice,* G. Palomba, Naples, Fondo, 1798; *Proserpine,* M. Guillard (after Quinault), Paris, Opéra, 28 March 1803; *I pittagorici,* V. Monti, Naples, San Carlo, 19 March 1808; *Epilogue for Mayr's Elise,* 1807.

Paisiello was perhaps the most prominent of the Italian composers whose works formed the basis for Mozart's operatic achievement. In fact, the talent, facility, and operatic successes of such wily Italians as Piccinni, Paisiello, Cimarosa, and Salieri made it difficult for Mozart to find the court position that could have made his career secure. No composer in that era of courtly patronage was to please more royal masters longer and more felicitously than Giovanni Paisiello.

Trained under Durante in Naples, Paisiello began his career in Bologna and Modena before returning to Naples and establishing his reputation with such operas as *L'idolo cinese* (1757) and *Socrate immaginario* (1775). Awkwardness in the control of rhythm, a limited harmonic vocabulary, and characters that seldom rise above stereotypes suggest that the young composer's success in *L'idolo cinese* rested heavily on pleasing melodies and a strong libretto by the estimable Giambattista Lorenzi. Musically, the opera displays a curious mixture of styles, ranging from highly ornamented serious arias in the fashionable manner of Hasse to simple comic songs that frequently rely too much upon literal repetition of short contrasting motives. Although present at the ends of acts, ensembles do little more than offer the characters singing in turn or in simple homophony. *Socrate immaginario,* composed on another unusual libretto by Lorenzi, reveals substantial progress in the technique of dramatic composition. Even so, the moments that linger in memory are those in act II when, none too subtly, Paisiello parodies the scene in Gluck's *Orfeo* in which Orpheus entreats the Furies.

From 1776 to 1784, Paisiello served as court composer to Catherine II in St Petersburg, his major achievement being *Il barbiere di Siviglia* (1782). This opera reveals not only a mastery of aria, ensemble, finale, and orchestration, but also full possession of a gift for musical characterization that was to influence contemporaneous composers. Despite regular reappointment, Paisiello became displeased with his duties at the Russian court. Without revealing his intention not to return, he took a leave of absence (with pay), and made his way to Vienna, where a significant success with *Il re Teodoro in Venezia* (1784) consolidated his favor with Emperor Joseph II. In addition, Alfred Einstein suggests that *Il re Teodoro a Venezia* had considerable bearing on Mozart's *Le nozze di Figaro* (1786) *(Essays on Music).*

During the last period of his life, with the exception of several years (1801-1804) spent in Paris as court composer and great favorite of Napoleon, Paisiello repeatedly refused invitations to compose abroad, preferring to remain in Naples in the service of King Ferdinand IV. Partly by inclination and certainly in deference to courtly taste, the composer turned increasingly to the composition of serious opera and sacred music. A successful setting of Metastasio's *Antigono* in 1785 led to a significant number of *opere serie,* among them *Pirro* (1787), which Paisiello claims was the first opera of its kind to use introductions and ensemble finales. Two collaborations with Gluck's influential librettist Raniero di Calzabigi followed (*Elfrida* and *Elvira*), both of them apparently distinguished by such elements of Gluckian reform as simpler arias and more expressive recitatives.

Despite the success in Naples of the composer's serious operas, Paisiello's international reputation rested then, as now, on his comedies. Two of the most played works from his later years are *L'amor contrastato* (better known as *La molinara*) and *Nina. La molinara* remains noteworthy for its parody of serious opera in the music of Calloandro and for the generally popular qualities of its melody and sentiment, which may be heard at their best in the aria "Nel cor piu non mi sento" (made famous through Beethoven's set of variations) and in the memorable quartet (praised by Stendhal in his *Vie de Rossini*). *Nina* is distinguished by a pervading lachrymose sentimentality that at times (as in Nina's "Il mio ben") foreshadows the melancholy vein of Donizetti's *L'elisir d'amore*. It has been called "one of the best examples of sentimental comedy in the whole period" (Donald J. Grout, *A Short History of Opera*). It seems significant that Paisiello, once an influence on Mozart, appears in both *La molinara* and *Nina* to have been influenced by Mozart. For example, it does not seem possible to hear Lindoro's "Questo e dunque" *(Nina)* without being reminded of Mozart's music for Don Ottavio (*Don Giovanni*, 1787).

After a long and noteworthy career that produced more than eighty operas and an old age replete with honors, the elderly Paisiello finally fell victim to the patronage system that had served him so well. Not once, but twice he chose to remain in Naples when Ferdinand IV was forced to abandon the city in the rapidly changing world of Napoleonic politics. The second time he even composed an opera, his last (*I pittagorici*, 1808), which alluded to the revolution of 1799 and was in fact commissioned by the reigning monarch, Joseph Buonaparte. When his Bourbon master returned, Paisiello had to live out the remainder of his days in disgrace.—DAVID POULTNEY

Palestrina

Composer: *Hans Erich Pfitzner.*

Librettist: *Hans Erich Pfitzner.*

First Performance: *Munich, Prinzregententheater, 12 June 1917.*

Roles: *Palestrina (tenor); Pope Pius IV (bass); Giovanni (baritone); Bernardo (tenor); Cardinal Madruscht (bass); Carlo (baritone); Cardinal from Lorraine (bass); Abdisu (tenor); Anton (bass); Luna (baritone); Bishop of Budoja (tenor); Theophilus (tenor); Avosmediano (bass-baritone); Ighino (soprano); Silla (mezzo-soprano); Bishop Ercole Severolus (bass-baritone); chorus.*

Palestrina, Pfitzner's three-act "musical legend," was published with an epigraph from the nineteenth-century German philosopher Schopenhauer, asserting the independence of intellectual and artistic life from the "bloodstained" history of man's political and social development. This viewpoint is elaborated in an interesting, if ultimately compromising, manner in Pfitzner's distinguished libretto, which concerns Palestrina's fabled rescue, through his *Missa Papae Marcelli,* of polyphonic choral music from an ecclesiastical ban. Pfitzner's treatment was elaborated from a careful reading of the history of the period. *Palestrina* is less a historical grand opera, however, than a post-Wagnerian drama of ideas about creativity and inspiration in the context of the pressure exerted upon artists by political controversy and social fashion.

In keeping with its setting at the time of the concluding sessions of the Council of Trent in 1563, the opera's broadly Wagnerian musical language is tempered by stylized effects of spare sixteenth-century harmony and contrapuntal figures. The long first act focuses upon Palestrina and his refusal to compose an exemplary mass for Cardinal Borromeo, with which the latter might persuade the council against an interdiction on polyphonic music. A ghostly visitation by ancient German masters, who press Palestrina to fulfil his artistic mission, is succeeded by a miraculous revelation of the angelic host, ecstatically singing music based on leading motifs from the historical *Missa Papae Marcelli*. In accordance with the legend, Palestrina writes the mass down in a sustained flow of divinely-dictated inspiration (we subsequently learn that it is taken to the authorities by his son Ighino—a travesty role for soprano—only after the composer has been imprisoned for his disobedience to Cardinal Borromeo). Act II presents, with great brilliance and some intentional humor, the relevant session of the Council of Trent, whose pedantic arguments conclude in chaos and brutal physical violence (a satire on democratic debate was apparently intended). The shorter concluding act finds Palestrina returned to his home, wearily awaiting the council's decision on the mass, which is being performed before Pope Pius IV. The work is received favorably, and the Pope himself arrives to thank Palestrina. Neither papal commendation nor the adulation of the crowd in the street below greatly interest the weary composer, however. He is finally left alone on stage, improvising on a chamber organ as he devoutly consigns his remaining days to God.

The work's musical construction depends upon an elaborate repertoire of leitmotifs and a deliberate contrast between the introspective, "spiritual" music of the outer, Roman acts and the more dynamic style of the grandly ceremonial and "worldly" second act. Palestrina's pupil Silla (a friend of Ighino and similarly a travesty role) is also given music affecting the new style of secular song-composition which he intends to go to Florence to study, forsaking his current master. The opera rapidly established itself in Germany and Austria as a worthy successor to *Parsifal,* but Pfitzner himself, in conversation with the novelist Thomas Mann, referred to it as an autumnal version of *Die Meistersinger.* Mann had been strongly impressed by the first performances of *Palestrina* in Munich under Bruno Walter, finding much to sympathize with in its nobly pessimistic reflection of the current state of the German spirit in the midst of the First World War. Mann was later, however, to distance himself from Pfitzner's chauvinistic conservatism, which Mann regarded as readier to engage with "bloodstained" political debates than *Palestrina*'s idealism appeared to warrant.

Mann thus began to appreciate the historical role of *Palestrina* as a work which revealed the mysterious nexus between artistic ideals and cultural ills that would occupy him in his 1947 novel, *Dr. Faustus.* Guided by his interest in the work, we may regard it as historically important not for its immediate attractiveness or theatricality, nor for its place in any mythically "progressive" development of Western musical style, but for its movingly self-reflexive dramatization of some of the conservative sentiments which would fuel the dark chapters of Germany's cultural history in the 1930s and 40s. The post-Romantic notion of transcendent art is here presented revealingly (if unintentionally) as a precisely contextualized and historically-oriented *musical,* as well as intellectual, construction.—PETER FRANKLIN

Parsifal

Composer: *Richard Wagner.*

Librettist: *Richard Wagner.*

First Performance: *Bayreuth Festspielhaus, 26 July 1882.*

Roles: *Kundry (soprano); Parsifal (tenor); Amfortas (baritone); Gurnemanz (bass); Klingsor (bass); Titurel (bass); First and Second Knights of the Grail (tenor and bass); Four Esquires (soprano, contralto, tenors); Flower Maidens (six sopranos); chorus (SSSAAATTTTBBBB).*

Parsifal is Wagner's final work, and the culmination of his long and turbulent career; the composer himself once described it as his "last card," in recognition of both his failing health and of the fact that *Die Sieger* (*The Victors*), the work that was to have followed *Parsifal,* would never be composed. Wagner's preoccupation with *Parsifal* stretched over almost four decades, from his first inspiration for the subject at Marienbad in 1845, and his later notion, soon rejected, of introducing the character of Parsifal into the third act of *Tristan,* to the writing of the first prose draft in 1865 and eventual completion of the poem in April 1877. The composition of the music was begun tentatively in 1876 and sustained over the period from August 1877 to April 1879, with the writing of the full score and revision or insertion of certain passages occupying Wagner until January of 1882. Recent research on Wagner's manuscripts has shown that the last extended musical passage he conceived was actually the second half of the transformation music in act I, which was added to his drafts in March 1881. *Parsifal* was painstakingly rehearsed and given a series of exemplary performances to reopen the Bayreuth Festival in July and August 1882, six months before Wagner's death. Wagner called it a *Bühnenweihfestspiel* ("stage consecration festival play") and meant to confine performances of the work to Bayreuth.

The text is based mainly on the medieval epic poem *Parzifal* by Wolfram von Eschenbach, but Wagner characteristically departed from his sources to create a highly concentrated drama heavily laden with symbolic import. He viewed the wounded Grail king in *Parsifal,* Amfortas, as analogous to the wounded Tristan in act III of *Tristan und Isolde* but with an enormous dramatic intensification. Amfortas' wound will not heal because it is the outward symbol of his inward state of moral impurity, and whenever he serves his duty of revealing the Holy Grail the wound opens afresh. This dilemma of Amfortas threatens to cause the downfall of the Order of Knights and bring the Grail into the hands of the diabolical Klingsor, who has already seized the Holy Spear and covets the Grail as well. Amfortas' inability to perform his office after the communion scene in the second half of act I eventually causes the death of his father Titurel, founder of the Grail Temple, whose funeral procession forms the transformation music at the change of scene in act III. Only the intervention of Parsifal as redeemer reverses this dissipation of the Order of the Grail in the final moments of the drama, as Parsifal returns the Spear, heals Amfortas' wound and assumes the role of leader of the Order.

The drama of *Parsifal* thus turns on the conflict between two opposing and incompatible realms. The crucial encounter that decides the outcome of this struggle is Kundry's attempt to seduce Parsifal in Klingsor's magic garden in act II. Only in this great duet scene, moreover, are the deeper layers of symbolic meaning unveiled. Kundry, the sole

The final scene from *Parsifal,* wood engraving after Theodor Pixis, 1882

female figure in *Parsifal* and perhaps the most fascinating and complex of all Wagner's characters, was developed as an amalgam of characters in Wolfram von Eschenbach's poem: in act I she is a wild heathen, distrusted by the knights but nonetheless bound to serve Amfortas for some undisclosed reason; in act II, she is an irresistible temptress and unwilling agent of the evil Klingsor in his magic castle; and in act III, she is a penitent who attains release through death in the opera's closing moments. As Kundry eventually reveals, she is under a curse and has experienced untold reincarnations through history, as Herodias and others. The cause of her curse and domination by Klingsor, was her spiteful laughter at the redeemer on the cross. Paradoxically, she can only be set free of her curse if her seductive charms are resisted, but no such "redeemer," with an insight transcending the sway of the senses, ever emerges until Parsifal. The seduction attempt, centered on the delivery of Kundry's poisoned kiss to Parsifal, acts like a replay of her earlier seduction of Amfortas, which led to his loss of the Spear and his wounding by Klingsor. Unlike Amfortas, Parsifal resists the temptation of her seduction because his capacity for compassion, as predicted in the prophecy of act I ("Knowing through Compassion, the Pure Fool"), enables him to identify with the agony of Amfortas, and gradually to grasp the significance of his calling to the Grail. Since the seduction has failed, and the protective shield of Parsifal's purity remains intact, the Spear when thrown by Klingsor cannot harm him. As Parsifal makes the sign of the cross with the Spear, Klingsor's realm is destroyed. Parsifal's return journey to the Grail is tortuous, since his path has been cursed by Kundry. His eventual return to the Grail, on Good Friday, coincides with Kundry's final reincarnation, and his first duty as redeemer is to baptise her. Act III concludes, as had act I, with the Communion service and revelation of the Grail, now no longer under threat from Klingsor.

The music of *Parsifal* assumes great dramatic weight and importance, especially in view of the ritualistic nature of the Grail scenes, the sparsity of text in portions of act III, which approach pantomime, and the inward, psychological nature of the Parsifal-Kundry encounter in act II. The largest single vocal part, on the other hand, is given to the narrator, Gurnemanz. At a formative stage in composition, Wagner described the "core of the drama" as the first Grail scene, and it is indeed the music for this section that is anticipated in the prelude to act I and eventually reinterpreted and resolved in the concluding Grail scene of act III. Noteworthy in this respect is Wagner's control of tonal relations on different levels of the musical structure. The opening Communion or Last Supper theme thus begins and ends in A-flat major, but turns prominently to C minor in its third bar, in a motivic gesture later associated with Amfortas' wound and hence with the threat to the Grail. Wagner also employs this A-flat/C axis to generate the ensuing tonal sequence of the entire theme beginning in C minor, with its internal dissonances intensified; and on the most gigantic level he plans the entire first act to modulate to the major mode of C at the entrance into the Grail Temple, where this tonality is affirmed by the fixed pitches of the temple bells. A grim reinterpretation of the fixed pitches of the bells occurs during the funeral procession in act III, in the key of E minor.

The music associated with Kundry and Klingsor, with Amfortas' agony, and with Parsifal's tortuous journey back to the Grail in the third-act prelude, displays a chromaticism sometimes even more advanced than in *Tristan* but which nevertheless retains contact with the music of the Grail. The so-called Magic motive, heard when Kundry delivers her kiss to Parsifal, outlines the dissonant interval of the tritone, instead of rising through the perfect fifth to the major sixth, as does the Communion theme; its intervallic configuration is constructed as a chromatic distortion of the latter. At Parsifal's response to Kundry's kiss, furthermore, this chromatic material is juxtaposed with the familiar dissonant inflection within the Communion theme itself, which enables the listener to hear that material with new insight as a "chromatic contamination"—stemming from Kundry's earlier seduction of Amfortas—of the otherwise diatonically pure music of the Grail. This "chromatic contamination" is purged from the music of the Grail in act III, after Parsifal's return of the Spear, as the head of the Communion theme receives a new ascending resolution. The enormous time-scale of Wagner's drama requires an appropriately massive musical resolution of tensions, which is supplied in part in the "Good Friday" music and capped by the closing music to act III, with its choral text "Erlösung dem Erlöser!" ("Redeemed the Redeemer!"). Here the various themes and motives heard successively in the first-act prelude are combined in a larger formal synthesis symbolizing the wholeness of the redemption.

The controversy that has always surrounded *Parsifal* is connected in part to its close relationship to Christianity. "Christus" is never mentioned by name, however, and there is no need to interpret *Parsifal* within a Christian framework. (To be sure, the analogy between "Adam and Eve: Christ" and "Amfortas and Kundry: Parsifal" lies close at hand, and was drawn by Wagner himself.) *Parsifal* is a major monument to the aesthetic of the sublime and to Wagner's conviction that art could "salvage the kernel of religion" through its "ideal representation" of mythical religious images. The theme of redemption, which obsessed Wagner throughout his career, is developed and radicalized here to concern not just individuals but a collective society. The resulting political and ideological overtones have seemed sinister to some commentators, especially in view of subsequent German history. Nevertheless, Parsifal's qualities of pity and renunciation are incompatible with fascism, and performances of the work at Bayreuth were discontinued during the Second World War.

Yet another critical problem is the imbalance between *Agapē* and *Eros;* the brotherhood of knights leaves no place for sexuality, and the "redemption" of Kundry renders her dumb before eliminating her. As Josef Chytry has pointed out, *Die Sieger* would have confirmed the compatibility of *Agapē* and *Eros,* but it remained unrealized.

It is above all the music of *Parsifal* that represents a summation of Wagner's achievement, in its exquisite textures and orchestration, richness of allusion, in the gigantic simplicity of its large-scale formal relations, and as an unconsummated symbol for those aspects of the drama that transcend action and concepts to embrace the ineffable and the numinous.—WILLIAM KINDERMAN

Pasta, Giuditta

Soprano. Born Giuditta Maria Costanza Negri, 26 October 1797, in Saronno, near Milan. Died 1 April 1865, in Blevio, Lake Como. Studied with Bartolomeo Lotti and Giuseppe Scappa; made debut in 1815; appeared in Scappa's Le tre Eleonore at the Teatro dei Filodrammatici di Milano, 1816; Paris debut in Paer's Il principe di Taranto, Théâtre-Italien, 1816; London debut as Telemachus in Cimarosa's Penelope, King's Theatre, 1817; appeared in Venice, Padua, Rome, Brescia, Trieste and Turin; appeared as Rossini's Desdemona at the Théâtre-Italien, Paris, 1821; appeared in Vienna, 1829; in St Petersburg, 1840; created title roles in Pacini's Niobe (Teatro San Carlo, Naples, 1826), Donizetti's Anna Bolena (Milan, 1830), Bellini's Norma (Teatro alla Scala, 1831) and Amina in Bellini's La sonnambula (Milan, 1831).

Giuditta Pasta was one of three great sopranos who helped mould the first years of the romantic period of opera. At a time when London opera house managers could afford to pay the highest fees, Pasta, Sontag and Malibran were the super-stars, to be followed by Grisi and Lind. Arguably, in comparison with her rivals Pasta had much the least "romantic" life and career, but for many contemporaries she remained on a pedestal. She also has unique historic importance as one of the first great interpreters of the three greatest Italian romantic composers—Rossini, Bellini, Donizetti—creating various of their works, including two which remain central to the repertoire—Norma and Amina in *La Sonnambula*.

After a debut in Brescia, Pasta made a false start to her international career at the Théatre des Italiens in Paris in 1816 and the King's Theatre in London in 1817. She made little impact and returned to Italy for further study with Scappa and appearances all over Italy, often in minor houses and mostly in long since forgotten works of minor composers.

Giuditta Pasta (Culver Pictures)

During these years and subsequently Pasta slowly moulded her voice, which she both lengthened and strengthened. Ebers, impressario of the King's commented on her appetite for hard work—"she leaves nothing to chance." He labeled her voice a mezzo soprano: "its present excellence is in great measure due to cultivation, its natural tone being far from perfect." Stendhal describes a register extending from low A to high C or even D, but draws attention to the different registers of voice. Indeed many contemporaries refer to the veiled quality of the middle register. Given the range and scope of Pasta's repertoire—Amina and Semiramide which we associate with lyric coloratura; Norma and Anna Bolena, true dramatic soprano territory; and Tancredi, bravura mezzo—the critics could easily have been describing Maria Callas! Indeed there are striking similarities in their careers, separated by nearly a century and a half.

From her reappearance in Paris in 1821 Pasta attained the status of international stardom and from 1824, when she again sang in London, she was for some years unrivaled. During this period she also appeared in Vienna, Naples, Milan and other centres, culminating in her 'creations'—Rossini's *Viaggio a Reims* in 1825, Anna Bolena in 1830, Norma and Amina in 1831 and the leading roles in Donizetti's *Ugo, conte di Parigi* in 1832 and Bellini's *Beatrice di Tenda* in 1836. Ultimately her repertoire extended to over 50 roles, including at least eleven by Rossini.

That Pasta's success was as much due to her acting as to her singing is another point of similarity with Callas. Chorley points to the way in which Pasta would first create and then maintain her interpretation, but though he knew what was coming both in terms of ornamentation and histrionically, Pasta's genius was such that he always felt as if he were seeing something quite new. From her first entry she was riveting. As late as 1837, when her voice had markedly deteriorated, he wondered "where has ever been seen any greater exhibition of art" than in her performance of Medea in Mayr's opera. Ebers felt "there is no perceptible effort to resemble the character she plays . . . . she comes upon the stage the character itself transformed into the situation."

The creation of Norma was the climax of Pasta's career. In June 1833 she sang the role in London and if the critics were initially lukewarm about the opera, there was no doubt about the heroine. "She (Pasta) was in grand voice and sang with a purity of intonation, with a truth of expression, with an intensity of feeling perfectly unrivalled." Pasta had carried the opera: "no other artiste now in existence could have produced a similar result."

Pasta's career began to wane by the late 1830s, although in 1840 and 1841 when she was only forty-four she appeared extensively in Eastern Europe, touring to Berlin, Moscow, St. Petersburg, Vienna and Warsaw. Once again there is a premonition of the Callas career, for nine years later Pasta reappeared in London in an ambitious program of arias and scenes, including the taxing finale of *Anna Bolena*. Chorley gives an evocative account of the heart-rending spectacle of a great voice in ruin, its owner unable to recapture past glory, and he ends with an unforgettable quotation from another witness—Pauline Viardot, sister of Malibran and then at the peak of her own career: "You are right! It is like the Cenacolo of da Vinci at Milan—a wreck of a picture, but the picture is the greatest picture in the world." The single epithet "greatest" given by the younger artist at such a moment is the final acknowledgement of Pasta's status.—STANLEY HENIG

Patti, Adelina

Soprano. Born 19 February 1843, in Madrid. Died 27 September 1919, in Craig-y-Nos Castle, near Brecon, Wales. Married: 1) Marquis de Caux, 1868 (divorced); 2) tenor Ernesto Nicolini, 1886 (died 1898); 3) Baron Rolf Cederström, 1899. Studied in New York with her half-brother Ettore Barilli, then toured as a prodigy; opera debut as Lucia di Lammermoor, 1859; Covent Garden debut as Amina in La sonnambula, *1861; in Berlin, 1861; Brussels, 1862; Paris, 1862; Vienna 1863; in Italy, 1865-66, then in Russia; appeared at the Teatro alla Scala, 1877-78, first as Violetta; appeared at Paris Opéra, 1874, 1888; presented at Metropolitan Opera, 1887; Covent Garden farewell season, 1903-04; appeared in recital until 1914.*

Born in Madrid of Italian parentage, Adelina Patti was taken to the United States where, aged seven, she began her career, then after giving some 300 concerts retired at ten to allow her voice to develop without risk of becoming strained. Six years later, Patti made an impressive debut as Lucia in New York. She had from the start the facility of learning a new part completely by singing it two or three times *sotto voce*, and once she sang it in public she never forgot it, proving her best in roles with opportunities for the display of exuberance and her natural gift for comedy. The longevity of her voice was due to her avoiding overexertion, helped perhaps, when once established, by her refusal to attend rehearsals. Making an immediate impact at her Covent Garden debut as Amina in 1861, she was hailed as Grisi's successor. Enthusiasm even surpassing that roused by Jenny Lind in 1848 followed the final cadenza in the Mad Scene when Adelina sang Lucia. She next became the youngest Violetta London had ever seen in *Traviata;* James H. Davison, critic of *The Times,* judged her acting "more elaborately finished than any previous impersonation of the character we remember." By the close of the season she had sung twenty-five times in six operas within eleven weeks, ending with Rosina in *Il barbiere di Siviglia,* which was destined to be the role in which she excelled.

Patti went on to establish herself in all the capitals of Europe. Wilhelm von Lenz, the Russian music critic, called her "the Paganini of voice virtuosity." When he originally heard her, he was struck at once with the fact that she launched a tone in a manner characteristic only of great instrumentalists. "She attacks the first note with a security and an exactness of intonation which the majority of singers achieve only in the course of a cantilena."

In Vienna, the distinguished critic Eduard Hanslick attended all Patti's major performances. He thought that as she grew older her understanding of her roles deepened, and he noticed in particular the greater fullness of her lower notes which resembled "the dark tones of a Cremonese violin." Her singing as Violetta was admirable, but the performance suffered from an inability to convince one that this was a courtesan. Patti made her first entrance like a high-spirited child, for whom lilies would have been more appropriate than camellias to wear in her corsage. All the same, in the last scene, she was most moving. Such exquisite transition from *piano* to expiring *pianissimo,* as when Violetta lay dying, and

Adelina Patti as Carmen (Culver Pictures)

from *mezza voce* to *fortissimo,* as in her duet with Alfredo, he had never before witnessed. Verdi had no reservations; Patti always was to him the ideal singer of his great role.

Hanslick thought Adelina failed to portray convincingly Marguerite's tranquil unworldliness in *Faust*. She was too lively, with her features continually in motion, but her singing of the "King of Thule" and of the "Jewel Song" were flawless. He was present once when the latter aria was followed by demands for an encore. Suddenly, without signalling the orchestra, Patti took up again the trill on B—they joined her in the next bar, and there was not the slightest difference in the pitch.

Patti's friendship with the Empress Eugénie led to her marriage in 1868 to the Marquis de Caux, equerry to Napoleon III, and eighteen years her senior. It soon proved a mistake, and pursued by a Don Juan of a tenor, Ernesto Nicolini, whom she first detested, Adelina eventually yielded and eloped with him. When in 1876 *Aïda* had its Covent Garden premiere with her in the title role and Nicolini as Radamès, Hermann Klein, the critic, who was present, called the first night the most exciting in her whole career. "There was a new note of tragic feeling in the voice; there were shades of poignant expression in the 'Ritorna vincitor' and the three superb duets . . . that seemed to embrace the whole gamut of human misery and passion."

The critic of the *Daily Telegraph* wrote in a similar vein. On no other occasion had he witnessed at Covent Garden anything "more impassioned than her acting, declamation and singing." The truth undoubtedly was that she had experienced a grand passion for the first time in her life and it was for the tenor originally so hated. Eventually they married and it was because he longed to lead the life of an English country squire that she bought her mock Gothic castle, Craig-y-Nos in South Wales.

It was there in 1905 when Patti was sixty-two and gramophones were in their infancy that the Gaisbergs recorded her singing for posterity. An excellent assessment of these historic discs is given by J.B. Steane in *The Grand Tradition—Seventy Years of Singing on Record*. His overall impression is of "an imaginative interpreter, an accomplished technician with a warm middle voice and a remarkable, sometimes disconcerting fund of energy." He compares her recording of "Ah, non credea mirarti" ("Scarcely could I believe it") from *La sonnambula* with those of other prima donnas and finds hers the most richly varied. "She colours with more emphasis than Callas. . . . The elderly lady singing into the old horn gives one some uneasy moments: a sudden forte in one phrase, a loose bit of timing in another . . . But Callas in her prime and with all EMI at her service gives more." On the whole, Steane prefers Patti who in addition to an intimate feeling for the music has retained some accomplishments—"swift turns, the trill with its fantastically fine texture and lightness—that few of the others have ever really acquired."

When Bernard Shaw, in his guise as the music critic, "Corno di Bassetto," heard Patti sing at the Albert Hall at the age of forty-seven, he disapproved of the program. There were few things more terrible to a seasoned musician than to have "Within a Mile" tacked on to "Ombra leggiera" or "Home, Sweet Home" introduced by "Il bacio." But he could not help wanting to hear those florid arias of the old school "on that wonderful vocal instrument, with its great range, its bird-like agility and charm of execution, and its unique combination of the magic of a child's voice with the completeness of a woman's."—CHARLES NEILSON GATTEY

Pavarotti, Luciano

Tenor. Born 12 October 1935, in Modena. Studied with Arrigo Pola in Modena and Ettore Campogalliani in Mantua; debut as Rodolfo in La bohème, *Reggio Emilia, 1961; same role for debuts in Vienna (1963), Covent Garden (1963), Naples (1964) and the Teatro alla Scala (1965); appeared as Idamante in* Idomeneo *in Glyndebourne, 1964; toured Australia with Sutherland, 1965; Metropolitan Opera debut as Rodolfo, 1968; Chicago debut in same role, 1973.*

Luciano Pavarotti has in the last few decades been billed variously as "the greatest singer in the world," "the world's greatest tenor," and "the greatest tenor since Caruso." He has taken to singing in stadiums, large parks, and other vast arenas such as the Baths of Caracalla in Rome with fellow tenors José Carreras and Placido Domingo during the 1990 World Soccer Cup match; this concert of "The Three Tenors" subsequently became a best-selling video. He has appeared in a movie ("Si, Giorgio," which was quickly dubbed "No, Luciano" by several critics) and frequently on talk shows. He has sponsored a singing competition based in Philadelphia and made a number of popular albums that have become best-sellers by any standard, not just those by which recordings by classical artists are judged.

None of these activities—many of which were practiced by his illustrious tenor predecessors Enrico Caruso and John McCormack in the early part of this century—should divert attention from the seriousness with which Pavarotti has studied and practiced his art. His vocal qualities come across strongly in his many gramophone recordings: his is a silvery, Italianate tenor voice with a ringing top, a fine *pianissimo,* smooth legato, a beguiling *mezza voce,* and liquid Italian diction. Like his tenor idol, Giuseppe di Stefano, Pavarotti has the passion of Italy in his voice, yet his is a sound unlike the dark tone of di Stefano. As Pavarotti notes, "Occasionally I worry that my voice is not 'brown' and rich enough . . . [but] I really want to have a clear voice, with a strong metallic sound." Thus, in terms of vocal timbre, Pavarotti is not in the line of Caruso, di Stefano, or his own contemporary, Placido Domingo, but has more in common with Beniamino Gigli, Giacomo Lauri-Volpi, and Jussi Bjoerling.

Allied with stunning natural vocal equipment—which Pavarotti comes by naturally from his baker father who sang tenor and owned a good collection of tenor recordings—is the indefinable factor of Pavarotti's great charm, his obvious enjoyment of life, and his ability to communicate human emotions to vast numbers of people through his singing. John Steane notes a "kind of tension in his singing which, for one thing, focuses interest . . . and more important, enforces the urgency of the music and the conviction that this is . . . *the* performance." But there has also been a great deal of hard work, beginning with seven years of study in his native Modena and in nearby Mantua, first with Arrigo Pola, who refused to let him indulge in excessive *portamenti,* and then with Ettore Campogalliani, who also trained Pavarotti's childhood friend from Modena, Mirella Freni. From the first, Pavarotti was fascinated by every technical detail of *bel canto* singing and was determined to learn it correctly and thoroughly. "Many singers find studying voice—the *solfeggio,* the endless vocalizing, the exercises—very boring . . . [but] I became intrigued with the process." Pavarotti describes *bel canto* mastery as "agility, elasticity, a smooth, even flow of liquid, well-focused sound, uniform of color, the ability to spin long, expressive legato lines without recourse to *portamenti* and, most important, without ever overdoing anything or giving the impression that you are over-exerting yourself, something you can do in *verismo.*"

Many fellow musicians and critics realized that the young tenor had indeed mastered the art of singing when Pavarotti began his career as Rodolfo in Puccini's *La bohème* at Reggio Emilia in 1961. This remains, along with Nemorino in Donizetti's *L'elisir d'amore,* one of Pavarotti's two favorite roles. As Rodolfo he eventually made debuts at La Scala, San Francisco, the Metropolitan,

Luciano Pavarotti as Nemorino in *L'elisir d'amore,* **Royal Opera, London, 1990**

the Paris Opéra, and at Covent Garden, where he replaced di Stefano in 1963 after having been heard and "discovered" by Joan Ingpen in Dublin. After this break, two important engagements occurred: the first was his involvement in the tenor version of Idamante in Mozart's *Idomeneo* at Glyndebourne; second was the 1965 tour of Australia with Joan Sutherland and Richard Bonynge. The noted accompanist Geoffrey Parsons heard Pavarotti at Glyndebourne: ". . . there was this glorious voice! I'd never heard anything like it before in my life. A really astonishing, silvery, yet full-bodied sound that possessed a wonderful, sweet quality." Pavarotti considers learning Idamante an invaluable experience: "I learned to sing in the Mozart style—piano and legato. Also, the Glyndebourne people have a very pure, almost cold approach to opera; this was a good counterbalance to some of my Italian excesses." It was, however, his connection with the illustrious Sutherland that brought Pavarotti's name before the opera world at large. Since that 1965 tour, the soprano and tenor have sung and recorded together extensively, matching each other in vocal brilliance and physical size. Ever serious about the study of singing, Pavarotti was astonished by Dame Joan's consistently high quality of performance night after night; from her he learned better breath support by, as Bonynge explains, putting "his hands on my wife's tummy trying to figure out . . . how she breathed." Good breathing, Pavarotti believes, "amounts to eighty per cent of the art of singing because leaning on the diaphragm, . . . a strong and highly elastic muscle, removes the strain from the vocal cords and ensures the sound will come out as it should."

The role that Pavarotti sang with Dame Joan that catapulted him into the realm of the legendary was Tonio in Donizetti's *La fille du régiment,* where in numerous live performances and on their Decca recording he poured out without obvious strain the nine high C's in Tonio's air, "Pour mon âme." Pavarotti has in fact been dubbed "King of the High C's," yet there are qualities he considers much more important for a tenor. "To make so much of the high C is silly. Caruso didn't have it. Neither did Tito Schipa . . . [who] was a great singer. He had a great line. For producing music, that is ten times more important."

In the 1960s Pavarotti was the perfect example of the *tenore di grazia,* turning down any large roles that might harm his voice, such as Cavaradossi, Arnold in Rossini's *Guillaume Tell,* Manrico, Radamès, Rodolfo in *Luisa Miller,* Ernani, and especially Verdi's Otello, instead concentrating on Tonio, Pinkerton, Arturo in *I Puritani,* Nemorino, Elvino in *La sonnambula,* and the Duke of Mantua. He has since sung most of these heavier roles, finally adding Otello to his repertoire in 1990 in concert performances with Sir George Solti and recorded on Decca. With the addition of the bigger parts there has been somewhat of a decline in Pavarotti's pure *bel canto* style, but at the same time his interpretive powers have increased. While his Radamès and Otello were only partially successful, by far his best *spinto* role has been Riccardo in Verdi's *Un ballo in maschera.* He has recorded it twice on Decca, the first time with Renata Tebaldi and again with Margaret Price.

Pavarotti considers Elvino the most difficult *bel canto* role, one that "requires great phrasing in the *mezza voce* as well as an easy top." The real measure of a tenor according to Pavarotti, however, is the Duke in Verdi's *Rigoletto.* He has made stylish and exciting recordings of most of his roles. The following complete recordings with Dame Joan Sutherland may be especially recommended: *La fille du régiment* (1967); *I Puritani* (1973) with its falsetto high f; *Rigoletto* (1972); *L'elisir d'amore* (1970); *Lucia di Lammermoor* (1971); and *Turandot* (1972). With Mirella Freni he has made affecting recordings of Puccini's *La bohème* and *Madama Butterfly,* Mascagni's *L'amico Fritz,* and Boito's *Mefistofele.* Pavarotti and Montserrat Caballé have appeared together in recordings of Verdi's *Luisa Miller,* Ponchielli's *La Gioconda,* and Giordano's *Andrea Chénier.* Of the many recital albums, his debut album of Verdi and Donizetti arias (Pavarotti considers Verdi the greatest dramatic composer but "my voice likes Donizetti"), *Primo Tenore,* and *O Sole Mio* give special pleasure.—STEPHEN A. WILLIER

Pears, Peter

Tenor. Born 22 June 1910, in Farnham, England. Died 3 April 1986, in Aldeburgh, England. Studied with Elena Gerhardt and Dawson Freer, 1934-38; studied with Thérèse Behr and Clytie Hine-Mundy, 1938-40; sang with the BBC Singers, 1934-38; sang with the New English Singers, 1936-38; first joint recital with Benjamin Britten in 1937; first tour in the United States in 1939; opera debut as Hoffmann in Offenbach's Les contes d'Hoffmann *at the Strand Theatre in London, 1942; premiered Britten's* Peter Grimes, *1945; premiered the role of the Male Chorus in Britten's* The Rape of Lucretia, *1946; premiered Britten's* Albert Herring, *1947; co-founded the Aldeburgh Festival, 1948; other Britten premiers include:* Billy Budd, *1951,* Gloriana, *1953,* The Turn of the Screw, *1954,* A Midsummer Night's Dream, *1960,* Curlew River, *1964,* The Burning Fiery Furnace, *1966,* The Prodigal Son, *1968,* Death in Venice, *1973; made a Commander of the Order of the British Empire, 1957; knighted, 1978.*

Peter Pears was an influential figure in British opera from 1945 until his death in 1986, not only as a performer but as an inspiration to composers and other singers. In *The Grand Tradition* John B. Steane suggests that Pears may be the best representative of the "educated modern singer," whose musicality and intelligence must embrace the music of all periods. Certainly, Pears's wide-ranging activities would support such a claim. He was particularly associated with Benjamin Britten, who wrote a dozen operatic roles for him—fourteen, if one adds the realizations of *The Beggar's Opera* and *Dido and Aeneas.* Pears also sang *Oedipus Rex* under Stravinsky, created Pandarus in Walton's *Troilus and Cressida* (1954) and Boaz in Berkeley's *Ruth* (1956), and appeared in important productions of Holst's *Savitri* (1956) and Poulenc's *Les mamelles de Tirésias* (1957). His activities were not restricted to contemporary music. As a young singer he sang the standard lyric tenor repertoire, appearing in leading roles with the Sadler's Wells Opera (1943-45) in *Il barbiere di Siviglia, Rigoletto, Die Zauberflöte, Così fan tutte, The Bartered Bride, La traviata,* and *La bohème;* he appeared at Covent Garden as Tamino and as David in *Die Meistersinger von Nürnberg* in the 1950s and added Idomeneo to his repertoire at Aldeburgh as late as 1969. To this marked versatility in opera should be added an even more striking range of music in concert work: he was a distinguished interpreter of the works of the English lutenists, Purcell, Schütz, Bach, and the great nineteenth-century Lieder composers. In addition, the archives at the Britten-Pears Library indicate that he sang the first performances of more than ninety non-operatic works, many of them written specifically for him.

The voice itself was not conventionally beautiful. It could sound unsteady at times (although this trait seems to have been more pronounced in recordings than in the concert hall), and it lacked richness. This rather vulnerable-sounding timbre, together with an unusually high register break and a well-developed capacity for pianissimo singing, was often exploited in the music written for him, particularly moments that present the character as a victim or a visionary.

Among the most famous instances that call upon this unique sound are "Now the Great Bear" and "What harbour shelters peace" in *Peter Grimes*.

Pears's many recordings demonstrate the sensitivity to words and music that made him such a sought-after interpreter. His last operatic recording (*Death in Venice*) provides many illustrations. For example, his handling of the rising interval at the end of the phrase "Should I go too beyond the mountains?" is a lesson in avoiding false accentuation (moun*tains*) while maintaining the musical line. Everywhere the text is evocatively colored: the caressing tone at "low-lying clouds, unending grey," the delivery of "Ah, here comes Eros" (scene v, besotted already), the physical decay of "O Aschenbach . . . Famous as a master," the numbed clarity of the Phaedrus passage. Pears's interpretation, however, is never fussy, and the performance never lapses into a demonstration of the role.

In addition, Pears was a gifted comic actor as well. His flair for sung comedy is evident on records in his operatic performances as Albert Herring and (even more subtly) Nebuchadnezzar in *The Burning Fiery Furnace*. That his abilities extended to the legitimate stage can be heard in his recorded portrayal of Feste in Shakespeare's *Twelfth Night* and, during his last years, in his readings at the Aldeburgh Festival.

Pears's contributions to musical life were not limited to his career as a performer. One of the founders (with Britten and Eric Crozier) of the Aldeburgh Festival, he contributed many witty and informative notes to its program books, and, with Britten, adapted Shakespeare's text for *A Midsummer Night's Dream*. In 1972 he and Britten established the Britten-Pears School for Advanced Musical Studies, where he was director of singing studies, a duty he shared with Nancy Evans after 1976. There he worked with promising young singers from all over the world, helping them establish careers.—JOE K. LAW

Les pêcheurs de perles [The Pearlfishers]

Composer: *Georges Bizet.*

Librettists: *Michel Carré and Eugène Cormon.*

First Performance: *Paris, Théâtre-Lyrique, 30 September 1863.*

Roles: *Léïla (soprano); Nadir (tenor); Zurga (baritone); Nourabad (bass); chorus (SATTBB).*

Bizet was only twenty-four in late March or April 1863 when Léon Carvalho, then director of the Théâtre-Lyrique in Paris, commissioned him to write a three-act score on a libretto by Eugène Cormon and Michel Carré. Rehearsals were to begin in August for an anticipated premiere in mid-September. To meet the tight schedule, the young composer borrowed from the earlier, incomplete *Ivan IV* and may well have cannibalized much of his now lost one-act *opéra comique, La guzla de l'Émir*. During rehearsals, he made numerous revisions and composed recitatives for acts I and II so that *Les pêcheurs de perles*, at that time entitled *Léïla*, no longer contained spoken dialogue. The premiere was postponed until 30 September due to the soprano's illness.

Most reviewers in 1863 pointed to passages they felt were derived from the work of established composers (notably Gounod, David, Verdi, and Wagner). And since Bizet was already identified as a leader of the younger generation, the critics also mounted their standard attack against "noisy" orchestration and unnatural harmonies; however, in the *Journal des débats* Berlioz testified to finding a "considerable number of beautiful pieces full of fire and rich coloring." The libretto was universally condemned. Though the work had a *succès d'estime* in certain circles, the public failed to embrace it, and *Les pêcheurs de perles* disappeared from the stage after eighteen performances that autumn. It was not performed again until the 1880s, when *Carmen's* popularity induced directors to look at other works by Bizet.

The plot, centered on the traditional operatic love triangle and set in exotic Ceylon, is driven and resolved by coincidence. Léïla and Nadir are lovers pitted against the jealous and powerful Zurga; the dynamics of the triangle are complicated by a long-term friendship between the two men and by Léïla's oath before the pearlfishers to forswear all men. Nadir comes to the isolated camp where he is welcomed as a long-lost friend by Zurga, who has just been chosen leader of the pearlfishers. The two reminisce about the evening when both saw and fell in love with a beautiful "goddess" at the temple in Kandi; both had then pledged to avoid her rather than jeopardize their friendship. In the next scene the same woman (Léïla) appears, veiled, and is sworn in as the chaste, solitary Hindu priestess who will pray for the safety and good fortune of the pearlfishers. Before the end of act I Léïla and Nadir have recognized one another, for Nadir had broken his oath to Zurga and returned to hear her songs in Kandi. The lovers meet that night (act II), but are discovered by the high priest Nourabad and are then condemned to death at sunrise by the furious Zurga. At the opening of act III, Zurga is tormented by guilt about sentencing his dear friend to death and thinks, too, of Léïla's great beauty; but when Léïla enters to plead for Nadir's life and confesses her love for him, she ignites Zurga's jealousy once more. Before leaving she asks him to give her necklace to her mother. He discovers that it is the very necklace he had given to a brave girl who had saved his life many years earlier. Zurga's jealousy evaporates, and he starts a fire in the camp, to distract the bloodthirsty pearlfishers and permit the lovers to escape.

In an effort to improve the dramatic impact of the score, posthumous editors (c. 1885, 1893) felt free to tinker with both music and plot in the final scene and elsewhere. The original form of these sections was not widely available until 1975 when Choudens issued a corrected score. Since the autograph manuscript has been lost, Arthur Hammond used the first-edition piano-vocal score and orchestrated sections missing since the 1880s. The strongest of the ensembles, the tenor/baritone duet from act I ("Au fond du temple saint"), has ironically become widely popular in a non-authentic posthumous version that discards the original triple meter closing allegro in praise of "sacred friendship" for a dramatically nonsensical return to the goddess theme ("Oui, c'est elle, c'est la déesse"). This wonderfully memorable goddess theme is first introduced in an effective flute and harp scoring and recurs, perhaps too often, whenever Bizet wishes to call attention to Léïla's effect on the men's friendship; it is effectively used, however, in the original version of the final scene after Zurga has saved the lovers from imminent death.

Very little of the score predicts that Bizet would write *Carmen* a little more than a decade later, but there is a good deal of lovely music for the soloists. Each has at least one strong aria, but the finest of them are Zurga's dramatically expressive recitative and aria in act III ("L'orage s'est calmé"/"O Nadir, tendre ami de mon jeune âge"); Nadir's exotic act II Chanson ("De mon amie"); and Nadir's often excerpted Romance in act I ("Je crois entendre encore"). Bizet supports the haunting Romance melody with an equally memorable scoring: the plangent English horn, muted violins, and two solo cellos that provide a rocking figure for the lullaby.

Choral music occupies a fairly substantial portion of the opera. It succeeds nicely in some places and sounds banal or dated in others. At their best the choruses help create the exotic setting, as in the opening choral dance for act I ("Sur la grève en feu"), where energetic rhythms are combined with interesting modulations; or in the offstage chorus opening act II, where simple choral parts and an ostinato rhythm in the male voices contrast with striking harmonies interjected by shrill piccolos. One of the weakest choral passages, judged embarrassingly old-fashioned even in 1863, accompanies Léïla's coloratura at the end of act I.

Only a few operas from Second Empire France are now more widely performed than *Les pêcheurs de perles,* and even fewer works by twenty-four-year-old composers have earned a place in the repertory. Though Bizet's distinctive musical personality emerges only occasionally and the more dramatic situations fall short of truth and power, this more than creditable score often transcends its weak libretto, largely due to Bizet's gift for melody and his colorful and effective orchestration.—LESLEY A. WRIGHT

Peerce, Jan

Tenor. Born Jacob Pincus Perelmuth 3 June 1904, in New York. Died 15 December 1984, in New York. Married: Sara Tucker. Sang at Radio City Music Hall, 1932; then studied with Giuseppe Boghetti; debut in Baltimore, 1938; became regular tenor soloist for Toscanini's broadcasts; Metropolitan Opera debut as Alfredo, 1941; on staff at Metropolitan Opera until 1966 and appeared there 1967-68; retired 1982.

"Between the high notes," said Jan Peerce, "there's something to be said in the middle of the aria." The middle of the aria often means the middle of the voice, and one of Peerce's most celebrated characteristics was his tonal consistency, a virtue he shared with some great cantors, with Giovanni Martinelli, and also with Aureliano Pertile, Toscanini's earlier "favorite tenor" at the Teatro alla Scala. For Peerce, to sing well was to breathe well; one senses immediately in his work not only responsible musicianship but total physical support. It was a luscious, forward sound, lyric in size but dramatic in quality, and crammed with texture. He gave to his Puccini roles and Don Ottavio a Verdian rectitude—quite the opposite of (for example) Beniamino Gigli, who often sentimentalized Verdi and Mozart as if they were Puccini. Peerce's forthright manner lent substance to all his Bach Aria Group performances and to his *Rigoletto* Duke in the opera house, and his earnest concern and full lyric voice made him a distinguished Alfredo and a vibrant Rodolfo, if not flirtatious in the manner of Ferruccio Tagliavini or Giuseppe di Stefano. Though his voice became drier, it remained steady and full until a stroke felled him in his seventies: he maintained strong vocal health as long as any other tenor of the century. His stage acting was dutiful, but his singing tone sounded even more persuasive in the opera house than on most of his records, which in RCA Victor's Studio 8H emphasized blatancy and harshness. In the house these were softened by distance, and his exceptional evenness of emission, now and then monotonous on record, meant in a live event that one heard *all* of his role very richly sung— an effect he shared with Jussi Bjoerling, who had a very different sort of voice.

Peerce knew his limits of volume and style, and refused to sing Wagner, even for his beloved Toscanini, who originally engaged him (after hearing Peerce's first and only concert performance of the first act of *Die Walküre!*) two years before the tenor's contract with the Metropolitan Opera. One understands the conductor's enthusiasm for the full, rattling voice, the dramatic commitment, and the rhythmic alacrity and clean musicianship of this dedicated tenor. Such qualities must have recalled his days in the twenties reshaping the Teatro alla Scala company with Pertile and others. Peerce and Toscanini performed together for fifteen years.

Aside from his Toscanini performances, Peerce made many records throughout his long career. Among them are some splendid moments of *La forza del destino*'s Alvaro, whose manly lyricism suits him very well, and his 1941 final scene from *Lucia di Lammermoor,* a performance of great richness and dramatic drive (hear his articulation of "No! No! No!" as he stabs himself) under complete artistic control. Perhaps his most representative work is in the Toscanini *La bohème,* ringing in tone, not subtly poetic but musically scrupulous and driven by passion, and wholly persuasive in its own special terms. Here, in short, was an artist whose musical style and vocal means were uniquely complementary and who fought for a repertoire which gave scope to his prodigious gifts without destroying them.—LONDON GREEN

Pelléas et Mélisande

Composer: *Claude Debussy.*

Librettist: *Claude Debussy (after Maeterlinck).*

First Performance: *Paris, Opéra-Comique, 30 April 1902.*

Roles: *Mélisande (soprano); Pelléas (tenor or high baritone); Golaud (baritone); Arkel (bass); Geneviève (mezzo-soprano); Yniold (soprano); Physician (bass); Shepherd's Voice (baritone); Serving Women (mute); chorus (AATBB).*

Pelléas et Mélisande is Debussy's only completed opera score. It is a slightly adapted version of Maeterlinck's play by the same title. Debussy began working on *Pelléas* in 1892, and the work was completed a decade later.

The opera takes place in an imaginary period, in the imaginary kingdom of Allemonde. While hunting, Golaud, a member of the royal family, finds a mysterious and lovely woman, Mélisande, weeping beside a well. The two of them become enamored of each other, and Mélisande agrees to go back to the kingdom and marry Golaud, who is a widower with a small son. Golaud announces that he must go get his son, Yniold, and asks Pelléas, his brother, to accompany Mélisande while he is away. While out walking with Pelléas, Mélisande drops her wedding ring in a fountain whose waters are said to cure the blind. Golaud returns home to find that Mélisande is not wearing the ring. She explains that she lost it in a cave on the seashore, and he insists that she go look for it at once, taking Pelléas for protection. A romance grows between Pelléas and Mélisande which devastates Golaud. Pelléas decides he must leave the kingdom and asks Mélisande for one last meeting, at which they confess their love and embrace for the first and last time. Golaud has been spying on them from the shadows and now leaps forward, running a sword through his brother. The final act of the opera takes place in the castle shortly after Mélisande has given birth to a daughter. Mélisande is dying, and the grieving, jealous Golaud asks whether she betrayed him with Pelléas. She never seems to understand him and dies without replying.

When Debussy had finished the opera, Albert Carré, the director of the Opéra-Comique, was alarmed at the language and the dramatic structure of the work. The premiere was a tense occasion: Maeterlinck had quarreled with both Debussy and the theater management because his wife was not chosen to play the heroine. The Scottish singer Mary Garden had been chosen instead. Maeterlinck publicly wished failure on the opera, and indeed its novel style of music outraged the public initially. Despite the public's first reaction, the opera played for fourteen nights, and gradually the hostility died down.

The style of *Pelléas et Mélisande* is unique. Debussy took the scenes just as he found them, making few cuts from Maeterlinck's play, which he set in reticent declamation over a subtle, shadowy layer of music. Musically, Debussy utilized modal, whole-tone, or pentatonic melodies and harmonies. He also used seventh and ninth chords, often in organum-like parallel movement.

The vocal line is murmuring, with much monotone recitation, and few sudden rhythms. By means of the slightest deviations of pitch and rhythm, Debussy was able to capture natural speech patterns.

Debussy linked the scenes all together within the acts through the use of musical interludes, a technique that deepens the mood and intensifies the concentration needed on the part of the audience. In addition, each scene has its own theme which is a subtle variant of the overall mood. *Pelléas* contains leitmotives in the Wagnerian tradition: short, flexible recurring fragments, associated with a person, or an idea.

Pelléas is considered one of the great works in opera literature and truly holds a significant place in opera development. It was this work that made Debussy a leader of a school, and brought about his revered position in music history. On the other hand, some say that this opera suffers because the drama is constructed out of ideas instead of persons and action. Nonetheless, the work has been closely examined and frequently performed, and will continue to be for quite some time.—KATHLEEN A. ABROMEIT

Penderecki, Krzysztof

Composer. Born 23 November 1933, in Debica, Poland. Married: Elzbieta Solecka, 1965 (one son, one daughter). Studied privately with F. Skoyszewski; studied theory with Artur Maawski and Stanisaw Wiechowicz at the Superior School of Music in Cracow, 1955-58; taught at the Superior School of Music, 1958-66; UNESCO award for Threnos, 1961; taught at the Folkwang Hochschule für Musik in Essen, West Germany, 1966-68; faculty member at Yale University, 1973-78; honorary member of the Royal Academy of Music in London, 1974, of the Arts Academy of West Berlin, 1975, of the Arts Academy of the German Democratic Republic, 1975, and of the Royal Academy of Music in Stockholm, 1975; honorary member, Accademia di Santa Cecilia, 1976; member of the Academia Nacional de Bellas Artes, Buenos Aires, 1982. Penderecki has been the recipient of numerous international composition awards and prizes.

Operas   *The Devils of Loudon*, [*Diably z Loudon*]. Penderecki (after Huxley/Whiting), 1969, Hamburg, Staatsoper, 20 June 1969; *Paradise Lost* [*Raj utracony*] C. Fry (after Milton), 1975-78, Chicago, Lyric Opera, 29 November 1978; *Die schwarze Maske*, after G. Hauptmann, 1984-86, Salzburg, 15 August 1986.

Krzysztof Penderecki, a Polish composer who shot to international attention after the "thaw" of Stalinist repression in Poland in the early 1960s, has to date written three operas.

Only the first, *The Devils of Loudon,* first performed in 1969, represents the aggressive avant-garde style (featuring dense tone-clusters, wide-ranging *glissandi* and garish tone-colors) with which his name is still most closely associated. By the mid 1970s, Penderecki had abandoned his *enfant terrible* attitude and with it his trademark orchestral effects. Like so many of his contemporaries, he attempted a rapprochement with such traditional musical devices as singable melody, periodic rhythm and clear-cut tonal centers. Whereas *The Devils of Loudon* is a deliberately harsh and pungent treatment of Aldous Huxley's novel about alleged witchcraft and demonic possession in central Europe in the seventeenth century, the 1978 *Paradise Lost* is a lushly orchestrated, unabashedly tonal treatment (rich in references to hymnody and E major brilliance) of the biblical story of creation as told in verse by the seventeenth century English poet John Milton.

If Penderecki can be said to have become a neo-Romantic with *Paradise Lost* and such other works as the 1972 Violin Concerto, the 1979 Te Deum and the 1980 Symphony No. 2, he can be said to have turned into something of a neo-Expressionist with his 1986 *The Black Mask.*

Based on the 1929 play of the same title by the German dramatist Gerhart Hauptmann, *The Black Mask,* like Penderecki's first two operas, has a religious subject with ties to the seventeenth century. Its setting is the well-stocked but seriously troubled home of the Dutch-born mayor of a small town in the state of Silesia on the German-Polish border; the action takes place in the winter of 1662, shortly after the Thirty Years' War and on the eve of an epidemic of bubonic plague. The cast of characters (including the Calvinist mayor, his Catholic wife, their Huguenot and Jansenist servants, a Jewish merchant, a Lutheran clergyman) is a metaphor for the region's troubled political situation. The gathering only appears to be friendly and civil; beneath the surface of pleasant chit-chat runs a deep stream of ugly hatreds. The stream floods over in the last act when a mysterious villain, to whom the mayor's wife once bore an illegitimate child, visits the house; he is a black man, dressed as a black masquer, and he presents the household not only with guilt but also with death.

The music of *The Black Mask* is turbulent, with dissonant harmonies and angular melodic lines. The score is freely atonal; in its extreme moments, it calls to mind both the dynamic intensity and the actual sounds of Schoenberg's *Erwartung.*—JAMES WIERZBICKI

Krzysztof Penderecki

Pergolesi, Giovanni Battista

Composer. Born 4 January 1710, in Iesi, near Ancona, Italy. Died 16 March 1736, in Pozzuoli. Studied with Francesco Santi, choir director at Iesi Cathedral; entered the Conservatorio dei Poveri in Naples as the result of a stipend given to him by the Marchese Cardolo Pianetti; studied violin with Domenico de Matteis, theory with Gaetano Greco, and later studied with Durante, Vinci, and Feo at the Conservatorio; first performed work the oratorio La conversione di San Guglielmo d'Aquitania *at the monastery of Sant' Angelo Maggiore, summer 1731; commissioned by the municipal authorities of Naples to write a Mass (after a series of violent earthquakes), December, 1732; in Rome, May 1734; in Pozzuoli, where he died of consumption, 1736.*

Operas *Salustia,* Sebastiano Morelli? (after Zeno, *Alessandro Severo*), Naples, San Bartolomeo, January 1732; [untitled intermezzo], Domenico Caracajus [performed with *Salustia;* lost]; *Lo frate 'nnamorato,* Gennarantonio Federico, Naples, Teatro dei Fiorentini, 27 September 1732; revised, Naples, carnival 1734; [untitled work performed with *Lo frate 'nnamorato*]; lost]; *Il prigionier superbo,* Naples, San Bartolomeo, 5 September 1733; *La serva padrona* (intermezzo), Gennarantonio Federico [performed with *Il prigionier superbo*]; *Adriano in Siria,* Metastasio, Naples, San Bartolomeo, 25 October 1734; *La contadina astuta* (intermezzo), Tommaso Mariani [performed with *Adriano in Siria*]; *L'Olimpiade,* Metastasio, Rome, Tordinona, 8 or 9 January 1735; *Il Flaminio,* Gennarantonio Federico, Naples, Nuovo, fall 1735.

Few composers in the history of western art music have been more misunderstood than Giovanni Battista Pergolesi, whose short productive career was followed by a posthumous rise in fame and mystique that culminated in his canonization as an early master of expressive affect (De Brosses) and of divine inspiration (Rousseau). He was championed as embodying the perfection of the Italian style during the so-called *Querelle des Bouffons,* in which the perennial Parisian battle of French versus Italian music and language was once again fought through a barrage of pamphlets and articles. Hundreds of misattributed compositions appeared under Pergolesi's name, often with music completely incongruous with his style and time; works such as the twelve concertini (by von Wassanauer) and *Il maestro della musica* (Auletta) still sometimes appear under Pergolesi's name. The proper estimation of Pergolesi places him with Vinci, Leo, and others, as a composer instrumental in transforming the contemporary musical language of the early eighteenth century through opera, a transformation that led to many of the characteristic features of the Classic style, such as a slow harmonic rhythm and melodies built of motivic repetition. At his best, he achieved high drama, generally through either the most expressive pathos or an inspired comic characterization.

Pergolesi's first public operatic work, a *dramma sacro* for the monastery of Sant' Angelo Maggiore on the conversion of William of Acquitaine, came at the end of his study in one of the famous Neapolitan music conservatories of the eighteenth century, the Conservatorio dei Poveri di Gesù Cristo, where he had studied for at least six years (and perhaps as many as ten) under the supervision of Gaetano Greco, Leonardo Vinci, and Francesco Durante. *San Guglielmo* is a limited work, but flashes of Pergolesi's soon-to-blossom genius are evident, particularly in the *buffo* scenes. The opera, overall, was tentative and less developed than those that would soon appear. Pergolesi's schooling must have gone well, for he was not required to pay tuition (as he led one of the conservatory's orchestras for hire), and the commission for *San Guglielmo* was arranged and performed by the conservatory, an honor reserved for only the best students. The boy was apparently a versatile and refined violinist, whose improvisations amazed even his fellow musicians (as reported by Villarosa), but he also may have studied voice—at least a set of solfeggi attributed to Pergolesi is found in the Naples Conservatory library.

From 1732 through 1735 a series of Pergolesi's operas appeared in Naples and Rome. Of his four serious operas, *Adriano in Siria* and *L'Olimpiade* (which borrowed heavily from *Adriano* and which was likely prepared in a rush) are the most developed. *Adriano* is one of his greatest works, at least in part inspired by his cast, which included the great Caffarelli in its ranks; Caffarelli's arias (such as the gorgeously lyric "Lieto così tal volta," with obbligato oboe, and the tumultuous "Torbido in volto e nero," with double orchestra) received his most careful and expressive treatment. Extensive alterations in the Metastasio libretto are everywhere to be found. *L'Olimpiade* was particularly singled out in contemporary accounts for its lyric beauty and passionate expression. Megacle's (the *primo uomo*) parlante aria, "Se cerca, se dice," which forms the centerpiece of the tragedy, was singled out as an "aria classicus" by later writers. Its poignant, sighing melodic line, reinforced by an orchestral "agitato" accompaniment, was in fact widely imitated in other settings of the same text in years to follow. *Salustia,* an adaptation of Zeno's *Alessandro Severo,* was plagued by sudden, last-minute cast changes (the *primo uomo,* Nicolini, died only days before the scheduled premiere), and the surviving scores suggest at least two possible performance formats. His second serious opera, *Il prigionier superbo,* was written for a rather undistinguished cast, although the orchestral writing is more secure. Both of these earlier operas seem tentative compared to the last two works.

The comic intermezzo written to separate the acts of *Salustia* is lost, but the two written for *Prigionier* and *Olimpiade, La serva padrona* and *La contadina astuta (Livietta e Tracollo),* are masterworks of comic writing. *La serva padrona,* whose renewed revival in Paris in 1752 precipitated, or at least encouraged, the *Querelle,* stands as a nearly unique example of an intermezzo largely unaltered in its transference and revival across European stages in the eighteenth century. *Livietta* brings to life its commedia dell'arte origins in a lively way, while the sometimes poignant arias of *La serva padrona* encourage a marvelously expressive dramatic flow.

Of his full-length operas, his most famous and successful works were his two *commedie musicali, Lo frate 'nnamorato* and *Flaminio.* Both works were revived on numerous occasions. The famous duet, "Per te ho io nel core," from the finale of *Flaminio* was later inserted into *La serva padrona* (one of its few alterations). *Flaminio* is closely modeled on the opera seria tradition, both in its dramaturgical design and its choice of cast. When *Lo frate* was revived in the Teatro Nuovo in Naples in 1748, it was reported that the opera had been sung in the streets for the previous twenty years (sic). It is a wonderful amalgam of music, from serious arias in a high style to lower, apparently popular tunes and allusions—references (both in music and text) that, though obvious in intent, are sometimes unidentifiable today. It is one of the earliest complete Neapolitan dialect comedies and represents an important transition in the history of Italian comic opera. It was such works as this, traveling through Rome to Venice, that inspired the development of other full-length comic works there in the 1740s and eventually led to the birth of the *dramma giocoso.*—DALE E. MONSON

Peri, Jacopo

Composer. Born 20 August 1561, in Rome. Died 12 August 1633, in Florence. Studied with Cristoforo Malvezzi in Lucca; maestro at the court of Fernando I and Cosimo II de' Medici, Florence; maestro at the court of Ferrara, 1601; member of the Florentine Camarata, formed by the counts Bardi and Corsi. Peri's setting of Rinuccini's Euridice *composed for the marriage of Maria de' Medici and Henry IV of France, 6 October 1600.*

Operas *La favola di Dafne* (with J. Corsi), O. Rinuccini, Florence, carnival 1598; revised, 1598-1600; *L'Euridice* O. Rinuccini, Florence, Palazzo Pitti, 6 October 1600; *Tetide*, F. Cini, for Mantua, 1608 [not performed]; *Lo sposalizio di Medoro e Angelica* (with M. da Gagliano), A. Salvadori, Florence, Palazzo Pitti, 25 September 1619; revised, c. 1622; *Adone*, J. Cicognini, 1611, for Mantua, May 1620 [not performed]; *La Flora, overo Il natal di Fiori* (with M. da Gagliano), A. Salvadori, Florence, Palazzo Pitti, 14 October 1628; *Iole ed Ercole*, A. Salvadori, for Florence, 1628 [not performed].

Despite the fact that historians practically from the very start have dubbed Peri the "inventor" of opera, the composer himself seems to have viewed his ground-breaking efforts in an altogether more modest light. Indeed, he later categorized his earliest work in the genre, *Dafne* (first performed during carnival 1598; all music lost save six numbers), as nothing more than a "simple trial." But however fortuitous his role may have been in setting in motion the new art form, there is no mistaking the fact that he envisioned his labor as a joining of the old and new: on the one hand a backward glance at the courtly entertainments and philosophical speculations of the Renaissance, on the other, an experimental first step toward the emergence, in music, of the Baroque. Ottavio Rinuccini, librettist of *Dafne,* in fact touched on both points when he wrote in the preface to *Euridice* (1600), his next collaboration with Peri: "It has been the opinion of many . . . that the ancient Greeks and Romans, in representing their tragedies on stage, sang them throughout. But until now this noble manner of recitation has been neither revived nor (to my knowledge) even attempted by anyone, and I used to believe this was due to the imperfections of modern music, by far inferior to the ancient. But the opinion thus formed was wholly driven from my mind by Jacopo Peri, who . . . set to music with so much grace the fable of *Dafne* ([the words of] which I had written solely to make a simple test of what the music of our age could do), that it gave pleasure beyond belief to the few who heard it."

Rinuccini was not alone in praising Peri's achievement. Marco da Gagliano, a colleague of Rinuccini's and Peri's who in 1608 composed his own setting of the poet's *Dafne* text, enthusiastically recalled "the pleasure and astonishment" afforded by the "novel spectacle" of *Euridice* and how it "aroused admiration and delight" in those who heard it. Arguably an even greater tribute had already taken place in 1607 when Claudio Monteverdi, in creating his first opera, *Orfeo,* modeled much of the style of his dialogues and monologues on those of *Euridice* (to judge by the evidence of his reliance on them, the passages of Peri's score that most captivated Monteverdi are those that first strike listeners today: Daphne's narration in which she recounts Euridice's death; Orpheus's response; Orpheus's plea in the underworld). Nevertheless, at least one contemporary listener found Peri's most novel accomplishment, that is, his "noble manner of recitation," rather tedious—"like the chanting of the passion."

Curiously, given both his contemporaneous fame and the prominence accorded him by posterity, most twentieth-century historians have shown a greater interest in the theories that gave rise to Peri's work than in the music he actually composed. Along with *Dafne* and *Euridice,* Peri composed five other operas between 1608-28 although three of them seem never to have been performed; the two others were written in collaboration with Gagliano. While with the lost *Dafne* this is unavoidable, with *Euridice* it can only be regretted.

Who was this shadow figure whose name is mentioned in all opera histories worthy of the name but whose music is so little known? As the musical scholar Tim Carter has written, in two important articles impressive for the way they build on original archival research and a review of existing information, Peri was "a singer and composer in rather routine, and for his part diffident, service at the Medici court. Some of his music is of the first order; but it needs to be seen in the context of his life and times." Part of that context is provided by the only other work of Peri's besides *Euridice* to have been published during his lifetime, the 1609 *Le varie musiche* (*The True Music;* 2nd ed., 1619), a volume of eighteen chamber songs containing fourteen for solo voice and two each for two and three voices with poetic forms running from the sonnet, madrigal, aria and a single example of strophic variation. From the literary point of view, the collection is especially telling in that it reveals the composer's tastes to have tended toward the conservative, with texts not only by Rinuccini but four by Petrarch, the latter inspiring songs of intense emotionalism that show Peri to have been the master of a compositional control matched by few of his contemporaries.

All told, Peri was at his most successful with highly-charged, dramatic texts. Although he was obviously drawn to the plaintive, the charge of "lugubrious" brought against him during his day has been shown to have been the vituperative handiwork of the pupils of Giulio Caccini, a fellow Florentine singer and composer who on more than one occasion seems to have delighted in impeding Peri's creative undertakings. While it is true that the lament on the death of Euridice along with Orpheus's first invocation in the underworld are among the most impressive moments of *Euridice,* these are not the only things treated in the opera, a point borne out variously by the vitality of the pastoral dances or the aristocratic mien given to the character of Pluto. Throughout the whole of the work one is aware of an unerring sense of proportion and drive. Howard Mayer Brown, describing *Euridice* in 1970, has elegantly and lovingly written that the work is one that "deserves repeated hearings and study, not merely for its historical significance as the first extant opera, but because it is capable of moving listeners even today." Brown himself has responded to the work with what one reviewer has termed "a landmark edition of early Baroque music" (Recent Researches in the Music of the Baroque, vol. 36, Madison, Wisconsin, 1982). Brown's words, but even more his edition of Peri and Rinuccini's unfaded allegory of music's power to influence and alter our lives, remain challenges not often enough taken up. Nowhere is that more apparent than in the continued need for a recording that does the work justice.—JAMES PARSONS

Peter Grimes

Composer: *Benjamin Britten.*

Librettist: *M. Slater (after the poem "The Borough," by George Crabbe).*

First Performance: *London, Sadler's Wells, 7 June 1945.*

Roles: *Peter Grimes (tenor); Ellen Orford (soprano); Captain Balstrode (baritone); Auntie (contralto); Niece (I and II, both soprano); Bob Boles (tenor); Swallow (bass); Mrs.*

Nabob Sedley (mezzo-soprano); Rev. Horace Adams (tenor); Ned Keene (baritone); Hobson (bass); Dr. Thorp (mute); Boy (mute); chorus (SSAATTBB).

Benjamin Britten's *Peter Grimes* occupies a unique place in the history of British music. A Koussevitsky Foundation commission had enabled Britten to devote himself to its composition. The Sadler's Wells Opera Company boldly decided to re-open its theater after World War II with a new work by a British composer. The resulting production drew together the composer's return from America to his English roots, the postwar sense of national rejuvenation, and the hope of a new era for English opera. Generally applauded, *Peter Grimes* rapidly established itself in the international repertoire.

The fisherman, Peter Grimes, appears in "The Borough," a poem describing English small-town life by George Crabbe, a native of Aldeburgh not far from Britten's own birthplace of Lowestoft. Montagu Slater's libretto, however, depicts a radically different Grimes from Crabbe's villainous monster. The protagonists in the opera are Peter Grimes himself, and (individually and collectively) the Borough as a whole. In the Prologue, an inquest pronounces the death of Grimes's apprentice to have been accidental, but Borough gossip continues to implicate him. In act I the townsfolk for the most part shun Grimes, but Ellen Orford (the schoolmistress) braves opposition to help him acquire a new apprentice and clear his name. With a storm raging outside, the Borough's superficial social life is depicted in The Boar pub, as Grimes, in a great lyrical aria, reveals his more profound sensitivity. But the following Sunday (act II), evidence of Grimes's harshness towards John, the new apprentice, in pursuit of his ambition, alienates Ellen (whom he had hoped to marry). As she deserts him, he defiantly resolves to go his own way, provoking a chorus of suspicion from the Borough, who angrily march to his hut. In the hut Peter and the apprentice are preparing to go to sea, but at the approach of the Borough Peter hurries the boy through the cliffside door. We hear his cry as he falls, but the crowd finds nothing. The final act begins with the conviviality of a town ball, but evidence of the boy's death emerges, causing suspicion against Grimes to intensify. A venomous manhunt ensues. Grimes re-appears, distraught to madness by his sufferings, and on the advice of the sea captain Balstrode he commits suicide.

Britten set out to compose a "numbers" opera of the traditional kind, with set-pieces defining key moments in the action, linked by continuous music. Six orchestral interludes depict both the natural elements, sunshine and storm, against which the community labors for its existence and the psychological tensions of the plot. Notable among those interludes is the passacaglia on Grimes's theme in act II, delineating Grimes's mental turmoil. The oscillation in the presentation of the minor characters, between individual expressions of musical personality and their merging in the collectivity of the crowd, reflects the fearful hold of mass psychology, while the extended choruses of mob fury are developed with great power. They contrast with the calm beauty of the reflections given to those (Ellen, the women, Balstrode) who stand aside from the hounding of a scapegoat, and the combination of strength, sensitivity, and destructive self-pity in the music of Peter himself.

Britten said that the opera concerned "a subject very close to my heart—the struggle of the individual against the masses. The more vicious the society, the more vicious the individual." Within that framework, Grimes has been interpreted as "an ordinary weak person, at odds with society, who offends against the conventional code"; "a maladjusted aggressive psychopath"; "a spiritual visionary"; "a misunderstood aesthete"; or "a rejected homosexual." As Philip Brett has shown, preliminary libretto drafts suggest that the last-mentioned view was in mind as the opera took shape. But overt suggestions of homoeroticism were steadily expunged as work progressed. Grimes is a harsh taskmaster, but hardly merits death on that account, and since the opera intends, I think, to absolve him of responsibility for the deaths of his apprentices, his enforced suicide requires explanation. British society may have ignored or even denigrated the unconventional, the visionary or the aesthete, but it has not pressurized them into suicide. For the homosexual, the sense of guilt arising from society's rejection has all too often had just that outcome. The dynamics of Grimes's relationship with the Borough reflect this experience.

The vignettes of the townsfolk reveal their various infringements of "morality" so that, confronted by Ellen Orford, none "dare throw the first stone." Like Grimes, "each one's at his exercise." Judged by this parallel, a homicidal tendency is too extreme to constitute Peter Grimes' "exercise"; but homosexuality would readily fill the bill. Moreover, the proposal for rehabilitation through financial success and a marriage of convenience is (in the 1940s) understandable in regard to a despised homosexual. When, at the mid-point of the opera, Grimes makes his defiant affirmation of his right to go his own way: "So be it! . . . ," the townsfolk, in the ensuing chorus, take up the *same* musical theme. This parallelism makes a profound dramatic point. If Grimes is asserting his self-identity, the Borough likewise asserts (however hypocritically) *its* right "to keep its standards up." Britten's answer to this unresolvable conflict of values is the plea for understanding expressed by the women (act II:1). Incapable of such understanding, the men of the Borough sink their individual judgment in a hysterical chorus, powerfully expressive of homophobia. Astoundingly, even Balstrode (earlier, Peter's friend) comes to endorse the mob's rejection. Grimes, on the other hand (in Brett's illuminating analysis) internalizes in self-hatred his rejection by society, and buckles under the strain to the point of self-destruction.

Writing his first opera in the 1940s, when homosexual acts were still criminal, Britten could hardly be explicit. Yet the unmentioned theme of homosexuality aptly fits the psychological dynamics of the work, and supplies the missing key to a full interpretation. For those who find such psychologizing not to their taste, the opera still works as a moving statement of the universal theme of the individual against society.—CLIFFORD HINDLEY

Peters, Roberta

Soprano. Born Roberta Peterman, 4 May 1930, in New York. Married: Robert Merrill (divorced). Studied with William Pierce Hermann; debut as replacement in role of Zerlina in Don Giovanni *at the Metropolitan Opera, 1950, where she remained for thirty-five seasons; sang Arline in* The Bohemian Girl *at Covent Garden, 1951; appeared at Salzburg, 1963; appeared as Violetta in* La traviata *at the Bolshoi Opera, 1972; has appeared in recital, musical comedy, and film.*

There are relatively few persons in opera whose fate in singing seems to have been established during their teenage years. Roberta Peters, however, was one who appeared to control the direction of her career at a very early age. Her desire to sing gained support from her parents, both of Austrian descent, although neither parent was musically inclined. Her father was a shoe salesman and her mother a milliner. As Roberta Peterman, she came into serious vocal study as a result of a contact made by her grandfather. He had a prestigious position in a hotel located in the Catskill Mountains that was often frequented by the tenor Jan Peerce. When Peters was yet very young, Peerce was asked by her grandfather to listen, assess, and make a recommendation about Peters' musical training. Peerce, though impressed, was hesitant to endorse any talent, let alone one so young and inexperienced; however, he did help the family arrange for voice lessons with William Pierce Hermann, teacher of Patrice Munsel.

Because Peters was a native of New York City, all her training began and revolved around tutors in this metropolitan area. Hermann almost immediately recognized the potential in his young, energetic singer. After Peters completed junior high school, Hermann was able to persuade her parents and school officials that she should withdraw from the public schools and continue her formal musical education with him. From the age of thirteen until her audition with the Metropolitan Opera at the age of nineteen, she learned a total of twenty operatic roles under his guidance. The first she learned was Lucia in Donizetti's *Lucia di Lammermoor*. Hermann arranged additional lessons in other areas essential in her preparation for a career in opera. These included ballet, acting, French, German, and Italian.

Even though she was given an opportunity to appear on Broadway at the age of sixteen, she declined because she was interested only in opera. Three years later Jan Peerce, who had checked on her progress throughout the years, took her to Sol Hurok, who, in turn, signed her to a contract and arranged auditions for her. In January of 1950, Max Rudolf heard her sing, and a week later Rudolf Bing engaged her to sing the Queen of the Night (*Die Zauberflöte*) and Rosina (*Il barbiere di Siviglia*) in performances scheduled nearly a year later. Her debut at the Metropolitan Opera did not wait until then, however. Because of her command of numerous roles and her participation in the Kathryn Turney Long program at the Metropolitan, she was able to replace an indisposed Nadine Conner as Zerlina in Mozart's *Don Giovanni* on six hours notice in November of 1950 without ever having performed an opera role on any stage.

As a result, she endeared herself to the critics, and the media immediately helped her to become an overnight sensation and a name known by virtually everyone in American operatic circles. Other demanding roles she has successfully assumed on short notice at the Metropolitan Opera include Gilda (*Rigoletto*), Sophie (*Der Rosenkavalier*), Susanna (*Le nozze di Figaro*), and Adele (*Die Fledermaus*). She created the role of Kitty in the American premiere of Menotti's *The Last Savage*. Her frequent appearances on television, on film, and in musical comedy have kept her name constantly before the American public.

The longevity of her career substantiates the artistic qualities present in her singing as a result of her meticulous preparation. Those persons who theorize that the singing of demanding operatic literature at an early age damages the human vocal instrument must ignore the ingredients of Peters' successes. In her youth she tackled a difficult coloratura repertory, beginning at the age of thirteen, and she maintained a rigorous and strenuous schedule thereafter in developing all facets of a singing career. She never pampered herself, but she was never without the help of a constant, trained technician. She studied with Hermann five and six days every week. She was proud of her command of exacting coloratura cadenzas, but she was also able to perfect the demanding Klosé clarinet studies for additional agility.

There are those who criticize her failure to create both warmth and excitement in her tone. At the height of her career, Peters was rather unfavorably compared, at first, to the fiery and passionate Maria Callas and later on to the dramatic and spectacular Joan Sutherland. In spite of the success of these two singers, Peters maintained an approach to coloratura singing which was more popular in the earlier part of this century and which was used by such singers as Galli-Curci and Pons. The demand for Callas and Sutherland in European venues possibly precluded any lasting acclaim for Peters on the international scene. Her appearances in 1951 in a gala performance at Covent Garden (*La bohème* under Beecham), in 1963 at Salzburg (*Die Zauberflöte*), in 1963 at Vienna (*Rigoletto*), and in 1972 in Russia at the Bolshoi Opera (*La traviata*) are highlights of her European performances.

Peters steadfastness as a performer is evidenced by the fact that by the end of her thirty-fifth anniversary with the Metropolitan Opera (1985), she had sung over three hundred sixty performances of twenty-three roles. Setting house records for her roles of Zerlina, the Queen of the Night, Oscar, and Gilda, she has experienced a career characterized by dependability, charm, and a perennial Cinderella quality which resulted from her fairy-tale debut at the Metropolitan Opera at the age of twenty.—ROSE MARY OWENS

Pfitzner, Hans Erich

Composer. Born 5 May 1869, in Moscow. Died 22 May 1949, in Salzburg. Married: daughter of James Kwast, in England, 1899. Studied piano with James Kwast and composition with Iwan Knorr at the conservatory in Frankfurt; taught piano and theory at the Conservatory of Coblenz, 1892-93; assistant conductor of the Municipal Theater in Mainz, 1894-96; on the faculty of the Stern Conservatory in Berlin, 1897-1907; conductor at the Theater des Westens, 1903-06; conducted the Kaim concerts in Munich, 1907-08; municipal music director of Strasbourg and dean of the Strasbourg Conservatory, 1908-18; conductor at the Strasbourg Opera, 1910-16; conducted at the Munich Konzertverein, 1919-20; master class at the Berlin Academy of Arts, 1920-29; taught composition at the Akademie der Tonkunst in Munich, 1929-34. Pfitzner stood trial for his supposed involvement with the Nazis in 1948, but was exonerated.

Operas *Der arme Heinrich,* James Grun (after a medieval epic poem by Hartman von Aue), 1891-93, Mainz, Municipal Theater, 2 April 1895; *Die Rose vom Liebesgarten* (prologue), James Grun, 1897-1900, Elberfeld, Munich, Municipal Theater, 9 November 1901; *Das Christ-Elflein,* Ilse von Stach and Pfitzner, [incidental music, Munich, 1906, recast as a "Spieloper," Dresden 1917]; *Palestrina,* Pfitzner, 1912-15, Munich, Prinzregententheater, 12 June 1917; *Das Herz,* Hans Mahner-Mons, 1930-31, Munich and Berlin, State Opera, 12 November 1931.

Although associated with the "modernists" of the pre-World War I era, Pfitzner was steeped in the traditions of both Viennese classicism and German romanticism, and his idealism expressed itself in a deliberately retrospective way. Whether as a composer, a conductor, a teacher or a polemical pamphleteer, he held himself aloof from what he regarded as wrong-headed "futuristic" experimentation, as well as from any inclination to seek easy, popular success in the theater.

Pfitzner's first opera, *Der arme Heinrich,* is a somewhat gloomy but finely wrought essay in Romantic medievalism in which a command of post-Wagnerian chromatic harmony and orchestral color is controlled by a dramatic ethos related more closely to *Tannhäuser* and *Lohengrin* than to the Wagner of *Tristan* or the *Ring* operas. The central character of this "music drama" after Hartman von Aue is an early twelfth-century German knight who suffers from a mysteriously debilitating malady that can supposedly be cured only by the sacrifice of a pure young girl. Agnes, the fourteen-year-old daughter of Heinrich's servant, devotedly offers herself, but Heinrich's cure is effected by his remorse as the sacrifice is about to be carried out under religious supervision in the monastery of Salerno. He intervenes and saves Agnes, who becomes the focus of the final tableau of transfigured renewal in the light of the rising sun.

The formal declamatory style of *Der arme Heinrich* and its use of clearly characterized leitmotivic material established the fundamental Wagnerian mode of Pfitzner's later dramatic development, which made its boldest inroad into his *fin de siècle* style and preoccupations in his second "Romantic opera", *Die Rose vom Liebesgarten*. Here the legacy of *Parsifal* is more strongly felt in the composer's treatment of a perhaps over-complex and turgid libretto by his friend James Grun. Rosicrucian symbolism and Romantic nature mysticism give birth to the idealized Germanic nobles of the Garden of Love and Siegnot, Guardian of the Gate of Spring, who is enticed into the subterranean realm of the mysterious Night-Sorcerer. There he meets his death, only to be restored to life in the Garden of Love through the quasi-divine intervention of the Star-Maiden, to whom Siegnot returns the mystic rose with which she had entrusted him. First performed in 1901, the opera was given an influential production, designed by Roller, in Vienna in 1905 under Gustav Mahler (who regarded it as having emotional appeal but too stuffy and "stagnant" a mystical atmosphere).

In the following year (1906) Pfitzner wrote incidental music for a children's Christmas play by Ilse von Stach. This infused pagan fairy tale material (anthropomorphic fir trees and elves) with sentimental bourgeois Christianity. In 1917 Pfitzner recast the work as the "Spieloper" (though still with spoken dialogue) *Das Christelflein*. The manner is that of Hans Andersen after Engelbert Humperdinck (*Hänsel und Gretel*), but von Stach's German nationalism combines with the deliberately simplified melodic style of Pfitzner's music to produce a work which, in retrospect, confirms the darker conservative implications detectable in his major opera, *Palestrina*.

Palestrina was to become Pfitzner's best known stage work, and was first performed in the same year as the revised *Das Christelflein* (1917); it had been composed between 1912 and 1915, to the composer's own libretto. In his depiction of the aging sixteenth-century composer, feeling himself to have become an irrelevant historical figure in his own lifetime, Pfitzner created an idealized operatic self-portrait that was as sympathetic as it was vulnerable. Palestrina's resignation and self-doubt are nobly expressed in the first act, but the transcendent idealism of his artistic philosophy is somewhat compromised by a haughtily anti-democratic chauvinism that reflected the cultural temper of the period in Germany. Pfitzner's subsequent polemical debates with Busoni and Paul Bekker revealed trenchantly nationalistic and even anti-semitic attitudes that led, with or without his consent, to official acclaim during the Nazi period.

For a variety of reasons—and a measure of critical self-awareness must have played its part—Pfitzner withdrew from the world in which he found himself caught between hostile modernist detractors and compromising Nazi admirers. As an opera director in Strasbourg before World War I, he had already begun to revive the works of earlier German Romantic opera composers—particularly Marschner—and his own final stage work of 1931, *Das Herz,* was appropriately in a Gothic-Romantic vein and set once more in a far away time (around 1700). Its black-magician hero, Daniel Athanasius, unintentionally sacrifices the heart of his own wife in order to restore the life of his master's son. Condemned and contrite, he is finally conducted into an elysian after-world by the astral figure of his wife, her glowing heart restored, even as the executioners arrive to lead him to the scaffold.

Although uneven in its quality and effectiveness, Pfitzner's operatic music, like that of his many concert and chamber works, was of wide imaginative and expressive range, for all the outward conservatism of its tonal language (acerbically contrapuntal, if at times given to Romantic lushness). Few composers have so argumentatively preached transcendent aesthetic values while so eloquently portraying their contingent and worldly self in their works. As a result, Pfitzner remains a composer of more than passing historical interest, for all that his ponderous and theatrically uncertain operas seem likely to remain unattractive to commercial-minded producers.—PETER FRANKLIN

Piccinni, Niccolò

Composer. Born 16 January 1728, in Bari, Italy. Died 7 May 1800, in Paris. Piccinni's father was a violinist at the Basilica di San Nicola in Bari, and his uncle Gaetano Latilla was an opera composer; the Archbishop of Bari, Muzio Gaeta, arranged for Piccinni to enroll at the Conservatorio di Sant' Onofrio in Naples, where he studied with Leo and Durante; instructor at the Conservatorio di Sant' Onofrio, 1755; produced operas in Rome and Naples; in Paris, December 1776; director of the Italian opera troupe in Paris, 1778; appointed maître de chant at the Ecole Royale de Chant et de Déclamation Lyrique in Paris, 1784; lost his position at the Ecole Royal de Chant after the Revolution, and returned to Naples; given a small pension by the King of Naples; returned to Paris, where he received honors and 5,000 francs, 1798; honorary position of sixth inspector, Paris Conservatory (Ecole Royal de Chant prior to the revolution); in Passy for the last months of his life.

Operas *Le donne dispettose,* A. Palomba, Naples, Teatro dei Fiorentini, fall 1754; *Il curioso del suo proprio danno,* A. Palomba, Naples, Nuovo, carnival 1755-56?; revised, with A. Sacchini, as *il curioso imprudente,* Naples, Teatro dei Fiorentini, fall 1761; *Le gelosie,* G.B. Lorenzi, Naples, Teatro dei Fiorentini, spring 1755; *Zenobia,* Metastasio, Naples, San Carlo, 18 December 1756; *L'amante ridicolo,* A. Pioli, Naples, Nuovo, 1757; *La schiava seria* (intermezzo) Naples, 1757; *Caio Mario,* G. Roccaforte, Naples, San Carlo, 1757?; *Farnace* (with D. Perez), M.A. Lucchini, Naples, San Carlo, 8 May 1757, or Messina?, 1753; *Nitteti* (G. Cocchi), Metastasio, Naples, San Carlo, 4 November 1757; *Gli uccellatori,* after C. Goldoni?, Naples/Venice, 1758; *Alessandro nelle Indie,* Metastasio, Rome, Torre Argentina, 21 January 1758; *Madama Arrighetta,* A. Palomba (after C. Goldoni, *Monsieur Petitone*), Naples, Nuovo, fall/winter 1758; *La scaltra letterata,* A. Palomba, Naples, Nuovo, winter 1758; *Siroe rè di Persia,* Metastasio, Naples, 1759; *Ciro riconosciuto,* Metastasio, Naples, San Carlo, November-December 1759; *La buona figliuola, ossia La Cecchina,* C. Goldoni, Rome, Teatro delle Dame, 6 February 1760; *L'Origille,* A. Palomba, Naples, Teatro dei Fiorentini, spring 1760; *Il rè pastore,* Metastasio, Florence, Teatro della Pergola, fall 1760; *La furba burlata,* P. di Napoli? (after A. Palomba), Naples, Teatro dei Fiorentini, fall 1760, or Naples, Nuovo, summer 1762; *Le beffe giovevoli,* after C. Goldoni, Naples, Teatro dei Fiorentini, winter 1760; *Le vicende della sorte* (intermezzo and comedy), G. Petrosellini (after C. Goldoni, *I portentosi effetti della madre natura*), Rome, Valle, 3 January 1761; *La schiavitù per amore* (intermezzo), Rome, Capranica, carnival 1761; *Olimpiade,* Metastasio, Rome, Teatro delle Dame, carnival 1761; *Tigrane,* V.A. Cigna-Santi (after C. Goldoni's revision of F. Silvani?), Turin, Regio, carnival 1761; *Demofoonte,* Metastasio, Reggio, Pubblico, May fair 1761; *La buona figliuola maritata,* C. Goldoni, Bologna, Formagliari, May 1761; *Lo stravagante,* A. Villani, Naples, Teatro dei Fiorentini, fall 1761; *L'astuto balordo,* G.B. Fagiuoli, Naples, Teatro dei Fiorentini, winter 1761; *L'astrologa,* P. Chiari, Venice, San Moisè, carnival 1761-62; *Amor senza malizia,* Nuremburg, Thurn und Taxis, 1762; *Artaserse,* Metastasio, Rome, Torre Argentina, 3 February 1762; revised, Naples, 1772; *Le avventure di Ridolfo* (intermezzo), Bologna, Marsigli-Rossi, carnival 1762; *La bella verità,* C. Goldoni, Bologna, Marsigli-Rossi, 12 June 1762; *Antigono,* Metastasio, Naples, San Carlo, 4 November 1762; *Il cavalier parigino?* (with Sacchini), Naples, Nuovo, winter 1762; *Il cavaliere per amore,* G. Petrosellini, Naples, Nuovo, winter 1762, or Rome, Valle, carnival, 1763; *Le donne vendicate* (intermezzo), after C. Goldoni, Rome, Valle, carnival 1763; *Le contadine bizzarre,* G. Petrosellini, Rome, Capranica, February 1763, or Venice, San Samuele, autumn 1763; revised as *La contadina bizzarra,* Naples, 1774; *Gli stravaganti, ossia La schiava riconosciuta* (intermezzo), Rome, Valle, 1 January 1764; *La villeggiatura,* after C. Goldoni?, Bologna, Formagliari, carnival 1764 [possible revision of *Le donne vendicate*]; *Il parrucchiere* (intermezzo), Rome, Valle, carnival 1764; *L'incognita perseguitata,* G. Petrosellini, Venice, San Samuele, carnival 1764; *L'equivoco,* L. Lantino [=A. Villani], Naples, Teatro dei Fiorentini, summer 1764; *La donna vana,* A. Palomba, Naples, Teatro dei Fiorentini, November 1764; *Il nuovo Orlando,* Modena, Rangoni, 26 December 1764; *Berenice?,* B. Pasqualigo, Naples, c. 1764; *Il barone di Torreforte* (intermezzo), Rome, Capranica, 10 January 1765; *Il finto astrologo* (intermezzo), after C. Goldoni?, Rome, Valle, winter 1765; *L'orfana insidiata* (with G. Astarita), Naples, Teatro dei Fiorentini, summer 1765; *La pescatrice, ovvero L'erede riconosciuta* (intermezzo), after C. Goldoni?, Rome, Capranica, 9 January 1766; *La baronessa di Montecupo* (intermezzo), Rome, Capranica, 27 January 1766; *L'incostante* (intermezzo), G. Palomba, Rome, Capranica, February 1776; *La molinarella,* Naples, Nuovo, fall 1766; *Il gran Cid,* G. Pizzi, Naples, San Carlo, 4 November 1766; *La francese maligna,* Naples, 1766-67, or Rome, 1769; *La fiammetta generosa* (with P. Anfossi?), Naples, Teatro dei Fiorentini, 1766; *La notte critica,* C. Goldoni, Lisbon, Salvaterra, carnival 1767; *La finta baronessa,* F. Livingni, Naples, Teatro dei Fiorentini, summer 1767; *La direttrice prudente,* Naples, Teatro dei Fiorentini, fall 1767; *Mazzina, Acetone e Dindimento,* Naples?, c. 1767?; *Olimpiade* [second setting], Metastasio, Rome, 1768; *Li napoletani in America,* F. Cerlone, Naples, Teatro dei Fiorentini, 10 June 1768; *La locandiera di spirito,* Naples, Nuovo, fall 1768; *Lo sposo burlato* (intermezzo), G.B. Casti, Rome, Valle, 3 January 1769; *L'innocenza riconosciuta,* Senigallia, 11 January, 1769; *La finta ciarlatana, ossia Il vecchio credulo,* Naples, Nuovo, carnival, 1769; *Demetrio.* Metastasio, Naples, San Carlo, 30 May 1769; *Gli sposi perseguitati,* P. Mililotti, Naples, Nuovo, 1769; *Cesare in Egitto,* G.F. Bussani, Milan, Ducale, January 1770; *Didone abbandonata,* Metastasio, Rome, Torre Argentina, 8 January 1770; *La donna di spirito,* Rome, Capranica, 13 February 1770; *Il regno della luna,* Milan, Ducale, spring 1770; *Gelosia per gelosia,* G.B. Lorenzi, Naples, Teatro dei Fiorentini, summer 1770; *L'olandese in Italia,* N. Tassi, Milan, Ducale, fall 1770; *Don Chisciotte,* G.B. Lorenzi, Naples?, 1770; *Il finto pazzo per amore,* Naples?, 1770; *Catone in Utica,* Metastasio, Naples, San Carlo, 1770, or Mannheim, 4 November 1770; *Antigono,* Metastasio, Rome, Torre Argentina, carnival 1771; *Le finte gemelle* (intermezzo), G. Petrosellini, Rome, Valle, 2 January 1771; *La donna di bell' umore,* Naples, Teatro dei Fiorentini, 15 May 1771; *La Corsala,* G.B. Lorenzi, Naples, Teatro dei Fiorentini, fall 1771; *L'americano* (intermezzo), Rome, Capranica, 22 February 1772; *L'astratto, ovvero Il giocator fortunato,* G. Petrosellini, Venice, San Samuele, carnival 1772; *Le trame zingaresche,* G.B. Lorenzi, Naples, Teatro dei Fiorentini, summer 1772; *Ipermestra,* Metastasio, Naples, San Carlo, 4 November 1772; *Scipione in Cartagena,* A. Giusti, Modena, Corte, 26

December? 1772; *Le quattro nazioni o La vedova scaltra,* after C. Goldoni's play, Rome?, 1773; *La sposa collerica* (intermezzo), Rome, Valle, 9 January 1773; *Il vagabondo fortunato,* P. Mililotti, Naples, Teatro dei Fiorentini, fall 1773; *Gli amanti mascherati,* Naples, Teatro dei Fiorentini, 1774; *Alessandro nelle Indie,* Metastasio, Naples, San Carlo, 12 January 1774; *Il sordo* (intermezzo), Naples, 1775; *L'ignorante astuto,* P. Mililotti, Naples, Teatro dei Fiorentini, carnival 1775; *I viaggiatori,* P. Mililotti (after C. Goldoni?), Naples, Teatro dei Fiorentini, fall 1775; *Enea in Cuma,* P. Mililotti, Naples, Teatro dei Fiorentini, spring? 1775; *La contessina,* Coltellini (after C. Goldoni?), Verona, Filarmonico, fall 1775; *Radamisto,* A. Marchi, Naples?, 1776; *Vittorina,* C. Goldoni, London, King's Theater in the Hay Market, 16 December 1777; *Roland,* J.-F. Marmontel (after Quinault), Paris, Académie Royale de Musique, 27 January 1778; *Phaon,* C.H. Watelet, Choisy, Court, September 1778; *Il vago disprezzato,* Paris, Académie Royale de Musique, 16 May 1779; *Atys,* J.-F. Marmontel (after Quinault), Paris, Académie Royale de Musique, 22 February 1780; *Iphigénie en Tauride,* A. de C. Dubreuil, Paris, Académie Royale de Musique, 23 January 1781; *Adèle de Ponthieu,* J.-P.-A. de R. de Saint-Marc, Paris, Académie Royale de Musique, 27 October 1781; revised (reset?), Paris, 1785 [not performed]; *Didon,* J.-F. Marmontel, Fontainebleau, 16 October 1783; *Le faux lord,* G.M. Piccinni, Fontainebleau, 6 December 1783; *Le dormeur éveillé,* J.-F. Marmontel, Paris, Comédie-Italienne, 14 November 1783; *Diane et Endymion* (with J.F. Espic Chevalier de Lirou), Espic, Paris, Académie Royale de Musique, 7 September 1784; *Lucette,* G.M. Piccinni, Paris, Comédie-Italienne, 30 December 1784; *Pénélope,* J.-F. Marmontel, Fontainebleau, 2 November 1785; *L'enlèvement des Sabines?,* Paris, 1787; *Clytemnestre,* L.G. Pitra, Paris, 1787 [not performed]; *La serva onorata,* Lorenzi?, Naples, Teatro dei Fiorentini, carnival? 1792; *Der Schlosser?,* 1793; *Le trame in maschera,* Naples, Teatro dei Fiorentini, carnival 1793; *Ercole al Termedonte,* Naples, San Carlo, 12 June 1793; *La Griselda,* after A. Anelli?, Venice, San Samuele, 8 October 1793; *Il servo padrone ossia l'amor perfetto,* C. Mazzolà, Venice, San Samuele, 17 January 1794; *I Decemviri. Il finto turco. Sermiculo? La pie voleuse, ou La servante de Valaiseau?*

One of the most inventive and popular composers of the mid-eighteenth century, Piccinni played a pivotal role in the development of both Italian and French opera. In his day he was almost universally in high regard; Burney placed Piccinni "among the most fertile, spirited and original," and La Borde found in his music "a vigour, a variety, and especially a new grace, a brilliant and animated style." He is frequently discussed today as a master of pathetic, sentimental affects, particularly in his Italian comedies. At his best he was brilliantly lyrical and emotive, yet Piccinni's music shows him to be much more than a writer of pretty melodies; he strove for a flexible approach to musical form and mood, and was unusually skilled in joining music and drama.

After Piccinni's education at the Sant' Onofrio Conservatory of Naples (where he studied under both Leo and Durante), his operas first began to appear in that city in 1754. His fame soon spread to other Italian houses, and within ten years he had written for Venice, Bologna, Reggio, Turin, and elsewhere. The vast majority of his works before 1776, however, were performed on the stages of Naples and Rome, including a large number of both comic and serious works. Among his youthful successes in comedy was his extremely popular *La Cecchina, ossia La buona figliuola,* produced in Rome on 6 February 1760 to a Goldoni libretto (first set in Parma with music by Dunì). From this moment his fame was assured. The often fickle Roman public finally deserted Piccinni for Anfossi in carnival 1776, however, during which Piccinni's *La capricciosa* was hissed from the stage—with no apparent musical motivation. Piccinni fell ill and returned to Naples.

With the promise of a royal pension in Paris from Marie Antoinette (the same enticement that had lured Gluck), Piccinni settled there on 31 December 1776, but found himself in another awkward, contrived rivalry, now with Gluck. The verbal battle between the "Gluckists" and the "Piccinnists" was only superficially over the merits of French and Italian music, however; in reality both Gluck and Piccinni represented a similar desire to join the two national styles. Gluck remained the more grand and was the master of high drama, and Piccinni excelled in versatility, adaptability, and melody. The debate first arose late in 1777; the poet Marmontel, in plot with the empress, sought to have Piccinni and Gluck simultaneously write for the same libretto, *Roland*. Gluck caught wind of the idea and destroyed his incomplete score. His *Armide* was produced instead, and was then held up by his admirers as a model that others were not likely to match; yet Piccinni's *Roland* early the next year was uncommonly successful. In February of 1778 Mozart summarized the French reaction: "My favourite type of composition, the chorus, can be well performed there [in Paris]. I am indeed glad that the French prize it highly. Their only objection to Piccinni's new opera *Roland* is that the choruses are too weak and thin, and that the music on the whole is a little monotonous; otherwise the work has been a success. To be sure they are used to Gluck's choruses in Paris."

Piccinni's French operas over the next ten years show remarkable inventiveness, but were not universally well received. An untimely staging of his *Iphigénie en Tauride* encouraged its poor reception (it followed by two years Gluck's version of the same story and is overall a less polished work). Still it abounds in expressive and coloristic effects, such as in Iphigénie's first act scene, "A la triste clarté de flambeaux palissants," in which swift changes of mode and key contribute greatly to the drama. He continued to experiment with a wide variety of musical styles and forms, with the rich orchestral palette of the French orchestra at his disposal (which Mozart also praised). Among his most successful, innovative, and influential works were *Atys* (a *tragédie lyrique* whose integration of French and Italian traits was perhaps his most successful), *Didon*, and *Pénélope*. In these operas, the advice and inspiration of his librettist, Marmontel (one of the loudest voices in the cries against French excesses in the Gluck/Piccinni controversy) was likely crucial.

Piccinni's popularity faded in the mid 1780s, and with the outbreak of the French revolution and the loss of his pension he left Paris and returned to Naples, where he settled in 1791. Falsely accused of political intrigue, he was placed under house arrest in 1794 for the next four years; upon his release he went again to Paris, but found little favor.—DALE E. MONSON

The Pilgrim's Progress

Composer: *Ralph Vaughan Williams.*

Librettist: *Ralph Vaughan Williams (after Bunyan).*

First Performance: *London, Covent Garden, 26 April 1951; revised, 1951-52.*

Roles: *The Pilgrim (baritone); John Bunyan (baritone); Evangelist (baritone); many lesser roles.*

Vaughan Williams completed his operatic "morality" based on John Bunyan's *The Pilgrim's Progress* in 1949. It represents the culmination of a fascination with this subject that occupied the composer intermittently for over forty years. A series of works composed over this time-span anticipate the finished score: incidental music provided for a dramatization of *The*

Pilgrim's Progress produced in 1906 at the Reigate Priory uses the hymn tune "York" which opens the opera; virtually the complete score of *The Shepherds of the Delectable Mountains* of 1922, a "pastoral episode" in one act, is incorporated into the fourth act; the incidental music of 1942 for a BBC radio adaptation of Bunyan's book employs music used in the opera; and the Fifth Symphony of 1943 is largely based on thematic material from the first act. Vaughan Williams adapted the libretto himself, skillfully interpolating passages of the Bible among scenes drawn from Bunyan, while paring down the elaborate Christian allegory to the essential framework of a spiritual quest. Further additions were made by the poet Ursula Wood (later Ursula Vaughan Williams). These are found primarily in the passages where Vaughan Williams revised and expanded the score in 1951-52.

The plot is developed in four concise acts with a prologue and epilogue, presented in a series of tableaux of gradually increasing intensity. After a prologue showing Bunyan in prison writing his book, the first act opens with the Pilgrim's cry "What shall I do to be saved?" An Evangelist appears and, despite the protests of conventional neighbors, encourages the Pilgrim to begin his quest. The Pilgrim journeys to the House Beautiful, where he receives absolution and inspiration. The second act consists of the Pilgrim's battle with the monstrous giant Apollyon, the hero's revival after defeating the giant, and the dark warnings of the Evangelist. In the next act, the Pilgrim encounters and rejects the worldly allurements of Vanity Fair, is tried and sentenced to death, but is miraculously freed from prison. The last act finds the Pilgrim among the shepherds of the Delectable Mountains. A Celestial Messenger arrives and summons him to the river of death; he crosses the river and enters into the Celestial City. As the radiant vision fades, Bunyan reappears in his cell and offers his book to the audience.

The Pilgrim's Progress does not conform to traditional expectations suggested by the term "opera"; Vaughan Williams recognized the unique quality of his score by titling it a "Morality." While acknowledging the origin of his material in seventeenth-century Puritanism, Vaughan Williams stressed its universality, and distanced his work from any specific set of beliefs: he pointedly changed his protagonist's name from Bunyan's "Christian" to the more general "Pilgrim." Thus *The Pilgrim's Progress* is neither an oratorio disguised as an opera nor an opera in the nineteenth-century tradition, but rather a music drama designed to appeal to the catholic beliefs of a wide audience. The premiere of *The Pilgrim's Progress,* given at Covent Garden on 26 April 1951 as part of the Festival of Britain, was marred by a hurried production, uninspired stage design, and an inexperienced conductor. Subsequent productions, such as those by Dennis Arundell at Cambridge and Geoffrey Ford at Charterhouse, and also the recording made by Sir Adrian Boult, have begun to tap the dramatic power and musical richness of this noble score.—BYRON ADAMS

Pinza, Ezio

Bass. Born 18 May 1892, in Rome. Died 9 May 1957, in Stamford, Connecticut. Studied voice with Ruzza and Vizzani at the Bologna Conservatory; debut as Oroveso in Norma *at Soncino, 1914; military service in World War I; appeared as Comte Des Grieux in Rome, 1920; Teatro alla Scala debut as Pimen in* Boris, *1922; selected by Toscanini to sing Tigellino in the premiere of Boito's* Nerone *at La Scala, 1924; Metropolitan Opera debut as Pontifex Maximus in Spontini's* La vestale, *1926; remained on the staff of the Metropolitan until 1947; also appeared in films.*

Pinza did much to restore the authority and importance of the operatic bass, especially at the Metropolitan Opera, in works such as *Don Carlos, Simon Boccanegra, Norma, Mefistofele* and *Boris Godunov.*

He was born in Rome, seventh among nine children of a poor family, but lived in Ravenna during his childhood years when he hoped to become a civil engineer. Having given up that idea, Pinza's father dissuaded him from being a racing cyclist and persuaded him to train for music. He underwent two years of vocal study in Bologna and made his debut in Soncino as Oroveso in *Norma.* He then took leading bass roles in smaller Italian opera companies until he was called up into the Italian artillery during the First World War. In 1920 he resumed his singing career at the Teatro Reale, Rome and two years later was called to the Teatro alla Scala.

His Milan debut was as Pogner in an Italian *Meistersinger,* and after that he was cast in the première of Pizzetti's *Deborah e Jaele.* Toscanini was so impressed with Pinza's voice and personality that he cast him as Nerone in Boito's opera of that name, which received its premiere in 1924.

This was the making of Pinza, who was immediately snatched by Giulio Gatti-Casazza for the Metropolitan Opera, where his debut performance was in Spontini's *La vestale* with Rosa Ponselle. Pinza's success that night assured his acceptance for the next twenty-two seasons.

He could sing Osmin in *Il seraglio* and had always wanted to be a *basso profundo,* but that was not to be. He was, instead, a *basso cantante* of sumptuous quality with an even tone over two octaves, a smooth legato with edge and carrying power, combined with a magnetic stage presence: handsome appearance and carriage, a good intelligence and the understanding to mould phrases with innuendo, humor, or malice.

Hence Don Giovanni, usually a baritone role, was not only possible for him vocally, but eminently suitable when related to his noble, dashing appearance that turned many a woman's head on and off stage. He sang it about two hundred times, although it took him a while to perfect the role. In 1929 at the Met (where Scotti had last sung it in 1908) Pinza was criticized for "lack of elegance, grace, adroitness and charm," which sounds biased; but he quickly amended these "faults," although it was not until he met Bruno Walter in Salzburg and sang it under him there, that Pinza admitted he was accomplishing all he could with the Don.

Toscanini was his other mentor, especially for general style, enabling Pinza to be considered the finest acting bass since Chaliapin, whose Italian repertoire he inherited. Pinza's favorite roles were Figaro and Boris Godunov. He first sang Pimen in the Mussorgsky opera at the Teatro alla Scala (with Vanni-Marcoux as the Czar), but then he made the title role his own, always singing it in Italian. They couldn't persuade him to do otherwise, even at the Met, where the rest of the cast sang in English.

He sang Figaro frequently at Salzburg—for the last time three days before the outbreak of war in 1939—as well as Don Giovanni, of course, and Basilio in *Il barbiere.* Salzburg welcomed him every season but one between 1934 and 1939.

After Pinza had mastered and sung almost one hundred major bass operatic roles (fifty-one of them at the Met) and could find no appropriate new ones, he became restless and left the Met for Broadway, appearing in the musicals *South Pacific* and *Fanny.* He also made a few films. But it was to the opera stage that he truly belonged.—ALAN JEFFERSON

Il pirata [The Pirate]

Composer: *Vincenzo Bellini.*

Librettist: *Felice Romani (after M. Raimond, Bertram ou le pirate).*

First Performance: *Milan, Teatro alla Scala, 27 October 1827.*

Roles: *Imogene (soprano); Ernesto (baritone); Gualtiero (tenor); Goffredo (bass); Itulbo (tenor); Adele (soprano); boy (mute); chorus (SSAATTBB).*

Bellini's *Il pirata, opera seria* in two acts with libretto by Felice Romani, was based on the three-act *mélodrame* by Raimond (Isidore J.S. Taylor) which was in turn based on Charles Robert Maturin's five-act gothic verse-play, *Bertram*. The title of the opera was undoubtedly taken from Walter Scott's *The Pirate* (1821). The story is set in the thirteenth century in and around the castle of Caldora in Sicily. With the Angevin victory, Imogene, although she loves Gualtiero, a fellow Swabian, has been forced to marry Ernesto, Duke of Caldora, to save her aged father's life. Gualtiero, forced by circumstances to become an outlaw and a leader of a band of pirates, has been defeated in a battle at sea by Ernesto. This is the background to the action. In act I, scene i, Gualtiero and his men are swept ashore near the castle during a raging storm. Imogene offers them aid, relates a strange prophetic dream that makes her ladies-in-waiting concerned for her slipping sanity, and fails to recognize Gualtiero. In scene ii, Gualtiero reveals his identity to Imogene. He is extremely distraught to find her married, for he had turned to piracy and battling the Angevins out of his love for her. Imogene explains the situation, whereupon Gualtiero decides to challenge the Duke to a duel. Ernesto returns triumphant to the castle after his victory over the pirates and reproves his wife for not sharing his joy. In act II Ernesto discovers that his old enemy Gualtiero is on the island. Discovering him in his wife's chambers, he draws a sword on him; in the ensuing duel Ernesto is killed. The knights of Caldora condemn Gualtiero to death. As the scaffold is erected for his execution, Imogene's latent madness blossoms fully: in an extended mad scene she runs a wide gamut of emotions, one moment singing tenderly to her son, the next calling on the sun to veil the sight of the fatal scaffold.

Although Romani acknowledged neither Raimond nor Maturin as a source for his libretto, the plot does not deviate far from its antecedents, even though for operatic purposes much of the length and complexity of the original had to be excised. In the opera, as might be expected, much is made of the opening storm at sea. It is impossible to discount the impression Bellini's music in this scene must have made on Verdi when he composed the opening storm scene of *Otello,* some sixty years later.

Imogene is the most fully-drawn character in both Maturin's play and in the opera. Between her opening dream sequence ("Sorgete; è in me dover"; "Lo sognai ferito") and her concluding mad scene one can trace the collapse of an already frail sensibility. The chorus is usually prominent in Bellini's operas, even in ostensibly solo scenes, where it provides affective commentary. Significantly, Imogene's dream narrative is interrupted several times by choral interjections, the chorus supplying the information, in the manner of Greek tragedy, that she has for some time exhibited a melancholy disposition. The fantastic nature of this dream aria allowed Bellini greater compositional freedom than arias dealing with more mundane matters. The form is nearly through-composed, and the melody is not as continuous or lyrical as in the preponderance of slow arias from the period. There is more musical continuity between recitative and aria style than was usual; the unsettled, rich harmonies help to underline the lamentations of the text, as do the orchestral coloring and the use of appoggiaturas on words such as "dolor" (sorrow).

In the final scene of the opera, Imogene's *gran scena di pazzia,* the dark timbre of the orchestra is paramount in painting the physical and psychological situations. To a harp accompaniment (the harp in this period suggests the unreal or fantastic, as in the fountain scene of Donizetti's *Lucia di Lammermoor*) of triplets and sustained viola chords, a long English horn solo (really a small orchestral tone poem) mirrors Imogene's bodily contortions and her mental fragmentation after she learns of Gualtiero's condemnation. Especially telling is the use of rhythm: on one level, tension is created by the contrast between the repeated triplets in the accompaniment and the simple duple meter of the solo line; the English horn melody itself is full of jarring rhythmic movement—dotted notes with or without preceding short appoggiaturas, double-dotted rhythms, gruppetti after longer-held notes, and smooth rhythms followed by jerky ones. Much of the sense of physical contortion comes from the use of repeated pitches that "twitch" back and forth; the dynamics also keep shifting. In the concluding fast aria, "Oh, Sole! ti vela di tenebre oscure," in which Imogene invokes the sun to blot out the scaffold, the ferocious rhythmic drive, jagged melodic contours, and projections of naked emotion become the prototype for subsequent scenes of madness and extreme anger, as in Anna's final cabaletta, "Coppia iniqua," from Donizetti's *Anna Bolena,* Lady Macbeth's part in Verdi's 1847 setting of *Macbeth,* and Abigaille's vocal lines in Verdi's *Nabucco.* This is one of the relatively few points in the opera that Bellini has invested with a great deal of embellishment (most of the vocal delivery in *Il pirata* is in unadorned, *declamato* style) and a wide melodic range in order to portray Imogene's state of delirium. Words such as "affanno" (anguish) and "angoscia" (distress) are repeated several times to long, semichromatic scalar runs.

Romani's libretto for *Il pirata* ends with an insurrection in which Gualtiero's band of pirates tries to save its leader. Gualtiero, however, rejects their assistance and throws himself from a bridge into an abyss. The opera as intended for performance, however, concludes with Imogene's mad scene. Although Bertram's onstage demise was suppressed in the case of *Il pirata,* Donizetti's *Lucia di Lammermoor,* composed a few years later, included both the heroine's mad scene and the hero's suicide in the church graveyard as Lucia's funeral cortege passes by. There are numerous ways in which the mad scene in *Lucia*—the *locus classicus* of the Romantic mad scene for a century and a half—is indebted to that of the extremely influential but relatively little known one in *Il pirata.* As the nineteenth-century composer Ferdinand Hiller noted, "*Lucia di Lammermoor* scarcely would have existed had there not been *Il pirata.*"—STEPHEN WILLIER

Ponchielli, Amilcare

Composer. Born 31 August 1834, in Paderno Fasolaro, Cremona. Died 16 January 1886, in Milan. Married: the soprano Theresa Brambilla. Studied at the Milan Conservatory, 1843-54; organist at Sant' Ilario in Cremona, later a bandmaster; professor at the Milan Conservatory, 1880; maestro di capella at the Cathedral of Bergamo, 1881-86. Puccini and Mascagni were among Ponchielli's students.

Operas *Il sindaco babbeo* (farsa) (with C. Marcòra, D. Cagnoni, A. Cunio), G. Giacchetti, Milan, Conservatory, March 1851; *I promessi sposi,* after Manzoni, Cremona, Concordia, 30 August 1856;

revised, E. Praga, Milan, Teatro dal Verme, 4 December 1872; *Bertrando dal Bormio,* 1858 [not performed]; *La Savoiarda,* F. Guidi, Cremona, Concordia, 19 January 1861; revised 1870; revised as *Lina,* C. D'Ormeville, Milan, Teatro dal Verme, 17 November 1877; *Roderico re dei goti,* F. Guidi (after R. Southey, *Roderick*), Piacenza, 26 December 1863; *La vergine di Kermo* (with ten others), F. Guidi, 1860, Cremona, Concordia, 22 February 1870; *Il parlatore eterno,* A. Ghislanzoni, Lecco, Sociale, 18 October 1873; *I Lituani,* A. Ghislanzoni (after Mickiewicz, *Konrad Wallenrod*), Milan, Teatro alla Scala, 6 March 1874; revised, Teatro alla Scala, 6 March 1875; *I Mori di Valenza,* A. Ghislanzoni (after Scribe, *Piquillo Alliaga*), 1874 [unfinished; act 4 completed by Annibale Ponchielli and A. Cadore], Monte Carlo, Opéra, 17 March 1914; *La Gioconda,* Tobia Gorrio [=Arrigo Boito] (after Hugo, *Angelo, tyran de Padoue*), Milan, Teatro alla Scala, 8 April 1876; revised, Venice, Rossini, 18 October 1876; *Il figliuol prodigo,* A. Zanardini, Milan, Teatro alla Scala, 26 December 1880; *Marion Delorme,* E. Golisciani (after Hugo, *Marion de Lorme*), Milan, Teatro alla Scala, 17 March 1885.

After taking his diploma with highest honors from the Milan Conservatory in 1854, Ponchielli began working in Cremona as organist and piano teacher. His goal was to conquer the Italian opera stage, which at that time meant challenging Giuseppe Verdi. To this end Ponchielli began working on a setting of Manzoni's *I promessi sposi,* to a libretto that he and several friends had devised. It was premiered in Cremona in 1856 at the Teatro Concordia; although the work was given fifteen times in Cremona, its success was purely local. Ponchielli's second opera, *Bertrando dal Bormio,* was slated for a premiere in Turin in 1858, but for unexplained reasons was not performed. His next effort, *La Savoiarda* (*The Girl from Savoy*), was given at Cremona; the revision, a return to the *opera semiseria* of the early nineteenth century renamed *Lina,* was heard in Milan in 1877.

In 1861 Ponchielli was appointed town band-master in Piacenza for three years, and his next opera, *Roderico re dei goti* (*Roderick, King of the Goths*), was given in 1863 at the Teatro Comunale. After his three-year stint in Piacenza, Ponchielli returned to Cremona as conductor of the town band. He also conducted operas there and was able to have one of his own ballets performed. It was a frustrating time for Ponchielli: he had not achieved his goal of becoming a recognized composer of opera; among other disappointments, Piave (the librettist of Verdi's *Rigoletto*) had agreed to write a libretto for him in 1867, but then had fallen ill.

Ponchielli's operatic success did not begin until his much revised *I promessi sposi,* now with libretto by Emilio Praga, was produced in December 1872 at the Teatro dal Verme in Milan. Soon after (in February of 1873), the Teatro alla Scala gave his ballet *Le*

Amilcare Ponchielli, 1887

due gemelle. Success was now Ponchielli's: Ricordi began to publish his music and to get it performed, and commissioned an opera from him for La Scala. This turned out to be *I Lituani,* to a libretto by Ghislanzoni, premiered at La Scala on 6 March 1874 and rearranged as *Aldona* for St Petersburg a decade later. This work is particularly notable for Ponchielli's attempts at Slavic coloring; it may profitably be compared with Musorgsky's *Boris Godunov* of the same year, an opera unknown to Ponchielli.

Ponchielli's greatest operatic triumph came in 1876 with *La Gioconda,* a melodrama set to a text by Boito (writing under the pseudonym Tobia Gorrio) based on Victor Hugo's *Angelo, tyran de Padoue.* However, *La Gioconda* was the apex of Ponchielli's operatic career. Subsequent works—such as *Il figliuol prodigo,* with its oriental coloring, and *Marion Delorme,* in the *opéra comique* tradition with bows to Verdi's *Traviata*—did not come close to the popularity of *La Gioconda,* which is the only opera by Ponchielli to have survived until the present.

Even *La Gioconda* is often maligned, although it has many strong points: vivid characters portrayed indelibly by musical means, sure and exact musical heightening of Venetian local color, seemingly inexhaustible melodic invention, and imaginative treatment of the orchestra. Many of Ponchielli's scores, even though each contains inspired pages and at the very least highly competent workmanship and a natural flair for drama, lack a strong musical personality, a facet of Ponchielli's own nature. As a man he was reticent, kindly, and passive to a fault.—STEPHEN WILLIER

Pons, Lily

Soprano. Born 16 April 1898, in Draguignan (near Cannes). Died 13 January 1976, in Dallas, Texas. Married: André Kostelanetz in 1938. Studied with Alberti de Gorostiaga at the Paris Conservatoire; debut as Lakmé at Mulhouse, 1928; Metropolitan Opera debut as Lucia in Donizetti's Lucia di Lammermoor, 1931; sang with the Metropolitan Opera, 1931-60; Covent Garden debut as Rosina in Rossini's Il barbiere di Siviglia, 1935; made several films, including I Dream Too Much, *and* That Girl from Paris.

Lily Pons was "Mr. Gatti's little Christmas gift from a kind providence." Thus wrote W.J. Henderson in the *New York Herald Tribune* of the petite French coloratura whom Metropolitan Opera general manager Giulio Gatti-Casazza put on, with no advance publicity, for an American debut as Lucia di Lammermoor on 3 January 1931. The success she scored then, which was nothing short of sensational, endured long after Pons had already become, in her unique way, a legend in her own lifetime.

In the eyes of both the operatic public and society at large, she was the very last of her voice type to be a full-fledged *prima donna.* Following the mid-twentieth-century advent of big-voiced Lucias such as Callas and Sutherland, it was no longer possible for a genuine *haute-colorature* to find consideration as an operatic "first lady." Voices of the size of Pons' became soubrettes for life, only rarely performing the "mad scene" heroines. And when they did, it was all too often not with the voices nature gave them but rather with instruments made wiry and intractable in the vain attempt to achieve feats that came naturally to their larger-voiced colleagues.

But Pons, following in the Galli-Curci tradition, knew better. She possessed style and sense and savvy and complete awareness of what she could and could not do. She stayed securely within the bounds of appropriate repertory. (She attempted Violetta only once, in her fifties, and did not return to it.) Moreover, she had a chic and bewitching kind of glamour that captivated the public at once.

During the 1930s Pons was the Metropolitan's principal box-office attraction, rivaled only by Kirsten Flagstad in the second half of the decade. And her influence upon her generation went beyond the excitement aroused in the public. Risë Stevens recalled that Pons singlehandedly made that era "a glamour time, when everyone dressed and was bejewelled. You were expected to be very glamorous. And we were."

Pons' voice, though small, was of utmost purity and carrying power. Beyond that, its quality was warm and appealing, not blanched and piercing like so many voices of the type, despite the brilliance that characterized it. The top range was so fluent that she always performed the *Lucia* mad scene transposed up a whole tone, in F, including the very last time she sang it (Fort Worth Opera, 30 November 1962, with Placido Domingo in his first Edgardo).

Although on the operatic stage she was never less than a serious and dedicated artist, her manipulation of the uses and possibilities of publicity was second to none. She made her first motion picture shortly after her American debut. At one point she acquired a pet ocelot, later donating it to the Bronx Zoo when it grew too large (both events were well covered in the press), and another time she was photographed eating a meal with some of the zoo's resident monkeys.

Like many other artists who left Europe before achieving real fame, Pons remained intensely loyal to the American public, which had regarded her as a star immediately. She sang rarely in her native land after her Metropolitan debut and not at all in opera after 1935. She visited Covent Garden for Rosina in the latter year and had made two brief stops at the Colón in Buenos Aires earlier (1932 and 1934).

Pons' profoundest effect was not as Lucia or Lakmé in the comfort and security of an opera house, however. She took her American citizenship in 1940 and during World War II spent a great deal of time traveling to entertain troops, enduring tremendous hardship and putting her own life in jeopardy continually. She performed in evening gowns in freezing cold at the Belgian front, in blistering heat in the Persian Gulf, and all temperatures between in China, Burma, India, Russia, Germany, Italy, and Africa. After the liberation of Paris she stood on the balcony of the Opéra, having been a full participant in the horror of the war, and before 250,000 of her compatriots sang the "Marseillaise." To the end of her days thousands of Allied servicemen who never went near an opera remembered with deep affection the tiny, plucky French nightingale who came to dangerous places to raise their spirits, often alone with only the pilot and her gown in the plane that transported her.

At her final appearance (in 1972, on a New York Phil-harmonic Promenade concert conducted by her former husband André Kostelanetz), Pons at seventy-four contrived not only to look as she had years before but to produce a sound almost palpably that of a much earlier day. Irving Kolodin's words then are a summation of the impact and appeal of Lily Pons, who "made an entrance that could only have been the product of nearly fifty years' practice in perfecting the unreality that is every *prima donna*. The exquisite way in which she was turned out assured her a triumph by sight alone." As a singer, "she had, literally decades ago, done herself less justice than she did this May 31. It was a kind of afterglow, a final flaring up of the barely smoldering vocal flame, a stirring about of the all but exhausted embers." It was equally the afterglow of a long bygone era, of which Pons herself was the symbol.—BRUCE BURROUGHS

Ponselle, Rosa

Soprano. Born 22 January 1897, in Meriden, Connecticut. Died 25 May 1981, in Baltimore. Married: Carle A. Jackson, 1936. Sang in cinema and vaudeville theaters with her sister Carmela; studied with William Thorner, Romano Romani; debut as Leonora in La forza del destino, *Metropolitan Opera, 1918, with Enrico Caruso; twenty-two roles at the Metropolitan Opera, including Norma, Aida, Violetta in* La traviata, *Donna Anna in* Don Giovanni; *created the role of Carmelita in Breil's* Legend, *1919; Covent Garden debut as Norma, 1929; sang Zoraima in American premier of* La notte di Zoraima *by Montemezzi, 1931; retired from opera stage, 1937. Served as artistic director of the Baltimore Civic Opera and taught; students include William Warfield, Sherrill Milnes, James Morris.*

Second only to that of Caruso, the voice of Rosa Ponselle has come to be regarded, simply, as the most beautiful in the history of recorded sound. Brash as such a valuation seems, more than half a century after the soprano's retirement, dissenters remain virtually unheard-of. The number of those living who actually saw her in performance has naturally dwindled, but, as with Caruso, the legion of her admirers only grows with time. The activating force behind this ongoing phenomenon is the same in both cases: the powerful legacy of a great singer's recordings.

Ponselle's career itself was hardly remarkable for length (two decades), nor was it really an international one. Except for three summer seasons at Covent Garden, a 1924 visit to Havana, and several performances at the 1933 Florence May Music Festival, it transpired entirely in the United States. Nonetheless, she is universally revered. For Tullio Serafin, she was one of only three "vocal miracles" in his lifetime (Caruso and Ruffo were the others). When Maria Callas made her Covent Garden debut (as Norma, 1952), Ernest Newman's astute summation was, "She's wonderful, but she is not a Ponselle."

The remarkable quality of her instrument allowed Ponselle to break every rule that existed for making an operatic career when she began. "Nobody taught me to sing," she said. "I was one of those fortunate few just 'born to sing'." American by birth (to Neapolitan immigrant parents), she was nonetheless an Italian singer in every respect. After a not exceptional amount of private study and coaching and a moderate accumulation of experience on the vaudeville stage, partnered by her older sister Carmela (also possessor of an exceptional voice), Ponselle sang in opera for the first time anywhere at the Metropolitan Opera. She was only twenty-one and made immediate history not only for the glory of her vocalism but for coming in as Leonora in the company premiere of Verdi's *La forza del destino* opposite Caruso (15 November 1918) without previous experience in anything approaching the demands of such an undertaking, let alone the then prerequisite apprenticeship in European opera houses. "Her voice disclosed a tonal beauty such as has not been surpassed by another soprano within memory. It is a big, luscious voice with a texture like a piece of velvet." Pierre Key's words presaged what would become the standard reaction to a voice darker, warmer, rounder, and richer than that of any recorded soprano predecessor, contemporary, or successor, whatever such other artists' manifest virtues.

With that voice, Ponselle was much more an instinctive than a calculated technician, and had from the beginning an inordinate fear where the top range was concerned. Moreover, as a performer she was beset by an excessive anxiety about getting on the stage at all, and this never abated. Set against these inseparable insecurities, which contributed not only to a vibrant dramatic temperament but also to a tendency toward emotional unreliability, was her devotion to work and study, her fanatical insistence on absolutely complete musical preparation. She demonstrated steady and admirable growth, maturing from the callow debutante with the golden voice into an artist for whom the Metropolitan Opera exhumed works long "dead." Most notable of these were *La vestale* and *Norma,* the revivals of which (in 1925 and 1927, respectively) have entered the realm of operatic legend.

The preservation on discs of the soprano's characteristic sound in such music, allied with her noble delivery, reposed legato, neatly articulated fioritura, and a trill quite exceptional for so large an instrument, has created not only a personal monument but a touchstone for the measurement of sheer beauty of voice. Commentary by those professional listeners who were of long experience when Ponselle was a beginner and who found her wanting, vocally and musically, must be taken somewhat on faith. If anyone before her possessed anything close to a timbre of such nurturing immediacy, the extant recording equipment was too primitive to do it justice, though one *can* discern more rarefied stylistic accomplishment, purer vowels, and more highly placed, radiant tone quality in certain older sopranos. No matter. Ponselle, just by having the voice she had and using it as eloquently as she did, superseded all previous models and became herself the one that female singers, from coloraturas to contraltos, want to sound like. Ponselle is the archetypal "modern" soprano, whose sound is a universal ideal, whose style and manner are broad and general enough (but not in any sense careless or unconscientious) not to reflect in some limiting or archaic way the era in which she herself performed. She is uniquely the Soprano for all Seasons.

She retired early, or so it seemed at least from the standpoint of chronological age. But by the mid-1930s, high notes that had felt precarious to her all along for the first time began to sound that way to the astute listener as well. For both that reason and what she felt to be a real temperamental affinity, Ponselle took on the title role of *Carmen.* There are no two opinions alike about this assumption (some said presumption) on her part; it was controversial from the start and remained so. When, in 1937, general manager Edward Johnson wanted her to return to Norma—in what turned out to be her last two seasons at the Metropolitan Opera she had sung only Carmen and Santuzza—Ponselle balked. She asked for a revival of *Adriana Lecouvreur* instead, and Johnson refused. Negotiations stalled and, over time, separation undramatically became divorce. Ponselle never appeared again at the Metropolitan Opera or anywhere else in an operatic role.

The quality of her sound was unaltered and retained its power to enthrall for two decades after her final appearance in opera, as visitors to her Baltimore home and an album recorded in her living room by RCA Victor in 1954 attested. (Numerous private recordings, several from as late as 1977, also exist.) In Aida Favia-Artsay's words, Rosa Ponselle's was "a perfectly phonogenic voice." Because of this fact, virtually everyone who comes to love opera eventually acquires also a special affection and admiration for that voice and for the particularly communicative artistry of its owner.—BRUCE BURROUGHS

Popp, Lucia

Soprano. Born 12 November 1939, in Uhorská Veš, Czechoslovakia. Studied at the Bratislava Academy, 1959-63; also studied in Prague, principally with Anna Hrušovska-Prosenková; debut at the Bratislava Opera, 1963; Vienna debut as Barbarina, Theater an der Wien, 1963; joined the Vienna State Opera, 1963, became principal member; appeared frequently at the Salzburg Festivals; Covent Garden debut as Oscar, 1966; Metropolitan Opera debut as the Queen of the Night, 1967; made an Austrian Kammersängerin, 1979.

To properly do justice to Lucia Popp we must really examine three careers, or at least three aspects of one remarkable career. In the beginning she was particularly celebrated for the clarity and freedom of her highest notes, and Popp followed an auspicious debut as the Queen of the Night by singing many of the German roles for coloratura soprano with great success. As her voice developed more bloom and richness, Popp went on to perform most of the soubrette parts in Mozart as well as much of the traditional lyric soprano repertoire. In the last decades, Popp's voice has continued to grow in size and depth, allowing her to take on challenges reserved for more powerful spinto voices. On records she has recently essayed with great success the essentially dramatic soprano part of Elisabeth in Wagner's *Tannhäuser,* and it seems reasonable to expect her stage repertoire to expand along similar lines.

So Popp has come full circle, now singing with equal success the heavier roles in operas whereas she once portrayed lighter heroines. There is a certain sense of balance in this; the great Queen of the Night in *Die Zauberflöte* of the 1960s has become one of the finest Paminas of the next decades, or in *Fledermaus,* as the sparkling Adele has been transformed into a suave, insinuating Rosalinde. Popp has more than mastered the hurdles posed in *Der Rosenkavalier:* an incomparable Sophie has become an equally distinguished Marschallin.

Popp is not the first singer to have made this transition successfully, but she is one of a very small number who have also matured as interpreters, so that the dramatic roles suit her today as well as the lyric repertoire did in years past. For the growth of Popp as a singer isn't merely vocal; as her instrument has developed in size and fullness she has also deepened as an artist. Lucia Popp today is not merely an accomplished virtuoso but one of today's important singing-actresses, and at this time—and her career is by no means over—there is every indication that she may join that select company of the century's greatest singers.

If it is Popp's interpretive intelligence that has been the great glory of her mature career, it must be said that she was able to build on a truly extraordinary natural gift, for there have been few if any voices in our time of more flawless quality and greater natural beauty. Popp's instantly recognizable soprano blends the natural creaminess found in the finest German singers with a distinctive Slavic edge, which lends a thrilling glamour to the tone color. From the start she has had the musical skills to deploy the voice like a virtuoso instrumentalist, and in fact her singing—perfect in intonation and sense of attack—often resembles great violin playing. And perhaps this is a bit of a drawback too, for in producing her voice like a string player Popp will sometimes "squeeze" the tone, draining it of all vibrato. Over the years this tendency has become more pronounced: often it is used effectively as a coloristic device, but sometimes Popp's singing can sound mannered and artificial, and very occasionally the sound is uncomfortably constricted and will not ring out freely. It should also be noted that although the basic timbre of Popp's voice has remained largely and amazingly unchanged over the nearly twenty-five years of her career, the highest notes have not come easily for several years now. But these small issues are comparatively insignificant in the face of such glorious singing and superb artistry.

We are fortunate that Popp has been and continues to be a prolific recording artist, and her discography abundantly supports her exalted reputation. Like Elisabeth Schwarzkopf, in whose distinguished steps she seems to follow, Popp is at her best in the operas of Mozart. She has preserved for posterity her Susanna, Despina, Zerlina, and Blondchen, and to each of these soubrette roles she brings not only the requisite bell-like tone but a sense of humor and humanity as well. As the Countess and Pamina, Popp invests her perfectly poised classical line with an almost unbearable poignancy and tonal beauty. And, in one of her first recorded performances, she remains an unbettered Queen of the Night: the staccati gleam with astonishing accuracy, the highest notes are not merely present but are integrated into the

William Warfield and Leontyne Price in *Porgy and Bess,* **1952**

body of the voice, and in the role's two short arias Popp paints an unusually detailed and sympathetic character: a wondrous and promising debut for this young singer, and the career that has followed has amply fulfilled the promise.—DAVID ANTHONY FOX

Porgy and Bess

Composer: *George Gershwin.*

Librettist: *DuBose Heyward (after DuBose and Dorothy Heyward,* Porgy, *with lyrics by Ira Gershwin).*

First Performance: *New York, Alvin Theater, 10 October 1935.*

Roles: *Porgy (bass-baritone); Bess (soprano); Sportin' Life (tenor); Crown (baritone); Clara (soprano); Serena (soprano); Maria (contralto); Jake (baritone); Mingo (tenor); Robbins (tenor); Peter (tenor); Frazier (baritone); Annie (mezzo-soprano); Lily (mezzo-soprano); Strawberry Woman (mezzo-soprano); Jim (baritone); Undertaker (baritone); Nelson (tenor); Crab Man (tenor); chorus (SSAATBB).*

Gershwin's enduring fame is based almost entirely on music he wrote for theatrical situations, yet the 1935 *Porgy and Bess* is his only contribution to the operatic literature.

Some would say that *Porgy and Bess* is not an opera, that it is, like Leonard Bernstein's *West Side Story* and recent efforts by Andrew Lloyd Webber, merely a "musical" that aspires to operatic status. That it was first produced not in an opera house but in a Broadway theater is less relevant to this argument than the song-like nature of its segments. *Porgy and Bess* indeed contains a bounty of solid numbers; most of them are easily extractable from the score, and many of them—"Summertime," "It ain't necessarily so," "There's a boat that's leavin' for New York"— have enjoyed dazzling success in the repertoire of pop and jazz performers. It remains, though, that *Porgy and Bess* is a through-composed work whose spotlit songs are connected more or less deftly with recitative and dialogue set over orchestral backdrops, as rich in atmosphere as it is in detail of plot and characterization, a tight-knit music-drama whose momentum flows consistently over its entire three-act course.

The lyrics for the song-like numbers are by Gershwin's brother Ira, but the libretto as a whole is by DuBose Heyward, based on his 1926 play *Porgy* and modeled loosely after real life characters in Heyward's native Charleston, South Carolina.

It is set in the city's Afro-American ghetto neighborhood near the harbor, once called "Cabbage Row" but renamed "Catfish Row" by the playwright. Porgy is a crippled beggar, in love with Bess, but troubled by Bess's involvements with various other members of the community. One of them is a thug named Crown, who loses his tyrannical hold on Bess only when he is killed by Porgy during a quarrel at the opening of act III. Another, a gambler named Sportin' Life, eventually convinces Bess to accompany him to New York. The opera ends with Porgy, undaunted, hitching up his goat-cart and setting off in pursuit, confident that with the help of Providence he will be reunited with Bess.—JAMES WIERZBICKI

Poulenc, Francis

Composer. Born 7 January 1899, in Paris. Died 30 January 1963, in Paris. Piano lessons with Ricardo Viñes; served in the French Army, 1918-21; studied composition with Koechlin, 1921-24; accompanist to the baritone Pierre Bernac, 1935; commissioned by Diaghilev to write for the Ballets Russes. Poulenc was one of "Les Six" that included Auric, Durey, Honegger, Milhaud, and Tailleferre.

Operas *Les mamelles de Tirésias,* Poulenc (after Guillaume Apollinaire), 1944, Paris, Opéra-Comique, 3 June 1947; *Dialogues des Carmélites,* Poulenc (after Georges Bernanos), 1953-56, Milan, Teatro alla Scala, 26 January 1957; *La voix humaine,* Poulenc (after Jean Cocteau), 1958, Paris, Opéra-Comique, 6 February 1959.

The music of Francis Poulenc presents few challenges, either to the critic or to the casual listener, for, though he continued writing well into the avant-garde period, his style remained resolutely tonal and accessible throughout his career. Despite an active interest in serialism and electronic music, he eschewed both, preferring to remain in the neo-classic and neo-romantic realms that had served him during his formative years (1916-1936). Poulenc reveled in eclecticism, borrowing unashamedly from Stravinsky, Debussy, Verdi, and Parisian music hall composers, and seeking stimulation from the parallel worlds of painting and poetry.

Poulenc launched his career with a *succès de scandale* of the kind dreamed about by every young composer, when his *Rapsodie nègre* outraged wartime audiences in December of 1917. He was soon grouped with five other young, audacious composers—Darius Milhaud,

Arthur Honegger, Georges Auric, Germaine Tailleferre, and Louis Durey—under the collective name "The Six," a title bestowed upon them by an obscure critic who compared them to "The Russian Five." The rhetoric surrounding each of their concerts, and their association with Erik Satie and Jean Cocteau, did much to launch successful careers for four of the six.

In 1958, Poulenc wrote to his friend and collaborator of more than twenty years, singer Pierre Bernac, saying: "I am decidedly a man of the theater." Though he was often guilty of hyperbole when speaking of his loves and pursuits, he was not exaggerating in this statement. His enthusiasm undoubtedly sprang from the fact that he was in the midst of composing his third, and final, opera, *La voix humaine,* which also turned out to be his last stage work. By that time, in addition to three operas, he also had to his credit three ballets, nine of the ten sets of incidental music he was to compose, music for five films, and minor contributions to three other stage works.

Though Poulenc had the intention of writing an opera early in his career (he toyed with setting Raymond Radiguet's *Paul et Virginie* in the early 1920s), he, like many other composers, was unable to find the "right" libretto. His first opera, *Les mamelles de Tirésias,* was thus not written until the summer of 1944, prompted by a new encounter with the play, which Guillaume Apollinaire had written in 1917. The two-act *opéra-bouffe* enjoyed a lengthy run at the Opéra-Comique and has been performed frequently in the ensuing years; it remains one of Poulenc's most popular works. His two other operas, *Dialogues des Carmélites* and *La voix humaine,* were both written in the 1950s, his last full decade of composition.

If *Mamelles* and *Dialogues* represent throwbacks to the comic and serious operatic traditions of the nineteenth century, the former suggesting Offenbach or Chabrier and the latter deriving from Verdi, Moussorgsky and Debussy (to whom it was dedicated), then *La voix* falls into the twentieth-century tradition of shorter, more intense operatic monodramas, which began with *Erwartung.* All three are essentially seamless operas, with the predominant vocal style occupying a middle ground between accompanied recitative and lyric aria, though there are obvious "tunes" or "numbers" in *Mamelles,* and much of the vocal line in *La voix* is subdued, narrow, almost chant-like, with repeated notes abounding. In general, Poulenc treated the texts carefully in his operas, but allowed himself some freedom and lighthearted fun with prosody in *Mamelles.* A further characteristic which sets *Mamelles* apart from the others is in the use of the orchestra, for it is strictly accompanimental, with an occasional coloristic effect, in the *opéra-bouffe,* whereas it is called upon to enhance the drama, by setting or deepening a mood, or by providing unifying musical motives (often leading motives in *Dialogues*), in the two dramas.

Poulenc's skill as a prosodist (few twentieth-century composers have set the poetry of their time more successfully) and composer of solo songs served him well in his operas. *La voix* is little more than an extended art song, while the bulk of the vocal writing in the other two operas is for solo voice, or an occasional duet. There are few ensembles and no attempt to construct a scene with them. Choral writing plays a large part in *Mamelles* and *Dialogues:* in the former, the style of writing ranges from mock-serious (a comment on rapid repopulation, thanks to men giving birth, wrapped in Poulenc's sensuous sacred choral style) to boisterous finales for both acts; in the latter, the sensuous sacred style, which had been perfected in such works as the *Mass,* the *Lenten Motets,* and *Figure humaine,* is kept subdued until the exultant, dramatic "Salve Regina" of the final scene.

Poulenc chose his opera texts carefully, selecting three contemporary writers who meant a great deal to him. Guillaume Apollinaire and Jean Cocteau were poets to whom he turned often throughout his career. Though his choice of Apollinaire poems that he set as *mélodies* (art songs) ran the spectrum from whimsical, to obscure, to quite serious, he turned to Apollinaire's World War I farce about repopulation during the darkest days of another war, when the French were facing a similar concern and were once again in need of a lighthearted laugh. Poulenc's choice of *La voix humaine,* of all of Cocteau's plays, suggests that the composer, as he approached the age of sixty, was concerned with more serious matters, such as the anguish of being alone (Poulenc had lived that way his entire life). On the other hand, Georges Bernanos, author of *Dialogues,* spoke to Poulenc's devout, personal view of Roman Catholicism. In each case, he prepared his own libretto, deleting and altering where he felt it was necessary.

Though he was not an innovator—and it increasingly seems that radical innovation is slower to gain acceptance in opera than in other genres—Poulenc will certainly be recognized as an important opera composer for, apart from those like Britten, whose output has been largely in the operatic field, few composers of this century have produced three popular operas that have entered the repertory and that continue to hold musical and dramatic sway on stage.—KEITH W. DANIEL

Prey, Hermann

Baritone. Born 11 July 1929, in Berlin. Married: Barbara Pniok, two daughters, one son. Sang with Berlin Mozart Choir as a child; studied with Günter Baum at Berlin Academy for Music 1948-51; also studied with Harry Gottschalk; debut as Moruccio in Tiefland *at the Hessische Oper, Wiesbaden, 1952; at Hamburg Opera 1953-60 in a number of contemporary operas; debuts at the Vienna State Opera, 1957, the Bavarian State Opera, Munich, 1957, and the Salzburg Festival, 1959; Metropolitan Opera debut as Wolfram von Eschenbach in* Tannhäuser, *1960; Bayreuth debut in same role, 1965; Covent Garden debut as Figaro in* Il barbiere di Siviglia, *1973; directorial debut* Le nozze di Figaro, *Salzburg, 1988. Prominent Lieder singer.*

Although most noted as a distinctive interpreter of German Lieder, the baritone Hermann Prey has also had an extensive and illustrious operatic career. In his native Germany he is also known as a comedian, an operetta singer, and a popular television personality. In opera he has sung an astonishingly wide repertoire ranging from Monteverdi and his contemporaries, Telemann, Bach, Mozart, Rossini, to Wagner and Alban Berg. Even though most of his extensive recording career has been devoted to Lieder (most of these recordings are unfortunately currently unavailable) rather than major operatic roles, Prey has made quite a few opera and oratorio recordings, a number of them of rather unusual works. These include Cavalieri's *La rappresentazione di anima e di corpo* with Troyanos, Zylis-Gara, and Adam; C.P.E. Bach's *Israel in Egypt* with Geszty and Häfliger; Schubert's *Alfonso und Estrella,* an EMI recording with Mathis, Schreier, and Fischer-Dieskau, which sounds like a *Liederabend;* Weber's *Die drei Pintos* (completed by Gustav Mahler) with Popp and Hollweg; a true classic of the gramophone, EMI's monaural version of Cornelius' *Der Barbier von Bagdad* with Schwarzkopf and Gedda, conducted by Leinsdorf; Weinberger's *Schwanda the Bagpiper* from 1981 in German translation with Popp and Jerusalem, conducted by Heinz Wallberg; Humperdinck's *Königskinder,* an opera even more Wagnerian than his *Hänsel und Gretel,* with Donath, Dallapozza, and Ridderbusch; and Korngold's *Die tote Stadt* on RCA Victor with Neblett and Kollo, conducted by Leinsdorf.

In the more standard repertoire he has recorded most of the major Mozart baritone roles: Figaro in *Le nozze di Figaro* with Böhm in 1967 (although Prey normally performed Count Almaviva on the stage); Guglielmo in Böhm's third recording of *Così fan tutte* from 1984, and a fine Papageno in *Die Zauberflöte* with Solti conducting. Prey has also recorded the role of Figaro in Rossini's *Il barbiere di Siviglia* conducted by Abbado, but in this role his coloratura is somewhat inelegant.

Prey was born in Berlin in 1929 and sang in the Berlin Mozart Choir as a boy. In 1951 he won a singing competition sponsored by the Hesse State Radio and made his stage debut at the Wiesbaden State Theater in 1952. The next year he began working with Günther Rennert at the Hamburg State Opera. Various debuts followed: in 1957 at both the Bavarian State Opera in Munich and at the Vienna State Opera; in 1960 at the Metropolitan Opera as Wolfram von Eschenbach in Wagner's *Tannhäuser;* in the same role (one of his best) in 1965 at Bayreuth. Since 1959 Prey has been a regular at the Salzburg Festival, singing Rossini's Figaro and Mozart's Guglielmo and Papageno. His Covent Garden debut came in 1973 as Figaro in *Il barbiere.* As a young singer Prey sang several Italian roles in German, such as the Count di Luna in Verdi's *Il trovatore,* Don Carlo in *La forza del destino,* and the Marquis of Posa in Verdi's *Don Carlos.* His later concentration on the German roles include five parts in three Strauss operas: Arlecchino and the Musikmeister in *Ariadne auf Naxos,* Storch in *Intermezzo,* and Olivier and the count from *Capriccio.* Of the Wagnerian roles, in addition to Wolfram he has also made a great success of performing Beckmesser. In this role his interpretation runs counter to the traditional one. Prey considers Beckmesser a gentleman, an intellectual, a respectable town clerk whose tragedy comes from falling in love with Eva. Moreover, he really sings the role, paying special care to the coloratura demands. Prey refers to Beckmesser as "one of two peak achievements of my career," the other being his portrayal of Papageno. Other endeavors undertaken by Prey include Eisenstein in *Die Fledermaus* and works by Henze and other modern composers. He also recorded early on the role of Escamillo in German with Christa Ludwig as Carmen. According to Rodney Milnes, Prey's Escamillo has "charm in abundance and more edge to the voice than we hear from him nowadays."

As his career progressed Prey has been criticized for a tendency to droop with the voice, presumably in an effort to sound expressive. His instrument is naturally a beautiful one, more satisfying in its purely tonal resources and command of legato than his older contemporary, Dietrich Fischer-Dieskau. Like Fischer-Dieskau, Prey has a tendency to perform, in Lieder as well as opera, in a somewhat affected manner, overloading the music with a too emphatic expression. He will not often enough sing a simple line as do the baritones Willi Domgraf-Fassbänder or Gerhard Hüsch, and from this point of view his singing can sometimes fail to satisfy a basic requirement. On the positive side, much of Prey's artistry is based on spontaneity and immediacy. Unlike Fischer-Dieskau, who has a much more "set" interpretation of a song cycle such as Schubert's *Die schöne Müllerin,* Prey's performance will often depend on his own particular mood and the response from the audience.—STEPHEN A. WILLIER

Price, Leontyne

Soprano. Born 10 February 1927, in Laurel, Mississippi. Married: William Warfield in 1952; divorced in 1973. Studied at Juilliard School of Music with Florence Page Kimball and Frederic Cohen; sang in Virgil Thomson's Four Saints in Three Acts, *1952; sang in Gershwin's* Porgy and Bess *in the United States and in Europe, 1952-54; premiered Barber's* Prayers of Kierkegaard *in Boston, 1954; television debut as Tosca, 1955; Vienna debut as Aida, 1958; London debut as Aida, 1958; Teatro alla Scala debut as Aida, 1959; Metropolitan Opera debut as Leonora in* Il trovatore, *1961; premiered Barber's* Anthony and Cleopatra, *1966. Received Lifetime Achievement award from the National Academy of Recorded Arts and Sciences, 1989.*

Leontyne Price is the first American-born black prima donna in opera history. Although she is at times hesitant to accept accolades related to her race, her accomplishments helped to eliminate much of the prejudice prominent in opera at the beginning of the twentieth century. It is not surprising that one of her first significant musical impressions came to Leontyne (her name then spelled Leontine) when, at the age of nine, she heard Marian Anderson sing a concert in Jackson, Mississippi. Price, born in Laurel, Mississippi, was encouraged in music by her parents, both singers in the Methodist Church choir. Her father, a carpenter, and her mother, a midwife, influenced her musical training by providing piano lessons for Leontyne and encouraging her to sing in public school and at church. This family support was essential to Price as she pursued a performing career, her mother serving as a constant inspiration until her death.

Price's parents financed her attendance at the College of Education and Industrial Arts (now Central State College) in Wilberforce, Ohio, where she received a Bachelor of Arts with preparation to teach public school music. In these surroundings she made her solo singing a vital ingredient to her education by performing in the school glee club, participating in as many musical functions as possible, and singing solo performances on the radio, for civic clubs, and in churches.

A teaching vocation slipped into the background for Price, however, when she was offered a full scholarship to the Juilliard School of Music. A long-time family friend from Laurel, Mrs. Elizabeth Chisholm, provided financial aid to meet her additional living expenses. Four years of study with Florence Page Kimball established for Price a secure vocal technique. She was almost magnetically drawn to opera by seeing produc-

Leontyne Price as Leonora in *Il trovatore*, 1977

tions of *Turandot* at New York City Center and *Salome* at the Metropolitan Opera. Her personal introduction to singing opera came first as Nella in *Gianni Schicchi* and then as Mistress Ford in *Falstaff* in productions at Juilliard. Composer-critic Virgil Thomson, hearing her in *Falstaff,* engaged her to appear as Saint Cecilia in a revival on Broadway of his opera *Four Saints in Three Acts.* It was the role of Bess in Breen's production of *Porgy and Bess,* however, that launched first her national and then her international career. After the opera had played in several American metropolitan areas, it settled in the Ziegfeld Theatre in New York for a rather lengthy run before being taken throughout Europe under the auspices of the Department of State. William Warfield, who sang the role of Porgy in these performances, became her husband, their marriage lasting legally until 1973, even though the couple separated much earlier.

The enjoyment of singing Bess apparently evoked in Price a desire to continue pleasing listeners with her appealing, quality-filled tone, which critics often describe as *dunkel* (dark). Price seemed unrestricted by registers in her voice, the vocal range forming a unit rather than being segmented.

Premier performances of works by Igor Stravinsky, Lou Harrison, Henri Sauguet, William Killmayer, and John LaMontaine helped to establish her as a singer of contemporary music, but meeting Samuel Barber had a more direct impact on her American career. Barber had begun his *Hermit Songs* in 1953 before he heard Price sing. Those he completed after meeting her were composed for her. In later years, at the pinnacle of her success, Price was chosen to sing the role of Cleopatra in Barber's new opera *Antony and Cleopatra* for the opening of the Metropolitan Opera House at Lincoln Center in 1966.

Beginning in 1955 she accomplished something significant to her career almost annually. That year the National Broadcasting Company Opera, under Peter Herman Adler, cast her in *Tosca,* making her the first black singer to appear in a major operatic role on television. In 1957 she sang her first staged opera in a major house. After debuting as Madame Lidoine in the America premiere of Poulenc's *Dialogues des Carmélites* with the San Francisco Opera, she went on to sing Leonora (*Il trovatore*), Aïda, and both Donna Elvira and Donna Anna (*Don Giovanni*) with that company.

While Samuel Barber assisted her to fame in America, Price had the aid of another musical giant in establishing her career abroad. André Mertens, her personal manager, arranged a brief but significant meeting with Herbert von Karajan during his first tour to the States with the Berlin Philharmonic. Immediately charmed by her voice, Karajan became a springboard for her further success, especially in Europe.

In 1958 Price made her European debut as Aïda at the Vienna State Opera under Karajan. Triumphant performances followed at Covent Garden in London, Verona Arena, Brussels, and Yugoslavia. With her debut at the Teatro alla Scala in Milan, Price became the first black singer to perform a major role in an Italian opera in that house. Performances of Liù (*Turandot*) and Thaïs at Chicago in 1959 gave her further preparation for her debut at the Metropolitan Opera in 1961. Her premiere performance there came as Leonora (*Il trovatore*) in January, quickly followed by performances of Aïda, Donna Anna, Liù and Cio-Cio-San. Even though she was the fifth black singer to sing on the stage in this famous house, she was the first to attain stardom. Her performances, both live and recorded, have not, however, escaped criticism. There are those who fault the quickness of her vibrato, often more noticeable in recordings than in live performances, even though it displays a uniqueness that has been a trademark of her singing.

Her failure to execute all the Mozart roles she attempted, especially Fiordiligi (*Così fan tutte*), in the style expected has gathered some disapproval for her interpretations. It has been her Verdi performances, however, that have reached the hallmark of her profession. Reviewers and audiences were eager to praise her singing of these parts, many calling her the greatest Verdi soprano of the century. Her ability to execute the soaring phrases while capturing astonishing, sudden pianissimo throughout the vocal range without losing her delectable tone is a feat not often attained even over the span of an entire career. Luckily, recordings have captured her development as a singer and serve as a chronicle of her vocal artistry.

One of her most significant achievements was that she sang in virtually every major opera house in the world. Except for brief explorations of unsuitable roles, she remained selective in those parts she undertook. This selectivity was a true strength of her entire tenure in opera. Although her performances at the Metropolitan and in opera were somewhat sporadic, she continued her reign as one of America's greatest divas during this century until her retirement from the stage in 1985. Her receipt of numerous national and international awards attests to her preeminence as a singer.—ROSE MARY OWENS

Price, Margaret

Soprano. Born 13 April 1941, in Tredegar, Wales. Studied with Charles Kennedy Scott, 1956-60; sang with the Ambrosian Singers, 1960-62; debut as Cherubino in Le nozze di Figaro, *Welsh National Opera, 1962; Covent Garden debut as Cherubino, 1963; U.S. debut as Pamina in* Die Zauberflöte, *San Francisco Opera, 1969; Metropolitan Opera debut as Desdemona in Verdi's* Otello, *1985. She was made a Commander of the Order of the British Empire in 1982.*

Margaret Price is one of the finest sopranos of the second half of the twentieth century. She made her professional debut as Cherubino (Mozart's *Le nozze di Figaro*) in 1962, and for the first decade of her career her repertory focused on Mozart; in the 1970s, as her voice matured in richness and size, she expanded her repertory to include nineteenth-century opera, especially Verdi. Price is not slim: her weight has made her reluctant to take on some roles. She could sing Violetta (in Verdi's *La traviata*) and Mimi (in Puccini's *La bohème*) beautifully, from a musical point of view, "but whoever heard of a consumptive my size?" she asked an interviewer in 1985.

As a student Price hoped to become a concert and recital singer; the operatic stage had little attraction for her. She has always moved audiences more with her voice than with her acting or appearance. Price is not an especially lively actress: she lacks the high-energy passion of Callas; nor does comedy come naturally to her. Her stage persona is noble, dignified; as a portrayer of tragic heroines she is unsurpassed.

Among Price's Mozart roles are the Countess (*Le nozze di Figaro*), Constanze (*Die Entführung aus dem Serail*), Pamina (*Die Zauberflöte*) and Fiordiligi (*Così fan tutte*). She has also made a recording of some of Mozart's greatest concert arias, conducted by James Lockhart, in which it is possible to hear some of her most attractive qualities. Hers is a warm, rich voice, yet without the excessive vibrato that mars the singing of so many twentieth-century operatic voices. In Price's performance of such arias as "Vorrei spiegarvi, oh Dio!" we can admire her *p*

OPERA

extraordinary accuracy of pitch, her lovely legato and the ethereal splendor of her high coloratura.

Some of Price's Mozart performances have left critics searching desperately for ways to describe her adequately; thus Brian Magee (in *Opera*), trying to put into words his reaction to Price's portrayal of Fiordiligi in *Così fan tutte* (Vienna, 1977), described her as "looking and sounding like pears and cream—each of her arias stopped the show." This was not the first time that the image of cream had come up in connection with Price's voice. A critic praised her "full, creamy tone," when she performed Donna Anna (*Don Giovanni*) in Paris in 1974. When she sang the title role of Bellini's *Norma* at Covent Garden in 1987, a critic described her voice as "rich, creamy, even from top to bottom." There is a combination of richness, smoothness and purity in Price's voice that makes critics think of cream when they hear her sing.

Price has won much applause as a singer of Verdi's heroines, most notably Desdemona (a role that she first sang in 1976) and Aida (which she first sang in 1979). In a recording of *Otello* made under Solti in 1977 we can hear the qualities that make her such a successful Desdemona. Her light, perfectly pure high notes sometimes remind us of Teresa Stich-Randall at her best. Her rendition of the Willow Song is memorable: when she sings the word "cantiamo" for the last time her vibratoless tone is of truly angelic beauty.—JOHN A. RICE

Prince Igor [Kniaz' Igor']

Composer: *Alexander Borodin (completed by Rimsky-Korsakov, Liadov and Glazunov).*

Librettist: *Alexander Borodin (after a scenario by V.V. Stasov based on the medieval chronicle Tale of Igor's Campaign).*

First Performance: *St Petersburg, Marinsky, 16 November 1890.*

Roles: *Yaroslavna (soprano); Konchakovna (contralto); Vladimir (tenor); Prince Igor (baritone); Khan Konchak (bass); Galitsky (bass); Khan Gzak (bass); Ovlour (tenor); Sulka (bass); Eroshka (tenor); Nurse (soprano); Maiden (soprano); chorus (SSAATTTTBBBB).*

Based primarily on the "Slovo o polku Igoreve," a mysterious and famous (at least to Slavicists) medieval Russian poem, *Kniaz' Igor' (Prince Igor)*, Alexander Borodin's only opera, tells the oddly inconclusive tale of the defeat of Prince Igor Sviatoslavich (1151-1202) of Novgorod-Seversk at the hands of the nomadic Polovtsy tribe in 1185. Borodin began *Igor* at the urging of nationalist critic Vladimir Stasov, who prepared the original libretto from the "Slovo" ("The Tale of Igor's Campaign") and early Russian chronicles. Though fragmentary, unwieldy, and dramatically unfocused, the subject offered the composer rich opportunities to draw on his country's history, folk songs, and folk music, and to stress the glories of the Russian past. Stasov believed it "met all the demands of Borodin's talent and artistic nature: broad epic motives, nationalism, variety of characters, passion, drama, the oriental." The subject also conformed with the aesthetic of the *moguchaia kuchka* ("mighty handful"), whose five members—including Borodin—came together in the 1860s largely in an attempt to build a native Russian operatic repertoire.

If Borodin had followed Stasov's original outline, the opera would surely have benefited. But the part-time composer (and full-time chemist) never even bothered to write an actual libretto. Instead, he produced *Igor* in fits and starts over a period of 18 years, drawing rather haphazardly on Stasov's scenario and on his own research, jumping between acts and scenes as his whims dictated, proceeding on impulse, responding to the spirit, not the details of the Igor story. As a result, when Borodin died in 1887 while attending a costume ball in Russian national dress, the opera remained far from finished. According to Alexander Glazunov, Borodin had completed in piano-vocal score only the Prologue; act I, scene i; and the whole of act IV. He had managed to orchestrate even less: only ten numbers. It fell, therefore, to Glazunov and Nicolai Rimsky-Korsakov (a fellow member of the *kuchka*) to flesh out the remaining sections, relying on the piles of fragments and sketches their colleague left behind. Glazunov restored act III and the Overture, and Rimsky-Korsakov the rest.

The opera opens on the main square of the southern Russian city of Putivl. In the Prologue, Igor and his Christian army prepare to march against the pagan Polovtsy, despite the omen of an eclipse. Yaroslavna, Igor's wife, bids a tearful farewell to her noble husband. In the first scene of act I, Yaroslavna's lascivious brother, Prince Galitsky, egged on by the comic characters Skula and Eroshka (invented by Borodin), stirs up trouble in Igor's absence, threatening to take over the kingdom. In the second, Yaroslavna struggles to defend her husband's throne and the honor of her violated female subjects.

Acts II and III unfold in the exotic Polovtsian encampment, where Igor and his son Vladimir are being held captive after the rout of their Russian forces. Against a background of much "Oriental" choral singing and dancing, the Polovtsian ruler, kindly Khan Konchak, befriends Igor. As act III ends, Igor escapes, but Vladimir stays behind, enchanted by Konchak's daughter Konchakovna, with whom he has fallen in love. (Act III has frequently been cut in performances and recordings, even though its omission robs the narrative of what little sense it makes.) Back in Putivl, act IV opens with one of the opera's most successful and famous arias, Yaroslavna's lament, inspired by the Russian folk tradition of the *plach*. At last, Igor returns to her waiting arms, amidst general rejoicing. The city's fate remains unclear, however, for as the curtain falls, the Polovtsy are approaching. Supported by his valiant and virtuous countrymen, Igor vows to defeat them.

More a collection of colorful scenes than a coherent dramatic whole, the scenario leaves many basic conflicts unresolved. Prince Galitsky plays a central role in act I but disappears thereafter; Vladimir and Konchakovna suddenly vanish after act III. Igor is also absent from the stage for long periods, and emerges as a considerably less dominant and psychologically less compelling character than Tsar Boris in Musorgsky's *Boris Godunov*.

Where Borodin excells, however, is in his use of the chorus, which assumes a dramatic and musical role so important as to become the work's real protagonist. The lengthy patriotic choruses (*"Slava"*—"Glory") of the people *(narod)* of Putivl in the Prologue and act IV; the plaintive songs of the maidens in act I; and the languid celebrations of the Polovtsy in acts II and III are the heart and soul of *Prince Igor*. The prominence of the choral episodes, which fill the stage with hundreds of colorfully costumed singers and dancers, also contributes to the opera's "Russianness," and sets it apart from those composed by Borodin's European contemporaries.

At the same time, Borodin's writing for the solo voice, unlike Musorgsky's, draws heavily on Italian *bel canto* models. In this and other features, he was following in the footsteps of his Russian predecessor Mikhail Glinka, whose operas *A Life for the Tsar* and *Ruslan and Lyudmila* had combined Russian subject matter and folk tunes with an Italianate style. From Glinka, too, Borodin inherited a fascination with the exotic East. In *Igor*, the scenes set in the Polovtsian encampment grabbed most of the composer's attention and inspiration. Himself the illegitimate son of an elderly Caucasian prince, Borodin had already given evidence of his special affinity for "Oriental" material in "The Steppes of Central Asia" (1880). Significantly, about one-half of the sections of *Igor* which Borodin managed to orchestrate belong to the Polovtsian scenes, including the opera's most celebrated pages: the wild and often-recorded "Polovtsian Dances" which end act II.

Similarly, the characters of the noble Konchak and the seductive, spontaneous Konchakovna receive such vivid musical and dramatic embodiment that Igor and Vladimir—and even the Russian people back in Putivl—almost pale by comparison. Whereas Borodin allows the Polovtsy to be decisive, romantically appealing figures, he portrays the Russians as a fractious, debauched, and querulous bunch of crybabies. Only Yaroslavna, in her act I arioso and her haunting act IV lament, achieves genuine heroic stature. For a supposedly patriotic Russian opera, *Prince Igor* is surprisingly defeatist.—HARLOW ROBINSON

Prokofiev, Sergei

Composer. Born 27 April 1891, in Sontzovka, near Ekaterinoslav, Russia. Died 5 March 1953, in Moscow. Married: the soprano Lina Llubera [=Carolina Codina], 1923 (two sons). Studied with Glière in Moscow; studied composition with Rimsky-Korsakov, Wihtol, and Liadov, piano with Mme Essipova, and conducting with Nicolas Tcherepnin at the St Petersburg Conservatory, graduating 1914; Anton Rubinstein Prize for his First Piano Concerto; first performance of his Classical Symphony, 1918; traveled to Siberia, Japan, and then the United States; performed concerts of his music in New York, Chicago, and other American cities; in Paris, 1920, where he composed for Diaghilev's Ballets Russes; Koussevitzky commissioned several works from Prokofiev; in Chicago for the production of his opera, Love for Three Oranges, 1921; concertized in Russia, 1927, 1929, 1932; last United States visit, 1938.

Operas   *The Giant* [*Velikan*], 1900 [unorchestrated]; *On Desert Islands* [*Na pustinnikh ostrovakh*], 1900-02 [unfinished]; *A Feast in the Time of Plague* [*Pir vo vremya chumi*], after Pushkin, 1903 [unorchestrated]; revised, 1908-09; *Undina,* M. Kilstett (after de la Motte Fouqué), 1904-07; *Maddalena,* after M. Lieven, 1911-13 [unfinished]: orchestrated by E. Downes and performed for the British Broadcasting Company, London, 25 March 1979; *The Gambler* [*Igrok*], Prokofiev (after Dostoevsky), 1915-17, revised 1927-28, Brussels, Théâtre de la Monnaie, 29 April 1929; *The Love for Three Oranges* [*Lyubov'k tryom apel'sinam*], after Gozzi, 1919, Chicago, Auditorium Theater, 30 December 1921; *The Fiery Angel* [*Ognenniy angel*], after V. Bryusov, 1919-23, revised, 1926-27, act II concert performance, Paris, 14 June 1928; concert performance, Paris, Champs Elysées, 25 November 1954; staged performance, Venice, La Fenice, 14 September 1955; *Semyon Kotko,* V. Katayev, Prokofiev (after Katayev), 1939, Moscow, Stanislavsky, 23 June 1940; *Betrothal in a Monastery* [*Obrucheniye v monastire*], Prokofiev and Myra Mendel'son (after Sheridan), 1940-41, Leningrad, Kirov, 3 November 1946; *Khan Buzay,* 1942-[unfinished]; *War and Peace* [*Voyna i mir*], Prokofiev (after Tolstoy), 1941-43, concert performance Moscow, 16 October 1944; revised, 1946-52; complete performance Moscow, Stanislavsky, 8 November 1957; *The Story of a Real Man* [*Povest'o nastoyashchem cheloveke*], Prokofiev and Myra Mendel'son (after B. Polevoy), 1947-48, private concert performance, Leningrad, Kirov, 3 December

1948; staged performance, Moscow, Bol'shoy, 8 October 1960; *Distant Seas* [*Dalyokiye morya*], Prokofiev (after V.A. Dïkhovichnïy), 1948- [unfinished].

French critic Rostislav Hofman may have been guilty of overstatement when he wrote that "musically speaking, Prokofiev's operas have nothing in common." But no one could argue that it is easy to reconcile the vast aesthetic differences between the early *The Gambler,* a radical application of Musorgskian principles to an intensely psychological subject, and the late *War and Peace,* a loose collection of patriotic military-domestic tableaux heavily indebted to Borodin and Tchaikovsky. Much of the explanation for the erratic course of Prokofiev's operatic career lies in the peculiar circumstances of his life: born and trained in Tsarist Russia, he lived in the West from 1918 to 1936, then returned to Stalin's Russia where he died in 1953. As a result, he composed for several different operatic markets and audiences, achieving at best limited public success. Ignoring the warnings of countless critics, including his countrymen Sergei Diaghilev and Igor Stravinsky, that full-length opera was *passé,* Prokofiev devoted great time and effort to this genre. Sadly, his work in the field has never achieved the popularity or recognition of his ballet, symphonic, film or piano music, and even today his operas, full of his trademark ironic humor, strong illustrative sense and quirky originality, all too rarely take the stage.

Obstacles and disappointment dogged Prokofiev throughout his operatic career. While still a student at St Petersburg Conservatory, he finished a charming (and uncharacteristically romantic) one-act opera, *Maddalena,* in piano score, but orchestrated only the first of its four scenes and failed to find a producer. His first completed mature opera, *The Gambler,* was written for the Mariinsky Theater in St Petersburg on the eve of the 1917 Bolshevik Revolution, but received its belated premiere in Brussels more than ten years later. His second, and by far most successful, *Love for Three Oranges* was commissioned and produced (in 1921) by the Chicago Opera and soon went on to international fame. His third, *The Fiery Angel,* was intended for a 1927 Berlin Staatsoper production, but reached the stage (in Florence) only in 1955, two years after Prokofiev's death.

One of the factors that led Prokofiev to return to the Soviet Union was his belief that it would be easier for him to get his operas produced there. Language had always been a problem in Europe and America. Moreover, because of the more conservative and closely controlled cultural climate, opera in the Soviet Union had remained a prestigious and viable form that attracted talented performers, directors and designers. Operating with huge state subsidies, the Kirov in Leningrad and the Bolshoi in Moscow seemed to represent great opportunities. And yet the harsh and ever-changing realities of Soviet history and cultural policy created a new set of problems no less vexing. Not a single one of Prokofiev's four "Soviet" operas traveled a smooth road to the stage.

Semyon Kotko fell out of the repertoire very soon after its 1940 Moscow premiere, tainted by its controversial portrayal of German participation in the 1918 Civil War in the Ukraine. The happily escapist *Betrothal in a Monastery* was produced in 1946, six years after it was completed. Prokofiev spent nearly 13 years working on his epic *War and Peace,* the opera he hoped would bring him official recognition, but this, too, proved problematic to the enforcers of Socialist Realism, and the composer died without seeing it staged in full. Nor did the composer live to see *Story of a Real Man* produced, for it, too, fell afoul of Stalin's censors in 1948 and reached the stage only in 1960. Of Prokofiev's four "Soviet" operas, only *War and Peace* and

Betrothal in a Monastery (which deserves to be better known) have achieved any measure of international success.

Prokofiev also left two of his last operas unfinished. The most nearly completed, *Khan Buzay,* begun in the early 1940s, was a "lyric-comic opera" based on folk legends and folk songs of Kazakhstan. In 1948, Prokofiev began an "opera-vaudeville," *Distant Seas,* inspired by a comedy by the Soviet playwright Dïkhovichnïy, but abandoned the project in the preliminary stages.

Of Prokofiev's seven mature operas, only *Love for Three Oranges* has managed to establish itself—and even then just barely—in the standard international repertoire. Like all of them, it is far from a singers' opera, and demands strong acting, tight ensemble work and a physical, highly imaginative production to succeed (The one directed by Frank Corsaro and designed by Maurice Sendak for Glyndebourne in 1982 is a good example). Intended at least in part as a parody of outmoded operatic conventions, *Oranges* also exemplifies the fierce and unresolved conflict between tradition and innovation that drives all of Prokofiev's best music, including his operas. Here and elsewhere, the composer attacks the very values he cherishes, alternating between nasty sarcasm and boyish lyricism. This uncertainty of tone (should we laugh or sympathize?) can also undermine the emotional impact of Prokofiev's operas; *The Fiery Angel* provides a good example, veering between vicious caricature of Catholic prelates and Renata's self-inflicted psychological torment.

One thing all of Prokofiev's operas share is an unusual respect for and fidelity to their literary sources. Only one, *Betrothal in a Monastery* (also known as *Duenna*), uses a non-Russian source. To some extent this marks the continuation of a tradition among nineteenth century Russian operatic composers of turning to the masterpieces of the national literature for libretti. What sets Prokofiev apart from them, however, is a preference for large works of narrative prose. Five of his operas (all except *Betrothal* and *Oranges*) use hefty pieces of fiction. Two come from the Russian nineteenth century literary mainstream: Dostoevsky's short novel *The Gambler* and Tolstoy's mammoth *War and Peace. The Fiery Angel* uses a Decadent novel of the same title by the twentieth century Russian Symbolist Valery Bryusov. The remaining two are from bland "official" works of Soviet Socialist Realism, by authors contemporary with Prokofiev. *Semyon Kotko* is based on Valentin Katayev's *I Am a Son of the Working People,* and *Story of a Real Man* on a novel of the same title about a brave Soviet fighter pilot by the hack journalist Boris Polevoy.

Unlike Stravinsky or Shostakovich, both of whom—for different reasons—paid considerably less attention to opera, Prokofiev authored or coauthored all his mature libretti. (Three were his own, four were collaborations.) Initially, he detested "libretto verse," insisting as much as possible upon prose, which guaranteed greater dramatic truth and power. He was encouraged in this belief by his friend and collaborator the avant-garde Russian stage director Vsevolod Meyerhold (1874-1940), a sworn enemy both of Wagnerism and of *verismo* melodrama who saw in Prokofiev the new hope of twentieth century operatic theater. Meyerhold also suggested the subject of *Oranges* and was collaborating with Prokofiev on a production of *Semyon Kotko* when he was arrested on Stalin's orders in 1939.

In *The Gambler,* Prokofiev followed the example set by Musorgsky in his experimental opera *The Marriage.* He transferred unedited chunks of Dostoevsky's text into the libretto, setting them to an uncompromisingly declamatory vocal line surrounded by a dense, dissonant and dynamic orchestral texture. Forward movement and dramatic truth were his early goals, which he hoped to achieve by virtually eliminating pauses in the action for arias, ensembles and choruses. Unfortunately, Prokofiev's "Scythian" orchestration (heavy, brassy and full of brilliant pictorial effects, like the spinning of the roulette wheel created by the woodwinds and xylophone) frequently upstaged the text and plot, and made the going rough for singers.

As was the case with Musorgsky himself, Prokofiev's early radical championship of the word in the word-music relationship modified as time went on. While still highly "literary," and placing great emphasis on dramatic values, *Oranges* and *The Fiery Angel* make greater concessions to the singers and to the audience's need for the emotional breathing space provided by arias, ensembles and choruses. When Prokofiev came back to revise *The Gambler* in 1927-28, he similarly incorporated some of the lessons he had learned in the meantime as an operatic composer.

Although Musorgsky's music exerted the central influence on Prokofiev during the time he was working on *The Gambler*, other Russian composers also played a role in the development of this highly impressionable composer's operatic style. One was Rimsky-Korsakov, the author of ten operas, and Prokofiev's teacher at the St Petersburg Conservatory. In his diary, Prokofiev remarked that he especially loved *The Legend of the Invisible City of Kitezh and the Maiden Fevronia, Sadko,* and *Snegurochka,* which he saw as a student. This interest in the devils and spirits of Rimsky's fairy-tale operas later turned up, with a strongly satirical twist, in *Oranges* and *The Fiery Angel,* as well as in the ballets *Chout, Cinderella* and *The Stone Flower.*

The operas of Borodin and Tchaikovsky also influenced Prokofiev. Certain features (a sense of color and visuality, a strong melodic gift, Orientalism) had always linked Prokofiev and Borodin, but these became more prominent in the operas he wrote after returning to the USSR in the late 1930s, at a time when Borodin was being held up to Soviet composers as a model to be followed. *Semyon Kotko, War and Peace,* and, to a certain extent, *Story of a Real Man,* share with *Prince Igor* a strongly patriotic message; a dramatic structure loosely constructed around a series of historical "tableaux"; imitation of folk music as an integral part of the style; and many important scenes for the chorus. *War and Peace,* of course, owes the most to *Prince Igor,* concerned as it is with huge military/historical issues stretching across an entire country.

Prokofiev came later to Tchaikovsky. Although he knew both *Eugene Onegin* and *The Queen of Spades* as a young man, his own early operas, especially *Oranges* and *The Fiery Angel,* represent a firm rejection of the "pretty," highly sentimental style Tchaikovsky brought to Russian opera (Prokofiev once remarked that he considered *The Queen of Spades* to be "in very bad taste.") After his return to the Soviet Union in the late 1930s, however, Prokofiev's attitude towards Tchaikovsky became more positive. *War and Peace* even includes scenes directly modeled on scenes in Tchaikovsky's operas: scene i, the duet between Natasha and Sonya, refers to the Polina-Lisa duet in act I, scene ii of *The Queen of Spades,* and scene ii, Natasha's first ball, refers to act II of *Eugene Onegin.* As was the case with Prokofiev's renewed interest in Borodin, his apparent reappraisal of Tchaikovsky stemmed in part from the demands of Soviet cultural policy, which looked increasingly to the nineteenth-century classics as the appropriate models for Soviet composers.

Oddly enough, then, Prokofiev, who lived abroad for almost twenty years, long enough to become a suspicious "cosmopolitan" in the eyes of Stalin's cultural officials, remained strongly Russian in his operatic aesthetic. Showing little use for or interest in twentieth-century European opera, he claimed to particularly dislike Richard Strauss (although *Maddalena,* his 1913 student one-act opera, shows a definite Straussian influence in its decadent theme and lush harmonic language). In his voluminous writings, Prokofiev showed no knowledge of Janáček, blamed Wagner for killing the vitality of opera, and displayed little enthusiasm for or curiosity about the music (operatic or otherwise) of Schoenberg, Berg and Webern.

In the final analysis Prokofiev's love for opera remained unrequited and his legacy uncertain. Every one of his operas boasts marvelous moments, from the fetching lament of the princesses in *Oranges* to Andrei's harrowing death-bed scene in *War and Peace,* from the wild convent orgy that concludes *The Fiery Angel* to the ironic music-making scene in *Betrothal in a Monastery.* For the most part, however, they remain isolated moments. Strangely, Prokofiev never achieved once in opera the complete artistic synthesis of the ballet *Romeo and Juliet,* remarkable precisely for its infallible dramatic sense, compassion and psychological insight. One of the most instinctive and "natural" of composers, Prokofiev had to work too hard at opera.—HARLOW ROBINSON

Le prophète [The Prophet]

Composer: *Giacomo Meyerbeer.*

Librettist: *Eugène Scribe.*

First Performance: *Paris, Opéra, 16 April 1849.*

Roles: *Berthe (soprano); Fidès (mezzo-soprano); Jean de Leyden (tenor); Count Oberthal (bass or bass-baritone); Jonas (tenor); Mathisen (bass); Zacharias (bass); Two Children (soprano, mezzo-soprano); Two Peasants (tenor, bass); Soldier (tenor); Two Bourgeois (tenors); Two Officers (tenor, bass); chorus (SSAATTBB).*

When *Le prophète* was finally produced in 1849, thirteen years had elapsed since Meyerbeer's last great success at the Paris Opéra, *Les Huguenots.* Plans for the new opera had begun in 1837, again with the accomplished playwright-librettist Eugène Scribe, and the score was largely completed by 1841, but a number of factors conspired to cause long delays: casting problems, administrative difficulties at the Opéra, the composer's tenure as Generalmusikdirektor in Berlin from 1842-46, and the political turmoil of 1848, to name a few. Such a long period of anticipation may actually have contributed to the eventual triumph of the opera, as did the performance of the famed Pauline Viardot-Garcia in the maternal role of Fidès (she was only twenty-eight at the time). Scribe's libretto, based on events surrounding the early sixteenth-century Anabaptist leader John (here named Jean) of Leyden, afforded a variety of picturesque scenes, splendid tableaux, and dramatic *coups de théâtre* such as Parisian audiences had come to expect. The underlying theme of popular rebellion, furthermore, had a timely appeal for European audiences in the wake of the revolutions of 1848-49.

The motivating force behind the action is the group of three Anabaptist preachers— Zacharie, Jonas, and Mathisen—who prey on the discontents of the peasant class to garner support for the political ambitions of their sect (act I). When the impending marriage of the innkeeper Jean to the orphan girl Berthe is thwarted by the tyrannical and rapacious Count Oberthal (who invokes his feudal *droits du seigneur*), Jean is convinced to act as leader of the Anabaptists, who notice his resemblance to a holy image in the Münster cathedral. He is forced to yield his fiancée to Oberthal in order to save his mother, Fidès (act II). In act III the Anabaptist faction succeeds in capturing Oberthal, but Jean is encouraged to pursue his chosen path still further and help them take the city of Münster. Act IV finds Jean on the point of being crowned Prophet-King of the victorious Anabaptists. Berthe and Fidès fortuitously encounter one another in Münster and resolve to avenge themselves against the false "prophet" whom they believe to be responsible for Jean's death. Amidst a grand coronation ceremony, Fidès recognizes the prophet as her son, but Jean is forced to deny his mother in his role as the new Messiah. In the final act Berthe is attempting to infiltrate the palace at Münster in order to set fire to a munitions storeroom and destroy the Anabaptist leader. On discovering his identity, she kills herself. When he learns that he has been betrayed and the emperor's troops are approaching to suppress the heretical rebellion, Jean himself determines to have Berthe's plan carried out. While the prophet and his court indulge in a riotous bacchanale, the enemy troops arrive, as does Fidès, to pardon her son. But all perish together as the hall collapses in the sudden conflagration.

Le prophète was the principal target of Wagner's famous diatribe against its composer in *Opera and Drama,* written soon after the opera's triumphant premiere and during a time when it was conquering nearly all the stages of Europe—unlike Wagner's own scores. Meyerbeer himself made no apologies about tailoring his music to the strengths of his cast, nor about taking full advantage of the resources offered by the Opéra. It may be an inevitable consequence of the long gestation period of Meyerbeer's later operas and the endless tinkerings to which this perfectionist craftsman subjected these scores that they appear more heterogeneous than organic. Yet despite the unconcealed artifice of the work, and Meyerbeer's obvious delight in experimenting with novel, often isolated instrumental effects, *Le prophète* is unified, in a sense, by several distinctive styles. The first two acts, for instance, set in a bucolic Dutch landscape near the river Meuse (Maas), are characterized by a pastoral idiom: the echoing of solo clarinets in the introduction (suggesting a rustic *chalumeau* sound), the "Valse villageoise" beginning act II, and an array of double-drone effects ("Choeur pastoral," entrance of Fidès, duo-romance for Berthe and Fidès in act I; the "Valse villageoise" and Jean's "Pastorale" in act II). The opening pastoral chorus includes a kind of ritornello scored for high pizzicato strings and arpeggiated parallel woodwind triads (with triangle), which produces a striking "polytonal" effect. On the other hand, the soprano cavatina ("Mon coeur s'élance et palpite") inserted after this chorus at the request of the first Berthe, Jeanne Castellan, is a blatant vocal display piece, demonstrating Meyerbeer's willingness to sacrifice stylistic continuity to singers' demands.

Meyerbeer himself cited a "somber and fanatic" tone as characteristic of *Le prophète*. This is achieved in part by the recurring Anabaptist chant, "Ad nos, ad salutarem undam," with its mock-antique modal idiom. The use of four bassoons (in another parody of the sacred style) to accompany the entrance of the Anabaptist trio is another example of this "somber" tone. The "fanatic" element—related to the "Benediction of the Daggers" scene in *Les Huguenots*—is well represented by the Anabaptist chorus opening act III, combining a trumpet-like call-to-arms, a fragment of choral prayer and an orgiastic, bloodthirsty rhythmic refrain ("Dansons sur leur tombe—du sang!"). The antiphonal off-stage trumpet calls introducing this number define yet another tone, dominant in the later acts. This character, appropriate to the military camp setting of act III, is manifested in numerous march rhythms so favored by the genre of grand opera and in opulent brass scoring in the larger choral scenes.

Aside from the use of roller skates for the ice-skating chorus and divertissement in act III and the innovative application of electric light to effect the sunrise at the end of this act ("Hymne triomphal"), the fame of this opera is concentrated on the great coronation scene of act IV. Many ingredients of the scene—grand march, Latin hymns with organ, the solo prayer—were already hallmarks of the genre. New elements here include the addition of children's chorus and the mezzo/contralto role (Fidès) as focal point. The powerful moment of Jean's enforced denial of his mother is possibly undermined by the somewhat trivial tune that dominates the closing ensemble (introduced by Fidès: "L'ingrat, il ne me reconnait pas"). Nevertheless, Scribe's compelling dramaturgical conception and Meyerbeer's exploitation of Viardot-Garcia's impressive range and theatrical presence contribute to one of nineteenth-century opera's most effective scenes, deeply admired by Verdi, among many others.—THOMAS S. GREY

Puccini, Giacomo

Composer. Born 22 December 1858, in Lucca. Died 29 November 1924, in Brussels. Married: Elvira Gemignani, 1904 (one son). Puccini came from a long line of musicians; studied with Carlo Angeloni at the Istituto Musicale of Lucca; church organist in Mutigliano, 1875; organist at San Pietro in Somaldi; submitted his cantata Juno *to a contest in Lucca, but did not win, 1877; studied with Antonio Bazzini and Amilcare Ponchielli at the Milan Conservatory, 1880-83;* Edgar *commissioned by the publisher Ricordi, 1884; lived in Torre del Lago from 1891; in New York for the American premiere of* Madama Butterfly, *1907;* La fanciulla del West *commissioned by the Metropolitan Opera of New York.*

Operas   *Le villi,* Ferdinando Fontana, Milan, Teatro dal Verme, 31 May 1884; revised, Turin, Regio, 26 December 1884; *Edgar,* Ferdinando Fontana (after de Musset, *La coupe et les lèvres*), Milan, Teatro alla Scala, 21 April 1889; revised, Ferrara, 28 February 1892; further revised, Buenos Aires, 8 July 1905; *Manon Lescaut,* Leoncavallo, Marco Praga, Domenico Olivia, Luigi Illica, and Giuseppe Giacosa (after Prévost), Turin, Regio, 1 February 1893; *La bohème,* Giuseppe Giacosa and Luigi Illica (after Murger), Turin, Regio, 1 February 1896; *Tosca,* Giuseppe Giacosa and Luigi Illica (after Sardou), Rome, Costanzi, 14 January 1900; *Madama Butterfly,* Giuseppe Giacosa and Luigi Illica (after the drama by David Belasco based on the story by John Luther Long), Milan, Teatro alla Scala, 17 February 1904; revised, Brescia, Grande, 28 May 1904; revised, London, Covent Garden, 10 July 1905; revised, Paris, Opéra Comique, 28 December 1906; *La fanciulla del West,* Guelfo Civinini and Carlo Zangarini (after David Belasco, *The Girl of the Golden West*), New York, Metropolitan Opera, 10 December 1910; *La rondine,* Giuseppe Adami (translated from a German libretto by Alfred Maria Willner and Heinrich Reichert), Monte Carlo, 27 March 1917; *Il trittico:* 1) *Il tabarro,* Giuseppe Adami (after Didier Gold, *La houppelande*), 2) *Suor Angelica,* Giovacchino Forzano, 3) *Gianni Schicchi,* Giovacchino Forzano (scenario based on lines from Dante, *Inferno*), New York, Metropolitan Opera, 14 December 1918; *Turandot,* Giuseppe Adami and Renato Simoni (after Gozzi), Milan, Teatro alla Scala, 25 April 1926 [unfinished; completed by Franco Alfano].

The phenomenon of Puccini's success from the period of *Manon Lescaut* (1893) until his death in 1924, a popularity that has if anything increased since then, sets him off from his chief contemporaries, the other members of what used to be called La Giovane Scuola or The Generation of the '90s. These composers, men like Mascagni, remembered primarily for *Cavalleria rusticana,* or Leoncavallo, regarded as another one-opera figure with *I pagliacci,* or Francesco Cilea with *Adriana Lecouvreur,* made their mark with a single major success that they

**Giacomo Puccini (left) with Giuseppe Giacosa
and Luigi Illica, c. 1905**

could never, try as they might, quite equal. Why should one man have an almost unbroken string of triumphs and leave his rivals far behind? To provide some answers to this question, to try to isolate some of the strengths of Puccini's talent that were less prominent in the others provides one way to take some measure of this phenomenon.

Puccini had, usually, a powerful sense of theater, of dramatic timing, and he would hone his works, even after they had been first introduced, modifying them as he experienced them in the opera house until they satisfied his discriminating taste. For instance, after the opening run of *Manon Lescaut* he rewrote the ending of act I. He expanded the Café Momus scene in *La bohème*. He tightened up the second act of *Tosca*. Over a period of three years (1904-07), he pared away at *Madama Butterfly*, modifying it and focusing more fully on his heroine. Up until the final *Turandot*, which was left incomplete at his death, there is not one of his operas that did not undergo some later revision. This acute sensibility for dramatic effect, kept alive through his personal supervision of a number of local premieres of his works, shows up in other ways as well.

Puccini was notorious for giving his librettists a hard time. His first two operas, *Le villi* and *Edgar* (although he revised them both, and the second on several occasions) suffered from weak texts. When he worked on *Manon Lescaut*, it took six people's efforts to come up with the scenes and diction adjusted as he wanted them. He participated actively in the preparation of the librettos he set, asking for revisions and then revisions of revisions, because he knew how much the viability of an opera depended upon its emphasis and timing. There is little evidence that any of his contemporaries were nearly as demanding or as discriminating about the fine tuning of the plots they had chosen or as fussy about the words they set to music.

Mascagni's *Cavalleria rusticana* (1890) is famous for introducing *verismo,* the operatic equivalent of naturalism in literature, to the musical theater. In contrast to the romantic *melodrama* that had dominated the Italian opera stage for most of the nineteenth century, the veristic approach involved a lessening of the aesthetic distance between the action on the stage and the audience. Part of the appeal of *La bohème* is that it is about ordinary people, although removed in time, being set in Paris of the 1830s, the period of Louis-Philippe. The neatly adjusted mixture of light-heartedness and pathos in this work helped to assure its popularity. Leoncavallo composed a setting of *La bohème* to his own libretto that appeared one year after Puccini's opera; he derived his text from the same source Puccini had turned to, but Leoncavallo's work is heavy-handed and lacks the clarity of dramatic focus of Puccini's setting. Not surprisingly, Puccini's opera is performed with great frequency, while Leoncavallo's is revived only very occasionally as a curiosity.

In *Madama Butterfly* Puccini sought to make an exotic setting vivid by employing some Japanese music as well as composing his own Japanese-style music, a course he would later follow with Chinese music in *Turandot:* borrowing some and inventing some, even imitating the sounds of Oriental instruments on occasion. Orientalizing, however, was not Puccini's only move in this direction; settings closer to home were important to him as well. The locations of the three acts of *Tosca,* for example, each involve historic landmarks of Rome, and Puccini was concerned enough with detail that he found out the note sounded by the great bell of St Peter's (low E) so that he might introduce it into the prelude of act III of *Tosca*.

The only simon-pure example of *verismo* among Puccini's output is the one-act *Il tabarro,* with its action involving working-class characters taking place upon a barge on the river Seine. Puccini understood the poignancy of the aspirations of poor or defenseless people and could give such feelings memorable musical expression in such arias as "Mi chiamono Mimì" from *La bohème* and "Un bel dì" from *Butterfly*. Puccini would occasionally exploit the sordid or violent aspects of *verismo* (a movement that spent its momentum fairly rapidly), but he understood how to counter-balance them with genuine sentiment and moments of pathos.

The creation of atmosphere, an effort to make as palpable as possible the physical and emotional climate in which the action takes place, was always a matter of close concern to Puccini. The dancing lesson in act II of *Manon Lescaut,* with its aura of minuets and other court dances, establishes a sense of eighteenth-century Parisian luxury. The snowy scene at the opening of act III of *La bohème* provides a background for a scene in which love has grown cold. Verdi had provided an example for his followers of how effective a strikingly evocative setting could be in the storm scene in the last act of *Rigoletto* and the raging tempest depicted at the opening of *Otello,* or the moonlight on the rippling Nile at the beginning of act III of *Aïda*. None of Puccini's contemporaries, however, could equal him in the sheer variety and poetic appropriateness of the scenic atmosphere he developed. A wonderful example of this is the opening of *Il tabarro* that summons up a sense of Seine-side sound and movement as vivid as any Utrillo cityscape of Montmartre.

There is a lighter side to Puccini's art as well, a range that eluded most of his contemporaries. Only Wolf-Ferrari among them could match his deftness. *La rondine* is a work that started out to be a Viennese-style operetta and ended up as a sentimental comedy with a slightly acerbic outcome; in it Puccini's flair for humor and charm shows up not only in the wonderful act II quartet but in the many examples of dance music in this score. His greatest comic achievement, thanks in no small measure to Forzano's pungent text, is the one-act *Gianni Schicchi,* with its sharply etched characters and its comic afflatus humanized by brief flights of lyric expansiveness. Among his other major works, there is not one that does not have some humorous or light-hearted moment to contrast with its more serious conflicts. A brilliant example of this is the trio of Ministers, Ping, Pang and Pong, in *Turandot*. One problem with *verismo* operas is that violent plots too easily tend to find expression in strident and over-vehement music, a defect that afflicted Puccini's contemporaries with embarrassing frequency, but his keen sense of proportion and his ability to make a deft transition from one mood to another, as at the end of "Nessun dorma" (Let no one sleep) in act III of *Turandot,* saves him from the worst of the excesses of the Generation of the '90s. Puccini understood the utility of occasional understatement as well as the precise position for a climax. His mental theatrical clock was more finely adjusted than the sense of stage time demonstrated by his rivals.

It is only comparatively recently that Puccini has become critically respectable. Not so long ago he was regarded with suspicion and jealousy just because of his great popularity, and the fact that he did not aim at grandly tragic or epic material was held against him. His music was faulted for appealing too directly to carnal emotions and less to spiritual values. It has taken time, however, to realize that Puccini had a profound instinctive feeling for the epoch in which he lived and possessed a combination of artistry and sensitivity to give it lasting expression to a degree that none of his contemporaries could match.—WILLIAM ASHBROOK

Purcell, Henry

Composer. Born c. 1659, in London. Died 21 November 1695, in Dean's Yard, Westminster. Married: Frances Peters, c. 1681 (six children). In the choir of the Chapel Royal under the direction of Cooke and Humfrey, 1669; studied with John Blow; appointed Assistant Keeper of the Instruments for the Chapel Royal, 1673; composer to the King's Band, 1677; succeeded Blow as the organist of Westminster Abbey, 1679; activity as a composer of dramatic music beginning 1680; organist of the Chapel Royal, 1682; Keeper of the King's Wind Instruments, 1683. Purcell is buried in the north aisle of Westminster Abbey.

Operas *Dido and Aeneas*, Nahum Tate, London, Josias Priest's Boarding School for Young Ladies, Chelsea, December 1689; *The Prophetess, or The History of Dioclesian* (semi-opera), Thomas Betterton (after J. Fletcher and P. Massinger), London, Dorset Gardens Theatre, spring 1690; *King Arthur, or The British Worthy* (semi-opera), John Dryden, London, Dorset Gardens Theatre, spring 1691; *The Fairy Queen* (semi-opera), Elkanah Settle? (after Shakespeare, *A Midsummer Night's Dream*), London, Dorset Gardens Theatre, April 1692; *The Indian Queen* (semi-opera) (with Daniel Purcell), John Dryden and R. Howard, London, Drury Lane Theatre, 1695; *The Tempest or The Enchanted Island* (semi-opera), T. Shadwell (after Shakespeare), c. 1695.

Henry Purcell II, alias 'Orpheus Britannicus, was born between 22 November 1658 and 10 June 1659, probably in Westminster. His father, Henry Purcell I, who served as a singing man and Master of the Choristers at Westminster Abbey, died on 11 August 1664. Soon thereafter, young Henry was adopted by his paternal uncle, Thomas Purcell, Gentleman of the Chapel Royal, Musician for Lute, Viol and Voice, Composer for the Violins, leader of the band of violins, and Groom of the Robes to Charles II.

Within a few years of his father's death, Henry Purcell joined the Children of the Chapel Royal, serving steadily until age fourteen, when his voice broke, and he was discharged, in 1673. Of his education otherwise, we know only that he held a "Bishop's Boy" scholarship at St Peter's, Westminster from 1678 to 1680, and that he complained publicly, in the preface to his *Sonatas of 1683,* that his education was inadequate.

Purcell did receive excellent musical training under Captain Henry Cooke and Pelham Humfrey, however, both of whom studied music abroad. He also was taught by Matthew Locke, John Blow, and Christopher Gibbons, organist. Further, he served for fourteen years as apprentice to John Hingeston, Keeper and Repairer of His Majesty's Instruments. Hingeston was also his godfather, as we know from his will, which, incidentally, identifies Henry Purcell as son of Elizabeth Purcell, who was wife to the elder Henry Purcell.

In 1677, upon the death of his mentor, Matthew Locke, Purcell was appointed Composer in Ordinary for the Violins at the Chapel Royal. Two years later, in 1679, he assumed duties as Organist at Westminster Abbey. Thus, even before finishing his twentieth year, Purcell held three important posts, and a scholarship as well.

About 1681, Purcell married Frances Peters, daughter of Captain John Baptist Peters, wealthy citizen of Westminster. Altogether, six children were to be born of the marriage; but only Frances, Edward and Mary Peters survived their father, the latest by a scant few weeks.

Already by 1680, Purcell's reputation as a rising musical genius had begun to spread. In 1677 he had made his debut as a composer of instrumental music for theater, with *The Stairre-Case Overture,* and also attracted favorable attention with his wonderfully affective "Elegy on the Death of his worthy Master, Matthew Locke" (*What shall we do, now he is gone?*) During this period, Purcell's songs began to appear in all the major published collections. Many of these were theater songs, which together with his instrumental pieces reflected Purcell's rapid rise to popularity with London's theater public. Some Purcell songs, like "Now the fight's done," and "Britons, strike home," reached a much broader popular audience once they were established as the tunes to which various nationalistic, political, or downright scurrilous texts were circulated daily throughout England.

Further clear evidence of Purcell's mastery of the art of composition appeared in the summer of 1680, when he composed most of his ingeneous fantazias and *In nomines* for consorts of from three to seven instruments. In these elegant, deeply conceived creations, Purcell not only revived England's oldest and most important instrumental tradition. He climaxed that tradition with works of such expressive power and beauty as former generations had never known. Purcell's fantazias and *In nomines* closed a century and a half's tradition of England's finest instrumental polyphony, as developed by such famous masters as Tye, Tallis, Taverner, Byrd and Gibbons. Though still a youth, Purcell appears here as a master among masters.

From the same period, Purcell's anthems, royal welcome songs and odes for various occasions continue the British tradition, despite their more modern Italianate and "Frenchyfied" trappings, which had been the vogue in England from the time or Charles I onward. By 1660, when Charles II renewed the Stewart monarchy, the music of Bassani, Carissimi, Gratiani, Lully and Lelio Colista had become part of British musical culture. Performers, such as Niccolo Matteis, virtuoso violinist, and Giovanni Battista Draghi, harpsichordist, soon popularized this new repertoire, which thereafter profoundly influenced England's musical life. From Purcell's use of forms and techniques characteristic of the works of these composers, as well as from elements of stylistic influence apparent in his own works, it is clear that the new Italian style had caught his fancy. But there is even more persuasive direct evidence, in the meticulous study scores of various Italian masters which Purcell copied during these years, most particularly in his close study of some of the revolutionary madrigals of Claudio Monteverdi, principal pioneer of this new, affective Italian style of the Baroque.

Purcell's most overtly Italianate works were his twenty-two trio sonatas. In a century in which Italianate trio-sonata publications proliferated in every quarter of the musical world, these trio sonatas are unique creations, the foremost of their kind. Paradoxically these twenty-two compositions, even while bringing the latest Italianate styles, forms and techniques to the English public, still retained the essence of the old English praxis.

Meanwhile, various problems had complicated Purcell's life, both at court and at home. His uncle, Thomas, who had fulfilled the role of father to him for nearly two decades, died suddenly, on 31 July 1682. Just a week after the burial of his uncle, Purcell then attended the birth of a new son, John Baptist, who survived only two months of infancy. As if all this were not enough, on 4 February 1683, Purcell was required to take the Sacrament according to the Church of England, before witnesses. It is not known whether Purcell was suspected of being a Papist, or merely was undergoing a formality contingent upon his new appointment as organist to the Chapel Royal, as of 14 July 1682.

Nevertheless, Purcell continued to compose industriously. After seeing the first set of trio sonatas through the press in June of 1683, he composed eight songs for Playford's *Fourth Book of Choice Ayres and Songs,* seven more for the fifth book in the same series, and a royal ode of thanksgiving for the King's providential delivery from the assassins of the Rye House Plot. The ode, "Fly bold rebellion" shows considerable advances in Purcell's skill of fusing the new Italianate instrumental style with a more traditional English vocal style, as do the three St Cecilian odes composed at this time—"Welcome to all the pleasures," "Raise, raise the voice" and "Laudate Ceciliam" and the ode celebrating the marriage of Princess Ann and Prince George of Denmark, "From hardy climes."

The year 1684 found Purcell involved in a widely discussed organ competition between Bernard Smith, Purcell's candidate, and Renatus Harris, in which, after much heat and a certain amount of skulduggery, Smith was awarded the palm. That year, too, his long and patient service under John Hingeston was rewarded, upon the latter's death, with the award of a livery and annual salary to Purcell as Keeper of His Majesty's Instruments. Throughout the year, he continued to produce odes, anthems, chamber music and theatrical music apace.

Then quite suddenly, on 3 February 1685, King Charles II died of an apoplectic stroke. As the nation mourned, Purcell wrote another touching funeral lament, "If prayers and tears," a warmly personal setting of an evocative text, published with an affective sub-title, "Sighs for our late sovereign, King Charles the second." The accession of James II brought no change in Purcell's official position. Musically, however, Purcell's compositions began to show new strength of inspiration and grander style and design. "My heart is inditing," the anthem he composed for James II's coronation on 23 April, breathes a new air of courtly grandeur, in the Lullian manner. The same sort of style animates his birthday ode for James II, "Sound the trumpet, beat the drum," and the anthem "Blessed are they that fear the Lord," which, according to a rubric in the John Gostling part-books at York Minster, was "Composed for the Thanksgiving appoint'd to be observed in London and 12 miles around and upon the 29th following over England for the Queen's being with child."

Purcell's stylistic development was not restricted to these forms, however, as may be seen in the twenty-nine songs published just then in the four books of *The Theatre of Music,* printed by John Playford and published by his son, Henry, during the years 1685 and 1686, or in the catches and duets that appeared in the same period. One of Purcell's most impressive small masterpieces was the pastoral threnody, "Gentle shepherds, you that know" set to verses penned by Nahum Tate (according to William Cummings, the piece was occasioned by the sudden, tragic death not of "Honest John Playford," but rather of his son, John Jr). It is a fine composition, in the newly developed style, as are Purcell's anthems and sacred songs appearing at that time in Henry Playford's *Harmonia Sacra,* along with several masterful anthems such as "O, sing unto the Lord" and "The Lord is King, the earth may be glad." All reveal him in full mastery of the late, expanded style mentioned above.

For Purcell himself the signal event of the year was the birth of his daughter Frances, one of three children who were to survive him. But he was also surely pleased that, with the fall of James II at the end of 1688 and the establishment of William and Mary as monarchs of Great Britain, he received a new appointment at court as Gentleman of the Private Music. Seemingly, this was a sinecure, adding to his fees without heavily increasing his responsibilities. From a charming anecdote first reported by Hawkins, we learn that his new duties involved performing chamber works for Queen Mary. Apparently the Queen, growing tired of Purcell's songs as sung by John Gostling and accompanied by Arabella Hunt on the lute, asked Hunt to sing the old Scots ballad "Cold and raw." Purcell, biding his time, set the tune as bass to a movement of his next birthday ode for the Queen, to the suggestive couplet: "May her blest example chase/Vice in troops out of the land."

These events coincided with Purcell's rise to preeminence as the foremost composer for the stage in London. His popularity in this realm was soon to be greatly expanded by the entirely new activity he entered into as an opera composer. His first operatic venture was to set Nahum Tate's libretto, *Dido and Aeneas* as an opera, with a great deal of dance intermixed, to satisfy the needs of the Royal choreographer Josias Priest, who had an active dance program at a boarding school for young ladies in Chelsea. These elements were not uncommon in seventeenth-century opera, particularly in France, so it seems clear that Purcell and Tate had studied the field carefully. What was unusual about Purcell's approach to *Dido and Aeneas* was that he should have attempted to perform such a work with amateurs, an attempt that is all the more astonishing in view of the superb quality of the music and the drama itself.

Although quite short, the opera has more dramatic power than any yet heard on the English stage and measures up in this regard to anything performed on any stage in Europe up to that time. Its four principal characters—Dido, Aeneas, Belinda and the Sorceress—are clearly drawn and dramatically convincing. The dramatic pace, greatly abetted by the seventeen intercalated dances, moves quickly and forcefully to the denouement, and the melodic beauty and general musical inspiration are profoundly moving.

Each year after the premiere of *Dido and Aeneas* (1689) until his death, Purcell mounted one major operatic event for the London season (these actually were called "semi-operas," since dialogue, dance and pantomime were included in their performances). First, in 1690, came *The Prophetess, or The History of Dioclesian,* with a plot paralleling the fall of James II. Musically, *Dioclesian* was a resounding success, being the first example of Purcell's new resplendant orchestral style, replete with trumpets and drums, which characterized all his productions during the reign of William and Mary.

King Arthur (1691) was less successful, perhaps due to an incomprehensible story line. But Purcell's music for *King Arthur* is all clarity and delight, expressed again in his resplendant, late style. This fact, added to its excellent adornment "with scenes and machines . . . and dances made by Mr. Jo: Priest" brought great success to the company. Unfortunately, Purcell's autograph score was lost, so that no further performances were possible until the work was reconstructed for presentation at Drury Lane Theatre in 1770.

Purcell's opera for the next season, the longest of his works in this genre, was reported as follows by Peter Motteux in *Gentleman's Journal* for May, 1692: "The opera of which I have spoken to you in former hath at last appeared, and continues to be represented daily; it is called *The Fairy Queen*. The drama is originally [that of] Shakespeare, the music and decorations are extraordinary. I have heard the dances commended, and without doubt the whole is very entertaining." Aesthetically, the production was a great success, but financially, it did not do well, as Downes observes: ". . . in ornaments [it] was superior to the other two; especially in clothes for all the singers, and dancers, scenes, machines and decoration, all most profusely set-off; and excellently performed, chiefly the instrumental and vocal part composed by the said Mr. Purcell and dances by Mr. Priest. The Court and the town were wonderfully satisfied with it; but the expenses in setting it out being so great, the company got very little by it."

Purcell's last semi-opera, *The Indian Queen,* is filled with irrational, even paradoxical qualities. Musically it is one of the most imaginative, and expressive of all of Purcell's stage works. His penchant for the occult and the mystical, demonstrated from the very beginning of his career, here found profoundly effective expression. In terms of musical composition and style, it is modern beyond belief. However its libretto is the most old-fashioned of all his major works, harking back to the early Restoration period when the London stage was showing the first feeble signs of revival. The plot is bizarre, and filled with historical inaccuracies: Howard set the play against a background of wars between Mexico and Peru as if these were neighboring principalities. Such total disregard of history and geography would have been totally uncharacteristic of Dryden. Nor would Dryden have created such an improbable cardboard villainess as Queen Zempoalla, as depicted in the original play, nor been responsible for the vast amounts of bombast with which the original was stuffed.

However, as Curtis Price suggests, his might well have been the skilful hand that revised the play as an opera for the production of 1695, for which Henry Purcell provided music. He set all but the additional act, which death prevented him from completing, and which consequently was passed on to his brother, Daniel. Whatever the truth here, Purcell rose magnificently to the challenge. Indeed he somehow managed to turn the weaknesses of the original play into sources of remarkable musical power, with new musical characterizations, awesome scenarios, and orchestral music that marks the pinnacle of his career as a dramatic composer.

During the last five or six years of his life, Purcell's creative development manifested itself not only in the sudden appearance of the English semi-opera, but in many other forms as well. Of the forty-three plays for which Purcell provided incidental music, all but half a dozen were written during this final period. These, too, reflect the rapid maturation and fulfillment of style which are so impressive in the semi-operas, as do several anthems, his numerous songs and dialogues, and his odes and welcome songs. Of the latter variety are his five birthday odes for Queen Mary and his last great St Cecilia Ode, "Hail, bright Cecilia." In the latter, a tour-de-force of instrumental and vocal virtuosity, Purcell is said to have sung the counter-tenor solo, " 'Tis Nature's voice," with the "incredible graces" he himself had written.

Amidst all this creative flow, Purcell died on the eve of another annual St Cecilia's Day celebration, which he had done so much to maintain and enrich during the whole tradition of the London society that he had helped to found. The exact cause of death is not known. Hawkins reports that he died because his wife locked him out to punish him for late-night carousing, but this may be dismissed as mere gossip. Several modern physicians to whom I have shown late portraits of Purcell suggest that he may have suffered from a thyroid ailment. However, Westrup's conjecture that he may have died of consumption is perhaps as plausible as any.

From the rudely scrawled signature to his will, and from the obvious haste in which this document was drawn up it is clear that death came unexpectedly. And yet from the annotations to two songs, Altisidora's "From rosy bowers," *Don Quixote* III and "Lovely Albina's come ashore," it seems that Purcell had been ill for quite some time when he died.

Buried in Westminster Abbey near the organ he once played and took care of, Purcell still lives in the memory of his countrymen and of some few beyond the seas, as "the British Orpheus." His reputation on the continent had impressed no less a musician than Archangelo Corelli who, according to Cummings, was actually on his way to England to visit Purcell personally when news of his death turned him back. Elsewhere on the continent, Purcell was

663

equally popular; witness the following statement from *Mackays's Journey Through England* of 1722: "The English affect more the Italian than the French music, and their own compositions are between the gravity of the first and the levity of the other. They have had several great masters of their own. *Henry Purcell's* works in that kind are esteemed beyond Lully's everywhere."—FRANKLIN B. ZIMMERMAN

I Puritani [The Puritans]

Composer: *Vincenzo Bellini.*

Librettist: *Carlo Pepoli (after Jacques-Arsène Ancelot and Joseph Xavier Boniface, Têtes rondes et cavaliers).*

First Performance: *Paris, Théâtre-Italien, 24 January 1835.*

Roles: *Elvira (soprano); Arturo (tenor); Riccardo (baritone); Giorgio (bass); Lord Walton (bass); Enrichetta (soprano or mezzo-soprano); Sir Bruno Robertson (tenor); chorus (SSATTBB).*

The action of *I Puritani* takes place in a fortress near Plymouth during the English civil war. The residents of the fortress prepare to celebrate the forthcoming wedding of Elvira, the daughter of the governor of the fortress, Lord Gualtiero Walton, a supporter of Cromwell. Riccardo, a rejected suitor, laments that he has lost Elvira. Elvira's uncle Giorgio tells her that her father has given permission for her to marry the man she loves, Arturo Talbo, although he is a supporter of the Stuarts. Arturo enters the fort and discovers that Enrichetta, the widow of Charles I, is being held prisoner there. He disguises her in Elvira's wedding veil and the two of them flee, urged on by Riccardo. When Elvira discovers her bridegroom has run off she lapses into madness.

In act II, Giorgio describes Elvira's aberrant behavior to the residents of the fortress. Riccardo announces that Arturo has been proscribed by the Parliament; if he is caught he will be executed. Elvira wanders in, at first melancholic over Arturo's disappearance but then manic as she enacts the start of the wedding ceremony. Giorgio tells Riccardo he must find a way to save Arturo or there will be two victims—Arturo and Elvira. They unite in a paean to their country, to victory, and to honor.

Act III takes place three months later. Arturo returns to the fortress, in the midst of a storm, pursued by soldiers. Hearing Elvira singing his love song, he goes to her and explains why he had abandoned her. The search party draws closer and Arturo tries to hide, but the possibility of Arturo running off again unhinges Elvira's mind. Arturo stays with her, is caught, and condemned to death. Just then it is announced that the war has ended and there is a general amnesty.

I Puritani, Bellini's last opera, contains many ravishing melodies, supported by lush chromatic harmonies; it is the most carefully orchestrated of all his works. Recitative is reduced, replaced by arioso and parlante—still flexible but musically more substantial means of setting the text. Free-standing solo pieces are minimized—neither Elvira nor Arturo has a traditional aria. Instead there are a number of ensembles which show imaginative experimentation with form, allowing both greater fluidity and greater control over larger units of time. Thus it is unfortunate that *I Puritani* makes use of the weakest libretto Bellini ever set. For all of his other mature operas Bellini set libretti written for him by Felice Romani. For *I Puritani* Bellini recruited

Count Carlo Pepoli who, according to Bellini, possessed "a talent for good verse and the facility to use it." However, Pepoli had no experience writing for the stage, and Bellini undertook to be his guide. The libretto they created together was full of touching situations and opportunities for expressive music. Unfortunately, it is peopled with stock characters and lacks dramatic consistency.

I Puritani shows Bellini at his most expansive, both in his abilities as a composer and in his willingness to let the music, rather than dramatic necessities, determine the course of the opera. For example, the second act contains four musical numbers—each one a gem. A chorus laments ("Ahi! dolor"), Giorgio describes Elvira's unhappy state ("Cinta di fiori"), Elvira appears for a mad scene ("Qui la voce"), and Giorgio and Riccardo assert their patriotism ("Il rival salvar tu dei"). A study of any one of these numbers reveals Bellini's richer and surer handling of form, melody, harmony, and orchestration. But it must be noted that at the end of the second act the dramatic action has not advanced at all. A plot summary which omitted the second act would be no less coherent than one which included it.

Before *I Puritani* received its premiere in Paris, Bellini agreed to revise and adapt it for a performance at the Teatro San Carlo in Naples. Thus Bellini was in the unusual position of working on two different versions of the opera at the same time. The Paris version was composed for Grisi, Rubini, Tamburini, and Lablache; the Naples version was to star Malibran, Duprez, Pedrazzi, and Porto. That is, instead of soprano, high tenor, baritone, bass, the Naples version is written for mezzo soprano, tenor, tenor, baritone. As things turned out, the Naples version was never performed in the nineteenth century. In the past decade there has been a certain amount of critical debate about the relative merits of these two versions. The changes made for Naples—some music added, some taken out, transpositions and adjustments made to accommodate different singers—are musical ones; dramatic issues are not addressed. Since it can certainly be argued that dramatic issues are the most problematic ones in the opera, it can also be argued that these musical changes do not make an essential difference in the value of the work.—CHARLOTTE GREENSPAN

OPERA

The Queen of Spades [Pikovaya dama]

Composer: *Piotr Ilyich Tchaikovsky.*

Librettists: *M. and P. Tchaikovsky (after Pushkin).*

First Performance: *St Petersburg, Mariinsky, 19 December 1890.*

Roles: *Lisa (soprano); Countess (mezzo-soprano); Herman (tenor); Count Tomsky (baritone); Prince Eletsky (bass); Pauline (mezzo-soprano); Governess (mezzo-soprano); Mascha (soprano); Chekalinsky (tenor); Surin (bass); Chaplitsky (tenor); Narumov (bass); Master of Ceremonies (tenor); Characters in interlude at the masked ball: Chloe (soprano); Daphnis (Pauline); Plutus (Tomsky); chorus (SSSAATTBB).*

The tense overture to *The Queen of Spades*, full of foreboding, introduces several themes to be heard later on in the work; it leads directly into act I, which takes place in the Summer Garden, St Petersburg, where children are playing, accompanied by their nurses and governesses. Two soldiers, Surin and Chekalinsky, discuss their melancholy friend, Herman, who is obsessed by gambling, yet never makes a bet. Tomsky cannot understand Herman's incessant gloom, and Herman explains that he has fallen in love with a girl whose name he does not know. Tomsky tells him that he must make every effort to learn this, but Herman is afraid that a difference in social rank will make any relationship impossible.

Herman states that if his pursuit of the unknown woman fails, he will commit suicide. Prince Eletsky, Chekalinsky, and Surin appear. The prince is elated over his recent engagement; his mood contrasts with Herman's wretchedness, and their conflicting emotions are expressed in a duet. The prince greets his fiancée, Lisa, who is accompanied by her grandmother, the countess. To his horror, Herman recognizes that Lisa is the girl with whom he has become infatuated. Lisa and the countess note Herman's strange looks as they, along with Herman, Tomsky, and the prince, sing an ensemble.

Tomsky then tells the story of the countess, who was once a celebrated beauty, though passionately addicted to cards. In a ballad he describes how, after she had lost everything at the tables, the Count St Germain gave her the secret of three cards, which would enable her to regain her fortune. She was successful and passed the secret on to two others. She was warned in a dream that if she ever conveyed the secret to a third party, however, she would die. Surin and Chekalinsky jokingly suggest that Herman should try to secure the countess's secret himself. A storm breaks and Herman, left alone on the stage, muses over what has been said and resolves to win Lisa from the prince.

Act II opens in a luxurious home where a ball is in progress. The master of ceremonies invites the guests into the garden to see the fireworks, and Chekalinsky and Surin decide to play a trick upon Herman. The prince is upset by Lisa's depression and, in a well-known aria, expresses his love and respect. Herman appears with a letter from Lisa requesting a meeting. As he thinks of the three cards, Chekalinsky and Surin whisper to him in such a way that he thinks he has heard a ghost. Lisa slips Herman a key which will give him access to her room via that of the countess. Herman insists on coming to see her that night. The scene ends with a triumphal chorus to mark the arrival of Empress Catherine.

The next scene takes place in the countess's bedroom at midnight. Herman hides himself while the countess is escorted to her boudoir by her maids and Lisa. When all is quiet and the servants have departed, Herman enters and looks at the countess, who stares back terrified. Herman beseeches her to tell him the secret of the cards, but she remains silent. To try to persuade her he draws out a pistol, and she falls back dead. Lisa enters and is convinced that Herman did not love her but was using her for his own ends. The scene now changes to the barracks, where Herman is reading a letter from Lisa forgiving him and requesting a midnight rendezvous. As the wind howls and a funereal chorus is heard, the countess's ghost appears and tells him that he must marry Lisa and that the cards he seeks are the Three, The Seven, and the Ace.

The next scene takes place at the canal near the Winter Palace where Lisa waits anxiously for Herman and expresses her feelings in a powerful aria. As the clock strikes midnight, Herman arrives and they express their love in an impassioned duet. But the illusion is shattered when he announces that they are going to the gaming table. Herman's wild obsession is too much for Lisa, and she drowns herself in the canal. The final scene takes place in the gambling house, where men are having supper. All are surprised to see the prince, whose engagement with Lisa has been broken off. Herman enters and, playing against Chekalinsky, wins twice with the Three and the Seven. He sings an aria about fate. Recklessly he calls for another opponent. The prince volunteers, but when Herman turns up a card saying that it is the Ace, it proves to be the Queen of Spades. The ghost of the countess appears, Herman stabs himself and, as he dies, begs the prince's forgiveness. The chorus sings a prayer for Herman's soul.

Obsessed with the element of fate, Tchaikovsky could not help but be fascinated by Pushkin's story. The opera is a masterpiece of the highest order in which, from the very beginning, a feeling of apprehension and foreboding is never far from the surface. The audience's attention is sustained by a series of contrasting scenes in which normalcy vies with abnormality, such elements sometimes occurring simultaneously as in the duet of Herman and the prince in act I. The opera abounds in fine numbers, which provide an almost inexhaustible repertoire for opera singers. The system of fate motives, especially those associated with the three cards, runs like a thread throughout the whole work, binding and fusing it together in a most effective manner. *The Queen of Spades* must be considered one of Tchaikovsky's outstanding achievements.—GERALD SEAMAN

OPERA

The Rake's Progress

Composer: *Igor Stravinsky.*

Librettists: *W.H. Auden and C. Kallman (after Hogarth's series of engravings).*

First Performance: *Venice, La Fenice, 11 September 1951.*

Roles: *Anne (soprano); Tom Rakewell (tenor); Nick Shadow (baritone); Baba the Turk (mezzo-soprano); Trulove (bass); Mother Goose (mezzo-soprano); Sellem (tenor); Keeper of the Madhouse (bass); chorus (SATB).*

Stravinsky first saw prints of William Hogarth's engravings depicting the life of an eighteenth-century libertine at the Chicago Art Institute in 1947. He had long wanted to write an opera with an original text in English, and Hogarth's pictures immediately suggested to him a succession of operatic scenes. His friend Aldous Huxley suggested W.H. Auden as a librettist, and the two worked together instinctively from the start. Hogarth's scenes are not followed closely in the opera, which adds to the simple story depicted in the engravings a mythic dimension ranging from the Greek myths of Venus and Adonis to the Faust legend with the introduction of Nick Shadow, who is none other than the devil himself. The libretto is a masterpiece of balance and symmetry, with moralizing counterbalanced by the element of chance, Hogarth's pregnant servant girl replaced by the chaste Anne, the ne'er-do-well rake by the innocent but fatally weak Tom (more reminiscent of Faust than Don Juan) and the element of evil personified by Nick Shadow.

The opera is cast in the mold of an eighteenth-century "number opera," with a succession of separate arias, recitatives, duets, trios, choruses, and instrumental interludes. Although in the earlier scenes the action is carried forward by the *secco* recitatives, as the opera progresses, the story unfolds almost entirely in song. While Stravinsky limited his outside listening during the work's composing almost exclusively to Mozart's *Così fan tutte,* there is little direct resemblance between the two works. Accused of avoiding the complex issues facing the twentieth-century composer by escaping into neoclassicism, Stravinsky always maintained that it was possible for a *v*

OPERA

composer to re-use the past and still move forward, and he asked listeners to focus instead on discovering the real qualities of the opera.

Throughout his life, Stravinsky was known to have an extraordinarily sensitive ear, and his preoccupation with harmony and color are ever-present in *The Rake*. The degree of control over the tonal organization is almost without precedent. The opera rises tonally to the dominant E, the dramatic turning point, with each episode in Tom's progress centered on an ever higher key area. As the action unfolds, Tom has moments of insight and doubt indicative of a psychologically complex character, and these points are distinguished musically by the use of keys outside the main tonal framework. The use of key circles within each act is close to Mozart's in *Così fan tutte*, the source of the more easily attributable derivations. Tom's cavatina "Love, too frequently betrayed" uses an opening motive from "Un aura amorosa," the arioso and terzettino are modeled on "Vorrei dir," and the whores' chorus seems inspired by the quintet "Di scrivermi ogni giorno." The harpsichord figurations for the card-playing scene, on the other hand, come from Tchaikovsky's *The Queen of Spades*, an opera Stravinsky must have known from his youth in Russia, rather than from any baroque model. The entire Bedlam scene was likely suggested to Hogarth by the popular ballads on the "Mad Tom of Bedlam" theme, so ubiquitous that one was included in a collection of Purcell songs.

Whatever the final verdict, Stravinsky's opera is no mere exercise in musical antiquarianism. Its music is vital and compelling, and it supports the drama in terms of both comedy and tragedy—the same elements Mozart fused so powerfully in *Don Giovanni*. As to why *The Rake* has been somewhat neglected since its initial flurry of performances, one may ask whether our craving for originality and hunger for the new has blinded us to this and other neoclassic works. It is true that Stravinsky declined a second Auden libretto, thinking that it would have meant composing a sequel to *The Rake*. After the premiere, Stravinsky began to turn toward serial composition, which was rapidly gaining the attention of the avant garde among the musical establishment.—ROBERT H. DANES

Rameau, Jean-Philippe

Composer. Born 25 September 1683, in Dijon. Died 12 September 1764, in Paris. Attended the Jesuit College of Dijon, 1693-97; in Italy, 1701; with a traveling French opera troupe as a violinist; assistant organist at Notre Dame in Avignon, and organist at Clermont-Ferrand, 1702; succeeded his father as church organist at the cathedral in Dijon, 1709; organist in Lyons, 1713; organist at the cathedral in Clermont-Ferrand, 1715-23; Traité de l'harmonie *published in Paris, 1722; organist at Sainte-Croix-de-la-Bretonnerie, 1732;* Nouveau système de musique théorique, *1726; music master to the wife of La Pouplinière, through whom he obtained the libretto for* Samson *from Voltaire; composer of the King's chamber music; granted a patent of nobility. Rameau was the subject of numerous vigorous debates comparing his music and his theories to those of previous generations of musicians, most notably those of Lully.*

Operas *Samson*, Voltaire, 1733; *Hippolyte et Aricie*, S.-J. Pellegrin, Paris, Opéra, 1 October 1733; revised, 11 September 1742; *Les Indes galantes* (opéra-ballet), L. Fuzelier, Paris, Opéra, 23 August 1735; revised 10 March 1736, 28 May 1743, 8 June 1751, and 14 July 1761; *Castor et Pollux*, P.-J. Bernard, Paris,

Opéra, 24 October 1737; revised, 8 June 1754; *Les fêtes d'Hébé* (opéra-ballet), A.G. de Montdorge, Paris, Opéra, 21 May 1739; *Dardanus,* C.-A. Le Clerc de la Bruyère, Paris, Opéra, 19 November 1739; revised, 23 April 1744; *La princesse de Navarre* (comédie-ballet), Voltaire, Versailles, 23 February 1745; revised as *Les fêtes de Ramire,* Versailles, 22 December 1745; *Platée,* J. Autreau and A.-J. Le Valois d'Orville, Versailles, 31 March 1745; libretto revisions, 9 February 1749; *Les fêtes de Polymnie* (opéra-ballet), L. de Cahusac, Paris, Opéra, 12 October 1745; *Le temple de la gloire* (opéra-ballet), Voltaire, Versailles, 27 November 1745; *Les fêtes de l'Hymen et de l'Amour, ou Les Dieux d'Egypte* (ballet-héroïque), L. de Cahusac, Versailles, 15 March 1747; *Zaïs* (ballet-héroïque), L. de Cahusac, Paris, Opéra, 29 February 1748; *Pygmalion* (acte de ballet), Ballot de Savot (after A.H. de La Motte, *Le triomphe des arts*), Paris, Opéra, 27 August 1748; *Les suprises de l'Amour,* J.-P. Bernard, Versailles, 27 November 1748; *Naïs,* L. de Cahusac, Paris, Opéra, 22 April 1749; *Zoroastre,* L. de Cahusac, Paris, Opéra, 5 December 1749; revised, 19 January 1756; *Linus,* Le Clerc de la Bruyère, c. 1752; *La guirlande, ou Les fleurs enchantées* (acte de ballet), J.-F. Marmontel, Paris, Opéra, 21 September 1751; *Acante et Céphise, ou La symphathie,* J.-F. Marmontel, Paris, Opéra, 19 November 1751; *Daphnis et Eglé,* C. Collé, Fontainebleau, 30 October 1753; *Lysis et Délie* (pastorale), J.-F. Marmontel, October 1753 [not performed; lost]; *Les Sybarites* (acte de ballet), J.-F. Marmontel, Fontainebleau, 13 November 1753; *La naissance d'Osiris, ou La fête Pamilie* (acte de ballet), L. de Cahusac, Fontainebleau, 12 October 1754; *Anacréon* [i] (acte de ballet), L. de Cahusac, Fontainebleau, 23 October 1754; *Anacréon* [ii] (acte de ballet), P.-J. Bernard, Paris, Opéra, 31 May 1757; *Le procureur dupé sans le savoir,* 1758-59 [private performance]; *Les Paladins* (comédie-ballet), D. de Monticourt, Paris, Opéra, 12 February 1760; *Abaris, ou Les Boréades,* L. de Cahusac, intended for fall 1763; *Nélée et Myrthis* (acte de ballet) [not performed]; *Zéphyre* [*Les nymphes de Diane*] (acte de ballet) [not performed]; *Io* (acte de ballet) [not performed].

Jean-Philippe Rameau is regarded, along with Lully and Gluck, as one of the finest composers of pre-revolutionary opera in France. He is equally renowned for his theoretical works, especially the monumental *Traité de l'harmonie.* Though he made important contributions to other genres, including harpsichord solos, motets, cantatas, and instrumental music, his thirty operas bear the most vivid stamp of his musical personality.

Rameau fostered an early interest in the stage, but it was not until his fiftieth year that his first *tragédie, Hippolyte et Aricie,* was produced at the *Académie Royale de Musique* (later the Paris Opèra) in Paris. Despite the novelty of his music to eighteenth-century listeners, his operas are closely bound to the traditions of French opera found in works by Lully, Collasse, Campra and others. The *tragédies* include a mythological prologue, five acts, declamatory recitative, vocal airs, and prominent use of chorus and dancing in each act. Rather than transform these traditional elements, Rameau invigorated them with orchestral writing of an astonishing variety and often used instruments in new ways, either by giving them prominent solos or using them in pairs (such as flute and bassoon). Other tragedies, including *Dardanus* and *Zoroastre,* contain some of Rameau's finest music, but they suffer from poor librettos, and their success in both cases rested upon significant revisions undertaken by both librettist and composer for later revivals. Rameau's last tragedy, *Les Boréades,* was rehearsed in 1763 but was not performed.

Of the other operatic genres in which Rameau wrote, the most important is the *opéra-ballet,* usually containing a prologue and three separate acts or *entrées.* In these works dance, costumes, and exotic locales are featured, and the music has a freshness and expressiveness completely removed from tragedy. Among the finest works in this genre are *Les Indes galantes* and *Les fêtes d'Hébé.* Rameau's only *comédie lyrique, Platée,* is a burlesque with a lovesick nymph (sung by a man), a bravura air for Folly in imitation of an Italian aria (act II, scene 4), and other comic music such as animal sounds in the overture and prologue. An occasional work written for the marriage of the Dauphin in 1745, it was greeted with praise by virtue of its novelty, but twentieth century writers have viewed its libretto more critically as a grotesque satire.

Among the most memorable music in Rameau's oeuvre are the extended vocal solos (*ariettes*) and duets, most of which were written for Marie Fel (soprano) and Pierre Jélyotte (*haute-contre* = high tenor). His instrumental dances are often marked by irregular phrase lengths and unusual instrumental timbres (such as musettes or clarinets), while the chaconnes, usually found at the end of an opera, are grand and extended pieces of unusual diversity. Some of the overtures, such as those in *Hippolyte et Aricie* and *Castor et Pollux* retain the traditional two-part Lullian form, to which Rameau added piquant harmonies and solo instrumental textures; the overtures to *La princesse de Navarre* and several later works are Italianate (fast-slow-fast), and still others are programmatic, including those in *Acante et Céphise* and *Zoroastre.* A particularly unusual one is the overture to *Zaïs,* which depicts the "unravelling of chaos." Its irregular phrasing and jarring harmonies were judged by some to be "shocking and disagreeable" when first performed, but despite the initial reservations Rameau's works sometimes encountered, they usually achieved successful first runs, and many remained in the repertoire long after his death.—MARY CYR

Ramey, Samuel E.

Bass. Born 28 March 1942, in Colby, Kansas. Married: Carrie Ramey. Studied with Arthur B. Newman at Wichita State University, then with Armen Boyajian in New York City while working as an advertising copywriter; debut as Zuniga in Carmen, *New York City Opera, 1973; various debuts as Figaro in* Le nozze di Figaro: *Glyndebourne (1976), Teatro alla Scala (1981), Covent Garden (1982); Metropolitan Opera debut as Argante in* Rinaldo, *1984.*

American bass Samuel Ramey's operatic career began when, after being a finalist in the Metropolitan Opera auditions in 1972, he made his operatic debut at the New York City Opera in the small role of Zuniga in Bizet's *Carmen,* followed at the end of the season by the substantially larger role of Don Basilio in Rossini's *Il barbiere di Siviglia.* At the time, the reigning bass at the company was Norman Treigle; upon Treigle's death in 1975, Ramey stepped into several of his roles, most notably Mefistofele in Boito's opera. But it was in the bel canto repertoire that Ramey made his mark, in roles such as Lord Walton in Bellini's *I puritani,* and especially in the florid roles of Rossini (of which he has now sung a large number, including Mustafa in *L'italiana in Algeri,* Selim in *Il turco in Italia,* Lord Sidney in *Il viaggio a Reims,* Moïse, Maometto II, and Assur in *Semiramide*) and early Verdi—*Attila* especially stands out. It was as Argante in Handel's *Rinaldo* that Ramey first appeared—belatedly, to many—at the Metropolitan Opera. Largely restricting himself to the Italian and French repertoire, Ramey has increased his range of roles to encompass Massenet's *Don Quichotte,* Nick Shadow in Stravinsky's *The Rake's Progress,* both Leporello and Don Giovanni in Mozart's opera, Figaro in Mozart's *Le nozze di Figaro,* Philip II in Verdi's *Don Carlos,* Méphistophélès in Gounod's *Faust,* and Bluebeard in Bartók's *Bluebeard's Castle,* and he has now appeared at Covent Garden, Salzburg, Aix-en-Provençe, Pesaro, the Deutsche Oper in Berlin, the Théâtre de la Monnaie in Brussels, the Chicago Lyric Opera, the

Vienna Staatsoper, the Hamburg Opera, the Netherlands Opera, Glyndebourne, and the Teatro alla Scala.

Ramey, a *basso cantante,* possesses a formidable technique for the coloratura bass roles—the requisite agility as well as the ability to spin out a long line. With a voice clearly focused throughout its wide range (from D below the stave to G above, although the tone loses color, but not volume, at the very bottom), a vibrant, sensual sound, substantial stage presence, and both good diction and skill with languages, Ramey lacks little to command the roles of his repertoire.

Ramey tries to maintain a balance between acting and singing. He prefers dramatic characters to comic ones—his skills are greater in conveying drama than comedy—and, in his more florid roles, he feels it is essential to understand the reasons behind the ornamentation in order to keep it from being empty vocal display.

Ramey's voice is notable for its authority, virility, and sturdiness. He is especially successful in conveying the combination of power and resignation that characterizes many of the kingly roles in his repertoire. What he somewhat lacks is introspection, charm, gentleness, sentiment, and humor when these characteristics are called for. He can sometimes seem rather detached, his characters appearing deficient in spiritual depth.

Ramey possesses one of the necessary, if not sufficient, elements of a great singer: a distinctive, recognizable timbre. What he does not possess, at least not in abundance, is the ability to differentiate his various characters; he fits his characters to his voice rather than fitting his voice to the characters. Nor does one look to him to find revelations of character; one finds instead incidental interpretive touches, sudden vivid illuminations created through a variation of vocal color or accent. These may seem relatively superficial rather than growing out of a holistic conception of the character, but as Ramey employs them they are nonetheless effective in projecting and underscoring the meaning of the text.

Ramey's contributions to recordings of complete operas (other than those taken from staged performances) include Angelotti in Puccini's *Tosca* (1976, under Colin Davis), Jacopo Loredano in Verdi's *I due Foscari* (1976, under Gardelli), Mustafà (1980, under Scimone), Figaro (1982, under Solti), Douglas d'Angus in Rossini's *La donna del lago* (1983, under Pollini), Nick Shadow (1984, under Chailly), Don Giovanni (1985, under Karajan), Banquo in Verdi's *Macbeth* (1988, under Chailly), Bluebeard (1988, under Fischer), Oroveso in Bellini's *Norma* (1988, under Bonynge), and Sarastro in Mozart's *Die Zauberflöte* (1989, under Marriner).—MICHAEL SIMS

Raskin, Judith

Soprano. Born 21 June 1928 in New York. Died 21 December 1984, in New York. Married: Raymond Raskin in 1948; two children. Studied at Smith College, and then with Anna Hamlin in New York; debuted in the title role of Douglas Moore's The Ballad of Baby Doe *in Central City, Colorado, 1956; television debut as Susanna in Mozart's* Le nozze di Figaro *with the NBC Opera, 1957; New York City Opera debut as Despina, 1959; Metropolitan Opera debut as Susanna, 1962; sang at the Metropolitan Opera, 1962-72; European debut, Glyndebourne, 1963; taught at the Manhattan School of Music from 1975; taught at Mannes College of Music from 1976.*

Few singers arriving on the American operatic scene successfully in the 1950s did so without first establishing a career in Europe. Judith Raskin, however, a native of New York City, was able to circumvent the need for overseas performances. In addition to this unusual aspect of her career, Raskin's development as a singer began later than usual. Both of her parents were educators. Her father was the chairman of the music department of a high school in the Bronx, and her mother was an elementary teacher. Because of his knowledge of music, her father did not want her to overtax what he felt was a fine young singing voice. As a result Raskin studied only violin and piano as a child. Raskin's studies at Smith College in Northampton, Massachusetts, continued with the same emphasis until her piano teacher heard her sing and realized she was concentrating on the wrong musical instrument. She immediately began studying voice with Anna Hamlin, herself once a student of Marcella Sembrich. The close alliance Raskin felt with her teacher did not end with her college days; her serious vocal study continued for several years after her graduation in 1949. During her senior year in college, Raskin married Dr. Raymond A. Raskin, a physician. Although she devoted most of her time to her husband and two young children for nearly ten years, she never relinquished her goal of becoming a singer.

Solo singing in synagogues and other sporadic musical engagements comprised her vocal development until 1957, when she successfully auditioned for George Schick, music coordinator of National Broadcasting Company Opera. Her debut on the stage came that same year with her portrayal of Susanna (*Le nozze di Figaro*) in Ann Arbor, Michigan, in a live performance with the NBC Opera. It was evident in her initial tour with this company that her interpretation of Mozart was excellent because of the thought and preparation she brought to her performances. As a result of her successes on the tour, Raskin was cast in Poulenc's *Dialogues des Carmélites* in an NBC telecast at the end of 1957. Performances with companies in Santa Fe, Dallas, Washington, D.C., Central City, Colorado, and in New York with the American Opera Society and Juilliard School of Music followed in the next two years.

Her debut at New York City Opera in 1959 and the Metropolitan Opera in 1962 were both in Mozart roles. Her European debut came in the 1963 summer season of the Glyndebourne Festival. The role she sang then and the following summer was Pamina (*Die Zauberflöte*). A repeat of this performance on British Broadcasting Corporation TV gave her talent greater exposure to the public.

Raskin's performances were not limited to Mozart. Notable roles she portrayed included Ann Brice in the world premier of Leonard Kastle's *Deseret*, the Wife in Menotti's *The Labyrinth* for television, the title role in *The Ballad of Baby Doe*, Nannetta in Verdi's *Falstaff* (produced by Franco Zeffirelli and conducted by Leonard Bernstein), Sophie in *Der Rosenkavalier* and Micaëla in *Carmen*. One of her most prestigious recordings is Anne Truelove in Stravinsky's *The Rake's Progress* under the baton of the composer.

Raskin was a very popular singer with colleagues, audiences, and critics. Her vocal purity and agility resulted in her being compared to the singer Elisabeth Schumann. Her interpretations were readily understood because of her absolute command of any language she was singing. The clarity of her English dispelled for many the rationale that only tone is important in opera. Although it is often difficult to understand words sung in the higher range of a soprano, this was not true with Raskin. In addition, her precise use of the language allowed her to effectively manipulate the shaping of the musical phrases. These two emphases—her ability to communicate well and her shaping of phrases—along with her vocal and physical attractiveness, worked hand in hand to reveal her as a consummate artist. Ill health necessitated Raskin's early departure from the operatic stage, but her loss of physical energy did not prevent her from giving occasional recitals and teaching at varying music schools in New York City until shortly before her death in 1984.—ROSE MARY OWENS

Ravel, (Joseph) Maurice

Composer. Born 7 March 1875, in Cibourne, Basses-Pyrénées. Died 28 December 1937, in Paris. Studied piano with Henri Ghis and harmony with Charles René; studied piano with Anthiome and Charles de Bériot (won first prize, 1891), and harmony with Emile Pessard at the Paris Conservatory, beginning 1889; studied composition with Fauré and counterpoint and fugue with Gédalge, 1897; debut as a conductor leading a performance of his Shéhérazade *with the Société Nationale, Paris, 27 May 1899; second place Prix de Rome for his cantata* Myrrha, *1901; served in the ambulance corps, 1914; visited Amsterdam and Venice, 1922; in London, 1923; in Sweden, England, Scotland, 1926; American tour as conductor and pianist, 1928; honorary D. Mus honoris causa, Oxford University, 1928.*

Operas *L'heure espagnole,* Franc-Nohain, 1907-09, Paris, Opéra-Comique, 19 May 1911; *L'enfant et les sortilèges,* Colette, 1920-25, Monte Carlo, 21 March 1925.

Maurice Ravel has been hailed as the leading French composer of his generation, but

during his lifetime he was a subject of controversy, and with good reason: he had a flair for upsetting French complacencies. Nothing that this great provocateur wrote was as strange and shocking as his two tiny operas, *L'heure espagnole* and *L'enfant et les sortilèges.*

Before *L'heure espagnole,* Ravel's first opera, there was a play of the same name, which in itself was scandalous stuff. The author was Franc-Nohain, pen name for Maurice-Etienne Legrand (1873-1934), who wrote several one-act comedies. This one-act *comédie bouffe* takes place in a Spanish clockmaker's shop and is about the amorous affairs of the clockmaker's wife, aptly named Concepcion. Every Thursday, while her husband Torquemada is away from the shop for an hour, Concepcion receives her lovers on the sly. On this particular Thursday there is young Gonzalve, who gushes poetical nonsense, and then Don Inigo Gomez, a fat, middle-aged banker who struts about like a peacock. Neither lover can satisfy Concepcion upstairs in her bedroom, so she ultimately

Maurice Ravel, 1937

sets her cap on a bumbling but sturdy mule driver named Ramiro, who does. The play concludes with a moral from Boccaccio: "There comes a moment in the pursuit of love when the muleteer has his turn."

Franc-Nohain wrote not only a sex comedy, but also a paradoxical tale in which the characters are so shrewd and calculating that they resemble clockwork, rather than people with any real feelings. The craftiest of the lot may well be Torquemada: upon returning toward the end of the play and catching two of his wife's lovers hiding inside his grandfather clocks, he is hardly upset but seizes the moment to sell the clocks. On account of the play's comic vision, however, the many intrigues never have tragic results.

In his adaptation of the play, Ravel left the story basically intact, since it was already tailor-made to his personal musical style and to aspects of his autobiography. Surely, Torquemada's occupation and the Spanish setting reminded him of his own heritage. His father was a Swiss civil engineer who, like his son, had an interest in all things mechanical. His mother was a Basque, and it was from her that Ravel inherited a lifelong attachment to Spanish folk music. In this opera he made use of several quintessential Spanish rhythms, like those of the jota, malagueña, and habanera.

The paradoxical aspect of the story, of humans behaving like machines, also must have appealed to him since he himself was an expert at drawing paradoxes. In the extraordinary orchestral introduction he inserted ticking clocks and whirring automatons that practically vibrate with a life force. Conversely, the characters sound wooden and unmusical since Ravel instructed the singers to give the impression of speaking, rather than of singing, their parts (the one exception is the role of Gonzalve, which is "affectedly lyrical"). There are all too few solo arias and ensembles, the customary places where singers vent their feelings. The characters simply chatter incessantly throughout the twenty-one little scenes, like puppets in a puppet play.

Ravel's primary aim in writing *L'heure espagnole* was to resurrect eighteenth-century Italian *opera buffa,* and in so doing, he created a suitable musical counterpart to Franc-Nohain's *comédie bouffe.* The dry "quasi parlando" vocal style relates to *buffo* recitative, and the concluding habanera, in which all five members of the cast take part, resembles *buffo* ensemble finales. There is even a *basso buffo,* the portly Don Inigo Gomez, who chirps falsetto "cuckoos" when stuffed inside the grandfather clock.

Ravel also captured the comic spirit of the *buffo* tradition, and made it his own, by writing funny music that enhanced the wittiness of the text. Often, his sense of humor is quite subtle and satirical. A case in point is his punctuation of Gonzalve's dramatic question, "Isn't [love] stronger than death?" with a plain C major chord, a chord that sounds so banal here that it instantly deflates the earnestness of the remark.

Predictably, the 1911 premiere of the opera drew a fair amount of controversy, and several critics faulted the work. A "miniature pornographic vaudeville" was how one writer described the libretto. Other critics liked the opera and praised Ravel's daring and original orchestration, especially that of the "symphony of clocks" in the introduction. *L'heure espagnole* went on to become a resounding success and remains to this day a delightful and entertaining comedy, as long as the shady side of the characters—their heartlessness and cunning—are not taken too seriously.

As for *L'enfant et les sortilèges,* it dates from 1916 when the famous author Colette (1873-1954) sent Ravel a copy of her eighteen-page libretto in the hope that he would set it to music. At this time of course the world was at war, and Ravel, a fervent patriot, had enlisted in the French army and was driving an army truck, sometimes near the front at Verdun. Apparently, the libretto was lost, for he never received it. Colette had to wait another three years before he agreed to collaborate, and another six years before the opera had its premiere. It was worth the long wait, however, for their joint efforts resulted in one of the most imaginative and enchanting operas of the twentieth century.

In brief, Colette's libretto, which is in two scenes, is a magical fairy tale about a naughty little boy who learns the meaning of compassion the hard way. When we first see him, he is ensconced in a cozy room; it is late afternoon and he is in a perverse mood. Not only does he refuse to do his homework, but the little brat also sticks his tongue out at his mother. For punishment he is confined to the room, whereupon he has a temper tantrum and wreaks havoc on nearly everything in it. But then the room comes under a spell of sorcery, and all the objects of his fury magically take on life to seek retribution.

The nightmare gets worse in the second scene, which is set in a moonlit garden outside his house. There the boy discovers that the trees, insects and animals are angry with him as well, and they take him to task for a whole host of other crimes, from pinning a dragonfly to the wall, to bashing a bat to death with a stick. The tension quickly escalates to the point where the garden becomes a battleground. All the animals encircle the terror-stricken child, jostle him back and forth, and then claw at each other in a terrible brawl. At the height of the frenzy, a squirrel is injured and the boy, filled with a new compassion, attempts to heal its wounded paw. Because of this one small act of kindness, the animals stop fighting and forgive him. The story comes to an end as he calls out softly for his mother. He has learned his lesson, the wicked spell is broken, and the natural order restored.

Magical as it is, Colette's story is more than just a fable for children. To be sure, behind the fairy-tale façade is a wartime story, and the implied message it carries is that war is triggered by hostile behavior while peace is ensured by love and compassion. Still deeper, and running through all aspects of the story, is a motif of progression and expansion that testifies to Colette's penetrating and coherent mind: the setting shifts from a small room to an outside garden, from afternoon to night; an act of aggression leads to chaos; a child develops; the pageant of bewitched characters begins with inanimate objects (from chairs to arithmatic homework), moves to plant life (trees), and then to more complex life forms (dragonflies, bats, frogs, squirrels). The exceptions to the overall progression are the two cats that appear in both scenes and merely ignore the child.

In short, Colette's libretto is multivalent, and Ravel understood this. To depict the fantastic side of the story, he broke it up into individual episodes—each distinguished by its own musical style and unrelated to the surrounding ones—and strung them all along in one continuous flow. He constructed, in effect, a musical dreamscape which, like our own dreams and fantasies, has a bizarre and haphazard sequence of events. In one memorable episode, a black Wedgwood teapot, representing an African-American boxer, and a Chinese teacup dance to a ragtime/foxtrot tempo and are accompanied by a contemporary jazz band. By contrast, in the following episode a tempestuous soprano, personifying "Fire," sings a coloratura aria that brings to mind eighteenth- and nineteenth-century opera arias.

To translate conflict and disorder in musical terms, Ravel relied on a wide variety of musical procedures. A standout is the temper tantrum episode where he inserted clashing bitonal passages to convey the boy's oppositional and perverse nature. There are plenty of examples of growth and expansion in the score; witness the orchestration of the openings of the two scenes. The first, which takes place in the child's room, suggests a sense of compression because the orchestra hovers over the boy's part, thereby blanketing him and emphasizing his smallness. The beginning of the second scene, which takes place in the moonlit garden, gives the opposite impression, that of depth and of the vast expanse between the ground and stars. Here, the muted strings, altogether sweeping an airy five-octave range, sound in the background, while the slide flute and piccolo (birds and crickets) are heard in the foreground.

Clearly, each opera in its own way is unique. *L'heure espagnole* is a dry and earthy comedy without an ounce of sentimentality. *L'enfant et les sortilèges* is a lyric fantasy that has traces of tenderness and real feeling. At the same time, the two operas may be viewed as opposite sides of the same coin. Both operas have similar formal designs that consist of a succession of brief scenes or episodes, and each lasts only an hour. Both give evidence that Ravel was drawn to stories with multiple layers of meaning, with the superficial layer on top and the darker or more serious layers underneath. His music as a whole is well-constructed, and he would spend years planning a new piece in his mind before writing a single note (the composition of *L'heure espagnole* is an exception to the rule as it was completed in about six months). In this light, it is hardly surprising that this finicky perfectionist only finished two operas and that his total output is rather limited.

Finally, both operas highlight Ravel's penchant for inconsistencies and paradoxes: pulsing clocks and heartless people, beastly child and humane animals. For him, the remarkable balance of contradiction, surprise, and technical perfection was the goal to which he always aspired. For us, that balance is a key to the understanding of his music.—TERESA DAVIDIAN

Resnik, Regina

Soprano and mezzo-soprano. Born 30 August 1922, in New York. Studied with Rosalie Miller and Giuseppe Danise; concert debut at the Brooklyn Academy of Music, 1942; sang opera in Mexico, 1943; Metropolitan Opera debut as Leonore in Il trovatore, 1944; sang regularly with the Metropolitan, turning to mezzo-soprano roles in 1955; appeared as Sieglinde at Bayreuth, 1953; Covent Garden debut as Carmen, 1957; sang there until 1972; active as an opera producer from 1971.

We so strongly think of Regina Resnik as a mezzo that it comes as a surprise to realize that this was really a second career, for she began as a soprano. Yet a soprano she was, and not as a brief, incidental foray into a repertoire which was abandoned early on; after her debut (as Lady Macbeth, no less) Resnik sang for a number of years such major and unequivocally soprano roles as Tosca, Aida, Butterfly, both Donna Anna and Donna Elvira in *Don Giovanni,* and—most interestingly—Chrysothemis in *Elektra,* the opera in which she would later score such a great success in the contralto part of Klytemnestra.

Indeed, that we tend to forget about these early years is not at all a negative comment on Resnik's achievements as a soprano; radio broadcasts preserve her in several of these roles and reveal a bright, shining instrument secure throughout the range and coping easily with top notes. It is instead that her achievements as a character mezzo are considerable, and the voice is the real thing—no topless-voiced soprano trying to maintain a career in a new repertoire, but a genuine mezzo of a particularly ripe and fruity color. This "second voice" is, in fact, so dark and formidable—and Resnik's sense of identification in mezzo roles is so complete and commanding—that it seems inconceivable that she was once an altogether different kind of singer.

Take, for example, the aforementioned role of Klytemnestra, in which she had few if any equals. Whether on records (the Decca performance under Georg Solti) or on the stage, Resnik's characterization is absolutely vivid, portraying the arrogance, rage, and ultimately terror and pathos of this character with unrivaled intensity and authority. She meets every arduous demand that Strauss makes with an instrument that is absolutely steady, although it should be said also that—here as elsewhere—Resnik is willing to use the voice for maximum dramatic impact. This means she will frequently bear down and force the tone, so that the dark color becomes almost suffocating, and the timbre will curdle a bit; at its most extreme, the sound can be really rather ugly and she can seem quite the harridan. This is always used in an appropriate and artistic way, but though it is eminently suitable for some roles—Ulrica in *Ballo in maschera,* for example, or the Principessa in *Suor Angelica*—it is rather less desirable in *Carmen* or as Eboli in *Don Carlo,* where a handsomer and more sensuous voice better suit these characters.

That Resnik has impersonated Carmen and Eboli with considerable success is yet another testimonial to her fine artistry. Records preserve her Carmen under less than ideal circumstances—del Monaco and Sutherland are in poor form and Resnik herself was past her best years for this role—but her distinction is still in evidence. Although without her handsome stage presence this Carmen sounds rather matronly, Resnik's word-painting is exceptionally fiery and full of innuendo—for once, she really sounds as though she might have worked in a cigarette factory. Later, when Carmen achieves a certain nobility, Resnik's conception of the part pays off especially well with a maturity and richness that are strikingly in contrast with her hoydenish early scenes. And turning from this to her wonderfully comical Mistress Quickly in Bernstein's superb recording of *Falstaff* is to see yet another remarkable facet of the art of this singing actress.

Resnik continues to make use of her dramatic skills. At the time of this writing a number of years have passed since she retired from singing opera and concerts, but she has performed to excellent reviews and predictably positive audience response in musicals, including a Broadway revival of *Cabaret*. Resnik has also achieved considerable success as a director of opera, and it is encouraging to realize that the stage instincts which made her such a memorable singer are still serving the opera world.—DAVID ANTHONY FOX

Rethberg, Elisabeth (Lisbeth Sättler)

Soprano. Born 22 September 1894, in Schwarzenberg, Germany. Died 6 June 1976, in Yorktown Heights, New York. Married: baritone George Cehanovsky, 1957. Naturalized as an American citizen, 1939. Studied piano, then voice at the Dresden Conservatory with Otto Watrin, 1912; debut at Dresden Hofoper, 1915; at Dresden 1915-22; Salzburg debut, 1922; Metropolitan Opera debut as Aida, 1922; at the Metropolitan Opera 1922-42, 30 roles including Sieglinde, Eva, Elsa, Madama Butterfly, Elisabeth, Aida, Desdemona;

Covent Garden debut as Aida, 1925; also sang in Rome, Milan, Paris, Florence, San Francisco, Chicago; created the title role of Die ägyptische Helena, *Dresden, 1928.*

Few singers of the inter-war years were celebrated in such grand terms, and with such abandon, as Elisabeth Rethberg. Testimonials to the beauty of her voice and the breadth of her technique abound in her legend. Toscanini is said to have compared her voice to a Stradivarius, insisting that she was the world's greatest soprano. She was made an honorary member of the State Theaters of Saxony in a 1930 tribute at the Dresden Opera. She was even subjected to the kind of beauty-contest pageantry typical of the times—in 1928, the New York Guild of Vocal Teachers bestowed upon her a gold medal for "Perfection in Singing," and a year later the New York Society of Singers proclaimed her's the world's "most perfect voice." Is it any wonder that when her singing teacher, Otto Watrin, assumed a modest teaching post at a small midwestern college in 1929, his arrival in America was reported in the *New York Times?*

The surviving recorded evidence, which is fairly plentiful, does little to contradict the extravagance of these claims. In its prime, roughly between 1924 and 1935, Rethberg's voice was indeed of surpassing beauty. Its large compass, even scale, absolute consistency of tone, and melting legato were further complemented by an effortless production rare even among great singers. Her legendary precision, the product of musical instincts as acute as her training was thorough, made all the standard deceptions unnecessary, for she had few inadequacies to hide and still fewer to overcome. What she seems to have lacked in spontaneous passion and depth of character penetration—charges frequently leveled against her—she made up for in the intelligence and tastefulness with which her voice was used, and in her consuming obligation to the composer's written intentions. Rethberg's was a simple and direct style of singing in the best sense, unburdened by contrivance, and guided by what seems to have been a faultless intuition. The absolute control she exerted over her instrument made her as adept an interpreter of Handel as of Richard Strauss, and allowed her voice to meet the boisterous demands of *verismo* as easily, if not as convincingly, as it dealt with the subtleties of Mozart.

Rethberg's repertory was primarily Italian and German, but her functional command of languages, aided by a prodigious memory, enabled her to maintain a familiarity with more than 100 of the most demanding lyric and dramatic soprano roles. It was boasted that she had committed 1000 songs to memory in their original languages, and had more than a passing acquaintance with the large-scale sacred works of Bach, Handel, Haydn, Mozart, and Brahms, many of which she performed throughout her career.

Born into a musical family, Rethberg showed great promise at an early age, singing and playing the piano with some proficiency by the time she was four—indeed, she was said to have performed the entire *Winterreise* cycle of Schubert by the age of seven. Her first formal musical instruction began at the Dresden Conservatory in 1912, where she studied voice with Otto Watrin. Watrin was himself a pupil of August Iffert (1859-1930), whose vocal method stressed breath control above all else. This was a revelation to Rethberg, and having mastered it to her own satisfaction, she undertook no further study. In the spring of 1915, and at the urging of then assistant conductor Fritz Reiner, she successfully auditioned for a contract at the Dresden Opera, and remained there for seven formative seasons. She quickly assumed many of the leading roles that would remain prominent in her repertory: Michaela in *Carmen,* Mimi in *La bohème,* Butterfly, Octavian and Sophie in *Der Rosenkavalier,* and Tosca. Guest performances in Vienna,

Berlin, and Milan followed, and included notable appearances with the Berlin Philharmonic and Leipzig Gewandhaus Orchestras under Artur Nikisch's direction.

From 1922 until her retirement in 1942, Rethberg was an outstanding fixture at the Metropolitan Opera in New York, singing some thirty roles over twenty consecutive seasons. Her debut as Aida on 22 November 1922 received sturdy if not unrestrained notices. Richard Aldrich's review in the *New York Times* noted that, despite her obvious nervousness, her "crude costuming" and the stentorian vocal demands placed upon her in the noisier segments of the score, Rethberg was, in all "essentials," a success. She became possibly the leading Aida of her generation, performing the role fifty-one times at the Metropolitan Opera alone. The role also served as her debut vehicle at Covent Garden, a last-minute engagement during the 1925 Grand Opera Season. There, she was hailed as the freshest interpreter of the role that house had seen in years. Her subsequent appearances at Covent Garden were surprisingly few, amounting to less than ten roles during the 1934-1936 and 1939 Royal Opera Seasons. Upon the invitation of Lilli Lehmann, she first appeared at the Salzburg Festival in 1922, and even after her American debut, continued to appear regularly in Europe—at the Salzburg Festivals of 1933 and 1939, in Italy, and in her native Dresden, where she created the title role in Strauss' *Die Ägyptische Helena* on 6 June 1928. She performed frequently with the San Francisco and Chicago Opera companies as well. In her prime, Rethberg's fame in Mozart was unmatched, but her stage repertory came also to stress Verdi and the lighter Wagnerian heroines—an exception being what Irving Kolodin considered a disastrous Brünnhilde (Siegfried), foolishly undertaken during her final season. Her retirement from the Metropolitan Opera, which brought her stage career to an end, was ostensibly the result of a contract dispute, but almost undoubtedly this was the culmination of her numerous quarrels with the management over repertory. An Aida on 6 March 1942, served as a quiet, surprisingly uneventful farewell. There followed only a few more years of concert and radio activity. By then, her powers had declined dramatically: her tone had become forced, its previous warmth sacrificed for volume; even her intonation was at times unpredictable.

Rethberg recorded somewhat discontinuously between 1920 and 1939, but her prime is well documented. Her earliest recordings were made in Berlin for Odeon when she was still singing at the Dresden Opera, and included duets with tenor Richard Tauber. Later sessions for that company in 1928 and 1933 yielded more pleasing results, though the operatic repertory she recorded, much of it Italian, was burdened by the German translations. Her first American recordings, made for Brunswick in Chicago between 1923 and 1925 are perhaps her best, for they preserve the voice as it was at the dawn of her prime—still fresh and miraculously responsive. Thereafter, her studio output, at least the operatic portion of it, tended to be repetitious, confining her to only a small portion of her vast repertory. Certain of her most prominent roles are scarcely represented at all. There is a fairly substantial amount of Baroque music by which to judge her activities in oratorio, but on the whole, the recordings are dominated by Mozart and Verdi, especially Aida (in addition to several versions of the two major arias, she recorded the entire third-act Nile Scene with Giacomo Lauri-Volpi and Giuseppe De Luca in 1929 and 1930). She often appeared on the radio throughout the 1930s and early 1940s, and a good many of her recitals and opera broadcasts have survived in transcription, including a matinee of *Otello* from 12 February 1938 with Giovanni Martinelli and Lawrence Tibbett, the original principals from the Metropolitan Opera's heralded 1937 revival of the work. Much of this off-the-air material, especially the performances dating from the final years of her career, has done her reputation a tragic disservice, documenting her decline with cruel efficiency.

—WILLIAM SHAMAN

Ricciarelli, Katia

Soprano. Born 18 January 1946, in Rovigo, Italy. Studied with Iris Adami-Corradetti at the Venice Conservatory; debut as Mimì in Mantua, 1969; U.S. debut as Lucrezia in I due Foscari, Chicago, 1972; Covent Garden debut as Mimì, 1974; Metropolitan Opera debut as Mimì, 1975; appeared as Desdemona in Zeffirelli's film version of Otello.

Of a clutch of Italian sopranos to emerge in the post Callas/Tebaldi era, Katia Ricciarelli is perhaps the most important. A pupil of Iris Adami-Corradetti, herself an outstanding lyric soprano of the thirties, Ricciarelli emerged onto the world operatic stage through winning no less than three major vocal competitions—at Milan, Parma and one organized by Italian radio and television to mark the seventieth anniversary of the death of Verdi. Within months she made her debut in *La bohème* at Mantua with the equally youthful and unknown José Carreras.

Within two years Ricciarelli was singing all over Italy and further afield—Verdi's *Il corsaro* in Venice and his *Giovanni d'Arco* in Rome, Puccini's *Suor Angelica* at Teatro alla Scala and Verdi's *I due Foscari* in Chicago. In 1974 she made her first appearances at both Covent Garden and the Metropolitan Opera.

In the high pressure world of international opera, Ricciarelli's career suggests the superstar. For twenty years she has sung all over the world; she has regularly partnered the tenor trio of Carreras, Domingo and Pavarotti and she has made a formidable number of recordings, particularly of complete operas. Nonetheless as was pointed out in a major profile in *Opera* her performances have been controversial throughout her career. Of her first Leonora in *Trovatore*, Giorgio Gualerzi spoke of "the smoothness of her warm and luminous timbre, the firmness of her high register." However, within months another critic spoke of "lack of real musical preparation. . . . phrasing is unvaried and monotonous" in a performance of Violetta in *La traviata*. Later in the 1970s Andrew Porter offered a balanced assessment of her Desdemona: "serious in intention, subtle and musical, not always limpid in timbre yet more satisfying than those who are sweeter in voice but not alert to the shades of Verdi's music."

Ricciarelli's very first LP disc was an ambitious Verdi recital, mostly little-known arias. Apart from some slightly tentative high notes, it is stunning—perhaps one of the finest first recordings. Her voice is expressive and much of the singing is of the greatest beauty. This pure beauty is still very much in evidence in a complete recording of *Luisa Miller* and in some fine duets with Carreras, where there is an almost magical quality to items from Verdi's *Lombardi* and Donizetti's *Poliuto*. On the other hand, she seems quite simply wrongly if not over-parted in her recordings of *Aida, Tosca* and *Turandot*. One criticism of the latter considers it more "sensuously feminine than usual" and goes on to argue that "Ricciarelli is a far more vulnerable figure than one expects of the icy princess, and the very fact that the part strains her beyond reasonable vocal limits adds to the dramatic point, even if it subtracts from the musical joys." As a recorded performance this is frankly best forgotten, but the conductor was Karajan. Ricciarelli in the same *Opera* interview admitted that she did not think such roles suitable for her voice, "but when Abbado or Karajan asks you to sing them, what do you do?" We can only speculate what equivalent stars of an earlier generation might have done or said! Ricciarelli's next comment goes some way perhaps to explaining her relationship to the world of musical criticism: "I don't regret anything. I relied on my instinct, and I really don't mind what anybody says."

Although Ricciarelli has more than sixty roles in her repertoire, her instinct now seems to be telling her to concentrate on the early Italian romantic repertoire—Rossini, Donizetti, Bellini and early and middle Verdi, plus Desdemona in Verdi's *Otello*. Indeed it is in this last role that she will be remembered best by the general public. Opposite Domingo in the filmed version of *Otello*, Ricciarelli is an expressive, vulnerable and beautiful Desdemona.

Afficionados may prefer to turn to her stunning 1986 Anna Bolena at the Bregenz festival—"she works miracles with her piano phrases which here assumed a Tebaldi-ish glow and shimmer. . . . the most complete performance of a role I have ever experienced from this variable singer. . . . if the real Anna Bolena had pleaded only half so eloquently . . . no male jury in all the world would judge her guilty." Significantly, the conductor was not Abbado or Karajan, but the under-rated Giuseppe Patanè who was one of the most sensitive and idiomatic of Italian maestri. Later that same year there was a superb performance at Pesaro of Rossini's *Bianca e Falliero* in which Ricciarelli's voice blended in perfect harmony with that of Marilyn Horne in one of the truly great operatic performances.—STANLEY HENIG

Riders to the Sea

Composer: *Ralph Vaughan Williams.*

Librettist: *Ralph Vaughan Williams (after J.M. Synge).*

First Performance: *London, Royal College of Music, 1 December 1937.*

Roles: *Maurya (contralto); Bartley (baritone); Cathleen (soprano); Nora (soprano); A Woman (mezzo-soprano); chorus (SSAA).*

As a composer, Ralph Vaughan Williams was an outdoorsman. His musical wanderings through the English countryside led him twice to the sea. First came the vast Sea Symphony for chorus and orchestra (1903-09) based on poems of Whitman. Sixteen years after its completion, Vaughan Williams began to sketch *Riders to the Sea,* a thirty-five minute opera based on Synge's seminal one-act play. Despite its modest forces (five singing roles, a small women's chorus, and an orchestra with mostly single winds), the work took him seven years to compose. He even asked his composer friend Gustav Holst for technical advice, knowing that this compact opera transcended his three full-length operas in theme and substance. Its chief player is the sea itself, never visible but ubiquitous and everlasting. We sense its cadence, its moods, and its boundless eminence.

The opera is set in a cottage on an island off the west coast of Ireland. It is the weathered home of a dwindling family. The sea has claimed father, grandfather, and five of the six sons. Remaining with Maurya, the mother, are two daughters, Cathleen and Nora, and their brother Bartley. As the curtain rises, the sisters are about to open a bundle containing a shirt and stocking taken from a drowned man whose body was washed ashore far to the north. The garments may belong to Michael, a brother lost only nine days before. But Maurya wakes from her nap, and the sisters hide the bundle, afraid of distressing their mother.

The wind is strong and the sea rising. Bartley prepares to transport a red mare and a grey pony by boat to Galway Fair. Fearing that he too will not return, Maurya tries to dissuade him from going, asking "What is the price of a thousand horses against a son where there is one son only?" But the determined young man goes forth, without his mother's blessing and his bit of bread forgotten. Apprehensive on both counts, the sisters send Maurya after Bartley with the bread. Left to themselves, they open the bundle, recognize Michael's clothes, and quickly hide them.

Maurya returns, lamenting distractedly. She has given Bartley neither bread nor blessing, for she saw Michael, wearing fine clothes, astride the pony Bartley was leading as he passed her. This portends disaster. The deaths of all but one of her men haunt Maurya's thoughts as women's voices mourn offstage. A procession of old women enters the cottage. They carry in Bartley's drowned body and lay it on the table. One of the women tells the tale: "The grey pony knocked him into the sea, and he was washed out where there is a great surf on the white rocks." Now Maurya finds peace. There is no man left for the sea to take from her. She asks God's blessing on the souls of the dead and the living. The last of her sons soon will rest in a fine white coffin. "No man at all can be living for ever, and we must be satisfied." The curtain falls on the fading music of the sea.

Critics have received *Riders to the Sea* more warmly than most prestigious opera companies have. Some attribute its exclusion from the basic repertoire to the scarcity of short operas suitable for performance on the same bill. It has, however, been paired with Pasatieri's *Signor Delusa,* and placed between Debussy's *The Prodigal Son* and Ibert's *Angélique.* Vaughan Williams' somber work thrived in both productions, evidence that contrast outweighs affinity when programming a monolithic opera.

Vaughan Williams has left the text of Synge's play almost unaltered. The music's blending modes and sloping melodic contours derive from British folk music, the composer's perpetual inspiration. The vocal lines commingle arioso style with recitative, supported by sustained orchestral counterpoint rather than disjointed rhetorical figures. This textural relation of voices and orchestra owes much to Debussy, although the musical locution is steadfastly British. The slow-paced tertial harmonies are often double-layered, their components diverging and converging to form polychordal dissonances. Parallel triads abound, giving the orchestral current a ponderous mobility reminiscent of the sea. Although Vaughan Williams threads a few motives through the score, his concentrated style provides a single-minded intensity that congeals the music as a single thought. No opera is more homogeneous or less diverting.

Maurya is the only character given lyric music or cause for lyricism. She has lived so long bound with the sea that it has crept into her soul. Those nurtured by the sea love the sea as a mother. It draws them back time and again and cradles them in eternal sleep. It is the matriarch of earthly life. In time its will prevails, for it outlasts the headstrong resolutions of men. It rolls with a majestic and unyielding pulse, but its melody is doleful and ancient as music. And Maurya, ageless in maternal grief and impassive to the untamed brunts of nature, keens like the sea.—JAMES ALLEN FELDMAN

Rienzi, der Letzte der Tribunen [Rienzi, the Last of the Tribunes]

Composer: *Richard Wagner.*

Librettist: *Richard Wagner (after E. Bulwer-Lytton and M.R. Mitford).*

First Performance: *Dresden, Königliches Hoftheater, 20 October 1842; revised, 1843.*

Roles: *Cola Rienzi (tenor); Irene (soprano); Steffano Colonna (bass); Adriano (mezzo-soprano); Paolo Orsini (bass); Raimondo (bass); Baroncelli (tenor); Cecco (bass); Messenger of Peace (soprano); Herald (tenor); chorus (SSSATTBB).*

Rienzi, der Letzte der Tribunens, first performed at the Dresden Court Opera on 20 October 1842, made Richard Wagner famous. Intended for the Paris Opéra, *Rienzi* augmented the grand operatic tradition of Meyerbeer and Spontini. The young Wagner, his ego aflame, hoped to overwhelm even the most seasoned operagoers with a prodigious extravaganza. Aggrandized by luxuriant choruses, processions, and an imposing ballet, *Rienzi* did just that. Dresden audiences loved the work despite its excessive length. (The premiere lasted five and a quarter hours.) Wagner himself suggested cuts which the management declined, and for a while *Rienzi* was given split performances on two successive nights. The first published score, however, trimmed the mammoth opus to Wagner's specifications, but the version most used in twentieth-century productions is based on a redaction by Wagner's wife Cosima and the conductor Julius Kneise. Unhappily, the original manuscript, a prized item among Hitler's personal possessions, has disappeared, preventing reconstruction of the opera as Wagner initially conceived it.

In various abridgments, productions of *Rienzi* abounded throughout Europe during the last half of the nineteenth century, with almost two hundred performances given in Dresden alone. Most opera companies, however, have long since dismissed it as a long-winded blaze of youthful immodesty. Yet *Rienzi* is far more, for Wagner's musical prowess matures from act to act, laying the seeds for his music dramas and consummating his transition from journeyman to master. He was already an accomplished orchestrator and found in the Germanic style of Weber the sinewy vitality he needed. The orchestra for *Rienzi* is exceptionally large, including a serpent, four horns (two with valves), four trumpets (two with valves), three trombones, an ophicleide, and enough percussion to busy four players. Although the music in acts I and II is derivative and often tedious, the remainder of the score sounds distinctively Wagnerian. We hear proliferating chromatic harmonies, remote key relations, subordinate counterpoint in the orchestra, and melodic adumbrations of works to come. Arias, ensembles, and choruses expand climactically in an upsweeping curve, while recitatives shed their formality and become melodically compelling.

Wagner based *Rienzi* on Bulwer-Lytton's novel of the same name (1835) about the fourteenth-century Roman notary who successfully led the plebeian citizens in an insurrection against the dissolute patricians, and briefly ruled the city, hoping to restore the freedom and glory of the ancient republic. Though he first tried to interest Eugène Scribe in providing a libretto, Wagner wrote the dramatic verse himself (as he always did), constructing it in five acts and sixteen scenes with rhymed quatrains for the traditional vocal pieces.

The curtain rises on a street in Rome. It is night. The patrician Paolo Orsini and friends are abducting Rienzi's sister, Irene; but Steffano Colonna, a rival patrician, and a party of men including his son Adriano, Irene's suitor, intercept the marauders. (Following eighteenth-century practice, Wagner composed Adriano's music for a mezzo-soprano.) A fight breaks out with both factions wielding their weapons until Rienzi appears and lays down the law to the nobles. He invokes the civic pride and allegiance of the citizens and wins their support, as well as sanction from a papal legate who has witnessed and tried to stop the skirmish. The patricians plan to resume combat at dawn outside the city. Their departure prompts Rienzi to lock the gates and rally the people against the miscreant nobles until they agree to abide by Roman law.

Word of the incident spreads quickly, and soon all the Roman commoners champion Rienzi. They offer him the crown, but he prefers the republican title of Tribune. Appointing Adriano as Irene's protector, Rienzi urges the young man to join the plebeian cause, but Adriano's loyalty to his family prevents him from endorsing Rienzi's ideals.

Disdaining their gratuitous subservience, the patricians plot Rienzi's assassination despite Adriano's attempts to dissuade them. At a festival procession in front of the Capitol, Orsini attacks Rienzi with a dagger, but the wary tribune has girded himself in chain-mail and the weapon pierces only his robe. The outraged citizens demand death for the conspirators. Rienzi orders their executions but changes his mind when Adriano and Irene plead for leniency to save Colonna's life. Forced to accept Rienzi's terms, the patricians speciously swear fealty to the new government.

The deposed patricians raise an army in the provinces and march on Rome, determined to regain their former power. Adriano appeals for conciliation, but Rienzi, exasperated by the patricians' disloyalty, will not hear of it. He rouses his Romans to a bellicose frenzy, leads them in battle, and returns triumphant with the bodies of many slain patricians, including Orsini and Colonna.

The patricians now resort to political intrigue, convincing the Pope and the German emperor that Rienzi's rebellion is heretical and dangerous to the sovereignty of Rome. The emperor recalls his ambassadors, and the Vatican censures Rienzi by issuing a papal ban against him. The tribune suddenly finds himself friendless and defenseless. Adriano, who in vengeance set out to murder Rienzi but lost his nerve, urges Irene to desert her brother before it is too late. Irene, however, will not leave Rienzi to face peril alone and sends Adriano away. He returns to entreat her more affectingly, only to receive the same reply.

Rienzi's faith in God and in Rome remains unshattered, but Rome has lost faith in him. He appears with Irene on a balcony of the Capitol to address the unruly Romans who stone them both and set fire to the building. As Adriano tries to rescue Irene, the balcony tower crashes down, burying him with the woman he loves and the man he has come to despise.

The story of Rienzi contains several themes and character types found in Wagner's subsequent stage works: the visionary hero, the self-sacrificing woman, the discomfited and ineffectual patriarchs, the betrayal of greatness, the volatility of judgment, the supersedure of the old order by the new, the sublimity of freedom and democracy, the fragility of transcendent morality, the tenacity of convention, and the inclination of the people to destroy its saviors. Rienzi, composed between 1838 and 1840, was the third and most egocentric of Wagner's early operas. It is a vast parable, a critical prospectus on politics, society, and the arts. A bold leader must arise to marshal the people or they will not venture forth, but his supremacy will make him a tragic figure, persecuted and ultimately brought down by his inferiors.

Wagner's score exalts its hero, probably the first operatic role requiring a *Heldentenor,* unless we so consider Florestan in Beethoven's *Fidelio.* Rienzi's music is titanic and wholly explicit. The thoughts behind his words, like the musings of Heracles or Theseus, remain unknown. Of the opera's nine characters, only Adriano shares with us something of his inner life. The others declaim but rarely intimate, leaving the music nothing to express beyond the categorical meaning of the text. The libretto exhibits the kind of histrionic dialogue that typified early Romantic drama. Learning to channel the indirect currents of metaphor and irony that charge the later music dramas took the composer another ten years. *Rienzi* brought to a close Wagner's artistic adolescence and compelled the prevailing motif of his music dramas: redemption through suffering, love, and spiritual enlightenment.—JAMES ALLEN FELDMAN

Rigoletto

Composer: *Giuseppe Verdi.*

Librettist: *Francesco Maria Piave (after Hugo, Le roi s'amuse).*

First Performance: *Venice, La Fenice, 11 March 1851.*

Roles: *Duke of Mantua (tenor); Gilda (soprano); Rigoletto (baritone); Sparafucile (bass); Maddelena (mezzo-soprano or contralto); Count Monterone (bass); Giovanna (mezzo-soprano); Count Ceprano (baritone); Borsa (tenor); Marullo (baritone); Countess Ceprano (mezzo-soprano or soprano); A Page (mezzo-soprano); chorus (SATB); chorus (TTBB).*

Rigoletto, a hunchbacked jester, encourages his young master, the libertine Duke of Mantua, to debauch the wives and daughters of his courtiers, all the while hiding his own innocent young daughter, Gilda. The courtiers, in turn, plot revenge after discovering the hiding place of Gilda, whom they take to be Rigoletto's mistress. The venerable Count Monterone publicly protests the dishonoring of his own daughter by the duke. Rigoletto mocks him, and the old nobleman curses both duke and jester. Tricking Rigoletto into helping them, the courtiers seize Gilda for the duke, who has already pledged his love to her and she to him. Rigoletto mistakenly believes the curse to have been fulfilled.

His daughter dishonored, Rigoletto swears vengeance. Gilda, still in love with the duke, tries to dissuade her father. A month later, Rigoletto arranges for the duke to visit a dilapidated tavern occupied by an assassin, Sparafucile; the nobleman is now in pursuit of the assassin's attractive sister, Maddelena. The jester brings Gilda to watch; she does and is griefstricken. Rigoletto then sends her away and pays the assassin to murder the duke; but Gilda returns and dies in his place. Rigoletto finds that the true curse, far more terrible than dishonor, is the death of his daughter.

For Verdi, Triboulet (Rigoletto) in Victor Hugo's drama *Le roi s'amuse* was a character worthy of Shakespeare, the composer's favorite dramatist; and the play inspired him to write an opera, his seventeenth, which he considered to be the finest of his early and middle period operas.

Avoiding a number of the conventions of Italian operas in his day (for example, in *Rigoletto* there is no large ensemble finale), Verdi used the orchestra and wind band brilliantly. There are no female or mixed choruses in the opera, but a male chorus is used to astonishing effect. It serves in the first and second acts to represent the courtiers of the Duke of Mantua who, as a group, rival the principals in dramatic importance. In act III the same chorus hums offstage to help create the effect of wind during a storm. The storm and the drama build simultaneously in the music. Their gradual development is brilliantly portrayed by the composer: lightning by rapid arpeggios played on the piccolo and flute; additional wind sounds produced by the cellos and double basses. At the climax of the storm comes the climax of the drama: the stabbing of Gilda.

Verdi once said that the second act of an opera should be better than the first and the third should be the best of all. In none of his operas is this crescendo of excellence more visible than in *Rigoletto*. The third act is incomparably masterful. It opens with a brief, soft prelude, followed by the duke's song "La donna é mobile," one of the most famous arias in all opera. Next comes the equally famous quartet, a tour-de-force of individual characterization, together with the extended storm scene described above. Finally, there is Rigoletto's exultant monologue, and the closing duet during which the buffoon discovers his dying daughter in a sack supposed to contain the body of the duke. Not a moment of the act is extraneous, and the tension never relaxes.

Highly successful from its premiere, *Rigoletto* is the first of Verdi's stage works to establish itself permanently in the operatic repertory; and, as one of the most popular operas in history, it has been translated and performed in almost every European language.

The composer first asked Salvadore Cammarano to prepare the libretto, but the Neapolitan poet refused, fearing the censors. Subsequently Francesco Maria Piave undertook the by no means simple task of converting Hugo's five-act play into a three-act opera libretto; and he did so with relative fidelity to the original. The opera is sometimes performed in four acts, with an intermission between the Introduction and remainder of the act. However, this weakens considerably the psychological and tonal connections between the two parts so vital to the drama and the music.

As Cammarano had foreseen, there were serious problems with *la censura* both while Verdi was writing the music and after the premiere. The composer was compelled to sacrifice the title he wanted, *La maledizione* (The Curse), to change the names of the characters, and to alter the venue from Paris at the time of Francis I to Mantua during the reign of the Gonzagas. He also had to forego Hugo's scene for Blanche and Francis in the latter's bedroom. This created a problem for the beginning of the second act of the opera that was never really solved. The duke's lament on the disappearance of Gilda strikes a false note dramatically. Some of the changes by the censor were not replaced by the text Verdi originally intended until the 1983 critical edition by Martin Chusid.

For a decade after the first performance, until the unification of Italy, censors in many Italian cities regularly altered the libretto of *Rigoletto,* in some cases deleting segments of the music as well. The changed texts were usually accompanied by new titles of which *Viscardello* was the most common. *Lionello* was performed in Naples and surrounding areas, and *Clara di Perth* in Naples alone. It was less the political aspect—the attempt to assassinate a ruler—that disturbed the censors than their perception that both play and opera shared a low moral tone. They objected to the failure of either the libertine duke or the assassin to be punished, and they were especially bothered by the fate of the innocent Gilda. In some versions the kidnapping of the heroine could not be shown on stage, and the first act ended with the chorus "Zitti, zitti." At times, Giovanna accompanied the girl into the duke's bedroom; and in several versions Gilda does not die of her wounds. Rigoletto then sings of Heaven's clemency with exactly the same music to which he had sung "la maledizione" in the version set by Verdi.—MARTIN CHUSID

Rimsky-Korsakov, Nicolai

Composer. Born 18 March 1844, in Tikhvin, near Novgorod, Russia. Died 21 June 1908, in Liubensk, near St Petersburg. Studied at the Naval School in St Petersburg, 1856-1862; studied piano with Théodore Canillé, who introduced him to Balakirev; served on the clipper Almaz, 1862-65; first symphony premiered at the Free Music School in St Petersburg with Balakirev conducting, 31 December 1865; professor of orchestration and composition at the St Petersburg Conservatory, 1871; inspector of the military orchestras of the Russian Navy, 1873-1884; assistant director of the court chapel, and conductor of the chorus and orchestra, 1883-94; conducted the annual Russian Symphony concerts sponsored by the publisher Belaieff, 1886-1900; elected a corresponding member of the French Academy, succeeding Grieg, 1907. Rimsky-Korsakov's students included Glazunov, Liadov, Arensky, Ippolitov-Ivanov, Gretchaninov, Nicolas Tcherepnin, Maximilian Steinberg, Gnessin, Miaskovsky, and Stravinsky.

Operas *The Maid of Pskov* [*Pskovityanka*], Rimsky-Korsakov (after L.A. Mey), 1868-72, St Petersburg, Mariinsky, 13 January 1873; revised 1876-77, 1891-92 (St Petersburg, Panayevsky, 18 April 1895), and 1898 [one new aria]; *Mlada* (with Borodin, Cui, Musorgsky, and Minkus) (opera-ballet), V.A. Krïlov, 1872 [unfinished]; *May Night* [*Mayskaya noch*], Rimsky-Korsakov (after Gogol), 1878-79, St Petersburg, Mariinsky, 21 January 1880; *The Snow Maiden* [*Snegurochka*], Rimsky-Korsakov (after A.N. Ostrovsky), 1880-81, St Petersburg, Mariinsky, 10 February 1882; revised, c 1895, St Petersburg, 1898; *Mlada* (opera-ballet), Rimsky-Korsakov (after Krïlov), 1889-90, St Petersburg, Mariinsky, 1 November 1892; *Christmas Eve* [*Noch' pered Rozhdestvom*], Rimsky-Korsakov (after Gogol), 1894-95, St Petersburg, Mariinsky, 10 December 1895; *Sadko*, Rimsky-Korsakov and V.I. Bel'sky, 1894-96, Moscow, Solodovnikov, 7 January 1898; *The Barber of Baghdad* [*Bagdadskiy borodobrey*], Rimsky-Korsakov, 1895 [sketches]; *Mozart and Salieri* [*Motsart i Sal'yeri*], after Pushkin, 1897, Moscow, Solodovnikov, 7 December 1898; *Boyarïnya Vera Sheloga*, Rimsky-Korsakov (after L.A. Mey), 1898, Moscow, Solodovnikov, 27 December 1898; *The Tsar's Bride* [*Tsarskaya nevesta*], after L.A. Mey (one scene by I.F. Tyumenev), 1898, Moscow, Solodovnikov, 3 November 1899; revised 1899 [one new aria]; *The Tale of Tsar Saltan* [*Skazka o Tsare Saltane*], V.I. Bel'sky (after Pushkin), 1899-1900, Moscow, Solodovnikov, 3 November 1900; *Serviliya*, Rimsky-Korsakov (after L.A. Mey), 1900-01, St Petersburg, Mariinsky, 14 October 1902; *Kashchey the Immortal* [*Kashchey bessmertnïy*], Rimsky-Korsakov (after E.M. Petrovsky), 1901-02, Moscow, Solodovnikov, 25 December 1902; conclusion revised, 1906; *Pan Voyevoda*, Tyumenev, 1902-03, St Petersburg, Conservatory, 16 October 1904; *Legend of the Invisible City of Kitezh and the Maiden Fevroniya* [*Skazaniye o nevidimom grade Kitezhe i deve Fevronii*], V.I. Bel'sky, 1903-05, St Petersburg, 20 February 1907; *The Golden Cockerel* [*Zolotoy petushok*], V.I. Bel'sky (after Pushkin), 1906-07, Moscow, Solodovnikov, 7 October 1909; *Sten'ka Razin*, V.I. Bel'sky, 1906 [sketches]; *Heaven and Earth* [*Zemlya i nebo*], after Byron, 1906 [sketches].

Rimsky-Korsakov's interest in the fantastic and exotic elements of Russian folklore is evident in his choice of opera subjects and in his musical treatment of those subjects. He was one of the five Russian composers responsible for the movement toward the development of national Russian music during the second half of the nineteenth century, and his operas cover a wide range of folk topics as well as a number of historic episodes, reflecting his preoccupations with pre-Christian societies as well as with particular historical figures (most notably Ivan the Terrible). At the same time, Rimsky-Korsakov was also influenced by the works of western European composers, so that his operas contain nationalist Russian elements in both music and text as well as western operatic elements.

Rimsky-Korsakov's stylistic development as an opera composer is clearly visible in his scores. The first few operas are not as lyrical as his later works, although none come close to *The Maid of Pskov* in terms of monotonal recitative. With the opera-ballet *Mlada* (composed in collaboration with Borodin, Cui, Musorgsky, and Minkus), Rimsky-Korsakov's numbers become more lyrical, as in the big set pieces found in the dance music, the divertissements, etc. A gradual change of style can be discerned, however, in *May Night* and *The Snow Maiden,* in which Rimsky-Korsakov blurs the distinction between recitative and aria, and does not include the large set pieces as found in his earlier operas. From this point on in Rimsky-Korsakov's opera composition, number opera is abandoned in favor of a continuous, through-composed approach.

The influence of Glinka, who in turn had been influenced by French grand opera, is evident in Rimsky-Korsakov's use of thematic recurrence functioning as identification motives in many of his works. These motives or themes rarely are used as a means of symphonic development, since most of them are never altered. The theme associated with the *The Snow Maiden,* for example, is constant, except for its transformations in act IV to show Leshii fooling Mizgir. Even in this instance, however, the thematic transformations are more closely related to those found in the works of Liszt and Berlioz than they are to the leitmotive technique developed by Wagner.

Wagner's influence on Rimsky-Korsakov is evident, however, in his orchestration and in some of the motives he employs. This is particularly noticeable in the opera-ballet *Mlada,* in which both orchestral techniques and motives can be linked to Wagner. In addition, Rimsky-Korsakov seems to have been particularly attracted to Wagner's nature music; there is Rhine-like music in *Sadko* (which uses an octatonic rather than a diatonic scale as its basis), as well as forest murmurs in *The Tale of Tsar Saltan.*

With the composition of the first of his last two operas, *Legend of the Invisible City of Kitezh,* Rimsky-Korsakov drew most successfully on Wagnerian theories. He interwove two legends to produce a tone poem based setting for a medieval miracle play (called "a Russian *Parsifal*"). Here, Rimsky-Korsakov delineated his characters, particularly the maiden Fevronia of Murom, with evocative expression, unlike his previous dramatizations.

Alexander Pushkin's works had influenced Rimsky-Korsakov's earlier experimental short opera *Mozart and Salieri.* In his final opera, Rimsky-Korsakov derived *The Golden Cockerel* from Pushkin's verse *Fairy Tales,* using poetic ridicule of aristocrats for a thinly-veiled satire of current officials. Rimsky-Korsakov deftly blended myth, Orientalism, fantasy, Wagnerism and originality. His melodic themes at last created both scenes and characters worthy of his technical scholarship, and it is fitting that *The Golden Cockerel* marked the end of both Rimsky-Korsakov's work and the fifty-year era of "The Five."—GREGORY SALMON

Rinaldo

Composer: *George Frideric Handel.*

Librettist: *Giacomo Rossi (after a scenario by A. Hill based on Tasso,* La Gerusalemme liberata*).*

First Performance: *London, Queen's Theatre in the Haymarket, 24 February 1711; revised 1717, 1731.*

Roles: *Goffredo (contralto); Almirena (soprano); Rinaldo (contralto); Argante (bass); Armida (soprano); Eustazio (contralto); Christian Magician (contralto); Herald (tenor); Two Mermaids.*

Rinaldo introduced both George Frideric Handel and newly composed Italian opera to London. Its libretto resulted from a collaboration of English and Italian hands. Aaron Hill, as he writes in the preface, was given the responsibility "to frame some Dramma," after which Giacomo Rossi proceeded "to fill up the Model I had drawn" into Italian verse.

Hill based his story on Torquato Tasso's *Gerusalemme liberata* (*Jerusalem delivered*) of 1581. His intent, as explained in his preface, was to address two issues: the desirability, first, of having a resident composer write specifically for a group of resident singers and, second, of imbuing Italian opera with the conventions of English musical theater. The presence of Handel and the resident singers answered the first need; the second was addressed by adding the spectacle that Italian opera, at that time mostly heroic and historical, lacked. As a result, *Rinaldo* is based not simply on Tasso's epic poem, but on recent English dramatic operas (operas in English with spoken text, elaborate spectacle, and extensive musical interludes) with the same or similar story line including both heroism and sorcery, such as *King Arthur* (1691) with music by Henry Purcell, *Rinaldo and Armida* (1699) with music by John Eccles, and *The British Enchanters* (1706) with music by Eccles and others.

The Hill-Rossi-Handel *Rinaldo* follows Tasso loosely. Goffredo, chief of the Christian armies, is engaged in a crusade to liberate Jerusalem from pagan forces, led by the warrior Argante. Rinaldo, one of Goffredo's most heroic knights, is enchanted by the sorceress Armida. Only by securing his release and return to battle is Jerusalem delivered.

In Tasso, Rinaldo, enchanted, dallies with Armida. Argante is killed, and Armida, repentent, continues to love Rinaldo. He returns her love, and they are reconciled. In Hill's version, on the other hand, Argante is King of Jerusalem, who is in love and in league with Armida. Goffredo has a daughter Almirena who is promised to Rinaldo on the condition that Jerusalem is delivered to the Christians. Almirena is abducted by Armida, and Rinaldo, while seeking to recover her, is captured himself through the siren call of singing mermaids. Rinaldo successfully repulses Armida's advances and with the help of Goffredo and his brother, who arrive in the nick of time, overpowers Armida. The Christians ultimately win Jerusalem, and the captured Argante and Armida convert to Christianity. Almirena and Rinaldo are united.

Two-thirds of Handel's music for this opera derives from his earlier works, mostly from Italy. There are two obvious reasons for this. First, Rossi states in his introduction that the opera was composed in fourteen days, so that the pressures of time may have encouraged Handel to borrow. Secondly, however, Handel may have wanted his first major work for London to offer an anthology of his best music. Thus, although the music is not always dramatically apt, it is generally of the highest quality.

Certain arias stand out as extraordinary, even within their new dramatic context. "Lascia ch'io pianga" ("Leave me to weep") is one of Handel's most beautiful melodies. The saraband dance rhythm (in slow triple time with a secondary accent on the second beat) lends a nobility and grace to the lament of Almirena in captivity. This air comes to *Rinaldo* from *Almira* (1705) through *Il trionfo del tempo* (1707; *The Triumph of Time*); nevertheless, it fits its new dramatic position perfectly. The same may be said of Rinaldo's lament at the moment of Almirena's abduction, "Cara sposa" ("Dear betrothed"). Its long vocal lines set against an intertwining string accompaniment capture the sense of tragedy. In the second section, Rinaldo breaks out of his shock just long enough to rail angrily at the gods, before falling back into despair and a repetition of the first section. Based on the aria in *La resurrezione* (1708; *The Resurrection*), "Caro figlio" ("Dear son"), in which S. Giovanni (St. John) describes Mary's reaction to seeing the resurrected Christ, "Cara sposa" has many of the same serious and intense qualities, but its angry middle section and string accompaniment are entirely new. Charles Burney, the late eighteenth-century music historian, proclaimed this aria "by many degrees the most pathetic song, and with the richest accompaniment, which had been then heard in England."

In addition to its music, *Rinaldo* succeeded because of its spectacle. Act I opens with the city of Jerusalem under full siege. Soon after, Armida arrives "in the Air, in a Chariot drawn by two huge Dragons, out of whose Mouths issue Fire and Smoke." When the scene then changes to "A delightful Grove," live sparrows were released into the theater. Shortly thereafter Almirena is abducted in a black cloud "all fill'd with dreadful Monsters spitting Fire and Smoke on every side." Acts II and III demand similar displays. In act III, for example, a full war is waged between the Christians and the supernatural spirits: "Godfrey, Eustatio [his brother] and the Soldiers, having climb'd half way up the Mountain, are stopp'd by a Row of ugly Spirits, who start up before 'em; The Soldiers, frighted, endeavour to run back, but are cut off in their Way by another Troop, who start up below 'em. In the midst of their Confusion, the mountain opens and swallows 'em up, with Thunder, Lightning, and amazing Noises."

The triumph of *Rinaldo* led detractors of Italian opera to ridicule the extravagant spectacle. Sir Richard Steele wrote in March of 1711 that the performance he attended had "but a very short Allowance of Thunder and Lightning, . . . [that] the Sparrows and Chaffinches at the Hay-Market fly as yet very irregularly over the Stage; and instead of perching on the Trees and performing their Parts, these young Actors either get into the Galleries or put out the Candles, . . . [and that] the Undertakers forgetting to change their Side-Scenes, we were presented with a Prospect of the Ocean in the midst of a delightful Grove." Nevertheless, *Rinaldo* was performed more in Handel's lifetime than any other of his operas.—ELLEN T. HARRIS

Der Ring des Nibelungen [The Ring of the Nibelung] (*Das Rheingold* [The Rhinegold]; *Die Walküre* [The Valkyrie]; *Siegfried*; *Götterdämmerung* [Twilight of the Gods])

Composer: *Richard Wagner.*

Librettist: *Richard Wagner.*

First Performances: *Das Rheingold:* Munich, Königliches Hof- und Nationaltheater, 22 September 1869; *Die Walküre:* Munich, Hof- und Nationaltheater, 26 June 1870; *Siegfried:*

Bayreuth Festspielhaus, 16 August 1876; Götterdämmerung: Bayreuth Festspielhaus, 17 August 1876; performance of the entire cycle, Bayreuth Festspielhaus, 13, 14, 16, 17 August 1876.

Roles: *Das Rheingold:* Fricka (mezzo-soprano); Loge (tenor); Wotan (baritone); Alberich (baritone); Freia (soprano); Erda (mezzo-soprano); The Rhinemaidens (sopranos or mezzo-sopranos); Froh (tenor); Donner (baritone); Mime (tenor); Fasolt (baritone); Fafner (bass); Nibelungs (shout, groan, etc., but do not sing).

Die Walküre: Sieglinde (soprano); Brünnhilde (soprano); Siegmund (tenor); Wotan (baritone or bass-baritone); Fricka (soprano or mezzo-soprano); Hunding (bass); Helmwige (soprano); Ortlinde (soprano); Gerhilde (soprano); Waltraute (mezzo-soprano); Siegrune (mezzo-soprano); Rossweise (mezzo-soprano); Grimgerde (mezzo-soprano); Schwertleite (mezzo-soprano).

Siegfried: Brünnhilde (soprano); Siegfried (tenor); Mime (tenor); Der Wanderer (bass or bass-baritone); Alberich (bass); Fafner (bass); Voice of the Forest Bird (soprano); Erda (contralto).

Götterdämmerung: Brünnhilde (soprano); Siegfried (tenor); Hagen (bass); Gutrune (soprano); Gunther (bass or bass-baritone); Alberich (bass); Waltraute (mezzo-soprano); Three Norns (contralto, mezzo-soprano, soprano); The Rhinemaidens (soprano, mezzo-soprano, contralto); chorus (STTBB).

Perhaps the greatest operatic work ever composed, the tetralogy *Der Ring des Nibelungen*

***Siegfried,* from Patrice Chéreau's Ring cycle, 1976**

creates a mythic world encompassing both tragedy and comedy. A universe in itself, the Ring cycle deserves study for its richness of characters, situations, themes, and leitmotifs, and for the development of its ideas.

Das Rheingold opens in the river Rhine as the Rhinemaidens celebrate (and guard) the Rhinegold. Into this world comes the dwarf Alberich, who tries to seduce the lovely Rhinemaidens. They laugh and tease him, and finally reject him. He then notices the Rhinegold and asks about it; they explain that whoever renounces love, steals the gold, and forms the gold into a ring will have power over the whole world. Rejected repeatedly in his quest for love, Alberich now curses it and steals the gold.

In the second scene of *Das Rheingold* the gods find themselves in a quandary. They have given their sister, the goddess of love Freia, to the giants Fasolt and Fafner in return for building them their fortress Valhalla. The god of fire, Loge, suggests that the newly stolen ring, made from the Rhinegold, would be a suitable substitute for Freia to pay the giants.

In the third scene of *Das Rheingold* Alberich has enslaved his brother Mime and the other Nibelung dwarves and forced them to make golden trinkets only for him. But Wotan and Loge enter Nibelheim and capture Alberich along with his magical ring. In the final scene of the opera, Wotan steals the ring from Alberich, who then puts a curse of death on whoever owns it. Wotan is very tempted to keep the ring because of its ultimate power, but finally—at the urgings of Erda, the Earth Mother—gives the ring to the giants and leads the gods into Valhalla.

Die Walküre presents the story of the Wälsungs (children of Wotan), specifically of Sieglinde, married to Hunding, but in love with a stranger—who turns out to be her brother Siegmund. Their love horrifies Fricka, the goddess of marriage, who successfully urges Wotan to kill Siegmund as an incestuous adulterer. Wotan unhappily orders his daughter, the Valkyrie Brünnhilde, to let Siegmund die in battle against Hunding. When she goes to Siegmund to announce his fate, he threatens to commit suicide rather than abandon his sister. Brünnhilde then promises to help him in his battle against Hunding. She tries to do this but Wotan intervenes, and in the end first Siegmund and then Hunding are killed.

In the last act of *Die Walküre*, Brünnhilde leads Sieglinde to her sister Valkyries for protection against the angry Wotan. They fear him but try to protect their sister and Sieglinde (who is now pregnant with Siegfried). However, Wotan furiously enters and orders them off. His final confrontation with his disobedient daughter Brünnhilde results in a compromise: Wotan will take away her godhead because of her disobedience and then put her in a magic sleep, but he will protect her from cowards by a circle of fire. Whoever kisses her will awaken her and can have her as a wife.

Siegfried involves the young manhood of Siegfried, the son of Siegmund and Sieglinde. Because of his mother's death, he has been raised by a Nibelung dwarf named Mime (brother of Alberich) and raised for the purpose of getting the ring from the dragon Fafner who is guarding it. Through a series of adventures, Siegfried kills the dragon, gets the powerful ring, but outsmarts Mime and keeps the ring himself. The opera's final act involves his climbing through the fire, finding Brünnhilde, and kissing her into consciousness and love. The opera ends with their wonderful duet.

The tetralogy ends with *Götterdämmerung,* which opens with the three Norns predicting the action of the opera: the death of all the characters and the final end of this greedy struggle for the all-powerful ring. The next scene presents Siegfried and Brünnhilde, joyfully in love. Siegfried then goes off on heroic adventures, leaving Brünnhilde on her mountain. Siegfried next comes to the land of the Gibichungs, ruled by Gunther, his sister Gutrune, and their half-brother Hagen (who is the son of Alberich, the original thief of the ring). The Gibichungs give Siegfried a sleeping potion which makes him forget Brünnhilde and fall in love with Gutrune. Gunther then proposes a marriage—Gutrune will marry Siegfried if he can find a suitable wife for Gunther. Gunther then proposes Brünnhilde, whom Siegfried seizes while disguised as Gunther.

The second act of *Götterdämmerung* begins with Hagen plotting with his father Alberich for their possession of the ring. The next scene involves a wedding celebration which becomes a public humiliation. Gunther marches in with the captive Brünnhilde, and Siegfried happily enters with Gutrune. Brünnhilde immediately accuses Siegfried of betrayal and demands revenge. By the end of the act Hagen, Gunther, and Brünnhilde have vowed to revenge themselves with Siegfried's death.

The final act of *Götterdämmerung,* perhaps the most glorious in the whole cycle, begins with comedy as the Rhinemaidens enter and try to tease Siegfried into returning their ring. When this fails, they leave, saying they will get their ring back by the end of the day in any case. In the next scene, Hagen, Gunther, and the Gibichungs enter, and Hagen kills Siegfried. His body is taken back to the hall of the Gibichungs, with the famous Funeral Music playing. Gutrune tries to claim his body, but Brünnhilde claims to be his real wife. In the fight over the ring, which is still on Siegfried's hand, Gunther is killed. Ultimately, Brünnhilde takes the ring from Siegfried's finger, sings her famous Immolation scene, and starts a fire which burns up first the hall of the Gibichungs and then Valhalla. The Rhine then overflows, bringing with it the Rhinemaidens who get their ring back at last. The evil of the ring has been purged through fire and water, and the gold is finally back where it belongs, in the waters of the river.

In the fairy-tale world of the Ring cycle exist first of all the gods—Wotan, Fricka, Freia, Donner, and Froh; there are also creatures who serve the world of the gods—the Valkyries, especially Brünnhilde and Waltraute, their mother Erda, and the Rhinemaidens. While the gods are creatures of the air and the Rhinemaidens live in water, underground are the Nibelung dwarves, including Alberich and his brother Mime. The creatures who live on the earth are the human beings, the Wälsungs, primarily the brother and sister Siegmund and Sieglinde and their son Siegfried, but also the giants Fasolt and Fafner, and the Gibichungs. The Rheingold lies at the bottom of the Rhine, adding beauty to the river while the swimming Rhinemaidens praise and guard the precious metal. But the person who makes the gold into a ring and renounces love will have power over the entire complex world of gods, dwarves, giants, and people. The cycle involves the power struggles through these various segments of the population to take possession of the ring and its awesome power, but with it the curse of a loveless life.

In the process we see the corruption of various characters and their altering situations as the moral and political issues connected with the powerful ring affect their lives and those around them. Wotan, the god who originally coveted the gold and stole it from Alberich, appears in three of the four operas and changes from an arrogant young god into an older, wiser god who desires the end of the conflict and his own death. His daughter Brünnhilde begins as a warrior-maiden, a Valkyrie, who sees the grief of her father Wotan and the despair of Siegmund when told that he will have to leave his sister and lover Sieglinde when ordered to Valhalla. Brünnhilde ultimately becomes the humanized, all-wise woman at the end of this vast tetralogy who sings the famous Immolation scene, hoping that by her death and the sacrifice of her husband Siegfried, the world will finally be rid of the evil ring so love and happiness can return.

Siegfried begins as an innocent though sometimes cruel adolescent, yet becomes a helpless and naive victim of the ring's power. He is accused of treacheries that he is unaware of having committed, thereby constituting the suffering innocent who will become the scapegoat for all the evil plotters around him. His murder will ultimately cause the return of the ring to the Rhine and its rightful owners, the Rhinemaidens. Only when in the Rhine, giving off beautiful reflected light to the river's flowing waters, does the Rhinegold provide any goodness for the universe. Human beings and the other creatures of this world can now begin again with hope.

This magnificent work lends itself to many moral, political, religious, philosophical, psychological, and ecological interpretations. The conflict of love and power, one of the recurrent themes in Western literature, finds operatic embodiment in the Ring cycle. To enter the world of Wagner's Ring is to enter a uniquely fascinating place, a place of both magical fairy-tale and profound philosophy, and that fascination will repay study with musical and dramatic enjoyment.—JOHN LOUIS DIGAETANI

Il ritorno d'Ulisse in patria [The Return of Ulysses to the Homeland]

Composer: *Claudio Monteverdi.*

Librettist: *G. Badoaro.*

First Performance: *Venice, 1640.*

Roles: *Human Frailty (soprano); Time (bass); Fortune (soprano); Love (soprano); Jove (tenor); Neptune (bass); Minerva (soprano); Juno (soprano); Ulysses (tenor); Penelope (soprano); Telemachus (tenor); Antinous (bass); Peisander (tenor); Amphinomus (contralto); Eurymachus (tenor); Melantus (soprano); Eumete (soprano); Irus (tenor); Eurykleia (soprano); chorus.*

Unfortunately, nothing is known of the public's reception of *Il ritorno d'Ulisse in patria*. Nor, if truth be told, is it certain that all of the work was composed by Monteverdi. The story, as worked into a libretto from the last twelve books of Homer's *Odyssey* by the amateur Venetian author, Giacomo Badoaro, is quite simple and straightforward: Act I opens at the Royal Palace in Ithaca, where Penelope mourns the absence of her husband, Ulysses, who even then is nearing home, though she is unaware of the fact. Her immediate concern is that in his absence, numerous suitors for her hand—she calls them hostile rivals—have gathered at the palace, and she fears for her safety. In the next scene Ulysses, born homeward by Phaeacian sailors, awakens on an unknown shore to discover that his mentors, terrified by Neptune's anger, have abandoned him. However, he learns from Minerva, who appears disguised as a shepherd, that he has been cast ashore near Ithaca. She transforms him into an old, bald beggar, and guides him towards his old residence. On the path he meets Eumete, an old, faithful servant who encourages him to the palace even though he does not recognize him as Ulysses. The bald beggar prophesies that Ulysses will return.

Act II begins as Ulysses' son, Telemachus, who is returning to Ithaca to assist his mother, encounters Eumete and the beggar. Soon Ulysses reveals to Telemachus that he is his father, and they proceed happily to the palace. There they find Penelope, surrounded by suitors, Antinous, Peisander and Amphinomus, who, upon learning of Telemachus' presence, and the impending return of Ulysses, redouble their efforts to seduce the queen. Actually, Ulysses is there already, disguised as the bald beggar, and immediately challenges Irus, another suitor, to a fight, in which Ulysses is the victor. Penelope, inspired by Minerva, then produces Ulysses' bow, suggesting that the rival suitors engage in an archery contest. All fail in their attempts to string the bow except the bald beggar, who with deadly aim promptly dispatches all the suitors. In act III, Ulysses at last convinces Penelope that he truly is her husband, by describing an embroidered sheet that earlier had graced their connubial bed, and they are blissfully reunited.

Monteverdi's handiwork is readily identifiable throughout most of the opera. No longer are the scenes so short-coupled as in *Orfeo,* but the stamp of his genius is clearly apparent. Formally and technically, the composition is more highly developed, the phrases longer, the sequences more intricate, and the musical characterization elaborated in greater detail through- out. The arias, the duets, and the ensembles reflect not only the old principles of *seconda prattica,* but also the innovations of *bel canto,* showing that Monteverdi had grown with the times and was ably competing with his brilliant students, such as Cavalli, Fedeli, Manelli, and Sacrati. It has been suggested that one or more of these may have collaborated with Monteverdi in the composition of *Il ritorno d'Ulisse.* Given that only one complete manuscript is now extant, further sources will have to be discovered before this interesting suggestion may be fully investigated.—FRANKLIN B. ZIMMERMAN

Robert le diable [Robert the Devil]

Composer: *Giacomo Meyerbeer.*

Librettists: *Eugène Scribe and G. Delavigne.*

First Performance: *Paris, Opéra, 21 November 1831.*

Roles: *Robert le Diable (tenor); Albert (baritone); Raimbaut (tenor); Bertram (bass- baritone); Alice (soprano); Isabella (soprano); Herald (tenor); Provost (tenor); Priest (baritone); Lady of Honor (mezzo-soprano); Helen (mute); Cavaliers (two tenors, baritone, bass); chorus (SSATTBB).*

Meyerbeer, whose Italian operas *Margherita d'Anjou* and *Il crociato in Egitto* had made the composer's name known in Paris, came to the French capital from Italy in 1826, having learned much about writing for the voice, but yearning for libretti that would allow him to extend the drama into the orchestra as well. His meeting with Eugène Scribe, soon to be the librettist of the first "grand opera," Auber's *La muette de Portici,* resulted in an agreement to collaborate on a three-act opéra comique based on the legend of Robert, Duke of Normandy, spawn of the devil and a mortal woman, saved from hell by his foster-sister.

The story itself was well known; it had played on the Paris stage as early as 1815. Had Meyerbeer gone ahead with staging the original version, it might, thanks to his gifts as a melodist, have become a period piece such as Boieldieu's *La dame blanche,* and the history of opera would have been far different. Instead, thanks in part to extrinsic circumstances, he urged Scribe to turn the story into a full-fledged five-act work which could be through-composed, like *La muette de Portici.* Armed with his understanding of how Mozart and Weber had treated drama in music, and with his understanding from his Italian operas of the capacities of the voice,

Meyerbeer produced a work which changed the face of opera and influenced even those who would later become the composer's musical adversaries.

With *Robert,* Meyerbeer and Scribe indicated the direction that opera would take for the next forty years. Perhaps Meyerbeer's most lasting contribution (though he himself had borrowed the idea from both Weber and Gluck) was the use of the orchestra as dramatic protagonist. His latter-day detractors sneer at his "effects for their own sake," but his method of enhancing and underscoring dramatic situations through the use of unusual instruments and instrumental combinations in *Robert* has been exhaustively analyzed by Hector Berlioz, whose reputation as a musician, unlike Meyerbeer's, has survived the same kind of criticism.

Meyerbeer diminished the importance of the solo aria in his French operas, beginning with *Robert.* The tenor of the title has no aria at all, the occasionally recorded "Sicilienne" being a short solo passage in an ensemble. The second tenor, Raimbaut, a folksinger who sets the stage for the opera's events, has a strophic tune for the legend of Robert the Devil, but even here Meyerbeer uses the simplicity of the first two verses as a foil for the inventive orchestration of the third. Isabelle, the princess Robert loves, and Bertram, his fiend-father, both have two "arias" apiece, but they reflect the beginning of a particularly Meyerbeerian treatment of solo melody, neither in classical ABA form nor in the development of a single tune, but rather a succession of undeveloped tune-forms which change at the bidding of the text's changing emotions, instead of forcing themselves on a text compelled by a single melodic development. Fitfully, especially in the injection of the demonic chorus beneath the stage, Meyerbeer also began to develop his idea of the chorus as a protagonist on its own, one he was later to perfect in *Les Huguenots* and *L'Africaine.*

In sum, *Robert le diable* is a laboratory from which Wagner took the idea of the orchestra as a coequal participant in the drama (and Tannhäuser as a character is obviously patterned on Robert); Berlioz the impact of unexpected, original orchestral effects; Gounod the structure for the final trio in *Faust;* Verdi the concept of human drama played out against historical perspective. Perhaps only a time-traveler from whose memory all subsequent musico-dramatic developments had been erased could appreciate the impact of *Robert le diable* as it was first played. Like Beethoven's *Eroica* Symphony and Stravinsky's *Le sacre du printemps,* it changed the course of its own musical form irrevocably.—WILLIAM J. COLLINS

Roméo et Juliette [Romeo and Juliet]

Composer: *Charles Gounod.*

Librettists: *Jules Barbier and Michel Carré (after Shakespeare).*

First Performance: *Paris, Théâtre-Lyrique, 27 April 1867; revised to include ballet, Paris, Opéra, 28 November 1888.*

Roles: *Juliette (soprano); Roméo (tenor); Mercutio (baritone); Friar Laurence (bass); Stephano (soprano or mezzo-soprano); Gertrude (mezzo-soprano); Tybalt (tenor); Count Capulet (bass); Gregory (baritone); Benvolio (tenor); Duke of Verona (bass); Count Paris (baritone); chorus (SATB).*

There are more than eighty operas based on Shakespeare's *Romeo and Juliet,* including Bellini's version in which the part of Romeo is sung by a woman. It is, of course, impossible to equal Shakespeare's beauty of language or to preserve the complicated sub-plots and large number of characters. Gounod's librettists adopted a bold approach and reduced the play to the barest and most important elements. The narrative becomes a straightforward tale of tragic love between two young and attractive people, while the remaining characters—Friar Laurence, Gertrude, Capulet, and so on—are kept firmly in their places as minor cogs in the machinery of the plot.

Roméo et Juliette is, in effect, a series of four love duets. The madrigal sung by the lovers at their first meeting, "Ange adorable" ("Adorable angel"), is a stylized piece with an attractive archaic flavor, the mannered style justified by the preciosity of Shakespeare's language at this point. The balcony scene of act II opens with Roméo's "Ah! lève-toi soleil!" ("Ah! rise o sun!"), a cavatina that reproduces the spirit of the soliloquy "Arise, fair sun, and kill the envious moon." The second love duet, "O nuit divine," mingles recitative and aria and changes of mood and rhythm with a suppleness of style that mirrors every fluctuating emotion. Fully half of act IV is taken up with the duet portraying the fearful joy of the two lovers when Roméo visits Juliette by night. Their mellifluous "Nuit d'hyménée!" is suddenly shot through with anguish when Roméo hears "the lark, the herald of the morn." The final duet that leads to double suicide is underlined by solemn music that changes with the speed of April weather into a triumphant affirmation of love.

But the love duets, although they provide the basic structure of the opera, are by no means the whole of the story. A happy stroke gives us a prologue sung by unaccompanied voices with

Jean De Reszke and Adelina Patti in *Roméo et Juliette,* Paris, 1888

occasional interjections from the harp. The harmonies, strangely novel for the time and austere only in their prophecy of later developments in French music, wander tragically through unusual modulations. More traditional is Friar Laurence's "Dieu qui fit l'homme à ton image" ("God who made man in thy image"), an aria which recalls Sarastro in *Die Zauberflöte*. Mercutio is also given a fine opportunity with the Queen Mab song, all quicksilver and urgent rhythms. So is Stephano, a character not found in Shakespeare, who, as a soprano *en travesti,* sings an Italianate *chanson.*

Apart from such minor blemishes as the waltz song and the pompous Second Empire mazurka that booms unrepentantly throughout the ball at the Capulets' in act I, *Roméo et Juliette* is notable for the consistency of its inspiration. The orchestral writing is fluently responsive to the demands that are made on it. Moods and atmosphere are quickly established with economy. While composing the opera Gounod lived like a man possessed, sorrowing with his characters and rejoicing in their pleasure. He believed passionately in what he was creating, and he felt, he said, like a young man of twenty again. This fresh quality, this keenness of feeling unblunted by the cynicism of middle age or the disillusionment of the years, are what give *Roméo et Juliette* a vitality and a spontaneity which keep it alive in performance today.—JAMES HARDING

La rondine [The Swallow]

Composer: *Giacomo Puccini.*

Librettist: *Giuseppe Adami (translated from a German libretto by Alfred Maria Willner and Heinz Reichert).*

First Performance: *Monte Carlo, 27 March 1917.*

Roles: *Magda de Civry (soprano); Lisette (soprano); Ruggero Lastouc (tenor); Prunier (tenor); Rambaldo Fernandez (baritone); Périchaud (bass or baritone); Gobin (tenor); Crébillon (bass or baritone); Yvette (soprano); Bianca (soprano); Suzy (mezzo-soprano); Rabonnier (bass); a Butler (bass); a Singer (soprano); a Grisette (soprano); a Student (tenor); chorus (SSTTBB).*

By 1913, Puccini was firmly established as the leading figure in Italian opera. His latest work, *La fanciulla del West,* which was premiered at the Metropolitan Opera in 1910, had scored remarkable successes around the world. In October of 1913, it was given in Vienna, and Puccini attended the production. It was during this stay in Vienna that he was approached by Harry Berté and Otto Eisenschütz, the directors of the *Karltheater,* at that time the foremost operetta theater in Vienna. Out of this encounter grew a commission for a new operetta, which is to say a piece consisting of separate numbers interspersed with spoken dialogue. This would have been a new and unaccustomed genre for Puccini; indeed, after some objections on his part, it was decided that the new piece would be a full-scale opera, with music throughout. The result was *La rondine.*

The genesis of the libretto is remarkable. The operetta text was to be provided for Puccini in German, and Puccini was to arrange for a translation into Italian. He would then set the music, and the finished result would be re-translated into German. Eventually, when the decision was made that spoken dialogue would be altogether omitted, Giuseppe Adami became in essence the sole librettist, and the two Viennese writers, Willner and Reichert, who had supplied the original German text, were to translate the finished result into German.

The story of *La rondine* is set in Paris and on the French Riviera during the Second Empire. Magda, concubine of the wealthy Parisian banker Rambaldo, is hosting a party with Rambaldo at her salon in Paris. Ruggero, the son of an old school friend of Rambaldo, appears at the party. As it is the first time Ruggero is in Paris, the guests suggest several dance halls to him as suitable places for a first night's entertainment. Lisette, Magda's maid, suggests that he visit *Chez Bullier*. When Ruggero and the guests have left, Magda, who had barely noticed Ruggero, decides to spend the evening at *Bullier's* as well.

Magda, wearing her maid's dress so as to remain incognito, chances upon Ruggero, who does not recognize her. She introduces herself as Paulette, and in the course of the evening they fall in love. Magda decides to break up with Rambaldo and leaves with Ruggero to live on the Riviera. One day, Ruggero tells Magda that he has asked his mother's permission to marry Magda. His mother has sent a letter in which she approves of the marriage, provided that Magda is a pure and virtuous woman. When Magda reads this letter, she is deeply moved and decides to reveal her past to Ruggero. Against his protests, she tells him that she cannot marry him; she can be his mistress, but not his wife. She leaves him to return to Rambaldo.

As is all too clear, the story shows remarkable parallels to *La traviata,* except that Magda, unlike Violetta, does not die in the end. Upon closer examination, however, it is difficult to regard *La rondine* as having the same seriousness of intent as *La traviata*. Clearly, the work was never intended as a tragedy, given its original conception as an operetta. At the same time, it is not light-hearted enough to pass as a comedy, and therein lies its greatest flaw. It is difficult to feel empathy for any of the characters because the emotional appeal is not strong enough; on the other hand, not enough room is given for any comic development. The lack of commitment to either dramatic option in *La rondine* ultimately fails to involve the listener in the story.

Overall, *La rondine* is one of Puccini's most disappointing operas. Its greatest weakness lies in the libretto, and it is hard to avoid the conclusion that Puccini was uninspired by it himself. But the score is certainly not without merit. In a letter to Sybil Seligman from September 1914, Puccini writes regarding *La rondine:* "it's a light sentimental opera with touches of comedy—but it's agreeable, limpid, easy to sing, with little waltz music and lively and fetching tunes . . . it's a sort of reaction against the repulsive music of today—which, as you put it so well, is very much like the war!"

The characterization is fitting. The score contains some exquisite melodies in the typical Puccinian mold, the most famous example being Prunier's/Magda's aria "Chi il bel sogno di Doretta." While the harmonic style is mostly straightforward, there are some conspicuous passages of bolder invention, with expanded harmonies, unresolved dissonances, instances of bitonality, and unmitigated harmonic shifts. The orchestration is skillfully handled and delicately scored. Despite the opera's dramatic shortcomings, Puccini's attention to musical detail is noticeable throughout the score.—JÜRGEN SELK

Der Rosenkavalier [The Knight of the Rose]

Composer: *Richard Strauss.*

Librettist: *Hugo von Hofmannsthal.*

First Performance: *Dresden, Court Opera, 26 January 1911.*

OPERA

Roles: *Princess von Werdenberg, The Marschallin (soprano); Octavian (mezzo-soprano or soprano); Sophie (soprano); Baron Ochs von Lerchenau (bass); Herr von Faninal (baritone); Singer (tenor); Marianne (soprano); Valzacchi (tenor); Annina (contralto); Police Commissioner (bass); Marschallin's Majordomo (tenor); Faninal's Majordomo (tenor); Attorney (bass); Innkeeper (tenor); Three Noble Orphans (soprano, mezzo-soprano, contralto); Milliner (soprano); Animal Vendor (tenor); Four Footmen (two tenors, two basses); Four Waiters (tenor, three basses); Scholar, Fluteplayer, Hairdresser, His Assistant, a Widow, Mahomet (all mute); chorus (SAATTBB).*

"That summer, the summer of 1914, it seemed as if the whole of London was a ballroom. . . . The dance tunes continued until the end to sound through the windows: fox-trots, tangos, and waltzes. And though that summer the waltzes were fewer in number when compared with other rhythms, nevertheless one of them reigned supreme in every ballroom, the waltz from *Rosenkavalier,* that mocking parody of the old order, that triumph of Ritz-Eighteenth Century. With its seductive rhythms, its carefully hidden cleverness, it was the last song of an era. . . ." Thus Osbert Sitwell wrote in his novel *Those Were the Days,* a chronicle of British high society life. In the summer of 1914, *Der Rosenkavalier* was only three years old, yet it already symbolized a pleasant past in which slightly scandalous intrigue flourishes but young love conquers all.

Der Rosenkavalier, **production by Herbert von Karajan, 1983**

Strauss' favorite librettist, the poet Hugo von Hofmannsthal, set his plot in the Vienna of Maria Theresa (i.e., mid-eighteenth century). A field marshal's wife (the Marschallin), still beautiful but beginning to age, is having a dalliance with the 17-year-old Octavian. The Marschallin's country-bred cousin, the boorish Baron Ochs, is about to marry the lovely Sophie, daughter of a wealthy bourgeois, von Faninal. According to local custom, Ochs requires a young cavalier to present a silver rose to his intended, and the Marschallin recommends Octavian for the task. When the actual presentation takes place, in act II, Octavian and Sophie fall forthwith in love. In act III, Octavian, dressed as a girl, entices the philandering baron to an inn to expose his true character. All ends happily, with the two young lovers singing an ecstatic duet (to which the sound of the celesta lends an ethereal quality) while Ochs decamps and the Marschallin is left to face the realization that the ravages of time are coming ever closer.

For all the skill and variety of Hofmannsthal's libretto, it is Strauss' richly lyrical and psychologically apt score that has elevated *Der Rosenkavalier* to its generally accepted rank as an operatic comedy that can bear comparison to such masterpieces as Mozart's *Le nozze di Figaro,* Wagner's *Die Meistersinger* and Verdi's *Falstaff.* As in all of Strauss' works, the orchestra is not least among his protagonists. The work opens with a near-symphonic episode designed to depict, before the curtain rises, the passionate nature of the affair between Octavian and the Marschallin. Similarly, act III is preceded by a brilliant instrumental *fugato* suggesting the conspiratorial activities of Valzacchi and Annina, two intriguers hired by Ochs to aid his amatory pursuit of the disguised Octavian. The orchestra is even accorded the final music of the opera, which ends with a black pageboy scampering across an otherwise empty stage to pick up a handkerchief dropped by Sophie.

It also is Strauss' delectable music rather than the sometimes convoluted stage action that saves the day in several drawn-out episodes during which a listener might be tempted to remark, with Christopher Sly: "'Tis a very excellent piece of work. . . . Would 'twere done!" A case in point is a good portion of act III, in which the farcical antics of Valzacchi and Annina grow wearisome, perhaps because one is impatiently awaiting the incadescently beautiful trio in which Octavian, with Sophie at his side, takes final leave of the Marschallin, who quietly and resignedly calls for God's blessing on the young couple.

Despite the sexual innuendo of its opening scene (in which Octavian and the Marschallin are practically discovered in bed), *Der Rosenkavalier* breathes a more wholesome air than either of Strauss' previous operatic successes, *Salome* and *Elektra.* It also is far longer (well over three hours) and musically expansive, with a huge cast and an orchestra of over one hundred. Ironically, Hofmannsthal had originally proposed it as a short comic opera, even including a ballet. The character of the Marschallin was not in the original *dramatis personae,* but once she entered she took over as the dominant personality. As the work expanded in size, it developed a radiant and robust quality of its own. The ballet episode never came to pass, but in its place there is a good deal of lusty stage business, most notably the Marschallin's act I *levée,* a madcap reception in her salon in which she receives a motley crowd of petitioners, supplicants, entertainers (including an Italian tenor who sings a fine aria), salespersons, attendants, and household staff—an enchanting and vivid portrayal of eighteenth-century Viennese society as it may or may not have existed.

In addition to its period flavor and scenic variety, *Der Rosenkavalier* flourishes in opera houses throughout the world because of its rich musical characterizations. The Marschallin, Ochs, and Octavian are all unmistakably identifiable by the music they sing. Strauss wanted the

Marschallin not to be depicted as decrepit, superannuated or even past her prime. "Octavian is neither her first lover nor her last," he wrote, suggesting that she display sorrow in one eye and gaiety in the other as their affair comes to an end. He also wanted her to exhibit "Viennese grace and lightness" and expressed the hope that conductors wouldn't give her draggy tempos. She is a woman afraid not of life, but of time. Her most moving words of all (are there any simpler in all opera?) are the cryptic "Ja, ja!" with which, at the close, she replies to Faninal's hearty but not very original observations that young people will be young people. Finding just the right way to sing those words is a constant challenge for Marschallins.

Ochs, too, is a more complicated character than he seems. It is a mistake for singers to present him as an out-and-out buffoon; he is, after all, an aristocrat, even if rough around the edges, and he is hopelessly out of his depth among a courtly coterie of sophisticated intriguers and voluptuaries whose moral level really isn't much higher than his. Strauss' music for Ochs, with its bluff heartiness, broad melodic appeal and artful touches of vulgarity, limns his character perfectly.

Octavian is frequently compared to Cherubino in *Le nozze di Figaro,* and indeed Strauss, after completing *Elektra,* had announced his intention of composing a Mozartean opera. No doubt there are certain resemblances: the mezzo voices, the fact that both are trouser-roles, the ease with which many singers slip from one part to the other. Yet the differences are significant: Cherubino has a quality of innocence lacking in the worldly Octavian, and he certainly is less discursive. Still, who is to say that the two "boys" might not enjoy comparing notes—and not necessarily musical ones?—HERBERT KUPFERBERG

Rossini, Gioachino

Composer. Born 29 February 1792, in Pesaro, Italy. Died 13 November 1868, in Paris. Married: 1) Isabella Colbran, soprano, 16 March 1822 (divorced 1837); 2) Olympe Pélissier, 16 August 1846. Studied French horn with his father and singing with the local canon in Lugo; studied singing, harpsichord, and music theory with Padre Tesei in Bologna; served as maestro al cembalo in local churches and opera houses; studied voice with the tenor Matteo Babbini; studied singing and solfeggio with Gibelli, cello with Cavedagna, piano with Zanotti, and counterpoint with Padre Mattei at the Liceo Musicale in Bologna, beginning 1806; received a prize from the Liceo Musicale for his cantata Il pianto d'Armonia sulla morte d'Orfeo, *performed 11 August 1808; his successful early opera compositions led to a commission from the Teatro alla Scala, 1812; commissioned by the impresario Barbaia, 1814; numerous operas, 1814-1822, including* Il barbiere di Siviglia *(1816); met Beethoven in Vienna, 1822; received in London by King George IV of England, 1823; director of the Théâtre-Italien in Paris, 1824;* Il viaggio a Reims *composed for the coronation of King Charles X, 1825; met Meyerbeer in Paris; Premier Compositeur du Roi and Inspecteur Général du Chant; contract with the government of Charles X to compose operas for the Paris Opéra, 1829 (invalidated with the outbreak of the revolution of 1830); consultant to the Liceo Musicale in Bologna, 1836-1848; in Florence, 1848; in Paris, 1855.*

Operas *Demitrio e Polibio,* V. Viganò-Mombelli, c. 1809, Rome, Valle, 18 May 1812; *La cambiale di matrimonio,* G. Rossi (after Camillo Federici), Venice, San Moisè, 3 November 1810; *L'equivoco stravagante,* G. Gasparri, Bologna, Teatro del Corso, 26 October 1811; *L'inganno felice,* G. Foppa (after G. Palomba), Venice, San Moisè, 8 January 1812; *Ciro in Babilonia, ossia La caduta di Baldassare,* F. Aventi, Ferrara, Comunale, 14? March 1812; *La scala di seta,* G. Foppa (after Planard, *L'échelle de soie*), Venice, San Moisè, 9 May 1812; *La pietra del paragone,* L. Romanelli, Milan, Teatro alla Scala, 26 September 1812; *L'occasione fa il ladro,* L. Prividali, Venice, San Moisè, 24 November 1812; *Il Signor Bruschino, ossia Il figlio per azzardo,* G. Foppa (after A. de Chazet and E.-T. Maurice Ourry, *Le fils par hazard*), Venice, San Moisè, January 1813; *Tancredi,* G. Rossi and L. Lechi (after Voltaire), Venice, La Fenice, 6 February 1813; *L'italiana in Algeri,* A. Anelli (for L. Mosca), Venice, San Benedetto, 22 May 1813; *Aureliano in Palmira* G.-F. Romani, Milan, Teatro alla Scala, 26 December 1813; *Il turco in Italia,* F. Romani (after Caterino Mazzdà), Milan, Teatro alla Scala, 14 August 1814; *Sigismondo,* G. Foppa, Venice, La Fenice, 26 December 1814; *Elisabetta, regina d'Inghilterra,* G. Schmidt (after Carlo Federici), Naples, San Carlo, 4 October 1815; *Torvaldo e Dorliska,* C. Sterbini (after J.-B. de Coudry, *Vie et amours du chevalier de Faubles*), Rome, Valle, 26 December 1815; *Almaviva, ossia L'inutile precauzione* (*Il barbiere di Siviglia*), C. Sterbini (after Beaumarchais and G. Petrosellini), Rome, Torre Argentina, 20 February 1816; *La gazzetta,* G. Palomba (after C. Goldoni, *Il matrimonio per concorso*), Naples, Teatro dei Fiorentini, 26 September 1816; *Otello, ossia Il moro di Venezia,* F. Berio di Salsa (after Shakespeare), Naples, Teatro del Fondo, 4 December 1816; *La Cenerentola, ossia La bontà in trionfo,* G. Ferretti (after Perrault, *Cendrillon,* C.-G. Etienne, and F. Fiorini), Rome, Valle, 25 January 1817; *La gazza ladra,* G. Gherardini (after d'Aubigny and Caigniez, *La pie voleuse*), Milan, Teatro alla Scala, 31 May 1817; *Armida,* G. Schmidt (after Tasso, *La Gerusalemme liberata*), Naples, San Carlo, 11 November 1817; *Adelaide di Borgogna,* G. Schmidt, Rome, Torre Argentina, 27 December 1817; *Mosè in Egitto,* A.L. Tottola (after F. Ringhieri, *L'Osiride*), Naples, San Carlo, 5 March 1818; revised as *Moïse et Pharaon, ou Le passage de la Mer Rouge,* L. Balocchi and E. de Jouy, Paris, Opèra, 26 March 1827; *Adina,* G. Bevilacqua-Aldobrandini, 1818, Lisbon, Saõ Carlo, 22 June 1826; *Ricciardo e Zoraide,* F. Berio di Salsa (after Niccolò Forteguerri, *Ricciardetto*), Naples, San Carlo, 3 December 1818; *Ermione,* A.L. Tottola (after Racine, *Andromaque*), Naples, San Carlo, 27 March 1819; *Eduardo e Cristina,* G. Schmidt (revised by Bevilacqua-Aldobrandini and A.L. Tottola), Venice, San Benedetto, 24 April 1819; *La donna del lago,* A.L. Tottola (after Scott, *The Lady of the Lake*), Naples, San Carlo, 24 September 1819; *Bianca e Falliero, ossia Il consiglio dei tre,* F. Romani (after A. van Arnhault, *Blanche et Montcassin*), Milan, Teatro alla Scala, 26 December 1819; *Maometto II,* C. della Valle (after his *Anna Erizo*), Naples, San Carlo, 3 December 1820; revised as *Le siège de Corinthe,* L. Balocchi and A. Soumet, Paris, Opèra, 9 October 1826; *Matilde di Shabran, ossia Bellezza, e cuor di ferro,* G. Ferretti (after F.-B. Hoffmann, *Euphrosine,* and J.M. Boutet de Monvel, *Mathilde*), Rome, Apollo, 24 February 1821; *Zelmira,* A.L. Tottola (after Dormont de Belloy), Naples, San Carlo, 16 February 1822; *Semiramide,* G. Rossi (after Voltaire), Venice, La Fenice, 3 February 1823; *Il viaggio a Reims, ossia L'albergo del giglio d'oro,* L. Balocchi (after Staël, *Corinne*), Paris, Théâtre-Italien, 19 June 1825; partial revision as *Le Comte Ory* E. Scribe and C.G. Delestre-Poirson (after their play), Paris, Opèra, 20 August 1828; *Guillaume Tell,* E. de Jouy, H.-L.-F. Bis et al. (after Schiller), Paris, Opéra, 3 August 1829.

Rossini's operatic career was short but intensely busy and productive. Only 19 years separated the composition of his first complete opera (*La cambiale di matrimonio,* 1810) from his last (*Guillaume Tell,* 1829); those nineteen years saw the composition of thirty-eight operas (not including the very early *Demetrio e Polibio,* the extent of Rossini's contribution to which is not clear). Rossini's career took him from Bologna, where he studied, first to the major theaters of northern Italy, then to Naples, and finally to Paris. This geographical progress coincided with three phases of Rossini's career and of the development of his operatic art. During the first and most prolific phase, 1810-1815, he wrote thirteen operas, most for the theaters of Venice and Milan. Many of these were one-act comic operas; the full-length operas, like those of Rossini's great eighteenth-century predecessors Cimarosa and Paisiello, were about evenly divided between *opera buffa* and *opera seria.* Naples witnessed the second phase of Rossini's career (1815-1822), devoted almost exclusively to serious opera, but with trips to Rome for the composition of two of his greatest comic operas, *Il barbiere di Siviglia* (1816) and *La Cenerentola* (1817). The third and final phase (1823-29) brought Rossini to Paris, saw a brief return to comic opera (*Le Comte Ory,* 1828), and culminated in his last opera, *Guillaume Tell.*

Rossini wrote many of his earliest works for the Teatro San Moisè in Venice. This theater specialized in one-act *farse,* comic operas that required simple staging, a small orchestra, no chorus and few rehearsals: perfect conditions for a young and inexperienced composer to try out new works. Rossini's early comic *farse* are infused with the spirit of late eighteenth-century *opera buffa.*

La cambiale di matrimonio is a conventional story along the lines of Cimarosa's *Il matrimonio segreto.* One can sense in Rossini's music his eagerness to challenge what was regarded at the time as a twenty-year-old classic. The entrance aria of Slook, a rich man engaged in absentia to the young heroine Fanny, was an open invitation for Rossini to match Cimarosa's

"Senza tante cerimonie." "Dite presto dove stà," the duet for the two comic basses Slook and Sir Tobia (Fanny's father), rivals Cimarosa's duet "Se fiato in corpo avete." To these and other conventional dramatic situations Rossini responded with his own effortless inventiveness. Sometimes a single delightful idea brings an entire number to life: this happens near the end of the duet "Dite presto dove stà," when, at the words "grazie tante," a pretty sequential passage suffuses everything with unexpected charm.

From the beginning of his career Rossini revealed himself to be a skillful and original composer of overtures. Using the same sonata form that the Viennese masters used for the first movements of their symphonies, Rossini created overtures that were totally different from anything written in Vienna—or in Italy, for that matter—and were instantly recognizable as products of his particular mind. Rossini's crescendos earned the disdain of Berlioz and Wagner, but others have felt and appreciated the excitement and

Gioachino Rossini, c. 1816

originality of Rossini's overtures. When Bernard Shaw attended a concert in celebration of the centenary of Rossini's birth in 1892, he reported of the performance of several of Rossini's overtures: "Nobody was disgusted, à la Berlioz, by 'the brutal crescendo and big drum.' On the contrary, we were exhilerated and amused; and I, for one, was astonished to find it all still so fresh, so imposing, so clever, and even, in a few serious passages, so really fine."

With *Tancredi* and *L'italiana in Algeri* (both first performed in Venice in 1813) Rossini began to establish an international reputation as a brilliant composer of both *opera seria* and *opera buffa*. Everywhere in these operas one finds evidence of Rossini's extraordinary melodic and harmonic gifts. Working comfortably within the musical conventions of his time, Rossini managed to bring subtle originality to his melodic lines and their harmonic underpinnings. Also admirable is Rossini's endless supply of imaginative orchestral figuration with which he accompanied both long, lyrical lines and parlando passages.

In 1815 Domenico Barbaia, the impresario of the Teatro San Carlo in Naples, persuaded the 23-year-old Rossini to settle in Naples as the music director of San Carlo. During the next seven years Rossini devoted most of his compositional efforts to the genre which predominated at San Carlo, *opera seria*. Rossini's Neapolitan operas show him taking inspiration from the operatic conditions that confronted him, and not only in terms of operatic genre. The ample and well-trained chorus of San Carlo encouraged Rossini to give the chorus an increasingly important role in his music dramas. The large and fine orchestra of the Teatro San Carlo caused him to use orchestral color to great dramatic effect. Rossini's first opera for Naples, *Elisabetta, regina d'Inghilterra* (1815) was also his first opera to abandon simple recitative in favor of orchestrally accompanied recitative throughout.

Rossini's flair for orchestral music, already evident in the overtures for many of the earlier operas, takes on new vigor and grandeur in the Neapolitan operas. Not only overtures, but marches, orchestral interludes, and long introductions (often with beautiful and elaborate solos), enrich *Otello* (1816), *La donna del lago* (1819) and *Maometto II* (1820); even as early as *Elisabetta,* Rossini made effective use of San Carlo's orchestral resources, coloring Leicester's prison scene with two English horns and strengthening the orchestration of the overture that he had composed for *Aureliano in Palmira* (1813) and now reused for *Elisabetta*. The fine canonic quintet near the beginning of *Mosè in Egitto* (1818), with harp, low strings (no violins), horns, and delicate touches of woodwind color may serve as one example of Rossini's orchestrational genius as it was inspired by the orchestra of San Carlo.

The availability of certain singers also shaped Rossini's art, as, for example, when the presence of several talented tenors in Naples caused Rossini to write three major tenor parts in *Otello* and to represent the conflicts between Otello and Rodrigo on the one hand and between Otello and Iago on the other as contests between tenors. In other Neapolitan operas too much of the drama is a product of the way in which Rossini engineered the relationship between the great virtuosos for whom he wrote and the audience that heard them sing. Rossini's genius was theatrical as well as musical. Arsace's entrance in *Semiramide* (Venice, 1823), preceded by a long orchestral introduction, is a great *coup de théâtre* in which the composer presented the singer to the audience at La Fenice, "Eccomi alfine in Babilonia" ("Here I am finally in Babilonia"). An innocuous platitude becomes, in Rossini's hands, one of the most memorable and dramatic moments in all of opera.

In 1821, the impresario Barbaia left Naples and took over the direction of the Court Opera in Vienna. Rossini accepted Barbaia's invitation to come to Vienna to present his operas there; this trip was followed by another to Paris and London (1823). The successes that Rossini achieved abroad encouraged him to take up the position of music director at the Théâtre Italien in Paris the following year, but not before composing one more opera for the city that saw most of his earliest successes. *Semiramide*, Rossini's last opera for Italy, was first performed at La Fenice, Venice, in February 1823, ten years almost to the day after *Tancredi* was first performed in the same theater.

Rossini arrived in Paris a celebrity whose musical supremacy was acknowledged by most of Europe; yet, as often in the past, he felt a need to rework older material. Rossini based most of his Parisian operas on Italian works: his Neapolitan opera *Maometto II* served as the basis for *Le siège de Corinthe* and *Mosè in Egitto* as the basis for *Moïse*. But to *Guillaume Tell* he devoted all his creativity and originality, recasting his musical style in the service of grand opera at its finest.

Everything in *Guillaume Tell* is on a grand scale. The splendid overture, so overplayed that it has, for modern audiences, lost much of the effect with which it must have stunned and delighted early audiences, shows Rossini to have been fully in command of the resources of the Opéra's large and disciplined orchestra. In the first-act duet "Où vas-tu? Quel transport l'agile" for Arnold and Guillaume we can see how Rossini could use the extraordinary flexibility of structure that he learned, above all, in the composition of ensembles for *opera buffa*, to construct a serious, dramatic confrontation between a young lover and a mature patriot. The duet for the lovers Arnold and Mathilde "Oui, vous l'arrachez à mon ame" (act II) is on a similarly enormous scale, but lacks some of the inventiveness and pure theatrical excitement that animates some of the ensembles in Rossini's earlier operas. Arnold's aria "Asile hérétidaire" (act IV) is a grandiose display of tenor heroics, a rousing call to arms that makes some of Rossini's earlier tenors (Edward in *La cambiale di matrimonio*, Lindoro in *L'italiana in Algeri*, even Otello) sound a little boyish in comparison. As one listens to *Guillaume Tell*, with its astonishing richness of invention, one is tempted to believe that Rossini thought it likely, as he wrote this opera, that he would compose no more operas after it. He lavished all his craft, all his dramatic power, on a last, triumphant spectacle.—JOHN A. RICE

Ruffo, Titta

Baritone. Born 9 June 1877, in Pisa. Died 5 July 1953, in Florence. Studied with Senatore Sparapani, Venceslao Persichini, and Lelio Casini. Debut as the Herald in Lohengrin, *at the Teatro Costanzi in Rome, 9 April 1898; appeared in Chile, 1900; appeared at Teatro Massimo in Egypt, 1901, Covent Garden in 1903, and as Rigoletto at Teatro alla Scala in 1904; United States debut as Rigoletto in Philadelphia, 1912; served in Italian army 1917-18; debut at Metropolitan Opera as Rossini's Figaro, 1922, and remained at Met until 1929.*

Titta Ruffo (Ruffo Cafiero Titta) was born in Pisa, on 9 June 1877. His father, Oreste, was an iron worker and young Ruffo, never allowed to attend school, started to work in his father's shop when he was ten years old. As he was growing up, his older brother Ettore, a music student at the time, took young Ruffo to a performance of *Cavalleria rusticana*. He was so impressed by the performance that upon returning home from the theater, he begged Ettore to play the "Siciliana" on his flute. As Ruffo later recalled, almost unaware of what he was doing, he began to sing "in a tenor voice of such beauty and spontaneity that when the music ended we looked at each other with astonishment. [Ettore] could not explain where my voice came from, and clasping his flute with trembling hands exclaimed: 'This is a miracle!' "

Years later, fellow baritone and colleague Giuseppe de Luca expressed the same sentiment. Asked to comment on Titta Ruffo's voice, he said: "That was no voice—it was a miracle!" This assessment is borne out by all contemporary reviews and the recordings. Ruffo's voice had a natural placement, and it only needed schooling and refinement. Senatore Sparapani taught him the rudiments of singing and breath control; he then attended the classes of Venceslao Persichini at the Accademia di Santa Cecilia of Rome for about six months. After quitting the Academy, he received sporadic private instruction from the baritone Lelio Casini. With his funds depleted, he could wait no longer: he either had to obtain an engagement or give up the dream of a singing career. After a series of auditions he was engaged to sing the Herald in *Lohengrin* at the Teatro Costanzi in Rome. He made his debut on 9 April 1898, under the name of Titta Ruffo, reversing his given and family name upon the suggestion of an impresario who found it more euphonious.

Ruffo's first engagements were in the Italian provinces, and he advanced slowly to larger and more important theaters. His first South American engagement took him to Chile, from July through October 1900. On the long sea voyage he met mezzo-soprano Adelina Fanton Fontana (1867-1907), a member of the company, who had a lasting influence on his life and career. She helped him artistically and became his companion until her premature death.

Titta Ruffo (Culver Pictures)

A series of important milestones followed. Ruffo appeared at the Teatro Massimo of Palermo and in Egypt in 1901, Buenos Aires and Montevideo in 1902, Covent Garden and La Fenice in Venice in 1903, the Teatro alla Scala in 1904, Russia and Paris in 1905, Vienna in 1906, and the San Carlo of Naples in 1908. During his Russian tours (1905-07) he sang in Moscow, St Petersburg, Kiev, Odessa, and Khar'kov. In 1908 he took part in the inaugural season of the Teatro Colón in Buenos Aires, and he returned to that city for the next three summers (and five more seasons between 1915 and 1931). He made his North American debut as Rigoletto in Philadelphia, on 4 November 1912, and his success prompted the company to rent the Metropolitan Opera House for a single performance of Ambroise Thomas' *Hamlet,* a great personal triumph for Ruffo. He then moved on to Chicago where he first appeared on 29 November 1912, again in *Rigoletto.* He soon became a local favorite and returned there for several seasons before and after the war.

Ruffo served two years in the Italian army (1917-18) and after resuming his career he rejoined the Chicago company in 1920. He became a member of the Metropolitan Opera Company in the season following Caruso's death, and made his debut as Rossini's Figaro on 19 January 1922. He remained a member of the company until 1929, singing seven roles in 55 performances, 47 of those in the house. After leaving the Met he returned to North America once more, to participate in the festive opening program of Radio City Music Hall (27 December 1932).

Between his extended engagements, Ruffo toured extensively. He sang in most major cities, opera houses, and auditoriums of Europe, and North and South America. He sang most often in Argentina, where he was lionized by his devoted public. During his best years his fees were the highest among baritones, ranking with those of Caruso and Chaliapin. He took part in five world premieres; on 13 December 1920 he created the title role of Leoncavallo's *Edipo re* in Chicago, a role that was expressly composed for him.

Lacking any formal education, Ruffo was an autodidact. He had a great interest in the arts, and he read extensively, particularly about the historical characters he was to impersonate and the period in which they lived. Purely fictional characters he would occasionally model on real persons. One of his most successful creations, Tonio in *Pagliacci,* was based on a poor retarded man he met several times in a forest near the place where he was vacationing. His other widely acclaimed roles were Rigoletto, the title role of *Hamlet,* and Figaro. His large repertoire included 56 roles, among them the major Verdi, Puccini, Leoncavallo, and Giordano roles; from the French repertory Hamlet, Escamillo, Nelusko, Athanael, Valentin and Méphistophèles *(Faust);* from the Russian repertory Boris Godunov, Eugene Onegin, and the title role of Rubinstein's *Demon.* His only Mozart role was Don Giovanni. Ruffo's versatility extended to the legitimate theater as well: in 1915 he participated in a stage performance of *Amphion* at the side of actor Gustavo Salvini. Ruffo spoke pure Italian with exemplary diction, which can be heard in his two recorded monologues from Shakespeare's *Hamlet.*

Because of overuse, the prodigal voice began to fail by the time Ruffo reached fifty, and he was obliged to retire in his mid-fifties. Some maintain that he was forced into early retirement because he never learned to sing properly, but logic suggests otherwise. His steady engagements lasted from 1898 until the end of 1932, and a thirty-four year time-span is anything but a short career. Furthermore, a faultily produced voice could not have withstood the relentless demands imposed upon it for over three decades.

Ruffo's voice was unique in every respect. It had extraordinary power without parallel in his lifetime, a highly individual and appealing timbre with a brilliant sheen and an incisive vibrato. He produced the voluminous sound with a free, unobstructed throat, and the voice, like Caruso's, seemed to open up and gain in brilliance with every note moving up on the scale. In his best years Ruffo had an easy top to a recorded high A and a privately witnessed high C. The forward placement of the voice, "in the mask," gave it unique resonance, supported by a spectacular breath control that made his cadenza of the *Hamlet* "Drinking Song" a perennial show-stopper. Although the voice was perfectly equalized, the recordings show that the lowest notes of his range were less secure, and they noticeably weakened toward the end of his career.

Titta Ruffo was an honest, ethical man, a staunch anti-fascist who suffered great indignities at the hands of the fascist regime. Plaques commemorating his appearances in Pisa and Terni were vandalized by the blackshirts; before an appearance in Marseille he was attacked by fascist thugs; his passport was revoked and he was even briefly incarcerated on the orders of

Mussolini. The socialist leader Giacomo Matteotti, kidnapped and assassinated by the fascists in 1924, was the husband of his sister Velia. Restricted in his movements, Ruffo spent most of his retirement years in his native Pisa, and he died in 1953. He left a recorded legacy against which all other baritones are measured. The recordings have a lasting appeal and have been frequently reissued, most recently in a two-album set containing all of his records, including unpublished takes. He made fifteen sides for Pathé in 1904, and thereafter recorded only for the Gramophone Company ("His Master's Voice") in Milan and London, and the Victor Talking Machine Co. in Camden, N.J. and New York. His records show the maturing of his interpretations and the development, zenith, and eventual decline of his immense voice that Andrès de Segurola likened to the "imposing mass of the Niagara Falls—no end in sight."—ANDREW FARKAS

Rusalka

Composer: *Antonin Dvořák.*

Librettist: *J. Kvapil.*

First Performance: *Prague, National Theater, 31 March 1901.*

Roles: *Rusalka (soprano); Prince (tenor); Watersprite (bass); Jezabibaba (contralto); Foreign Princess (soprano); Hunter (baritone); Gamekeeper (tenor); Kitchenboy (soprano); Three Dryads; chorus (SATB) (SSAA).*

The ninth of Dvořák's ten operas, *Rusalka* was composed in 1900, the same year in which Puccini's *Tosca* and Gustave Charpentier's *Louise* were first performed. And yet in contrast to the verismo, or realistic, treatment of everyday life in *Tosca* and *Louise* (in the case of the former some have said overly realistic, most notably Joseph Kerman when he penned his oft-quoted assessment of the opera as "that shabby little shocker" dressed up in "café-music banality"), *Rusalka,* like Humperdinck's *Hänsel und Gretel* which reached Prague five years earlier in 1895, is a reaction against the blood-and-guts violence of verismo. Dvořák in fact called *Rusalka* a "lyric fairy-tale in three acts." His librettist, Jaroslav Kvapil (not to be confused with the composer of the same name, a pupil of Janáček's), in fashioning the opera's sequence of dreamlike scenes, noted that he was inspired to take up the subject "in the land of [Hans Christian] Andersen, on the island of Bornholm, where I was spending my summer holidays. The fairy-tales of Karel Jaromír Erben and Božena Němcová accompanied me to the seashore, and there merged into a single tale in the manner of Andersen." As it happens, the sea had a profound effect on Kvapil, for what he produced was another version of the ancient French story of Mélusine, the Lorelei, Friedrich de La Motte-Fouqué's *Undine,* Andersen's *The Little Mermaid,* and the Ruthie in Gerhardt Hauptman's *Sunken Bell,* all of which tell of the doomed love of a water nymph and a mortal man.

Kvapil's account, praised by no less a master librettist than Hugo von Hofmannsthal (librettist of six of Richard Strauss's operas) for its "pleasing musical verse, full of tender, shimmering and shadowy moods, the work of an artist who was also a fine connoisseur of the stage and its requirements," opens not by the shore of some large sea, but rather at the edge of a forest lake. There the water nymph Rusalka sings of her love for a handsome prince. She describes her love to the old Water Sprite, whom she calls father, in unequivocally sensual terms: "He comes here often, reposes in my embrace, he leaves his clothes on the shore and plunges into my arms. Yet I am just a wave, he cannot sense my being." And so Rusalka yearns to be made human, to "live in the sunshine," so that she might love. Her wish is granted by the witch Ježibaba, but for a price: in human form she must remain mute, and should she be rejected in love both she and her lover will be cast into the lake in "eternal damnation." Although Rusalka has been taken by the prince to his castle by act II, we soon discover that her embrace "is always cold," that she does not "burn with passion." Thus the prince turns his attention to a lovely foreign princess. At the start of act III, rejected by the prince, Rusalka sits again at the edge of the forest lake, her youth vanished, her hair turned white. Ježibaba emerges from her cottage and sings, "Short has been your honeymooning, long will be your lamenting." Rusalka again asks the witch to grant her a wish: return her to her life as a water nymph. Once more there is a price. She must slay her seducer. Her refusal prompts Ježibaba to deliver a jeering rebuke: "Into silly human form you have been lured—and now you lack the strength to spill human blood. Man attains manhood only when he has dipped his hand in blood, when moved by passion he becomes drunk with his neighbor's blood." Rusalka seeks refuge in the lake but is rebuffed by her former sisters, the three Dryads. "Do not descend to us," they ominously intone, lest "with the will-o'-the-wisps you play, to entice people to their graves!" At the opera's end it is the prince who now approaches the lake's edge, the place where he first met Rusalka. She suddenly appears, lighted by the glow of the moon. The prince ardently begs her for a kiss. She warns him, "If I kiss you now, you are lost for all time." Staggering toward her he repeats the request. At last she yields. To his now mute and lifeless body she sings: "Because you loved, because you were humanly fickle, because of all that makes up my fate—God have mercy on your human soul!" The curtain falls as Rusalka returns at last to the depths of the forest lake.

Lovingly and intelligently produced, the "sweet sadness"—as one critic has aptly put it—at the heart of *Rusalka* can make for an intensely moving theatrical experience. (Despite its success and undeniable merit, one must wonder if the English National production, available on videotape, set as it is by David Poultney in an Edwardian nursery replete with incestuous undertones, is really in touch with the story envisioned by its creators.) The score, rich and ample in its orchestration, contains some of the most beautiful melodies Dvořák would ever compose. His use of recurring motives for the principal characters, a system he appears to have conceived independently of Wagner or of Smetana, is as ingenious as it is subtle. His bewitching tone-painting of the moonlight forest is capable of holding a modern, cough-prone audience in rapt silence. Evocations of nature clearly brought out the very best in Dvořák. The only one of his operas to win a place in the international repertory, *Rusalka* nevertheless deserves to be known by a far greater number of listeners than the record collector who occasionally puts on Rusalka's lovely aria "O silver moon" or those lucky enough to live near operatic companies dedicated to adventurous fare. Opera houses—and their audiences—in need of a rest from the same handful of war-horses could do well by *Rusalka*. Dvořák at his very best can be glorious indeed.—JAMES PARSONS

Rysanek, Leonie

Soprano. Born 12 November 1926, in Vienna. Married: musicologist E.L. Gausmann. Studied at Vienna Conservatory, with Alfred Jerger, Rudolf Grossman, and Clothilde Radony von Ottean; debut as Agathe in Der Freischütz, *Innsbruck, 1949; sang Sieglinde in first postwar Bayreuth Festival, 1951; Bavarian State Opera, Munich, 1952-54; Covent Garden debut as Danae, 1953; Vienna State Opera debut, 1954; American debut as Senta in* Der fliegende Holländer, *San Francisco, 1956; Metropolitan Opera debut as Lady Macbeth, 1959; Metropolitan Opera Gala celebrated her 25th anniversary with the company, 1984; her twenty roles there include Elisabeth, the Marschallin, Tosca, Salome, Aida, Elsa, and Desdemona.*

Throughout her forty-year career, Leonie Rysanek has garnered some of the warmest accolades imaginable from critics, the public, and from her fellow singers. Not only has she been acclaimed as one of the most exciting actresses to mount the opera stage; not only has her voice not deteriorated over the decades but actually grown stronger in terms of the middle voice; not only has she never lost the soaring, gleaming top that allows her to excel in a number of Strauss roles; but she has constantly expanded her repertoire until it encompasses an astonishing diversity of parts. With the heights have, admittedly, come also the depths. In addition to the early problems with the insecurity of the middle voice, there was initially no low register to speak of. In her own words, however, she had "two things by nature: an extremely good top and extremely easy pianissimo, . . . and fortissimo up there, from the G up." It was not until her early forties (around 1970) that the middle voice was suddenly there.

Inevitably Rysanek is compared to her Germanic predecessors. It has been pointed out that with her glorious top register, she was able to assume the Strauss roles associated with the glamorous Maria Jeritza, and John Steane hears in her something of the creamy quality of Tiana Lemnitz. Rysanek's is a voice to experience above all in the theater. On recordings the unsteady middle voice, the lack of bite sometimes apparent, and the overt histrionics do not always make for a satisfying listening experience. Fortunately a number of her recordings are products of the theater rather than the studio. In her 1967 Sieglinde for Karl Böhm at Bayreuth she is, as in a number of recordings, not in the best vocal estate but, as always, expressive, and her high notes are exhilarating. One can hear the "coital scream" she unleashes in act I as Siegmund wrenches the sword from the tree. Her Kundry from Bayreuth, where she sang frequently, exists in a nearly complete version with Siegfried Jerusalem under Janowski. Although she made a studio recording of *Die Frau ohne Schatten* under Böhm in conjunction with the 1955 Vienna staging, a more vital one exists, also under Böhm (whom she has termed her "musical father"), live from the Staatsoper in 1977. Rysanek in this performance typically takes a portion of the evening to warm up but is very impressive in the power and radiance she brings to the high-lying role, especially when one considers that she had been singing this difficult music for nearly twenty-five years and only doing it better with the passage of time.

Other Rysanek recordings were made in the studio, yet were, as with the early *Frau,* associated with concurrent stagings. Such was the 1959 Lady Macbeth under Leinsdorf, made when she substituted for Callas in the Metropolitan Opera production. Rysanek's Lady is beautifully sung and typically thrilling dramatically. In addition to Sieglinde, the Empress in *Die Frau ohne Schatten* (a role in which no one could challenge her), and Kundry, Rysanek's other greatest roles were Senta and Elisabeth. It should be noted that she declined certain parts, e.g., Isolde, Turandot, Elektra, and Brünnhilde, because she considered that Birgit Nilsson did them to perfection. Yet she and the Swedish soprano were good colleagues, appearing together not only in *Die Frau* but also in *Elektra,* in which Rysanek took on the soaring soprano role of Chrysothemis. She was slated to do this part for Solti's recording of *Elektra* with Nilsson, but had to cancel.

Recorded documents exist of Rysanek's greatest roles. In addition to the 1967 Bayreuth Sieglinde, she made one in the studio in 1954 with Furtwängler in which she begins act I poorly but ends triumphantly, giving a tantalizing glimpse of how inspired she was on the stage; there is also an act III from 1951 with Karajan that includes a thrilling "O hehrstes Wunder." In 1961 she recorded Senta with George London as the Dutchman; here she displays her gorgeous pianissimo singing, although she is not overall in best voice. Her arias from *Tannhäuser* probably most readily display the quality of Lemnitz that can be heard in the voice.

Additional Germanic roles include the Marschallin, captured on a 1955 highlights disc with the Berlin Philharmonic under Schuchter, a famous revival of *Die ägyptische Helena* in Munich under Keilberth (which was for Harold Rosenthal the finest soprano singing he heard that year, 1956), Salome, Leonore, and Ortrud. Her rapturously confident top register can be heard to good advantage in a 1958 recording of Leonore in *Fidelio* under Fricsay. Of the Italian repertoire, in addition to Lady Macbeth there is an early Abigaille at the Metropolitan Opera, as well as Tosca, Aida, Gioconda, Elisabetta in *Don Carlos, Un ballo in maschera,* and *La forza del destino.* There is a sumptuous recording of Verdi's *Otello* with Jon Vickers and Tito Gobbi, conducted with great love and mastery by the veteran Tullio Serafin. Other notable roles undertaken by Rysanek included Medea, and Kostelnicka in Janáček's *Jenůfa.*

There is no doubt that in everything she performed, Rysanek gave the utmost of herself. She was a singing-actress who gambled mightily and when that gamble paid off, as it often did, she was supreme.—STEPHEN WILLIER

OPERAs

St François d'Assise [St Francis of Assisi]

Composer: *Olivier Messiaen.*

Librettist: *Olivier Messiaen (after the anonymous 14th-century* Fioretti *and* Contemplations of the Stigmata*).*

First Performance: *Paris, Opéra, 28 November 1983.*

Roles: *The Angel (soprano); St Francis (baritone); The Leper (tenor); Brother Leon (baritone); Brother Massée (tenor); Brother Elie (tenor); Brother Bernard (bass); Brother Sylvester (bass); Brother Rufin (bass); chorus.*

It is perhaps surprising that a composer who in his early days took an intense interest in opera and the plays of Shakespeare should not have embarked on writing an opera himself until the age of sixty-six. By his own admission, he would not have started such a project even then had it not been for the insistence of Rolf Liebermann of the Paris Opéra, who commissioned the work. Messiaen himself felt that he had no gift for the theater, in spite of his early interest in works written for it. The choice of subject was the composer's own, and it was natural, in the light of his own religious convictions, that he should choose St Francis of Assisi as his subject. In addition, the legend of St Francis preaching to the birds gave Messiaen the opportunity to indulge his own love of birdsong as part of the musical material of the opera. The libretto is by the composer himself, who began work on the poem in the summer of 1975. The music was composed between 1975 and 1979 and orchestrated from 1979 to 1983.

The opera does not attempt to present the complete story of St Francis' life, but consists rather of a series of tableaux representing events or episodes which were crucial in St Francis' spiritual development as based on *Fioretti* and *Contemplations on the Stigmata* by anonymous Franciscan friars of the fourteenth century. The work contains three acts, the first two divided into three tableaux each and the third into two tableaux. In the first tableau, *La croix* (The Cross), Francis explains to a fellow-friar, Brother Leon, that it is essential to endure all sufferings with patience for the love of Christ. In the second tableau, *Les laudes* (Lauds), after the morning office, Francis asks God to let him meet a leper and make him capable of loving him. The third tableau,

714

Le baiser au lépreux (The Kissing of the Leper) fulfils Francis' prayer. He visits a leper hospital and meets a leper. Francis eventually overcomes his revulsion and embraces the man, thus curing him of his leprosy. Simultaneously with the cure of the leper, Francis experiences grace; this is the point, says Messiaen, at which Francis achieves sanctity and becomes Saint Francis.

The fourth tableau, *L'ange voyageur* (The traveling angel), at the beginning of the second act, is the only one in which St Francis does not appear. An angel, who is taken for a traveler by the characters in the opera, appears outside the friary. He knocks at the door with a loud noise (symbolizing the inrush of grace) and asks a question about predestination. In the fifth tableau, *L'ange musicien* (The Angel as Musician), the angel appears to St Francis and plays to him on the viol (represented by three ondes martenot in the orchestra) in order to give him a foretaste of heavenly bliss. The sixth tableau, *Le prêche aux oiseaux* (The Sermon to the Birds), takes place at Carceri in Assisi. The birds reply to St Francis' sermon with a grand chorus. In this section Messiaen exploits a new technique in his treatment of birdsong. Although the rhythms are notated exactly, some songs commence at a signal from the conductor and are played at their own tempo, independent of the rest of the orchestra.

Act III begins with the tableau in which St Francis receives the stigmata (*Les stigmates*). Five luminous rays shine out from the cross and pierce both hands and feet and the right side of St Francis, accompanied by the same hammer-blows from the orchestra which were used for the angel's knock on the door of the friary. The five wounds are the divine seal of the sanctity of St Francis. The last tableau, *La mort et la nouvelle vie* (Death and New Life), portrays Francis' death as he sings the last verse of his *Canticle of Creatures*. Surrounded by his brethren, the angel and the leper, he dies. Bells toll, everyone disappears, and while the chorus sings of the Resurrection, a spot of light, which increases to blinding intensity, shines on the place where the body of St Francis lay.

Theatrically, the work is very static, but it nevertheless makes a powerful impact, and the music contains some of Messiaen's most imaginative and inventive. While there is no use of *leitmotiv* in the Wagnerian sense, the main characters are symbolized by themes associated with them, varying according to the theatrical context. St Francis has five themes: a violin melody (the principle one), a harmonic theme consisting of a cluster followed by a trombone chord which accompanies his solemn pronouncements, a Decision theme, a theme of Joy, and in particular the song of the blackcap (*fauvette à tête noire*). Messiaen made a special journey to Carceri (the scene of the sermon to the birds) in order to note the song of the local blackcap which would have been familiar to St Francis.

In addition to birdsong, color (as in other works of Messiaen) plays an important role. The composer prescribes the color of the angel's wings, in particular, with great precision, and all the costumes are described in detail. Much of the inspiration comes from the frescoes and altarpieces of Fra Angelico in Florence; the angel is modeled on one of the Annunciations of Fra Angelico in the San Marco Museum.—ROBERT SHERLAW-JOHNSON

The Saint of Bleecker Street

Composer: *Gian Carlo Menotti.*
Librettist: *Gian Carlo Menotti.*
First Performance: *New York, 27 December 1954.*

Roles: *Annina (soprano); Desideria (mezzo-soprano); Michele (tenor); Don Marco (bass); Assunta (mezzo-soprano); Carmela (soprano); Maria Corona (mezzo-soprano); Salvatore (baritone); chorus (SSAATTBB).*

The Saint of Bleecker Street was written four years after *The Consul,* in the same period as *Amahl* and Menotti's first major works for the concert hall. It won a Drama Critics Award and the Pulitzer Prize (his second for both awards) and is the one composition of Menotti's that can possibly be classified as "verismo." The human emotions characterized here are devoid of supernatural imagery and dream sequences, and the people are real. To quote John Ardoin, "religion and faith are no longer side issues or subplots but the main event—the opera's heart and soul." The chorus is not just a vehicle for commentary, but a protagonist in its own right.

Michele and Annina, brother and sister, live in a cold-water flat on Bleecker Street, in the Little Italy section of New York's Greenwich Village. Annina, a young woman of extremely fragile health, has religious visions accompanied by bleeding stigmata in her hands, and is considered by the neighborhood to be a saint with miraculous powers, occasionally effecting miracle-healings. Her brother is a sceptic; to him the hysterically adoring mob and the Church's clerics have only exacerbated his sister's poor health, and were she (and they) rich, there would be no visions. His all-consuming love for and protective stance toward his sister border on incest, a situation he has never admitted to himself until confronted with it by Desideria, his girlfriend and lover. Evicted by her mother because of her liason with Michele, Desideria longs for marriage or at least a live-in arrangement, and in her fury at Michele's refusal, she accuses him of incestuous love for Annina. In a blind rage, he stabs Desideria in the back, an act that is witnessed by the celebrants leaving Carmela's and Salvatore's wedding reception. Michele flees for his life as his lover dies.

In a clandestine meeting, Annina begs Michele to turn himself in and accept his punishment, and reveals that she is determined to take holy orders and become a nun. Michele is desperate; he tells his sister that she is all he has to live for, and his need is greater than God's. Failing to win his argument, he curses her, shoves her away, and disappears into the subway, while Annina collapses in tears.

The final scene is back in Annina's tenement flat; pale and extremely ill, she is wrapped in a shawl and is resting in an armchair, surrounded by a nun and several women friends, including Carmela. To the latter Annina confides that her voices have told her she will take the veil today, and she asks Death to postpone his coming until permission arrives from Rome for her investiture. When Annina worries about having the required white dress and veil, Carmela produces her own wedding gown which she has brought for that purpose. Don Marco receives the letter from Rome, and relays the joyful news that Annina's wish has been granted, so the nun and Carmela help her to the bedroom to dress. Just then word comes that the ceremony might be interrupted by Michele, who is still determined to prevent her from becoming a nun. He does indeed arrive but is too late to prevent the investiture. Annina, in a holy trance, does not hear his outcry, and Michele can only stand staring as the initiate's hair is cut off and the ceremony draws toward an end. As Don Marco extends the gold wedding ring by which Annina becomes the Bride of Christ, she falls to the floor and dies as the priest kneels to place the ring on her finger.

The Saint marked the last of Menotti's works with which he tried to present opera as a self-sustaining financial endeavor. Although it ran for three months to packed houses, this theater piece never made money. Its autobiographical elements portray the ongoing conflict within

Menotti between his Catholic upbringing and subsequent lack of faith. Menotti considers Michele and Annina as opposing parts of himself.—JEAN C. SLOOP

Saint-Saëns, (Charles-) Camille

Composer. Born 9 October 1835, in Paris. Died 16 December 1921, in Algiers. Married: Marie Truffot, 1875 (separated 1881; two sons who died in infancy). Studied piano with his great-aunt, Charlotte Masson; studied with Stamaty, beginning 1842; debut as a pianist at the Salle Pleyel, 6 May 1846; studied harmony with Pierre Maleden; studied organ with Benoist and composition with Halévy at the Paris Conservatory; two unsuccessful attempts to win the Prix de Rome, 1852 and 1864; first prize of the Société Sainte-Cécile for his Ode à Sainte-Cécile, *1852; first symphony performed, 11 December 1853; organist at the church of Saint-Merry, Paris, 1853-57; succeeded Lefébure-Wély as organist at the Madeleine, 1857-76; taught piano at the Ecole Niedermeyer, 1861-65; Chevalier of the Legion of Honor, 1868; one of the founders of the Société Nationale de Musique, 1871; elected to the Institut de France, 1881; Officer of the Legion of Honor, 1884, Grand-Officier, 1900; in the United States, 1906; Grand-Croix of the Legion of Honor, 1913; tour of South America, 1916; honorary Mus. D. from Cambridge University; gave many of his manuscripts and belongings to the municipal museum in Dieppe, where they are preserved in a special section. Pupils included André Messager and Gabriel Fauré.*

Operas *La princesse jaune,* L. Gallet, Paris, Opéra-Comique, 12 June 1872; *Le timbre d'argent,* J. Barbier and M. Carré, Paris, National-Lyrique, 23 February 1877; *Samson et Dalila,* F. Lemaire, Weimar, Hoftheater, 2 December 1877; *Etienne Marcel,* Lyons, Grand Théâtre, 8 February 1879; *Henry VIII,* Détroyat and A. Silvestre, Paris, Opéra, 5 March 1883; *Proserpine,* L. Gallet (after V. Vacquerie), Paris, Opéra-Comique, 14 March 1887; *Ascanio,* L. Gallet (after P. Meurice), Paris, Opéra, 21 March 1890; *Phryné,* L. Augé de Lassus, Paris, Opéra-Comique, 24 May 1893; *Frédégonde* (with E. Guiraud), L. Gallet, Paris, Opéra, 18 December 1895; *Les barbares,* V. Sardou and P.B. Gheusi, Paris, Opéra, 23 October 1901; *Hélène,* C. Saint-Saëns, Monte Carlo, 18 February 1904; *L'ancêtre,* L. Augé de Lassus, Monte Carlo, 24 February 1906; *Déjanire,* Saint-Saëns (after L. Gallet), Monte Carlo, 14 March 1911.

Saint-Saëns was an unusually prolific musician who wrote in every medium, so it is not surprising that he should have been attracted to opera, which, in his day, was the surest way to fame and riches for the composer lucky enough to succeed. He wrote, in all, thirteen operas on a wide variety of subjects. They range from the charming little one-act *La princesse jaune* to the blood-boltered melodrama of *L'ancêtre,* from the pageantry of *Henry VIII* to the musical comedy frivolity of *Phryné.* His best-known opera is, of course, *Samson et Dalila,* although it took nearly twenty years to establish itself. When it did, however, it became one of the most popular items in the repertory—much to Saint-Saëns's annoyance when he reflected on how much it overshadowed his eleven other operas, none of which achieved real success.

The reason why Saint-Saëns never won fame as a major opera composer was that he had little sense of theater. Prodigiously gifted in every branch of music and endowed with a Mozartian facility, he lacked that precious instinct which his detested rival Massenet possessed in abundance. When he embarked on *Etienne Marcel,* an ambitious historical opera based on the leading figure in the struggles between the medieval guilds of Paris and the king, he tackled a subject to which only the grandiose and flashy technique of Meyerbeer could have done full justice. The music, as always, is elegant and skillfully shaped, but it fails to make its point on the stage. As in *Henry VIII,* for which he studied sixteenth-century manuscripts in the then music library at Buckingham Palace, the most telling passages are the more intimate moments: the love duets, the occasional meditative aria, the limpid ballet music. The attempt at Wagnerian grandeur does not come off.

The same verdict applies to *Les barbares,* in which, despite the collaboration with Victorien Sardou, the day's most successful playwright, Saint-Saëns failed to create an epic drawn from French history in the way Wagner had utilized the heroic legends of his own country. The story of a vestal virgin of ancient Gaul who breaks her vow to save a town from pillaging barbarians remains lifeless and unmoving. *Ascanio* will never rival Berlioz's opera *Benvenuto Cellini* which has the same hero, and it now belongs to the obscurity that shrouds *Déjanire* and *Proserpine.* The most successful, and the most deserving of revival, are the smaller works that do not call for extended inspiration or for accomplished stage technique. The best of them is *La princesse jaune,* an attractive example of *Japonaiserie* spiced with an amusingly Parisian brand of exoticism, deftly orchestrated and wittily written.

There remains the paradox of *Samson et Delila.* It has survived because, here, for once, the quality of inspiration rarely fails Saint-Saëns, and, more important still, the opera could almost as well be performed as an oratorio without harming any of the effect. It also has at least three big arias which are a gift for star singers, besides a colorful ballet familiar as an independent suite in the concert hall. Given these advantages, the only survivor of Saint-Saëns's operas shows no signs of losing its popularity.—JAMES HARDING

Salome

Composer: *Richard Strauss.*

Librettist: *Richard Strauss (based on H. Lachmann's translation of Oscar Wilde's play).*

First Performance: *Dresden, Court Opera, 9 December 1905.*

Roles: *Salome (soprano); Herod (tenor); Herodias (mezzo-soprano); Jokanaan (baritone); Narraboth (tenor); Page of Herodias (contralto); Five Jews (four tenors, bass); Two Nazarenes (tenor, bass); Two Soldiers (two basses); Cappadocian (bass); Slave (soprano).*

Strauss was not the first to use the story of the death of John the Baptist as the basis of a dramatic work, nor was Oscar Wilde, the author of Salome's literary source. Indeed, images of the beheading of John the Baptist are scattered throughout the visual as well as literary art of the latter nineteenth century. Wilde was drawn to the story by the paintings of Gustave Moreau, and the cruel, sultry illustrations produced by Aubrey Beardsley for Wilde's play are famous. Violent biblical women were a current source of subject material, Klimt having already painted Judith (from the Apocrypha) more than once. The art of Gustav Klimt, leader of the Viennese Secession, shows an obsession with beautiful, sensuous, and frighteningly cruel women, thoroughly congruent with the aesthetic of *Salome.*

The character of the daughter of Herodias in these artistic imaginations evolved considerably beyond the mindless girl of the brief biblical tale. The new Salome—determined, mature, beautiful, chaste, perverse—acts quite independently of any vengeful designs on the part of her mother. Yet in all its gory psychotic perversion, *Salome* is a brilliant reflection of the artistic tenor of Austria and Germany at the turn of the century, and deeply rooted in the currents of nineteenth-century literary Decadence, with its contorted language and macabre imagery, and its interest in death, the occult, and the erotic.

The story of the opera runs as follows: Herod the tetrarch holds John the Baptist imprisoned. Salome, daughter of Herod's wife Herodias, is obsessed with the captive, admiring his voice, his body, hair, and above all his mouth. When John sternly rebuffs her, she becomes obsessed. Herod in his turn is obsessed with Salome, insisting that she dance for him the dance of the seven veils. After Herod swears to give her whatever she asks, Salome agrees, afterwards demanding the head of John. In a lurid apostrophe to the head, Salome exults in her triumph, ecstatically kissing the severed head. The horrified king orders his soldiers to kill Salome.

With the very opening line "How beautiful Princess Salome is tonight!" the opera dives into the realm of sexual obsession, and the tension only builds from that moment until the end. The obsessive and neurotic atmosphere is underscored by the weird repetitive nature of the text. John drones on with his imprecations, the Jews bicker over the nature of John, and Herod in his overpowering anxiety repeatedly worries that "something terrible" will happen. The recurrence

The first production of *Salome,* with Marie Wittich as Salome, Karl Burian as Herodes, and Irene von Chavanne as Herodias

of textual themes, together with the visual motif of the moon and the constantly recurring musical motifs, is not only suggestive of obsession, but eerily reminiscent of biblical language.

Strauss' score forms a brilliant exegesis of the neurotic, sensual obsessions of the characters on the stage. Opening directly, without a prelude, the music is a dense network of tense *Leitmotifs* which appear over and over, altered in rhythm, harmony, and color as they recur in a changing web of meaning and association. The crisp and memorable motives developed in Strauss' tone poems are here employed to devastating effect, moving far beyond such musical depictions as Don Quixote's harmless obsession or Till Eulenspiegel's death knell. *Salome's* motifs are nagging, uneasy, piercing, vicious. By the end, the *idée fixe* of Salome's obsession, piercing through a veil of harsh trills, is scarcely endurable.

Despite the execution of Salome at the end, there is no moral judgment passed on her behavior. A desperate and amoral hunt for pure sensation and novelty, characteristic of Decadence, leads inevitably away from moral strictures. When sensation is all that matters, rules do not apply: not to the linguistics of poetry, the harmony of music, or the morals of social behavior. An oblique theological justification is advanced by one of the bickering Jews, who says, "God is in what is evil even as He is in what is good." But Wilde himself wrote, "I myself would sacrifice everything for a new experience, and I know there is no such thing as a new experience at all . . . I would go to the stake for a sensation and be a sceptic to the last!"

Certainly not everyone was sympathetic to the sentiments, aesthetic or otherwise, expressed in *Salome*. The 1905 premiere in Dresden caused a terrific scandal. In London and in Berlin, where Strauss was conductor of the Royal Court Opera, premieres were delayed and the opera censored. When *Salome* was given at the Metropolitan Opera House in New York, in 1907, it was withdrawn after one performance. "Bestial!" "corrupt!" "blasphemous!" cried viewers. But the opera did not die. Perhaps it was irresistible precisely because it was such an accurate reflection of its time; indeed, *Salome* is remarkable for expressing so clearly so many contemporary cultural currents. Herodias' crazed daughter is a vision at once compelling and troubling of Old Testament society, reinterpreted for the modern age and given vivid expression by musicians, artists, and writers alike, united in the multi-media genre of opera.

Salome triumphed in spite of, or perhaps because of, the scandal and shock it caused, to become Strauss' first operatic triumph and one of the most influential works of the time. As Strauss later commented wryly, "Wilhelm II once said, 'I am sorry Strauss composed this *Salome*. I really like the fellow, but this will do him a lot of damage.' The damage enabled me to build my villa in Garmisch."—ELIZABETH W. PATTON

Samson et Dalila [Samson and Delilah]

Composer: *Camille Saint-Saëns.*

Librettist: *F. Lemaire.*

First Performance: *Weimar, Hoftheater, 2 December 1877.*

Roles: *Samson (tenor); Dalila (mezzo-soprano or contralto); High Priest to Dagon (baritone); Abimelech (bass); An Old Hebrew (bass); chorus (SSAATTBB).*

The plot of *Samson et Dalila* closely follows the story of Samson as told in Chapter XVI of the Book of Judges. The only main change is that Dalila hands Samson over to the Philistines for patriotic reasons and not, as in the Bible, for eleven hundred pieces of silver—an alteration probably introduced to avoid offending the susceptibilities of opera audiences at the time. The work had originally been intended as an oratorio, but the librettist, a Creole poet named Ferdinand Lemaire who was distantly related to Saint-Saëns by marriage, insisted that it should be an opera. Portions of the second act were quickly written in 1867, but, when tried out privately, they met with little enthusiasm. Then, on a visit to Liszt in Weimar, Saint-Saëns was encouraged by the remark: "Finish your opera. I will have it performed in Weimar." Liszt was as good as his word: in 1877 he sponsored the world premiere in that town. But French impresarios remained uninterested since they traditionally regarded biblical subjects as box-office poison, and *Samson et Dalila* had to wait a long time before reaching the Paris Opéra in 1892.

It is Saint-Saëns' only successful opera, largely because its oratorio-like form and uncomplicated story line enabled him to concentrate on the purely musical aspects instead of seeking after theatrical effect. The many gifts Saint-Saëns possessed did not include a highly developed sense of theater, which is why none of his other stage-works survives today. In *Samson et Dalila* this lack of feeling for the stage did not matter greatly, and Saint-Saëns could give full rein to his musical genius. He was an eclectic composer able to assimilate a wide variety of different styles, absorb them, and turn them deftly to his own use. As an early enthusiast of Handel, whose music was then little known in France, he brought a sombre Handelian power to the choral writing, notably in the laments of the oppressed Hebrews, and his contrapuntal style is, as always, impeccable. Samson's impassioned arias—"Arrêtez, ô mes frères," for example, and "Israël romps ta chaîne,"—are an inspired continuation of Meyerbeer at his most stirring. *Samson et Dalila* is historically important too in that it brings exoticism into French music. However facile the oriental languors of the ballet music may seem today, it should be remembered that prior to Saint-Saëns none of his insular compatriots, with the possible exception of that minor figure Félicien David, had sought inspiration very far beyond the frontiers of their own country.

Most important of all, Saint-Saëns rose to the occasion by giving Dalila melodies of a delectable but subtle sensuality. Passion is not normally a strong point of his music, yet in depicting the great temptress he drew on reserves of unexpected voluptuousness. "Printemps qui commence" is full of an amorous yearning which flames into raging desire with "Amour viens aider ma faiblesse," where Dalila's sexual longing mingles ardently with feelings of patriotism. "Mon coeur s'ouvre à ta voix" is one of the most famous arias ever written, a love song in which the effect is skillfully ensured by chromatic variation of the melodic line. Dalila's music alone, together with the sensational climax when Samson brings the pillars of the temple crashing down, is enough to guarantee the continued success of the work.—JAMES HARDING

Sayão, Bidú (Balduina de Oliveira Sayão)

Soprano. Born 11 May 1902, in Niteroi, near Rio de Janeiro. Married: 1) impresario Walter Mocchi, 1927 (divorced); 2) baritone Giuseppe Danise, 1947 (died 1963). Studied in Rio de Janeiro and in Bucharest with Elena Theodorini, and later with Jean de Reszke, Lucien Muratore, Reynaldo Hahn, and Luigi Ricci; operatic debut as Rosina in Il barbiere di Siviglia, Rome, 1926; Opéra-Comique debut, Paris, 1926; Teatro alla Scala debut as Rosina, 1930; created the role of Rosalina in Giordano's Il rè, Rome, 1930; Metropolitan Opera debut as Manon, 1937; seventeen roles at the Metropolitan opera, including Mimi,

Gilda, Violetta, Zerlina, Mélisande, Susanna; Chicago Opera, 1941-45; San Francisco, 1946-52; retired 1957.

As a child, Bidú Sayão had set her mind on a career as an actress, but because of family objections and her early love of music, she settled on a career as a recitalist. Fortunately, the great Rumanian opera singer Elena Theodorini had retired and opened a singing school in Rio, and she was persuaded to accept Bidú as a pupil at the age of fourteen. Initially the voice was of very limited range, but Theodorini began to build it. By the end of World War I, when the teacher decided to move back to her native Rumania, Sayão had made such spectacular progress that she felt she could not possibly change teachers, so she (accompanied by her mother) followed, and resumed lessons in Bucharest.

Sayão later studied with Jean de Reszke, and after the latter's death in 1925 Sayão's mother agreed that the young soprano should consult the famous Emma Carelli (1877-1928) who, along with teaching singing, was co-manager, with her husband Walter Mocchi (1870-1955), of the Teatro Costanzi in Rome. From 1910, when they took over the operation of the Teatro Costanzi until the theater was nationalized in 1926, Carelli and Mocchi were powerful figures on the Italian operatic scene.

In 1925, Carelli placed Bidú Sayão under the tutelage of Maestro Luigi Ricci to learn repertoire. "The voice is limited," she commented, "but sometimes it is the tiny birds who fly the greatest distances and for the longest times!" Sayão's operatic debut took place as Rosina in *Il barbiere di Siviglia* at the Costanzi on 25 March 1926; this was followed by Gilda in *Rigoletto* and Carolina in *Il matrimonio segreto*. This was the final season at the Costanzi under the Carelli-Mocchi ageis. Walter Mocchi had long been associated with opera management in South America; in 1926 he accepted the post of director of the Teatro Municipal in São Paulo which also included an opera season each year in Rio. He drew many of his artists from the Costanzi, among them Bidú Sayão.

Sayão's debut in her native Rio was as Rosina on 15 July 1926. She was also heard in two Brazilian operas, as Mario Maria in Carlos de Campo's *Un caso singular* and as Margarida in her uncle Alberto Costa's *Soror Madalena*. The Rio season was interwoven with the season at the Teatro Municipal in São Paulo, where Sayão was heard in the same roles.

In 1927 Bidú Sayão became Mrs. Walter Mocchi, a marriage which the singer said later in an interview "lasted . . . until 1934, with the divorce coming later." The singer made Rome her base, making many extended concert tours throughout Europe, with occasional opera appearances. In 1928 and 1929 she was heard at the Teatro Colón in Buenos Aires in *Il barbiere di Siviglia, Rigoletto, Il rè,* and *Lucia di Lammermoor*. On 24 January 1930 she was chosen by Giordano to create Rosalina in his new opera *Il rè* for its first performance in Rome. She then made extensive engagements in Europe and South America.

Bidú Sayão had sung frequently with the veteran baritone Giuseppe Danise (1882-1963), especially in South America. In an interview with Lanfranco Rasponi in 1979, Sayão said that Danise "took me in hand to steer me gradually into some of the lyric roles. He was fantastic as a teacher, and tremendously strict. . . . Watching me like a hawk, he ignored my pleas to take on Desdemona, Fiora, and Butterfly. He allowed me to try Violetta . . . and then Mimi, Mélisande, and Manon. I had sung Marguerite in *Faust* at the Opéra in Paris, but Danise did not approve, for he considered the Church Scene too heavy, so I dropped it. At the end of my career, I appeared in

San Francisco as Margherita in *Mefistofele,* and as Nedda [in *Pagliacci*], but by then I was willing to take risks. . . . It was Danise who was totally responsible for my American career [for] in 1936 he persuaded me to accompany him to New York.''

In New York Sayão was introduced to Toscanini, who at the time was looking for a soloist for Debussy's *La damoiselle élue;* she was given the part, and made her debut with sensational critical acclaim at Carnegie Hall in April 1936. The Sayão-Danise timing for a New York debut could not have been more perfect: Lucrezia Bori had left the Metropolitan on 29 March, and the question as to who could possibly replace her seemed to be automatically answered. Sayão returned to the local seasons at Rio and São Paulo with a Metropolitan contract for the 1936-37 season in her pocket. If there were any doubts about Sayão's ability to replace Bori, they were quickly dispelled at her Metropolitan debut as Manon on 13 February 1937.

Sayão remained with the Metropolitan Opera for sixteen seasons, during which she sang twelve roles, including Violetta, Mimi, Juliet, Susanna (in *Le nozze di Figaro*), Norina, Zerlina, Adina, Mélisande and Serpina (in *La serva padrona*). Of her 226 performances in New York and on tour with the company, a total of thirty-six were broadcast, and recordings thus exist of all of her Metropolitan roles except Serpina. During 1939, 1940, and 1946, she also took part in seasons in Rio, São Paulo and Buenos Aires, and she was a great favorite on the Pacific Coast where she sang with the San Francisco Opera Company, both at its home base and on tour, during 1939-42, 1946-48, and 1950-52.

With the advent of Rudolph Bing at the Metropolitan Opera (1950), Sayão's performances were drastically reduced, and she was only offered a few performances of *La bohème.* When a new production of *Pelléas et Mélisande* was mounted in November 1953, the role with which Sayão had been so closely identified was given to Nadine Conner. It did not take Danise (whom she had married in 1947) to tell her that it was time to leave the Metropolitan and concentrate on concerts, for which her services were in great demand throughout the United States and Canada. Her final performance at the Metropolitan Opera was as Mimi on 26 February; her last with the company was on tour in Boston, as Manon, on 23 April 1952.

Sayão's voice was that of a true lyric coloratura. It was even throughout its extensive range, and had a peculiar sweetness. Perhaps most distinctive was the singer's ability to change the color of the tone. This feature of the Sayão voice was especially effective during a song recital and was a technique she had learned from Jean de Reszke. Another feature of her voice was its projection: although small, it could always be heard in solo or ensemble from the back of a large hall, perhaps again because it could be colored in a distinctive way and thus the ear could separate it from other sounds and voices. But Sayão did not live by voice alone. She was a fine actress: as Mélisande she seemed an ethereal thing that could glide rather than walk; as Zerlina she was a country girl who could give as well as take; as Manon her mood changed as the story developed: the audience would be laughing with her at one minute and crying with her the next.

Bidú Sayão's first commercial recordings were made by RCA Victor in Brazil in 1933. Only two selections from *Il Guarany* received world circulation. After Sayão's arrival in New York, she continued to record for Victor, at sessions late in 1938, 1939 and 1940. In 1941 she went with Columbia, with whom she recorded a complete *La bohème* in 1947 (with Tucker). She stayed with Columbia until 1950. Her only other commercial recording was made after her retirement, when she was persuaded by Villa-Lobos to record his last composition, released on the United Artists label in 1959. Of her Metropolitan Opera roles which were broadcast, one, a performance

723

of *Romeo et Juliette* on 1 February 1947 with Jussi Bjoerling, has been officially released by the Metropolitan; many others have found their way into circulation.—WILLIAM R. MORAN

Scarlatti, Alessandro

Composer. Born 2 May 1660, in Palermo. Died 22 October 1725, in Naples. Married: Antonia Anzalone, 1678 (10 children, including the musicians Pietro Filippo and the famous composer Domenico). Studied with Carissimi in Rome, 1672; referred to as maestro di cappella to Queen Christina of Sweden on a manuscript copy of his opera Il Pompeo, *25 January 1683; taught at the Conservatorio di Santa Maria di Loreto in Naples, 1689; maestro to the Viceroy at Naples, 1694; assistant maestro to Foggia at Santa Maria Maggiore in Rome; succeeded Foggia as first maestro at Santa Maria Maggiore, 1707; resigned in 1709 and returned to Naples; maestro of the Royal Chapel, Naples. Among Scarlatti's private pupils was J.A. Hasse, 1724.*

Operas *Gli equivoci nel sembiante,* D.F. Contini, Rome, Capranica, 5 February 1679; *L'honestà negli amori,* F. Parnasso, Rome, Palazzo Bernini, 6 February 1680; *Tutto il mal non vien per nuocere,* G.D. de Totis, Rome, Palazzo Rospigliosi, 1681; *Il Pompeo,* N. Minato, Rome, Colonna, 25 January 1683; *La guerriera costante,* F. Orsini, Rome, palace of Duchess of Bracciano, carnival 1683; *L'Aldimiro o vero Favor per favore,* G.D. de Totis, Naples, Palazzo Reale, 6 November 1683; *La Psiche o vero Amore innamorato,* G.D. de Totis, Naples, Palazzo Reale, 21 December 1683; *Olimpia vendicata,* A. Aureli, Naples, Palazzo Reale, 23 December 1685; *La Rosmene o vero L'infedeltà fedele,* G.D. de Totis, Rome, Palazzo Doria Pamphili, carnival 1686; *Clearco in Negroponte,* A. Arcoleo, Naples, Palazzo Reale, 21 December 1686; *La santa Dinna* (with Alessandro Melani and B. Pasquini), B. Pamphili, Rome, Palazzo Doria Pamphili, carnival 1687 [lost]; *Il Flavio,* M. Noris, Naples, Palazzo Reale, 14? November 1688; *L'anacreonte tiranno,* G.F. Bussani, Naples, San Bartolomeo, 9 February 1689; *L'Amazzone corsara [guerriera] o vero L'Alvilda,* G.C. Corradi, Naples, Palazzo Reale, 6 November 1689; *La Statira,* P. Ottoboni, Rome, Tordinona, 5 January 1690; *Gli equivoci in amore o vero La Rosaura,* G.B. Lucini, Rome, Palazzo della Cancelleria, December 1690; *L'humanità nelle fiere o vero Il Lucallo,* Naples, San Bartolomeo, 25 February 1691 [lost]; *La Teodora augusta,* A. Morselli, Naples, Palazzo Reale, 6 November 1692; *Gerone tiranno di Siracusa,* A. Aureli, Naples, Palazzo Reale, 22 December 1692; *L'amante doppio o vero Il Ceccobimbi,* Naples, Palazzo Reale, April 1693 [lost]; *Il Pirro e Demetrio,* A. Morselli, Naples, San Bartolomeo, 28 January 1694; *Il Bassiano o vero Il maggior impossibile,* M. Noris, Naples, San Bartolomeo, spring 1694 [lost]; *La santa Genuinda, o vero L'innocenza difesa dall'inganno* (with G.L. Lulier and C.F. Cesarini), B. Pamphili, Rome, Palazzo Doria Pamphili, 1694; *Le nozze con l'inimico o vero L'Analinda,* Naples, San Bartolomeo, 1695; *Nerone fatto Cesare,* M. Noris, Naples, Palazzo Reale, 6 November 1695; *Massimo Puppieno,* A. Aureli, Naples, San Bartolomeo, 26 December 1695; *Penelope la casta,* M. Noris, Naples, San Bartolomeo, 23? February 1696; *La Didone delirante,* F.M. Paglia (after A. Franceschi), Naples, San Bartolomeo, 28 May 1696; *Comodo Antonino,* F.M. Paglia (after F. Busani), Naples, San Bartolomeo, 18 November 1696; *L'Emireno o vero Il consiglio,* F.M. Paglia, Naples, San Bartolomeo, 2 February 1697; *La caduta de' Decemviri,* S. Stampiglia, Naples, San Bartolomeo, 15 December 1697; *La donna ancora è fedele,* D.F. Contini (revised), Naples, San Bartolomeo, 1698; *Il prigioniero fortunato,* F.M. Paglia, Naples, San Bartolomeo, 14 December 1698; *Gl'* *inganni felici,* A. Zeno, Naples, Palazzo Reale, 6 November 1699; *L'Eraclea,* S. Stampiglia, Naples, San Bartolomeo, 30 January 1700; *Odoardo* (with the intermezzo *Adolfo e Lesbiana*), A. Zeno, Naples, San Bartolomeo, 5 May 1700; *Dafni,* F.M. Paglia (after E. Manfredi), Naples, Casino del Vicerè a Posillipo, 5 August 1700; *Laodice e Berenice,* after M. Noris, Naples, San Bartolomeo, April, 1701; *Il pastor di Corinto,* F.M. Paglia, Naples, Casino del Vicerè a Posillipo, 5 August 1701; *Tito Sempronio Gracco* (with the intermezzo *Bireno e Dorilla*), S. Stampiglia, Naples, San Benedetto, carnival? 1702; *Tiberio imperatore d'Oriente,* G.D. Pallavicino, Naples, Palazzo Reale, 8 May 1702; *Il Flavio Cuniberto,* M. Noris, Pratolino, Villa Medicea, September 1702; *Arminio,* A. Salvi, Pratolino, Villa Medicea, September 1703; *Turno Aricino,* S. Stampiglia Pratolino, Villa Medicea, September 1704 [lost]; *Lucio Manlio l' imperioso,* S. Stampiglia, Pratolino, Villa Medicea, September 1705 [lost]; *Il gran Tamerlano,* A. Salvi (after Pradon), Pratolino, Villa Medicea, September 1706 [lost]; *Il Mitridate Eupatore,* G. Frigimelica Roberti, Venice, San Giovanni Grisostomo, carnival, 1707; *Il trionfo della libertà,* G. Frigimelica Roberti, Venice, San Giovanni Grisostomo, carnival 1707; *Il Teodosio,* V. Grimani?, Naples, San Bartolomeo, 27 January 1709 [lost]; *L'amor volubile e tiranno,* G.D. Pioli and G. Papis, Naples, San Bartolomeo, 25 May 1709; *La principessa fedele,* D.A. Parrino? (after A. Piovene), Naples, San Bartolomeo, 8 February 1710; *La fede riconosciuta,* B. Marcello?, Naples, San Bartolomeo, 14 October 1710; *Giunio Bruto o vero La caduta dei Tarquini* (with C.F. Cesarini and A. Caldara), G. Sinibaldi, intended for Vienna [unperformed]; *Il Ciro,* P. Ottoboni, Rome, Palazzo della Cancelleria, carnival 1712; *Il Tigrane o vero L'egual impegno d'amore di fede,* D. Lalli, Naples, San Bartolomeo, 16 February 1713; *Scipione nelle Spagne* (with the intermezzo *Pericca e Varrone*), A. Zeno and N. Serino (intermezzo by Salvi?), Naples, San Bartolomeo, 21 January 1714; *L'amor generoso* (with the intermezzo *Despina e Niso*), G. Papis and S. Stampiglia, Naples, Palazzo Reale, 1 October 1714; *Carlo re d'Allemagna* (with the intermezzo *Palandrana e Zamberlucco*), F. Salvani, Naples, San Bartolomeo, 30 January 1716; *La virtù trionfante dell' odio e dell' amore,* F. Silvani, Naples, San Bartolomeo, 3 May 1716 [lost]; *Telemaco,* C.S. Capece, Rome, Capranica, carnival 1718; *Il trionfo dell'onore,* F.A. Tullio, Naples, Teatro dei Fiorentini, 26 November 1718; *Il Cambise,* D. Lalli, Naples, San Bartolomeo, 4 February 1719; *Marco Attilio Regolo* (with the intermezzo *Leonzio e Eurilla*), Rome, Capranica, carnival 1719; *La Griselda,* after A. Zeno, 1720; revised, Rome, Capranica, January 1721.

The aristocratic tradition of Italian opera that was established about 1600 in Florence and Mantua reached its culmination after 1700 in the works composed for Rome and Naples by Alessandro Scarlatti. His operas continue to touch the heart today even while expressing the stylized words and doctrinal affections of his Baroque poets and their ever more schematicized libretti. To appreciate the masterpieces of Scarlatti's maturity, one must accept their unlikely circumstances of plot (as in modern adventure films) as situations contrived to test the mettle of the principal characters. Unlike films, however, the *dramma per musica* centered not on exciting actions but largely on the characters' emotional states, creating an internal drama in the heart and mind such as must often have engaged those occupying the higher rungs of the era's tightly structured social order.

Audiences readily accepted the use of the greatest singers of the time—the castrati—to express their own idealized responses to the situations presented in the *dramma per musica.* The largest obstacle to the acceptance of modern performances of these works is not the improbable plots (often based on events from Roman history very freely embellished) or the unbelievable disguises, but the well-intended modern attempts at realism, whether in the

Alessandro Scarlatti

replacement of the male sopranos with natural male voices (generally employed at the time only in minor or comic roles) or in realistic stage action not in keeping with a character's station.

Scarlatti established his reputation in Rome, where he forged relationships with aristocratic patrons that endured throughout his subsequent court appointments in Naples and brought him commissions for many of his approximately 800 cantatas, 40 oratorios, and 30 serenatas. His first opera, *Gli equivoci nel sembiante* (Rome, 1679), proved to be one of the most successful works of his career. An unpretentious pastoral drama, it perfectly suited the varied small-scale forms of Scarlatti's early period and his inclination to draw his music from the rhythms and inflections of the words. Unlike the later libretti, scenes unfold freely and the verse forms allow the composer to write expanded binary and ground-bass arias as well as small-scale ternary forms. Arias can even change meter and tempo for contrasting sections (act II, scene 6: "V intendo, si"), and the music can rise to considerable eloquence at moments of climax, as in the duet "Ecco l'alma ti dono" (act III, scene 8). It is also true, however, that in Scarlatti's early operas the singers seem to bear the burden of varying an undue amount of literal repetition, as in the habitually repeated phrases and sections of an aria written in ternary form that is also given an identical second strophe. Of the early operas, Donald Grout (*Alessandro Scarlatti,* Berkeley, 1979) named *Rosmene* (Rome, 1686) "certainly one of the best, if not the very best."

Most of Scarlatti's eighty-five or so operas (of which about thirty are extant) were written for Naples, where the composer served the court three times (1684-1702, 1708-18, and 1722-25). It was in Naples that the composer's operatic language underwent transformation, the bass line gradually changing from a contrapuntal role to a mainly harmonic one and the melody being differentiated from the chamber style of the cantata by its greater breadth and virtuosity. Instead of expressing faithfully every nuance of the words, Scarlatti comes to stress the primary affection of the aria, allowing the melody to unfold freely and breaking up the poetic lines and fitting words to the motives when necessary.

In *Tigrane* (Naples, 1713), for example, far from being daunted by a libretto that provides almost exclusively *da capo* arias and scenes that seldom consist of more than a recitative and an aria, the composer seizes the opportunity of working within a fixed form to expand his range of aria types and styles and to extend his musical language with wider-ranging modulations, more varied rhythms, and a new attitude towards tone-painting that raises it to an integral facet of his art. In addition, he makes greater use of accompanied recitatives and independent instrumental pieces, including the three-movement Italian overture (which he had established in 1697); he even differentiates the thematic material of the instruments from that of the voice, as in the act I *aria concertata* entitled "All acquisto di gloria" (the first known use of horns in opera). Other significant operas of Scarlatti's mature years include *Mitridate Eupatore* (Venice, 1707), and *La principessa fedele* (Venice, 1710).

The composer's last years found his music falling out of fashion in the public theaters of Naples but still in demand by his Roman patrons and, more significantly, growing ever more expressive within his established parameters. Grout found *Telemaco* (Naples 1718) "one of Scarlatti's most interesting operas." *Griselda,* composed in 1720 on a story from Boccaccio's *Decameron* and revised in 1721 for performance in Rome, also offers great depth of musical richness, including more independent instrumental writing (as in the act III simile aria "Come va l'ape"). Perhaps its most striking moment occurs when the ever faithful Griselda reacts to a threat on her son's life with a dramatic aria (act II, scene 4: "Figlio! Tiranno!") whose agitated style *(stile concitato)* and declamatory power place Scarlatti firmly within the distinguished tradition established by Monteverdi.

The operas of Alessandro Scarlatti represent a variety of musical styles and dramatic types, ranging from the *dramma per musica* (which required comic scenes in Naples) to the *commedia (Tutto il mal)* and including as well the pastoral *(Gli equivoci nel sembiante)* and even the *tragedia in musica (Mitridate Eupatore).* They deserve revival, if only in concert performances (which would eliminate many of the obstacles to successful performance), because they reveal as does no other medium the spirit and character of their age.—DAVID POULTNEY

Schipa, Tito

Tenor. Born Raffaele Attilio Amadeo Schipa, 2 January 1888, in Lecce, Italy. Died 16 December 1965, in New York. Studied with A. Gerunda in Lecce and E. Piccoli in Milan; debut in Verdi's La traviata *in Vercelli, 1910; Teatro alla Scala debut, 1915; premiered Ruggero in Puccini's* La rondine, *Monte Carlo, 1917; joined the Chicago Opera, 1919-32; Metropolitan Opera debut as Nemorino in* L'elisir d'amore, *1932; toured extensively until he retired from opera in 1954; farewell concert in New York in 1961; he was the teacher of Cesare Valletti.*

During the last half of the nineteenth century the repertoire of the major opera houses of the world underwent a substantial change. In Italy during the first half of the century the dominant composers were Rossini, Bellini, Donizetti and Verdi, all of whom followed the principles of *bel canto* (beautiful singing—a style characterized by brilliant vocal display and purity of tone). By the 1870s the concepts of music drama, exemplified by Wagner, had become the new critical standard of opera composition. These changes produced the *verismo* school of Italian composers and resulted in the last great period of Italian opera composition. The vocal category most affected by this change was that of the tenor, and the singer who popularized the new style of singing was Enrico Caruso. The emphasis was now on dramatic declamation and sheer power. The tenor who was accepted as the foremost exponent of the older *bel canto* tradition during his career (1911-1950) was Tito Schipa.

The light, lyric tenor, in the older tradition, was termed a *tenore leggiero* (light, agile, nimble). All voice ranges from bass to soprano were required to develop the technique of what is called coloratura—the ability to sing runs and trills, and to ornament and decorate the music with aspects of vocal virtuosity. By Schipa's time coloratura had become almost the exclusive property of the high soprano. In the operas that remained in the repertoire—principally Rossini's *Il barbiere di Siviglia,* Bellini's *La sonnambula,* Donizetti's *L'elisir d'amore, Lucia di Lammermoor* and *Don Pasquale,* along with Verdi's *La traviata* and *Rigoletto,* which constituted the basic Italian repertoire that Schipa sang during his career—tenor *cabalettas,* which were written to display vocal virtuosity, were traditionally cut out and not performed. Schipa's operatic repertoire was extended into the French lyric school, Delibes' *Lakmé,* Thomas' *Mignon,* Massenet's *Manon* and *Werther.* The Mozart revival of the late 1920s provided him with the role of Don Ottavio in *Don Giovanni.* These thirteen operas constituted the basic repertoire that he sang during his long career. At the outset of Schipa's career, however, he did sing in operas of the newer *verismo* school: Mascagni's *Cavalleria rusticana,* Leoncavello's *Zaza,* Cilèa's *Adriana Lecouvreur* and Puccini's *Tosca,* and even recorded arias from *Cavalleria* and *Tosca* in his earliest series of recordings (1913/14). By about 1920 he had wisely abandoned that repertoire.

Michael Scott in *The Record of Singing, Volume Two 1914-1925* states that "Schipa was never, not even at the beginning of his career, a *bel canto* singer." By the traditional definition of the term, Scott is probably correct; however, Schipa's reputation as a master of *bel canto* can be defended by noting the change in the critical attitude toward the term. No longer was the *leggiero* aspect of the method considered important. Indeed the light, lyric tenor was by then defined as a *tenore di grazia,* gracefulness replaced agility as the touchstone of the *bel canto* method.

Schipa's own recordings give evidence to the fact that he was primarily a *tenore di grazia.* In 1916 he recorded the original version of "Ecco ridente in cielo" on two sides of a ten inch disc for Pathé. The tempo is slow and the runs are breathy and labored. In 1926 when he again recorded the aria for Victor, he was content with the then current simplified version. In both his commercial (c1927) and later air check (1941) of "Il mio tesoro" from *Don Giovanni,* he again chooses an inordinately slow tempo and comes to grief on the long run.

Schipa's reputation as a *bel canto* artist is justified by the fact that he was, first, a highly trained musician; second, because he had an instinctive, intuitive sense of rhythm—a sense of knowing just how a phrase should go; and finally because he had adopted and mastered the art of equalization of tone quality throughout the range. This aspect of singing became the most important touchstone of the newer definition of *bel canto.* In Schipa it produced a seamless *legato* and a command of breath control, gracefully and tastefully used.

Schipa's voice, while not remarkable in either range or power, was unique and totally distinctive. He was what is termed a "short" tenor. Although early recordings show that he had a high C, his top notes disappeared about 1920. In fact, he was famous for transposing arias down to accommodate his limited range. But within that limited range his command of nuance and purity of tone enabled him to encompass all aspects of the music he sang. He was a prime example of the fact that pure, resonant projection of the voice, rather than simply volume, is the touchstone of audibility—that a relatively small voice, purely produced will carry, even in a large opera house, better than a louder, larger, unfocused voice.

John Freestone testifies to the special qualities of Schipa in a record note: "He possessed, like McCormack, the truly miraculous ability of making a perfect crescendo and dimuendo on one note. He possessed a whole armory of superbly subtle effects and though the voice seemed small in scale and a little lacking in range, he seemed incapable of uttering an ill-balanced note." Furthermore, one is always impressed by Schipa's ease of production; the voice floats in an effortless stream of sound, and the purity of tone enabled him to modulate from the pure soft head voice to a ringing, passionate fortissimo. Rodolfo Celletti notes that Schipa's voice "had also just a trace of that guttural quality which somehow recalls Spanish tenors, and gives a rare and exotic sound to the voice."

Schipa's recorded output in the operatic repertoire began in 1913 and concluded in 1942. Unfortunately he only recorded one complete role, that of Ernesto in *Don Pasquale* (1933). Air checks issued on private recordings exist of excerpts from *Manon, Werther,* and *Don Giovanni* and Cimarosa's *Il matrimonio segreto* from the Teatro alla Scala in 1949. He was equally famous as a singer of Neapolitan and Spanish songs of the more popular vein and recorded extensively in this area as well as classical *arie antiche.* In the popular songs his intuitive sense of rhythm and delicacy of phrasing convinces the listener that even the most simple song sounds like a work of artistic merit.

After his retirement from the opera stage he continued to concertize and also devoted himself to teaching voice. His pupil, Cesare Valletti, was his successor in the basic repertoire of the *tenore di grazia.*

The fact that Schipa preserved his voice over a span of more than fifty years is attributable to his perfect technique, and that, once having found his *Fach,* he never ventured into the heavier tenor repertoire. At the age of 73 in 1962 he gave a farewell concert tour. The recording issued of his New York concert gives proof of the fact that the unique timbre, the nuance and phrasing remained intact. Even at that age the distinctive voice could have issued from no other throat.—BOB ROSE

Schönberg, Arnold

Composer. Born 13 September 1874, in Vienna. Died 13 July 1951, in Los Angeles. Married: 1) Mathilde von Zemlinsky (1877-1923), 1901 (two children); 2) Gertrud Kolisch, 1924 (three children). Studied at the Realschule in Vienna; learned the cello and the violin; first work, three piano pieces, 1894; studied counterpoint with Alexander Zemlinsky, and played in his instrumental group Polyhymnia; public performance of his first String Quartet in D major, Vienna, 17 March 1898; in Berlin, 1901, where he and E. von Wolzgen, F. Wedekind, and O. Bierbaum started a cabaret called Überbrettl; string sextet Verklärte Nacht *performed, Vienna, 18 March 1902; met Richard Strauss, who recommended him for a Liszt stipend and a teaching position at the Stern Conservatory; met Mahler in Vienna, 1903, who helped Schönberg establish his career; Vereinigung Schaffender Tonkünstler organized for the performance of new music; symphonic poem* Pelleas und Melisande *performed 26 January 1905;* Kammersymphonie *performed 8 February 1907, but not well received; began painting seriously, 1907; took on Alban Berg, Anton von Webern, and Egon Wellesz as private students; appointed to the faculty of the Vienna Academy of Music, 1910; instructor at the Stern Conservatory, Berlin, 1911; his* Fünf Orchesterstücke *premiered in London, under the direction of Sir Henry Wood, 3 September 1912;* Pierrot Lunaire *premiered in Berlin, 16 October 1912, and condemned by critics; Verein für Musikalische Privataufführungen formed by Schönberg for the performance of new music at the exclusion of critics, 1918-22; taught a master class at the Prussian Academy of Arts in Berlin, 1925; taught at the Malkin Conservatory of Boston, 1933; professor of music at the University of Southern California, 1935; professor of music at the University of California at Los Angeles, 1936-44; turned down for a Guggenheim fellowship; United States citizenship, 11 April 1941; Award of Merit for Distinguished Achievements from the National Institute of Arts and Letters, 1947.*

Operas *Erwartung* (monodrama), M. Pappenheim, 1909, Prague, Neues Deutsche Theater, 6 June 1924; *Die glückliche Hand,* Schönberg, 1910-13, Vienna, Volksoper, 14 October 1924; *Von Heute auf Morgen,* M. Blonda [=G. Schönberg], 1928-29, Frankfurt, Opernhaus, 1 February 1930; *Moses und Aron,* Schönberg, 1930-32 [unfinished: act III never composed], partial performance, Darmstadt, 2 July 1951; concert performance of acts I and II, Hamburg, 12 March 1954; staged performance of acts I and II, Zurich, Stadttheater, 6 June 1957.

During army service in World War I, Arnold Schönberg was asked by an officer if he was that controversial composer of the same name, to which he replied: "Somebody had to be, and nobody else wanted the job, so I took it on myself." That answer neatly encapsulates his sense of the inevitability of his creative mission, and the belief that personal wishes had little to do with it. He was in many ways an unwilling revolutionary, driven by the need for continual clarification of his emotional and artistic concerns. Pursuing his ideals, he effected the most profound transformation of the terms of musical discourse; a revolution that forced a revaluation of all aspects of musical creativity.

Schönberg was virtually self-taught, apart from some tuition from Alexander von Zemlinsky (himself a prolific composer of operas), who became his brother-in-law and lifelong friend. Both of them, in the early 1900s, were befriended and supported by Mahler, who as conductor of the Vienna Hofoper was enormously influential, and whose opera performances were of great significance to younger Viennese musicians. As early as 1897 Schönberg collaborated with Zemlinsky on the libretto of the latter's first opera, *Sarema,* and prepared the vocal score.

Schönberg's own music, which soon began to outpace Zemlinsky's in the swiftness of its stylistic development, first acquired a personal profile by an exceptionally thorough-going synthesis of Brahmsian contrapuntal texture and motivic development with Wagnerian chromaticism, harmonic ambiguity and large compositional spans. This idiom attained its magnificent early flowering in the *Gurrelieder,* a cantata for five singers, reciter, large chorus and enormous orchestra, composed to texts by Jens Peter Jacobsen in 1900-1, but not fully scored until 1911. Although designed for concert performance, its equally intense dramatic and lyrical features refer back constantly to the world of Wagnerian music-drama, especially *Tristan* and *Götterdämmerung.*

It is notable that the work owes almost nothing to Richard Strauss, whose style is only very occasionally hinted at in subsequent pieces, such as the symphonic poem *Pelleas und Melisande* (written at Strauss's suggestion, and in ignorance of Debussy's opera). This was the first of several scores in which Schönberg began to compress four movement symphonic schemes into a single unbroken span, while radically increasing the degree of contrapuntal and motivic development of every thematic element—a kind of rage for maximum communication that was already, as far as his contemporaries were concerned, causing serious difficulties for comprehension of his purpose.

The emotionally and intellectually supercharged style of these works of the early 1900s exploded, after 1908, into the music of Schönberg's "Expressionist" phase, where he strove to represent extreme states of mind and feeling more or less directly, without any intervening decorum of form. His ideal, he once said, was a music "without architecture, without structure. Only an ever-changing, unbroken succession of colors, rhythms and moods." His works of this period are accordingly characterized by an unprecedented degree of harmonic ambiguity, asymmetry of melody and phrase-lengths, wide and dissonant melodic intervals, abrupt contrasts in register, texture, stasis and dynamism. All twelve notes of the chromatic scale occur with extreme frequency; consequently the harmonic language shifts away from any kind of diatonic hierarchy towards a state of total chromaticism—an "emancipation of dissonance" which does not, however, prevent the covert and allusive operation of tonal functions, and so belies the popular misnomer of "atonality" which is so often applied to this idiom.

The apotheosis of musical Expressionism was attained in two extraordinary short operas, the monodrama *Erwartung* and the "Drama with Music" *Die glückliche Hand* (the virtually untranslatable title ironically combines the concepts of "A happy knack" with "The hand of fate"). Both works have more often been presented in the concert-hall than on stage—not inappropriately, as both inhabit what are essentially regions of the unconscious mind.

Schönberg once described *Erwartung*—composed and scored at fantastic speed in a creative brainstorm of uncompromising intensity and freedom—as an *Angsttraum* (anxiety dream), a slow-motion representation of a single second of maximum spiritual stress. Its action is purely psychological, and the moonlit forest through which the female protagonist moves is the stage embodiment of her unconscious fears. Apprehensive, somnambulistic, she wanders in search of her lover, giving voice in broken, discontinuous sentences analogous to a stream of consciousness. Eventually she discovers his corpse, but it remains unclear whether she herself may have done the deed, or whether the entire episode is taking place in her fevered imagination. Despite the chaos of the protagonist's mind, however, the score of *Erwartung* is not in any sense chaotic. There is a willed unity of atmosphere, created through a myriad of intensely imagined details, which could only have been achieved under iron control. Yet the daring juxtapositions of lyricism, violence, anguish and *Angst*-ridden terror attain the effect of high-pressure improvisation, and the solo part demands a tremendous variety of expression, from near-*Sprechstimme* to big moments of Valkyrie-like power and stamina.

Schönberg, himself an "amateur" painter of near-genius within severe technical limitations, discerned a kinship between what he was doing in works like *Erwartung* and the art of the contemporary Expressionist painters, above all Kandinsky, whom he came to know personally. The parallels are perhaps even clearer in *Die glückliche Hand,* a new kind of *Gesamtkunstwerk* in which music, staging, movement and especially color (achieved by "orchestration" and "color modulation" of the lighting) are expected to play equal parts in a symbolic drama. There are striking similarities to Kandinsky's own contemporary stage-work *Der gelbe Klang,* though it is now known that the two works were conceived entirely independently. "I called it, in my own private language, *making music with the media of the stage,*" Schönberg commented in a lecture preceding a production in Breslau in 1928: "This kind of art, I don't know why, has been called Expressionist: it has never expressed more than was *in it!* I also gave it a name, which did not become popular . . . I said that it is the *art of the representation of INNER processes.*"

Die glückliche Hand is a symbolic representation of the eternal struggles of any creative artist, and as such probably contains a strong autobiographical element. The action again centers on a single unnamed protagonist, male in this case, who is the only vocal soloist. Other characters—his unattainable *innamorata,* a wealthy gentleman, metalworkers, and a monstrous "mythical beast," presumably an exteriorization of the protagonist's self-lacerating consciousness, which has him pinioned to the ground at the beginning and end of the drama—are mimed. A small choir of twelve voices performs the role of a Greek chorus, commenting on the action in a complex vocal texture combining song and *Sprechstimme*. Even more than in *Erwartung,* the sung text is dreamlike, fragmentary, a short verbal index of the inner emotional drama expressed through the medium of the orchestra. On the other hand the structure is, after *Erwartung,* comparatively easy to grasp, and the orchestration has a wonderful iridescence. However, since the solo baritone part of the Man offers far fewer attractions than *Erwartung*'s great soprano role, and the other technical difficulties are no less fearsome, *Die glückliche Hand* has been far less often performed.

No sooner had the Expressionist style attained its climacteric than Schönberg was concerned to reintroduce "architectural" principals into his music, aware that the supremely intuitive, quasi-improvisational achievement of *Erwartung* was by definition unrepeatable, and that his linguistic revolution had for the moment put traditional means of large-scale organization beyond his grasp. The problems are already reflected in the three years it took to compose *Die glückliche Hand* (as against *Erwartung*'s three weeks) and its more consciously patterned and symmetrical structure. Most of his works of the next decade were vocal, the text helping to determine the progress of the form. At the same time he began to concentrate on intensive development of the constituent tones of principal thematic ideas, and cultivated a wide range of canonic and other "ancient" structural devices to provide structural backbone.

All these tendencies appear in *Pierrot Lunaire* (1912) for instrumental ensemble and *Sprechstimme* ("Speech-song," i.e. half-sung recitation), an ironic cycle of rondel-settings with elements of an Expressionist cabaret. However, they reached a new density, and an impasse, in the unfinished oratorio *Die Jakobsleiter* (1917-22), which grew out of a project for a gigantic choral symphony dealing with modern man's spiritual problems, but which began to assume operatic proportions with a large number of clearly-characterized soloists taking the parts of souls undergoing judgment in purgatory, justice being dispensed by the Angel Gabriel. Though it remains a 40-minute torso (completed for performance after Schönberg's death by his pupil Winfried Zillig), *Jakobsleiter* brings his musical, philosophical, and religious dilemmas into sharp focus with extraordinary power, and contains the seeds of the idea that would resolve his creative difficulties.

Schönberg's central problem was how to accept and assimilate the "traumatic" forces of Expressionism as a natural extension and enrichment of the existing scheme of musical discourse: to "objectify" the intense subjectivity of the new idiom within an enlarged musical language which he could apply consciously—not merely intuitively—in further works. We should observe that his pupil Alban Berg found a personal solution to this conundrum, somewhat ahead of Schönberg, in *Wozzeck* (1917-22), where total chromaticism is balanced by passages with fairly strong tonal orientation, and the large-scale form is articulated by building each scene upon an "abstract" or traditional classical form—passacaglia, sonata, invention on one note, and so on. Berg, however, was always a slow and painstaking worker: Schönberg's problem was different in kind as well as degree, for he desired a solution that would give him the means to recapture his spontaneity of inspiration.

Schönberg's approach to this problem, characteristically, was far more radical than Berg's: he developed the "method of composition with twelve tones related only to each other"; the "twelve-note method", or "twelve-note serialism" for short. A fixed series of all the notes of the chromatic scale, derived from the initial melodic and harmonic ideas for a particular work, becomes the kernel, the essence, the germinating cell of that work's unique tonal properties. The series is developed continually through transposition, inversion, retrograde motion, in whole or in part, in melodic lines and in chords, in "punning" similarities between different segments (which, at different transpositions, may employ identical pitches), to provide an inexhaustible and self-consistent source of invention.

Schönberg developed the techniques of twelve-note serialism progressively through the 1920s in the revivification of classical forms, beginning with dance-movements (in the op. 23 Piano Pieces and op. 25 Suite for Piano), and working up through large-scale chamber scores (Wind Quintet, String Quartet no. 3) and orchestral compositions (Variations for Orchestra). His logical goal was opera, and the one-act comic opera *Von heute auf morgen* (1928-9, to a libretto by his second wife Gertrud, writing under the pseudonym of 'Max Blonda') and the three-act biblical parable *Moses und Aron* (1930-2, to his own libretto) remained his largest twelve-note scores, even though the latter was nominally unfinished.

The oddity of Schönberg writing a comic opera is lessened when one recalls his Viennese background and his unashamed enthusiasm for the operettas of Franz Lehar. *Von heute auf morgen* is a domestic comedy, reputedly inspired by the home-life of Schönberg's Berlin colleague Franz Schreker, and a satire on fashionable modernity in social life. A bourgeois couple, dissatisfied with their ordinary lives, become involved with a sophisticated woman-friend and a famous tenor, a sort of Richard Tauber figure, whose smartness and "up-to-dateness" they envy. A night's flirtation with the idea of adopting the latter pair's standards gives way by morning to a reaffirmation of the virtues of a stable marriage. The score is musically almost over-rich, the tone benevolently satirical, with some sharp parodic touches that range from Wagner through Puccini to jazz. Seldom staged, it needs careful handling to bring it alive in the theater—yet it is one of Schönberg's most humane and positive works, and was clearly invaluable preparation for his operatic masterpiece, *Moses und Aron*. It is that work above all (discussed separately in this dictionary) which sums up a lifetime's musical development and applies it to dramatic ideas of the epic, religious and philosophical scope towards whose expression Schönberg's genius had always struggled.—MALCOLM MACDONALD

Schorr, Friedrich

Bass-Baritone. Born 2 September 1888, in Nagyvárad, Hungary. Died 14 August 1953, in Farmington, Connecticut. Studied law at the University in Vienna, and music with Adolf Robinson; minor roles with the Chicago Opera, 1911-12; major debut as Wotan in Die Walküre, *Graz, 1912; in Graz, 1912-16; in Prague, 1916-18; in Cologne, 1918-23; Berlin State Opera, 1923-32; Metropolitan Opera debut as Wolfram in* Tannhäuser, *1924; at Metropolitan Opera, 1924-43, singing eighteen roles, primarily Wagner; Covent Garden debut in* Das Rheingold, *1924; Bayreuth debut as Wotan, 1925; at Bayreuth, 1925-31; sang Daniello in American premiere of* Jonny spielt auf, *1929; at San Francisco, 1931-38; sang in American premiere of Weinberger's* Schwanda, *1931; appointed vocal advisor to Wagner department at the Metropolitan Opera, 1938; taught at The Manhattan School of Music and Hartt School of Music, 1943-53; advisor on German opera, New York City Opera, 1950. Became United States citizen.*

Friedrich Schorr's career spanned over forty years and two continents. He sang Lieder and sacred music as well as opera, but he was above all a Wagnerian. Schorr gave his first performance singing Wotan, and in his final performance he sang the Wanderer in *Siegfried*. At the end of his career, he coached and taught Wagnerian singers at the Metropolitan Opera and elsewhere. As J.B. Steane said in his book *The Grand Tradition,* "It is in Wagner, particularly as Sachs and Wotan, that Schorr is most himself and irreplaceable." He was a true *Heldenbariton,* and it was said that his impressively noble Wotan spoiled his audiences for any other performer.

Schorr began his long career in 1912 in Graz, Austria, debuting as Wotan; that same year he also sang several small roles with the Chicago Opera company in the United States. He sang in Europe—mostly Graz, Prague, and Berlin—for a decade before his Metropolitan Opera debut, again as Wotan, in 1924. Although he concentrated on Wagnerian roles, he sang in other operas as well, including Beethoven's *Fidelio,* Strauss's *Rosenkavalier,* Puccini's *Tosca,* and lesser known works like Weinberger's *Schwanda* and Krenek's *Jonny spielt auf.* In 1938, he was made vocal advisor to the Metropolitan Opera's Wagnerian singers. After he retired from the company in 1943 and until his death in 1953, he taught singing at The Manhattan School of Music in New York City, and at Hartt School of Music, in Hartford, Connecticut.

Audiences loved Schorr. Arthur Notcutt, who saw his debut at Covent Gardens in 1924, wrote later: "His singing in *Rheingold* on the opening night at once stamped him as an artist of outstanding gifts. The commencing phrase when Wotan is asleep and dreaming, 'Der Wonne seligen Saal' was sung in the softest of tones—followed later by the full opulence of his voice in his address to the castle, 'Vollendet das ewige Werk.' One could sense the reaction of the audience immediately. *Die Walküre* on the following evening confirmed one's initial impression." Both his vocal quality and his acting were lavishly praised. Notcutt mentioned the "ravishing beauty of his mezza-voce" and described his "nobility of . . . expression, his intensity and dramatic fire, and [his] melting tenderness and pathos." His first New York season was equally well-received, and he continued to reap such praise. In 1934, New York critic W.J. Henderson wrote of him: "He sang all the music like a great artist and some of it as it had never been sung."

Schorr left a large recorded legacy. He did, of course, record a substantial amount of Wagner, but he recorded other literature as well. His recordings of the difficult excerpts from Beethoven's *Fidelio* are masterful, while his recording from Weber's *Der Freischütz* is not his most successful. He recorded passages from Bach's *Mass in B Minor,* Mendelsohn's *Elijah,* and Hayden's *The Seasons,* as well as some Lieder.

While many of Schorr's Wagnerian predecessors had sung in a generally dry and declamatory style, Schorr's voice was pure velvet. His fortes were powerful, steady, and smooth, not shouted. He never obscured the pitch with excess vibrato. His quiet singing was beautifully controlled and always focused; the effect was rich and dignified. The recordings made towards the end of his life do show some signs of age—he sings the higher notes with more care, but the voice is still free of excess wobble, and retains its warmth and color. An even legato and a command of the messa di voce always underlay his singing; while he always sang expressively, he never sacrificed the musical line for the drama.

Schorr's recordings show the same interpretive care and dramatic ability ascribed by critics to his live performances. His Wagnerian recordings demonstrate a constant sensitivity to the smallest nuances, handling the changes of mood and tempo with great expressive effect. In all of his opera recordings, from his evil and energetic Pizarro in *Fidelio* to his warm-hearted Sachs in *Die Meistersinger von Nürnberg,* he portrays a variety of moods. Boris Semeonoff, in his commentary on Schorr's discography, described Schorr as "a noble and impressive Wotan," yet he showed the proper resignation when required. Schorr's recordings of sacred music are simple and reverent. His Lieder recordings are slightly less successful, but while some of them may fail to come to life, he does great justice to the dramatic *Prometheus* of Wolf.

As a teacher, Schorr had very strong ideas about singing and teaching. "Personally, I think non-professional singers are not capable of teaching voice. They aren't able to *show* their students the pros and cons of singing," he said in an interview with *Opera News.* "People who have never done strenuous parts like Otello or Isolde or Wotan aren't able to instruct their students as to vocal economies so that they will be fresh to the very end—no matter how hard the role." He taught careful Wagnerian singing: "Some say that singing Wagner spoils the voice. That is not true. If a voice is fundamentally of the right volume and trained properly, the voice will not be hurt at all by singing Wagner . . . A singer with a sound voice and correct vocal production shouldn't be afraid to sing anything." The secret, he continued, was to learn how "to conserve and preserve the voice." He was a nurturing teacher, attentive to all aspects of a student's development. "The teacher has to develop not only voice but personality of each student."

Although Schorr died several decades ago, his name and reputation live on. He holds a notable place in the history of Wagnerian singing, and his Wotan and Sachs are still held up as examples. His recordings are regularly re-issued and re-released in the newest formats, standing up solidly to more recent recordings of higher electronic fidelity made by younger singers. He still holds interest for music critics, and his performances, both live and recorded, are still discussed in print. He will not soon be forgotten, for, as J.B. Steane says, "no one who carries in his head Schorr's singing . . . in [for example] *Das Rheingold,* is likely to hear another performer without some yearning to get back to the gramophone and listen again to Friedrich Schorr."—ROBIN ARMSTRONG

Schreier, Peter Max

Tenor. Born 29 July 1935, in Meissen, Germany. Sang in the Dresden Kreuzchor; studied with Polster in Leipzig from 1954-56, and with Winkler at the Dresden Musikhochschule, 1956-59; as a child, he sang as one of the three boys in Mozart's Die Zauberflöte *at Dresden's Semper Opera House, 1944; debut as the First Prisoner in Beethoven's* Fidelio, *Dresden State Opera, 1959; joined the Dresden State Opera, 1961; joined the Berlin State Opera, 1963; Metropolitan Opera debut as Tamino in* Die Zauberflöte, *1967; began conducting in 1970.*

During a long and busy singing career that has spanned the 1960s, 70s and 80s, Peter Schreier has won recognition as one of the world's leading lyric tenors. He has been particularly successful as an interpreter of Mozart's tenor roles, but he has also won applause for his performances in nineteenth-century German opera.

Schreier's portrayals of Mozart's Belmonte, Ottavio, Ferrando and Tamino are among the best in recent times; and his Mozart interpretations have not been limited to young lovers. He has performed the title role of *La clemenza di Tito* (Berlin, 1978); his recording of arias from that opera shows him to be an exciting and sympathetic emperor and makes one wish that he had performed the role more often. In 1987 he took on the role of Idomeneo for the first time. (He had previously sung Arbace and Idamante). In singing this role only late in his career Schreier followed in the footsteps of the first Idomeneo, the tenor Anton Raaff, who created the role at the end of his career, when he was sixty-six years old.

Schreier's voice is distinctive, lyrical yet virile, with a touch of baritone quality to it. His enunciation is admirably clear and vivid. He is at his best in gentle, lyrical passages. High notes and loud passages sometimes strain his voice. For example, in his recorded portrayal of Tamino (under Sawallisch), the "Portrait aria" is on the whole elegant and expressive, but at the word "Götterbild" Schreier shouts out the A flat harshly. Much the same criticism can be leveled at his portrayal of the hero Gomatz in Mozart's rarely performed Singspiel *Zaide* (recorded under Bernhard Klee). When Schreier relaxes and sings lyrically his voice is remarkably beautiful, but when he sings loudly an unpleasant, harsh tone enters his voice (as, for example, in the aria "Rase, Schicksal").

Schreier is a master of recitative, especially in German. One can hear this in the long orchestrally accompanied recitative in act I of *Die Zauberflöte* (again as recorded under Sawallisch), where he brings the text to life with his vivid and emphatic delivery. Characteristically for Schreier, this vividness comes, to some extent, at the expense of pure beauty of tone. But how sweetly and movingly he projects the line "Man opferte vielleicht sie schon?" as he expresses his fear for Pamina's life.

Schreier has shown little interest in nineteenth-century Italian opera, preferring opera in German. His recorded performance of Max (*Der Freischütz*) shows that his voice is not entirely suitable to the interpretation of Romantic heroes; the strain that is heard only rarely in his portrayals of Mozart's heroes is much more obvious here. But his performances of lesser and lighter roles in German Romantic opera, like David (*Die Meistersinger*), have been praised for their strong acting as well as their fine singing. (Schreier's David can be heard in a recording of *Die Meistersinger* under Karajan). In a rare revival of Strauss's *Die ägyptische Helena* (Vienna 1971), Schreier won applause for his portrayal of Da-ud. Among his other nineteenth-century roles are Baroncelli in *Rienzi* (a fine portrayal recorded under Hollreiser), Fenton in Nicolai's *Die lustigen Weiber von Windsor* and Lensky in *Eugene Onegin* (a German version presented in Vienna in 1974).

As Schreier's vocal power declined in recent years, he has directed much of his musical energy to operatic conducting; in this new phase of his career he seems to have made an auspicious start.—JOHN A. RICE

Schumann, Elisabeth

Soprano. Born 13 June 1885, in Merseburg, Germany. Died 23 April 1952, in New York. Studied with Natalie Hänisch in Dresden, Marie Dietrich in Berlin, and Alma Schadow in Hamburg; debut as the Shepherd in Tannhäuser, *Hamburg Opera, 1909; remained on roster there until 1919; Metropolitan Opera debut as Sophie in* Der Rosenkavalier, *1914; principal member of the Vienna State Opera, 1919-38; concert tour of the U.S. with Richard Strauss, 1921; lived in the U.S. after 1938; taught at the Curtis Institute of Music in Philadelphia; became naturalized citizen, 1944.*

Elisabeth Schumann was born in Merseburg, Thuringia in 1885 (not 1888 as she claimed) and was descended from the German soprano Henriette Sontag, who had created Euryanthe for Weber in 1823 and had also been the first solo soprano in Beethoven's Mass in D and in his Ninth Symphony. Sontag's voice was described as being "clear, bright, and used with exquisite taste"—these words describe Schumann's voice equally well. Her personality was full of fun and mischief, but she was astute enough to preserve the voice's youthful qualities until the late 1940s.

Schumann's parents always intended that she should become a singer and provided her with sound training in Dresden, whence she went to Marie Dietrich (a Pauline Viardot pupil) in Berlin. As soon as she finished her studies, she was given a contract by the Hamburg State Theater where she made her debut as the Shepherd Boy in *Tannhäuser*. The audience was entranced by the sweetness and brilliance of her tone and by the purity of sound.

In the following season, Schumann was the Sophie in Hamburg's first production of *Der Rosenkavalier,* a role with which later gramophone records have always associated her. No other Sophie has produced such crystal notes, especially in the act II Presentation Scene. This is the character of Sophie personified, all sweetness and virginity. In Hamburg she also sang a number of the same roles as Lotte Lehmann: Eva in *Die Meistersinger,* Mimi and one performance of Octavian as the result of a romantic scandal in which she was involved with the conductor, Otto Klemperer.

Schumann sang for one season at the Metropolitan Opera in 1914-15 and her debut there was as Sophie. "A clear and high soprano of pure quality and agreeable timbre, a voice possessing the bloom of youth," said a critic that night. She also sang Musetta, Gretel and Papagena in New York. Her London debut was again as Sophie, ten years later when, it was said, "for sheer beauty of tone and perfection of technique she towered above the rest of the cast," which included Lotte Lehmann and Richard Mayr.

Despite these positive assessments of Schumann's voice, it has been stated (by Michael Scott) that she suffered from "technical inadequacy," that "the voice was not fully developed and lacked support." Considering her training and immense success in all major opera houses, this view seems difficult to uphold. Of course it was not a large voice and could even be called soubrettish without any intended slur. Her Adele in *Fledermaus* when heard in Paris and admitted reluctantly to Covent Garden by Bruno Walter—both in 1930—was certainly a soubrette role, but how magically she did it!

In 1919 Richard Strauss, who was very partial to Schumann's voice and personality, engaged her for the Vienna Opera, especially to sing Mozart. He also took her to Salzburg for four of the Festivals between 1922-36 where she gave memorable characterizations of Despina, Susanna, Zerlina and Blondchen, and one performance of Marzelline in *Fidelio*. In Vienna, where she remained until 1937, she sang Micaela, Nedda and Norina, together with her usual Mozart roles and Ilia in Strauss's adaptation of *Idomeneo*—and of course Sophie.

When the Anschluss came, Elisabeth Schumann went to the USA, a refugee on account of her Jewish husband, the conductor Karl Alwin. She gave up the stage and devoted the rest of her life to *Lieder* and to teaching. But she often demonstrated how to sing operatic roles, and her voice was still capable, pure, and fresh as ever.—ALAN JEFFERSON

Schumann-Heink, Ernestine

Contralto. Born Ernestine Rössler, 15 June 1861, in Lieben, near Prague. Died 17 November 1936, in Hollywood. Married: 1) Ersnt Heink, 1882 (divorced, 1893), three sons, one daughter; 2) Paul Schumann, 1893 (died), two sons, one daughter; 3) William Rapp, Jr., 1905 (divorced, 1914). Studied with Marietta von Leclair in Graz, then with Karl Krebs, Franz Wüllner and G.B. Lamperti; debut as Azucena in Il trovatore, Dresden, *1878; in Dresden 1878-82; in Hamburg 1882-97; performed in a London production of* Der Ring des Nibelungen *under Gustav Mahler, 1892; Bayreuth debut in* Der Ring des Nibelungen, *1896; Berlin Opera, 1898; at Covent Garden 1897-1900; American debut as Ortrud in* Lohengrin, *Chicago, 1898; Metropolitan Opera debut as Ortrud, 1899; created the role of Klytemnestra in* Elektra, *Dresden, 1909; also a performer in musical comedy, radio, and films. Naturalized as an American citizen 1908.*

Ernestine Rössler, later known to the world as Ernestine Schumann-Heink, was born in Lieben, on the outskirts of Prague, in what was then Austria. While her mother had been well educated in Italy, her father had to support his family on a soldier's pay. Ernestine was raised around the army barracks wherever her father happened to be stationed, eventually in Graz where she was heard by an ex-singer who offered to give her lessons. At the age of fifteen she made her first public appearance, singing the alto part in the Beethoven Ninth from memory as she could not read music. The soprano, Marie Wilt of the Vienna opera, was so impressed with her little colleague that she arranged an audition in Vienna. Funds had to be borrowed for the trip, but the thin, scrawny girl in a made-over dress and army boots failed to impress. She was advised to go home and become a dressmaker. Ernestine was broken-hearted; fortunately her case was taken up by Amalie Materna who arranged an audition in Dresden, and this time she was successful. Her debut, on 15 October 1878, was as Azucena in *Il trovatore*. She was seventeen. She continued to sing a variety of small parts, from Puck in *Oberon* to Martha in *Faust;* from Merceedes in *Carmen* to the Shepherd in *Tannhäuser*. She also sang in the services at the Dresden Cathedral and had the opportunity to study seriously with Franz Wüllner and other musicians who lived in the city.

In 1882, Ernestine married Ernst Heink, a secretary at the opera. Their marriage was without the consent of the management, which was required by contract, and they were dismissed from the Dresden opera. After several months of bleak despair, Tini Rössler, now Frau Heink, obtained an engagement at the Hamburg Opera. As her biographer James McPherson put it, "during her first four years at Hamburg, Ernestine had nothing but bit parts and babies. To the latter category belonged August, Charlotte and Henry. When a fourth child grew imminent, Ernst Heink fled back to Saxony." In spite of her pleas with the management at Hamburg for larger and more substantial roles (and higher fees) Frau Heink continued to sing small roles, night after night, often giving as many as twenty-two performances in one month. At last, in 1889, the break finally came: Marie Goetze, the principal contralto of the opera, had a fit of temperament and refused at the last minute to go on as Carmen. In desperation, the management turned to Heink. Could she sing the opera? "I'll sing it if I die on the stage" was her answer, and sing it she did, in spite of no rehearsal and an improvised costume. She was a sensation, and Goetze was so put out that she cancelled her next appearance, Fidès in *Prophet*. Frau Heink came through again. The drudgery experienced on the lower rungs of the ladder had paid off. Then followed appearances at the Hofoper in Berlin, a tour of Scandinavia, and Paris. In 1892 she appeared in London, opening with Heink as Erda and Max Alvary as Siegfried. There the company performed two *Ring* cycles, two *Tristan und Isolde,* and England's first performances of *Der Trompeter von Sackingen,* in which the critics found special praise for Frau Heink.

In 1896 Schumann-Heink (she had in the meantime married Paul Schumann) was coached by Cosima Wagner at Bayreuth in the roles of Erda, Waltraute and the First Norn. She participated in five complete *Ring* cycles in July and August, and then back to Hamburg where she took part in 128 performances between September and May. Now most of the parts were major ones, and her repertory was enlarged by roles in several new operas, including *Rienzi, Andrea Chénier,* Meyerbeer's *Star of the North, The Bartered Bride, Hänsel und Gretel,* Kreutzer's *Verschwender,* Kienzl's *Evangelimann,* and even Gilbert & Sullivan's *Mikado.* In 1897, she returned to Covent Garden, Bayreuth, and without a break, back to Hamburg with still new operas like *Bohème, Cavalleria, Gioconda, Aida, Odysseus, Undine,* and *Fra Diavolo.*

With the death of the intendant of the Hamburg Opera in November 1897, the contract which had regulated Schumann-Heink's life for the past fourteen years was broken. She began accepting engagements in Berlin and elsewhere, and wrote "Ende—Finis" to Hamburg in her performance log on 31 May 1898. She was in London in June and July, and in August signed a new contract with the Berlin Hoftheater. Next it was the Metropolitan: the company was on tour, and Schumann-Heink made her debut in Chicago as Ortrud, with Eames, Dippel, Bispham and Edouard de Reszke, and received twenty curtain calls. There was a second triumphant Ortrud on the 10th, followed by Fricka in *Walküre* on the 18th and 23. Her New York debut was again in *Lohengrin,* this time with Nordica, Bispham, Jean and Edouard de Reszke.

For the next four years, she spent winters in New York and the balance of the year in Berlin and elsewhere. In the spring of 1903, Maurice Grau retired from the Metropolitan, and Schumann-Heink decided it was time for a change. A comic opera called *Love's Lottery* with book by Stanislau Stange and music by Julian Edwards, cast the singer as a Hausfrau laundress and ran for fifty performances on Broadway after its opening on 3 October 1903. After the Broadway closing, the show went on tour: the opening night in Boston brought the news of Paul Schumann's death in Dresden. Leaving the children in the care of their grandmother, Ernestine finished the tour, which was a great financial success. Events moved rapidly. The singer took out American citizenship, married her business manager, William Rapp Jr., brought the children to the United States, purchased a new home at Singac, New Jersey, and began a 40,000-mile concert tour in the United States. The great love affair between Ernestine Schumann-Heink and the American people had begun. During the next few years there were many such tours, both in the United States and in Europe, with an occasional appearance at an opera house squeezed in. The Metropolitan saw her again in 1907 when she sang ten performances, including the Witch in *Hänsel und Gretel;* there was an *Il trovatore* for Hammerstein in 1908; and she created Klytemnestra in Strauss' *Elektra* in Dresden, 25 January 1909. Now and again there were Bayreuth performances until the war, with occasional visits to the operatic stage in Boston and Chicago. In February and March 1926, to celebrate her "Golden Jubilee" as a singer, she sang Erda in *Das Rhinegold* and *Siegfried* at the Metropolitan; another *Rhinegold* followed in February 1929; and in 1932, she sang Erda in *Das Rhinegold* and *Siegfried* in her 71st year.

When World War I broke out, Schumann-Heink's eldest son August joined the German navy; shortly after, her son Hans contracted typhoid and died. When America entered the war, her youngest three boys enlisted in the American forces, and Schumann-Heink plunged into war work. Paying concerts were cancelled. She turned her home, then in Chicago, into a servicemen's canteen. She began an endless procession of appearances in hospitals and military camps; between these visits, she sang for Liberty Loan drives. She became known as "Mother Schumann-Heink" to countless service men. Actually, the work for "her boys" went on until her death, as she made it known that she was always available at no fee to any group of disabled veterans or the American Legion, no matter how inconvenient the engagement to the aging singer.

In 1926 Schumann-Heink made her first venture into radio; in the following year she made three Vitaphone shorts, and there was talk of "retirement" which was ended abruptly by the stock market crash of 1929. She was supporting a small army of relatives and hangers-on, and she desperately needed funds. The only way seemed to be vaudeville engagements in a nation-wide tour of motion picture houses, and radio appearances, including her weekly "show" for a maker of canned baby food, during which she told yarns about her career and sang a few songs. In 1935 she was signed to play herself in a "musical" film featuring Nino Martini called *Here's to Romance*. She turned out to be the hit of the show, and suddenly she was assailed by offers to make her own feature film. Unfortunately, it was not to be: she was taken ill in November 1936, returning from a Disabled Veterans convention in Milwaukee. She died of leukemia in Hollywood on 17 November. Two days later, the American Legion held a funeral service at their Hollywood post.

Schumann-Heink has left us some remarkable recordings, even though her voice had had some twenty-five years' hard usage before she made her first commercial discs for Columbia, early in 1903. In 1906, she began her long association with Victor, which ended in 1931, some forty-three years after her debut. Regretfully, her great Wagnerian roles are poorly represented, but the 1908 recording of "Gretcher Gott" from *Rienzi* must stand as a model of declamation and style. Her Erda's warning from *Das Rhinegold* can be compared in her acoustical version of 1907 and the electrical recording made in 1929 which, in spite of her age, commands tremendous respect. There are excellent examples of her coloratura in the Arditi "Bolero" (1907), in the aria from Mozart's *La clemenza de Tito* (1909), the two-part prison scene from *Le prophète*, and there are the famous renditions of the *Lucrezia Borgia* "Brindisi" with extended trills and two-octave leaps. She has left us "Ah mon fils" in both German and French, several versions of the *Samson* arias, and some Schumann, Schubert, Strauss and Brahms Lieder, the latter being especially important as she was given (she said) these songs by the composer. While some of her concert songs are of little lasting value, others are miniature works of art. Most will agree that her recordings of "Stille Nacht" have never been surpassed, and playing one of these recordings on Christmas Eve is still an important ritual in many American homes. A good deal of her fabulous personality comes through in the four sound films of 1927 and 1935, brief as her appearances in them are.—WILLIAM R. MORAN

Schwarzkopf, Elisabeth

Soprano. Born 9 December 1915, in Jarotschin, near Poznan. Married: record producer Walter Legge, 1953 (died 1979). Studied with Lula Mysz-Gmeiner at the Berlin Hochschule für Musik, and later with Maria Ivogün and her husband, accompanist Michael Raucheisen; joined Berlin Städtische Oper in 1938, making debut as a Flowermaiden in Parsifal; *gave successful recital at Beethoven Saal in Berlin, 1942, and was subsequently asked by Karl*

Böhm to join the Vienna Staatsoper; Covent Garden debut as Donna Elvira during Staatsoper's visit there in 1947, and remained with the Covent Garden company five seasons; at Salzburg Festival, 1947-64, and Teatro alla Scala, 1948-63; created role of Anne Trulove in Stravinsky's The Rake's Progress, *Venice, 1951; also in 1951 sang Eva and Woglinde at Bayreuth; San Francisco debut as Marschallin in* Der Rosenkavalier, *1955; debut at Paris Opéra (1962) and Metropolitan Opera (1964) in same role; from the 1950s recorded extensively, usually in collaboration with husband; retired from opera in 1972 and from concerts in 1975; holds honorary Doctorate from Cambridge University and the Grosses Verdienst-Kreuz der Bundesrepublik Deutschland.*

In Mozart and as Richard Strauss's Marschallin and Countess Madeleine (*Capriccio*), Elisabeth Schwarzkopf may lay claim as the most significant interpreter in our time. Yet she antagonizes as many listeners as she pleases, so that the distinguished critic John Steane will write of a Schwarzkopf performance that "what one hears is the most beautiful legato, the finest of lightenings, the least fussy and most sensitive of interpretations," while the equally respected Robin Holloway describes "narcissism to the point of incest . . . this isn't renunciation; it's a pettish *grande dame* with migraine."

What is the reason for such contradictory opinions? Certainly not in dispute is the quality of Schwarzkopf's natural talents: Holloway himself rather grudgingly admits to her "singing of extraordinary technical accomplishment; it is perfect, even great, in its way." Indeed, few singers in our time have been so prodigiously gifted. A great physical beauty, Schwarzkopf also possessed a superb lyric soprano voice—instantly recognizable and managed with the precision of an instrumentalist. Although over time the top of the voice hardened somewhat, Schwarzkopf's technical mastery and canny artistic intelligence allowed her to mask this weakness and even turn it to her advantage; the lighter, slightly crooning quality employed in some of her later recordings has the suggestion of elegant and sophisticated artistic choice. If this fact reveals a degree of calculation, perhaps we have arrived at the source of the controversy. Much has been written about Schwarzkopf's marriage to record producer and EMI executive Walter Legge, a union of two perfectionists with seemingly insatiable appetites for refinement. Their collaboration meant that music, text and interpretation were prepared with the meticulous care of a diamond-cutter. The resulting performances had a specificity and richness of detail which are quite unique, but a certain lack of naturalness and spontaneity could also characterize the finished product.

Ultimately one's reaction to Schwarzkopf is very much a matter of personal taste. Like Maria Callas in a rather different repertoire, Schwarzkopf is an artist of bold choices, and audiences tend to be deeply factionalized about her work. Some cannot tolerate her often fussy diction and find her insufferably arch and mannered in almost every role. Others think Schwarzkopf incomparable in achieving a unification of dramatic insight and superb vocalism. For the latter group of listeners, Schwarzkopf ranks with Callas as one of the complete operatic artists of our time—as much actress as singer.

Certain operas suited Schwarzkopf's aristocratic approach better than others, and in her mature career she cagily restricted her stage portrayals to a limited number of roles which she performed internationally. The music of Mozart figured prominently. She brought a towering, tragic stature to Donna Elvira, a part which in lesser hands can seem merely hectoring and pathetic, and her singing of the difficult music—demanding a perfectly controlled legato line as

741

well as a formidable florid technique—was superb in every way. Schwarzkopf's touching Countess in *Figaro* was equally distinguished. As Fiordiligi, she revealed a delicious flair for comedy and sang the fiendishly difficult music as well as it has been sung in recent memory: year after year, her portrayal was one of the highlights of the Salzburg Festival.

Even Schwarzkopf's most virulent detractors allow that she has few peers as the Marschallin, a role which needs a singer who can provide a steady outpouring of beautiful tone as well as illuminate the profound, often difficult and abstract poetry of Hofmannsthal's masterly libretto. Since the premiere performance of *Der Rosenkavalier* in 1911, only a few sopranos have really made the part their own. The great Lotte Lehmann was indelibly identified with the opera in the 1930s and 1940s, and, since the 1950s, it is Schwarzkopf's portrayal which has become legendary. Many first-class singers have performed the Marschallin with distinction since Schwarzkopf's retirement—the list includes Elisabeth Söderström, Kiri Te Kanawa, Lucia Popp and others—but none has displaced her memory in the part.

Although Elisabeth Schwarzkopf retired from singing in the late 1970's, she continues to play a significant role in the musical world. In 1976, she and Walter Legge offered a highly successful series of Master Classes at the Julliard School in New York City. Since Legge's death in 1979, Schwarzkopf has continued her career as a master teacher in venues around the world. Among her students have been the American baritone Thomas Hampson; soprano Margaret Marshall, whose cultivated assumptions of the Mozart heroines are very much in the tradition of her mentor; and Mitsuko Shirai, the noted Japanese concert singer. As a teacher Schwarzkopf continues to promote the exacting standards which made her one of the century's greatest singers.—DAVID ANTHONY FOX

Scotti, Antonio

Baritone. Born 25 January 1866, in Naples. Died 26 February 1936, in Naples. Studied with Ester Triffani-Paganini and Vincenzo Lombardi; debut as Amonasro in Aida, *Malta, 1889; major debut as Cinna in* La vestale, *Naples, 1889; Teatro alla Scala debut as Hans Sachs, 1899; Covent Garden debut as Don Giovanni, 1899; Metropolitan Opera debut as Don Giovanni, 1899; at Metropolitan Opera, 1899-1933, roles including Scarpia, Falstaff, Rigoletto, Iago, Tonio; created the role of Chim-Fen in Leoni's* L'oracolo, *Covent Garden, 1905; his Scotti Opera Company toured the United States for four years; retired in 1933.*

On 20 January 1933, five days before his sixty-seventh birthday, Antonio Scotti, seeming even older than his years, stood alone in front of the great gold curtain at the Metropolitan Opera and said to the assemblage, "I do not want to leave you, but I must." The role he had just performed at this official farewell was that of Chim-Fen in Leoni's *L'oracolo,* one which he had created at Covent Garden (1905) and of which he had been sole interpreter at the Metropolitan (in a total of fifty-five performances between 1915 and 1933).

Scotti's honest remark to his final audience acknowledged that his voice, never his most important asset and eventually his greatest liability, would simply no longer bear the strain of performance. Perhaps the body, too, was at last in rebellion against the histrionic requirements of his signature roles—Scarpia, Marcello, Sharpless—parts that he "owned" in New York from the first moment he brought them to life there. Scotti's 217 Scarpias with the Metropolitan constitute an unbreakable record: the most performances of a leading role by any artist in the company's history.

What kept Scotti onstage for so many years beyond his time of prime vocal accomplishment was his almost unparalleled sense of the theater, impossible to part with until there was absolutely no choice but to do so. He had debuted in Naples as Cinna in *La vestale* in 1889, and followed this with a decade of hard singing throughout Italy, as well as in Spain, Portugal, Poland, Russia, and South America. He came both to London and New York in 1899 (in each case as a dapper Don Giovanni), singing in a smoothly produced, well-schooled *bel canto* style, supported by a high level of musical understanding that gave him rank even though his voice was quite the least of those baritone instruments that emerged from Italy at the end of the nine-

Antonio Scotti as Falstaff

teenth century. Battistini, De Luca, Ancona, Ruffo, and Amato, all of whom were prominent at various points during Scotti's lengthy time before the public (the first two enjoyed similarly long careers), all possessed voices either larger or of much greater natural beauty, and all were much more suited to the high-lying *cantilena* of early and middle-period Verdi, for instance.

But Scotti was completely aware of his strengths and limitations and began to specialize in verismo roles, along with occasional others (Iago, Falstaff) wherein his command of characterization and dramatic nuance went largely unchallenged. In 1924, W.J. Henderson wrote of Scotti that "now when his voice has passed its meridian his skill in impersonation, which years ago became the chief part of his stock, still chains the interest of operagoers." Despite the considerable, nearly Verdian, vocal hurdle posed for him by the "Prologue" (from which he omitted the two stand-out high notes), Scotti retained the otherwise verismo part of Tonio in *I pagliacci* in his repertory all the way up until 1930, simply because it appealed to him so much from the dramatic standpoint.

Even though the evidence of Scotti's recordings, being strictly aural, belies for some commentators his high historical standing (William Albright has written that Scotti "is a singer whose legendary status tends to elude me. I find his tone dry, hooded, and stiff, his legato gluey"), the impression he made in person was overpowering. Max Smith described his Chim-Fen as "a gruesomely realistic characterization of the villainous Chinaman, every detail of his portrayal, even to the forward inclination of his head, the indrawing of his shoulders and elbows and the ghastly limpness of his pendulous fingers, showing careful study and elaboration. Few persons are likely to forget the uncanny sight Scotti presented as he sank, loose and spineless, under the onslaught of his murderer, and later as he flopped forward in a heap and rolled over on the stage."

Offstage, Scotti possessed a sophistication and innate elegance that his fellow Neapolitan and frequent colleague Enrico Caruso lacked, particularly in matters of dress. But Caruso, "natural man" that he was, endured unfavorable comparisons with good humor, perhaps privately noting that he had considerably more success in matters of the heart than Scotti: urged on by William J. Guard, the Metropolitan's publicist, the New York papers in 1911 carried a statement containing "the annual announcement of [Geraldine] Farrar's rejection of Scotti's proposal of marriage." Whatever their differences in character, Caruso and Scotti were lifelong friends, and left to posterity recordings of duets from *Don Carlo*, *La forza del destino*, *La bohème*, and *Madama Butterfly* that stand among the most important documents in operatic history.

Scotti could not live without the stage, and he had an ego, too. One of the most celebrated incidents in Metropolitan annals occurred at the 1925 revival of *Falstaff*. When the audience clamored for the young American baritone Lawrence Tibbett, who was singing Ford, following the act II inn scene, Scotti mistook the applause as being for himself and insisted on bowing again and again with Tibbett ("the modest Mr. Tibbett evidently did not want to get between the limelight and Mr. Scotti," wrote Lawrence Gilman). But the opera was not allowed to proceed until Tibbett finally showed himself alone before the curtain. His compatriots "split the roof" and created a new star simultaneously.

Scotti retired, poverty-stricken (a fact known only to a faithful servant), to his native Naples. Death came within three years to the man we still honor as the greatest Italian operatic actor of his day.—BRUCE BURROUGHS

Scotto, Renata

Soprano. Born 24 February 1934, in Savona. Started to study music in Savona at age fourteen; studied in Milan with Emilio Ghirardini, Merlini, and Mercedes Llopart; debut as Violetta, Savona, 1952; formal debut in same role, Milan, Teatro Nuovo, 1953; sang at Teatro alla Scala; U.S. debut as Mimi, Chicago Lyric Opera, 1960; Metropolitan Opera debut as Madama Butterfly, 1965; won wide recognition as Mimi in the "Live from Lincoln Center" telecast of La bohème, *1977.*

In the opera house a diva creates her own world. Whatever the means, she obliterates for the moment any other realization of the role she is playing: she fills you with herself. The effect is quite unlike the reasoned appreciation roused by an accomplished professional performance. Renata Scotto was, by common consent, a diva. She brought to the operatic stage at first a truly beautiful lyric voice, full of unexpected light and shadow. She had curiosity, intelligence, and the gift of perception; her *Trittico* heroines, for example, were works of great skill as well as great art.

Scotto also had a dangerous audacity. Against strong advice she went on in the second half of her career to sing dramatic soprano roles such as Gioconda, Norma, and Lady Macbeth. Her dramatic gifts illuminated some of them—one thinks particularly of Gioconda—but she destroyed her voice and sometimes seriously compromised the music in the process, a fate predicted for her by a number of major Italian sopranos of the previous generation, from Pagliughi to Caniglia to Tebaldi.

Scotto's voice had everything: a forward lyric quality, a silvery edge that did not belie warmth, the brilliant high range and mobility to conquer Lucia, and, when she wished it, a fascinating darkness that qualified her for a lovely Violetta, the role in which she made her debut at age eighteen. She also had discipline. Seeing herself in the Met's televised *Bohème* of 1977, she decided to lose thirty pounds, did so, and never regained it. She was a graceful, if slight, stage figure. She was the subtlest vocal actress of the post-Callas period in not one but three repertories (bel canto, Verdi, and verismo), and the only one to provide a conviction and a complexity of dramatic effect sufficient to recall the occasional glories of the previous two generations. Typically, Mafalda Favero, one of the great La Scala lyric sopranos of the thirties and forties, called Scotto the finest of the later Italians.

Early recordings of *La serva padrona* and *Lucia* show her in splendid voice, with lovely phrasing and an exquisite projection of both vitality and warmth in characterization. As Lucia, even in 1959, before she had sung the role onstage, she had a technique and beauty of tone to match any of her later rivals except possibly the young Sutherland, and a concept excelled in subtlety and romantic fervor only by Callas. The very way she sings the word "Ascolta!" ("Listen!") before her first aria draws us in to hang upon her mysterious tale. From the beginning, her Lucia's love is unconditional, and expressed with a noble economy of means which is in itself a comment on Lucia's character: color, phrasing, and just a hint of hysteria in the tone. The mad scene is deliciously warm, though it settles for pathos and misses the tragic: that was to come later. Of her mature recordings the 1966 Butterfly is typically memorable: beautifully voiced save for a few top notes, grave and yet youthful, shy but sensual, full of humor but never coy, intimate and yet somehow far more tragic in its effect than the creations of darker voices, and rich with a thousand fine-grained vocal effects.

Scotto was especially impressive when actually seen on the stage. Her three roles in Puccini's *Trittico*—rather dull when done by three other sopranos in the same production previously in New York, were gripping in her live performance. The restless despair of Georgetta, the ecstatic purity of Suor Angelica, and the charm of young Lauretta were separately winning and together overwhelming. Only Scotto among modern sopranos could build the second half of *Suor Angelica* in such a way as not to lose dramatic tension in sentimentality. On television she made of the melodrama *Gioconda* a genuine tragedy. One of the few great operatic videotapes is of her *Manon Lescaut*, conducted by Levine, directed by Menotti, beautifully set and costumed, and also featuring Placido Domingo in one of his most fervent performances. Scotto herself is in fine voice. Her skill and spontaneity, and the mystery, frivolity, and passion of her performance are in heartbreaking balance. It is, in short, the diva experience.—LONDON GREEN

Seefried, Irmgard

Soprano. Born 9 October 1919, in Köngetried, Germany. Died 24 November 1988, in Vienna. Married: violinist Wolfgang Schneiderhan, 1948; two daughters. Studied with her father, with Albert Meyer at the Augsburg Conservatory, and with Paola Novikova; debut as Gretel at age 11; adult debut as Priestess in Aida, Aachen, 1940; at Aachen 1940-43; Vienna State Opera debut as Eva in Die Meistersinger von Nürnberg, 1943; at Vienna State Opera 1943-76; Covent Garden debut as Fiordiligi in Così fan tutte, 1947; Teatro alla Scala debut as Susanna in Le nozze di Figaro, 1949; Metropolitan Opera debut as Susanna, 1953; after 1976, performed some character parts at the Deutsche Volksoper and taught.

Seldom is a world-famous soprano as much liked by her colleagues as she is by her public, but Irmgard Seefried never acted the prima donna. She was born in Bavaria in 1919 of Austrian parents, both musical, and her father became her first teacher, training her thoroughly in piano and violin. She became a vocal student in Augsburg and later at the Munich Music Academy with such success that she was engaged for the 1940-41 season at Aachen Opera by its director, Herbert von Karajan. While there, she also sang in the Cathedral Choir and learned a great deal from its director, Dr. Theodor Rehmann. It was indirectly through him that Seefried was invited by Karl Böhm as a guest artist to Dresden. When Böhm moved to Vienna in 1943, Seefried went as a contract member of Vienna's famous opera company. Her debut was as Eva in *Die Meistersinger,* though her career was to become centered on Mozart.

In 1944, Richard Strauss asked that Seefried be cast as the Young Composer in his 80th Birthday Festival performance of *Ariadne auf Naxos;* she subsequently sang Octavian in *Der Rosenkavalier,* and in both of these trouser roles she displayed great gusto, even though she was innately feminine and graceful.

Seefried appeared with the Vienna Staatsoper at Covent Garden in 1947 as Fiordiligi in *Così fan tutte* (its first appearance at that house) and also as Susanna in *Figaro* which, together with Pamina in *Die Zauberflöte* and Zerlina in *Don Giovanni,* were to be her staple roles at Salzburg and elsewhere for the next twenty years.

Irmgard Seefried was a very intelligent musician and has left several perceptive indications of the way in which she approached Mozart. She particularly liked singing Pamina: "there is no greater test for the production of smooth legato. Some of my colleagues found her dull; I never did." And "Zerlina suited my voice and sense of comedy. She is really the audience's key to understanding what the Don is like." About Fiordiligi: "She is hard to sing, but in my estimation one must think of her as a violin. Although many people think the role is ideal for an Italian soprano, that is not true."

Later in her career, Seefried filled out her repertoire with contrasting roles: Blanche in *Les dialogues des Carmélites,* Cleopatra in Handel's *Giulio Cesare* and Marie in *Wozzeck*—probably the most appealing Marie on any stage, sung from a firm Mozartian technique and not screamed.

She was always full of admiration for other great singers, which indicates total self-confidence in her own artistry. The voice was, as the roles she sang indicate, full of expression, warm and sunny like her nature, and thoroughly trained always to produce the very best. The frequency with which she sang her Mozart roles added to, rather than detracted from, their impression on audiences; she was not only seeking fresh insights into her characters and new, convincing ways round vocal difficulties (with which they abound) but was always prepared to adapt to other singers' needs when in ensemble.

Seefried had a successful marriage with Wolfgang Schneiderhan, leader of the Vienna Philharmonic Orchestra throughout the war and afterwards, and was vocally, as well as personally, a happy, relaxed and grateful singer whose gifts were given generously.—ALAN JEFFERSON

Semiramide

Composer: *Gioachino Rossini.*

Librettist: *G. Rossi (after Voltaire).*

First Performance: *Venice, La Fenice, 3 February 1823.*

Roles: *Semiramide (soprano); Arsace (contralto); Assur (baritone); Idreno (tenor); Oroe (bass); Azema (soprano); Mitrane (tenor); chorus (SSATB).*

Although the plot of *Semiramide* seems and in fact is overwhelmingly complex, it is nonetheless comprehensible. The story takes place in ancient Babylon. Queen Semiramide has years earlier plotted but failed to kill Ninias, the son she bore King Nino. Nino, however, has himself been assassinated by the wicked Semiramide and her lover Prince Assur. Now that the oracle has declared that a new king will be designated, Arsace, the commander of the army, has returned to Babylon. In love with Princess Azema, Arsace angers Assur because Assur also loves Azema and plans to make her his queen once he has taken over the throne. The Indian King Idrino also loves Azema.

Misinterpreting a divine oracle, Semiramide has now fallen in love with Arsace. She arranges for Idreno to marry Azema and for herself to marry Arsace, who would thereby become king. The ghost of Nino declares that Arsace will indeed become king once certain ancient crimes have been atoned. (At its premiere in 1823, this much of the opera—act I—reportedly lasted two and one-half hours.)

In act II Arsace is told by the High Priest (Oroe) that it was Semiramide and Assur who had murdered Nino and that he, Arsace, is in fact Ninias, the long-lost son of Nino and rightful heir to the throne. When Arsace confronts Semiramide with her crime, she confesses, but he is unable to avenge his father's death on his own mother. In the dark of Nino's tomb, however, Arsace mistakes his mother for Assur and kills her instead. Arsace nobly contemplates suicide, but when all is revealed, Assur is arrested, and the people declare as their new king Arsace, who finally makes Azema his queen.

Set design by Alessandro Sanquirico for the sanctuary scene in *Semiramide*

The legend of Semiramis can be traced back to an historical Assyrian queen, Sammuramat, wife of Shamshi-Adad V, who lived during the late ninth century B.C. On the other hand, the popularized legend of Semiramis was promulgated in Italy by Muzio Manfredi as early as 1593, set as an opera in 1648, and was reworked by Metastasio in the eighteenth century. Rossini's libretto, based on Voltaire's treatment of the legend in 1748, was written again by Gaetano Rossi, the same librettist who had rendered Rossini a libretto for Voltaire's *La cambiale di matrimonio* in Venice some years before at the outset of his career. Remarkably (but characteristically), Rossini claims and seems to have completed the opera in less than forty days.

The premiere at La Fenice on 3 February 1823, was well received, although the extraordinary length of the first act had the audience at first somewhat perplexed. Nonetheless, the finale of the first act was captivating, and Rossini's reputation did not suffer. The opera was repeated almost nightly for an entire month and played well subsequently in France, Germany, and England. Chronologically, however, *Semiramide* was the last opera Rossini wrote in Italy. After returning to Bologna that spring, Rossini and Mme Colbran-Rossini signed a contract to work in London, an arrangement which ultimately brought them to Paris. For the new Parisian production of *Semiramide* in 1825, Rossini stretched out the quickly unfolding events at the end of act II by extending Semiramide's death scene.

The splendidly atmospheric music Rossini composed for Arsace's visions in Nino's tomb, for the finale of act I, and even for the substantial overture typify his particular ability at composing a convincing *opera seria* in the mystical world of (what was then called) the Orient with an obviously Italian idiom. Previous examples include *Ciro in Babilonia, Aureliano in Palmira, Otello, Mosè in Egitto*, and *Maometto II*.—JON SOLOMON

Shirley, George

Tenor. Born 18 April 1934, in Indianapolis. Married: artist and educator Gladys Lee Ishop, 1956; one daughter, one son. Studied with Amos Ebersole, Edward Boatner at Wayne State University; also with Themy S. Georgi, Cornelius Reid; debut as Eisenstein in Die Fledermaus, Woodstock, New York, 1959; Italian debut as Rodolfo at Teatro Nuovo, Milan, 1960; New York City Opera debut as Rodolfo, 1961; Metropolitan Opera debut as Ferrando in Così fan tutte, 1961; at Metropolitan Opera, 1961-73, singing twenty-seven roles including Ottavio, Alfredo, Pinkerton, Tamino, Romeo, Almaviva; Glyndebourne debut as Tamino, 1966; Covent Garden debut as Don Ottavio, 1967; Alwa in Lulu, Santa Fe, 1973. On the faculty of Staten Island Community College; Artist-in-Residence, Morgan State College, Baltimore.

The American tenor George Shirley sang in a wide variety of operas during a relatively short career that unfolded primarily during the 1960s and 1970s. His repertory was remarkable for the extent to which it went beyond the standard repertory of late eighteenth- and nineteenth-century classics. Shirley was as successful with Haydn and Britten as he was with Mozart, Wagner and Debussy.

One of Shirley's best Mozart roles was the title role of *Idomeneo*, which he performed under Colin Davis at Covent Garden. He was less successful in some of his performances of Mozart tenor roles that require a gentler touch. His portrayals of Ferrando (in *Così fan tutte*)

earned mixed reviews. Shirley was praised for the passion and nobility he brought to the role, but was criticized for the tightness of voice that one could hear in his rendition of "Un' aura amorosa", an aria that demands more delicacy and tenderness than Shirley could convey.

Wagner's operas offered Shirley roles well suited to his voice. His portrayals of Loge in the *Ring* were much applauded at Covent Garden during the 1970s. One critic praised his performance as "subtle and musical"; another praised his "dazzling portrayal of Loge"; others called him "eloquent," even "superb."

Writing of Shirley's Loge, a critic noticed in his voice "a baritonal sound." He was referring no doubt to a dark quality that was characteristic of Shirley's voice and to his tessitura, which was lower than those of some other tenors. Shirley was a tenor, not a baritone, but he was never completely comfortable with high notes. One could hear this in one of his best roles, that of Pélleas in Debussy's *Pelléas et Mélisande*. When he performed the role with the Scottish Opera in 1975 he was praised for his portrayal, but also criticized for the strain perceptible in his voice.

Pelléas was not Shirley's only successful role with the Scottish Opera. He won much applause for his portrayal of Quint in Britten's *Turn of the Screw* when the Scottish Opera presented the opera at the King's Theatre in 1979. *Opera* praised his performance as "insinuating, physically threatening and mesmerizingly sung."

Shirley's portrayal of the title character in Haydn's *Orlando paladino*, recorded under Dorati, gives listeners some idea of the singer's weaknesses and strengths. This is a very strong, vivid depiction of the violent, love-crazed Orlando. But Shirley sometimes goes too far, seemingly forcing his character on the audience. In such arias as "D'Angelica il nome" we can admire the beauty of Shirley's voice in lyrical passages, but in louder passages he sometimes shouts rather than sings. He seems to be able to express his character's rage only with a harsh fortissimo. Shirley's voice sounds like a high baritone rather than a tenor; high notes sometimes sound forced. A tremulous vibrato often mars the gentler, more lyrical passages. And yet we remember this character. Shirley's passion, energy and enthusiasm stay with us, as the rest of the performances in this recording fade from memory.—JOHN A. RICE

Shostakovich, Dmitri

Composer. Born 25 September 1906, in St Petersburg. Died 9 August 1975, in Moscow. Early musical training from his mother, a professional pianist; studied piano with Nikolayev and composition with Maksimilian Shteinberg at the Petrograd Conservatory, 1919-25 (piano degree, 1923; composition degree, 1925); his first symphony performed by the Leningrad Philharmonic, 12 May 1926.

Operas *The Gypsies,* after Pushkin, before 1918 [destroyed by the composer]; *The Nose [Nos].* E. Zamyatin, G. Yonin, and A. Preis (after Gogol), 1927-28, Leningrad, 18 January 1930; *The Lady Macbeth of Mtsensk District [Ledi Makbet Mtsenskogo uezda].* A. Preis (after Leskov), 1930-32, Leningrad, 22 January 1934; revised as *Katerina Izmailova,* 1956-63, Moscow, 8 January 1963; *The Gamblers [Igroki]* after Gogol, 1941 [unfinished]; *Moscow, Cheremushki [Moskva Cheremushki]* (operetta), V. Mass and M. Chervinsky, 1958, Moscow, 24 January 1959.

A single newspaper article blighted one of the most promising operatic careers of the twentieth century and diverted the entire operatic tradition of a nation. On 28 January 1936, *Pravda* denounced Dmitri Shostakovich's *The Lady Macbeth of Mtsensk District* as "Chaos instead of Music." The article was unsigned, and there have been disputes as to its authorship, but it clearly carried the authority of Stalin, who had seen a production of the opera the previous month. As the Soviet intellectual community had already discovered, the price of such disapproval could be loss of livelihood, victimization of relatives, internal exile, imprisonment, or even death.

Shostakovich abandoned his planned operatic trilogy (later announced as a tetralogy) about heroic Russian and Soviet women, and he never completed another serious opera; instead his dramatic instincts were redirected and he became one of the great twentieth century symphonists. Meanwhile Soviet composers, if they ventured into musical drama at all, took refuge in nationalistic song operas of the kind known to appeal to Stalin. Here the approved model was Ivan Dzerzhinsky's *The Quiet Don* (after Sholokhov's novel), which ironically enough had been completed under Shostakovich's artistic supervision.

Lady Macbeth was a huge popular and critical success in Leningrad and Moscow, notching up nearly 200 performances in 1934 and 1935. It was also performed all over Europe and in both American continents, where its reception was more mixed. Russian and Western commentators alike saw its emotional excesses as a product of Soviet society, although their reasons for drawing this conclusion were very different. It would almost certainly be wrong to see *Lady Macbeth* as dissident or even consciously non-conformist, even if later events made it seem so. By the time of the opera's completion in 1932 the Party's policy directives for the arts had only just been formulated, and their relevance to music was far from clear. *Lady Macbeth* was almost certainly an attempt to influence the direction of that policy rather than a gesture of either compliance or defiance. Its subject matter (an indictment of the merchant class in nineteenth-century Russia) and its dramatic tone (summed up by the composer as "tragedy-satire") represented considerable modifications of Leskov's original story, in line with what might have been understood as Socialist/Realist principles at the time.

Shostakovich's early musical development was remarkable. His First Symphony, finished at the age of 18, was an international sensation, and on the strength of it he was acclaimed as the first significant composer to have spent his formative years under the Bolsheviks. Among the juvenilia he burned after his graduation in 1925 was an opera *The Gypsies,* after Pushkin, probably composed before 1918—three vocal numbers survive, but are unpublished.

In the ideological battlefield of Soviet music in the 1920s, Shostakovich sided with those who favored increased contact with new Western music. His satirical opera *The Nose* (1927-28) has many features in common with the burlesque tone of Prokofiev's *The Love for Three Oranges,* the atonal caricatures in Berg's *Wozzeck,* and the music hall elements of Krenek's *Der Sprung über den Schatten,* all produced in Leningrad in 1926 and 1927. Shostakovich always played down their influence, however, and it is probable that his imagination was fired more intensely by the work of the famous actor-director Vsevolod Meierkhold, with whom he lodged during the composition of *The Nose.* The eighty-odd solo roles in this work are something of an obstacle to staged performance, and the first Soviet production had great difficulties coping with Shostakovich's musical demands. Nevertheless the score, which includes parts for domra and balalaika and an interlude for percussion alone, is brilliantly inventive and succeeds in matching Gogol's text in its refusal to allow any single interpretation of its meaning.

Much of Shostakovich's work between *The Nose* and *Lady Macbeth* consisted of ballet and film scores and incidental music for the theater. The thirty-five numbers for the music hall review *Conditionally Killed* (1931) make this virtually a full blown operetta; in 1929 he supplied two additional movements for the opera *Columbus* by the young German composer Erwin Dressel; and in 1932 he began work on a comic opera to Nikolai Aseev's *The Great Lightning,* whose nine published numbers (rediscovered in 1980) suggest the influence of Weill's *Die Dreigroschenoper.* All of these activities left their mark on the music of *Lady Macbeth*—less avant-garde than that of *The Nose,* but still immensely vivid. Subsequently there are two film scores—for the cartoons *The Tale of the Priest and his Servant Balda* (1933-34) and *The Silly Little Mouse* (1939)—which Shostakovich regarded as "little operas," since the films were put to the music rather than vice versa.

Shostakovich's rehabilitation after *Lady Macbeth* came with the Fifth Symphony in 1937 and was consolidated with the Seventh (the "Leningrad") in 1941. His interest in the stage was kept alive, however, by his edition and orchestration of Musorgsky's *Boris Godunov* in 1939-40, and in 1942 he started work on the Gogol play *The Gamblers.* His word-for-word setting of the latter was abandoned at the end of act I, ostensibly because it was becoming unmanageable, but more importantly because there were no realistic prospects of performance, still less of approval (a posthumous three-act completion has been made by his Polish pupil, Krzysztof Meyer).

In 1944, Shostakovich completed the orchestration of the 40-minute one-act opera *Rothschild's Violin* (a Chekhov short story) by his pupil Veniamin Fleishman who had died at the battlefront. This encounter with Jewish folk idioms was to bear fruit in many of Shostakovich's later instrumental works, as well as in the general enrichment of his modal harmonic style; there are direct echoes of Fleishman's music in the Twenty-four Preludes and Fugues (1950-51) and the Tenth Symphony (1953).

Shostakovich's operetta (or musical comedy) *Moscow, Cheremushki* (1958) deals with the lives of workers in a Moscow suburb and incorporates at least half a dozen folk and popular songs of the 1920s, as well as references to his own songs of that period. In an explanatory article he professed admiration for the work of Offenbach, Lecocq, Johann Strauss, Kálmán and Lehár (the notorious invasion music of the "Leningrad" Symphony is based partly on a snatch of melody from Lehár's *The Merry Widow*). In the same year he prepared an edition and orchestration of Musorgsky's *Khovanshchina,* originally undertaken for a film version of the opera. Between 1956 and 1963 he worked on a revision of *Lady Macbeth,* toning down its most lurid extremes. His closest musical associates consider the revisions politically rather than artistically motivated. The new version was entitled *Katerina Izmailova.*

Throughout his career, Shostakovich was offered various operatic projects and in some cases made sketches. These include Ilf and Petrov's *The Twelve Chairs* (1937-38), *Quiet Flows the Don* (mentioned in the Soviet press between 1965 and 1970) and, perhaps most tantalizing of all, Chekhov's story *The Black Monk,* which he was considering in his last years and which he claimed was a sub-text to the Fifteenth Symphony of 1971.—DAVID FANNING

Le siège de Corinthe [The Siege of Corinth]

Composer: *Gioachino Rossini.*

Librettists: *L. Balocchi and A. Soumet (after della Valle's libretto for Rossini's Maometto II, 1820).*

First Performance: *Paris, Opéra, 9 October 1826.*

Roles: *Mahomet II (bass); Pamira (soprano); Néoclès (tenor); Hiéros (bass); Adraste (tenor); Omar (tenor); Ismène (soprano); Cléomène (tenor); chorus.*

Le siège de Corinthe is a reworking of Rossini's Neapolitan opera *Maometto II*. It was his debut at the Paris Opéra, for which Rossini was apparently as yet reluctant to write a completely new work in French (his first opera for Paris, the Italian *Il viaggio a Reims,* was performed at the Théâtre-Italien in June of 1825).

The plot of the opera basically follows that of *Maometto II,* but the place, time, and names of characters as well as some details are changed. It is based on the historical Turkish victory at Corinth in 1459 (in *Maometto II* the Turks conquer the Venetians at Negroponte in 1476). Cléomène (Paolo Erisso in *Maometto II*), the Greek governor of Corinth, has called his council to determine whether to fight the Byzantines who have besieged the city for two months or to surrender. The young officer Néoclès (Calbo), to whom Cléomène has promised the hand of his daughter Pamira (Anna), encourages the Greeks to resist. However, Pamira is in love with a man named Almanzor (Uberto), whom she met in Athens, and refuses to wed Néoclès. Cléomène gives her a dagger with which to kill herself if the city is captured. The Turks breach the wall of the city, and Mahomet confides to his friend Omar (Selimo) that while traveling under the name of Almanzor he met a Greek girl whose memory makes him feel clemency toward her compatriots. Cléomène is brought before him and Mahomet and Pamira recognize each other. Still rejecting Néoclès, Pamira brings her father's wrath upon herself.

The second act opens in Mahomet's tent as the Turkish maidens exhort Pamira to enjoy the delights of love. Torn between love for Mahomet and loyalty to her country, she prays to her dead mother to watch over her destiny. Mahomet, trying to lessen her sorrow, offers her his crown and says they will appease her father's anger. Pamira's confidante, Ismène, and the chorus joyfully anticipate the wedding, dancing and singing a marriage hymn. Néoclès tries to prevent the wedding, and to save him Pamira tells Mahomet that he is her brother; Omar interrupts them to say the Greek women and soldiers are defending the citadel. Pamira says she loved Almanzor but will die for her country.

In the final act, Néoclès brings Pamira to her father in the catacombs, where the Greeks have prepared their last defense, and convinces him to forgive her; Cléomène then unites them in marriage. Cléomène and Néoclès go to join the Greeks in battle as Pamira and the Greek women pray. When Mahomet and the victorious Turks burst in, Pamira stabs herself. Flames engulf the stage, for the Greeks have set fire to their city, leaving only ruins to the conquerors.

Rossini's approach to the revision ranges from minor changes of the Italian originals to composition of entirely new pieces. *Maometto II* was a work in which he had pushed his musical techniques to new limits, using richly elaborated vocal lines and forms that expand into long continuous musical and dramatic units. He himself coined the term "Terzettone" (big trio) for its astounding trio. *Le siège de Corinthe* is reworked to moderate both the vocal floridity and the formal innovations. The "Terzettone" is reduced to a more conventional form, and the solo arias for Mahomet, Pamira, and Néoclès are adapted to what Rossini perceived to be French dramaturgy. The new music for the French stage includes an overture, which the Italian original had lacked (the thematic material, to be sure, is derived from earlier works). There are grand numbers in which the chorus joins the soloists as a dramatic character, as in the second finale. True to French taste, dance and patriotic spectacle are provided. The score, more uniform in style than that of *Maometto II,* lacks the boldness which characterized the earlier version.—PATRICIA BRAUNER

Siepi, Cesare

Bass. Born 10 February 1923, in Milan. Studied at the Milan Conservatory; debut as Sparafucile in Verdi's Rigoletto, *Schio, near Vicenzo, 1941; Teatro alla Scala debut as Zaccaria in Verdi's* Nabucco, *1946; sang at La Scala, 1946-58; Metropolitan Opera debut as Philip II in* Don Carlo, *1950; sang at the Met, 1950-73; sang at Covent Garden 1962-73.*

The first season of Rudolf Bing's regime at the Metropolitan Opera, which commenced on November 6, 1950 with an innovative production of Giuseppe Verdi's *Don Carlo,* served to introduce to the New York scene the bass Cesare Siepi. Originally, Siepi was not to have been cast as King Philip and was engaged when Boris Christoff could not acquire the proper visa to enter the country. The premiere was to be televised and along with Siepi, the powerhouse Italian mezzo-soprano Fedora Barbieri, the Argentinian soprano Delia Rigal and the young American soprano Lucine Amara were all scheduled to make their debuts in company with the "veterans," Jussi Björling, Robert Merrill and Jerome Hines. It was a triumph for everyone concerned and especially for Siepi, whose delivery of King Philip's, "Ella giammai m'amò," brought the entire proceedings to a halt with a thunderous ovation. It did not take long for the newspapers to want to know more about this new bass, and soon it was discovered that under the grey exterior of the aging monarch was a young man of twenty-seven years who could rival any of Hollywood's matinee idols in appearance. The reign of Siepi began at the Metropolitan where he was thought of as the natural heir to Ezio Pinza, who concluded his twenty-two year association with that house in 1948.

The similarities between Pinza and Siepi are striking; physically both were tall, athletically built men who could dominate a stage by their presence alone. However, it is in their voices where they were most similar, but certainly not because they could ever be mistaken for one another. Each had a unique sound which is immediately identifiable by hearing just one note. Their voices had a lushness and a warmth which imparted an aura of palpable sensuality. Siepi's voice was the more evenly produced of the two, giving him the edge over Pinza in legato singing. Both excelled as Mozart's Don Giovanni and Figaro. Siepi's "Là ci darem la mano" was a veritable textbook of *bel canto* singing, his "Se vuol ballare" a showcase for the many faceted shadings and colors in his voice.

There was another side to Siepi, the romantic lead, and that was the consummate comedian. His Don Basilio in *Il barbiere di Siviglia* was a comic masterpiece of subtle timing and innuendo. For those not old enough to have seen Pinza and the great *buffo* Salvatore Baccaloni as Don Basilio and Don Bartolo, the pairing of Siepi with Baccaloni's successor, Fernando Corena, as the two Dons left nothing to be desired. The master artist Eugene Berman who created designs for the Metropolitan's *Il barbiere di Siviglia* in the 1953-1954 season gave each a chair in the second act which conformed to the figures of the characters they played. The expansive, rotund one for Bartolo and the spindly ladder-back for Basilio could certainly have been abstractions of the singers themselves, and each made the most of the prop he was given.

Cameo roles such as Colline, Sparafucile, and Ramfis were etched as carefully as was the tortured Boris Godunov (performed in English, which he took great pains to enunciate clearly). Siepi's death of Boris was not only heart-rending but also hair-raising when he toppled head first down a staircase at its conclusion. When playing opposite Maria Callas in *Norma,* his granite exterior as the implacable Oroviso visually crumbled under her pleadings for forgiveness for her children and gave the audience the soul-stirring experience of two great singing-actors playing off one another. No less effective was his Méphistophélès in Gounod's *Faust* with its proper blend of elegance and evil so often overlooked by others.

Siepi was no stranger to the recording studios and the old Cetra-Soria label championed his cause early on when they issued two albums devoted to him, one of arias and another of Italian songs. The collection of songs in particular remains a treasured part of any collector's holdings as does his anthology of Cole Porter which is rendered in delightfully (and ever so lightly) accented English. Fortunately, he recorded a number of operatic roles and his Don Giovanni, Figaro, Mefistofele, Alvise, Padre Guardiano, among others, have been preserved.

Siepi came upon the operatic scene when good, even great, voices were plentiful. That he dominated his surroundings speaks volumes for the singular abilities which made him an international star of the first magnitude. When Pinza chose to leave the Metropolitan, Siepi followed two years later, and he remains irreplaceable.—JOHN PENNINO

Silja, Anja

Soprano. Born 17 April 1940, in Berlin. Married conductor Christoph von Dohnányi, 1979; one son, one daughter. Studied with her grandfather, Egon van Rijn; debut as Rosina in Il barbiere di Siviglia, *Berlin, 1956; at Brunswick, 1956-58; American (Chicago) and Bayreuth debuts as Senta in* Der fliegende Holländer, *1960; London debut as Leonore in* Fidelio, *1963; Metropolitan Opera debut as Leonore in* Fidelio, *1972; directed Lohengrin, Brussels, 1990.*

Silja's early career is inextricably bound up with that of her mentor, Wieland Wagner. In his productions she became the most famous Lulu and Salome of her time, and, transcending modern ideas about what one singer's repertoire might be, seemed to sing everything from The Queen of the Night and Zerbinetta to Brünnhilde and Isolde.

Silja's ambition was from the beginning directed towards the Wagner roles, something that seemed unlikely considering that she made her debut, still in her teens, as Rosina in Rossini's *Il barbiere di Siviglia* in Brunswick. Only four years later Wieland Wagner brought her to Bayreuth to sing Senta. Silja's voice as a young singer was very high—she claims to have been able to sing a whole octave above top C ("like Yma Sumac"). Many eyebrows were raised at the casting for the 1960 Bayreuth Festival, but after her debut, William Mann wrote in the London *Times* that if Silja were to attempt more Wagner she would "light those roles with a glorious new flame." That was precisely what happened. Returning every summer to Bayreuth until Wieland Wagner died in 1966, she sang Elisabeth and Venus in *Tannhäuser,* Elsa in *Lohengrin* and Eva in *Die Meistersinger.* Elsewhere she also sang Isolde and the three Brünnhildes (notably in Cologne with George London as Wotan). But after Wieland's death, she at first said she wanted to abandon her career: "I didn't want to sing any more and I couldn't think of anything that was not connected with him. Even the operas I'd sung that he hadn't staged, still there was a connection in my eyes."

Under the influence first of Otto Klemperer, however, who chose her to be his Senta and Leonore in *Fidelio* for London, and later Christoph von Dohnányi (whom she married) she expanded her repertory, first turning to French roles. She sang all three soprano parts in Offenbach's *Les contes d'Hoffmann,* the title role in *Carmen* and Cassandre in *Les troyens.* Later she concentrated on Russian and Czech roles—*Katya Kabanová,* Emilia Marty in *The Makropoulos Case* and Shostakovich's *Lady Macbeth of Mtsensk.*

Just as Callas had seemed for many a throw-back to the times of Pasta and Grisi, so Silja seemed to be the successor to Wilhelmine Schroeder-Devrient, Wagner's adored "Queen of Tears." In conventional terms, Silja's voice had not equipped her to be a recording or concert artist, it being essential to see and hear her. (From this point of view it is sad that almost nothing of her work with Wieland was video-taped, except one performance of *Lulu,* although she did film both Jenny in *Mahagonny* and the title role in *Fidelio.*) A totally committed stage actress, no one who saw her as Fidelio at Covent Garden in 1969, with Klemperer conducting, is likely to have forgotten the moment when, at "Tot erst sein Weib!" she tore off the grey prison-cap (designed by Wieland), and her red-gold tresses tumbled to her shoulders. Her command of the stage, her ability to carry off supremely melodramatic gestures within the confines of the drama continued to be hers for three decades. When she took on the role of Kostelnicka in Lehnhoff's memorable production of *Jenůfa* at Glyndebourne in 1989, she revealed a voice that had gained in power and strength in the lower register. She claimed to have added an octave at the bottom, having discarded the notes *in alt,* and became for a new generation one of the most powerful singing actresses. The dangerous quality in her tone, a whining sound and apparent insecurity on the high notes, makes hers an art that will always provoke extreme controversy, but as Harold Rosenthal wrote of her Salome in the 1960s, "her voice is not beautiful by any stretch of the imagination, but it is clearly projected, and every phrase carries its overtones—psychological not musical—which suggests the child-like degenerate, over-sexed princess in all too clear a manner. Her nervous, almost thin body is never still; she rolls on her stomach and her back; she crawls, she slithers, she leaps, she kneels . . . There is no denying that this is one of the great performances of our time."—PATRICK O'CONNOR

Sills, Beverly

Soprano. Born Belle Miriam Silverman, 25 May 1929, in Brooklyn. Married: Peter B. Greenough, 1956; one son, one daughter. Child prodigy, sang on radio; studied with Estelle Liebling from age 11; debut as Frasquita in Carmen, *Philadelphia, 1947; toured with the Charles Wagner Company; San Francisco debut as Elena in* Mefistofele, *1953; at New York City Opera, 1955-79, debuting as Rosalinde; Vienna debut as the Queen of the Night in* Die Zauberflöte, *1967; Teatro alla Scala debut as Pamira in* Le siège de Corinthe, *1969; Covent Garden debut as Lucia di Lammermoor, 1970; Metropolitan Opera debut as*

Pamira, 1975; sang in premier of Menotti's La Loca, *San Diego, 1979; celebrated as Violetta; retired from stage, 1979; director of New York City Opera 1979-89.*

To many of those who saw Beverly Sills in performance or who listen to her records, she was unquestionably one of the greatest—some would claim *the* greatest—bel canto sopranos of the nineteen-sixties and seventies. While audiences everywhere adored her, there were ongoing reservations from some critics. Peter Davis in the Sills entry in the *New Grove Dictionary of Music and Musicians* can be taken as representative of this reserve when he describes her mainly in terms of drawbacks, as lacking the dramatic weight of Callas or the sheer tonal beauty of Sutherland or Caballé, as not dramatically commanding and with a stage personality that is merely ingratiating. While no one is likely to question Callas's supremacy, J.B. Steane is nearer the mark when he describes Sills as achieving "profundity perhaps more genuinely" than her rivals, and remarks about her, "The interesting thing, finally, is that Sills is so satisfying, not as a sweet-sounding, highly-trained nightingale, but as a singer of remarkable intellectual and emotional strength."

Sills's career as a radio child-prodigy is as well-known as the fact that she began her serious vocal training at age 11 with Estelle Liebling, who had been a pupil of Mathilde Marchesi and who remained Sills's only teacher. A debut in Philadelphia as Frasquita (1947) was followed two years later by a tour as Violetta during which she sang the role fifty-four times in nine weeks; it was to become one of her most celebrated roles, one which she was to sing more than three hundred times in the course of her career. A contract with the New York City Opera singing a variety of roles eventually led to her appearance in 1958 as the heroine of Douglas Moore's *The Ballad of Baby Doe,* a high-soprano role which brought considerable recognition and which became identified with her. But it was eight more years and many more roles—her repertoire eventually totalled more than seventy—before her appearance as Cleopatra in Handel's *Giulio Cesare* (1966) brought her international acclaim.

Sills then entered on a period of intense activity both abroad—debuts in Vienna, the Teatro alla Scala, Covent Garden, Teatro Colón quickly followed—and at home in America. Her debut at the Metropolitan Opera in Rossini's *Le siège de Corinthe* (1975) was delayed by Rudolph Bing until after his departure from the house. The New York City Opera remained her home base, at which she appeared as the three heroines in *Les contes d'Hoffmann,* the Queen in Rimsky-Korsakov's *Le coq d'or,* Manon, Elvira in *I puritani,* Lucia, *La Fille du Régiment, Lucrezia Borgia,* and, in some ways her most important achievements, the so-called Donizetti three queens trilogy—*Roberto Devereux, Maria Stuarda,* and *Anna Bolena.*

Onstage, Sills enjoyed a considerable dramatic advantage over her rivals; Sutherland, never at ease with her own physicality, overcame her awkwardness to achieve a measure of sincerity onstage, while Caballé belonged to the philosophy of stage deportment associated with Zinka Milanov, whose baroque acting style was once described by Irving Kolodin in the *Saturday Review* as a cross between Eleanora Duse and Mack Sennett. Sills, like Sutherland, is a tall woman but one who is at home with the fact; allying her natural acting ability to a shrewd practical training resulted in a series of highly skilled and moving stage impersonations.

Sills sang many of the Italian roles associated with the bel canto revival of the fifties and sixties, as well as remaining a Mozart singer—Donna Anna, Donna Elvira, Constanze—and also specializing in the French repertoire—she sang Marguerite, Manon, Thaïs, Louise, the three heroines in *Les contes d'Hoffmann,* Philine in *Mignon,* among others. She was always willing to push herself vocally and histrionically, and this led to her assuming roles which in some ways were, as she herself acknowledged, unwise for her. Her middle voice, though evocative in timbre, could betray signs of stress under pressure; but it was her high voice that was her claim to glory. Although some perceived it as shallow in tone, her high singing in the theatre was extraordinarily telling; it had carrying power, flexibility, brilliance, and, thanks to excellent pitch, accuracy. Again J.B. Steane goes to the heart of the matter when he remarks that there is "something exalted, non-pedestrian, even crazy, about the high notes of the soprano voice (so far above the pitch of the woman's normal speaking voice), especially when taken in context with fast passage-work. No 'coloratura' seems quite to have sensed this as Sills has done." He proceeds on this basis to analyze her recording of Lucia's first aria in terms of the eerie supernatural chill she evokes, and provides a number of other examples from her *Roberto Devereux*. Her recording of Olympia's aria from *Les contes d'Hoffmann* can be seen to provide a zany version of the same phenomenon, including a perfectly tuned running-down as the doll unwinds.

At the same time, one cannot overlook the sheer beauty of sound evidenced in many of Sills's recording. In the St Sulpice scene from Manon she spins a gossamer web of erotic magnetism; in "O luce di quest'anima" (*Linda di Chamonix*) the staccatos are feathery light; in Mozart's lullaby, "Ruhe sanft, mein holdes Leben" (*Zaïde*) her tone is preternaturally beautiful, in Strauss's "Breit über mein Haupt" full of unbearable pathos. It is not an exaggeration to say that she scarcely ever made a recording which does not provide exquisite moments.

It is typical that Sills chose to end her career with a challenge—the premiere of Menotti's *La Loca* (1979); indeed in later interviews she attributed her decision to retire comparatively early to two factors, the first an operation for cancer in 1972 which robbed her of perfect security in her breath control, and second, the decision to take on roles like *Norma* which she knew perfectly well were too heavy for her voice, consequently shortening her vocal life, but which she felt were worth doing. It was, indeed, that very desire to rise to the great artistic challenges available to her and if possible to go beyond them that made her one of the formidable figures of the lyric stage of her day.—PETER DYSON

Simionato, Giulietta

Mezzo-soprano. Born 12 May 1910, in Forli. Studied with Locatello and Palumbo; won first place in a bel canto competition in Florence, 1933; sang in premiere of Pizzetti's Orsèolo at Florence Festival, 1935; Teatro alla Scala debut in Puccini's Suor Angelica, 1936; appeared regularly at La Scala until 1966; British debut as Cherubino at 1947 Edinburgh Festival; appeared as Adalgisa, Amneris, and Azucena at Covent Garden in 1953; in 1954 a revival of Bellini's I Capuletti ed i Montecchi was staged for her in Palermo; made United States debut in Chicago in same year, and sang for the Metropolitan Opera, 1959-65; made farewell appearance (as Servilia in La clemenza di Tito) at the Piccola Scala, 1966.

For many opera-goers of the 1950s one of the greatest voices and most beloved personalities of that decade was the mezzo-soprano Giulietta Simionato. She seemed to combine the coloratura agility of Conchita Supervia with the lush authority of manner of Ebe Stignani into the ideal versatile mezzo-soprano. Her voice exhibited the richness of a contralto's with the upward extension of a soprano's—indeed she sang some soprano roles (Donna Elvira, Ännchen, Fedora, and Santuzza) early on, but on a number of occasions wisely resisted taking on others. She turned down offers of Norma, Lady Macbeth, and Minnie; she agreed to learn Leonora in *Il trovatore,* but Antonino Votto eventually dissuaded her from performing it.

Simionato's range of roles was nevertheless astonishing. She undertook the coloratura repertoire, represented by the operas of Handel, Rossini, Bellini, Donizetti, and Verdi; lyric mezzo roles such as Mignon, Octavian, Dorabella, and Cherubino; and the heavy, dramatic characters such as Dalila, Azucena, Amneris, Eboli, Leonora in *La favorita,* the Aunt in Puccini's *Suor Angelica,* and the Princess in *Adriana Lecouvreur.* Some of her roles were curiosities from the past, as when she appeared in Alessandro Scarlatti's *Mitridate Eupatore* at Piccolo Scala with Victoria de los Angeles in 1956. At La Scala, where she debuted in 1936, she also sang, in addition to many of the roles mentioned above, Dido in Berlioz's *Les Troyens,* Gluck's *Iphigénie en Aulide,* and undertook the soprano role of Valentine in a renowned 1962 production of *Les Huguenots* with Sutherland and Corelli. A well-circulated pirate recording exists of this production in which Simionato sings in a grand veristic style that is not true to Meyerbeer or the period but is nevertheless exciting. The enjoyment of the La Scala audience is palpable. Also from La Scala with Sutherland during the same period is a live performance of Rossini's *Semiramide.* Yet another famous La Scala production in which Simionato took a prominent part, and for which recorded documentation exists, was the 1957 revival of Donizetti's *Anna Bolena* for Maria Callas, a soprano with whom Simionato often appeared. Simionato is in splendid form in the role of Jane Seymour; she is perhaps all the more forthright and unsubtle in contrast to Callas's vulnerability.

Much of the admiration and respect accorded Simionato comes from those who heard her often and regularly on the stage; her regal timbre, great versatility, and endearing physical presence made her a beloved operatic personality. Yet the recordings reveal problems, some of them basic. It must also be admitted that some of the flaws—such as the sharp register breaks and unequalized tone—are intentional products of her training, and owe something to the fact that she was an Italian singer performing during a certain era. Blatant aspirates and lack of a seamless scale clearly are more acceptable at certain times and in certain places than others. If one compares Simionato to Marilyn Horne in such parts as Arsace (*Semiramide*), Rosina in *Il barbiere di Siviglia,* and Isabella in *L'Italiana in Algeri,* Simionato emerges a distinct second-best in technical accuracy. Horne is near perfect in this regard, with Simionato displaying all of the problems mentioned above to a blatant degree. Then there is the matter of charm. Horne's fioriture sparkle and delight; even for all Simionato's agility, which is quite considerable, Simionato rarely charms or delights in a Rossini comic role. We hear her instead as an Azucena or a commanding Amneris who is, astonishingly, able to toss off roulades with an amazing degree of accuracy. Many of these recordings were admittedly made when Simionato was rather mature, such as the *La Cenerentola* from 1964 when she was fifty-four years old. Even in Simionato's Verdi recordings there are shortcomings: she rarely follows Verdi's copious and explicit expressive markings, although in the several recordings that display her Amneris, Ulrica (when this recording was made in 1961 she could no longer adequately sustain the low notes necessary for the role), Preziosilla, and Dame Quickly, she is almost always in sumptuous, authoritative-sounding voice. This assessment holds true of her Laura, sung to Anita Cerqueti's Gioconda, and her Aunt to Renata Tebaldi's Suor Angelica.

Simionato retired without fanfare in the mid-1960s without any discernible deterioration in vocal quality. She left the opera stage a greatly beloved singer; when she retired she perhaps left an older era behind her.—STEPHEN WILLIER

Simon Boccanegra

Composer: *Giuseppe Verdi.*

Librettists: *Francesco Maria Piave and G. Montanelli (after Antonio García Gutiérrez).*

First Performance: *Venice, La Fenice, 12 March 1857; revised, Arrigo Boito, Milan, Teatro alla Scala, 24 March 1881.*

Roles: *Amelia Grimaldi (soprano); Gabriele Adorno (tenor); Simon Boccanegra (baritone); Fiesco (bass); Paolo Albiani (baritone); Pietro (baritone); Maid (soprano or mezzosoprano); A Captain (tenor); chorus (SSAATTTBB).*

Although this vast, complicated, and much-revised melodrama has never been very successful, *Simon Boccanegra* has great historical importance in Verdi's career in that it helped to bring the composer out of his post-*Aida* retirement to compose his great Shakespearean operas, *Otello* and *Falstaff*. There are two main versions of *Simon Boccanegra:* one which premiered as a fiasco at the 1857 Venice carnival season (and received minor revisions over the next several years), and a substantially revised version which premiered in the 1881 Teatro alla

Kiri Te Kanawa and Michael Sylvester in *Simon Boccanegra*, **Royal Opera, London, 1991**

Scala season, which Verdi prepared with the assistance for the first time of the most gifted librettist of the day, Arrigo Boito, and which is the version heard in theaters today.

Based on a complex political melodrama by the Spanish playwright García Gutiérrez (also the source of Verdi's *Il trovatore*), *Simon Boccanegra* deals with the conflict between the patrician and plebeian parties in the fourteenth-century sea-going republic of Genoa. In brief, the prologue presents us with the famous pirate Simon Boccanegra, as he returns from hiding to accept election as Doge of Genoa in a vote controlled by Paolo, an organizer of the plebeians. Simon accepts the position in the hope that it will allow him to reunite with his beloved Maria, daughter of the patrician Fiesco, as well as unwed mother of their lost child, also named Maria. Twenty-five years later in act I, the mysteriously adopted Amelia Grimaldi (actually the young Maria) loves the young patrician Gabriele Adorno; they receive permission to marry from her guardian Andrea, who is actually Fiesco in disguise. But meanwhile, Paolo has asked Simon the political favor of interceding on his behalf and courting Amelia. During their encounter Simon and Amelia realize they are father and daughter, and Simon desists from pleading Paolo's case, after which the angry Paolo avenges himself by having Amelia abducted. In act I, scene ii (completely revised from the original plot), Simon is meeting with his council when Gabriele breaks onto the scene, followed by a plebeian mob, which is enraged that he has murdered one of their members, Lorenzin. Admitting to the murder, Gabriele reveals that Lorenzin conspired in the abduction of Amelia (but he suspects that Simon was behind the abduction). Amelia, having secured her own release, calls for peace among the warring factions. Suspecting Paolo as the perpetrator of the abduction, Simon calls on him to curse the abductor (himself), and the act closes on the crowd's repetition of the curse.

In act II the vengeful Paolo secretly poisons Simon's cup and tries to persuade Fiesco/Andrea and Gabriele to kill him as well. Gabriele agrees, responding mainly to Paolo's hints of a romantic relationship between Simon and Amelia, who have been together frequently. He hides in Simon's private chamber, preparing to strike. Amelia finds him, and pleads with him to accept peace with Simon, but refuses to explain her own relationship with the doge. Next, Amelia begs for Simon's consent to her marriage with Gabriele, and he reluctantly agrees, provided that Gabriele repents his opposition. Alone, Simon unknowingly drinks Paolo's poison, and falls asleep. Gabriele rises from hiding to strike him, but Amelia appears again and stops him just as Simon awakens and reveals that Amelia is his daughter. As the act closes, Simon gives his blessing for the marriage of Gabriele and Amelia, and Gabriele decides to join Simon's side in the upcoming battle he has helped to brew with the patricians. In act III, Simon has won the battle, but Fiesco/Andrea learns from the condemned Paolo that Simon will nonetheless die from poisoning, Paolo's revenge. Fiesco/Andrea then confronts Simon for a last accusatory scene, but instead learns from a gratified Simon of his granddaughter Amelia/Maria. Simon dies as the opera ends, and Gabriele is proclaimed Doge.

In letters to his librettist for the first version of *Simon Boccanegra,* Francesco Maria Piave, Verdi had insisted that "the layout of the libretto, of the numbers, etc. etc. must be as original as possible," in keeping with the unusual features of the drama. But the fact that Piave's work, never superior, was especially convoluted cannot be blamed on the librettist alone, since he closely followed the prose sketch which Verdi himself had prepared from the Gutiérrez drama, and since the worst problems in the opera were inherent in the political complexity of the subject—a complexity little suited to the lyrical language of Italian opera. Besides, the aspect of *Simon Boccanegra* that most troubled audiences in 1857 was not the text but rather the music, which was considered overly somber and lacking in lyrical vocal melody. In fact, Verdi had taken special pains to avoid conventional set pieces in the scenes he considered particularly dramatic, including the prologue and act III scenes between Simon and Fiesco. Moreover there is no real aria for the central figure of Simon (one of the main reasons he fails to achieve the necessary weight in the 1857 version of the opera), and there is very little in words or music to convey Paolo's crucial role in the drama. On the other hand, there are many conventional set pieces for the less central characters and situations, including three cavatina-cabaletta pairs in act I, scene i for Amelia, Amelia and Gabriele, and Amelia and Simon respectively.

The 1881 revisions reveal Boito's skill at refocusing the weight of the dramatic action onto the central characters of Simon and Paolo, and they also show the remarkable evolution in Verdi's compositional style between 1857 and 1881, a twenty-four-year gap in which the composer had blended the vocal traditions of Italian opera with the French emphasis on scenography and orchestral accompaniment, as well as with his own unique brand of melodic vigor and characterization. Grafting this blend onto a twenty-four-year-old dramatic failure was no easy matter, and many of Verdi's solutions were weak compromises. For instance, he made very few changes in acts II and III, and, although he cut a cabaletta for Amelia in act I, he only lightly revised the remaining two, at a time when the cabaletta was considered terribly outdated and dramatically stifling. However, there are two sections of the opera, the beginning of the prologue and the Council Chamber scene (act I, scene ii) which are largely new. In these sections, the orchestra unifies the drama with large-scale tonal symmetries and thematic recurrences, similar to those found in the later operas *Otello* and *Falstaff*. Vocal melody is perhaps less prominent than usual here, but that is owing to the dark, political nature of these scenes. Still, when Simon has a heroic moment in his efforts to unite the Genoan people in the Council Chamber after Amelia's abduction, Verdi gives him full lyrical opportunity with the dramatic "Plebe! Patrizi! Popolo!" ("Plebeians! Patricians! People!"). Some parts of the score foreshadow the style of *Otello*, particularly in the Council Chamber scene, where Amelia's melodic plea for peace resembles that of Desdemona in act III of *Otello*, and the brass fanfare and trill accompanying Paolo's self-cursing is a harbinger of Iago's act II "Credo."

The revised *Simon Boccanegra* of 1881 brought mixed reviews, ranging from Filippo Filippi's claim of "A Triumph" following the La Scala premiere, to Eduard Hanslick's assessment at the 1882 Vienna debut that "The old Verdi is distracted, tired, and in a bad mood." Still, the revision succeeded in gaining a place for *Simon Boccanegra* in the modern repertory; the somber, heavily masculine tone of the opera is so unique and so uniquely Verdian that it has developed a following among the composer's most avid fans.—CLAIRE DETELS

Slezak, Leo

Tenor. Born 18 August 1873, in Mährisch-Schönberg (now Sumperk), Moravia. Died 1 June 1946, in Egern am Tegernsee, Germany. Married: Elsa Wertheim. Studied with Adolf Robinson, Jean De Reszke; debut as Lohengrin in Brno, 1896; in Berlin, 1898-99; Breslau, 1899; Vienna State Opera as Guillaume Tell, 1901, remained until 1933; Covent Garden debut as Lohengrin, 1900; Teatro alla Scala debut, 1902; Metropolitan Opera debut as Otello, 1909; Boston Opera, 1911-13; retired from opera, 1933; continued to act in film; his son was actor Walter Slezak.

Slezak, having studied initially with baritone Adolf Robinson, had a rise to prominence was fairly rapid, with few significant setbacks. His earliest professional activity at Brno and Berlin was not especially distinguished, but neither was the repertory that was entrusted to him. At Breslau he was given more demanding roles, but he still seemed to show more promise than accomplishment. A British tour of the Breslau company afforded him the opportunity of making his Covent Garden debut during the 1900 Royal Opera Season as Lohengrin to Milka Ternina's Elsa. Bitter political developments managed to distract his audience, considerably diminishing his impact, but an invitation to sing before Queen Victoria at Buckingham Palace during his stay provided some consolation. Guest appearances in Vienna followed in 1901, when he attracted the attention of Gustav Mahler, and the twenty-eight-year-old tenor was offered a contract to sing in the conductor's extraordinary ensemble of principals at the Vienna State Opera.

If his manner was in many ways rather typical of the German vocal style, Slezak's repertory was international, made up primarily of the brash, pre-*verismo* Italian and French dramatic heroes: Raoul (*Les Huguenots*), Jean (*Le prophète*), Arnold (*Guillaume Tell*), Gounod's Faust, Des Grieux (*Manon*), Gerald (*Lakmé*), Eléazar (*La juive*), and Julien (*Louise*); Canio (*I pagliacci*) and Rodolfo (*La bohème*); Flotow's Alessandro Stradella and Goldmark's Assad (*Die Königin von Saba*); Hermann (*The Queen of Spades*); Radames (*Aida*), Manrico (*Il trovatore*), the Duke (*Rigoletto*), and Otello. His reputation as a Wagnerian is surprising, for he generally confined himself to that composer's less taxing vehicles, those which his voice could accommodate. An early, unhappy flirtation with the young Siegfried, a role he first sang at Brno, ended abruptly with a poorly-received 1900 Covent Garden performance. Thereafter he wisely limited himself to Walther (*Die Meistersinger*), Lohengrin, and Tannhäuser.

Unable to negotiate a suitable contract with Mahler's successor, Felix Weingartner, Slezak left the Vienna Opera temporarily after Mahler's departure in 1907, and spent the next six years abroad. Though already well established, he clearly had his sights set upon an international career, which led him to study the non-German repertory that same year with Jean De Reszke in Paris and Lieder interpretation with Reynaldo Hahn. Sporting a new-found refinement that did not go unnoticed, he made an auspicious second debut at Covent Garden on 2 June 1909 as Otello, though his Radames that season was not similarly well received. Under Toscanini's direction, he made his Metropolitan Opera debut, also as Otello, on 17 November 1909, and this was an unqualified success. His portrayal of the Moor received excellent notices, and despite "a certain huskiness at times in his voice" attributed to nervousness, Henry Krehbiel was impressed with the "fine power" of his voice, and the "more than ordinary discretion" with which it was used.

Slezak's success in America was altogether remarkable, owing as much to his overwhelming physical stature as to his singing. Certainly, at over six feet, Slezak cast an enormous, almost menacing presence, but his bearing was anything but clumsy, prompting Krehbiel to remark that he presented "such a figure as would have delighted the audience that once applauded the heroics of Tommaso Salvini"—high praise indeed, bestowed at a time when the haunting memory of the great Italian tragedian still lingered. Unlike many European artists, whose soft tones and subtle manner were more or less wasted on a public accustomed to the more robust Italian wing already so well-established in America, Slezak had no difficulty making a profound and lasting impression. Both his voice and his physical stature were of the same vast proportions as his repertory, and he enjoyed immediate favor. At the Metropolitan Opera he sang Radames, Manrico, Stradella, Hermann, Gounod's Faust, Walther, and Lohengrin, and added Tamino (*Die

Zauberflöte) during his last season. He was given relatively little to do during his two seasons with the Boston Company, and was obliged to share his major roles—Otello, Manrico, and Radames—and even some peripheral ones—Julien, Faust, and the Duke—with Boston's own leading tenors. In the 1912-1913 Boston season he was called upon only once for a single Otello, substituting for Giovanni Zenatello.

Slezak returned to Europe in 1913, and remained there for the rest of his career, undertaking successful tours of Sweden, Russia, Holland, and the Scandinavian countries. His final appearance at the Vienna State Opera, his artistic home until 1928, was made as Canio on 26 September 1933, by which time he had already established himself with equal success as a singer of operetta and as a character actor in films.

In addition to his records, there are four delightful volumes of memoirs that have long served as testimonials to his wit; indeed, mention of him in the literature has seldom resisted the temptation of recalling some clever remark or further embellishing one of the particularly mischievous backstage pranks for which he was famous.

At his best, Slezak was a singer of the first rank. His voice could be as attractive as it was robust, and richly expressive. He could shade his voice as sensitively as the most renowned Italian and French stylists, aided by what must have been among the most beautifully-contrived head voices in the tenor business—a *voix mixte* as rich in tone as it was well-controlled. Examples of it abound in his records, exerting an almost magic presence—the ending high Cs of his 1905 *Lakmé* "Fantaisie," the 1905 "Magische Töne" from *Der Königin von Saba,* and the celebrated 1905 "Viens, gentille dame" from Boieldieu's *La dame blanche.* Accounts vary, but it would appear that Slezak was not so great an *actor* as he was an effectively dramatic *singer*—something he had in common perhaps with Caruso and Martinelli, both of whom shared his repertory and experienced a similar histrionic growth over the course of their respective careers.

Between about 1901 and 1931 Slezak left nearly 400 souvenirs of his voice, among them operatic excerpts drawn from the four corners of the international tenor repertory, and an imposing number of superbly-executed Lieder. Generally, they maintain a consistency of quality comparable to that of other prolific recorders. His huge voice recorded exceptionally well from the very beginning, as many big voices did, and it remained more or less unchanged over a period of some forty years, enabling him to record electrically with great effectiveness. His many recordings for the Gramophone Company, made between 1901-1912, are among his best, and give a thorough accounting of his behavior in the repertory in which he clearly excelled. This notwithstanding the often brutal German translations. Only rarely did he record the non-German repertory in its original language, which makes the few items he recorded for American Columbia during his seasons with the Boston Opera especially precious. Perhaps the most extraordinary of all his records are the Lieder, the best of which were made when he was already past his sixtieth year. These are as expressively sung as any on disc, and help us to understand Richard Aldrich's observation after a 1912 Carnegie Hall recital that "Mr. Slezak has an unusual power of giving apt and significant expression to a variety of moods, expression that is gained by subtle means in the molding of a phrase, the color of the voice, the suggestion of dramatic or emotional motive." Herman Klein, reviewing a batch of Slezak's recorded Lieder in the April 1927 issue of *The Gramophone,* wrote that "For my part I do not want to hear a more perfect or more poetic diction, better phrasing, an apter sense of colourful contrast, clearer rhythm, or greater depth and purity of expression."

As a whole, Slezak's records impress us with a voice of distinctive timbre and clarion strength. He was not above forcing his voice, however, with the kind of senseless abandon characteristic of the worst exponents of the German school, hence the slow wobble, and coarseness of tone so frequently encountered among his records. His interpretations, especially those of his Verdi specialties, can be overwhelmingly dramatic, yet at the same time keenly perceptive. His many recordings from *Otello* suggest that, with Zenatello, he was clearly one of that generation's most striking exponents of the role, certainly ranking high among its definitive interpreters. It is perhaps significant that Slezak was the last to sing Otello at the Metropolitan (on 31 January 1913) until the opera was revived for Martinelli in December 1937, a suitable replacement having taken nearly a quarter of a century to appear.—WILLIAM SHAMAN

Smetana, Bedřich

Composer. Born 2 March 1824, in Leitomischl. Died 12 May 1884, in Prague. Married: Katharina Kolař (died 1859), pianist, 1849. Studied piano with Proksch in Prague; music teacher to the family of Count Thun; financially disastrous piano tour 1848; aided by Liszt in opening a piano school, 1848; conductor of the Philharmonic Society of Göteborg, Sweden, 1856; returned to Prague to support the nationalist artistic movement, 1861; composition of nationalist operas, 1863-74; conductor of the Provisional Theater, 1866; symphonic poems collectively entitled Má vlast composed 1874-79; further opera composition from 1876-82.

Operas *The Brandenburgers in Bohemia* [Braniboři v Čechách], K. Sabina, 1862-63, Prague, Provisional Theater, 5 January 1866; various revisions up to 1870; *The Bartered Bride* [Prodana nevěsta], K. Sabina, 1863-66, Prague, Provisional Theater, 30 May 1866; revised, 1869, Prague, Provisional Theater, 29 January 1869; revised, 1869, Prague, Provisional Theater, 1 June 1869; revised, 1869-70, Prague, Provisional Theater, 25 September 1870; *Dalibor*, J. Wenzig (Czech translation by E. Špindler), 1865-67, Prague, New Town Theater, 16 May 1868; revised, 1870; *Libuše*, J. Wenzig (Czech translation by E. Špindler), 1869-72, Prague, National Theater, 11 June 1881; *The Two Widows* [Dvě vdovy], E. Züngel (after P.J.F. Mallefille), 1873-74, Prague, Provisional Theater, 27 March 1874; revised, 1877, Prague, Provisional Theater, 15 March 1878; *The Kiss* [Hubička], E. Krásnohorská (after K. Světlá), 1875-76, Prague, Provisional Theater, 7 November 1876; *The Secret* [Tajemství], E. Krásnohorská, 1877-78, Prague, New Czech Theater, 18 September 1878; *The Devil's Wall* [Čertova stěna], E. Krásnohorská, 1879-82, Prague, New Czech Theater, 29 October 1882; *Viola*, E. Krásnohorská (after Shakespeare, *Twelfth Night*), 1874, 1883-84 [unfinished].

Until the end of the World War I, the Czech regions—Bohemia, Slovakia and Moravia—remained provinces of the Austro-Hungarian Empire. In common with all members of the Czech middle classes during the earlier nineteenth century, Bedřich Smetana was educated and brought up speaking the "official" language, which was German. His musical training was classical, in the German and Italian traditions. The emergence of Czech nationalism caught Smetana's imagination, and he determined to help create a distinctively national musical style, using opera as its central focus. Among the challenges that this commitment brought was that of learning his native language; for instance, it was not until the age of thirty-two that Smetana could summon the confidence to write a letter in Czech. A little later, in 1860, he wrote: "I am not ashamed to write in my mother tongue, however imperfectly, and am glad to be able to show that my fatherland means more to me than anything else."

Smetana did not gain early recognition in his homeland, however, and he worked in Gothenburg in Sweden for the six years from 1856. The opportunity he needed to achieve a breakthrough came from a competition set up by Count Jan Harrach to encourage the creation of new Czech operas. Two types of opera were suggested: one to be based upon the history of the Czech people, the other to be "of lighter content and taken from the national life of the people in Bohemia and Moravia." This development made Smetana aware of the new potential for the arts in his homeland, especially when in 1862 the Provisional Theater was opened in Prague, for opera as well as drama, in order to stage performances in Czech.

The two types of work stipulated in the competition regulations reflect the two basic approaches Smetana was to follow in his eight completed operas. Czech history was a natural subject for nationalist opera, as was the life of the people, which reflected the rural communities and their peasant customs as well as the preservation of the Czech language. In order to become a significant and lasting phenomenon, however, any emergent national trend had to gain a composer of genius, as had previously been the case with Glinka in Russia. Smetana's Czech predecessors were worthy but mediocre, and his duty became the creation of the repertory of opera which his homeland lacked.

In 1863, Smetana submitted the score of *The Brandenburgers in Bohemia* to the competition judges. It won the first prize and in due course received a triumphant premiere in the Provisional Theater. The opera is set at a time when Bohemia was overrun with foreign troops, its dramatic potential captured and enriched by Smetana's music. The experience already gained in his symphonic poems on literary subjects enabled him to create vivid scenes and rounded characters, which he combined with writing for the chorus that is both subtle and assured.

The premiere of a second opera, *The Bartered Bride* (which has proved to be Smetana's most popular work for the stage) fulfilled the second of the competition's options, being in a lighter style. The composer claimed he wrote it "not out of vanity but for spite, because I was accused after *The Brandenburgers* of being a Wagnerian who was incapable of writing anything in a lighter vein." At first, *The Bartered Bride* was not well received, but various revisions up to 1870 transformed it, particularly by means of the addition of distinctive material such as the dances and "beer chorus," in which the national element really came to the fore. However, the characterization is strong and so too are the dramatic pacing and the melodic invention. The piece was performed more than one hundred times during Smetana's

Bedřich Smetana

lifetime, although its style was not always understood; when he was accused of modeling it on the operettas of Offenbach, his indignant response was: "Did none of those gentlemen realise that my model was Mozart's comic opera?" Smetana much admired *The Marriage of Figaro,* and in its general features his opera has similarities to it: its bubbling presto overture, as well as its plot, structure and basic themes. There are two pairs of lovers in each case, as well as an identical resolution of the drama, brought about by the discovery of a long-lost son.

Yet Smetana believed that more important tasks awaited him, for his next two operas, *Dalibor* and *Libuše,* are concerned with heroic and epic themes. *Dalibor* presents the story of the hero of the title, who stood bravely and selflessly for the cause of right and for the most noble aspirations. Having avenged the murder of his beloved friend Zdeněk, Dalibor is imprisoned, but despite the efforts of his enemy's sister Milada to rescue him, the opera ends tragically. Thus the moral stance taken by Beethoven in *Fidelio* is adapted by Smetana for his own ends, one of which was surely the nationalist vision of freedom from oppression.

The composer was bitterly disappointed by the adverse critical response to *Dalibor,* caused largely by the misconception that it was deliberately Wagnerian. In fact, if an influence is at work it is that of Liszt's "transformation of themes," a procedure already evident in Smetana's symphonic poems. The chorus, representing the Czech people, has some stirring music, and the range of emotion and balance of dramatic urgency and release of tension show *Dalibor* to be a masterpiece of the first order.

Libuše, designed as a national epic, was composed by 1872 but held back for a further nine years in order to coincide with the opening of the new National Theater. The music has a special festive quality, in keeping with Smetana's intention that it should celebrate the Czech nation itself. Its plot treats the legendary creation of the Přemsylid dynasty, an historical episode of great symbolic significance. Libuše herself is the Queen of Bohemia, and her abdication by marriage allows the firm rule of Přemsyl to unite the conflicting elements within the nation. Smetana described this opera as "a glorious tableau animated by musical drama," and decreed that its performance should be reserved for ceremonial occasions. This patriotic scheme immediately preceded the completion of his cycle of six symphonic poems, *Ma Vlast* (*My Homeland*), and the two works are intimately linked in their imagery.

Throughout his career as an opera composer, Smetana continued to diversify his approach to the medium. *The Two Widows* is a lively comedy in which subtleties of characterization are enhanced both by the vocal writing and the role of the orchestra. Stylistically this work is very advanced for its time, with an intimate story in which one widow pretends to be in love with the landowner Ladislav in order to encourage the other to commit herself to him. It is set as a number opera with linking recitatives, the latter replacing the original spoken dialogue in a subsequent revision, and among its strongest admirers was Richard Strauss, who may even have used it as the model for his own opera *Intermezzo.*

By 1875-76, when Smetana composed his sixth opera, *The Kiss,* he had become completely deaf. This was his first collaboration with the excellent librettist Eliska Krásnohorská, and though the plot, based upon a lovers' quarrel, may seem slight, the humanity with which it is treated transcends the surface level by virtue of wide-ranging characterization and the atmospheric creation of mood in the contrasting scenes.

Smetana could by now work only slowly, and for no longer than an hour at a time, since the concentration required when composing had the effect of intensifying the buzzing sensation in his ears. Despite the distress these circumstances caused him, his will remained strong, as he explained in a letter to Krásnohorská written during October 1877, while he was working on *The Secret,* their second collaboration: "I am afraid my music is not cheerful enough for a comedy. But how could I be cheerful? Where could happiness come from when my heart is heavy with trouble and sorrow? I should like to be able to work without having to worry. When I plunge into musical ecstasy, then for a while I forget everything that persecutes me so cruelly in my old age." Yet this new three act opera was completed within nine months, and warmly received. Set in the Bohemian countryside in the eighteenth century, its dramatic situation, characterization and musical structure are more sophisticated than in *The Kiss.* The vocal writing, particularly for the principal soprano, Kalina, is wide-ranging and often declamatory, and the musical flow is continuous rather than in separate numbers. Accordingly, the orchestral writing is distinguished, and dramatically the tensions build until they release large scale ensembles with splendid choral contributions.

Smetana described *The Devil's Wall* as a "comic-romantic opera," a strange terminology stemming from the fact that it is a parody set in the age of chivalry, when men of the church plotted in order to acquire power and wealth. In this, his last completed opera, there are few indications of musical weakness, though the complex plot does not avoid confusions. One fundamental and forward-looking aspect of this work is that one of the leading characters appears simultaneously as two different personalities, with two different singers onstage, one representing the hermit Beneš and the other his alter-ego, the devilish Rarach, though the other characters see them as one and the same person. Rather more than elsewhere, Smetana used recurring themes, perhaps to unify the potential confusions inherent in the drama.

At the time of his death Smetana was working on *Viola,* an adaptation by Krásnahorská of Shakespeare's *Twelfth Night,* but he only reached the stage of preliminary sketches, since his condition deteriorated rapidly during his final months. He complained frequently of "a pounding and intense hissing in the head, day and night without ceasing, as if I were standing underneath a huge waterfall." His mind gave way, and he was eventually taken to the Prague lunatic asylum on 23 April 1884, where he died nearly three weeks later.

Apart from *The Two Widows,* based on a French comedy but reset in Bohemia, all Smetana's completed operas are thoroughly Czech in subject matter. He succeeded in establishing a national operatic tradition, and his firm commitment to opera ensured the achievement of this goal. Yet each of his operas brings its own approach and its own identity within his style. Perhaps the most clearly Czech elements in these works are the folklike peasant choruses and the vigorous dances, but these features are less significant than his extraordinary and often intensely personal expressive range, from historical epic grandeur to light lyric comedy. In retrospect, Smetana must be viewed as one of the giants of nineteenth century opera.—TERRY BARFOOT

Söderström, Elisabeth

Soprano. Born 7 May 1927, in Stockholm. Married: Sverker Olow, 1950; three sons. Studied with Andrejeva von Skilondz and at Royal Academy of Music and Opera School in Stockholm; debut as Mozart's Bastienne at Drottningholm Court Theater, 1947; joined Swedish Royal Opera, 1949; Glyndebourne debut as the Composer in Ariadne auf Naxos, *1957; debut at Metropolitan Opera as Susanna, 1959; debut at Covent Garden, with Royal*

Swedish Opera (as Daisy Doody in Blomdahl's Aniara*), 1960; sang Ellen Orford in* Peter Grimes *at Metropolitan, 1983; sang in premiere of Argento's* The Aspern Papers, *Dallas, 1988; appointed artistic director, Drottningholm Court Theater, 1990.*

Söderström, like her near contemporaries Kerstin Meyer, Nicolai Gedda and Birgit Nilsson, had the benefit of belonging to the company at the Royal Opera in Stockholm and being part of a tightly-knit ensemble, before launching out on an international career. Like Nilsson, Söderström first came to Great Britain to sing at Glyndebourne, where she made a specialty of Strauss roles, the Composer in *Ariadne,* the title-role in *Der Rosenkavalier,* the Countess in *Capriccio* and Christine in *Intermezzo.*

The mantle of Schwarzkopf descended upon Söderström to an extent once, after 1965, Schwarzkopf began to withdraw from the opera stage. Whereas Schwarzkopf's interpretations depended upon her analytic approach to the text and music, something which she continued to develop in her Lieder recitals, Söderström's great theatricality and obvious spontaneity—by her own admission she found it difficult to hold back tears on stage—and her intense desire to include the audience in her confidence made her one of the most fascinating singing actresses of the day. Consequently, her recording career was slow to take off, and despite the allure of her recordings of the three great Janáček parts, Jenůfa, Kat'a and Emilia Marty, they might have benefited from being caught a little earlier.

Söderström's voice was essentially a lyric soprano; when she undertook heavier roles such as Leonore in *Fidelio,* Emilia Marty and the Marschallin, in the theatre one became conscious of her need always to negotiate the music fairly cautiously. But as Tatyana, the *Capriccio* Countess and Jenůfa she was unsurpassed in her time. She brought to these roles the same qualities which distinguish her singing in the enormous repertory of Lieder, Mélodies and folk-songs that she included in her recitals. A quiet intensity, the ability to make the audience feel that she was abandoning herself completely to each moment in the music and drama, was added to a voice which although neither large nor conventionally beautiful had an individual quality, a quick vibrato in the middle range and a silver purity on the highest notes, plus exemplary diction in German, English, Italian, French and Swedish.

Söderström was an accomplished comedienne and mimic, as can be heard in her performance as Octavian—unfortunately not recorded complete, but a souvenir of each act is to be heard on the disc of highlights conducted by Varviso, with Crespin as the Marschallin. Like the singers of the nineteenth century, Söderström was always willing to learn and sing the music of living composers. In 1969 she claimed that her favorite role was that of the Governess in *The Turn of the Screw.* Equally memorable was her Jenny in Richard Rodney Bennett's *The Mines of Sulphur,* Daisie Doody in Blomdahl's *Aniara,* Elisabeth Zimmer in Henze's *Elegy for Young Lovers,* and her final role, as the aged primadonna in Argento's *The Aspern Papers.* To all of these she brought that same responsive, alert enthusiasm mixed with a wry femininity that made her more a Countess in *Figaro* than a Fiordiligi. It was this very warmth that told against the total success of her Mélisande; Mélisande has seldom seemed so vibrant, and it is not really conceivable that such a vivid presence can succumb to the gloomy inevitability of the plot.

Because her career was so diversified, Söderström never had the international fame or notoriety that lesser singers have achieved. She was one of the last of the true ensemble singers and a great star in her own right.—PATRICK O'CONNOR

Die Soldaten [The Soldiers]

Composer: *Bernd Alois Zimmermann.*

Librettist: *Bernd Alois Zimmermann (after Lenz).*

First Performance: *Cologne, 15 February 1965.*

Roles: *Wesener (bass); Marie (soprano); Charlotte (mezzo-soprano); Wesener's Old Mother (contralto); Stolzius (baritone); Stolzius' Mother (contralto); Obrist (bass); Desportes (tenor); Pirzel (tenor); Eisenhardt (baritone); Lt Mary (baritone); Major Haudy (baritone); Countess de la Roche (mezzo-soprano); Count de la Roche (tenor); Three Young Officers (tenors); several lesser roles; chorus.*

Bernd Alois Zimmermann's *Die Soldaten* (1958-60; revised 1963-64) stands at a particularly important juncture in the history of opera. It represents the first major effort in the genre by a composer of the post-World War II *avant-garde,* and it is considered to be the most significant opera by a German composer since those of Alban Berg. Zimmermann's debt to Berg is as often cited as it is over-rated. The similarities between *Die Soldaten* and Berg's *Wozzeck* (1921) are due as much to Georg Büchner (the author of *Woyzeck* [1836], Berg's source for *Wozzeck*) as to Zimmermann. Büchner based characters and themes in *Woyzeck* on the play *Die Soldaten* (1775) by J.M.R. Lenz, the same play which forms the basis for Zimmermann's opera. The similarity between Marie of *Die Soldaten* and the title character of Berg's other opera, *Lulu* (1935), is perhaps coincidental, since the character in Zimmermann's opera is no different from that in Lenz's play.

Zimmermann's real contribution is that he successfully integrates several of the innovative techniques pioneered by European composers at mid-century—including integral serialism, textural "sound-mass" effects, and *musique concrète* (the technique of manipulating tape-recorded sounds through cutting, splicing, and other methods)—into a newly conceived operatic framework. By re-working the narrative of J.M.R. Lenz into an increasingly fragmentary and mercurial braid of fifteen scenes, some of which overlap in simultaneous montages of visual and aural images, Zimmermann was able to effect a formal revolution in the drama analogous to, and in concordance with, that which originates in the music.

The libretto deals with the immoral behavior of soldiers in relation to the society that they are supposed to protect. During the course of the opera, Marie—the beautiful but flighty daughter of a merchant, M. Wesener—becomes the object of several knavish soldiers' amorous intents. Her downfall, and that of her spurned suitor Stolzius, is linked to the failure of society to protect itself adequately from its own protectors: the soldiers. Marie is, in a sense, sacrificed by a society which depends on an unnatural separation between several classes. The soldiers and their immoral behavior are creations of society; as a result of her social ambitions, Marie becomes entangled in an uncontrollable sequence of events.

The innovative features for which the opera is famous—the quotation of pre-existing music (Bach chorales, Gregorian chant, Jazz), the simultaneous presentation of disparate "scenes" in separate stage locations, the use of multi-media through projection of film and recorded sound playback—are all representative of the composer's pluralistic attitude toward time which he summed up in the novel concept "Kugelgestalt der Zeit" (sphere-form of time). This may briefly be described as an opening up of the present to include the past and the future. Zimmermann's quotation of older music, combined always with his "own" music, is the result of this opening up. It presents another layer of significance to the drama, which is itself opened up through the gradual breakdown of the barriers between temporally and spatially separate localities, as well as the erosion of any causality implied by traditional narrative structure.

The first scene of act IV is perhaps the single most representative realization of these innovations. Zimmermann's depiction of the action takes on completely the characteristically fragmentary and overlapping presentation in which the classical unities of time and place are discarded in favor of the more contemporary view that reality is closer to the confused, the contingent, and the fortuitous than to any clearly delineated straight-line narrative. While Zimmermann's techniques in this scene are thoroughly innovative in terms of operatic treatment, the composer couches the action in the age-old dramatic scenario of the dream. Marie has a dream in which various scenes from her past, present, and future are simultaneously entangled. The persons who have been a part of this dream finally come together in a tribunal to pass judgment on her behavior.

In the final scene of the opera, Zimmermann makes a significant alteration over Lenz's original. In Lenz's play, the penultimate scene shows Wesener accosted by his daughter Marie, who has become unrecognizable to him as a destitute beggar. Wesener finally recognizes Marie and they are reunited. Zimmermann opts for the completely desolate alternative in which Wesener pushes Marie away without recognition. This underscores Zimmermann's apocalyptic and thoroughly twentieth-century ending in which images projected on screens depict soldiers marching in endless columns, shouting orders in several languages, only to be stopped when an atomic explosion ends the opera.—RICHARD BLOCKER

La sonnambula [The Sleepwalker]

Composer: *Vincenzo Bellini.*

Librettist: *Felice Romani (after a ballet-pantomime by Eugène Scribe and Jean-Pierre Aumer).*

First Performance: *Milan, Teatro Carcano, 6 March 1831.*

Roles: *Amina (soprano); Lisa (soprano); Elvino (tenor); Rodolfo (bass); Teresa (mezzo-soprano); Alessio (bass); Notary (tenor); chorus (SSATTBB).*

La sonnambula is set in a Swiss village at some unspecified time. The villagers are preparing to celebrate the betrothal of Amina, an orphan, to Elvino, a prosperous farmer. The only unhappy person at the gathering is Elvino's former flame, Lisa, the innkeeper. The notary and Elvino arrive and the betrothal ceremony takes place. A stranger arrives, on his way to the castle. As evening approaches, the villagers warn the stranger of their local phantom. He decides to spend the evening at the inn and offers a few courteous compliments to the bride-to-be, provoking a jealous response from Elvino.

The scene changes to the stranger's room in the inn. Lisa tells him that the villagers have learned he is the new Count; they will soon be coming to offer their respects. Amina wanders in through the window; she is sleepwalking. Dreaming, she converses with Elvino and enacts the wedding ceremony. The Count, not wanting to compromise Amina, leaves. The villagers appear and find Amina, in her nightgown, in the Count's room. Amina's foster mother Teresa wraps Amina in the shawl Lisa had left in the room. Elvino denounces Amina and calls off the wedding.

In the second act the villagers decide to go to the castle to ask the Count directly if Amina is innocent, as she protests she is. Elvino angrily rejects Amina and declares he will marry Lisa instead. Teresa accuses Lisa of having been in the Count's room and produces Lisa's shawl as evidence. When the Count arrives and explains that Amina is an innocent sleepwalker Elvino refuses to believe him. Amina appears, perilously sleepwalking across the roof of the mill, sorrowing over Elvino who has so unjustly rejected her. Amina wanders onto safe ground, Elvino awakens her by slipping a ring on her finger, and the villagers once again prepare to celebrate a wedding.

La sonnambula is not a typical Bellini opera. An *opera semiseria,* it dispenses with heroic gestures and historic trappings. Instead the work celebrates romanticized pastoral virtues— rustic innocence, naivete, simplicity. References to the supernatural are tongue-in-cheek. What we are meant to take completely seriously, however, are the sentiments of the protagonists— Amina's pure love for Elvino, Elvino's passionate love for Amina and his equally passionate sense of betrayal, the Count's affection for his homeland and his general good will. There are no villains in *La sonnambula,* only misunderstandings which are relatively easily set right.

La sonnambula shows almost no conflict between dramatic ends and musical means. Bellini composed it quickly (in approximately two months) after he discontinued work on a projected *Ernani.* Unlike most of his operas, Bellini produced *La sonnambula* seemingly effortlessly. The work has an abundance of set numbers that do not strain against the received Rossinian formulas. All of the characters are well served with arias: Amina has two full-scale

Set design by Alessandro Sanquirico for the final scene of *La sonnambula,* 1831

double arias, Elvino and the Count one double aria each; even Lisa has two arias, though of more modest size and shape. Elvino is not given an entrance cavatina but he dominates both of the act I duets he sings with Amina. The first duet begins with his action of giving Amina a ring ("Prendi l'anel ti dono") and the second duet begins by discussing his feelings of jealousy ("Son geloso del zeffiro errante"). He also leads off the second-act quartet. In all of the set numbers, the sentiments stated, their musical expression, and their appropriateness to the characters and action are in perfect balance.

In *La sonnambula* the characters seem to be notably at ease with their status as musical beings. In her first duet Amina complains, with no irony intended, that she cannot find words to express her feelings—but of course, expressing feelings through words is not what this preeminently lyrical opera is about. Indeed, the opening chorus hardly bothers with a text at all; an occasional "Viva Amina" punctuates the pervasive "la, la, la." The chorus is on stage for more than half of the opera. It functions as a kind of collective comic character, a useful balance for the sentimentalized principal characters.

The abundance of numbers in compound time or with accompaniments with triplet subdivision helps establish and maintain the pastoral atmosphere. Indeed, only Lisa's and Elvino's arias in the second act—sung when pastoral contentment is at the point of greatest disruption—are entirely free from triplet rhythms.

Critical opinion on *La sonnambula* is divided. For some, this is a very silly work. For others it is Bellini's finest opera—"Bellini's genius at its purest." In order to enjoy it, one needs to suspend not only disbelief but sophistication. But if one can enter its idyllic, pastoral world, one is rewarded by gifts of beauty and kindliness.—CHARLOTTE GREENSPAN

Spontini, Gaspare

Composer. Born 14 November 1774, in Majolati, Ancona. Died 24 January 1851, in Majolati, Ancona. Married: the daughter of Jean-Baptiste Erard, 1810. Studied singing with Tritto and composition with Sala at the Conservatorio della Pietà de' Turchini in Naples, 1793; commissioned by the Teatro della Pallacorda in Rome, 1796; aided by Piccinni in the composition of his second opera, L' eroismo ridicolo; composed three operas for the Neapolitan court, 1800; in Rome, 1081, Venice, 1802, and Naples and Paris, 1803; appointed "compositeur particulier" by the Empress Josephine of France; with La vestale, won the prize offered by Napoleon (and judged by Méhul, Gossec, and Grétry) for best dramatic work, 1807; director of the Italian Opera in Paris, 1810-12, where he staged the Paris premiere of Mozart's Don Giovanni; appointed court composer to Louis XVIII, 1814; court composer and general music director to King Friedrich Wilhelm III, Berlin, 1820-41; knight of the Prussian Ordre pour le Mérite; member of the Berlin Akademie, 1833; member of the French Institut, 1839; returned to Paris, 1842, and then retired to his birthplace; given the rank and title of Conte de Sant' Andrea by the Pope, 1844; Ph.D. from Halle University.

Operas *Li puntigli delle donne,* Rome, Teatro della Pallecorda di Firenze, carnival 1796; *Il finto pittore,* Rome, 1797-98 [lost]; *Adelina Senese, o sia L'amore secreto,* after G. Bertati, *La principessa d' Amalfi,* Venice, San Samuele, 10 October 1797; *L'eroismo ridicolo,* D. Piccinni, Naples, Nuovo, carnival

1798; *Il Teseo riconosciuto*, C. Giotti, Florence, Intrepidi, spring 1798; *La finta filosofa*, D. Piccini?. Naples, Nuovo, summer 1799; revised, Paris, Théâtre-Italien (Salle-Favart), 11 February 1804; *La fuga in maschera*, G. Palomba, Naples, Nuovo, carnival 1800; *I quandri parlante*, Palermo, Santa Cecilia, 1800 [lost]; *Gli Elisi delusi*, M. Monti, Palermo, Santa Cecilia, 26 August 1800 [only act I survives]; *Gli amanti in cimento, o sia Il geloso audace*, Rome, Valle, 3 November 1801 [lost]; *Le metamorfosi di Pasquale, o sia Tutto è illusione nel mondo*, G. Foppa, Venice, San Samuele, carnival 1802 [lost]; [*Che più guarda meno vede*, Florence, 1798?; *La petit maison*, A.M. Dieulafoy and N. Gersaint, Paris, Opéra-Comique (Feydeau), 12 May 1804; *Milton*, E. de Jouy and Dieulafoy, Paris, Opéra-Comique (Feydeau), 27 November 1804; *Julie, ou Le pot de fleurs*, A.G. Jars, Paris, Opéra-Comique (Feydeau), 12 March 1805; *La vestale*, E. de Jouy, Paris, Opéra, 15 December 1807; *Fernand Cortez, ou La conquète du Mexique*, E. de Jouy, J.A. d'Esmenard, Paris, Opéra, 28 November 1809; revised, Paris, Opéra, 8 May 1817; *Pélage, ou Le roi et la paix*, E. de Jouy, Paris, Opéra, 23 August 1814; *Les dieux rivaux ou Les fêtes de Cythère* (opéra-ballet, with Kreutzer, Persuis, and Berton), A.M. Dieulafoy and C. Briffaut, Paris, Opéra, 21 June 1816; *Olimpie*, A.M. Dielafoy and C. Briffaut (after Voltaire), Paris, Opéra, 22 December 1819; revised as *Olympia*, revised and translated by E.T.A. Hoffman, Berlin, Opera, 14 May 1821; *Nurmahal, oder Das Rosenfest von Caschmir*, C.A. Herkotz (after T. Moore. *Lalla Rookh*), Berlin, Opera, 27 May 1822; *Alcidor*, G.M. Théaulon de Lambert (after Rochon de Chabannes, translated into German by C.A. Herklotz), Berlin, Opera, 23 May 1825; *Agnes von Hohenstaufen*, S.B.E. Paupach, performance of act I, Berlin, Opera, 28 May 1827; revised, Berlin, Opera, 12 June 1829; revised, Lichtenstein, Berlin, Opera, 6 December 1837.

The Italian composer Gaspare Spontini was a major international figure during the first part of the nineteenth century. He worked in Naples and other Italian centers until around 1800, gaining considerable operatic experience. Throughout his life, opera dominated his creative work. Most of his early operas have been lost; however, the most successful of them, *Li puntigli delle donne,* gave him a reputation in comic opera.

It was his move to Paris after 1802 which proved the decisive factor in Spontini's career, since it enabled him to fulfill his potential in new directions. His first Parisian works were in fact *opéras comiques;* they were, however, badly received, to some extent because of anti-Italian resentment in the city's musical fraternity. In 1804 his *opéra comique Milton* revealed a tendency towards the French preference for a noble style and serious subjects, and the following year Spontini confirmed this trend by composing *La vestale* to a libretto by Etienne de Jouy, a text already rejected by Boieldieu, Cherubini and Méhul, three leading contemporaries.

La vestale was a *tragédie lyrique* written for the Paris Opéra, and its triumph there in 1807 revived the flagging fortunes of that institution and established Spontini as a major figure in the operatic world. Its style is founded on Gluck, but updated to suit the tastes of Napoleonic audiences through its melodrama and spectacle. It remains an impressive achievement, with a brilliantly paced drama built around the perennial operatic issue, the conflict between love and duty.

Although Spontini wrote some two dozen operas, only three—*La vestale, Fernand Cortez* and *Olimpie*—have become established enough to form the basis for his reputation. *Fernand Cortez* was another collaboration with Jouy, and it has been suggested that Napoleon himself put forward the subject, hoping that an opera dealing with the conquest of Mexico might reflect favorably upon his Spanish campaign. However, the work only became popular several years later, following substantial revisions. This version, first staged in 1817, received hundreds of performances during Spontini's lifetime.

In *Fernand Cortez* the hero is a complex character who falls in love with his enemy's daughter. Therefore it is mistaken to view this opera merely as a grand historical epic, even though its staging was particularly spectacular. There is a cavalry charge stipulating seventeen horses, the burning of the Spanish fleet, and the destruction of the Aztec temple in the final scene. The chorus understandably plays a central role, the two sides characterized by march-like music and exotic percussion effects.

Spontini had a typically Italian gift for vocal melody and a sure command of the orchestra. He used the full modern orchestra of his day, preferring to separate the roles of cellos and basses, and to divide the violas as Mozart had done. His woodwind writing was distinctive, especially as an aid to developing character, and he was fond of the spatial potential of the on-stage band and the exotic sounds of tam-tam, bells and other percussion. The next generation recognized his special talent, as the words of Berlioz confirm: "Spontini's orchestration has no antecedents. Its special colour is achieved by a use of wind instruments which contrasts skillfully with that of the strings. The frequent stressing of weak beats, dissonances whose resolution is transplanted into a different part, bass figures rising and falling majestically beneath the bulk of the orchestra, the sparing but ingenious use of trombones, trumpets, horns and timpani, the almost total exclusion of the very top register of piccolos, oboes and clarinets—all this gives Spontini's great works a grandiose character, an incomparable power and energy, and often a poetic melancholy."

Spontini's last *tragédie lyrique, Olimpie,* was begun in 1815 but only performed four years later. Despite being his most grand conception, it remained in the repertory for only a few performances (Spontini's ability to make enemies contributed to his downfall). This disappointment led to his accepting an offer from the King of Prussia to direct the Berlin Opera, and one of his first decisions was to stage *Olimpie* using E.T.A. Hoffmann as an adviser. This 1821 production was a success, but it was soon overshadowed by Weber's *Der Freischütz,* which was premiered only a month later.

The formal pageantry of Spontini is at its height in *Olimpie.* For instance, it ends with a lengthy divertissement, a spectacle which comes after the resolution of the plot; and the hero is directed to make his entry riding on an elephant, as indeed he did in the Berlin production.

Spontini responded to his new circumstances by incorporating fairy-tale supernaturalism, so effective in Weber's *Freischütz,* into his own opera *Nurmahal.* But he could hardly have expected to create a real German romantic opera, especially since his music drew heavily on earlier works, even from his Italian period. Then, in *Agnes von Hohenstaufen,* he adapted a medieval German subject in his efforts to respond to the taste of his Berlin audience. This opera has massive ensemble scenes of great formal complexity, as in *Olimpie,* but his position in Berlin was declining by this stage, and in 1842 he returned to Paris, where he tried unsuccessfully to rekindle past glories. In 1850, just a year before his death, he returned to Italy.

Spontini had much in common with Meyerbeer, whose rise to prominence he resented, but who continued the tradition of grand opera which he had largely established. Despite his reputation as a creator of spectacle, it is for his music that Spontini should be remembered. He was an important influence on Weber and Wagner as well as on Berlioz, who believed him to be the greatest composer he ever met, the "genius of the century." Most of all, Spontini followed

Gluck's precedent as a composer of powerful operas, whose chief concern was the expression of human passions.—TERRY BARFOOT

Steber, Eleanor

Soprano. Born 17 July 1916, in Wheeling, West Virginia. Died 3 October 1990, in Langborne, Pennsylvania. Attended New England Conservatory in Boston, and studied privately with Paul Althouse and William Whitney; debut as Senta, Boston, 1936; in 1940 won Metropolitan Opera radio auditions, which led to Metropolitan debut (as Sophie) in same year; remained at Metropolitan until 1962, singing Violetta, 1943, Konstanze in Metropolitan premiere of Die Entführung aus dem Serail, *1946, the Marschallin, 1949, title role in American premiere of* Arabella, *1955, title role in world premiere of Barber's* Vanessa, *1958, and Marie in Metropolitan's first* Wozzeck, *1959; appeared at Edinburgh Festival, 1947, as Elsa at Bayreuth, 1953, in Vienna, 1953, and in Florence, as Minnie, 1954; sang in first performance of Barber's* Knoxville: Summer of 1915, *1948; sang Miss Wingrave in American premiere of Britten's* Owen Wingrave, *Santa Fe, 1973; in later years appeared frequently in musical comedies and as concert artist, and was active as teacher at Cleveland Institute and Juilliard School, among other schools.*

One of the most renowned operatic sopranos of the twentieth century, Eleanor Steber was born on 17 July 1916 in Wheeling, West Virginia. She studied at the New England Conservatory and won the 1940 Metropolitan Opera auditions. Steber's lengthy career at the Met (1940-1962) and other operatic venues established her as a singer of astonishing breadth and depth. Steber's popularity may be gauged by the fact that she had a very active fan club with numerous chapters throughout the United States which even published a regular newsletter entitled "The Silvertone." A noted performer of Richard Strauss (especially the roles of Sophie, the Marschallin, and Arabella) and Mozart (including but not limited to the roles of Donna Anna, Donna Elvira, Pamina, and Fiordiligi), Steber also successfully tackled more modern roles such as Marie of Berg's *Wozzeck* and Miss Wingrave of Britten's *Owen Wingrave.*

Steber's flexibility as a singer and her stage presence contributed greatly to the development of an uniquely American approach to opera singing, with a much greater emphasis placed on the singer as actor. Convincing characterization was an essential element of this approach and led Steber as her career matured to take successively older roles in operas in which she had already starred in younger roles.

Steber's singing was particularly associated with the music of the American composer Samuel Barber. She premiered the title role of Barber's *Vanessa* (1958) and also commissioned and premiered the composer's well-known *Knoxville: Summer of 1915* (1948) based on a text by the American writer James Agee. Steber's championing of American music was paralleled in her great concern for correct instruction in English diction, which the singer believed was not being properly taught in European conservatories.

After her retirement from the Met in 1962, Steber continued to perform in operas and solo recitals. One of the most notable performances of her post-Met career was as old Miss Wingrave in the Santa Fe (New Mexico) Opera's production of *Owen Wingrave*

Steber dedicated her later years to teaching (at the Juilliard School of Music in New York City, Temple University in Philadelphia, the New England Conservatory in Boston, and the Cleveland Institute of Music, among other institutions) and providing financial support to aspiring singers through the agency of the Eleanor Steber Music Foundation, which is dedicated to financing, in Steber's words, "the no man's land that lies between school training and big-time debut."—WILLIAM E. GRIM

Stevens, Risë

Mezzo-soprano. Born 11 June 1913, in New York. Married: Walter Surovy, 1939. Studied at the Juilliard School of Music with Anna Schoen-René; studied in Salzburg with Marie Gutheil-Schoder and Herbert Graf; debut in Thomas's Mignon, *Prague, 1936; sang Octavian in Strauss's* Der Rosenkavalier, *1938; Metropolitan Opera debut as Octavian, 1938; sang at the Glyndebourne Festival, 1939; films include* The Chocolate Soldier, *1941, and* Going My Way, *1944; sang at the Met, 1938-61; Teatro alla Scala debut, 1954; retired from the stage in 1964; co-director of Metropolitan Opera National Company, 1965-67; president, Mannes College of Music, 1975-78; managing director, Metropolitan Opera Board, 1988.*

Possessor of one of the most sensuous mezzo-soprano voices of her generation, Risë Stevens virtually owned the roles of Carmen and Dalila at the Metropolitan Opera during the 1940s and 1950s. Her vocal texture was pure velvet, not meant for the heavy dramatic mezzo heroines of Verdi and Wagner. She had the good sense to drop Amneris, as well as her weighty Wagnerian sisters, Fricka and Erda, early in her career. From the start Stevens was more suited to the classic line of Gluck's Orfeo than the heroic outpourings of Beethoven's Leonore—a role she was offered by Bruno Walter and wisely declined.

Like several of her opera colleagues—Gladys Swarthout, Lawrence Tibbett, Grace Moore and Lily Pons—Stevens built a career notable for its diversity. She was a popular star of radio and television, an appealing recitalist, an opera singer of the first rank, a much sought after concert performer, a film actress (who had the good fortune to be in *Going My Way*), and a recording artist whose extensive output included classical, semi-classical, Broadway and popular songs. Her rendition of Cole Porter's "Ev'rything I love" ranks with the best, and the excitement generated in her final scene from *Carmen* with Raoul Jobin leaves all others far behind (even her own later version with Jan Peerce). Her occasional pairing with the dynamic Italian tenor and congenial colleague, Mario Del Monaco at the Metropolitan, produced superlative performances of *Carmen* and *Samson et Dalila* which set standards unchallenged to this day. Recorded highlights of *Samson et Dalila* with these two artists preserve the chemistry which existed between them.

Carmen was Stevens's most famous role because she willed it to be. She molded herself to a part which actually was wrong for her. The Nordic-American beauty which was hers is light years away from that of a Spanish Gypsy's. At first, her interpretation followed conventional lines, but after her encounter with Tyrone Guthrie, who directed a production of *Carmen* at the Metropolitan Opera done especially for her, she completely changed her conception of the central character. Stevens's Carmen was not pretty, but rather hard, calculating, tough and one step away from a prostitute. This approach was a gamble, for she walked a fine line between characterization and caricature. To her credit, she completely avoided the obvious and probed deeper and deeper into the role. The death of Carmen, set in the grimy dressing room of Escamillo, with her defiant rejection of Don José constitutes one of the greatest moments of theater.

As with anyone who is so closely identified with a part, we tend to forget that Stevens was also brilliant as Octavian. Her early collaboration with Lotte Lehmann in *Der Rosenkavalier* is what operatic legends are made of. She was one of the very few who could bring Dalila to vivid realization, present an Orfeo of compelling beauty and pathos, a Prince Orlofsky of endearingly wacky charm, a beguiling Cherubino and a bewitching Mignon. That she also received critical acclaim as Laura in *La Gioconda,* Marfa in *Khovanshchina* and Marina in *Boris Godunov* further defines the versatility she possessed.

When speaking of Stevens, one can not avoid the word "multi-faceted." She excelled in a wide variety of forms of entertainment; today's "superstars" would be hard pressed to duplicate her achievements. Her greatest asset was her uncanny ability to communicate. No matter if it was in the large expanse of an opera house or the intimacy of the television screen, Stevens could give the impression that she was singing to you alone.—JOHN PENNINO

Stich-Randall, Teresa

Soprano. Born 24 December 1927, in West Hartford, Connecticut. Studied voice at the Hartford School of Music and at Columbia University; created role of Gertrude Stein in Thomson's The Mother of Us All, 1947; sang under Toscanini and NBC Symphony Orchestra as the Priestess in Aïda, 1949, and Nannetta, 1950; European debut as Mermaid in Oberon, Florence, 1952; Vienna State Opera debut, 1952; Metropolitan Opera debut as Fiordiligi in Così fan tutte, 1961; first U.S. singer to be named Austrian Kammersängerin, 1962.

The American-born soprano Teresa Stich-Randall made an early and auspicious debut: in 1947, while still a student at Columbia University she created the role of Gertrude Stein in Virgil Thomson's opera *The Mother of Us All.* By 1950 she had been recruited by Arturo Toscanini, who, no doubt impressed by her pure tone and secure intonation, cast her as the Priestess in *Aida* and Nanetta in *Falstaff* in his NBC broadcasts of these operas. These performances, still available on records, testify to Stich-Randall's excellence even then—particularly in *Falstaff* where, surrounded by a formidable cast, she shines by virtue of the flute-like purity of her tone.

Stich-Randall's voice, basically a lyric soprano with some bloom, was notable for a concentrated silvery sharpness which could penetrate large orchestrations with ease, creating the illusion of a dramatic size which was perhaps not hers by nature. Also striking was a remarkable sense of attack: the voice moved in even the fastest and most complex passagework with the uncanny accuracy of an instrument, always—or nearly always—landing in the dead center of a note. If the instrumental analogy suggests efficiency more than poetry, that is probably just: Stich-Randall's singing is often distinguished more by its brilliance and gleam than by its humanity. In addition, particularly in the latter part of her career, the virtuosic florid singing could sound mannered and mechanical. A recorded recital includes performances of arias from *I Puritani* and *La traviata*. Here the tempi are almost freakishly fast, and the manic precision of the scale work becomes comically inappropriate. In fact, none of the arias as recorded (all from the French and Italian repertoires) really satisfies. The glinting tone seems much better suited to German music, and although Stich-Randall's stage repertoire encompassed Gilda and even Norma it is unsurprising that she is best known for her significant contributions to the music of Strauss and Mozart. The EMI recording of *Der Rosenkavalier* (conducted by Herbert von Karajan) in which Stich-Randall sings Sophie introduced her to many listeners, and the performance remains justly celebrated; there have been more human, vulnerable Sophies but none who negotiates the rise to the soft B flat in the Presentation of the Rose with such superb ease.

As an interpreter of the music of Mozart, Stich-Randall left many significant recorded souvenirs of her artistry. Among the operatic roles she was perhaps best known as Donna Anna (*Don Giovanni*), and her performance recorded live at Aix-en-Provence captures the fleet, shining voice at its best—as well as a memorable impersonation, alive to every nuance of the chimerical, neurotic character. This vividness of interpretation is the exception rather than the rule among Stich-Randall's recorded performances, and although critics and audiences who saw her in the theater invariably comment on her fine acting, her records tell a somewhat different story. Her Fiordiligi in *Così fan tutte*, for example, barely hints at the critical change of heart which is foreshadowed in "Per pietà," although the arching legato line is masterly. In "Come scoglio," the fearsome leaps are negotiated with almost impudent ease—but the critical sense of fun is absent. Similarly, Stich-Randall's recording of the Countess in *Le nozze di Figaro* is a first-rate piece of singing but a leaden and unmemorable interpretation placed against those of Elisabeth Schwarzkopf, Lisa Della Casa, Sena Jurinac and other contemporaries. Several recital records of Mozart opera arias include, in addition to the roles noted above, characters as diverse as Pamina (*Die Zauberflöte*, Ilia (*Idomeneo*) and Constanze (*Die Entführung aus dem Serail*)—all are sung with care and artistry, shining tone, musicianly attention to detail, and all are indistinguishable from one another as personalities.

The concert arias of Mozart require less specific insights, and Stich-Randall's recordings of these show her at her marvelous best. The extended motet *Exsultate, Jubilate* with its celebrated "Alleluja" (taken here at an especially brisk pace) is sung with gorgeous tone and invigorating accuracy, the extreme difficulties of "Ah, se in ciel benigne stelle" are tossed off with seeming ease, and in the long legato lines of "Bella mia fiamma" the instrumental purity is a joy to hear. All of these preserve the remarkable artistry at its finest, and all go far to justify the inclusion of Stich-Randall in the pantheon of great Mozart singers of the middle of our century.—DAVID ANTHONY FOX

Stiffelio

Composer: *Giuseppe Verdi.*

Librettist: *Francesco Maria Piave (after E. Souvestre and E. Bourgeois).*

First Performance: *Trieste, 16 November 1850; revised as Aroldo,* Rimini, Nuovo, 16 August 1857.

Roles: *Stiffelio (tenor); Lina (soprano); Stankar (baritone); Jorg (bass); Raffaele (tenor); Dorotea (mezzo-soprano); Federico (tenor); chorus.*

In the few years since Julian Budden's description of *Stiffelio* as Verdi's most unjustly neglected opera—he was writing after the 1968 Parma performances of the opera, the first in more than a hundred years—little has happened to alter its status except perhaps a remarkable 1985-86 staging (in tandem with *Aroldo,* Verdi's 1857 reworking of *Stiffelio*) by Pier Luigi Pizzi at La Fenice. The neglect up until 1968 is understandable given that Verdi used the autograph score of *Stiffelio,* as the manuscript for the *Aroldo* revisions and ordered other copies destroyed; consequently no autograph exists for *Stiffelio,* and it was only with the discovery of two copyists' full scores in the 1960s that performance became possible once again. Considering that it was composed between *Luisa Miller* and *Rigoletto,* the comparative lack of interest still shown for *Stiffelio* is extraordinary.

The frustration which led Verdi to abandon *Stiffelio* as unperformable in his day stemmed primarily from censorship difficulties. The subject was the most contemporary Verdi had tackled; the play on which it was based, *Le pasteur, ou L'évangile et le foyer* by Emile Silvestre and Eugène Bourgeois, had premiered in Paris only the year before. The adultery of a Protestant clergyman's wife was bewildering to the Italian public, who were unused to clergymen having wives, let alone adulterous ones, while the Church censors found it presumptuous and offensive on numerous grounds. Verdi had to agree unwillingly to changes—indeed some of them made nonsense of the drama—to get it onstage at all. The alterations to the climax in act III, scene i, for example, when Lina, the erring wife, having failed to move Stiffelio to listen to her as a husband, suddenly asks him to hear her confession as a minister, rendered it pointless. A bowdlerized version, *Guglielmo Wellingrode,* made the rounds for a few years, but Verdi's detestation of it brought about the decision to revise it into *Aroldo.*

Act I begins with Stiffelio's return from his travels to be greeted by his wife, Lina, her father, Stankar, and his elderly colleague, Jorg. Magnanimously refusing to investigate a possible adulterous liaison brought to his attention, Stiffelio soon has reason to suspect that the liaison is in fact his wife's. Her father discovers the truth and challenges Raffaele, the lover, to a duel in the graveyard of the castle that night, where act II takes place. Lina, waiting to warn Raffaele, prays at the grave of her mother. He enters, followed by Stankar; they fight, bringing Stiffelio out of the church onto the scene. Stankar informs him that Raffaele is Lina's lover; enraged, Stiffelio moves to revenge himself on Raffaele. Suddenly the congregation in the church is heard singing "Non punirmi, Signor, nel tuo furore" ("Do not punish me, O Lord, in thine anger"); Jorg, appearing at the church door, persuades Stiffelio to renounce his anger and reenter the church. Act III, scene i brings the confrontation between Stiffelio and Lina; he offers her a divorce freeing her to marry Raffaele but refuses to listen to her. She eventually signs the document but swears she loves him and that she was Raffaele's victim. Stiffelio, again enraged, is about to take vengeance on Raffaele but is forestalled by Stankar, who enters announcing that *he* has killed Rafaele. The concluding scene is set in the church, where the congregation, singing the same psalm begging for mercy, waits for Stiffelio to preach. He enters and, not perceiving Lina, mounts the pulpit praying for guidance; at Jorg's urging he opens the Bible for inspiration and, finding himself at the story of the woman taken in adultery, reads the passage aloud, forgiving his wife before the congregation.

There are problems in the libretto, chiefly the necessity of compressing the very complicated action of the play; in effect, Piave dramatized only the last two acts of the four-act drama. The chief loss is a clear sense of the context of Lina's adultery, of her motivation apart from a sense of guilt so that her music alone has to establish her as a figure with whom the audience can identify unquestioningly. Today's audiences may also have difficulty accepting that the modern society depicted could hold to a moral code in which the "wronged" husband

and father assume the right to murder the seducer while remaining reluctant to forgive the "fallen" woman.

Much of the music, as one would expect at this point in Verdi's career, is extraordinarily mature. Opening the opera with Jorg's sombre meditation on the holy book ("O santo libro") rather than with the more usual chorus, establishes the elder preacher as the drama's voice of moral aspiration. The septet following Stiffelio's entrance is unable to distinguish the characters and their relative positions very satisfactorily, but Stiffelio's aria, "Vidi dovunque gemere," establishes him as a kind of tenor character different from any Verdi had yet tackled: a balanced man of mature years, a kind of early Otello-figure, whose struggle will be between his magnanimity and his impulses. Lina's aria after Stiffelio's suspicions are awakened, "A te ascenda," leads to a splendidly varied duet with her father, "Dite che il fallo a tergere," in which the true Verdian baritone vents its fury while the soprano's fragmented laments anticipate Gilda's vocal line in the soon-to-be-completed *Rigoletto* quartet. Act II works well both dramatically and musically, moving from Lina's opening aria, "Ah daglie scanni eternei" (whose luminous accompaniment looks forward to Amelia's first-act act aria in *Simon Boccanegra*) into a powerful quartet, "Ah, era vero." However, it is the act-III duet between husband and wife ("Opposto è il calle") that realizes their full stature and marks the greatness of the work. The musical austerity of the final scene, from the simple organ opening through the choral psalm punctuated by Stankar's prayer for mercy and Lina's hopeful cries, gradually builds up a tremendous tension which is released only by the ensemble's repeated cry of "Perdonata."—PETER DYSON

Stockhausen, Karlheinz

Composer. Born 22 August 1928, in Mödrath, near Cologne. Studied piano and music education at the Hochschule für Musik in Cologne, 1947-51; studied composition with Frank Martin at the Hochschule, 1950-51; studied with Olivier Messiaen at the Paris Conservatory, musique concrète at Pierre Schaeffer's Club d'Essai, and privately with Darius Milhaud in Paris, 1951-53; production assistant, Studio for Electronic Music, WDr. Cologne, 1953-63; summer seminars for the Ferienkurse für Musik in Darmstadt, 1953-74; lecture tour of Canadian and American Universities, 1958; founder and artistic director of the "Cologne Courses for New Music," 1963-68; artistic director, Studio for Electronic Music, WDr. Cologne, 1963-75; visiting professor at the University of California, Davis, 1966-67; public lectures in England, 1969-71; performances at the World's Fair in Osaka, Japan, 1970; professor of composition at the Hochschule für Musik, Cologne, 1971-77; Ernst von Siemens Music Prize, 1986; honorary membership, the Royal Academy of Music, London, 1987; honorary membership, the American Academy of Arts and Sciences, 1989.

Operas *'Atmen gibt das Leben . . .'* (choral opera), 1974-77, Cologne, Cologne Radio, 10 February 1979; *Licht: die sieben Tage der Woche,* 1977—) *Der Jahreslauf* (scene from *Dienstag aus Licht*), 1977; 2) *Donnerstag aus Licht,* 1978-80, Milan, 1981; 3) *Samstag aus Licht,* 1981-84, Milan, 1984; *Montag aus Licht,* 1984-88, Milan, 1988.

The cultural environment in which Stockhausen grew up was hardly the comfortable life of regular opera-going, but a real world of Germany in the 1930s, in which material deprivation, spiritual anguish, state persecution, the threat and reality of war, the solace of music and the saving grace of religion all played a part. As a youthful conscript he played the piano to the wounded and dying in a camp hospital, then when the war was over he worked for two years as operetta *repetiteur* in Blecher, a country town, which led to his directing Humperdinck's *Hansel and Gretel*. His philosophy and music studies in Cologne were paid for by working as a nightclub pianist and accompanist to a touring magician, capitalizing on his skills at jazz improvisation. In 1950, he co-authored and composed *Burleska,* a pantomime extravaganza for speaker, solo singers, choir and chamber ensemble. It was his nearest venture into opera for twenty-seven years.

The avant-garde composing milieu in which Stockhausen rapidly assumed a leading role had little sympathy for either the social or the narrative conventions of traditional operatic entertainment, thriving instead on the ritual of the concert platform and a music of deliberately cryptic codes and utterances as well as dazzling instrumental effects. The taboo against representational elements, forbidding the use of a conventional tonal language, continuous narrative or recognizable characters, arose from a desire to reinvent music from ground zero, and it led to a style of spiritual abstraction strangely similar in inspiration to the mathematical patterning of traditional Islamic art. Nevertheless, the ecstatic verbal confusion of *Gesang der Jünglinge* (1955-56) for five-channel electronic sound incorporating a boy soprano's voice, had undeniable dramatic impact as an image of the biblical fiery furnace and its divinely-protected survivors, and the cantata *Momente* (1961-64; revised 1971-74), an accompanied stream-of-consciousness monologue for soprano solo, though static and essentially radiophonic in conception, betrayed a well-developed sense of comedy and impressive emotional and dramatic range.

After 1970, elements of visible ritual, often parodying the stiffness of concert-hall behavior, but always in strict obedience to the underlying musical agenda, gradually infiltrated Stockhausen's instrumental and orchestral compositions. Anecdotal events from everyday musical life provide comic relief in *Trans* (1971), in *Tierkreis* (1975) and the choir opera '*Atmen gibt das Leben . . .*' (1974-77) the musical form is translated into through-composed and choreographed stage actions. The underlying motive of his visionary cantata *Sirius* (1975-77) for soprano, bass, trumpet and bass clarinet is self-evidently the same kind of visitation celebrated by Steven Spielberg in the movie *Close Encounters of the Third Kind*. The increasingly visual choreography of all of Stockhausen's music during this time (and retrospectively in his revivals of earlier compositions) can be regarded in part as a gradual progress toward finding a gestural and scenic vocabulary; but it can equally be seen as a shrewd pre-emptive tactic to ensure control of the visual presentation of his works in a new age of video and interpretative license in opera generally.—ROBIN MACONIE

Stratas, Teresa

Soprano. Born Anastasia Strataki, 26 May 1938, in Toronto. Studied with Irene Jessner at Toronto Conservatory; from age twelve sang at nightclubs and at father's restaurant in Toronto; debut as Mimi with Canadian Opera, Toronto, 1958; won 1959 Metropolitan Opera Auditions of the Air and made Metropolitan debut that year as Poussette in Manon;

created title role in Glanville-Hicks's Nausicaa, *Athens Festival, 1960; Covent Garden debut as Mimi, 1961; sang Queen Isabella in Falla's* Atlántida, *Teatro alla Scala, 1962; sang Susanna in* Figaro *in Salzburg, 1972-73; sang* Salome *for German television, 1974; has made regular appearances in Munich, Hamburg, Paris, and at the Bol'shoy Theater; performed title role in first three-act production of Berg's* Lulu, *Paris, 1979; was Violetta in Zeffirelli's film version of* La traviata *(1983); was subject of film portrait by Harry Rasky,* StrataSphere; *Broadway debut in musical* Rags, *1986; made an Officer of the Order of Canada, 1972.*

When Stratas auditioned for the Opera School at the Royal Conservatory of Music, University of Toronto in 1954, she was completely untrained, her only singing experience having been in the clubs and cafes of the local Greek community. She was nevertheless accepted, so striking was her natural ability, and she studied there for four years with Irene Jessner, her only teacher. Her progress was remarkably swift and unfolded with the intensity that has characterized everything she has done. In 1958 she made an impressive professional debut in Toronto as Mimi in *La bohème,* joined the Metropolitan Opera in October 1959, sang Cio-Cio-San at Vancouver in 1960, and in 1961 made her Covent Garden debut as Mimi. Through the 1960s she appeared at most of the principal opera houses in Europe and America in roles as varied as Yniold in *Pelléas et Mélisande,* Tatyana in *Eugene Onegin,* the Composer in *Ariadne auf Naxos,* and Despina in *Così fan tutte.* During this period she maintained about fifteen roles in her active repertoire, roles that covered a great vocal and dramatic range.

The alluring timbre of her voice has been described as "smoky" but that alone does not convey the tension in the sound. It is by no means a big voice, but it is especially well-focussed and projected with great power. In the Puccini roles in which she first established her reputation it is foregone that one of the requirements is beautiful, even voluptuous singing, but mere beauty of voice is only the starting point for a Stratas portrayal. More important are the shadings of the voice, the textual inflections, the exclamations that give varied insights into the character of the role. Although diminutive in stature (something that allowed her to play soubrettes and youths so convincingly) she has great presence on stage, and has developed an acting ability of extraordinary subtlety and detail to make her one of the greatest and most affecting actress/singers on the operatic stage.

In 1974 she sang the title role in *Salome* for German television in a performance that records everything that makes Stratas so remarkable. Vocally she is able to rattle off the chatter of the girlish Salome, to express the bewilderment and growing sensuality when she first encounters Jochanaan, and finally to give free rein to Salome's depraved rapture in the final scene. Visually Stratas depicts with flashing detail the broad development of Salome from a naive, puzzled and spoiled child to a woman overwhelmed by sensual desire. At the climactic moments she does not hesitate to push her voice to the emotional edge to project the intensity of the action.

In the 1970s Stratas sharply curtailed her appearances and became more and more selective about what and when she would sing. She did allow herself one of her greatest triumphs in the title role in the full three-act premiere of Berg's *Lulu* at Paris in 1979, and later that same year she appeared at the Metropolitan as Jenny in Weill's *Aufstieg und Fall der Stadt Mahagonny.* Through the latter work she came to know Weill's music and when, in the 1980s she had virtually stopped singing in public, she devoted herself to the recording of his songs. She did appear in Zeferelli's 1983 film of *La traviata* where the exaggerated production could not diminish the riveting tension, the vulnerability and desperation that she brought to the role of Violetta.

Her interest in exploring new avenues brought her to the Broadway show *Rags,* which had a disastrously short run but which brought Stratas a Tony Award for the best actress in a musical, and to the recording of Julie in Jerome Kern's *Showboat.* Stratas was always unpredictable and with the passing of time she had more and more the need to live her own life privately. The self-evaluation and the exhaustive scrutiny with which she considered any role have had the result of fewer Stratas performances, but she has maintained the finesse, the shading, and the conviction of her performances.—CARL MOREY

Strauss, Richard

Composer. Born 11 June 1864, in Munich. Died 8 September 1949, in Garmisch-Partenkirchen. Married: the singer Pauline de Ahna, 10 September 1894. Studied piano with A. Tombo, harpist of the court orchestra, 1868; studied the violin with Benno Walter, concertmaster of the court orchestra, 1872; studied music theory and instrumentation with F.W. Meyer, court conductor, 1875-1880; graduated from the Gymnasium, 1882; went to lectures on philosophy at the University of Munich, 1882-83; Symphony in D minor performed in Munich, conducted by Hermann Levi, 30 March 1881; violin concerto performed in Munich by Benno Walter, 5 December 1882; American premiere, Symphony in F minor, conducted by Theodore Thomas and performed by the New York Philharmonic, 13 December 1884; in Berlin, 1883-84; assistant conductor to Bülow's orchestra in Meiningen, then principal conductor, 1885; in Italy, spring 1886; a conductor of the court opera in Munich, 1886-89; conductor of the Weimar court orchestra, 1889-94; tone-poem Don Juan *premiered 11 November 1889; in Greece, Egypt, and Sicily, 1892-93; conductor of the Berlin Philharmonic, 1894-95; conducted his own works in Brussels, Liège, various German cities, and Moscow, 1896; visited Amsterdam, Paris, London, and Barcelona, 1897; worked for the Berlin Opera, 1898-1918; honorary Ph.D., University of Heidelberg, 1903; premiere of* Symphonia domestica *in the United States, 1904; co-director (with Franz Schalk) of the Vienna State Opera, 1919-24; concert tour in America, 1921; V.P.O. concert tour of South America, 1923; president of the Reichsmusikkammer under the Nazi regime, 15 November 1933 (resigned 1935); concert tour in London, 1936; Gold Medal of the London Philharmonic Society; English concert tour, 1947; faced the post-war court in Munich for collaborating with the Nazis, but was not found guilty.*

Operas *Guntram,* Strauss, 1892-93, Weimar, Court Theater, 10 May 1894; revised, Weimar, Deutsches Nationaltheater, 29 October 1940; *Feuersnot,* E. von Wolzogen, 1900-01, Dresden, Court Opera, 21 November 1901; *Salome,* O. Wilde (translated H. Lachmann), 1904-05, Dresden Court Opera, 9 December 1905; *Elektra,* H. von Hofmannsthal, 1906-08, Dresden, Court Opera, 25 January 1909; *Der Rosenkavalier,* H. von Hofmannsthal, 1909-10, Dresden, Court Opera, 26 January 1911; *Ariadne auf Naxos,* H. von Hofmannsthal, 1911-12, Stuttgart, Court Theater, 25 October 1912; revised, 1916, Vienna, Court Opera, 4 October 1916; *Die Frau ohne Schatten,* H. von Hofmannsthal, 1914-18,

Vienna, Staatsoper, 10 October 1919; *Intermezzo*, Strauss, 1918-23, Dresden, Staatsoper, 4 November 1924; *Die ägyptische Helena*, H. von Hofmannsthal, 1923-27, Dresden, Staatsoper, 6 June 1928; revised (act II), L. Wallerstein, 1932-33, Salzburg, Festspielhaus, 14 August 1933; *Arabella*, H. von Hofmannsthal, 1929-32, Dresden, Staatsoper, 1 July 1933; *Die schweigsame Frau*, S. Zweig (after Jonson), 1933-34, Dresden, Staatsoper, 24 June 1935; *Friedenstag*, J. Gregor, 1935-36, Munich, Staatsoper, 24 July 1938; *Daphne*, J. Gregor, 1936-37; Dresden, Staatsoper, 15 October 1938; *Die Liebe der Danaë*, J. Gregor (after H. Hofmannsthal), 1938-40, Salzburg, Festspielhaus, dress rehearsal for canceled premiere, 16 August 1944; first performance, Salzburg, Festspielhaus, 14 August 1952 [posthumous]; *Capriccio*, Krauss and Strauss, 1940-41, Munich, Staatsoper, 28 October 1942.

In terms of continuity and output, Richard Strauss, whose work dominates the first four decades of this century, must be considered one of the most successful—and by implication one of the most important—of twentieth-century opera composers. His first music drama, *Guntram,* was completed in 1893, his last opera, *Capriccio,* in 1941, while *Die Liebe der Danaë* (1940) despite the Salzburg General probe of 1944, was not officially premiered until 1952, four years after his death. Strauss came to opera relatively late (he was 29 when he wrote *Guntram*), but the Munich environment, the growing influence upon him of Wagner's music and the spirit of times heady with post *Tristan*-esque romanticism and Nietzschean polemic inevitably drew him to opera.

The goal of opera was approached by Strauss, perhaps subconsciously, through the medium of the tone poem where, continuing the Berlioz/Liszt tradition, he demonstrated a mastery of large-scale formal procedures and orchestration as well as, prophetically enough, an astounding dramatic flair. The overcomplexity of which he was accused was a symptom of an exuberance which swept him into a position, alongside Gustav Mahler, as one of Europe's most avant-garde composers. His palette of unconventional sounds, together with the opulent forces involved in works such as *Also Sprach Zarathustra* (1896) and *Ein Heldenleben* (1898), raised establishment eyebrows and stamped him as something of an *enfant terrible* in late nineteenth century music.

Encouraged by his mentor, the Wagnerian Alexander Ritter, and having conducted *Tristan* for the first time (Weimar, 1892), he was, when he set out upon *Guntram* in 1892, both orchestrally and formally "armed at all points," even, in true Wagnerian tradition, writing his own text for the work. In itself *Guntram* is, perhaps, relatively unimportant. It does, however, identify Strauss's Wagnerian starting point and (despite miscalculations from which he was quick to learn), together with *Feuersnot* (1901), acts as a palpable link with a tradition upon which he was to build and to which in the fullness of time he was to return.

The climax of the first phase of Strauss's operatic career arrived with *Salome* and *Elektra* (1905 and 1908 respectively), single act works which, eclectic in nature, project the salient features of the symphonic tone poem into the field of music drama. Strauss's absolute confidence and consequent success in this one-act format stems from a clear-headed objectivity which subsequently never left him: an ability to learn from past errors, and to exploit—in this case by transference of technique from one medium to another—universally acknowledged strengths. *Salome,* highly illustrative in musical effect, employs an orchestrally motivated symphonic design as well as firmly establishing what was to become an almost legendary predilection for the soprano voice.

Strauss saw *Elektra,* his first collaboration with Hugo von Hofmannsthal, as a logical extension of the *Salome* line. The notorious success of *Salome,* which utilized flagrantly expressionist devices to interpret the psychological conflict of the drama, confirmed his avantgarde position in the eyes of his contemporaries. Once committed to Hofmannsthal, however, Strauss's horizons manifestly broadened as the poet, assuming the role of "cultural arbiter," guided him in an up to then unforeseen direction. He encouraged Strauss to adopt his own, admittedly somewhat rarified, aestheticism and to renounce a Wagnerian heritage which was, nonetheless, to retain a powerful hold upon the composer's imagination.

The path, from *Elektra* to *Arabella* (the last Hofmannsthal/Strauss collaboration), was unpredictable to Strauss's peers. The perceived stylistic U-turn which fueled the romantic "classicism" of *Rosenkavalier*

Richard Strauss, 1933

(1910) was labeled retrogressive, by implication an opting out, a symptom of artistic complacency. Nevertheless, posterity has uniquely benefited from the Strauss/Hofmannsthal theatrical experiments of the 1920s and 30s which in the search for a new rationality of form, means, and expression attempted to establish a working balance between the musical, literary, visual and psychological elements of the drama. The ultimate achievement, which transcended Hofmannsthal's tragic death in 1929, was substantial.

Hofmannsthal's first "purpose built" Strauss libretto, *Der Rosenkavalier* (*Elektra* was adapted from the already existing stage play), deliberately sought to win the composer away from the "through-composed" Wagnerian style to a more "classical" format which would provide for set pieces in the traditional manner. The lyrical moments of the score emerge naturally from a recitative-like, conversational medium, a technique enabled by the rhythmic fluidity of Hofmannsthal's text. It was this flexibility, centered as it was upon a conceptual equality of "word" and "music" that was new. From it developed the parlando manner whose pace and expressivity contributed greatly to *Rosenkavalier's* success and which was to be further refined in *Ariadne* (1912), *Intermezzo* (1923) and *Arabella* (1932).

It was the *direction* in which Hofmannsthal pointed Strauss that had such important implications. *Ariadne*—written for Max Reinhardt—looked forward, in its later "prologue" version, towards the developed "conversational" style of *Intermezzo* (for which, once again, Strauss provided his own text). The pace and modernity of this work, with its cinematographically inspired scenic "takes," is remarkable. Even Hofmannsthal, who deplored its bourgeois domesticity, recognized that it took the "new style" of *Rosenkavalier* and the *Ariadne* Vorspiel one step further. Their last opera, *Arabella,* sought to reconcile the parlando "extreme" of *Intermezzo* with the more popular lyricism of *Rosenkavalier.* Here, the marriage, on equal terms, of text and music operates with even greater flexibility than heretofore. Its "fined-down" romanticism, orchestral restraint, lyrical charm, and artistry create a stylistic synthesis that is the ultimate achievement of the collaboration, establishing a new genre of music theater—the "conversation" opera.

It is surely here, in the obsession with "conversation opera" that Strauss's longterm significance lies. That is not, however, to discount works of a more eclectic nature such as *Salome, Elektra* or *Die Frau ohne Schatten;* they also played an important part in the development of his *oeuvre*. Masterpieces in their own right, they bear out, viewed in context, Strauss's own admission that the specific nature and form of each work is dictated by the resolution of technical problems propounded by text, ethos, environment and musical-theatrical resource. Bound together by a common cultural ideal and heritage, Strauss and Hofmannsthal realized a unique (great poet/great composer) collaboration. Working out of a clearly defined tradition, the starting point for *Rosenkavalier* was Mozart's *Marriage of Figaro*. *Ariadne* (based on Molière's *Le bourgeois gentilhomme*) has pronounced neo-classical overtones derived from Baroque opera, while *Die Frau ohne Schatten* (1918), links the world of Wagner to that of *The Magic Flute*. It is, perhaps, significant that *Die ägyptische Helena* (1927), which has no obvious antecedents, has proved—despite its music and craftsmanship—their least successful work.

Hofmannsthal's death was a bitter blow to Strauss. A new unexpectedly fortuitous liaison with the gifted Austro/Jewish writer Stefan Zweig seemed to hold out new collaborative hopes, but these were soon dashed by the political turmoil of the 1930s. The fruit of this brief but happy partnership, Strauss's only truly Italian-inspired opera, *Die schweigsame Frau* (1934) (based on Ben Jonson's play *The Silent Woman*) was banned in Germany on anti-semitic grounds after only four performances. Condemned to self-exile but still anxious to serve, Zweig provided a successor, his friend Joseph Gregor, who texted three operas for Strauss, the first of which was the Zweig-inspired *Friedenstag* (closely modeled on Beethoven's *Fidelio*). Here, the woman, Maria, is the catalyst; as a "peace" advocate she transcends religious enmity and engineers universal reconciliation. *Friedenstag* (1936) was, for the reclusive Strauss of the late 1930s, a rare "political" document—a plea, albeit fruitless, for peace and brotherhood at a crucial time in European history.

Of the two remaining Gregor works, *Daphne* (1937) is a psychological version of the Greek myth worked on post-Nietszchean lines, and *Die Liebe der Danaë,* (1940) another mythological subject, summarizes the cultural influences which had guided the composer throughout his life. Deeply read, historically aware and culturally literate, Strauss retreated into his shell in these late years, disassociating himself from the insanity of the contemporary world. His works of the period demonstrate a reassessment of longheld cultural beliefs, a reaffirmation of aesthetic values, and an attempt to renew his identification with, and to salvage something from, a tradition which he saw endangered in the bigoted, war-torn world of the 1940s. It was upon this tradition, he believed, that the future depended. Evidence suggests that he regarded *Die Liebe der Danaë,* which in its final act integrates Classical (Mozartian) and Romantic (Wagnerian) impulses, as something of an artistic testament, while *Capriccio* occupies itself exclusively with the central problem of his career, that of the relationship between words and music. As a philosophical treatise upon relativity in theater-related arts, *Capriccio,* designated by its authors Strauss and Clemens Krauss as a "Konversationsstück" (conversation piece), confirms, reinforces and justifies the stylistic thrust discernible from *Rosenkavalier* onwards.

It is all too easy to theorize about Strauss's operas. His work is, indeed, characterized by superb craftsmanship and by a consummate and practical instinct for theater. His level of musical intelligence is phenomenal—every effect is calculated and where effect failed, he was himself the first to recognize the fact. In his treatment of the soprano voice, he reaches his greatest inspirational heights. His range of operatic heroines from Salome to Madelaine still challenge, and are as roles still coveted by, the greatest singing artists of today. New productions of his operas are significant and prestigious events calling for the most advanced production techniques and demanding the ultimate in vocal and instrumental virtuosity. He ranks high among musical lyricists and it is, indeed, melody that dominates the last period works (which include his final incomplete "school" opera *Des Esels Schatten*). Strauss's own hope that he might merit "an honourable place at the end of the rainbow" of tradition has been amply realized—from a total of fifteen operas at least ten are regularly performed while seven (a conservative estimate), undisputed mainstays of the repertoire, are universally regarded as classics of the genre.—KENNETH BIRKIN

Stravinsky, Igor

Composer. Born 18 June 1882, in Oranienbaum, near St Petersburg. Died 6 April 1971, in New York. Married: 1) Catherine Nossenko (died 1939), 24 January 1906 (four children); 2) Vera de Bosset (died 1982), 9 March 1940. Stravinsky's father was Feodor Stravinsky, a famous bass at the Russian Imperial Opera. Studied piano with Alexandra Snetkova and then with Leokadia Kashperova; studied music theory with Akimenko and then Kalafati, 1900-03; studied law at St Petersburg University, 1901; traveled to Germany, 1902; composition of a piano sonata for Nicolai Richter, 1903-04; lessons in orchestration from Rimsky-Korsakov, 1905; commission from the impresario Diaghilev to compose a work for the Ballets Russes, which resulted in The Firebird, *performed in Paris, 25 June 1910; became a resident of Paris, 1911, and composed numerous works for the Ballets Russes, including* Pétrouchka, *1911, and* Le sacre du printemps, *1913; work on* Les noces, *1914-18; piano concerto commissioned by Koussevitzky and performed by Stravinsky, 22 May 1924; commissioned by the Elizabeth Sprague Coolidge foundation, which resulted in* Apollon Musagète, *performed at the Library of Congress, 27 April 1928;* Symphony of Psalms *composed for the fiftieth anniversary of the Boston Symphony Orchestra, 1930, but premiered in Brussels; the Violin Concerto commissioned by the violinist Samuel Dushkin, 1931; the melodrama* Perséphone *commissioned by the ballerina Ida Rubenstein; became a French citizen, 1934;* Dumbarton Oaks *concerto commissioned by Mr. and Mrs. Robert Woods Bliss, 1938; Charles Eliot Norton lecturer at Harvard University, 1939-40; became an American citizen, 1945; composed* Circus Polka *on a commission from Ringling Brothers; worked with George Balanchine, who choreographed a number of his ballets; the choral work* Canticum Sacrum *his first attempt at serial composition for the theater; visited Russia, 1962, where some of his works were finally accepted.*

Operas   *Le rossignol* [*Solovey*], Stravinsky and S. Mitusov (after Anderson), 1908-09, 1913-14, Paris, Opéra, 26 May 1914; *Mavra*, B. Kochno (after Pushkin, *The little house in Kolomna*, 1921-22), Paris, Opéra, 3 June 1922; *Oedipus Rex* (opera-oratorio), J. Cocteau (translated into Latin by J. Danielou), 1927, concert performance, Paris, Sarah Bernhardt, 30 May 1927; staged performance, Vienna, 23 February 1928; revised 1948; *The Rake's Progress*, W.H. Auden and C. Kallman (after Hogarth's series of engravings), 1947-51, Venice, La Fenice, 11 September 1951.

Stravinsky's life-work falls, both stylistically and historically, into three periods: Russian, neoclassical and serial. His four operas belong to the first two periods, *Le rossignol* and *Mavra* being Russian works, *Oedipus Rex* and *The Rake's Progress* neoclassical. He did not write a serial opera, being primarily concerned in the later stage of his life with religious choral music and the style and structure appropriate for that. But it is through the theater (using the term in its widest sense) that Stravinsky has most profoundly affected the twentieth century. He belonged to the theater by birth, by tradition, and by inclination. Never was there a composer less willing to repeat himself, and each of his eighteen major theater works represents a different solution to a different problem. With each, he altered the face of his music.

Stravinsky disliked many aspects of opera. He was disenchanted with the aesthetic basis on which, since Wagner, it rested. "Music-drama" was an idea to which he was antipathetic, while the conception of "endless melody" was for him a contradiction in terms. The composition of opera, therefore, presented aesthetic problems to him which did not exist in the case of ballet. The path to the discovery of a new classicism appropriate to ballet was unimpeded, but classicism in opera had been practically obliterated by the "inflated arrogance" of the Wagnerian conception of "music-drama," which represented no tradition and fulfilled no musical necessity. The operas of Stravinsky's maturity, particularly *Mavra* and *The Rake's Progress,* may be seen as his solutions to this problem.

His first opera, *Le rossignol,* which he calls "a lyric tale," stands midway between opera and ballet, with a marked leaning to the latter. It seeks a solution to the opera problem along Debussy's path of lyric drama; it is the only one of his operas capable of being adapted into a symphonic poem for concert use with a minimum of alteration. It was concerned not with action or character but with a story, and a disembodied, tongue-in-cheek fairy story at that. It was also a spectacle, sumptuous and impressive, the last to be staged by Diaghilev before Europe was plunged, two months later, into war.

The opera is short (only forty-five minutes), and the story, which hardly qualifies as a plot, concerns the miraculous power of the Nightingale's song, which in the end restores the dying Emperor to health and vigor. The chief moment of this stage spectacle is the Emperor of China's march, which so affected the designer Alexandre Benois that for the first time in his life he felt genuinely moved by one of his own creations. Stravinsky had the model before him of the coronation scene in Musorgsky's *Boris Godunov*; as for the love of things oriental, this was something that was equally strongly felt in Paris and St Petersburg at this time.

Mavra is more of an opera than *Le rossignol,* and has clean, formal divisions into solos, duets, and ensembles. It is in one act, lasting less than thirty minutes, and marks the end of Stravinsky's Russian period. It is an *opera buffa,* a charming take-off of the *romances sentimentales* of nineteenth century Russian composers, built around a Russo-Italian melodic line. The music stays within the hundred-years-old tradition of Glinka and Dargomizhsky, not in an attempt to reestablish that tradition, but to realize the form of *opera buffa,* which was so well suited to the subject. The plot tells of a hussar who dresses up as a cook (Mavra) to obtain admission into the household of his betrothed (Parasha), only to be discovered shaving by Parasha's mother and a neighbor. The joke contained in Kochno's libretto, based on the Pushkin story *The little house in Kolomna,* is well matched by the wit contained in Stravinsky's music: on to the long melodic lines of bel canto with frequent repetition of words and phrases, the composer has grafted his recently minted metrical discoveries. The score thus has a freshness, a subtlety, which the nineteenth century period and the Italian influence cannot conceal, only offset. In this respect, although the joke fell distinctly flat at the first performance, the opera marks a turning point in Stravinsky's creative thought. Its stylistic successor, though not for thirty years, was *The Rake's Progress*.

Although *Oedipus Rex* was completed in 1927, only some five years after the completion of *Mavra,* the contrast between these two operas could hardly be greater. Stravinsky had felt the desire to write a large-scale dramatic work for some time; one might almost speculate that this desire was itself a reaction to the smallness of *Mavra*. The story of *Oedipus Rex* is the universal, timeless Greek myth of Oedipus. The composer's choice of the Latin language and his use of the oratorio procedure whereby the characters address not each other but the audience combine to give the work its uniqueness. The events themselves are concentrated in the music, and the only stage movements are entrances and exits; moreover the moving characters (Speaker, Tiresias, Messenger, Shepherd) are secondary figures: the agents of Destiny, not its victims. Nothing could afford a greater contrast to the lightweight, charming, satirical *Mavra*.

Oedipus Rex is static, monumental, archetypal drama. Just as Greek tragedy was itself a compound of drama, history and myth, with the action taking place off-stage, so Stravinsky's work is part profane (opera), part sacred (oratorio). With the chorus stretched across the stage, the singers appear like statues, at different heights, in masks which restrict their movements. With the use of stage lighting, they can be made to appear disembodied; *Oedipus Rex* invites multi-media production. Conceptions such as these, combined with the narrator in contemporary dress and the use of a dead language combine to hold the audience at a distance, and to portray nervous energy and mystery; indeed the themes of detachment and alienation are Brechtian concepts.

The music too has a monumental quality, and is tonally and harmonically simple. The rhythms are four-square, unlike earlier works, and are more static and regular as they follow the rhythms of Sophocles's choruses (an idea which Stravinsky was to pursue further in his next stage work, *Apollo*). Moreover, unlike Stravinsky's earlier vocal style, accentuation is decided by musical, not linguistic, considerations. The second syllable of "Oedipus" is a case in point. The word "oracula" also gives rise to an insistent rhythmic pattern. As for the *melos,* a minor tonality predominates, gradually dropping, but is offset by the occasional section in the major, such as the music for Creon's first appearance, and the sudden outburst of C major on the word "gloria" at the end of the first act. The harmony and the orchestral sonority are built up from the bass line, as Handel would have done. For this reason, the texture has a firmness and a classical solidity. There is also a strong Verdi influence, particularly in the use of the chorus.

Twenty years after *Oedipus Rex, The Rake's Progress* (1947-51) marks the end of Stravinsky's neoclassical period. Not only is it the longest and most substantial of the four operas, lasting 150 minutes, it also uses a libretto which is a work of art in its own right (by a leading poet, W.H. Auden). Its first production in Venice was a spectacular success; its subsequent popularity has been unbroken. With this opera, Stravinsky resumed consideration of the operatic problem where he had left it with *Mavra*. In the meantime, Berg's *Wozzeck,* whose premiere took place in December 1925, had moved twentieth century European opera even further away from pre-Wagnerian clichés. Stravinsky did not set out to outflank Berg as a "reformer"; instead he returned to the very clichés of the Italian-Mozartian Classical style that the contemporary German composers had sought to supersede.

Stravinsky maintained a lifelong acquaintance with opera; such works as *Un ballo in maschera* and *Rigoletto* were familiar to him beyond the point where criticism of their obvious absurdities made any difference. While he was working on *The Rake's Progress,* Mozart's *Così fan tutte* was his musical diet. He deliberately sought to revitalize the conventions of a period that many might have imagined were long since dead. The structure is built round arias, recitatives, choruses, and ensembles, with a definite scheme of tonality. Generally speaking, prose is used for the recitatives, while the arias and ensembles are in verse. The orchestra is correspondingly small. As so often before, Stravinsky strove for a period piece; in this case the conventions of ostinato accompaniment were more appropriate for the eighteenth century than polyphony, whose effect could be timeless or hieratic, as in *The Symphony of Psalms.*

The presence of Mozart is pervasive throughout *The Rake's Progress.* Not only is the orchestra one of classical proportions, including a harpsichord for the recitatives, but the demonic atmosphere of the churchyard scene, as Rakewell and Shadow play cards, and the moralizing epilogue with which the opera ends, all point unmistakably to one model—*Don Giovanni.*

The Rake's Progress marked both the end and the culmination of that "incubation" period of Stravinsky's work known as neoclassicism. This was a universal musical phenomenon, to which diverse composers subscribed, particularly (but not exclusively) those of the Franco-Russian tradition. In the case of this opera, the origins both of the score and the libretto are well documented in primary sources, chiefly the correspondence between Auden and Stravinsky. Comparing it with the earlier operas, the composer said: "*The Nightingale* seems more remote to me now than the English operas of three centuries ago, or than the Italian-Mozartian opera which has been so neglected and misunderstood by the world of the musical dramatists. In so far as *Mavra* suggests any comparison to my present work, it is in my conception of opera. I believe 'music drama' and 'opera' to be two very, very different things. My life work is a devotion to the latter."—FRANCIS ROUTH

Susannah

Composer: *Carlisle Floyd.*

Librettist: *Carlisle Floyd.*

First Performance: *Florida State University, Tallahassee, 24 February 1955.*

Roles: *Susannah Polk (soprano); Sam (tenor); Olin Blitch (bass-baritone); Lil Bat McLean (tenor or speaking); Elder McLean (bass); Elder Gleaton (tenor); Elder Hayes (tenor); Elder Ott (bass); Mrs. McLean (mezzo-soprano); Mrs. Gleaton (soprano); Mrs. Hayes (soprano); Mrs. Ott (contralto); chorus.*

When Carlisle Floyd's *Susannah* premiered, the critical reaction was overwhelmingly favorable. Here is an opera in which the subject matter is thoroughly American in flavor although the story is based on the Biblical tale of "Susannah and the Elders" from the *Apocrypha*. Stories of Bible Belt preachers and their shenanigans have precedence in Mark Twain, Sinclair Lewis, and more recently television evangelism. Even though it is an old subject, the treatment in this case—operatic, or as "musical theater" as Floyd prefers to name it—is fresh and vital mainly because the story yields two flesh and blood characters in Susannah, a vivacious, pretty girl, and Olin Blitch, a traveling preacher. Using hymn tunes, modality, and folk song sources, the musical structure is straightforward. With non-polyphonic textures, it communicates easily and is not difficult to execute.

Susannah gains the attention of Rev. Olin Blitch, who is to preach at the local church. When she returns home, she sings "Ain't it a Pretty Night" and is answered by her brother, Sam, who lives with her. Later he sings "Jaybird sittin' on a hick'ry limb." The next day the four elders discover Susannah bathing nude in the creek where they propose to hold a baptism. Scandalized, they vow punishment of Susannah. Li'l Bat, a feeble minded friend, tells Susannah of the elders' plan. However, she attends the revival service where Blitch preaches a hell-fire sermon, a musically powerful scene, which moves from spoken dialogue to singing. Susannah refuses to be "saved," and Blitch comes to her house later. He tells her of his loneliness and succeeds in seducing her. The next day as the baptism proceeds, Sam returns to hear the whole story from Susannah. Infuriated and somewhat drunk, he takes a gun and goes to the baptism. Susannah hears shots; Blitch is killed. The townspeople want to hang Sam and run Susannah out of the Valley. She stands them off with a gun, laughing defiantly, as the curtain falls.

Floyd has fashioned a piece that is dramatically and musically viable. The libretto is a mixture of words spoken, spoken on pitch and in rhythm, and full singing voice—all of this with a fluidity that respects natural speech rhythms and dramatic intensity. Floyd is striving to create a more viable musical theater, and in some respects he has. *Susannah* moves with a logical development and feeling for the situation of the characters, who are allowed space in which to move emotionally as they build the story. However, Floyd, a Methodist minister's son with a background of church music, employs orchestration and musical development that is thin and lacking in resourcefulness. But this opera is good theater and connects with the audience, an ideal Floyd respects. It has been produced repeatedly at the New York City Opera as well as in many professional and university opera companies.—ANDREW H. DRUMMOND

Sutherland, Joan

Soprano. Born 7 November 1926, in Sydney. Married: pianist/conductor Richard Bonynge, 1954; one son. Studied piano and voice with her mother; later studied with Joan and Aida Dickens in Sydney and, in London, with Clive Carey at the Royal College of Music and at the Opera School; won first of many singing competitions at age 19; sang first operatic role, Dido in Dido and Aeneas, in concert performance at Lyceum Club in Sydney, 1947; operatic debut at Sydney Conservatorium, in title role of Goosens's Judith, 1951; Covent Garden debut as First Lady in Die Zauberflöte, 1952; while with the company sang Aida (1954), Jennifer in Tippett's The Midsummer Marriage (1955), Gilda in Rigoletto and the title role in Alcina (both 1957); greatest triumph of the period came with Zeffirelli's production of Lucia di Lammermoor (1959); Teatro alla Scala and Metropolitan Opera debuts, both as Lucia, 1961; returned to Australia for 1965-66 season; later made many appearances there while husband was director of Australian Opera in Sydney, 1976-86; farewell appearance at Sydney in Les Huguenots, 1990; made Dame Commander of the Order of the British Empire, 1979.

Joan Sutherland's early career as a member of the company at the Royal Opera House, Covent Garden, during the 1950s is particularly interesting and relevant when one considers her later position as the most celebrated and popular coloratura soprano in the world. She achieved a three-decade-long succession of triumphs with the public, a great deal of it in the face of quite hostile criticism from the music critics of the English-speaking world.

During the decade that led to her most famous performance, her debut in the title role of Donizetti's *Lucia di Lammermoor* on 17 February 1959, she had built up a repertory that included not only roles by Handel, Mozart, Donizetti and Verdi—parts that she continued to sing for the rest of her career—but also Weber, Wagner, Britten, Tippett, Poulenc, Bizet and heavier Verdi roles (such as Amelia in *Ballo in maschera* and Aida). This career as member of a company, something which few of her successors have had the chance to develop to such an extent, laid the foundations for her formidable technique and assurance, which meant that even past the age of sixty she still took on new roles, maintaining to an impressive degree the flexibility and security for which she was most prized. Of her early roles, one which she allegedly disliked was that of Jennifer in the world premiere of Michael Tippett's *The Midsummer Marriage*. In her recording of this work, one can hear that as early as January 1955 all of Sutherland's characteristics were already there: the agility and brilliant attack on staccato notes *in alt,* especially in the passage beginning "Then the congregation of the stars began to dance" and the legato that made the longest arching phrases seem easy. Her English diction was then at its best. The low-lying passages obviously pose a problem, as they were always to do. It is hard to imagine now that there were people who considered that Sutherland should have taken on the heaviest Strauss and Wagner parts; her future obviously lay in the lyric-coloratura range.

Sutherland's career will always be inseparable from that of her husband, Richard Bonynge, who is usually credited with encouraging her to study the early nineteenth-century Italian repertory, especially the operas of Bellini and Donizetti. Once her position as leading soprano of the Covent Garden company had been established, with her singing of Pamina, Desdemona, Gilda and the three soprano roles in *Les Contes d'Hoffmann,* her assumption of Lucia seemed inevitable. Here Sutherland owed a great deal to the example of Callas, approaching the role as one of dark drama instead of the prettiness that sopranos of the previous generation, Pons and Robin among them, had been said to bring to it. The 1959 performances of *Lucia* at Covent Garden, repeated shortly afterwards in Paris, Milan and other Italian cities, and her assumption of the role of Elvira in *I Puritani* at Glyndebourne in 1960 marked the very peak of the early Sutherland style. One hears in it the complete freedom and purity of her voice, unimpaired by the swooping portamenti and the veiled diction that later marred it for so many. This sound differs from that which she developed in the early 1960s, in which in the middle and lower registers her enunciation had a "thick" quality in contrast to the mercurial quality which she always found for the upper registers.

It is idle to speculate where Sutherland's career would have gone without Bonynge. His coaching, their exploration together of the nineteenth-century opera and song repertory and the many recordings that resulted gained for them a huge and loyal following. If critics in the late 60s were inclined to carp, referring to their set-up as "a circus," and to criticize her poor diction, which in fact was no worse than most other coloraturas, they seemed always to ignore the very things which made her performances such a pleasure: the total security, accuracy of pitch, retention of the natural quality of her voice right up to the highest regions, and her always generous stage presence.

If Sutherland's acting never had the spontaneous or psychological insight that, say, Silja or Callas seemed to bring to their roles, she was always engaged in the role, was a commanding figure on stage, and moved with grace and often surprising swiftness. After her success as Norma at the New York Metropolitan Opera in 1970, Sutherland began to move into somewhat heavier, more dramatic-soprano roles. Donizetti's Maria Stuarda, Lucrezia Borgia and eventually Anna Bolena, Massenet's Esclarmonde and Leonora in *Il trovatore*, all challenged her voice. Of these parts the Lucrezia seemed to suit her the best, although her Maria Stuarda had some impressive moments dramatically, her vehement "Vil bastarda!" quite the equal of Gencer, Caballé or Sills, all of whom were performing the role at the same time.

Always noticeable, even as late as her 1988 Anna Bolena at Covent Garden, was the rhythmic pulse and energy that she could put into ensemble passages. However, she never achieved to the same degree as her contemporaries Caballé and Leontyne Price the melting smoothness when holding on to the long, sad lines of a Verdi aria such as "Tacea la notte."

Sutherland was an accomplished comedienne, and in Donizetti's *La fille du Régiment*, Strauss's *Fledermaus* and Lehàr's *Merry Widow*, she demonstrated her good-natured personality (as she did in the television series "Who's Afraid of Opera?," in which she added the roles of Rosina in *Il barbiere di Siviglia* and Offenbach's *La Périchole*, neither of which she sang on the stage).

If one wished to analyze Sutherland's particular greatness, the best role to examine is not Lucia, the most famous, but her own favourite, that of Violetta in *La traviata*. Her last London performances of this, in 1975, found her in the best possible voice, her diction better than ever, and her ability to bring off the staccato high Cs in the Tetrazzini variations which she interpolated into the second verse of "Sempre libera," a pulse-racing crescendo on the final E flat, all superb. If the drooping, mooning quality was still there in the second-act duet with Germont père, her total commitment to the death scene, in which she seemed to have found a perspective on the slowness of the dying woman's movements, as well as a stream of solid, golden tone that had not only pathos but variation in color within individual notes, made even her harshest critics sit up in surprise.

Sutherland has left a formidable recorded legacy. All her records made up to and including *Lucrezia Borgia,* issued in 1980, have fascination and provide great pleasure; the later ones are inclined to accentuate the greater beat in the voice, the absence of the remembered radiance in her tone, and a sameness of characterization. This did not seem so apparent when one heard her in the opera house. Of those roles she sang only for the gramophone, supreme is the title-role in *Turandot,* conducted by Mehta, and a very enjoyable Adina in *L'elisir d'amore.*—PATRICK O'CONNOR

Svanholm, Set

Tenor. Born 2 September 1904, in Västerås, Sweden. Died 4 October 1964, in Saltsjö-Duvnäs, near Stockholm. Studied as baritone with John Forsell at the Opera School of the Stockholm Conservatory; debut, as baritone, as Silvio in I Pagliacci, *Stockholm, 1930; tenor debut as Radames, Stockholm, 1936; appeared at the Salzburg Festival and the Vienna State Opera, 1938, the Berlin State Opera, Teatro alla Scala, 1941-42, and Bayreuth Festival, 1942; appeared as Tristan in Rio de Janeiro, 1946, and as Lohengrin in San Francisco, 1946; Metropolitan Opera debut as Siegfried, 1946; remained on roster of the Metropolitan until 1956; also sang at Covent Garden, 1948-56; director of the Royal Theater in Stockholm, 1956-63.*

Like a number of distinguished dramatic tenors before him—Jean De Reszke, Giovanni Zenatello, Lauritz Melchior, Eric Schmedes, and Renato Zanelli among them—Set Svanholm came to opera as a baritone. Having studied with the eminent Swedish baritone John Forsell at the Stockholm Conservatory (Björling was a fellow Forsell pupil), he made his debut in 1930 at the Royal Opera of Stockholm in the same role in which Melchior had made his—Sylvio in *I Pagliacci*. Six years later he successfully re-emerged a tenor, singing Radames in a well-received *Aïda*. He remained a principal at the Royal Opera until 1956, and by the late 1930s had already assumed a busy schedule of guest appearances that would continue throughout his career. He was offered a Metropolitan Opera contract as early as 1940, but the volatile political climate of the times prevented him from accepting it. He remained in Europe during the war, and appeared with some success at the Teatro alla Scala and Bayreuth. The post-war restoration of the Wagnerian repertory finally brought him to Britain and the United States. His Metropolitan Opera debut on 15 November 1946 received impressive if not spectacular notices, but he came eventually to sing seventeen roles there in 105 performances between 1946 and 1956, the majority of them Wagnerian. In similar roles, he was also a regular guest at Covent Garden between 1948 and 1956, and finished his career as an innovative director of the Royal Opera of Stockholm, with a strong commitment to a wide and varied repertory.

Svanholm was appreciated most for his energy, his youthful appearance, and his good looks. Clearly, the physical illusion he created was far more considerable than any lasting vocal or dramatic impression he may have made. Ernest Newman for example, was genuinely taken with his young Siegfried, which "really looked and behaved like the young boy Wagner had in mind," but had misgivings about his Tristan, one of the singer's most important and popular roles, which Newman dismissed as "musical but unpoetical."

Svanholm's musicianship was reputed to be as impeccable as his faithfulness to the composer's written intentions, but his singing seems always to have lacked the drama and individuality of those heldentenors to whom he was hastily proclaimed a natural successor, notably Melchior. His reviews, like his performances, were remarkably consistent throughout his career, both cast from a palette of few colors, which says something about his limitations and his inability to transcend them. Olin Downes' account of Svanholm's 1946 Met debut, which noted that he was obviously "a sound musician who sings his part accurately as written," that he was "youthful in action as well as in song," and that dramatically, "his conception was fully rounded and always significant" was, in retrospect, a virtual prototype for the majority of reviews that would follow.

Svanholm was a diligent craftsman, always intelligent and determined even at his least inspired. His voice was outstanding for its vitality and for a clean, open tone uncommon to even the best singers normally associated with his repertory, but in the more intimate resources of warmth, vibrance and sweetness, it was somehow deficient. His repertory, developed prior to his post-war triumphs, was large and international in scope, and included many of the heaviest Italian and French dramatic roles along with a complement of German specialties—Florestan (*Fidelio*), Herod (*Salome*), Eisenstein (*Die Fledermaus*), and Aegisth (*Elektra*). But it was as a Wagnerian that he is best remembered. Given such a diverse repertory, he suffered remarkably few setbacks, Lohengrin being perhaps the most perplexing.

His most successful roles, Siegfried, Siegmund, Tristan, Florestan, and Aegisth, certainly stand alongside the better post-war intrepretations, as he does generally among the better post-war interpretors, and these have all survived in extensive recorded segments and even complete performances, some of them commercial studio recordings, others live broadcasts taken off the air. His celebrated partnership with Kirsten Flagstad was as persistent in the studio as it was on the stage, and is exceedingly well documented. It is most unfortunate that no recordings of him as a baritone seem to have been made: considering that his timbre lacked virtually any trace of latent baritone weight and resonance, it would be especially interesting to compare the before with the after. That he had the physical resources to meet the demands of such taxing heldentenor roles is unquestionable, and this is borne out not only by the length of his career, but by the fact that his voice underwent little significant change between 1946 and the assumption of his administrative duties in Stockholm a decade later. The same youthful but manly sound, albeit a bit dryer, is as evident in his last studio recordings of the late 1950s as it is in his earliest ones for Victor just after the war.—WILLIAM SHAMAN

Szymanowski, Karol

Composer. Born 6 October 1882, in Timoshovka, Ukraine. Died 28 March 1937, in Lausanne. Studied with Gustav Neuhaus in Elizavetgrad; studied with Noskowski in Warsaw, 1901; in Berlin composing symphonic music, 1906-08; returned to Warsaw, where his first symphony was performed, 26 March 1909; second symphony completed 1911; in Vienna, 1912-14; in Timoshovka, 1914-17, where he composed his third symphony; performed his violin works with the violinist Paul Kochanski in Moscow and St Petersburg; in Elizavetgrad, 1917-19; settled in Warsaw, 1920; visited Paris, London, and New York, 1921; director of the Warsaw Conservatory, 1927-29; rector of the Warsaw Conservatory, 1930-32.

Operas *Lottery for a husband [Loteria na mezów]* (operetta), J. Krewiński-Haszyński, 1908-1909; *Hagith,* after F. Dörmann, 1912-13, Warsaw, 13 May 1922; *Król Roger,* Szymanowski and J. Iwaszkiewicz, 1918-24, Warsaw, 19 June 1926.

Apart from childhood pieces—*Roland, Złocisty szczyt* ("The Golden Summit"—which have been lost without trace, Szymanowski's first stage work was the operetta *Loteria na mežów* ("Lottery for a husband"), composed to a libretto by Juliusz Krewiński-Haszyński in 1908-09, shortly after the composer's student days in Warsaw. Undoubtedly his least happy artistic venture ("I decided to finish it with clenched teeth"), the work remains unpublished and unperformed.

Szymanowski's first major opera, the one-act *Hagith,* was composed to a German libretto by Felix Dörmann (Polish translation by Stanisaw Baracz) in 1912-13. Based on oriental legends of King David as well as on the bible, its central theme is the demand for the sacrifice of Hagith's young body to restore youth and strength to the old king. Her refusal to make the sacrifice (because of her love for the young prince) results in Hagith being stoned to death. The libretto was modeled on Hofmannsthal and the music—by the composer's own admission—on the Strauss of *Salomé* and *Elektra.* "I often fall into the Straussian manner," he conceded in a letter to his friend Stefan Spiess. At times the music veers alarmingly from Straussian frenzy to banal echoes of Puccini, as in the love-duet between Hagith and the young prince. Wagner is also echoed here, and again in Hagith's final love-death. Yet at the dramatic climax of the work—the final duet between Hagith and the Old King—there is music of genuine power, already foreshadowing the world of *Król Roger* (King Roger).

Hagith was followed by a year of extensive travel (including Sicily and North Africa) in the course of which Szymanowski steeped himself fully in the worlds of classical and oriental mythology, as well as in the history and culture of the Arab lands. On his return to Poland in 1915, he found himself as a composer, achieving (belatedly) full creative maturity and branching out in quite new aesthetic directions, inspired both by his travels and by his extensive reading. His most prolific period followed, coinciding almost exactly with the war years and culminating in his masterpiece *Król Roger,* begun in 1918. In some ways, *Król Roger* may be regarded as an autobiographical statement, exorcising the creative crisis which Szymanowski experienced in 1917, when his private world of composition was brutally shattered by the Russian Revolution, which totally destroyed the Szymanowski estate in the Ukraine.

Already before the completion of *Król Roger* in 1924 Szymanowski's music began to take a new turn, evidenced in the simpler idiom of the ballet-pantomime *Mandragora* (1920) and the folk-influenced ballet *Harnasie* (1923). Apart from some incidental music to Tadeusz Miciński's drama *Kniaź Patiomkin* ("Prince Potemkin") (1925), these were his only other stage works. His later music was broadly nationalist in tone, responding to the new-found political independence of Poland with music much indebted to the folk music of the southern Tatra highlands. In addition to *Harnasie* there is a cycle of mazurkas, the song-cycle *Słopiewnie* ("Word-songs"), a *Stabat Mater* and several extended instrumental compositions.

In later life Szymanowski was dogged by ill health and straitened circumstances. Following an unhappy period as director of the Warsaw Conservatory (1927-29), during which he wrote extensively about music, he was appointed Rector of the State Academy of Music in Warsaw, a post which did even more to fray his nerves. He was dismissed, along with others, in a controversy of monumental proportions in 1932 and spent his remaining years trying to make a living through concert performances. He died of tuberculosis in a Lausanne sanatorium at the age of fifty four.—JIM SAMSON

Tagliavini, Ferruccio

Tenor. Born 14 August 1913, in Barco, Reggio Emilia. Died 28 January 1995. Married: soprano Pia Tassinari (divorced). Studied with Brancucci in Parma and Amadeo Bassi in Florence; debut as Rodolfo in La bohème, *Florence 1938; at Teatro alla Scala, 1942-53; U.S. debut in Chicago, 1946; at Metropolitan Opera, 1947-54 and 1961-62; sang Nemorino in* L'elisir d'amore *during La Scala's 1950 visit to Covent Garden; also appeared in London as Cavaradossi in* Tosca *and Nadir in* Les pêcheurs de perles; *retired from opera in 1965.*

While Italy's reputation as "The Land of Song" is not as indisputable as it once was, we still look to Italy for one type of voice in particular: the tenor. At its best the warmth of the Italian sun pervades its timbre and, when combined with the forward placement and rounded vowel sounds of the language, results in a tonal quality that is unique in its beauty. Ferruccio Tagliavini, whose voice was typical of the genre, achieved glory over a long and brilliant career.

When Tagliavini made his debut, there was no shortage of great Italian tenors: Martinelli was at his zenith; Lauri-Volpi and Pertile had seen their greatest triumphs but were by no means at the end of their careers; Gigli, who had already won every accolade in his outstanding career, would still sing with honor for almost two more decades. To triumph in the face of such formidable competition may have seemed an awesome task, yet Tagliavini achieved the status of his older colleagues.

It was Gigli whom Tagliavini most resembled in quality and weight of voice. Tagliavini began as a lyric tenor; the voice not overly large but well-produced and even throughout its range. Its greatest asset was its sweetness of timbre and a lovely mezza-voce (half-voice) of ravishing quality.

In the early years of his career he wisely did not stray from roles suitable for the light lyric tenor: Rodolfo (*La bohème*), The Duke (*Rigoletto*), Fritz (*L'amico Fritz*), Elvino (*La sonnambula*) and Almaviva (*Il barbiere di Siviglia*). Tagliavini scored over his contemporaries because of an innate sense of style which he brought to his interpretations, at once placing him on a plane above most Italian tenors.

Tagliavini conquered all the important operatic stages of the world, none more so than the Metropolitan Opera, and at a time when several fine tenors such as Jussi Björling, Richard Tucker and Jan Peerce were already firmly established there. Of his debut role, Rodolfo, Virgil Thompson (*New York Herald Tribune*) wrote "Not in a very long time have we heard tenor singing at once so easy and so adequate." Irving Kolodin (*New York Sun*) waxed even more poetic: "(He) was the best the old house has had in a decade at least. A quantity of listeners limited only by the fire laws took Tagliavini to their hearts almost immediately, and he responded by charming their hearts away by the beauty of his voice and the artistry of his singing. The suggestions in his record were supported by the airy brightness of his vocal quality, the style and verve which he used it to make Rodolfo a tangible figure on the stage. Not by any means the largest tenor voice the work has had (even this season) it floats superbly, and reaches the ear with ring and vibrance at all levels of force. As if being an Italian tenor who is also a musician is not enough, Tagliavini added a lively sense of stage action. . . ." His singing elicited similar reactions wherever he appeared.

Fortunately for collectors, Tagliavini recorded extensively, both solo items and several complete recordings. His earliest Cetra recordings from the 1940s are treasures indeed, the voice ravishing in its lyricism, stylish and of beautiful quality. As a general rule, the earliest recordings are the ones to seek out. Of the complete recordings, most have much to commend them; only the very late Supraphon *L'elisir d'amore* is to be avoided: recorded at the very end of his career, the voice is coarse and unattractive. His complete recording of *L'amico Fritz* is particularly worth searching for: for not only was Tagliavini a famous interpreter of Fritz, but the performance is conducted by the composer. It is a document of true historic value and a worthy testimony to a glorious career.—LARRY LUSTIG

Talvela, Martti

Bass. Born 4 February 1935, in Hittola, Finland. Died 22 July 1989, in Juva, Finland. Studied at the Lahti Academy of Music, 1958-60, and then with Carl Martin Oehmann in Stockholm; debut as Sparafucile in Verdi's Rigoletto, *Stockholm, 1961; joined Berlin's Deutsche Opera, 1962; Metropolitan Opera debut as the Grand Inquisitor in* Don Carlos, *1968; sang many Verdi and Wagner roles; artistic director of the Savonlinna Festival, 1972-80.*

Although few artists ever achieve the status of national hero in their homeland, basso Martti Talvela was so venerated in Finland. His untimely death at the age of 53 while dancing at his daughter's wedding was considered a national calamity. Having been the director of the Savonlinna Opera Festival for many years, and after instigating the Finnish National Opera's 1983 triumphant appearance at the Metropolitan Opera House in New York, he had been appointed to lead the National Opera into their newly built home in Helsinki when death intervened.

A former heavyweight boxing champion, he was an immensely imposing man, six feet eight inches tall and weighing almost 300 pounds, and had a large beard. He loved his farm.

He was working as a schoolteacher when his voice developed: he then studied with Carl Martin Ohman in Stockholm. His debut was as Sparafucile in Helsinki, 1960, but he then sang regularly with the Royal Opera in Stockholm. The Berlin Opera called, and so did Bayreuth, where Talvela sang many roles. He also sang at the Salzburg Festival and performed many times at Covent Garden. He came to the Metropolitan Opera in 1968 and immediately became a favorite there. The Teatro alla Scala, Paris, Moscow, Leningrad and further music centers experienced his opera roles and concerts.

Talvela possessed a large, commanding voice. The Finnish opera *The Last Temptations* by Joonas Kokkonen allowed the opportunity for one of Talvela's greatest roles, the itinerant preacher Paavo Ruotsalainen, a Finnish historical figure. Other roles in which he excelled were Hunding, Pimen, the *Don Carlo* Inquisitor, Rocco, Daland, and King Marke. He also widely sang Boris Godunov, King Philipp, Sarastro, and other leading roles, but did not reach the supreme excellence in those that he did in the others. He was also a dedicated concert singer, offering extremely serious programs.

Talvela's many recordings range from Finnish folk songs to the role of Boris Godunov in Musorgsky's original orchestration. He has also recorded Musorgsky's cycle *Songs and Dances of Death* in an orchestration he commissioned from Kalevi Aho, Schubert's *Winterreise,* the Wagner roles, and a Sarastro from Salzburg.—BERT WECHSLER

Tancredi

Composer: *Gioachino Rossini.*

Librettists: *G. Rossi and L. Lechi (after Voltaire).*

First Performance: *Venice, La Fenice, 6 February 1813.*

Roles: *King Argirio (tenor); Orbazzano (bass); Amenaide (soprano); Tancredi (mezzo-soprano); Isaura (mezzo-soprano); Roggiero (tenor); chorus.*

Tancredi was the first opera composed by Rossini for La Fenice, Venice's leading theater. Its success confirmed Rossini's newly-won reputation as one of Italy's leading operatic composers. He was then twenty-one years old.

The action, loosely based on Voltaire's tragedy *Tancrède,* takes place in Syracuse, on Sicily, during the middle ages. After an unsuccessful rebellion against King Argirio, Orbazzano swears allegiance to Argirio; the king, to celebrate their reconciliation, promises his daughter Amenaide to Orbazzano in marriage. But Amenaide loves Tancredi, an exiled hero. Tancredi, returning to Syracuse in secret, presents himself to the audience in a memorable *scena* that anticipates in some respects the appearance of Arsace in act 1 of *Semiramide* (1823). He reveals his identity only to Amenaide, with whom he sings a passionate love duet ("L'aura che intorno spiri"). As Amenaide is led toward the nuptial alter, Orbazzano enters with a love letter by Amenaide and addressed, he believes, to Solamir, ruler of the Saracens who threaten Syracuse; the first act ends with all expressing their astonishment, confusion, anger, and fear.

In the second act Argirio condemns his daughter to death for treason. Even Tancredi believes her to be unfaithful and, in despair, he goes off to court death in battle with the Saracens. The drama comes to a climax in the final scenes, set in a Romantically conceived forest with gullies, caves, and waterfalls (cf. Weber's Wolf Glen). Tancredi leads his troops against the enemy; victorious, he hears from the dying Solamir that Amenaide is innocent. Argirio happily blesses the marriage of Tancredi and Amenaide as the opera ends.

With *Tancredi* Rossini came of age as a composer of *opera seria*. Craftsmanship and inspiration are at a consistently high level throughout. The music breathes freshness and vitality. Tancredi's arrival in act I, with its celebrated caballetta "Di tanti palpiti," has tended to overshadow the opera's many other beauties. Argirio's accompanied recitative "Dall patria ogni nemico" (also in act 1) is full of the excitement of battle. The aria that follows, "Pensa che sei mia figlia," conveys a sense of energy, even violence, with music that is splendidly heroic and dramatic. The king's confusion and indecision, as he condemns his daughter to death in the great recitative and aria (with chorus) "Oh Dio crudel!" (act II) is vividly expressed by rests between syllables and sudden modulations, by coloratura and extremes of vocal range. In the quiet passage at the words "Ma, la figlia," we can feel Argirio's remorse.

No less successful is Amenaide's prison scene, which begins with a long, atmospheric oboe solo over throbbing strings. The beautiful orchestration of Amenaide's aria, with English horn, clarinet and flute, anticipates the wonderful orchestral experiments of Rossini's Neapolitan operas. Rossini's ability to differentiate characters is apparent in the first-act duet for Amenaide and Tancredi. Amenaide's disjunct line reveals her distracted state of mind; Tancredi's smoother line helps Amenaide (and us) believe him when he says confidently "Contra il destin crudele / Trionferà amor" ("Against cruel destiny love will triumph").—JOHN A. RICE

Tannhäuser und der Sängerkrieg auf Wartburg [Tannhäuser and the Song Contest at the Wartburg]

Composer: *Richard Wagner.*

Librettist: *Richard Wagner.*

First Performance: *Dresden, Königliches Hoftheater, 19 October 1845; revised, text alterations with C. Nuitter, Paris, Opéra, 13 March 1861; revised, Munich, Königliches Hof- und Nationaltheater, 5 March 1865; revised, Vienna, Hofoper, 22 November 1875.*

Roles: *Elisabeth (soprano); Venus (soprano or mezzo-soprano); Tannhäuser (tenor); Wolfram von Eschenbach (baritone); Hermann (bass); Walther von der Vogelweide (tenor); Biterolf (bass); Heinrich der Schreiber (tenor); Reinmar von Zweter (bass); Young Shepherd (soprano); Four Noble Pages (sopranos, altos); chorus (SSAATTBB).*

Tannhäuser, a medieval minstrel, has deserted his beloved Elisabeth and the cliffed castle of the Wartburg and fled to the pagan goddess of love and her underground Venusberg. But when he hears a distant churchbell, he tells Venus that he is weary of a life of the senses and longs to return to a life of striving, piety, and pain. The goddess' spell over him is broken when he invokes the Virgin Mary. He wakes in the green valley of the Wartburg and is found there by the minstrels he had deserted.

In the Wartburg's hall of song, Landgrave Hermann holds a contest for the hand of Elisabeth. The pious minstrel Wolfram sings the praises of courtly love, and Tannhäuser answers him with a song about his erotic encounter with Venus. The court is shocked, and the men draw their swords. Elisabeth intervenes, and the landgrave orders the repentent Tannhäuser to make a pilgrimage to Rome and ask pardon from the Pope.

Later in the year, the pilgrims return without Tannhäuser, and Elisabeth, after a prayer to the Virgin, dies of grief. As the evening star appears in the sky, the faithful Wolfram meets Tannhäuser in the Wartburg valley and hears that the Pope has denied him absolution: sooner will the papal sceptre put forth green leaves than such a sinner will find redemption. The disillusioned Tannhäuser is about to return to Venus when Wolfram tells him that Elisabeth has died and is interceding for him in heaven. Tannhäuser, shattered by the revelation, dies in Wolfram's arms as messengers arrive from Rome carrying the Pope's staff which, in a miracle of grace, has blossomed in green leaves.

The complete title, *Tannhäuser und der Sängerkrieg auf der Wartburg,* underlines the fact that Wagner blended two figures to make his hero—the legendary Tannhäuser who sinned with Venus, and the quasi-historical Heinrich von Ofterdingen who competed in song with Wolfram von Eschenbach and other Minnesingers in the Wartburg. The opera itself exists in two main versions, the earlier written for Dresden in 1845, the latter a revision, especially of the Venusberg scene, for the Paris Opéra in 1861. Its stormy reception there was perhaps the greatest musical scandal of the nineteenth century. The Paris version has passages of post-*Tristan* complexity, but in either version *Tannhäuser* is a more or less traditional blend of arias, duets, ensembles, choruses, and even a ballet. One remarkably prophetic moment is the hero's "Rome Narrative," which anticipates the powerful narratives of the music dramas to follow.

Tannhäuser has lost some of its popularity as Wagner's later scores have come to be better known, and is now often regarded as a melodious but simplistic conflict between good and evil. This verdict does the work a grave disservice. *Tannhäuser* is set in a historical era of some complexity, a time when a stable Christian society, confident of its political and spiritual values, was challenged by a renascent paganism. The opera's hero is a man torn not between good and evil so much as between two opposing sets of values, each important and essential to him, and he rises above his two experiences to achieve a new synthesis of them. His redemption (to use Wagner's word) is won through what Goethe had called *das Ewig-Weibliche,* the ability of a woman intuitively to understand a man and lead him upwards (like the famous "evening star" of Wolfram's song). Tannhäuser's victory is sounded on the score's last page when, to quote the composer, "The music of the Venusberg sounds amid the hymn of God." The greening of the papal sceptre is a sign of the integration of medieval and Renaissance sensibilities promised in the fifteenth century, and a sign too of what twentieth-century Jungians would call the healing of the psyche.

The opera may thus be seen as a kind of psycho-biographical statement by a young Romantic composer defying the society he knows and seeking to change it, a neo-pagan unable to win a hearing for his music because of his unorthodoxy, an idealist soon to be driven into exile and forced to act out the scenario he has written. But ultimately the opera's hero is anyone who has had to relate a new world of intellectual or spiritual or sensual awareness to the traditional values of the world in which he is placed. *Tannhäuser* represents that human struggle in mythic symbols and in music that, to listeners as varied as Hanslick and Baudelaire, came as a kind of self-revelation. "It seemed to me," the latter said, "that I already knew this music. It seemed to me it was my *own* music."—M. OWEN LEE

Tauber, Richard

Tenor. Born 16 May 1891, in Linz. Died 8 January 1948, in London. Married: 1) soprano Carlotta Vanconti; 2) actress Diana Napier, 1936. Studied conducting and composition at Frankfurt Conservatory, and voice with Carl Beines at Frieburg; debut as Tamino in Die Zauberflöte, *at the Chemnitz Neues Stadt-Theater, where his father was director, 1913; his success prompted a five-year contract with the Dresden Opera; debut at German Opera House in Berlin as Bacchus in* Ariadne auf Naxos, *1915; member Vienna Staatsoper, 1922-28 and 1932-38, and Berlin State Opera, 1923-33; sang to great acclaim at Mozart Festivals in Munich and Salzburg, appearing as Tamino, Belmonte and Don Ottavio; after 1925 began appearing frequently in light opera, singing in Lehár's* Das Land des Lächelns *at Drury Lane in 1931; Covent Garden debut as Tamino, 1938; in 1947 made final operatic appearance (as Don Ottavio) during a visit of the Vienna Staatsoper to Covent Garden; became a naturalized British citizen in 1940.*

The development of the phonograph in the first half of the twentieth century made it possible for the first time for singers to achieve popularity with a large section of the public. The phonograph record can be used as a valid yardstick to measure the popularity of singers, and during this period three tenors stand out above all others. First, the immortal Enrico Caruso, whose records outsold all others; second, the peerless John McCormack, the most prolific recording artist of all time with over 800 recorded titles to his credit; and third, the Austrian, Richard Tauber, second only to McCormack in the quantity of records produced—over 700 titles. All three singers were idolized by the public and were held in high esteem by critics—the only negative critical opinion that was voiced in regard to them was their common fondness for popular, less serious, music.

Of the three, Tauber was undoubtedly the most versatile. Caruso was primarily an opera singer, while McCormack was principally a concert artist, although he appeared in opera. Tauber, whose formal musical education was more thorough, achieved recognition not merely as a singer but also as a composer and conductor. From 1913, when he contracted to appear with the Dresden Opera, until 1922, Tauber devoted himself to opera, not only at Dresden, but at principal opera houses in Berlin and Vienna. From 1923 up to the time he fled to England in the mid-1930s to escape Nazi persecution, Tauber divided his time between opera and operetta. In the final years of his career he sang principally in concerts and appeared in films.

Tauber possessed a unique, utterly distinctive voice that was instantly recognizable. During his career several colleagues achieved a degree of celebrity because they supposedly "sounded like Tauber," but none succeeded in approximating Tauber's vocal personality. Apart from its individualistic *timbre*, Tauber's voice was not remarkable either in power or in range. It was a lyric tenor, modeled on the old *bel canto* tradition, aided and abetted by consumate musicianship, technical proficiency marked by impeccable intonation, outstanding breath control, and a seamless *legato*. In order to produce the distinctive resonant quality that characterizes his voice, Tauber sacrificed the highest notes of the tenor range, and is generally considered a "short" tenor because he had no high C from the chest register. Thus he reverted to the older tradition of singing high notes in either the pure head voice, or the mixture of head and chest resonance, a technique that came from the French lyric tradition and known as the *voix-mixte*. Nor did he eschew the use of the vocal technique known as *falsetto*.

Henry Pleasants defines *falsetto* as "a kind of vocal production, now normally applied only to males, by which the upper range is extended and takes on the character of the female (or boy) alto or soprano." Pleasants adds "Nor does everyone agree on just where a 'legitimate' head voice ends and *falsetto* begins." One of the earliest works on the technique of singing is Piero Francesco Tosi's *Opinion d' cantori antiche e moderni o siano osservazioni sopra il canto figurato* published in 1723. Tosi considered the use of *falsetto* necessary for successful singing. Throughout the early period of opera up to the early nineteenth century, tenors traditionally sang high notes in either the head voice or *falsetto*. It was Gilbert-Louis Duprez who first sang the high C from the chest in a performance of Rossini's *Guillaume Tell* in 1837. Rossini detested the sound and preferred the traditional use of the head voice. But gradually other tenors began to emulate Duprez and by the end of the nineteenth century the ringing chest voice tenor high notes were critically and publicly acclaimed. Conversely the use of the *falsetto* fell into critical disapproval. Thus critics applying modern standards have criticized Tauber for his use of the technique, which he employed more often in operetta and popular songs than he did in opera. However, the quality and resonance of the tone which Tauber produced by the use of this technique, even in the softest *pianissimo,* overcomes all objections.

From 1920-25, during the acoustical era, Tauber recorded twenty-six operatic arias for Odeon. With the advent of electrical recordings, he made another forty-two operatic recordings from 1925 to 1947. Of these only eight were repeats of arias which he had previously recorded. Thus out of his recorded legacy of 725 records only 86 were of operatic music. He followed the contemporary custom of singing almost exclusively in German, notable exceptions being two arias from *Don Giovanni* in Italian, the flower song from *Carmen* and an aria from Lalo's *Le Roi d'Ys* in French. His operatic recorded repertoire ranged from Rossini to Wagner, but he achieved his greatest acclaim as a Mozart specialist. Critics noted that his personal magnetism and vocal brilliance transformed Don Ottavio in *Don Giovanni* into a major role, and his success as Tamino in *Die Zauberflöte* was so brilliant that both critics and colleagues referred to the opera as "*Tauberflöte*."

Tauber's early acoustical recordings consist of arias and duets from twenty-one operas, ten of which are from Italian opera, with the emphasis on Verdi and Puccini. Because of his command of *legato* and *bel canto* style, his singing of Italian opera is not severely compromised by the constant use of a German text. A notable example is his recording of the drinking song from *La traviata,* which he sings as a solo. Despite the language, Tauber's instinctive rhythmic sense captures the essence of the music. During this period he ventured into the dramatic tenor repertoire, recording duets from *Aida* and arias and duets from *Il trovatore*. Unfortunately his lack of a chest voice high C necessitated his lowering the pitch in the aria "Di quella pira" a full tone. However, his recordings of Puccini arias are justly admired. Six operas are represented from German opera, only one from Mozart, a recording of "Dalla sua pace" from *Don Giovanni,* also sung in German. Two recordings are of Wagner operas which he never sang on stage. The list is completed by three arias from French opera, one each from Russian and Czech.

In his later electrical recordings the emphasis shifts to German opera. Only the *Tosca* arias are repeated from the Puccini canon, and he forsakes Verdi, except for a duet from *La forza del destino* with Benno Zeigler. His most critically acclaimed recordings are his Mozart arias from *Die Entführung aus dem Serail, Die Zauberflöte* and *Don Giovanni*. From the latter opera he sings the correct Italian text. All of his electric operatic recordings are noteworthy, the most outstanding being his two arias from Offenbach's *Les contes d'Hoffmann,* which are examples of his most ravishing style despite the use of a German text. His recording of "Durch die Wälder, durch die Auen" from Weber's *Der Freischütz* is justly considered to be the classic version.

During his early career, Tauber's impact was so exceptional that he reinstituted an older tradition in a new genre. Nineteenth-century composers invariably wrote operas for specific singers to create the roles. By the twentieth century this practice had become obsolete, but Tauber's relationship with composers of operetta, notably Franz Lehár and Emmerich Kálmán, was such that both composers wrote operetta specifically for him. Every operetta had to have a "Tauberlied," the most famous of which is "Dein ist mein ganzes herz" (Yours is my heart alone) from Lehár's *Das Land des Lachlens* (The Land of Smiles).

Tauber was undoubtedly the most versatile tenor of all time. He sang and recorded nearly everything: "pop" tunes of Irving Berlin and Jerome Kern, Strauss waltzes, Irish songs, Neapolitan songs, operetta, oratorio arias, German lieder, and grand opera. Whatever the music, he brought to it his inimitable musical style. He was gifted with an instinctive, intuitive feeling for rhythm, perfect pitch, exemplary breath control, and a unique sound.

In addition to his voluminous output of commercial recordings, air checks have been published of various radio broadcasts. Also published is a private recording of Tauber's own operetta *Old Chelsea* as well as a record of the sound-track from his film of *Pagliacci*. Twenty-seven commercial recordings have been issued with Tauber as the conductor of various orchestras.

His legacy of recordings prove that his voice did not deteriorate with age. On 27 September 1947, already stricken with lung cancer, he sang his final operatic performance of *Don Giovanni* at Covent Garden as a guest artist with the visiting Vienna State Opera Company. Air checks of a duet and his two principal arias reveal that, in spite of his illness, singing on virtually one lung, he still produced the resonance and vocal quality that made him unique.—BOB ROSE

Tchaikovsky, Piotr Ilyich

Composer. Born 7 May 1840, in Votkinsk, Viatka district. Died 6 November 1893, in St Petersburg. Married: Antonina Milyukova, 18 July 1877. Became a government clerk, 1859; studied music with Lomakin; studied harmony and counterpoint with Zaremba and composition with A. Rubinstein at the music school established by Rubinstein (ultimately the St Petersburg Conservatory), 1861-65; silver medal for his cantata on Schiller's Hymn to Joy; *professor of harmony at the Moscow Conservatory, 1866-78; composition of orchestral works, 1866-1870; music criticism for Moscow newspapers, 1868-74; world premiere of his Piano Concerto by Hans von Bülow in Boston, 25 October 1875; numerous trips to Paris, Berlin, Vienna; covered the first Bayreuth Festival for the Moscow newspaper* Russkyie Vedomosti, *1876; in Italy, Switzerland, Paris, and Vienna, 1877-78; in America, 1891; concert tour of Russia, Poland, and Germany, 1892. Tchaikovsky was financially supported throughout much of his life by the patronage of Nadezhda von Meck.*

Operas *Voyevoda*, Ostrovsky and Tchaikovsky (after Ostrovsky, *Son po Volge*), 1867-68, Moscow, Bol'shoy, 11 February 1869 [destroyed by the composer; reconstructed by Pavel Lamm]; *Undina*, V. Sollogub (after Zhukovsky's translation of F. de la Motte Fouqué), 1869, excerpts performed Moscow, 28 March 1870 [destroyed by the composer]; *Mandragora*, S. Rachinsky, 1870, Moscow, 30 December 1870 [unfinished; one chorus only]; *Oprichnik*, Tchaikovsky (after I. Lazhechnikov), 1870-72, St Petersburg, Mariinsky, 24 April 1874; *Vakula the Smith* [*Kuznets Vakula*]. Ya. Polonsky (after Gogol, *Noch'pered rozhdestvom*), 1874, St Petersburg, Mariinsky, 6 December 1876; revised as *The Slippers* [*Cherevichki*] (comic-fantastic opera), 1885, Moscow, Bol'shoy, 31 January 1887; *Eugene Onegin* [*Evgeny Onegin*], K. Shilovsky and Tchaikovsky (after Pushkin), 1877-78, Moscow, Maliy, 29 March 1879; *The Maid of Orleans* [*Orleanskaya deva*]. Tchaikovsky (after Zhukovsky's translation of Schiller, *Die Jungfrau von Orleans*), 1878-79, St Petersburg, Mariinsky, 25 February 1881; revised, 1882; *Mazeppa*, V. Burenin, revised by Tchaikovsky (after Pushkin, *Poltava*), 1881-83, Moscow, Bol'shoy, 15 February 1884; *The Sorceress* [*Charodeyka*], I. Shpazhinsky, 1885-87, St Petersburg, Mariinsky, 1 November 1887; *The Queen of Spades* [*Pikovaya dama*]. M. and P. Tchaikovsky (after Pushkin), 1890, St Petersburg, Mariinsky, 19 December 1890; *Iolanta*, M. Tchaikovsky (after V. Zotov's translation of H. Hertz's *King René's Daughter*) 1891, St Petersburg, Mariinsky, 18 December 1892.

Although *Eugene Onegin* and *The Queen of Spades* are the only operas by Piotr Ilyich Tchaikovsky that are regularly performed in the West today, he composed ten operas, and no genre spans his career quite so neatly. Tchaikovsky's opera composition demonstrates a wide range of aesthetic and compositional approaches, from works based on the French grand opera tradition as represented by Meyerbeer (usually with a nationalist bent) to attempts at realism (inspired by Balakirev and his circle). His influences were both from traditional western European opera and from the attempts of "The Five" (Balakirev, Borodin, Cui, Musorgsky, Rimsky-Korsakov) to create a genuinely nationalist Russian opera. Like Rubinstein, however, Tchaikovsky's works remain on the more traditional, conservative, and heavily western-based side of the equation.

All of Tchaikovsky's operas are number operas, but in spite of this conservative approach, there is at times considerable originality to its use in relation to dramatic structure, such as in *Eugene Onegin,* for example. Tchaikovsky was a great admirer of Gounod's (he said that he valued Gounod's *Faust* above any other opera) and was influenced by his lyricism, although, unlike Gounod, Tchaikovsky frequently allows his lyricism to dominate dramatic considerations. In keeping with his primarily musical rather than dramatic aesthetic, Tchaikovsky was frequently accused of being a symphonist in his operas rather than a true dramatic composer (especially by Cesar Cui, an experienced if not successful opera composer who could hardly let a critique pass without summoning the epithet). This symphonism is evident in numerous facets of his operas, from some of the most effective passages (such as the near leitmotivic manipulation of the love theme in *Eugene Onegin*) to the weakest moments (such as the excessive filigree in some of the choruses in *The Maid of Orleans*).

None of Tchaikovsky's operas are without fine musical moments; unfortunately, however, these moments do not always coincide with the drama. In *The Sorceress,* for example, the opening genre numbers, which are musically some of the best in the opera, have nothing to do with the drama, and the real dramatic events fall so weakly in the midst of it all that act II is barely explainable. Similarly, Tchaikovsky's orchestration is at his best in the dances, where he is able to free himself from the constraints of accompanying and supporting the voice. He also excelled

t

OPERA

Piotr Ilyich Tchaikovsky, c. 1890

at divertissements, the style of which provide much of the best music in *The Queen of Spades,* and at melodrama, which in *Oprichnik* is surprisingly well paced and well-balanced musically.

Tchaikovsky was very fond of connecting numbers within an opera by quoting a previous tune as a transition to the next piece, perhaps as an attempt at continuity within the segmented number opera format. This tendency toward melodic self-quotation is also evident in the echo voice over a measure of rest in both accompanied recitatives and arias. His operas also frequently contain mad scenes, such as in *Mazepa* and *The Sorceress,* the latter of which was probably influenced by the Mad Miller in Dargomyzhsky's *Rusalka.* His dramatic music was also influenced by Ostrovsky; his first opera, *Voyevoda* was based on Ostrovsky's *A Dream on the Volga,* and he composed an overture for Ostrovsky's play *The Storm,* as well as incidental music for *The Snow Maiden* and other Ostrovsky plays. Perhaps the most puzzling omission in Tchaikovsky's works, however, particularly in the context of post-*Ruslan* Russian opera, is the almost total absence of Orientalism. The part of the Moorish doctor in *Iolanta,* added to the *Nutcracker,* and a slight touch of Orientalism in the *Mazepa* overture is the extent of its use in Tchaikovsky's works.

Tchaikovsky's choice of librettos was not always fortunate; he was given some weak librettos and prepared a few himself. The success of *The Queen of Spades,* for example, is largely in spite of its libretto rather than because of it. Tchaikovsky's librettos do span a wide range of subjects, however, from Pushkin to historical and political topics to melodrama and fantasy.

In general, Tchaikovsky excelled in the musical parts of his operas (song, ballet), but not in the dramatic aspects. He is at his best in the purely domestic scenes (as in much of *Eugene Onegin*) and genre numbers, but he does not always succeed in building musico-dramatic tension. He had a real lyric gift rather than a genuine dramatic sense, and as a result, individual numbers work very well and could easily be lifted from one work and placed in another without any real loss of effect (as Tchaikovsky did in *Oprichnik,* using several numbers from *Voyevoda*). Tchaikovsky's operatic strength was therefore rooted in his abilities as a lyricist, which is not surprising in light of the fact that his international reputation and fame rested primarily on his symphonic and instrumental compositions.—GREGORY SALMON

Tebaldi, Renata

Soprano. Born 1 February 1922, in Pesaro. Studied with Brancucci and Campogalliani at the Parma Conservatory, 1937-40; studied with Carmen Melis and Giuseppe Pais at the Pesaro Conservatory, 1940-43; debut as Elena in Mefistofele, *Rovigo, 1944; among the artists chosen by Toscanini to reopen the Teatro alla Scala in 1946; sang at La Scala until 1954; British debut as Desdemona with the visiting La Scala company, Covent Garden,*

1950; U.S. debut as Aïda, San Francisco, 1950; Metropolitan Opera debut as Desdemona, 1955; sang at Metropolitan until 1973.

Assessment of Tebaldi's career will always be influenced by two extramusical factors: the misinterpretation of a remark by Arturo Toscanini and the fact that her twenty-nine years on stage spanned the shorter, more intense career of Maria Callas. Toscanini, having accepted Tebaldi as the only young singer to participate with pre-war veterans in the 1946 reopening of the Teatro alla Scala, had, for his performance of Verdi's *Four Sacred Pieces,* positioned her in the organ loft for her brief contribution. At rehearsal, partly in tribute to her beauty of voice but mainly making a pun on her location high above the orchestra, he exclaimed "Ah! La voce d'angelo!" (Ah, the voice of an angel). The offhand play on words soon transformed via the operatic grapevine into a benediction of her artistry by the world's leading conductor, but to hear the voice in the Trio from Rossini's *Mosé,* recorded at that reopening concert, one can believe Toscanini had meant it more seriously. Tebaldi's sound, full, clear, and seamless, agile and fresh, does sound "angelic," a sound she would retain well into the late years of her career.

Her role vis-à-vis Callas did not have such positive results. It originated in Rio de Janeiro in 1951, when Callas had the role of Tosca taken from her after a sub-par performance and given to Tebaldi, who had been 400 miles away in Sao Paulo and thought she was replacing a different singer entirely (Elisabetta Barbato) when she returned to Rio. Callas saw a conspiracy where none had existed. Back in Italy, fueled by hysterical fans of both singers (called by the Italian press "tifosi," a word otherwise used only to describe rabid football fans and typhoid fever sufferers), Tebaldi became identified with the traditional, antidramatic, voice-for-its-own-sake school of singing, while Callas was seen as the wind of change, the exponent of opera as theater, of voice in the service of art. According to the myth, Callas revived forgotten operas and revealed their hidden greatness, while Tebaldi regurgitated the mainstream repertoire in admittedly golden but psychologically empty tones.

In fact, in the early years of their coincident careers, Tebaldi had been as active in reviving long-buried operas as Callas: Rossini's *Le siège de Corinthe,* Spontini's *Fernando Cortez* and *Olympie,* Handel's *Giulio Cesare.* They had both made excursions into Wagner and Tebaldi had even created a contemporary work, Casavola's *Salammbô.* But to some extent the myth created by Callas and by the tifosi, and fanned by the Italian newspapers, whose critics almost to a man were in the Callas camp, became a reality. Tebaldi retreated to a small group of traditionally popular operas in the mid-1950s. At the same time Callas gave up a number of soprano parts in which sheer beauty of voice and effortless emission were worth more than psychological nuance or subtle coloration. Only with the virtual withdrawal of Callas from the stage in the early 1960s did Tebaldi once again venture into more dramatic parts: Minnie in *La fanciulla del West,* Gioconda, and Adriana Lecouvreur (a meaty dramatic role Callas strangely never sang).

Tebaldi's recordings span almost her entire career. Her earliest 78s reveal a youthful freshness well suited to lyric roles such as Mimi. The most thoroughly satisfying discs from this period are those of her complete *Giovanna d'Arco.* "O fatidica foresta" demonstrates a perfect command of legato, as do her duets with Carlo Bergonzi, in which she rises to the climaxes without apparent effort, the purity of tone at the core of the sensuous overall sound reflecting the conflicting emotions of a saint in love. Tebaldi's Verdi heroines (leaving aside Elisabeth in *Don Carlos* and Amelia in *Un ballo in maschera* which she never sang on stage and recorded late in her career) are her most satisfying. She recorded *Aida* twice; the second recording, under

Karajan, shows off her aristocratic style and ability to convey emotion in purely vocal terms, though her voice is much more voluptuous in a third act duet with Mario Filippeschi from a 1954 Rio de Janeiro broadcast which has not yet been put on disc.

From that same year come several recordings of complete performances of *La forza del destino,* of which the best is the commercial Decca/London release. In the duet with the Father Guardian she demonstrates that the agility of the 1940s has not left her, especially in the "Plaudite, o cori angelici" passage. At "Voi mi scacciate? Voi?" she displays her opulent chest voice and an aristocratic projection which illuminates the character's nobility and desperation. Her "Pace, pace, mio Dio" must rank with Ponselle's for pure beauty of sound and the phenomenal breath control which supports long phrases without apparent effort. One's choice will probably depend on whether one prefers the duskiness of Ponselle or the brighter Tebaldi sound.

She was equally at home in the spinto-dramatic roles of Puccini, though most of her studio recordings of that repertoire date from the period in which she sacrificed, to some extent, characterization to sound. On stage at this time she could be unusually variable. Under a conductor such as Karajan, her Tosca could thrill an audience not only vocally, but with an underplayed intensity and economy of gesture which conveyed a character as well-conceived as the more celebrated Callas interpretation, though less vulnerable as a human being. Given a more indulgent conductor and costars, her *Tosca* could turn into a concert in costume, its arias and duets directed at the audience.

Tebaldi had little empathy for 18th-century music, though she obstinately included it in recital throughout her career. Despite reports that her Countess in *Le nozze di Figaro* was excellent, most of her pre-Rossini repertoire has a sameness which, despite the beautiful sounds, is empty of commitment. At the other chronological extreme of her repertoire, she sang *canzone* of the post-verismo composers with an understanding of style that makes it all the more tragic that, despite its being announced for both Florence and San Francisco, she never sang in her one-time teacher Zandonai's *Francesca da Rimini,* only recording the love duet long after her smoothness of emission had become a mechanical chore rather than a natural attribute.

Representing, as she did for a generation of operagoers, one pole of a controversy as to the nature of operatic singing, Tebaldi's contributions to that art have been both praised and castigated for the wrong reasons. At her best, she demonstrated how the possessor of a magnificent sound could serve the text without sacrificing the sheerly sensual appeal of that sound. Even at less than her best, she exemplified how much pleasure could be gained from hearing an Italian dramatic-lyric role sung by the finest pure voice of its generation—or, so far, since.—WILLIAM J. COLLINS

Te Kanawa, (Dame) Kiri Janette

Soprano. Born 6 March 1944, in Gisborne, Auckland. Married: company director Desmond Stephen Park, 1967; one daughter, one son. Studied with Sister Mary Leo, Auckland; at London Opera Centre; and with Vera Rosza; debut as Carmen, Northern Opera, 1968; London debut as Idamante in Idomeneo, *Chelsea Opera Group, 1968; Covent Garden debut as Blumenmädchen in* Parsifal, *1971; major debut as Countess Almaviva in* Le nozze di Figaro, *Covent Garden, 1971; Glyndebourne debut, 1973;*

t

≡≡OPERA

Metropolitan Opera debut as Desdemona, 1974; Paris debut as Elvira, 1974; Dame of the British Empire, 1982.

New Zealand-born soprano Kiri Te Kanawa received her early vocal training (as a mezzo-soprano) in New Zealand, but her first performances in staged opera took place in England: Idamante in Mozart's *Idomeneo* for the Chelsea Opera Group in 1968, Ellen in Rossini's *La donna del lago* at the Camden Festival in 1969, and a Bridesmaid in Mozart's *Le nozze di Figaro* at the Royal Festival Hall in 1970 under the baton of Otto Klemperer. Small roles followed at Covent Garden: a Flowermaiden in Wagner's *Parsifal,* the High Priestess (an offstage role) in Verdi's *Aida.* Her breakthrough came in December 1971 with a performance of the Countess Almaviva in *Le nozze di Figaro.* Desdemona in Verdi's *Otello* and Micaela in Bizet's *Carmen* followed, and to these roles were soon to be added Amelia in Verdi's *Simon Boccanegra* and Donna Elvira in Mozart's *Don Giovanni.* Signed to make her Metropolitan Opera debut as Desdemona in 1974, she made an unscheduled early debut when the announced Desdemona, Teresa Stratas, canceled. The performance was well received and launched her American career.

Te Kanawa has had particular success in the Mozart and Strauss repertoire, most notably as the countess in *Le nozze di Figaro* and Fiordiligi in *Così fan tutte,* and in the title role of *Arabella,* which she first sang in 1977, the Marschallin in *Der Rosenkavalier,* which she added in 1981, and the countess in *Capriccio.* She brings to the Strauss roles the soaring top notes, if not quite the careful attention to the text, that these roles ideally require.

Te Kanawa is less suited to the Verdi and Puccini roles, although she has sung Puccini's Mimi, Tosca, and Manon Lescaut, and Verdi's Desdemona, Amelia, and Violetta in *La traviata;* she lacks sufficient expansiveness, heft, and dramatic thrust, as well as the combination of *spinto* strength and agility needed to negotiate the difficulties of many of these parts, nor does she have the strong chest register needed for verismo roles. She has had greater success in the French and German repertoires; among her French roles are Marguerite in Gounod's *Faust,* while her German roles include Rosalinde in Johann Strauss's *Die Fledermaus.*

Primarily a lyric soprano, Te Kanawa possesses a creamy, silky sound, a clear, plangent vocal tone with a shimmery brightness allied to physical beauty and poise, a combination that, for many, more than compensates for some failings in intonation and dramatic projection. Her voice is free from an obtrusive vibrato, and she avoids the common fault of scooping into notes. She has the ability to sing softly and is at least proficient in floating her piano high notes, notes that have extended to the high E-flat.

Te Kanawa's detractors find her an unimaginative singer, prone to swallowing her words and creating generalized portrayals. They complain about her lethargic delivery of the vocal line and the text, a droopy quality to her phrasing, an imperturbability that persists even in the most dramatic situations. Her projection of the words is not strong; her enunciation tends to be cloudy and her pronunciation of German and French is not ideally idiomatic, resulting in the production of sounds that, while lovely in an abstract sort of way, do not incisively project the music, the text, or the emotions of the character she is portraying. Her Italian roles are compromised by a lack of fire. Nor is she particularly able to differentiate one of her characters from another—they all appear to be cast in the same, rather passive, unemotional mold, if an exceptionally beautiful one. It is this characteristic combination of vocal beauty and emotional remoteness that makes Te Kanawa a frustrating singer for some.

Kiri Te Kanawa in *Capriccio*,
Royal Opera, London, 1991

Early in her career, Te Kanawa performed tiny roles in some recordings of complete operas. She was heard, if briefly, as the groom Dmitri in Gardelli's recording of Giordano's *Fedora* in 1969, was the Countess Ceprano in Bonynge's recording of Verdi's *Rigoletto* in 1972, and was a Flowermaiden in Wagner's *Parsifal* (also in 1972, under Solti's baton). Once her international career had been launched, she was assigned to major roles in numerous recordings, especially in her specialty roles of Mozart and Strauss. Her complete operatic recordings include her portrayals of the Countess Almaviva (1973, under Colin Davis; 1978, under Solti; and 1991, under Levine); Donna Elvira (1973, under Colin Davis, and 1978, under Maazel); Micaela in Bizet's *Carmen* (1975, under Solti); Fiordiligi (1977, under Lombard, and 1989, under Levine); the Sandman in Humperdinck's *Hänsel und Gretel* (1978, under Pritchard), Pamina in *Die Zauberflöte* (1978, under Lombard, and 1989, under Marriner); Magda in Puccini's *La rondine* (1983, under Maazel), Tosca (1986, under Solti); Manon Lescaut (1988, under Chailly); Amelia (1989, under Solti), Arabella (1987, under Tate); Mademoiselle Silberklang in Mozart's *Der Schauspieldirektor* (1990, under Pritchard), Rosalinde (1991, under Previn); the Marschallin (1991, under Haitink); and the Woodbird in Haitink's recording of Wagner's *Ring* cycle.—MICHAEL SIMS

Tetrazzini, Luisa

Soprano. Born 29 June 1871, in Florence. Died 28 April 1940, in Milan. Married: 1) Alberto Scalaberni, c. 1890; 2) Pietro Vernati, 1926. Studied at the Istituto Musicale in Florence with Contrucci and Cecherini, and with her sister Eva, herself a soprano and wife of conductor Cleofonte Campanini; debut at the Teatro Pagliano in Florence, as Inez in L'Africaine, 1890; toured throughout Europe, as well as Russia and Latin America; U.S. debut in San Francisco, 1905; Covent Garden debut as Violetta, 1907, and sang for the summer seasons there from 1908 to 1912; New York debut as Violetta at the Manhattan Opera House, 1908; sang there until 1910; sang for 1911-12 season at the Metropolitan Opera and the 1911-12 and 1912-13 seasons in Chicago; was recorded extensively between 1903 and 1914; toured widely after World War I, singing only concerts; made final appearances in New York in 1931 and London in 1934; in later years was active as a teacher in Milan.

Luisa Tetrazzini made her debut in Florence at the Teatro Pagliano (now the Verdi) in 1890 as Inez in Meyerbeer's *L'Africaine*. After singing at the Argentina, Rome, and touring Italian cities, she joined Tomba's opera company at the San Martin, Buenos Aires, in October, 1892, and returned every season until 1895, singing also in Rosario and Mendoza, as well as Uruguay and Brazil. In 1896 she sang in Portugal, Italy, Poland, and Spain. In early 1987 she sang in St Petersburg before returning to Madrid in the spring, where she sang Amina in *La sonnambula*, Lucia, and the *Jollie fille de Perth*'s title role at the Prince Alfonso Theatre. She showed serious signs of vocal decline in *Ugonotti* but fully recovered to win acclaim at the Dal Verme, Milan, the same year, then in 1898 at the Teatro Brunelli, Bologna, and the Teatro de la Opera, Buenos Aires. From the start of 1899 to the spring of 1903 she sang in Warsaw, Moscow, St Petersburg, Berlin, and occasionally in Italy where she triumphed in *Puritani* at the Teatro Adriano, Rome, in April, 1900. From summer 1903 to early 1905 she was mostly in Mexico. Engaged by W.H. Leahy to sing at the Tivoli, San Francisco, for two seasons, she created a furor, as she did at her Covent Garden debut as Violetta in 1907, returning there every season until 1912. She made an equally brilliant debut in the same role in 1908 at the Manhattan, New York, returning every year until 1910. When Hammerstein disbanded his company, she sang for a few performances at the Metropolitan Opera. She reacted against his lawsuit to prevent her singing for other managements by announcing that she would sing in the streets of San Francisco. As a result, she gave her famous Christmas Eve open air concert there in 1910 attended by nearly 250,000 people who heard her clearly without any form of amplification.

After World War I, Tetrazzini ceased appearing in opera and sang instead in popular concerts in Britain and America. In 1925 she starred in the first British Broadcasting Corporation concert heard world-wide.

In 1926, Tetrazzini married Pietro Vernati, twenty-four years younger than she, but they parted after only three years together. She then became involved with charlatans who exploited her obsession with spiritism. Foolish and generous, Tetrazzini squandered her fortune of five million dollars by the mid-1930s and was reduced to giving singing lessons to pupils who boarded with her in Milan, the most successful of these being Lina Pagliughi. According to Harry Higgins, who ran Covent Garden for some thirty years, she was the greatest prima donna of his time. He said nothing ever excelled the brilliance of her attack and the abandon of her cadenzas.

John McCormack, who often sang with Tetrazzini at Covent Garden and in New York, was a discerning judge. Above E flat, she was superb, he thought, her chromatic scales upward and downward being marvels of clarity, and her trill unrivalled. "She could get an amazing amount of *larmes dans la voix,* far more than I ever heard from any other coloratura soprano." On the other hand, "the middle of her voice was white and breathy, probably from overwork as a young singer." This criticism refers to what W.J. Henderson of the *New York Sun* described after her Manhattan debut as her worst shortcoming—"the extraordinary emission of her lower medium notes" which were sung with "a pinched glottis and with a color so pallid and a tremolo so pronounced that they were often not a bad imitation of the wailing of a cross infant."

The "tremolo" was probably caused by first night nerves, for this complaint was rarely again made. The distinguished critic John Pitts Sanborn observed that when Tetrazzini returned the following season "the crudities had largely disappeared, and her medium register, previously deficient, she had recovered or developed." He thought this improvement due to singing under her brother-in-law Cleofonte Campanini's guidance. Writing in 1912, Sanborn states: "But the apotheosis of Tetrazzini came last spring when, after a year's absence, she returned here to sing in concert. Then the voice was almost perfectly equalised, a glorious organ from top to bottom. Even in the lowest register she was ready with a firm, rich tone. . . . She not only sang great florid arias with perfect command of voice technique and style; she sang Aida's 'Ritorna vincitor' as scarcely a dramatic soprano has sung it here. She sang Solvejg' song from *Peer Gynt* like a true Lieder singer, and the page's song from *Figaro* with . . . the most wonderful display of vocal virtuosity since Patti. . . . Her 'Voi che sapete' was the finest piece of Mozart singing I have ever heard, and I have heard both Melba and Sembrich sing the same piece." In his opinion, she was, one of the last exponents of a perfect trill—"two golden hammers beating a faultless interval."

Fortunately, Tetrazzini made many recordings. Her singing of the Carnival of Venice and other examples of her art were included in the "Great Recordings of the Century" LP (Angel COLH 136) issued in 1964. Gerald Fitzgerald in *Opera News* for 12 December that year commented that, like most of her records, "it belies many of the criticisms raised against her, especially the deficiency in the lower region of her voice, which bounds forth jubilantly. . . . More than singing, however, one senses a vibrant personality—generous, uninhibited, warm and joyous that establishes immediate rapport with the listener."—CHARLES NEILSON GATTEY

Thaïs

Composer: *Jules Massenet.*

Librettist: *Louis Gallet (after Anatole France).*

First Performance: *Paris, Opéra, 16 March 1894.*

Roles: *Thaïs (soprano); Athanael (baritone); Nicias (tenor); Crobyle (soprano); Myrtale (mezzo-soprano); Albine (mezzo-soprano); Servant (baritone); Palemon (bass); La Charmeuse (soprano); chorus (SSSATTTTBB).*

The once immensely popular *Thaïs* does not figure prominently in today's repertoire; the late 1970s saw a resurgence of interest in the opera, but questions remain as to the overall quality of the drama and the score. Most criticism has centered on the dated subject matter, on Louis Gallet's shallow adaptation of the novel by Anatole France, and, ultimately, on Massenet's inability to delineate the principal characters in musical terms. Roger Pines writes: "*Thaïs* is a little much for us today. . . . One struggles to care about the fate of Massenet's troubled courtesan and the crazed monk who loves her. The score . . . has not worn as well as either *Manon* or

Illustration from the first production of *Thaïs*, 1894

Werther; moments of inspiration alternate all too often with tedium." Robert Lawrence, otherwise a defender of Massenet, finds Thaïs to be "a courtesan whose rates and prestige have declined by now."

The opera's insubstantiality may be due in large part to its libretto, which oversimplified Anatole France's novel and was sharply attacked from the start (most notably by France himself). Andrew Porter notes that though France "ranged far beyond the simple moral drama and handled the history in no pious way. . . . There could be no place for this in the opera. Louis Gallet, Massenet's librettist, omitted the irony, the kaleidoscope of daring speculations, and all the jokes. The tone was quite altered."

For Martin Cooper, who wrote the article on Massenet for *The New Grove Dictionary of Music and Musicians,* Massenet's music also lacks a true dramatic quality: "When Massenet attempted the portrait of . . . Thaïs, he was handicapped by his conventionality. Inasmuch as Thaïs is a real person, she is simply a reincarnation of Manon." Furthermore, Cooper notes, though Athanael's "divided personality, and his passion for Thaïs inspired Massenet with some of his rare impassioned music . . . the absence of any comparatively powerful music to express Athanael's asceticism . . . leaves his character and the work unbalanced."

Other critics find the opera still worthy of interest, especially when it is presented well. Despite his negative criticism, Pines also notes that "in the right hands, [the] music still offers some rewards. It is certainly worth enduring a great deal of languid dialogue and quaint salon exoticism in order to savor Thaïs' arias and large chunks of her duets with Athanael. Here Massenet exploits the lyricism and dramatic flair that helped to sustain his immense popularity." And though Porter thought the Met's 1978 revival was marred by poor staging, he found the work to be "a pretty opera, and very skillfully written."

A final assessment seems dependent as well on one's willingness to accept *fin-de-siècle* French culture. As Martin Cooper notes: "the figure of the reformed courtesan . . . was given a devotional tinge very much in line with certain currents in contemporary French Catholicism. . . . The climax of this particular genre was reached with *Thaïs.*" Going even further, Gary Lipton feels that Massenet's (and Anatole France's) "special vision of Egyptian antiquity . . . reflects the volatile discussion of equality, social justice and progress in evidence since the literary debates of French Enlightenment figures."—DAVID PACUN

Thomas, (Charles Louis) Ambroise

Composer. Born 5 August 1811, in Metz. Died, 12 February 1896, in Paris. Studied piano with Zimmermann and harmony and accompaniment with Dourlen at the Paris Conservatory, beginning 1828; studied piano privately with Kalkbrenner, harmony privately with Barbereau, and composition privately with Lesueur; Grand Prix de Rome for his cantata Hermann et Ketty, *1832; spent three years in Italy and visited Vienna; returned to Paris and began composing opera; elected to the Académie, 1851; professor of composition at the Paris Conservatory, 1856; director of the Paris Conservatory, 1871.*

Operas *La double échelle,* F.A.E. de Planard, Paris, Opéra-Comique, Salle des Nouveautés, 23 August 1837; *Le perruquier de la régence,* F.A.E. de Planard and P. Dupont, Paris, Opéra-Comique, Salle des Nouveautés, 30 March 1838; *Le panier fleuri,* A. de Leuven and L.L. Brunswick, Paris, Opéra-

Comique, Salle des Nouveautés, 6 May 1839; *Carline*, A. de Leuven and L.L. Brunswick, Paris, Opéra-Comique, Salle des Nouveautés, 24 February 1840; *Le comte de Carmagnola*, Eugène Scribe, Paris, Opéra, 19 April 1841; *Le guerillero*, T. Anne, Paris, Opéra, 22 June 1842; *Angélique et Médor*, T.M.F. Sauvage, Paris, Opéra-Comique, Salle Favart, 10 May 1843; *Mina, ou Le ménage à trois*, F.A.E. de Planard, Paris, Opéra-Comique, Salle Favart, 10 October 1843; *Le caïd*, T.M.F. Sauvage, Paris, Opéra-Comique, Salle Favart, 3 January 1849; *Le songe d'une nuit d'été*, J.B. Rosier and A. de Leuven, Paris, Opéra-Comique, Salle des Nouveautés, 20 April 1850; *Raymond, ou Le secret de la reine*, J.B. Rosier and A. de Leuven, Paris, Opéra-Comique, Salle Favart, 5 June 1851; *La Tonelli*, T.M.F. Sauvage, Paris, Opéra-Comique, Salle Favart, 30 March 1853; *La cour de Célimène*, T.M.F. Sauvage, Paris, Opéra-Comique, Salle Favart, 11 April 1855; *Psyché*, J. Barbier and M. Carré, Paris, Opéra-Comique, Salle Favart, 26 January 1857; revised, 21 May 1878; *Le carnaval de Venise*, T.M.F. Sauvage, Paris, Opéra-Comique, Salle Favart, 9 December 1857; *Le roman d'Elvire*, A. Dumas père and A. de Leuven, Paris, Opéra-Comique, Salle Favart, 4 February 1860; *Mignon*, J. Barbier and M. Carré (after Goethe, *Wilhelm Meister*), Paris, Opéra-Comique, Salle Favart, 17 November 1866; *Hamlet*, J. Barbier and M. Carré (after Shakespeare), Paris, Opéra, 9 March 1868; *Gille et Gillotin*, T.M.F. Sauvage, 1859 (as *Gillotin et son père*), Paris, Opéra-Comique, Salle Favart, 22 April 1874; *Françoise de Rimini*, J. Barbier and M. Carré (after Dante), Paris, Opéra, 14 April 1882.

Although Ambroise Thomas is a relative unknown today, in the second half of the nineteenth century he was a major force in French music. His twenty operas appeared on all of Paris's leading lyric stages from 1837 onward, and thanks in large measure to the enormous successes of his two masterworks from the 1860s, *Mignon* and *Hamlet*, Thomas served as director of the Paris Conservatory from 1871 until the end of his life. There, for better or for worse, he was in a position to influence the course of French music during the last decades of the century.

Thomas's parents were both music teachers in Metz, and they sent their son to Paris in 1828 to complete his musical education at the Conservatory. He compiled an enviable student record at the august institution, culminating in the Prix de Rome for composition in 1832. During his mandatory three years in the Eternal City, Thomas absorbed well the Italian vocal style, as evidenced by the 1835 collection of six songs *Souvenirs d'Italie,* his first published work and the earliest of nearly forty solo songs he composed throughout his life. Almost immediately upon his return to Paris, Thomas began to write for the lyric stage, at that time the only promising avenue open to a young French composer.

His first attempt in 1837 was *La double échelle,* a one-act comedy premiered at the Opéra-Comique and generously reviewed by Berlioz in the press. Berlioz especially noted Thomas's skill with orchestration (high praise indeed), an important part of Thomas's musical assets. The next year began a series of seven mostly mediocre works that did little to advance Thomas's career. But in 1849 he succeeded with *Le caïd,* a Rossinian comedy, and in 1850 with *Le songe d'une nuit d'été* which, despite its title, is decidedly non-Shakespearean. Here Falstaff, Elizabeth I and Shakespeare himself appear as characters in the opera, the last-named with a severe drinking problem. Another dry spell followed: six unremarkable operas in nine years. In 1856 Thomas joined the Conservatory faculty as teacher of composition, replacing Adolphe Adam. He turned his creative attention to male choruses, composing about a dozen in the late 1850s and the 1860s. These choruses, sturdy and well crafted, along with the solo songs and operas form the bulk of Thomas's entire output. His other works include three ballets and a quantity of sacred and chamber music.

In 1866 Thomas returned to the boards with *Mignon,* derived from the first part of Goethe's *Wilhelm Meister. Mignon* received immediate acclaim, and enjoyed its 1000th performance at the Opéra-Comique by 1894. Less than two years after *Mignon, Hamlet* was an even greater success at the Opéra, and consolidated Thomas's position as the leading composer of French opera on the eve of the Franco-Prussian War.

After assuming the directorship of the Conservatory, Thomas's new responsibilities left little time for composing large-scale works. His final two operas included one that had been composed before 1870, and his last, *Françoise de Rimini* (1882), was a critical failure said to be the biggest disappointment in Thomas's long life. At the Conservatory, Thomas was a careful and conscientious administrator who raised faculty salaries, improved instructional standards, and expanded the local branch conservatories in the provinces. In 1894, two years before his death, Thomas was awarded the Legion of Honor by the French government.

Mignon and *Hamlet* are still performed today, if infrequently. Thomas's most enduring contribution to musical history has to be considered his pioneering development of a new genre of French opera, opéra-lyrique, midway between opéra-comique and grand opera. Opéra-lyrique was to find full maturity in the works of the next generation of French composers, particularly Bizet, Délibes, Lalo and Thomas's favorite pupil Massenet.—MORTON ACHTER

Thomson, Virgil

Composer. Born 25 November 1896, in Kansas City, Missouri. Died 30 September 1989, in New York City. Served in the United States Army, World War I; studied music with E.B. Hill and A.T. Davison at Harvard University, 1919-23; studied piano with Heinrich Gebhard and organ with Wallace Goodrich in Boston; studied with Nadia Boulanger in Paris, 1921-22; studied composition with Rosario Scalero in New York; organist at King's Chapel in Boston, 1923-24; in Paris, 1925-40; director, Society of Friends and Enemies of Modern Music, 1934-37; music critic of the New York Herald Tribune *1940-54; Pulitzer Prize for his score to the film* Louisiana Story, *directed by R. Flaherty, 1948; sixteen honorary doctorates including Harvard University, 1982; awarded the sixth Annual Kennedy Center Honor for lifetime achievement, 1983.*

Operas *Four Saints in Three Acts,* G. Stein, 1927-28, 1933, Hartford, Connecticut, 8 February 1934; *The Mother of Us All,* G. Stein, 1947, New York, 7 May 1947; *Lord Byron,* J. Larson, 1966-68, New York, Juilliard School of Music, 20 April 1972.

Although he studied in Paris with Nadia Boulanger and spent fifteen years composing and writing as an expatriate in stimulating pre-World War II Paris, Virgil Thomson never wholly shed the influences of a boyhood and early youth spent in the very center of the United States. His music with its wit, clever simplicity, and occasional dips into the downright homespun, is American to its heart. An omnivorous reader throughout his life and the author of many books, Thomson was also the deftest of composers for voice, and singers everywhere delight in his wonderfully expressive and apt declamation. His three unconventional operas are testaments to his skill and to his rich and complex American style.

Soon after Thomson met fellow expatriate Gertrude Stein in Paris in 1926, the two began collaborating on the strangely compelling *Four Saints in Three Acts*. Thomson worked at the piano with Stein's stream-of-consciousness text to produce crisply rhythmic, basically diatonic music of enormous vitality. Containing roughly thirty saints in four acts, the setting is the Spain Stein recalled from her travels. Thomson, however, had never been there and leaned heavily on his Southern Baptist upbringing for the religious flavor of the music. Although there are episodes of Anglican chant, his instrumentation and melodies often echo American revivalist meetings, hymn tunes, and even popular dance rhythms. The Hartford, Connecticut premiere on February 8, 1934 featured an all black cast with sets imaginatively designed by Florine Stettheimer of cellophane, crystal, seashells, feathers, and colored lights. The work was an infamous success and the tour of New York and Chicago firmly launched the young composer's career.

Thomson remained in Paris until just before the German occupation in 1940. Arriving in New York with little money and few prospects, he was engaged as music critic for the *New York Herald Tribune* almost immediately and held the post for fourteen years. During this time he also managed to compose a great deal, including the 1946 *The Mother of Us All*. Less abstract than *Four Saints in Three Acts,* the opera's theme is the women's suffrage movement as represented by leader Susan B. Anthony. The nostalgia-tinged music seems familiar since Thomson evokes marches, bugle calls, parlor songs, waltzes, and hymn tunes in the pastiche method which serves him so well. However, with the exception of "London Bridge is Falling Down," all the melodies are original, bearing witness again to Thomson's ever acute ear for musical Americana.

Unable to find an inspiring libretto or librettist, Thomson's third and last opera was not begun until the 1960s. For seven years Thomson worked with poet Jack Larson on the less successful *Lord Byron,* which was premiered in New York at the Juilliard School in 1972. Framed by a choral elegy upon the return of the poet's body to England from Greece and a semi-chorus of welcoming Poets' Corner shades, the opera presents a series of flashback scenes covering Lord Byron's life. Thomson's sensitive and meticulous attention to prosody is evident here too, as well as his playfulness and affinity for deceptively complex simplicity.

Thomson wrote music in all genres with varying degrees of success. He took the musical portrait, a category to which little attention had been paid except for brief essays by Couperin, Schumann, Elgar, and a few others, and made it his own with more than 150 works. However, it was opera that really challenged him and drew upon his musical skills most fully. In general, Thomson's free-wheeling American style may at times lack a deeply personal expressiveness, but there is always an abundance of conviction of some sort, careful craftsmanship, and open-handed wit.—MICHAEL MECKNA

Tibbett, Lawrence

Baritone. Born 16 November 1896, in Bakersfield, California. Died 15 July 1960, in New York City. Married: Grace Mackay Smith, 1919 (divorced 1931); two sons. Studied with Frank La Forge and Basil Ruysdael; began career as actor; also sang in church and light operas, and with a travelling quartet; opera debut as Amonasro, Los Angeles, 1923; Metropolitan Opera debut as Lavitsky in Boris Godunov, *1923; first major success came there with role of Ford in* Falstaff, *1925; remained at Metropolitan for twenty-seven seasons, singing in premieres of Taylor's* The King's Henchman *(1927) and* Peter Ibbetson *(1931), Gruenberg's* The Emperor Jones *(1933), Hanson's* Merry Mount *(1934), and Seymour's* In the Pasha's Garden *(1935), and took part in first Metropolitan performances of* Jonny spielt auf *(1929),* Simon Boccanegra *(1932) and* Peter Grimes *(1949); created title role in Goossens's* Don Juan de Mañara *at Covent Garden (1937); sang at San Francisco (1927-49), Chicago (1936-46), and Cincinnati (1943-46); made last Metropolitan appearance in Mussorgsky's* Khovanshchina, *1950; toured extensively throughout the world and appeared on Broadway and in films; president, American Guild of Musical Artists, 1937-53.*

Lawrence Tibbett is generally recognized as the first American-born, American-trained male opera singer to achieve star status without prior European stage experience.

Tibbett's father, the sheriff of Kern county (California), was killed by an outlaw when Larry was seven years old. His mother then moved with her four children to Los Angeles where Larry grew up. As a youngster he took part in school productions, and after graduation he found various engagements in musicals and plays in the Los Angeles area. For a short while he toured with the Shakespearean company of Tyrone Power, Sr, eventually attracting the attention of the poet Rupert Hughes. Recognizing his talent, Hughes raised a $2,500 loan among his wealthy friends to send Tibbett to New York to study with Frank La Forge. Soon after Tibbett began his studies in 1922, impresario Charles Wagner hired him to replace Giuseppe de Luca on the Metropolitan Quartet, and he toured with Frances Alda, Giovanni Martinelli, and Carolina Lazzari from 1922 through 1925.

In January 1923, La Forge arranged an audition for Tibbett with the Metropolitan Opera. It was unsuccessful, but in May he tried again and was hired at $60 a week. His inconspicuous debut with the Met followed on 24 November 1923, as Lovitsky in *Boris Godunov* with Chaliapin in the title role. He learned his next role, Valentin in *Faust* (again with Chaliapin), in three days when he had to step in for an ailing Vincente Ballester.

Tibbett sang several small roles in his first season, and his second season started the same way. His big break came when he was asked to take over the role of Ford, again for Ballester, in a new production of *Falstaff* with Antonio Scotti in the title role. Left alone onstage to deliver Ford's monologue, "I let myself go with all I had," he wrote later of that first night on 2 January 1925. "In my aria . . . I tore my heart out." The audience went wild. The ovation lasted for over ten minutes and the performance could not proceed until Tibbett was called back for a solo bow. The incident was written up in all the major newspapers and magazines, and Tibbett became a celebrity overnight.

As Tibbett developed artistically, he was given more challenging assignments. He sang Wolfram, Telramund, Amonasro, Scarpia. In 1926, he took over the role of Neri from Titta Ruffo in *La cena delle beffe* (Giordano), and in 1929, the role of Jonny from Michael Bohnen in Krenek's *Jonny spielt auf*. The first production mounted specifically for him was the Metropolitan premiere of Verdi's *Simon Boccanegra* on 28 January 1932. The performance was a great personal success for Tibbett, and the opera was chosen to open the following season.

Tibbett sang several seasons with the Chicago and San Francisco opera companies, but his artistic home remained the Metropolitan where he performed 442 times in the house, 160 times on tour. During his twenty-seven seasons there he sang forty-nine roles in thirty-seven operas, at times graduating from comprimario to leading roles, from Morales to Escamillo, from Silvio to Tonio, from the Herald to Telramund. He also earned high praise for his portrayals of Rigoletto, Iago, and Falstaff. Equally at home on the concert platform, Tibbett gave solo recitals in many cities throughout the United States. He made his first international tour in 1937, appearing in opera (*Rigoletto, Otello*) and concert in England, France, Hungary, and the Scandinavian countries, to enthusiastic audience reception and critical acclaim. He toured Australia and New Zealand in 1938, Italy in 1946, and London and South Africa in 1947.

In 1940, Tibbett's voice was afflicted by some still undisclosed illness and his gradual vocal decline is traceable to that time. He continued to sing at the Metropolitan until 1950; his last performance in opera

Lawrence Tibbett as Rigoletto

was as Ivan Khovansky in *Khovanshchina,* on 24 March 1950. He then appeared in Broadway plays and musicals, and in 1956, he replaced Ezio Pinza in the Broadway production of *Fanny*. He pioneered opera on television and sang the elder Germont in a condensed TV version of *La traviata* in 1950.

His film career began in 1930, with *The Rogue Song,* and in the same year he made his second film, *New Moon,* with soprano Grace Moore. Of his other four films the most interesting from a musical standpoint is *Metropolitan* (1935) with a handful of complete opera arias and songs. Concurrently with his films, Tibbett launched his radio career, and the triple exposure—stage, film, radio—made him a national celebrity.

As contemporary criticism and posterity agree, Lawrence Tibbett's powerful, virile voice ranks with the best of this century. A true bass-baritone with an even scale from a high B natural down to a low F, it was equal to the demands of all the roles in his large repertory. In his best years he could reduce his rich and resonant voice to an exquisite pianissimo or project it over a full orchestra. Although he sang in five languages, Tibbett never learned to speak any of them and had to learn his roles by rote. At the same time his dramatic and expressive phrasing is interpretatively correct, leaving no doubt that he was thoroughly familiar (in translation) with the texts he sang. Giving the right inflection and texture to the words, he was able to weave a magical aura around an aria, a song, a ballad, entering into the psyche of the character. He consistently earned high praise for his acting, and the large number of commercial recordings and airchecks demonstrate that Tibbett was an imaginative performer and an accomplished vocalist who could act with his voice as well. He was a successful interpreter of a wide range of music, equally at home in nineteenth century operas and in new, modern compositions. Some of his recordings, notably his model interpretations of the Toreador Song from *Carmen* and the Te Deum from *Tosca* are arguably in a class by themselves, and his selections from *Porgy and Bess,* sung in dialect and recorded under the supervision of the composer, are interpretative gems.

Tibbett's 78 rpm recording career was exclusively with the Victor Talking Machine Co. and RCA Victor. These recordings captured his voice at its peak, spanning the years 1926 to 1940. The long playing records of songs and arias he made for the Royale and other labels ca. 1955, show the deterioration of his voice and do a great disservice to his memory. Fortunately, an extraordinary number of his radio performances and live Metropolitan Opera broadcasts have survived. Many of these have been privately issued on "The Golden Age of Opera" and UORC labels. These give a fair idea of Tibbett's remarkable talent and great versatility as a singing actor. His exceptionally beautiful and manly speaking voice is preserved on film and in interviews.

Not forgetting his personal and musical origins, Tibbett championed the cause of American artists. He took part in several world premieres: Deems Taylor's *The King's Henchman* (1927) and *Peter Ibbetson* (1931); Louis Gruenberg's *The Emperor Jones* (1933), a great artistic triumph for Tibbett; Howard Hanson's *Merry Mount* (1934); and J.L. Seymour's *In the Pasha's Garden* (1935). In 1937, he created the title role in Eugene Goossens' *Don Juan de Mañara* at Covent Garden. Wanting to protect all performers regardless of status, he organized the American Guild of Musical Artists (AGMA), a national labor union. He became its first president in 1937, and he held the office until 1953.

Because of his language handicap, he could easily identify with the American opera-goer, and he was a lifelong advocate of opera in English. His sunny, open, down-to-earth personality is well captured in his chatty autobiography, *The Glory Road*. But that was in 1933, near the crest of his fame. The downhill slide began seven years later, and his vocal problems and diminished powers reportedly had a destructive effect on his personal life, the details of which have been kept private by his family. Following an automobile accident, Tibbett was operated on 27 June 1960; he later lapsed into a coma and died on 15 July 1960, in New York City. Fortunately, the many facets of his unique talent have been preserved on recordings and film; they show the quintessential American operatic artist, the first of many who followed in his pioneering footsteps.—ANDREW FARKAS

Tippett, (Sir) Michael (Kemp)

Composer. Born 2 January 1905, in London. Studied composition with Charles Wood and C.H. Kitson at the Royal College of Music in London, 1923-28; studied piano with Aubin Raymar and conducting with Sir Adrian Boult and Sir Malcolm Sargent; studied counterpoint and fugue with R.O. Morris, 1930-32; directed the South London Orchestra at Morley College, 1933-1940; music director at Morley College, 1940-51; served a three month term in jail for his refusal to serve in the military, 21 June to 21 August 1943; broadcasts for the British Broadcasting Corporation, 1951; director of the Bath Festival, 1969-74; Commander of the Order of the British Empire, 1959; visited the United States, 1965, 1972, 1989, 1991; knighted, 1966.

Operas *The Village Opera*, realization of the ballad opera by C. Johnson (1729) with added music, 1928; *Robin Hood* (with D. Ayerst and R. Pennyman), Tippett, D. Ayerst, and R. Pennyman, 1934; *The Midsummer Marriage*, Tippett, 1946-52, London, Covent Garden, 27 January 1955; *King Priam*, Tippett, 1958-61, Coventry, Belgrade, 29 May 1962; *The Knot Garden*, Tippett, 1966-69, London, Covent Garden, 2 December 1970; *The Ice Break*, Tippett, 1973-76, London, Covent Garden, 7 July 1977; *New Year*, Tippett, 1985-88, Houston, Grand Opera, October 1989.

It is not too much to claim that Michael Tippett's five operas are among his most powerful statements about his belief in humanity, a belief that has consistently informed all his works. To know the operas is to know the composer: his aesthetic creed, the scope of his literary and philosophical influences, the force of his musicianship, and the warmth of his personality.

The operas have appeared at the rate of one in each decade of the sixty years of his career as composer. They reveal significant philosophical and musical thinking and have been influenced by or have influenced works around them in his output.

Tippett's first oratorio, *A Child of Our Time* (1939-1941), focuses on the Jungian idea of human duality, the shadow and light of human nature, and considers the consequences of deeds governed by our darker inclinations. The first opera, *The Midsummer Marriage* (1946-1952), followed soon after and is considered by Tippett as a pendant to the oratorio. It is a lyric, symbolic opera about the reconciliation between our light and dark forces and the ultimate acquisition of wholeness. In its turn, this opera became a powerful source of inspiration for two subsequent orchestral works. The *Piano Concerto* (1952-1955) reflects the opera's "magic" music and the "ascent" music of the heroine as she begins her search for wholeness. The *Second Symphony* (1957) is the orchestral counterpart of the opera, manifesting sound akin to the operatic score and using a Stravinsky-like developmental process that reflects the ritualistic atmosphere of the opera.

The dramatic necessities of Tippett's second opera, *King Priam* (1958-61), an opera about human choice and the relentless consequences thereof, drove Tippett to a drastic change of style. All the works written in the shadow of that opera reflect the change. *The Lullaby for Six Voices* (1960) uses musical ideas that appear in the opera. Its bitonality, for example, foreshadows that of the scene between Paris and Helen in the opera. The *Concerto for Orchestra* (completed in 1963) issued directly out of the opera in that its layered instrumental sounds depict various dramatic ideas, a dramaturgical technique used everywhere in the opera. The form of the *Second Piano Sonata* (1962) is derived from the formal procedures of *King Priam*. The music of the sonata, like that of the opera, proceeds now by flow, now by rest, and the unity comes from constant variation and repetition of new material.

The creative impulse of the third opera, *The Knot Garden* (1966-1969), sheds its light on surrounding works too. Two of the three *Songs for Ariel* that Tippett wrote for a performance of *The Tempest* in 1962 are quoted in the opera. Their use occurs in a scene where, like Prospero in the Shakespeare play, Mangus has the six other characters enact charades in order to help them be reconciled to one another. The first work that stems directly from *The Knot Garden* is *The Songs for Dov* (1970). In the opera, Dov, the white male of a homosexual couple whose black lover has rejected him, is the only one of seven characters whose characterization is incomplete at the opera's end. The *Songs* draw Dov's journey into personal discovery more fully. *Symphony No. 3* (1972) owes the world of its sound to *The Knot Garden*. To give but one example, the Symphony uses the blues both as a stylistic element and, as in the opera, a dramatic means of speaking about human love and understanding.

Tippett's fourth opera, *The Ice Break* (1973-1976), is one of his most realistic and certainly the most violent. If the music of the first three operas is metaphorical for reconciliation and renewal of the human spirit, the realism of the gun shots, police sirens, and foot stomping in *The Ice Break* shows "the extent to which Tippett was prepared to divest his music of metaphor and make his message as clear as possible" (Kemp, 1984, p. 462). The message is for us to abandon

t

OPERA

faith in the false gods that abound in our time and place it in our own humanity—a constant concept in Tippett's credo. What is unique in *The Ice Break* is the harsh sounds of the chorus as mob-worshipping stereotypical idols constantly breaking into the gentler sounds of the soloists who portray the fear and hope of the individual. Remembrance of the "musique concrète" of the mob scenes almost obviates the gentleness of the ethereal music of hope at the opera's end.

The Ice Break appears to have no direct musical descendants. Having uttered in this opera his strongest statements of distrust of modern society's false gods, Tippett next enters a new world of expression. With *Symphony No. 4* (1976-1977)—already in his mind as *The Ice Break* was being finished—the *Triple Concerto* (1978-1979), the second oratorio *A Mask of Time* (1980-1982), *The Blue Guitar* (1982-1983), *Piano Sonata No. 4* (1983-1984), and the fifth opera *New Year* (1985-1988), Tippett's vision has become both more expansive and more serene, his musical style as challenging as ever, yet more appealing.

Since *The Knot Garden*, jazz and blues-inspired harmony and instrumentation have become a factor in each opera. In *The Ice Break*, use of off-stage electronically projected sounds entered Tippett's "scoring." In *New Year*, Tippett increases his use of electronic sound. He writes taped electronic music that is used to accompany the take-off and landing of a space ship traveling between "today" and "tomorrow." The influence of musical theater is also very significant: there is exciting dance music depicting the energy of street crowds and a character acting as narrator whose singing is pop, not classical.

As with the earlier operas, in *New Year* Tippett once again dramatizes the search for full human potential. Situations, characters, and musical techniques here recall the same in earlier operas; in this fifth opera they appear more gently or more exuberantly handled and in many ways more appealing. The heroine Jo Ann, for example, reminds one of Jenifer in *The Midsummer Marriage*: each must find her true identity by undergoing ritualistic purification. The arias of both heroines bear the stamp of melismatic vocalism typical of Tippett's style for significant characters, but Jo Ann's is a simpler, more easy-going lyricism, depicting a gentler character than that of Jenifer. Donny, Jo Ann's black adoptive step-brother, is strongly reminiscent of Mel, the black homosexual in *The Knot Garden*. Both represent a kind of primitive who mocks the real world because he does not fit in. Tippett gives to Donny some of the most interesting vocal music and certainly the most physically and musically exciting solo dance music of any that he has written. He thus depicts, in more memorable detail than in *The Knot Garden*, a human being at odds with himself.

Nowhere are the comparisons and contrasts between the operas more significant than in Tippett's messenger figures. Each opera has one. In *The Midsummer Marriage*, the messenger is Sosostris, stunningly assured in her role as visionary. In *King Priam*, the messenger is Hermes, detached but appealing intermediary between the divine and human worlds. Mangus in *The Knot Garden* would untangle the complex web of others' failing relationships but must finally admit that he is no wiser than they. In *The Ice Break*, the androgynous messenger figure, Astron, excels only at self-mockery and tells us to forego the myth of blind hero worship. Pelegrin, the messenger figure in *New Year*, is at the center of the drama, its hero. As space-pilot mediating between "tomorrow" and "today," he seeks out the heroine Jo Ann. Through his disinterested yet deeply loving guidance, she is led from fear of her world to the self-assurance she needs to face its realities.

The messenger figure in his operas is, of course, a metaphor for the composer himself. In 1965, Tippett admitted that Hermes stood for the artist, "for myself—the go-between one world and another . . ." ("Music and Poetry," *Recorded Sound,* January, 1965, 292). He must surely say the same again in 1989 of Pelegrin, the most significantly dramatized messenger figure of his career.

The integrity of Tippett's vision and the unique eclecticism of his musical style point to a man of strong individuality and catholicity of interests. His individuality manifested itself early in his training. While a student of conducting and composition at the Royal College of Music (1923-1928), he taught himself Renaissance counterpoint and the music of the English madrigalists, and arranged to direct a choir to put his study to practical use. In the 1930s he was introduced to left-wing politics, but decided before the decade was out that an active role in politics would stand in the way of his role as musician. So strong was his belief in that role that he endured a three-month prison term in 1943 during the war rather than conform to rules that he considered did not apply to composers who were conscientious objectors.

As Director of Music at Morley College (1940-1951) and Artistic Director of the Bath Festival (1969-1974), Tippett manifested his genius for working well with colleagues, maintaining a cordial atmosphere for music-making and conducting, and developing highly musical and enterprising concert programs.

The inspiration for his varied works springs in part from his catholicity of interests as well as from friends and artistic mentors. The operas alone reflect the breadth of his reading: Shakespeare, Goethe, Frazer, Jung, Fry, Eliot, Pasternak and Solzhenitsyn, to name but a few. T.S. Eliot was the most significant artistic mentor in Tippett's life. Over the years, their considerations of verse and drama finally led Tippett, at Eliot's insistence, to be his own librettist for the oratorios and operas. Since his student days, his voracious appetite for a wide variety of musical styles has influenced his own style. Madrigals, rap, the musical *Fame,* gamelan music, the music of Purcell, Wagner, Stravinsky, Beethoven—he has studied each and assimilated and used them as he saw fit. The continuing vigor of his musical style attests to his enduring capacity to be inspired and—what is more significant—to be inspiring. In 1958 in *Moving into Aquarius,* Tippett stated that his role in this new age is to ". . . try to transform the everyday by a touch of the everlasting . . . to project into our mean world music which is rich and generous." In the last three decades, every major work has fulfilled that pledge.—MARGARET SCHEPPACH

Tosca

Composer: *Giacomo Puccini.*

Librettists: *Giuseppe Giacosa and Luigi Illica (after Sardou).*

First Performance: *Rome, Costanzi, 14 January 1900.*

Roles: *Floria Tosca (soprano); Mario Cavaradossi (tenor); Scarpia (baritone); Cesare Angelotti (bass); Sacristan (baritone); Spoletta (tenor); Sciarrone (bass); a Jailer (bass); a Shepherd Boy (boy soprano); chorus (SSATTBB).*

Based on a very popular play Victorien Sardou wrote as a vehicle for Sarah Bernhardt, *Tosca* is a thriller with great situations, characters, and philosophical and religious ideas. The libretto by Luigi Illica and Giuseppe Giacosa shortens and tightens the drama of the play. The opera, set in Rome during the revolutionary Napoleonic period, features a famous opera singer in love with the political revolutionary Mario Cavaradossi. Tosca meets her lover in the church of Sant' Andrea della Valle as he paints a scene of Mary Magdalene. But before she arrives, he has helped to hide a political prisoner, Angelotti. Baron Scarpia, the chief of police, enters looking for the political prisoner. By the end of the act, Cavaradossi is implicated and Scarpia decides to question Cavaradossi about the whereabouts of Angelotti.

The second act takes place in the Palazzo Farnese, where Cavaradossi is being tortured to force him to reveal the hiding place of Angelotti. When Tosca enters to negotiate with Scarpia, she hears Mario's screams under torture. Scarpia proposes a deal—if she'll spend the night with him, he will release her lover. In her desperation, she agrees. Scarpia says, however, that he can't release him openly and there will be a sham execution, after which she and Mario will be free to leave Rome. When Scarpia rushes to Tosca for his sexual demands, she stabs him to death instead. In the final act Mario Cavaradossi, imprisoned in Castel Sant' Angelo, is awaiting execution. Tosca rushes in to tell him that she has killed Scarpia, and that the execution will be done with blanks, after which they will be free to leave Rome forever. However, the act ends with Mario's execution and Tosca's suicide.

Thematically, the core of the opera is the conflict between Tosca's belief in God and the Catholic Church and Mario Cavaradossi's agnosticism, perhaps atheism. Between these two ideological poles moves the powerful Baron Scarpia, who outwardly expresses a devout belief in God and the Church but in actuality is a hypocrite who uses his powers as Rome's chief of police to destroy the rebellion against the old regime in any way expedient, and who also uses his political power to force women to go to bed with him.

Tosca's killing of Scarpia in the second act is preceded by her famous aria, "Vissi d'arte," which is at the philosophical core of the opera. She says that she has lived for art and love, and to do good in the world, and she asks God why He is putting her in such a horrible situation. Her prayer includes that most profound question: Why does God allow the suffering of the innocent? Her only response is Scarpia's renewed demands for her favors in exchange for the life of Cavaradossi.

In the last act, Mario sings his final aria, "E lucevan le stelle"—his thoughts before he dies are of the beauty of Tosca's body and the intensity of his love for her. Tosca thinks she has outsmarted Scarpia and that this execution will only be a sham, but she is sadly mistaken. The bullets are real, and Mario is killed; Tosca's final words and suicide in the opera suggest that she does not want to continue living in a world where Mario's philosophy of life prevails.
—JOHN LOUIS DIGAETANI

Die tote Stadt [The Dead City]

Composer: *Erich Wolfgang Korngold.*

Librettist: *Paul Schott [=E.W. and J. Korngold] (after Georges Rodenbach, Bruges la morte).*

First Performance: *Hamburg and Cologne, 4 December 1920.*

Roles: *Paul (tenor); Marietta (soprano); Frank (baritone); Fritz (tenor); Count Albert (tenor); Brigitta (contralto); Vision of Marie (soprano); Juliette (soprano); Lucienne (mezzo-soprano); Gaston (tenor); Victorin (tenor); chorus (SATB).*

Critics call it kitsch, but members of the Erich Wolfgang Korngold Society call *Die tote Stadt* the composer's best opera, possibly even his best work. This opera, his third, premiered when Korngold was only twenty-three years of age; the boy-genius had composed two others while still in his teens. Although *Die tote Stadt* was initially received well, its lush, romantic style grew out of favor, and the work was ignored for years. It was revived in the mid 1970s to mixed reviews, and has maintained a modest place in the operatic repertoire since.

The libretto was based on Georges Rodenbach's novel *Bruges la morte,* a symbolist work about death and decay. In the quiet, almost deserted grey city of Bruges, the hero Hughes has lost his beloved wife, but he cannot accept her death; he begins each day by worshipping at the altar he built to honor her relic—a plait of her hair. One day, he meets a dancer who strongly resembles his dead wife. After spending the night with her, Hughes becomes consumed with guilt, and when she mocks his altar and the sacred tress of hair, he kills her and collapses, muttering that everything is death in Bruges.

The young Erich Korngold and his father, music critic Julius Korngold, wrote the libretto under the name of Paul Schott: Paul for their hero's name (changed from Hughes to Paul) and Schott for Erich's publishing firm, B. Schott's Söhne in Mainz, to whose senior partner, Ludwig Stecker, the composer dedicated his opera. Korngold took the dark story and lightened it with his youthful perspective. The opera opens in Paul's apartment. Brigitta is showing Frank the altar Paul has made to his dead wife Marie. An excited Paul enters claiming that he has found Marie alive, and tells them how he met Marietta, the dancer, who is the very image of his wife. Frank tries to dissuade him from his fantasy. He leaves, and Paul begins to rhapsodize about his Marie. Marietta appears to pick up the umbrella she left behind. She stays for a while, singing and dancing for Paul. After she leaves, Paul imagines he sees Marie step out from the frame of her portrait. Later, Marietta returns from performing with her troupe. She taunts Paul by dancing with the braided hair of his wife from the altar, and he kills her, and collapses. Then, the door opens, and Marietta appears to ask Paul for her umbrella: he has been dreaming. This time when she asks to stay, he tells her to leave. He has learned from his dream to live in the present, not the past.

Korngold used a rich, expressionistic musical language for his opera. While tonal, the work is filled with rich chromaticisms and dissonances. His orchestration calls upon a large orchestra that includes bass trumpet, two harps, celesta, piano, harmonia, and pipe organ. As a brilliant melodist, he wrote vocal lines of splendid tunes that show off the voices. The work is lush and sonorously luxuriant.

In 1920, *Die tote Stadt* premiered with much fanfare and praise. Two opera companies, one in Hamburg and one in Colgone, gave it its world premiere on the same night, and much was made of the composer's youth. During the following years, it appeared in over eighty opera ·houses throughout the world, including the Metropolitan Opera in New York in 1921. It received rave reviews. One critic from Hamburg wrote: "The music grows so powerfully out of the text that it determines the significance of the work and turns it into one of the most important operas written in a long time. The intellectual content . . . does not prevent Korngold from writing a thoroughly musicianly work in which genuine melody comes into its own again, without neglecting progressive art and its laws. This combination turns the opera into a musical masterwork and also gives us new hope for the future of German art." But as the serial method of composition rose in favor, Korngold's tonal language became unfashionable, and the opera was dropped. At the outbreak of World War II, Korngold left Europe for Hollywood and put his fine musical drama skills to work for the movies. At the end of the war when he began writing absolute music again, he could not get his works performed. Not only was his music the wrong style, he was further stigmatized as a film composer and was no longer regarded as a "serious composer." It took thirty years—fifteen years after his death—for interest in his music to renew.

In 1972, RCA released a recording of Korngold's film music. Audiences at once recognized the quality of his work and a general revival of his music followed. In 1975, New York City Opera produced *Die tote Stadt;* this production was followed by others throughout Europe. The work is still occasionally performed today. While there has been enough interest to keep it in the repertoire, critics do not all agree as to its quality. Ann Lingg, writing in *Opera News,* called Korngold "a master of surging melody," and praised the opera's "full sonorities, telling leitmotifs, uncanny musical characterization and bold harmonies that never manage to offend the ear." Yet others were less pleased at the revivals. Martin Bernheimer, the Los Angeles critic, called the work "a masterpiece of Junk." He thought the music was "grandiose, overblown, big-band kitsch." The libretto, he wrote, "lent new depths of meaning to such words as mawkish and maudlin." James Helme Sutcliffe, writing in *Opera,* agreed that "with its over-used glockenspiel and ever-present harp and piano glissandos, Korngold's *Die tote Stadt* may not be musically to everyone's taste."

Erich Korngold the child prodigy did not lose his popularity by peaking early and losing his creative edge. Rather, he was a victim of radically changing tastes. Likewise, his opera was dropped from the repertoire not through lack of quality or any intrinsic flaw, but because the lush sound fell out of favor. When the pendulum of fashion swings the other way, the work may become a firm part of the operatic canon.—ROBIN ARMSTRONG

Traubel, Helen

Soprano. Born 20 June 1899, in St Louis. Died 28 July 1972, in Santa Monica, California. Studied with Vetta Karst; concert debut with St Louis Symphony Orchestra; Metropolitan Opera debut as Mary Rutledge in Damrosch's The Man without a Country, *1937; first major role with the Met was as Sieglinde in 1939; remained there until 1953; also appeared in Chicago and San Francisco.*

It seems that Helen Traubel will be remembered as the "other" great Wagnerian soprano of her time, for her career almost directly parallels that of the legendary Kirsten Flagstad. Traubel's Metropolitan Opera debut, in fact, was in *Die Walküre* where she sang Sieglinde to Flagstad's Brünnhilde. And it was the departure of Flagstad for Europe in 1941—amidst a flurry of rumors of Nazi collaboration—which finally opened to Traubel the preeminent position among female Wagnerians at the Metropolitan Opera.

That Traubel's career is somewhat overshadowed by Flagstad should not, however, imply that she was an inferior singer, for in fact Traubel's was a remarkable voice, warm and golden-toned, of great size and solidly placed—a true dramatic soprano. It is only by comparison with Flagstad that she perhaps is found wanting, and then only to a degree. Traubel's top notes, for example, do not satisfy as they should—the powerful and gleaming middle of the voice leaves us anticipating a glorious climax which is not always forthcoming. This flaw became more pronounced as she grew older, but it was noticeable from the start, as off-the-air recordings show her shying away from exposed high passages, and we read that in her Met performances of Isolde she left out the written high Cs.

Like Flagstad, Traubel was not always an involving actress. Her recording of the Narrative and Curse from *Tristan und Isolde,* for example, is among the most impressive pieces of singing on record, but there are many colors and moods to Isolde's character which here are generalized into one. Later, in the love music from the same opera, the shining tone and firmness cannot be faulted, but where passion and involvement are called for, Traubel offers instead an unrelenting, statuesque grandeur.

Perhaps this lack of dramatic spirit explains why she didn't choose to pursue much operatic music outside of the Wagnerian repertoire. Traubel made some records of Italian arias, often not ideally chosen for her (entirely apart from her dramatic gifts, she was never a natural Desdemona or Norma) and again the amplitude and brightness of the voice give much pleasure, but roles like Santuzza and Donna Anna need a passion that just isn't forthcoming.

This said, there are many great records which preserve Traubel at her magnificent best. Her performance of Brünnhilde's Immolation Scene, conducted by Toscanini with all the excitement we would expect, is still among the best ever—here the high notes give her no trouble and at last there is the nobility and excitement which we wanted all along. And there are some lovely souvenirs of Traubel as a recitalist, notably a spacious and superbly secure performance of Richard Strauss' "Zueignung" as well as some Beethoven arrangements of English folksongs where the crisp enunciation and personal warmth are especially pleasing.

What may have limited Traubel's career far more than her few vocal problems was her own overwhelming and rather hearty personality, and in particular her insistence on maintaining a high profile in the popular arts. She appeared frequently on television, and even recorded some comic duets with Jimmy Durante, where her vivid personality fairly jumps off the disc and she reminds us of Sophie Tucker—where is this singer in all of her opera roles? She even developed her own nightclub act, centered around a heavily orchestrated and really quite unappetizing arrangement of "Saint Louis Blues." This secondary career met with substantial disapproval from the Met's general manager, Rudolf Bing, and, after a rather well publicized skirmish between the two, Traubel left the Met in 1953, never to return. This did not end her remarkable career; in 1955 she even appeared in a Broadway musical, *Pipe Dream,* which has the dubious distinction of being the shortest running show in the Rodgers and Hammerstein canon. She had little of the proper manner for this material—some late recordings of American popular song are, like the original cast album of *Pipe Dream,* better left unheard. They are certainly not representative of the soprano who, at her formidable best, may be counted as one of the great Wagner singers of our age.—DAVID ANTHONY FOX

La traviata [The Strayed Woman]

Composer: *Giuseppe Verdi.*

Librettist: *Francesco Maria Piave (after Dumas fils, La dame aux camélias).*

First Performance: *Venice, La Fenice, 6 March 1853.*

Roles: *Violetta Valéry (soprano); Alfredo Germont (tenor); Giorgio Germont (baritone); Flora Bervoix (soprano or mezzo-soprano); Baron Douphol (baritone); Gastone (tenor);*

Marquis D'Obigny (bass); Doctor Grenville (bass); Annina (mezzo-soprano); Joseph (tenor); Commissionaire (bass); Flora's Servant (bass); chorus (SSATTBB).

After a delicate prelude, which foretells the opera's tragic theme in its simple but expressive, tender pathos, *La traviata* opens with an exuberant celebration in the luxurious apartments of Violetta Valéry. Musically and affectively, the contrast is extraordinary. Verdi employs similar emotive contrasts to underscore various ironies throughout the plot. Violetta is a popular figure in *demi-mondaine* Paris. Beautiful, carefree, and secure in the protection of Baron Douphol, she is devoted to her frivolous existence, and unaware that one of the guests, young Alfredo Germont, has been deeply in love with her for more than a year. But he soon makes known to her the depth of his feeling, first in a magnificent toast before the assembled guests, and then again in an impassioned aria. This aria, *"Di quell' amor ch'e palpito dell' universo"* ("With that love that is the very breath of the universe") becomes the central melody of the opera, symbolic of Alfredo's genuine love for Violetta and, eventually, of hers for him. Verdi plays on the nostalgic quality of this beautiful melody with magnificent psychological effect later, when estrangement and then death separate the lovers.

Reluctant to break off relations with Baron Douphol, and still enamored of her free and easy life, Violetta is at first unwilling to make the total commitment Alfredo seeks. However, his innocence, sincerity, and intensity at last win her over. She accepts both his love and his offer to care for her for the rest of her life. Already, her frequent coughing spells and fits of weakness reveal that she suffers poor health.

Three months later, Violetta and Alfredo are happily living together in a country estate which she has rented. Here, Verdi's music conjures up an idyllic bliss, which also will provide for musical flash-back when tragedy occurs. Upon discovering that Violetta is on the brink of bankruptcy, as a result of the expenses of their new life together, Alfredo hurries away to Paris to draw upon his inheritance and so stave off financial disaster. By mischance, Alfredo's father, Giorgio Germont, arrives during Alfredo's absence. He has come on a special mission, which is to persuade Violetta to end her affair with Alfredo. She resists Germont's arguments, until at last he explains that her past reputation not only is harming Alfredo's prospects, but will inevitably destroy his sister's forthcoming marriage to a young man from a fine family. Faced with this argument, she capitulates, agreeing to leave Alfredo for good at once. This scene is a *tour de force* of impassioned musical declamation, coupled with apt characterization.

Alfredo returns from Paris just as Violetta is finishing her farewell note. (Already she has asked Baron Douphol to take her back.) She conceals its contents from Alfredo until the Baron's carriage has come for her. When she is on her way, a messenger delivers the note, which explains, falsely, that she no longer loves him, and is returning to her former lover. Alfredo's father returns from the garden just then and prevents him from following after Violetta. Alfredo is unwilling to listen to his father's reasoning.

Still nursing his jealous anger, Alfredo attends unbidden a fête at the home of Flora Bevon, Violetta's former friend and confidante. Alfredo gambles recklessly and wins large sums of money, mainly from Baron Douphol, who meanwhile had arrived with Violetta. Alfredo then humiliates Violetta, denouncing her perfidy, and throwing all his winnings at her. His father upbraids him severely for his churlishness, his stern anger bringing Alfredo to his senses. But repentance comes too late to ward off the Baron's challenge to a duel.

Several months later, Violetta, lying on what soon will be her deathbed, receives a letter from Giorgio Germont explaining that the duel has taken place, the Baron has been wounded but recovering, and Alfredo has gone abroad. Alfredo's father has explained her sacrifice, and the two have reconciled. Soon both men visit her, hoping to make amends and start anew. Alfredo renews his vow of love and promises to take Violetta to the country again, where they may live in happiness forever after. But Violetta, sensing the approach of death, gives him a medallion portrait of herself, asking him to show it to the young lady who will one day win his heart. With a brief return of energy, Violetta rises from her bed, only to be overcome by death.

Having startled his public by presenting a plot based on free love, and having broken with convention in choosing a contemporary subject, Verdi composed for *La traviata* one of the deepest and most psychologically revealing scores of his career. The impassioned melody of the aria "Di quell' amore" becomes a veritable *idée fixe,* which at various points in the unfolding story recalls states of former happiness, contrasting these most poignantly with current woes of the main protagonists. Not until he composes *Otello* towards the end of his life will Verdi again find such psychological depth in depicting human tragedy.—FRANKLIN ZIMMERMAN

Treemonisha

Composer: *Scott Joplin.*

Librettist: *Scott Joplin.*

First Performance: *New York, 1915.*

Roles: *Treemonisha (soprano); Monisha (soprano); Lucy (soprano); Remus (tenor); Andy (tenor); Cephus (tenor); Zodzetrick (baritone); Ned (bass); Luddud (bass); Simon (bass); Parson Alltalk (bass); chorus.*

Joplin's progress in composition and his disassociation from ragtime is extremely evident in the opera *Treemonisha,* his final extended composition. Although essentially a folk opera, it is conceived in a "grand" manner. An overture precedes the first act and a prelude precedes each of the other two acts. Within the opera there are no spoken parts. Recitatives, arias, and ensembles abound, and in each situation the type of performance sought is indigenous to the story of the opera.

Preparations for *Treemonisha* began early in Joplin's career, perhaps soon after he composed *A Guest of Honor.* Around 1907 Eubie Blake met Joplin in Washington, D.C., and mentioned that Joplin was seeking copyright for the opera. In 1908, Joplin is known to have played portions of the opera for Joseph F. Lamb. However, *Treemonisha* was not published until 1911, and then Joplin had to set up his own publishing company in order to secure publication. It was during this time that Joplin and his publisher John Stark had a serious misunderstanding concerning the awarding of royalties. Between 1911 and 1915, Joplin looked long and in vain for backers, supporters, and producers. An informal performance held in a small Harlem theater in 1915 failed, and the failure apparently broke the back of the "King of Ragtime," for he was soon after committed to a state hospital. Nevertheless, today we have a fine recording and a video of the opera by the Houston Grand Opera company.

As the opera begins the conjurors are intent upon controlling the Negro community, but Treemonisha aims to thwart their purposes. Later Treemonisha is captured by the conjurors, who plan to cast her in the wasps' nest; however, Remus and other men from the community capture the conjurors and rescue Treemonisha, whereupon all proceed back to the plantation. The Negro community wishes to punish the conjurors, but Treemonisha and Remus persuade the people to forgive them. The community hails Treemonisha as their leader, so that they may be free from the plight of conjuring and superstition.

The overture to the first act, the introduction to the second act, and the prelude to the third act of the opera are conceived in a rhapsodic manner, but formal coherence is achieved by the reiteration of themes which express the story and the emotional content of the opera. Several themes from various parts of the opera are heard in the overture, which opens with the theme that Joplin claims is the principal strain in the opera. It appears when Monisha explains why she has named her little girl Treemonisha, and when Treemonisha is rescued from the conjurors. The introduction to the second act and the prelude to the third act of the opera are fairly programmatic in conception, since both signify in their mood the coming events. The somber nature of the introduction to the second act suggests the ensuing conjurors' meeting at the wasps' nest, and the prelude to the third act literally defines the impending joy and utter relief of Treemonisha's mother and father when she is returned to the community. The type of syncopation that occurs in the rags of Joplin may be noticed in the prelude to the third act, but it is softened by a moving bass line rather than the "oompah" bass usually associated with ragtime. Also novel is that each of the instrumental selections that precede an act are closed in structure, rather than open as in a ragtime composition.

The vocal writing in *Treemonisha* makes one overlook what many consider a weak libretto, for it is here that Joplin demonstrates his genius. The vocal writing comprises choruses, recitatives, arias, and ariosos, and in one instance Joplin employs a through-composed aria for one soloist. This is "The Sacred Tree" sung by Monisha when she explains to the community why they must not harm the tree that grew in front of her home. The aria, which is quite lengthy, displays melodic variety and harmonic subtleties of a very high order. Another magnificent aria is "Wrong Is Never Right" sung by Remus after the conjurors have been captured. Though strophic in conception and closing with a choral rendition of the aria, the manner in which Joplin handles the roulades of the aria is particularly astounding.

A particularly striking example of Joplin's genius occurs in the ensemble section entitled "Confusion," which closes the first act of the opera. To express the horror of Treemonisha being captured by the conjurors, Joplin used the device called *Sprechstimme* (speech-song) initiated by Engelbert Humperdinck in 1897 and further developed by Arnold Schoenberg between 1910 and 1913. Joplin gives directions in the score that women should indicate crying, and that the crying should start on a high pitch and the sound gradually diminish. The men speak in crying tones indicated by headless notes. Joplin also indicates that the crying need not be in strict time, but the accompaniment must be. This is surely an innovative step by Joplin, suggesting his enormous creative ability and giving him a seminal position in music history.—ADDISON W. REED

Treigle, Norman

Bass-baritone. Born 6 March 1927, in New Orleans. Died 16 February 1975. Studied with Elizabeth Wood at Loyola University; debut as Duke of Verona in Gounod's Roméo et Juliette *with New Orleans Opera Association, 1947; New York City Opera debut as Colline*

in La bohème, *1953, and remained with the company until 1973; appeared at Covent Garden, 1974; also appeared in Hamburg and Milan.*

Norman Treigle (baptized as Adanelle), the youngest of five children of Wilfred and Claudia Treigle, was born in New Orleans, on 6 March 1927. His mother, an accomplished pianist and organist, was responsible for his early interest in music, and he joined the church choir as a boy soprano at the age of nine. Later on, he took part in musical events in high school, where, as an honor student, he graduated at the age of 16. Following a two-year tour of duty in the Navy, he entered Loyola University on a scholarship as a voice major, where he studied with Elizabeth Wood. After winning the New Orleans Opera Auditions of the Air, he made his debut with the New Orleans Opera Association as the Duke of Verona in Gounod's *Roméo et Juliette* on 23 October 1947.

To support himself and to build up some cash reserves, Treigle accepted singing engagements at the First Baptist Church in New Orleans and in nightclubs. He appeared at the Blue Room of New Orlean's Roosevelt Hotel with the bands of Horace Heidt, Jimmy Dorsey, Joe Reichman, and Red Nichols, and toured the American south as a revival singer with the Baptist preacher Rev. Bob Harrington. Described as a devout Baptist and "an intensely religious man," Treigle continued to sing in church and recorded three albums of religious music.

After moving to New York City, Treigle was engaged by the New York City Opera where he made his debut as Colline in *La bohème,* on 28 March 1953. During his twenty years with the City Opera, he sang some thirty of the sixty-two major and minor roles in his repertoire, often working with the best directors the company could attract, among them Christopher West, Tito Capobianco, and Frank Corsaro. Although he appeared with many other opera companies in the United States, the City Opera was the scene of his greatest triumphs. His most successful portrayals were Gounod's diabolically fascinating, elegant, and menacing Mephistopheles; Boito's detached, evil, frightening, snake-like Mefistofele; the grotesquely comic King Dodon of *The Golden Cockerel;* the four villains in *Les contes d' Hoffmann;* and the title roles in *Don Giovanni, Giulio Cesare, Boris Godunov, Le nozze di Figaro,* and *Gianni Schicchi.* But he could make an indelible mark even in such brief parts as the toreador in *Carmen.* This reviewer wrote of his Escamillo (*Opera,* 1973) that "he looked and behaved like a toreador; tall, lean, nimble, agile, self-assured, lustful, arrogant—a born winner unafraid of man and beast, at home in the bull-ring and boudoirs, and equally doused in bull's blood and perfume. Vocally Treigle was nothing less than shattering." Arthur Jacobs, reviewing his Mefistofele at the Royal Festival Hall (*Opera,* 1974), wrote of his "marvelously expressive and infinitely malleable voice," calling his performance "spellbinding."

Treigle was equally at home in the modern compositions of Walton, Orff, von Einem, Dallapiccola, Copeland, and Floyd. He created the role of Grandpa Moss in Aaron Copland's *The Tender Land,* and Reverend Hale in Ward's *The Crucible.* He first assumed the role of Olin Blitch in Carlisle Floyd's *Susannah* on 27 September 1956, giving the role a definitive portrayal. He and Phyllis Curtin, creator of the title role, took the performance to the Brussels World's Fair in 1958, to great critical acclaim. In later years, Treigle created three roles composed explicitly for him by Floyd, who called him "an actor-singer with no superiors and few equals . . . an extravagantly gifted man. I am greatly and happily in his debt as a composer."

Opera to Treigle was music drama, with emphasis on the drama. "To me the most important thing is to be an actor who sings," was his artistic credo. *Newsweek* called him

"Probably the finest singing actor in opera" (1969), which makes it all the more remarkable that he never appeared at the Metropolitan, only a few hundred yards away from his home theater.

Treigle's voice was a finely grained, well-modulated, and perfectly equalized true bass with an extension that enabled him to sing the most coveted roles of the bass-baritone literature. His timbre, though somewhat reminiscent of the young Pinza, had a color and character of its own, easily recognizable and distinguishable from all others. One of its most remarkable features was its awesome power, wholly unexpected of a 5'11" man weighing only 140 pounds. The best creations in Treigle's repertoire were extraordinary portrayals, unique interpretations that set the singer apart from other exponents of his roles. He was a dynamic, electrifying performer who could fill the stage, dominate a scene, and reduce his less accomplished colleagues to animated props. His conceptions were characterized by a strong sense of theater, and giving proper weight and emphasis to every word he sang, he projected a role physically as well. At times a mere posture or an evocative gesture of his could linger in one's memory as long as the sound of his voice. The recordings that captured his singing—always more impressive in a live performance than in the studio—actually preserved only half of his art.

Treigle recorded for Angel, RCA, ABC, Columbia, Westminster, and some lesser labels. His Mefistofele, Julius Caesar, and Hoffmann villains have been preserved on commercial records. In addition to operatic and religious recital records, there are "private" recordings and tapes of live performances of his Olin Blitch, Mephistopheles, Gianni Schicchi, Cardinal Brogni of a concert performance of *La Juive;* one performance of his King Dodon was issued on records and another is known to exist on videotape.

Treigle believed in the company he served so faithfully for two decades, and when, in his perception, the City Opera was becoming a "glamour house," he resigned to pursue an international career. He partially realized his ambition with an acclaimed concert performance of *Mefistofele* at the Royal Festival Hall (18 March 1974), followed by his Covent Garden debut in *Faust* (22 November 1974), and appearances in Hamburg and Milan. Soon after, on 16 February 1975, he was found dead in his apartment. The New York City Opera honored his memory by establishing in 1975 the Norman Treigle Memorial Fund, with the aim of two permanent scholarships for young American singers. His premature death just two weeks short of his 48th birthday deprived him and the opera world of a fitting climax to a distinguished career.—ANDREW FARKAS

Triptych (Einstein on the Beach, Satyagraha, Akhnaten)

Composer: *Philip Glass.*

Librettists: Einstein on the Beach, *Philip Glass (opera composed with Robert Wilson);* Satyagraha, *C. DeJong (after* Bhagavad Gita*); Akhnaten, Philip Glass and others.*

First Performances: Einstein on the Beach, *France, Avignon, 25 July 1976;* Satyagraha, *Rotterdam, 5 September 1980;* Akhnaten, *Stuttgart, 24 March 1984.*

Roles: Einstein on the Beach: *various voices and instruments;* Satyagraha: *M.K. Gandhi (tenor); Miss Schlesen (soprano); Kasturbai (contralto); Mr. Kallenbach (baritone); Parsi Rustomji (bass); Mrs. Naidos (soprano); Mrs. Alexander (contralto); Lord Krishna (bass); Prince Arjunabar; Count Leo Tolstoy, Rabindranath Tagore, Martin Luther King Jr (all non-singing roles);* Akhnaten: *Akhnaten (counter tenor); Nefertiti (contralto); Queen Tye* *(soprano); Horembab (baritone); Aye (bass); The High Priest of Amon (tenor); Akhnaten's six daughters (female voices); Funeral Party (eight men's voices); Tourist Guide (voice-over).*

Although the three operas gathered under the title *Triptych* have on only one occasion been presented in tandem (in Stuttgart in the summer of 1989), Philip Glass has often stated that he did conceive his 1976 *Einstein on the Beach,* his 1980 *Satyagraha* and his 1983 *Akhnaten* as a unit. Each of them, he says, is a "portrait" of an individual whose ideas have changed the course of world events, and together, he says, they form a sort of triptych. Their similarities are more philosophical than musical or theatrical.

Satyagraha, which concerns the life of the Indian pacifist Mohandas K. Gandhi, and *Akhnaten,* which deals with the Egyptian pharaoh who supposedly invented the concept of monotheism, indeed seem cut from the same cloth; both feature sumptuously lyric singing set over often soft-textured orchestral accompaniments, and both are cast in the form of vignettes which, although they are presented in something other than chronological order, are comparable in structure to the traditional opera scene. *Einstein on the Beach,* in marked contrast, is a highly abstract work representative of Glass's earlier, more aggressive Minimalist style. The rhythmically insistent score is played for the most part at high volume levels by an ensemble of synthesizers and electronic organs, and the vocal materials are limited to monotone recitations and choral chantings of numbers and solfège syllables. Just as significant, the various segments are not so much scenes as stage pictures, intended as showcases for the virtuosity of designer Robert Wilson. Because of the order in which they are presented, the events portrayed in *Satyagraha* and *Akhnaten* are perhaps hard to follow, but at least they are events clearly based on episodes in the protagonists' lives; in *Einstein on the Beach,* there is very little that in the conventional sense seems narrative.

As different as the first item in the triptych is from its successors, however, all three works are ultimately powerful for the same reason. Even in the more traditionally structured *Satyagraha* and *Akhnaten,* the communication to the audience of text is not an issue; in the one opera the libretto is in Sanskrit, and in the other it is in a variety of archaic languages, and for productions of both the composer has specifically requested that the audience not be provided with translations. The result, as in *Einstein on the Beach,* is a removal of literal meaning from that which is sung; the words have only a cumulative effect, comparable to that of a litany prayed *en masse* in a resonant cathedral. In combination with the aural consistency of Glass's deliberately repetitious, harmonically static scores, the effect—even without vivid stage imagery—can be quite overwhelming.—JAMES WIERZBICKI

Tristan und Isolde [Tristan and Isolde]

Composer: *Richard Wagner.*

Librettist: *Richard Wagner.*

First Performance: *Munich, Königliches Hof- und Nationaltheater, 10 June 1865.*

Roles: *Isolde (soprano); Tristan (tenor); Brangäne (mezzo-soprano or soprano); Kurwenal (baritone); King Marke (bass); Melot (tenor); A Shepherd (tenor); A Steersman (baritone); A Sailor's Voice (tenor); chorus (TTBB).*

In 1857 Wagner interrupted the composition of *Siegfried* to write *Tristan und Isolde.* He chose a different kind of verse from the alliterative style of *Der Ring,* though his verse was nevertheless criticized as "bombastic" and as "stammering speech, murderous to thought and language" (Hanslick). The opera preserves little of the original legend, using the theme of love to explore the conflict between Will and Circumstance. It thus comes close to the ideals of Schopenhauer, whom Wagner had read in 1854.

In his letters to Liszt, Wagner had talked of developing a kind of drama expressed purely through music, while to Marie Wittgenstein he wrote: "For the moment, music without words: several things I would rather treat in music than in verse." His libretto does indeed call for very little stage action. Where such action is necessary he confines it to the ends of acts: in act I, Tristan and Isolde's embrace; in act II, Tristan's wound; in act III, Tristan's death. The inner drama is portrayed through the orchestra.

The prelude at once projects the listener into a world of mystery and uncertainty. This uncertainty is increased by a feeling of yearning, an element which continues throughout the work until the final bars.

Act I takes place on the ship in which Isolde is being carried to Cornwall to marry the aged King Marke. To her attendant Brangäne, Isolde expresses her rage and humiliation at being taken to an unwelcome marriage by Tristan, the enemy whom she had nursed back to strength even though he had killed her former betrothed. She orders Brangäne to prepare a poisoned potion and offers it to Tristan, as if in atonement. Quickly realizing that it is poisoned, he nevertheless accepts the drink, since he knows his love for Isolde can never be fulfilled. Brangäne, however, has substituted a love potion in place of the poison. The lovers are overcome with longing and embrace each other passionately, oblivious of their arrival in Cornwall.

In act II, Tristan and Isolde meet at night by Marke's castle while the king is away hunting. In a long scene they curse the day that keeps them apart: only at night can their love flourish. Their duet moves to an overwhelming climax, in which the text is reduced to mere pairs of words; its final note, however, is cut short by the arrival of Tristan's squire, Kurwenal. Despite Kurwenal's warning, the lovers are discovered by the king as dawn breaks. Marke gives vent to

Jon Vickers and Helge Dernesch in *Tristan und Isolde,* 1972

his grief at Tristan's lack of faith. Melot, a courtier, challenges Tristan with his sword, and during their fight Tristan suddenly lowers his guard and is gravely wounded.

Act III is set on the coast of Brittany, in a deserted ruined castle at Kareol. Tristan survives only in the hope that Isolde might arrive. From delirium, he eventually sinks into unconsciousness. This long monologue is punctuated by a strange, mournful phrase first heard on a shepherd's pipe at the opening of the act. The sound of the pipe changes to joy as Isolde's boat is seen, at which Tristan's outbursts become more and more frenzied. As Isolde enters, he collapses into her arms (a moment emphasized with a musical recollection of their drinking of the love potion) and dies. A second boat arrives bearing King Marke. His agonizing statement of forgiveness is answered only with Isolde's farewell to life, the *Liebestod,* at the end of which she sinks down onto Tristan's body.

Tristan und Isolde was initially conceived to be easily performable by an ordinary opera company, avoiding the difficulties posed by *Der Ring* with its huge orchestra and powerful voices. This ambition was, however, not fulfilled. The first production in Vienna was abandoned after over seventy rehearsals, and it took four years before *Tristan* received its first performance, in Munich. The reasons can easily be explained. While the musical style of the secondary characters follows the established diatonic manner, that for Tristan and Isolde inhabits another world, its highly chromatic idiom so original that even today it can seem unsettling. Moreover, Tristan's delirium in act III is intensified by means of unorthodox rhythmic patterns, including passages of five (5/4) and even seven (4/4 + 3/4) beats, all of which contemporary singers found alien. As Nietzsche commented in *Nietzsche contra Wagner* (1888), these methods produce the effect of music moving in water, without any point of reference.

The use of a smaller orchestra did little to help, since Wagner's approach to the voice remained close to that which he had employed in *Der Ring.* Tristan's role, initially conceived as a "lyric" part, became closer to that of the *Heldentenor* (heroic tenor), and the role is made especially difficult since the singer is on stage for almost the entire work. The relationship between voice and orchestra differed from that of conventional opera: the music is written on a contrapuntal basis where the vocal line is but one of many melodic strands. Nor is the voice necessarily the leading part, for at times it becomes obscured in the overall sound.

Leitmotives are used in *Tristan,* but in a different manner than in *Der Ring.* There are only a small number of them, and they represent not characters or objects but wishes and emotions. The work's structure is strengthened by such features as the parallel construction of acts I and III and the points of analogy between Tristan's two long monologues in act III. Further coherence comes from the fact that the three acts emphasize in turn the work's three interlocking main themes: love, night, and death.

Such formal organization is all the more necessary in view of the tonal instability of the work's musical language, an instability encapsulated in the famous "Tristan" chord, first heard in the opening phrase of the prelude and unresolved until the final bars. Furthermore, the work avoids closed musical forms, preferring a style that Nietzsche characterized as "infinite melody." Wagner acknowledged this, claiming that his finest art was "the art of transition, for my whole texture consists of such transitions."—ALAN LAING

Il trittico

Composer: *Giacomo Puccini.*

Librettists: Il tabarro: *Giuseppe Adami (after Didier Gold,* La houppelande*);* Suor Angelica: *Giovacchino Forzano;* Gianni Schicchi: *Giovacchino Forzano (scenario based on lines from Dante,* Inferno*).*

First Performance: New York, Metropolitan Opera, 14 December 1918.

Roles: Il tabarro: *Giorgetta (soprano); Michele (baritone); Luigi (tenor); Frugola (mezzo-soprano); Tinca (tenor); Talpa (bass); Two Lovers (soprano, tenor); Song Vendor (tenor); chorus (STBB).*

Suor Angelica: *Sister Angelica (soprano); The Princess (contralto); The Abbess (mezzo-soprano); The Monitor (mezzo-soprano); Mistress of Novices (contralto); Sister Genevieve (soprano); Sister Osmina (mezzo-soprano); Sister Dolcina (mezzo-soprano); Nursing Sister (mezzo-soprano); Two Attending Nuns (mezzo-soprano); Two Novices (mezzo-sopranos); Two Lay-Sisters (soprano, mezzo-soprano); chorus (SSSTB).*

Gianni Schicchi: *Lauretta (soprano); Rinuccio (tenor); Gianni Schicchi (baritone); Zita (mezzo-soprano); Gherardo (tenor); Nella (soprano); Betto (baritone); Simone (bass); Marco (baritone); La Ciesca (soprano); Master Spinelloccio (bass); Amantio di Nicolso (bass); Gherardino (mezzo-soprano or boy soprano); Pinellino (bass); Guccio (bass).*

Il trittico consists of three one-act operas bound together by recurrent themes and images. The first of the operas, *Il tabarro,* is based on a play by Didier Gold, with a libretto by Giuseppe Adami. The most *verismo* of Puccini's many operas, it involves adultery, revenge, and murder, all involving poor people. The opera is set on a barge on the river Seine in Paris. Michele, the

A scene from the first production of Puccini's *Gianni Schicchi,* from *Il trittico,* Metropolitan Opera, New York, 1918

captain of the barge, is madly in love with his wife Giorgetta, and they have recently suffered the death of their only child. But Giorgetta, much younger than her husband, is having an affair with a young worker, Luigi, on board her husband's barge. Ultimately, and after much suffering, Michele discovers who his wife's lover is and murders him.

The second opera, *Suor Angelica,* has a libretto by Giovacchino Forzano and was based on his own idea. The opera is set in a convent in Italy during the seventeenth century. Convents were places where the Italian nobility stashed away daughters and other females who had caused disgrace to the family. In this case, Suor Angelica has had a child out of wedlock. In the opening of the opera, she and the other nuns sing of their life in the convent, with mixed reactions to their incarceration. Suddenly a relative of Suor Angelica enters, the Zia Principessa, and asks to speak to Angelica alone. She wants her niece to sign some documents involving the family estate, which Angelica obediently does, but she is desperate for news of her son. Her aunt coldly informs her that the child has died, and then hastily leaves. The opera ends with Angelica committing suicide in the hope that God will save her and her son.

Gianni Schicchi, also to a text by Forzano, is based on a few lines from Dante's *Inferno,* concerning the character of Gianni Schicchi, who is placed in hell for falsifying a will. The opera is set in Florence in 1299, and the Donati household is in mourning as their relative, old Buoso Donati, dies. Their grief becomes much more genuine once they find the old man's will and discover that they have all been disinherited—Donati willed his entire estate to a local monastery. In their desperation, the family call upon a lawyer with a dubious reputation, Gianni Schicchi, at the advice of their son Rinuccio, who is in love with Schicchi's daughter, Lauretta. Schicchi then hatches a plot: the family will call in a notary, Schicchi will pretend he is the old and dying Buoso Donati and dictate a new will leaving them everything. This they do, but he outsmarts them by giving them some property while keeping the bulk of the estate for himself. The opera ends with Gianni Schicchi throwing them out of his house, and giving it to the young lovers so they can marry.

All three of the *Trittico* operas involve the themes of death, revenge, and inter-family conflicts. In terms of symbolism, the operas use imagery of water, money, growth, death, and social conflict. Puccini wanted all three operas performed together as a single unit, but very soon after the premiere *Gianni Schicchi* became the audience favorite and is often done without the other two operas. *Gianni Schicchi* has been called the best Italian operatic comedy since Verdi's *Falstaff* and it undoubtedly is, though the other two operas are very fine as well. Recently, some opera companies have staged all three *Trittico* operas together, as Puccini wanted.
—JOHN LOUIS DIGAETANI

Troilus and Cressida

Composer: *William Walton.*

Librettist: *Hassall.*

First Performance: *London, Covent Garden, 1954; revised, 1975-76.*

Roles: *Cressida (soprano); Troilus (tenor); Pandarus (tenor); Diomede (baritone); Calkas (bass); Evadne (mezzo-soprano); Antenor (baritone); Horaste (baritone); Woman's Voice (speaking); Two Priests (tenor, baritone); Two Soldiers (tenor, baritone); Three Watchmen (offstage; tenor, two baritones); chorus (SSSSAAAATTTTBBBB).*

The story of *Troilus and Cressida* concerns the love of Troilus, Prince of Troy, for Cressida, the daughter of Calkas, High Priest of Pallas, at a time when the Greeks are besieging the city. Act I reveals Calkas, subsequently to be proven a traitor, trying to persuade the Trojans that further resistance is useless. Against this background Troilus meets Cressida and falls in love with her. Pandarus, brother of Calkas, acts as matchmaker. In act II he unites the lovers, but the sudden arrival of Diomede, Prince of Argos, interrupts their new-found happiness. He has come to take Cressida to her father, who has deserted to the Greeks, in exchange for Antenor, Captain of Trojan Spears, whom the Greeks have captured.

Act III shows Cressida in the Greek camp, anxiously awaiting news of Troilus but unaware that her father has arranged for all his messages to be intercepted by Evadne, her servant. Believing herself to be abandoned, she yields completely to Diomede's advances. Then Troilus and Pandarus, admitted through the Greek lines in an hour of truce, come upon Evadne and urge her to fetch Cressida, whose ransom is being arranged. When Troilus reclaims Cressida, Diomede commands her to renounce him, but she refuses. He fights with Diomede, but is mortally wounded in the back by Calkas. Diomede orders Calkas back to Troy, declaring that Cressida must stay behind as a prisoner without privilege. She escapes her fate by taking her own life.

Shortly after finishing the opera, Walton wrote that the theme had commended itself to him because of the human situations which, though set in prehistoric times, were of a universal kind. "If my aim here was a close union of poetic and music drama, it was also my concern to recreate the characters in my own idiom as an example of English *bel canto,* the parts carefully designed to bring out the potentialities of each voice according to its range—in the hope of adding another 'singer's opera' to the repertory."

In fact, Walton had created a masterpiece in which he did indeed establish the principal characters with the sureness of a master's touch. Much of the music is written in his strong romantic lyrical vein (Cressida's arias "Slowly it all comes back to me" and "At the haunted end of the day" are good examples), although some commentators felt that the opera was not full-blooded or romantic enough. Walton's writing for massed voices demonstrates here his ability to create great dramatic effect as he had previously done in such works as *Belshazzars's Feast.* He uses a large orchestra, including triple wind, two harps, celesta and a large percussion section, but the scoring is extremely delicate and colorful. Indeed, he acquired in the composition of this opera new skills and sounds, many of which were to be echoed in subsequent works.

Walton was always dissatisfied with Hassall's libretto, which has been described as too "flowery." Hassall had written libretti for Ivor Novello, and Walton thought that his style had been ruined as a result. Cuts were made in each act for a revival in April 1955, and further incisions in April 1963 accounted for about eight more minutes of music being discarded.

Yet somehow the opera still failed to establish itself as a favorite, even in 1976 when yet further cuts were made and the soprano line lowered to suit Dame Janet Baker's mezzo voice. Nevertheless, many felt that the revisions were ill-considered and that Walton had made a cardinal error in transposing the part. One may therefore look forward to the promised recording of the original version in the complete Chandos series which will use the high soprano of Walton's original conception.—STEWART R. CRAGGS

Trouble in Tahiti and A Quiet Place

Composer: *Leonard Bernstein.*

Librettist: Trouble in Tahiti, *Leonard Bernstein;* A Quiet Place, *Stephen Wadsworth.*

First Performance: Trouble in Tahiti, *Waltham, Massachusetts, Brandeis University, 12 June 1952;* A Quiet Place, *Houston, Houston Grand Opera, 17 June 1983 [revised 1984].*

Roles: Trouble in Tahiti: *Dinah (mezzo-soprano); Sam (bass-baritone); Trio (soprano or mezzo-soprano, tenor, baritone).* A Quiet Place: *Funeral Director (tenor); Bill (baritone); Susie (mezzo-soprano); Analyst (tenor); Doc (bass); Mrs. Doc (contralto); Dede (soprano); François (tenor); Junior (baritone); Sam (bass).*

Although Leonard Bernstein had already ventured into the theatrical medium in the 1940s, *Trouble in Tahiti* (1952) represents his initial effort in the operatic genre. Several years earlier he had made his mark in the musical theater with the scores for the ballet *Fancy Free* (1944) and the Broadway musical *On the Town* (1944, derived from the ballet). It should not seem surprising then that elements from the musical styles of these works emerge in the score for *Trouble in Tahiti,* particularly the jazz-influenced timbres and rhythms, and such popular-song style musical numbers as the opening radio commercial-inspired trio. Bernstein dedicated *Trouble in Tahiti* to Marc Blitzstein, whose caustic influence on the text is felt throughout the work.

Trouble in Tahiti chronicles a single day in the troubled marriage of Sam and Dinah. Sam is self-indulgent and ambitious; Dinah consults an analyst to clarify the desperate circumstances of her life. Caught in the middle is young Junior, who must suffer the neglect of his self-absorbed and uncommunicative parents. Neither Sam nor Dinah can bridge the ever-increasing gap that separates them. In the end both fail in their mutually groping attempts to talk about their estrangement. They escape its consequences by going to a movie together, *Trouble in Tahiti,* where they will not have to confront the bleakness of their shared lives.

Bernstein successfully merges and contrasts elements of the popular musical theater and the conventional opera house in *Trouble in Tahiti.* For example, he employs elements of scat singing in the jazz-inspired Trio—situated either downstage or off-stage—that comments on the action. In contrast, Dinah's aria "There is a Garden," although written in a popular song form and idiom, reveals Bernstein's close attention to details of larger operatic form and nuance. He interrupts the verses of her aria with brief digressions for Sam and the orchestra. The section then concludes with an elaborate duet for them that paraphrases one of Erik Satie's *Gymnopédies.* This entire section reflects the work's character as an opera perhaps better than any other in the work and represents its musical and dramatic coup.

Less successful however is the merging of styles in *A Quiet Place.* In 1980 Bernstein and Stephen Wadsworth began a collaboration on a sequel to *Trouble in Tahiti* that would eventually become *A Quiet Place.* Along the way to this sequel Bernstein had written *Candide* (1956), *West Side Story* (1957), *Mass* (1971), and even a work entitled *Songfest* (1977), "a study for an American opera." As Wadsworth explains, both men wanted to revitalize and rejuvenate the waning American musical theater and opera, so they worked closely together on the project, revising, rewriting, and trying to recapture the spirit of the earlier work.

A Quiet Place opens with Sam's family in attendance at Dinah's funeral, following her death in an automobile accident. All three acts describe in lurid detail the disintegration of their family over the years, the attempts to bring it together again, and the final, somewhat ambiguously achieved reconciliation.

In its original version *A Quiet Place* consisted of one act with four scenes; it had followed *Trouble in Tahiti* on a double bill. At the urging of conductor John Mauceri, and after poor reviews from the preview in Houston, Bernstein and Wadsworth rewrote *A Quiet Place*. This subsequent version integrates *Trouble in Tahiti* much more thoroughly and ingeniously by incorporating it as two flashbacks (act II) in Sam's mind as he reads through Dinah's diary and later recalls his past.

Much of *A Quiet Place* derives from *Trouble in Tahiti*, both musically and textually, either as a direct quotation, harmonic progression, or musical/textual phrase that clearly alludes to the earlier work. For example, the opening musical passage in the prologue quotes fragments from *Trouble in Tahiti*. By integrating thematic and dramatic elements from *Trouble in Tahiti* into *A Quiet Place*, the collaborators have attempted to magnify and expand on the original idea. One of the most successful examples of this integration occurs in Sam's act I aria "You're Late," which blends textual and motivic elements from *Trouble in Tahiti* with the more contemporary musical idiom of *A Quiet Place*. Ultimately, however, this procedure represents both a strength and weakness of the opera. Whereas it achieves a sense of cohesion between the two temporally and stylistically incongruous works, it also calls attention to the disparity in musical idiom and language. *Trouble in Tahiti*, which works well as a self-sufficient opera in its own right, intrudes upon the textual and compositional style of *A Quiet Place*.

While Bernstein and Wadsworth have endeavored to integrate the two works through the use of common musical motives and textual allusion, they do not realize the dramatic or musical unity and continuity of the earlier opera. Much that fails in *A Quiet Place* should be blamed on the inadequacies of the libretto. Only in isolated instances does the libretto attain the dramatic intensity and concision of the earlier work. By incorporating many of the worst melodramatic elements of ordinary soap opera, it becomes increasingly ineffectual and prosaic on repeated hearings.

Both *Trouble in Tahiti* and *A Quiet Place* contain many autobiographical elements (as Joan Peyser points out in her controversial biography of Bernstein). However, both librettos can and should be interpreted as much wider and serious indictments of contemporary Western/American society, mores, and culture. Although the works are frequently mired in pretentiousness and obscure allusion, their social commentary has not yet received its due recognition. Perhaps the unsavoriness of the material and its peculiar representation have undermined its message.—WILLIAM THORNHILL

Il trovatore [The Troubadour]

Composer: *Giuseppe Verdi.*

Librettists: *Salvadore Cammarano and L.E. Bardare (after García Gutiérrez, El trovador).*

First Performance: *Rome, Apollo, 19 January 1853.*

Roles: *Manrico (tenor); Count di Luna (baritone); Leonora (soprano); Azucena (contralto or mezzo-soprano); Ferrando (bass); Inez (mezzo-soprano); Ruiz (tenor); chorus (SATB).*

During the civil wars in fifteenth-century Spain, Ferrando, the captain of the di Luna forces, tells his soldiers how, years before, a gypsy hag was found bending over the cradle of the family's newborn boy, Garzia, and how, when the baby's health began to fail, they hunted the gypsy down and burned her at the stake. Then the gypsy's daughter avenged her mother by stealing the baby from his cradle, and the family, after a frantic search, found only a half-charred infant skeleton on the spot where the old woman had been burned. The lost baby's father died of grief, but not before he had made his other son swear he would never stop searching for his brother.

The son has grown up to be the Count di Luna, enamored of the lady Leonora, who in turn loves a mysterious troubadour. Beneath Leonora's window, the count clashes with the troubadour, who lifts his visor and reveals himself as a political enemy of the di Lunas, Manrico. Later the rivals face each other again in the battle of Pelilla, where Manrico is left for dead.

In the mountains of Biscay, Manrico has been nursed back to health by his mother, the gypsy woman Azucena, who tells him how, long ago, she had stolen the di Luna baby and, with her own infant at her breast, returned to the spot where they had burned her mother, and in crazed confusion cast into the fire there her own infant. The horrified Manrico then wonders about his own identity. He clashes again with the Count di Luna at the convent where Leonora, who has presumed him dead, is about to become a nun. He is finally captured by the count when the di Lunas seize Azucena and he rushes to defend her.

Leonora, in desperation, offers herself to the count in return for Manrico's life. The count assents, then finds that Leonora has secretly taken poison. In fury he orders Manrico's immediate execution, dragging Azucena to the prison window to watch. When the ax falls, Azucena shrieks to the Count what we have feared even to suspect—that he has killed the brother he had sought for all his life. The gypsy woman falls lifeless with the cry, "Mother, you are avenged."

The plot of *Il trovatore,* often unjustly maligned, reflects Verdi's furiously pessimistic view of the world. When he himself was a baby, his mother fled with him in her arms to escape the sabres of a vindictive Russian regiment. He saw his own two children die of illness within the span of a few months, followed in time by their young mother. The year before he wrote *Il trovatore,* his own mother died. His librettist died in the midst of writing it. When the opera appeared, Verdi wrote, "People say that it is too sad, that there are too many deaths in it. But death is all there is to life. What else is there?"

Leontyne Price and Piero Cappucilli in *Il trovatore,* **1977**

Il trovatore's chaotic text is, on close inspection, full of subtleties, ironies, patterns of imagery. Manrico, for example, is associated in Leonora's first aria with the moon, and the moon emerges from the clouds to reveal his face as he lifts his visor, though no one present knows that his real name is Garzia di Luna (Garzia of the Moon), and eventually he goes to his death never knowing who he was. The four main characters, caught as they are in fixed attitudes, are emotionally charged symbols of life's ironies—Manrico of the inability of any man to know himself, the count of the destructiveness of human passion, Leonora of the futility of self-sacrifice, Azucena of the relentless and confused operation of instinct in a universe that is overwhelmingly cruel to its creatures.

Verdi brought the terrifying story to vivid musical life. Manrico's "Ah sì, ben mio" and Leonore's "D'amor sull' ali rosee," which draw on past *bel canto* traditions, are among the most beautiful arias he ever wrote, while the count's "Il balen" illustrates his new and demanding way of writing for high baritone, and Azucena's music looks forward to the dramatic intensity of his later work. But the source of *Il trovatore*'s strength lies in more than its famous melodies. Francis Toye has said of it, "Something emerges and hits you, as it were, between the eyes, something elemental, furious, wholly true."—M. OWEN LEE

Troyanos, Tatiana

Mezzo-soprano. Born 12 September 1938, in New York. Died 21 August 1993. Studied with Hans Heinz and at the Juilliard School of Music; debut as Hippolyta in A Midsummer Night's Dream, *New York City Opera, 1963; member of the Hamburg State Opera, 1965-75; created role of Sister Jeanne in Penderecki's* The Devils of Loudon, *1969; Covent Garden debut, 1969; engaged by Paris Opéra, 1971; Metropolitan Opera debut as Octavian in* Der Rosenkavalier, *1976.*

Tatiana Troyanos is an increasingly rare example of a singer who seems identified in the public's mind with a particular theater—in this case, the Metropolitan Opera. Although she had a major international career, New York audiences (for whom she performed regularly since the 1960s) feel a particular sense of pride in her accomplishments. Troyanos has become almost a latter-day Risë Stevens, much beloved by fans who virtually heard her "grow up" at the Met and develop—through nearly three decades and several management regimes—into a mature and special artist, gifted with a burnished mezzo-soprano voice and a vibrant theatrical sense.

These vocal and theatrical attributes were with Troyanos from the start; over the years her passionate involvement only increased, while her voice remained remarkably unchanged. Her voice retained a unique throaty quality which is instantly recognizable, and although the sound darkened a bit over time, the top remained as bright and assured as that of many sopranos.

It is the glory of her upper register that made Troyanos such a successful exponent of roles that lie somewhere between soprano and mezzo. Santuzza in *Cavalleria rusticana,* Adalgisa in *Norma,* Giulietta in *Les contes d'Hoffmann,* the Composer in *Ariadne auf Naxos,* Venus in *Tannhaüser* and Kundry in *Parsifal* are just a few examples of these parts: Troyanos, possessed of a perfectly even voice over a wide range, encompassed them all with ease, and brought to each a fervor and ardor which were hers alone. Actually she scored one of her earliest triumphs when she created the soprano role of Sister Jeanne in Penderecki's *Teufel von Loudun,* whose high tessitura and difficult musical intervals say much for Troyanos' vocal skills and musicianship. Her intense portrayal was an acting triumph as well, and it is tempting to find in Troyanos—a New York born singer of Greek descent—links with her heritage, for her flashing brunette good-looks, the dark glow of her mezzo-soprano and her fiery stage presence remind us of another great singer with a similar background: Maria Callas.

And, like Callas's, there was a distinctive strength and color to Troyanos's lower register as well, and she used this marvelously shadowy sound to superb dramatic effect. Her physical and vocal gifts made her a natural as Carmen; there as elsewhere the persistent pulse of her vibrato (which, it should be said, was not to every listener's taste) became a vital part of the character and one sensed a fiercely elemental life force as it rises and ultimately ebbs away. Her Eboli (*Don Carlos*) and Dido (*Les Troyens*) achieved a similar stature and feeling of commitment.

Yet as successful as these assumptions have been, it would do Troyanos a disservice to characterize her as a specialist in the world of fervent and doomed heroines. Her excellent training and technique gave her real skills in florid music. Troyanos chose not to sing much Rossini but gave admirably fluent performances of Romeo in Bellini's *I Capuleti ed i Montecchi* and Sesto in Mozart's *La clemenza di Tito*. In later years, she also became a noted Handel stylist, and in addition to a distinguished reading of *Ariodante*, Troyanos must be one of very few singers to have taken on both the roles of Cleopatra and Caesar in *Giulio Cesare*. And she has a marvelous flair for comedy—her Dorabella in *Così fan tutte* was a delight.

Although she inexplicably never made a recital record, Troyanos had a long and fruitful recording career. Many of these discs capture her faithfully—or, more properly, as faithfully as is possible without her marvelous physical presence. Her performances as Carmen and the Composer, both with Georg Solti, are worthy souvenirs of these monumental portrayals, and in rather a different vein her recording of Cleopatra under Karl Richter reveals Troyanos' liquid sensuality of tone and ease in coloratura. In fact, she never made a bad record, and—artist that she was—in every case Troyanos contributed something unique and memorable.—DAVID ANTHONY FOX

Les Troyens [The Trojans]

Composer: *Hector Berlioz.*

Librettist: Hector Berlioz (after Virgil).

First Performance: *Paris, Théâtre-Lyrique, 4 November 1863 (part II); first complete performance in German, as* Die Eroberung Trojas, *Carlsruhe, 5 and 6 December, 1890.*

Roles: *Part I—*La Prise de Troie: *Cassandra (soprano); Choroebus (baritone); Aeneas (tenor); Helenus (tenor); Ascanius (soprano); Hecuba (mezzo-soprano); Pantheus (bass); Priam (bass); Ghost of Hector (bass); Polyxena (soprano); Andromache (mute); Astyanax (mute); chorus (SSATTBB).*

      *Part II—*Les Troyens à Carthage: *Dido (mezzo-soprano or soprano); Anna (contralto); Aeneas (tenor) Ascanius (soprano); Narbal (baritone); Pantheus (bass); Iopas (tenor); Hylas (tenor); Mercury (baritone); Two Soldiers (baritone, bass); Ghost of Cassandra (soprano); Ghost of Choroebus (baritone); Ghost of Hector (baritone); Ghost of Priam (bass); chorus (SATBB).*

Part I: *La Prise de Troie*. In the tenth year of the Trojan War, the Greeks appear at last to have sailed away, and the Trojans are jubilant. Only the prophetic princess Cassandra believes that the city is still in danger. She pleads in vain with her lover Choroebus to save himself. Despite her warnings, the Trojans escort into the city a huge wooden horse which the Greeks have left, supposedly as a votive offering, on the shore. That night, as Greek troops pour out of the horse and open the gates of Troy, the Trojan hero Aeneas is warned in a dream by the ghost of the dead prince Hector to escape with what people he can and found a new city in Italy. Cassandra and the Trojan women slay themselves rather than submit to the victorious Greeks.

Part II: *Les Troyens à Carthage*. Aeneas and the survivors of the Trojan War, shipwrecked off the coast of Carthage, are received by Queen Dido. Though she has sworn fidelity to her dead husband Sychaeus, she falls in love with Aeneas when he defends her city against the Numidians and tells her of all the dangers he has passed. They consummate their love in a cave when their royal hunt is interrupted by a storm. But Aeneas, warned by the mysterious cry of the god Mercury and by apparitions of the dead Trojans he has left behind, sets sail again for Italy. Dido, on a terrace by the sea, curses him, falls on his sword, and immolates herself, predicting amid the flames that an avenger (Hannibal) shall rise from her ashes, but seeing too a vision of the imperial Rome that eventually will be the fulfillment of Aeneas' mission.

Virgil was a main source of inspiration for Hector Berlioz, who, named after the noblest Trojan of them all, was moved to tears when, as a boy, he construed the *Aeneid* in Latin with the help of his father. In *Les Troyens*, he limits himself mainly to the first four books of Virgil's twelve-book epic. But the song of the young sailor in the masthead, written by Berlioz with his own sailor son in mind, is derived from the famous Palinurus incident in Book V; Aeneas' touching solo "Others, my son, will teach you to be happy" comes from Book XII; and there are echoes of Virgil's earlier *Eclogues* and *Georgics* in the song of the minstrel Iopas, the figure in the opera who may be thought to represent Virgil himself.

Virgilians will also detect the sound of the dactylic hexameter, "the stateliest measure ever moulded by the lips of man," in such passages as the chorus sung by the Trojans when they first appear, and in the whispering orchestral nocturne that accompanies the love duet of Dido and Aeneas. Another main influence, Shakespeare, enters at that moment, as the lovers trade mythic reminiscences ("In such a night . . .") as Jessica and Lorenzo do in the moonlit night in *The Merchant of Venice*. On many pages of the score, Berlioz shows his extraordinary sensitivity to the suggestive powers of instruments, while his long-lined melodies remain, after a century, absolutely unique.

Les Troyens was regarded as eccentric and unperformable in Berlioz' day, and he never saw his five-and-a-half-hour epic staged complete. Its rejection was a source of immense sorrow to him, and Gounod remarked that, like his namesake, Hector Berlioz died beneath the walls of Troy. The first publication of the complete score in 1969, the performance that year at Covent Garden, and the subsequent complete recording under Colin Davis, are among the most important musicological events of this century. *Les Troyens* is now rightly thought to be *the* classic of French opera.—M. OWEN LEE

Tucker, Richard

Tenor. Born 28 August 1913, in New York. Died 8 January 1975, in Kalamazoo, Michigan. Studied with Paul Althouse; debut as Alfredo in Verdi's La traviata *with the Salmaggi Opera, New York, 1943; Metropolitan Opera debut as Enzio in* La Gioconda, *1945; sang at the Met from 1945 until 1975 in 30 leading roles; European debut in* La Gioconda *at the Verona Arena, 1947.*

Richard Tucker was a leading member of the generation of singers who, during World War II, produced a kind of American golden age of vocalism at the Metropolitan Opera in New York. Even among such artists as his fellow tenor (and brother-in-law) Jan Peerce, baritones Leonard Warren and Robert Merrill, and sopranos Eleanor Steber and Risë Stevens, he was distinguished by the beauty and power of his voice and the fervor and enthusiasm of his style. During his thirty seasons at the Metropolitan Opera he never gave an indifferent performance, skillfully utilizing a *lirico-spinto* tenor voice that could encompass the forcefulness of Canio in *Pagliacci* and the suavity of Ferrando in *Così fan tutte.* He sang some thirty roles and over 400 performances at the Metropolitan, becoming one of its most dependable performers and distinctive personalities. Many regarded him as the finest operatic tenor ever produced by the United States. Among his warmest admirers was Metropolitan Opera general manager Rudolf Bing, who made Tucker one of the bulwarks of his regime. "Caruso, Caruso, that's all you hear!" Bing said in 1956. "I have an idea that we're going to be proud some day to tell people we heard Richard Tucker."

Tucker was born 28 August 1913 in Brooklyn, New York, the son of poor Jewish immigrants from Bessarabia. His name at birth was Reuben Ticker; he changed it about the time he was beginning his adult singing career, although his family and intimate friends always called him "Ruby." His first job was as a boy alto at the age of six in a Lower East Side Manhattan synagogue, and he later sang at weddings and bar-mitzvahs. After leaving high school (before graduating) he went into the business of making silk linings for fur coats, while pursuing vocal studies with Paul Althouse, the veteran Wagnerian tenor.

Tucker began his professional career as a cantor, conducting services at the Brooklyn Jewish Center, one of the city's largest synagogues. In 1941 he entered the Metropolitan Opera Auditions of the Air, but was not selected as a winner. However, three years later Althouse persuaded Edward Johnson, then the general director of the Metropolitan Opera, to visit the Brooklyn temple to hear him. As Tucker remembered it, Johnson offered him a contract and remarked, "If you can hold an audience of 2,000 in a synagogue, you can hold an audience of 3,600 in an opera house."

Johnson proved to be an accurate prophet, for when Tucker made his Metropolitan Opera debut as Enzo Grimaldo in *La gioconda* on 25 January 1945 he received ovations after "Cielo e mar" and at the conclusion of the opera. Henceforth, he proceeded methodically and with growing artistry through the Italian repertory, and also undertook successfully such French roles as Don José in *Carmen* and Hoffmann in *Les contes d'Hoffmann.* In 1951 Bing asked him to sing Ferrando in an English-language production of *Così fan tutte.* Tucker at first was reluctant to sing Mozart but eventually consented. "I'm glad I did," he said afterward, "it was like honey to my voice." He participated in the Metropolitan Opera recording of *Così,* one of many recordings (including several solo collections) he made.

Possessing a strong and stocky build (he had been an athlete in high school) Tucker was a natural if unpolished actor, who plunged into each new role with unbridled eagerness. He also developed a reputation in the house as a prankster, once inserting a nude picture into the small casket which baritone Robert Merrill was to open during act III of *La forza del destino*. On another occasion he surprised Mr. Bing and the audience by bursting into Italian for the aria "M'apparì" in an English-language performance of Flotow's *Martha*.

Tucker remained an ordained cantor throughout his life; in 1967 during the Vietnam War he conducted Passover Seder services for Jewish servicemen in Saigon, and his foreign tours took him to Israel as well as to Italy. His religious sensibilities prevented him from wearing a crucifix in operas requiring him to play the roles of priests or prelates. One famous story at the Met tells of the time he was rehearsing the role of Don Alvaro in the final scene of *La forza del destino*. As he lay prostrate in grief and penitence at the feet of Padre Guardino, bass Jerome Hines, playing the monk, unthinkingly began making the sign of the cross over him. Indignantly, Tucker leaped to his feet and shouted: "Not over my dead body, you don't!"

However, Tucker felt honored to be asked to sing César Franck's *Panis Angelicus* at St Patrick's Cathedral at the funeral of Robert Kennedy, and he held honorary degrees from two Roman Catholic universities, Notre Dame and St John's. He seldom appeared with other American companies, but made an exception to sing at Carnegie Hall in a concert version of Halévy's *La Juive,* an opera he vainly tried to persuade Bing to stage for him at the Metropolitan Opera. "He said it was old-fashioned," complained Tucker. "So what opera isn't?" On the 25th anniversary of his debut, the Metropolitan Opera did him the rare honor of holding a Richard Tucker Gala, during which he appeared opposite Leontyne Price, Joan Sutherland and Renata Tebaldi in one act of three different operas.

Tucker was deeply attached to his wife Sara and inordinately proud of his three sons, a doctor, a lawyer and a stockbroker. At least one, and sometimes all, of the family was in the house whenever he sang. "So far as I am concerned," Tucker once said, "an artist can live on better through a family's love and memories than in annals and archives. That is the real immortality."

Richard Tucker was still in full career when he died of a heart attack on 8 January 1975 as he prepared to give a concert in Kalamazoo, Michigan. His family has established in his honor the Richard Tucker Award which gives an annual stipend of $20,000 to a promising young singer. The annual prize-giving takes place at a Carnegie Hall concert in which many of today's Metropolitan Opera stars participate. It is a memorial very much in the spirit of Richard Tucker.—HERBERT KUPFERBERG

Turandot

Composer: *Giacomo Puccini.*

Librettists: *Giuseppe Adami and Renato Simoni (after Carlo Gozzi).*

First Performance: *Milan, Teatro alla Scala, 25 April 1926 [unfinished; completed by Franco Alfano].*

Roles: *Turandot (soprano); Calaf (tenor); Liù (soprano); Timur (bass); Ping (baritone); Pang (tenor); Pong (tenor); Emperor Altoum (tenor); Herald (baritone); chorus (SATTB).*

t

OPERA

In March 1920, a meeting between Puccini, Giuseppe Adami (librettist of *La rondine* and *Il tabarro*), and Renato Simoni (a critic at the *Corriere della sera*) brought forth the idea to consider *Turandotte,* a play by the Venetian playwright Carlo Gozzi (1720-1806) for a new opera. *Turandotte* as the model for an opera was by no means a new idea; several composers before Puccini, including Ferruccio Busoni and Antonio Bazzini, one of Puccini's teachers at the Milan conservatory, had already written operas on the subject, with varying degrees of success. Puccini's first introduction to the play was in the form of an Italian translation by Andrea Maffei of Friedrich Schiller's German adaptation of Gozzi's play. He was sufficiently impressed by his reading of the play that he decided to request a libretto from Adami and Simoni. Initial work on the libretto progressed quickly, but many painstaking revisions caused *Turandot* to become Puccini's most fussed over opera since *Manon Lescaut.* In fact, not until September 1924 did Puccini finally receive a version for the final duet that suited him, and this late date is most responsible for Puccini's inability to complete the score before his death.

Adami's and Simoni's libretto, while maintaining essential aspects of Gozzi's play, offers a completely new text which simplifies Gozzi's convoluted plot and adds elements not found in Gozzi. The Princess Turandot, daughter of the Chinese Emperor Altoum, has taken a vow that she will only be the bride of a royal suitor who can solve three riddles which she will pose. The punishment for any suitor who fails to solve all three riddles is death by beheading. Her reason for this vow, as Turandot will explain, is to avenge her ancestress Lo-u-Ling, who was abducted thousands of years ago by the King of the Tartars, who had defeated China in battle. Many suitors have tried to win Turandot, but all have failed, their heads, impaled on stakes, serving as grim reminders of their fate.

At the beginning of the first act, the crowd witnesses the proclamation of a mandarin announcing Turandot's law and the upcoming execution of the Prince of Persia, the latest suitor who has failed to solve all three riddles and is to be executed the same night. Among the crowd are Timur, the old Tartar King, deposed by the Chinese, and his companion, the slave-girl Liù. They soon discover Calaf, Timur's son, whom they had believed was killed in battle with the Chinese. Thus, both Calaf and Timur find themselves fugitives in the country of their enemies.

After the Prince of Persia is led to his execution, Calaf, who at first had cursed Turandot for her cruelty, catches a glimpse of her and falls madly in love. He resolves to conquer her by solving the three riddles. All efforts by Liù (who loves Calaf), by Timur, and by the three courtiers, Ping, Pang, and Pong, to dissuade Calaf, fail, and Calaf strikes the gong as a signal that a new suitor is ready to accept the challenge.

In act II, Calaf is subjected to the three riddles and solves them. The stunned Turandot begs her father not to give her to the unknown stranger, but Altoum explains that the oath is sacred and must be fulfilled. Calaf, who does not want to win Turandot without gaining her love, offers to release her from the oath, if she will solve one riddle he will pose: if by dawn she can discover his name, he will offer her his life.

In the third act, all efforts on Turandot's part to determine the stranger's name fail. When it becomes known that Liù knows his name, she, fearful that she might reveal Calaf's name under torture, takes her own life in order to protect him. Thus, Turandot's last chance to exact the stranger's name has disappeared. In the course of her subsequent encounter with Calaf, he kisses her, and Turandot finally succumbs to her feelings of love for Calaf. Acknowledging defeat, she begs Calaf to leave and to take the mystery of his identity with him. Calaf, by now

Lawrence Winters, Luigi Vellucci, and Nathaniel Sprinzena in
Turandot

certain of her love, reveals his name to her, thus putting himself entirely at her mercy. Turandot, instead of demanding his life for having solved his riddle, proclaims that she has discovered the stranger's name: it is "Love."

Very early in the planning process to the opera, Puccini expressed his intention to find some "authentic" musical source material, just as he did while working on *Madama Butterfly.* In a letter to Adami, apparently from the spring of 1920, Puccini writes: "I shall get some old Chinese music too, and descriptions and drawings of different instruments which we shall put on the stage (not in the orchestra)." As it turns out, Puccini derived some of his "Chinese" material from two sources. One of them was a Chinese music box belonging to Baron Fassini, a friend of Puccini's, who had lived in China for a number of years. It played two tunes, both of which Puccini utilized in the opera. The other source was a book, entitled *Chinese Music,* by J.A. van Aalst. Puccini drew four tunes from this book.

Turandot became the most "exotic" of Puccini's operas, not so much for incorporating a few original tunes as for Puccini's fabrication of *couleur locale* through unorthodox orchestration and freely invented, "exotic" thematic material. Puccini creates *chinoiserie* partly through the use of a greatly expanded percussion section, consisting of fourteen different instruments. Some of these are to be found in Chinese music as well, but the exotic effect does not just emanate from them; rather, it is the size of the percussion section which imitates the large percussive apparatus of Chinese cult and court music. In only a few instances is percussion absent from the score, and combinations of several percussive instruments are frequent.

The basis of the Chinese tonal system is essentially an hemitonic pentatonicism; this characteristic can be observed in the original melodies which Puccini made use of. It is not surprising, therefore, that those "exotic" melodies in *Turandot,* which are freely invented by Puccini, are also by and large pentatonic. Needless to say, large portions of the score are steeped in the expanded tonality of late Romanticism, and it is in these passages that the instrumentation is likewise more conventional—"Puccinian." In such sections, for instance, the strings are usually the main carriers of the melody. This is true in particular for the more melodious passages of the main characters, whose parts are then doubled by the strings, a technique for which Puccini is often, strangely enough, criticized. It is important to note that virtually all pentatonic melodies are supported not by *legato* (as opposed to *pizzicato*) strings, but rather by winds and percussion.

Aside from the pentatonically structured passages and the more conventional, tonally expanded sections, Puccini also uses a more purely dissonant mode of expression, as at the beginning of the opera, where two unrelated triads (D minor and C-sharp major) are superimposed. The function of such dissonant passages, similar to the "exotic" sections, often is to create an "alienation effect," portraying the unusual, shocking, or barbaric aspects of the story.

When Puccini died, he had completed the entire score, including orchestration, up to and including Liù's cortège in act III. For the remainder of the opera, the libretto was completed, and Puccini left thirty-six pages of sketches. With the aid of these, Franco Alfano, commissioned by Toscanini and the Ricordi publishing house, embarked on the task of completing the score. His original completion of the opera, which incorporated much of the sketch material left by Puccini, also contained much original music. Toscanini was not pleased with the result, and insisted on changes and cuts. Thus the reduced version (which is the one published in the scores and usually performed today) is not only 109 measures shorter, but has also retained ungainly transitions from one passage to another where cuts were performed without smoothing over the edges.

Amazingly, Alfano did not inspect Puccini's orchestration until shortly before he had completed his own score. This certainly accounts for the break in orchestral color, most strongly felt in the complete absence of percussion in the final scene. Much criticism has been directed at Alfano's conclusion, and much of it unfairly. The cut-and-paste job of the second version, having been forced upon Alfano, is a reflection more upon his disillusionment with the project than upon his inability to write a coherent score. There is much of merit in Alfano's completion, even though his failure to absorb Puccini's orchestration is perhaps Alfano's greatest shortcoming.

Ever since its premiere in 1926 at the Teatro alla Scala in Milan, *Turandot* has maintained itself in the repertory. Reactions to the opera have always been mixed, and Turandot as an operatic heroine has caused many reviewers considerable problems. She certainly is not a character who arouses genuine empathy. Unlike other Puccini heroines, such as Mimi, Manon, Butterfly, or Minnie, Turandot appears to be an inhuman character, aloof and cruel. She is not a heroine who sincerely moves us (as Mimi or Butterfly do); that role is left to Liù. To many reviewers, Turandot's coldness and cruelty appear unmotivated, her transformation into a loving woman illogical and unconvincing.

But it is too simple to dismiss Turandot as the frigid queen, whose attributes are grossly exaggerated for mere effect, with no dramatic rationale behind the characterization. Turandot is not an Aristotelian heroine whose suffering arouses pity. Nor is *Turandot,* the opera, music drama in the sense that the actions of the protagonists, be they mythical or verisimilar, are dramatically plausible. There is little that is plausible in *Turandot.* It is false, however, to conclude that for this reason, myth in *Turandot* is emptily employed.

Turandot is arguably Puccini's greatest accomplishment. The work illustrates his complete mastery of orchestration, his unsurpassed melodic inventiveness, and his thorough knowledge of harmonic vocabulary. His unfailing gift to create atmosphere has made *Turandot* a most impressive piece of musical theater; the work may well be considered the apex of Italian opera.—JÜRGEN SELK

Il turco in Italia [The Turk in Italy]

Composer: *Gioachino Rossini.*

Librettist: *F. Romani (after Caterina Mazzolà).*

First Performance: *Milan, Teatro alla Scala, 14 August 1814.*

Roles: *Selim (bass); Fiorilla (soprano); Geronio (bass); Narciso (tenor); Prosdocimo (bass); Zaida (soprano); Albazar (tenor); Isaura (soprano); chorus (SATTB).*

The plot of *Il turco in Italia* unfolds within the framework of Prosdocimo the Poet's attempt to write a libretto for an *opera buffa.* Within this conceit, the poet can see every episode as a possible number for his opera, and he is not above manipulating the situation for his own ends. A camp of gypsies provides him with an opening chorus and introduces Zaida, the exiled fiancée of a Turkish prince, and Geronio, husband of the flirtatious Fiorilla. Selim, a Turk (and coincidentally Zaida's former fiancé), happens to be visiting Italy, and the poet plans to arrange a meeting between him and Zaida; however, Fiorilla encounters Selim first and invites him to coffee. In a delightful trio ("Un marito sciumunito": An idiotic husband), the poet presents an opera plot about a foolish husband, a capricious wife, and a lover thrown over for a handsome Turk; Geronio and Narciso (who is in love with Fiorilla) are both insulted and Narciso proposes that the hypothetical poet be beaten. In the lively quartet that follows ("Siete Turchi": You are a Turk), husband, wife, Narciso, and the Turk argue and protest the nature of love and fidelity in the two cultures. Geronio will have none of Fiorilla's willfulness. Selim and Fiorilla have planned an elopement; while he waits for her, he is discovered by Zaida. Narciso, Fiorilla and her friends, and then Geronio arrive: the poet is delighted with the ensuing brawl of a sextet ("Ah! che il cor non m'ingannava": Ah! that my heart was not deceiving) as a first finale.

In the second act the Turk tries to buy Fiorilla from Geronio. The two women want Selim to choose between them, but he is unable to decide. Later at a masked ball Zaida dresses as Fiorilla and Narciso as Selim. The identical couples mistakenly pair with their more appropriate partners, leading to a marvelous *buffo* quintet in which the befuddled Geronio desperately tries to discover and claim his wife. Finally, prompted by the poet, Geronio pretends to divorce Fiorilla and send her home to her parents; she is chastened and reconciled with Geronio. The happy ending sees Selim and Zaida returning together to Turkey and Narciso pardoned.

Despite the suggestion of the title that *Il turco in Italia* was capitalizing on the success of *L'italiana in Algeri* (*The Italian Girl in Algiers*), the plot is not derivative of the earlier work; and despite the fact that the first Milanese audiences felt that Rossini had cheated them by borrowing from himself, almost all of the music is newly composed. It must be noted that an anonymous collaborator wrote not only all the *secco* recitatives of the opera (a typical practice), but also arias for Geronio ("Vado in traccia d'una zingara": I'm looking for a gypsy) and Albazar ("Ah! sarebbe troppo dolce": Ah! it would be too sweet) and the entire second finale. For Rossini the first-act finale is a musical highpoint. His concern centered on the interaction of characters, dramatically and musically, in the unresolved complexities of the mid-point of the opera. The expression of the characters' satisfaction with the resolution of those conflicts at the end of the opera could be entrusted to a collaborator. Indeed, the denouement of some of Rossini's serious operas occurs so swiftly that a tragic ending could be changed to a happy one with minimal disruption to the rest of the opera: he provided both *Tancredi* and *Otello,* for example, with revised endings which reverse the fortunes of the previous one.

Unfortunately, *Il turco in Italia* was published in the nineteenth century as a Parisian *pastiche:* apparently a one-act reduction Rossini made for the Théâtre-Italien was refleshed with numbers from other operas. The delights of the original version were essentially unknown for a century until its revival with Maria Callas in 1950.

Il turco in Italia is carefully constructed and reveals the strong influence Mozart's comic operas had on the young Rossini. The opera depends largely on its ensembles to develop the dramatic and comic situations as well as to reveal the psychological dimensions of the characters. Their various encounters in sentiment, anger, and confusion inspire Rossini to some of his liveliest music, as in the quintet's canonic passage, "Questo vecchio maledetto": This accursed old fellow), or the trio for Geronio, Narciso, and the poet. There are also lovely moments of reflection, as in the unaccompanied passage of the quintet ("Deh! raffrena, amor pietoso, tanti affetti del cor mio": Ah! gentle love, restrain the abundant feelings of my heart). Fiorilla's aria "Squallida veste, e bruna" (Drab, dark garments), in which she repents her treatment of her husband, reveals an unexpected, deeper level of this apparent coquette's personality.—PATRICIA BRAUNER

t

OPERA

The Turn of the Screw

Composer: *Benjamin Britten.*

Librettist: *M. Piper (after Henry James).*

First Performance: *Venice, La Fenice, 14 September 1954.*

Roles: *Governess (soprano); Mrs. Grose (soprano); Miss Jessel (soprano); Peter Quint (tenor); Miles (boy soprano); Flora (soprano).*

The Turn of the Screw adapts one of the world's most celebrated ghost stories for the operatic stage. The compelling events of Henry James's novella are narrated through a series of 16 scenes, interwoven with orchestral interludes—a taut, integrated construction, typical of Britten's chamber operas, and particularly appropriate to this psychological mystery. The central character is an inexperienced and unworldly Governess, who comes to a remote country house to take charge of two young children. She gradually becomes convinced that they are in communication with the previous governess and a manservant—both dead. Her attempts to save the children from these malign influences result in the death of one child, and the fact that there is a second child whose fate is unresolved at the close of the opera gives the chilling drama, in James's words, "another turn of the screw."

Critics still squabble over whether Britten's opera preserves the ambiguities essential to James's story. James leaves open the dual possibilities that either the children are indeed being corrupted by the ghosts, or that their creepy commerce with the dead is only a figment of the Governess's imagination. The continuing controversy suggests that Britten succeeded in reproducing James's puzzle: from the first performance onwards, there have been sufficient champions for both interpretations to prove that the opera tells no less subtle a tale than its source.

In fragmentary sentences and elusive language, close to James's original text, Myfanwy Piper's libretto provides both the everyday exchanges of the schoolroom, and the sweet seduction of ghostly voices, real or imagined. (Giving the ghosts voices, and words to sing, is one of the most criticized aspects of the opera. A producer needs a little ingenuity to preserve the possibility that they are creations of a hysterical brain.) Terse conversations, set-piece songs and the occasional impassioned flare-up of emotion call for a wide range of lyrical and declamatory vocal styles: Britten has them all in his vocabulary, and unifies them with striking consistency, so that the boy Miles is as surely characterized when singing his Latin exercises as when romping with his sister, or flirting timidly with the Governess. The opera does not deal exclusively with horrors: it is also a love story, and delicately hints at the Governess's infatuation with the children's absent guardian, transformed at one moment into a destructive passion for her pupil, at another to a morbid obsession with the dead manservant who also loved the boy.

The opera is a study in tensions. Few operas have matched score and story to such purpose. Each of the two acts runs continuously. The orchestral interludes are no mere "mood music" but comprise a theme and variations for the thirteen instrumentalists that make up the chamber orchestra. The theme is the opera's "screw," using all twelve notes of the chromatic scale, and the variations "turn" it through all the keys, developing in intricacy and menace as the story unfolds. For the listener, the effect is far more than an ingenious technical tour-de-force: the dazzling colors of the score exploit a range of timbres appropriate to a ghost story—rippling celesta arpeggios announce an appearance of the male ghost, Quint, an ominous gong warns of the dead governess, Miss Jessel, a nocturne of birdsong fills the garden at night, and church bells accompany the ironic churchyard scene. *The Turn of the Screw* is among Britten's most important operas, a worthy analogue of a literary masterpiece, a memorable score, and superb theater.—PATRICIA HOWARD

Turner, (Dame) Eva

Soprano. Born 10 March 1892, in Oldham, England. Died 16 June 1990, in London. Studied with Dan Roothan, Giglia Levy, Edgardo Levy, Mary Wilson, and Albert Richards-Broad; debut as a Page in Wagner's Tannhäuser, *London, 1916; sang with the Carl Rosa Opera Company, 1916-24 in roles that included Santuzza, Tosca, and Brünnhilde; Teatro alla Scala debut as Freia in Wagner's* Das Rheingold, *1924; sang at Covent Garden, 1928-48; taught at the University of Oklahoma, 1949-59; joined the faculty at the Royal Academy of Music, 1959. Was made a Dame Commander of the Order of the British Empire in 1962.*

Relatively few English-born sopranos of the twentieth century have achieved international fame. Considering the scarcity of truly great dramatic sopranos in this century, it is even more amazing that Eva Turner, born in Oldham, Lancashire, could circumvent so many odds and achieve for herself such a notable place in opera performance. Although her father was a cotton mill engineer and her mother a housewife, her parents considered music essential to Turner's education. In Bristol, her home city during school days, she studied voice with Daniel Rootham, teacher of another renowned English singer, Dame Clara Butt. Hearing a concert version of Wagner's *Die Walküre* and seeing a performance of Verdi's *Il trovatore* kindled young Turner's intense interest in opera.

With five years of study at the Royal Academy of Music with Edgardo Levi and Gigia Levi, she was prepared to audition for the Carl Rosa Opera Company in 1915. Although she began as a chorus member, by asserting herself she was soon able to learn and sing smaller roles. It was during her first year with this company that Turner met and began study with Albert Richards-Broad. Richards-Broad, a member of the Carl Rosa management, was an Australian singing master recognized as an authority on vocal production. With constant work, Turner soon established herself as the prima donna of this provincial English touring ensemble.

In 1924 one of Arturo Toscanini's assistants, having heard Turner in London, urged her to sing for the Maestro at the Teatro alla Scala in Milan. Toscanini engaged her immediately, and from her first performances in Italy her singing commanded the respect of audiences, colleagues, and conductors. Her singing of operatic roles throughout England, Western Europe, Brazil, Argentina, Venezuela, and the United States during the inter-war years was notable in that she was the only English-born dramatic soprano to achieve this status. She performed such roles as Aida, Santuzza, Sieglinde, Agathe, and Isolde; but persons knowledgeable of her contributions to opera and singing continue to speak and write of her singing of the lead in Puccini's *Turandot*. Her performance of the title role in this work remains the yardstick by which all others are measured.

She first sang the role of Princess Turandot in the Teatro Grande at Brescia, Italy, in 1926, where she gained almost instant recognition. Alfano, who had completed the score of this work following Puccini's untimely death, later stated that Turner was perfect for the role. She first sang it in England in 1928 and eventually retired from the operatic stage after a series of performances of *Turandot* at the Royal Opera House, Covent Garden during the 1947 and 1948 seasons.

Commentators on Turner's career often focus on her huge success in the role of Turandot, ignoring the vast repertoire she presented to audiences throughout her career. Early on, she displayed the musicianship and eagerness to learn contemporary works such as *Le chant fatal* by Georges d'Orlay and *Thais and Thalmae* by Colin Campbell. Her Italian repertoire included, in addition to roles mentioned earlier, such parts as Amelia (*Un ballo in maschera*), Leonora (*Il trovatore*), Musetta (*La bohème*), Donna Anna (*Don Giovanni*), Cio-Cio-San (*Butterfly*), Nedda (*I pagliacci*), Tosca, and Isabeau (from Mascagni's *Isabeau*). Her German repertory was represented by such roles as Venus and Elisabeth (*Tannhäuser*), Elsa (*Lohengrin*), Brünnhilde (*Siegfried* and *Die Walküre*), Eva (*Die Meistersinger*), and Leonora (*Fidelio*).

Turner's first recordings come during 1926 in Italy, where she, along with other soloists and the chorus from the Teatro alla Scala, put on disc the Triumphant Scene from *Aida* and the ensemble from the end of act III of *La gioconda*. Further recordings preceded her famous 1928 recordings in London. These sessions were unique in that Central Hall, Westminster, was used rather than the traditional studio. Turner said that the space given her voice in this setting provided surroundings similar to those of an opera house. Hearers of these recordings in England, Europe, and the Americas longed to hear this voice in person. Those fortunate enough to do so never ceased talking about the beauty of her full-bodied, trumpet-like tone, which was capable of carrying over chorus and orchestra in stunning fashion. Unable to fault her tone, some critics of Turner, however, cited her failure to deliver the language clearly and her inability to modulate her voice adequately. Those seeing her icy portrayal of Turandot were somewhat reluctant to admit that her acting abilities could encompass the warmth needed for such roles as Aida, Santuzza, and Isolde, but reviews testify that she did achieve a variety of emotions that reflected her sensitivity as an actress.

Another contribution Turner made in the field of opera was in her teaching. In 1949, following her retirement from singing, she was employed by the University of Oklahoma. She remained in this position for ten years before returning to teach at her alma mater, the Royal Academy of Music, and to teach privately in her home. Today Turner's students who serve as singing professors continue teaching the technique she imparted. Several singers she taught or coached have attained success in opera, including Amy Shuard, Pauline Tinsley, Elizabeth Vaughan, Janet Coster, and Linda Esther Gray.

Her highest non-singing honor came in 1962 when Queen Elizabeth II conferred upon her the title of Dame Commander of the British Empire.

Followers of Turner's career were sorely disappointed that she failed to perform Turandot at the Metropolitan Opera. At the height of her successes, both Kirsten Flagstad and Marjorie Lawrence held firm contracts with this house. One cannot help wondering if the situation would have been different if Turner had used someone other than Richards-Broad to serve as her manager. Many of her contracts evolved from what appeared to be casual meetings rather than carefully negotiated and orchestrated business dealings. Although she signed with the agency of Harold Holt, Richards-Broad continued as her manager/teacher until his death in 1940. Shortly after this Turner committed herself to remaining in England for the duration of World War II. By the end of the war, resuming an international career was impossible because of her age.

When she died in June 1990 at the age of ninety-eight, Turner had become almost a legendary figure due to her personality and longevity. Her death left a void in opera. Fortunately, however, her singing has become accessible to audiences by means of compact discs. In 1988 a digitally remastered compact disc containing excerpts from her 1937 performance of *Turandot* was issued with amazing results. Another compact disc containing most of the selections from her older 78s plus two arias from her German repertory was also made available in 1989 in the Great Recordings of the Century series. It would appear that these presentations will continue to allow listeners an opportunity to judge her worth and contributions to opera.—ROSE MARY OWENS

t

OPERA

OPERA V

Der Vampyr [The Vampire]

Composer: *Heinrich Marschner.*

Librettist: *Wilhelm August Wohlbrück (after the melodrama by Charles Nodier, François Adrien Carmouche, and Achille de Jouffroy).*

First Performance: *Leipzig, 29 March 1828.*

Roles: *Lord Davenaut (bass); Malwina (soprano); Edgar Aubrey (tenor); Lord Ruthven (baritone); Sir Berkley (bass); Janthe (soprano); George Dibdins (tenor); John Perth (speaking part); Emmy (soprano); James Godshill (tenor); Richard Scrop (tenor); Robert Green (bass); Thomas Blunt (bass); Suse (mezzo-soprano); Vampire Master (speaking part); Berkley Servant (bass); chorus.*

Marschner's first real operatic success, *Der Vampyr* capitalized on the popularity of Weber's recent *Der Freischütz* (1821), with its mixture of German folk elements and demonic motifs, as well as that of the widespread vampire literature in the wake of Polidori's "The Vampyre: A Tale" of 1819, originally attributed to Byron. From the variety of existing stage versions, the librettist Wohlbrück, Marschner's brother-in-law, drew primarily on Heinrich Ludwig Ritter's *Der Vampyr oder die Todten-Braut*, based in turn on an 1820 French melodrama by Charles Nodier with music by Louis-Alexandre Piccinni (grandson of Niccolò Piccinni).

To prolong his earthly existence by another year, the vampire Lord Ruthven swears to the vampire-master and assembled spirits that he will provide them with three sacrificial brides within twenty-four hours. After an expository recitative and aria describing his bloodthirsty lifestyle, he quickly dispatches his first victim, Janthe, who has rushed out for a nocturnal tryst with him. A posse led by the girl's father discovers the murder and stabs Ruthven. But the vampire is unwittingly rescued by Aubrey, once the beneficiary of Ruthven's aid, who carries his body into a patch of moonlight. Aubrey is forced to swear an oath of secrecy until the new day is past. The scene changes to a hall in the castle of Lord Davenaut. Aubrey greets his beloved Malwina, the Lord's daughter, only to discover that she has been promised to the wealthy Earl of Marsden, in whom he recognizes—to his dismay—the vampire Ruthven.

Act II finds Emmy and George, peasants belonging to the estate of Marsden, preparing to celebrate their wedding. Emmy's ballad of the "pale man" (*Romanze*, "Sieh, Mutter, dort den bleichen Mann") is ominously interrupted by the appearance of Ruthven. Neither George nor Aubrey (still under oath) is able to prevent the vampire's seduction and murder of Emmy, whom he has enticed away from the festivities. A bullet wound inflicted by George is counteracted by the curative force of the moonlight, once again. In the following scene more wedding festivities are underway in the Davenauts' castle. Aubrey does all he can to dissuade Malwina from this unwanted match and later to hinder the nuptial ceremonies themselves. Both he and Malwina stall for time until finally, as the clock strikes one, Aubrey reveals the horrible identity of Lord Ruthven, who is struck down by a lightning bolt. Thus rescued from an infernal fate, Malwina is given to Aubrey in marriage amidst general rejoicing.

Der Vampyr has often been cited as a link between *Der Freischütz* and Wagner's *Der fliegende Holländer*. Like Weber's opera, it is grounded in the traditions of the *Singspiel* and the recent dramatic *opéra comique*, bringing more fully developed solo and ensemble numbers and extended finales in the manner of recent Italian opera to the older mix of spoken dialogue and simple strophic songs. The vampire story enables Marschner to place the demonic character center stage, unlike Weber's Kaspar, end even to endow him, at least faintly, with qualities of the alienated Byronic anti-hero divided against himself. Ruthven's character stands somewhere between that of two related baritone roles: the amoral seducer Don Giovanni (whose ultimate fate he shares) and Wagner's tragically cursed Dutchman, whose search for salvation also involves repeated sacrifices of innocent young women. His startling appearance at the close of Emmy's F-minor *Romanze* (ballad) has often been cited as a model for the Dutchman's appearance following Senta's ballad, although the sinister narrative romance or ballad type was not itself new (both *Der Freischütz* and Boieldieu's *La dame blanche* had already treated the type with an element of parody).

Numerous melodic and instrumental details of Marschner's score recall Weber, particularly the second theme of the overture (closely resembling that of the *Euryanthe* overture) and the recurring motive of "infernal laughter"—repeated downward leaps in flute, piccolo, or other woodwinds in thirds over a diminished harmony—modeled on a similar gesture associated with Kaspar in *Der Freischütz*. Marschner also makes effective use of melodrama (spoken text to orchestral accompaniment) in act I. The Vampire-Master's brief admonition in the Introduction (over timpani and low string tremolo, resolving to F-sharp minor) is obviously inspired by Samiel in the Wolf's-Glen scene. A more extended piece of melodrama closes the first scene, when Aubrey discovers the wounded Ruthven and carries him to the moonlit hillside. Finally, the various folk-like numbers—the two drinking choruses in act II and the festive music in both finales—recall elements of *Der Freischütz* and *Euryanthe*, respectively.

Marschner's ensembles, however, tend to be more extensive than Weber's, often involving a greater amount of action, as in the chorus of Lord Berkley's nocturnal posse in the first scene ("Wo kann sie sein?"). A desire for increased musical continuity, despite the dialogue format, is manifested in the *attacca* connection of separate numbers, as with the duet (no. 3) following the aforementioned chorus of Berkley's men, or the scene and aria of Malwina (no. 6) and her subsequent duet with Aubrey. Similarly progressive is the extended *grosse Szene* (no. 14) between Aubrey and Ruthven in its discursive treatment of tonality and freely gestural accompaniment; this, again, connects directly with the ensuing aria ("Wie ein schöner Frühlingsmorgen").

V

OPERA

Der Vampyr remained current on smaller German stages throughout the nineteenth century, although not reaching the larger theaters of Vienna and Berlin until the end of the century. The score was revised by Hans Pfitzner in the 1920s, who retouched the orchestration and liberally cut what he considered the "weaker passages." Pfitzner also suggested playing the overture *after* the first scene, while the scenery is shifted (an idea he borrowed from Marschner's own procedure in *Hans Heiling*). This revision has served as the basis for a number of modern revivals.—THOMAS S. GREY

Van Dam, José (Joseph Van Damme)

Bass-baritone. Born 25 August 1940, in Brussels. Studied with Frédéric Anspach at the Brussels Conservatory from 1953 to 1960; debut as Basilio, Liège, 1960; Paris Opéra debut as the Voice of Mercury in Les Troyens, *1961; in Paris at Opéra and Opéra-Comique 1961-65; at Geneva Opera 1965-67; sang in premiere of Milhaud's* La mère coupable, *Geneva, 1966; debut at Deutsche Oper, Berlin, 1967; various debuts as Escamillo: Santa Fe, 1967; San Francisco, 1970; Covent Garden, 1973; Metropolitan Opera, 1975; also at Metropolitan Opera sang Golaud, Colline, Wozzeck, Figaro, Jokanaan; sang title role in the world premiere of Messiaen's* St François d'Assise, *Paris Opéra, 1983.*

José Van Dam possesses one of the most attractive bass-baritone voices of recent decades, coupled with great interpretive intelligence. His range of roles is enormous, encompassing not only the bass-baritone repertoire but some purely baritone and bass roles as well. His greatest roles include Amfortas, Jokanaan, Wagner's Dutchman, Don Alfonso in Mozart's *Così fan tutte,* and Wozzeck. Van Dam tends to play parts for melancholy; his Dutchman is extremely brooding, for which he has been criticized. He does not find, for example, Mozart's Figaro to be a comic role, explaining that ". . . after five minutes onstage Figaro learns his best friend may be sleeping with Susanna, and I don't think that's funny."

Van Dam considers his ultimate working relationship to have been with Herbert von Karajan, who invited him to the Salzburg Easter Festival for many productions. Van Dam feels that Karajan's "rapport with his singers amounts to a metaphysical marriage." On recordings Van Dam may be heard in a number of roles under Karajan. He is the Jokanaan on Karajan's *Salome* with Behrens in the title role and manages to invest the prophet with some dramatic interest for once. He sings the part of the monk on Karajan's *Don Carlos* from the Salzburg Easter festival of 1978, sounding at once suitably aged yet steady of tone. On Karajan's *Pelléas et Mélisande* Van Dam sings gloriously as Golaud, managing to elicit sympathy from the listener in a role normally associated with monstrous cruelty. Van Dam's Figaro, an example of great singing and subtle character portrayal by any standards, is featured on the Karajan Decca recording of *Le nozze di Figaro* with a cast that was featured in the Jean-Pierre Ponnelle production at Salzburg. Van Dam is excellent on Karajan's 1984 recording of *Der fliegende Holländer,* displaying gorgeous tone, eloquent phrasing, clear diction, long breath, and a perfect legato in the exquisitely soft singing of "Wie aus der Ferne." For all his admiration of Karajan, Van Dam has turned down a number of roles the maestro proposed to him: Sarastro, Telramund, and Pizarro.

Perhaps Van Dam is an iconoclast in his interpretation of many of the roles he undertakes. Even his Leporello, seen in the Joseph Losey film of *Don Giovanni,* is not a particularly comic character, yet it is a rich interpretation, with many subtleties in the Catalogue aria. The score is conducted by Lorin Maazel, another conductor with whom Van Dam likes to work. Early in his career, Van Dam was invited by Maazel to join the Deutsche Oper, Berlin. There, his first big success was as Paolo in Verdi's *Simon Boccanegra,* a role he recorded on the incomparable DGG set conducted by Claudio Abbado. In Berlin Van Dam also performed, among others, Leporello, Figaro, Attila, Boris, Gianni Schicchi, and Philip in *Don Carlos.* He sang in the 1965 DGG recording of Ravel's *L'heure espagnole* conducted by Maazel. Georg Solti, becoming aware of Van Dam's talents, engaged him as Escamillo at Covent Garden, a role that he subsequently recorded under Solti on Decca and the one in which he made many of his debuts around the world. Van Dam also recorded Berlioz' *La Damnation de Faust* with Solti.

Born in Brussels in 1940, Van Dam sang in a neighborhood church where his voice was discovered by a Jesuit priest. At age 13 he went to Professor Frédéric Anspach at the Brussels Conservatory, where he received a diploma in Lyric Art in 1960. He was then hired by the Paris Opéra, remaining there for four years singing such roles as Marcello, Colline, and Angelotti before leaving for the Geneva Opera for two years and then for Berlin, where his main career may properly be said to have begun. Van Dam is a particularly quick learner but likes to spend a great deal of time preparing a new role, ideally a year between learning and performing. He prefers to read extensively about his characters. In preparing for the role of the devil in Berlioz's Faust setting, for example, he discovered the delights of Goethe's *Faust.* Wozzeck, Van Dam feels, is his most arduous role: "It's more of an actor's part than a singer's. . . ." In an *Opera News* interview in 1980 Van Dam revealed that growing up he admired Bjoerling, Warren, Pinza, Siepi, Wunderlich, and, among the ladies, Leontyne Price. "She has a fantastic instrument, a beautiful line." He also looks to instrumentalists for that line, such as Rostropovich, Perlman, Zukerman, and Menuhin. Other notable recordings by Van Dam include Don Alfonso in Muti's 1983 Salzburg *Così fan tutte,* a Massenet *Manon* with Cotrubas and Kraus under Plasson, and a superb Father in *Louise* with Sills and Gedda.—STEPHEN A. WILLIER

Vanessa

Composer: *Samuel Barber.*

Librettist: *G.-C. Menotti.*

First Performance: *New York, Metropolitan Opera, 15 January 1958.*

Roles: *Vanessa (soprano); Erika (mezzo-soprano); Anatol (tenor); Doctor (baritone or bass-baritone); Baroness (contralto); Nicholas, Majordomo (bass); Footman (bass); Pastor (mute); chorus (SATB).*

Samuel Barber's *Vanessa,* completed in 1957 and premiered at the Metropolitan Opera in 1958, was the composer's most ambitious work of the 1950s. Following its premiere, the opera was presented at the Salzburg Festival on 16 August 1958—the first time in history that the Festival presented an American opera and in English. The Metropolitan also staged the work two other seasons, 1958-59 and 1964-65. Thus, *Vanessa* became one among only a few moderately successful American operas to have emerged in the international performance repertoire. However, critics have pointed out that it is an American opera only because the composer was native-born, and not in any nationalistic sense, since neither the libretto nor the score is based on any American "mores or musical lore."

Vanessa, an attractive middle-aged woman who has been grieving over a lost love affair, has withdrawn from the world and lives isolated in a baronial house with her niece Erika "in a northern country." As the opera opens Vanessa awaits the return of her beloved Anatol after twenty years. However, the Anatol who arrives is not her lover but his son, who is an opportunistic adventurer seeking the good life. When Vanessa leaves the scene in disappointment, the young Anatol proceeds to seduce the lonely Erika, who soon realizes he is not serious. In act II, sensing Erika's doubt, Anatol turns his attentions to Vanessa and revives her illusions of youthful love. When the couple's betrothal is announced at the ball in act III, Erika, who is pregnant, attempts suicide. In the final act, Erika is rescued, suffers a miscarriage, and renounces her relationship to Anatol. As Vanessa rides off with Anatol, Erika orders the house be shut up again as she, waiting for love, assumes Vanessa's former role.

Barber had been seeking a libretto for years, discussing opera projects with Dylan Thomas, Thornton Wilder, and Stephen Spender, among others. He was delighted when his friend Gian-Carlo Menotti, who had an excellent working knowledge of the theater as both composer-librettist and stage director, offered to write a text for him. Although Menotti modestly defined a libretto as a "pretext for music," Barber, in his total immersion in any poetry he set, appreciated the economy of Menotti's verbal expression, his pronounced simplicity, and unique theatrical timing—all elements imperative for the singing stage. According to Barber, composer and librettist discussed twists and turns of plot and character but Barber changed very few words, and sometimes requested additional text, including an extra aria for the doctor, to be

The first production of Barber's *Vanessa*, with Eleanor Steber and Regina Resnik, Metropolitan Opera, New York, 1958

sung by Giorgio Tozzi. Menotti's text, filtered through Barber's musical personality, produced high-style bravura duets, a delightful waltz, as well as pastoral dance tunes, a brilliant coloratura aria for Vanessa, a soliloquy for the doctor, and in the final act, a transporting quintet.

With a Chekhovian quality, *Vanessa* is a subtle character study with recognizable prototypes in the literature of the period. Vanessa's music, through high tessitura and virtuosic demands, reveals her high-strung emotionalism. Erika as a pivotal character has many opportunities—her opening aria, her renunciation of Anatol, and her suicide attempt—for a compelling performance. Anatol, though not so fully developed, reveals a marked weakness. The old Doctor serves as a contrast to the leading participants, and the Baroness—silent and immobile most of the time—must project in her negativity an ominously powerful minor character.

The world premiere under the baton of Dmitri Mitropoulos—the first time in ten years that the Metropolitan Opera had mounted an American opera—was greeted with a standing ovation. Encouraged by this reception, the European premiere in the Festspielhaus at the Salzburg Festival was meticulously planned. Although cordially greeted by an international audience, *Vanessa* was "brutally condemned" by the Austrian and German critics. According to Raymond Ericson's report in *Musical America* (September 1958, vol. 78 no. 10), "Unfortunately, all the best efforts of these distinguished artists could not persuade the critics that Menotti's libretto was not foolishness and that Barber's music was not a pastiche of ideas borrowed from Puccini and Strauss."

However, because of Barber's knowledge and empathy for the human voice, his extraordinary technical skills combined with his inventiveness in infusing formal structures with dramatic content and lyrical expansion, *Vanessa* has survived in the performance repertoire in spite of this evaluation.—MURIEL HEBERT WOLF

Vaughan Williams, Ralph

Composer. Born 12 October 1872, in Down Ampney, Gloucestershire. Died 26 August 1958, in London. Married: 1) Adeline Fisher, 1897 (died 1951); 2) the poet Ursula Wood, 7 February 1953. Played violin and viola in the orchestra of the Charterhouse School, London, 1887-90; studied harmony with F.E. Gladstone, theory with Parry, and organ with Parratt at the Royal College of Music, London, 1890-92; studied composition with Charles Wood and organ with Alan Gray at Trinity College, Cambridge, receiving a Mus. B. in 1894 and a B.A. in 1895; studied with Stanford at the Royal College of Music; studied with Max Bruch in Berlin, 1897; Mus. D., Cambridge University, 1901; member of the Folk Song Society, 1904; conductor of the Leith Hill Festival in Dorking, 1905; studied with Ravel in Paris, 1909; served in Salonika and France as a medical orderly and later as an artillery officer in the British Army, 1914-18; professor of composition at the Royal College of Music, 1919-38; conductor of the London Bach Choir, 1920-28; A Pastoral Symphony completed 1921; in the United States, 1922; Gold Medal of the Royal Philharmonic Society of London, 1930; lectured at Bryn Mawr College, 1932; Order of Merit from King George V, 1935; composition of his fourth through ninth symphonies, 1931-58; lecture tour of several American universities, 1954.

Operas/Masques *Hugh the Drover, or Love in the Stocks,* H. Child, 1910-14, London, His Majesty's, 14 July 1924; revised, 1956; *The Shepherds of the Delectable Mountains,* Vaughan Williams (after Bunyan), 1921, London, Royal College of Music, 11 July 1922 [incorporated into *The Pilgrim's Progress*]; *On Christmas Night* (masque), A. Bolm and Vaughan Williams (after Dickens), 1926, Chicago, Eighth Street, 26 December 1926; *Sir John in Love,* Vaughan Williams (after Shakespeare), 1924-28, London, Royal College of Music, 21 March 1929; *Job* (masque), G. Keynes and G. Raverat (after Blake), 1927-30, London, Cambridge Theatre, 5 July 1931; *The Poisoned Kiss* (romantic extravaganza), E. Sharp (after R. Garnett), 1927-29, Cambridge, Arts Theatre, 12 May 1936; revised, 1956-57; *Riders to the Sea,* Vaughan Williams (after J.M. Synge), 1925-32, London, Royal College of Music, 1 December 1937; *The Bridal Day* (masque), U. Wood (after Spenser), 1938-39, British Broadcasting Corporation, 5 June 1953; revised, 1952-53; *The Pilgrim's Progress,* Vaughan Williams (after Bunyan, et al.), 1949; London, Covent Garden, 26 April 1951; revised, 1951-52.

Ralph Vaughan Williams, son of an Anglican clergyman, came from a well-to-do middle class background of considerable intellectual distinction, being descended from the Darwins and the Wedgewoods on his mother's side and from a line of professional people on his father's. He showed a talent for music and an interest in the theater from his early childhood; he had a toy theater as a boy at Leith Hill Place in Surrey and composed small pieces to accompany the plays "performed" in it. Titles of some of these have been preserved: *The Ram Opera,* for example, and *The Galoshes (sic!) of Happienes (sic),* found in a musical exercise book dating from the year 1882.

After leaving Charterhouse school in the summer of 1890, the boy went to Munich before entering the Royal College of Music as a student. There, he heard Wagner's *Die Walküre* for the first time; he described the experience as "a feeling of recognition as of meeting an old friend." Two years later, in June 1892, he heard in London a visiting company from the Hamburg opera under Gustav Mahler perform *Tristan und Isolde* and was profoundly affected by the music.

In the autumn of 1895, having graduated in History and having obtained his Bachelor of Music degree at Trinity College, Cambridge, he returned to the Royal College of Music, studying composition with C.V. Stanford. Stanford was not only a fine teacher, scholar and "academic" composer of choral and orchestral music, but also much interested in opera. He had conducted the English premieres of Cornelius's *Barber of Baghdad,* of Schumann's *Genoveva,* and of Delibes's *Le roi l'a dit* earlier in the 1890s. He greatly admired both Verdi and Wagner and composed seven operas himself, including *Shamus O'Brien,* on an Irish theme, first performed in March 1896, which had a successful run of over 100 performances.

Although Vaughan Williams liberated himself from the Brahmsian idiom of his irascible teacher, his operas follow the more traditional kind favored by Stanford himself rather than the Wagnerian music drama. He had discovered the appeal of English folk song, was excited by the freshness of the great Tudor and Stuart composers from Tallis to Purcell, and responded to the beauty and power of Anglo-American literature (Walt Whitman's verse was an early and lifelong enthusiasm). Like many young English musicians of his time, he realized that "second-hand off-scourings of the classics," as he himself put it, were not the way to establish a vital school of English composition. This did not mean, however, that he felt either folk song or a return to the past was the be-all and end-all of any musical renaissance in England. Something more was needed, in his own case, at any rate. He therefore spent three months in Paris in 1908 studying with Maurice Ravel.

In April 1905, music by Vaughan Williams for a masque based on Ben Jonson's *Pan's Anniversary* had been performed at Stratford-on-Avon; another pointer to the future came in 1909, when he composed music for a performance of a dramatized version of Bunyan's *Pilgrim's Progress* at Reigate Priory. Music for a number of Greek plays including *Iphigenia in Tauris, The Bacchae* and *Elektra* followed, but undoubtedly the most successful of these scores was that composed for a production at Cambridge in November 1909 of Aristophanes' *The Wasps.* In 1913, he composed music for other plays, including Maeterlinck's *The Death of Tintagiles* and (for F.R. Benson's Shakespearean season that year at Stratford-on-Avon) *The Merry Wives of Windsor* (to which he was to return for the source of his second full-length opera), *King Richard II, King Henry IV, Part II, King Richard III* and *King Henry V.* Benson also produced Shaw's *The Devil's Disciple,* set in the American colonies in revolt against George III, to which Vaughan Williams contributed the incidental music.

Vaughan Williams was now regarded as the leading English composer of the post-Elgar generation with works such as the *Fantasia on a Theme by Thomas Tallis* (1910), the impressionistic and highly dramatic song cycle *On Wenlock Edge* (1909, poems by A.E. Housman), the *Sea Symphony,* and the *Five Mystical Songs* (1911; poems by George Herbert). By 1910, he felt that he was ready to try his hand at an opera, regardless of whether it might ever reach the stage.

The origin of his first opera, *Hugh the Drover,* was ostensibly the result of a desire to set a prize fight to music, and the boxing match in the first act of *Hugh* is evidence of the fact. Vaughan Williams also wanted to compose a modern equivalent of the ballad operas of the eighteenth century, of which *The Beggar's Opera* had been the first and of which the Savoy operettas of Gilbert and Sullivan were a direct descendant.

The book of *Hugh the Drover* was by Harold Child, a writer on the staff of the London *Times.* "The duty of the words," Vaughan Williams had written in 1902, "is to say just as much as the music has left unsaid and no more." From about August 1910 over a period of years, he gently bullied Child into reshaping his text to do this, and the piece was virtually finished just before the outbreak of war in August 1914.

Despite his age (nearly 42), Vaughan Williams volunteered for military service, first in the Royal Army Medical Corps and then in the Royal Artillery, serving in the Balkans and on the western front. After the armistice, he became Director of Music for the British First Army, and on demobilization in February 1919, he set about revising his *London Symphony* (composed in the years before the war) and *Hugh the Drover.* He also started work on his third (*Pastoral*) symphony, some of the musical ideas for which had occurred to him when in military service. That year, he joined the staff of the Royal College of Music, teaching composition.

Vaughan Williams's music of this period is notable particularly for a ruminatively lyrical strain, evident not only in the *Pastoral Symphony,* but in such works as *The Lark Ascending* (1920) for violin and orchestra (completed before the war but revised after it) and his second opera, *The Shepherds of the Delectable Mountains,* (1922) a one-acter adapted from an episode in Bunyan's *Pilgrim's Progress* and incorporated many years later into the full-length opera he composed on Bunyan's book. In the same year that he composed *The Shepherds,* he also paid his first visit to the United States, to conduct a performance of his *Pastoral Symphony* at the Litchfield County Music Festival, Norfolk, Connecticut. It is amusing to note that he was far more impressed by the bustle of New York than he was by Niagara Falls!

V
OPERA

The 1920s saw a broadening and deepening of his idiom. He absorbed something of the neo-classicism of Stravinsky and the brash brightness of "Les Six," but he remained in general true to his own musical past, with works such as the Mass in G minor (1922), the *English Folk Song Suite* for military band (1923) and the Violin Concerto (1926). 1926 also saw the composition of two works in which the power and passion latent in his music reached a new intensity of expression: the oratorio *Sancta Civitas* and the haunting *Flos Campi,* for solo viola, wordless chorus and small orchestra. In the meantime, *Hugh the Drover* reached the professional stage, being produced by the British National Opera Company at His Majesty's Theatre, London, on 14 July 1924.

The success of *Hugh the Drover* stimulated the composer to work on other operatic ventures. The first of these to achieve public performance (on 21 March 1929 at the Royal College of Music) was *Sir John in Love,* a Falstaff opera based on Shakespeare's *The Merry Wives of Windsor,* the text arranged by the composer. The opera marks a distinct advance in stagecraft and musical sophistication over *Hugh,* and the main reason why this delightfully lyrical and strongly characterized piece has not become more popular is probably the sheer number of singers required. It certainly stands up well to the comparison it inevitably courts with Verdi's great masterpiece on the Falstaff story.

There followed what is probably the composer's operatic masterpiece, his setting of J.M. Synge's one-act tragedy *Riders to the Sea.* Work on this began in the 1920s, and although the piece was completed by 1932, it was not performed until 1 December 1937. The taut action and restrained musical idiom of *Riders,* its simplicity and terseness have caused it to become a problem opera; its quality and stageworthiness are indisputable, but because it lasts a mere thirty-five minutes and is difficult to provide with a complementary work of the right scale to fill the rest of the evening, it has been unjustly neglected.

Growing recognition abroad led to a further visit to the United States, this time to lecture at Bryn Mawr University on "National Music." Every new work was now eagerly awaited. The massive "masque for dancing" *Job* (1930, first staged at the Cambridge Theatre, London, 5 July 1931), the powerful Piano Concerto (1931), the violent F minor Symphony (1935) and numerous choral works, including the racy *Five Tudor Portraits* of 1935 and the sombre *Dona Nobis Pacem* (1936) testified to his versatility. Further evidence of this is found in the comic opera *The Poisoned Kiss,* first performed on May 12 1936 at the new Arts Theatre in Cambridge. This work suffers from an irredeemably arch libretto, but it contains some fine music, dramatically apt and lighter in touch than is usually the case with Vaughan Williams. Unlike his other operas and in keeping with its somewhat farcical subject matter, *The Poisoned Kiss* has spoken dialogue.

The Second World War and after saw Vaughan Williams exploiting new fields as well as continuing to cultivate old ones. He composed music to the film *49th Parallel* in 1940-41, the first of many film scores (elements from at least two of which found their way into symphonic compositions), and in 1943, at the age of 70, he produced his luminous and visionary Fifth Symphony, incorporating elements from his unfinished operatic version of *The Pilgrim's Progress.* Many took the Fifth to be his final symphonic testament; but four more symphonies were to follow it, including the pungent and disquieting sixth (1948) and the *Sinfonia Antarctica* (No. 7, 1953), the themes of which were in large measure developed from his music to the film *Scott of the Antarctic.*

Vaughn Williams' final completed opera (he was working on a further operatic project, based on an English folk ballad, when he died) was the *The Pilgrim's Progress,* first performed at the Royal Opera House, Covent Garden, on 26 April 1951. The subject matter and the absence of any conventional operatic love interest and intrigue failed to impress the audience, and a gimmicky production presented the opera in the worst possible light. None the less, the score contains some of his finest music, with a telling theatrical contrast between the sinister mechanical monotone of Apollyon, the Hogarthian ribaldry of the Vanity Fair scene, the laid-back vapidity of the By-Ends episode and the radiant visionary quality of the central figure's apotheosis at the end.

Vaughan Williams is an outstanding figure in the history of twentieth century English music. Basically traditionalist, the individuality, power, depth and intensity of his music at its best have few equals.—JAMES DAY

Les vêpres Siciliennes [The Sicilian Vespers]

Composer: *Giuseppe Verdi.*

Librettists: *Eugène Scribe and Charles Duveyrier.*

First Performance: *Paris, Opéra, 13 June 1855; revised as Giovanni di Guzman,* later called *I vespri siciliani,* Milan, Teatro alla Scala, 4 February 1856.

Roles: *Montforte (baritone); Henri (tenor); Hélène (soprano); Procida (bass); Bethune (bass); Count Vaudimont (bass); Ninetta (contralto); Daniele (tenor); Tébald (tenor); Robert (bass); Manfred (tenor); chorus (SATTB); chorus (TB).*

For his first commission from the Paris Opéra, Verdi chose the librettist preferred by Meyerbeer and Halévy, the reigning monarchs of that stage: Eugène Scribe. Though Scribe was supposed to offer an original work, he in fact merely rewrote a libretto Donizetti had attempted to set fifteen years earlier, but failed to complete before succumbing to the venereal disease which eventually killed him. At that time the libretto was called *Le duc d'Albe,* and dealt with Spanish oppression in the Lowlands under the eponymous Duke of Alva. Scribe transferred the oppression to thirteenth-century Sicily, converted the Duke into Guy de Montfort, the cruel governor, changed Amelia, sister of the martyred Count of Egmont, into Hélène, sister of the martyred Regent of Sicily, and Marcel, a revolutionary whom the duke has just discovered to be his illegitimate son, into Henri, Montfort's son under the same circumstances. The major addition to the original libretto is its setting at the moment of a well-known historical event, the uprising of the Sicilians and their massacre of the French as the bells tolled vespers on Easter Sunday, 1282. Verdi also added a character, Procida, who existed in history but seems to have been a diplomat without portfolio rather than the terrorist fanatic the opera makes of him.

Verdi, with his uncanny sense of what would and would not "play," put his finger on a central problem of the libretto. Writing to the Paris Opéra's director, he observed that "M. Scribe offends the French, because Frenchmen are massacred; he offends the Italians by altering the historical character of Procida into the conventional conspirator." Scribe, however, made no alterations, and the opera was given a surprisingly warm reception, the urbane Parisians apparently caring less about seeing their ancestors portrayed as villains than about hearing a good, Meyerbeerian plot realized with Italianate verve. The Italians were denied an opportunity to express themselves on the slandering of Procida, because the Austrians occupying Italy would

865

not permit an opera depicting an Italian nationalist uprising, especially a successful one. For the Italian performance, the action was transferred to the Iberian peninsula, as *Giovanna da Guzman,* with Portuguese patriots and Spanish brutality.

Verdi's criticism of the libretto is cogent, but those of subsequent commentators must be treated with some reservation, since by and large their references are to the eventual Italian translation which, like all Italian translations of the French libretti set by Verdi, Rossini, and Donizetti, reflect a banality of concept and trivialization of motive not found in the originals.

Independent of his reservations about the libretto, Verdi was faced with a difficult task, the writing of "French" music for a Meyerbeerian grand opera. His successful adaptation of *I Lombardi* into the more subtle *Jerusalem* in 1847 had been critically acclaimed in Paris, but there he had adapted an existing score. Now he would have to test himself where both Rossini and Donizetti had succeeded before him, not only in composing music to a libretto in a foreign language (which he, like they, spoke and understood well enough), but also in modifying the essential directness of the Italian operatic idiom into the subtler harmonies, more complex ensembles, and less easily excerptable solo passages preferred by the Parisian public. One hesitates to call this style "French," except geographically: it had its origins in the German Gluck's ideas, while its form had been dictated primarily by the Germanized Italian Spontini and the Italianized German Meyerbeer. Though Verdi would eventually master its requisites perhaps better than anyone else in *Don Carlos* (1867), *Les vêpres siciliennes* can be seen as a laboratory in which Verdi tests his capacity for French expression. Those who know the opera only from its most often played and recorded excerpts, the overture, Procida's act II aria, and Hélène's act V bolero, have heard only the most Italianate parts of the score. Montfort's act III aria and duet with Henri are identifiably Verdian, but more contemplative, less direct than similar pieces from his most recent Italian operas. Henri's aria, proceeding from a complex recitative without the obligatory musical break, is unlike anything Verdi had written up to this time, and can only be compared with the tenor's music in *Stiffelio.* Hélène's act I aria, with its four-movement structure (andante, largo, allegro moderato, allegro giusto) has no model in earlier Verdi, resembling much more closely Fidès' scena in Meyerbeer's *Le prophète.* But it is in the great ensembles concluding the second and fourth acts in which Verdi entirely masters the French style (to the incidental benefit of his later Italian works, especially *Simon Boccanegra* and *La forza del destino*). *Les vêpres siciliennes* is, finally, not a great opera, but it has great passages, is crucial to Verdi's development, and is fascinating in comparison with both Verdi's later works and the immensely popular works of Meyerbeer and Halévy that the Italian master sought to match in popularity.—WILLIAM J. COLLINS

Verdi, Giuseppe

Composer. Born 9 or 10 October 1813, in Le Roncole, near Busseto, Duchy of Parma. Died 27 January 1901, in Milan. Married: 1) Margherite Barezzi, daughter of Verdi's patron, 4 May 1836 (died 18 June 1840); 2) the renowned soprano Giuseppina Strepponi, 29 August 1859 (died 1897). Studied at a very early age with the church organist Pietro Baistrocchi; music lessons with Ferdinando Provesi, director of the municipal music school in Busseto; resident at the home of the merchant Antonio Barezzi, 1831, who paid Verdi's way to Milan for further musical instruction; denied admission to the Milan Conservatory; private study of counterpoint, canon, and fugue with Vincenzo Lavigna;

maestro di musica in Busseto, 1834; first opera, Oberto, *completed 1838, which was accepted and performed at the Teatro alla Scala in Milan, 1839; further opera composition for the Teatro alla Scala, 1839-43; premieres of operas in Venice, Florence, London, St Petersburg, and Paris, 1844-47; elected to and served in the first Italian Parliament, 1861-65; elected to the Académie des Beaux Arts in Paris, 1864; premiere of* Aida *in Cairo, 1871, an international event; nominated a senator of the Italian Parliament, 1875; last operas,* Otello *(1887) and* Falstaff *(1893), composed after years of retirement; the King of Italy named Verdi "Marchese di Busseto," 1893, but Verdi did not accept the title; founded the Casa di Riposo per Musicisti in Milan, 1897.*

Operas *Oberto, Conte di San Bonifacio,* Temistocle Solera? (after A. Piazza, *Rocester, Lord Hamilton*), Milan, Teatro alla Scala, 17 November 1839; *Un giorno di regno, ossia Il finto Stanislao,* Felice Romani, revised Temistocle Solera? (after Romani, *Il finto Stanislao* 1812), Milan, Teatro alla Scala, 5 September 1840; *Nabucodonosor* (shortened to *Nabucco*), Temistocle Solera (after the ballet by A. Cortesi, 1838), Milan, Teatro alla Scala, 9 March 1842; *I Lombardi alla prima crociata,* Temistocle Solera (after Tommaso Grossi), Milan, Teatro alla Scala, 11 February 1843; revised as *Jérusalem,* Gustave Vaëz and Alphonse Royer, Paris, Opéra, 26 November 1847; *Ernani,* Francesco Maria Piave (after Hugo, *Hernani*), Venice, La Fenice, 9 March 1844; *I due Foscari,* Francesco Maria Piave (after Byron, *The Two Foscari*), Rome, Torre Argentina, 3 November 1844; *Giovanna d'Arco,* Temistocle Solera (after Schiller, *Die Jungfrau von Orleans*), Milan, Teatro alla Scala, 15 February 1845; *Alzira,* Salvadore Cammarano (after Voltaire), Naples, San Carlo, 12 August 1845; *Attila,* Temistocle Solera and Francesco Maria Piave (after Z. Werner), Venice, La Fenice, 17 March 1846; *Macbeth,* Francesco Maria Piave and Andrea Maffei (after Shakespeare), Florence, Teatro della Pergola, 14 March 1847; revised, Piave, French translation by Charles Nuitter and A. Beaumont, Paris, Théâtre-Lyrique, 21 April 1865; *I masnadieri,* Andrea Maffei (after Schiller, *Die Räuber*), London, Her Majesty's, 22 July 1847; *Il corsaro,* Francesco Maria Piave (after Byron, *The Corsair*), Trieste, Grande, 25 October 1848; *La battaglia di Legnano,* Salvadore Cammarano (after J. Méry, *La bataille de Toulouse*), Rome, Torre Argentina, 27 January 1849; *Luisa Miller,* Salvadore Cammarano (after Schiller, *Kabale und Liebe*), Naples, San Carlo, 8 December 1849; *Stiffelio,* Francesco Maria Piave (after E. Souvestre and E. Bourgeois), Trieste, Civico, 16 November 1850; revised as *Aroldo,* Rimini, Nuovo, 16 August 1857; *Rigoletto* (originally, *La maledizione*), Francesco Maria Piave (after Hugo, *Le roi s'amuse*), Venice, La Fenice, 11 March 1851; *Il trovatore,* Salvadore Cammarano, some changes and additions by L.E. Bardare (after Garcia Gutiérrez, *El trovador*), Rome, Apollo, 19 January 1853; *La traviata,* Francesco Maria Piave (after Dumas fils, *La dame aux camélias*), Venice, La Fenice, 6 March 1853; *Les vêpres siciliennes,* Eugène Scribe and Charles Duveyrier, Paris, Opéra, 13 June 1855; [revised as *Giovanni di Guzman,* later called *I vespri siciliani,* Milan, Teatro alla Scala, 4 February 1856]; *Simon Boccanegra,* Francesco Maria Piave and G. Montanelli (after Antonio García Gutiérrez), Venice, La Fenice, 12 March 1857; text revised, Arrigo Boito, music revised by Verdi, Milan, Teatro alla Scala, 24 March 1881; *Un ballo in maschera* (originally *Gustavo III*), Antonio Somma (after Eugène Scribe, *Gustave III*), Rome, Apollo, 17 February 1859; *La forza del destino,* Francesco Maria Piave (after Angelo Pérez de Saavedra, *Don Alvaro, o La fuerza de sino,* and Schiller, *Wallensteins Lager*), St Petersburg, Imperial Theater, 10 November 1862; text revised, A. Ghislanzoni, music revised by Verdi, Milan, Teatro alla Scala, 27 February 1869; *Don Carlos,* François Joseph Méry and Camille Du Locle (after Schiller, W.H. Prescott, *History of Philip II,* and E. Cormon, *Philippe II, roi d'Espagne*), Paris, Opéra, 11 March 1867; translated into Italian by A. de Lauzières and A. Zanardini, with musical revisions by Verdi, for

867

Milan, Teatro alla Scala, 10 January 1884; *Aida,* Antonio Ghislanzoni (after a scenario by François Auguste Ferdinand Mariette as sketched in French by Camille Du Locle), Cairo, new Opera House, 24 December 1871; *Otello,* Arrigo Boito (after Shakespeare), Milan, Teatro alla Scala, 5 February 1887; *Falstaff,* Arrigo Boito (after Shakespeare, *The Merry Wives of Windsor* and *King Henry IV*), Milan, Teatro alla Scala, 9 February 1893.

Verdi showed talent and a great love of music early in his life, and was given keyboard lessons as a child. At ten he played the organ in church well enough to replace his teacher, the village organist Pietro Baistrocchi, at the latter's death. By this time Verdi was boarding in Busseto, where he attended school and (in 1825?) began studying music with the composer and organist Ferdinando Provesi, director of the town's church music, the municipal music school and the local philharmonic society.

As a teenager, Verdi began assisting his master as organist and in the music school, and he also began writing and arranging for the philharmonic group (marches, overtures, serenades, cantatas, arias, duets, terzets and church music). He also wrote concertos and piano variations to play at the group's concerts. The gifted youth became a protegé of the philharmonic organization's president, the wealthy merchant Antonio Barezzi, and gave music lessons to his daughter Margherita, whom he ultimately married.

Primarily with the financial aid of Barezzi but also with support from the Monte di Pietà of Busseto, Verdi applied for admission to study piano at the Milan Conservatory in 1831. This was denied because of his age (eighteen), the fact that he was not a citizen of Lombardy, and poor positioning of his hands at the keyboard. He was advised to study composition privately and from 1832-1835 did so with Vincenzo Lavigna, composer and *maestro al cembalo* at the Teatro alla Scala for many years. These studies were mainly in counterpoint; but the young Verdi also subscribed to the opera, rented scores and analyzed music with Lavigna. After Provesi's death in 1833, an apparently reluctant Verdi was persuaded to apply for his former teacher's several positions and a protracted struggle ensued between the young musician's supporters, mainly members of the town's philharmonic society, and his detractors, for the most part officials of the church.

After some time had elapsed (Verdi's application had not yet arrived), the clerical faction hired an organist from a neighboring town as director of church music. An attempt to have him made director of the philharmonic society and municipal school of music was foiled by a petition to the Duchess of Parma, Marie Louise. After delaying a year,

Giuseppe Verdi, 1886

she ordered a competition for the municipal positions (to take place in February 1836) which Verdi won easily. Before this event Verdi completed his studies with Lavigna and successfully directed, from the keyboard, Haydn's *Creation* (April 1834) and Rossini's *La Cenerentola* (April 1835) at the Teatro Filodrammatico in Milan. In the process he made powerful friends among the Milanese nobles who sponsored these events.

Verdi's new position in Busseto allowed him to marry Margherita, and he attended to his responsibilities well enough. But his primary interest was in opera and he wrote a work entitled *Rocester* which many authorities believe formed the basis for his first performed stage work, *Oberto, Conte di san Bonifacio.* As soon as his first contract expired, Verdi resigned his position in Busseto and took his wife and an infant son to Milan (February 1839). A daughter, the first born, had died some months earlier. Shortly before the relatively successful premiere of *Oberto,* Verdi's son also died (November 1839). Misfortune continued to plague the young composer and he lost his wife while writing his second opera, *Un giorno di regno* (later *Il finto Stanislao*), a farce which proved unsuccessful (September 1840).

Verdi's fortunes turned with *Nabucodonosor* (now universally called *Nabucco,* March 1842), in which his future second wife, Giuseppina Strepponi, sang the role of Abigaille. Strepponi, whose voice declined after a relatively short career as one of Italy's leading dramatic sopranos (1835-1842), was not effective in the difficult role, and the truly phenomenal success of the opera dated from its second season at La Scala, that summer, with an almost entirely new cast of principals. A remarkable string of additional successes followed. The first of these was *I Lombardi alla prima crociata* (February 1843), a sprawling work of little dramatic cogency but with many effective musical numbers. In addition, just as audiences had identified with the Hebrews in their Babylonian captivity in *Nabucco,* they did so no less with the Italian crusaders freeing the Holy land in *I Lombardi.*

Ernani (La Fenice, Venice, March 1844), based on Victor Hugo's play, was the composer's fifth opera and his most successful stage work until *Trovatore.* This was followed the same year by *I due Foscari* (Torre Argentina, Rome November 1844), an intimate, melancholy work based on Byron which had considerable success in the 1840s and 50s, and was still to be heard in the 1860s before disappearing from the repertory.

Verdi returned once more to La Scala with *Giovanna d'Arco* (February 1845), the first of his quartet of operas based on plays by Schiller, and unquestionably the weakest of the four. It was much less successful than its immediate predecessors, although it was heard occasionally in Italy and elsewhere for about twenty years. Verdi believed it to have been poorly staged at La Scala, a complaint he voiced about all his operas performed there in the 1840s and 50s. As a result, he broke off relations with Italy's premier house for almost twenty-five years. Later that year the composer traveled to Naples to direct *Alzira* (August 1845), a work he later considered to be one of his weakest. The following year Verdi returned to Venice to direct *Attila* (March 1846), one of the most successful of the earliest operas, with two lines—Roman Ezio's remark to Attila, "You may have the universe, leave Italy to me"—calculated to enflame the patriotic sensibilities of Italian audiences. Police censors in some Italian cities, in fact, changed these verses.

Verdi's next opera, *Macbeth* (Florence, March 1847), the first of his stage works based on a play by his beloved Shakespeare, is the most original and ambitious of his early operas. Later in life (1875), during a discussion of Wagner, Verdi called *Macbeth* his own attempt to write music drama. During the late nineteenth century, *Macbeth* had more success in its original version than in Verdi's revision for Paris (April 1865). This may be attributed to a more rapid and effective denouement, the concise manner in which the composer treated the battle music and death of Macbeth in the first version.

Verdi then left Italy, composing first *I masnadieri* for London (July 1847). Although the opera was not particularly successful in England, it did quite well in Italy. In Paris that summer, Verdi began living with Giuseppina Strepponi, his companion and later his wife (1859) for fifty years. He also signed a contract for *Jérusalem* (November 1847), an extensive revision of *I Lombardi* to a French text with the obligatory ballet required by France's premier house. Performed with modest success in cities where French was spoken (e.g. Paris, Brussels and New Orleans) it failed in a retranslation to Italian as *Gerusalemme* (La Scala, December 1850).

Verdi grudgingly fulfilled a contract he had made with the publisher Lucca by writing *Il corsaro* (Trieste, October 1848). Although much of the music is beautiful, this is one of Verdi's less dramatically effective operas. In a departure from his usual habit, the composer refused to direct the premiere. Just days before the proclamation of the short-lived Roman Republic, Verdi joined Giuseppe Mazzini and Giuseppe Garibaldi in Rome where he directed his most blatantly patriotic opera, *La battaglia di Legnano* (January 1848). The story of the defeat of the German emperor Frederick Barbarossa by a league of northern Italian knights, the opera was hampered by censorship in the period after the failure of the revolutions of 1848-49. It had a brief period of success during the early years of the unification of Italy (1859-61) but not thereafter.

With the more intimate *Luisa Miller* (Naples, December 1849), a work for which he had particular affection, Verdi turned away from operas with a political message. The injustices of society, however, especially as they affected individuals, continued to concern him. Here, it is the misuse of unbridled power by a nobleman, Count Walter. In his next opera, *Stiffelio* (Trieste, November 1850), Verdi came to the defense of a minister's wife who commits adultery, but still loves her husband. While there is beautiful music in both works, *Luisa Miller* entered the repertory but *Stiffelio* did not; at least in part it was because of the inherently more logical dramatic development of the former.

With the famous triad of *Rigoletto* (March 1851), *Il trovatore* (Rome, January 1853) and *La traviata* (March 1853), Verdi reached a new level of artistic maturity. He now had full command of the compositional resources of early and mid nineteenth century Italian opera, and he focused these resources on better dramas. Most notably, the characters in these and his later operas are often less stereotypical than in previous operas; they are sometimes grotesque, but they are always intensely human, with well-motivated actions.

Les vêpres siciliennes (June 1855) was Verdi's first completely new opera for Paris. It was followed there a year and a half later by *Le trouvère*, a French translation and revision of *Trovatore* with added ballet. If Verdi's music up to and including *Traviata* may be said to have been mainly influenced by Italian composers such as Rossini, Bellini, Mercadante and especially Donizetti, much of the music he wrote for the stage after *Traviata* may be considered to reflect the influence of French grand opera composers, particularly Meyerbeer. This may be discerned not only in *Les vêpres* and *Don Carlos* (March 1867), both written to French texts specifically as grand operas, but also in such Italian works as *La forza del destino* (St Petersburg, November 1862), *Aida* (Cairo, December 1871) and *Otello* (February 1887). All of these show the massive scale, the greater importance of the drama, the lavish scenery, costumes and staging, the expanded orchestra and richer accompaniments, the rhythmic flexibility (for example, there are far fewer cabalettas with their stereotyped Polonaise or march rhythms) and the approach to structure that stresses the larger, through-composed or tripartite subdivisions that characterize grand opera. The emphasis in these works tends to be less on the soloists, their arias and duets, and more on the ensembles and crowd scenes. Verdi, aware of this changed approach, called his operas of the decade 1862 to 1871 (*Forza, Don Carlos* and *Aida*) his "modern" operas and distinguished them from the earlier operas which he called "cavatina" operas. He specifically included *Traviata* among the "cavatina" operas in which the soloists and their *convenienze* or conventions where stressed. Two of Verdi's operas of the late 1850s, the first version of *Simon Boccanegra* (March 1857) and *Un ballo in maschera* (Rome, February 1859) show elements of both styles. Of the two, *Ballo* is the more brilliant, closer to the older style and was then, and is now, far more successful at the box office (Verdi's measure of an opera's success). Among the reasons for *Ballo*'s success are the fact that the dramatic thread is clearer in *Ballo* than in *Simon Boccanegra*, and the scenes with the secondary characters, Oscar and Ulrica, provide welcome changes of pace, but in addition are crucial for the plot. In Verdi's revision of *Simon Boccanegra* (for La Scala, March 1881), twenty-four years later, the most exciting change occurs with the introduction of a council chamber scene into the finale of act I. Written while the composer was thinking about *Otello*, the music of this scene foreshadows the power and emotional intensity of Verdi's last tragic opera.

Falstaff (February 1893), the composer's final stage work, was written by a mellowing Verdi as he approached eighty, and was undertaken to prove to a doubting musical world that he could successfully set a comedy. Thanks in large part to a brilliant libretto by Arrigo Boito, a composer in his own right who also wrote the librettos for *Otello*, the revision of *Simon Boccanegra* and the *Inno delle nazione, Falstaff* is more tightly constructed than Shakespeare's *Merry Wives of Windsor* on which it is largely based. The opera has magical orchestration, quicksilver melodic ideas and a surprisingly wide range of emotions. It also has a convincing continuity of movement between the individual scenes found consistently only in the final acts of *Aida* and in *Otello*.

As his letters to librettists show, to a certain extent Verdi shared in the construction of his librettos. Sometimes he prepared the *programma*, the summary prose draft of a libretto with which the composer and librettist began their collaboration. This is especially clear in the manuscript materials for the never completed *King Lear* and especially those for *Aida* presently at Verdi's estate, Sant'Agata, where his heirs reside. In two instances the composer literally taught the craft of writing librettos to poets, and the results were successful operas. The works are *Ernani*, Francesco Maria Piave's first libretto, and *Un ballo in maschera*, Antonio Somma's only libretto.

Despite the enormous popularity of most of his operas from *Rigoletto* through *Aida*, it was not until Verdi had written the Manzoni Requiem (1873-74), the finest of his nonoperatic works, and later *Otello* and *Falstaff*, that musicians in Northern Europe and the United States recognized him to be one of the major composers in the history of Western music.—MARTIN CHUSID

Verrett, Shirley

Soprano. Born 31 May 1931, in New Orleans. Studied with Anna Fitziu and Hall Johnson, and with Mme Szekely-Freschl at Juilliard; debut as Lucretia in Britten's The Rape of Lucretia, *Yellow Springs, Ohio, 1957; New York debut as Irina in Weill's* Lost in the Stars,

1958; European debut in Rasputins Tod *by Nabokov, 1959; Teatro alla Scala debut as Carmen, 1966; Metropolitan Opera debut as Carmen, 1968; has sung with the Metropolitan Opera since 1968.*

American diva Shirley Verrett's mid-career transition from mezzo-soprano to soprano has divided critical and popular opinion. Some see the change as an appropriate step for this singer, whose theatrical flair has led her to seek out ever more challenging roles. Others hear the transformation as accompanied by a serious decline in vocal quality and range, and cite her example as a cautionary tale for other mezzos contemplating a similarly reckless path.

Both arguments are valid. Verrett's soprano roles have included at least one portrayal—Verdi's Lady Macbeth—about which critical opinion is almost entirely positive, as well as others (Tosca, even Norma) in which, by and large, she has met the vocal challenges with success, and which have been illuminated by her dramatic presence. At the same time, it is difficult not to hear and regret a separation of vocal registers and substantial wear on the velvety timbre which was such a notable characteristic of one of the most beautiful mezzo-soprano voices of the 1960s and early 70s.

The voice and repertoire of Verrett in her prime were unequivocally those of a mezzo-soprano, although we can hear in the easy upper register the promise of a "higher calling." Verrett's mezzo assayed a large number of roles from coloratura to lyric and dramatic, and to all she brought her instantly recognizable velvety sound as well as a sincerity and nobility of manner which were equally distinctive.

It may be this very diversity that makes Verrett more difficult to characterize than some of her contemporaries. She is not identified as a *bel canto* specialist, for example, unlike her celebrated compatriot Marilyn Horne, though Verrett achieved real distinction in this repertoire, notably in the Metropolitan Opera's production of Rossini's *L'assedio di Corinto* which was also the house debut of Beverly Sills. Neither do we instantly think of Verrett as a Verdi singer, the way we do of Fiorenza Cossotto, though her Azucena, Ulrica and particularly Eboli are among the finest portrayals of those roles in our time.

Perhaps it is in the French repertoire that Verrett has made her most visible and lasting contribution. Her Dalila is notable for a voluptuous exoticism and superbly sensual vocalism, and she has performed to great acclaim both Didon and Cassandre in *Les Troyens,* where her statuesque grandeur is especially welcome. Audiences who saw Verrett as Carmen (a role she sang in most

Shirley Verrett as Dalila in the Royal Opera production of *Samson et Dalila,* 1981

major international theaters) will never forget her sensuality and fire. Alas, Verrett was not record this role.

As Lady Macbeth, a crucial role in her transition to soprano, Verrett came into her own. The voice itself was rather soft-grained for this taxing part, but Verrett's technical security allowed her to negotiate the difficulties with seeming ease; moreover, her powerful physical and vocal acting were precisely right for this flamboyant part. Critics who attended her first performances of the role at the Teatro alla Scala found her the most compelling interpreter of the part since Callas. Fortunately, Verrett's Lady Macbeth was recorded under near ideal circumstances (Claudio Abbado conducting the forces of the Scala revival), and this document goes a long way toward suggesting the impact, both vocal and dramatic, that Verrett can make in the theater. More recent assumptions of soprano roles (including Amelia in *Un ballo in maschera*, and *Aida*) have yielded mixed results, the dramatic thrust and commitment not entirely compensating for increasingly threadbare vocalism—though it should be said that at present Verrett is still a formidable figure on the operatic scene, even if the opulent voice shows unmistakable signs of decline. For a souvenir of that voice at its finest, her Orfeo recorded under the sympathetic baton of Renato Fasano shows Verrett's singing at its richest, the steady tone gleaming with a dark brilliance that few singers have matched.—DAVID ANTHONY FOX

Vickers, Jon

Tenor. Born 29 October 1926, in Prince Albert, Saskatchewan. Married: Henrietta Outerbridge, 1953; three sons, two daughters. Studied with George Lambert at the Royal Conservatory of Music in Toronto; debut as Duke in Rigoletto, *Toronto, 1952; sang regularly for Canadian radio; Covent Garden debut as Riccardo in* Un ballo in maschera, *1957; at Covent Garden until 1969; sang Siegmund at both Bayreuth and London, 1958; sang Siegmund, Don José, Radames, and Canio at Vienna Staatsoper, 1959; Metropolitan Opera debut as Canio, 1960; remained there for twenty seasons; sang Peter Grimes at Metropolitan in 1967, and repeated role in London in 1969, 1971, and 1975; sang in U.S. premiere of Handel's* Samson, *Dallas, 1976; retired in 1988; was made Companion of Honor of the Order of Canada, 1969.*

From the beginning of his career in the mid-1950s until 1988, Jon Vickers was without peer as a dramatic tenor. The character of his voice was atypical and strikingly individual— rugged, sinewy, tough, but capable of great warmth and lyrical beauty—and the range of vocal colors that he commanded allowed him to be equally persuasive in the English, Italian, French, and German repertoires.

During his early years of study in Toronto, the brilliant ring of his voice was evident, but his teacher, George Lambert, laid a vocal foundation for Vickers with the music of Bach, Handel and Purcell. While far from the dramatic repertoire in which Vicker's became famous, this music provided a source to which he returned throughout his career. As he once put it in an interview, "Last season, after singing Siegmund, I felt my voice crying out for an antidote of Handel and Bach." In the 1950s in Canada he had the opportunity to sing such diverse roles as the Duke in *Rigoletto,* Alfredo in *La traviata,* Ferrando in *Così fan tutte,* Troilus in *Troilus and Cressida,* the Male Chorus in *The Rape of Lucretia,* as well as radio performances of Act I of *Die Walküre* and the final scene of *Parsifal,* and oratorios of Handel and Haydn. By the time he reached Covent

Garden and the international stage in 1957, he was vocally accustomed to a variety of musical demands, and he had the experience and the interest to maintain that variety.

Throughout his long career Vickers sang with virtually every major conductor, singer, and director of the time. He developed a particularly fruitful relationship with Herbert Von Karajan. Although he appeared in all the great opera houses of Europe and America, he nevertheless severely restricted the number of his performances in any one season, and he chose carefully when he would add a role to his repertoire and when he would leave it. His resources were maintained and nourished, and when he closed his career with the second act of *Parsifal* at Kitchener, Ontario, in 1988, he did so with the compelling, full-throated affirmation that had distinguished his performances for thirty-five years.

Vickers did not record or publicly perform single arias to show off his voice and beguile the public, because for him the voice was to be at the service of the music, not the reverse. For Vickers, an aria would make sense only in the context of the drama to which it belonged, and almost all his operatic recording is of complete works. His recorded legacy is, in fact, relatively small considering his prominence and stature. Recordings in any case convey only inadequately a Vickers performance. Vocal effects such as his use of half-voice or head-tone, or a tendency to portamento, can stand out on a recording as vocal mannerisms, but they could have tremendous effect in the theater because they were so dramatically motivated. Moreover, Vickers is a powerfully built man whose physical presence in itself carries great force, and on the stage he understood fully how to express in external gesture and movement his understanding of the inner feelings and motivations of the characters he portrayed.

Vickers could produce a heroic sound, but he could also sing quietly with sensual beauty and intimacy, and he could accomplish this dynamic range without a break in timbral continuity. He used this range to extraordinary effect, and this is something that can be grasped from his recordings. The final act of *Tristan und Isolde* he sang like chamber music, as if offering to the listener the chance of merely overhearing the interior musings of the delirious Tristan, but the arrival of Isolde would bring forth a torrent of sound, only to die literally in his mouth as Tristan himself dies. Similarly in *Peter Grimes,* Vickers makes Peter's final monologue a *tour de force* of expressive singing as Peter's emotions and reminiscences thrash about, from the rage of "Now is gossip put on trial" to the distant and heart-breaking quietness of the phrase "Turn the skies back and begin again."

The song recital played a relatively small part in Vickers's career, but his ability to adjust the vocal scale of his performance was especially evident there. A recording of songs that he made for the Canadian Broadcasting Corporation in 1969 is sung with compelling simplicity and a directness of communication from singer to listener. His performances of Schubert's *Die Winterreise* were a highly personal interpretation of those often bleak songs, with an intimacy that demanded the utmost concentration of the listener.

Vickers included among his greatest roles the monumental figures of Otello, Tristan, Parsifal, Siegmund, Aeneas and Peter Grimes, but he was as convincing in lesser masterpieces such as *Samson et Dalila, I pagliacci, The Bartered Bride,* or *Carmen* because of the complete conviction and understanding that he carried to a performance. Since opera was not for him merely entertainment, he had to find in a role some moral force, whether it be Tristan's struggle to overcome desire or the consequences of Samson's broken vows. It was this conviction, the absolute certainty of his own understanding, and uncompromising standards that he brought to his performances and which made them so thrilling.—CARL MOREY

A Village Romeo and Juliet

Composer: *Frederick Delius.*

Librettist: *Frederick Delius (after Gottfried Keller, Romeo und Julia auf dem Dorfe).*

First Performance: *Berlin, Komische Oper, 21 February 1907.*

Roles: *Manz (baritone); Marti (baritone); Sali (tenor); Vreli (soprano); Dark Fiddler (baritone); Two Peasants (baritones); Three Women (contralto, two sopranos); Ginger-Bread Woman (soprano); Wheel-of-Fortune Woman (soprano); Cheap Jewelry Woman (contralto); Showman (tenor); Merry-Go-Round Man (baritone); Shooting-Gallery Man (bass); Slim Girl (soprano); Wild Girl (contralto); Poor Horn Player (tenor); Hunchback Bass Fiddler (bass); Three Bargemen (two baritones, tenor); chorus (SATBB).*

The original story from which Delius fashioned the consistently beautiful score for *A Village Romeo and Juliet* was drawn from a real life occurrence. On 3 September 1847, a Zurich newspaper had reported the deaths of two youths whose bodies had been found in a field. Children of poor background from a village near Leipzig, they had not been allowed to marry because of enmity between their families. After dancing one night at a nearby inn, they had shot themselves. The story caught the attention of the Swiss author Gottfried Keller, who jotted down in his diary shortly afterwards a possible motive for the feud: a dispute over a strip of land between the farms of the respective families. In 1885 this peasants' dispute and the Romeo and Juliet theme were interwoven by Keller to become the subject of his most famous novella, *Romeo und Julia auf dem Dorfe,* published the following year in the first of the two volumes which comprised the collection of stories entitled *Die Leute von Seldwyla.*

When Delius first encountered Keller's tale is not known, but a friend noted in September 1897 that the composer "had long had it in mind to use it as an opera." Earlier, in 1894, Delius had written: "I have a vague idea of writing 3 works: one on the Indians *[The Magic Fountain],* one on the Gypsies and one on the Negroes and quadroons *[Koanga].*" It may well be that the loose group of wanderers and social outcasts who appear towards the end of Keller's novella represent in Delius's opera the vestigial gypsies of that projection.

The principal characters of *A Village Romeo and Juliet* are Salomon (Sali) Manz and Vrenchen (Vreli) Marti. Delius presents the two as young children in just the first scene of his "lyric drama in six scenes." Scene ii takes place six years later, and the remaining action probably just some months after that. The dispute between the farmers Manz and Marti, which results in ruinous litigation between them, is contained within the first two scenes of the opera, whereas the quarrel and its aftermath play a major role continuing well into the second half of Keller's original. Delius, however, wished his Romeo and Juliet to take center stage as early as possible, with the result that for the purposes of the opera the farmers' wives and other subsidiary characters in Keller are excised completely from the score. On the other hand, the role of the Dark Fiddler—the true but dispossessed inheritor of the strip of "wildland" that is at the root of the whole tragedy—is much expanded in Delius's hands. The grandson of the original owner of the now-disputed land, he has never been able to prove title to it (Delius adopts the device of illegitimacy to explain why), and he appears in the first scene of the opera, while the children are playing on the wildland that is gradually being ploughed into by each father, to warn them that time may well avenge him. Following his departure, farmers Manz and Marti quarrel and separate the children, who must no longer play together.

Six years later, their fathers now impoverished, Sali finally seeks out Vreli again. Love dawns. They agree to meet secretly on the wildland where, however, the Dark Fiddler disturbs them once again. He bears them no ill will, though he finds a grim satisfaction in their fathers' downfall and suggests that as they too have become reduced to such beggarly circumstances, they should join him in his wanderings. Even if they choose not to do so, "We'll meet again, no doubt, further down the hill." Left alone, the lovers take their first kiss, but are seen by Marti, looking for his daughter. While trying to drag her away he is knocked unconscious by Sali. The blow has terrible consequences: Marti is from then on confined in an asylum in the nearby town of Seldwyla. Vreli is left alone.

Time passes, and Vreli is spending her last night in the family home, now sold to pay her father's debts. As the twilight deepens, Sali returns and vows never to leave her again. They talk until darkness and then fall asleep in each other's arms. Each dreams of their wedding. Early next morning they take their leave of the house and make their way to the annual September fair at the village of Berghald. Wandering around the booths and stalls, they find their happiness cut short when they are recognized by other fairgoers from Seldwyla. Miserably self-conscious in their poor clothing, they decide to move on and at twilight reach an old riverside inn, the *Paradiesgärtlein*. Although here, at least, they do not expect to be recognized, they soon find that the inn is frequented by the Dark Fiddler and the vagabonds who are his friends. Welcomed by the group, Sali and Vreli again have temptation put in their way. Should they not after all join the fiddler and his companions in their nomadic life, free of all bourgeois moral restraints? Vreli has, after all, sung earlier of wandering "like gypsies on the great road." The youngsters' innate innocence and integrity will not, however, permit them to do so. They rather choose to consummate their love and die. Sali sees a hay-barge moored nearby, lifts Vreli into it and casts off. He will sink the boat and the lovers will drown in each other's arms.

Like all of Delius's operas, with the exception of the fairy tale *Irmelin,* the emphasis of *A Village Romeo and Juliet* is on alienation—between individuals, classes, or races. One or another set of circumstances decrees that the principal actors on Delius's stage will be outcasts, with death usually the outcome. The wellspring of tragedy in *The Magic Fountain* is racial conflict, as it is again in *Koanga*. In the one case it is the North American Indian, in the other the Afro-American whose downfall is brought about, willingly or unwillingly, by the white man. The outcasts of *Margot la Rouge* are the apache underclass of Parisian society. *Fennimore and Gerda* too is in major part the story of the alienation (for the first and only time on a bourgeois level in Delius's operas) between the three people at the heart of the main "Fennimore" episode. In *A Village Romeo* the alienation of each of the principal characters is virtually complete. Society rejects them all. Through their greed for land, Manz and Marti become impoverished and are then the direct cause of the years of separation between their children. The Dark Fiddler has long been a social outcast: interestingly, he remains so throughout, the only character who has adjusted to his life and achieved some kind of happiness. Sali and Vreli are innocent outcasts who end by being completely unable to relate to the world around them. They elect to die because they can envision this quite clearly, and not because they take a nihilistic or fatalistic view of the world. Triumphantly, the process of alienation is brought to an end by the unity of their love and death.

In 1897 and 1898 Delius had two writer friends make separate attempts to produce a libretto from Keller's story. The first was C.F. Keary, *Koanga's* librettist, the second Karl-August Gerhardi, who started to fashion a suitable German text. Neither satisfied Delius, who, beginning to see the shape of his opera, decided in the autumn of 1899 to write his own libretto, which he swiftly completed. By November he was hard at work on the music, several successive months going into composition. After various interruptions, the opera was completed in 1901. Thomas Beecham, who gave it in London in 1910 and again in 1920, made with Delius's agreement certain revisions to the text, and this is the work's authentic libretto. The fresh English libretto (or "new translation") commissioned for the opera's revival in 1962 derived from the mistaken belief that Jelka Delius's excellent German translation of Delius's text was in fact the original libretto. It was finally—and one hopes irrevocably—abandoned when the 1989 film of the opera largely reverted to the Delius/Beecham version.

Peter Weigl's film has in fact confirmed what Frank Corsaro's 1970s production of *A Village Romeo,* with its cinematographic commitment to the scenic qualities as well as the moods evoked by the music, had already suggested: that Delius wrote, as it were, a film scenario and then composed an almost seamless stream of ravishingly beautiful music to mirror and amplify it. Claus Helmut Drese, at the time of his Zurich production in 1980, spoke of the challenge presented by the fact that some forty minutes of the score were purely orchestral. There is for most of this time comparatively little stage action. It is this kind of almost wilful disregard for the expectations of conventional operagoers that has received wry acknowledgement by successive (and largely sympathetic) commentators on *A Village Romeo and Juliet.* In 1923 Heseltine first hinted at the possibilities the gramophone may open up for the work; in 1948 Hutchings saw radio broadcasting as providing its most effective future; in 1970 Jefferson wrote of the possibility of its "triumphing" as a film. It is perhaps not surprising that earlier critics were disappointed at this lack of action. After all, in spite of requiring a large orchestra, the piece has at its core little more than the intimate interaction of the two young lovers who hold the center of the stage throughout. This rather static quality—shared in many respects with Debussy's *Pelléas et Mélisande*—is likely to demand more from an audience than, say, most of its verismo contemporaries, and the finest productions have been those in which the quality of the acting, as well as the singing, of the Sali and Vreli characters has served to draw the audience deeply into the taut intimacy of the drama, a drama impelled to its tragic conclusion by Delius's extraordinarily cogent and sinuous score. The composer, incidentally, always insisted on his singers' acting "from the music and not from the stage."

A Village Romeo and Juliet is to all intents and purposes the fruit of the happy circumstance of compositional maturity reached at the same time as the discovery of a virtually perfect vehicle for the composer's genius. The descriptive power of Delius's music, particularly in relation to the kind of pantheism that so attracted him, was already evident in his earliest orchestral works dating from the later 1880s and was fully assured by the time of the composition of the symphonic poem *Paris,* immediate predecessor of *A Village Romeo.* All of Delius's rich harmonies are there, as indeed are longer melodic lines than his previous operas have tended to give us, together with a characteristic translucence in the scoring. The score is in fact remarkably faithful to its source, and those very qualities of restraint, indeed reticence, that characterize Keller's economically-expressed story are also present in the music. Apart from the opportunity offered by the village fair music, with its striking pre-echoes of Stravinsky's *Petrushka,* there are remarkably few "theatrical" effects, and indeed some productions have given emphasis scenically to a perceived dream-like character inherent in the work—a character that may obviously be epitomized as the very antithesis of verismo. We are indeed far from Verona with this almost Nordic Romeo and Juliet, and there is no doubt that Delius saw his work to some extent as a psychological drama pointing the way to the J.P. Jacobsen-inspired *Fennimore and Gerda* a few years later. But whereas in the main "Fennimore" episode there is a darker, more troubled and even claustrophobic aspect to this later score, it is the quality of freshness and light which predominates in *A Village Romeo*. From the opening orchestral outburst (already giving us one of the opera's main leitmotifs) in all its sun-drenched vigor, evoking the dazzling beauty and the vibrant late-summer air of the countryside, to the final passionate duet, lit by moonlight, the elemental forces of nature and, with them, the oneness of human life are evoked, giving us some of Delius's finest music. Each of the opera's six scenes has its prelude, the first five being purely orchestral, the last taking the form of a distant mixed chorus set against the lower strings and followed by echoing horn-calls, and among them are ravishing examples of Delius's evocative use of woodwind, horns and strings (see particularly the transition between scenes ii and iii leading to Sali and Vreli's meeting on the wildland). Otherwise the best-known of the orchestral interludes is "The Walk to the Paradise Garden," only composed in 1907 when the scene-changing exigencies of Hans Gregor's production at Berlin's newly-founded Komische Oper demanded its interpolation.

The number of European productions in the 1980s has given scope for a full reassessment of *A Village Romeo and Juliet,* and Weigl's film of the opera has at last provided us with a view of the work as nearly as possible as Delius would have wished to see it. Those earlier critical views of Delius' characters as little more than prototypes or symbols, moving in dreamlike sequence to their predestined end, are seen to be very wide of the mark: the lovers are flesh and blood, and their passion, so long held in check and finally fully released, is committed, believable and deeply moving. Heseltine was right from the start: "There is never any disparity between the music and the action. . . . If opera be defined as perfect co-relation between music and action, then *A Village Romeo and Juliet* is one of the most flawless masterpieces that have ever been given to the world."—LIONEL CARLEY

Vinay, Ramón

Tenor and baritone. Born 31 August 1912, in Chillán, Chile. Died 4 January 1996. Studied engineering in France, voice in Mexico City with José Pierson; baritone debut as Count di Luna in Il trovatore, *Mexico City, 1938; tenor debut as Don José in* Carmen, *Mexico City, 1943; New York City Opera debut as Don José, 1945; Metropolitan Opera debut as Don José, 1946; at Metropolitan Opera, 1946-62 and 1965-66; Teatro alla Scala debut as Otello, 1947; Salzburg debut, 1951; at Bayreuth, 1952-57; Covent Garden debut, 1955; Paris debut, 1958; artistic director of The Santiago Opera, 1969-71.*

Fairly early in his career, Ramón Vinay staked out his operatic territory and took psychological siege. There was heroic agony in his sound, but sorrow and tenderness, too. He could suggest the noble pain of a tenor like Giovanni Martinelli, but with an intellectual frenzy all his own. Vinay's was a dark voice of medium size, called rich on good nights and thick on problematic ones, shadowed and occasionally unsteady but at its peak possessing great warmth, like sunlight in a thicket. In the theater it lacked a cutting edge, the *squillo* of Mario del Monaco or Franco Corelli, but it had a complexity of color that gave his Otello vulnerability, his Don José tragic stature, and his Wagnerian roles spiritual profundity. The lower range connoted authority and the upper an implacable yearning.

Like Renato Zanelli, Lauritz Melchior, and Set Svanholm, Vinay began as a baritone. His international career, though, started in 1944 with a Mexican performance of Verdi's *Otello*. In two years his "Rembrandtian tone quality" (as Arthur Bloomfield put it) led him to the Metropolitan Opera in this and other tenor roles, and then to Bayreuth for half a dozen seasons in Wagner, and meanwhile to Salzburg, San Francisco, Holland, London, and Italy, singing his famous Moor and Don José, Samson, Canio, Radames, Tannhäuser, Siegmund, Tristan, Parsifal, and Herod. In the 1960s he returned to lower roles: Falstaff, Telramund, Iago, Scarpia, Dr. Schoen, and even Bartolo (*Il barbiere di Siviglia*), Varlaam (Lord Harewood reportedly thought it the best characterized he had ever seen), and the Grand Inquisitor in *Don Carlo*. He closed his singing career in Chile singing tenor one more time, in the final act of *Otello*.

As can be seen, Vinay had his triumphs in roles of the greatest motivational complexity. The voice was best heard in a house the capacity of Bayreuth—about 2000; faced with Wagner at the Metropolitan Opera (nearly twice that size), he might push. His expressive qualities were already finely developed in his first studio recording, some highlights from *Carmen* done with Gladys Swarthout in 1946. Pride and intimate yearning shape his performance. His Flower Song is deeply committed rather than declamatory, his reading of "Carmen, je t'aime" at its conclusion an exposed private moment. Vinay's characterization in the final duet is equally adult: forgiving and demanding, desperate, restrained, and impossible all at once, without either vulgarity or pretension, but suggesting more fully than any later singer but Jon Vickers the nobility of Don José's sexual passion.

These qualities dominated Vinay's other roles, too. His Otello under Toscanini (1947) may lack some of the suffocating tenderness of Martinelli's, but it too is profoundly indicative of both public valor and private frailty. Under Fritz Busch's direction at the Metropolitan Opera (1948) he deepens the frenzy, and with Furtwängler in Salzburg (1951) the element of reverie.

By that time Vinay had begun his forays into Wagner with an initial Tristan in San Francisco with Kirsten Flagstad (1950), and his Bayreuth career in tenor leads was about to begin. Some of those performances may be even more satisfying on records than they were in the opera house, where the visceral impact of the voice was less and the details could be lost in a single hearing. One would expect him to enact the frenzies of Tristan's third act movingly, but the erotic passion of act II is more difficult for a voice blunt in tone, a little tight at the climaxes, and not always free. Nevertheless, in a Bayreuth performance of July 1952 a despairing idealism always illuminates the mature sound, and towards the end of the love duet Vinay's spiritual quietude highlights amazingly the ensuing ecstasy of the climax. By contrast, the Melchior performance of 1936 (Covent Garden)—a touchstone—is incomparably beautiful in timbre: a tender seduction unequaled in my experience of this opera, but without the rapturous pain that makes the Vinay version an endless stimulation. Likewise, Melchior's subsequent appeal to Isolde to follow him into death is infinitely comforting, but Vinay's remains filled, uniquely, with exhausted longing. These traits are also found in his 1954 Bayreuth Tannhäuser. As one might expect, he sounds more industrious than joyful in the Venusberg salute, but the Rome Narration, chronicling the hero's damnation, has all the rage and sorrow implicit in the music and demonstrates most strikingly Vinay's special gifts. His revelation is one of increasing anguish. In this performance, the words of the Pope are indeed the words of anathema and the call to Venus a final cry of spiritual exhaustion. In his 1957 Parsifal, the voice is even older, but his response to seduction by Kundry is movingly agonized and the final redemption suffuses his tone with joy.

Vinay's baritone period is not so fully documented, though his Telramund and Iago (both 1962) show strong musical profile if not much vocal glamour. In the Verdi, he uses rhythm as a dramatic weapon and brings immense energy and craft to his work. "Era la notte" is strikingly intimate *and* obscene, and the duets with the Otello of Del Monaco are interesting for their differently projected voices: Del Monaco's is a sword and Vinay's a truncheon.

A commanding man onstage, Vinay was a singing actor of profound feeling in his French and Italian roles, and the subtlest and most heroic in spirit of the tenors of the Bayreuth renaissance in the early 1950s. His characterizations remain unique, but some of his work reminds one fondly of Jon Vickers, who has expressed deep admiration for Vinay's accomplishments.—LONDON GREEN

Vishnevskaya, Galina

Soprano. Born 25 October 1926, in Leningrad. Married: cellist/conductor Mstislav Rostropovich, 1955; two daughters. Studied in Leningrad with Vera Garina; debut in operetta, 1944; toured with Leningrad Light Opera Company, 1944-48; soloist with the Leningrad Philharmonic, 1948-52; joined Bol'shoy Theater in Moscow, 1952 (debut as Tatyana in Eugene Onegin*); Metropolitan Opera debut as Aida, 1961; Covent Garden debut in same role, 1962; Teatro alla Scala debut as Liù in* Turandot, *1964; appeared in film of Shostakovich's* Katerina Izmaylova *(1966) and sang in first performance of his Symphony No. 14 (1969); left USSR with husband in 1974; Soviet citizenship stripped in 1978 but restored in 1990.*

Since first becoming a soloist with the Bol'shoy Theatre in 1952, Galina Vishnevskaya's name has become increasingly well known throughout the musical world. Following an international tour in 1955 embracing Eastern Europe, Yugoslavia, Italy, Austria, France, England, the United States, Australia, New Zealand, and Japan, her performances of such roles as Tatyana and Lisa in Tchaikovsky's *Eugene Onegin* and *The Queen of Spades,* Kupava and Marfa in Rimsky-Korsakov's *The Snow Maiden* and *The Tsar's Bride,* Aida and Violetta in Verdi's *Aida* and *La Traviata,* Madama Butterfly and Tosca in Puccini's operas of the same titles, Leonora in Beethoven's *Fidelio,* Cherubino in Mozart's *Le nozze di Figaro* and the solo part in Poulenc's *La voix humaine*—all have been highly commended. She was the first performer of the role of Katarina in Shebalin's *The Taming of the Shrew* at the Bol'shoy in 1957, of Natasha Rostova in Prokofiev's *War and Peace* in 1959, of Marina in Muradeli's *October* in 1964, and of Sofiya Tkachenko in Prokofiev's *Semen Kotko* in 1970. In 1966 she sang the title role in the screen adaptation of Shostakovich's opera *Katerina Izmaylova* (a modified version of the earlier opera *The Lady Macbeth of the Mtsensk District*).

Vishnevskaya's superb artistry has often been a source of inspiration to composers. Benjamin Britten dedicated to her and her husband, Mstislav Rostropovich, his song cycle to words of Pushkin, *The Poet's Echo.* For her also was intended the soprano part in Britten's *War Requiem.* Shostakovich dedicated to her his Seven Romances, op. 127, likewise including a part for cello, and she was also a performer in the premiere of his Symphony No. 14 (1969).

Since 1974, following the emigration of Vishnevskaya and her husband to the West, both artists have been tremendously active often in joint projects (Rostropovich acting either as conductor or piano accompanist). In Britain alone both have appeared regularly at the Edinburgh Festival, the Aldeburgh Festival, Covent Garden, the Royal Festival Hall, and at the more recent Rostropovich Festival in Snape. Galina Vishnevskaya is a master in the art of creating mood, and it has been frequently stated that, even if the listener lacks an understanding of Russian, in her performance the underlying meaning of a song or aria could still be felt.

While Vishnevskaya's acting (influenced, like her singing, by Russian traditions) has on occasion been criticized as being a little "old-fashioned" (some critics consider her interpretation of Tatyana in Tchaikovsky's *Eugene Onegin* to be somewhat stylized), critics are unanimous in acknowledging the superb quality of her voice and the beauty of her tone. Equally at home in Russian, English, French, and Italian, she captures the essential features of each composer, be it Shostakovich, Britten, Poulenc or Verdi. Her performance as the passionate Katerina in Shostakovich's *Katerina Izmaylova* in the HMV recording of the work must certainly be regarded as one of her masterpieces; the *Gramophone* reviewer writes of "the moments of tenderness beautifully controlled, the voice coloured in great effect to convey a whole range of moods. . . . With Vishneskaya the character achieves a truly tragic stature." Impressive, too, is her portrayal of Pushkin's naive and guileless Tatyana in Tchaikovsky's *Eugene Onegin,* in which her interpretation is equally telling in its psychological insight. Though Vishnevskaya has occasionally been criticized for unevenness of performance, her voice is one that commands our attention and thus our emotions: in the final analysis, her supreme artistry prevails.—GERALD SEAMAN

Vivaldi, Antonio

Composer. Born 4 March 1678, in Venice. Died (buried) 28 July 1741, in Vienna. Studied violin probably with his father, Giovanni Battista Vivaldi, violinist at San Marco; commenced training for the priesthood 1693, ordained 1703; violin teacher at the Ospedale della Pietà in Venice 1703-9, 1711-17, 1735-8; music director at the court in Mantua of Prince Philip of Hesse-Darmstadt 1718-20; invited to Vienna by Charles VI, to whom he dedicated his twelve violin concertos entitled La cetra, *1727; composed many operas for Venice and other cities both inside and outside Italy.*

Operas *Ottone in villa,* D. Lalli, Vicenza, Teatro delle Garzerie, May 1713; *Orlando finto pazzo,* G. Braccioli, Venice, Sant' Angelo, fall 1714; *Nerone fatto Cesare,* M. Noris, Venice, Sant' Angelo, carnival 1715 [lost]; *La costanza trionfante degl' amori e de gl'odi,* A. Marchi, Venice, San Moisè, carnival 1716 [lost]; revised as *L'Artabano, re de' Parti,* Venice, San Moisè, carnival 1718; revised as *L'Artabano,* Mantua, carnival 1725; revised? as *Doriclea,* Prague, Sporck, carnival 1732; *Arsilda, regina di Ponto,* D. Lalli, Venice, Sant' Angelo, 27/28 October 1716; *L'incoronazione di Dario,* A. Morselli, Venice, Sant' Angelo, 23 January 1717; *Tieteberga,* A.M. Lucchini, Venice, San Moisè, 16 October 1717 [lost]; *Scanderbeg,* A. Salvi, Florence, Teatro della Pergola, 22 June 1718 [lost]; *Armida al campo d'Egitto,* G. Palazzi, Venice, San Moisè, carnival 1718 [act 2 lost]; revised, Mantua, Arciducale, 1718; revised?, Lodi, 1719; revised as *Gl'inganni per vendetta,* Vicenza, Teatro delle Grazie [lost]; *Teuzzone,* Zeno, Mantua, Arciducale, carnival 1719; *Tito Manlio,* M. Noris, Mantua, Arciducale, carnival 1719; *Tito Manlio* (pasticcio) (with G. Boni and G. Giorgio), Rome, Teatro della Pace, carnival 1720 [lost]; *La Candace o* *siano Li veri amici,* F. Silvani and D. Lalli, Mantua, Arciducale, carnival 1720 [lost]; *La verità in cimento,* G. Palazzi and D. Lalli, Venice, Sant'Angelo, 26 October 1720; *Filippo, re di Macedonia* (with G. Boniventi), D. Lalli, Venice, Sant' Angelo, 27 December 1720 [lost]; *La Silvia,* E. Bissari?, Milan, Ducale, 28 August 1721 [lost]; *Ercole su'l Termodonte,* G.F. Bussani, Rome, Capranica, 23 January 1723 [lost]; *Giustino,* N. Berengani, Rome, Capranica, carnival 1724; *La virtù trionfante dell'amore e dell'odio overo Il Tigrane* (with B. Micheli and N. Romaldi), F. Silvani, Rome, Capranica, Carnival 1724; *L'inganno trionfante in amore,* M. Noris and G.M. Ruggieri, Venice, Sant' Angelo, fall 1725 [lost]; *Cunegonda,* A. Piovene, Venice, Sant' Angelo, 29 January 1726 [lost]; *La fede tradita e vendicata,* F. Silvani, Venice, Sant' Angelo, 16 February 1726 [lost]; revised as *Ernelinda* (pasticcio) (music mostly by F. Gasparini, B. Galuppi and Vivaldi), F. Silvani, Venice, San Cassiano, carnival 1750 [lost]; *Dorilla in Tempe,* A.M. Lucchini, Venice, Sant'Angelo, 9 November 1726; revised?, Prague, Sporck, 1732; revised, Venice, Sant' Angelo, 1734; *Ipermestra,* A. Salvi, Florence, Teatro della Pergola, carnival 1727 [lost]; *Siroe, re di Persia,* Metastasio, Reggio Emilia, Pubblico, May 1727 [lost]; revised, Ancona, Fenice, 1738; revised, Ferrara, Bonacossi, 1739; *Farnace,* A.M. Lucchini, Venice, Sant' Angelo, 10 February 1727; revised, Venice, Sant' Angelo, 1727; revised?, Prague, Sporck, 1730; revised, Pavia, Omodeo, 1731; *Orlando,* G. Braccioli, Venice, Sant' Angelo, fall 1727; revised?, Este, Grillo, 1740; *Rosilena ed Oronta,* G. Palazzi, Venice, Sant' Angelo, carnival 1728 [lost]; *L'Atenaide o sia Gli affetti generosi,* Zeno, Florence, Teatro della Pergola, 29 December 1728; *Argippo,* D. Lalli, Prague, Sporck, fall 1730 [lost]; *Alvilda, regina de' Goti,* Prague, Sporck, spring 1731 [lost]; *La fida ninfa,* S. Maffei, Verona, Filarmonico, 6 January 1732; *Semiramide,* Zeno, Mantua, Arciducale, carnival 1732 [lost]; *Motezuma,* G. Giusti, Venice, Sant' Angelo, 14 November 1733 [lost]; *L'Olimpiade,* Metastasio, Venice, Sant' Angelo, 17 February 1734; *L'Adelaide,* A. Salvi, Verona, Filarmonico, carnival 1735 [lost]; revised?, Graz, Tummelplatz, 1735; *Griselda,* Zeno (additions by C. Goldoni), Venice, San Samuele, 18 May 1735; *Tamerlano* (*Bajazet*) (pasticcio), A. Piovene, Verona, Filarmonico, carnival 1735; revised? as *Bajazette,* Vicenza, Teatro delle Garzerie, 1738; *Ginevra, principessa di Scozia,* A. Salvi, Florence, Teatro della Pergola, January 1736 [lost]; *Catone in Utica,* Metastasio, Verona, Filarmonico, May 1737 [act 1 lost]; revised?, Graz, Tummelplatz, 1740; *L'oracolo in Messenia,* Zeno, Venice, Sant' Angelo, 30 December 1737 [lost]; revised, Vienna, Kärntnertor, 1742; *Rosmira* (pasticcio), S. Stampiglia, Venice, Sant' Angelo, 27 January 1738; revised?, Graz, Tummelplatz, 1739; *Feraspe,* F. Silvani, Venice, Sant' Angelo, 7 November 1739 [lost].

Were one to take the date of Vivaldi's first opera, *Ottone in villa* (Vicenza, 1713), as the deciding factor, one would conclude that he came late to the genre, at the age of thirty-five. This impression is misleading, however, since both he and his violinist father were actively involved with opera as performers and in management long before then; in fact, already in 1708 Vivaldi had composed a dramatic cantata for five voices, *Le gare del dovere,* that deploys the full range of musical resources found in opera.

Having made his debut outside his native Venice, Vivaldi concentrated his operatic efforts during the years up to 1718 on his native city. Much of the time he acted not only as composer but also as arranger (of other men's operas), musical director and impresario. From 1713 to 1717 he worked at the little Sant' Angelo theater, in 1717-18 at the hardly more pretentious San Moisè house. Although Vivaldi did not enjoy the prestige and patronage that came from activity in Venice's premier theaters (the Venetian nobles who controlled them tended to despise him as a parvenu), his wearing of so many "hats" at once—impossible in the larger houses—enabled him to develop an integrated view of opera that, while in no sense revolutionary, allowed his musical language to develop in fruitful ways.

The function of music in Italian opera of the early eighteenth century was more modest than that to which we have grown accustomed from Gluck onwards. Whereas in a modern opera music is a full partner in the drama and is expected to make a contribution to it independent of (and even sometimes in opposition to) the words and stage action, in late baroque "heroic" opera (*opera seria*) music is expected—like scenery, stage machinery, and costume—to provide appropriate "clothing" for a pre-existing drama that essentially inheres in the poet's libretto alone. The task of the composer is to set the words efficiently, with respect for accent and poetic meter (this especially in recitatives), to reflect in music the imagery and feelings of the text by drawing on traditional figures and devices, to satisfy the singers' need for vocal display (paying careful attention to the special qualities of each singer and the relative status of each), and to control the pace of the action so that the stage effects succeed.

Vivaldi fulfilled this basic set of requirements with great skill, but he also brought to opera the experience of a composer who had already distinguished himself in orchestral music. His first set of violin concertos (*L'estro armonico* Op. 3, 1711) had created a sensation all over Europe and was the object of much admiration and imitation. As one might expect, Vivaldi introduced the same degree of liveliness, complexity and feeling for sonority into the accompaniments of his operatic arias. The backbone of his orchestra was the string section, but every opera contains one or two arias featuring one or more "novelty" instruments such as recorder, bassoon, viola d'amore or a pair of horns. In these Vivaldi demonstrates his keen sense of tone color and idiomatic instrumental writing. On occasion, the orchestral writing in his arias is so elaborate and prominent that one almost has the sensation of a Wagnerian texture in which the instruments supply the foreground and the voice—weaving a free counterpoint against them—the background. Not that Vivaldi's vocal writing is undistinguished; particularly in arias of a more "popular" type he evinces real flair and produces melodies of true memorability. It is, however, true that his attentiveness to accuracy of word-setting and sensitivity of word-painting is sometimes found wanting. This is often the result of a concern to develop motives to the full, which may lead him to persist in using the opening musical ideas of an aria even when they are no longer metrically or dramatically apposite.

As in all Italian opera of his time, two well-defined types of musical setting predominate: recitative and aria (ensembles and choruses are rare, and the latter are often very perfunctory). Recitative is the core of the drama, carrying the action forward in a musical language that, although neutral and conventional in its basic form, is able through harmony, modulation and vocal inflection subtly to reflect the dramatic situation. Arias are conceived as static "moments" illustrating a character's feelings at a given point. They are like stills in a moving picture. In consequence, their structure is non-dynamic and nearly always has recourse to the "da capo" plan in which following a middle section the opening section returns in unvaried form, except for the addition of improvised vocal embellishment. Vivaldi is always content to accept the traditional division of labor between recitative and aria, although on occasion he will employ special varieties of recitative (such as instrumentally accompanied recitative and arioso) for emotionally charged scenes.

Vivaldi continued along the same path during the three-year period (1718-20) he spent at the court of Mantua as director of secular music. Soon after his return to Venice, Benedetto Marcello's pamphlet *Il teatro alla moda* (*The Fashionable Theater*) appeared, a mordant satire

OPERA

on contemporary Italian opera. It has been thought that Vivaldi was a particular target of Marcello, but today the general opinion among scholars is that the satirist included Vivaldi merely as the most prominent representative of the general operatic practice of his time. Marcello criticizes, for example, the frequent use of unison writing in the orchestra, a device that Vivaldi certainly liked and which several other composers had taken up under his influence. The pamphlet did nothing to impede his career as a composer of opera during the 1720s, which saw him at the height of his productivity and reputation. During this decade he received several commissions from houses in other cities such as Rome and Florence, and several of his works were revived inside and outside Italy, often without his active participation. He also began to act as a roving impresario, taking opera (his own works included) to provincial centers.

Musically, however, the 1720s were a decade of crisis for Vivaldi. In the middle years composers of Neapolitan origin including Vinci, Porpora and Leo became dominant on the Venetian stage. Their musical language reasserted the primacy of the singer, whose part became ever more ornate and finely nuanced, and pushed the orchestral accompaniment into the background. To some extent Vivaldi accommodated this new fashion, though he never repudiated totally the personal style that he had already forged. It is notable how rarely he set libretti by Metastasio, the poet *par excellence* of the Neapolitan school; the latter's bias towards reflection rather than action was perhaps at odds with Vivaldi's preference for a more vigorous approach. His later operas show a greater variety of treatment than his earlier ones, but at some cost to stylistic integrity. Several of them include ensembles of great distinction (the quartet in *Farnace* differentiates the characters as finely as Mozart would have done), while one (*Giustino*) has a powerful final chorus styled as a full-length chaconne.

Following his return from a visit to central Europe in 1729-30, Vivaldi, now aging, found it impossible to maintain his pre-eminent position in Venetian opera. Increasingly, his opportunity to compose operas became dependent on his parallel activity as a freelance impresario, since commissions had become less frequent. The focus of his activity gravitated away from Venice, now firmly in the grip of the Neapolitans, towards the minor operatic centers of the Italian mainland. His operatic projects met by turns with spectacular success and miserable failure, and their financial returns fluctuated correspondingly. He was particularly unlucky in Ferrara, where three consecutive seasons (1737-39) ended in frustration for him (on one occasion because, as a priest, he was forbidden by the papal legate to direct the performances). Nevertheless, a late opera such as *Catone in Utica* (*Cato in Utica,* Verona, 1737) shows few signs of waning inspiration. It is symptomatic of the precarious nature of Vivaldi's operatic activity at the end of his life that he journeyed from Venice to Vienna, leaving behind a legal tussle arising from one opera (*Feraspe*), only to find that the work he had planned for Vienna could not be staged because of a compulsory period of public mourning following the unexpected death of Emperor Charles VI. Cast adrift in the imperial capital, he died in great poverty.

Always given to exaggeration, Vivaldi claimed in 1739 to have composed ninety-four operas. Fewer than fifty have been identified, and of these only sixteen survive in a complete enough form to make their revival possible today. In fact, the "survival rate" evidenced by those figures is remarkably high for its time. It arises, first, from the fact that in his role as impresario Vivaldi was able to retain the scores that he had supplied to himself as composer (rather than give them up to the commissioning opera house) and, second, from the near-miraculous survival of his collection of his own manuscripts, today preserved in the Foà and Giordano bequests in the Biblioteca Nazionale, Turin.

The old view that Vivaldi's operas were "concertos in vocal dress" is discredited, and the musical value of his operas, as of all his vocal music, is nowadays generally recognized. That said, they do not depart in the least from the norms of Italian *opera seria* as practiced in the age of Zeno and Metastasio, and their appreciation on the stage depends greatly on the modern audience's acceptance of the underlying conventions, in particular those pertaining to the poetry and dramaturgy of the literary text. It is a mistake, for example, to imagine that a da capo aria can successfully be turned into a forward-moving event by means of the anachronism of cleverly devised accompanying action; it is far better to accept, and capitalize on, its intentionally static character. Given the importance to the drama of the recitative, it is desirable to cut it as little as possible and deliver it in a swift, unexaggerated and continuous manner.

Of the pre-1720 operas *L'incoronazione di Dario, La verità in cimento* and *Tito Manlio* have all been presented successfully in modern times; of the later operas *Giustino, Farnace, Orlando (furioso), La fida ninfa, Griselda* and *L'Olimpiade* have all been revived. The early *Ottone in villa* and *Orlando finto pazzo* have not yet been given modern performances but deserve them. Although Vivaldi cannot claim the artistic and historical importance of Handel or even Alessandro Scarlatti in the domain of opera, he is a figure with a distinct and attractive voice.—MICHAEL TALBOT

La voix humaine [The Human Voice]

Composer: *Francis Poulenc.*

Librettist: *Francis Poulenc (after Jean Cocteau).*

First Performance: *Paris, Opéra-Comique, 6 February 1959.*

Roles: *The Woman (soprano).*

Barely a year after the January 1957 premiere of *Dialogues des Carmélites,* Francis Poulenc's second opera, he was approached by the Paris director of Ricordi, the company that had commissioned and published *Dialogues,* with a suggestion for a new project. Would Poulenc, who was now a recognized musical dramatist, be interested in setting Jean Cocteau's monodrama, *La voix humaine?* Poulenc agreed quickly and enthusiastically, but rejected an additional suggestion that the single role in the opera (a character known simply as "Elle" ["She"]) be created for Maria Callas; instead, Poulenc had in mind his now-favorite leading lady, Denise Duval. The forty minute, one-act "tragédie-lyrique" was composed quickly, between February and June 1958, and Cocteau himself worked closely with Poulenc on the libretto, as well as handling design and production for the premiere.

For the second time in five years, Poulenc was obsessed by a composition, as he had been with *Dialogues,* writing to a friend that he composed *La voix* "in a trance." It was the intense mood of grief and solitude pervading *La voix* that caused Poulenc's state of agitation: "I think that I needed the experience of spiritual and metaphysical anguish in *Dialogues* so as not to betray the terribly human anguish of Jean Cocteau's superb text."

Cocteau's 1930 monodrama reveals to us a young, attractive woman who has been jilted by her lover. As the only character on stage, she prowls around her bedroom like a caged animal, pouring out her mixed emotions in a telephone conversation with this lover, whom we neither see nor hear. A disturbing intrusion upon this already pathetic monologue are the notorious hazards of the French telephone system at that time: the conversation is actually cut off twice and

OPERA

v

interrupted once. Because of this and because it represents her sole link to her lover, the telephone receiver almost becomes a second on-stage character. These problems only intensify the woman's anxiety. She is barely coherent at times; she is mad with jealousy and suspicion; she has attempted suicide; she soars to ecstasy and descends to despondency; and her voice rises to a cry of anguish as the opera ends and she realizes she will never speak to her lover again.

Since this is an opera for a single character, we can focus our attention on the style and contour of the vocal line. The following characteristics are observed: repeated notes abound; intervals greater than a fifth are rare, while stepwise motion and thirds predominate; rhythm and accents are designed to reflect actual speech patterns, particularly the pauses and hesitations of a telephone conversation. Thus, much of the vocal writing suggests plainchant, and the restrained style is appropriate since the main character is trying to contain her emotions throughout most of the conversation. She gives her feelings free rein only three times: during a particularly dramatic passage in which she laments losing the intimacy they shared with each other; and two lyric passages, when she speaks fondly of a happy occasion the two of them had shared, and when she speaks of her suicide attempt and her pathetic dream. This latter passage must be considered the most emotional part of the opera, and in it the vocal line finally becomes lyrically shaped and tonally stable.

Indeed, *La voix humaine* is one of Poulenc's most tonally unstable, ambiguous works, for it is filled with nonfunctional progressions, unresolved dissonances, particularly sevenths and ninths, diminished sevenths which do not resolve in a conventional manner, and progressions of chords related chromatically. Tonality is established definitively only in the most lyric passages, or by short orchestral motives based on functional harmonies.

This is but one way in which the orchestra serves to hold this fragmentary, declamatory opera together. A series of orchestral motives—not leading motives since they have no single dramatic reference—serves to unify the work. Many of these motives, nine of which are readily identifiable, can be traced back to similar or identical passages in *Dialogues des Carmélites,* the seminal work of Poulenc's mature style. In addition, the orchestra portrays the ringing of the telephone with repeated notes on the xylophone; it expresses the singer's agitation and confusion while trying to reach her former lover; it even suggests the jazz which she hears in the background over the phone. Most importantly, however, the orchestra fills in the voids created by the inherently dry, disjointed vocal line. If *La voix humaine* succeeds as a piece of music, it is because of the orchestral framework. Poulenc himself, in a preface to the opera, says: "The entire work should be bathed in the deepest orchestral sensuality."

Ultimately, then, Poulenc saw *La voix humaine* as an expressive, romantic work. It is certainly a fine, challenging vehicle for a singing actress and, though major opera companies seldom perform this, or any other, solo opera, there seems to be a place for Poulenc's last opera in the hands of a serious dramatic soprano.—KEITH W. DANIEL

von Stade, Frederica

Mezzo-soprano. Born 1 June 1945, in Somerville, New Jersey. Married: singer Peter Elkus (divorced). Studied with Sebastian Engelberg, Paul Berl, and Otto Guth at Mannes College, New York; debut as the Third Boy in Die Zauberflöte, *Metropolitan Opera, 1970; Paris debut as Cherubino in* Le nozze di Figaro, *1973; Glyndebourne debut as Cherubino,*

1973; sang Penelope in the American premiere of Il ritorno d'Ulisse in patria, *Washington, 1974; Covent Garden debut as Rosina in* Il barbiere di Siviglia, *1975; created the role of Maria in Villa-Lobos's* Yerma, *Santa Fe.*

In an age when most leading opera singers specialize in some relatively restricted repertory, Frederica von Stade's repertory covers two centuries and extends into two more; she has brought to her portrayal of Monteverdi's Penelope (*Il ritorno d'Ulisse in patria*) as much dramatic intensity and musicality as she displayed in her performances, at the Metropolitan Opera and several of the world's other leading houses, of Debussy's Mélisande.

Von Stade has brought comic and tragic roles to life with equal vividness. One can hear and see this clearly in her portrayals of Rossini heroines, both comic and serious. In the performances of Rossini's *Il barbiere di Siviglia* with which she made her Covent Garden debut in 1975, she sang Rosina with liveliness, sweetness, and a command of Rossinian coloratura; in a recording of Rossini's rarely performed opera seria *Otello,* she sang the role of Desdemona with a touching sense of tenderness and vulnerability. Von Stade displayed a stunningly beautiful legato in Rossini's Willow Song and the recitative that precedes it, spinning out Rossini's lines with perfect artistry.

Von Stade has won much applause for her performances of nineteenth-century French opera. Charlotte (*Werther*) is among several Massenet roles that she has performed with particular beauty and dramatic effect; she contributed much to a recording (under Rudel) of Massenet's *Cendrillon.* She has also sung the role of Béatrice in Berlioz's *Béatrice et Bénédict* with great success.

Von Stade is clearly an adventurous and ambitious singer, constantly expanding her repertory and seeking new roles. At the same time she has remained faithful to certain roles and types of roles with which she has been successful through most of her career. Von Stade is comfortable wearing trousers. Her slim figure, handsome face and bright, silvery high mezzo-soprano voice have helped her become the busiest female portrayer of boys and young men in all opera. Idamante (Mozart's *Idomeneo*), Stephano (Gounod's *Roméo et Juliette*), Fréderic (Thomas's *Mignon*), Octavian (Strauss's *Rosenkavalier*) and Hänsel (Humperdink's *Hänsel und Gretel*) are among her roles; but it is especially as Cherubino (in Mozart's *Le nozze di Figaro*) that von Stade has won applause throughout her career, bringing to that role just the right combination of sensuality and innocence, of mischief and charm. Her Cherubino was praised by one critic near the beginning of her career (San Francisco, 1972) as "nimble, milky-toned, vocally aristocratic." Fifteen years later she was still singing the role to universal applause, welcomed at the Metropolitan in 1987 as a "wonderous Cherubino." She has also sung the role at Glyndebourne, the Paris Opéra, and many other theaters.

One can hear much of what makes von Stade so successful in one of her lesser-known trouser roles, that of Annio in Mozart's *La clemenza di Tito* (as recorded under Colin Davis). Annio is not one of the opera's leading roles; yet von Stade is an exciting, interesting Annio; she brings all her musical and dramatic energy to the part, coloring words and phrases vividly. Listen, for example, to the way in which she gives a tragic quality to the words "il nostro dolore" in the aria "Tu fosti tradito." Only a quivering, almost constant vibrato detracts from an otherwise perfect performance.—JOHN A. RICE

OPERA

W

Wächter, Eberhard

Baritone. Born 9 July 1929, in Vienna. Died 29 March 1992. Studied with Elisabeth Rado in Vienna; debut as Silvio in I pagliacci, Vienna Volksoper, 1953; joined Vienna State Opera, 1955; Covent Garden debut as Count Almaviva in Le nozze di Figaro, 1956; Salzburg debut as Arbaces in Idomeneo, 1956; Covent Garden debut as Count Almaviva, 1956; Bayreuth debut as Amfortas in Parsifal, 1958; Paris debut as Wolfram in Tannhäuser, 1959; Teatro alla Scala debut as Count Almaviva, 1960; Metropolitan Opera debut as Wolfram, 1961; sang in first performances of Martin's Der Sturm (1956), Einem's Der Besuch der alten Dame (1971), in Vienna; director of Vienna Volksoper and the Vienna State Opera, 1991-; son Franz also a baritone.

Eberhard Wächter, the Austrian dramatic baritone, was born in Vienna on 9 July 1929. After completing his Abitur in 1947, he studied piano and music theory at the Vienna Hochschule für Musik and in 1950 began his voice studies with Elisabeth Rado. Wächter made his operatic debut in 1953 at the Vienna Volksoper as Silvio in *I pagliacci*. In 1955 he became a member of the Vienna State Opera. From then on his career became a series of important international successes with guest performances in Italy, at Milan's Teatro alla Scala and in Rome, at Covent Garden (the Count in *Le nozze di Figaro* in 1956 and Amfortas and Renato in *Un ballo in maschera* in 1959), as well as in Munich, Stuttgart, Wiesbaden, Berlin, and Brussels. Beginning in 1956, Wächter was a regular guest at the Salzburg Festival where his outstanding portrayals in Mozart's baritone repertoire included Arbaces in *Idomeneo* in 1956 and 1961, the Count in 1958, Don Giovanni in 1960 and 1961, and the role of Orest in Richard Strauss' *Elektra* in 1964.

Eberhard Wächter was also engaged for the Edinburgh and Glyndebourne Festivals, and in 1960 he performed in both Dallas and San Francisco. His debut at New York's Metropolitan Opera took place in 1961. The Bayreuth Festival during the years 1957-59, 1962-63, and 1966 saw his outstanding portrayals of Amfortas in *Parsifal* and as Wolfram in *Tannhäuser*.

Wächter took part in the first performances of Frank Martin's *Der Sturm* on 17 June 1956 and Gottfried von Einem's *Der Besuch der alten Dame* on 23 May 1971 at the Vienna State Theater. Other roles included Rodrigo in *Don Carlos*, Simon Boccanegra, the Count di Luna in *Il trovatore*, and the name role in *Dantons Tod*. Besides his great successes as an opera singer, Eberhard Wächter's expressive singing led him to have an almost equally rewarding career in concert and recitals.

Among Wächter's many recordings are complete versions of *Tristan und Isolde* and *Der Freischütz* on the DGG label; *Salome, Arabella, Das Rheingold, Die Fledermaus, Wozzeck,* and *Lulu* on Decca; *Le nozze di Figaro, Don Giovanni, Die Fledermaus, Der Rosenkavalier,* and *Capriccio* on Columbia; *Don Giovanni, Tannhäuser,* and *Tiefland* on Philips; *Cavalleria rusticana* on Ariola-Eurodisc; Dallapiccola's *Il prigioniero* on Italia; and a third *Die Fledermaus* for RCA. His performances in opera highlights are to be found on Replica (the Heerrufer in *Lohengrin* from the 1958 Bayreuth recording), on Melodia (*Parsifal* and *Lohengrin,* Bayreuth 1958 and 1960), on Movimento Musica (*Fidelio, Die Zauberflöte,* and from the Salzburg Festivals of 1960 and 1961, *Don Giovanni* and *Idomeneo*).

Wächter's son Franz is also a baritone. In 1991-92 Eberhard Wächter was named Intendant of both the Vienna Volksoper and the State Opera.—SUZANNE SUMMERVILLE

Wagner, (Wilhelm) Richard

Composer. Born 22 May 1813, in Leipzig. Died 13 February 1883, in Venice. Married: 1) Christine Wilhelmine ("Minna") Planer, actress, 24 November 1836; 2) Cosima Liszt, daughter of the composer and piano virtuoso Franz Liszt and former wife of the famous conductor Hans von Bülow, 25 August 1870 (one daughter, one son). Student at the Dresden Kreuzschule, 1822-27; studied piano with Humann and violin with Robert Sipp, 1825; studied classics with his uncle Adolf Wagner; entered the Nikolaischule in Leipzig, 1828; studied harmony with Christian Gottlieb Müller; entered the Thomasschule, 1830; his Overtüre *in B-flat performed at the Leipzig Theater, conducted by Heinrich Dorn, 24 December 1830; studied composition and counterpoint with Theodor Weinlig, cantor of the Thomaskirche; music director of Heinrich Bethmann's theater company, Magdeburg, 1834; director of the Königsberg town theater, 1 April 1837; music director of the theater in Riga, 1837-39; met Meyerbeer in Boulogne; arranged piano scores for operas and wrote for the* Gazette musicale *in Paris, 1839-42; in debtor's prison, 28 October-17 November 1840;* Rienzi *accepted for production in Dresden, 1842; named second Hofkapellmeister in Dresden, 1843; an order for Wagner's arrest was issued for his participation in the Dresden uprising, 1849; met Liszt in Weimar; in Zurich by July, 1849; received loans for the production of his operas from the merchant Otto Wesendonck, 1854; conducted concerts of his own music in London, 1855, where he met Queen Victoria; moved to Venice, 1858; in Lucerne, still escaping the Dresden government, 1859, and then in Paris; Napoleon III ordered the director of the Paris Opéra to produce Wagner's* Tannhäuser, *1860; partial amnesty by Dresden authorities, 1860 (total amnesty given 1862); moved to Biebrich, 1862; offered unlimited patronage by King Ludwig II of Bavaria, 1864; cornerstone of the Bayreuth Festspielhaus laid, 22 May 1872; premiere of the* Ring *cycle conducted by Hans Richter and attended by Kaiser Wilhelm I, among others, 1876; Wagner's grave is at his family home, the villa* Wahnfried *at Bayreuth.*

Operas *Die Hochzeit,* Wagner, after J.G. Büsching: Ritterzeit und Ritterwesen, 1832-33, Leipzig, Neues Theater, 13 February 1938 [partially lost]; *Die Feen,* Wagner (after C. Gozzi, *La donna serpente*), 1833-34, Munich, Königliches Hof- und Nationaltheater, 29 June 1888; *Das Liebesverbot, oder Die Novize von Palermo,* Wagner (after Shakespeare, *Measure for Measure*), 1834-36, Magdeburg, 29 March 1836; *Rienzi, der Letzte der Tribunen,* Wagner (after E. Bulwer Lytton and M.R. Mitford), 1837-1840, Dresden, Königliches Hoftheater, 20 October 1842; revised, 1843; *Der fliegende Holländer,* Wagner (after Heine, *Aus den Memoiren des Herrn von Schnabelewopski*), 1841, Dresden, Königliches Hoftheater, 2 January 1843; revised, 1846; revised, 1852; *Tannhäuser und der Sängerkrieg auf Wartburg* (originally *Der Venusberg*), Wagner, 1843-45, Dresden, Königliches Hoftheater, 19 October 1845; revised, text alterations with C. Nuitter, 1860-61, Paris, Opéra, 13 March 1861; revised, 1865, Munich, Königliches Hof- und Nationaltheater, 5 March 1865; slightly revised, 1875, Vienna, Hofoper, 22 November 1875; *Lohengrin,* Wagner, 1845-47, Weimar, Hoftheater, 28 August 1850; *Der Ring des Nibelungen,* Wagner, first text draft 1848; 1) *Das Rheingold,* 1851-54, Munich, Königliches Hof- und Nationaltheater, 22 September 1869; 2) *Die Walküre,* 1851-56, Munich, Königliches Hof- und Nationaltheater, 26 June 1870; 3) *Siegfried* (originally *Der junge Siegfried*), 1851-71, Bayreuth Festspielhaus, 16 August 1876; 4) *Götterdämmerung,* 1850-74, Bayreuth Festspielhaus, 17 August 1876; performance of the entire cycle, Bayreuth Festspielhaus, 13, 14, 16, 17 August 1876; *Tristan und Isolde,* Wagner, 1856-59, Munich, Königliches Hof- und Nationaltheater, 10 June 1865; *Die Meistersinger von Nürnberg,* 1845, 1865-67, Munich, Königliches Hof- und Nationaltheater, 21 June 1868; *Parsifal* (originally *Parzival*), Wagner, 1857, 1865, 1876-82, Bayreuth Festspielhaus, 26 July 1882.

In the works of Wilhelm Richard Wagner elements of the tradition of German romantic opera stemming from Mozart's *Zauberflöte* and Weber's *Der Freischütz* were incorporated into a highly original artistic synthesis often described as *Musikdrama,* although that term was disowned by Wagner himself. The influence of Wagner has been immense and many-faceted, extending beyond opera and drama into aesthetic theory, literature, politics, and performance practice. A prolific writer, Wagner composed the texts as well as the music of his works, adapting material from medieval epics such as the *Nibelungenlied,* the *Edda,* Gottfried von Strassburg's *Tristan,* and Wolfram von Eschenbach's *Parzifal.* Wagner's music shows major innovations in its form, orchestration, and harmonic language. In the works of his most advanced style, beginning with *Tristan und Isolde,* an expanded tonal practice based on the twelve chromatic modes, a richly allusive, polyphonic motivic texture, and a formal control over vast temporal spans all contribute to an artistic synthesis in which the music assumes a central if not dominant role. In order to realize his ideals, Wagner founded a center for performance of his works at Bayreuth, Germany, where a theater was constructed according to the composer's specifications, and festivals have continued since 1876.

Wagner's earliest operas reveal comparatively little of his originality. The most important of these, *Rienzi,* owes much to the grand opera of Spontini and Meyerbeer. Wagner later polemicized vigorously against "opera," but some features of grand opera style nevertheless reemerge in certain of his ripest works, such as *Die Meistersinger* and *Götterdämmerung.* It was in the first of his German romantic operas, *Der fliegende Holländer* of 1841, that Wagner successfully developed material from legend centered on his favorite theme of redemption, involving here an accursed sea captain seeking release through the unconditional love of a woman, Senta.

Der fliegende Holländer and Wagner's succeeding works from the 1840s also show some important musical innovations. Wagner goes beyond the strict sectional divisions and stereotyped conventions of opera in his treatment of Senta's ballade, with its startling interruption of the spinning song and its powerful evocation of the chromatic music in the minor associated with the Dutchman, with whom she is obsessed. That music, in turn, is first heard at the beginning of the overture, where its open fifths in D minor, projected in the string tremoli and ghostly horn call, recall the opening of Beethoven's Ninth Symphony. In the two following operas written while he was Kapellmeister at Dresden, *Tannhäuser* and especially *Lohengrin,* Wagner tended to blur or eliminate divisions between successive set-numbers, and merge the functions of recitative and aria

Richard Wagner, 1871

into an arioso-like *Sprechgesang,* or "speech song," while imposing a unity of tone on the whole, in part through the resourceful use of recurring motives in the orchestra. In *Lohengrin* not only themes and motives but also keys assume consistent dramatic associations: the A major of the prelude, for instance, is linked with Lohengrin and the Grail, and F# minor with Ortrud.

During the 1840s Wagner also identified the dramatic material for all of his later works except *Tristan,* thereby setting out the major goals of his career long in advance. *Die Meistersinger von Nürnberg* was originally conceived as a comic pendant to *Tannhäuser,* whereas the mythological material for *Lohengrin* is closely associated with *Parsifal.* (In the medieval sources, Parzifal is Lohengrin's father.) Wagner was keenly aware of such interconnections between his works, and sometimes deliberated for years over the necessary adaption and compression of his source material, making prose sketches well in advance of the writing of the dramatic poems. It was during the 1840s as well that Wagner assimilated some of the vocabulary and conceptual apparatus of Hegelian dialectics, with its questionable indulgence in sweeping generalization based on evolutionary historicism. This ideological approach surfaces in many of Wagner's prose writings, from his famous polemic about the end of the symphony after Beethoven's Ninth to his infamous pronouncements about the Jews in *Judaism in Music* of 1850, a treatise Wagner reissued in 1869. Wagner's antisemitism needs to be understood in an historical context, but the issue has done much damage to his reputation, and points of connection do exist between his legacy of Bayreuth and the murderous regime of Hitler.

Wagner's involvement with the unsuccessful revolutionary uprisings at Dresden in 1849 led to a call for his arrest, and with Liszt's help, he fled to Switzerland, where he spent several years occupied not with musical composition but with prose writings and the poem of his gigantic cycle *Der Ring des Nibelungen.* The most central of his theoretical writings is *Oper und Drama* of 1851, the doctrines of which correspond closely to the earlier parts—but not the last third—of the *Ring.* The *Ring* cycle consists of the prologue *Das Rheingold* and three main dramas, *Die Walküre, Siegfried,* and *Götterdämmerung.* The works were initially conceived in reverse order, the oldest being *Siegfried's Tod,* the original title of *Götterdämmerung,* but

Wagner soon resolved to expand the project to unprecedented dimensions. The subject of this cycle of epic dramas thus begins not with the tale of Siegfried but with the theft of the Rhine gold—or rape of nature—committed by the Nibelung Alberich, who foreswears love to gain power. Wotan, leader of the gods, seizes Alberich's ring and hoard in order to discharge his financial obligations for the building of the palace of Walhalla, but increasingly loses his ability to control events, and ultimately Walhalla—symbol of the established order—is consumed in flame at the dawn of a new era, as the ring is returned to the Rhinemaidens. The story is rich in political overtones, and parts of it have been interpreted as a socialist allegory.

For the music of this vast cycle, Wagner devised a large number of motives and themes that have often been labeled as *leitmotives* or "leading motives." The term *leitmotive* does not stem from Wagner, however, and the familiar labels have little meaning in themselves and can easily mislead, by giving the false impression of a fixed and constant symbolic association. Actually, Wagner's motives tend to evolve in their dramatic associations as well as in their intervallic configuration, so their significance is usually dependent on the larger context.

The central innovation of Wagner's *Ring* and later works is his abolishment of set-numbers as such, and his equation of the development of music with the development of the entire drama. The slow pacing and enormous time-scale of Wagner's music makes possible this identification, whereby, in Wagner's words from one of his later treatises, "the music spreads itself over the entire drama, and not just over small, isolated, arbitrarily separated parts of the whole." One is reminded of Beethoven's imposition of a tighter musical and dramatic interconnection between the successive movements of pieces like the Fifth and Ninth Symphonies; Wagner could claim with some justification to be Beethoven's heir in this respect.

The constant recall of short motives and more extended themes—however important—would not always suffice to articulate the major events of the drama on such a massive time-scale, and Wagner also relies not infrequently on extended, varied musical recapitulation. In the *Ring,* these recapitulatory elements are especially prominent in *Götterdämmerung,* which begins and ends with references to the beginning of the cycle, and culminates in a great recapitulation from the preceding drama leading to a new outcome. The opening of its prelude, for example, recalls not only the chords from Brünnhilde's awakening in *Siegfried* but also the rising motivic arpeggiations from the outset of *Das Rheingold.* The very first vocal theme of the cycle, the Rhinemaidens' "Weia! Waga! Woge, du Welle, walle zur Wiege!" (an extreme example of the alliteration which replaces end-rhyme in the *Ring* poem) recurs for the last time near the close of *Götterdämmerung,* where Flosshilde's music at the recovery of the ring corresponds closely, even in its pitch level, to the initial appearance of this theme from the prologue; the theme is then transposed, and combined and juxtaposed with other motives as the Rhinemaidens swim into the depths with their prize. The setting of Siegfried's final narrative, death and funeral procession earlier in the last act of *Götterdämmerung,* on the other hand, involves a massive varied recapitulation of material drawn from both acts II and III of the preceding drama, *Siegfried,* which is even grouped into a modulatory structure passing from E to C that recalls and transforms the tonal progression from Brünnhilde's awakening in *Siegfried.* Such modulatory structures often assume an important dramatic and architectural role in the later works, but as Robert Bailey has shown, Wagner had determined an overall framework of tonalities with dramatic associations already at a formative stage in the composition of the *Ring.*

Other innovations of the *Ring* include the use of the so-called Wagner tubas—instruments specifically designed for this work and later employed by Bruckner and Richard Strauss—

and the curtailment of duet and ensemble singing in those portions of the cycle composed up to 1857, namely *Das Rheingold, Die Walküre,* and the first two acts of *Siegfried.* The music of the later portions of the *Ring* was composed only in 1869-74, following a twelve-year hiatus during which Wagner wrote *Tristan und Isolde* and *Die Meistersinger von Nürnberg.* There is consequently a noticeable stylistic shift within the *Ring* to a more advanced and polyphonic musical style in the last act of *Siegfried* and in *Götterdämmerung,* whose text is nevertheless the oldest and the most conventionally operatic. A somewhat analogous stylistic discontinuity was introduced into the final version of *Tannhäuser* written for Paris in 1861, when Wagner added chromatic music in a Tristanesque style to the Venusberg scene, in striking contrast to the rest of the score.

As a culminating monument to romanticism and a starting-point of modern music, *Tristan und Isolde* assumes a pivotal position in music history. The initially unexpressed love of Tristan and Isolde grows after the drinking of the potion into a passion and longing for night, and ultimately into a metaphysical separation from outward existence as symbolized in Isolde's concluding transfiguration and apparent death. Such a symbolic treatment of "Night" as an alternative realm builds upon literary models such as Novalis's *Hymnen an die Nacht,* and celebrates the triumph of the suprarational through the articulating power of music. The famous chromatic music of the prelude embodies the unfulfilled yearning of the lovers not only through its use of the harmonically ambiguous "Tristan" chord (a minor triad with added sixth), rising semitone motion, and the melodic intensity and rich contrapuntal texture of its "infinite" melody—to use Wagner's term—but also through its tonal context: a tonal center of A minor is implied, but its actual triad is withheld. In the structural unit comprising the first seventeen bars, the music outlines a chromatic ascent through the octave from G# to G# an octave higher—leading tones of the implied tonic—while the chords at the phrase endings sound the dominant-seventh chords of the triad degrees of A minor. Here, as elsewhere, the cadence at the end of the progression is deceptive, since a resolution to the implied tonic would break the tension and disrupt the musical continuity, and furthermore would be dramatically unmotivated. This example shows how Wagner's dramatic effects can be embedded in the larger musical structure, and not only reflected in referential motives. Wagner's later music, in becoming more autonomous and less dependent on the text in specific details, often becomes thereby an ever greater and more generalized function of the drama.

Wagner restates this entire progression at several important junctures of the drama (at the drinking of the love potion in act I, at Tristan's confrontation with King Marke in act II, and at Tristan's death in the final act). Most consequential for the drama as a whole, however, is Wagner's transformation of the structural basis for the passage at the climax of the love-duet in act II, and again in the closing moments of Isolde's transfiguration in act III (this conclusion of *Tristan* is often described as her *Liebestod* or "Love-Death," but Wagner used that word only in reference to the first act prelude, and his description of the conclusion as a *Verklärung* or transfiguration is more fitting). In these passages, the idea of the chromatic ascent through the octave from G# is retained in a new texture of more ecstatic character, and the harmonic support to the G# is altered through the substitution of one pitch—F# for Fb—purging thereby the mysterious ambiguity of the "Tristan" chord. The resulting appoggiatura chord then becomes the stable tonic of B major, but only at the conclusion of Isolde's transfiguration is the cadence, with its accompanying large-scale rhythmic resolution, supplied. Isolde's text in this section is allied solely with the inward, metaphysical action, since she finds Tristan "awake" and describes the "ringing sound"—that is, the music—that envelopes her. The great cadence, treated as the culmination of a large-scale recapitulatory gesture, is Wagner's means of symbolizing Isolde's ascent into Night, and the all-encompassing nature of the resolution is underlined by his recall of the "Tristan" chord in the final moments. The revolutionary chromaticism of *Tristan* still depends crucially on the diatonic background of this resolution, which signals the dramatic breakthrough as the lovers disappear, as it were, from the level of the visible action.

Wagner completed *Tristan* in 1859, while still in exile, and the years that followed were some of the most difficult of his life. The breaking-off of Wagner's relationship with Mathilde Wesendonck (who acted as an inspiration behind the composition of *Tristan*), his inability to mount performances of the work, his usual problems with debts, and the *Tannhäuser* scandal at Paris in 1861 all tended to undermine his tenacity. Wagner did much conducting of his own works in various cities during this period (his contributions to the art of conducting were substantial, and include the important treatise *On Conducting* published in 1869). Then, on 3 May 1864, in an astonishing turn of events, he was summoned by the eighteen-year-old Ludwig II, the new King of Bavaria, who supported Wagner financially and placed the musical resources of Munich at his disposal, opening up the last and most successful phase of Wagner's career. Yet in spite of Ludwig's support, less than two years later Wagner was forced to leave Munich. One of the main reasons was his relationship with the wife of his conductor Hans von Bülow, Liszt's daughter Cosima, whom Wagner married in 1870. Wagner left Munich for Tribschen, Switzerland (near Lucerne), where he finished *Die Meistersinger* in October of 1867. *Tristan* had already been given its successful premiere at Munich in 1865 and *Die Meistersinger* followed in 1868. By that time, however, Wagner's plans for a festival theater for the performance of the *Ring* in Munich were doomed to failure, and his attention was soon to turn to Bayreuth.

Die Meistersinger, Wagner's major work of the 1860s and the only comic opera of his maturity, centers on the relation between art and society. The singing contest between Walther von Stolzing—a "natural" genius—and Beckmesser—sterile pedant and caricature of Viennese critic Eduard Hanslick—reflects just one aspect of the theme. The only one of the masters who fully understands art is Walther's instructor, the widower Hans Sachs, who is sorely tempted to join the contest for Eva Pogner's hand, but does not do so out of a gesture of "bitter resignation" and commitment to the "angel" who holds him in an artistic "paradise" counterposed to the *Wahn* or "delusion" of earthly existence. Carl Dahlhaus has observed how the predominant diatonicism of *Die Meistersinger*—with social roots in its chorales, marches, and dances—is rendered fragile through a juxtaposition with chromaticism, and this is nowhere more evident than in the scenes for Eva and Sachs in act III, culminating in an explicit quotation from *Tristan*. The influence of Schopenhauer is felt here no less than in *Tristan,* both in the idea of denial of the will to life and in the elevation of musical art, which for Schopenhauer represented no less than "the inner nature, the in-itself of all phenomena," a cosmic force unifying the spiritual and material poles of existence. The final choral scene of *Die Meistersinger* has been misused for chauvinistic purposes, but it actually glorifies not the state, but art ("should the Holy Roman Empire dissolve in mist, there would remain the holy German Art!"), and was criticized for precisely this reason in Germany during the Second World War.

After the completion of the *Ring* and its first performance at Bayreuth in 1876, Wagner succeeded in finishing one remaining work, the *Bühnenweihfestspiel* ("stage consecration festival play") *Parsifal.* (Another projected work based on Buddhist sources, *Die Sieger* was left unrealized.) *Parsifal* is the only one of Wagner's major works composed at Bayreuth, and its orchestral subtleties take full advantage of the sunken orchestra pit and superb acoustics of the

Bayreuth Festival Theater. Performances of *Parsifal* reopened the Bayreuth Festival in 1882, after several years when the future of the project was in financial jeopardy.

Parsifal is perhaps the most advanced and controversial of all Wagner's works. The theme of redemption takes on a more radical, collective character in *Parsifal,* as aspects of Christianity are assimilated into Wagner's temple of art. Thus the "transfiguration" of the central protagonist(s) occurs not as an end point to the action, as in *Der fliegende Holländer* or *Tristan,* but begins already in act II, as Parsifal recoils from Kundry's seduction attempt, with its musical embodiment in the contaminating chromaticism of her music. Parsifal's denial of the temptation of the senses is connected to his capacity for compassion; Agapē overcomes Eros. Musically, there can be no resolution of chromaticism into diatonicism here, as in *Tristan,* but rather a purification *from* chromaticism of the diatonic themes and motives of the Grail, which are integrated and combined for the first time in the closing recapitulatory synthesis at the end of act III, after Parsifal appears as redeemer and reveals the Grail. At the same time, the wound of the Grail King Amfortas—outward symbol of his sinful condition—is healed by Parsifal, and Kundry, whom he has baptized, is released from her curse through death. The symbolism of *Parsifal* is especially complex, and resists unambiguous interpretation, but the indispensable essence of the drama is conveyed in the music. *Parsifal* is a major monument to the aesthetic of the sublime and to Wagner's conviction, expressed in *Religion and Art* of 1880, that art could "salvage the kernel of religion" through its "ideal representation" of mythical religious images. Wagner's attempts to express the inexpressible, or at least the extraordinary, were carried to their limits in *Parsifal,* and not surprisingly, it proved difficult if not impossible for subsequent composers of opera to build further on this line of approach. In recognition of its exhaustive character, Debussy once described Wagner's legacy as "a beautiful sunset that was mistaken for a dawn."—WILLIAM KINDERMAN

La Wally

Composer: *Alfredo Catalani.*

Librettist: *Luigi Illica (after the novella by Wilhelmine von Hillern* Die Geyer-Wally*).*

First Performance: *Milan, Teatro alla Scala, 20 January 1892.*

Roles: *Wally (soprano); Stromminger (bass); Walter (soprano); Giuseppe Hagenbach of Sölden (tenor); Vincenzo Gellner of Hochstoff (baritone); Afra (mezzo-soprano); Wanderer (bass); chorus (SSATTBB).*

In 1878, the Lombard artist Tranquillo Cremona provoked something of a scandal with a painting of the twenty-four-year-old Alfredo Catalani. Cremona and his subject were fellow *scapigliati* (roughly "bohemians"), disaffected adherents of a Milanese artistic movement. The disturbing portrait, a canvas entitled *L'edera* ("Ivy"), depicted the pale and sickly Catalani—he would die of tuberculosis—desperately clinging to a robust but aloof Milanese beauty, Elisa Cagnoli. Glacial indifference is only one aspect of the *femme fatale,* a figure that resonated in the arts throughout the period of the "decadence." The *femme fatale* was equally apt to figure as the predatory female, whether in the paintings of Gustave Moreau, the poetry of Stéphane Mallarmé, or the operas of Catalani. If the *femme fatale* tended to take on the aspect of Salomé or the Sphinx in France, Catalani's deep involvement with German Romanticism led him to discover her image in German folklore. In Catalani's penultimate opera, *Loreley* (1890), the hero struggles with the conflicting passions he experiences for his beloved, a mortal girl, and the water nymph Loreley. For his last opera, Catalani turned to a novella by Wilhelmine von Hillern, *Die Geyer-Wally* or *The Vulture Wally,* which was serialized in a Milanese newspaper.

In the libretto that Luigi Illica prepared for Catalani—Illica was later the co-librettist for a number of Puccini's operas—the vulturine aspects of Catalani's eponymous heroine are notably downplayed. Unlike the novella, the opera ends with the destruction of ill-fated lovers at Nature's hands, as Boito had suggested it should. Like the novella's heroine, however, the opera's heroine is closely identified with nature. *La Wally* is set in the village of Hochstoff in the Tyrol, where the wealthy landowner Stromminger's seventieth birthday is being celebrated. When Hagenbach and other huntsmen from neighboring Sölden turn up to boast of their exploits, Stromminger and Hagenbach come to blows. Stromminger's untamed daughter Wally intervenes, but Hagenbach and Wally are immediately smitten with one another, to Stromminger's chagrin. Stromminger promises Wally's hand to his bailiff, Gellner, but Wally spurns Gellner's advances and is exiled from her father's estate. At the feast of Corpus Christi a year later, Gellner taunts Wally, who has inherited her father's estate, with the information that Hagenbach is engaged to marry Afra. When Wally insults Afra, Hagenbach is urged to avenge Afra by stealing a kiss from Wally during the torrid kissing dance, the *Walzer del bacio*. Dancing with Wally rekindles Hagenbach's passion for her, however, and, oblivious of the crowd, he wrests a passionate kiss from her. The crowd cheers, publicly humiliating Wally, and Hagenbach is dragged away by his companions before he can assure Wally of his true feelings. Wally promises Gellner her hand if he will kill Hagenbach. That night Gellner pushes Hagenbach into a deep ravine and leaves him for dead. Regretting the events she has set in motion, Wally manages the dangerous feat of climbing down into the ravine and rescuing the unconscious Hagenbach. Wally retires to the seclusion of the mountains where Hagenbach ultimately pursues her. Hagenbach defends his kiss as a token of his true feelings for Wally, who confesses her role in Hagenbach's near-fatal accident. A violent snowstorm has developed and Hagenbach is killed in an avalanche. Wally leaps from a precipice, joining Hagenbach in death.

Although Illica's characters remain paste-board, his libretto afforded Catalani abundant opportunity for rendering nature and for bringing the atmosphere of a Swiss mountain village vividly to life. Catalani certainly possessed the evocative power necessary for such atmospheric effects. Throughout the opera, Wally and her relationship to nature are simply yet effectively suggested with horn fifths and tremolo strings. With its Alpine setting, the fourth act in particular provided Catalani with opportunities for evoking nature. The act opens with an atmospheric prelude suggesting the endless desolation of the Alps and Wally's own isolation within them. Essentially a ternary form, the prelude is spun out of a somber and modally inflected motive. Catalani drew upon a number of sources within his immediate Italian tradition for a vivid depiction of the brewing snow storm later in the act. From the last act of Verdi's *Rigoletto,* Catalani borrowed the device of an offstage chorus humming in imitation of the sound of the wind. With the duet of the reunited Wally and Hagenbach ("Vieni, vieni; una placida vita"), Catalani managed a synthesis of the "Lontano, lontano" duet from Boito's *Mefistofele* and the duet for Helen of Troy and Faust from the same opera.

Catalani's real allegiance was to German Romantic opera of the pre-Wagnerian variety, and he was sometimes hampered by the framework of the conventions that he inherited from the Italian tradition in which he labored, yet the operas of Carl Maria von Weber that he so much admired no more provided a model for Catalani's symphonic continuities than did the operas of

Catalani's Italian predecessors. Catalani was a master of transitions and atmospheric effects, but he was less successful in spinning out the sort of formal melodies necessary for creating fully convincing set pieces. Consequently, *La Wally*'s set pieces can seem inert within the context of so flexible a continuum. In *La Wally* Catalani made supple and effective use of all of those forms of musical declamation intermediate between aria and recitative, of various effects of *arioso* and *parlando*. There is a measure of true motivic development in the opera, too, as in the opening tableau with its villagers and hunters, where horn calls and fragments of folk melody are woven into a developing contrapuntal fabric. In addition to other forms of melodic reminiscence and recall, Catalani even used what can only be considered a Wagnerian leitmotiv for the music expressing the love at first sight of Wally and Hagenbach, which is transformed on its successive reappearances. Such developmental and motivic processes required the freedom to be found in the varied patches between the opera's set pieces, and the quasi-symphonic continuity throughout much of *La Wally* is remarkable not only for its originality, but for its independence from the alternative models provided by Wagnerian music drama and Verdi's *Otello*. At the same time, *La Wally* is not without full-blown lyrical melody, as its most famous excerpt, "Ebben? Ne andrò lontana," serves to confirm, although Catalani adapted this aria from a *Chanson groenlandaise* he had composed in 1876. This aria has found a wide public in recent years through Jean-Jacques Beineix's 1981 film, *Diva*.—DAVID GABLE

Walton, (Sir) William (Turner)

Composer. Born 29 March 1902, in Oldham, Lancashire. Died 8 March 1983, in Ischia, Italy. Married: Susana Gil Passo. Enrolled in the Cathedral Choir School at Christ Church, Oxford; entered Christ Church, but never graduated; string quartet performed at the International Society for Contemporary Music, 1923; composed Crown Imperial March *for the coronation of King George VI, 1937; honorary doctorate from Oxford University, 1942; knighted in 1951; composed* Orb and Sceptre *for the coronation of Queen Elizabeth II, 1953.*

Operas *Troilus and Cressida,* Hassall, 1947-54, London, Covent Garden, 1954; revised, 1975-7; *The Bear* (extravaganza), P. Dehn (after Chekhov), 1965-67, Aldeburgh, 1967.

Walton, in his long career, wrote only one full-length opera, *Troilus and Cressida* (1947-1954), and one comic opera, *The Bear* (1964-1967). In addition, however, he had begun a correspondence with Cecil Grey in May 1941 about the possibility of collaborating on an opera. The composer Carlo Gesualdo, Prince of Venosa, who in 1590 had murdered his wife and lover, was their chosen subject. This collaboration lasted until the end of 1942 when Walton's interest began to fade.

Three events may have helped to re-kindle his interest in opera after World War II. The first was the production of Britten's *Peter Grimes* at Sadler's Wells in June 1945; the second was the acceptance of a commission from the British Broadcasting Corporation in February 1947 for an opera for broadcasting; and the last was the encouragement of Alice Wimbourne, who brought Walton in contact with his librettist, Christopher Hassall.

Lady Wimbourne died the following year, and Walton later traveled to Buenos Aires for a Performing Right Society conference. Here he met Susana Gil, and, despite parental opposition, married her. They returned to England and decided to settle on the island of Ischia in the Bay of Naples. Here Walton returned to the writing of *Troilus and Cressida* with renewed vigor.

The Mediterranean atmosphere consequently had a bearing on *Troilus and Cressida* which relates to the operatic tradition of Verdi and Puccini more than to any other. The treatment of the opera's subject is derived from Chaucer (Shakespeare's play was the least helpful version of the legend) and resulted in the romantic theme of a lonely, frightened individual seeking shelter from an alien world.

The opera contains some of Walton's best music and may be regarded as the culmination of his composing career. Many features of his previous music re-appear: the vocal and dramatic intensity of *Belshazzar's Feast* (Walton brought a superb sense of theater to the opera); the tension and the ferocity of the First Symphony; the sensuousness, beauty and brilliance of both the Viola Concerto and the Violin Concerto. The music of Pandarus also includes elements from *Façade,* besides being influenced by Britten.

Walton was always anxious to write another opera, and indeed announced, in May 1963, that he was beginning work on a new opera, again with Christopher Hassall as librettist. Alas, this was not to be because of Hassall's untimely death.

In October 1958, however, Walton had been offered (and accepted) a commission by the Koussevitsky Music Foundation in the Library of Congress for an opera which finally resulted in his one-act extravaganza, *The Bear.* The idea of turning Chekhov's play into an opera originated with Peter Pears, who had suggested to Walton that he should read Chekhov's three vaudevilles or jests. From these, he chose *The Bear.*

Walton started to compile his own libretto, but then decided that he required the services of a professional, and Paul Dehn, one of the most versatile writers of his generation, was brought in. Work on the opera was brought temporarily to a halt in January and February 1965 because of Walton's grave ill-health, and it was not until the summer that he was really fit to work again.

Composition continued until April 1967 when it was decided that the first performance should be given at the Aldeburgh Festival the following June. The opera contains much satirical wit and parody; indeed, among the composers parodied are Offenbach, Tchaikovsky, Poulenc, Verdi, Britten (*A Midsummer Night's Dream*), and Walton himself (*Troilus and Cressida* and *Façade*).

Walton always wanted to write a companion piece for *The Bear* and eventually found a suitable librettist, the writer Alan Bennett, in 1980. It was originally hoped that the English Music Theatre Company might perform the proposed opera at Aldeburgh, in celebration of the composer's 80th birthday in March 1982. Unfortunately, this plan had to be abandoned.

—STEWART R. CRAGGS

War and Peace [Voyna i mir]

Composer: *Sergei Prokofiev.*

Librettist: *Sergei Prokofiev (after Tolstoy).*

First Performance: *concert performance, Moscow, 16 October 1944; complete performance, Moscow, Stanislavsky, 8 November 1957; revised, 1946-52.*

Roles: *Prince Andrei Bolkonsky (baritone); Count Rostov, Ilya (bass); Natasha (sopra-no); Pierre (tenor); Hélène (contralto or mezzo-soprano); Anatole (tenor); Dolokhov (bass); Prince Kutuzov, Michael (bass); Denisov (baritone); Prince Bolkonsky, Nicolai (bass); Princess Marie (mezzo-soprano); Sonya (mezzo-soprano); Princess Mariya Akhrosimova (soprano); Karataev (tenor); more than fifty additional lesser roles, many of which may be doubled; chorus (SSATTBB).*

Prokofiev's *War and Peace* occupied his attention from 1941 until his death in 1953, during which time it underwent several transformations, including placing greater emphasis on melody and on the part played by Kutuzov and the Russian army of 1812. Lasting over four hours if given in its entirety, *War and Peace,* like its literary counterpart, is one of the great Russian epics.

The opera opens with an overture, though this is often replaced by a choral epigraph, using Tolstoy's and Denis Davydov's original words extolling the strength of the Russian people in the face of aggression. Scene i opens in the house and garden of Count Rostov at Odradnoe in May 1809. Prince Andrei Bolkonsky, recently widowed, reads by the window, but is roused from his melancholy by the sound of young girls' voices. The lyrical duet of Natasha and Sonya, as they comment on the beauty of the spring night, fills Andrei with fresh hope. Scene ii takes the form of a ball given by a grandee of Catherine's day in St Petersburg, 1810. As a chorus is sung, Count Rostov appears with Natasha and Sonya, followed by Count and Countess Bezukhov (Pierre and Hélène). Pierre Bezukhov approaches his old friend Prince Andrei and suggests that he invite Natasha to dance with him. Natasha has already attracted the attention of the dissolute Prince Anatole Kuragin (Hélène Bezukhov's brother).

The next scene takes place a year later, in February 1812. Natasha is engaged to Prince Andrei, who has been obliged by his father, who is opposed to the marriage, to spend a year abroad. In a soliloquy Natasha expresses her love for Andrei. In scene iv, Anatole gives Natasha a letter in which he suggests that they elope.

In scene vi, which takes place in the house of Mariya Akhrosimova where Natasha and Sonya are staying in the count's absence, Dunyasha the chambermaid warns Natasha that Sonya has told Mariya about the intended elopement. When Anatole appears, his way is barred by the butler; after a struggle, Anatole and Dolokhov make their escape. Akhrosimova remonstrates with Natasha, who runs off in tears. Pierre Bezukhov enters and on Mariya's instigation tries to talk to Natasha, telling her that Anatole is already married. Natasha, overwhelmed with remorse and shame at her stupidity, tries to commit suicide but is saved by Sonya. Scene vii takes place in Pierre's study the same night. When alone with Anatole, Pierre demands that Natasha's love letter agreeing to the elopement be handed over to him, which is done. In a soliloquy Pierre muses on the uselessness of his life and confesses that he himself loves Natasha. News is brought in that Napoleon is at the Russian frontier.

Part II: War opens on the Field of Borodino, preceding the battle on 25 August 1812. Against a background of patriotic soldiers' songs, Prince Andrei and Lieutenant-Colonel Denisov discuss the possibility of cutting Napoleon's lines of communication with a partisan detachment. Andrei's thoughts go back to Natasha and the unhappiness she has brought him. While two German generals discuss military strategy, Andrei tells Pierre that the Russians will win since they are defending their homeland. They embrace. Field Marshall Kutuzov appears and is acclaimed by his men, whom he inspires. The battle commences.

Scene ix takes place later the same day in the French camp, where Napoleon's confidence is shaken as reports indicate that the battle is not going as expected. Scene x occurs two days later in a peasant hut at Fili, where Kutuzov is discussing tactics with his generals. Is it better to try to defend Moscow and possibly risk total defeat, or to abandon Moscow and keep the army intact? Kutuzov decides to sacrifice the old capital. Left alone he expresses his patriotism in a moving aria.

Scene xi takes place in September-October. Moscow, captured by the French, has been set on fire. The soldiers are looting. Pierre learns that the Rostovs have left the city with some of the wounded, among whom (though unknown to Natasha) is Andrei. Pierre himself is arrested and sentenced to death as an arsonist; though reprieved, he remains a prisoner. Napoleon walks through the city, saddened by the outcome, though marveling at the Russian people's resilience and courage.

In scene xii Prince Andrei is lying in a hut outside Moscow, mortally wounded. In his delirium he dreams of Natasha, Moscow, his country. Natasha enters, dressed in white, and begs for forgiveness. They reaffirm their love and, in a poignant scene, he dies.

The final scene takes place in November 1812 on the road to Smolensk. A blizzard is raging, and at the end of Napoleon's retreating army is a column of Russian prisoners, among whom are Pierre and Karataev. Karataev falls to the ground exhausted and is shot. However, partisans appear who attack the French and free Pierre, followed by a group of women partisans. In the final moments Kutuzov and soldiers enter. "The enemy is beaten" cries the Field Marshall, "Russia is saved." All join in a final patriotic chorus.

It is a tribute to Prokofiev's skill that he was able to condense Tolstoy's enormous work into a coherent whole and produce an opera that nearly always holds one's attention. To achieve this, the action is interspersed with a variety of numbers—orchestral interludes, dances, arias, duets, and choral items, including some of the composer's most lyrical numbers. The splendid duet in scene i, Natasha's soliloquy in scene iii, Pierre's monologue in scene vii, Kutuzov's aria in scene x are only some of the impressive numbers, while mention must be made of the numerous choruses in a distinctive national idiom which give the opera a unique flavor. Running through the opera is a series of motto themes, knowledge of which enhances one's understanding of what is taking place, since the motives are sometimes used in the manner of the Wagner *Leitmotiv* to refer to characters not present on the stage or to convey general concepts, such as the idea of patriotism and victory. Though *War and Peace* is inferior to Prokofiev's earlier works such as *The Love for Three Oranges* and *The Fiery Angel,* it is not only an outstanding example of the Soviet ideological thinking of the time but manages to transcend national boundaries. Prokofiev himself, rightly or wrongly, regarded it as his finest work.—GERALD SEAMAN

Ward, Robert

Composer. Born 13 September 1917, in Cleveland. Studied with Howard Hanson and Bernard Rogers at the Eastman School of Music; B. Mus. from Eastman, 1939; studied composition with Frederick Jacobi and conducting with Albert Stoessel at the Juilliard School of Music; M. A. from Juilliard, 1946; taught at the Juilliard School, 1946-56; Vice President and Managing Editor of Galaxy Music Corporation, 1956-66; Pulitzer Prize for The Crucible, 1962; chancellor of the North Carolina School of the Arts, 1967-72; elected to the National Institute of Arts and Letters, 1967; Mary Duke Biddle Professor of Music at Duke University, 1979.

Operas *Pantaloon* [later, *He Who Gets Slapped*], B. Stambler (after Andreyev), 1955, New York, City Center Opera Company, 1959; revised, 1973; *The Crucible*, B. Stambler (after A. Miller), New York, 1961; *The Lady from Colorado*, B. Stambler (after H. Croy), Colorado, Central City Opera, summer 1964; *Claudia Legare*, B. Stambler (after Ibsen, *Hedda Gabler*), 1973, Minneapolis, Minnesota Opera Company, 14 April 1978; revised, 1978; *Abelard and Heloise*. J. Hartman, Charlotte, North Carolina, Charlotte Opera Association, 1981; *Minutes till Midnight*, Ward and D. Lang, 1978-82, Miami, New World Festival of the Arts, June 1982.

Robert Ward's emergence as an opera composer did not occur until 1956 when the opera *Pantaloon* was given in New York by the Juilliard School where Ward was an instructor. The opera was based on the play *He Who Gets Slapped* by Leonid Andreyev. A colleague at Juilliard, Bernard Stambler, collaborated with Ward in adapting the play for an opera. The work was later published under the original play title and also performed by the New York City Center Opera Company in 1959. For many of Ward's admirers this opera remains one of his finest operatic works, and Ward stated much later that it was "still as good an opera an any I've written."

The success which Ward and Stambler had with *He Who Gets Slapped* led them to collaborate on three more works: *The Crucible* (1961), *The Lady from Colorado* (1964), and *Claudia Legare* (1978). Most important was *The Crucible,* which was premiered in 1961. This opera was based on Arthur Miller's play of the same name and recreates the atmosphere of the New England witch trials of colonial America. The work has become Ward's most successful and important opera and received the 1962 Pulitzer Prize and the New York Music Critics' Circle Award. *The Lady from Colorado* was based on a book by Homer Croy. Commissioned by the Central City (Colorado) Opera House, the opera was performed fifteen times during the 1964 summer season. The work was an attempt to blend serious opera with light, musical comedy and the result received mixed reviews. Ross Parmenter wrote in the *New York Times,* "The "Lady" is nearly all corn. Its chief characters are stereotyped and the music, far from having naivete of genuine innocence, has the professionalism of opera companies turning their hands to a "paint your wagon" type of Broadway show." In contrast, Allen Young's review in *Musical America* states "the melodies are expansive and goodnatured, its rhythms supple and varied achieving a consistently mobile and buoyant texture."

It is perhaps the disappointment in the reception of *The Lady from Colorado* that Ward turned his attention away from opera for several years. However, in the 1970s, he resumed his operatic compositions and completed *Claudia Legare,* a commission from the New York Center Opera Company, in 1977. The work was based on the play *Hedda Gabler* by Henrik Ibsen. The opera was first given 14 April 1978 in Minneapolis by the Minnesota Opera Company. A large work of four acts, the opera was revised into a chamber version in 1978 to be more accessible for performance. Ward maintains his conservative, tonal style in this work.

Ward's next opera was *Abelard and Heloise,* which was a commission from the Charlotte (North Carolina) Opera Association. The premiere was given in 1982 by the Charlotte Opera Association. The librettist was Jan Hartman and the story deals with the famous love affair in the Middle Ages between Abelard and his beloved Heloise. Ward's musical style is well-suited for this story and the result is a romantic and dramatic opera which may be compared to *The*

Crucible for its favorable critical reviews. Claire McPhail of the Charlotte Post wrote, "It is romantic, dramatic, poignant and completely theatrical. Visually, dramatically and aurally the opera reaches a majestic height in the Cathedral of Sens."

Ward's most recent opera is *Minutes till Midnight*. A large work of nine scenes in three acts, the opera was commissioned by the Southeast Bank of Florida and was given its premiere at the New World Festival of the Arts in Miami, June 1982. The librettist was Daniel Lang. For the first time Ward was challenged by a story which deals with a current topic. The main character is Emil Roszak, a physicist, who worked on the atomic bomb and is on the threshold of completing a formula for the use of cosmic energy. His assistant, Chris, envisions this new energy source as the panacea for the world's ills. Unfortunately Roszak is summoned to the White House to develop his cosmic energy into a cosmic bomb as the enemy is also working on one. Roszak is tormented by the idea that the world will be destroyed, and he boldly publishes his formula in an international journal. The message of the opera appears to be that all information, especially that which can endanger mankind, should be made available to all. The opera received considerable criticism in that "the music is too lyrical and sweet to underscore such mind-boggling consequences as global destruction and the annihilation of mankind." It is hoped a revival of the opera will enable further consideration of the work and its importance as an American opera.

Robert Ward has made considerable contributions to the American operatic repertoire. He has shown his ability to project a definite nationalistic character into his operas and deserves consideration as one of the outstanding composers of American opera. Although his musical style is conservative, his eclecticism enables him to utilize not only American jazz, cowboy songs, and non-western melodies but also moments which can only be attributed to the influence of Arnold Schoenberg and his followers. The resultant operatic works have been accessible to most audiences and his style offers a link with the past. It is difficult to make a critical judgment on the totality of Ward's operas at this point in time, but there is general agreement that his Pulitzer Prize winning opera *The Crucible* is an important contribution to the American repertoire of the twentieth century.—ROBERT F. NISBETT

Warren [Varenov], Leonard

Baritone. Born 21 April 1911, in New York City. Died 4 March 1960, on the stage of the Metropolitan Opera House, New York City, during a performance of La forza del destino. *Studied with Sidney Dietsch, Giuseppe De Luca, Giuseppe Pais, and Riquardo Picozzi. Sang in Radio City Music Hall chorus; Metropolitan Opera debut as Paolo in* Simon Boccanegra, *1939; for twenty-two seasons, the company's leading "Italian" baritone; twenty-six roles included Rigoletto, Iago, Germont, Escamillo, Falstaff, Macbeth, Simon Boccanegra, Scarpia; created the role of Ilo in Menotti's* Island God, *1942; at San Francisco, 1943-56; Chicago, 1944-46; Teatro alla Scala debut, 1953; Soviet tour 1958.*

Before American baritone Leonard Warren made his Metropolitan Opera debut (as Paolo in Verdi's *Simon Boccanegra* in 1939), he had virtually no operatic experience. His only previous appearance on the operatic stage was in excerpts from Verdi's *La traviata* and Leoncavallo's *I pagliacci* the previous year. After Paolo, his roles at the Metropolitan Opera, in the order in which he assumed them, were Rangoni and Shchelkalov in Musorgsky's *Boris Godunov* (1939), Valentin in Gounod's *Faust* (1939), the Herald in Wagner's *Lohengrin* (1940), Amonasro in

Verdi's *Aida* (1940), Barnaba in Ponchielli's *La gioconda* (1940), Escamillo in Bizet's *Carmen* (1940), Alfio in Mascagni's *Cavalleria rusticana* (1941), the High Priest in Gluck's *Alceste* (1941), the High Priest in Saint-Saëns's *Samson et Dalila* (1941), Giorgio Germont in Verdi's *La traviata* (1942), Ilo in Menotti's *The Island God* (1942), Enrico in Donizetti's *Lucia di Lammermoor* (1942), Count di Luna in Verdi's *Il trovatore* (1943), Carlo in Verdi's *La forza del destino* (1943), Renato in Verdi's *Un ballo in maschera* (1943), Tonio in Leoncavallo's *I pagliacci* (1943), Verdi's *Rigoletto* (1943), Verdi's *Falstaff* (1944), Iago in Verdi's *Otello* (1946), Verdi's *Simon Boccanegra* (1949), Gérard in Giordano's *Andrea Chénier* (1954), Scarpia in Puccini's *Tosca* (1955), Don Carlo in Verdi's *Ernani* (1956), and Verdi's *Macbeth* (1959). In 1944 he participated in the legendary Red Cross benefit performance at Madison Square Garden of the final act of *Rigoletto*, conducted by Arturo Toscanini. By the end of his career, which was cut short by his death on the stage of the Metropolitan Opera House in 1960 during a performance of Verdi's *La forza del destino*, Warren had become the company's leading Verdi baritone. Although his career took him to a number of other opera houses, notably in Rio de Janiero, in Mexico City, and at the Teatro alla Scala, as well as on a tour of Russia in 1958, the overwhelming majority of Warren's performances were at the Metropolitan Opera.

Warren was one of a long line of American baritones; many saw him as the successor to Lawrence Tibbett, and such latter-day American baritones as Sherrill Milnes have acknowledged Warren's influence on their careers.

With a voice marked by a beautiful, rich tone, a firm line, power, and an easy upward extension beyond high A, Warren was a nearly ideal singer for the Verdi baritone roles, most of which lie relatively high, and it was largely in these parts, notably Iago, Rigoletto, Simon Boccanegra, and Macbeth, that his fame lies. His greatness lay in the sheer sound of his voice. His virtues were more vocal than dramatic, although his voice had a basically dramatic sound; he worked hard—with success—to improve his acting ability as his career progressed. The sound of his voice has been described as mellifluous, generous, imposing, and sympathetic. The voice was employed with a mastery of phrasing founded on a solid, confident technique. He was adept at producing soft notes that retained their body, as well as powerful, ringing high notes. Toward the end of his career, his voice became somewhat dryer, with a more pronounced vibrato, but the overall sound was retained. The beauty and smoothness of Warren's voice reaped benefits outside the Verdi canon as well, not least in the verismo roles he sang, as seen, for example, in the chilling elegance he brought to Puccini's Scarpia.

Warren made relatively few recordings of complete operas, The roles he did record include Rigoletto (1950, under Cellini), Count di Luna (1952, under Cellini, and 1959, under Basile), Renato (abridged, 1955, under Mitropoulos), Amonasro (1955, under Perlea), Macbeth (1959, under Leinsdorf), Giorgio Germont (1956, under Monteux), Scarpia (1957, under Leinsdorf), Barnaba (1957, under Previtali), and the Don Carlo in *La forza del destino* (1958, under Previtali).—MICHAEL SIMS

Weber, Carl Maria, Freiherr von

Composer. Born 18 November 1786, in Eutin, Oldenburg. Died 5 June 1826, in London. Married the singer Caroline Brandt. His first teacher was his stepbrother Fritz, a student of Haydn; studied piano with J.P. Heuschkel in Hildburghausen, 1796; studied counterpoint

with Michael Haydn in Salzburg, 1797; studied singing with Valesi (J.B. Wallishauser) and composition with J.N. Kalcher in Munich, 1798-1800; further study with Michael Haydn in Salzburg, 1801; studied the works of previous masters under the tutelage of the Abbé Vogler in Vienna, 1803; conductor of the Breslau City Theater, 1804; Musik-Intendant to Duke Eugen of Württemberg at Schloss Carlsruhe, 1806; private secretary to Duke Ludwig in Stuttgart, and music teacher to his children, 1807; his opera Silvana, *Frankfurt 1810, successful; piano concert tours of Frankfurt, Würzburg, Nuremberg, Bamberg, Weimar, Gotha and other German cities; conductor of the German opera in Prague, 1813; asked by the King of Saxony to take over the German Opera Theater in Dresden, 1817; treated for tuberculosis in Marienbad, 1824; led the enormously successful performances of his* Oberon *in London.*

Operas *Die Macht der Liebe und des Weins* (Singspiel), 1798 [lost]; *Das Waldmädchen,* C. von Steinsberg, Freiburg, 24 November 1800 [fragments]; *Peter Schmoll und seine Nachbarn,* J. Türk (after C.G. Cramer), 1801-02, Augsburg, March? 1803; *Rübezahl,* J.G. Rhode, 1804-05 [fragments]; *Silvana,* F.C. Hiemer (after *Das Waldmädchen*), 1808-10, Frankfurt am Main, 16 September 1810; *Abu Hassan* (Singspiel), F.C. Hiemer (after *The 1001 Nights*), 1810-11, Munich, Residenz, 4 June 1811; *Der Freischütz,* F. Kind (after J.A. Apel and F. Laun, *Gespensterbuch*), 1817-21, Berlin, Schauspielhaus, 18 June 1821; *Die drei Pintos,* T. Hell (after C. Seidel), 1820-21, Leipzig, Neues Stadt-Theater, 20 January 1888 [unfinished; finished by G. Mahler]; *Euryanthe,* H. von Chezy, 1822-23, Vienna, Kärntnertor, 25 October 1823; *Oberon,* J.R. Planché (after C.M. Wieland), 1825-26, London, Covent Garden, 12 April 1826.

As the son of a theater director and a singer, Weber grew up with the theater in his blood, and composed his first *Singspiel* (in other words, a German play mostly set to music) when he was eleven, while as a precocious seventeen-year-old he took charge of a Breslau theater and trod on a number of toes by initiating what he saw as necessary reforms, from repertory to his orchestra's seating arrangements. After he was laid low for some weeks by his strange accident of poisoning himself with engraving acid, he found that his many enemies had reversed most of his innovations and he resigned. Already by the age of twenty he was an experienced man of the theater, although he was inclined to be disillusioned about human nature, and he went on to hold a number of important positions in major opera houses, conducting standard repertory and introducing new pieces in a way that gave him an unrivaled knowledge of opera as it existed at the time in northern Europe.

The vigor of Weber's activities as a conductor and composer was sustained throughout his comparatively short life, and it undoubtedly contributed to the brevity of his life. Indeed, it belied his uncertain health and the fact that he walked with a slight limp (and perhaps some pain also) owing to a damaged hip, and the personality expressed in his music is a genial and attractive one as well as abounding in energy and imaginative force. He was still in his twenties when he first came across the story of his most famous work, *Der Freischütz,* and when the opera was produced in 1821 it was clear that he offered a new genre of "romantic opera" (as it was designated). In *Der Freischütz,* ordinary people plausibly confront mysterious powers of good and evil in a story of love and ambition set in a Bohemian village. The music has a folk-like idiom in some numbers such as the choruses of huntsmen and bridesmaids, but in the celebrated Wolf's Glen scene in which the magic bullets are cast, the composer's orchestral mastery is to the fore (for example, in his use of horns and drums) along with his capacity for tellingly sinister harmonies. Such Gothic horrors were much to the taste of a new German middle-class audience, particularly when they were fairly sure that all would be resolved in a happy ending.

To understand what Weber aimed at, we need to have some idea of what he meant by "romantic opera," a term he applied also to his *Euryanthe* and *Oberon*. The concept of romanticism itself is vast, but one definition that this composer might have agreed with was "the addition of mystery to beauty," and folk-lore, ballads and fairy tales of all kinds provided him with supernatural and exotic elements in plenty. He called *Euryanthe* a "grand heroic-romantic opera," and it is a complex tale of love and intrigue set in twelfth century France. Its music is continuous, unlike that of *Der Freischütz* with its occasional spoken dialogue, and in it he also went **Carl Maria von Weber** further with the technique of relating persons or dramatic concepts to musical "motives" (small but recognizable melodic and rhythmic fragments) or tone colors in a way that was to flower fully half a century later with Wagner, who indeed acknowledged German music's debt to Weber. *Oberon* is really something of a pantomime, a thirteenth-century story, telling of chivalry, magic, fairies, pirates and mermaids and set in locations as far afield as Baghdad and Tunis. Weber was no stranger to such armchair travel, and even his early one-act *Singspiel* called *Abu Hassan* takes its story from the Arabian collection called *The Thousand and One Nights*.

Such adventurousness has dangers as well as advantages. We may well feel that Weber's penchant for the exotic prevented him from creating the really believable human characters we look for in opera, except perhaps for the lovers Max and Agathe in *Der Freischütz*. The craggy heroes of Wagner's operas are not for him, nor the heroines such as we find at the center of Puccini's or Massenet's, nor, for that matter, Mozart's social comment or the political and psychological insights of Verdi. But with his pioneering imaginative writing for voices and his mastery of the orchestra he is a central figure in the development of German opera, and one above all who paved the way for Wagner, not least in his use of folk-lore, and the way in which he told of the supernatural and its interaction with human beings.—CHRISTOPHER HEADINGTON

Weikl, Bernd

Baritone. Born 29 July 1942, in Vienna. Studied economics at the University of Mainz and started vocal studies in 1965. Graduated from Hanover Hochschule für Musik, 1970; debut as Tsar Peter in Lortzing's Zar und Zimmermann, *Düsseldorf, 1970; appeared as Melot in Karajan's* Tristan *production, Salzburg Easter Festival, 1972; appeared at Bayreuth 1972-92; Vienna Volksoper debut as Billy Bigelow in* Carousel; *Covent Garden debut as Figaro in* Il barbiere di Siviglia, *1975; Metropolitan Opera debut as Wolfram, 1977; appeared in Tokyo in 1980 and Paris in 1982; Teatro alla Scala debut as Iago, 1990; has also appeared on film and television.*

From his first appearance in Bayreuth as Wolfram in Götz Friedrich's 1972 production of *Tannhäuser,* Bernd Weikl appeared upon the operatic firmament as a special presence, and this only two years after graduating from the Hanover School of Music. His development from lyric baritone (Lortzing, Donizetti) to roles requiring more spinto heft (Onegin, Rossini's Figaro, Hans Heiling) to Wagner's most lyrical baritone role took place so rapidly that some may have anticipated an early demise of his bright voice, even timbred through an extraordinary range, perhaps because of the rapid, expressive vibrato which gives it its special appeal and can be shaded or colored for any dramatic situation. They would not have been reckoning with the absolute control which he has exercised over every stage of his career, feeling that a voice must develop in its own way and within its own time span, never being artificially darkened or pushed for more volume. For this reason, he allowed himself much time before singing dramatic baritone roles, partly because he at first had difficulty finding the kernel or vocal center of gravity, as he describes it. In search of this personal ideal he has sought out the most distinguished teachers in several centers, forces himself to test his own development by the most rigorous standards and regularly returns to a famous vocal coach to have the state of his art analysed. Waiting until he was vocally and spiritually ready for a role has been a first principle. His first Hans Sachs was at thirty-nine. Though Wagner's was thirty-three, Weikl was determined not to open himself to the charge of being too young for the role, although Sachs has to be young enough to make Eva's attraction to him believable. His first Holländer was at forty-eight. By then he had left some roles behind—Rossini's Figaro, Eisenstein and Falke—and added some: Boccanegra and Iago. Nabucco may lie in the future, perhaps even Scarpia. Wotan never, although conductors constantly beleager him. He has twice been under contract to sing Falstaff, which he feels to be the great Italian counterpart of Sachs, but in each case he has cancelled because he felt his voice was too young, and he was searching for a great conductor to work on the characterization of the role with him.

Weikl is the averred enemy of jet-set opera, approving of stagione and festivals because they allow a singer to develop a role over a series of performances. He feels the best performance is often the fifth or seventh, and refuses to alternate roles in repertory that requires different vocal color.

He has made passionate appeals in print for designers to create sets which help a singer project the voice, and condemnations of directors who know nothing about vocal technique and therefore require action which hampers breath control or positions which make support of the vocal tone impossible. He wishes more conductors would discuss their roles with the singers, learn to phrase vocally, breathe with the singers and adjust orchestral volume to the characteristics of each voice. Opera, he feels, must be approached (by the artist) with love, not egomania or calculating commercialism.—JAMES HELME SUTCLIFFE

Weill, Kurt

Composer. Born 2 March 1900, in Dessau. Died 3 April 1950, in New York. Married: singer/actress Lotte Lenya. Studied privately with Albert Bing in Dessau, 1914-18; studied with Humperdinck and Krasselt at the Berlin Hochschule für Musik, 1918; opera coach in Dessau; conductor at the theater in Lüdenscheid; studied privately with Busoni in Berlin, 1921; completed his Berliner Symphonie, *1921; collaboration with Brecht on* Die Dreigroschenoper, *Berlin 1928 (200 years after the premiere of Gay and Pepusch's* The

Beggar's Opera*); in Paris, London, and then the United States, 1935; United States citizen, 1943.*

Operas and Musicals *Der Protagonist,* G. Kaiser, 1924-25, Dresden, 27 March 1926; *Royal Palace* (ballet-opera), Goll, 1925-26, Berlin, Staatsoper, 2 March 1927; *Na und?,* F. Joachimson, 1926-27 [not performed; lost]; *Der Zar lässt sich photographieren,* Kaiser, 1927, Leipzig, 18 February 1928; *Mahagonny* (Songspiel), B. Brecht, 1927, Baden-Baden, 17 July 1927; revised as *Aufstieg und Fall der Stadt Mahagonny,* 1927-29, Leipzig, Neues Theater, 9 March 1930; *Die Dreigroschenoper* (play with music), B. Brecht and E. Hauptmann (after John Gay, *The Beggar's Opera*), 1928, Berlin, Theater am Schiffbauerdamm, 31 August 1928; *Happy End* (play with music), E. Hauptmann and B. Brecht, 1929, Berlin, Theater am Schiffbauerdamm, 2 September 1929; *Der Jasager* (school opera), B. Brecht, 1930, Berlin Radio, 23 June 1930; *Die Bürgschaft,* C. Neher, 1930-31, Berlin, Städtische Oper, 10 March 1932; *Der Silbersee,* G. Kaiser, 1932-33, Leipzig, Altes Theater, 23 February 1933; *Der Kuhhandel* (operetta), R. Vambery, 1934 [not performed]: revised as *A Kingdom for a Cow* (musical comedy), R. Arkell and D. Carter, London, Savoy, 28 June 1935; *Der Weg der Verheissung* (biblical drama), Werfel, 1934-35 [not performed]; revised as *The Eternal Road,* L. Lewisohn, 1935-36, New York, Manhattan Opera House, 7 January 1937; *Johnny Johnson* (fable), P. Green, 1936, New York, 44th Street, 19 November 1936; *Knickerbocker Holiday* (operetta), M. Anderson, 1938, New York, Ethel Barrymore, 19 October 1938; *Ulysses Africanus* (play with music), M. Anderson, 1939 [incomplete]; *The Firebrand of Florence* (operetta), E.J. Mayer and I. Gershwin, 1944, New York, Alvin, 22 March 1945; *Street Scene* (Broadway opera), E. Rice and L. Hughes, 1946, New York, Adelphi, 9 January 1947; *Down in the Valley* (college opera), A. Sundgaard, 1945-48, Bloomington, Indiana, School of Music, 15 July 1948.

Kurt Weill's music occupies a unique position in the history of musical theater and opera, and he represents to scholars of theatrical music one of the most enigmatic figures in twentieth century music. While in the midst of a highly successful career in the European theater, where he was regarded as one of the bright lights of contemporary German composition, Weill fled his native continent, came to America in 1935, and radically altered his compositional style to accommodate the musical idiom of the Broadway stage. As a result of his attempt to integrate his personal style effectively into the popular American musical theater and to compose "the American opera," we possess a series of works that often transcend the usual boundaries of plot/ theme and musical sophistication found on the Broadway stage. Because of this extraordinary adjustment in idiom and technique, Weill presents to the music critic one of the most difficult of all careers to assess.

Weill's earliest works, including the opera *Der Protagonist* (1925) with which he established his reputation, utilize a complex contrapuntal and harmonic vocabulary influenced by the Germanic/Austrian musical language inherited and developed by Arnold Schoenberg and his followers. However, with his next work, *Der neue Orpheus* (1925, cantata for soprano, solo violin and orchestra), he embarked on a "new type of expression" that embraced sociological goals and a simpler musical idiom incorporating popular elements. His next opera, *Royal Palace* (1927), incorporated these new materials into a theatrical work for the first time. For the remainder of the 1920s and the early 1930s he made a conscious effort to write his works in a more accessible vein for a wider audience. Each of these introduces popular musical styles and forms, and shows, to a small extent, the influence of jazz. Eventually this shift in emphasis proved to be the turning point in his theatrical career, and helped bind together many of the seemingly disparate elements that appear in his work.

Two of Weill's most widely known operas date from this time: *Die Dreigroschenoper* (1928) and *Aufstieg und Fall der Stadt Mahagonny* (1929), both with librettos by Bertolt Brecht. Also during this time Weill wrote the first of his school operas, *Der Jasager* (1930, also with Brecht), a work that has affinities with the "Gebrauchsmusik" idiom of Paul Hindemith and the didactic operas of Hanns Eisler. Together with Brecht, he helped develop a kind of socially relevant musical theater, *Zeitoper,* and laid the groundwork for the "epic theater." His later American works would further explore and exploit the popular styles introduced here, but within the context of the Broadway theater.

With the world premiere of the three-act opera *Die Bürgschaft* in 1932, Weill believed he had again created the foundation for a new opera form, the promise of which was unfortunately thwarted by the political situation that eventually sent Weill on to America.

In September, 1935, Weill and his wife Lotte Lenya arrived in New York City for the production of his Biblical drama *The Eternal Road*. Undoubtedly one of the most significant sights he saw in those first few months in America was a rehearsal of George Gershwin's *Porgy and Bess* (1935). When he had completely absorbed the production before him, he recognized immediately that his vision of writing an American opera presented a real possibility.

Kurt Weill with his wife, Lotte Lenya, 1928

Certain aspects of Weill's European thought became integral to his theoretical approach in America. Similarly, many of his goals for the theater remained constant, such as trying to write music accessible to a wide variety of listeners. It should come as no surprise then that when Weill arrived in America he chose to work primarily in the Broadway theater. He realized wisely that if he wanted to write relevant works for the dramatic stage comparable to those he had already done in Europe, his outlet for performances would be restricted to that on Broadway. No other medium in this country could compare favorably with the subsidized theater in which he had worked in Europe. The Metropolitan Opera at that time was not in the habit of staging or commissioning commercial fare of the type he wanted to write. Rather than accept Broadway as a limiting medium, he utilized it to attempt his own new brand of musical theater that could offer new possibilities and forms for integrating text and music. Clearly, his thought processes and musical instincts for the theater remained steadfast despite the obvious change in perspective.

One of Weill's primary goals in the United States was to write a definitive American opera, using indigenous American materials and sources. He believed that this could be achieved only in the "living American theater," that is, on the Broadway stage. As Weill modified his musical language for the Broadway stage, he nevertheless maintained a concern for socially relevant themes, and wrote works that, for the most part, belie the mainstream of the traditional Broadway musical theater. Weill's search for the right combination of elements and circumstances for an opera production became quite determined, almost obsessive at times. His folk opera *Down in the Valley* (composed 1945-48, and originally conceived as a radio opera) certainly contained the indigenous raw material for an American opera, utilizing as it did five representative folk songs, but it failed to satisfy his desire for a professional opera on Broadway. Ultimately he believed that *Street Scene* (1947) fulfilled this role.

Perhaps the most important and influential decision Weill made early in his European career was to work primarily with playwrights, so that he could take advantage of the modern theatrical techniques they offered. Similarly, in America, Weill generally eschewed the traditional Broadway approach toward collaboration which brought together established lyricists and book writers. He had already worked with several of Europe's most outstanding playwrights, such as Bertolt Brecht (*Die Dreigroschenoper*), Georg Kaiser (*Der Protagonist*), and Caspar Neher (*Die Bürgschaft*) (to name a few), and was to collaborate with some of the finest American playwrights of the 1930s and 1940s, such as Paul Green (*Johnny Johnson*), Maxwell Anderson (*Lost in the Stars*), and Elmer Rice (*Street Scene*), among others. This decision unquestionably influenced his choice of librettos and helped develop in him a theatrical experience and acumen deliberately calculated for operatic diversity.

While most critics tend to divide Weill's career into two radically independent stages, it now seems much more evident that the American career evolved almost inevitably from his European one. Weill confirmed this view near the end of his life when he succinctly summarized his personal objectives as a composer. In his notes to the recording of his Broadway opera *Street Scene* he stated: "Ever since I made up my mind, at the age of 19, that my special field of activity would be the theatre, I have tried continuously to solve, in my own way, the form problems of the musical theatre, and through the years I have approached these problems from all different angles." This remark represents one of the most important and fundamental considerations for understanding Weill's entire career. If his relationship to opera and musical theater in general is viewed as a constant effort to develop new directions and paths, then this statement throws into relief the wide variety of works he composed for the theater.

W

OPERA

Weill was never satisfied with the musical theater as he had inherited it, and he was never satisfied completely with his own efforts on its behalf. When he stated in the same notes cited above that all of his works prior to *Street Scene* represent "stepping stones" toward that work's composition, he implied that all of his works are integrated in some manner. Each individual work along the way reveals through its form a link in his continued search for an adequate means to express his artistic vision. It also explains why, in an attempt to convey the underlying meaning of that form, his works display such a wide variety of descriptive titles and genres.

Nearly all of Weill's theatrical works skirt or straddle the lines between the usually accepted genres. To consider any of his European works as operas in the traditional sense of the word would alter its meaning almost beyond comprehension. Likewise none of his Broadway works falls into any traditional type; rather they tend to create their own autonomous categories. In fact, he usually designated his operas by various distinctive titles to suggest their general form and means of expression: *Die Dreigroschenoper* was called a "Play with music"; *Der Jasager* a "School opera"; *Down in the Valley* a "Folk-opera"; and *Street Scene* "An American Opera." The generic description functions as a reminder that the works stand outside the usual boundaries prescribed by opera.

Weill scholar Kim Kowalke has demonstrated in his book *Kurt Weill in Europe* that Weill's application of certain compositional elements and techniques unite the European works. It should not seem surprising that some of these same elements appear, albeit somewhat altered, in the American works, thus transcending their original purpose. In addition, Weill's highly sophisticated musical vocabulary provided him with a means of organization and musical variety not always available to the popular songwriter. As a result, the musical continuity of his American works—*Street Scene* in particular—suggests a direct influence from his earlier theatrical career in Europe. In fact, the mixture of popular elements, jazz-derived idioms, and cliché, and the attempt at tight musical organization, represents in some ways a remarkable continuation of his late European technique.

Superficially, the popular musical techniques remain his most faithful and consistent strain between the two musical worlds of the European and America theater. However, some of the compositional procedures in *Street Scene* vividly recall the more complex European techniques discussed in detail by Kowalke. Also, because both the European and American careers embrace many of the same ideological goals, the connection between them is less tenuous than often perceived, despite the disguise of a different musical language and medium. It is these connections, rather than the disparities, that make of Weill's music and career one of the most influential, innovatory, adventurous, and original contributions to twentieth century opera and musical theater.

From 1925 until his death in 1950, Weill wrote a series of works which run the gamut of theatrical subject matter and musical style, ranging from the expansive *Aufstieg und Fall der Stadt Mahagonny* and *Die Bürgschaft*, to his school operas *Der Jasager* and *Down in the Valley*, and finally to the combination of Broadway and traditional operatic elements in *Street Scene*. The result was a dramatic legacy distinguished by its diversity, innovative intentions, and ultimately by its overall musical content.—WILLIAM THORNHILL

Welitsch, Ljuba

Soprano. Born Ljuba Veličkova, 10 July 1913, in Borissovo, Bulgaria. Studied with Gyorgy Zlatov in Sofia, and in Vienna with Lierhammer; debut at Sofia Opera, in small part in Louise, *1934; sang at Graz, 1937-40; at Hamburg, 1941-43; at Vienna Volksoper, 1940-44; at Munich, 1943-46; sang in special Vienna performance of Strauss's* Salome, *with the composer conducting, 1944; joined Vienna Staatsoper, 1946, and made debut at Covent Garden (as Salome) during a visit by the company in 1947; sang Donna Anna in* Don Giovanni *(1948) and Amelia in* Un ballo in maschera *(1949) in Edinburgh with Glyndebourne Opera; Metropolitan Opera debut as Salome, 1949, and appeared there for four seasons; sang* Queen of Spades *at Covent Garden, 1953; final operatic role was in Egk's* Der Revisor, *Vienna, 1959; took the speaking part of the Duchess of Crakentorp in Met production of* La fille du régiment *(1972).*

Welitsch's name is associated above all with the role of Salome, one that she studied with the composer and sang under his direction. In London she was also particularly remembered for her performance of this opera in a once notorious production by Peter Brook, with decor by Salvador Dali. Although in retrospect this seems a fairly mild-mannered interpretation of the opera, at the time it was received by a conservative public and press, unused to any form of experimental reinterpretation, as if it were scandalous.

In her years as a member of the ensemble at Graz, and later in Munich and Vienna, Welitsch sang a large number of parts encompassing much of the soprano repertory from Cherubino in *Le nozze di Figaro* to Aida, Tosca, Senta and Salome. Because her career reached its peak during the Second World War and its immediate aftermath, Welitsch's international renown was consequently shortlived. Her debut at the Metropolitan Opera was in 1949; by 1955 she had virtually retreated from large roles, although she continued to perform in Vienna both as an actress in drama and in character roles at the Volksoper. It is tempting to ascribe this cessation of her singing career, like that of Callas in her forties, to misuse of the natural range of her voice, stretching it from lyric to dramatic roles.

Those who heard Welitsch in her prime describe a voice of apparently limitless resources, a musicality that was of instrumental purity, wedded to a stage presence of enormous charm, warmth and fascination. Lord Harewood wrote in *Opera* (Feb 1953): "A more full-blooded and generous performer probably does not exist today" and of her Aida, "the way she dominated the great ensemble of the Triumph scene seemed to me nothing short of uncanny, and older operagoers have confirmed that they had perhaps never heard that part of the role so well realised."

On records Welitsch's generosity of breath, phrasing, for instance, "Vissi d'arte" with wonderful swelling and diminishing of tone, and seeming to employ her intake of breath for purely dramatic purposes, and her victorious attack on the repeated high notes and runs in the Csardas from *Die Fledermaus,* confirm the contemporary reports. Her top notes were compared by the conductor Boyd Neel to "a saw-mill," a characteristically unromantic description of something of the relentless security she seemed to be able to muster. The critic Philip Hope-Wallace chose her as "The most beautiful woman I know" and described her "princely/feline stride, red-gold hair, that *strahlende sopran* . . . Welitsch sang on her nerves—clear stream of tone like Rethberg, a diamond top C like the evening star."

Of the few complete recordings of operas with Welitsch that survive, her Chrysothemis in a Beecham-conducted *Elektra,* Donna Anna in a Furtwängler *Don Giovanni* with Gobbi in the title role, and a *Salome* from the Metropolitan Opera, all confirm that hers was a supremely theatrical voice and presence. Her Mozart performances were received in their time as models of style, though today they would be considered somewhat sketchy; that she could refine her art and produce an intimate, less flamboyant mood can be heard on some records of lieder, notably an impassioned *Im Walde* by Schubert, recorded in 1947, and nearly fifteen years later, her last record, as a guest in the party scene of Karajan's direction of *Die Fledermaus,* when she sings a beautifully phrased though insecure, "Wien, Wien nur du allein." Welitsch inspired the sort of adoration in public and critics that is accorded to few, when in 1953 she returned to Covent Garden as Lisa in *The Queen of Spades.* While already her voice was beginning to present her with problems, William Mann wrote, "The flexibility, the melting purity of tone and the artistry are perhaps even more mature than before. Even if the voice proves to have lost its carrying power, I would rather hear and see Welitsch in her own repertory than any other living singer."—PATRICK O'CONNOR

Werther

Composer: *Jules Massenet.*

Librettist: *Édouard Blau, Paul Milliet, and Georges Hartmann (after Goethe) [libretto translated into German by Max Kalbeck].*

First Performance: *Vienna, Court Opera, 16 February 1892.*

Roles: *Charlotte (mezzo-soprano); Sophie (soprano); Werther (tenor); Albert (baritone); Le Bailli (baritone or bass); Schmidt (tenor); Johann (baritone or bass); chorus (SSAA).*

When a Viennese operatic commission came Massenet's way, he had a subject ready in Goethe's novel *Die Leiden des jungen Werthers,* a profoundly influential work of the Romantic movement, which he had read while traveling in Germany. It tells of a young intellectual who suffers and dies for love, whose repudiation of common sense and convention stirred many thinking people in a period when much of the social and moral order was being questioned and found wanting.

Like Puccini, Massenet usually liked to have a woman as his central character in an opera, and his Hérodiade, Manon, and Thaïs are all memorable characters in the works which bear their names. Here, the protagonist is a man, a young German poet aged twenty-three, but he is no ordinary strong hero in the Wagnerian sense, and in that, perhaps, he resembles Tchaikovsky's Eugene Onegin; certainly he shares with that character a difficulty in knowing his own mind. The prelude to the opera, in D minor and then D major, perhaps describes him in being contemplative and passionate by turns. Then at the start of the opera, set around 1780 in Frankfurt, we find that he is in love with Charlotte, but that she, while returning something of his affection, is to be married to his friend Albert, who is a year or two older than he and seen by her respectable bourgeois family as a practical man and not the dreamer that Werther is. It becomes clear that the

W

OPERA

decision as to Charlotte's future is a firm one and that Werther must accept it, though he cries in despair, "she'll be another man's wife!"

Werther has moved out of Charlotte's life, but having done so he finds himself unable to forget her, and in act II he returns to find her and Albert happy after three months of marriage. Albert sees him sitting disconsolately and generously greets him and welcomes him. Again Werther realizes that he should stay away, and resolves to respect his friend's marriage, but as soon as he is alone with Charlotte he renews his declaration of love and she begs him to go, at least until Christmas. When he rather dramatically tells her younger sister Sophie that he is departing "never to return," Sophie tells Charlotte and Albert, who now realizes with certainty and distress that Werther is still in love with his wife.

By the beginning of act III, set at Christmas time, Werther is writing love letters to Charlotte, who responds in spite of herself and is deeply disturbed and tearful although she does her best to hide her feelings from those around her, praying for strength to bear her difficult situation. Finally, Werther appears, saying that he could no longer stay away; the two of them reminisce about happy times past, he sings the despairing aria with harp obbligato, "Pourquoi me réveiller?" and finally they embrace. But now Charlotte is overwhelmed by her feelings and rushes off to a locked room. Albert returns, having heard of Werther's return and at once fearing the outcome. A servant enters with a message from Werther, asking for the loan of his pistols, and Albert coldly tells Charlotte to hand them over, which she does as if in a dream. Act IV which is relatively short, serves as an epilogue. Werther, who lies dying, is contented when Charlotte tells him, in some of the most passionate music of the opera, that he has always had her love. The voices of children celebrating Christmas in a joyful carol in G major are heard as the opera ends.

The story of *Werther,* though deeply touching, is somewhat thin in itself to be spread over a whole opera, and there are of course skilful dramatic tributaries. The family atmosphere of Charlotte's parental home is well drawn, and Werther himself sings of it in his A flat major aria "O spectacle idéal d'amour et d'innocence." Albert has a quiet domestic exchange with his wife in act II, and he is most effective when he hands the pistols to Charlotte to be given to Werther and leaves the room with an angry gesture. However, inevitably his is not a very sympathetic or fully drawn role compared to that of his less stable but dramatically more interesting rival. One feature of the opera that even a seasoned operagoer may find hard to swallow is that the last exchange between Charlotte and Werther occupies no less than twenty pages of the opera's vocal score.

One could argue that Massenet, with his occasional sentimentality, was not the ideal composer for this powerful and passionate German story, and that Verdi or Richard Strauss might have handled it more strongly—just as it might be suggested of the famous treatment of Goethe's *Faust* by another French composer, Gounod. But whatever the case, Massenet's music is invariably elegant and often moving, and its moments of tenderness are not confined to the lovers. Indeed, the family scenes and the final children's carol are among the most evocative and touching in the opera, while the writing for the solo voices is always fluent, skilful, and sweet, Werther's role being especially demanding.—CHRISTOPHER HEADINGTON

Windgassen, Wolfgang

Tenor. Born 26 June 1914, in Annemasse, Haute Savoie. Died 8 September 1974, in Stuttgart. Married: singer Lore Wissman. Studied with his father, tenor Fritz Windgassen;

with Maria Ranzow and Alfons Fischer, Stuttgart Conservatory; debut as Alvaro in La forza del destino, *Pforzheim, 1941; Stuttgart, 1945-72; at Bayreuth, 1951-70, debuting as Parsifal; Teatro alla Scala debut as Florestan in* Fidelio, *1952; Paris Opéra debut, 1954; Covent Garden debut as Tristan, 1954; regularly sang Siegfried in* Ring *cycles at Covent Garden; Metropolitan Opera debut as Siegmund, 1957; director of Stuttgart Opera, 1972-74.*

For most of the 1950s and 1960s, Wolfgang Windgassen was the greatest living Heldentenor. As John Steane notes in *The Grand Tradition,* Windgassen "came on the scene just as the hunger for a listenable Heldentenor was reaching starvation point." After studying with his father Fritz Windgassen, a leading tenor, Wolfgang completed studies at the Stuttgart Conservatory with Maria Ranzow and Alfons Fischer and made his debut as Alvaro in Verdi's *La forza del destino* in 1941. Wolfgang's mother was likewise a singer, the coloratura soprano Vally van Osten (1882-1923). Windgassen was a regular member of the Stuttgart Opera from 1945 until 1972; from 1972 until his death in 1974 he served as director of that company. Initially specializing in relatively lighter roles such as Hoffmann, Tamino, Don José, Max in Weber's *Der Freischütz,* and in works by Lortzing, Windgassen soon moved into the Wagnerian roles that comprised his main career. He gained international attention in the role of Parsifal at Bayreuth at its reopening in 1951 and returned there nearly every summer until 1970. At Bayreuth he performed nearly all the major tenor roles, including Siegmund, Siegfried, Tristan, Loge, Lohengrin, Walther von Stolzing, Erik in *Der fliegende Holländer,* and Tannhäuser. For much of his career he specialized in Siegfried and Tristan. He had also a repertoire of Italian operas that he performed in German, Verdi's *Otello,* for example. His best roles outside of Wagner were, in addition to Otello, Adolar in Weber's *Euryanthe,* the Emperor in Strauss's *Die Frau ohne Schatten,* and Florestan in *Fidelio.* Windgassen sang only six performances at the Metropolitan Opera in New York but was a regular singer at the Teatro alla Scala from 1952, the Paris Opéra from 1954, and at Covent Garden from 1954. He was also a regular guest at the Staatsoper in Vienna.

Windgassen's abilities are well documented on a fairly large number of recordings both live and commercial. He is perhaps at his lyrical best in the 1953 *Lohengrin* from Bayreuth with Eleanor Steber as a radiant Elsa, conducted by Keilberth. At times Windgassen is somewhat unsteady, but in the Narrative and in other passages calling for bel canto singing, the voice is firm and beautiful. In Solti's *Ring* cycle on Decca his Siegfried is sufficiently heroic but also human, intelligent, and affecting. It remains one of the very best examples of this thoughtful singer's work. Windgassen also recorded Siegfried for Philips's *Ring* cycle under Karl Böhm. Windgassen's Parsifal is preserved in his 1951 debut performance from Bayreuth, conducted by Hans Knappertsbusch. This is widely considered to be one of the greatest of all opera recordings, both for the level of singing and because of Knappertsbusch's sense of musical architecture.

During his Bayreuth years Windgassen became a believable actor under the guidance of Wieland Wagner. For Windgassen Wagner directed a production of his grandfather's seldom-performed *Rienzi* in Stuttgart. The 1966 Bayreuth *Tristan und Isolde* production with Birgit Nilsson and Windgassen, under the direction of Wieland Wagner with Karl Böhm conducting, was recorded by DGG. Windgassen's third act is especially compelling, the tenor making up for vocal deterioration by interpretive greatness. In the first two acts he seems not to have yet fully assumed the role. From 1961 there are highlights of the famous Bayreuth *Tannhäuser* with De Los Angeles as Elisabeth and Grace Bumbry as Venus. Here Windgassen is not in his best vocal estate; his singing is at times rough and he resorts too often to aspirates. For DGG Windgassen made complete recordings of Walther in *Die Meistersinger von Nürnberg* and Erik in *Der fliegende Holländer.* In the latter, recorded in 1955 under Fricsay, Windgassen gives an eloquent performance. His reliability in this role may also be judged in live Bayreuth recordings. A 1953 recording of *Fidelio* for HMV under Furtwängler finds Windgassen's Florestan well sung but lacking conviction and heroic stature. In highlights from Verdi's *Otello* sung in German, Alan Blyth finds the tenor "a taxed but moving Moor."

By the standards of Windgassen's predecessor, the incomparable Lauritz Melchior, Windgassen's voice lacked the ultimate force and volume needed for these Wagnerian roles, yet, in the words of Steane, he "has been as scrupulous a lyricist as any Wagnerian singer of the earlier generation," and he was "the most human and humane of Siegfrieds." In hundreds of performances of these roles throughout his career, Windgassen proved to be steady and reliable. Because of the vocal demands of Wagner he sometimes tended to save himself for the big moments and if there is a lack of thrust and bite needed for passages such as Siegfried's Forging Scene, his 1974 obituary in *Opera* noted that "Few Tristans or Siegfrieds were able to sing the lyrical portions of their music with as much beauty of tone and at the same time rise to the more dramatic moments of the score."—STEPHEN A. WILLIER

Wozzeck

Composer: *Alban Berg.*

Librettist: *Alban Berg (after Georg Büchner).*

First Performance: *Berlin, Staatsoper, 14 December 1925.*

Roles: *Marie (soprano); Captain (tenor); Drum Major (tenor); Wozzeck (baritone); Doctor (bass); Margaret (mezzo-soprano or contralto); Andres (tenor); Child (child soprano); Two Apprentices (bass and baritone); Fool (tenor); Soldier (tenor); Townsman (tenor); chorus (SATTBBBB).*

Wozzeck, a soldier of the lowest rank, is ridiculed by his Captain, his fellow soldier Andres, and the Doctor, for whose bizarre dietary experiments Wozzeck acts as a subject in order to supplement his meagre income. All these are his intellectual and spiritual inferiors, and none has his acute appreciation of social injustice. Marie, the mother of Wozzeck's child, is unable to resist the charms of the shallow Drum Major and is seduced by him. His attention having been drawn to Marie's infidelity, Wozzeck challenges her to admit it, but she refuses. Her spiteful reaction ("Rather a knife in my body than a hand laid on me") and the sight of her dancing openly with the Drum Major arouse Wozzeck's imagination. He kills Marie before she has an opportunity to convey her repentance to him. Guilt and terror lead Wozzeck back to the scene of the crime, where he drowns himself. Their child, on hearing of his mother's death, is drawn by innocent curiosity to look at the body.

Berg's first essay in operatic composition was not only a resounding commercial success on its appearance in 1925 but has maintained its place in the repertoire throughout the post-war period. Regarded by some as atonal, its musical language is perhaps best thought of as an eclectic blend which draws on the resources heard in Schoenberg's *Erwartung* while maintaining strong links with the expanded tonality characteristic of Strauss's *Elektra.* Its musico-dramatic orientation also embodies compromise, coming close to Expressionism at some points—notably Marie's murder—but essentially naturalistic in the manner of Berg's Austrian contemporaries. His literary source, Büchner's *Woyzeck,* was the product of a revolutionary sensibility which stressed the plight of the working class and held bourgeois values up to ridicule, and thus through a fortunate accident of history needed no major reinterpretation in order to mesh with the aesthetics of Krausian Vienna.

Only judicious cuts were needed for Berg to adapt the text of his libretto from Franzos's masterly realization of Büchner's hastily written drafts. In devising the format of the opera, however, he showed a sense of musico-dramatic vision which compares with Boito's. The fifteen short scenes are organized, according to Berg's own description, through abstract musical forms: baroque suite, rhapsody, military march, lullaby, passacaglia and rondo (act I); a five-movement symphony (act II); inventions on a theme, a note, a rhythm, a chord, a key and a *moto perpetuo* (act III). That this well known account of the work is slightly forced merely underlines its quality of deliberation and artifice, which complements the music's wide-ranging harmonic and motivic language. But closer study also reveals a careful web of cross-references within the musical substance, including literalistic leitmotives of the Straussian kind as well as a more abstract system of organization which arguably supports the consistency of forceful expression that is the opera's hallmark.

Despite the organization of the opera into discrete formal units, an impression of through-composed music-drama is generated by the orchestral interludes which link the scenes of each act. These tend either to summarize the music of the preceding scene through abbreviated and concentrated recapitulation, producing an effect of heightened reflection, or to introduce a complex musical texture—as with the off-stage military music (act I, scene 3) or the dance music of the large tavern scene (act II, scene 4)—so as to establish a rich context for the vocal exchanges of the following scene. After the scene of Wozzeck's death, the final orchestral interlude—which begins in a clear D minor—carries the entire burden of his tragedy, and the children's scene which follows is also sustained by the orchestra's glinting *moto perpetuo*. The post-Wagnerian credentials of Berg's approach to operatic composition are also confirmed by the absence of arias and other set pieces, despite the apparent reliance on conventional forms. This is true even of Marie's famous lullaby (act I, scene 3) and her other intimate exchanges with the child (act II, scene 1; act III, scene 1), and of the stylized folk songs sung by Andres (act I, scene 2; act II, scene 4), all of which are conceived as indicators of social status and projected as stage music by a recognizable simplification of musical language.

Berg reserves the effect of alienation, which one may easily read into Büchner's drama throughout, for the final scene of the opera, in which the children greet the news of Marie's death much as they might the arrival of a traveling showman. Elsewhere, the narrative focus and the play of motivic musical materials project a sympathy for Wozzeck—famously enhanced by Fischer-Dieskau in his recorded performance (1965)—which is thought by some to distort the play. The other roles are less troublesome, and all are well characterized; those of Wozzeck and Marie are notable in their own right. The opera makes sensitive use of *Sprechstimme,* together with sung delivery of all kinds including *bel canto. Lulu*—a very different opera—is now regarded as the composer's masterpiece, but *Wozzeck's* historical position is no less assured.—ANTHONY POPLE

Wunderlich, Fritz

Tenor. Born 26 September 1930, in Kusel, Germany. Died 17 September 1966, in Heidelberg. Studied with Margarethe von Winterfeldt at the Freiburg Hochschule für

Musik; debut as Tamino in Die Zauberflöte, *Freiburg, 1954; sang in Stuttgart, 1955-58, Frankfurt, 1958-60, and in Munich from 1960; also sang in Vienna from 1962; Covent Garden debut as Don Ottavio, 1965.*

The outstanding German lyric tenor of his generation, Fritz Wunderlich was first and foremost a melodist. Although he played many operatic roles in his brief career (which ended in a tragic accident) they were those in which qualities of sweetness were more important than those of strength. In some ways the role of Mozart's Prince Tamino, the hero of *Die Zauberflöte,* seemed tailor-made for him, and it is appropriate that he began and ended his work in the opera house with it. Tamino is an innocent figure who nevertheless has the character and courage to face the unknown in a series of trials that lead him to love and a more mature understanding of himself, and while Schikaneder's story and libretto in themselves can seem a little silly, it can convince us fully when allied to Mozart's music sung by an artist such as Wunderlich.

It was in Mozart, and as Tamino above all, that Wunderlich was seen at his finest, and also as an actor who characterized his role with his voice as much as with his physical presence. Although he could elicit sympathy as Don Ottavio, the lover of Donna Anna in *Don Giovanni,* inevitably the baritone who played Giovanni dominated the stage proceedings. In fact, many of the roles that Wunderlich played, and played well, did not allow his qualities of firmness and essential goodness to shine fully: another example is his portrayal of Onegin's friend Lensky in Tchaikovsky's *Eugene Onegin.* Still, both Don Ottavio and Lensky take up moral attitudes against an unscrupulous man, and in this respect the roles suited him. As Alfredo in Verdi's *La traviata* he could also show a devoted earnestness and fidelity of character. In Pfitzner's *Palestrina,* he played the Italian Renaissance composer himself, a leading role though not a romantic one. Palestrina is shown here as undergoing various uncertainties of mind and feeling external pressures but ultimately saving the art of liturgical music for the Catholic Church. The opera is set in 1563, when the real Palestrina was approaching forty; Wunderlich himself was in his mid-thirties and identified well with the role of an artist seeking to serve his God in an imperfect world, while the spirituality of his voice made a deep impression on those who heard these Vienna performances in 1965.

With his sweet, firm, yet sensitive tone and an easy stage presence, Wunderlich was also effective in the comedy role of the young actor Henry in Strauss's *Die Schweigsame Frau* and the Greek shepherd boy Leukippos in the same composer's *Daphne.* He also sang successfully in operetta. At the time of his death, he was considering singing some of the major Wagnerian roles, and the idea of him as Parsifal in Wagner's opera is perhaps one of the major might-have-beens in the history of 20th-century opera; here his performance might have been a revelation. Nor do we have memories or recordings of Wunderlich as the apprentice David in *Die Meistersinger,* although tantalizingly, the richness of his expressive characterization in the deeper kind of German music is to be heard outside opera in his recorded performance with Klemperer of Mahler's *Das Lied von der Erde.*

Fritz Wunderlich made a number of recordings, including Tamino in *Die Zauberflöte,* Wozzeck's soldier friend Andres opposite Dietrich Fischer-Dieskau in Berg's gloomy and powerful opera *Wozzeck,* and Jenik in Smetana's *The Bartered Bride.* There are too few recordings of entire operas with Wunderlich, however, and they do not always feature him in important roles. He may have been happier in his recorded recitals of individual numbers from opera and operetta which feature such composers as Handel, Mozart, Donizetti, Verdi, Puccini, Lortzing, Johann Strauss, Lehár and Kálmán.—CHRISTOPHER HEADINGTON

Zandonai, Riccardo

Composer. Born 30 May 1883, in Sacco Trentino. Died 5 June 1944, in Pesaro. Married: soprano Tarquinia Tarquini, 1917. Studied with Gianferrari at Rovereto, 1893-98; studied with Mascagni at the Liceo Rossini in Pesaro, 1898-1902; international success with Conchita, *1911; involved in a political movement for the return of former Italian provinces during World War I; director of the Liceo Rossini in Pesaro, 1939.*

Operas *La coppa del re,* G. Chiesa (after Schiller), c. 1906 [unperformed]; *L'uccellino d'oro* (children's opera), G. Chelodi (after Grimm), Sacco di Rovereto, 1907; *Il grillo del focolare,* C. Hanau (after Dickens), Turin, 1908; *Conchita,* M. Vaucaire and C. Zangarini (after P. Louÿs), Milan, 1911; *Melenis,* M. Spiritini and C. Zangarini (after L. Bouillet), Milan, 1912; *Francesca da Rimini,* d'Annunzio (abridged by T. Ricordi), Turin, 1914; *La via della finestra,* G. Adami (after Scribe), Pesaro, 1919; revised, Trieste, 1923; *Giulietta e Romeo,* A. Rossato (after da Porto and Shakespeare), Rome, 1922; *I cavalieri di Ekebù,* A. Rossato (after S. Lagerlöf), Milan, 1925; *Giuliano,* A. Rossato (after J. da Varagine), Naples, 1928; *Una partita,* A. Rossato (after Dumas père), Milan, 1933; *La farsa amorosa,* A. Rossato (after Alarcón), Rome, 1933; *Il bacio,* A. Rossato and E. Mucci (after G. Keller), 1940-44 [unfinished].

Riccardo Zandonai belonged to what was later to be called the "eighties generation" *(generazione dell'ottanta)* by the musicologist Massimo Mila. These composers were linked by little more than their dates of birth; in fact they display all the diversity of Italian music in the first half of the twentieth century. While most reflected the contemporary desire in Italy to change the balance of music from opera to instrumental music (chiefly on Austro-German models), others were content to expand on the elements of Austro-German music which had already been adopted in Italian opera.

Just as in 1890, when the tradition of opera composition in Italy seemed to receive new impetus with the work of Mascagni and the other members of the "young school" *(giovane scuola),* so in 1914 a new start seemed likely with Zandonai's *Francesca da Rimini.* On the eve of the First World War, operatic life in Italy was about to change from a repertoire based on contemporary works to the situation which has held for the rest of the century—a repertoire based on classic works from the past. Zandonai was the choice of the most powerful music publisher, Ricordi, to continue their prestigious line of composers and be "Puccini's successor."

Arrigo Boito personally recommended Zandonai to Giulio Ricordi in 1907 and the composer was immediately contracted to write an opera with a ready-made libretto on Dickens's *The Cricket on the Hearth*. Next he was offered Pierre Louÿs's *La femme et le pantin*, a subject with a Spanish setting which Puccini had already turned down. Zandonai was not daunted by a piece which so strongly echoed *Carmen*, and Ricordi sent him to Spain to capture the atmosphere for his work.

A letter from Seville to Ricordi in 1909 records Zandonai's strong impression of Spanish folk music and the declaration that "even Bizet neglected the most interesting types of Spanish song." Zandonai was determined that his *Conchita* (as the opera was eventually called) should be "really Spanish-speaking." Other comments in this letter give hints about Zandonai's approach to composition and show how a composer who feels himself to be part of a living tradition can confidently find musical material from extra-musical stimuli. He writes about the great buildings of Seville as "grandiose tone-poems" and the little alleys with their "incredibly white building and little balconies" being "little snatches of music which an artist can capture and reproduce."

Following the successful production of *Conchita* and the far less popular *Melenis*, Zandonai's moment of glory came with *Francesca da Rimini*. Here he catches perfectly the precious medievalism of D'Annunzio's text, and creates a magically colored score of passion and refinement. It was his only significant international success, and is still occasionally revived in Italy and elsewhere. Thereafter the story of Zandonai's career is one of decline. A single collaboration with Giuseppe Adami brought into existence the comic opera *La via della finestra*, and later the composer found a long-term collaborator in the journalist Arturo Rossato. Their first work together (and Rossato's first libretto) was *Giulietta e Romeo*, effectively a return to the terrain and manner of *Francesca*. Zandonai felt that he had reached his compositional maturity with their later opera *I cavalieri di Ekebù*, with its Nordic setting. The composer's last years were spent in Pesaro, where he succeeded his teacher Mascagni as the Director of the Conservatory. After the fall of Mussolini and the German occupation, he and his wife took refuge in a monastery above Pesaro, where he worked on an opera, *Il bacio*, incomplete at his death.

Zandonai was effectively trapped by the passing of the Romantic period in music. His inheritance was the symphonically structured operatic idiom that held sway in Italy after Verdi's *Falstaff* (1893). His scores are shaped by the orchestral web, into which the vocal lines are woven. His orchestral sound is profoundly colored by the work of Strauss and Debussy, while the vocal delivery is essentially that of the *verismo* opera, robust declamation and lyrical passages alike being supported by a weighty orchestral sound.

Zandonai's harmony is still tonal, but harmonic movement is by way of parallels, altered dominants and subdominants. Modal and whole-tone passages sit side by side, while passages in a specific key may be qualified by a "foreign" chord: D flat major—G flat major—A flat major—G7—D flat major. Textures are created out of a selection of motifs attached to characters and ideas in the general Italian post-Wagner manner ("Wagner explained to the masses," in the words of Rubens Tedeschi). The motifs themselves are generally well-characterized, and steer clear of the obvious immediacy and occasional vulgarity of some of the *verismo* composers.

Zandonai's vocal writing accepts the norms of *verismo:* the tenor lover, soprano heroine and evil baritone. In each case the writing makes extreme demands on the singer in terms of tessitura and sheer power and weight. A feature of some of Zandonai's operatic scores is the extended descriptive orchestral passage, like the third-act prelude in *Conchita* (an impression of the Sevillian night) and the "Cavalcata" in *Giulietta e Romeo,* which describes Romeo's frantic ride back to Verona. Zandonai also wrote a number of orchestral pieces in their own right, often with a descriptive intention, such as *Primavera in Val di Sole* (Spring in the Val di Sole), and *Concerto andaluso* (Andalusian concerto).

With the passing of this late-Romantic style and the establishment of the Fascist state after 1922, Zandonai's aesthetic was well in tune with the provincial and backward-looking nature of much music during the period. In 1932 he was one of the co-signatories of Alceo Toni's Manifesto of Italian Musicians for the Tradition of Nineteenth-Century Romantic Art. This unequivocally expressed the desire to turn away from the experimentation current in Western music elsewhere in favor of the standards of the turn of the century. While a totalitarian, repressive state is not a necessary condition of provincialism and regression in music, the opportunism of the period created the backdrop against which Zandonai's later works were composed.—KENNETH CHALMERS

Die Zauberflöte [The Magic Flute]

Composer: *Wolfgang Amadeus Mozart.*

Librettist: *Emanuel Schikaneder.*

First Performance: *Vienna, Theater auf der Wieden, 30 September 1791.*

Roles: *Queen of the Night (soprano); Pamina (soprano); Tamino (tenor); Papageno (baritone); Sarastro (bass); Papagena (soprano); Monostatos (tenor); Three Ladies (sopranos, mezzo-soprano); Three Genii (soprano, mezzo-soprano, contralto); Speaker of the Temple (bass); Two Priests (tenor, bass); Two Men in Armor (tenor, bass); chorus (SATTBB).*

Labeled simply a *Grosse Oper* (Grand Opera), *Die Zauberflöte* is Mozart's last opera. Made in collaboration with an old friend, Emanuel Schikaneder (1751-1812), director of the Theater auf der Wieden (Freihaus Theater) since 1789, it is a *Singspiel* consisting of musical numbers and spoken dialogue.

Set in Egypt, colored by Enlightenment ideals and Masonic precepts, and seasoned with comic episodes, magic, and stage machinery, the plot hinges upon a theme of trial and purification, a quest for wisdom guided by friendship and supported by love. Pursued by a frightful serpent, the foreign prince Tamino rushes on stage and faints, most unheroically. Three ladies rescue him. Their mistress, the Queen of the Night, implores Tamino to rescue her beautiful daughter Pamina from the wicked sorcerer Sarastro. Inspired by love, armed with magic bells and a magic flute, and accompanied by the comic bird-catcher Papageno, Tamino embarks upon his journey. Having reached Sarastro's realm, Tamino discovers not a sorcerer but an enlightened ruler. With the truth revealed, Tamino readily agrees to undergo the trials which will make him an initiate of the Sun Temple. United after much tribulation, Tamino and Pamina successfully pass the tests of fire and water. Papageno finds his Papagena, the Queen and her minions are vanquished, and the community rejoices, praising the victory of strength, beauty, and wisdom.

No other Mozart dramatic work has such a complicated early history. Frustratingly little is known about the circumstances that led to the opera's creation. No contract survives. No correspondence chronicles Mozart's creative process. Never before had a libretto been compiled from such a remarkable range of sources: books, contemporary stage works, Masonic ritual and numerology (especially the number three), Schikaneder's earlier works and his Shakespearean experience, and prior compositions of Mozart (e.g., *Zaide, Thamos, König von Ägypten,* and *Die Entführung aus dem Serail*). Selecting ideas, scenes, characters, and plot details, the collaborators assembled from these disparate elements an action-packed entertainment, filled with suspense, spectacle, low comedy, and lofty idealism.

Generally discredited now is the theory that Schikaneder and Mozart reversed the plot in midstream, changing Sarastro from a sorcerer to an enlightened ruler and the Queen of the Night from a sorrowing mother to a destructive force. Generally accepted, on the other hand, is the view that while others such as Karl Ludwig Giesecke or Pater Cantes may have contributed details, Schikaneder was the guiding force who wrote the bulk of the text. A more intriguing question cannot be answered: what was Mozart's share in the fashioning of the libretto? The text—simple in diction, pictorial, intelligible, and often inspiring—stands well above the average German opera libretto of its time. Surface inconsistencies notwithstanding, it fired Mozart's musical imagination. Within its frame, his music could unfold fully.

Aligned on the sides of darkness and light, the seven principal characters form a hierarchy. At the bottom, Monostatos (Italian *opera buffa* style) opposes Papageno and Papagena (folklike German songs). At the top, the Queen of the Night (Italian *opera seria* style) opposes the wise Sarastro (simple, exalted hymn style). In the middle, with no counterparts on the side of darkness, stand the central characters, the noble lovers Tamino and Pamina, whose expressive arioso style unites Italian lyricism with German intensity. Not only are these characters memorable individuals; they are also symbols. *Die Zauberflöte* is an allegory depicting the triumph of light over darkness and of good over evil, the victory of virtue and brotherhood, and extolls universal love and friendship. Although Schikaneder and Mozart left no hints, commentators soon believed that the characters embodied other meanings or represented real people in politics, Freemasonry, or music.

For the opera's production, Schikaneder fully exploited the resources of his theater, transforming the often poetic stage directions into the spectacle that he and his public relished. Beyond an engraving of Schikaneder in his Papageno costume, little if anything survives to show how the production might have looked.

A new serenity, a heightened sense of control, and a ceremonial/religious tone characterize Mozart's music for *Die Zauberflöte*. Propelled by march and dance rhythms, his melodies animate the characters and illuminate the dramatic situations. Enriching Mozart's basic harmonic vocabulary at crucial spots is an expressive chromaticism that heightens intensity or adds poignance, as appropriate. The inclusion of counterpoint in the Bach tradition evokes a time and place foreign to the Vienna of 1791. Not only does the fugal section of the overture foreshadow the trials to be endured by the lovers; almost paradoxically, the rapid repeated notes and bright orchestral colors of its theme presage the comic side of the proceedings. For the Two Men in Armor, who intone a paraphrase of a biblical text, Mozart exhumes the venerable Lutheran chorale-prelude, in which a hymn tune unfolds in slow note values above a more rapidly moving contrapuntal accompaniment.

Mozart knew his singers and understood their voices. A kaleidoscope of vocal color, *The Magic Flute* offers solos, ensembles ranging from duets to quintets, and choruses. Supplementing the adult male and female voices is the cool, serene sound of the Three Boys. Similarly, Mozart had at his disposal a capable orchestra of thirty-five players. In addition to the special effects of Glockenspiel and panpipes, he also includes solemn trombones and the basset horns associated with his Masonic music. The opera exhibits a dazzling variety of musical types. Distributed among its twenty-one numbers are folklike strophic songs, elaborate coloratura arias, expressive ariettes, a hymn, an instrumental march, numerous ensembles, choruses, an *introduzione,* and two enormous ensemble finales, each a *tour de force* of the dramatic composer's art.

The sharp contrasts of musical material are self-evident. More difficult to assess are the factors that forge this opera into such a powerful unity. Schikaneder's drama supplies the poetic kernal. Mozart furnishes the rest. Certain recurring musical figures, rhythmic patterns, and harmonic progressions are readily audible. Operative too is Mozart's singular ability to reconcile musical and dramatic demands. His key scheme, for example, makes sense musically and, at the same time, relates closely to the course of the drama and to the contents of the individual numbers. E-flat major (three flats) is the Masonic key, C minor (also three flats) represents the dark side, while C major, to the Age of the Enlightenment, is the key of light. He creates a unity of sound, bathing his characters in a radiant glow. Perhaps the greatest binding force is a unity of musical conception that mediates and ultimately resolves the conflicting opposites: dark-light, evil-good, masculine-feminine, sublime-ridiculous.

The Magic Flute quickly became Mozart's greatest success, a triumph he could relish for only two months. It proved to be Schikaneder's greatest success as well, the springboard to the fulfillment of his ultimate dream, the Theater an der Wien. Two centuries later, this enigmatic, sublimely beautiful opera remains a repertory staple.—MALCOLM S. COLE

Zemlinsky, Alexander von

Composer. Born 14 October 1871, in Vienna. Died 15 March 1942, in Larchmont, New York. Studied piano with Door and composition with Krenn, R. Fuchs and J.N. Fuchs at the Vienna Conservatory, 1887-92; joined the Tonkünstlerverein, 1893; involved with the orchestral society Polyhymnia, 1895, and became associated with Arnold Schoenberg; opera Es war einmal conducted by Mahler at the Vienna court opera, 1900; conductor of the Karlstheater in Vienna, 1900-06; conducted at the Theater an der Wien, 1903; principal conductor of the Volksoper, and organized with Schoenberg the Union of Creative Musicians, 1904; conductor of the German Opera in Prague and taught at the Prague College of Music, 1911; assistant conductor to Otto Klemperer at the Kroll Opera in Berlin, 1927; emigrated to the United States, 1938.

Operas *Sarema,* Adolph von Zemlinsky (after R. von Gottschall, *Die Rose vom Kaukasus*), c. 1895, Munich, Hofoper, 10 October 1897; *Es war einmal,* Drachmann, 1897-99, Vienna, Hofoper, 22 January 1900; *Der Traumgörge,* L. Feld, 1904-06; *Kleider machen Leute,* L. Feld (after G. Keller), c. 1908, Vienna, Volksoper, 2 October 1910; revised, 1922; *Eine florentinische Tragödie,* Wilde (translated by M. Meyerfeld), 1915-16, Stuttgart, 30 January 1917; *Der Zwerg,* G.C. Klaren (after Wilde, *The Birthday of* the Infanta), 1920-21, Cologne, 28 May 1922; *Der Kreidekreis,* after Klabund, 1932, Zurich, 14 October 1933; *Der König Kandaules,* Gide (translated by F. Blei), c. 1935 [unfinished].

Influential in turn-of-the-century Vienna as a modernistically-inclined composition teacher, Zemlinsky in fact devoted the major part of his creative energy to opera, both as an innovative conductor and as a composer. His seven completed works in the genre appeared at strategic points throughout his career (an eighth, *Der König Kandaules,* after Gide, was left uncompleted). They negotiate an interesting path between the demands of popular musical theater and an idealistic refinement of taste and purpose.

Zemlinsky was by nature inclined to the fairy-tale romanticism of Humperdinck as much as the more severe, expressionistic modernism of his close friend Arnold Schoenberg, whose experimental harmonic language was at times eclipsed by Zemlinsky's before the First World War. Strong though his sympathetic association with the Second Viennese School was, Zemlinsky came to admire the works of Gustav Mahler above those of his younger contemporaries. The senior composer was to play an important role in the development of Zemlinsky's career when he accepted his second opera, *Es war einmal,* for performance at Vienna's Hofoper in 1900.

Mahler had initially considered Zemlinsky's prize-winning first opera, *Sarema* (first performed in Munich, 1897) for performance in Vienna. This work was of the heroic post-Wagnerian type, was set in the eighteenth century on the Russian-Caucasian border and concerned the relationship between a Russian officer and a Caucasian girl, Sarema, who kills herself after struggling between love and loyalty to her oppressed people. In the event Mahler seems to have realized that Zemlinsky was more at home in the subtler world of *Es war einmal,* the preparation of whose final version Mahler supervised (making changes to the libretto and orchestration, lengthening the interlude following the prologue and recomposing the conclusion of act I). This work incidentally established a first, indirect connection between Mahler and his future wife, Alma Schindler, a pupil and near-fiancée of Zemlinsky's. It is not impossible that she played a part in Zemlinsky's attraction to Holger Drachmann's fairy-tale comedy in which a haughty princess is compromised into banishment by a "gypsy" who reveals himself as the Prince of Northland only after having tamed her shrewish ways and having inspired her passively submissive love.

The first act of *Es war einmal* is an impressive, state-of-the-art essay in post-Wagnerian style influenced not only by Humperdinck, but also Tchaikovsky and Rimsky-Korsakov (Dukas and Debussy subsequently attracted Zemlinsky; later still, Stravinsky and Weill). Statuesque Wagnerian rhetoric is replaced by a more naturalistic vocal declamation, borne upon a symphonically evolving and kaleidoscopically colored orchestral discourse. This is nevertheless always ready to retreat before the closed-form songs and dances that Zemlinsky incorporates (often of a characteristic or specifically "gypsy" nature).

Rehearsals for *Der Traumgörge* were shelved after Mahler's departure from Vienna in 1907 and this remarkable experiment in through-composed "magic realism" remained unperformed in Zemlinsky's lifetime. He seems to have sensed, however, that the virtuosity of its advanced orchestral and harmonic language, rarely permitting the crystallization of extended periodic melody, would not have attracted a wider audience. *Kleider machen Leute* (1910) seems deliberately to reintroduce clearer recurring melodic material and occasional closed forms. This gently comic opera, revised in 1922, was derived from the Seldwyla stories of Gottfried Keller (amongst which Delius discovered his *A Village Romeo and Juliet*). Wenzel

Strapinski, a ne'er-do-well tailor, encourages the social confusion caused by his fine clothes when he arrives in an unfamiliar village; he is taken for a Polish count before finding a little post-Wagnerian redemption in the arms of a girl who will love him even when his true identity is revealed. Although Leo Feld's libretto shares some of the faults of that for *Der Traumgörge* and detracted from the opera's complete success in its first, three-act version, Strapinski's melodically folksy (if harmonically sophisticated) little song provides a source of effective devices for focusing Straussian lushness in this satire upon petty-bourgeois self-deception.

Criticism of the opera's lack of strong effects nevertheless dogged *Kleider machen Leute* and may have led Zemlinsky to change direction somewhat in the two one-act operas he composed during his time in Prague. *Eine florentinische Tragödie* (1917) and *Der Zwerg* (1922—posthumously revived as *Der Geburtstag der Infantin*) explore more extreme areas of decadent emotionalism and were both based on Oscar Wilde (like Strauss's *Salome*). *Der Zwerg* is striking not least for its harrowing central role for the tenor: a grotesque dwarf whose natural innocence is shattered into expressionistic nightmare by the wilful, musically somewhat neoclassical Infanta (she would prefer a toy that does not have a heart). This powerful work successfully unites deliberately contrasted musical styles in a way that was still more elaborately explored in *Der Kreidekreis,* which drew on the same, originally Chinese, source as Brecht's *The Caucasian Chalk Circle*. Composed during Zemlinsky's Kroll Opera period in Berlin, it alluded to jazz (for the less savory characters) as well as something of the Brecht-Weill manner of closed-form "numbers" with spoken dialogue in its fusion of romantic idealism and sharp social criticism. It was successfully premiered in Zurich in 1933, although the events of history gave it no better chance of achieving the conclusive public success that had eluded Zemlinsky's earlier operas.—PETER FRANKLIN

Zimmermann, Bernd Alois

Composer. Born 20 March 1918, in Bliesheim, near Cologne. Died 10 August 1970, in Königsdorf. Studied philology at the universities of Bonn, Cologne, and Berlin; studied composition with Philipp Jarnach in Cologne; attended lectures by Wolfgang Fortner and René Leibowitz at Darmstadt; lecturer in composition at the Hochschule für Musik in Cologne, 1958.

Operas *Die Soldaten*, Zimmermann (after Lenz), 1958-60; revised 1963-64; *Medea*, H.H. Jahnn, [unfinished].

Bernd Alois Zimmermann's single opera, *Die Soldaten* 1958-60; revised 1963-64, has been widely recognized as one of the most significant contributions to the genre by a composer of Germanic origin since Alban Berg's *Wozzeck* (1921). Its historical importance derives from three factors: 1) it is the first opera composed by a person closely associated with the post-war avant garde; 2) it is the first opera in which techniques of integral serialism are utilized as an organizational basis; 3) quotation and collage are introduced as significant aspects of the dramatic and musical design.

This last aspect, the use of musical material borrowed from other sources in a manner similar to the technique of collage in the visual arts, is perhaps the single most innovative feature of the opera. Not only does Zimmermann quote composers of the past (primarily Bach) and allude stylistically to jazz and other "vernacular" idioms, he is able to integrate these materials into the musical and dramaturgical fabric. The barriers between past, present, and future are broken down through musical and dramatic juxtapositions; all of history is presented as completely present in a pluralistic and contemporary world view. One way this is achieved is through the simultaneous presentation of separate "scenes" on different levels of the stage; in this way, the dramatic stage presentation parallels the equally pluralistic attitude shown in the use of stylistic and material borrowings superimposed upon the composer's "own music."

Despite his limited operatic output, Zimmermann's primary musical orientation was toward the dramatic. Throughout his career, he displayed a keen interest in musical forms which are inherently dramatic: the solo sonata, the symphony, the ballet, and especially the concerto. He was also active as a composer of music for dramatic productions in radio and film. It would seem that this dramatic orientation was pivotal in his espousal of pluralistic techniques of collage and quotation for most of his works following *Die Soldaten*.

Zimmermann's first mature works were in the particular vein of neo-classicism which dominated Germany's musical life during the inter-war years. His earliest published composition, the five Extemporale für Klavier (1938-46), shows the influence of Hindemith in the use of unusual yet still diatonically derived harmonies. *Enchiridion: Kleine Stücke für Klavier* (1949-51) is similar, but incorporates the diatonic harmonies within a quickly moving chromatic linear design. This work is one of the first in which Zimmermann incorporated the twelve-tone techniques of Arnold Schoenberg which had recently begun to resurface following the suppression of Schoenberg's music by the Nazis.

Building on the models of his teachers Wilhelm Fortner and René Leibowitz, Zimmermann composed several works in which he attempted to reconcile Schoenberg's twelve-tone techniques with the dominant formal tradition of Central European music as exemplified by such composers as Igor Stravinsky, Béla Bartók, and Paul Hindemith. Typical of this period are his Violin Concerto (1949/50), and Oboe Concerto (1952), each of which adheres stylistically to neo-classicism, while incorporating thematic material derived from twelve-tone series. The renewed interest in Schoenberg's twelve-tone technique following the Second World War was reflected in the organization in 1946 of the "Darmstädter Ferienkurse für Neue Musik." These seminars were attended by many of the most talented young composers of the time, including Zimmermann in 1948 and 1950, and were pivotal in reacquainting composers and the public with the music of Schoenberg, Berg, and Webern. It was in Darmstadt that Zimmermann studied with Fortner, Leibowitz and Hindemith, who were among the first to be engaged as leaders of the composition seminars. It was also here that Zimmermann became associated with the somewhat younger composers of the post-war avant-garde who were just beginning to radically alter the course of European music.

By the mid-fifties, the attitudes of many composers in Europe had changed dramatically: twelve-tone serialism was no longer seen as simply the basis for the creation of themes within a neoclassical style, but as a systematic mode of organization to be applied to the entire musical fabric. This more thorough-going integration of serialism is evident in Zimmermann's works of the period, such as Perspektiven (1955/56), Canto di speranza (1953/57), and the Cello Sonata (1959/60). This last work also exemplifies Zimmermann's continuing occupation with music of a dramatic thrust. The structural rigor of serialism did not hinder Zimmermann's ability to create dramatic intensity. Like his earlier neo-classical concertos, the Cello Sonata is music requiring extreme virtuosity and dramatic flair from the performer.

Although Zimmermann's serial orientation would remain basically unaltered for the remainder of his career, he began increasingly to use stylistic and material quotation within serially structured works. He had already shown an openness to pre-existing materials in his work during the years when he was first exploring integral serialism. His Trumpet Concerto entitled *Nobody knows de trouble I see* (1954) uses, as the title suggests, the African-American spiritual of the same title as what Zimmermann terms its "geometrical center" (letter to Karl Amadeus Hartmann, 30 October 1956; quoted in Konold, 1986, p. 95). Even before this, in *Kontraste* (1953), the composer had called up the ghosts of such eminent forebears as Claude Debussy, Maurice Ravel and Johann Strauss to preside over this first in his series of "Imaginary Ballets."

Zimmermann would, however, go beyond the use of stylistic allusion—already evident, at any rate, in his earlier neo-classicism—in works such as *Die Soldaten* (1958/64), and *Dialoge* (1960/65). In these works, actual quotation of pre-existing material is used. In each case, the overall conception is serial and the quotations appear superimposed over one another along with Zimmermann's "own music." In one section alone of *Dialoge* the composer quotes Debussy's *Jeux*, Mozart's Piano Concerto in C Major, K.467, and the hymn *Veni creator spiritus*. In both *Die Soldaten* and *Dialoge*, quotation is confined to relatively small portions of each work. But in Zimmermann's most extreme use of quotation, his *Musique pour les soupers du roi Ubu* (1966), the composer pieces together a work consisting entirely of pre-existing music by himself and others. Zimmermann's quotations sometimes emerge as part of a continuous musical fabric, alluding to the past as simply another element available for a composer's use. At other times, they appear as interruptions, startling the music, as it were, as abrupt and foreign-sounding elements.

The pluralistic attitude which Zimmermann and others began to display in the 1960s toward the music of the past has been seen by some as a transformation of serial procedures. Robert P. Morgan has compared Zimmermann's careful manipulation of pre-existing material through "combinational and permutational methods" in *Musique pour les soupers du roi Ubu* to the use of serial procedures with more usual "pre-formed" materials such as pitch or rhythm (*Twentieth-Century Music*, New York 1991, 412).—RICHARD R. BLOCKER

This index includes references to all entries on individual operas (printed in boldface type) as well as references to all operas listed in the composer entries.

OPERA

Abromeit, Kathleen A. Public services librarian, Conservatory Library, Oberlin College. Author of articles on Ethel Smyth, *The Wreckers*, and Anna Bon. Author of CD-ROM reviews for *Mad River Review* and reviews for *Choice*.

Achter, Morton Professor of music and chairman of department of music, Otterbein College, Westerville, Ohio. Former chairman of Fine Arts at Bloomfield College; faculty appointments also at the University of Michigan and Boston University.

Adams, Byron Composer, conductor, and assistant professor of music, University of California, Riverside. Author of articles for *MLA Notes*, *Music and Letters*, and *Musical Quarterly*.

Anderson, David E. Doctoral candidate at the University of Chicago. Author of articles for *Music Review*, *The Opera Quarterly*, and *Notes*.

Antokoletz, Elliott Head of musicology division and professor of musicology, University of Texas, Austin. Editor of the *International Journal of Musicology*. Author of *The Music of Béla Bartók*, 1984, *A Guide to Béla Bartók Research*, 1988, and *Twentieth Century Music*, 1992.

Armstrong, Robin Free-lance writer. Contributor of articles to *Contemporary Musicians*, *Contemporary Black Biography*, and African-American Almanac.

Ashbrook, William Professor Emeritus of music, Indiana State University. Author of *Donizetti*, 1965, *The Operas of Puccini*, 1968, *Donizetti and His Operas*, 1982, and *Puccini's Turandot: The End of the Great Tradition*, with Harold Powers, 1991. Contributing editor for *The Opera Quarterly* and member of editorial board of *Cambridge Opera Journal*.

Backus, Joan Visiting assistant professor, University of Victoria, British Columbia, Canada. Author of articles on Liszt for *19th Century Music* and *Journal of the American Liszt Society*.

Barfoot, Terry Senior lecturer in history of music, The South Downs College, England. Coauthor of *Opera: A History*, 1987. Editor of *The Classical Music Repertoire Guide* and *Quarternote*. Feature writer for *Classical Music Magazine*, music critic for *The News* (Portsmouth), and author of program notes for various concert series and opera companies throughout England.

Birkin, Kenneth Free-lance writer and reviewer; musician. Author of *Richard Strauss's "Arabella,"* 1989, *"Friedenstag and Daphne": An Interpretative Study of the Literary and Dramatic Sources of the Richard Strauss Operas*, 1989, and editor of *Stefan Zweig/Joseph Gregor: Briefwechsel, 1921-1938*, 1991. Author of record sleeves as well as reviews and articles for *International Richard Strauss Gesellschaft-*

949

Wein, Music and Letters, Musical Times, Opera, and *Tempo*.

Blocker, Richard R. Lecturer in music, DePaul University. Former lecturer in music, The University of Chicago.

Brauner, Charles S. Professor of music history and literature, and chairman, department of theory, history, and composition, Chicago Musical College, Roosevelt University. Author of articles for *Journal of the American Musicological Society* and *Musical Quarterly*. Contributor of articles to *Studies in the History of Music, Volume 2*, 1988, and *Musical Humanism and Its Legacy*, 1992.

Brauner, Patricia B. Coordinator of the Center for Italian Opera Studies, University of Chicago; and musicological consultant and research associate, Fondazione Rossini. Author of articles on Gioacchino Rossini.

Burroughs, Bruce Editor-in-chief, *The Opera Quarterly*, Van Nuys, California. Author of articles for *The Houston Post, Musical Journal, Los Angeles Times*, and *Opera News*.

Bushnell, Howard Author of *Maria Malibran: A Biography of the Singer*, 1979.

Carley, Lionel Honorary archivist and adviser to Delius Trust, England. Author of *Delius: The Paris Years*, 1975, *Delius: A Life in Pictures*, 1977, *Delius: A Life in Letters*, with Robert Threlfall, 1988, and *Grieg and Delius: Marion Boyars—A Correspondence*, in press.

Carr, Maureen A. Professor of music theory, Pennsylvania State University. Author of *Sightsinging Complete*, 5th ed., with Bruce Benward, 1991, and *Introduction to Sightsinging and Ear Training*, 2nd ed., with Bruce Benward and J. Timothy Kolosick, 1992.

Carter, Tim Reader in music, Royal Holloway and Bedford New College, University of London, England. Author of *W.A. Mozart: "Le nozze di Figaro,"* 1987, *Jacopo Peri (1561-1633): His Life and Works*, 1989, and *Music in Late Renaissance and Early Baroque Italy*, 1992. Contributor *to The New Grove Dictionary of Opera* and *The Penguin Opera Guide*. Author of articles on late Renaissance music for many scholarly journals.

Chalmers, Kenneth Composer. Regular translator for *Opera* magazine.

Cherniss, Michael Essayist.

Chusid, Martin Professor of music and director of American Institute for Verdi Studies, New York University. Author of *A Catalog of Verdi Operas*, 1974, and *The Verdi Companion*, 1979. Author of articles for *Acta Musicologica, Mozart-Jahrbuch, Opera News, The Opera Quarterly*, and other journals. Editor of the *Verdi Newsletter* since 1984.

Clinkscale, Martha Novak Lecturer, University of California, Riverside. Author of *Makers of the Piano 1700-1820*, in press. Editor of *Journal of the American Musical Instrument Society*. Contributor to *The New Grove Dictionary of Opera*, 1992, and *Encyclopedia of Keyboard Instruments, in* press.

Cole, Malcolm S. Professor of musicology, University of California, Los Angeles. Author of *Armseelchen: The Life and Music of Eric Zeisl*, with Barbara Barclay, 1984, and *Guided Listening*, with Eleanor Hammer, 1992. Author of articles and reviews for *Journal of the American Musicological Society, Journal of Musicology*, and *Performance Practice Review*. Contributor to *The New Grove Dictionary of Music and Musicians*, 1980.

Collins, William J. Member of English department faculty, Kutztown University, Pennsylvania. Coauthor of *Black Bart: The True Story of the West's Most Famous Stagecoach Robber*, 1992, and *EJS: A Discography of the Private-Label Recordings of Edward J. Smith, in* press. Author of articles on opera for *The Record Collector*.

Corse, Sandra Associate professor of English, Georgia Institute of Technology. Author of *Opera and the Uses of Language*, 1987, and *Wagner and the New Consciousness*, 1989.

Craggs, Stewart R. Development services librarian, University of Sunderland Library, England. Author of catalogues for the works of William Walton and biobibliographic works on Arthur Bliss, Richard Rodney Bennett, and John McCabe. Author of articles for *Musical Times* and *Perspective in Music*.

Crohn, Harris N. Associate professor of music, piano faculty, Southern Methodist University. Active recitalist, chamber music performer, accompanist, and conductor.

Cyr, Mary Chair, department of music, University of Guelph, Quebec, Canada. Author of *Performing Baroque Music*, 1992. Editor of *Canadian University Music Review* and contributor to *The New Grove Dictionary of Opera,* 1992. Author of articles on Jean-Phillipe Rameau and eighteenth-century opera for *Early Music, Music and Letters,* and *Musical Times.*

Danes, Robert H. Associate professor of music and associate dean of College of Arts and Sciences, Washburn University, Topeka, Kansas. Author of articles for *Diapason and Washington Opera Magazine.*

D'Angelo, James Member of the faculties of Goldsmiths College, University of London, Webster University, and The Westminister Institute, England. Author of *Tonality Symbolism in Paul Hindemith's Opera "Die Harmonie der Welt,"* 1985, and *The Tuning of the Universe,* 1991.

Daniel, Keith W. Music teacher, Concord Academy, Concord, Massachusetts. Author of *Francis Poulenc: His Artistic Development and Musical Style,* 1982. Author of articles for *In Theory Only, American Choral Review,* and *Stagebill.*

Darcy, Warren Professor of music theory, Oberlin College Conservatory of Music. Contributor to *The Opera Quarterly* and *19th Century Music.*

Davidian, Teresa Visiting assistant professor, Bowdoin College. Author of articles for *Journal of Musicological Research* and *Theory and Practice.*

Day, James Free-lance writer and lecturer and former principal, Cambridge Eurocentre, England. Author of *Vaughan Williams,* 1961, *The Literary Background to Bach's Cantatas,* 1961, and *Music and Aesthetics in the 18th and 19th Century,* with Peter le Huray, 1981.

Dennis, Lawrence J. Professor of philosophy of education, Southern Illinois University. Reviewer for *Opera Canada.* Previously a pianist and teacher at McGill University, Canada, and reviewer for *Music and Musicians.*

Detels, Claire Associate professor of music, University of Arkansas. Author of articles for *Opera Journal* and *Yearbook of Interdisciplinary Studies in the Fine Arts.*

Digaetani, John Louis Associate professor of English, Hofstra University. Author of *Richard Wagner and the Modern British Novel,* 1978, *Puccini the Thinker,* 1987, *An Invitation to the Opera,* 1990, and *Penetrating Wagner's Ring: An Anthology,* 1990. Author of articles for *Opera Canada, Opera Digest, Opera News,* and *The Opera Quarterly.*

Drake, James A. Executive director, Greenville University Center, Clemson University. Author of *Ponselle: A Singer's Life,* 1982, *Richard Tucker: A Biography,* 1984, and *Rosa Ponselle: A Profile in Perspective,* in press. Author of articles for *High/Fidelity, Musical America, The Opera Quarterly,* and other periodicals.

Drummond, Andrew Professor of theatre arts, Kingsburough Community College of the City University of New York. Author of *American Opera Librettos,* 1973.

Dyson, Peter Associate professor of English, University of Toronto, Ontario, Canada. Reviewer and feature writer for *Opera Canada* and *Opera.* Author of articles on opera for *Current Musicology* and *Henry James Review.*

Elliott, Jonathan Composer and member of music faculty, Saint Ann's School, Brooklyn, New York. Contributing editor for MCR Productions, The Netherlands.

Ewans, Michael Associate professor of drama and warden of the Central Coast Campus of the University of Newcastle, New South Wales, Australia. Author of *Janáček's Tragic Operas,* 1977, *Wagner and Aeschylus: The "Ring" and the "Orestei,"* 1982, *Georg Büchner's Woyzeck: Translation and Theatrical Commentary,* 1989, and numerous articles and essays on Greek tragedy and opera.

Fanning, David Lecturer in music, Manchester University, England. Author of articles for *Royal Musical Association.*

Farkas, Andrew Director of libraries and professor of library science, University of North Florida. Editor, contributor, and translator of *Tita Ruffo: An Anthology,* 1984; author of *Opera and Concert Singers: An Annotated International Bibliography,* 1985; editor of *Lawrence Tibbett: Singing Actor,* 1989; and coauthor of *Enrico Caruso: My Father and My Family,* with Enrico Caruso, Jr. Author of articles for numerous publications, including *Opera, Opera News, The Opera Quarterly,* and *Record Collector.*

Feldman, James Allen Professor of music theory, Baldwin-Wallace College Conservatory, Berea, Ohio.

Fitzlyon, April Free-lance writer and translator. Author of *Lorenzo da Ponte,* 1956, *The Price of Genius,* 1964, and *Turgenev and the Theatre,* 1983. Contributor to *The New Grove Dictionary* *of Music and Musicians*, 1980. Author of articles for many periodicals.

Foltz, Roger E. Professor of music, University of Nebraska. Author of *Sight Singing and Related Singing*, 1973, 1978, and *Sight Singing: Melodic Structures in Functional Tonality*, 1978, both with Anne Marie de Zeeuw. Author of articles for *Clavier Magazine, Indiana Theory Review, Journal of Music Theory Pedagogy*, and other journals.

Fox, David Anthony Associate director, College of General Studies, University of Pennsylvania. Formerly director of special programs at University of California, Los Angeles. Author of reviews for *The Opera Quarterly, Pulse*, and other musical journals.

Franklin, Peter Lecturer in music, University of Leeds, England. Author of *The Idea of Music: Schoenberg and Others*, 1985, and *Mahler's Third Symphony*, 1991.

Freeman, John W. Associate editor for *Opera News*, New York. Author of *The Metropolitan Opera Stories of the Great Operas*, 1984, and *Toscanini: A Pictorial Biography*, with Walfredo Toscanini, 1987.

Furman, Nelly Professor of French and past director of women's studies program, Cornell University. Author of *La Revue des Deux Mondes et le Romantisme (1831-1848)*, 1975, and coeditor of *Women and Language in Literature and Society*, 1980.

Gable, David Doctoral candidate, Harper Fellow, The University of Chicago. Coeditor of *A Life for New Music: Selected Papers of Paul Fromm*, 1988, and *Alban Berg: Historical and Analytical Perspectives*, 1991. Author of articles for *Journal of Musicology* and *Journal of the American Musicological Society*.

Galante, Jane Hohfeld Chamber music pianist, and trustee, Morrison Chamber Music Foundation. Former music editor for *A Journal of Modern Culture* and instructor, history of opera at Mills College and the University of California, Berkeley.

Garlington, Aubrey S. Professor of music, University of North Carolina. Author of *Confraternity and "Carnivale" at San Giovanni Evangelista, Florence, 1820-1920*, 1991. Author of articles for *Journal of the American Musicological Society, Musical Quarterly*, and *Yearbook of Interdisciplinary Studies in the Fine Arts*.

Gattey, Charles Neilson Biographer, playwright, lecturer, and author. Author of *Queens of Song*, 1979, *The Elephant That Swallowed a Nightingale and Other Operatic Wonders*, 1981, *Peacocks on the Podium*, 1982, *and Foie Gras and Trumpets*, 1984. Regular contributor to *About the House.*

Gray, Timothy O. Legal proofreader, free-lance editor, and doctoral candidate, Loyola University of Chicago.

Green, London Professor of drama and stage director, Bishop's University, Quebec, Canada; writer, radio commentator, and stage director. Author of *Metropolitan Opera Guide to Recorded Opera*, in press. Author of articles for *Opera Canada, Opera News, The Opera Quarterly, Theatre Research International*, and *Theatre Journal.*

Greenspan, Charlotte Free-lance writer. Translator of *Haydn Keyboard Sonnets*, 1982. Contributor to *The New Harvard Dictionary of Music*, 1986. Editor of *Maria Malibran, Album Lyrique*, and *Dernières Pensées*, 1984.

Grey, Thomas S. Assistant professor of music, Stanford University. Contributor to *Analyzing Opera*, 1989, *Wagner Compendium*, 1992, and *Music and Text: Critical Inquiries*, 1992. Author of articles for *19th Century Music.*

Grim, William E. Assistant professor of music, Worcester State College, Massachusetts. Author of *The Faust Legend in Music and Literature*, vol. 1, 1988, vol. 2, 1992, *Max Reger: A Bio-Bibliography*, 1988, and *Haydn's Sturm und Drang Symphonies: Form and Meaning*, 1990. Editor of *Yearbook of Interdisciplinary Studies in Fine Arts.*

Guenther, Roy J. Professor of music and chairman of department of music, George Washington University, Washington, D.C. Music critic for the *Washington Post*. Author of *Musorgsky's Days and Works: A Biography in Documents*, 1983, and contributor to *Russian Theoretical Thought in Music*, 1983.

Gutman, David Senior Discographer (classical), National Discography, MCPS, England. Author of *Prokofiev*, 1988. Editor of *The Lennon Companion*, 1987, and *The Dylan Companion*, 1990, both with Elizabeth Thomson.

Harding, James Lecturer, broadcaster, and writer. Author of *Saint-Saëns and His Circle*, 1965, *Massenet*, 1970, *Rossini*, 1971, *Gounod*, 1973,

Folies de Paris: The Rise and Fall of French Operetta, 1979, *Jacques Offenbach*, 1980, *Maurice Chevalier: His Life*, 1982, *Ivor Novello*, 1987, *Gerald du Maurier: The Last Actor Manager*, 1989, and *George Robey and the Music Hall*, 1991.

Harris, Ellen T. Professor of music and associate provost for the Arts, Massachusetts Institute of Technology. Author of *Handel and the Pastoral Tradition*, 1980, and *Henry Purcell's "Dido and Aeneas,"* 1987. Editor of *Henry Purcell: "Dido and Aeneas,"* 1989, and *The Librettos of Handel's Operas*, 1989. Author of articles for *Händel-Jahrbuch* and *The Journal of Musicology*.

Hartwell, Robin Lecturer in music, Liverpool Institute of Higher Education. Former member of faculties of University of Sussex, University of Keele, and University of Liverpool.

Hatch, Christopher Previously a lecturer in music, Columbia University. Editor of *Music and Civilization: Essays in Honor—Paul Henry Lang*, with Edmond Strainchamps and Maria Rika Maniates, 1984, and editor of *Music Theory and the Exploration of the Past*, with David W. Burnstein, 1992. Author of articles for *Musical Quarterly* and *The Opera Quarterly*.

Headington, Christopher Composer, pianist, author, and teacher. Author of *The Bodley Head History of Western Music*, 1974, *Illustrated Dictionary of Musical Terms*, 1980, *The Performing World of the Musician*, 1981, *Britten*, 1981, and *Listener's Guide to Chamber Music*, 1982. Coauthor of *Opera: A History*, 1987, and *Sweet Sleep*, 1992.

Heller, Wendy Doctoral candidate, Brandeis University, Waltham, Massachusetts. Contributor to *The New Book of Knowledge*, in progress.

Henig, Stanley Head of Centre for European Studies, University of Central Lancashire, England. Former chairman, Court of Royal Northern College of Music and Secretary, Historic Masters Ltd. and Historic Singers Trust. Contributor to *Opera*.

Heyer, John Hajdu Dean, College of Fine Arts, Indiana University of Pennsylvania. Editor of *Gilles "Messe de morts,"* 1984, and *Lully and the Music of the French Baroque*, 1989. Contributor to *The New Grove Dictionary of Music and Musicians*, 1980.

Hindley, Clifford Independent scholar. Author of articles on Benjamin Britten and *Billy Budd* for *Music and Letters* and *Musical Quarterly*.

Howard, Patricia Tutor and lecturer in music, The Open University, England. Author of *Gluck and the Birth of Modern Opera*, 1963, *The Operas of Benjamin Britten: An introduction*, 1969, *Haydn in England*, 1980, *Mozart's "Marriage of Figaro,"* 1980, *C.W. Gluck: "Orfeo,"* 1981, *Benjamin Britten: "The Turn of the Screw,"* 1985, *Christoph Willibald Gluck: A Guide to Research*, 1987, *Music in Vienna 1790-1800*, 1988, and *Beethoven's "Fidelio,"* 1988.

Hunter, Mary Associate professor of music, Bates College, Lewiston, Maine. Contributor to *The New Grove Dictionary of Opera*, 1992, and to *Cambridge Opera Journal* and *Journal of Musicology*.

Jefferson, Alan Writer. Author of *Delius*, 1972, *Inside the Orchestra*, 1974, *The Glory of Opera*, 1976, *Sir Thomas Beecham*, 1979, *The Complete Gilbert & Sullivan Opera Guide*, 1984, *Der Rosenkavalier*, 1986, *Lotte Lehmann*, 1990, and several works on Richard Strauss. Past editor of *The Monthly Guide to Recorded Music*.

Kaufman, Thomas G. Author of *Annals of Italian Opera, Volume 1: Verdi and His Major Contemporaries*, 1990. Contributor of chronologies to several publications and to *Verdi's "Macbeth"—A Source Book*, 1984. Author of articles and reviews for *The Opera Quarterly* and *Journal of the Donizetti Society*.

Kinderman, William Professor of music, University of Victoria, British Columbia, Canada. Author of *Beethoven's Diabelli Variations*, 1989. Editor of *Beethoven's Compositional Process*, 1991. Author of articles on Wagner for *Archiv für Musikwissenschaft*, *Journal of Musicology*, and *19th Century Music*.

Kotze, Michael Professional singer.

Kupferberg, Herbert Senior editor, *Parade* magazine, New York. Author of *The Mendelssohns: Three Generations of Genius*, 1972, *Opera*, 1975, *Basically Bach*, 1985, *Amadeus: A Mozart Mosaic*, 1987, and *The Book of Classical Music Lists*, 1988. Past music critic for *Atlantic Monthly* and *National Observer*; contributor to many magazines.

Kushner, David Z. Professor of music and coordinator of musicological studies, University of

Florida. Contributor to *The New Grove Dictionary of Music and Musicians*, 1980, *The New Grove Dictionary of American Music*, 1984, and *Great Lives from History: Renaissance to 1900*, 1989. Music book reviewer for *American Music Teacher*.

Laing, Alan Lecturer, University of Hull, England, and composer. Author of articles for *Association of Teachers of Italian Journal;* composer.

Law, Joe K. Writing instructor, Texas Christian University. Author of articles on opera or opera and literature for *Opera Journal, The Opera Quarterly, Review of English Studies*, and *Twentieth Century Literature*.

Lee, M. Owen Professor of classics, St. Michael's College, University of Toronto, Ontario, Canada. Author of *Word, Sound, and Image in the Odes of Horace*, 1969, *Fathers and Sons in Virgil's "Aeneid,"* 1979, *Death and Rebirth in Virgil's Arcadia*, 1989, and *Wagner's Ring: Turning the Sky Round*, 1990. Author of many articles on classics and music for journals, including *Opera News* and *The Opera Quarterly*.

Lessem, Alan Deceased, February 1992. Former associate professor of music, York University, Ontario, Canada, and editor of *Canadian University Music Review*. Author of articles for *Journal of the Arnold Schoenberg Institute* and *Musical Quarterly*.

Lustig, Larry Editor, *The Record Collector*, Broomfield, England.

MacDonald, Malcolm Editor, *Tempo* magazine. Author of *Schoenberg*, 1976; *The Symphonies of Havergal Brian*, volume 1, 1974, volume 2, 1978, volume 3, 1983; *John Foulds: His Life in Music*, 1975; *Ronald Stevenson*, 1989; and *Brahms*, 1990. Compiler of *The Gramophone Classical Catalogue*, 1974-1978.

Maconie, Robin Composer and writer on music, and quotations manager, Dawson UK, Book Division, England. Author of *The Works of Karlheinz Stockhausen*, 1976, and *The Concept of Music*, 1990. Compiler and editor of *Stockhausen on Music*, 1989. Contributing music editor to Helicon (formerly Hutchinson Encyclopedias).

Meckna, Michael Associate professor of music, Texas Christian University. Author of *Virgil Thomson: A Bio-Bibliography*, 1986, and of articles for *American Music, Music Journal, Musical Quarterly*, and *Musical Times*. Con-

tributor *to The New Grove Dictionary of American Music*, 1984, and *The New Grove Dictionary of Opera*, 1992.

Mintzer, Charles B. Essayist.

Mitchell, Jerome Professor of English, University of Georgia. Author of *Thomas Hoccleve: A Study in Early Fifteenth-Century English Poetic*, 1968, *The Walter Scott Operas*, 1977, and *Scott, Chaucer, and Medieval Romance*, 1987.

Monson, Dale E. Associate professor of music, Pennsylvania State University. Former editor of *Current Musicology*. Contributor to *The New Grove Dictionary of Opera*, 1992. Author of articles for *International Review of the Aesthetics and Sociology of Music*, and *Pergolesi Studies*.

Moran, William R. Founder and honorary curator of the Stanford Archive of Recorded Sound, California. Author of *Melba: A Contemporary Review*, 1985, and *The Recordings of Lillian Nordica*. Contributor to *Opera and Concert Singers*, 1985. Author of articles, reviews and discographies for *High Fidelity, The Opera Quarterly, Record Collector, Record News, Recorded Sound*, and other journals.

Morey, Carl Jean A. Chalmers Professor of Music, University of Toronto, and director of Institute for Canadian Music, Ontario, Canada. Author of articles for *Opera Canada*. Contributor of articles to *The Concise Oxford Dictionary of Opera*, 1979, *Encyclopedia of Music in Canada*, 1981, *The Encyclopedia of Opera*, 1976, and *The New Grove Dictionary of Opera*, 1992.

Moshell, Gerald Associate professor of music, Trinity College, Hartford, Connecticut. Stage director and conductor of numerous productions of twentieth-century opera and musical theatre. Theatre critic and music critic for *The Hartford Courant*.

Nash, Elizabeth H. Professor of theatre arts, University of Minnesota. Author of *Always First Class: The Career of Geraldine Farrar*, 1981, and *The Luminus Ones: A History of the Great Actresses*, 1991.

Neumeyer, David Professor of music, Indiana University. Author of *The Music of Paul Hindemith*, 1986. Author of articles on Hindemith for *Hindemith-Jahrbuch, Journal of the Arnold Schoenberg Institute, Music Theory Spectrum*, and *Musik Theorie*.

Nisbett, Robert F. Chair and associate professor, department of music, theatre, and dance, Colorado State University. Contributor to *The New Grove Dictionary of Opera*, 1992. Author of articles for *American Music, Current Musicology*, and *Sonneck Society Bulletin*.

Nobusawa, Kiko Free-lance writer. Author of concert reviews and editorials for *The Vermont Times*.

O'Connor, Patrick Free-lance writer. Editor-in-chief, *Opera News*, and deputy editor, *Harpers & Queen*. Author of *Josephine Baker*, 1988, *Toulouse-Lautrec: The Nightlife of Paris, 1991*, and *The Amazing Blonde Woman*, 1991. Regular contributor to *Daily Telegraph, Literary Review*, and *Times Literary Supplement*.

Oglesby, Donald Associate professor of music, University of Miami, and artistic director and conductor, Miami Bach Society, Florida. Author of *A Conductor's Study of Marc-Antoine Charpentier's "Judicium,"* 1979, and *Score Preparation: A Study Guide for Conducting Students*, 1981.

Owens, Rose Mary Professor of music, Southwest Missouri State University. Author of *Eva Turner: The Grand Dame of Singing: A Study of her Life as a Singer and as a Teacher*, 1983, and *Study Guide to Accompany Stanley Sadie's Brief Guide to Music*, 1987. Regular reviewer for *The Choral Journal*.

Pacun, David E. Lecturer in music, University of Vermont; doctoral candidate, University of Chicago.

Parker, C. P. Gerald Music librarian, Bibliothéciare de Musique, University of Quebec, Montreal, Canada. Author of articles for *ARSC Journal, Fanfare, The Opera Quarterly, Spectrum*, and other journals.

Parsons, James Visiting assistant professor, department of music, University of Missouri. Contributor of essays to *Four Centuries of Opera: Manuscripts and Printed Editions in The Pierpont Morgan Library*, 1983. Author of articles and reviews for *Early Music, Journal of Musicology, Notes, Opera, Opera Canada, Opera News, Opera Journal, Opus*, and *Stagebill*.

Patton, Elizabeth W. Free-lance writer. Music critic for the *Ann Arbor News*.

Pennino, John Assistant archivist, Metropolitan Opera, New York. Author of articles for *The Opera Quarterly*.

Perlis, Vivian Director, Oral History, American Music, School of Music, Yale University. Author of *Charles Ives Remembered: An Oral History*, 1974, *An Ives Celebration*, 1977, *Copland: 1900 Through 1942*, 1984, and *Copland: Since 1943*, 1989.

Pople, Anthony Lecturer in music, Lancaster University, England. Editor of the journal *Musicus: Computer Applications in Music Education*. Author of *Skryabin and Stravinsky: Studies in Theory and Analysis*, 1988, and *Berg: Violin Concerto*, 1991. Author of articles for *Music Analysis, Music and Letters*, and *The Musical Times*.

Poultney, David Professor of music, Illinois State University. Author of *Studying Music History*, 1983, and *Dictionary of Church Music*, 1991. Author of articles for *Musical Quarterly*.

Reed, Addison W. Deceased, 1991. Former chair, department of music, Northern Kentucky University. Contributor to *The New Grove Dictionary of Music and Musicians*, 1980, *Black Journals of the United States*, 1982, and *Ragtime, Its History, Composers, and Music*, 1985. Author of articles for *The Black Perspective in Music* and *Piano Quarterly*.

Rice, John A. Assistant professor of music, University of Houston. Author of *W.A. Mozart: "La Clemenza di Tito,"* 1991. Author of articles and reviews for *Early Music, Haydn Yearbook, Music and Letters, Notes, Studi musicali*, and other periodicals.

Robertson, Patricia Connors Instructor of music, Ball State and Taylor universities, Indiana.

Robinson, Harlow Associate professor, Department of Slavic Languages and Literatures, State University of New York at Albany. Author of *Sergei Prokofiev: A Biography*, 1987. Regular contributor to *Musical America, New York Times, Opera News, The Opera Quarterly*, and *Stagebill*.

Rose, Bob Opera review critic, Davis Enterprise, Davis, California. Author of record sleeve notes, 1978-1991, for recordings of complete opera and operatic recitals for *Voce Records*.

Routh, Francis Composer. Author of *Contemporary Music*, 1968, *Contemporary British Music*, 1970, *Early English Organ Music*, 1973, and *Stravinsky*, 1975. Former editor of *Composer*. Author of articles for *The Annual Register*.

Runyan, William E. Assistant dean of the College of Arts and Liberal Arts, Colorado State University. Author of articles for *Brass Bulletin, Journal of the Conductor's Guild, Notes*, and *The Opera Journal.*

Rushton, Julian Professor of music, University of Leeds, England; past general editor of Cambridge Music Handbooks. Author of *W.A. Mozart: "Don Giovanni,"* 1981, *The Musical Language of Berlioz*, 1983, *Classical Music: A Concise History*, 1986, and *W.A. Mozart: "Idomeneo,"* in press. Editor of *New Berlioz Edition*, 4 vols., 1970-1991. Author of numerous articles, conference papers, and reviews.

Salmon, Gregory Died October 1991. Doctoral candidate, University of California, Berkeley.

Saloman, Ora Frishberg Professor of music, Baruch College of the City University of New York. Contributor of articles to *Music and Civilization: Essays in Honor of Paul Henry Lang*, 1984, and *The New Grove Dictionary of Opera*, 1992. Author of articles for journals, including *Acta Musicologica, American Music*, and *Journal of Musicology.*

Samson, Jim Professor of musicology, University of Exeter, England. Author of *Music in Transition: A Study in Tonal Expansion and Early Atonality 1900-1920*, 1977, *The Music of Szymanowski*, 1980, *The Music of Chopin*, 1985, and *Chopin: The Four Ballads*, 1992. Editor of *The Cambridge Companion to Chopin*, 1982, *Chopin Studies*, 1988, and *The Late-Romantic Era: Man and Music, Volume 7*, 1991.

Sansone, Matteo Lecturer in English, Conservatorio di Musica Luigi Cherubini, Florence, Italy. Author of *Italian and Maltese Music (1573-1809) in the Cathedral Museum of Malta*, with John Azzopardi, 1992. Author of articles for *Bulletin for the Society for Italian Studies, Italian Studies*, and *Music and Letters.*

Scheppach, Margaret Professor of music, College of Saint Rose, Albany, New York. Author of *Dramatic Parallels in the Operas of Michael Tippett*, 1990.

Schulken, Samuel B., Jr. Professor of music, Southwest Virginia Community College. Author of *Introduction to Music History-Appreciation Correspondence Study*, 1967.

Seaman, Gerald R. Associate professor of musicology, University of Auckland, New Zealand. Author of *History of Russian Music*, 1967, *and*

Rimsky Korsakov: A Bibliographical Research Guide, 1988. General Editor of *Encyclopaedic Dictionary of Russian and Soviet Music*, in press.

Selk, Jürgen Doctoral candidate and research assistant, Center for Italian Opera Studies, University of Chicago.

Sells, Michael Opera singer; professor of music and dean, Jordan College of Fine Arts, Butler University, Indianapolis, Indiana.

Shaman, William Librarian and assistant professor of librarianship, Bemidji State University, Bemidji, Minnesota. Author of *Discography of the Edward J. Smith Recordings*, 1992, and *Guiseppe De Luca: A Discography*, 1992. Contributor to *The New Grove Dictionary of Opera*, 1992. Author of many reviews for *American Music, The Journal of the Association for Recorded Sound Collections, Notes*, and *Record Collector.*

Sherlaw-Johnson, Robert Fellow, Worcester College, Oxford University, England. Author of *Messiaen*, 1976.

Simpson, Adrienne Research fellow, National Library of New Zealand. Author of *Opera in New Zealand: Aspects of History and Performance*, 1990, and *Southern Voices: International Opera Singers of New Zealand*, with Peter Downes, 1992. Contributor to *The New Grove Dictionary of Music and Musicians*, 1980, and *The New Grove Dictionary of Opera*, 1992. Author of numerous scholarly articles for journals in Europe and Australasia.

Sims, Michael Managing editor, The MIT Press, Cambridge, Massachusetts.

Sloop, Jean C. Professor of music, Kansas State University.

Smith, Carolyn J. Humanities bibliographer/associate professor, Kansas State University Library. Author of *William Walton: A Bio-Bibliography*, 1988.

Snowman, Daniel Writer and broadcaster, British Broadcasting Corporation, England. Author of *The Amadeus Quartet: The Men and the Music*, 1981, and *The World of Placido Domingo*, 1985. Former Chairman, London Philharmonic Choir. Author of articles and reviews for *Gramophone, The Musical Times, The Washington Opera Magazine*, and other newspapers and journals.

Solomon, Jon Associate professor of classics, University of Arizona. Associate editor of the *Greek and Latin Music Theory Series*, University of Nebraska Press. Author of articles for *American Journal of Philology, Classics and Cinema, Journal of Musicology*, and *Music and Letters*.

Steane, John B. Free-lance writer and broadcaster. Author of *The Grand Tradition: 70 Years of Singing on Record*, 1974, and *Voices: Singers and Critics*, 1992. Regular reviewer of vocal records for *Gramophone*. Frequent broadcasts for BBC Radio 3 and World Service. Author of articles for *The Musical Times, Opera, Opera News*, and *Opera Now* (monthly). Contributor to *The New Grove Dictionary of Opera*, 1992.

Stearns, David Patrick Music critic for *USA Today*; correspondent for *The Independent* in London; music commentator for National Public Radio; contributing editor of *Stereo Review*.

Stein, Louise Writer on opera, ballet, and films.

Stevens, Denis President, Accademia Monteverdiana. Author of *The Mulliner Book*, 1952, *Thomas Tomkins*, 1957, *Tudor Church Music*, 1966, *Musicology: A Practical Guide*, 1980, *The Letters of Claudio Monteverdi*, 1980, *Musicology in Practice*, 1987, and *The Joy of Ornamentation*, 1989. Editor of *Grove's Dictionary of Music*, 5th ed. and *A History of Song*, 1960.

Studwell, William E. Principal cataloger and professor, University Libraries, Northern Illinois University. Editor of *Music Reference Services Quarterly*. Author of *Adolphe Adam and Leo Delibes: A Guide to Research*, 1987. Author of many articles on library science and music for journals and other publications.

Summerville, Suzanne Professor of music, University of Alaska. Music director, Fairbanks Choral Society. Author of articles for *National Association of Teachers of Singing Bulletin, The Opera Quarterly*, and *Unitas Fratrum*.

Sutcliffe, James Helme Free-lance opera critic and composer. Regular contributor to *Musica, Musical America, Opera, Opera Canada, Opera News*, and *Opernwelt Zurich*.

Talbot, Michael Professor of music, University of Liverpool, England. Author of *Vivaldi*, 1978, *Antonio Vivaldi: A Guide to Research*, 1988, and *Tommaso Albinoni: The Venetian Composer and His World*, 1990. Author of articles on late Baroque Italian music for *Music and Letters, Music Review, Rivista italiana de musicologia, Soundings*, and other journals.

Thornhill, William Professor of music history, Ohio State University.

Wakeling, Dennis W. Deceased, May 1992. Former director of opera, College of Music, University of North Texas. Regular reviewer of books and records for *The Opera Quarterly*.

Weatherson, Alexander Principal lecturer in visual and performing arts, The Leeds Polytechnic, and chairman of the Donizetti Society. Editor of *The Journal of the Donizetti Society*. Author of *"Ugo, conte di Parigi": Its Source, and the "Convenienze Teatrali" Which Led to Its Short Life on the Stage*, 1985, and *"I fratelli Ricci": due compositori divisi dalla stessa opera*, 1989.

Wechsler, Bert Free-lance writer. Author of articles for *Dance Magazine, High Fidelity, New York Times, Opera News, Video Review*, and other newspapers and periodicals.

Whitton, Kenneth S. Professor Emeritus of European cultural studies and German, University of Bradford, England. Author of *The Theatre of Friedrich Dürrenmatt*, 1980, *Dietrich Fischer-Dieskau: Mastersinger*, 1981, *Lieder: An Introduction to German Song*, 1984, and *Dürrenmatt: Reinterpretation in Retrospect*, 1990.

Whyte, Sally Free-lance international arts writer, reviewer, and correspondent. Regular correspondent on music and the arts for *Ha'Aretz (The Nation)* and *Arts Review*, London.

Wierzbicki, James Music editor, *St. Louis Post-Dispatch*.

Willier, Stephen Professor of music history, Temple University. Lecturer and program annotator for the Opera Company of Philadelphia and the Pennsylvania Opera Theater. Author of articles and reviews for *Fontes artis musicae, Journal of the American Musicological Society, Opera News*, and *The Opera Quarterly*. Contributor to *The New Grove Dictionary of Opera*, 1992.

Willis, Stephen C. Head of archives, music division, National Library of Canada.

Wolf, Muriel Hebert Professor of music, State University of New York at Buffalo. Author of articles for *Overture, The Opera Journal*, and *The Opera Quarterly*.

Wright, Lesley A. Associate professor of musicology, University of Hawaii. Author of *Georges Bizet: Letters* in *the Nydahl Collection*, 1988. Contributor to *The New Grove Dictionary of Opera*, 1992. Author of articles for *English National Opera Guide, 19th Century Music*, and *Studies in Music*.

Wynne, Meredith Essayist.

Zimmerman, Franklin B. Professor of music, University of Pennsylvania, and director, Pennsylvania Promusica. Author of *Henry Purcell: An Analytical Catalog of His Complete Works*, 1963, *Henry Purcell: His Life and Times*, 1967, *Henry Purcell: An Index to His Complete Works*, 1971. *The Symphonies of C.F. Abel*, 1982, and *Henry Purcell: A Guide to Research*, 1988. Coauthor of other works on Purcell.

Zucker, Stefan Editor, *Opera Fanatic*, and host of the radio show of that name. Author of articles for *American Record Guide, La Follia, New World, New York Tribune, Opera News, The Opera Quarterly, Professione Musica*, and other publications.